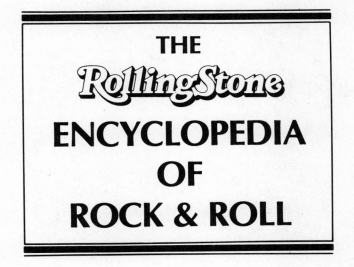

THE
Rolling Stone
ENCYCLOPEDIA
OF
ROCK & ROLL

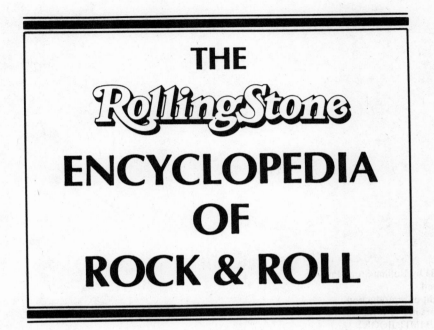

THE RollingStone ENCYCLOPEDIA OF ROCK & ROLL

Edited by

Jon Pareles
CONSULTING EDITOR

and

Patricia Romanowski

RollingStone

ROLLING STONE PRESS/SUMMIT BOOKS

NEW YORK

Copyright © 1983 by Rolling Stone Press
All rights reserved
including the right of reproduction
in whole or in part in any form
Published by SUMMIT BOOKS
A Division of Simon & Schuster, Inc.
Simon & Schuster Building
Rockefeller Center
1230 Avenue of the Americas
New York, New York 10020
SUMMIT BOOKS and colophon are trademarks of Simon & Schuster, Inc.
Designed by Stanley S. Drate

Manufactured in the United States of America

1 2 3 4 5 6 7 8 9 10

First Edition

Library of Congress Cataloging in Publication Data

Main entry under title:

The Rolling stone encyclopedia of rock & roll.

   1. Rock music—Dictionaries. 2. Rock Music—Bio-
bibliography. I. Pareles, Jon. II. Romanowski, Patricia.
III. Rolling stone.
ML102.R6R64   1983   784.5′4′00321   83-4791

ISBN 0-671-43457-8 cloth
0-671-44071-3 paperback

Acknowledgments

When we first began work on *The Rolling Stone Encyclopedia of Rock & Roll* over a year and a half ago, we knew there was a lot to do, but we had no idea how many people it would take to do it. This has been a collaborative effort in every sense of the term, and the editors would like to thank everyone who contributed.

We would like to thank the staff writers: Ken Braun, Jim Farber, Nelson George, Jeff Howrey, Ira Kaplan, John Milward, Mitchell Schneider and Michael Shore. Philip Bashe, Wayne King and Doug Tomlinson wrote additional pieces. The research, discography and fact-checking staff included Ken Braun, Jim Farber, Steve Futterman, Holly George, Jeff Howrey, Barry Jacobs, Wayne King, Jill Schoenstein and Doug Tomlinson. We also wish to thank Michael Ochs, Nelson George, Ira Kaplan and Jim Farber for contributing photographs.

For their help in typing the manuscript, we thank Iris Brown, Lori Carney, Elizabeth Collier, Debra Hurst, Nora and Ann Kerrigan and Mary Redstone. We also want to thank Janis Bultman and the Rolling Stone Press staff of assistants and interns: Kaija Berzins, Laura Fraser, Liza Handman, Bobby Miller, Johnetta Romanowski and Michael Silberman.

We are especially indebted to the countless anonymous record company and management personnel who answered questions and supplied materials and phone numbers. In addition, we would like to thank the following who provided assistance and advice: Billy Altman, Long John Baldry, Terry Barnes, Allen Betrock, Jay Black, T-Bone Burnett, Gene Chandler, Robert Christgau, Bobby Colomby, Felix De Palma, Simo Doe, Willis Draffen, Jr., Russell Driver, Robert Fripp, Randall Grass, Malu Halasa, Lister Hewan-Lowe, Richard Hogan, Elliott Hubbard, Jimmy Ienner, Scott Isler, Lynn Kellerman, Cub Koda, Bob Jones, Sherry Jones, Ida Langsam, Marilyn Laverty, David Lindley, Amelie Littell, Gary Lucas, Dave Marsh, Ernie Martinelli, Bonnie McCourt, Richard Nader, Barbara Pepe, Lavern Perry, Raleigh Pinsky, Sherry Ring-Ginsberg, Ira Robbins, Melanie Rogers, Pat Smith, Audrey Strahl, John Swenson, Jeff Tamarkin, Bill Troute and Barbara Venezia.

Jon Pareles would like to thank M. Mark, who did not type the manuscript.

The editors would also like to thank Jim Silberman, Jonathan Segal, Kate Edgar and Arthur Samuelson at Summit Books and Sarah Lazin and Jann S. Wenner at Rolling Stone Press.

Preface

There's no stopping rock & roll. It is the most vital, unpredictable force in pop culture, and the exception to every rule. Like all important popular art, it can speak to and from the public's heart of hearts even if it has been crafted by the most knowing artisans. And even at its most elaborate it hints at a rebel spirit: the idea that an outsider with something important to say can broadcast it to the world. At its best, rock can be entertainment, good business and catharsis all at once; at its worst, it's only rock & roll.

It is music that just can't be pinned down, a contradiction any old way you choose it. Rock can be both amateur and professional, innocent and slick, subtle and crass, sincere and contrived, smart and stupid. It is a happy bastard style, claiming a pedigree from jazz, blues, Tin Pan Alley, country, classical music, movies, television, sex, drugs, art, literature, electronics and out-and-out noise. It is rooted in real emotion; it is also rooted in racism, cynicism and greed.

Rock accepts everything its detractors say, only to laugh it off. Sure, its basics are stolen, and its ideas are often clichés. Yes, it tends to aim for a lowest common denominator and appeal to base, primal impulses. It is proud to be a commodity, one that brings in billions of dollars, with "artistic" success frequently measured in sales figures. It doesn't even have to be in tune. No matter—rock & roll moves people, in simple and sophisticated ways. And it never takes no for an answer.

The history of rock is a wild tangle, affected by changes in technology, media, demographics, politics and the economy as well as by the inspirations of packagers and musicians. Rock cheerfully accepts all its roles; it is product and spectacle and art, something for everybody, and its development and documentation are by no means orderly.

In the Fifties, pop was infiltrated by rockabilly from Memphis and blues from Chicago and rhythm & blues from New Orleans and doo-wop from city streetcorners, more like outbreaks of some mysterious contagion—rockin' pneumonia?—than a concerted artistic movement. The music business counterattacked with its own more malleable teen idols and girl groups, but by the early Sixties their records were rocking anyway. As baby-boom babies became America's largest population group, the Beatles and other British Invasion bands fed back Little Richard and Chuck Berry and teen-idol pop to an eager audience, and rock took over pop.

During the Sixties the music grouped and regrouped into an explosion of genres: folk rock, soul, Motown, psychedelic rock, hard rock, funk, blues rock, jazz rock, progressive rock, country rock, bubblegum. By the Seventies, a split had been established between singles buyers (who listened to bouncy AM pop) and album buyers, as genres solidified and subdivided; the early Seventies brought heavy metal, Southern rock, fusion, hard funk, singer/songwriters and classical rock. As rock record buying peaked in the later Seventies, disco and punk and reggae arose to reemphasize rhythm and energy, and in the Eighties those styles—and all the rest—helped foster new wave, rap and other genres yet unnamed. After all these years, rock is still wide open.

vii

But one kind of tension shows up in every phase of rock. That's the tension between convention and rebellion—between familiarity and freedom. In the music itself, musicians forge personal statements from a common "commercial" language; imitators become innovators because they can't help leaving fingerprints on the formula. Periodically, when genres become too familiar, new generations of rockers arrive with something tougher and simpler, shaking down the current conventions. That tension makes rock an eternal hybrid, testing and absorbing and mutating new ideas as the public listens.

The music business also sees battles between tradition and insurgency, between a pop-star careerism it understands and a rock-rebel goal it doesn't. Rock has always been a collision—and a marriage—of minority culture and majority tastes; new ideas pop out of unlikely places to threaten, then merge with, the mainstream. Virtually every rock genre has come out of nowhere—amateur musicians, independent record labels—to be taken up and marketed by major corporations when the coast is clear. As the music annexes ideas, the music business accepts new approaches.

Rock's most pervasive minority-to-majority connection has been to act out the tug-of-war between black and white culture in America. "If I could find a white man who had the Negro sound and the Negro feel," said Sam Phillips, who discovered Elvis Presley, "I could make a billion dollars." Rock has continually crisscrossed the color line, as each side borrowed the other's secrets and added a few tricks of its own, a constant process of thievery and homage and inexact imitation. In uncountable ways, rock is a metaphor for American culture—a vital, unpredictable mess of individualism and assimilation.

So much for my grand theories (which owe quite a bit to Greil Marcus, Ishmael Reed, Robert Palmer, Robert Christgau and others). With the information in this encyclopedia, you are welcome to assemble your own thesis, and you'll be able to base it on accurate, objective, salient information. This encyclopedia was designed to tell, as clearly and concisely as possible, the stories of the people who made the music. As in the music, the category of "rock" is open-ended. We have included entries on country, blues, jazz and even classical musicians who have left a mark on rock music. And since rock's commercial peaks don't always coincide with its artistic ones, we have included unsung (or perhaps unsold) innovators as well as hitmakers, Professor Longhair and Captain Beefheart along with Styx.

Why assemble another rock encyclopedia? Because, frankly, the others are inadequate. *The Rolling Stone Encyclopedia of Rock & Roll* covers more musicians in more depth than any other rock encyclopedia. In particular, we have made efforts to cover more black music, and more new music, than earlier encyclopedias; and we have made every effort to cut through the inaccuracies—from public-relations mythmaking to moralistic scare tactics—that have surrounded rock from the start. As popular culture, rock has always been considered kid stuff, too silly and capricious and rude to be seriously watched. Like other entertainers, rock musicians have been known to lie about their age, experience and background, and those distortions are willingly spread by a press that is often more interested in a good story than a true one. In some cases, there is no story at all, especially in early rock and in most black music. We have tried to include bands and musicians who are often ignored not for their failure to contribute to rock but for their lack of documentation. The facts are here.

So many people have been involved in rock that we were forced to make hard decisions about who was best to include in this encyclopedia. The criterion—which, like every critical standard in rock, is ultimately subjective—was that those people included had a direct impact on the music, through popularity or through influence on other musicians. We chose to include as many musicians as possible rather than businessmen or other rock scenemakers; those moguls, disc jockeys and others who receive full entries have had a direct effect on the music. And since this is a biographical dictionary, not a critical one, the length of an entry is not directly related to a musician's worth. Someone who makes great records and does nothing else in public is likely to receive less space than a band that breaks up every two months; we have chosen to use as few or as many words as it takes to get the story straight. Musicians tend to lead complicated lives, and the entries make sense of them as economically as the facts allow.

Naturally, some bands and musicians are left out; given the inevitable limitations of space, we chose those whom we considered most important. We would appreciate hearing about any sins of omission, but we have tried to err on the permissive side, as rock always does.

To read about these thousands of musicians, finally, is to be astonished at the combinations of creativity, ambition and recklessness it takes to make it in rock & roll. For every band in this encyclopedia, there are twenty whose records nobody heard, and hundreds that never recorded at all; there are musicians who practice in basements around the world trying to find that certain chemistry. As these entries show, a rock career can be as short as the trajectory of a single hit or as long as the reign of Chuck Berry or the Rolling Stones, and some factors are out of anyone's control. Still, musicians keep trying and keep breaking through—and the glory of rock & roll is that even now, anyone can try it.

JON PARELES

Introduction

The Rolling Stone Encyclopedia of Rock & Roll is a guide to the people who have made rock & roll. Each of the alphabetically arranged entries provides basic biographical information and, where appropriate, a selective discography or a discography plus group personnel chronology, followed by an essay that sums up the subject's life and career in music.

In researching, writing and fact-checking this book we learned a great deal about rock & roll and its history. But we also learned how poorly that history has been preserved: It is simply a mess. From its inception nearly three decades ago, rock & roll has been only rarely and sporadically documented. We began researching various sources, including newspapers, periodicals, books, fan magazines, press releases, press files, records, televised and broadcast interviews, and films and live performances. In addition, whenever possible, we collected information through telephone conversations and correspondence with subjects and/or their representatives, record company personnel, management and interested writers and collectors. Through all of this, we have sought corroboration among our best sources and attempted to glean the truth. It has not been easy. Except for the efforts of collectors, self-appointed archivists and fans, most of that history would have been lost years ago.

Just how difficult that history is to trace can be found in the constant difficulty we encountered whenever we sought information on the most important artifacts in a performer's history: his own records. Over the years, literally hundreds of record labels have come and gone; dozens of others have been taken over by larger corporations and their files either stored, lost or destroyed. The record business's current well-publicized economic problems have rendered almost impossible what was once merely difficult. Staffs in publicity and archive departments everywhere have been cut to a minimum. In most cases, record company personnel can just meet the demands for information on current acts. And with very few exceptions, once a performer or group leaves a record company (for another label or oblivion), all press releases and other sources of information simply disappear. Similarly, most record companies have little or no interest in providing information on a performer's earlier career unless it was unusually successful, in which case it's readily available elsewhere. Many major companies cannot even provide a complete discography on their most important acts (Bob Dylan for example).

Fortunately, our requests for information directed to managers, booking agents and the performers themselves were greeted with more enthusiasm. Sometimes a performer had changed managers or just could not be reached. But even when we found someone who was knowledgeable and willing to talk, the issue of a performer's public image frequently served to restrict and sometimes distort the information we did receive. This is not to say that everyone we contacted was evasive or uncooperative. However, on the average, 70 to 80 percent of our requests for a performer's date of birth were either refused, answered incompletely (day and month given, but without the year), or answered in a way that was—either deliberately or accidentally—inaccurate.

One of the more fascinating—and frustrating—aspects of rock & roll is that much of its appeal is based on legend. Performers gave as many as ten accounts of the same incident to ten different reporters, with the predictable result: ten different stories, all from the horse's mouth, all equally self-aggrandizing. We discovered performers whose "triple platinum" albums in fact never even went gold and kings of rock & roll with barely a chart showing. Given the degree of inaccuracy we found in such important primary sources, it's easy to see why most books on the subject present information that is often contradictory and sometimes wrong. Nonetheless, we have pooled our resources and knowledge in an attempt to provide a complete and accurate account of the life and work of each performer. We anticipate future revisons and welcome all comments, suggestions, additional information and corrections. These should be addressed to Rolling Stone Press, 745 Fifth Avenue, New York, New York 10151.

Where appropriate, each entry begins with a discography. In general, all discographies are selective. Even complete discographies list only LPs, unless otherwise noted. The criteria for selection are not based on the album's critical value but on its availability (either current or as a reissue or from secondhand record dealers and collectors), its importance in the context of the performer's career or within a particular genre or movement, or, in the case of performers like Johnny Cash, who may release as many as four LPs a year, how representative it is of all the performer's work. The date of release precedes the album title, and the label, in parentheses, follows. "N.A." means that the album's release date is unavailable. All dates, titles, labels and album contents refer to the U.S. release unless otherwise noted. Where a performer has released more than one album on the same label, the label is listed only once.

The same criteria apply to group discography/chronologies. For groups formed since the late Sixties, most discographies are complete for U.S. releases. Discographies also include a chronological listing of personnel additions (denoted by a plus, +) and personnel deletions (denoted by a minus, −). The personnel chronology lists only those musicians who either have recorded with the group or whose membership is clearly documented in published articles or press releases. Thus most guest musicians are not listed, although major ones are mentioned in the text. Where the discography is complete, the chronology indicates roughly which musicians appear on a given album. But because the chronology presents events in the order they occurred, it is not always possible to determine the exact personnel on a given album. With few exceptions, it was not until the late Sixties that groups listed musicians on their albums. Also, a surprising number of soul and disco groups still do not print this information on record sleeves and jackets. In these instances, or wherever a group has undergone dozens of personnel changes, we have listed the original, best-known or current lineup. In the case of a group that is actually dozens of musicians working under the same name (the Ritchie Family or Gong, for instance), we have discussed the most important members in the text.

Another problem in determining exactly who may be on an album is that the time between the recording date and its release date can be anywhere from a few weeks to decades. In that time, personnel changes, even deaths, may have occurred. The full entry will clarify the exact sequence of events. Also note that with reissues, greatest-hits albums and retrospectives, earlier lineups—sometimes several different ones—may all appear on the same LP. Changes like these are far too numerous and extensive to document without adding to the confusion.

All discography and personnel listings are current through May 1983. Chart positions are based on those published weekly in *Billboard* and are based on Joel Whitburn's Record Research for all dates through 1981, and for 1982 and 1983 on *Billboard* itself. Record Research books and pamphlets are available from Record Research, Inc., P.O. Box 200, Menomonee Falls, Wisconsin 53051. All figures used for chart positions refer to the Hot 100 or pop chart or its equivalent unless otherwise noted. The date following the chart positions is the date that the record peaked on the chart. All references to sales are based on published figures or figures that have been released by the record company. Except in cases where a performer's success warrants at least a gold certification, record companies often decline to release such information. In those cases, references to poor sales are based on low chart showings or published statements.

Gold and platinum record awards are based on lists compiled by the Recording Industry Association of America (R.I.A.A.), the organization that certifies these awards. For further information on exactly what constitutes a gold or platinum record, turn to the box on the R.I.A.A. on page 220. All statements regarding nominations and presentations of Grammy Awards are based on materials published by the National Academy of Recording Arts and Sciences, and are current through February 1982. A box listing performance Grammys awarded rock and related country, blues and jazz performers appears under each letter.

In addition to the biographical entries, we have included definitions, arranged alphabetically throughout the book, and featured boxes, in addition to the Grammy listings. The purpose of the boxes is to provide an overview of some of the more interesting phenomena in rock like rock festivals, rock on television, rock on Broadway and comedy about rock. Also included are lists of the great one-hit wonders and rock stars who have written books, as well as essays on producers and managers and their role in rock, the evolution of studio technology and the importance of dance in rock.

PATRICIA ROMANOWSKI

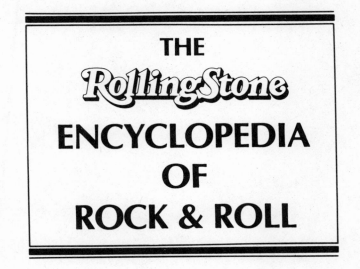

THE
RollingStone
ENCYCLOPEDIA
OF
ROCK & ROLL

ABBA

Formed 1973, Sweden

Benny Andersson (b. Dec. 16, 1946, Stockholm), kybds., synth., voc.; Björn Ulvaeus (b. Apr. 25, 1945, Gothenburg, Swed.), gtr., voc.; Agnetha "Anna" Fältskog (previously Ulvaeus; b. Apr. 5, 1950, Jönköping, Swed.), voc.; Anni-Frid "Frida" Lyngstad-Fredriksson-Andersson (b. Nov. 15, 1945, Norway), voc.

1974—Waterloo (Atlantic) 1975—Abba 1976—Greatest Hits, volume 1; Arrival 1977—The Album 1979—Voulez-Vous; Greatest Hits, volume 2 1980—Super Trouper 1981—The Visitors 1982—Abba, The Singles, The First Ten Years.

Easily the most commercially successful group of the Seventies in every country except the U.S., Abba's wholesome image and buoyant tunes made them international pop stars and the second most profitable corporation on the Stockholm stock exchange. Though Björn Ulvaeus and Benny Andersson's hook-laden singles ("Fernando" and "Money, Money, Money," 1976; "Knowing Me, Knowing You," 1977) often topped European charts, U.S. success has been limited to several hit albums and two gold singles: "Dancing Queen" in 1977 and "Take a Chance on Me" in 1978.

Each member was a solo star in Sweden before Abba (an acronym of their first initials) coalesced in 1973. "Waterloo" won the prestigious Eurovision Song Contest in 1974, a year after they began recording in English. Abba tours have been limited because of the difficulty of re-creating their densely layered sound in concert, though they mounted their first international tour in 1977 and appeared in the U.S. two years later.

Longtime live-in lovers Benny and Anni-Frid (who both have children from teenage marriages) were wed in 1978; they have since separated. That same year, Björn and Agnetha's marriage of six years ended in divorce. Abba's public image, however, remains harmonious. In 1982, Phil Collins produced Frida's post-Abba solo debut, Something's Going On.

A CAPPELLA

Generally believed to mean voices singing without instrumental accompaniment. While that is how the term is used today, a cappella is derived from the Italian, which translates literally as in the chapel style. In its original usage, a cappella referred to the singing done in church without instrumental accompaniment. Modern a cappella is generally associated with the doo-wop R&B of the late Fifties and early Sixties. The first a cappella/doo-wop hits were recorded by a New Haven–based group, the Nutmegs, in 1955: "Story Untold" and "Ship of Love." Since the genre's heyday, a cappella has become the almost exclusive province of two groups: the veteran Persuasions and the critically acclaimed newcomers 14 Karat Soul.

AC/DC

Formed 1973, Sydney, Australia

Angus Young (b. Mar. 31, 1959, Glasgow), gtr.; Malcolm Young (b. Jan. 6, 1953, Glasgow), gtr.; three months later, added Bon Scott (b. July 9, 1946, Kirriemur, Scot.; d. Feb. 19, 1980, London), voc.; after a succession of bassists and drummers, in 1974 added Phillip Rudd (b. May 19, 1946, Melbourne), drums; Mark Evans (b. Melbourne), bass.

1976—High Voltage (Atlantic) 1977—Let There Be Rock (− Evans; + Cliff Williams [b. Dec. 14, 1949, Rumford, Eng.], bass) 1978—Powerage; If You Want Blood, You've Got It 1979—Highway to Hell 1980—(− Scott; + Brian Johnson, voc.) Back in Black 1981—Dirty Deeds Done Dirt Cheap; For Those About to Rock, We Salute You.

Australian heavy-metal band AC/DC features knickers-clad guitarist Angus Young, who moons audiences regularly, and songs about sex, drinking and damnation. Their raucous image, constant touring and explicit lyrics in songs like "Big Balls" and "The Jack" helped make them one of the top hard-rock bands of the early Eighties. The Young brothers moved with their family from Scotland to Sydney in 1963. In 1973, they formed the first version of AC/DC with Bon Scott. After a year of working with temporary bassists and drummers they settled on drummer Phillip Rudd and bassist Mark Evans in 1974. Their first four albums were produced by ex-Easybeats Harry Vanda and George Young, Angus' older brother. The group had gained a solid reputation in their homeland early on, but it wasn't until 1979 with the platinum Highway to Hell (#17, 1979) that they became a presence on the American charts.

Within months of AC/DC's American success, vocalist Scott died from choking on his own vomit after an all-night drinking binge. He was quickly replaced by ex-Geordie vocalist Brian Johnson, and within a year, Back in Black began a year-long run on the U.S. charts, peaking at #4

(1980). *Dirty Deeds Done Dirt Cheap*, a 1981 reissue of a 1978 Australian LP, went to #3 in the U.S. *For Those About to Rock* became the group's first U.S. #1 LP in December, 1981. AC/DC have become international stars with record sales in the millions.

ACE

Formed 1973, London
Alan "Bam" King (b. Sep. 1946, London), gtr., voc.; Phil Harris (b. July 1948, London), gtr.; Paul Carrack (b. Apr. 1951, Sheffield, Eng.), kybds., voc.; Terry "Tex" Comer (b. Feb. 1949, Burnley, Eng.), bass; Steve Witherington, drums.
1974—(− Witherington; + Fran Byrne [b. Mar. 1948, Dublin], drums) *Five-A-Side* (Anchor) **1975**—*Time for Another* **1976**—(− Harris; + Jon Woodhead [b. San Francisco], gtr., voc.) **1977**—*No Strings*.

Ace became the best-known of London's pub-rock bands when "How Long," written and sung by Paul Carrack, became a #3 U.S. hit in 1975. The group had been founded the year before by Alan King and Phil Harris, and "How Long" was a product of their first recording session. What many listeners believed was a love song actually concerned Terry Comer's temporary departure from the band to work with the Sutherland Brothers and Quiver and his later decision to return to Ace.

The rest of the group's material failed to match the success of their debut single, and after a 1976 tour with Yes, they resettled in Los Angeles and soon disbanded. Carrack, Byrne and Comer joined Frankie Miller. Carrack later recorded with Roxy Music, Squeeze (he sings lead on "Tempted") and a short-lived backup band for Carlene Carter. In 1982 he joined Nick Lowe's Noise to Go. He has released two solo albums, *Nightbird* (1980) and *Suburban Voodoo* (1982).

JOHNNY ACE

Born John Alexander, Jr., June 29, 1929, Memphis; died December 24, 1954, Houston
1974—*Johnny Ace Memorial Album* (Duke).

Johnny Ace was one of the most popular balladeers of the early Fifties, but is perhaps most famous for the way he died: He shot himself while playing Russian roulette. Ace served in the Navy during World War II. After his discharge he joined Adolph Duncan's Band as a pianist; he often jammed with B. B. King and Bobby "Blue" Bland in Memphis' famed Beale Streeters. In 1953, he released his first single, "My Song," which became a big R&B hit. Like his subsequent releases, it featured his soothing baritone in a subdued arrangement similar to the style of Nat "King" Cole. On Christmas Eve 1954, Ace died backstage at Houston's City Auditorium. One of his biggest pop successes came with the posthumously released "Pledging My Love" in early 1955.

DAVID ACKLES

Born February 20, 1937, Rock Island, Illinois
1968—*David Ackles* (Elektra) **1970**—*Subway to the Country* **1972**—*American Gothic* **1973**—*Five and Dime* (Columbia).

David Ackles is a singer/songwriter whose work, particularly *American Gothic*, was briefly popular in the early Seventies. Ackles was born into a show-business family and began performing in vaudeville at age four. Later he starred in a series of B films with a dog named Rusty. He attended the University of Southern California and then the University of Edinburgh. Following his graduate work in film at USC, Ackles worked as a television writer and later began writing songs. On the strength of his song "Blue Ribbons" he was signed to Elektra Records. His third LP, *American Gothic*, was hailed by some critics as a masterpiece. But Ackles' success was short-lived. His brooding, sometimes Biblical songs were fairly popular in Britain but found little favor in the U.S. Ackles recorded one more album, *Five and Dime*, before he dropped from sight.

BARBARA ACKLIN

Born February 28, 1943, Chicago
1968—*Love Makes a Woman* (Brunswick) **1969**—*Seven Days of Night* **1970**—*I Did It; Someone Else's Arms* **1971**—*I Call It Trouble* **N.A.**—*Great Soul Hits of Barbara Acklin*.

Barbara Acklin is an R&B singer/songwriter whose late-Sixties hits include "Love Makes a Woman." After singing with a gospel choir during her teens, Acklin began her professional career as a background vocalist for St. Lawrence Records in 1964. She sang lead on a handful of singles under the pseudonym Barbara Allen and wrote songs (including Jackie Wilson's 1966 hit "Whispers [Gettin' Louder]") before signing with Brunswick around 1967.

There she recorded a string of duets with Gene Chandler (including "From the Teacher to the Preacher," #57, 1968), as well as solo sessions, writing much of her material herself or with her producer, Eugene Record of the Chi-Lites. An Acklin-Record composition, "Love Makes a Woman," reached #15 on the pop charts and #3 R&B in 1968. Her other R&B Top Forty hits include "Am I the Same Girl," "Just Ain't No Love" (1968) and "I Did It" (1970). During the late Seventies, she toured with Tyrone Davis. By 1981, she was recording with producer Gene Chandler for Chi-Sound Records in her hometown of Chicago, where she was also studying engineering.

ROY ACUFF

Born September 15, 1903, Maynardsville, Tennessee
1966—*Roy Acuff Sings Hank Williams* (Hickory)

1970—*Best of Roy Acuff* (Capitol) *The Great Roy Acuff; Songs of the Smoky Mountains; The Voice of Country Music.*

Singer, songwriter, fiddler, bandleader, music publisher, show-business booster, Roy Acuff has been called the "King of Country Music" for forty years. As a teenager he suffered a sunstroke, which prevented him from realizing his ambition to play pro baseball. He took up the fiddle and later joined a traveling medicine show that was passing through his Tennessee mountain hometown—only after he had been assured that he'd work only after sundown. In medicine and tent shows traversing the South he perfected an act that included old-time string-band music, hymns, a few popular contemporary songs and comedy routines (he was known for the yo-yo he played with onstage). In 1933, he formed the Tennessee Crackerjacks, with whom he performed on Knoxville radio. The next year, the group became the Crazy Tennesseans, and in 1936 they began recording. That same year Acuff recorded his two best-known hits, "Great Speckled Bird" (a million-selling record in 1943) and "Wabash Cannonball."

In 1938, he changed the group's name to the Smoky Mountain Boys. Acuff and the Boys began appearing regularly at Nashville's Grand Ole Opry, and Acuff became one of the Opry's first solo stars. His dry, high-pitched voice became familiar on such hits as "Night Train to Memphis," "Fire Ball Mail" and "Wreck on the Highway." His career sales total exceeds 25 million records.

In 1942, Acuff formed the Acuff-Rose Music Publishing Company with songwriter Fred Rose. Though Acuff continued to record, his success as a music publisher eclipsed that of his later recording career. Acuff-Rose eventually became one of the biggest country music publishing companies in the world, and in the process Acuff and Rose were mentors to many of Nashville's most successful songwriters and performers (Hank Williams, Marty Robbins, Boudleaux Bryant and others). Such was Acuff's popularity and influence that in 1944, 1946 and 1948 he ran for the governorship of Tennessee. A Republican in a traditionally Democratic state, he nonetheless came close to winning in 1948. In 1961, he became the first living musician elected to the Country Music Hall of Fame.

ADAM AND THE ANTS
Formed 1977, England
1979—First solid formation: Adam Ant (b. Stuart Goddard, Nov. 3, 1954, London), voc., gtr., piano; David Barbe (b. Eng.), percussion; Matthew Ashman (b. London), gtr., piano; Andrew Warren (b. Eng.), bass. *Dirk Wears White Sox* (Do-It Records) **1980**—(−Barbe; −Ashman; −Warren; +Marco Pirroni [b. Apr. 27, 1959, London], gtr.; +Terry Lee Miall [b. Nov. 8, 1958, London], drums; +Merrick [b. Chris Hughes, Mar. 3, 1954, London], drums; +Kevin Mooney [b.

Adam Ant

Eng.], bass; *Kings of the Wild Frontier* (Epic) **1981**—(−Mooney; + Gary Tibbs [b. Jan. 25, 1958, London], bass) *Prince Charming   Adam Ant solo LP* **1982**—*Friend or Foe.*

Though they were the undisputed leaders of Britain's short-lived fantasy-oriented New Romantic movement of the early Eighties, Adam and the Ants' impact in the U.S. was minimal until the wide dissemination of rock video clips. Their presentation of music as part of their self-contained make-believe universe (complete with self-promoting mottos like "Antmusic for Sexpeople" and its own vocabulary—fans were Antpeople) was not unique. Groups like Devo and Kiss had attempted the same thing with greater success. Starting in late 1980, Adam's fashion sense (which combined hero images of pirates, Western men and American Indians) took England by storm. His unusual music, which featured double-drum rhythms from Burundi and yodeling vocals, produced several British pop singles including "Ant Music" and "Dog Eat Dog" and a #1 LP, *Kings of the Wild Frontier.*

Ant, who had worked in various British bands since 1976, first came to national attention under the auspices of ex-Sex Pistols' manager Malcolm McLaren, who worked with the band on their debut LP, *Dirk Wears White Sox* (released in England only). McLaren left soon after, though, taking with him several Ants to form a more pliable New Romantic band, Bow Wow Wow. Ant then joined with ex-Siouxsie and the Banshees guitarist Marco Pirroni, and the pair developed the Antpeople image and wrote the songs for *Kings of the Wild Frontier*, the group's U.S. debut. Though the band received extensive media coverage in the U.S., their visual style never really caught on to the extent that it had in Britain, and as a result the album sold a disappointing 300,000 copies despite a well-publicized tour. In November 1981, *Prince Charming*, recorded with ex-Roxy Music bassist Gary Tibbs, repeated its predecessor's success in England, eventually spending over six months on the British charts, but it also failed to hit in the U.S. In 1982, the Ants disbanded, and Adam's debut solo effort, a single entitled "Goody Two Shoes," was #1 in England and Top Ten in the U.S.

FAYE ADAMS
Born Faye Scruggs
N.A.—*Shake a Hand* (Warwick)   **1980**—*Faye Adams* (Savoy).

Faye Adams was a blues shouter in the tradition of Big Maybelle and was best known for her 1953 hit, "Shake a Hand." She joined Joe Morris' Blues Cavalcade in the early Fifties, shortly before Herb Abramson signed the group to Atlantic Records. Abramson left to join the Army before the group had a chance to record, and the Cavalcade soon disbanded. Adams was then signed by Herald Records. "I'll Be True" (#1, 1953) and "Hurts Me to My Heart" (#1, 1954) followed "Shake a Hand."

Adams recorded over thirty tracks for Herald before moving to Imperial in 1957. From there her career faded, although she continued to record for Lido, Warwick, Savoy and Prestige, until her retirement in 1963.

JOHNNY ADAMS
1970—*Heart and Soul* (SSS Int'l).

Johnny Adams is a New Orleans–based R&B vocalist. Although his early style, which couched his big soulful croon in plush orchestral and choral arrangements, was much closer to pop than to late-Fifties New Orleans R&B, his early records on the Ric label—"Come On" (1960) and "A Losing Battle" (1960)—were big local hits, and the latter made the R&B Top Thirty.

Little is known of Adams' early life. In 1963, he changed labels (to Watch), but had no hits until 1969, when he made his comeback with four consecutive hits on the SSS International label: "Release Me," "Reconsider Me," "I Can't Be All Bad" and "I Won't Cry." Without the strings and choirs, his later style is earthier, drawing on country music and the blues. He continues to work and record in New Orleans.

MARIE ADAMS
Born Lyndon, Texas

During her twenty-year career, R&B vocalist Marie Adams has been successful both as a solo act and in collaborations with other performers. A gospel singer before she signed with Peacock Records in 1952, Adams had an R&B Top Ten hit with her first release, the very secular "I'm Gonna Play the Honky Tonks." That led to jobs with some of the biggest bandleaders of the Fifties—Cherokee Con-

yer, Pluma Davis and Johnny Otis (as a star of the Johnny Otis Show). One Otis group in which she took part was the Three Tons of Joy (Adams weighed over 260 pounds), a vocal trio with Sadie and Francine McKinley. The Three Tons' recording of "Ma, He's Making Eyes at Me" topped the British pop charts in 1957. A duet with Otis, "Bye Bye Baby," was a Top Twenty hit the following year.

Adams left the Johnny Otis group around 1960 and recorded as a solo act on the Sure Play and Encore labels. She rejoined the Three Tons of Joy for an album and a world tour with Johnny Otis in 1972.

AEROSMITH
Formed 1970, New Hampshire
Steven Tyler (b. Mar. 26, 1948, New York City), voc.; Joe Perry (b. Sep. 10, 1950, Boston), gtr.; Brad Whitford (b. Feb. 23, 1952, Winchester, Mass.), gtr.; Tom Hamilton (b. Dec. 31, 1951, Colorado Springs), bass; Joey Kramer (b. June 21, 1950, New York City), drums.
1973—*Aerosmith* (Columbia)   **1974**—*Get Your Wings*   **1975**—*Toys in the Attic*   **1976**—*Rocks*   **1977**—*Draw the Line*   **1979**—*Live! Bootleg; Night in the Ruts*   (− Perry; + Jim Crespo, gtr.)   **1980**—*Aerosmith's Greatest Hits*   **1981**—(− Whitford; + Rick Dufay, gtr., voc.)   **1982**—*Rock in a Hard Place*.

Fronted by Mick Jagger lookalike Steve Tyler and known for its aggressive blues-based hard-rock style, Aerosmith was the top American heavy-metal band of the mid-Seventies. The group was formed in 1970 by Joe Perry, Tom Hamilton and Tyler, who was then their drummer. Tyler left and the group was completed with Joey Kramer and Brad Whitford. Tyler then rejoined as lead singer. For the next two years, all five members shared a small apartment in Boston and played almost nightly throughout the area, occasionally venturing to New York. Clive Davis saw them perform at Max's Kansas City in New York and signed them to Columbia. A minor hit from their debut, "Dream On," strengthened their regional following, and it eventually rose to #6 in 1976. Meanwhile, Aerosmith began to tour widely. By the time "Walk This Way" (#10, 1977) was released, the band had become headliners. Their success was phenomenal but short-lived. A series of sold-out tours and platinum albums (including *Aerosmith, Get Your Wings, Toys in the Attic*) peaked in 1976.

By 1977, the group's constant touring began to take its toll. After months of rest, they recorded *Draw the Line* and appeared as the villains in Robert Stigwood's movie *Sgt. Pepper's Lonely Hearts Club Band;* their version of Lennon and McCartney's "Come Together" from the soundtrack was a minor hit. In 1979, Perry quit, admitting to long-standing personality and musical conflicts with Tyler, his songwriting partner. In 1980, Whitford departed to form the Whitford–St. Holmes band with ex–Ted Nugent sidekick Derek St. Holmes and was replaced by Jimmy Crespo. Rick Dufay joined, and in 1982 the group released *Rock in a Hard Place,* their first new recording in almost three years.

AFRICAN MUSIC

"Jungle music" is an epithet that has been applied to rock & roll since its beginnings, and though usually meant derisively, there is considerable truth in it: rock's pounding drums, jangling guitars, call-and-response vocals and sensual communal dance all bear more than incidental resemblance to tribal music and dance of tropical Africa. Rock & roll's roots extend firmly into Africa via its origins in the blues and in black gospel music, and musicians from Bo Diddley to James Brown to the Rolling Stones, Santana and Talking Heads have drawn from the source of those roots to reinforce the African presence in Western pop.

Since the Second World War, the intercontinental connection has gone full circle. Many of the styles popular in modern urban Africa are hybrids of traditional African elements and Afro-American elements. In the Fifties, Ghanaian bandleaders like guitarist E. K. Nyama and trumpeter E. T. Mensah developed *highlife,* a nightclub dance music influenced by calypso. At the same time, South African pennywhistle bands like the Solven Whistlers used swing jazz tunes and arrangements. In the Sixties, the Congolese *kasongo* and *kiri-kiri* of "jazz orchestras" like l'O.K. and Afrisan Internationale reflected the African taste for the Cuban rhumba, while the Kenyan *sukuma* of Nashil Pichen and Peter Tsotsi combined Congolese guitar styles with Arabian influences. South African *'smodern* groups like the Dark City Sisters and the Mahotela Queens forged a female vocal group style from Zulu polyphonic singing and Motown-like pop. In the Seventies, Nigerian *juju* musicians like Ebenezer Obey, Prince Nico Mbarga and King Sunny Adé added multiple electric guitars to the ancient interplay of multiple drums, while saxophonist/keyboardist/orator Fela Anikulapo Kuti re-Africanized James Brown funk arrangements in a style known as *afro-beat.* These particular Nigerians—

Grammy Awards

The annual Grammy Awards should be taken with a grain of salt—or maybe a shakerful. Presented by the National Academy of Recording Arts and Sciences, the Grammys are as unpredictable as the Academy Awards for movies, and even less reliable as a guide to quality. They are influenced, but not guided exclusively, by sales;

the Song of the Year is always a top-selling single, but not necessarily the year's biggest hit. While many Grammy choices are downright baffling, they often reflect a pop sensibility. Songs that try for Tin Pan Alley goals of tunefulness and melodic sophistication—the kinds of songs old-fashioned music-business types

think of as "classy"—are generally rewarded, while harder rock and funk are treated as an aberration. Grammy categories also change from year to year, in puzzling ways that seem to be a vain attempt to keep up with the music. Listed below are the Grammys awarded for best song, record, album, performance and best new artist.

Alabama
1982 Best Country Performance by a Duo or Group with Vocal: *Mountain Music*

Herb Alpert
1965 Record of the Year; Best Instrumental Performance, Non-Jazz: "A Taste of Honey" (with the Tijuana Brass)
1966 Best Instrumental Performance (Other Than Jazz): "What Now My Love" (with the Tijuana Brass)
1979 Best Pop Instrumental Performance: "Rise"

Amazing Rhythm Aces
1976 Best Country Vocal Performance by a Duo or Group: "The End Is Not in Sight (The Cowboy Tune)"

America
1972 Best New Artist of the Year

Asleep at the Wheel
1978 Best Country Instrumental Performance: "One O'Clock Jump"

Chet Atkins
1967 Best Instrumental Performance: *Chet Atkins Picks the Best*
1970 Best Country Instrumental Performance: *Me and Jerry* (with Jerry Reed)
1971 "Snowbird"
1974 *The Atkins-Travis Traveling Show* (with Merle Travis)
1975 "The Entertainer"
1976 *Chester and Lester* (with Les Paul)
1981 *Country—After All These Years*

immensely popular in their country—attracted considerable attention in Europe and America.

Contemporary African musicians have, from time to time, been accepted into the American mainstream. South African singer Miriam Makeba and trumpeter Hugh Masekela put "Pata Pata" and "Grazing in the Grass," respectively, on AM radio in the mid Sixties. Osibisa, a predominantly Ghanaian band, sold around 100,000 copies of each of their first two albums to Americans in the early Seventies. A couple of years later, Cameroonian saxophonist Manu Dibango made a prototypical disco hit with "Soul Makossa." African musicians perform fairly frequently in the more cosmopolitan American cities.

AIR SUPPLY
Formed 1976, Australia
Graham Russell (b. June 1, 1950, Eng.), voc., gtr.;
Russell Hitchcock (b. June 15, 1949, Melbourne), voc.;
Ralph Cooper (b. April 6, 1951, Coffs Harbour, Austral.), drums; David Moyse (b. Nov. 5, 1957, Adelaide), gtr.; David Green (b. Oct. 30, 1949, Melbourne), bass;
Rex Goh (b. May 5, 1951, Singapore), gtr.; Frank Esler-Smith (b. June 5, 1948, London), kybds.
1980—Lost in Love (Arista) 1981—The One That You Love 1982—Now and Forever.

Air Supply is an Australian group whose light pop-rock hits have earned them several gold LPs and singles worldwide. The group originally consisted of lead vocalists Russell Hitchcock and Graham Russell, backed by studio musicians. As such, they had several hit singles in Australia, including "Love and Other Bruises" (1976), "Empty Pages" and "Do What You Do" (both 1977), and two gold albums. After forming a band to record their third LP, they came up with one of the U.S.'s biggest hits in 1979, "Lost in Love" (#3, 1979). A string of Top Ten hits followed: "Every Woman to Me" (#5, 1980), "The One That You Love" (#1, 1981) and "Even the Nights Are Better" (#6, 1982). Russell does the bulk of Air Supply's songwriting.

LAUREL AITKEN
Born Cuba

Cuban-born Laurel Aitken emigrated to Jamaica in the early Fifties and began recording in the incipient local record industry. His records were popular throughout the West Indies and eventually reached Britain when his 1953 single "Little Sheila" (on Melodisc Records) became the first Jamaican record issued in the U.K. Subsequent releases in a variety of styles (the bluebeat of "Bartender," the old-fashioned gospel of "Daniel Saw the Stone") were popular among England's West Indian immigrants, and in the early Sixties, Aitken moved to London.

As one of the stars of Melodisc's Bluebeat label (a specialty line catering to the transplanted West Indian population), Aitken—along with Prince Buster, Derrick Morgan and others on Bluebeat—pioneered ska in England. Songs such as "Bugaboo," "You Was Up," "Fire in Your Wire" and "The Rise and Fall of Laurel Aitken"—distinguished by Aitken's low, gruff voice and unabashed sexual humor—popularized ska with British white youth while fomenting a sub-genre of ska called "rude" songs, with lyrics as brash and raucous as the music. Occasional tracks in a serious vein, such as "Lion of Judah," "Judgment Day" and "Landlords and Tenants," proved Aitken could appeal to other than prurient interests, but one of his biggest hits, "Pussy Price" in 1968, was as rude a song as has ever been recorded.

ALABAMA
Formed 1969, Fort Payne, Alabama
Jeff Cook (b. Aug. 27, 1949, Fort Payne), gtr., fiddle, voc.; Randy Owen (b. Dec. 13, 1949, Fort Payne), gtr., voc.; Teddy Gentry (b. Jan. 22, 1952, Fort Payne), bass, voc.; Mark Herndon (b. May 11, 1955, Springfield, Mass.), drums.
N.A.—Wild Country (LSI) Deuces Wild; Alabama 3
1980—My Home's in Alabama (RCA) 1981—Feels So Right 1982—Mountain Music.

Alabama was one of the biggest-selling country-rock groups of the early Eighties with a string of hit singles and LPs. The group was originally formed as a trio in 1969 by cousins Jeff Cook, Randy Owen and Teddy Gentry in their hometown. Then known as Young Country, they performed on weekends at a local amusement park, Canyonland. In 1973, they moved to Myrtle Beach, South Carolina, and there, with drummer Rich Scott, began playing their own songs in clubs. By this time, they had changed their name to Alabama.

After a few self-produced singles, they signed with GRT Records in 1977. Their first release, "I Want to Be with You," made the country Top 100, but subsequent releases failed to match even that standing. In 1979, they went to MDJ Records of Dallas, but before they began to record, Scott left and was replaced by Mark Herndon. Their first MDJ single, "I Wanna Come Over," reached #32 on the country charts in 1980, and its follow-up, "My Home's in Alabama," made #17. Their first RCA single, "Tennessee River," hit #1 in 1980. Their debut album went gold; their second album, platinum.

ALESSI
Billy and Bobby Alessi born 1954, Long Island, New York
1977—Alessi (A&M) 1978—All for a Reason; Driftin'
1979—Words and Music 1982—Long Time Friends
(Warner Bros.).

Identical twins Billy and Bobby Alessi grew up on Long Island, where as children they taught each other to play guitar, and during their teens played in a number of amateur bands. While still in high school, the two worked as jingle writers for Lucas and McFaul; the Mellow Yellow song is theirs. After studying theater for two years at Nassau Community College, they both got roles in the Broadway play *Hair*. There they met fellow cast member Peppy Castro, who persuaded them to form a band with him. That group, Barnaby Bye, lasted three years and recorded only two albums, but enjoyed something of a cult following in the New York area. In 1977, the pair left to perform as a duo. Prolific songwriters, the Alessis supported themselves on their compositions, which have been recorded by Olivia Newton-John, Peter Frampton, Richie Havens and Frankie Valli.

With the release of their 1977 debut album, the Alessis became international teen idols and "O Lori" went to the Top Ten in Europe. But that success was not matched in the States and was never repeated. After three more albums, the duo returned to jingle writing and only recorded their songs to circulate them among other artists and music publishers. One tape made for that purpose attracted the interest of Michael Ostin and Quincy Jones, who, along with Christopher Cross, produced Alessi's Warner Bros. comeback in 1982.

ARTHUR ALEXANDER
Born 1942, Sheffield, Alabama
1962—*You Better Move On* (Dot) 1972—*Arthur Alexander* (Warner Bros.).

Country-soul vocalist Arthur Alexander wrote and recorded the 1962 hit "You Better Move On." He began singing in church as a child, and during his teens belonged to a group called the Heartstrings. In 1961, he was working a day job as a bellhop and recording occasionally. Early the next year, his song "You Better Move On" hit #24 on the pop charts. Not only was it Alexander's first and most successful single, but the first hit to come out of Rick Hall's Muscle Shoals studios. Dot Records unwisely attempted to market Alexander as a pop singer, and such follow-up releases as the Barry Mann–Cynthia Weil composition "Where Have You Been (All My Life)" and his own "Anna (Go to Him)" (both 1962) were well sung but commercially unsuccessful.

His records had more impact in England, though; and his songs were later recorded by the Beatles, the Rolling Stones and the Bee Gees. In 1972, Alexander's eponymous album on Warner Bros. drew critical kudos but low sales. A few years later, he reentered the pop charts with "Everyday I Have to Cry Some" (#45, 1975).

LEE ALLEN
Born July 2, 1926, Pittsburg, Kansas
1958—*Walkin' with Mr. Lee* (Ember).

Although the closest Lee Allen ever came to getting a hit for himself was "Walking with Mr. Lee" (#54, 1958), his tenor saxophone session performances and arrangements were integral to numerous hits by Fats Domino, Little Richard and others who recorded in New Orleans in the Fifties and early Sixties. He first performed professionally with Paul Gayten's band, one of the pioneer New Orleans R&B bands, in the early Fifties. In 1956, he joined Dave Bartholomew's band, which recorded and toured with Fats Domino during Domino's peak years. At that time Allen also worked as a session musician and arranger; he and baritone saxophonist Alvin "Red" Tyler led New Orleans' most in-demand session ensemble, the Studio Band, which included drummers Earl Palmer and Charles "Hungry" Williams, guitarists Ernest McLean and Justin Adams, pianists Salvador Doucette, Edward Frank and Allen Toussaint, bassist Frank "Dude" Fields and trumpeter Melvin Lastie.

Bumps Blackwell hired the Studio Band to back Little Richard on some of his hit records—"Tutti Frutti," "Long Tall Sally," "The Girl Can't Help It" and others. Allen also played behind Shirley and Lee ("Let the Good Times Roll"), Huey Smith and the Clowns ("Rockin' Pneumonia and the Boogie Woogie Flu"), Sam Cooke, Lowell Fulson, Charles Brown and Jimmy Clanton.

In 1957, Allen signed a solo contract with Herald Records. His first single was "Walking with Mr. Lee," a #1 hit in New Orleans, followed by "Tic Toc" and a tour of the U.S. in the late Fifties. He then returned to the New Orleans studios to work for $42 per session on hit records that sold millions of copies. He retired in the early Sixties, but returned in 1982 to tour with the Blasters.

PETER ALLEN
Born February 10, 1944, Tenterfield, Australia
1971—*Peter Allen* (Metromedia) 1972—*Tenterfield Saddler* 1974—*Continental American* (A&M) 1976—*Taught by Experts* 1977—*It's Time for Peter Allen* 1979—*I Could Have Been a Sailor* 1980—*Bi-Coastal* 1982—*The Best*.

Singer/songwriter/pianist Peter Allen became a popular cabaret-style performer in the late Seventies. He began playing piano and singing in local clubs at age eleven; within three years he was performing the day's rock hits in hotels. By his eighteenth birthday, he'd left school for Sydney, where he met Chris Bell (who changed his last name to Allen). Together the duo toured the world as Chris and Peter Allen. Judy Garland saw them perform in Hong Kong and hired them as her opening act. The duo made twenty appearances on "The Tonight Show" and toured the U.S. In 1964, Allen and Garland's daughter, Liza Minnelli, were engaged; they married in 1967. In 1970, the couple separated on the same day that Allen broke up his partnership with Chris Bell (Allen and Minnelli were divorced in 1973).

Allen recorded two albums for Metromedia (*Peter Allen* and *Tenterfield Saddler)*, both of which attracted favorable reviews but sold poorly. His big break came in 1974, when a song he cowrote, "I Honestly Love You," became a #1 hit for Olivia Newton-John and later won a Grammy for Best Record. Allen has since recorded several hits including "I Go to Rio" (a minor U.S. hit, but #1 in France and Australia) and "Six-Thirty Sunday Morning." In 1981, Allen was one of four cowriters (including Burt Bacharach and Carole Bayer Sager) of the Grammy Award–winning theme song from the movie *Arthur*, "The Best That You Can Do," a #1 hit for Christopher Cross. Allen tours internationally, and in 1981 he did a series of shows in New York's Radio City Music Hall with the Rockettes. He resides in Tenterfield, Australia. A waltz he wrote, "I Still Call Australia Home," is popular there.

LUTHER ALLISON

Born August 17, 1939, Mayflower, Arkansas
1969—*Love Me Mama* (Delmark) 1974—*Luther's Blues* (Gordy) 1975—*Night Life* (Motown) N.A.—*Bad News Is Coming* (Gordy).

Blues guitarist Luther Allison is part of the generation of electric blues guitarists that came of age in the Sixties and was able to appeal both to old-line blues audiences and to younger, white rock audiences. Before he was ten years old, he sang with a gospel group, the Southern Travellers, on tours through the South. He moved with his family to Chicago around 1951 and took up guitar. He first performed as a blues guitarist with his elder brother's band, which played Chicago clubs between 1954 and 1957, then formed his own, the Rolling Stones, later renamed the Four Jivers, which lasted a year.

For the next ten years, Allison was a mainstay of the Chicago blues scene, often playing in the bands of Freddie King and Magic Sam. He made his first records for Delmark in 1967, the same year he took to the road with his group, the Tornados. In 1968, he toured and recorded for World Pacific with Shakey Jake, and began making annual appearances at the Ann Arbor Blues and Jazz Festival. In 1970, he began playing rock venues like San Francisco's Fillmore West, Los Angeles' Whiskey-a-Go-Go, and New York's Fillmore East and Max's Kansas City. In 1975, Allison recorded for Motown Records, and the following year cut the soundtrack to *Cooley High*. He toured Europe in 1976 and 1977.

MOSE ALLISON

Born November 11, 1927, Tippo, Mississippi
N.A.—*Allison* (Prestige) *Best of* (Atco).

Singer/pianist Mose Allison has been popular in jazz circles for over twenty years, and he is known in rock for his songs, which have been covered by the Who ("A Young Man Blues"), Bonnie Raitt ("Everybody's Cryin' Mercy"), John Mayall ("Parchman Farm") and many others. Allison began playing piano at age six, and later

took up the trumpet. He absorbed both jazz and country blues, and when he arrived in New York City in the late Fifties he played piano with "cool" jazzmen Al Cohn, Stan Getz, Gerry Mulligan and Zoot Sims, blending the simplicity of the blues with modernist harmonies. He began to sing in 1957, when he formed his own trio, and his understated and laconically cynical songs have been periodically rediscovered by the rock audience.

THE ALLMAN BROTHERS BAND

Formed 1968, Macon, Georgia
Duane Allman (b. Nov. 20, 1946, Nashville; d. Oct. 29, 1971, Macon, Ga.), gtr.; Gregg Allman (b. Dec. 8, 1947, Nashville), kybds., gtr., voc.; Berry Oakley (b. Apr. 4, 1948, Chicago; d. Nov. 11, 1972, Macon, Ga.), bass; Dickey Betts (b. Dec. 12, 1943, West Palm Beach), gtr., voc.; Jai Johanny Johanson, a.k.a. Jaimoe (b. John Lee Johnson, July 8, 1944, Ocean Springs, Miss.), drums; Butch Trucks (b. Jacksonville), drums.
1969—*The Allman Brothers Band* (Capricorn) 1970—*Idlewild South* 1971—*At Fillmore East* 1972—(− D. Allman) *Eat a Peach* (+ Chuck Leavell, kybds.; − Oakley; + Lamar Williams [b. 1947; d. Jan. 1983, Los Angeles], bass) 1973—*Brothers and Sisters* 1974—*Beginnings* 1975—*Win, Lose or Draw; The Road Goes on Forever* 1976—*Wipe the Windows—Check the Oil—Dollar Gas* 1978—(− Leavell; − Williams; + Dan Toler, gtr.; + Rook Goldflies, bass) 1979—*Enlightened Rogues* 1980—*Reach for the Sky* (Arista) 1981—*Brothers of the Road* 1982—(+ Leavell; − Johanson).

The Allman Brothers Band blended strains of Southern music—blues, R&B, country and gospel—into a flexible, jam-oriented style that reflected the emergence of the "New South" and set the style for Lynyrd Skynyrd, the Marshall Tucker Band and many other Southern rockers.

Brothers Gregg and Duane Allman formed the Kings in Daytona Beach, Florida, in 1960 and played in various bands until 1965, when they formed the Allman Joys. After their version of Willie Dixon's "Spoonful" failed as a single, the two brothers and two other band members went to Los Angeles, where they signed with Liberty Records as the Hourglass. They recorded two albums of outside material (*Hourglass*, 1967 and *Power of Love*, 1968) before moving to Muscle Shoals, Alabama, to record at Fame Studios. Liberty rejected the resulting tapes, and Duane and Gregg returned to Florida.

Soon after they returned to Jacksonville in 1968, the two brothers joined the 31st of February, whose drummer was Butch Trucks. While preparing to record an album, Gregg was called back to Los Angeles to make good on the Liberty contract. (A 1973 Polydor album called *Duane and Gregg* consisted of demos made by the 31st of February.) While Duane stayed in Jacksonville, Gregg began

The Allman Brothers: Butch Trucks, Dickey Betts, Berry Oakley, Duane Allman, Gregg Allman, Jaimoe Johanny Johanson

playing with the Second Coming, which included Dickey Betts and Berry Oakley, veterans of Tommy Roe and the Romans. But before Duane became an established member of the Second Coming, Fame Studios owner Rick Hall asked him to return to Muscle Shoals to play lead guitar for a Wilson Pickett session. At Duane's suggestion, Pickett recorded Lennon and McCartney's "Hey Jude." Duane became Fame's primary session guitarist, recording over the next year with Aretha Franklin, King Curtis, Percy Sledge, Clarence Carter and Arthur Conley.

Atlantic's vice-president Jerry Wexler signed Duane to a solo agreement, and Allman assembled a group. He hired Jai Johanny Johanson, a Muscle Shoals drummer who had worked with Otis Redding, Percy Sledge, Joe Tex and Clifton Chenier. He went back to Florida and reconvened Trucks, Oakley, Betts and Gregg. Once assembled, the Allman Brothers Band moved to Macon, Georgia, where Phil Walden was setting up Capricorn Records.

The Allman Brothers Band, their debut LP, was well received only in the South. After its release, Duane continued to play on sessions with Boz Scaggs, Laura Nyro, Otis Rush, Delaney and Bonnie, Ronnie Hawkins and John Paul Hammond. He appears with Eric Clapton on Derek and the Dominos' *Layla.* (His session work is collected on *Anthology, volumes 1 and 2.*)

On the strength of a growing reputation as a live band, the Allmans' second album sold well. In March 1971, a concert at New York's Fillmore East was recorded for release as a live double LP set in July. By the time the album reached the Top Ten, the Allman Brothers Band was being hailed in print as "America's best rock & roll group."

But on October 29, 1971, less than three months after *At Fillmore East*'s release, Duane was killed in a motorcycle accident in Macon. The group played at his funeral and decided to continue without a new guitarist. Three songs on their next LP, *Eat a Peach,* had been recorded before Duane's death, and with live material from the March Fillmore East concert, the double LP was released in February, entered the charts in the Top Ten and rose to #4. In 1972, Oakley was killed in a motorcycle crash three blocks from the site of Duane's accident a year earlier. Lamar Williams took Oakley's place.

Dickey Betts, by then the band's unofficial leader, wrote and sang "Ramblin' Man," the band's first and biggest hit single (#2, 1973); *Brothers and Sisters* went to #1. Reissued as *Beginnings,* the first two albums more than doubled their original sales. The group returned to the road after two years (with Leavell on keyboards, Gregg joined Betts for the twin guitar lines). In Watkins Glen, New York, 600,000 people gathered in July 1973 for an all-day concert by the Allman Brothers Band, the Grateful Dead and the Band.

There was growing dissension in the group, however. Gregg and Betts began to disagree over schedules and musical direction. In 1974, they each recorded a solo album (Allman's *Laid Back* and Betts's *Highway Call*), and Allman formed the Gregg Allman Band with Johanson, Leavell, Williams and others to tour and record *The Gregg Allman Tour.* The subsequent Allman Brothers Band album, *Win, Lose or Draw,* sold well, but it was four years before the next album of new material; *The Road Goes on Forever* and *Wipe the Windows* are both live collections. By 1975, Allman was involved in an on-again, off-again marriage to Cher. They had a son, Elijah Blue, in 1976.

But the greatest blow to the group occurred in 1976, when Allman testified against Scooter Herring, his personal road manager, charged with dealing narcotics. He was subsequently sentenced to 75 years in prison. Allman's action, the others said, betrayed the fraternal loyalty that had sustained them; they vowed never to work with him again.

Betts formed Great Southern, duplicating the original Allman Brothers lineup with two guitars, two drums, bass and keyboards and vocals. *Dickey Betts and Great Southern* was released in 1977, *Atlanta's Burning Down* in 1978. Gregg and Cher Allman, billed as Allman and Woman, released *Two the Hard Way* in 1977. Allman then regrouped the Gregg Allman Band, with no help from any former Brothers, and put out *Playin' Up a Storm* in 1977. The other members also remained active: Trucks studied music at Florida State University for two years and formed an experimental group, Trucks. Leavell, Williams and Johanson, with guitarist Jimmy Nalls, formed the fusion-oriented Sea Level.

In 1978, the Allman Brothers Band regrouped. After Allman, Trucks and Johanson joined Betts and Great Southern onstage in New York in 1978, Great Southern guitarist Dan Toler and bassist Rook Goldflies also joined the new Allman Brothers Band. *Enlightened Rogues* was gold within two weeks of its release. 1981's *Brothers of the Road* gave the group a minor hit single, "Straight from the Heart." In 1983 Lamar Williams died of cancer.

HERB ALPERT

Born March 31, 1937, Los Angeles
1962—*The Lonely Bull* (A&M) **1963**—*Herb Alpert's Tijuana Brass, volume 2* **1964**—*South of the Border* **1965**—*Whipped Cream & Other Delights; Going Places* **1966**—*What Now, My Love; S.R.O.* **1967**—*Sounds Like; Herb Alpert's Ninth* **1968**—*The Beat of the Brass; Christmas Album* **1969**—*Warm; The Brass Are Comin'* **1970**—*Greatest Hits* **1971**—*Summertime* **1972**—*Solid Brass* **1973**—*Four Sider* **1974**—*You Smile—The Song Begins* **1975**—*Coney Island* **1976**—*Just You and Me* **1978**—*Herb Alpert and Hugh Masekela* (Horizon) **1979**—*Rise* (A&M) **1980**—*Beyond* **1981**—*Magic Man* **1982**—*Fandango*.

Herb Alpert rose to fame in the mid-Sixties as the king of South of the Border MOR, or as it was called, "Ameriachi." Alpert has since become a music industry force, both as a performer (he's sold more instrumental records than any artist in history) and as cofounder and vice-chairman of A&M Records.

Alpert was raised in L.A. and began playing trumpet at age eight. After returning from the Army, he had a brief acting career and then recorded as Dore Alpert for RCA. During the late Fifties, he produced Jan and Dean, and with songwriting partner Lou Adler recorded a cover version of the Hollywood Argyles' "Alley Oop" under the name Dante and the Evergreens. In 1962, he and Jerry Moss (b. 1946) founded A&M Records. A shoestring operation out of Alpert's garage on Westbourne Drive in L.A., A&M eventually became the nation's largest independent record company, largely on the strength of Alpert's Tijuana Brass hits such as "The Lonely Bull" (#6, 1962), "A Taste of Honey" (#7, 1965) and "The Mexican Shuffle" (#85, 1964), later used in chewing gum commercials as the "Teaberry Shuffle." In 1965, the group had five LPs in the Top Twenty and in 1966 sold 13 million records.

Around 1969, Alpert stopped performing and turned his attentions to overseeing A&M. He returned to the charts in 1979 with the biggest record of his career, "Rise." It was only Alpert's second #1 hit, the other being a rare vocal outing, 1968's "This Guy's in Love with You."

ALPHA BAND

Formed July 1976, Tesuque, New Mexico
Steven Soles (b. New York City), gtr., voc.; David Mansfield (b. N.J.), gtr., mandolin, voc.; T-Bone Burnett (b. St. Louis), gtr., voc.; David Jackson, bass. **1977**—*Alpha Band* (Arista) (− Jackson; + David

Miner [b. Los Angeles], bass; + Billy Maxwell [b. Oklahoma City]; + Matt Betton, drums) *Spark in the Dark* **1978**—*Statue Makers of Hollywood*.

The Alpha Band were so genuinely eccentric and joyfully eclectic—borrowing from every American pop style, especially the Southwest's blues, swing and rockabilly—that their born-again Christianity was rarely obtrusive. The band's core—Steven Soles, David Mansfield and T-Bone Burnett—played together as part of Bob Dylan's Rolling Thunder Revue in 1975; they reportedly influenced Dylan's conversion to Christianity. Before the Revue, Burnett had lived in Fort Worth, and he worked as a producer in Los Angeles with Delbert (McClinton) and Glen. After a short stint with Delaney and Bonnie Bramlett, he joined B52, whose tour led him to New York and Rolling Thunder. Soles (who claims to have kissed Marilyn Monroe when he was nine) worked with Happy and Artie Traum and Eric Kaz in Bear, who did the soundtrack for Brian de Palma's film *Greetings* (1968). He also worked as a staff songwriter for Jeff Barry and backed up Melvin van Peebles. The classically trained Mansfield was a member of Quacky Duck and His Barnyard Friends, who released one Warner Bros. album. After the Revue, the three stayed together and picked up a rhythm section. They recorded three albums (Ringo Starr appears on *Spark in the Dark*), toured the U.S., and performed a series of acoustic-instrument concerts live in radio stations around the country, but they broke up in 1979. Burnett released two solo efforts, *Truth Decay* on Takoma in 1980 and an EP, *Trap Door*, on Warner Bros. in 1982. Mansfield wrote the score for and appeared in Michael Cimino's *Heaven's Gate* (1981).

AMAZING RHYTHM ACES

Formed 1974, Knoxville
Russell Smith (b. Lafayette, Tenn.), gtr., harm., voc.; Butch McDade (b. Tenn.), drums, voc.; Jeff Davis (b. Tenn.), bass; Billy Earhart (b. Tenn.), kybds.; James Hooker (b. Tenn.), kybds., voc.; Barry "Byrd" Burton, gtr., dobro, mandolin, voc., pedal steel gtr. **1975**—*Stacked Deck* (ABC) **1976**—*Too Stuffed to Jump; Toucan Do It, Too* **1978**—*Burning the Ballroom Down* **1979**—*Amazing Rhythm Aces* (− Byrd; + Duncan Cameron, gtr., voc.) **1980**—*How Do You Spell Rhythm* (Warner Bros.).

The country-rock Amazing Rhythm Aces were formed as an informal assemblage headed by guitarist/lead singer/main songwriter Russell Smith, who had learned how to sing country blues while working as a teenage disc jockey on station WEEN in his native Lafayette. The group was temporarily sidetracked in the early Seventies when several members joined Jesse Winchester's backup band, but they then regrouped. Their debut, *Stacked Deck*, featured a mixture of country, gospel, rock and bluegrass and yielded a hit single, "Third Rate Romance" (#14, 1975). Despite continuous touring, however, that success was never repeated, even though subsequent efforts like "The End Is Not in Sight" (1976) and "Amazing Grace (Used to Be Her Favorite Song)" (1976) placed on the country charts. The band has had a turbulent managerial history; in 1979, their album *Amazing Rhythm Aces* appeared first on ABC, then on Columbia when their contract changed hands. In early 1982, Smith released a self-titled solo album on Capitol Records.

AMBROSIA
Formed 1971, Southern California
David Pack (b. 1952), gtr., voc.; Joe Puerta (b. 1952), bass, voc.; Burleigh Drummond (b. 1952), drums, voc.; Christopher North (b. 1952), kybds., voc.
1975—*Ambrosia* (20th Century–Fox) **1976**—*Somewhere I've Never Travelled* (Warner Bros.) **1978**—(– North) *Life Beyond L.A.* **1980**—*One Eighty* **1982**—*Road Island*.

Ambrosia play pop with classical flourishes and are best known for their late-Seventies hit singles. The group was formed in 1971 in the Los Angeles area. David Pack and Joe Puerta met in high school and were later joined by Burleigh Drummond and Christopher North. Three months later, while helping check a new sound system in the Hollywood Bowl, Gordon Parry heard them play and arranged for them to perform at UCLA. Parry arranged for Los Angeles Philharmonic conductor Zubin Mehta to attend the performance, and Mehta then invited the group to participate in his All American Dream Concert in the Hollywood Bowl soon thereafter. In 1973, Ambrosia performed in the debut of Leonard Bernstein's *Mass* at the Kennedy Center for the Performing Arts in Washington, D.C.

The four members play a total of 72 instruments, and their songs often contain literary allusions such as "Nice, Nice, Very Nice," a line from Kurt Vonnegut's *Cat's Cradle*. The group contributed to the soundtrack of *All This and World War II*. Their hit singles include "Holdin' on to Yesterday" (#17, 1975), "How Much I Feel" (#3, 1978), "You're the Only Woman" (#13, 1980) and "Biggest Part of Me" (#3, 1980).

AMEN CORNER
Formed 1966, Cardiff, Wales
Andy Fairweather-Low (b. 1948), voc., gtr.; Neil Jones, gtr.; Blue Weaver, organ; Clive Tayler, bass; Dennis Byron, drums; Allen Jones, baritone sax; Mike Smith, sax.
1968—*Round Amen Corner* (Deram) **1969**—*National Welsh Coast Live* (Immediate) *Farewell Magnificent Seven World of Amen Corner* (Decca) **1975**—*Amen Corner and Small Faces* (New World) **1976**—*Return of the Magnificent Seven* (Immediate) **1978**—*Greatest Hits*.

Amen Corner was one of the last British mod bands. Led by Andy Fairweather-Low, they had their first British Top Twenty hit in 1967 with "Gin House," an R&B song, and subsequent hits included a cover of the American Breed's "Bend Me, Shape Me" and "High in the Sky," both of which went Top Ten in 1968. Their only #1 hit came in 1969 with "(If Paradise Is) Half as Nice"; "Hello Suzie" was a Top Five hit later that year.

Their label, Immediate, folded at the height of the group's popularity, and without a commercial outlet Amen Corner was overhauled, the two horn players were dropped, and the name was changed to Fairweather. They had a 1970 Top Five single with "Natural Sinner," but disbanded soon thereafter. Byron played briefly with the Bee Gees, and Weaver worked with the Strawbs. Fairweather-Low went on a sabbatical of several years before beginning a solo career in 1974.

AMERICA
Formed 1969, England
Dewey Bunell (b. Jan. 19, 1952, Yorkshire, Eng.), gtr., voc., drums; Dan Peek (b. 1950, Fla.), gtr., voc.; Gerry Beckley (b. Sep. 12, 1952, Tex.), gtr., voc.
1971—*America* (Warner Bros.) **1972**—*Horse with No Name; Homecoming* **1973**—*Hat Trick* **1974**—*Holiday* **1975**—*Hearts; History* (greatest hits) **1976**—*Hideaway Harbor* **1977**—*Live* (– Peek) **1980**—*Alibi* (Capitol) **1982**—*View from the Ground*.

America was one of the most popular American folk-rock groups of the early Seventies. Sons of U.S. servicemen stationed in England, America's members were schoolmates in London's Central High when they began composing and performing together. Three years later "A Horse with No Name" hit #1 in March 1972, followed a month later by their debut LP. A string of gold and platinum singles ("I Need You," #9, 1972; "Ventura Highway," #8, 1972; "Tin Man," #4, 1974; "Sister Golden Hair," #1, 1975; "Lonely People," #5, 1975) and albums (*Harbor, Hat Trick, Hearts, Hideaway*) followed.

America's sound featured breezy acoustic guitars, high vocal harmonies and smooth production; since *Holiday*, their producer has been George Martin. After Peek's departure in May 1977 (he has since become a born-again Christian), America continued as a duo, but with less success. In late 1981, the pair was the subject of controversy when they toured South Africa, ignoring the "cultural boycott" of that country that the United Nations had instituted to protest the nation's apartheid policies. In 1982, they returned to the Top Ten with "You Can Do Magic."

THE AMERICAN BREED

Formed 1966, Chicago

Al Ciner (b. May 14, 1947, Chicago), gtr.; Gary Loizzo (b. Aug. 16, 1945, Chicago), gtr., voc.; Lee Graziano (b. Nov. 9, 1943, Chicago), drums; Charles Colbert (b. Aug. 30, 1944, Chicago), bass; later added Kevin Murphy, kybds.

1967—*American Breed* (Dot)   1968—*Bend Me, Shape Me;   Pumpkin, Powder, Scarlet and Green* (Atlantic) *Lonely Side of the City.*

With five hit singles in 1967 and 1968, the American Breed were one of Chicago's top pop bands. Originally called Gary and the Nite Lights, they became favorites at local dances and recorded one unsuccessful single for MGM entitled "I Don't Think You Know Me." After signing with Acta, a Dot subsidiary, they changed their name to the American Breed and rereleased the song, thus beginning a short but successful string of hits including "Step Out of Your Mind" (#24, 1967), "Green Light" (#39, 1968) and the song for which they are best remembered, "Bend Me, Shape Me" (#1, 1968). Following their peak years, Kevin Murphy, along with Andre Fischer (a later member) and Chaka Khan founded Rufus in 1972.

AMON DUUL II

Formed 1968, Munich, Germany

Permanent members: Renate Knaup-Kroetenschwanz, voc.; John Weinzierl, gtr., voc.; Chris Karrer, gtr., saxes, violin. Sometime members: Dave Anderson, bass; Falk U. Rogner, kybds., synth.; Peter Leopold, drums; Lothar Meid, bass; Karl-Heinz Hausmann, kybds.; Danny Fischelscher, drums; David Heibl, bass; Olaf Kubler, sax.

1969—*Phallus Dei* (Liberty)   1970—*Yeti*   1971—*Dance of the Lemmings* (United Artists)   1972—*Carnival in Babylon;   Wolf City*   1973—*Live in London;   Lemmingmania*   1974—*Vive la Trance;   Hi Jack* (Atlantic) 1975—*Made in Germany* (Atco). (These are the U.S. releases only; other releases in France and Germany.)

With their doomsday visions, heavy deployment of electronic gadgetry and touches of the avant-garde, Amon Duul II was the first German rock group to make an impression on the rest of Europe. The band originated in a counterculture commune outside Munich. In 1968, they split into two factions: the more politicized Amon Duul I, which made one album before disbanding, and the more musically adventurous Amon Duul II. With Knaup-Kroetenschwanz, Weinzierl, and Karrer forming the nucleus, and a constantly shifting auxiliary personnel, Amon Duul II made nearly a dozen albums.

ERIC ANDERSEN

Born February 14, 1943, Pittsburgh

1965—*Today Is the Highway* (Vanguard)   1966—*'Bout Changes 'n' Things*   1968—*'Bout Changes 'n' Things, Take 2;   More Hits from Tin Can Alley;   A Country Dream*   1969—*Avalanche* (Warner Bros.)   1970—*Eric Andersen*   1971—*The Best of Eric Andersen* (Vanguard)   1973—*Blue River* (Columbia)   1974—*Stages* 1975—*Be True to You* (Arista)   1976—*Sweet Surprise!*   1977—*The Best Songs.*

Folksinger/songwriter Eric Andersen was active in Cambridge, Massachusetts, and Greenwich Village folk circles in the mid-Sixties. He is best known for his compositions like "Thirsty Boots," "Violets of Dawn," "Be True to You" and "Is It Really Love At All." Andersen, who began playing guitar at age eight, attended Hobart College in Geneva, New York. He traveled (via freight car) to the West Coast in search of a music publishing deal; nothing developed and he returned East. While living in Cambridge in 1963, he became part of the burgeoning folk scene (which then included Joan Baez, Bob Dylan, Richard and Mimi Fariña) and met folksinger and club owner Deborah Green, whom he later married. In 1964, he moved to Greenwich Village, where he performed at Gerde's Folk City and the Gaslight Cafe, garnering enthusiastic reviews in the *New York Times* and elsewhere. Several days after his arrival, he had secured a recording contract with Vanguard Records.

With the 1965 release of his debut album and his frequent appearances in New York and at the Newport and Cambridge folk festivals, Andersen became established on the folk circuit. Though he has never had a hit single, most of his albums have been well received, particularly *Blue River*, his best-selling album to date. Release of the long-awaited followup to *Blue River* was delayed when the master tapes were lost; by the time they were found, Andersen had rerecorded the entire album and signed to Arista. He continues to tour. Among the artists who have recorded his songs are Judy Collins; Peter, Paul and Mary; Merrilee Rush; Joan Baez; and Johnny Cash.

LAURIE ANDERSON

Born 1947, Chicago

1982—*Big Science* (Warner Bros.).

Avant-garde performance artist Laurie Anderson had a British pop hit with her 1981 recording "O Superman" (b/w "Walk the Dog"). Like all her music, "O Superman" was just one aspect of a larger multimedia oeuvre—in this case a seven-hour work in four parts called *United States,* which premiered early in 1983. With background music performed on various electronic keyboard instruments and woodwinds, and Anderson's speaking and singing voice (sometimes also electronically treated), "O Superman" was one of the year's more unusual hits.

Anderson studied violin through her teens, and moved from Chicago to New York in 1967. She earned a BA in art history from Barnard College in 1969 and an MFA in sculpture from Columbia University in 1972. She then taught art history and Egyptian architecture at City College. Anderson's works incorporate graphics, sculpture, film, slides, lighting, music, mime and spoken and printed language. She claims that all her pieces are based on words and their declamation. In 1973, she began giving public performances of her works, and by 1976 she was performing in museums, concert halls and art festivals around the United States and in Europe. "O Superman" sold over 30,000 copies in Europe in 1981, reaching #2 in Britain, and Anderson signed for an album with Warner Bros. The American response to the single was considerably milder. In 1982, Warner Bros. released her debut album, *Big Science*.

ANGEL

Formed 1975, Washington, D.C.
Frank DiMino (b. Oct. 15, 1951, Boston), voc.; Greg Giuffria (b. July 28, 1951, Gulfport, Miss.), kybds.; Punky Meadows (b. Feb. 6, 1950, Washington, D.C.), gtr.; Mickey Jones (b. Dec. 17, 1952, Washington, D.C.), bass; Barry Brandt (b. Nov. 14, 1951, Washington, D.C.), drums.
1975—*Angel* (Casablanca) 1976—*Helluva Band* 1977—*On Earth As It Is in Heaven* (– Jones; + Felix Robinson [b. ca. 1952], bass) *White Hot* 1979—*Sinful*.

Angel was designed as the dressed-in-white counterpart of Casablanca labelmate Kiss, but its stagy heavy metal was never blessed with comparable sales figures. Formed in 1975 from the wreckage of several East Coast bands—including Max (Mickey Jones, Barry Brandt, Frank DiMino), the Cherry People (Punky Meadows, Barry Brandt), who had recorded for MCA, and Bux (Mickey Jones, Punky Meadows), a Capitol act—Angel moved to Los Angeles, where Kiss frontman Gene Simmons introduced them to Casablanca president Neil Bogart. Enough venture capital was provided to give Angel a spectacular stage show, with lasers, flash pots and a giant holographic face (their logo) that appeared to speak as it hovered above the stage. Even package tours with Kiss failed to bring Angel's screechy heavy metal any closer to teenagers' hearts, although Frank Zappa invoked Punky Meadows' name repeatedly in "Punky's Whips," when Angel seemed to be on the verge. Angel was last heard from in the Casablanca Film Works movie *Foxes* (1979).

ANGEL CITY

Formed 1975, Australia
Doc Neeson, voc.; John Brewster, gtr., voc.; Rick Brewster, gtr.; Graham "Buzz" Bidstrup, drums; Chris Bailey, bass.
1980—*Face to Face* (Epic) *Darkroom* 1982—*Night Attack*.

Hard-rockers Angel City are a major draw in their native Australia, still seeking a U.S. audience. Doc Neeson and the Brewster brothers started the band in 1975 as a folk trio, the Moonshine Jug and String Band. A year later, they switched to electric instruments, added a drummer, changed their name to the Keystone Angels and moved from Adelaide to Sydney. Their Fifties-style rock & roll led to a stint as Chuck Berry's backup band on an Australian tour, while they worked on original material that eventually came to the attention of Australian rock magnates Harry Vanda and George Young (Easybeats). Vanda and Young produced a single and an album for the band, now calling itself the Angels. The band shifted its lineup and toured for three years, while their second album, *Face to Face*, stayed in Australia's Top 100 for 67 weeks. It became Australia's best-selling album in 1978 and fourth-best (two places below their third LP, *No Exit)* in 1979.

CBS Records (Epic in the U.S.) signed the Angels to an international contract, and released a compilation culled from their Australian albums, entitled *Face to Face*. To avoid confusion with Angel, the group added City to its name for American use. They toured the U.S. in 1980 and 1981 as an opening act for Cheap Trick and the Pretenders.

THE ANGELS

Formed 1961, Orange, New Jersey
Barbara Allbut (b. Sep. 24, 1940, Orange, N.J.), voc.; Phyllis "Jiggs" Allbut Meister (b. Sep. 24, 1942, Orange, N.J.), voc.; Linda Jansen (b. Hillside, N.J.), voc.
1962—(– Jansen; + Peggy Santiglia McGannon [b. May 4, 1944, Bellview, N.J.]) 1963—*My Boyfriend's Back* (Smash) *A Halo to You* 1970s—(– Barbara Allbut; + Lana Shan).

The Angels were one of the most successful of the early-Sixties girl groups. Originally known as the Starlits, they were formed when Barbara and Jiggs Allbut, who had sung together in high school, began doing backup vocal work in New York with Linda Jansen. After they were signed to Caprice, Jiggs dropped out of college and Barbara (who arranged the group's early records) ended her studies at the Juilliard School. Shortly before their first release, " 'Til," they drew the name Blue Angels out of a hat, then dropped the *Blue*. Their debut single went to #14 in 1961; after their third; "Cry Baby Cry" in 1962, lead vocalist Jansen left and was replaced by Peggy Santiglia, who had sung commercial jingles and appeared on Broadway in *Do Re Mi*.

After moving to Smash, they released the million-selling "My Boyfriend's Back" (#1, 1963), cowritten by producer Richard Gottehrer. After a few minor followups—"I Adore Him" (#25, 1963), "Thank You and Goodnight" (1963) and "Wow Wow Wee (He's the Boy for Me)" (1964)—the group faded from the limelight. They continued to record for RCA and Polydor until 1974. They still perform in nightclubs and at rock revival shows.

THE ANIMALS
Formed 1963, Newcastle upon Tyne, England
Alan Price (b. Apr. 19, 1942, County Durham, Eng.), kybds.; Eric Burdon (b. Apr. 5, 1941, Newcastle upon Tyne), voc.; Bryan "Chas" Chandler (b. Dec. 18, 1948, Newcastle upon Tyne), bass; John Steel (b. Feb. 4, 1941, Gateshead, Eng.), drums; Hilton Valentine (b. May 21, 1943, North Shields, Eng.), gtr.

1964—*The Animals* (MGM) **1965**—*On Tour; Animal Tracks* **1966**—*Best of the Animals; Animalization; Animalisms* (− Price; + Dave Rowberry [b. Dec. 27, 1943, Newcastle upon Tyne], kybds.; − Steel; + Barry Jenkins [b. Dec. 22, 1944, Leicester, Eng.], drums) **late 1966**—(Eric Burdon and the New Animals: − Valentine; − Chandler; − Rowberry; + Johnny Weider [b. Apr. 21, 1947, Shepherd's Bush, Eng.], gtr.; + Vic Briggs [b. Feb. 14, 1945, Twickenham, Eng.], gtr.; + Danny McCullough [b. July 18, 1945, London], gtr.) **1967**—*Eric Is Here; Best of Eric Burdon and the Animals, volume 2 Winds of Change; Twain Shall Meet; Every One of Us* (− McCullough; − Briggs) **1969**—*Love Is; The Greatest Hits of Eric Burdon and the Animals* **1975**—*Eric Burdon and the Animals* (Polydor) **1977**—*Before We Were So Rudely Interrupted* (United Artists).

Of the original British Invasion bands, the Animals were the most influenced by black American R&B rather than blues. Originally the Alan Price Combo (formed in 1958), they became the Animals shortly after the addition of lead vocalist Eric Burdon in 1962. By 1964, under the wing of U.K. producer Mickie Most, they had recorded their second single, "House of the Rising Sun," a #1 hit on both sides of the Atlantic in summer 1964.

More hits followed through 1966: "Don't Let Me Be Misunderstood" (#15, 1965), "We Gotta Get Out of This Place" (#13, 1965), "It's My Life" (#23, 1965). In late 1965, Price left the band (the result of tension between him and Burdon) for a solo career. That, and frequent drug use by members, shook the band up somewhat, but Price was replaced by Dave Rowberry, and the band had another hit ("Inside Looking Out," #34, 1966) before John Steel left. With Barry Jenkins (formerly of the Nashville Teens) replacing Steel, the band had several more hits (including the Rowberry-penned "See See Rider," #10, 1966, and "When I Was Young," #15, 1967), but by this time Chas Chandler had left (he became the Animals' and Jimi Hendrix's manager) and Hilton Valentine had gone on to pursue a solo career. Steel became Chandler's assistant.

In 1966, the group was billed as Eric Burdon and the Animals. They endorsed psychedelia with "San Franciscan Nights" (#9, 1967), "Monterey" (#15, 1968), "Sky Pilot" (#14, 1968) and "White Houses." Burdon carried on with backup by the "New Animals," an unstable lineup that briefly included future Police guitarist Andy Summers, before embarking on an intermittently successful solo career. The original Animals reunited for a Christmas show at City Hall in Newcastle in 1968. In 1969, Valentine recorded a solo album entitled *All in Your Head*. The original band reunited in 1976 to record a one-shot LP, *Before We Were So Rudely Interrupted*. In April 1983 they announced plans to reunite once more.

PAUL ANKA
Born July 30, 1941, Ottawa
1960—*Paul Anka Sings His Big 15* (ABC) *Paul Anka Sings His Big 15, volume 2* **1961**—*Anka at the Copa* **1962**—*Young, Alive and in Love* (RCA) *Let's Sit This One Out* **1963**—*Paul Anka's 21 Golden Hits* **1969**—*Goodnight My Love; Life Goes On* **1971**—*Paul Anka* (Buddah) **1972**—*Jubilation* **1974**—*Anka* (United

The Animals: John Steel, Dave Rowberry, Eric Burdon, Chas Chandler, Hilton Valentine

Artists) **1975**—*Feelings; Times of Your Life* **1976**—
The Painter **1977**—*The Music Man* **1978**—*Listen to
Your Heart* (RCA) *Paul Anka—His Best.*

Unlike most Fifties teen idols, Paul Anka was not only a
performer but a successful songwriter. After his string of
early hits ended, Anka concentrated on writing and performing more adult-oriented works, like Frank Sinatra's
theme song, "My Way." Son of a Lebanese restaurateur,
Anka began performing at age ten, singing and doing
impersonations. Four years later, Anka's father paid for a
trip to Hollywood, where, in September 1956, Anka recorded "I Confess" (backed by the Cadets) for Modern.
Anka returned to Canada and later, though underage,
worked a nightclub in Gloucester, Massachusetts. In 1957,
he won a contest for saving soup-can labels. First prize
was a trip to New York City, and in May of that year Anka
auditioned for ABC with "Diana," a song he had written
about a girl he knew. Within a year, "Diana" was a #1 hit.

Throughout his career, Anka composed many of his
hits, including "You Are My Destiny" (#7, 1958), "Crazy
Love" (#15, 1958), "Put Your Head on My Shoulder"
(#2, 1959), "Puppy Love" (#2, 1960), "Lonely Boy" (#1,
1959) and "Hello Young Lovers" (#23, 1960). In 1962, he
purchased all of his masters from ABC and signed with
RCA. Although his Top Twenty hits ended temporarily in
1962, he continued to write and record in French, German
and Italian. In 1970, he signed with Buddah. In 1974, his
controversial "(You're) Having My Baby," a duet with his
protégée Odia Coates, became his first #1 since 1959.

Over 400 of his compositions have been recorded,
including "It Don't Matter Anymore" (Buddy Holly),
"My Way" (Frank Sinatra) and "She's a Lady" (Tom
Jones). He wrote "The Tonight Show" theme and has
composed film scores for *The Longest Day* and others. He
has amassed over forty hit singles, 18 gold records and
sales in excess of 100 million.

AOR

This abbreviation stands for both "album-oriented rock"
and "album-oriented radio." The terms are interchange-
able, which in itself explains the peculiar marketing effect
of a broadcasting format that fosters a rigidly codified
musical genre, and vice versa. AOR music is played all the
time because it's popular; it remains popular because it's
played all the time. AOR grew up from the ashes of once-
"progressive" "free-form" FM radio. When FM had, by
the early Seventies, garnered enough of an audience that it
could no longer be considered "underground," it maintained commercial status by limiting the choice of music to
a certain playlist, abetted in some instances by the consul-
tations of ex–disc jockey firms like Burkhart-Abrams.

Through AOR, FM radio became almost as conservative as the AM radio of the Sixties to which FM had been
an alternative. An AOR radio station plays album cuts

rather than commercially released singles; it ultimately
renders the LP an extended single-style marketing device,
since in most cases AOR stations play only certain album
cuts in an AM-style playlist rotation.

Stylistically, AOR bands derive from the musical genres
that had found success on pre-AOR FM radio. AOR stars
like Styx, Kansas and Foreigner incorporate the high-
harmony vocals (derived by Yes from Crosby, Stills and
Nash), instrumental virtuosity, pseudoclassical keyboard
orchestrations and epic themes of British progressive
rock; REO Speedwagon trades on heavy-metal mixes; .38
Special is based in guitar-heavy Southern boogie-rock;
Toto refers to laid-back California studio rock, and Journey to San Francisco rock. Like a sponge, the AOR
format can easily include everyone from onetime new
wave artists like Blondie and the Go-Go's to pure pop
singers like Olivia Newton-John (who only a few years
earlier had been disdained by AOR's huge audience of
predominantly white adolescent males).

Usually scorned by music critics, AOR has remained a
successful sales institution through the Seventies and into
the Eighties; in the form of MTV/Music Television, the
first 24-hour cable-rock video channel, AOR even took
over "rock video."

AOR stations showed flagging ratings in the early Eighties, and consultant Lee Abrams admitted his format had
become "boring."

APRIL WINE

Formed 1970, Montreal
Lineup as of 1977: Myles Goodwyn (b. June 23, 1948,
Woodstock, Can.), piano, gtr., voc.; Gary Moffet (b.
June 22, 1949, Ottawa), gtr.; Brian Greenway (b. Oct.
1, 1951, Ontario), gtr., voc., kybds.; Steve Lang (b.
Mar. 24, 1949, Montreal), bass; Jerry Mercer (b. Apr.
27, 1939, Montreal), drums.
1970—*April Wine* (Big Tree) **1971**—*On Record*
1973—*Electric Jewels* (Aquarius) **1974**—*Live* **1975**—
Stand Back (Big Tree) **1976**—*The Whole World's Goin'
Crazy* (London) *Forever for Now* (Aquarius) **1977**—
April Wine Live at the El Macambo (London) **1979**—
First Glance (Capitol) **1980**—*Harder . . . Faster*
1981—*Nature of the Beast* **1982**—*Power Play.*

April Wine became one of the top Canadian heavy-metal
bands of the Seventies through frequent touring and a
basic hard-rock sound. They earned ten gold LPs in
Canada and are one of the few acts ever to have a
Canadian release, *The Whole World's Goin' Crazy,*
shipped platinum. In the U.S., after attracting attention
with *First Glance,* they earned their first American gold
LP with *The Nature of the Beast* (#26, 1981), which
featured eleven originals by leader Myles Goodwyn. The
group has gone through extensive personnel changes, and
by 1978 Goodwyn was the only remaining original member.

THE ARCHIES
Archie (Ron Dante) born August 22, 1945, Staten
Island, New York
1969—*Everything's Archie* (RCA) *Jingle Jangle*
1970—*Sunshine* (Kirshner) *Greatest Hits.*

The Archies were a make-believe group based on the
comic book and mid-Sixties cartoon series of the same
name. Their #1 hit, "Sugar, Sugar," was the biggest-
selling single of 1969, with six million copies sold
worldwide. A Don Kirshner creation, the Archies were
studio musicians hired to provide the soundtrack for a
popular Saturday morning cartoon series. Other hits included "Bang-Shang-a-Lang" (#2, 1968), "Jingle Jangle"
(#10, 1969) and "Who's Your Baby" (#40, 1970). Ron
Dante, the voice of Archie, later produced several Barry
Manilow hits in the Seventies, and in 1971 he became
editor of the literary magazine *Paris Review*.

ARGENT
Formed 1969, England
Rod Argent (b. June 14, 1945, St. Albans, Eng.), kybds.,
voc.; Jim Rodford (b. July 7, 1945, Eng.), bass; Robert
Henrit (b. May 2, 1945, Eng.), drums; Russ Ballard (b.
Oct. 31, 1947, Eng.), gtr., voc.
1970—*Argent* (Epic)   1971—*Ring of Hands*   1972—*All
Together Now*   1973—*In Deep*   1974—*Nexus*   (−
Ballard; + John Grimaldi, gtr.; + John Verity, gtr.,
voc.) *Encore*   1975—*Circus; Counterpoint*   1976—
Anthology.

After the Zombies broke up in 1967, keyboardist Rod
Argent started his own band just in time to capitalize on
the Zombies' postmortem hit, "Time of the Season" (#1,
1969). Argent had heavier rhythms than the Zombies,
while continuing that band's penchant for minor keys and
mysterious lyrics. Although their debut album was their
most consistent, the group peaked commercially with
"Hold Your Head Up" (#1, 1972). In 1974, songwriter
Ballard left, and after expanding to a quintet, Argent
folded in mid-1976. Ballard and Argent went on to solo
careers, although Ballard was more successful as a songwriter ("Come and Get Your Love," "Liar," "Since
You've Been Gone," "New York Groove," "So You Win
Again") and producer (Roger Daltrey, Leo Sayer) than as
a performer. John Verity, Jim Rodford and Robert Henrit
formed Phoenix, which recorded briefly for Columbia. By
1978, Rodford had joined the Kinks.

ARMAGEDDON
Formed 1975
Keith Relf (b. Mar. 22, 1943, d. May 14, 1976), voc.,
harmonica; Martin Pugh, gtrs.; Bobby Caldwell,
drums; Louis Cennamo, bass.
1975—*Armageddon* (A&M).

Armageddon was a mid-Seventies rock group composed
primarily of already-known British blues-rock musicians.
The group was formed when Martin Pugh and Louis
Cennamo, members of Steamhammer, a highly acclaimed
but short-lived band of the early Seventies, met former
Yardbirds lead singer Keith Relf. Cennamo and Relf had
founded the original Renaissance in 1969, and Relf was
interested in joining Steamhammer. But since Steamhammer was in the process of disintegrating, Pugh and Cennamo invited Relf to join their new group.

Concerned that their reputations in Britain would inflate
expectations, they went to America to find a drummer and
a recording contract. They found Bobby Caldwell—who
had drummed for Johnny Winter, Edgar Winter and Captain Beyond—in a Los Angeles club. A&M's Jerry Moss
heard a jam session and signed them to his label. The
group disbanded soon after their debut LP's release, and
Relf was in the process of putting together a new group
called Illusion with Yardbird drummer Jim McCarty when
he was accidentally electrocuted in his home in May 1976.
With Relf's sister Jane, McCarty formed Illusion after
Relf's death.

JOAN ARMATRADING
Born December 9, 1950, St. Kitts, West Indies
1974—*Whatever's for Us* (A&M)   1975—*Back to the
Night*   1976—*Joan Armatrading*   1977—*Show Some
Emotion*   1978—*To the Limit*   1979—*How Cruel;
Steppin' Out*   1980—*Me, Myself, I*   1981—*Walk under
Ladders*   1983—*The Key.*

Joan Armatrading's synthesis of folk, reggae, soul and
rock has made her a critical and cult favorite in America
and a major star in Europe. She left the West Indies and
moved to England with her family while still a child. She
began her professional career in 1972 in collaboration with
lyricist Pam Nestor (born April 28, 1948, Guyana), but by
the mid-Seventies the two had parted.

A distinctive vocalist and lyricist, Armatrading has
worked with producers Gus Dudgeon, Glyn Johns, Richard Gottehrer and Steve Lillywhite, but generally does her
own arranging. Her backup bands have included alumni of
Fairport Convention and Little Feat, and guitarist Albert
Lee.

ART ENSEMBLE OF CHICAGO
Formed 1969, Paris
Roscoe Mitchell (b. 1940, Chicago), saxes, flute,
clarinet, oboe, bassoon, misc.; Lester Bowie (b. 1941,
Frederick, Md.), trumpet, misc.; Malachi Favors, a.k.a.
Magoustous (b. 1937, Lexington, Miss.), bass, percus-
sion; Joseph Jarman (b. 1941, Pine Bluff, Ark.), saxes,
flute, clarinet, oboe, bassoon, voc., misc.
1969—*People in Sorrow* (Nessa)   *Reese and the
Smooth Ones* (BYG)   *A Jackson in Your House;*

Message to Our Folks (Polydor) *Tutankhamun* (Freedom) **1970**—(+ Dougoufana Famoudou [b. Don Moye, 1946, Rochester, N.Y.], drums, xylophones, percussion) *Certain Blacks* (America) **1971**—*Les Stances à Sophie* (Nessa) *Home* (Galloway) *Art Ensemble with Fontella Bass* (America) *Phase One; Chi-Congo* **1972**—*Baptizum* (Atlantic) *Live at Mandel Hall* (Delmark/Trio) **1973**—*Fanfare for the Warriors* (Atlantic) **1978**—*Nice Guys* (ECM) *Kabalaba* (AECO) **1980**—*Full Force* (ECM) **1982**—*Urban Bushmen.*

The Art Ensemble of Chicago was the most innovative jazz group to emerge in the Seventies. Their compositions and collective improvisations draw from all sorts of world music: traditional and avant-garde jazz, rhythm & blues, African music, twentieth-century European art music, even rock & roll, gospel, martial music, jug band music and the natural sounds of human and animal voices. The quintet has been known to employ five hundred instruments in a concert, which might also include a slide show, dance or vaudeville schtick.

The Ensemble evolved from collective jazz experiments in Chicago in the early and mid-Sixties. Roscoe Mitchell (who played at one time with John Coltrane) and Malachi Favors (who had played with Dizzy Gillespie, Freddie Hubbard and Archie Shepp) first played together in Muhal Richard Abrams' Experimental Band in 1961. Along with Abrams, the two were charter members of the Association for the Advancement of Creative Music, founded in 1965 with such jazz experimentalists as Anthony Braxton and the members of Air. Lester Bowie (who had played R&B with Little Milton and Albert King) was also an AACM member. In 1968, the Roscoe Mitchell Art Ensemble (including Mitchell, Bowie, Favors, and drummer Phillip Wilson) began gigging and earned a local reputation for both their music and their integration of music and conceptual theater.

Before the end of 1968, Wilson had joined the Paul Butterfield Blues Band. The Ensemble continued without a drummer, but the addition of Joseph Jarman (who had studied under John Cage and Indian classical musicians) kept them a quartet. In 1969 they moved to Paris. During their two years there they recorded eleven albums and three film scores, performed hundreds of concerts and met Don Moye. They returned to the U.S. in 1971 to tour. Atlantic signed the Art Ensemble in 1972, but it took a grant from the National Endowment for the Arts to finance their second Atlantic album. Since then they have recorded for both large and small labels and have formed their own AECO Records.

Each of the members has recorded solo and with other musicians, including Anthony Braxton, Henry Threadgill (of Air) and Jack DeJohnette. Abrams and singer Fontella Bass (who had a #1 soul hit with "Rescue Me" in 1965;

she is Bowie's wife) have performed frequently with the Art Ensemble. From the late Seventies onward, Art Ensemble members have spent six months each year on solo projects and six months as a group.

PETER ASHER
Born June 22, 1944, London

After his 1961-68 stint as half of Peter and Gordon (with Gordon Waller), Asher became one of the most influential producers of the Seventies, virtually inventing the style that was later known as adult contemporary: a restrained, perfectionistic mix of country, folk and black-and-white pop. Following the breakup of Peter and Gordon, Asher was hired by his sister Jane's boyfriend, Paul McCartney, as A&R head for Apple Records in 1968. He resigned from Apple a short time later, and then left for Los Angeles. James Taylor, whom he had produced and managed for Apple, soon moved to L.A. as well, and Asher resumed handling Taylor's career and recording. In 1973, Asher began working with Linda Ronstadt, and with their first production, the platinum *Heart Like a Wheel* (1974), both Ronstadt and Asher achieved massive success. Asher has produced all of Ronstadt's and Taylor's albums since, and continues to manage them both. He has also produced albums by Bonnie Raitt, John Stewart and Kate Taylor.

ASHFORD AND SIMPSON
Nickolas Ashford born May 4, 1943, Fairfield, South Carolina; Valerie Simpson born August 26, 1948, Bronx, New York
1973—*Keep It Comin'* (Tamla) (re-released in 1977) *Gimme Something Real* (Warner Bros.) **1974**—*I Wanna Be Selfish* **1976**—*Come As You Are* **1977**—*Send It* **1978**—*Is It Still Good to Ya?* **1979**—*Stay Free* **1980**—*Musical Affair* **1981**—*Performance* **1982**—*Street Opera.*

During the late Sixties, writer/performer/producers Nickolas Ashford and Valerie Simpson wrote and produced some of Motown's greatest hits, and since the early Seventies they've also become successful performers. The son of a construction worker, Ashford grew up in Willow Run, Michigan, where he sang in the church choir as a child. He spent one semester at Eastern Michigan College before dropping out. Against his parents' wishes, he left home and moved to Harlem (with only $57). He worked as a busboy and began attending the White Rock Baptist Church in Harlem, where, in 1964, he met Simpson, then 17 years old. She had recently graduated high school and was studying music at Chatham Square School.

They began writing songs together (the first bunch of which they sold for $75), and two years later, when Ray Charles had a hit with their "Let's Go Get Stoned," they signed on with Berry Gordy's Motown organization. As

Nickolas Ashford and Valerie Simpson

Motown staff writers and producers, they were responsible for many hits, including Marvin Gaye and Tammi Terrell's "Ain't No Mountain High Enough" and "You're All I Need to Get By" and Diana Ross's "Reach Out (and Touch Somebody's Hand)." While at Motown, Simpson recorded two solo LPs (*Exposed!*, 1971 and *Valerie Simpson*, 1972), both of which were produced by Ashford. Although neither album sold well, the pair were anxious to concentrate on performing (which Gordy discouraged) and recorded *Keep It Comin'* just before leaving Motown in 1973 for Warner Bros. They lived together for a few years before they were married in 1974, she for the second time. Their daughter, Nicole, was born two months later.

Their hit singles include "So, So Satisfied" (#27, 1977) and "Is It Still Good to Ya?" (#12, 1978). *Send It, Is It Still* . . . and *Stay Free* have been certified gold. Ashford and Simpson continue to work frequently as independent writers and producers, and their clients include Diana Ross (*The Boss*), Gladys Knight and the Pips (*About Love*), and Chaka Khan ("I'm Every Woman"). They also contributed original material to the soundtrack of *The Wiz*. Simpson's brother, Ray Simpson, was a lead vocalist for the Village People.

ASHTON, GARDNER AND DYKE
Formed circa 1968, England
Tony Ashton (b. Mar. 1, 1946, Blackburn, Eng.), kybds., voc.; Kim Gardner (b. Jan. 27, 1946, Dulwich, Eng.), bass; Roy Dyke (b. Feb. 13, 1945, Liverpool), drums.
1969—*Ashton, Gardner and Dyke* (Polydor)   **1971**— *The Worst of Ashton, Gardner and Dyke* (Capitol) **1972**—*What a Bloody Long Day It's Been*.

Ashton, Gardner and Dyke were all veteran English session musicians before they decided to form a group. Their hard-rock style won immediate support from Eric Clapton, and George Harrison produced a track on their debut LP. The band toured widely in 1970 and in 1971 had their only U.S. hit, "Resurrection Shuffle." Success proved brief, and by 1973 each had returned to session work.

In 1976, Tony Ashton joined yet another alliance, Paice, Ashton and Lord, with Jon Lord and Ian Paice, formerly of Deep Purple. They lasted together about a year and released one album, *Malice in Wonderland* (another LP was never released), and toured Europe extensively. Ashton resurfaced in December 1979 as part of the all-star contingent at the benefit Concert for the People of Kampuchea. By 1980, Kim Gardner was playing bass in Billy Burnette's backup band.

ASIA
Formed 1981, Los Angeles
Carl Palmer (b. Mar. 20, 1951, Birmingham, Eng.), drums; John Wetton (b. 1950, Derby, Eng.), bass, voc.; Steve Howe (b. Apr. 8, 1947, London), gtr.; Geoffrey Downes (b. Eng.), kybds.
1982—*Asia* (Geffen).

The first supergroup of the Eighties, Asia is composed of famous musicians whose earlier work in major rock groups virtually guaranteed their success. Carl Palmer had been a member of Emerson, Lake and Palmer; Steve Howe and Geoffrey Downes had both belonged to Yes, and Downes had worked with the Buggles; John Wetton had been bassist for King Crimson, U.K., Family and Roxy Music. Though criticized for what many considered pedestrian musicianship, Asia was instantly accepted by radio programers. Their debut LP, *Asia*, went #1 and sold two million copies.

ASLEEP AT THE WHEEL
Formed 1970, Paw Paw, West Virginia
Ray Benson (b. Ray Benson Seifert, Mar. 16, 1951, Philadelphia), gtr., voc.; LeRoy Preston, drums, gtr.; Lucky Oceans (b. Reuben Gosfield), pedal steel gtr. (Since its inception, the group has undergone over 55 personnel changes.)
1973—*Comin' Right at Ya* (United Artists)   **1974**— *Asleep at the Wheel* (Epic)   **1975**—*Fathers and Sons; Texas Gold* (Capitol)   **1976**—*Wheelin' and Dealin'; Texas Country* (United Artists)   **1977**—*The Wheel* (Capitol)   **1978**—*Collision Course*   **1979**—*Served Live*   **1980**—*Framed*   **1981**—*American Band 3*.

The current lineup of Asleep at the Wheel is Benson; Chris O'Connell (born March 21, 1952, Hagerstown, Maryland), vocals and guitar; Paul Anastasio (born April 12, 1953, Chicago), fiddle; Tom Anastasio (born February 19, 1958, Bellingham, Washington), bass; Falkner Evans (born October 5, 1953, Tulsa), keyboards; Michael Francis (born June 25, 1951, Yuma, Arizona), sax; Ron McRorey (born

February 22, 1953, Dallas), drums; Wally Murphy (born August 26, 1954, St. Louis), pedal steel guitar.

The group is dedicated to reviving, with slight modernization, the Western swing pioneered by Bob Wills in the Thirties and Forties, a hybrid of country, big-band jazz, Cajun fiddling and be-bop. Through the Seventies, with frequent—over 55—personnel changes, Asleep at the Wheel has become a dependable attraction in country circles, skirting the rock mainstream. The group was founded by three Easterners: lead guitarist/vocalist Ray Benson, rhythm guitarist/vocalist/songwriter LeRoy Preston and pedal steel guitarist Lucky Oceans; female singer Chris O'Connell joined them for their debut album. At first they mixed satiric originals with Western swing standards, to the incomprehension of their early record companies.

After a few years in San Francisco, they resettled in Austin, Texas, in 1974. In 1975, they signed with Capitol and began to reach the country market with such deadpan songs as "The Letter That Johnny Walker Read" (#10 C&W, 1975) and their versions of "Bump Bounce Boogie" (#31 C&W, 1975) and "Nothin' Takes the Place of You" (#35 C&W, 1976). Each of their Capitol releases since 1976 has garnered at least one Grammy nomination; they finally won in 1978 when their version of Count Basie's "One O'Clock Jump" won for Best Country Instrumental Performance. In 1980, they appeared on the soundtrack for *Roadie*.

THE ASSOCIATION
Formed 1965, Los Angeles
Jules Alexander (b. Chattanooga), gtr., voc.; Terry Kirkman (b. Salinas, Kan.), kybds., voc.; Brian Cole (b. 1944, Tacoma; d. Aug. 2, 1972, Los Angeles), bass, voc.; Ted Buechel, Jr. (b. San Pedro, Calif.), drums; Jim Yester (b. Birmingham, Ala.), gtr., voc.; Russ Giguere (b. Oct. 18, 1943, Portsmouth, N.H.), gtr., voc.
1966—*And Then . . . Along Came the Association* (Valiant) **1967**—*Renaissance* (— Alexander; + Larry Ramos [b. Kauai, Hawaii], gtr., voc., harm.) *Insight Out* (Warner Bros.) **1968**—*Birthday* **1969**—(+ Alexander) *Greatest Hits; Goodbye Columbus* (soundtrack) *The Association* **1970**—"*Live*" (— Giguere; + Richard Thompson [b. San Diego], gtr., voc.). **1971**—*Stop Your Motor* **1972**—*Waterbeds in Trinidad* (CBS).

A primarily soft-rock and ballad band, the Association sold over 15 million records in the Sixties. The group first formed when Terry Kirkman, who had played in several bands, including Zappa's Mothers of Invention, and Jules Alexander recruited Brian Cole and Jim Yester (whose brother Jerry was a member of the Lovin' Spoonful). Russ Giguere and Ted Buechel joined soon after, and following six months of rehearsal the band debuted in Pasadena. The hits, most written by various group members, began a few

months later in 1966 with their first single, "Along Comes Mary" (which some listeners believed was an ode to marijuana) and continued with the more romantic songs for which the group is best remembered, "Cherish" (#1, 1966), "Windy" (#1, 1967), "Never My Love" (#2, 1967) and "Everything That Touches You" (#10, 1968). Their singles, including the theme song from the movie *Goodbye Columbus* (1969), continued to chart but never again reached the Top Thirty. After an unsuccessful try at progressive rock from 1969 through 1973, the group faded from the charts and began working nightclubs. In early 1981, most of the band's original members (except for Cole, who died in 1972 of a drug overdose) regrouped for a comeback attempt.

CHET ATKINS
Born June 20, 1924, Luttrell, Tennessee
1958—*Chet Atkins at Home* (RCA) **1959**—*Session with Chet Atkins* **1960**—*Mister Guitar; Teensville* **1961**—*Most Popular Guitar* **1962**—*Back Home Hymns* **1963**—*The Pops Goes Country* **1964**—*Best of Chet Atkins* **1965**—*My Favorite Guitars* **1966**—*From Nashville with Love* **1967**—*Guitar World* **1968**—*Solid Gold 68* **1969**—*Solid Gold 69* **1970**—*By Special Request; Yestergroovin'* **1972**—*Nashville Gold; Chet Atkins Picks the Hits* **1974**—*Superpickers* **1976**—*The Best of Chet and Friends* **1977**—*Me and My Guitar; A Legendary Performer* **1978**—*Guitar Monsters*.

Principally a country artist, legendary guitarist Chet Atkins played a noteworthy role in the formative years of rock & roll. Atkins' family lived in poverty, but he received musical training from his parents and an older half-brother. At age 18, Atkins was working at Knoxville

Chet Atkins

country radio station WNOX as guitarist and fiddler with Bill Carlisle and his Dixieland Swingers. By the late Forties, he had performed at the Grand Ole Opry and recorded as a session musician and a solo artist. Atkins became vice-president in charge of RCA's Nashville operations in the late Fifties. As such, he was involved—both as a player and a producer—in the early development of Eddy Arnold, Perry Como, Elvis Presley, Roy Orbison, the Everly Brothers and others. He has recorded over thirty albums and in 1973 was elected to the Country Music Hall of Fame.

ATLANTA RHYTHM SECTION
Formed 1970, Doraville, Georgia
Barry Bailey (b. June 12, 1948, Decatur, Ga.), gtr.; Rodney Justo, voc.; Paul Goddard (b. June 23, 1945, Rome, Ga.), bass; Robert Nix, drums; J. R. Cobb (b. Feb. 5, 1944, Birmingham, Ala.), gtr.; Dean Daughtry (b. Sep. 8, 1946, Kinston, Ala.), kybds.
1972—*Atlanta Rhythm Section* (MCA)   (– Justo; + Ronnie Hammond [b. Macon, Ga.], voc.)   1973—*Back Up Against the Wall*   1974—*Third Annual Pipe Dream* (Polydor)   1975—*Dog Days*   1976—*Red Tape*   1977—*A Rock and Roll Alternative*   1978—*Champagne Jam* (– Nix; + Roy Yeager [b. Feb. 4, 1946, Greenwood, Miss.], drums)   1979—*Are You Ready!;   Underdog* 1980—*The Boys from Doraville*   1981—*Quinella* (Columbia).

Former sessionmen, the Atlanta Rhythm Section smoothed out Southern rock's rough edges with studio sophistication. J. R. Cobb, Dean Daughtry and producer/ manager Buddy Buie had been members of the Classics IV. (Daughtry had also been in the Candymen.) They met the other Section members while working together on a Roy Orbison session in 1970. Soon after, they formed the group, adding lead vocalist Ronnie Justo for their debut LP. He was soon replaced by Ronnie Hammond, a former recording engineer. Though hampered by the lack of a distinctive frontman or a group identity, frequent touring helped establish them as a major group in the late Seventies. Their hit singles included "So In to You" (#7, 1977), "Imaginary Lover" (#7, 1978) and "I'm Not Gonna Let It Bother Me Tonight" (#14, 1978). *A Rock and Roll Alternative* has been certified gold; *Champagne Jam*, platinum.

BRIAN AUGER
Born July 18, 1939, London
1967—*Open* (Marmalade)   1968—*Definitely What*   1969—*Streetnoise*   1970—*Befour* (RCA)   1971—*Brian Auger's Oblivion Express;   A Better Land*   1972—*Second Wind*   1973—*Closer to It*   1974—*Straight Ahead;   Live Oblivion, volumes 1 and 2*   1975—*Genesis* (Polydor) (early Steampacket recordings)   *This Is* (Metronome)   *Reinforcements*

(RCA)   1977—*Happiness Heartaches* (Warner Bros.) *Best of Brian Auger* (RCA)   1978—*Encore*.

British keyboardist Brian Auger helped lay the groundwork for fusion with his jazz-rock hybrids in the Sixties and early Seventies. In 1964, he abandoned pure jazz and upright piano for R&B and a Hammond organ. He soon formed the Brian Auger Trinity with bassist Rick Brown and drummer Mickey Waller. Within a few months the group was renamed Steampacket and included vocalists Long John Baldry, Rod Stewart and ex-model Julie Driscoll. Each had a spotlight segment during the group's live shows, which also featured jazzy R&B instrumentals highlighting Auger's keyboards. By mid-1966, Stewart and Baldry had left, and the group dissolved.

Auger then organized Trinity with bassist Dave Ambrose (born December 11, 1946, London), drummer Clive Thacker (born February 13, 1940, Enfield, England), guitarist Gary Boyle (born Bihar, India) and Driscoll. In 1969 they had hits in Europe ("Save Me") and England (a cover of Dylan's "This Wheel's on Fire"). Subsequent singles floundered, and during a 1969 U.S. tour, Driscoll quit the group. (She later married pianist Keith Tippetts and continues to record occasionally under the name Julie Tippetts.) Further hampered by contractual and management problems, Trinity broke up in mid-1970 after releasing *Befour*.

Auger reemerged late in the year with the four-piece Oblivion Express (at one time including the late Robbie McIntosh, who later joined the Average White Band), a Santana-influenced jazz-rock band that released several albums but failed to crack the U.S. market. The group's latter-day vocalist was Alex Ligertwood, later of Santana. By 1977, Auger was playing synthesizers as well, and in 1983 he did a reunion album with Julie Tippets—*Encore*. As the Seventies closed, Auger was without a recording contract and was living in San Francisco. He wrote "Happiness Is Just around the Bend," a minor hit in 1974 for the Main Ingredient.

AUTOMATIC MAN
Formed 1975, San Francisco
Michael Shrieve (b. San Francisco), drums, electronic percussion; Bayeté, kybds., synth., voc.; Pat Thrall (b. San Francisco), gtr., voc.; Doni Harvey (b. San Francisco), bass, voc.
1976—*Automatic Man* (Island)   (– Shrieve)   1977— *Visitors*.

Automatic Man, whose music was an intriguing combination of psychedelic guitar (like Jimi Hendrix), futuristic funk (like Weather Report and Herbie Hancock) and intelligent pop (Roxy Music), was formed by Michael Shrieve in 1975, two years after he left Santana. He had worked in the interim on Stomu Yamashta's *Go* and on an unreleased solo album. Bayeté, who had studied classical piano and graduated from Oxford University, had recorded two albums on Fantasy. Pat Thrall was a Bay Area guitar instructor and sessionman, and Doni Harvey had been working with a San Francisco band, Stratus. After their debut album, Shrieve left rock, returning in 1981 with Novo Combo. The band broke up after their second album; Thrall later played with Pat Travers.

FRANKIE AVALON
Born Francis Avallone, September 18, 1939 (or 1940), Philadelphia
N.A.—*Sixteen Greatest Hits* (Trip).

Teen idol Frankie Avalon was originally a trumpet-playing prodigy when, at age eighteen, he joined a group called Rocco and the Saints (which then included Bobby Rydell). He began making appearances on local television, and in 1958 his debut single, "DeDe Dinah" was #7. Through the late Fifties and up until 1960, Avalon had six Top Ten hits: "Ginger Bread" (#9, 1958), "Bobby Sox to Stockings" (#8, 1959), "A Boy Without a Girl" (#10, 1959), "Just Ask Your Heart" (#7, 1959), "Venus" (#1, 1959), and "Why" (#1, 1960). He was a regular on Dick Clark's "American Bandstand," appeared in several beach-party movies with Annette Funicello (including *Beach Blanket Bingo*), and also appeared in *Disc Jockey Jamboree* (1957), *Guns of the Timberland* (1960) and *The Carpetbaggers* (1962). By the Seventies, he was appearing regularly on the resort club circuit and occasionally had TV roles in such shows as "Love, American Style." His 1976 disco remake of "Venus" peaked at #46.

AVERAGE WHITE BAND
Formed 1972, Scotland
Alan Gorrie (b. July 19, 1946, Perth), bass, voc.; Onnie McIntyre (b. Sep. 25, 1945, Lennox Town, Scot.), gtr., voc.; Roger Ball (b. June 4, 1944, Dundee), kybds., saxes; Malcolm "Molly" Duncan (b. Aug. 24, 1945, Montrose, Scot.), tenor sax; Robbie McIntosh (b. 1950, Scot.; d. Sep. 23, 1974, Los Angeles), drums; Hamish Stuart (b. Oct. 8, 1949, Glasgow), gtr., voc.
1973—*Show Your Hand* (MCA) **1974**—*AWB* (Atlantic) (– McIntosh; + Steve Ferrone [b. Apr. 25, 1950, Brighton, Eng.], drums) **1975**—*Cut the Cake; Put It Where You Want It* (MCA) **1976**—*Soul Searching* (Atlantic) *Person to Person* **1977**—*Benny and Us* **1978**—*Warmer Communications* **1979**—*Feel No Fret* **1980**—*Shine* (Arista) *Volume VIII* (Atlantic).

The Average White Band's derivative but convincing funk crossed the Atlantic and the color line, heralding the arrival of disco in the mid-Seventies. Each of the members had been active in various English and Scottish bands before Alan Gorrie founded the group. Robbie McIntosh had been with Brian Auger's Oblivion Express; Roger Ball

and Malcolm Duncan had been members of the Dundee Horns.

After opening for Eric Clapton at his January 1973 Rainbow Theatre comeback concert, they released an unnoticed debut album. The next year, they began abbreviating the band name as AWB, and a 1974 album produced by Arif Mardin yielded a Grammy Award–winning disco hit, "Pick Up the Pieces" (#1, 1975). The group was shaken by drummer McIntosh's death of accidental heroin poisoning at a Hollywood party but regrouped for a second gold album, *Cut the Cake* (which was dedicated to McIntosh). Since 1975, they have recorded less often and have worked as sidemen, including backup work for Chaka Khan in 1978. Their 1977 LP, *Benny and Us*, featured soul singer Ben E. King.

HOYT AXTON
Born March 25, 1938, Duncan, Oklahoma
1962—*The Balladeer* (Horizon) **1963**—*Thunder 'n' Lightnin'; Saturday's Child* (reissued 1964) **1964**—*Hoyt Axton Explodes* (Vee Jay) *The Best of Hoyt Axton; Greenback Dollar* (reissue of *The Balladeer*) *Hoyt Axton Sings Bessie Smith* (Exodus) (rel. 1974) *Bessie Smith . . . My Way* (Vee Jay) (reissued as *Long Old Road*, 1977) **1965**—*Mr. Greenback Dollar Man* (Surrey) **1969**—*My Griffin Is Gone* (CBS) (reissued 1974) **1971**—*Joy to the World* (Capitol) *Country Anthem* **1973**—*Less Than a Song* (A&M) **1974**—*Life Machine* **1975**—*Southbound* **1976**—*Fearless* **1977**—*Road Songs* **1978**—*Snowblind Friend* (MCA) *Free Sailin'* **1979**—*A Rusty Old Halo;* (Jeremiah) **1980**—*Where Did the Money Go*.

Singer/songwriter Hoyt Axton's most famous songs are those, like "Joy to the World," "Greenback Dollar" and "The Pusher," that have been hits for other artists. The son of Mae Axton, who wrote "Heartbreak Hotel," and a blues-singer father, Axton moved frequently during his childhood. He began performing in West Coast folk clubs in the late Fifties. In 1962, he signed with Horizon Records and recorded his debut, *The Balladeer*, live at Los Angeles' Troubadour; and later that year, the Kingston Trio's version of "Greenback Dollar" became the first of his hit credits. Other cover versions include Steppenwolf's "The Pusher" (1968), Three Dog Night's "Joy to the World" (#1, 1971) and Ringo Starr's "No No Song" (#1, 1975).

Axton acquired and eventually kicked a ten-year cocaine habit. In 1979, he appeared in the movie *The Black Stallion* and founded his own record label, Jeremiah. Axton continues to tour and perform, particularly in the Southwest.

KEVIN AYERS
Born August 16, 1945, Herne Bay, England
1970—*Joy of a Toy* (Harvest) **1971**—*Shooting at the*

Moon **1972**—*Whatevershebringswesing* **1973**—
Bananamour **1974**—*Confessions of Dr. Dream*
(Island) *June 1st, 1974* **1975**—*Sweet Deceiver; Joy
of a Toy/Shooting at the Moon* (Harvest) **1976**—*Old
Ditties* **1977**—*Yes, We Have No Mañanas* **1978**—
Rainbow Takeaway.

Cheerfully eccentric Kevin Ayers has been active in British progressive rock since 1963, when he and some friends from Canterbury founded the Wilde Flowers. In 1966, Ayers and Robert Wyatt left to start Soft Machine. He played bass with them until 1968, then began his ongoing solo career. Singing in a deep bass voice and making quiet jokes about moons and bananas—his specialty is pataphysical humor, the British equivalent of Zen koans—Ayers has played alongside Mike Oldfield (who first recorded on Ayers' albums), Steve Hillage, John Cale, Brian Eno and Andy Summers (Police). In 1980, Ayers made some concert appearances in the U.S. He spends most of his time at his estate in Majorca.

ROY AYERS
Born September 10, 1940, Los Angeles
1972—*He's Coming* (Polydor) **1973**—*Virgo Red*
1974—*Change Up the Groove* **1975**—*Ubiquity; A
Tear to a Smile; Mystic Voyage; Red, Black and
Green* **1976**—*Daddy, Bug and Friends* (Atlantic)
Vibrations (Polydor) *Everybody Loves the Sunshine*
1977—*Life Line* **1978**—*Starbooty* (Elektra/Asylum)
Let's Do It (Polydor) *You Send Me; Step into Our
Life* **1979**—*Fever; The Best of Roy Ayers* **1980**—*No
Stranger to Love* **1981**—*Africa, Center of the World;
Love Fantasy* **1982**—*Feeling Good.*

Vibraphonist Roy Ayers crossed over from jazz to pop and found commercial success in the mid-Seventies with what he calls "disco jazz." He learned to play piano at an early age; at five, his playing impressed Lionel Hampton, who gave him a pair of mallets. Ayers began playing vibes professionally with West Coast jazz bands in the late Fifties. In 1965, he formed his own quartet, but disbanded it when Herbie Mann invited him to join his band. He recorded and toured with Mann from 1966 to 1970, and Mann produced three Ayers solo albums.

Around 1970, Ayers began experimenting with electronics and rock rhythms. He was probably the first vibraphonist to electrify his instrument and certainly the first to employ such devices as the wah-wah pedal and effects like fuzztone. In 1970, he formed the Roy Ayers' Ubiquity, a fully electrified ensemble aiming to fuse jazz, rock, Latin, pop and R&B. Guest soloists with Ubiquity have included drummer Billy Cobham, flutist Herbert Laws, guitarist George Benson, trombonist Wayne Henderson of the Crusaders, Nigerian saxophonist Fela Anikulapo Kuti (with whom he toured in Africa in 1979) and vocalist Dee Dee Bridgewater.

Beginning in 1976, Ayers' records hit the charts after receiving radio and disco play. "Running Away" made the R&B Top Twenty in 1977. "The Freaky Deaky" inspired a dance step of the same name in 1978.

BABY HUEY AND THE BABYSITTERS
Formed 1963, Chicago
Baby Huey (b. James Ramey, 1944, Richmond, Ind.; d. Oct. 28, 1970, Chicago), voc.; Othello Anderson, alto sax, flute; Dave Cook, organ; Reno Smith, drums, percussion; Byron Watkins, tenor sax; Rick Marcotte, trumpet; Alton Littles, trumpet; Dan O'Neil, gtr.; Dan Alfano, bass; Plato Jones, bongos.

Baby Huey, a Chicago-based R&B singer, was just beginning to find an audience when he died in 1970 from a heart attack brought on by sustained drug abuse. Four-hundred-pound Huey was still in his teens when he left his hometown of Richmond, Indiana, and moved to Chicago to start the Babysitters. In 1963, they began working regularly at a North Side bar called Thumbs Up. By the late Sixties, the Babysitters were playing regularly on both coasts. On one trip to New York for college and club dates, they were seen by a member of the Rothschild family and were promptly shipped to Paris to play at the Baron de Rothschild's daughter's debutante party.
  In 1968, the group recorded "Mighty, Mighty Children," a song written and produced by Curtis Mayfield. It never reached the charts. Shortly before his death, Baby Huey completed his only album. Always sensitive about his weight (caused by glandular dysfunction), Huey became increasingly despondent and started to use hard drugs in his final years. He began missing performances and was hospitalized more than once for detoxification. He was found dead on a bathroom floor in a South Side Chicago motel.

THE BABYS
Formed in 1976, London
John Waite (b. July 4, 1955, Eng.), bass, voc.; Wally Stocker (b. Mar. 17, 1954, London), gtr., voc.; Mike Corby (b. July 3, 1955, Eng.), voc., kybds., gtr.; Tony Brock (b. Mar. 31, 1954, Bournemouth, Eng.), drums, voc.
1976—The Babys (Chrysalis) 1977—Broken Heart (− Corby) 1978—Head First (+ Jonathan Cain, kybds.; + Ricky Phillips, bass) 1980—Union Jacks 1981—On the Edge (− Cain) Anthology.

Power pop with a veneer of youthful vibrancy made the Babys a hot act on FM rock radio in the late Seventies. Formed in London as a teen-oriented act, the Babys signed with Chrysalis in late 1976 on the strength of one of the first video demos. Conceived by producer Mike Mans-field, it showed off their looks, gleaming smiles and wardrobes. The Babys appeared on several American television programs in 1977 to support their debut (produced by Bob Ezrin) and, aided by massive advertising, had such hits as "Isn't It Time" (#13, 1977). As the Seventies drew to a close, the Babys experimented with a more synthesizer-oriented style on Head First and 1980's Union Jacks, which bore two moderate hits, "Back on My Feet Again" (#33, 1980) and "Midnight Rendezvous." Jonathan Cain joined Journey in early 1981, and the Babys disbanded. Chrysalis released lead singer John Waite's solo debut, Ignition, in 1982.

BURT BACHARACH
Born May 12, 1929, Kansas City, Missouri
1967—Reach Out (A&M) 1969—Make It Easy on Yourself 1971—Burt Bacharach 1973—Living Together 1974—Burt Bacharach's Greatest Hits 1977—Futures 1979—Woman.

Composer Burt Bacharach's songs (many of which were abetted by Broadway veteran lyricist Hal David) played a major role in Sixties mainstream pop. The son of syndicated columnist Bert Bacharach, Burt was born in the Midwest but grew up in New York City. He studied theory and composition at McGill University in Montreal and was awarded a scholarship to the Music Academy of the West in Santa Barbara. He worked regularly as piano accompanist for Vic Damone and Steve Lawrence.
  Bacharach began composing with David (b. May 25, 1921) in 1958 and immediately had hits with Marty Robbins ("The Story of My Life," 1957) and Perry Como ("Magic Moments," 1958). Bacharach and David were eventually responsible for hundreds of compositions, including hits for Jackie DeShannon ("What the World Needs Now," #7, 1965), the Fifth Dimension ("One Less Bell to Answer," #2, 1970), Jerry Butler ("Make It Easy on Yourself," #20, 1962), the Carpenters ("[They Long to Be] Close to You," #1, 1970) and many others.
  Bacharach worked extensively with the Drifters, arranging horn and string parts and collaborating with lyricist Bob Hilliard on the group's 1961 singles "Mexican Divorce" and "Please Stay" (#14). At a Drifters session, he met Dionne Warwick, whose voice proved to be well suited to his material. Beginning in 1962 with "Don't Make Me Over" (#21), Bacharach-David provided Warwick with 39 chart records in ten years, eight of them Top Ten hits: "Walk On By," "Anyone Who Had a

Heart," "I Say a Little Prayer," "You'll Never Get to Heaven," "Message to Michael," "Trains and Boats and Planes," "Do You Know the Way to San Jose?" and "Promises, Promises."

As the Sixties closed, Bacharach and David teamed up for a Broadway musical, *Promises, Promises* (1968). The title song was a hit for Warwick, and the play ran for three years. Through his wife, actress Angie Dickinson (whom he divorced in 1982 after 12 years of marriage), Bacharach moved into film scores. His credits include *What's New, Pussycat?* (its title song was a Top 5 hit for Tom Jones in 1965), *Casino Royale* (1967), *Lost Horizon* (1973) and *Butch Cassidy and the Sundance Kid* (1969), which spawned "Raindrops Keep Fallin' on My Head," a #1 hit for B. J. Thomas in 1970. The score brought Bacharach two Oscars (Best Score and Best Theme Song).

Bacharach has sporadically recorded on his own since 1963 with moderate success. In 1979, he released *Woman*, featuring the Houston Symphony. Bacharach, Carole Bayer Sager, Peter Allen and Christopher Cross cowrote the 1981 hit theme from the film *Arthur*. Recorded by Christopher Cross, "Arthur's Theme (Best That You Can Do)" was a #1 hit and won an Academy Award for Best Song. In April 1982, Bacharach married Sager.

BACHMAN-TURNER OVERDRIVE
Formed 1972, Winnipeg, Canada
Randy Bachman (b. Sep. 27, 1943, Winnipeg), gtr., voc.; Tim Bachman (b. Winnipeg), gtr.; Robbie Bachman (b. Feb. 18, 1953, Winnipeg), drums; C. F. (Fred) Turner (b. Oct. 16, 1943, Winnipeg), bass, voc.
1973—*Bachman-Turner Overdrive* (Mercury) *Bachman-Turner Overdrive 2* (− Tim Bachman; + Blair Thornton [b. July 23, 1950], gtr.) 1974—*Not Fragile* 1975—*Four Wheel Drive; Head On* 1976—*Best of Bachman-Turner Overdrive* 1977—*Freeways* (+ Jim Clench, bass, voc.; − Randy Bachman) 1978—*Street Action; Rock 'n' Roll Nights.*

Bachman-Turner Overdrive parlayed workmanlike heavy metal, a blue-collar image and nonstop touring into nearly seven million records sold in the U.S. by 1977. Guess Who founders Chad Allan and Randy Bachman had left that group in 1965 and 1969 respectively, and after Bachman made a solo album (*Axe*, 1970), he teamed up with Allan and younger brother Robbie Bachman in *Brave Belt*. After two albums, Tim Bachman and vocalist/bassist Fred Turner—both Mormons like Randy—replaced Allan, and Brave Belt became Bachman-Turner Overdrive, named in part after the truckers' magazine *Overdrive*.

The band was rejected by twenty-five record companies before Mercury released their 1973 debut album, but extensive touring netted BTO several hit singles including "Taking Care of Business" (#12, 1974) and "You Ain't Seen Nothin' Yet" (#1, 1974). In 1975, Tim Bachman left

to become a producer. That year Warner Bros. rereleased *Brave Belt II* under the title *As Brave Belt*. With Randy Bachman's departure in 1978 for a solo career, BTO's momentum slowed considerably, although they did release two more LPs. The group disbanded in 1979. Randy Bachman has done solo work since.

BAD COMPANY
Formed 1973, England
Paul Rodgers (b. Dec. 17, 1949, Middlesborough, Eng.), voc.; Mick Ralphs (b. Mar. 31, 1948, Herefordshire, Eng.), gtr.; Simon Kirke (b. July 28, 1949, Wales), drums; Boz Burrell (b. Raymond Burrell, 1946, Lincolnshire, Eng.), bass.
1974—*Bad Company* (Swan Song) 1975—*Straight Shooter* 1976—*Run with the Pack* 1977—*Burnin' Sky* 1979—*Desolation Angels* 1982—*Rough Diamonds.*

The members of Bad Company were stars before their first concert in March 1974. Paul Rodgers and Simon Kirke had been members of Free, Mick Ralphs had been Ian Hunter's main sidekick in Mott the Hoople and Boz Burrell had played with King Crimson. Their self-titled debut album, recorded in only ten days with a minimum of overdubs in Ronnie Lane's mobile studio, eclipsed all that by going #1 worldwide with the single "Can't Get Enough."

Playing sparse, elemental hard rock dominated by Rodgers' husky vocals and Ralphs's power chords, Bad Company has sold more than 12 million records worldwide. Their 1975 release, *Straight Shooter*, yielded the Top Ten single "Feel Like Makin' Love" (#10, 1975), while their third platinum LP, *Run with the Pack*, stayed on the charts for over nine months.

On *Desolation Angels* (which included the Rodgers-penned hit "Rock and Roll Fantasy," #13, 1979), Bad Company added synthesizers and strings. Indicative of their increasingly sporadic activities, three years elapsed between *Angels* and *Rough Diamonds*.

Despite frequent critical pans and the pressure of various musical trends of the past decade, Bad Company has remained steadfastly true to its original hard-rock formula. Like Free before it, Bad Company proves that there is always a market for riffy blues rock.

BADFINGER
Formed mid-1960s, England
Peter Ham (b. Apr. 27, 1947, Swansea, Wales; d. Apr. 23, 1975, Weybridge, Eng.), voc., gtr., piano; Joey Molland (b. June 21, 1948, Liverpool), voc., gtr., kybds.; Tom Evans (b. 1947, Liverpool), voc., bass; Mike Gibbins (b. 1949, Swansea, Wales), drums.
1970—*Magic Christian Music* (Apple) *No Dice* 1971—*Straight Up* 1973—*Ass* 1974—*Badfinger*

(Warner Bros.) *Wish You Were Here* 1975—
(— Molland; — Ham) 1978—(+ Peter Clarke,
drums; + Tony Kaye, kybds.) *Airwaves* (Elektra)
1981—*Say No More* (Radio).

Badfinger was a popular British pop-rock band of the early
Seventies. Originally called the Iveys, the group signed
with Apple Records in late 1968. In the fall of 1969, Paul
McCartney supervised their soundtrack work on the
Ringo Starr–Peter Sellers film, *The Magic Christian,* for
which he wrote "Come and Get It," Badfinger's first hit
(#7, 1970).

During the early Seventies, Badfinger had three more
hit singles: "No Matter What" (#8, 1970), "Day after
Day" (#4, 1972) and "Baby Blue" (#14, 1972). Peter Ham
and Tom Evans' "Without You" was covered by Harry
Nilsson on *Nilsson Schmilsson* and became a #1 single in
February 1972. The group frequently backed the ex-
Beatles on tours and records, appearing at George Harri-
son's benefit concert for Bangladesh and on *All Things
Must Pass,* on John Lennon's *Imagine* and on Ringo
Starr's "It Don't Come Easy."

Badfinger left Apple after their fourth album, *Ass.* In
1973, they signed with Warner Bros. for a reported $3
million advance, but neither of their two Warner Bros.
albums reached the Top 100. The poor sales of *Wish You
Were Here* prompted Joey Molland to quit in late 1974.
Despondent over personal as well as professional problems, leader and main songwriter Ham hanged himself in
April. Badfinger collapsed. A third album, recorded before Ham's suicide, was never released.

Soon thereafter, Molland formed a group called Natural
Gas in Los Angeles with former Humble Pie drummer
Jerry Shirley; Evans returned to England to join the
Dodgers. By 1977, Molland was working as a carpet
installer and Evans was a draftsman. In 1978, they re-
formed Badfinger, with the addition of drummer Peter
Clarke, formerly of Stealer's Wheel, and keyboardist
Tony Kaye, who had worked with Yes and David Bowie.
Say No More enjoyed moderate chart success in 1981,
with one minor hit single, "Hold On."

JOAN BAEZ

Born January 9, 1941, Staten Island, New York
1960—*Joan Baez* (Vanguard)   1961—*Joan Baez 2*
1962—*In Concert*   1963—*In Concert 2*   1964—*Joan
Baez 5*   1965—*Farewell Angelina*   1966—*Noel;
Portrait*   1967—*Joan*   1968—*Baptism; Any Day
Now*   1969—*David's Album*   1970—*One Day at a
Time; First Ten Years*   1971—*Blessed Are*   1972—
Carry It On; Come from the Shadows (A&M)   *The
Ballad Book* (Vanguard)   1973—*Where Are You Now,
My Son?; Hits, the Greatest and Others* (Vanguard)
1974—*Gracias a la Vida (Here's to Life)* (A&M)   1975—
Diamonds and Rust; Live in Japan (Vanguard)

Joan Baez

1976—*Love Song Album; From Every Stage* (A&M)
Gulf Winds   1977—*Blowing Away* (Portrait)   *Best of
Joan Baez* (A&M)   1979—*Honest Lullaby* (Portrait)
Country Music (Vanguard).

Singer/songwriter Joan Baez was the perfect symbol of the
early-Sixties folk revival: young, sincere, technically
gifted and equally committed to traditional songs and
social action. In the Seventies, she found it increasingly
difficult to be both commercial and socially conscious. She
became involved with political issues while attending
Boston University in the mid-Fifties. Baez emerged from
the 1959 Newport Folk Festival acclaimed for the purity of
her voice. In the early Sixties, she released several influential albums of sparsely arranged traditional folk material
and—largely through her association with the anthemic
"We Shall Overcome"—she became a voice of the early-
Sixties civil rights movement.

Baez also played an important role in the rise of Bob
Dylan by recording his songs and sharing concert bills
with him in the early Sixties. From 1963 through 1965,
they were virtually inseparable. Nearly a decade later
their romance provided the subject matter for Baez's hit
"Diamonds and Rust." By 1975, the two were reconciled,
and they sang duets in Dylan's Rolling Thunder Revue,
captured on the fall 1976 TV special "Hard Rain." Baez
also appeared in Dylan's 1978 feature film, *Renaldo and
Clara.*

By 1965, politics had become Baez's main concern. In
that year, she founded the Institute for the Study of Non-
Violence in Carmel, California, signaling her increasing
preoccupation with U.S. involvement in Vietnam. In 1968,
she married student protest leader David Harris, who was
jailed for draft evasion a year later, fueling Baez's antiwar

fervor (reflected in *David's Album* and *One Day at a Time*). The marriage fell apart in 1971, two years after the birth of their son, Gabriel.

Baez's career suffered under the burden of her political commitment. At the height of her anti-war activities, she devoted the second side of *Where Are You Now, My Son?* to a quasi-documentary account of a U.S. bombing raid of Hanoi. But in the early Seventies, she also made some of the most commercial music of her career, including her #3 rendition of the Band's "The Night They Drove Old Dixie Down" (a gold single in 1971) and *Diamonds and Rust*. Her voice had become lower and richer than in her folk phase.

Baez has remained politically active. In 1973, she was a vocal opponent of the coup in Chile and the assassination of Socialist president Salvador Allende. In August 1981, Baez toured Latin America and was met with bomb threats and harassment. Later in the year, she met with U.S. government officials in Washington, D.C., to discuss human rights in South America. A ninety-minute TV special on the tour was scheduled for 1982, but was not shown.

In 1968, Baez published an autobiography, *Daybreak*. Her sister Mimi was married to novelist and songwriter Richard Fariña.

GINGER BAKER

Born Peter Baker, August 19, 1939, Lewisham, England
Ginger Baker's Air Force: 1970—*Air Force* (Atco)   *Air Force 2*. **Ginger Baker: 1972**—*Fela Ransome-Kuti and Africa '70 with Ginger Baker* (Signpost)   *Stratavarious* (Polydor)   *Ginger Baker at His Best*   **1977**—*Eleven Sides of Baker* (Sire)   **1980**—*Kuti and Africa*.   **Baker-Gurvitz Army: 1975**—*Baker-Gurvitz Army* (Janus)   *Elysian Encounter* (Atco)   **1976**—*Hearts on Fire*.

In the adulation that outlasted Cream, Ginger Baker was touted as a great drummer; his splashy style paved the way for a decade of heavy-metal drum solos. As a teenager, Baker played with traditional jazz bands, but he got his first taste of R&B with Alexis Korner's Blues Incorporated when Charlie Watts left the group to join the fledgling Rolling Stones in 1962. A year later, Baker and two other group members, singer Graham Bond and bassist Jack Bruce, formed the Graham Bond Trio (later, Organisation). He and Bruce remained until forming Cream with Eric Clapton in mid-1966. Over the course of two years, Cream became a supergroup. After Cream split up in November 1968, Baker joined the short-lived Blind Faith.

Ginger Baker's Air Force debuted in January 1970. The percussion-dominated group was loosely structured, both in arrangements and personnel, which in various permutations included Stevie Winwood, Rick Grech, Bond, Denny Laine and Remi Kabaka, one of three full-time drummers.

Phil Seaman and the members of Air Force encouraged Baker's growing interest in African music, and in 1971 the drummer moved to Lagos, Nigeria, to build the first 16-track studio in West Africa. For the next few years he played with local talent, formed the group Salt, and ran his recording studio. Paul McCartney recorded *Band on the Run* there in 1973, by which time Baker had been musically inactive for many months. In 1974, he reemerged with the Baker-Gurvitz Army, which recorded three jazz-rock albums before disbanding in the late Seventies. By then, Baker was reportedly spending a lot of his time playing polo.

Baker was not in the news again until 1982, when it was reported that he was leaving England because of tax debts that British authorities claimed exceeded £100,000. He moved to Milan, Italy, where he signed with CGD Records, formed a band with American musicians and set up a drum school in a small mountain village.

LAVERN BAKER

Born November 11, 1929, Chicago
1970—*Let Me Belong to You* (Brunswick)   **1971**—*LaVern Baker: Her Greatest Recordings* (Atco).

LaVern Baker was a major R&B vocalist during the Fifties. Born in Chicago, where she sang gospel as a girl, Baker got her first professional experience in Detroit, where she appeared in the late Forties as Little Miss Sharecropper. She was soon signed by Columbia, but her recordings for that label were unsuccessful, as were her efforts for King beginning in 1952. Her luck changed with the emerging Atlantic label in 1953, where she did tunes like "Tweedle Dee," "Bop-Ting-a-Ling" and "Play It Fair."

Ahmet Ertegun and Herb Abramson, who produced most of her sessions, started getting her stronger material in 1956. Rocking items like "Jim Dandy," "Jim Dandy Got Married" and "Voodoo Voodoo" established her as a major international R&B star in the late Fifties, although her sales were perpetually hampered by white acts' cover versions. (At one point, the competition was so fierce that Baker fired off a letter to her Detroit congressman. All she got back was publicity.) Her only big pop hit came in 1959 with the ballad "I Cried a Tear" (#6). The followup, "I Waited Too Long," only reached #33. Although continuing to score minor hits through the early Sixties ("Tiny Tim," "Shake a Hand," "Bumble Bee," "You're the Boss," "Saved," "See See Rider"), by the time she switched to Brunswick in 1963, her career was on the decline.

LONG JOHN BALDRY

Born Jan. 12, 1941, East Maddon-Doveshire, England
1966—*Looking for Long John* (United Artists)   **1971**—*It Ain't Easy* (Warner Bros.)   *Long John's Blues*   **1972**—

Everything Stops for Tea   **1974**—*Heartaches (Golden Hour) (Pye)*   **1976**—*Baldry's Out (EMI)   Welcome to Club Casablanca (Casablanca)*   **1977**—*Good to Be Alive*   **1980**—*Long John Baldry*   **1981**—*Rock with the Best (Capitol, Canada).*

Although sustained commercial success has eluded him, blues vocalist John Baldry's influence in the Sixties on future British superstars was considerable. He grew up in the English countryside and began playing guitar at age 15. He played in Dixieland bands before becoming a solo performer on the English folk-club circuit. After touring Europe with Ramblin' Jack Elliott between 1957 and 1961, he turned to the blues and R&B.

Baldry (nicknamed Long John because of his six-foot-seven frame) came to prominence in Britain's early-Sixties blues-rock scene. He played in Alexis Korner's Blues Incorporated (which at times included Jack Bruce, Ginger Baker, Mick Jagger and Charlie Watts) until 1962, when he toured Germany with a jazz band for a few months. Upon his return to England, he joined the Cyril Davies R&B All-Stars, and when Davies died in January 1964 from leukemia, Baldry recruited some of the All-Stars to start his own band, the Hootchie Coochie Men, which included Rod Stewart. The following year Baldry formed Steampacket with Stewart, Brian Auger, Julie Driscoll, drummer Mickey Waller (later with Jeff Beck) and guitarist Vic Briggs (later with the Animals). In 1966 he formed Bluesology; its roster included keyboardist Reg Dwight, who would later change his name to Elton John.

Beginning in 1967, Baldry had several hit pop ballads in the U.K. ("Let the Heartaches Begin," "Mexico"), but he turned to blues and rock in 1971 and recorded *It Ain't Easy.* Former protégés Elton John and Rod Stewart each produced one side of the disc, which yielded a U.S. Top 100 single, "Don't Try to Lay No Boogie-Woogie on the King of Rock 'n' Roll." After spending a couple of months in a mental institution in 1976, Baldry released an LP titled *Baldry's Out* (1976). Through the late Seventies, Baldry toured the U.S. and Canada. He became a Canadian citizen in 1980.

HANK BALLARD
Born November 18, 1936, Detroit

Hank Ballard earned distinction as a rock pioneer by laying sexually explicit lyrics on top of raw gospel-derived rhythms. With his backup group the Midnighters, he recorded several successful sides for the King label in the early Fifties. In his best year, 1954, he had three R&B Top Ten hits with the "Annie" trilogy—"Work with Me, Annie," "Annie Had a Baby" and "Annie's Aunt Fanny"—each of which sold over a million copies internationally despite being widely banned from the airwaves. They made Ballard a top draw on the R&B circuit, although he

did not have another major hit until "Teardrops on My Letter" in 1958.

While recording "Teardrops," he quickly composed a B-side novelty dance tune called "The Twist." In 1960, Chubby Checker's slicker version became one of early rock's best-selling singles. Ballard and the Midnighters had two hits in 1960, "Finger Poppin' Time" (#7) and "Let's Go, Let's Go, Let's Go" (#6). When the group broke up in the mid-Sixties, he embarked on a solo career. By then, his fortunes had waned, and he returned to playing soul clubs. Befitting a man whose biggest successes were risqué records, Ballard tried to promote his 1974 song "Let's Go Streaking" by recording it in the nude. He continues to perform in clubs.

THE BAND
Formed 1967, Woodstock, New York
James Robbie Robertson (b. July 5, 1944, Toronto), gtr.; Richard Manuel (b. Apr. 3, 1945, Stratford, Can.), piano, voc.; Garth Hudson (b. Aug. 2, *ca.* 1943, London, Can.), organ, sax; Rick Danko (b. Dec. 9, 1943, Simcoe, Can.), bass, voc.; Levon Helm (b. May 26, 1942, Marvell, Ark.), drums, voc., mandolin.
1968—*Music from Big Pink* (Capitol)   **1969**—*The Band*   **1970**—*Stage Fright*   **1971**—*Cahoots*   **1972**—*Rock of Ages*   **1973**—*Moondog Matinee*   **1975**—*Northern Lights—Southern Cross*   **1976**—*The Best of the Band*   **1977**—*Islands*   **1978**—*The Last Waltz* (Warner Bros.)   **1978**—*Anthology* (Capitol).

With their rock-ribbed, austerely precise arrangements and a catalogue of songs that link American folklore to primal myths, the Band—four Canadians and a Southerner—made music that was both earthy and mystical, still unsurpassed in its depth and originality. They had been playing together for most of a decade before they recorded their first album in 1968. Beginning with Robbie Robertson, they joined rockabilly singer Ronnie Hawkins' Hawks one by one, and by 1960 the future Band had all been with Hawkins on and off, an association that continued until 1963. They then began working on their own, variously as Levon and the Hawks, or the Crackers, or the Canadian Squires. Singer John Hammond, Jr. (John Paul Hammond) heard them in a Canadian club in 1964 and asked them to perform and record with him in New York City, Chicago and Texas. Once active in Greenwich Village they attracted Bob Dylan's attention. Robertson and Levon Helm were in the electrified backup band at Dylan's controversial Forest Hills concert of August 28, 1965. Despite a falling out between Dylan and Helm, Dylan hired the Hawks—with drummer Mickey Jones in lieu of Helm—for his 1965-66 world tour, inaugurating a longtime collaboration.

After Dylan's 1966 motorcycle accident, the group settled near the suddenly reclusive star in the Woodstock,

The Band: Rick Danko, Levon Helm, Richard Manuel, Garth Hudson, Robbie Robertson

New York, area. Helm rejoined, and while recording extensively with Dylan (the much-bootlegged sessions were released in 1975 as *The Basement Tapes*), they began working on their own material, most of it written by Robertson and Richard Manuel. Recorded in a basement studio in their house (Big Pink) in West Saugerties, the material made up the Band's debut album. With its unflashy sound and enigmatic lyrics, *Music from Big Pink* was a revolutionary album; although its long-term influence was enormous, it has yet to be certified gold.

The group moved to Hollywood, but their second album, *The Band,* was a celebration of rural life and the past. It was their masterpiece and their commercial breakthrough, and they did a national tour on their own to support it. Robertson was emerging as chief songwriter as well as producer, and his impressions of the road inspired the Band's third album, *Stage Fright.* After 1971's *Cahoots* (with an appearance by Van Morrison) the Band recorded a tribute to early rock & roll (*Moondog Matinee,* named after Alan Freed's radio show) and a double live LP, *Rock of Ages.*

With the exception of a joint appearance in 1969 at the Isle of Wight Festival in Britain, the Band rarely worked with Dylan in the early Seventies. But shortly after the Band played at the Watkins Glen concert in July 1973, they joined Dylan in the studio to record his *Planet Waves.* The next year, they toured together and did the live album *Before the Flood.*

The Band's output continued to slow down through the Seventies. In November 1975, they released their first new material in four years, *Northern Lights—Southern Cross,* followed two years later by their final studio album,

Islands. Robertson had produced an album for Neil Diamond, *Beautiful Noise,* in 1976. After 16 years together, the Band called it quits with a gala concert on Thanksgiving Day 1976. The Band and guests (including Dylan, Morrison, Neil Young, Muddy Waters, Joni Mitchell, Neil Diamond and others) performed at San Francisco's Winterland (the site of their first concert as the Band in 1969) for *The Last Waltz,* filmed by Martin Scorsese.

Since the breakup, Helm has continued to record and tour, with the RCO All Stars, the Cate Brothers, and Danko. He made his film debut in 1980 in *Coal Miner's Daughter.* Robertson starred in and composed part of the score for 1980's *Carny,* and wrote music for Scorsese's *The King of Comedy.* Danko has a solo contract with Arista and has toured with a group that has sometimes included Manuel and Garth Hudson, and he has done occasional session work.

THE BARBARIANS
Formed circa 1965, Boston
N.A. *The Barbarians* (Laurie)   **1979**—*The Barbarians* (Rhino).

A classic mid-Sixties protopunk garage band, the Barbarians boasted a drummer named Moulty who had a hook for a left hand. He sang many of the band's songs, including the autobiographical "Moulty" (#90, 1966). The group had a minor hit with "Are You a Boy or Are You a Girl" (#55, 1965) a reference to the band's prepsychedelic long hair. The Barbarians appeared in the mid-Sixties documentary *The T.A.M.I. Show.*

BARCLAY JAMES HARVEST
Formed 1967, England
Stewart "Wooly" Wolstenholme (b. Apr. 15, 1947, Oldham, Eng.), kybds., voc.; Melvyn John Pritchard (b. Jan. 20, 1948, Oldham, Eng.), drums; John Lees (b. Jan. 13, 1948, Oldham, Eng.), gtr., voc.; Les Holroyd (b. Mar. 12, 1948, Oldham, Eng.), bass, voc.
1970—*Barclay James Harvest* (Capitol) 1971—*Once Again* (Sire) 1972—*Early Morning Onward* (EMI) *Barclay James Harvest* (Sire) 1973—*Baby James Harvest* (Capitol) 1974—*Live* (Polydor) *Everyone Is Everybody Else* 1975—*Time Honoured Ghosts* 1976—*Octoberon* (MCA) 1977—*Gone to Earth* 1978—*Live Tapes* (Polydor) *Number 12* 1979—*Best of, Volume 2* (Harvest) (– Wolstenholme) 1980— *Eyes of the Universe* (Polydor).

This is an English art-rock band that has developed a loyal cult following in its homeland. With a remarkably smooth personnel record for a veteran band that's never been financially successful, BJH carries on as it nears the end of its fifteenth year. Like the nascent Pink Floyd, with whom they were often compared, BJH were a hard-rock group with classical overtones when they were signed to EMI/ Parlophone in 1968. The band was formed by art-school classmates, John Lees and Stewart Wolstenholme. Beginning in 1970, EMI released its albums on a subsidiary label, Harvest, which was named after the promising BJH. But the promise never panned out, leaving BJH as a minor British attraction supported by an enthusiastic but limited cult.

THE BAR-KAYS
Formed mid-1960s, Memphis
Jimmy King (b. 1949; d. Dec. 10, 1967); Ron Caldwell (b. 1948; d. Dec. 10, 1967); Phalin Jones (b. 1949; d. Dec. 10, 1967); Carl Cunningham (b. 1949; d. Dec. 10, 1967); Ben Cauley, trumpet; James Alexander, bass.
N.A.—*Soul Finger* (Atco) 1969—*Gotta Groove* (Stax) 1982—*Night Cruisin'* (Mercury).

The Bar-Kays were part of the Stax-Volt roster in the mid-Sixties and had one big hit, "Soul Finger" (#17), in 1967. Their career seemed finished when four members died in the icy plane crash that also killed Otis Redding in 1967. The two surviving members, James Alexander and Ben Cauley, re-formed the group in late 1968 and have had sporadic success since. They backed Isaac Hayes on *Hot Buttered Soul* and the award-winning "Shaft" (#1, 1971). In the early Seventies, the Bar-Kays were a featured act at a huge outdoor concert in Watts sponsored by Stax. The concert was filmed and released as *Wattstax*.

Still regarded as one of soul's premier backing bands, the Bar-Kays worked in the early Seventies with such artists as the Staple Singers, Albert King, Carla Thomas

and Johnnie Taylor. In 1976, following a three-year hiatus caused by managerial and record company problems, they signed with Mercury and placed several records on the soul charts, and even scored a pop hit with "Shake Your Rump to the Funk" (#23, 1976). While personnel have changed frequently in recent years, several excellent R&B musicians have passed through the Bar-Kays' ranks, including longtime vocalist Vernon Burch and drummer Willie Hall, who went on to play in Hayes's band for several years and then joined the revamped Booker T. and the MGs in 1975.

SYD BARRETT
Born January 6, 1946, Cambridge, England
1970—*The Madcap Laughs* (Harvest) *Barrett* 1974— *The Madcap Laughs/Barrett.*

British singer/songwriter/guitarist Syd Barrett was an art school student in London when he founded and named Pink Floyd in 1964. He wrote "See Emily Play" and *Piper at the Gates of Dawn* for the group, and his acid-inspired lyrics were the quintessence of London's 1967 Summer of Love. Barrett was dismissed from the band in April 1968 because of his drug-induced personality problems; Dave Gilmour was his replacement. Barrett has subsequently spent time in a mental ward and lived as a recluse. He has released two solo albums, assisted by members of Pink Floyd, who dedicated a popular 1975 song, "Shine On, You Crazy Diamond," to their eccentric founder.

JEFF BARRY
Born April 3, 1938, Brooklyn, New York

As songwriters and producers, Jeff Barry and his wife, Ellie Greenwich, were a major force in early-Sixties pop. Between 1959 and the time he met Greenwich in 1962, Barry had recorded over ten singles with minimal success. He fared better writing for other artists, scoring with the macabre "Tell Laura I Love Her," a big hit for Ray Peterson in 1960, and Gene McDaniels' Top Ten outing in 1962, "Chip Chip,"

After he and Greenwich married in 1963, their tunes were recorded by Lesley Gore, the Exciters, the Shirelles, the Chiffons and the Phil Spector stable. Their hits for Spector's groups included "Da Doo Ron Ron" (also a big hit in the Seventies for Shaun Cassidy), "Then He Kissed Me" for the Crystals, "Be My Baby" and "Baby I Love You" for the Ronettes and "Chapel of Love" for the Dixie Cups as well as hits for Darlene Love, Bobb B. Soxx and Ike and Tina Turner.

In 1963, Barry and Greenwich recorded for Jubilee Records as the Raindrops and had hits with "What a Guy" and the Top Twenty "Kind of Boy You Can't Forget." They continued their success with Leiber and Stoller's Red Bird label in 1964, working with the Shangri-Las,

Dixie Cups and Jelly Beans; and their writing partnership outlived their marriage by a few years. By 1966, they were at Bert Berns's Bang records with Neil Diamond, for whom they produced five LPs and several hits like "Cherry Cherry" and "Solitary Man." They continued to score freelance hits like the infectious "Do Wah Diddy Diddy," a Top Ten item for Manfred Mann, and the chart-topping bubblegum teaser "Hanky Panky" (originally a Raindrops B side resurrected by Tommy James, with whom Barry worked in the late Seventies). Barry also produced the Monkees' #1 hit, Diamond's "I'm a Believer."

As the Sixties came to a close, Greenwich became an independent producer, and Barry recorded some unsuccessful singles for United Artists before striking it rich with the Archies, writing the 1969 blockbuster hits "Jingle Jangle" and "Sugar Sugar," which sold six million records.

Barry moved to L.A. in 1972 and remains sporadically active. He wrote the theme song to "The Jeffersons" TV series and produced and cowrote Olivia Newton-John's 1972 smash "I Honestly Love You."

LEN BARRY

Born Leonard Borisoff, December 6, 1942, Philadelphia
1965—*1-2-3* (Decca) **N.A.**—*Len Barry Sings with the Dovells* (Cameo) *My Kind of Soul* (RCA) *Ups and Downs* (Buddah).

Len Barry was a latter-day Philadelphia teen idol whose several mid-Sixties hits included "Like a Baby," "Somewhere" and "1-2-3," which rose to #2. A mainstay of the Philly scene in its peak, Barry sang on the Bosstones' 1958 hit "Mope-Itty Mop" and sang lead with the Dovells, who were regularly on the charts from 1961 through 1963 with songs like "The Bristol Stomp." Barry's greatest success, "1-2-3," was produced by Leon Huff, later a soul-music producer. Barry was known for a manic, wild stage manner modeled after James Brown's. When the hits stopped coming, he toned down his style considerably and hit the supper-club circuit.

DAVE BARTHOLOMEW

Born December 24, 1920, Edgard, Louisiana

An architect of the New Orleans sound of the Fifties, Dave Bartholomew produced many artists, most notably Fats Domino, with whom he also frequently collaborated on songs. His father, tuba player Louis Bartholomew, encouraged his interest in music from an early age, and while still in his teens, Dave played trumpet in Fats Pichon's band on a Mississippi riverboat.

Following World War II military service, he returned to New Orleans in 1946 and started his own band, playing R&B, jazz and standards. Bartholomew hand-picked his talent and in the late Forties signed a young pianist named Fats Domino. Bartholomew recorded regularly (his "Country Boy" sold almost 100,000 in 1949) and began producing for others. In the early Fifties, he worked regularly for Imperial Records, where he recorded Domino. Their first release, "The Fat Man," was the first of many Top Ten hits ("Blueberry Hill," "I'm Walkin' ") for Domino.

Bartholomew also produced or arranged singles by a variety of New Orleans–based artists including Jewel King ("3 x 7 = 21"), Lloyd Price ("Lawdy Miss Clawdy"), Shirley and Lee ("I'm Gone"), Smiley Lewis ("I Hear You Knockin' "), Bobby Mitchell ("Try Rock and Roll"), and many others. His band also backed up Little Richard on his early recordings. Though Bartholomew continued to record on his own through the early Sixties, his reputation is primarily based on his work for others.

BAY CITY ROLLERS

Formed 1967 (as the Saxons), Edinburgh
Alan Longmuir (b. June 20, 1953, Edinburgh), bass; Eric Faulkner (b. Oct. 21, 1955, Edinburgh), gtr.; Derek Longmuir (b. Mar. 19, 1955, Edinburgh), drums; Leslie McKeown (b. Nov. 12, 1955, Edinburgh), voc.; Stuart "Woody" Wood (b. Feb. 25, 1957, Edinburgh), gtr.
1975—*Bay City Rollers* (Arista) **1976**—*Rock 'n' Roll Love Letter; Dedication* (− Alan Longmuir; + Ian Mitchell [b. Aug. 22, 1958], gtr.; Wood switched to bass; − Mitchell; + Pat McGlynn [b. Mar. 31, 1958, Edinburgh], gtr.) **1977**—*Greatest Hits* (− McGlynn) **1978**—*Strangers in the Wild.*

The Bay City Rollers were touted as the "new Beatles." Actually, the Rollers were cute young musicians who were vigorously promoted to a market of teenagers. Probably the most successful act ever to emerge from Scotland, they scored their first English hit in 1971. Through the next few years, under the guidance of mentor/manager Tam Paton (who named the group by arbitrarily sticking a pin in a U.S. map and hitting Bay City, Michigan), they slowly expanded their predominantly female audience. Clad in tartan uniforms highlighted by knicker-length pants, they eventually inspired a genuine outbreak of teenage frenzy reminiscent of Beatlemania in the early Sixties.

Rollermania spread to the U.S. briefly in spring 1976 with the group's first Stateside concerts and a #1 single, "Saturday Night." The Rollers sang the words but didn't always play the instruments on their records. Their close-knit, wholesome image was tarnished somewhat in the late Seventies with the disclosure that they had all regularly taken Valium to help them cope with the rigors of superstardom and life on the road and that two members (Faulkner and Mitchell) had been treated for overdoses in apparent suicide attempts. By the early Eighties they were a quartet playing bars in the U.S., still wearing their tartan plaid.

THE BEACH BOYS

Formed 1961, Hawthorne, California.
Brian Wilson (b. June 20, 1942, Hawthorne), voc., bass, piano; Dennis Wilson (b. Dec. 4, 1944, Hawthorne), voc., drums; Carl Wilson (b. Dec. 21, 1946, Hawthorne), voc., gtr.; Mike Love (b. Mar. 15, 1941, Los Angeles), voc., misc., percussion; Al (Alan) Jardine (b. Sep. 3, 1942, Lima, Oh.), voc., gtr.
1962—(– Jardine; + David Marks [b. Hawthorne], gtr.) *Surfin' Safari* (Capitol) **1963**—*Surfin' USA; Surfer Girl; Shut Down; Little Deuce Coupe* **1964**—*Shut Down, volume 2 All Summer Long; The Beach Boys' Christmas Album* (– Marks; + Jardine) *The Beach Boys' Concert* **1965**—*The Beach Boys Today; Summer Days (and Summer Nights) The Beach Boys' Party!* (+ Bruce Johnston [b. June 24, 1944, Chicago], gtr., voc.) **1966**—*Pet Sounds; Best of the Beach Boys, volume 1* **1967**—*Best of the Beach Boys, volume 2 Smiley Smile; The Beach Boys Deluxe Set; Wild Honey* **1968**— *Friends; Best of the Beach Boys, volume 3 Stack o' Tracks* **1969**—*20/20; Close Up* **1970**—*Sunflower* (Brother/Reprise) **1971**—*Surf's Up* **1972**—*Pet Sounds* (– Johnston) *Holland* (Reprise) *The Beach Boys in Concert* (Brother/Reprise) **1974**—*Endless Summer* (Capitol) *Wild Honey* and *20/20* (Reprise) *Friends* and *Smiley Smile; Pet Sounds* (Capitol) **1975**—*Spirit of America; Good Vibrations: Best of the Beach Boys* (Brother/Reprise) **1976**—*15 Big Ones; Beach Boys '69 (The Beach Boys Live in London)* (Capitol) **1977**— *The Beach Boys Love You* (Brother/Reprise) **1978**— *M.I.U. Album* (+ Johnston) **1979**—*L.A. (Light Album)* (Caribou) **1980**—*Keepin' the Summer Alive* (originally *All Summer Long*, 1964) **1981**—*Ten Years of Harmony.*

In their early-Sixties hits, the Beach Boys virtually invented California rock. Brian Wilson's songs celebrated an idealized California teenhood—surfing, driving, dating—and his productions were a glossy, perfectionistic, ultra-smooth blend of guitars and vocal harmonies, with their experiments concealed. While the Beach Boys attempted more grown-up topics and more obvious progressivism in the late Sixties, they survived into the Eighties as America's premier nostalgia act. They have sold over 65 million records worldwide, most of which are their early hits and repackages of them.

The three Wilson brothers were encouraged by their parents, Murray and Audree, to try music and sports. Brian was a varsity baseball player at suburban Hawthorne High when he began to work seriously on music. His first band included brothers Dennis and Carl (who eventually got expelled from Hawthorne High for going to the bathroom without permission), cousin Mike Love, and friend Al Jardine. As the Pendletones, Kenny and the Cadets (Brian was "Kenny") or Carl and the

The Beach Boys: Al Jardine, Dennis Wilson, Brian Wilson, Carl Wilson, Mike Love

Passions, the group played local gigs. On Dennis' suggestion, Love and Brian wrote "Surfin'," which became a regional hit on the soon defunct Candix label in December 1961, while the group was calling itself the Beach Boys. Like most of their early songs, "Surfin'" used Chuck Berry guitar licks with vocal harmonies (arranged by Brian) recalling Fifties pop groups like the Four Freshmen.

Murray Wilson, who managed his sons' band, got them a contract with Capitol, and their hits began: "Surfin' Safari" (#14, 1962); "Surfin' U.S.A." (#3, 1963), a note-for-note copy of Berry's "Sweet Little Sixteen" with new lyrics; and "Surfer Girl" (#7, 1963), all of which launched and capitalized on the "surf music" fad, although only Dennis surfed regularly. *Surfer Girl* marked Brian's emergence as a producer, with its complex vocal harmonies and sophisticated pop chords.

The next two years established the Beach Boys' legacy: "I Get Around" (#1, 1964); "Fun, Fun, Fun" (#5, 1964), written by Brian and Love in a taxi to the Salt Lake City airport; "Help Me, Rhonda" (#1, 1965); "California Girls" (#3, 1965); and such ballads as "In My Room" (#23, 1963) and "Don't Worry, Baby" (#24, 1964). Early in 1965, Brian Wilson had a nervous breakdown and decided to quit touring. The first result was *Pet Sounds* in March 1966, which included "Wouldn't It Be Nice" and "God Only Knows" but sold comparatively poorly; it ushered in the era of studio experimentation, predating the Beatles' *Sgt. Pepper's Lonely Hearts Club Band.* The highlight of the Beach Boys' borderline psychedelic period was "Good Vibrations" (#1, 1966), Wilson's production masterpiece. It took six months and cost $16,000 to make, with several distinct sections and such exotic instruments as Jew's harp, sleighbells, harpsichord and theremin.

Brian's ambitions, neuroses and drug intake were increasing. He and Van Dyke Parks began collaborating on *Smile* in late 1966, but after a mysterious fire at the studio where they were working, Wilson reportedly destroyed most of the tapes in a fit of paranoia. Several *Smile* songs have appeared since; the Wilson-Parks "Heroes and Villains" (#12, 1967) appeared on *Smiley Smile*, and the title cut of *Surf's Up* was also a *Smile* composition. The *Smile* debacle, and *Smiley Smile*, marked the end of Brian's reign as the Beach Boys' sole producer.

On *Wild Honey, Sunflower* and *Holland*, other group members shared writing and production, along with Bruce Johnston, who had joined the touring Beach Boys after Brian retired from the road. (Johnston replaced Glen Campbell after a brief stint.) Johnston has been associated on and off with the Beach Boys, primarily as producer, ever since. The Beach Boys' late-Sixties touring band also included Daryl Dragon (later the Captain of the Captain and Tennille) on keyboards, Blondie Chaplin (later with Rick Danko and others) on guitar, bass and vocals, and Ricky Fataar (later of Joe Walsh's band) on drums. In 1968, the Beach Boys became the first major American rock band to play behind the Iron Curtain when they performed in Czechoslovakia.

The Beach Boys got a custom label, Brother Records, with Reprise; their first album under the deal, *Sunflower*, inaugurated a five-year hiatus for Brian, although he tried one live show in early 1970 at the Whisky-a-Go-Go in Los Angeles. While the band continued to release new material, the bulk of their live repertoire from the early Seventies onward has been their mid-Sixties hits, which went platinum in the repackages *Endless Summer* and *Spirit of America. Holland*, recorded during a six-month stay in Amsterdam, returned the Beach Boys to the charts with "Sail on Sailor."

Meanwhile, efforts continued to coax Brian out of his mansion (which included a sandbox as well as a recording studio) in Bel Air. In the late Sixties, he had briefly run a West Hollywood health food store, the Radiant Radish; and in 1972 he produced an album by his wife, Marilyn, and her sister Diane Powell, as Spring (or American Spring). In 1976, after a much-publicized rehabilitation, Brian rejoined the band for *15 Big Ones*, which included oldie remakes (Chuck Berry's "Rock and Roll Music," which went to #5) and Brian Wilson originals, such as "Johnny Carson."

In 1977, open personality clashes (primarily between Dennis Wilson and Mike Love) jeopardized the band's future as they switched labels; eventually, Mike's brothers Stan and Steve Love were removed from Beach Boys management. For the Beach Boys' first Caribou album, *L.A. (Light Album)*, Johnston was back as co-producer; in the mid-Seventies he had left the band to write songs (including Barry Manilow's hit "I Write the Songs") and make a solo album, *Going Public* (1977). Early in 1982, the Beach Boys were back on the charts with a remake of the Del-Vikings' "Come Go with Me."

In Brian's absence the other Beach Boys gained some prominence. Dennis Wilson's writing and singing surfaced on *20/20* in 1969, while he was friendly with Charles Manson. In 1971, Dennis appeared in *Two Lane Blacktop* with James Taylor, and in 1977 he released a solo album, *Pacific Ocean Blue*. By 1979, he was romantically involved with Fleetwood Mac's Christine McVie. Carl Wilson has had a songwriting credit on nearly every Beach Boys album since 1967, and did a solo tour in support of 1981's *Carl Wilson*. Mike Love was featured on Celebration's "Almost Summer" (#28, 1978). Al Jardine, who along with Love has practiced Transcendental Meditation since 1967, has supplied Beach Boys songs for over a decade, including "Lady Lynda," a tribute to his wife.

THE BEATLES
Formed 1959, Liverpool
John Lennon (b. Oct. 9, 1940, Liverpool; d. Dec. 8, 1980, New York City), gtr., voc., harmonica, kybds.; Paul McCartney (b. June 18, 1942, Liverpool,), bass, voc., gtr., kybds.; George Harrison (b. Feb. 25, 1943, Liverpool), gtr., voc., sitar; Stu Sutcliffe (b. 1940, Edinburgh; d. Apr. 10, 1962, Hamburg), bass; Pete Best (b. 1941, Eng.), drums.
1962—(− Best; + Ringo Starr [b. Richard Starkey, Jr., July 7, 1940, Liverpool], drums, percussion, voc., misc.) **1963**—*Please Please Me* (Parlophone, U.K.) *With the Beatles* (U.K.) **1964**—*Meet the Beatles* (Capitol) *The Beatles' Second Album; The Beatles' Story; Something New; A Hard Day's Night* (United Artists) *Beatles '65* **1965**—*Early Beatles; Beatles VI; Help!; Rubber Soul* **1966**—*Yesterday . . . and Today; Revolver* **1967**—*Sgt. Pepper's Lonely Hearts Club Band; Magical Mystery Tour* **1968**—*The Beatles* (Apple) **1969**—*Yellow Submarine* (Capitol) *Abbey Road* **1970**—*The Beatles Again; Let It Be* (Apple) **1973**—*The Beatles 1962–1966* (Capitol) *The Beatles 1967–1970* **1976**—*Rock 'N' Roll Music* **1977**—*Love Songs; Live at the Hollywood Bowl; Live at the Star Club in Hamburg, Germany, 1962* (Atlantic) **1980**—*Rarities* **1982**—*Reel Music.*

The impact of the Beatles—not only on rock & roll but on all of Western culture—is simply incalculable. As musicians, they proved that rock & roll could embrace a limitless variety of harmonies, structures and sounds; virtually every rock experiment has some precedent on

Beatles records. As a unit, they were a musically synergistic combination: Paul McCartney's melodic bass lines, Ringo Starr's slaphappy no-rolls drumming, George Harrison's rockabilly-style guitar leads, John Lennon's assertive rhythm guitar—and their four fervent voices. One of the first rock groups to write most of their material, they inaugurated the era of self-contained bands, and forever centralized pop. And as personalities, they defined and incarnated Sixties style: smart, idealistic, playful, irreverent, eclectic. Their music, from the not-so-simple love songs they started with to their later perfectionistic studio extravaganzas, set new standards for both commercial and artistic success in pop. Although many of their sales and attendance records have since been surpassed, no group has so radically transformed the sound and meaning of rock & roll.

Lennon was performing with his amateur skiffle group, the Quarrymen, at a church picnic on July 6, 1957, in the Liverpool suburb of Woolton when he met McCartney, whom he later invited to join his group; soon they were writing songs together, such as "The One after 909." By the year's end, McCartney had convinced Lennon to let Harrison join their group, whose name was changed to Johnny and the Moondogs in 1958. The next year, an art school friend of Lennon's, Stu Sutcliffe, became their bassist. Sutcliffe couldn't play a note but had recently sold one of his paintings for a considerable sum, which the group, now rechristened the Silver Beatles (from which "Silver" was dropped a few months later), used to upgrade their equipment. Tommy Moore was their drummer until Pete Best replaced him in August 1960.

Once Best had joined them, the band made their first of four trips to Hamburg, Germany. In December, Harrison was deported back to England for being underage and lacking a work permit, but by then their thirty-set weeks on the stages of Hamburg beerhouses had honed and strengthened their repertoire (mostly Chuck Berry, Little Richard, Carl Perkins and Buddy Holly covers), and in January 1961 they debuted at the Cavern Club on Mathew Street in Liverpool, beginning a string of nearly 300 performances there over the next couple of years.

In April 1961, they again went to Hamburg, where Sutcliffe (the first of the Beatles to wear his hair in the long, shaggy style that came to be known as the Beatle haircut) left the group to become a painter, while McCartney switched from rhythm guitar to bass. The Beatles returned to Liverpool as a quartet in June. Sutcliffe died from a brain hemorrhage in Hamburg less than a year later.

The Beatles had been playing regularly to packed houses at the Cavern when they were spotted in late 1961 by Brian Epstein. After being discharged from the British Army on medical grounds, Epstein had attended the Royal Academy of Dramatic Art in London for a year before returning to Liverpool to manage his father's record store.

The Beatles: (top) Paul McCartney, Ringo Starr, (bottom) George Harrison, John Lennon

The request he received for a German import single entitled "My Bonnie" (which the Beatles had recorded a few months earlier in Hamburg, backing Tony Sheridan and billed as the Beat Boys) convinced him to check out the group. Epstein was surprised to discover not only that the Beatles weren't German but that they were one of the most popular local bands in Liverpool. Within a month he became their manager. Epstein cleaned up their act, eventually replacing black leather jackets, tight jeans and pompadours with collarless gray Pierre Cardin suits and mildly androgynous haircuts.

Epstein landed a contract with EMI's Parlophone subsidiary after the Beatles were rejected by nearly every label in Europe. Producer George Martin (b. Jan. 3, 1926, North London) auditioned the group in June 1962, and signed them to a contract the next month. Pete Best (then considered the group's undisputed sex symbol) was asked to leave the group on August 17, 1962, and Ringo Starr, drummer with a popular Liverpool group, Rory Storme and the Hurricanes, was added shortly before their first session for Parlophone. On September 11, they cut "Love Me Do" b/w "P.S. I Love You," which became their first U.K. Top Twenty hit in October. In early 1963, "Please Please Me" went to #2, and they recorded an album of the same name in one 13-hour session on February 11, 1963. With the success of their third English single, "From Me to You" (#1), the British record industry coined the term

"Merseybeat" for groups like Gerry and the Pacemakers, Billy J. Kramer and the Dakotas, and the Searchers, who also hailed from Liverpool on the Mersey River. By midyear, the Beatles were given billing over Roy Orbison on a national tour, and the hysterical outbreaks of "Beatlemania" had begun. Following their first tour of Europe in October, they moved to London with Epstein. Constantly mobbed by screaming fans, the Beatles required police protection almost any time they were seen in public. Late in the year, "She Loves You" became the biggest-selling single in British history. In November 1963, the group performed before the Queen Mother at the Royal Command Variety Performance.

EMI's American label, Capitol, had not released the group's 1963 records (which Martin licensed to independents like Vee Jay and Swan with little success), but was finally persuaded to release their fourth single, "I Want to Hold Your Hand," and *Meet the Beatles* (identical to the Beatles' second British album, *With the Beatles*) in January 1964 and to invest $50,000 in promotion for the then-unknown British act. On February 7, screaming mobs met them at New York's Kennedy Airport, and more than 70 million people watched each of their appearances on "The Ed Sullivan Show" on February 9 and 16. In April 1964, "Can't Buy Me Love" became the first record to top American and British charts simultaneously, and in the same month the Beatles held the top five positions in *Billboard*'s singles chart ("Can't Buy Me Love," "Twist and Shout," "She Loves You," "I Want to Hold Your Hand," "Please Please Me").

Their first movie, *A Hard Day's Night* (directed by Richard Lester), opened in America in August; it grossed $1.3 million in its first week. The band was aggressively merchandised—Beatle wigs, Beatle clothes, Beatle dolls, junk food, lunch pails, a cartoon series—from which, because of Epstein's ineptitude, they made surprisingly little. The Beatles also opened the American market to such British Invasion groups as the Dave Clark Five, the Rolling Stones and the Kinks.

By 1965, Lennon and McCartney rarely wrote songs together, although by contractual and personal agreement songs by either of them were credited to both. In 1965, the Beatles toured Europe, North America, the Far East and Australia. Their second movie, *Help!* (again directed by Lester), was filmed in England, Austria and the Bahamas in the spring and opened in the U.S. in August. On August 15, they performed to 55,000 fans at New York's Shea Stadium, setting a record for largest concert audience. McCartney's "Yesterday" (#1, 1965) would become one of the most often covered songs ever written. In June the Queen had announced that the Beatles would be awarded the MBE (Member of the Order of the British Empire). The announcement sparked some controversy—some MBE holders returned their medals—but on October 26, 1965, the ceremony took place at Buckingham Palace. (Lennon returned his medal in 1969.)

With 1965's *Rubber Soul,* the Beatles' ambitions began to extend beyond love songs and pop formulas. Their success led adults to consider them, along with Bob Dylan, spokesmen for youth culture; and their lyrics grew more poetic and somewhat more political. During the summer of 1966, controversy erupted when a remark Lennon had made to a reporter months before was widely reported in the U.S. The quotation—"Christianity will go. It will vanish and shrink. I needn't argue about that, I'm right and will be proved right. We're more popular than Jesus Christ right now"—incited denunciations and Beatles record bonfires. Lennon later apologized.

The Beatles gave up touring after an August 29, 1966, concert at San Francisco's Candlestick Park and made the rest of their music in the studio, where they had begun to experiment with exotic instrumentation ("Norwegian Wood," 1965, had featured sitar) and tape abstractions such as the reversed tracks on "Rain." With "Taxman" and "Love You To" on *Revolver,* Harrison began to emerge as a songwriter.

It took four months and $75,000 to record *Sgt. Pepper's Lonely Hearts Club Band* using a then state-of-the-art four-track tape recorder and building each cut layer by layer. Released in June 1967, it was hailed as serious art for its "concept" and its range of styles and sounds, a lexicon of pop and electronic noises; such songs as "Lucy in the Sky with Diamonds" and "A Day in the Life" were carefully examined for hidden meanings. On June 25, 1967, they appeared on international television to an audience of 200 million viewers.

On August 27, 1967—while the four were in Wales beginning their six-month involvement with Transcendental Meditation and the Maharishi Mahesh Yogi (which took them to India for two months in early 1968)—Epstein died alone in his London flat from an overdose of sleeping pills, later ruled accidental. Shaken by Epstein's death, the Beatles retrenched under McCartney's leadership in the fall and filmed *Magical Mystery Tour,* which was aired by BBC-TV on December 26, 1967, and later released in the U.S. as a feature film. Although the telefilm was panned by British critics, fans and Queen Elizabeth herself, the soundtrack album contained their most cryptic work yet in "Strawberry Fields Forever"—an astonishing display of electronically altered sounds—and "I Am the Walrus," both Lennon compositions.

As the Beatles' late 1967 single "Hello Goodbye" went to #1 in both the U.S. and Britain, the group launched the Apple clothes boutique in London. McCartney called the retail effort "Western communism," but the boutique closed in July 1968. Like their next effort, Apple Corps Ltd. (formed in January 1968 and including Apple Records, which signed James Taylor, Mary Hopkin and Badfinger), it was plagued by mismanagement. In July, the group faced its last hysterical crowds at the premiere of *Yellow Submarine,* an animated film by German poster artist Heinz Edelmann featuring four new Beatles songs.

In August they released McCartney's "Hey Jude," backed by Lennon's "Revolution," which sold over six million copies before the end of 1968—their most popular single.

Meanwhile, they had been working on the double album *The Beatles* (frequently called the "White Album"), which showed their divergent directions. The rifts were artistic—Lennon moving toward brutal confessionals, McCartney leaning toward pop melodies, Harrison immersed in Eastern spirituality—and personal as Lennon drew closer to his wife-to-be, Yoko Ono. Lennon and Ono's *Two Virgins* (with its full frontal and back nude cover photos) was released the same month as *The Beatles*.

The Beatles attempted to smooth over their differences in early 1969 at filmed recording sessions. When the project fell apart hundreds of hours of studio time later, no one could face editing the tapes (a project that eventually fell to Phil Spector) and "Get Back" (#1, 1969) was the only immediate release. Released in spring 1970, *Let It Be* is essentially a documentary of their breakup, including an impromptu rooftop concert at Apple Corps headquarters, their last public performance.

By spring 1969, Apple was losing thousands of pounds each week. Over McCartney's objections, the other three brought in manager Allen Klein to straighten things out; one of his first actions was to package non-album singles as *The Beatles Again* (a.k.a. *Hey Jude*). With money matters temporarily out of mind, the four joined forces in July and August 1969 to record *Abbey Road,* featuring an extended suite as well as more hits, including Harrison's much-covered "Something" (#3, 1969). While its release that fall spurred a "Paul Is Dead" rumor based on clues supposedly left throughout their work, *Abbey Road* became the Beatles' best-selling album. Meanwhile, internal bickering persisted. In September, Lennon told the others, "I'm leaving the group, I've had enough. I want a divorce," but he was persuaded to keep quiet while their business affairs were untangled. On April 17, 1970, McCartney released his first solo album and publicly announced the end of the Beatles. Throughout the Seventies as repackages of their music continued to sell, the four were hounded by bids and pleas for a reunion. Lennon's murder on December 8, 1980, ended those speculations.

THE BEAU BRUMMELS
Formed 1964, San Francisco
Sal Valentino (b. Sal Spampinato, Sep. 8, 1942, San Francisco), voc.; Ron Elliott (b. Oct. 21, 1943, Healdsburg, Calif.), gtr., voc.; Declan Mulligan (b. County Tipperary, Ire.), bass; John Petersen (b. Jan. 8, 1942, Rudyard, Mich.), drums; Ron Meagher (b. Oct. 2, 1941, Oakland, Calif.), gtr.
1965—(– Mulligan; Meagher shifts to bass) *Introducing the Beau Brummels* (Autumn) (– Petersen; no permanent drummer added) **1966**—*Beau Brummels* (Pye) *Beau Brummels '66* (Warner Bros.) **1967**—*Best of the Beau Brummels* (Vault) *Triangle*

Rock Musicians Who Have Written Books

JOAN BAEZ
Daybreak (1968)
And Then I Wrote . . . (1980)
EXENE CERVENKA and LYDIA LUNCH
Adulterers Anonymous (1982)
LEONARD COHEN
Let Us Compare Mythologies (1956)
Spice Box of Earth (1961)
The Favorite Game (1963)
Flowers for Hitler (1964)
Parasites of Heaven (1966)
Beautiful Losers (1966)
Poems 1956–68 (1968)
BOB DYLAN
Tarantula (1970)

RICHARD FARIÑA
Been Down So Long It Looks Like Up to Me (1966, 1983)
WOODY GUTHRIE
Bound for Glory (1968)
GEORGE HARRISON
I Me Mine (1981)
IAN HUNTER
Autobiography of a Rock Star (1974)
LENNY KAYE (and DAVID DALTON)
Rock 100 (1977)
JOHN LENNON
In His Own Write (1964)
A Spaniard in the Works (1965)
BETTE MIDLER
A View from a Broad (1980)
JIM MORRISON
The Lords and the New Creatures (1971)

YOKO ONO
Grapefruit (1968)
JOHNNY OTIS
Listen to the Lambs (1970)
PATTI SMITH
Seventh Heaven (1973)
With a Book of Poems (1973)
Kodak
Ha! Ha! Houdini (1973)
Babel (1979)
CHRIS STEIN and DEBORAH HARRY
Making Tracks: The Rise of Blondie (1982)
IAN WHITCOMB
After the Ball: A History of Pop (1972)

(Warner Bros.) **1968**—*Bradley's Barn* **1974**—(+ Dan Levitt, gtr.) **1975**—*The Beau Brummels* **1982**— *Introducing the Beau Brummels* (Rhino) (reissue).

The Beau Brummels were the first nationally successful rock act to emerge from San Francisco. With the exception of their Irish-born bassist, Declan Mulligan (who quit the group before their hits began and later sued for a piece of their earnings), all the members were Bay Area high school graduates. Their early performances featured covers of Beatles and Rolling Stones songs as well as Ron Elliott's originals. San Francisco disc jockey Tom Donahue signed them to his Autumn Records. Their first release, the Sly Stone–produced "Laugh, Laugh," went to #15 in 1965, only a few months after they had played their first live show together. Their next single, "Just a Little" (#8), was their only Top Ten hit. None of their subsequent releases—"You Tell Me Why," "Don't Talk to Strangers," "Good Time Music" (1965) and "One Too Many Mornings" (1966)—entered the Top Thirty.

In 1965, Autumn went out of business and the group's contract was sold to Warner Bros. They failed to regain commercial favor, but produced interesting failures, including 1967's progressive *Triangle* (recorded after Petersen had left to join Harper's Bizarre) and one of the first country-rock albums, *Bradley's Barn* (recorded in Nashville in 1968 by Valentino and Elliott). Neither LP sold well, and by the end of 1968 the Beau Brummels moniker was retired. Valentino then recorded a couple of singles for Warner Bros. before assembling Stoneground. Elliott released a solo album entitled *The Candlestick Maker* in 1969 and then took a lengthy sabbatical before resurfacing with a group called Pan in the early Seventies. In 1974, the original Beau Brummels regrouped, augmented by guitarist Dan Levitt. They released *The Beau Brummels* in April 1975, but the LP met with little success, and the group disbanded.

BEAVER AND KRAUSE
Formed 1967, San Francisco
Bernard L. Krause (b. Detroit); Paul Beaver (b. 1925, d. 1975).
1969—*Ragnarok Electronic Funk* (Limelight) **1970**—*In a Wild Sanctuary* (Warner Bros.) **1971**—*Gandharva* **1972**—*All Good Men* **1975**—*Guide to Electronic Music* (Nonesuch).

Paul Beaver and Bernard Krause helped introduce the synthesizer into rock. Before they teamed up in 1967, Krause had gained some distinction as an itinerant folkie (he was a member of the Weavers), while Beaver had worked as a jazz keyboardist. Beaver also wrote soundtrack music for *Catch-22, The Graduate, Candy, Rosemary's Baby* and *Performance*. Their session credits include work with the Rolling Stones, the Beatles, the Beach Boys, the Doors, Neil Young, the Byrds, Leon

Russell, and Simon and Garfunkel. Krause accused Beatle George Harrison of using one of his recorded performances to fill up one side of his 1969 *Electronic Sound* LP. Beaver died from a stroke in 1975.

BE-BOP DELUXE
Formed 1972, England
Bill Nelson (b. Wakefield, Eng.), gtr., voc., kybds.; Robert Bryan (b. Eng.), bass; Nicholas Chatterton-Dew (b. Eng.), drums; Ian Parking (b. Eng.), gtr.; Richard Brown (b. Eng.), kybds.
1974—(– entire original group, except Nelson; + Milton Reame-James, kybds.; + Paul Jeffreys, bass; + Simon Fox, drums) *Axe Victim* (Harvest) (– Reame-James; – Jeffreys; + Charles Tumahai, bass) **1975**— *Futurama* (+ Andrew Clark, kybds.) **1976**—*Sunburst Finish; Modern Music* **1977**—*Live in the Air Age* **1978**—*Drastic Plastic* **1979**—*The Best and the Rest of Be-Bop Deluxe.*

Bill Nelson was an accomplished guitarist by his late teens and began his professional career in his early twenties. With a Yorkshire-based group, Gentle Revolution, he recorded two locally distributed albums. On his own, he recorded a home-produced LP entitled *Northern Dream* in 1971. He put together Be-Bop Deluxe, styled after David Bowie's science-fiction rock efforts, in early 1972. Though a modest success in England, the band failed to attract large audiences in America, and Nelson retired its name in 1979. His next group, Bill Nelson's Red Noise, produced a 1979 LP entitled *Sound on Sound.* He has since been active as a soloist, releasing almost a dozen singles, EPs and albums in Europe in 1980 and 1981. 1981's *Quit Dreaming and Get off the Beam*, a double LP, hit the English Top Ten. He has continued his experimental work, including *Das Kabinet* in 1981. He has also worked as a producer with A Flock of Seagulls on their "Telecommunication." His 1982 solo releases include an LP (*The Love That Whirls*, PVC) and an EP (*Flaming Desire and Other Passions*, PVC).

JEFF BECK
Group formed 1967, England
Jeff Beck (b. June 24, 1944, Surrey, Eng.), gtr.; Rod Stewart (b. Jan. 10, 1945, London), voc.; Ron Wood (b. June 1, 1946, Hillingdon, Eng.), bass; Aynsley Dunbar (b. 1946, Liverpool), drums.
1967—(– Dunbar; + Mickey Waller, drums) **1968**— (+ Nicky Hopkins, kybds.) *Truth* (Epic) (– Waller; + Tony Newman, drums) **1969**—*Beck-Ola* **1971**— (new group: Max Middleton, kybds.; Cozy Powell [b. Dec. 29, 1947, Cirencester, Eng.], drums; Clive Chaman, bass; Bobby Tench, voc.) *Rough and Ready* **1972**—*The Jeff Beck Group* (new group; Tim Bogert, bass; Carmine Appice, drums) **1973**—*Beck, Bogert*

and Appice **1975**—*Blow by Blow; Truth/Beck-Ola*
1976—*Wired* **1977**—*Jeff Beck with the Jan Hammer Group—Live* **1980**—*There and Back.*

One of the most influential lead guitarists in rock, Jeff Beck has helped shape blues rock, psychedelia and heavy metal. Beck's groups have been short-lived, but his aggressive style—encompassing screaming, bent sustained notes, distortion and feedback, and crisply articulated fast passagework—has been more important than his material.

After attending Wimbledon Art College in London, Beck backed Lord Sutch before replacing Eric Clapton in the Yardbirds. He established his reputation with that band, but he left in late 1966 and after a short sabbatical released a version of "Love Is Blue," played deliberately out of tune. In 1967, he founded the Jeff Beck Group with Ron Wood and Rod Stewart; the band's reworkings of blues-based material laid the groundwork for Seventies heavy metal. Clashing temperaments broke the group up after two acclaimed LPs and several U.S. tours. Stewart and Wood went on to join the Small Faces, and Stewart continued to use drummer Mickey Waller on his solo albums until 1974.

Beck was planning to form a band with Vanilla Fudge members Tim Bogert and Carmine Appice when he was sidelined for 18 months with a fractured skull he sustained in a car crash. When he recovered, Bogert and Appice were busy in Cactus, so Beck assembled a second Jeff Beck Group, and put out two albums of Memphis funk laced with heavy metal. When Cactus broke up in late 1972, Beck, Bogert and Appice returned Beck to a power-trio format, but weak vocals hampered the band and it dissolved in early 1974. Beck went into hibernation until 1975, when he reemerged in an all-instrumental format, playing jazzy tunes. He toured as coheadliner with the Mahavishnu Orchestra, and started an on-again, off-again collaboration with former Mahavishnu keyboardist Jan Hammer in 1976 with *Wired.* During the later Seventies, Beck reportedly spent most of his time on his seventy-acre estate outside London. He and Hammer worked together on the 1980 album *There and Back,* but Hammer did not join Beck for his 1980 tour, Beck's first in over four years. In 1981, Beck appeared at Amnesty International's Secret Policeman's Ball.

THE BEE GEES
Formed 1958, Brisbane, Australia.
Barry Gibb (b. Sep. 1, 1947, Isle of Man), voc., gtr.;
Robin Gibb (b. Dec. 22, 1949, Isle of Man), voc.;
Maurice Gibb (b. Dec. 22, 1949, Isle of Man), voc., bass, kybds.
1967—*Bee Gees First* (Atco) **1968**—*Horizontal; Rare Precious and Beautiful; Rare Precious and Beautiful, volume 2; Idea* **1969**—*Odessa; Best of the Bee Gees* (Polydor) **1970**—*Cucumber Castle* (Atco)

Sound of Love (Polydor) **1971**—*2 Years On* (Atco) *Trafalgar* **1972**—*To Whom It May Concern* **1973**—*Life in a Tin Can* (RSO) *The Best of the Bee Gees, volume 2* **1974**—*Mr. Natural* **1975**—*Main Course; Portrait* **1976**—*Children of the World; Bee Gees Gold* **1977**—*Here At Last . . . Live; Saturday Night Fever* (soundtrack) **1979**—*Spirits Having Flown; Bee Gees Greatest* **1981**—*Living Eyes.*

In twenty years of latching onto trends, the Bee Gees became one of the wealthiest groups in pop. The three Gibb brothers, sons of English bandleader Hugh Gibb, started performing in 1955, going under names like the Rattlesnakes and Wee Johnny Hays and the Bluecats, entertaining crowds between shows at a Manchester movie house for a shilling each. They moved with their parents to Brisbane in 1958 and worked talent shows and other amateur outlets, singing sets of Everly Brothers songs and an occasional Barry Gibb composition, by this time calling themselves the Bee Gees (for Brothers Gibb). They signed with Australia's Festival Records in 1962 and released a dozen singles and two albums in the next five years. Then as now, close high harmonies were the Bee Gees' trademark, and the Gibbs wrote their own material.

They hosted a weekly Australian TV show, but their records went unnoticed until 1967, when "Spicks and Specks" hit #1 after the Bee Gees had relocated in

The Bee Gees: Maurice Gibb, Barry Gibb, Robin Gibb

England. There they expanded to a quintet with drummer Colin Peterson and Vince Melouney (both Australians) and found themselves a new manager, Robert Stigwood, then employed by the Beatles' NEMS Enterprises. Their first Northern Hemisphere single, "New York Mining Disaster 1941," was a hit in both the U.K. and the U.S. (#14, 1967), and was followed by a string of equally popular ballads: "To Love Somebody" (#17, 1967), "Holiday" (#16, 1967), "Massachusetts" (#11, 1967), "Words" (#15, 1968), "I've Got to Get a Message to You" (#8, 1968) and "I Started a Joke" (#6, 1969). Their clean-cut neo-Edwardian image and their English-accented harmonies were a variation on the Beatles' approach, although the Bee Gees leaned toward ornate orchestration and sentimentality.

Cracks in their toothsome facade began to show in 1969, when the non-family members left the group (Peterson claiming the Bee Gees name for himself) and reports of. excessive lifestyles and fighting among the brothers surfaced. From mid-1969 to late 1970, Robin tried a solo career, while Barry and Maurice recorded *Cucumber Castle* as a duo and cut some singles individually. The trio reunited for two more hit ballads—the million-sellers "Lonely Days" (1970) and "How Can You Mend a Broken Heart" (1971)—before bottoming out with a string of flops between 1971 and 1975. Stigwood effected a turnabout by recruiting producer Arif Mardin, who steered them toward R&B and brought them to Miami to work out the funk-plus-falsetto combination that brought them their third round of hits. *Main Course*, including "Jive Talkin'" (#1, 1975) and "Nights on Broadway" (#7, 1975), caught disco on the upswing and gave the Bee Gees their first platinum album.

In 1976, Stigwood's RSO label broke away from its parent company, Atlantic, rendering Mardin unavailable to the Bee Gees. Engineer Karl Richardson and arranger Albhy Galuten took over as producers, and the group continued to record with Miami rhythm sections for hits like "You Should Be Dancing" (#1, 1976) and a ballad, "Love So Right" (#3, 1977), which recalled such black vocal groups as the Spinners rather than the Beatles. Stigwood, meanwhile, had produced the films of *Jesus Christ Superstar* and *Tommy*, and asked the Bee Gees for four or five songs he could use in the soundtrack of *Saturday Night Fever*. The soundtrack album, a virtual best-of-disco, included Bee Gees charttoppers "Stayin' Alive," "Night Fever" and "How Deep Is Your Love," and eventually sold 30 million copies worldwide. Barry, with Galuten and Richardson, also wrote and produced hits for Yvonne Elliman, Samantha Sang, Tavares, Frankie Valle, and younger brother Andy Gibb as well as the title tune for *Grease*.

In 1978, with *Saturday Night Fever* still high on the charts, the Bee Gees started Music for UNICEF, donating the royalties from a new song and recruiting other hitma-

kers to do the same. They also appeared in Stigwood's movie fiasco *Sgt. Pepper's Lonely Hearts Club Band* and continued to record. After *Saturday Night Fever*, even the platinum *Spirits Having Flown*, with three #1 hits—"Too Much Heaven," "Tragedy" and "Love You Inside Out"—seemed anticlimactic. As of 1979, the Bee Gees had made five platinum albums and more than twenty hit singles. Since then, however, their career has entered yet another dry season.

In October 1980, the Bee Gees filed a $200 million suit against Stigwood, claiming mismanagement. Meanwhile, Barry produced and sang duets with Barbra Streisand on *Guilty* (1980). The lawsuit was settled out of court, with mutual public apologies, in May 1981. *Living Eyes* was the Bee Gees' last album for RSO. Barry and Maurice have been living in Miami since 1977, while Robin still resides in England. In 1982, they were reportedly composing the soundtrack to *Saturday Night Fever*'s sequel, tentatively titled *Stayin' Alive*. Barry had also written and produced an album for Dionne Warwick, *Heartbreaker*.

BEES MAKE HONEY
Formed 1972, England
Ruan O'Lochlainn, gtr., piano, sax; Deke O'Brien, gtr., voc.; Bob Cee Benberg, drums; Barry Richardson, bass, voc.; Mick Molloy, gtr., voc.
1973—(− O'Lochlainn; + Malcom Morley, kybds.; − Benberg; + Fran Byrne, drums; − O'Brien; Richardson moved to sax; + Rod Demick, bass, voc.) *Music Every Night* (EMI) 1974—(+ Kevin McAlea, piano; + Ed Dean, gtr.; + Willie Finlayson, gtr., voc.).

A pioneering U.K. pub-rock band alongside Brinsley Schwarz and Ducks Deluxe, Bees Make Honey's main claims to fame are its two top-notch drummers. Bob Cee Benberg graduated to the big time with Supertramp, while his replacement, Fran Byrne, had a momentary taste of glory with Ace. The group recorded several albums, but only one was released. They disbanded in autumn 1974, a few months after the pub-rock scene ground to a halt.

ARCHIE BELL AND THE DRELLS
Formed mid-1960s, Houston
1969—*There's Gonna Be a Showdown* (Atlantic) 1977—*Dance Your Troubles Away* (Philadelphia International) *Hard Not to Like It* 1981—*I Never Had It So Good* (Becket) (solo album by Archie Bell).

Archie Bell and his group had the nation dancing in 1968 with the strutting "Tighten Up," which featured a choked guitar phrase. The Drells were frequently produced by noted Philadelphia soul stylist Bunny Sigler, although their follow-up hit, the Top Ten "I Can't Stop Dancing" in late 1968, was produced by the then-emerging black music titans Kenny Gamble and Leon Huff. They scored another

Top Thirty success in early 1969, but have since reached only a loyal black audience. In the late Seventies, they recorded extensively for the Philadelphia International label, releasing a discofied version of "Tighten Up." By 1981, Bell was recording solo for the Becket label.

THOM BELL
Born circa 1940, Philadelphia

Producer/arranger/songwriter Thom Bell was an architect of the "Philadelphia sound" that dominated black pop in the early Seventies. In the Sixties, he worked as a session pianist at Philadelphia's Cameo Records and was a member of Kenny Gamble and the Romeos. Bell was replaced on keyboards by Leon Huff, who subsequently became Kenny Gamble's production and business partner when they founded Philadelphia International Records. Gamble and Huff built a reputation as producers, and Bell often played on their sessions and supplied arrangements.

By the early Seventies, Bell was writing and producing on his own. His use of french horns, strings and light Latin percussion on hits by the Delphonics ("La La Means I Love You," "Didn't I [Blow Your Mind This Time]"), the Stylistics ("Betcha By Golly Wow," "You Are Everything") and the Spinners ("I'll Be Around," "Mighty Love" and "Games People Play") became his trademark.

In the late Seventies, Bell's productions included a three-song EP with Elton John, including "Mama Can't Buy You Love." More recently, Bell coproduced with singer/songwriter Deniece Williams her "My Melody" (1981) and "Niecy" (1982).

JESSE BELVIN
Born December 15, 1933, Texarkana, Arkansas; died February 6, 1960, Los Angeles

Jesse Belvin's untimely death came just as the singer was achieving success commensurate with his influence on West Coast black vocal music in the Fifties. He began his career as a 16-year-old vocalist for Big Jay McNeely's band. After a stint in the Army, he formed a vocal duo with Marvin Phillips—Jesse & Marvin—and scored an R&B Top Ten hit with "Dream Girl" in 1953. Over the next eight years, he served as unofficial leader of L.A.'s doo-wop groups, coaching them, writing and arranging their material, and using his influence with the city's independent companies to get them recorded. His biggest songwriting success was with "Earth Angel," a million-seller for the Penguins in 1954. He also sang with the Cliques, the Sharptones, Three Dots and a Dash, and the Sheiks. The Cliques had a 1956 hit with his "Girl of My Dreams."

Belvin recorded as a solo artist for numerous labels, including Specialty, Knight and Modern/Kent, but not until the mid-Fifties did Belvin, with his soft, careful enunciation and tasteful ballads, enjoy some solo success.

"Goodnight My Love" hit the R&B Top Ten in 1956. In 1958, Belvin was signed to RCA; in 1959, "Funny" made the Top Thirty and "Guess Who" went to R&B. Two months later, he died in an auto accident.

PAT BENATAR
Born Patricia Andrzejewski, 1953, Brooklyn, New York
1979—*In the Heat of the Night* (Chrysalis)   **1980**—*Crimes of Passion*   **1981**—*Precious Time*   **1982**—*Get Nervous.*

Hard-rock singer Pat Benatar grew up on Long Island, where at age 17 she began vocal training in preparation for study at the Juilliard School. She soon rebelled against the rigorous training and ended her studies. After turning 18, she married Dennis Benatar, a GI stationed in Richmond, Virginia. There she worked as a bank clerk before taking a job as a singing waitress. In 1975, the couple returned to New York; they were later divorced.

Benatar began working Manhattan's cabaret circuit in 1975 with a chanteuse style derived from Barbra Streisand and Diana Ross. At Catch a Rising Star, she attracted the attention of club owner Rick Newman, who became her manager. By 1978, she had switched to a more aggressive rock approach, and after being rejected by several labels was signed to Chrysalis.

Benatar's debut, co-produced by Mike Chapman and Peter Coleman, went platinum on the strength of the #23 single, "Heartbreaker." Her followup, *Crimes of Passion*, sold over a million copies in late 1980, yielding two hit singles, "Hit Me with Your Best Shot" (#9, 1980) and a cover of the Rascals' "You Better Run"(#42, 1980). Her third LP, *Precious Time* (also platinum), boasted "Promises in the Dark" (#38, 1981), "Fire and Ice" (#17, 1981) and "Treat Me Right" (#18, 1981).

Benatar writes many of her own lyrics, usually in collaboration with her guitarist and musical director, Neil Geraldo, whom she married in Hawaii in 1982. Besides Geraldo, her band consists of Roger Capps, bass; Scott St. Clair Sheets, guitar; and Myron Grombacher, drums. The *Get Nervous* single "Shadows in the Night" was a Top Ten hit in late 1982.

GEORGE BENSON
Born March 22, 1943, Pittsburgh
1964—*Benson and McDuff* (Prestige)   **1965**—*It's Uptown* (Columbia)   **1966**—*George Benson Cookbook*   **1967**—*Giblet Gravy* (Verve/MGM)   **1968**—*George Benson Goodies;   Shape of Things to Come* (A&M)   **1969**—*Tell It Like It Is;   The Other Side of Abbey Road*   **1971**—*Beyond the Blue Horizon* (CTI)   **1972**—*White Rabbit*   **1973**—*Body Talk*   **1974**—*Bad Benson*   **1976**—*Good King Bad;   Benson and Farrell;   Blue Benson;   In Concert;   Breezin'* (Warner Bros.)   **1977**—*In Flight;   Summertime* (Embassy)

1978—*Weekend in L.A.* (Warner Bros.) 1979—*Living inside Your Love* 1980—*Give Me the Night* 1981—*The George Benson Collection* 1982—*The Best* (A&M).

Jazz guitarist/vocalist George Benson's breakthrough came in 1976 when *Breezin'*, the biggest-selling "jazz" album to date, brought him into the pop mainstream. Benson began singing at an early age; at four he won a singing contest and later performed on radio as Little Georgie Benson. Though he started playing the guitar at age 8, he worked as a vocalist with numerous Pittsburgh R&B bands before playing the instrument in public at age 15. Soon he had gained a reputation as a guitar player and was working as a session guitarist outside Pittsburgh.

With his groups, the Altairs and George Benson and his All-Stars, he recorded for Amy Records. By the late Fifties, however, he had given up singing and was concentrating solely on the guitar. In 1965, he moved to New York, where he met his main influence, Wes Montgomery, and talent scout John Hammond, who signed him to Columbia. Though his LPs of mainstream jazz on Columbia, A&M and CTI helped establish his reputation among other musicians and jazz fans, sales were never outstanding.

In late 1975, Benson signed with Warner Bros., where for the first time in his recording career he was encouraged to sing. *Breezin'* was the first of several hits for Warner Bros. (all six Warner albums are gold; four of those are platinum). Featuring his understated pop funk and vocals modeled on Stevie Wonder and Donny Hathaway, his hits have included "On Broadway" (#7, 1978), Leon Russell's "This Masquerade" (#10, 1976), "The Greatest Love of All" (#24, 1977), "Love Ballad" (#18, 1979), "Give Me the Night" (#4, 1980) and "Turn Your Love Around" (#5 1981).

BROOK BENTON

Born Benjamin Franklin Peay, September 19, 1931, Camden, South Carolina

1960—*The Two of Us* (with Dinah Washington) (Mercury) 1961—*Brook Benton's Golden Hits; The Boll Weevil Song and 11 Other Great Hits; If You Believe* 1962—*Singin' the Blues* 1963—*Brook Benton's Golden Hits, volume 2* 1967—*Laura, What's He Got That I Ain't Got* (Reprise) 1969—*Do Your Own Thing* (Cotillion) 1970—*Brook Benton Today; Home Style* 1971—*The Gospel Truth* 1973—*Something for Everyone* (MGM) 1975—*Brook Benton Sings a Love Story* (RCA) 1976—*This Is Brook Benton* (All Platinum) 1977—*Making Love Is Good for You* (Olde Worlde).

One of a handful of black singers who wrote their own material in the early Sixties, Brook Benton has had four gold records and almost a score of Top Twenty hits over a lengthy and resilient career. Benton's hits feature his smooth baritone (in a style he learned from Nat "King" Cole and Billy Eckstine) and lush string backing. In the early Fifties, he sang with Bill Landford and the Golden Gate gospel quartets. By the middle of the Fifties, Benton had begun recording pop songs for Epic and then Vik Records, for whom he had a minor hit, "A Million Miles from Nowhere."

Collaborations with songwriter Clyde Otis and arranger Belford Hendricks produced 1958 hits for Nat "King" Cole ("Looking Back") and Clyde McPhatter ("A Lover's Question"). In 1959, Otis helped get Benton a contract with Mercury, and Benton began four years of success for the label, beginning with four Benton/Otis/Hendricks compositions: "It's Just A Matter of Time" (#3), "Endlessly" (#12), "Thank You Pretty Baby" (#16) and "So Many Ways" (#6).

Benton's early-Sixties hits included two duets with Dinah Washington, "Baby (You've Got What It Takes)" (#5, 1960) and "A Rockin' Good Way" (#7, 1960), as well as the folk-tinged "The Boll Weevil Song" (#2, 1961) and "Frankie and Johnny" (#20, 1961). Other hits included more standard soul-pop fare like "Think Twice" (#11, 1961), "Revenge" (#15, 1961), "Lie to Me" (#13, 1962), "Shadrack" (#19, 1962) and "Hotel Happiness" (#3, 1963). Thereafter, his Mercury releases fared noticeably poorer on the charts. He recorded for RCA (1965–67) and Reprise (1967–68) with meager results.

In 1970, he had one more big pop hit with a stirring version of Tony Joe White's "Rainy Night in Georgia" (#4, 1974) on Cotillion. As the decade progressed, he recorded for MGM, Brut, Stax, All Platinum and Olde Worlde.

BERT BERNS

Born Bert Russell, 1929; died December 31, 1967, New York City

As a songwriter, producer, talent scout and record executive, Bert Berns was an important behind-the-scenes figure in Sixties pop. After working as a record salesman, a music copyist and a session pianist, he began writing songs in 1960, collaborating with writers such as Phil Medley, Wes Farrell and Jerry Ragavoy. Among his best-known songs are "Twist and Shout" (the Isley Brothers, the Beatles), "Cry to Me" (Solomon Burke, the Rolling Stones), "Everybody Needs Somebody to Love" (Solomon Burke, Wilson Pickett, the Rolling Stones), "Here Comes the Night" (Ben E. King, Them), "Hang On Sloopy" (the McCoys), "Up in the Streets of Harlem" (the Drifters), "I'll Take Good Care of You" (Garnett Mimms), "Piece of My Heart" (Erma Franklin, Janis Joplin) and "Brown-Eyed Girl" (Van Morrison). He owned a publishing company, Webb IV, and record label, Keetch, but he also worked as a songwriter, producer, arranger and talent scout for Atlantic, United Artists, Cameo, Jubilee, Laurie and other companies. As a producer, he was responsible for such hits as the Jarmels' "A Little Bit of Soap," Barbara Lewis' "Baby I'm Yours," the Drifters' "Under the Boardwalk" and most of Solomon Burke's Atlantic catalogue.

In 1964, he moved to London to work for British Decca, for whom he discovered and then produced Lulu and Them (with Van Morrison). In 1965, he started Bang Records; the name was an anagram of the first names of Bert and his partners (and old Atlantic cohorts) Ahmet and Nesuhi Ertegun and Gerald Wexler. Bang had hits with Van Morrison, the McCoys, and Berns' last major discovery, Neil Diamond.

CHUCK BERRY

Born October 18, 1926 or 1931, St. Louis
1958—*After School Sessions* (Chess)   *One Dozen Berrys*   **1959**—*Chuck Berry Is on Top*   **1960**—*New Juke Box Hits*   **1964**—*Chuck Berry Greatest Hits*
1965—*Chuck Berry in London*   **1967**—*Golden Hits* (Mercury)   *Chuck Berry's Golden Decade* (Chess)
1972—*The London Sessions*   **1973**—*Golden Decade, volume 2*   **1974**—*Golden Decade, volume 3*   **1975**—*Chuck Berry 75*   **1979**—*Motorvatin'* (Atlantic)   *Rockit* (Atco)   **1982**—*The Great Twenty-eight* (Chess).

The archetypal rock & roller, Chuck Berry melded the blues, country and a witty, defiant teen outlook into songs that have influenced virtually every rock musician in his wake. In his best work—about forty songs (including "Round and Round," "Carol," "Brown-Eyed Handsome Man," "Roll Over Beethoven," "Living in the U.S.A.," "Little Queenie"), recorded mostly in the mid- and late Fifties—Berry matched some of the most resonant and witty lyrics in pop to music with a blues bottom and a country top, trademarking the results with his signature double-string guitar lick.

Berry learned guitar as a teenager. From 1944 to 1947, he was in reform school for attempted robbery; upon release, he worked on the assembly line at a General Motors Fisher Body plant and studied hairdressing and cosmetology at night school. In 1952, he formed a trio with drummer Ebby Harding and pianist Johnnie Johnson, his keyboardist on and off for the next three decades. By 1955, the trio had become a top St. Louis–area club band, and Berry was supplementing his salary as a beautician with regular gigs. He met Muddy Waters in Chicago in May 1955, and Waters introduced him to Leonard Chess. Berry played Chess a demo tape that included "Ida Red"; Chess renamed it "Maybellene," and sent it to disc jockey Alan Freed (who got a cowriting credit in the deal), and Berry had his first Top Ten hit.

Through 1958, Berry had a string of hits. "School Day" (#8 pop, #1 R&B, 1957), "Rock & Roll Music" (#8 pop,

Chuck Berry

#6 R&B, 1957), "Sweet Little Sixteen" (#2 pop, #1 R&B, 1958) and "Johnny B. Goode" (#8 pop, #5 R&B, 1958) were the biggest. With his famous "duckwalk," Berry was a mainstay on the mid-Fifties concert circuit. He also appeared in such films as *Rock, Rock, Rock* (1956), *Mister Rock and Roll* (1957) and *Go, Johnny, Go* (1959).

Late in 1959, Berry was charged with violating the Mann Act: He had brought a 14-year-old Spanish-speaking Apache prostitute from Texas to check hats in his St. Louis nightclub, and after he fired her she complained to the police. After a blatantly racist first trial was disallowed, he was found guilty at a second. Berry spent two years in federal prison in Indiana, leaving him embittered and his marriage ruined.

By the time he was released in 1964, the British Invasion was under way, replete with Berry's songs on early albums by the Beatles and Rolling Stones. He recorded a few more classics—"Nadine," "No Particular Place to Go"—although it has been speculated that they were written before his jail term. Since then, he has written and recorded only sporadically, although he had a million-seller with "My Ding-a-Ling" (#1, 1972), and 1979's *Rockit* was a creditable effort. Berry still plays concerts, often with pickup bands, and he appeared in the 1979 film *American Hot Wax.*

When not on the road, Berry stays at his amusement park in Wentzville, Missouri. The law continues to harass him. Shortly before a June 1979 performance for Jimmy Carter at the White House, the Internal Revenue Service charged Berry with income tax evasion, and he served a 100-day prison term in 1979.

B-52's

Formed October 1976, Athens, Georgia
Cindy Wilson (b. Feb. 28, 1957, Athens, Ga.), voc., percussion, gtr.; Keith Strickland (b. Oct. 26, 1953, Athens, Ga.), drums; Fred Schneider III (b. 1954, Newark, Ga.), voc., organ, kybds., gtr., toy piano, walkie talkie; Ricky Wilson (b. 1953, Athens, Ga.), gtr.; Kate Pierson (b. 1948, Weehawken, N.J.) organ, voc. **1979**—*The B-52's* (Warner Bros.) **1980**—*Wild Planet* **1981**—*Party Mix* **1982**—*Mesopotamia* **1983**— *Whammy*.

The gleefully eccentric party music of the B-52's— stripped-down, off-kilter funk without bass lines, topped by chirpy vocals and lyrics crammed with Fifties and Sixties trivia—garnered such a large following at dance clubs and colleges that their debut album sold 500,000 copies despite minimal airplay. Named for the tall bouffant hairdos worn on stage by the two female 52's, the band

The B-52's: Keith Strickland, Cindy Wilson, Ricky Wilson, Kate Pierson, Fred Schneider

claims it originated in a jam session under the influence of tropical drinks. Fred Schneider, Kate Pierson and Keith Strickland had had a little performing experience; the Wilson siblings had none. The B-52's debuted at a Valentine's Day party in 1977 in the college town of Athens, Georgia; they originally performed with taped guitar and drum parts, but preferred the sound when someone accidentally pulled the plug on the tape recorder.

Their first gig was at Max's Kansas City, and they soon attracted a New York cult, partly thanks to their stage image: miniskirts, go-go boots, toy instruments and demonstrations of such dance steps as the Camel Walk and the Shy Tuna. They pressed 2,000 copies of the single "Rock Lobster," which sold out rapidly, before signing in early 1979 to Warner Bros. Their debut album sold steadily as the band toured the U.S. and Europe. *Wild Planet*, which hit #18 in 1980, was even more successful, and songs from it reappeared in remixed, more danceable versions on the gold *Party Mix* EP. For 1982's *Mesopotamia*, the B-52's collaborated with producer David Byrne of Talking Heads, who brought in backup musicians to broaden the sound.

THE BIG BOPPER

Born J. P. Richardson, October 24, 1930, or October 29, 1932, Sabine Pass, Texas; died February 3, 1959, Iowa

The Big Bopper, a disc jockey moonlighting as a pop star, was killed in a plane crash with Buddy Holly and Richie Valens, leaving as his legacy the line, "Oh baby that's what I like!"

Richardson began working as a disc jockey at KTRM, Beaumont, Texas, while still attending high school, calling himself the "Big Bopper." Except for a two-year hitch in the Army (as a radio communications instructor), he worked at KTRM the rest of his life. He began writing songs during his Army years, and in 1957 he sent a demo of original material to a Houston record producer, who brought him to the attention of Mercury Records. He cut two country & western singles for Mercury under his real name and a novelty record called "The Purple People Eater Meets the Witch-Doctor" as the Big Bopper. The flip side was a rockabilly original called "Chantilly Lace," which became the international hit of 1958.

He followed "Chantilly Lace" with two modest singles, "Little Red Riding Hood" and "The Big Bopper's Wedding," and developed a stage show based on his radio persona. Buddy Holly, a longtime West Texas friend, invited him to accompany a Midwestern tour in the winter of 1959. On February 3, 1959, between concert stops in Mason City, Iowa, and Fargo, North Dakota, the tour plane flew into a snowstorm and crashed, killing all on board.

Richardson left little in the way of recordings. As a songwriter, however, he returned to the charts a year after his death with "Running Bear," which he wrote for Johnny Preston.

BIG BROTHER AND THE HOLDING COMPANY
Formed 1965, California
Peter Albin (b. June 6, 1944, San Francisco), bass, gtr., voc.; Sam Andrews (b. Dec. 18, 1941, Taft, Calif.), gtr.; James Gurley (b. Detroit), gtr.; David Getz (b. Brooklyn), drums, piano, voc.; Janis Joplin (b. Jan. 19, 1943, Port Arthur, Tex.; d. Oct. 4, 1970, Hollywood, Calif.), voc.
1967—*Big Brother and the Holding Company* (Mainstream) 1968—*Cheap Thrills* (Columbia) (− Joplin; − Andrews) 1970—(+ David Shallock, bass; + Nick Gravenites, voc.) *Be a Brother* (− Gurley; − Shallock; − Gravenites; + Andrews; + Michael Pendergrass, gtr.; + Kathy McDonald, voc.; + Mike Finnigan, kybds.) 1971—*How Hard It Is.*

While Big Brother and the Holding Company are remembered as Janis Joplin's band, they were active before Joplin joined them and after she left. Leader Peter Albin (a country-blues guitarist who had played with future founders of the Grateful Dead Jerry Garcia and Ron McKernan) met Sam Andrews (a jazz guitarist with classical training) and James Gurley (who had taught himself to play guitar on hallucinogenic sojourns through the California desert) at an open jam session hosted by entrepreneur Chet Helm in 1965. Helm encouraged them to form a group, found them a drummer and set up their first gig, at the Trips Festival of January 1966. In the Festival audience was art historian and amateur musician David Getz, who soon replaced the original drummer. Big Brother and the Holding Company became the house band at the Avalon Ballroom, but without a lead vocalist there was little to distinguish them from other bands. Helm recalled hearing Joplin the year before and contacted her in Texas. She returned to California in June 1966.

The Holding Company was basically a blues band, and Joplin at the time was more a folksinger than a blues singer. But Joplin's voice and presence, and the band's slapdash intensity, made them a Bay Area sensation. Their debut album spread their reputation, and their appearance at the Monterey Pop Festival in June 1967 gave them the national spotlight. New manager Albert Grossman brought them to Columbia Records, which issued their legacy, the live *Cheap Thrills*.

Cheap Thrills went to #1 with the help of "Piece of My Heart" (#12, 1968). Numerous observers convinced Joplin that she could use a more precise backing band, and at the end of 1968 she and Andrews left the group. After a year, Big Brother returned as a loose assemblage of four to eight musicians, which might include Gravenites (ex–Electric Flag), McDonald (a backup vocalist for Ike and

Tina Turner, Joe Cocker and Leon Russell), or no lead singer at all. Albin was the only regular member. In 1972, Big Brother disbanded.

BIG STAR
Formed 1971, Memphis
Alex Chilton (b. Dec. 28, 1950, Memphis), voc., gtr.; Chris Bell (b. Jan. 12, 1951, Memphis; d. Dec. 27, 1978, Memphis), voc., gtr.; Andy Hummell (b. Jan. 26, 1951, Memphis), bass; Jody Stephens (b. Oct. 4, 1952), drums.
1972—*#1 Record* (Ardent) 1973—(− Bell) 1974—*Radio City* 1978—*Third* (Aura) (reissue).

Big Star's combinations of Beatles-style melody, Who-like punch and Byrds-y harmonies defined power pop before the term (or an audience for it) existed. Ex–Box Tops Alex Chilton and songwriting collaborator Chris Bell founded the group; but Bell left in 1973, and after recording two more albums Big Star disbanded in 1975. Bell worked in Memphis until he died in a 1978 car crash. Chilton continues to be active; he toured with his own band in the late Seventies, released a solo EP, *Singer Not the Song*, in the U.S. in 1977 and solo albums in Japan (*One Day in New York*), Germany (*Bach's Bottom*) and Britain (*Like Flies on Sherbert*) in 1980. He also produced the Cramps' *Gravest Hits* (1979) and *Songs the Lord Taught Us* (1980) and recently appeared with Tav Falco's Panther Burns, a Memphis band, on an EP and an LP.

THE BIG THREE
Formed circa 1962, Liverpool
Brian Griffiths, gtr.; Johnny Gustafson, bass; Johnny Hutchinson, drums.

The Big Three were popular on the Liverpool club scene at the start of the Sixties. The group evolved out of an earlier Merseybeat outfit called Cass and the Casanovas. Although their handful of studio recordings were disappointing, they did record a powerful EP, *Live at the Cavern*. They were one of the many Liverpool groups managed by Brian Epstein, who got them their first contract with Decca and often had another of his prodigies, Cilla Black, sing with them. By 1964, mainstays Brian Griffiths and Johnny Gustafson (who went on to play with the Merseybeats, Quartermass, Hard Stuff and as part of Roxy Music's road band) had left. Despite stopgap additions like Paul Pilnick (who later played with Stealer's Wheel), the group quickly fell apart. In 1973, Griffiths and Gustafson re-formed for an album on Polydor, *Resurrection*, with assistance from Elton John's drummer, Nigel Olsson.

BIG YOUTH
Born Manley Buchanan, *circa* 1949, Kingston, Jamaica
1973—*Screaming Target* (Trojan) (All U.K. releases in

Seventies) **1976**—*Natty Cultural Dread; Hit the Road Jack* **1977**—*Reggae Phenomenon* (Big Youth) **1978**—*Dreadlocks Dread* (Klik) *Isaiah, First Prophet of Old* **1979**—*Everyday Skank* (best of) (Trojan) **1982**—*Some Great Big Youth* (Heartbeat) **1983**—*The Chanting Dread Inna Fine Style.*

A cabbie turned disc jockey, Big Youth was Jamaica's most popular "toaster" (a disc jockey who ad-libs over instrumental tracks) in the Seventies. His early records featured his rhymes, doggerel and scat singing over previously released tunes by other artists remixed to cut out the original voices and bring out the bass and drums. Like his first hit, "Ace 90 Skank" (1972), his songs frequently dealt with current events: When a heavyweight boxing championship was fought in Kingston in 1973, Youth took to the airwaves with "George Foreman" and "Foreman and Frazier."

Big Youth later adopted Rastafarianism as his religion, and his songs took on weightier topics, as in "House of Dreadlocks" and "Natty Cultural Dread." He also began writing his own music, recording with a band and singing in a high, breathy croon rather than toasting. "When Revolution Come," produced by Prince Buster, was his first of many Jamaican charttoppers through the mid-Seventies. He performs periodically in the U.S. and Great Britain.

ELVIN BISHOP
Born October 21, 1942, Tulsa, Okla.
1969—*Elvin Bishop* (Fillmore) **1970**—*Feel It* (Columbia/Epic) **1971**—*Rock My Soul; Applejack* **1972**—*Best of: Crabshaw Rising* **1974**—*Let It Flow* (Capricorn) **1975**—*Juke Joint Jump* **1976**—*Struttin' My Stuff; Hometown Boy Makes Good* **1977**—*Raisin' Hell* **1979**—*Best of.*

Although good-humored blues-rock was well-received live, ex–Paul Butterfield guitarist Elvin Bishop didn't establish his solo recording career until his 1976 smash hit single, "Fooled Around and Fell in Love"—sung by Mickey Thomas, who went on to join Jefferson Starship.

Bishop met Paul Butterfield at the University of Chicago. Though Bishop had just started playing guitar, he and Butterfield began jamming together at parties; Bishop also played the Chicago folk circuit by himself. Eventually, he and Butterfield jammed with Muddy Waters, Howlin' Wolf and other leading South Side bluesmen. Bishop and Butterfield played in bar bands with names like the Salt and Pepper Shakers and the South Side Olympic Blues Team. One winter, when times were especially hard, Bishop was jailed for stealing a preacher's coat from a restaurant.

He moved to New York, where he worked breaking toys (for manufacturers' discounts) at a department store, but returned to Chicago to join Butterfield's first Blues

Band as lead guitarist, switching to rhythm guitar a few months later when Mike Bloomfield joined. When Bloomfield left to form Electric Flag, Bishop moved back to lead guitar. After Butterfield's fourth LP, Bishop left to form his own band, settling in Mill Valley, California. He brought with him a Boston folk trio—Jo, Janice and Mary—Jo Baker was the only one to remain with the group. Bishop also jammed with Al Kooper at the Fillmore (when Bloomfield was ill). Bishop signed with Bill Graham's Fillmore Records and made several albums.

Dickey Betts of the Allman Brothers Band persuaded Capricorn's Phil Walden to sign Bishop. His first few Capricorn LPs sold fairly well, yielding near-hits in "Travelin' Shoes," "Juke Joint Jump" and "Sure Feels Good." His breakthrough finally came with *Struttin' My Stuff* and its #3 single, "Fooled Around and Fell in Love." Bishop hasn't had a real hit since, but his albums have continued to sell decently, supported by dogged touring.

BILL BLACK COMBO
Formed 1959, Memphis
Original personnel: Bill Black (b. Sep. 17, 1926, Memphis,; d. Oct. 21, 1965, Memphis), bass; Carl McAvoy, piano; Martin Wills, saxophone; Reggie Young, gtr.; Jerry Arnold, drums. *Ca.* 1961: + Bobby Emmons, piano; + Bob Tucker, gtr. Personnel *ca.* 1981: Bob Tucker, gtr.; Gil Michael, pedal steel gtr., fiddle; Bill Compton, drums; Robert Gladney, sax; Phil Munsey, bass.
N.A.—*Memphis Tennessee* (Hi) *Award Winners* **1960**—*Saxy Jazz* **1961**—*That Wonderful Feeling* **1962**—*Solid and Raunchy; Let's Twist Her; Record Hop* **1963**—*Untouchable Sound; Greatest Hits* **1964**—*Bill Black's Combo Plays the Blues; Tunes by Chuck Berry; Combo Goes West Combo Goes Big Band* **1965**—*More Solid and Raunchy; Mr. Beat* **1966**—*All-Timers* **1967**—*Black Lace; King of the Road* **1972**—*Juke Box Favorites* **1973**—*Rock 'n' Roll Forever* **1974**—*Bill Black Is Back* **1975**—*Solid and Country; World's Greatest Honky-Tonk Band.*

In 1954 in Memphis, Bill Black, a neighbor of guitarist Scotty Moore, happened to visit Moore's home one day when he and a young truck driver named Elvis Presley were playing together for the first time. Soon thereafter, Sam Phillips hired both Black and Moore to rehearse with Presley. Their first recording, "That's All Right," was Presley's first hit.

Black toured and recorded with Presley until 1959, when he formed the Bill Black Combo, an instrumental group. In 1959, "Smokie (Part 2)" sold over a million copies; as did "Josephine," "White Silver Sands" and "Don't Be Cruel" in 1960. During this time, Black became particularly popular in Europe. He retired from the band in 1962 and died three years later from a brain tumor. The Bill Black Combo, however, has continued to tour and record, and remains one of the most successful country instrumental bands, despite over 56 personnel changes (Bob Tucker, who has been with the band over twenty years, is not an original member).

CILLA BLACK

Born Priscilla Maria Veronica White, May 27, 1943, Liverpool
1968—*The Best of Cilla Black* (Parlophone)   **1969**— *Surround Yourself with Sorrow*   **1970**—*Sweet Inspiration.*

Singer Cilla White was a familiar figure on the Merseybeat scene. In 1962, she was working as a hatcheck girl at the Cavern Club, where she occasionally sat in as vocalist with Rory Storme and the Hurricanes (whose drummer was Ringo Starr). Soon White was singing with other groups, most notably with the Big Three, and occasionally performing solo, billed as Swingin' Cilla. The Beatles urged manager Brian Epstein to sign her. Epstein had her change her name to Cilla Black, and under his tutelage she became a British MOR star. Her 1963 recording debut was a version of John Lennon and Paul McCartney's "Love of the Loved." Minor American hits ("You're My World, #26, 1964; "It's for You," #79, 1964) followed. She last appeared on American charts in 1966 with a version of "Alfie." In England, however, she had over a dozen Top Twenty hits and a British cabaret career. She has since moved into acting, notably on BBC-TV.

BLACKFOOT

Formed in Jacksonville, Florida
Rick Medlocke, voc. gtr.; Jakson Spires, drums, voc.; Greg T. Walker, bass, voc.; Charlie Hargrett, gtr.
1975—*No Reservations* (Island)   **1976**—*Flyin' High* (Epic)   **1979**—*Strikes* (Atco)   **1980**—*Tomcattin'*   **1981**—*Marauder.*

Southern rock band Blackfoot came out of the Jacksonville, Florida, bar circuit that nourished the Allman Brothers Band and Lynyrd Skynyrd. For most of the Seventies, Blackfoot followed in Skynyrd's footsteps before moving toward British-style heavy metal.

Rick Medlocke (who was raised by his Sioux grandfather, folk musician and songwriter Shorty Medlocke) formed his first group with Jakson Spires and Greg T. Walker (both of Indian extraction) when he was ten. The group was joined by transplanted New Yorker Charlie Hargrett in the late Sixties. Calling themselves Fresh Garbage, they became regulars on the North Florida bar circuit. Not long after changing their name to Blackfoot, the group broke up to allow Medlocke and Walker to join Lynyrd Skynyrd as substitutes for departed members in

1971. After a year with Skynyrd, Medlocke reunited the original Blackfoot.

RITCHIE BLACKMORE/RAINBOW

Formed 1975, Los Angeles
Ritchie Blackmore (b. Apr. 14, 1945, Weston-super-Mare, Eng.), gtr.; Ronnie James Dio (b. Cortland, N.Y.), voc.; Gary Driscoll, drums; Craig Gruber, bass; Mickey Lee Soule, kybds.
1975—*Ritchie Blackmore's Rainbow* (Polydor) (− Driscoll; − Gruber; − Soule; + Cozy Powell [b. Dec. 29, 1947, Cirencester, Eng.], drums; + Tony Carey, kybds.; + Jim Bain, bass)   **1976**—*Rainbow Rising*   **1977**—*Onstage*   (− Carey; − Bain; + Bob Daisley, bass; + David Stone, kybds.)   **1978**—*Long Live Rock 'n' Roll*   (− Dio; − Daisley; − Stone) **1979**—(+ Roger Glover [b. Nov. 30, 1945, Brecon, S. Wales], bass; + Don Airey, kybds.; + Graham Bonnet, voc.)   *Down to Earth*   **1980**—(− Bonnet; − Powell; + Joe Lynn Turner, voc.; + Bob Rondinelli, drums)   **1981**—*Difficult to Cure*   (− Airey; + David Rosenthal, kybds.)   **1982**—*Straight between the Eyes* (Mercury).

Hard-rock guitarist Ritchie Blackmore began studying classical guitar at age 11, then switched to rock in his teens. He became a session player and worked with Screaming Lord Sutch before cofounding Deep Purple in 1968. Associates claim that Blackmore is often arrogant and belligerent, and after Purple had peaked, he left in 1975 amid rumors of dissension. He founded his own band, made up mostly of members of the upstate New York band Elf (which had frequently opened for Deep Purple), and it has been billed alternately as Rainbow or Ritchie Blackmore's Rainbow.

Over the years, the frquently changing lineup has included vocalist Ronnie James Dio (who later replaced Ozzy Osbourne in Black Sabbath) and drummer Cozy Powell (formerly of the Jeff Beck Group and later with the Michael Schenker Band). Ex–Deep Purple bassist Roger Glover joined Blackmore in 1979, and with vocalist Joe Lynn Turner and Blackmore he cowrote Rainbow's minor 1982 hit "Stone Cold."

BLACK OAK ARKANSAS

Formed 1969, Los Angeles
Jim Dandy Mangrum (b. Mar. 30, 1948, Black Oak, Ark.), voc.; Ricky Reynolds (b. Oct. 29, 1948, Manilan, Ark.), gtr.; Jimmy Henderson (b. May 20, 1954, Jackson, Miss.), gtr.; Stan Knight (b. Feb. 12, 1949, Little Rock, Ark.), gtr.; Pat Daugherty (b. Nov. 11, 1947, Jonesboro, Ark.), bass; Wayne Evans, drums.
1969—*The Knowbody Else* (Stax)   **1970**—*Black Oak Arkansas* (Atco)   **1972**—*Keep the Faith;   If an Angel Came to See You*   **1974**—*High on a Hog* (Atlantic)

Street Party; Hot and Nasty **1975**—*Raunch and Roll Live; Ain't Life Grand; X-Rated* (MCA) **1976**—*Balls of Fire; Live Mutha; 10 Year Overnight Success* (MCA) **1977**—*Race with the Devil* (Capricorn) *Best of; I'd Rather Be Sailing.*

Black Oak Arkansas was a Southern heavy-metal group whose boogie philosophy and long-haired, bare-chested front man, Jim Dandy Mangrum, were briefly popular in the early to mid-Seventies. All of the band's original members grew up in rural Arkansas near the small town of Black Oak. They were in a juvenile gang before becoming a band. (In a 1976 press release they boast of having stolen a p.a. system.) They toured the South as Knowbody Else and released one album on Stax before moving to Los Angeles in 1969 and changing their name to Black Oak Arkansas. They soon signed with Atlantic, the first of several labels they recorded for.

With almost constant touring, they eventually built up an enthusiastic following, composed mainly of young fans who appreciated the group's down-home Dixie boogie and quasi-mystical lyrics. In 1970, they made their national debut, but big-time success eluded them until *High on a Hog* (1974) and *Raunch and Roll* (1975) went gold. They also had a #1 radio hit with "Jim Dandy to the Rescue," which featured Dandy exchanging double entendres with a female singer, a sometime group member named Ruby Starr. By the mid-Seventies, the group was a huge draw on the U.S. concert circuit. The group has sustained numerous personnel changes, and by 1977, Mangrum was the only original member of the band left.

BLACK SABBATH
Formed 1968, England
Ozzy Osbourne (b. Dec. 3, 1948, Birmingham, Eng.), voc.; Geezer Butler (b. July 17, 1949, Birmingham), bass; Tony Iommi (b. Feb. 19, 1948, Birmingham), gtr.; Bill Ward (b. May 5, 1948, Birmingham), drums.
1970—*Black Sabbath* (Warner Bros.) **1971**—*Paranoid; Masters of Reality* **1972**—*Volume 4* **1973**—*Sabbath, Bloody Sabbath* **1975**—*Sabotage* **1976**—*We Sold Our Soul for Rock 'n' Roll; Technical Ecstasy* **1978**—*Never Say Die* **1979**—(− Osbourne; + Ronnie James Dio [b. Cortland, N.Y.], voc.) *Heaven and Hell* **1981**—(− Ward; + Vinnie Appice [b. Staten Island], drums) *Mob Rules.*

Mixing equal parts of bone-crushing volume, catatonic tempos and ominous pronouncements of gloom and doom, Black Sabbath were the heavy-metal kings of the Seventies. Despised by rock critics and ignored by radio programmers, Black Sabbath sold over seven million records.

The four original members, schoolmates from a working-class district of industrial Birmingham, first joined forces as Earth in 1968, playing pop-ish rock modeled

after the Move. The following year they moved to hard rock and changed their name to Black Sabbath. They were unknown in Britain until the release of their debut album, which hit the English Top Ten. A single, "Paranoid," from their forthcoming *War Pigs,* reached #4 (their only Top Twenty single ever), and they renamed the album after the song.

Sabbath first came to the States in 1970. In spite of their name, the crosses erected on their stages, and their songs dealing with apocalypse, death and destruction, their interest in the black arts was, they insisted, nothing more than innocuous curiosity (the sort that led Ozzy Osbourne to sit through eight showings of *The Exorcist*); and in time their princes-of-darkness image faded. Although Grand Funk Railroad then ruled the American heavy-metal scene, persistent touring paid off, and by 1974 Black Sabbath were considered peerless. They were bigger in the U.S. than in the U.K. and their albums regularly scaled the charts.

Osbourne quit the group to form his own Blizzard of Ozz. Sabbath could never be the same without him, although his replacement, Ronnie James Dio (formerly of Blackmore's Rainbow), was a soundalike. Sabbath lost much of their homeland following to the late-Seventies second wave of Anglo heavy metal (Judas Priest, Def Leppard, etc.), but they kept their hold in America; and the songwriting team of Tony Iommi (music) and Geezer Butler (lyrics) remained intact, even when Bill Ward took a long-term leave of absence.

BLACK UHURU
Formed 1974, Kingston, Jamaica
Derrick "Duckie" Simpson (b. June 24, 1950, Kingston), harmony voc.; Michael Rose (b. July 11, 1957, Kingston), lead voc.; Errol Nelson, harmony voc.
1977—*Love Crisis* (Prince Jammy's) (− Nelson) **1978**—(+ Sandra "Puma" Jones [b. October 5, 1953, S.C.], harmony voc. **1979**—*Showcase* (Taxi) **1980**—*Sensimilla* (Island) **1981**—*Red* **1982**—*Tear It Up; Chill Out* **1983**—*The Dub Factor* (Mango).

One of Jamaica's top reggae bands in the wake of Bob Marley and the Wailers, Black Uhuru use Jamaica's finest studio band to back songs made distinctive by "Puma" Jones's descant and melodies that suggest Hebrew cantillation. "Duckie" Simpson originally formed Uhuru (Swahili for "freedom") with Garth Dennis and Don Carlos. They played clubs around Jamaica but failed to attract much local attention despite their Top Cat Single, "Folk Songs." Dennis and Carlos quit soon after (Dennis to join the Wailing Souls), and Simpson brought Errol Nelson and Michael Rose to Uhuru. Their next singles, "Natural Mystic" and "King Selassie," found their way to England in 1977, and U.K. distributor Count Shelley issued their first album there.

Nelson left the group to join the Jayes, and Simpson and Rose recorded some singles as a duo a few months later. After cutting a couple of songs with producer Lee "Scratch" Perry, they teamed up with drummer Sly Dunbar (an old friend of Rose's) and his partner, bassist Robbie Shakespeare. Uhuru's "Observe Life" was the first single Sly and Robbie produced and the first issued on their Taxi label.

Simpson and Rose were then joined by Sandra Jones, an American with a master's degree in sociology from Columbia University who had come to Jamaica as a social worker. Her only professional experience had been as a dancer and backup singer with Ras Michael and the Sons of Negus. With Sly and Robbie the trio recorded their best-known singles, "General Penitentiary," "Guess Who's Coming to Dinner," "Plastic Smile," "Abortion" (which is anti—and was banned in Jamaica) and "Shine Eye Gal." *Showcase* followed. In late 1979, New York City radio station WLIB sponsored Uhuru's first appearance outside Jamaica, a concert at New York City's Hunter College, and Island Records signed them. *Sensimilla* (their American record debut) and *Red* were recorded in Jamaica with Sly and Robbie and their Taxi All-Stars (Keith Richard adding his guitar to the former). *Tear It Up*, a live set, was recorded in Europe. Black Uhuru's touring group has included Dunbar, Shakespeare and their studio band.

BOBBY "BLUE" BLAND
Born January 17, 1930, Rosemark, Tennessee
1960—*Barefoot Rock and You Got Me* (Duke)   **1961**—*Two Steps from the Blues*   **1962**—*Here's the Man*   **1963**—*Call on Me*   **1964**—*Ain't Nothing You Can Do*   **1968**—*Touch of the Blues*   **1973**—*His California Album* (ABC)   **1974**—*Dreamer;   B. B. King and Bobby Bland/ Together for the First Time . . .Live*   **1975**—*Get on Down with Bobby Bland*   **1976**—*Bobby Bland and B. B. King/Together Again . . . Live*   **1977**—*Reflections in Blue*   **1978**—*Come Fly with Me*   **1979**—*I Feel Good, I Feel Fine* (MCA)   **1980**—*Sweet Vibrations*   **1981**—*Try Me, I'm Real*   **1982**—*Here We Go Again;   Introspective Early Years.*

One of the patriarchs of modern soul singing, Bobby "Blue" Bland's distinctively grainy vocal style draws on gospel and blues. Raised in Memphis, he joined a gospel ensemble, the Miniatures, in the late Forties. He later met guitarist B. B. King and joined the Beale Streeters, an informal group of Memphis blues musicians that included King, Johnny Ace, Roscoe Gordon and Willie Nix. But not until 1954 (after working as King's chauffeur) did he land his first recording contract, when an executive of Duke Records heard him sing at a Houston talent show.

His first successful single, "It's My Life, Baby," was released in 1955. He played one-nighters around the country accompanied by his band, led by tenor saxophonist

Bill Harvey and trumpeter/arranger Joe Scott. Members of the band, under the pseudonym of Deadric Malone, wrote or cowrote most of Bland's material. His band was bigger and brassier than most current blues bands, and anticipated the rich sound of Sixties soul music while harking back to big-band jazz.

Since 1957, when "Farther Up the Road" was a #5 R&B hit, Bland has had over thirty R&B Top Thirty singles, including "I'll Take Care of You" (#2, 1959), "I Pity the Fool" (#1, 1961), "Don't Cry No More" (#2, 1961), "Turn on Your Love Light" (#2, 1961) and "That's the Way Love Is" (#1, 1963).

Most of Bland's records enjoyed only modest success in the pop market; only three singles ever made the pop Top Thirty. In the mid-Sixties, Bland adopted a slicker, more upbeat style, but his career stalled until Duke Records was taken over by ABC-Dunhill in 1972. Dunhill paired him with producer Steve Barri (the Four Tops), who guided Bland back to a bluesier vocal style while giving him contemporary material by Leon Russell and Gerry Goffin, as well as new material by Deadric Malone. *His California Album* and *Dreamer* introduced him to white audiences and proved to be the most popular LPs of his career.

While he never achieved the wide recognition of B. B. King (with whom he toured and collaborated on two LPs, *Together* and *Together Again*), he had a considerable influence on modern soul music. He continues to record and tour internationally.

CARLA BLEY
Born Carla Borg, May 11, 1938, Oakland, California
1972—*Escalator over the Hill* (JCOA)   **1974**—*Tropic Appetites* (Watt)   **1975**—*13 and ¾*   **1977**—*Dinner Music*   **1978**—*European Tour 1977*   **1979**—*Musique Mechanique*   **1981**—*Social Studies* (ECM)   **1982**—*Carla Bley Live!*

Composer Carla Bley has experimented with free jazz, punk rock, big bands, orchestras and forms and groupings of her own (like the "Chronotransduction" *Escalator over the Hill*). But while many of her pieces are tricky and eccentric, they are rarely less than tuneful, and her gift for bittersweet parody has earned her comparisons with Kurt Weill. Bley plays keyboards and sax, and occasionally sings, although her reputation rests on her tunes, her arrangements and the bands she has conducted.

The daughter of a piano teacher and choir director, she began composing at age nine. After she moved to New York in the late Fifties, her works were performed by pianists George Russell and Paul Bley (whom she married), and later by vibraphonist Gary Burton (who has done an entire album of Bley's pieces) and Charlie Haden's Liberation Music Orchestra (which reunited in 1982). She began performing in 1964, when she and her second husband, trumpeter Michael Mantler, formed the

Jazz Composers Orchestra, which has featured Cecil Taylor, Pharoah Sanders and others.

With lyricist Paul Haines, she began working on *Escalator over the Hill* in 1968 and completed it in 1972. To record it, she assembled an unlikely assortment of musicians, including Linda Ronstadt, Jack Bruce, John McLaughlin, Gato Barbieri, and Don Cherry and Charlie Haden from Ornette Coleman's quartet. Since then, she has continued to use both rock and jazz musicians. *Tropic Appetites* featured singer Julie Tippetts (who as Julie Driscoll was part of Brian Auger's Trinity); *Dinner Music* used R&B session players Stuff, and *Nick Mason's Fictitious Sports* (1981), although released under the name of Pink Floyd drummer Mason, used her band along with British progressive rockers.

In 1977, she formed the Carla Bley Band, which has included NRBQ pianist Terry Adams, Soft Machine bassist Hugh Hopper, Mothers of Invention keyboardist Don Preston and Modern Lovers drummer D. Sharpe. Bley has also been active in the dissemination of new music. In 1964, she was a charter member of the Jazz Composers Guild (with Cecil Taylor, Sun Ra and others), a cooperative to promote avant-garde music. In 1966 Bley and Mantler founded JCOA (Jazz Composers Orchestra Association) Records and in 1972 began the New Music Distribution Service, which handles hundreds of small independent jazz, classical and rock labels, among them Bley and Mantler's own Watt Records.

BLIND FAITH
Formed 1969, London
Steve Winwood (b. May 12, 1948, Birmingham, Eng.), kybds., gtr., voc.; Eric Clapton (b. Mar. 30, 1945, Ripley, Eng.), gtr., voc.; Ginger Baker (b. Aug. 19, 1939, Lewisham, Eng.), drums; Rick Grech, bass.
1969—*Blind Faith* (Atco).

Blind Faith's already famous personnel stayed together for one album and one arena-circuit tour before splitting up. Eric Clapton and Baker had been two-thirds of Cream, and Steve Winwood had led (and would return to) Traffic. Rick Grech was from Family, which had been considerably more popular in Britain than in the U.S. Blind Faith made their debut before 100,000 fans in London's Hyde Park, and played a sold-out American tour. Their one album included the FM hits "Can't Find My Way Home," by Winwood, and "Presence of the Lord," by Clapton. Its jacket, featuring a prepubescent nude girl, was deemed controversial in the U.S. and was replaced by a photograph of the band (a later U.S. reissue bore the original cover).

After Blind Faith, Clapton played sideman for Delaney and Bonnie and John Lennon, then secluded himself before reemerging as a leader in the late Seventies. Winwood regrouped Traffic, including Grech, then wrote and

did session work (Marianne Faithfull) and, beginning in the late Seventies, solo albums. Baker moved to Nigeria, where he operated a recording studio before returning to England and then moving to Italy.

BLODWYN PIG
Formed 1968, England
Mick Abrahams (b. Apr. 7. 1943, Luton, Eng.), gtr., voc.; Jack Lancaster, saxes, flute; Andy Pyle, bass; Ron Berg, drums.
1969—*Ahead Rings Out* (A&M)   1970—*Getting to This*.

Mick Abrahams quit Jethro Tull after one album to form Blodwyn Pig. A blues guitarist in the British style of Eric Clapton and Peter Green, he made Blodwyn Pig more blues-based than Jethro Tull. Like Ian Anderson, Jack Lancaster was influenced by Rahsaan Roland Kirk and played alto and soprano sax simultaneously à la Rahsaan. Pig's debut album was a distinctly British meeting of rock, blues and jazz.

Abrahams left the group after recording the second album to form the Mick Abrahams Band, while the remaining members of Pig enlisted guitarist Peter Banks (formerly of Yes) and guitarist/vocalist Barry Reynolds to take his place. The second lineup never recorded, and the group disbanded.

BLONDIE
Formed 1975, New York City
Deborah Harry (b. July 1, 1945, Miami), voc.; Chris Stein (b. Jan. 5, 1950, Brooklyn), gtr., voc.; Clem Burke, drums; Gary Valentine, bass; Jimmy Destri, kybds.
1976—*Blondie* (Private Stock)   (− Valentine; + Frank Infante, bass)   1977—(+ Nigel Harrison [b. Eng.], bass; Infante switched to guitar)   1978—*Plastic Letters* (Chrysalis)   *Parallel Lines*   1979—*Eat to the Beat* 1980—*Autoamerican*   1981—*The Best of Blondie* 1982—*The Hunter*.

Blondie started as an ironic update of trashy Sixties pop. By the end of the Seventies, they were far and away the most commercially successful survivors of the New York punk scene, with three platinum albums (*Parallel Lines*, *Eat to the Beat* and *Autoamerican*) and an international recognition factor for bleached-blond lead singer Deborah Harry. Blondie's repertoire, most of it written by Harry and boyfriend Chris Stein, was always on the melodic side of punk, and has grown increasingly eclectic, trademarked mostly by Harry's deadpan delivery.

Born in Miami, Harry was adopted at age three months by Richard and Catherine Harry, who now run a gift shop in Cooperstown, New York. She grew up in Hawthorne, New Jersey, and after graduating from high school moved to Manhattan. Harry joined a folk-rock band, the Wind in the Willows, which released one album for Capitol in 1968;

Blondie: Chris Stein, Frank Infante, Deborah Harry, Nigel Harrison, Jimmy Destri, Clem Burke

she worked as a beautician, a Playboy bunny, and a barmaid at Max's Kansas City. In the mid-Seventies, she became the third lead singer of a glitter-rock band, the Stilettoes, which also included future Television bassist Fred Smith. Stein, a graduate of New York's School of Visual Arts, joined the band in October 1973, and he and Harry reshaped it, first as Angel and the Snakes, then as Blondie.

By 1975, the band was appearing regularly at CBGB, home of the burgeoning punk underground. Their first single, "X Offender," was independently produced by Richard Gottehrer and Marty Thau, who sold it to Private Stock. Private Stock released Blondie's debut album in December 1976, also produced by Gottehrer. The group expanded their cult following to the West Coast with shows at Los Angeles' Whisky-a-Go-Go in February 1977, and opened for Iggy Pop on a national tour. A few months later, they made their British concert debut. In July, Gary Valentine left the band to form his own trio, Gary Valentine and the Know, which broke up in spring 1980.

After one album for Private Stock, and some legal wrangling, Blondie signed with Chrysalis in October 1977, and the label financed them on an international tour. Mike Chapman, a veteran of glitter pop, produced *Parallel Lines*, which was released in September 1978 and slowly made its way into the Top Five, breaking first in markets outside the U.S. Blondie's third single, the disco-style "Heart of Glass," hit #1 in April 1979 and established the group with a platinum album. Blondie maintained its

popularity and dabbled in black-originated styles, collaborating with Eurodisco producer Giorgio Moroder for the *American Gigolo* soundtrack ("Call Me," #1, 1980), covering a reggae tune "The Tide Is High" (#1, 1980) and writing a rap song, "Rapture" (#1, 1981), on *Autoamerican*. Harry also did the rounds as a celebrity, including an endorsement of Gloria Vanderbilt designer jeans in 1980.

As the group's success continued, there were reports that Stein and Harry were asserting more control; by 1981 some Blondie backing tracks were played by session musicians under Stein's direction. Burke produced the New York band Colors, and Destri released a solo album, *Heart on the Wall,* in 1982. In 1981, Harry released her solo *KooKoo.* Produced under the direction of Chic's Bernard Edwards and Nile Rodgers, *KooKoo* went gold.

Blondie has also worked in visual media. *Eat to the Beat* was made into an album-length videocassette, and Harry has appeared in a number of films: as a cameo singing "Lili Marlene" in Amos Poe's *The Passenger,* as a brunette housewife in the 1979 *Union City* and in 1982's *Videodrome.*

Early in 1982, Infante brought suit against the group, claiming they were out to destroy his career by excluding him from group meetings, rehearsals and recording sessions. The suit was settled out of court and Infante remained in the band. However, by late 1982, following a disastrous tour (Blondie was never known as a great live act), the group quietly disbanded. Harrison and Burke joined a group called Checkered Past, Stein continued producing acts for his Animal Records label, Destri began producing and Harry continued her solo career; she appeared Off-Broadway in a musical, *Teaneck Tanzi,* in 1983.

BLOODSTONE

Formed 1962, Kansas City, Missouri
Willis Draffen, Jr. (b. Kansas City), voc., gtr.; Charles Love, voc., gtr.; Charles McCormick, bass, voc.; Harry Williams, Jr. (b. Tupelo, Miss.), percussion, voc.; Roger Durham (b. 1946, d. 1973), percussion, voc.
1972—*Bloodstone* (Decca, U.K.) **1973**—*Natural High* (London) *Unreal* (− Durham) **1974**—*I Need Time; Riddle of the Sphinx* **1975**—*Train Ride to Hollywood* **1976**—*Do You Wanna Do a Thing?; Lullaby of Broadway* (Decca) **1979**—*Don't Stop* (Tamla) **1981**—(− McCormick; + Ron Wilson [b. Los Angeles], kybds., voc.; + Ronald Bell [b. Calif.] percussion, voc.) **1982**—*We Go a Long Way Back* (T Neck).

Bloodstone's pop music blended soul vocal harmonies with funk and Hendrix-inspired guitar flash. The five original members were high school classmates in Kansas City, where they formed an a cappella group, the Sinceres, in 1962. In 1968, they spent a year as a nightclub act in Las Vegas, then moved on to Los Angeles. There they decided to learn to play instruments themselves. They reappeared as Bloodstone in 1971, with a succession of drummers (including Edward Summers, Darryl Clifton and Melvin Webb) as associate members. On the advice of their manager, they moved to England, where in 1972 they teamed up with English producer Mike Vernon (John Mayall, Ten Years After, Savoy Brown) for their first five albums.

Their first single, "Natural High," went gold, reaching #4 on American soul charts and #10 pop in 1973. They followed it with a series of soul hits, including "Never Let You Go" (#7 R&B, 1973), "Outside Woman" (#34 R&B, #2 soul, 1974), "That's How It Goes" (#22 R&B, 1974), "My Little Lady" (#4 R&B, 1975), "Give Me Your Heart" (#18 R&B, 1975) and "Do You Wanna Do a Thing?" (#19 R&B, 1976).

In 1975, they produced and appeared in a feature movie entitled *Train Ride to Hollywood*, for which they also wrote the soundtrack. Among the songs covered in this musical comedy were "Toot Toot Tootsie" and "As Time Goes By," and like all of their albums since *Unreal*, the soundtrack also contained their versions of oldies like "Sh-Boom" and "Yakety Yak."

BLOOD, SWEAT AND TEARS

Formed 1968, New York City
Al Kooper (b. Feb. 5, 1944, New York), kybds., voc.; Steve Katz (b. May 9, 1945, Brooklyn), gtr., voc.; Fred Lipsius (b. Nov. 19, 1943, New York), alto sax, piano; Jim Fielder (b. Oct. 4, 1947, Denton, Tex.), bass; Bobby Colomby (b. Dec. 20, 1944, New York), drums; Dick Halligan (b. Aug. 29, 1943, Troy, N.Y.), kybds., trombone, flute; Randy Brecker, trumpet, flugelhorn; Jerry Weiss (b. May 1, 1946, New York) trumpet, flugelhorn. **1968**—*Child Is Father to the Man* (Columbia) (− Kooper; − Brecker; − Weiss; + Chuck Winfield [b. Feb. 5, 1943, Monessen, Penn.], trumpet, flugelhorn; + Lew Soloff [b. Feb. 20, 1944, Brooklyn], trumpet, flugelhorn; + Jerry Hyman [b. May 19, 1947, Brooklyn], trombone; + David Clayton-Thomas [b. Sep. 13, 1941, Surrey, Eng.], voc.) *Blood, Sweat and Tears* **1970**—*3* (− Hyman; + Dave Bargeron [b. Sep. 6, 1942, Mass.], trombone, tuba, trumpet) **1971**—*4* **1972**—*Greatest Hits* (− Lipsius; − Halligan; − Clayton-Thomas; + Lou Marini, Jr. [b. Charleston, S.C.], saxes, flute; + Georg Wadenius [b. Sweden], gtr.; + Larry Willis [b. New York], kybds.; + Jerry Fisher [b. Dekalb, Tex.], voc.) *New Blood* (− Katz; − Winfield; + Tom Malone, trumpet, flugelhorn, trombone, saxes) **1973**—*No Sweat* (− Fielder; − Soloff; − Marini; − Malone; + Ron McClure, bass; + Tony Klatka, trumpet, horn; + Bill Tillman, saxes, flute, clarinet; + Jerry LaCroix, voc., sax, flute, harmonica) **1974**—*Mirror Image* (− LaCroix; − Fisher; + Clayton-Thomas; + Joe Giorgianni, trum-

pet, flugelhorn) **1975**—*New City* (− Wadenius; − McClure; − Giorgianni; + Danny Trifan, bass; + Mike Stern, gtr.; + Forrest Buchtell, trumpet; + Don Alias, percussion) **1976**—*More Than Ever* (− Colomby; − Alias; + Roy McCurdy, drums) **1977**—*Brand New Day* (ABC).

Founder Al Kooper conceived Blood, Sweat and Tears as an experiment in expanding the size and scope of the rock band with touches of jazz, blues, classical and folk music. When Kooper went on to other experiments, BS&T became increasingly identified as a "jazz-rock" band, although their music was essentially easy-listening R&B or rock with the addition of brass.

Kooper formed BS&T after leaving the Blues Project in 1967. The nucleus of the original band was Steve Katz, also of the Blues Project; Jim Fielder, who had played with the Mothers of Invention and the Buffalo Springfield; and Bobby Colomby, who had drummed behind folksingers Odetta and Eric Andersen. The horn players were recruited from New York jazz and studio bands.

Child Is Father featured songs by Harry Nilsson, Tim Buckley, Randy Newman and Gerry Goffin and Carole King, along with Kooper originals and arrangements by Fred Lipsius for brass, strings and studio effects.

The band nearly broke up when Kooper, Randy Brecker and Jerry Weiss left (Brecker to join the Thad Jones–Mel Lewis Band). Regrouping under Katz and Colomby and fronted by David Clayton-Thomas (who had sung with a Canadian blues band, the Bossmen), BS&T entered a period of immense popularity. *Blood, Sweat and Tears* featured arrangements of music by French composer Erik Satie and jazz singer Billie Holiday, as well as by Laura Nyro, Steve Winwood and others. It was the #1 album for seven weeks in 1969, sold over two million copies and spawned three gold singles: "You've Made Me So Very Happy" (#2, 1969), "Spinning Wheel" (#2, 1969) and "And When I Die" (#2, 1969). It also received three Grammy Awards, including one for Album of the Year.

In 1970, the U.S. State Department sent the band on a goodwill tour of Yugoslavia, Romania and Poland. The album *3* duplicated the *Blood, Sweat and Tears* mix of styles and was almost as popular. Again, the album went to #1, and two singles "Hi-De-Ho" and "Lucretia MacEvil"—hit the Top Thirty.

But interest in the band began to wane. Their *4*, which contained almost all original material, barely made the Top Ten. In 1971, its single "Go Down Gamblin' " was their last hit. When Clayton-Thomas left for a solo career, BS&T's place on the charts was filled by similarly styled bands like Chicago, Chase and the Ides of March. Katz left the next year, first to join the short-lived American Flyer and then to an A&R position at Mercury Records.

BS&T became regulars in Las Vegas, with ever-changing personnel recruited largely from big bands like Maynard Ferguson's, Woody Herman's and Doc Severinsen's.

Vocalist Jerry LaCroix appeared between his tenures with Edgar Winter's White Trash and Rare Earth; distinguished jazz tenor saxophonist Joe Henderson was a member in 1972; guitarist Mike Stern later played with Miles Davis's early-Eighties band. Clayton-Thomas' return in 1974 briefly boosted the band's popularity. Columbia dropped them, and Colomby, the last original member, left in 1976. Colomby continued to influence BS&T as producer of *Brand New Day,* and, with Clayton-Thomas, as co-owner of the band's name and catalogue. Since 1975, the band has been billed as Blood, Sweat and Tears Featuring David Clayton-Thomas.

MICHAEL BLOOMFIELD

Born July 28, 1944, Chicago; died February 15, 1981, San Francisco

1968—*Super Session* (Columbia)   (with Al Kooper, Stephen Stills)   **1969**—*It's Not Killing Me;   The Live Adventures of Mike Bloomfield and Al Kooper*   **1973**—*Try It Before You Buy It;   Triumvirate*   **1976**—*Mill Valley Session* (Polydor)   **1977**—*If You Love These Blues, Play 'Em As You Please* (Guitar Player)   *Analine* (Takoma)   *Count Talent and the Originals* (Clouds)   *Michael Bloomfield* (Takoma)   **1980**—*Between the Hard Place and the Ground*   **1981**—*Cruisin' for A Bruisin';   Living in the Fast Lane* (Waterhouse).

Michael Bloomfield

As a teenager living on Chicago's North Shore, Michael Bloomfield ventured downtown to seek out the patriarchs of Chicago blues—Muddy Waters, Albert King and others—and he learned their guitar techniques firsthand. Playing Chicago blues and folk clubs with singer Nick Gravenites and harmonica player Charlie Musselwhite in the early Sixties, he attracted the attention of Paul Butterfield, whose band he joined in 1965. After recording their first album, Bloomfield and other members of the Paul Butterfield Blues Band accompanied Bob Dylan at the Newport Folk Festival on July 25, 1965, Dylan's first performance with an electric rock & roll group. Bloomfield played electric guitar on Dylan's "Like a Rolling Stone" and later that year on *Highway 61 Revisited.*

He left the Butterfield band after recording a second album with them, and formed the Electric Flag with Gravenites. While their concerts and debut album were well received, dissension within the group and Bloomfield's aversion to touring led him to quit the Electric Flag after one year. Thereafter he devoted himself mainly to studio work and solo ventures, including *Super Session* with Al Kooper and *Triumvirate* with John Hammond, Jr. (John Paul Hammond) and Dr. John (Mac Rebennack).

Bloomfield's last shot at stardom came in 1975 with KGB, an attempt by MCA Records to create a supergroup with Bloomfield, keyboardist Barry Goldberg, bassist Rick Grech, drummer Carmine Appice and singer Ray Kennedy. After one album, Bloomfield abandoned the group and the corporate music world. He supported himself by scoring pornographic movies. His previous movie soundtrack credits included *Medium Cool, Steelyard Blues* and *Andy Warhol's Bad.* In 1975, he returned to recording solo albums, releasing eight in the six years before his death (attributed to an accidental drug overdose). *If You Love These Blues, Play 'Em As You Please,* a blues guitar "sampler" produced by *Guitar Player* magazine, was nominated for a Grammy Award in 1977.

KURTIS BLOW

Born Kurt Walker, New York City
1980—*Kurtis Blow* (Mercury)   **1981**—*Deuce.*

Kurtis Blow's "The Breaks" was the record that popularized rap outside the form's native New York City. Blow was a disco DJ before he made records. He started out working at a Harlem disco in 1976, blatantly copping rhymed lines from an originator of rap, Deejay Hollywood (Anthony Holloway). Later he worked with one of the masters of instrumental track editing, Grandmaster Flash (Joseph Seddler). At an impromptu performance with Flash at a midtown disco party in 1979, Blow was spotted by two producers looking for a rapper. "Christmas Rappin' " was released at the end of 1979 and became—with the Fatback Band's "King Tim III" and the Sugar Hill Gang's "Rapper's Delight"—one of the first rap records on the market. It sold almost 400,000 copies; "The

Breaks" sold over 600,000 copies nationwide. By the end of 1980, Blow was performing around the country with his partner Davy D (David Reeves) at the turntables. In 1981 he toured Europe.

DAVID BLUE

Born S. David Cohen, February 18, 1941, Providence Rhode Island; died December 2, 1982, New York City
1966—*David Blue* (Elektra) **1968**—*These 23 Days in September* (Reprise) **1970**—*Me* (as S. David Cohen) **1972**—*Stories* (Asylum) **1973**—*Nice Baby and the Angel* **1975**—*Comin' Back for More* **1976**—*Cupid's Arrow.*

David Blue was better known for his friendship with Bob Dylan than for his own Dylan-influenced songs and recordings. He met Dylan and others on the Greenwich Village folk music scene—Phil Ochs, Fred Neil, Eric Andersen—after arriving in New York around 1960. By his own estimation a songwriter rather than a musician, he began writing songs in the Greenwich Village folk style but did not perform them publicly until after he had recorded his first album. He had cut several songs the year before for an Elektra compilation album called *Singer/Songwriter Project*, which also included Richard Fariña. At that point he changed his name from Cohen to Blue.

He moved to Los Angeles, where he formed a rock band, and in 1968 he recorded his first Reprise album. His second Reprise album was cut in Nashville with session musicians. *Nice Baby* was produced by Graham Nash and featured Dave Mason, Glenn Frey (Eagles), Chris Ethridge and John Barbata; the Eagles recorded Blue's "Outlaw Man" on *Desperado*. In 1975, Blue joined Dylan on the Rolling Thunder Revue and appeared in the resulting film, *Renaldo and Clara* (1978). He died while jogging in Greenwich Village.

BLUE CHEER

Formed circa 1966, California
Dickie Peterson (b. 1948, Grand Forks, N.Dak.), voc., bass; Paul Whaley, drums; Leigh Stephens, gtr.
1968—*Vincebus Eruptum* (Philips) *Outside Inside* **1969**—*New! Improved!* (– Whaley; – Stephens; + Norman Mayell [b. 1942, Chicago], drums; + Bruce Stephens [b. 1946], voc., gtr.; + Ralph Burns Kellogg, kybds.) *Blue Cheer* **1970**—*The Original Human Beings;* *Oh Pleasant Hope.*

Blue Cheer appeared in the summer of 1968 with a heavy-metal remake of Eddie Cochran's "Summertime Blues." One of the first hard-rock power trios, the group was named for an especially high-quality strain of LSD. Their manager, Gut, was an ex–Hell's Angel. Their first album, *Vincebus Eruptum*, hit #11 in 1968 and remains something of a heavy-metal landmark. In early 1979, leader Dickie Peterson regrouped Blue Cheer for a short time.

BLUE ÖYSTER CULT

Formed 1969, Long Island, New York
Eric Bloom, gtr., voc.; Albert Bouchard, drums, voc.; Joe Bouchard, bass, voc.; Allen Lanier, kybds., synth., gtr.; Donald "Buck Dharma" Roeser, lead gtr.
1972—*Blue Öyster Cult* (Columbia) **1973**—*Tyranny and Mutation* **1974**—*Secret Treaties* **1975**—*On Your Feet or on Your Knees* **1976**—*Agents of Fortune* **1977**—*Spectres* **1978**—*Some Enchanted Evening* **1979**—*Mirrors* **1980**—*Cultosaurus Erectus* **1981**—*Fire of Unknown Origin* (– Albert Bouchard; + Rick Downey, drums) **1982**—*Extraterrestrial Live.*

Semi-satiric exponents of the high-decibel apocalypse, Blue Öyster Cult forged an unlikely alliance between teen tastes and critical appeal and have been a major heavy metal band since the mid-Seventies. The group goes back to 1967, when future rock critic R. Meltzer and future Cult producer Sandy Pearlman decided to organize a band. Along with fellow Stony Brook university students Allen Lanier, Donald Roeser and Albert Bouchard, they formed Soft White Underbelly (a name the Cult still uses for club dates). Vocalist Meltzer was replaced by Les Bronstein, with whom they recorded one unreleased LP for Elektra, and several vocalists followed before Eric Bloom joined in 1969. With Bloom, the group's name changed to Oaxaca (a change prompted by a disastrous appearance at the Fillmore East and Pearlman's observation that the group's name was "mud"). By then, Bouchard's brother Joe had joined the band. They recorded another unreleased LP before changing the group's name from the Stalk-Forrest Group to Blue Öyster Cult.

They signed with Columbia in late 1971, and their debut album was released a few months later. There followed several years of extensive touring as Alice Cooper's opening act, picking up theatrical pointers along the way. Their show—featuring lasers and flash pots and Buck Dharma's guitar solos—built a small but loyal following that paved the way for their 1976 commercial breakthrough with the gold LP *Agents of Fortune* and its #12 hit single "(Don't Fear) the Reaper," a Buck Dharma composition. *Agents* also featured vocals and songwriting from Patti Smith, who was then Lanier's girlfriend. The Cult's performances have been captured on three live LPs: *On Your Feet or on Your Knees, Some Enchanted Evening* and *Extraterrestrial Live.*

The band's dark imagery is symbolized by their logo, the ancient symbol of Cronos, the Titan god who ate his son the Grim Reaper. A good deal of the band's success and their image can be credited to their longtime manager and occasional songwriter and producer Pearlman, who supposedly was inspired by having read a recipe for Blue Point oysters and so named the band. The group has also enjoyed the support of rock writers like Meltzer, who has also written songs for the band. In 1980 they coheadlined with Black Sabbath on the Black and Blue Tour. A feature length film of the Nassau (Long Island) Coliseum show entitled *Black and Blue* was released in 1981.

THE BLUES

The basic vocabulary of rock is the blues. The 12-bar song form, the bent notes and the basic attitude of the blues—that joyful music can come out of real pain—have filtered into rock directly, via the blues songs in the rock repertoire ("I'm So Glad," "Love in Vain," "Rollin' and Tumblin'," "Dust My Broom," "Hootchie Koochie Man") and indirectly, as a way of approaching a song.

The blues arose sometime after the Civil War as a distillate of the African music brought over by slaves. From field hollers, ballads, church music and rhythmic dance tunes called jump-ups evolved a music for a singer who would engage in call-and-response with his guitar; he would sing a line, and the guitar would answer it. The early blues were irregular and followed speech rhythms, as can be heard in the recordings made in the Twenties and Thirties by Charley Patton, Blind Lemon Jefferson, Robert Johnson and Lightnin' Hopkins. Radio broadcasts and records spread the blues across the South, and they became more regular, settling into a form in which one line of lyrics was repeated, then answered—AAB—over a chord progression of four bars of tonic, two of subdominant, two of tonic, one of dominant, one of subdominant, and two of tonic.

In the Thirties and Forties, the blues spread northward with the black migration from the South and filtered into big-band jazz; they also became electrified as the electric guitar became popular. In Northern cities like Chicago and Detroit in the later Forties and early Fifties, Muddy Waters, John Lee Hooker, Howlin' Wolf, and Elmore James amplified basic Mississippi Delta blues, built backing bands with bass, drums, piano and amplified harmonica, and began scoring national hits with songs based on simple but powerful repeated riffs. In the same period, T-Bone Walker in Houston and B. B. King in Memphis were perfecting a style of lead guitar playing that used the smoothness of jazz technique on the moaning, crying phrases of blues singing.

The urban bluesmen were "discovered" in the early Sixties by young white musicians in America and Europe; and their bands—the Paul Butterfield Blues Band, the Rolling Stones, the Yardbirds, John Mayall's Bluesbreakers, Canned Heat, Fleetwood Mac—brought the blues to young white audiences. Since the Sixties, rock has undergone periodic blues revivals, while rock guitarists from Eric Clapton and Jimi Hendrix to Eddie Van Halen have used the blues as a foundation for offshoot styles. Originators like Muddy Waters, John Lee Hooker and B. B. King—and their heirs Buddy Guy and Otis Rush in Chicago, Johnny Copeland in Texas—continue to make music in the blues traditions.

THE BLUES BROTHERS

Formed 1977, New York City
Jake Blues (b. John Belushi, Jan. 24, 1949, Chicago; d. Mar. 5, 1982, Los Angeles), voc.; Elwood Blues (b. Dan Aykroyd, July 1, Ottawa), harmonica, voc.
1978—*Briefcase Full of Blues* (Atlantic) **1980**—*Made in America; The Blues Brothers* (soundtrack) **1981**—*The Best of the Blues Brothers.*

What started as a joke on "Saturday Night Live" turned into million-selling records and a movie featuring comedians John Belushi (Jake Blues) and Dan Aykroyd (Elwood Blues). In fall 1977, Belushi and Aykroyd concocted the Blues Brothers as a preshow warmup act for "SNL" studio audiences. Dressed in baggy Fifties-style suits, narrow ties, fedoras and Ray-Ban sunglasses, Belushi sang Sixties soul songs and Aykroyd played middling harmonica. Once the Blues Brothers wangled their way onto actual "SNL" telecasts, they supplied an anachronistic image for young rock fans hungry for the golden era of soul and R&B.

Their top-notch backing band included such Memphis session musicians as guitarist Steve Cropper and bassist Donald Dunn, who'd performed on some of the original hits the Blues Brothers covered (Sam and Dave's "Soul Man" and "Hold On, I'm Comin' "). During a September 1978 engagement opening for comedian Steve Martin in Los Angeles, they recorded *Briefcase Full of Blues* live. With two hit singles—a cover of Sam and Dave's "Soul Man" (#14) and "Rubber Biscuit" (#37)—the album was platinum by 1979, although the Blues Brothers would be the first to admit that their versions were inferior to the originals they outsold. They toured occasionally, particularly to promote their 1980 film "biography," *The Blues Brothers,* which grossed over $32 million in its first two months of release. They had further hits with covers of the Spencer Davis Group's "Gimme Some Lovin'" (#18, 1980) and Johnnie Taylor's "Who's Making Love" (#39, 1980). Belushi died in Hollywood of an accidental drug overdose.

BLUES IMAGE

Formed 1966, Tampa, Florida
Malcolm Jones (b. Cardiff, Wales), bass; Mike Pinera (b. Sep. 29, 1948, Tampa), gtr.; Joe Lala (b. Tampa), drums, percussion; Manuel Bertematti, drums.
1968—(+ Frank "Skip" Konte [b. Canon City, Okla.], kybds.) **1969**—*Blues Image* (Atco) **1970**—*Open; Red, White, and Blues Image.*

Tampa-based Blues Image were one of the first groups to experiment with Latin-tinged rock and are best known for their 1970 #4 hit, "Ride Captain Ride." They signed with Atlantic in February 1969. *Open* contained their lone smash hit. The group disbanded two years later, with some of the members joining Manna in 1972. Lead guitarist Mike Pinera later joined Iron Butterfly, and conga player Joe Lala backed up Stephen Stills in Manassas and Joe Walsh on *The Smoker You Drink, the Player You Get.*

BLUES MAGOOS

Formed circa 1965, New York City
Ralph Scala (b. Dec. 12, 1947 Bronx), kybds., voc.; Ronnie Gilbert (b. Apr. 25, 1946, Bronx), bass, voc.; Peppy Castro (b. Emil Thielhelm, June 16, 1949, Bronx), gtr., voc.; Geoff Daking (b. Dec. 8, 1947, Del.), drums.
1966—*Psychedelic Lollipop* (Mercury) **1967**—*Electric Comic Book* **1968**—*Basic Blues Magoos* **1969**—*Never Goin' Back to Georgia* (ABC) **1970**—(Castro, Eric Kaz, others) *Gulf Coast Bound.*

A lightweight blues-rock band known to wear bell-bottoms trimmed with neon-filled plastic tubes, the Blues Magoos were popular at the height of psychedelia. They signed with Mercury in mid-1966 and scored Top Twenty albums with *Psychedelic Lollipop* and *Electric Comic Book*, which featured the gold single "We Ain't Got Nothing Yet" (#5, 1967). They played the Fillmores and opened tours for Herman's Hermits and the Who. A few months after they disbanded in 1969, Castro put together a halfhearted new version of the band (which included Eric Kaz) before joining Billy and Bobby Alessi in the soft-rock group Barnaby Bye.

THE BLUES PROJECT

Formed 1965, New York City
Danny Kalb, gtr., voc.; Roy Blumenfeld, drums; Andy Kulberg (b. 1944, Buffalo, N.Y.), bass, flute; Steve Katz (b. May 9, 1945, Brooklyn), gtr., harmonica, voc.; Tommy Flanders, voc.; Al Kooper (b. Feb. 5, 1944, Brooklyn), kybds., voc.
1966—*Live at the Cafe Au Go Go* (Verve/Forecast) (− Flanders) **1967**—*Projections; Live at Town Hall* (disbanded) **1968**—*Planned Obsolescence* **1971**— (regrouped: Kalb, Blumenfeld, +Don Kretmar, bass, sax) *Lazarus* (Capitol) **1972**—(+ Flanders; + David Cohen, piano; + Bill Lussenden, gtr.) (disbanded) **1973**—(reunited: Kalb, Blumenfeld, Kulberg, Katz, Kooper) *Reunion in Central Park* (MCA).

The Blues Project, along with the Paul Butterfield Blues Band, helped start the blues revival of the late Sixties. The group was formed in early 1965 with folk, bluegrass and pop musicians. Danny Kalb, formerly one of Dave Van Ronk's Ragtime Jug Stompers, and Roy Blumenfeld, a jazz fan, had discussed playing folk and country blues on electric instruments and drums. Blumenfeld brought in Andy Kulberg, who had studied modern jazz theory at the NYU School of Music, and Kalb rounded up guitarist Artie Traum and folksinger Tommy Flanders. Traum dropped out during rehearsals, and Steve Katz, who had played with the Ragtime Jug Stompers and Jim Kweskin's

Even Dozen Jug Band, replaced him. The final addition was keyboardist Al Kooper (one of the Royal Teens whose "Short Shorts" was a #3 hit in 1958), fresh from Bob Dylan's *Highway 61* sessions. The group made its debut at Greenwich Village's Cafe au Go Go in summer 1965, toured the East Coast, traveled to San Francisco in spring 1966, then played campus shows all the way back to New York.

They made their debut album in May 1966. Flanders then left for a solo career, and recorded *Moonstone* for Verve in 1969. The Project continued as a quintet, which did three open-air concerts in Central Park in the summer of 1966 and gigs as backup band for Chuck Berry.

Projections yielded FM standbys, including "I Can't Keep from Crying" and the instrumental "Flute Thing," but the Blues Project's popularity was limited to New York and scattered college towns. Chief arranger and songwriter Kooper left the group after a second live album had been recorded in the summer of 1967, Kalb mysteriously disappeared, and the group soon disbanded. Katz joined Kooper in Blood, Sweat and Tears, Kalb later returned to session work, and Kulberg and Blumenfeld went to California to form Seatrain. *Planned Obsolescence* was pieced together from recordings the Project had made as a quintet in 1967.

Kalb revived the Blues Project in 1971. Blumenfeld joined him and brought in Seatrain alumnus Kretmar. *Lazarus* was produced by Shel Talmy (the Kinks, the Who, Manfred Mann) but sold no better than previous Project releases. The eponymously titled followup found Flanders again singing with the group, which now included pianist David Cohen, once of Country Joe and the Fish, and guitarist Bill Lussenden. It was the last heard of the Blues Project, second edition. The next year, however, Kooper reunited the original group—minus Flanders—for a one-shot concert in Central Park, documented on the live *Reunion.*

ANGELA BOFILL

Born circa 1954, New York City
1978—*Angie* (GRP) **1979**—*Angel of the Night* **1981**— *Something About You* (Arista) **1983**—*Too Tough.*

Pop-jazz singer Angela Bofill grew up in the Bronx, the daughter of a French-Cuban father (a former bandleader) and a Puerto Rican mother. At age ten, she began studying piano and viola, and a few years later began writing her own songs. In high school she sang in the All-City Chorus and after hours with a group called the Puerto Rican Supremes. By graduation day, she was singing on the latino club circuit with the Group, Ricardo Morrero's popular salsa band. Meanwhile she studied voice at the Hartford Conservatory and the Manhattan School of Music. She developed an interest in jazz through friendships with Herbie Hancock, Joe Zawinul and Flora Purim. After earning her music degree, she was hired by the Dance Theater of Harlem as a singer, dancer, composer and arranger. She also wrote and performed a jazz suite premiered at the Brooklyn Academy of Music and sang with jazz masters Dizzy Gillespie and Cannonball Adderley and with the reggae group Inner Circle.

Through flutist Dave Valentin of the Group, she met Dave Grusin and Larry Rosen of GRP Records, who signed her to a seven-year contract in 1978. Her debut was a best-selling jazz album (#3, *Record World*'s jazz chart) and a promising soul and pop debut. "This Time I'll Be Sweeter" made #23 on the soul singles charts. Her second album moved her closer to widespread popularity, charting at #10 R&B.

It was two years before she made another record. In the interim she settled a royalty dispute with GRP by transferring her contract to Arista. She also toured North America, South America and the Orient. Her 1981 album was produced by Narada Michael Walden. She produced half of *Too Tough* herself.

MARC BOLAN (See T. Rex)

TOMMY BOLIN
Born 1951, Sioux City, Iowa; died December 4, 1976, Miami
1975—*Teaser* (Nemperor) **1976**—*Private Eye* (Columbia).

Guitarist/songwriter Tommy Bolin played in several hard-rock bands before his death of a drug overdose in 1976. After refusing to cut his hair, Bolin dropped out of high school in Sioux City in 1968. He drifted to Denver, where he joined the band Zephyr and later Energy. When Joe Walsh left the James Gang in 1973, he recommended Bolin as a replacement, and Bolin appears on the James Gang's *Bang* (1973) and *Miami* (1974), both of which contained many of his tunes. In 1973, Bolin played jazz-rock fusion on Billy Cobham's *Spectrum*. In 1975, he replaced Ritchie Blackmore in Deep Purple, in the interim completing his first solo album, *The Teaser*. He wrote seven songs on Deep Purple's *Come Taste the Band* (1975) and also appears on their *Last Concert in Japan* (1977) and *When We Rock We Rock* (1978) LPs. After Purple disbanded in the summer of 1976, Bolin returned to his solo career. He died in a Miami hotel room.

GRAHAM BOND
Born circa 1937, England; died May 8, 1974, London
1965—*The Sound of 65* (Columbia, U.K.) **1966**—*There's a Bond between Us* **1968**—*Mighty Graham Bond* (Pulsar, U.K.) *Love Is the Law* **1970**—*Solid Bond* (Warner Bros.) **1971**—*Holy Magick* (Vertigo, U.K.) **1972**—*This Is Graham Bond* (Philips, U.K.) **1974**—*We Put Our Magick on You* (Mercury).

Along with Alexis Korner and John Mayall, Graham Bond was a pioneer of British R&B. Initially a jazz musician, Bond earned his early reputation in the late Fifties playing alto sax with the Don Rendell Quintet. He left Rendell in 1962 to join Alexis Korner's R&B-rock band, Blues Incorporated. His discovery of the electric organ as a blues instrument led him to quit the group in 1963 and, with drummer Ginger Baker and bass player Jack Bruce, to form the Graham Bond Organisation, to which guitarist John McLaughlin was later added. When McLaughlin left the band in 1964 to join Brian Auger's Trinity, Bond replaced him with saxophonist Dick Heckstall-Smith, also late of Blues Incorporated. After Bruce's 1965 departure for Mayall's Bluesbreakers, Bond employed a succession of bassists. In 1966, Baker left to join Cream, and was replaced by Jon Hiseman. When Hiseman and Heckstall-Smith formed Colosseum in 1968, Bond dissolved his Organisation.

Bond tried working as a solo act, but was forced to take on session work. After reuniting with Ginger Baker in Air Force, Bond collaborated with lyricist Pete Brown on *Two Heads Are Better Than One* (1972).

He married British singer Diane Stewart, with whom he shared a fascination for the occult (he claimed to be the son of renowned Satanist Aleister Crowley). Together they formed Holy Magick. After that marriage failed, Bond formed Magus in 1973, with British folksinger Carolanne Pegg. The group broke up within the year because of Bond's financial mismanagement. He also had drug problems. After suffering a nervous breakdown, Bond spent a month in the hospital in 1973. He was eager to revive his career when he died. His body was discovered under the wheels of a stationary train.

GARY "U.S." BONDS
Born Gary Anderson, June 6, 1939, Jacksonville, Florida
1960—*Dance Till Quarter to Three* (Legrand) *Twist Up Calypso* **1961**—*Greatest Hits of Gary U.S. Bonds* **1981**—*Dedication* (EMI) **1982**—*On the Line; Certified Soul* (Rhino).

An early-Sixties hitmaker with a rough, expressive voice, Gary "U.S." Bonds had his career revived in 1981 by fan Bruce Springsteen. As a young streetcorner doo-wop singer named Gary Anderson, Bonds caught the attention of Norfolk, Virginia, music business jack-of-all-trades Frank Guida, who signed him to his Legrand Records. With Guida as producer, they released some of the most exuberant R&B singles of the day. Their first national release in late 1960, "New Orleans," was credited by Guida to one "Gary U.S. Bonds"; Anderson was not consulted. When the single became a hit, Anderson found himself with a new identity. For the next two years Bonds had a string of hits—"School Is Out" (#5, 1961) and "Dear Lady Twist" (#9, 1962), which peaked with the

May 1961 release of his #1 hit, "Quarter to Three." Though Bonds recorded for Legrand through the mid-Sixties, his last chart single of the decade was "Copy Cat" in 1962.

Bonds doggedly continued playing one-nighters as a lounge act until 1978, when Bruce Springsteen—of whom Bonds had never heard—showed up and jammed with him. Springsteen (who often climaxed his concerts with "Quarter to Three") later proposed making a comeback album. *Dedication*, produced by Springsteen's guitarist Steve Van Zandt, was a hit in 1981, and the Springsteen-penned "This Little Girl Is Mine" was a #8 single that same year—Bond's first hit in nearly twenty years.

KARLA BONOFF
Born 1952, Los Angeles
1977—*Karla Bonoff* (Columbia) **1979**—*Restless Nights* **1981**—*Wild Heart of the Young*.

Songwriter Karla Bonoff has written some of Linda Ronstadt's most effective ballads, including "Someone to Lay Down beside Me." She began playing Monday-night hoots at the Troubadour near her family's West L.A. home when she was 16. After briefly attending UCLA in the late Sixties, she was part of Bryndle, a short-lived group that included Wendy Waldman and Andrew Gold and recorded an unreleased album for A&M. Their bassist and longtime Bonoff associate Kenny Edwards introduced Bonoff to Ronstadt a few years later. Ronstadt included "Lose Again," "Someone to Lay Down beside Me" and "If He's Ever Near" on her *Hasten Down the Wind*. Bonoff's first solo album was released in late 1977. It sold respectably, but she was mercilessly compared to Ronstadt, and she took two years to assemble a second album. Her songs have also been recorded by Bonnie Raitt and Nicolette Larson.

THE BONZO DOG BAND
Formed 1965, London
Roger Ruskin Spear (b. June 29, 1943, Wormwood Scubbs, Eng.), kazoos, Jew's harp, various other musical and non-musical toys; Rodney Desborough Slater (b. Nov. 8, 1944, Lincolnshire, Eng.), saxes; Vivian Stanshall (b. Mar. 21, 1943, Shillingford, Eng.), voc., trumpet, ukulele; Neil Innes (b. Dec. 9, 1944, Essex, Eng.), voc., kybds.; Vernon Dudley Bohay-Nowell, gtr.; "Legs" Larry Smith (b. Jan. 18, 1944, Oxford, Eng.), drums; Sam Spoons (b. Martin Stafford), percussion.
1967—*Gorilla* (Liberty) **1968**—(+ Dennis Cowan [b. May 6, 1947, London], bass) *The Doughnut in Granny's Greenhouse* **1969**—*Tadpoles*; *Keynsham* (United Artists) **1972**—(− Spear; − Slater; − Bohay-Nowel; − Smith; − Spoons; + Bubs White, gtr.; + Andy Roberts, fiddle, mando-lin, gtr.; + Dave Richards, bass; + Dick Parry, flute; + Hughie Flint [b. Mar. 15, 1942, Eng.], drums) *Let's Make Up and Be Friendly*.

Originally the Bonzo Dog Dada Band, the group was the brainchild of art-college classmates Roger Spear and Rodney Slater, and its express purpose was to do to music—especially the jazz and popular music of the Twenties and Thirties—what Marcel Duchamp had done to art and Tristan Tzara to poetry: give it a good kick in the pants. Early versions of the group contained about thirty members, mostly fellow art students. By the time they began performing in pubs in 1965—the Dada in their name changed to Doo-Dah—they had been reduced to fewer than a dozen. Within a year, they were playing clubs and had broadened their act to include parodies of musical styles, surrealistic sight gags and comic skits in the punning, non-sequitur style of "The Goon Show." Their stage setup was cluttered with Spear's collection of useless gadgets, machines, mannequins and robots.

They cut two singles for Parlophone before signing with Liberty in 1967. *Gorilla* included gag advertisements and radio interviews sandwiched between parodies of Prohibition-era jazz, Tony Bennett, Rodgers and Hammerstein and Elvis Presley (most of the material written by Stanshall or Innes). It was Neil Innes' interest in electronic music, rock and drugs that lent subsequent LPs the psychedelic touches epitomized by "I'm the Urban Spaceman," a 1968 single written by Innes and produced by one Apollo C. Vermouth, a.k.a. Paul McCartney—a Top Five British hit. (The Bonzos appeared in *Magical Mystery Tour*.)

Despite growing popularity the Bonzos broke up in 1970. Larry Smith, Vernon Bohay-Nowell and Sam Spoons joined Bob Kerr's Whoopee Band, an outfit similar to the early Bonzos. Slater quit show business to become a government social worker. Innes and Cowan formed a group called World and made an album called *Lucky Planet* before Innes briefly joined McGuinness Flint. Stanshall, with Dennis Cowan, Spear and former Bonzo roadie "Borneo" Fred Munt (as percussionist and saxophonist) formed the Big Grunt. Spear left to put together the Kinetic Wardrobe, in which he was backed by a band of robots. He toured Britain and the Continent opening for the Who in the early Seventies. Stanshall led several other groups—the Human Beans, Gerry Atric and His Aging Orchestra, Viv and His Gargantuan Chums—boasting Eric Clapton and Keith Moon and John Entwistle of the Who as sidemen on occasional singles.

In 1972, Stanshall, Innes and Cowan revived the Bonzo Dog Band—or at least the name—for one album, *Let's Make Up*. In spite of contributions from Smith and Spear, old Bonzo fans did not take well to the new band, and there have been no further revival attempts. Spear returned to his Kinetic Wardrobe. Smith toured twice in

1974, supporting Elton John and Eric Clapton. Stanshall announced on Mike Oldfield's *Tubular Bells* and David Bowie's *Peter and the Wolf* as well as on his own BBC show, "Viv Stanshall's Radio Flashes." He has released two solo albums, 1974's *Men Opening Umbrellas Ahead* and 1979's *Sir Henry at Rawlinson End*. Innes has released solo albums (including 1973's *How Sweet to Be an Idiot*) and worked primarily as a composer for British television, most notably "Monty Python's Flying Circus" and "Rutland Weekend Television" with Python's Eric Idle. In 1977, he and Idle wrote, directed and performed in "The Rutles," a television special spoofing the Beatles. Innes played the John Lennon character, Ron Nasty.

BOOGIE

This term derives from the jazz-based "boogie-woogie," which generally referred to a style of piano playing that featured a "hot" rhythm based on eight-to-the-bar figures in the left hand. Boogie-woogie style is believed to have originated in Kansas City with such pianists as Pete Johnson and Joe Turner; other leading boogie-woogie pianists included Albert Ammons, Meade Lux Lewis, James P. Johnson and early Fats Waller.

The term "boogie-woogie" itself probably found its first expression in the phrase "booger-rooger," for a "hot" party or musical good time, used by Twenties Texas country bluesman Blind Lemon Jefferson. Through such blues guitarists as Albert Smith (with his post–World War II hit "Guitar Boogie") and John Lee Hooker (with his "Boogie Chillun") the phrase came to refer to guitar playing as well.

Although the Allman Brothers' expanded "boogie" jams incorporated blues, gospel, country and R&B, nowadays, the term refers to the simple, unadorned blues/R&B-based rock of white bands like Britain's Foghat, and latter-day southern rock groups like .38 Special. It also means a form of dancing in which one stands before a bandstand and moves one's hips to the beat. As an extension from the white heavy post-blues-rock application of the term, "to boogie" can also mean for a musician to play with enough rhythm to make an audience boogie.

JAMES BOOKER

Born December 17, 1939, New Orleans
1976—*Junco Partners* (Island, U.K.)   1981—*New Orleans Piano Wizard: Live!* (Rounder).

Although James Booker had only one hit, his keyboards on hits by Joe Tex, Fats Domino, Bobby Bland, Lloyd Price and Junior Parker, and his unpredictable temperament, made him a New Orleans legend. A child piano prodigy, the son of a minister and brother of gospel singer Betty Jean Booker, he made his first recordings for Imperial Records, working with Dave Bartholomew, when he

was 14. He also recorded for the Ace and Duke labels and toured with Joe Tex, Shirley and Lee, Huey Smith's Clowns (impersonating the road-weary Smith) and the Dovells.

In the late Fifties, Booker's value as a session musician—already high—rose when he became the first notable New Orleans R&B musician to play the organ. His R&B organ instrumental "Gonzo" (on Peacock Records) hit #3 on the national R&B charts and made the pop Top Fifty in 1960. He continued to work as a session musician and sideman with B. B. King, Little Richard and Wilson Pickett, among others, into the mid-Sixties, when he was sidelined by drug problems and a jail term. He began working again around 1968, most notably with Fats Domino, Dr. John and the Doobie Brothers. He toured Europe in 1977 (the Rounder live album was recorded in Zurich that year), then returned to regular engagements in New Orleans. The Clash covered his "Junco Partner" on their 1981 album, *Sandinista!*

BOOKER T. AND THE MGs

Formed 1961, Memphis
Booker T. Jones (b. Dec. 11, 1944, Memphis), organ; Lewis Steinberg, bass; Al Jackson (b. Nov. 27, 1935, Memphis; d. Oct. 1, 1975, Memphis), drums; Steve Cropper (b. Oct. 21, 1941, Willow Springs, Mo.), gtr. (1964: − Steinberg; + Donald "Duck" Dunn [b. Nov. 24, 1941, Memphis], bass).
1962—*Green Onions* (Stax)   1966—*And Now, Booker T. and the MGs*   1967—*Back to Back*   1968—*The Best of Booker T. and the MGs* (Atlantic)   *Doin' Our Thing* (Stax)   *Hip Hug-Her; Soul Limbo; Uptight*   1969— *The Booker T. Set*   1970—*McLemore Street*   1971— *Melting Pot*   1973—*Star Collection* (Warner Bros.) 1974—*Greatest Hits*   1975—*Memphis Sound* 1976—*Union Extended;   Time Is Tight* 1977—*Universal Language* (Asylum)   1978—*Try and Love Again* (A&M).

As the rhythm section of the Stax Records house band, Booker T. and the MGs were principal architects of the lean, punchy Stax sound. Though they had some instrumental hits on their own, they did invaluable backup work on hits by other Stax and Atlantic performers like Otis Redding, Sam and Dave, Wilson Pickett, Albert King, Eddie Floyd and Rufus and Carla Thomas. Steve Cropper also has writing credit on "Knock on Wood," "In the Midnight Hour," "Soul Man" and "(Sittin' on) The Dock of the Bay." Booker T. Jones was a teenage multiinstrumental prodigy who joined the Stax organization in 1960 as a saxophonist. Jamming with Mar-Keys guitarist Steve Cropper led to the formation of the MGs (Memphis Group) and to the recording of "Green Onions." "Green Onions" went to #3 and gold in 1962 and was followed by "Boot–Leg" (1965), "My Sweet Potato" (1966), "Hip

Hug-Her'' (1967), a cover version of the Rascals' "Groovin' " (#21, 1968), "Soul Limbo" (#17, 1968) and two film soundtrack hits in 1969, "Hang 'Em High" (#9) and "Time Is Tight" (#6).

The best-known version of the band was composed of Jones, Cropper, Jackson and Dunn. They toured sporadically as part of Stax/Volt Revue. The MGs proper were a very informal assemblage and played together only intermittently, partly due to Jones's frequent absences while completing his music major at Indiana University. Often limited to working only when Jones was available on weekends and vacations, the group eventually broke up in 1971.

Soon afterwards, Jones began working as a producer (for his since divorced wife, Priscilla Coolidge, among others), as a session player and as a solo vocal performer. Jackson also returned to session work, notably for Al Green. In 1973, he joined Dunn in a short-lived MGs reunion.

In 1975, Jackson was shot and killed on a Memphis street. Former Bar-Kays drummer Willie Hall took his place in reunion sessions with Jones, Cropper and Dunn between 1975 and 1978. In 1977, Jones, Cropper and Dunn toured with Levon Helm's RCO All Stars. Since then, Cropper and Dunn have been active as freelance musicians and producers, joining the Blues Brothers in 1978, while Jones has worked on his solo career. He had a disco hit with his 1982 A&M single "Don't Stop Your Love."

THE BOOMTOWN RATS
Formed 1975, Dun Laoghaire, Ireland
Bob Geldof (b. Oct. 5, 1954, Ire.), voc.; Johnny Fingers (b. Ire.), kybds.; Pete Briquette (b. Ire.), bass; Simon Crowe (b. Ire.), drums; Gerry Cott (b. Ire.), gtr.; Garry Roberts (b. Ire.), gtr.
1977—The Boomtown Rats (Mercury) 1979—A Tonic for the Troops (Columbia) The Fine Art of Surfacing 1981—(– Cott) Mondo Bongo 1983—Ratrospective.

Irish new-wavers, the Boomtown Rats have become full-fledged pop stars in Britain and Europe while being virtually ignored in the U.S. The band started in Garry Roberts' kitchen in Dun Laoghaire. Originally called the Nightlife Thugs, they changed their name to the Boomtown Rats after a gang in Woody Guthrie's Bound for Glory. They moved to London (and into a communal house in Chessington) in 1976. Their stage show attracted attention for Johnny Fingers, who always wears pajamas, and the Mick Jagger–David Bowie posturings of frontman Bob Geldof (who had previously worked as a meat worker, bulldozer operator, photographer and Melody Maker correspondent).

While most of London's punk bands were sneering at rich, selfish rock stars, Geldof announced his ambition to become one. The first Rats single, "Looking After No. 1,"

hit #11 in England in August 1977 (the first new wave single to be playlisted by the BBC) and the media discovered Geldof's willingness to utter controversial opinions on virtually any subject. The Rats' first album (recorded in Germany and released in England in late 1977) did well in the U.K. With A Tonic for the Troops ("She's So Modern") the group established a pattern of critical raves but poor sales in the U.S. In Britain, their success continued; by early 1981 they had nine consecutive Top Fifteen singles.

The group scored a minor U.S. hit with "I Don't Like Mondays" (#73, 1980), based on the case of a 17-year-old San Diego girl named Brenda Spencer who randomly shot eleven passersby (killing two) on Monday, January 29, 1979, and explained her actions by saying, "I don't like Mondays." The single was banned by some radio stations and prompted a lawsuit by the girl's parents who claimed it created adverse pretrial publicity.

The advent of the Eighties found the Rats continuing to tour internationally and release records, such as 1981's Mondo Bongo and the reggae single "Banana Republic." In 1982, Geldof played the lead role of Pink in a film of Pink Floyd's The Wall.

DEBBY BOONE
Born September 22, 1956, Hackensack, New Jersey
1977—You Light Up My Life (Curb/Warner Bros.)
1978—Midstream 1979—The Promise 1980—Love Has No Reason.

Debby Boone had the longest-running #1 hit single—ten weeks—with "You Light Up My Life" in 1977. One of singer Pat Boone's four daughters, Debby began performing with her sisters in 1969 as the Boone Girls. They toured with their father and recorded for the Lamb & Lion label. In 1977, producer Mike Curb persuaded Debby to record solo. The song he chose for her, "You Light Up My Life," theme song from a movie, won an Oscar for Best Song. Boone retired to start a family. She wrote an autobiography that chronicled her teenage "rebelliousness" and her life with Christ, entitled Debby Boone . . . So Far. She returned to performing in 1982, when she starred in the play Seven Brides for Seven Brothers, a hit around the country which closed within weeks of its Broadway debut.

PAT BOONE
Born June 1, 1934, Jacksonville, Florida
1962—Pat Boone's Golden Hits (Dot)

Singer Pat Boone claims to be a descendant of early American frontier hero Daniel Boone. He attended high school in Nashville, where he lettered in three varsity sports as well as serving as student body president and being elected the school's most popular boy. Following his graduation, he married country & western star Red Foley's daughter, Shirley. In the early Fifties, he attended David Lipscomb College in Nashville before transferring to North Texas State. There he won a local talent show, which led to an appearance on the Ted Mack program and then Arthur Godfrey's amateur hour, where Boone became a regular for a year.

By mid-decade, he had begun recording with some mildly successful singles for Nashville's Republic Records. In February 1955, he released his first single for Dot Records, "Two Hearts, Two Kisses." By the end of the year, he had his first of dozens of hits for the label, a relaxed cover of Fats Domino's "Ain't That a Shame," which hit #1.

Over the next seven years, Boone made 54 chart appearances, including many two-sided hits, and became one of the all-time biggest-selling pop singers. His Top Ten hits for Dot included "At My Front Door (Crazy Little Mama)" (#7, 1955), "I'll Be Home" (#4, 1956), "I Almost Lost My Mind" (#1, 1956), "Friendly Persuasion" (#5, 1956), "Don't Forbid Me" (#1, 1957), "Why Baby Why" (#5, 1957), "Love Letters in the Sand" (#1, 1957), "April Love" (#1, 1957), "A Wonderful Time Up There" (#4, 1958), "Moody River" (#1, 1961), and "Speedy Gonzales" (#6, 1962). At his peak, he was considered a rock & roller—a parent-approved alternative to Elvis, Jerry Lee Lewis and Chuck Berry in white buck shoes. He starred in films like *Bernadine* and *April Love* (both 1957) and *State Fair* (1962). From 1957 to 1960, he had his own television series on ABC.

In 1977, his daughter, Debby Boone, became a star in her own right.

EARL BOSTIC

Born April 25, 1913, Tulsa, Okla.; died 1965.
N.A.—*Best of Bostic* (King) *Bostic Rocks; Dance Time; Earl Bostic and His Alto Sax; Let's Dance with Earl Bostic.*

Grammy Awards

Burt Bacharach
1967 Best Instrumental Arrangement: "Alfie"
1969 Best Original Score Written for a Motion Picture or a TV Special:
Butch Cassidy and the Sundance Kid
Best Score From an Original Cast Show Album:
Promises, Promises (with Hal David)

The Beatles (see also: George Harrison, John Lennon, Paul McCartney, Ringo Starr)
1964 Best New Artist of 1964;
Best Performance by a Vocal Group:
A Hard Day's Night
1967 Album of the Year; Best Contemporary Album:
Sgt. Pepper's Lonely Hearts Club Band

The Bee Gees (see also: Barry Gibb)
1977 Best Pop Vocal Performance by a Duo, Group or Chorus:
"How Deep Is Your Love"

1978 Album of the Year; Best Pop Vocal Performance by a Duo, Group or Chorus:
Saturday Night Fever (with others)

Pat Benatar
1980 Best Rock Vocal Performance, Female:
Crimes of Passion
1981 Best Rock Vocal Performance, Female:
"Fire and Ice"
1982 Best Vocal Performance, Female:
"Shadows of the Night"

George Benson
1976 Record of the Year:
"This Masquerade"
Best Pop Instrumental Performance:
Breezin'
Best R&B Instrumental Performance:
"Theme from Good King Bad"
1978 Best R&B Vocal Performance, Male:
"On Broadway"

1980 Best R&B Vocal Performance, Male:
Give Me the Night
Best R&B Instrumental Performance:
"Off Broadway"
Best Jazz Vocal Performance, Male:
"Moody's Mood"

Blood, Sweat and Tears
1969 Album of the Year:
Blood, Sweat and Tears
Best Contemporary Instrumental Performance:
"Variations on a Theme by Erik Satie"

Debby Boone
1977 Best New Artist of the Year
1980 Best Inspirational Performance:
With My Song I Will Praise Him

Clarence "Gatemouth" Brown
1982 Best Traditional Blues Recording:
Alright Again

James Brown
1965 Best R&B Recording:
"Papa's Got a Brand New Bag"

Earl Bostic's alto sax propelled Lionel Hampton's big band into R&B in the late Forties and gave his own band a #1 R&B hit in 1951; his style was the cornerstone of rock and soul sax playing. Bostic began playing clarinet and tenor saxophone in high school. He studied music at universities in Omaha and New Orleans and, after receiving his degree, remained in New Orleans to play with Fate Marable's band. He moved to New York in the early Forties and played with Don Redman and Cab Calloway before joining Hampton. In 1945 he formed his own nine-piece band, which recorded on the Majestic, Gotham and King labels. He had his biggest hit with "Flamingo" (#1 R&B, 1951), following it the same year with "Sleep," a #9 R&B hit. He was active in jazz and R&B until he died of a heart attack in 1965.

BOSTON

Formed 1975, Boston
Tom Scholz (b. Mar. 10, 1947, Toledo), gtr., kybds.; Brad Delp (b. June 12, 1951, Boston), voc., gtr.; Barry Goudreau (b. Nov. 29, 1951, Boston), gtr.; Fran Sheehan (b. Mar. 26, 1949, Boston), bass; Sib Hashian (b. Aug. 17, 1949, Boston), drums.
1976—*Boston* (Epic)   **1978**—*Don't Look Back.*

In 1976, hard-pop group Boston had the fastest-selling debut album in rock. *Boston* was a slightly altered version of tapes made by guitarist Tom Scholz in his 12-track basement studio, characterized by what he calls "power guitars, harmony vocals and double-guitar leads." Scholz had a master's degree in mechanical engineering from MIT and was a senior product designer for Polaroid Corporation who made elaborate hard-rock tapes in his off-hours. Eventually, the tapes attracted the interest of Epic Records and they signed Scholz and a band of local musicians, Boston. Upon signing, the band recut some tracks on the West Coast with producer John Boylan, but their 1976 debut was essentially Scholz's basement tapes. As it sold 6½ million copies, Boston went almost directly to the arena circuit on tour.

Two years later, *Don't Look Back* presented the Boston formula virtually unchanged and sold a comparatively disappointing 3½ million copies, while less-than-sellout concert crowds suggested that audience interest was flagging. Barry Goudreau released a solo album in 1980. As of mid-1983, their third LP had not been released, but Scholz had invented a paperback-sized guitar amplifier with headphones, the Rockman.

DAVID BOWIE

Born David Robert Jones, Jan. 8, 1947, London
1967—*The World of David Bowie* (London/Deram)
1969—*Man of Words, Man of Music* (Mercury)   **1970**—*The Man Who Sold the World*   **1971**—*Hunky Dory* (RCA)   **1972**—*The Rise and Fall of Ziggy Stardust and the Spiders from Mars*   **1973**—*Aladdin Sane; Pin-Ups; Images 1966–67* (London/Deram)   **1974**—*Diamond Dogs* (RCA)   *David Live*   **1975**—*Young Americans*   **1976**—*Station to Station; Changes-OneBowie*   **1977**—*Low; "Heroes"*   **1978**—*Stage*   **1979**—*Lodger*   **1980**—*Scary Monsters*   **1981**—*ChangesTwoBowie; Christiane F* (soundtrack)   **1982**—*Cat People* (soundtrack)   *Baal* (EP)   **1983**—*Let's Dance* (EMI).

David Bowie has made his career a series of charged, contradictory images—androgyne, alien, decadent, star, fashion plate, traveler—while making increasingly avant-garde music. He has drawn on freely acknowledged sources, from Marc Bolan and the Velvet Underground to Brian Eno, put his own mark on them, then abruptly moved on, leaving behind imitators of each of his phases.

David Jones took up the saxophone at age 12, and when he left Bromley Technical High School to work as a commercial artist at an advertising agency three years later, he began playing in part-time bands (the King Bees, David Jones and the Buzz). A punch from high school chum George Underwood permanently paralyzed Jones's left pupil but didn't end their friendship; Underwood later designed two Bowie LP covers. Three of Jones's early bands—the King Bees, the Manish Boys (produced by Shel Talmy and featuring session guitarist Jimmy Page) and David Jones and the Lower Third—each recorded a single. In 1966, having changed his name to Bowie (after the knife) to avoid confusion with Monkees' Davy Jones, he recorded three singles for Pye Records, then signed in 1967 with London/Deram. Several London singles, notably "Love You Till Tuesday" and "The Laughing Gnome," hit the U.K. charts, and London issued *The World of David Bowie* (most of the songs on that album, and others from that time, were collected on *Images*).

But Bowie hadn't yet settled on pop music. He spent some weeks in a Buddhist monastery in Scotland, but decided not to take the monastic vows. He then apprenticed himself in Lindsay Kemp's mime troupe, exchanging musical scores for pantomime lessons, in 1967. He also acted on a 15-minute short (*The Image*), a feature (a bit part in *The Virgin Soldiers*), a commercial for ice cream bars and a BBC-TV play, *The Pistol Shot*. With his costar from the play, he started Feathers, a mime troupe, in 1968. American-born Angela Barnett met Bowie in London's Speakeasy and married him on March 20, 1970. (Son Zowie Bowie was born in June 1971.) After Feathers broke up, Bowie started the Beckenham Arts Lab in 1969 to experiment with theater and music. To finance the project, he signed with Mercury; *Man of Words, Man of Music* included "Space Oddity," an international hit at the time of the U.S. moon landing.

Marc Bolan, an old friend, was beginning his rise as a glitter-rocker in T. Rex, and introduced Bowie to his producer Tony Visconti; Bowie mimed at some T. Rex concerts, and Bolan played guitar on Bowie's "Karma Man" and "The Prettiest Star." Bowie, Visconti, guitarist Mick Ronson and drummer John Cambridge toured briefly as Hype. Ronson eventually recruited drummer Michael Woodmansey from his old blues band, the Rats, and with bassist Visconti they recorded *The Man Who Sold the World,* which included "All the Madmen," inspired by Bowie's institutionalized brother, Terry. *Hunky Dory* was Bowie's tribute to the New York City of Andy Warhol, the Velvet Underground and Bob Dylan, with Bowie's virtual theme song, "Changes."

By 1971, Bowie was working hard on his image. He told *Melody Maker* he was gay in January 1972, and enjoyed the idea of a cult growing around his androgynous image. New manager Tony DeFries gave Bowie accoutrements of stardom—limos, champagne, first-class hotels—and Bowie began to think about the star as character. Enter Ziggy Stardust, the doomed messianic rock icon. *The Rise and Fall of Ziggy Stardust and the Spiders from Mars* (the Spiders were Ziggy's band: Ronson, Woodmansey and bassist Trevor Bolder) made Bowie the star he was portraying. The live show, with Bowie in futuristic costumes, makeup and orange hair, was a sensation in London and New York, and "Starman" became a hit while *Ziggy Stardust* sold a million copies. Bolan and other British glitter-rock performers barely made the Atlantic crossing, but Bowie emerged a star. *Aladdin Sane* was a surrealistic diary of his first American tour, with hits in "The Jean Genie" (the title is a pun on playwright Jean Genet's name; the song is about singer Iggy Pop) and Bowie produced albums for his inspiration Lou Reed (*Transformer,* including "Walk on the Wild Side") and Iggy Pop (*Raw Power*) and wrote a glitter anthem for Mott the Hoople, "All the Young Dudes."

In l973, Bowie announced at a London concert that ended a sixty-date British tour that he would never again perform onstage. He disbanded the Spiders and sailed to Paris to record *Pin-Ups,* a collection of covers of mid-Sixties British rock. The retirement didn't last; Bowie videotaped an invitational concert for American TV, "The 1980 Floor Show" (broadcast on "The Midnight Special") with guests the Troggs and Marianne Faithfull.

Meanwhile, Bowie worked on a musical adaptation of George Orwell's *1984,* but was denied rights to the book by Orwell's widow. He rewrote the material for *Diamond Dogs,* and mounted a $250,000 extravaganza to tour America. Midway through the tour, however, he scrapped the sets and costumes and appeared thereafter in baggy Oxford trousers, without makeup, his hair trim and its natural blond. His sound, too, underwent revision: he toned-down the glitter-rock, hired a new band led by guitarist Earl Slick (former musical director for the Main Ingredient and an ex-James Brown sideman) and added soul music standards to his repertoire. The new Bowie

was an entertainer, the Thin White Duke (as he called himself in a song and an unpublished autobiography).

Bowie ended the 1974 tour by recording a live double set in Philadelphia (the then-current capital of black pop), then booked Philly's Sigma Sound Studios to cut *Young Americans* with guitarists Slick and Carlos Alomar, bassists Willy Weeks and Emir Ksasan and drummer Dennis Davis. Two singles from that album became favorites in discos, and "Fame" (cowritten by Bowie, Alomar and John Lennon) became Bowie's first American #1. Bowie moved to Los Angeles and became a fixture of American pop culture, appearing on TV's "Soul Train," Grammy Award ceremonies, the Dinah Shore show and a Cher special. He also played the title role in Nicolas Roeg's *The Man Who Fell to Earth* (1976).

After recording another album of what he called "plastic soul" with the *Young Americans* band, Bowie left Los Angeles, complaining that he had become predictable again. He returned to the U.K. for the first time in three years, then settled in Berlin, where he lived almost reclusively, painting, studying art and recording with Brian Eno. His work with Eno (*Low, "Heroes," Lodger*) took him into electronic music, and the occasional narrative song employed novelist William Burroughs' random "cut-up" writing technique.

David Bowie

Bowie revitalized Iggy Pop's career by producing *The Idiot* and *Lust for Life* and toured Europe and America unannounced in 1977 as Pop's pianist. While in America, he narrated Eugene Ormandy and the Philadelphia Orchestra's recording of Prokofiev's *Peter and the Wolf*. He spent most of the next year in Berlin acting with Marlene Dietrich and Kim Novak in *Just a Gigolo*. He then embarked on a world tour with a band that included Davis and Murray and, variously, violinist Simon House of Hawkwind, synthesizist Roger Powell of Utopia, and guitarist Adrian Belew, who had worked with Frank Zappa. A second live album, *Stage*, was recorded during the U.S. leg of that tour. Work on *Lodger*, his third collaboration with Eno, was begun in New York, continued in Zurich and completed in Berlin.

In 1979, Bowie returned to New York to record the paranoiac *Scary Monsters*, updating "Space Oddity" in "Ashes to Ashes (The Continuing Story of Major Tom)"; a 12-inch single distributed to radio stations only, segued "Space Oddity" into "Ashes to Ashes." Bowie also made some of the most innovative promotional rock videos with songs from *Lodger* and *Scary Monsters*. He spent 1980 in the title role of Bernard Pomerance's Broadway play *The Elephant Man* in Denver and Chicago and on Broadway. And while rockers awaited the latest new Bowie, he kept himself in royalties by collaborating with Queen on 1981's "Under Pressure" and providing lyrics and vocals on Giorgio Moroder's title tune for the soundtrack of Paul Schrader's 1982 film *Cat People*. His music provided the soundtrack for *Christiane F.*, the film biography of a young heroin addict. In 1982, Bowie appeared in a BBC-TV production of Bertolt Brecht's *Baal*. He portrays a 150-year-old man in the movie *The Hunger*. In 1983 he returned to recording with *Let's Dance*, produced by Nile Rodgers of Chic.

BOW WOW WOW

Formed in 1980, London
Annabella Lwin (b. Myant Myant Aye, ca. 1966, Rangoon, Burma), voc.; Matthew Ashman (b. London), gtr.; Dave Barbarossa (b. Mauritius), drums; Leroy Gorman (b. Eng.), bass.
1981—*See Jungle! See Jungle! Go Join Your Gang Yeah! City All Over, Go Ape Crazy* (RCA) *Your Cassette Pet* **1982**—*Last of the Mohicans* **1983**—*When the Going Gets Tough, the Tough Gets Going*.

After manager/entrepreneur Malcolm McLaren assembled the Sex Pistols, he followed up with Bow Wow Wow. He discovered Annabella Lwin (a young woman from Burma of a reportedly aristocratic family who arrived in England a refugee at the age of five) working in a dry cleaner's when she was fourteen. Although she didn't sing, she had the look, and he installed her in front of Matthew Ashman, Dave Barbarossa and Leroy Gorman,

whom he had separated from Adam and the Ants. The key to the group's sound was Barbarossa's percussion, a pounding tom-tom beat derived from Burundi ritual music (and the essence of Adam's Antmusic). With Annabella's girlish squeal, Bow Wow Wow's songs (mostly written by McLaren and the instrumentalists) were a heady concoction of African rhythms, Balinese chants, surf instrumentals and New Romantic pop melodies.

EMI released "C30, C60, C90 Go!" in fall 1980, and the song entered the U.K. Top Thirty despite EMI's refusal to promote it because it allegedly advocated home taping. The group's next release was one of the first commercial recordings to be released on tape but not on vinyl. *Your Cassette Pet* was a twenty-minute, eight-song cassette packaged to resemble a pack of Marlboro cigarettes, and became the first tape to place on the British singles charts. Songs like "Sexy Eiffel Tower" helped to win headlines suggesting that McLaren was promoting child pornography. EMI dropped Bow Wow Wow after issuing their second single, "W.O.R.K.," in the spring of 1981.

"W.O.R.K." became a best-selling import single in the U.S., and Bow Wow Wow signed with RCA. Just before a planned U.S. tour, Annabella's mother instigated a Scotland Yard investigation of alleged exploitation of a minor for immoral purposes. A magistrate granted permission to leave England only when McLaren and RCA promised not to publish a photograph of Annabella as the nude woman of Manet's painting *Déjeuner sur l'herbe* or to promote her as "a sex kitten."

Bow Wow Wow: (top) Matthew Ashman, Leroy Gorman, (bottom) Annabella Lwin, Dave Barbarossa

Shortly before the release of their debut album, Bow Wow Wow made their first appearance in the U.S. The group's entourage included a chaperone for Annabella (who was now fifteen) and two go-go dancers named Boo and Fifi. A 1982 EP (containing the single "I Want Candy," produced by Joan Jett's producer/manager Kenny Laguna), used the *Déjeuner sur l'herbe* photo on its jacket. Later albums moved away from the Burundi beat and toward heavy metal.

THE BOX TOPS
Formed circa 1966, Memphis
Alex Chilton (b. Dec. 28, 1950, Memphis), voc.; Bill Cunningham (b. Jan. 23, 1950, Memphis), kybds., bass; Tom Boggs (b. July 16, 1947, Wynn, Ark.), drums; Rick Allen (b. Jan. 28, 1946, Little Rock), organ, bass; Gary Talley (b. Aug. 17, 1947), gtr., bass.
1968—*The Box Tops: "The Letter"/"Neon Rainbow"* (Bell) *Cry Like a Baby* (Stateside) *Super Hits* (Bell) *Non-Stop* **1969**—*Dimensions* **1982**—*Greatest Hits* (Rhino).

The Box Tops came out of Memphis in the late Sixties with a string of blue-eyed-soul hits. Young Alex Chilton's raw lead vocals sparked million-selling singles "The Letter" (#1, 1967) and "Cry Like a Baby" (#2, 1968). Their success was partially due to producer/writer Dan Penn, who later released a solo album that was a Box Tops soundalike. The band toured infrequently (Chilton later described their live abilities as "terrible"), and its lineup was unstable (two members quit the group at the height of its success to return to college). After several albums for Bell and minor hits like "Sweet Cream Ladies" (#28, 1969), they disbanded in early 1970, and Chilton eventually formed Big Star.

TOMMY BOYCE AND BOBBY HART
Formed circa 1963, Los Angeles
Tommy Boyce (b. 1944, Charlottesville, Va.), Bobby Hart (b. 1944, Phoenix).
1967—*Test Patterns* (A&M) **1968**—*I Wonder What She's Doing Tonight; Which One's Boyce and Which One's Hart?; It's All Happening on the Inside.*

One of the top songwriting teams of the mid-Sixties, Boyce and Hart teamed up to write "Last Train to Clarksville," "Valleri" and "I'm Not Your Steppin' Stone" for groups like the Monkees and Paul Revere and the Raiders. They began working together in the early Sixties and their "Come a Little Bit Closer," a hit in 1964 for Jay and the Americans, led to a songwriting contract with Screen Gems. They wrote most of the material for Don Kirshner's made-for-TV Monkees. In May 1967, they began recording as a duo and a few months later enjoyed pop success

with "I Wonder What She's Doing Tonight" and "Alice Long (You're Still My Favorite Girlfriend)." They toured nightclubs through the late Sixties. In 1975, they teamed up with ex-Monkees Davy Jones and Mickey Dolenz for an album and tour. Boyce and Hart claim over 300 compositions and sales of more than 42 million records.

EDDIE BOYD
Born November 25, 1914, Mississippi
1967—*Eddie Boyd and His Blues Band* (Decca) **1968**—*7936 South Rhodes* (Epic) *Eddie Boyd Live* (Storyville) **1974**—*Legacy of the Blues, volume 10* (GNP).

Guitarist/keyboardist/singer Eddie Boyd was responsible for the 1952 #1 R&B hit "Five Long Years." Half-brother of Memphis Slim and first cousin of Muddy Waters, Boyd was born on a plantation in Coahoma County, Mississippi, where he worked until he ran away from home in 1928. He taught himself to play guitar and keyboards and began touring the Mississippi bar and juke joint circuit during the early Thirties. In 1936, he moved to Memphis, where he worked in Beale Street bars.

In 1937, he formed his first group, the Dixie Rhythm Boys, with whom he toured Tennessee and Arkansas before moving to Chicago in 1941. Quickly embraced by the Southside blues circles, he worked through the mid-Forties with Memphis Slim, Sonny Boy Williamson and his cousin Waters. He made his first recordings (with Williamson) for the Victor/Bluebird label around 1943, and has recorded for several labels over the years, including Chess Records from 1952 to 1957. He gave Chess two R&B Top Ten hits—"24 Hours" and "Third Degree"—in 1953.

By the start of the Sixties, Boyd was recording for small independent labels, but a blues and R&B resurgence led him to Decca in 1965. From mid-decade on, he frequently toured Europe and England with rock artists like John Mayall and recorded for various European labels. He lived in London, Paris, Finland and other foreign locations. He returned to America in 1977 and remains active both in recording and club work.

BRASS CONSTRUCTION
Formed 1968, Brooklyn, New York
Randy Muller, lead voc., kybds., flute, percussion; Wade Williamston, bass; Joseph Arthur Wong, gtr.; Morris Price, trumpet, voc., percussion; Wayne Parris, trumpet, voc.; Larry Payton, drums; Sandy Billups, voc., congas; Jesse Ward, Jr., sax, voc.; Michael Grudge, sax, voc.
1975—*Brass Construction* (United Artists) **1976**—*II* **1977**—*III* **1978**—*IV* **1979**—*V* **1980**—*VI* **1982**—*Attitudes* (EMI/Liberty).

Brass Construction was one of the horn-dominated big bands that ushered in the disco era of the mid-Seventies.

Formed by Randy Muller in Brooklyn in 1968, Brass Construction's cosmopolitan sound—a mix of Sly and the Family Stone funk, big-band jazz, Latin salsa and Caribbean upbeats—was underscored by its makeup: Muller was from Guyana, Joseph Wong from Trinidad, and Wayne Parris and Michael Grudge from Jamaica. By 1975, when United Artists signed them, their nine-man lineup was firm and remained consistent through their recording career.

With Muller as writer and arranger, the first album was mainly instrumental, with vocals used as choral embellishments. Their first single, "Movin'," hit #1 on the R&B charts in 1976 (pop #14). "Changin' " followed it at #24, and the album went platinum. The second album, which included "Ha Cha Cha" (#8, 1977) and brought the vocals into the foreground, sold gold. *III*'s single, "L-O-V-E-U," made only #18, but the album sold gold. Their subsequent releases included no more hit singles, although their albums continued to regularly place in the Top Forty.

Since 1979, Muller has divided his attentions between Brass Construction and another New York dance band, Skyy, for whom he is producer and songwriter. Skyy has been the beneficiary of his new ideas, while Brass Construction has continued to play according to established formulas; of the two, Skyy has been the more commercially successful in recent years.

BREAD
Formed 1969
David Gates (b. Tulsa), voc., gtr., kybds.; James Griffin (b. Memphis), voc., gtr.; Robb Reyer, kybds.
1969—*Bread* (Elektra) (+ Mike Botts [b. Sacramento], drums) **1970**—*On the Water* (Elektra) **1971**—*Manna* (Elektra) (− Reyer) (+ Larry Knechtel [b. Bell, Calif], kybds.) **1972**—*Baby I'm-A Want You* (Elektra) *Guitar Man* (Elektra) **1973**—*The Best of Bread* (Elektra) **1974**—*The Best of Bread, volume 2* **1977**— *Lost Without Your Love*.

Bread's mellow pop rock was an early-Seventies model for the "adult contemporary" sound. Led by guitarist and songwriter David Gates, the nucleus of Bread was made up of studio players who had been working as Pleasure Faire before they made their first album for Elektra in 1969. Their second album gained them the first of several gold singles, "Make It with You" in the summer of 1970 (#1). Buoyed by its success, they added permanent drummer Mike Botts (studio musician Jim Gordon had handled percussion on their first album) to play live concerts. Hits like "It Don't Matter to Me" (#10, 1970), "If" (#4, 1971), "Baby, I'm-A Want You" (#3, 1971), "Let Your Love Go" (#28, 1971) and "Guitar Man" (#11, 1972) continued until the group broke up in 1973. After three years together, Bread had earned six gold albums. Thereafter, only Gates has worked with moderate success as a solo

act. He had hit singles with "Never Let Her Go" (#29, 1975) and "Goodbye Girl" (#15, 1978). Bread re-formed in late 1976 to release a hit album and a single, "Lost Without Your Love" (#9, 1977) and disbanded once again.

BREWER AND SHIPLEY
Formed 1968, Los Angeles
Mike Brewer (b. 1944, Oklahoma City), gtr., voc.; Tom Shipley (b. 1942, Mineral Ridge, Oh.), gtr., voc.
1968—*Brewer and Shipley Down in L.A.* (A&M) **1969**—*Weeds* (Kama Sutra) **1970**—*Tarkio* **1971**— *Shake Off the Demon* **1972**—*Rural Space* **1974**— *Brewer and Shipley* (Capitol) **1975**—*Welcome to Riddle Bridge* **1976**—*Best of Brewer and Shipley* (Kama Sutra) **1978**—*Not Far from Free* (Mercury).

Folk-rockers Mike Brewer and Tom Shipley grew up in the Midwest and met in L.A. They signed songwriting contracts with A&M in 1965. Without the duo's approval, A&M released some of their demos as an album entitled *Down in L.A.* To counter that album, the pair, who had moved to a communal twenty-acre farm outside of Kansas City, released the first of several increasingly successful country-styled albums for Kama Sutra. *Tarkio* contained the hit "One Toke over the Line" (1971), which was the subject of some controversy when the FCC—then intent on banishing drug references from the airwaves—discovered the meaning of *toke*. Although the song was informally banned, it was a #10 hit that year. The duo switched to Capitol in 1974 but has had only marginal success since.

BRINSLEY SCHWARZ
Formed 1970, England
Brinsley Schwarz, gtr., voc., sax; Nick Lowe (b. Mar. 25, 1949), bass, voc., gtr.; Billy Rankin, drums; Bob Andrews (b. June 20, 1949), kybds., bass, voc.
1970—*Brinsley Schwarz* (Capitol) *Despite It All* (Liberty, U.K.) (+ Ian Gomm [b. Mar. 17, 1947, London], gtr.) **1972**—*Silver Pistol* (UA, U.K.) *Nervous on the Road* **1973**—*Please Don't Ever Change* **1974**—*New Favourites; Original Golden Greats* **1978**—*15 Thoughts of Brinsley Schwarz* **1979**—*Brinsley Schwarz* (Capitol).

Brinsley Schwarz were not successful outside the early-Seventies English pub circuit, but the later successes of its members have given the group semi-legendary status. Overzealous promotion almost nipped the band in the bud when a planeload of U.K. journalists was flown to the States to witness their Fillmore East debut and returned with tales of overpromotion that hounded the band until its death. Their good-time aura and country-flavored rock—a back-to-basics attitude in the wake of psychedelia—attracted ardent followers in England, but major success eluded them.

Their last album, *New Favourites,* was produced in 1974 by Dave Edmunds. After its release, Nick Lowe teamed up with Edmunds to form Rockpile, but not before he and Ian Gomm cowrote "Cruel to Be Kind," which eventually became Lowe's biggest U.S. hit (#12, 1979). Gomm himself scored an American hit in 1979 with "Hold On" (#18). Bob Andrews and Brinsley Schwarz earned subsequent kudos in the Rumour, primarily backing Graham Parker and later Garland Jeffreys. In 1979, Capitol released a Brinsley Schwarz double-album compilation.

BRITISH INVASION

Between 1964 and 1966—after the dominance of girl groups and doo-wop R&B, and just before the advent of psychedelia—British rock bands dominated the pop charts in both their homeland and the U.S. British Invasion bands included the Beatles, the Rolling Stones, Yardbirds, Kinks, Animals, Manfred Mann, as well as "Merseybeat" (so named because the Mersey River runs through Liverpool) bands like Gerry and Pacemakers (one of whose hits was "Ferry Cross the Mersey"), Billy J. Kramer and the Dakotas, Wayne Fontana and the Mindbenders, and Herman's Hermits, who further exploited the Liverpool-based softer pop rock the Beatles had first purveyed. The hallmarks of British Invasion and Merseybeat rock—jangly guitars, pleasant melodies, immaculate vocal harmonies and a general air of teenage romantic innocence—were later a direct influence on mid- and late-Seventies power-pop groups like the Raspberries, Big Star and the Knack.

DAVID BROMBERG

Born September 19, 1945, Philadelphia
1972—*David Bromberg* (Columbia) *Demon in Disguise* **1974—***Wanted Dead or Alive* **1975—***Midnight on the Water* **1976—***How Late'll Ya Play 'Til?* (Fantasy) **1977—***Best: Out of the Blues* (Columbia) *Reckless Abandon* (Fantasy) **1978——***Bandit in a Bathing Suit; My Own House; Hillbilly Jazz* (Flying Fish) **1980—***You Should See the Rest of the Band.*

As a virtuoso on guitar, mandolin, fiddle and other stringed instruments, David Bromberg has been a folk-rock mainstay for over a decade. He grew up in Tarrytown, New York, and studied at Columbia University before becoming part of the mid-Sixties Greenwich Village folk scene. He began playing sessions regularly in the late Sixties and has since appeared on over seventy albums, including ones by Bob Dylan, Ringo Starr, Tom Paxton, Chubby Checker, Sha Na Na, Carly Simon and Phoebe Snow. Bromberg's eclecticism embraces blues, jazz, rock, bluegrass, country and old-timey traditional music. He began releasing solo albums in 1970 and by 1976 had formed the David Bromberg Band. In 1978 and 1979, he toured extensively with fellow Fantasy Records artist

Ralph McTell. But upset with his persistent lack of commercial acceptance, Bromberg announced his retirement from performing in mid-1980 and began studying the craft of violin making. Nonetheless, he continues to perform occasionally, including annual concerts at New York's Bottom Line.

THE BROOKLYN BRIDGE

Formed 1967, Long Island, New York
Johnny Maestro (b. John Mastrangelo, May 7, 1939, Brooklyn), voc.; Fred Ferrara (b. 1945), voc.; Mike Gregorio (b. 1947), voc.; Les Cauchi (b. 1945), voc.; Tom Sullivan (b. 1946), musical director; Carolyn Woods (b. 1947), organ; Jim Rosica (b. 1947), bass; Jim Macioce (b. 1947), gtr.; Artie Cantanzarita (b. 1949), drums; Shelly Davis (b. 1950), trumpet, kybds.; Joe Ruvio (b. 1947), sax.
1969—*Brooklyn Bridge* (Buddah) **N.A.—***The Second Brooklyn Bridge; Bridge in Blue.*

The Del-Satins, a vocal quartet led by Johnny Maestro (formerly of the Crests), and the Rhythm Method, a seven-piece band led by Tom Sullivan, joined forces to become the Brooklyn Bridge when they found themselves rivals at a Long Island talent contest in 1967. They had their only hit with a Jim Webb song first recorded by the Fifth Dimension, "Worst That Could Happen"(#3, 1969), and continued to record for Buddah into the early Seventies. By 1975, when they signed with Private Stock, the group had been trimmed to a quintet, with Maestro still leading. In 1981, they were playing one-nighters in the New York–New Jersey metropolitan area and appearing at nostalgia shows.

ELKIE BROOKS

Born February 25, 1945, Manchester, England
1975—*Rich Man's Woman* (A&M) **1977—***Two Days Away* **1978—***Shooting Star* **1979—***Live and Learn.*

The sister of Billy J. Kramer, Brooks began singing professionally at age 15, billed as "Manchester's answer to Brenda Lee." She moved to London to sing with Eric Delaney's dance band, then with Humphrey Lyttleton's jazz band, and from there to Georgie Fame's Blue Flames. Over the next few years, she worked in clubs, theaters, studios, radio and television, though usually as an anonymous backup vocalist.

In the late Sixties, she joined Dada, a 12-piece band experimenting with jazz-rock fusion. Dada recorded one album in 1971 before becoming the R&B-styled Vinegar Joe the next year. In Vinegar Joe, Brooks shared vocals with Robert Palmer, and elicited comparisons to Janis Joplin and Tina Turner. Though Vinegar Joe's live appearances were well received, its three albums (*Vinegar Joe,* 1972; *Rock 'n' Roll Gypsies,* 1972; *Six Star General,* 1973) sold poorly, and in 1974 the band broke up.

Two singles from Brooks's *Two Days Away* (produced by Leiber and Stoller)—"Pearl's a Singer" (a Brooks original about Janis Joplin) and "Sunshine After the Rain"—made the British Top Ten in 1977. While she has yet to appear on American charts, Brooks continues to score in the U.K.

THE BROTHERS JOHNSON
George Johnson (b. May 17, 1953, Los Angeles), gtr., voc.; Louis Johnson (b. Apr. 13, 1955, Los Angeles), bass, voc.
1976—*Look Out for #1* (A&M) 1977—*Right on Time*
1978—*Blam!* 1980—*Light Up the Night* 1981—
Winners 1982—*Blast!*

The Brothers Johnson have been playing music together since they were seven and eight years old. They put together their first group, the Johnson Three + 1, with older brother Tommy on drums and cousin Alex Weir (later a member of the Brothers Johnson Band) on rhythm guitar. They worked their way up from school dances to opening L.A. shows for acts like Bobby Womack and the Supremes.

George had just graduated from high school when Billy Preston invited him to join his band, the God Squad, as lead guitarist. When Preston's bass player abruptly left in the middle of a tour, George persuaded Preston to hire Louis. In the two years that the Johnsons were with Preston, they contributed several songs to his albums, including his 1974 hit single "Struttin' " (#22 pop, #11 R&B).

The brothers left Preston in 1975 and spent almost a year writing songs, rehearsing and recording demo tapes. Quincy Jones hired the Johnsons for a tour of Japan. He later recorded four Johnson compositions on his *Mellow Madness* (#16, 1975) and, having signed the duo to an A&M recording contract of their own, produced their first four albums.

Look Out for #1 sold over a million copies, with two hit singles, "I'll Be Good to You" (#3 pop, #1 R&B, 1976) and "Get the Funk Out Ma Face" (#30 pop, #4 R&B, 1976). *Right on Time* went gold three days after its release and platinum three months later. "Strawberry Letter 23" (a Shuggie Otis song) was a hit single (#5 pop, #1 R&B, 1977) and "Q," the Brothers' tribute to Jones, was awarded the 1977 Grammy for Best Instrumental. With the eight-piece Brothers Johnson Band, George and Louis toured the U.S., Europe and Japan in 1977.

A departure from the nonstop dance format of their first two albums, *Blam!* contained the Johnsons' first ballad and "Ride-O-Rocket," a song written for them by Ashford and Simpson. The U.S. tour in support of that album took them to eighty cities. After a year's vacation, they returned to the charts in 1980 with *Light Up the Night* (#5 pop, #1 R&B) and its hit single "Stomp!" (#7 pop, #1

R&B). Their first self-produced album, 1981's *Winners*, was their first LP to sell fewer than a million copies.

ARTHUR BROWN
Born June 24, 1944, Whitby, England
1968—*The Crazy World of Arthur Brown* (Atlantic)
1972—*Galactic Zoo Dossier* (Polydor) 1973—*Kingdom Come* (Track, U.K.) *The Journey* (Polydor) 1975—
Dance with Arthur Brown (Gull).

The eccentric Arthur Brown had one U.S. hit, "Fire" (#2) in 1968. A trailblazer of theater rock, Brown capped his performances by igniting what appeared to be his hair (actually a metal helmet), and so became the rage in London during the summer of 1967. Pete Townshend gave him a record deal with the Who's Track label, but Brown proved unable to repeat his initial success, and by 1969 his band, the Crazy World of Arthur Brown (which included drummer Carl Palmer, later of Emerson, Lake and Palmer, and keyboardist Vincent Crane of Atomic Rooster), had broken up.

Brown has made several comeback attempts since. From 1970 to 1973, he fronted Kingdom Come, an electronic rock band, for *Galactic Zoo Dossier, Kingdom Come* and *The Journey*. After departing that group, he toured the Mideast, and upon returning to England he studied meditation. He played a small role in the movie version of Who's *Tommy* in 1975.

CLARENCE "GATEMOUTH" BROWN
Born April 18, 1924, Vinton, Louisiana
1974—*Clarence "Gatemouth" Brown Sings Louis Jordan* (Black and Blue) 1975—*Gate's on the Heat* (Barclay) *Down South in Bayou Country* 1976—
Bogalusa Boogie Man 1979—*San Antonio Ballbuster* (Charly) 1982—*Alright Again* (Rounder).

Although blues singer/guitarist Clarence "Gatemouth" Brown had only one chart single during his career, his mix of blues and country marks him as a Texas original. Born in Louisiana, he grew up in Orange, Texas. His father was a musician who taught him to play guitar when he was five; by age ten, he could play fiddle and mandolin as well, and in ensuing years he picked up drums, bass and harmonica. Nicknamed by a teacher for his big voice, "Gatemouth" Brown began singing at an early age. In the early Forties, he was a drummer for the Brown Skin Models. After serving in the Army Corps of Engineers, he returned to show business after World War II, working in big bands in San Antonio. He made his solo debut in 1945 when he sat in for an ill T-Bone Walker. That show introduced him to club owner Don Robey, who signed him to a management contract that bound him for the next twenty years.

Robey sent Brown to Los Angeles in 1947 to record for Aladdin Records. In 1949, Brown was the first to record for Robey's own company, Peacock Records; and that same year he cut "Mary Is Fine," his only hit. Either under his own name or as D. Malone, Robey took songwriter's credit on many of Brown's compositions; Brown's bitter "You Got Money" was written about Robey. Between 1947 and 1960, Brown recorded over fifty sides for Peacock, including "Pale Dry Boogie" and "Okie Dokie Stomp." He spent most of the Fifties leading two bands, a 23-piece black orchestra and a smaller group of white musicians. This arrangement allowed him to play both all-black clubs and white establishments where blacks were usually not allowed. His style combined elements of country, jazz, blues and Cajun music, and has influenced guitarists as diverse as Albert Collins, Frank Zappa, Roy Buchanan and Guitar Slim.

Brown broke free of Robey in 1964. In the remainder of the decade, he recorded for Cue, Cinderella, Pam, Chess and Heritage. In 1971, he went to France, where he enjoyed a strong following and recorded for French companies like Black and Blue, Barclay and Blue Star. He appeared at the Montreux Jazz Festival (1973), the Newport Jazz Festival (1973), the New Orleans Jazz and Heritage Festival (1974, '76, '77) and the Monterey Jazz Festival (1977). His half-brother, James "Widemouth" Brown, was also a singer until his death in 1971.

DENNIS BROWN

Born circa 1950, Kingston, Jamaica
N.A.—*Dennis Brown Meets Hippy Harry* (Golden Age) *Super Hits* (Trojan) **1975**—*Just Dennis* **1978**—*Visions of Dennis Brown* (Lightning) *Westbound Train* (Third World) **1979**—*Words of Wisdom* (Laser) *Live at Montreux;* *Wolf and Leopards* **1980**—*Spellbound* **1981**—*Foul Play* (A&M) **1982**—*Love Has Found a Way.*

Reggae singer Dennis Brown began his career in tourist clubs in Jamaica and other West Indian islands when he was nine. In his teen years, he became a protégé of Jamaican bandleader and producer Byron Lee and by the mid-Sixties he was recording regularly for such producers as Coxsone Dodd, Derrick Harriot and Joe Gibbs. He had a string of Jamaican hits in the late Sixties and Seventies, including "No Man Is an Island" (1968), "Silhouettes" (1968), "Baby Don't Do It" (1971), "Look of Love" (1971), "Things in Life" (1972) and "Money in My Pocket" (1972)—mostly conventional pop love songs set to reggae rhythms. In 1979, he rerecorded "Money in My Pocket" for issue in the U.K.; it reached #14 on the British charts and opened the way to Brown's international popularity. That year he toured Europe, and in 1980 he signed with A&M, his first major label. He toured North America, poised to reach for the pop market with such derooted numbers as "Foul Play" and "If I Ruled the World," both of which were given some airplay on black pop stations.

JAMES BROWN

Born 1928 in Tennessee, or 1933 in Georgia
1963—*The James Brown Show Live at the Apollo* (King) **1964**—*Pure Dynamite* **1965**—*Grits and Soul* (Smash) **1966**—*Soul Brother #1* (King) **1967**—*Raw Soul* **1968**—*"Live" at the Apollo, volume 2* **1969**—*It's a Mother* **1970**—*Ain't It Funky* **1971**—*Sho' Is Funky Down Here;* *Revolution of the Mind* (Polydor) **1975**—*Everybody's Doing the Hustle* and *Dead on the Double Bump* **1977**—*Mutha's Nature* **1978**—*Take a Look at Those Cakes* **1979**—*The Original Disco Man* **1980**—*Live and Lowdown at the Apollo, volume 1* (Solid Smoke).

Self-proclaimed "Soul Brother Number One," James Brown was perhaps the best-known and clearly the most successful black male vocalist of the Sixties and early Seventies; his polyrhythmic funk vamps of the Sixties virtually reshaped dance music. Brown was born into poverty in the deep rural South around the time of the Depression (some records give his birthdate as 1928; he claims it is 1933). As a child he picked cotton, shined shoes, danced for pennies in the streets of Augusta, Georgia—and stole. Convicted of armed robbery at age 16, he spent three years in a juvenile detention institution. On his release he turned to semi-professional sports, first as a boxer, then as a baseball pitcher. A leg injury ruined his chances of going pro, so—having sung in church choirs most of his life—he turned to music. With Bobby Byrd, whom he met in the Augusta Baptist Church choir, he sang gospel duets at church functions around Augusta and then joined a professional gospel group called the Swanees. Soon, however, he and Byrd transformed the Swanees (Johnny Terry, Sylvester Keels and Floyd Scott) into the Famous Flames. Each Flame sang, danced and played an instrument or two (Brown's were piano and drums).

From their base in Macon, Georgia, the Flames had been touring the South for two years when Ralph Bass, head of Federal Records, signed them in 1956. Their first single, "Please Please Please," was a big hit in Georgia and adjacent states, and eventually sold a million copies. Subsequent releases in the same gospel-influenced yet distinctly rougher R&B style made Brown a regional star, until "Try Me" became a national hit in 1958, charting #1 in R&B, #48 in pop.

By this time, Brown had become de facto leader of the Flames. Guided by Universal Attractions director Ben Bart, Brown created the James Brown Revue, complete with opening acts, his own emcee and a stage band—the J.B.s—in addition to the Famous Flames. The show was precisely choreographed, with Brown pumping his hips, twisting on one foot and splitting to the floor as the troupe executed their own intricate steps; night after night, he would feign heart failure before returning for an encore. Sweating off a purported seven pounds a night, and

James Brown

breaking box-office records in every major black venue in America, Brown earned the nickname "Mr. Dynamite" and the title "The Hardest Working Man in Show Business."

As the J.B.s became one of the tightest bands in the field (at one time they included Jimi Hendrix), Brown became dissatisfied with his predominantly vocal recordings with the Famous Flames. Federal refused to let him use the J.B.s in the studio, so he arranged for the band to record for another company as Nat Kendrick and the Swans. The resulting instrumental hit, "Mashed Potatoes," persuaded Federal's parent company, King, to take over Brown's contract and to sign up the J.B.s both for Brown's sessions and as a separate act. From then on, Brown concentrated on pared-down, jump-and-shout dance music ("Think," "Night Train"). If a new song made the concert crowd dance, he would record it that night, often in one take.

Brown's *Live at the Apollo, volume 2,* recorded in Harlem in 1962, sold a million copies, unprecedented for a black music album. In 1964, frustrated by King's failure to reach into the white market, Brown and Bart formed Fair Deal Productions. "Out of Sight," which Fair Deal released through Smash Records, hit #1 R&B, #24 pop, and fared even better in Britain, where Brown was popular with the Mods.

Brown's 1965 contract with King gave him complete artistic control. He revamped the J.B.s under the leadership of Nat James, and with his "Papa's Got a Brand New Bag" he became a world-class force in popular music. Disposing of the conventional verse-and-chorus structure, eliminating even chord progressions, he distilled his sound to its essence: rhythm. "Brand New Bag" topped the R&B charts, initiating a long streak of #1 R&B hits—"I Got You," "It's a Man's, Man's, Man's World," "Cold Sweat," "I Got the Feelin'," "Say It Loud, I'm Black and I'm Proud," "Give It Up or Turn It Loose," "Mother Popcorn" and "Superbad"—which were also Top Twenty (many of them Top Ten) pop hits.

The second half of the Sixties found James Brown a cultural hero, "Soul Brother Number One." As a black of wealth, independence and influence, he was a symbol of self-determination and triumph over racism. He took that responsibility seriously. Songs such as "Say It Loud," "Don't Be a Drop-Out," "America Is My Home" and "King Heroin" contained direct social messages. He sponsored programs for ghetto youth, toured high schools, invested in black businesses, performed for troops in Vietnam, and went on television to calm racial tensions after the assassination of Martin Luther King—a service for which he was ceremoniously thanked by Vice President Hubert Humphrey.

In 1971, Brown renovated his career almost completely. He became his own manager, signed up with an international record company, Polydor, and sold it his entire catalogue. He parted with most of the J.B.s, including Albert Ellis, musical director since 1967, with whom he had written some of his biggest hits; Clyde Stubblefield, drummer since 1967; and William "Bootsy" Collins, bassist since 1969. (Collins and four other ex-J.B.s joined George Clinton's Parliament-Funkadelic.) The revamped J.B.s were led by Fred Wesley and powered by guitarist Jimmy Nolan, trumpeter Maceo Parker and bassist Clair St. Pinckney. Brown's music became even less formal; as the instrumental sections dug into funk grooves, Brown spouted stream-of-consciousness verbiage summoned more for sound than sense. His records continued to sell by the millions: "Hot Pants," "Make It Funky," "Talking Loud and Saying Nothing," "Get on the Good Foot," "The Payback," "My Thang" and "Papa Don't Take No Mess" all topped the R&B charts but failed to crack the Top Thirty or Forty in pop.

Around 1975, his popularity began to wane. Because of financial difficulties, Brown was forced to sell his three black radio stations and his jet. The U.S. government claimed he owed $4.5 million in back taxes, a manager said Brown was part of a payola scandal, his son Teddy died in a car crash and his second marriage ended. Young record buyers favored imitators like the Ohio Players, Kool and the Gang and the Parliamentfunkadelic Thang (which now employed Wesley and Parker), and Brown channeled much of his energy into movies, scoring *Black Caesar* and *Slaughter's Big Rip-Off* (1973), and starring in *Come to the Table* (1974).

He was welcomed to Africa and Japan as a star, and at home he continued to work. When disco peaked, he promoted himself as "The Original Disco Man," which he was. When "It's Too Funky in Here" reached #15, it was called a "comeback." With a cameo role in the 1980 movie *The Blues Brothers,* Brown introduced his soul-church preaching to a new generation. Returning to American stages that year, he drew much of his audience from the white punk-funk faction, for whom he was the essence of polyrhythmic minimalism. Brown continues to outwork performers half his age.

ROY BROWN
Born September 10, 1925, New Orleans; died May 25, 1981, Los Angeles.
N.A.—*The Blues Are All Brown* (Bluesday) *Roy Brown Sings 24 Hits* (King) *Hard Luck Blues; Roy Brown and Wynonie Harris; Cheapest Price in Town* (Faith) **1973**—*Hard Times* (Bluesway) **1978**—*Good Rocking Tonight* (Route 66) *Laughing But Crying.*

Blues shouter Roy Brown had a major impact on early rock & roll. He wrote and recorded the jump-blues "Good Rocking Tonight" in 1947, and it became a national R&B hit the following year; Elvis Presley recorded it at one of his 1954 Sun Records sessions and had a hit. Brown followed "Good Rocking Tonight" with minor hits through the Fifties, including "Boogie at Midnight" and "Hard Luck Blues." Brown's big-band backups helped shape the New Orleans sound (Fats Domino, Allen Toussaint); his stage shows with his band, the Mighty Men, foreshadowed modern rock theatrics. B. B. King, Bobby "Blue" Bland and others have cited Brown's singing as an influence. Brown was still playing frequent club dates when he died of a heart attack in 1981.

RUTH BROWN
Born January 30, 1928, Portsmouth, Virginia
N.A.—*Along Comes Ruth* (Philips) *The Best of Ruth Brown* (Atlantic) *Gospel Time* (Philips) *Jim Dandy; Late Date with Ruth Brown* (Atlantic) *Miss Rhythm; The Real Ruth Brown* (Cobblestone) *Ruth Brown* (Atlantic) *Ruth Brown Sings; Teardrops from My Eyes* **1976**—*Sugar Babe* (President) **1982**—*The Soul Survives* (Flair).

Known as "Miss Rhythm," Ruth Brown was a major R&B star in the Fifties, briefly rivaling Dinah Washington as the era's leading black female singer. As a teenager, she sang in her church choir, then worked with jazz big bands in the Forties. She signed with fledgling Atlantic Records in 1949 and recorded over eighty songs for them between then and 1962, making her the label's most prolific and best-selling act in that period. At first her hits were confined to the R&B charts, which she topped with "Teardrops from My Eyes" (1950), "5-10-15 Hours" (1952), "(Mama) He

Treats Your Daughter Mean" (1953, with a band led by Ray Charles), "Oh What a Dream" and "Mambo Baby" (both 1954). In 1956, she began performing in Alan Freed's rock & roll shows and attracting a white youth audience. "Lucky Lips"—written by Leiber and Stoller—made #25 on the pop charts in 1957, followed the next year by "This Little Girl's Gone Rockin'," #24 pop.

In 1962, she left Atlantic for Philips. She had a couple of minor hits on that label, then retired. In the Seventies she came out of retirement to record for Cobblestone and President. She still appears occasionally at jazz festivals.

DUNCAN BROWNE
Born circa 1946, England
1968—*Give Me Take You* (Immediate) **1972**—*Journey* (RAK) **1977**—*Metro* (Sire) **1979**—*The Wild Places; Streets of Fire.*

Duncan Browne's music fuses English pop and folk styles with classical guitar technique and light electric jazz instrumentation. The son of a classical violinist, he studied clarinet and guitar from an early age. At the London Academy of Music and Dramatic Art, he met David Bretton, with whom he wrote the songs for his first album, a folkish set produced by Andrew Loog Oldham (the Rolling Stones) for his Immediate label. After Immediate folded, Browne was without a contract for four years, although he acted and performed in a late Sixties German film, *Zeit für Träume.*

In 1972, he teamed up with producer Mickie Most for his second album. *Journey*'s title song became a Top Thirty single in the U.K., putting Browne on British TV and the European tour circuit. After breaking with Most over commercial disagreements, he moved to France, where he met Peter Godwin. The two collaborated on songs and, with guitarist Sean Lyons, formed Metro in 1976. Metro recorded one album, disbanded, and Browne began putting together his own jazz-rock group with drummer Simon Phillips, a sometime member of the Jeff Beck band; keyboardist Tony Humas, who had worked with Beck, Jack Bruce and Stanley Clarke; and bassist John Giblin.

JACKSON BROWNE
Born October 9, 1948, Heidelberg, West Germany
1972—*Jackson Browne* (Asylum) **1973**—*For Everyman* **1974**—*Late for the Sky* **1976**—*The Pretender* **1978**—*Running on Empty* **1980**—*Hold Out.*

Singer/songwriter Jackson Browne's introverted, finely observed songs have made him one of the West Coast's most influential songwriters. Browne's songs infuse domestic sagas with a sense of romantic doom, making lovers into heroes. Browne's family moved to Southern California when he was young, and in his late teens he played guitar with an embryonic version of the Nitty

Gritty Dirt Band, which later performed his songs. He spent the winters of 1967 and 1968 in Greenwich Village, where he backed Tim Buckley and Nico; she did an early cover of Browne's "These Days." By 1969, he had begun to establish a reputation as a songwriter, and in the next few years Tom Rush, the Byrds, Bonnie Raitt, Linda Ronstadt and others performed his songs. Browne's solo debut produced a hit with "Doctor My Eyes" (#8, 1972) and eventually went gold, while Browne toured as an opening act for fellow West Coast acts Joni Mitchell and the Eagles. He cowrote the Eagles first hit, "Take It Easy."

With each album his following has grown, and *The Pretender* became his first platinum album; its sense of despair derived in part from the suicide of Browne's first wife, Phyllis, in 1976, three years after the birth of their son, Ethan. A 1977 tour produced *Running on Empty,* a live concept album about touring featuring new material recorded onstage, in hotel rooms and on the tour bus, including a hit remake of "Stay" (#20, 1978). *Hold Out* went to #1 in its first week of release.

Browne continues to tour internationally, and he has been active on the board of directors of MUSE (Musicians United for Safe Energy), which has organized benefits to fight nuclear power. He has produced albums for Warren Zevon and high school friend Greg Copeland, and he has collaborated with fellow West Coast songwriters, including J. D. Souther, Valerie Carter and the Eagles.

Jackson Browne

BROWNSVILLE STATION

Formed 1969, Ann Arbor, Michigan
Cub Koda (b. Oct. 1, 1948, Detroit), gtr., voc.; Michael Lutz, gtr., voc.; T. J. Cronley, drums; Tony Driggins, bass.
1971—(− Cronley; + Henry "H Bomb" Weck, drums) *No B.S.* (Warner Bros.) **1972**—*A Night on the Town* (Big Tree) (− Driggins) **1973**—*Yeah* **1974**—*School Punks* **1975**—(+ Bruce Nazarian, gtr., kybds.) *Motor City Connection* **1977**—*Brownsville Station* (Private Stock) **1979**—*Air Special* (Epic).

Brownsville Station was formed by Michael Lutz and Cub Koda. The two met in Al Nalli's parents' record store, and at Nalli's suggestion started the group; Nalli became their manager. A hard-rock act, Brownsville spent most of its ten years together working the Midwestern club circuit. Their 1973 hit single, "Smokin' in the Boys' Room," reached #3 in January 1974. Like much of their material, "Smokin'" was written by Koda. After the group disbanded in June 1979, Koda began a solo career; he has recorded three LPs, all on Baron Records (*Cub Koda and the Points,* 1980; *It's the Blues,* 1982; *That's What I Like About the South,* 1982), and is a columnist for the record collectors' magazine *Goldmine.*

JACK BRUCE

Born May 14, 1943, Lanarkshire, Scotland
1969—*Songs for a Tailor* (Atco) **1970**—*Things We Like* **1971**—*Harmony Row* **1972**—*Jack Bruce at His Best* (Polydor) **1974**—*Out of the Storm* (RSO) **1977**—*How's Tricks* **1980**—*I've Always Wanted to Do This* (Epic) **1983**—*Truce* (Chrysalis).

The punchy bass riffs and urgent tenor vocals Jack Bruce lent to Cream were widely imitated by the heavy-metal bands that followed. Although Bruce's virtuosity and arty inclinations led him to make jazzy, complex music after he left Cream, he has returned periodically to hard rock. At age 17 he won a scholarship to the Royal Scottish Academy of Music but dropped out after three months to play jazz in Glasgow. He moved to London in his late teens and played with British R&B pioneers Alexis Korner and Graham Bond. In 1965, he left the Graham Bond Organisation, whose drummer was Ginger Baker, for John Mayall's Bluesbreakers, a band that included guitarist Eric Clapton.

After a brief stint in Manfred Mann, Bruce joined Clapton and Baker in forming Cream in 1966. The three virtually invented a hard-rock trio style—complete with extended improvisations in which Bruce's bass chased Clapton's guitar—before breaking up in 1968. Most of Cream's hit singles were written by Bruce and lyricist Pete Brown.

Since Cream's breakup, Bruce has divided his efforts between fusion, hard rock and an ambitious, eccentric folk-rock-classical hybrid style of songwriting he tried on *Songs for a Tailor, Harmony Row* and *Out of the Storm.* Of those songs, "Theme for an Imaginary Western" became a hit for Mountain. Bruce's first post-Cream group, Jack Bruce and Friends, included jazz guitarist Larry Coryell and Jimi Hendrix Experience drummer Mitch Mitchell. In 1970 and 1971, Bruce was a member of the Tony Williams Lifetime, the pioneering fusion band that also included guitarist John McLaughlin. Bruce's *Things We Like* was a jam session with McLaughlin, Dick Heckstall-Smith and other British progressive jazzmen; Bruce also appeared (as vocalist) with McLaughlin on Carla Bley's 1972 *Escalator over the Hill,* and in 1979 he toured with McLaughlin and Mahavishnu Orchestra alumni Billy Cobham and Stu Goldberg.

On the hard-rock side, Bruce put together a power trio with Mountain's Leslie West and Corky Laing, which released albums in 1972, '73 and '74. He appeared on Frank Zappa's *Apostrophe* in 1974, and in 1975 he fronted the Jack Bruce Band, with keyboardist Bley and former Rolling Stones guitarist Mick Taylor, on a tour of Europe; they did not record. The 1980 version of Jack Bruce and Friends included drummer Cobham, ex–Humble Pie guitarist Clem Clempson and erstwhile Bruce Springsteen pianist David Sancious. In 1981, Bruce joined another power trio, B.L.T., led by Robin Trower; and in 1982 Bruce and Trower collaborated on *Truce.*

FELICE AND BOUDLEAUX BRYANT

Boudleaux Bryant (b. Feb. 13, 1920, Shellman, Ga.);
Felice Bryant (b. Aug. 7, 1925, Milwaukee).

Felice and Boudleaux Bryant are the husband-and-wife songwriting team responsible for most of the Everly Brothers' late-Fifties and early-Sixties hits. Boudleaux had studied classical violin and performed with the Atlanta Philharmonic before joining a jazz group. He and Felice married in 1948 and began writing songs together. The year after their first hit, "Country Boy," was recorded by Little Jimmy Dickens (1949), they moved to Nashville, where they wrote songs for Eddy Arnold ("The Richest Man") and Carl Smith ("Hey Joe"). In 1957, they began writing what would be the Everly Brothers' biggest hits: "Bye Bye Love," "Wake Up, Little Susie," "Problems," "Bird Dog," "All I Have to Do Is Dream," "Poor Jenny" and "Take a Message to Mary," each of which sold millions of copies. In 1959, their "Raining in My Heart" was a posthumous hit for Buddy Holly. Their compositions have been recorded by over 400 musicians.

PEABO BRYSON

Born April 13, 1951, Greenville, South Carolina
1976—*Peabo* (Bang) **1977**—*Reaching for the Sky* (Capitol) **1978**—*Crosswinds* **1979**—*We're the Best of Friends* **1980**—*Paradise; Live and More* **1981**—*I Am Love; Turn the Hands of Time* **1983**—*Don't Play with Fire.*

Peabo Bryson grew up on a farm in South Carolina, sang in a rural church and joined his first group, Al Freeman and the Upsetters, as a harmony singer at age 14. His first professional group was Mose Dillard and the Tex-Town Display, with whom he sang from 1968 to 1973, touring the U.S., the Caribbean and Vietnam. The group recorded on the Curtom and Bang labels. Bang president Eddie Biscoe encouraged Bryson to write and sing his own material, and in 1970, he signed a solo contract with Bang and moved to Atlanta, where he worked as a staff producer before recording his solo debut album. He had his first hit as guest vocalist with Michael Zager's Moon Band, whose "Do It with Feeling" made the R&B Top Thirty in 1976. On his own, he placed three singles in the R&B Top Thirty: "Underground Music" (1976), "Just Another Day" (1977) and "I Can Make It Better" (1977).

He signed with Capitol in 1977, and his debut album included R&B hit singles in the title song, "Reaching for the Sky" (#6, 1978) and "Feel the Fire" (#13, 1978). *Crosswinds* boasted a #2 single, "I'm So Into You." In 1979, Bryson toured with Natalie Cole; their studio collaborations yielded an album, *We're the Best of Friends,* and two R&B hit singles: "Gimme Some Time" (#8, 1979) and "What You Won't Do for Love" (#16, 1980). Later in 1980, after charting R&B Top Twenty with Michael McDonald's "Minute by Minute," he joined Roberta Flack for a concert tour and a live album that gave the duo a hit single, "Make the World Stand Still." All of Bryson's Capitol LPs, except for *Turn the Hands of Time,* a collection of early unreleased material from Bang, have been certified gold.

ROY BUCHANAN

Born September 23, 1939, Ozark, Ark.
1972—*Roy Buchanan* (Polydor) *Roy Buchanan Second Album* **1974**—*That's What I'm There For* **1975**—*Rescue Me; Live Stock* **1976**—*A Street Called Straight* (Atlantic) **1977**—*Loading Zone* **1978**—*You're Not Alone.*

Blues guitarist Roy Buchanan was considered a musician's musician in the Seventies for his impeccable Telecaster leads. The son of a Pentecostal preacher, he grew up in Pixley, California, and was a proficient guitarist by age nine. At 15, he played with rockabilly star Dale Hawkins ("Suzy Q"), with whom he toured for three years before joining Ronnie Hawkins. He moved to the Washington, D.C. area, where he still lives, and in the mid-Sixties did East Coast session work. In 1968, he formed the Soundmasters and worked clubs on the Eastern Seaboard regularly for the next several years. A *Rolling Stone* article in February 1971 inspired some interest in Buchanan; he claimed the Rolling Stones asked him to join in 1970 and he turned them down. In 1972, Buchanan signed his first solo recording contract. He continues to tour and record, although his following has never expanded beyond a cult.

THE BUCKINGHAMS
Formed 1966, Chicago
Marty Grebb (b. 1947, Chicago), multiinstr.; Carl Giammerse (b. 1948, Chicago), gtr.; Nick Fortune (b. 1948, Chicago), bass; John Poulos (b. 1947, Chicago), drums; Denny Tufano (b. 1947, Chicago), gtr., harmonica.
1967—*Kind of a Drag* (U.S.A.)   *Time and Charges* (Columbia) **1968**—*Portraits; In One Ear and Gone Tomorrow* **1969**—*Greatest Hits* **1975**—*Made in Chicago.*

The Buckinghams' one major hit, "Kind of a Drag" (#1, 1967), temporarily pulled them out of the Chicago club circuit; after a few follow-ups, the entire band was arrested on drug charges in 1968 and they faded from the scene. Producer James William Guercio went on to perfect the Buckinghams' pop-with-horns sound with Chicago. Drummer John Poulos later headed a Midwestern management firm.

TIM BUCKLEY
Born February 14, 1947, Washington, D.C.; died June 29, 1975, Santa Monica, California
1967—*Tim Buckley* (Elektra)   *Goodbye and Hello*
1969—*Happy Sad* **1970**—*Blue Afternoon* (Straight) *Lorca* (Elektra) **1971**—*Starsailor* (Warner Bros.)
1972—*Greetings from L.A.* **1974**—*Look at the Fool* (DiscReet) *Sefronia.*

Buckley was a highly respected singer/songwriter through the late Sixties. His professional career began in the early Sixties when he played frequently with bassist Jim Fielder (later of Buffalo Springfield and Blood, Sweat and Tears) and attracted the attention of Frank Zappa's manager Herb Cohen, who got him a deal with Elektra in 1966. (Buckley later signed with Cohen's Straight Records.) His second album, *Goodbye and Hello*, produced by the Lovin' Spoonful's Jerry Yester, made the Top Twenty.

Buckley soon began exploring avant-garde jazz, and later recorded in Swahili. After several label switches, he tried funky, danceable material in the mid-Seventies, but without success. On June 29, 1975, Buckley died of a heroin and morphine overdose; according to coroner's inquest testimony, he had snorted what he believed was cocaine. The man who owned the house where he died was later convicted of involuntary manslaughter.

BUFFALO SPRINGFIELD
Formed 1966, Los Angeles
Neil Young (b. Nov. 12, 1945, Toronto), voc., gtr.;

Stephen Stills (b. Jan. 3, 1945, Dallas), voc., gtr.; Richie Furay (b. May 9, 1944, Dayton), voc., gtr.; Dewey Martin (b. Sept. 30, 1942, Chesterville, Can.), voc., drums; Bruce Palmer (b. ca. 1946, Liverpool, Can.), bass.
1967—*Buffalo Springfield* (Atco)   *Stampede* (unreleased) (– Palmer; + Ken Koblun, bass; – Koblun; + Jim Fielder [b. Oct. 4, 1947, Denton, Tex.], bass; + Doug Hastings, gtr.;)   *Buffalo Springfield Again* (Atco) (– Palmer; – Fielder; – Hastings; + Jim Messina [b. Dec. 5, 1947, Maywood, Calif.], bass)
1968—*Last Time Around* **1969**—*Retrospective*
1976—*Buffalo Springfield.*

During its brief and stormy lifetime, the Buffalo Springfield broke ground for what became country rock. The subsequent success that several members found in Poco and Crosby, Stills, Nash and Young explains the group's current larger-than-life stature. Although several members had played together sporadically, mostly in New York and Canadian clubs, the group (named after a farm vehicle) wasn't formed until 1966, when its members independently converged on the West Coast. Originally called the Herd (not to be confused with Peter Frampton's first group), they had become the Buffalo Springfield by the time of their debut album in 1967.

After a long stint as the house band for the Whiskey-a-

The Buffalo Springfield: Richie Furay, Dewey Martin, Neil Young, Stephen Stills, Bruce Palmer

Go-Go, they toured extensively with the Byrds. Stills's "For What It's Worth" (#7, 1967) gave them their biggest hit. By the time their second album was released, they were a major group coming apart at the seams. After a number of personnel changes, and amid persistent squabbling between Stills and Young, the group disbanded in May 1968.

When *Last Time Around* was released later that year, all of the Springfields were on their own. Dewey Martin kept the band's name alive with some hired musicians, and then had an abortive solo career. Stills and Young were successful in the Seventies with CSN&Y and solo work. Short-term bassist Jim Fielder joined Blood, Sweat and Tears, while Messina and Furay formed Poco with pedal steel guitarist Rusty Young, who had played on the Springfield's final album.

JIMMY BUFFETT
Born December 25, 1946, Mobile, Alabama
1970—*Down to Earth* (Barnaby)   **1973**—*A White Sport Coat and a Pink Crustacean* (Dunhill)   **1974**—*Living and Dying in 3/4 Time;   A-1-A*   **1975**—*Havana Day-dreamin'* (ABC)   **1976**—*High Cumberland Jubilee* (Barnaby)   **1977**—*Changes in Latitudes, Changes in Attitudes* (ABC)   **1978**—*Live;   Son of a Son of a Sailor;   You Had to Be There*   **1979**—*Volcano* (MCA) *Before the Salt* (Barnaby)   **1981**—*Coconut Telegraph* (MCA).

Singer/songwriter Jimmy Buffett is known for humorous chronicles of a laid-back seafaring life; his philosophical outlook is encapsulated in tunes like "Why Don't We Get Drunk (and Screw)" and "My Head Hurts, My Feet Stink and I Don't Love Jesus."

Raised in the Deep South, Buffett attended Auburn University and then the University of Southern Mississippi, majoring in journalism (he later worked as a *Billboard* reporter). He moved to Nashville in the late Sixties, intent on becoming a country singer. His first album, 1970's *Down to Earth*, sold 324 copies. Barnaby Records then temporarily misplaced the master tape of his second album before its release. By 1972, Buffett had left both Nashville and a failed marriage, moving to Key West, where he helped to support himself by smuggling a little marijuana from the Caribbean. He signed to ABC-Dunhill, and his 1973 release, *A White Sport Coat and a Pink Crustacean*, found Buffett developing his drunken-sailor persona. Although he'd had minor hits, like 1974's "Come Monday," Buffett's commercial breakthrough came in 1977 with the platinum *Changes in Latitudes, Changes in Attitudes* and its hit single, "Margaritaville" (#8).

Buffett tours infrequently, spending most of his time living on his fifty-foot ketch *Euphoria II*. He frequently docks at Montserrat, where his 1979 LP *Volcano* was recorded.

He formed his Coral Reefer Band in 1975 with guitarist Roger Bartlett, harmonica player Greg "Fingers" Taylor, bassist Harry Dailey and drummer Phillip Fajardo. Bartlett and Fajardo were replaced later by Tim Krekel and Keith Sykes, and keyboardist Jay Spell was added. Buffett scored and acted in the 1974 film *Rancho Deluxe*, and appeared in the 1977 movie *FM*.

THE BUGGLES
Formed late 1970s, England
Trevor Horn, voc.; Geoffrey Downes, kybds.
1980—*Age of Plastic* (Island)   **1982**—*Adventures in Modern Recording* (Epic).

The electro-pop "Video Killed the Radio Star," written by Horn, Downes and Bruce Wooley, was a huge international hit in 1979. Keyboardist Downes and vocalist Horn went on to join Yes in 1980, appearing on *Drama* and in Yes's 1980–81 tour. Following Yes's 1981 breakup, Downes joined Asia.

CINDY BULLENS
Born 1953, West Newbury, Massachusetts
1978—*Desire Wire* (United Artists)   **1979**—*Steal the Night* (Casablanca).

Cindy Bullens is a singer and guitarist who started her career as a background singer. After five years of doing disco records (Disco Tex's "Get Dancin'," for example), movie soundtracks (three songs for *Grease*) and background singing for Elton John, Rod Stewart and Bob Dylan, she made her solo debut with 1978's *Desire Wire*.

Bullens spent the early Seventies on the Boston–New York bar-band circuit, then moved to Los Angeles, pumped gas for a year and started recording with producer Bob Crewe. A week after crashing a Rocket Records party and introducing herself to Elton John, she signed on for the first of three tours, and later sang on his *Blue Moves*. She had also sung on Stewart's *Atlantic Crossing* (1975), joined Dylan's Rolling Thunder Revue in 1975 for two dates and hooked up with the Alpha Band for a tour and vocals on two albums. At the end of 1977, Bullens devoted herself to songwriting, and she recorded a demo tape that led to a United Artists contract. *Desire Wire* yielded a moderate West Coast hit with the single "Survivor" (#56).

ERIC BURDON
Born May 11, 1941, Newcastle upon Tyne, England
Eric Burdon and War:1970—*Eric Burdon Declares War* (Polydor)   **1971**—*The Black Man's Burdon* (MGM) **1976**—*Love Is All Around* (ABC)   **Eric Burdon: 1971**—*Guilty* (MGM)   **1974**—*Ring of Fire* (Capitol)   *Sun Secrets*   **1975**—*Stop*   **1978**—*Survivor* (Polydor) **1982**—*Eric Burdon Band Live* (Germany).

Eric Burdon's rudely emotive vocals kept him on the charts through the British Invasion (as a frontman for the Animals), psychedelia (as a solo act) and early-Seventies funk (with War). He grew up in working-class Newcastle and went to art school, where he studied graphics and photography and was introduced to blues records. Unable to find a job, he became a musician and joined the Alan Price Combo in 1962, which became the Animals a year later. With their success, Burdon took to drinking, womanizing and shooting his mouth off. When the original band broke up in 1966, Burdon billed the new group as Eric Burdon and the Animals. Then, for several months, he toured with the New Animals, a backup band that at one point included future Police guitarist Andy Summers.

By the end of 1967, Burdon had been converted to flower power. He traded his denims for a Nehru jacket, moved to California and scored several hits, including "Monterey" (#15, 1968), "San Franciscan Nights" (#9, 1967) and "Sky Pilot" (#14, 1968). After his 1968 double album, *Love Is,* Burdon announced his retirement and left the public eye.

In late 1969, Burdon heard a funk band called Night Shift; they became War and backed him on his 1970 hit "Spill the Wine" (#1) and their debut album, *Eric Burdon Declares War.* After a second album together, Burdon became exhausted on a 1971 European tour, and War went on without him. Since then, Burdon has been only sporadically active, making an album with blues legend Jimmy Witherspoon *(Guilty)* in 1971 and an Animals reunion album, *Before We Were So Rudely Interrupted,* in 1977. ABC put out material recorded in 1970 by Burdon and War on a 1976 album, *Love Is All Around.* During the late Seventies, Burdon appeared in several European movies, and in 1981 he starred in and composed the soundtrack for a German film entitled *Come Back.*

SOLOMON BURKE

Born 1936, Philadelphia
1964—*Rock 'n' Soul* (Atlantic) **1965**—*The Best of Solomon Burke* **1966**—*King of Rock 'n' Soul* **1969**—*Proud Mary* (Bell) **1975**—*Music to Make Love By* (Chess) **1977**—*Back to My Roots; Greatest Hits* (Atlantic).

With his big, powerful voice and fervent-but-controlled emotionality, Solomon Burke was a pioneer of soul music in the early Sixties. By the age of nine, he was a preacher and choir soloist for his family's Philadelphia church, the House of God for All People. At 12, he began hosting his own gospel radio show, "Solomon's Temple," and touring the gospel circuits billed as the "Wonder Boy Preacher." In 1955, he began recording both religious and secular music for the Apollo label. He also recorded for Singular before signing with Atlantic in 1960.

At Atlantic, Burke made some of the first soul records by setting his gospel "preaching" style in song forms,

borrowed from R&B, rock & roll and other secular music. His second Atlantic release, "Just Out of Reach," was a country & western song, and it became his first hit when it reached #7 on the R&B charts in 1961. Burke called his big-beat dance songs "rock 'n' soul music," and he won crossover popularity with "Cry to Me" (#44 pop, #5 R&B, 1962), "If You Need Me" (#37 pop, #2 R&B, 1963), "Got to Get You off My Mind" (#22 pop, #1 R&B, 1965) and "Tonight's the Night" (#28 pop, #2 R&B, 1965). He was a primary influence on Mick Jagger, who covered Burke's "You Can Make It If You Try," "Everybody Needs Somebody to Love" and "Cry to Me" on early Rolling Stones albums. Burke was also covered by Otis Redding ("Down in the Valley").

He continued to record for Atlantic until 1969, when he moved to Bell and hit with a cover of John Fogerty's "Proud Mary" (#45 pop, #15 R&B, 1969). In the Seventies, he recorded with uneven results for MGM, Dunhill and Chess. In 1981, he toured with the Soul Clan, which included Don Covay, Wilson Pickett, Ben E. King and Joe Tex.

BILLY BURNETTE

Born May 8, 1953, Memphis
1971—*Billy Burnette* (Columbia/Entrance) **1979**—*Billy Burnette* (Polydor) *Between Friends* **1980**—*Billy Burnette* (Columbia) **1981**—*Gimme You.*

Son of Dorsey Burnette, nephew of Johnny Burnette and cousin of Rocky Burnette, Billy Burnette moved from Memphis to Los Angeles, where he made his recording debut at age seven, fronting the Ricky Nelson band for a session at Phil Spector's Gold Star Studios. His second record, "Just Because We're Kids," was written by Dr. Seuss (Theodor Seuss Geisel), produced by Herb Alpert and released on A&M Records when he was 11 years old. During his early teen years, he recorded for Warner Bros., made TV appearances and—at age 13—toured the Far East with the Brenda Lee show. He started playing guitar and writing songs at age 16; the next year he began an apprenticeship with producer Chips Moman (Elvis Presley, Aretha Franklin), who produced his first solo album.

Burnette spent most of the Seventies leading his father's band, playing guitar and singing with Delaney Bramlett, and writing songs for Charlie Rich, Loretta Lynn, Conway Twitty, Irma Thomas, Glen Campbell, Gary Stewart and Levon Helm. He made two country albums in 1979, but it was not until after his father died that year that he began playing rock & roll. His first Columbia album contained remakes of "Tear It Up" and "Honey Hush," two rockers made famous by his father's Rock 'n' Roll Trio.

DORSEY BURNETTE

Born December 28, 1932, Memphis; died August 19, 1979, Canoga Park, California
1963—*Dorsey Burnette* (Capitol) **N.A.**—*Dorsey*

Burnette (Dot)   *Dorsey Burnette's Greatest Hits* (Era)
Tall Oak Tree;   Things I Treasure (Calliope).

Dorsey played bass in brother Johnny Burnette's pioneering rockabilly group, the Rock 'n' Roll Trio. Following their brief fling with stardom in 1955–56, he moved with his brother from Memphis to Los Angeles. They wrote some successful tunes ("Waiting in School") for Ricky Nelson, and each had moderate solo success in the early Sixties. Dorsey's hits on Era Records included "Tall Oak Tree" (#23, 1960) and "Hey Little One." He was an active mainstream country artist until his death in 1979 from a heart attack. By then his son, Billy Burnette, had made his debut.

JOHNNY BURNETTE
Born March 25, 1934, Memphis; died 1964.
N.A.—*Dreamin'* (Liberty);   *Johnny Burnette;   Johnny Burnette Hits;   Johnny Burnette Sings;   The Johnny Burnette Story;   Johnny Burnette's Hits and Other Favorites;   Roses Are Red   1971—Johnny Burnette and the Rock 'n' Roll Trio* (Coral)   **1975**—*The Very Best of Johnny Burnette* (United Artists)   **1978**—*Johnny Burnette and the Rock 'n' Roll Trio Tear It Up* (Solid Smoke)   **1979**—*Stars of Rock 'n' Roll, volume 1* (MCA).

With his brother Dorsey, Johnny was a mid-Fifties rockabilly pioneer and had some solo success in the early Sixties. A guitarist/singer/songwriter, with Dorsey he put together the Rock 'n' Roll Trio along with guitarist Paul Burlison (who released his first solo album in 1981 on a small Memphis label). They had a couple of minor hits like "Train Kept a-Rollin' " with Burlison's breakthrough fuzz guitar riff, but disbanded in late 1956. (An album of their rockabilly ravers was reissued on Solid Smoke in the late Seventies.)

Johnny and Dorsey moved to Los Angeles, where they cowrote several hits for Ricky Nelson among others. Johnny got a solo contract with Liberty Records in the late Fifties, for whom he cleaned up his sound and image. He had the biggest hit of his career in November 1960 as a teen idol with the million-selling "You're Sixteen" (#8). With a couple of lesser hits in 1961, Johnny had his last taste of rock glory. He was plotting a comeback when he died in a boating accident in 1964.

ROCKY BURNETTE
Born June 12, 1953, Memphis
1979—*Son of Rock 'n' Roll* (EMI)   **1980**—*Rocky Burnette.*

After 26 years in the shadow of his father, Johnny, and uncle Dorsey Burnette, Rocky—the self-proclaimed "Son of Rock & Roll"—came into his own with a #8 hit single, "Tired of Toein' the Line." He began writing songs in his early teens and at age 14, three years after his father's death, became a songwriter with the Acuff-Rose publishing company. His songs were recorded by several minor

country singers. After finishing college, where he studied film and the Bible, he made some unreleased recordings for Curb Records. In January 1979, broke after leaving Curb, he traded the rights to a couple of his songs for the studio time to record "Clowns from Outer Space," which he sent to EMI in London. EMI released it as a single. Its B side, "Tired of Toein' the Line," was written in less than half an hour; EMI put it on the A side. It hit first in Europe and Australia, making the British charts in 1979, before crossing to America.

BURNING SPEAR
Winston Rodney, born 1947, St. Ann's Parish, Jamaica
1975—*Marcus Garvey* (Island)   **1976**—*Garvey's Ghost* (Mango)   *Man in the Hills* (Island)   **1977**—*Dry and Heavy* (Mango)   *Live* (Island)   **1979**—*Harder Than the Best*   **1980**—*Hail H.I.M.* (Tammi)   **1981**—*Social Living*   **1982**—*Farover* (Heartbeat).

Burning Spear's stark, hypnotic reggae is far removed from thoughts of love or sex or marijuana, the staples of pop reggae. Instead, Winston Rodney, a.k.a. Burning Spear, concerns himself with oppression—black Jamaicans' heritage of slavery—and mystical transcendence through Rastafarianism. Rodney, Burning Spear's sole member since 1977, was born and continues to live in the northern hill region of Jamaica. He formed Burning Spear with bass vocalist Rupert Willington in the late Sixties. (Burning Spear was a name given to Kenyan leader Jomo Kenyatta.) In 1969, the two cut their first singles for Clement "Sir Coxsone" Dodd. Second tenor Delroy Hines joined soon after, and Spear became a vocal trio in the popular Jamaican style, with a repertoire based on traditional songs and chants dating from slave times. They were not particularly popular, and between 1971 and 1974 the group virtually disappeared.

In 1974, however, a runaway hit single on Lawrence "Jack Ruby" Lindo's Fox label, "Marcus Garvey" (about the founder of Rastafarianism), was heard all over Jamaica, followed by "Slavery Days." Dodd rereleased three five-year-old singles—"Swell Headed," "Foggy Road" and "Ethiopians Live It Out"—and Britons as well as Jamaicans snapped them up, along with other singles and two import albums, *Burning Spear* and *Rocking Time*.

Marcus Garvey and its dub remix, *Garvey's Ghost*, which featured guitarist Earl "Chinna" Smith, bassist Robbie Shakespeare, drummer Leroy "Horsemouth" Wallace and keyboardist Tyrone Downie, found U.S. release. When Willington and Hines left Burning Spear in 1977, Rodney continued to record solo. He appeared in the film *Rockers* (made in 1977, released in the U.S. in 1980), in concert footage, and in an interview in the documentary *Reggae Sunsplash* (1980). He tours the U.S. regularly with his own band. In Jamaica he teaches cultural history at the Marcus Garvey Youth Club, which he founded.

THE BUS BOYS

Formed, late 1970s, Los Angeles
Brian O'Neal, kybds., voc.; Kevin O'Neal, bass, voc.;
Gus Louderman, voc.; Mike Jones, kybds., voc.;
Victor Johnson, gtr.; Steve Felix, drums.
1980—*Minimum Wage Rock & Roll* (Arista) **1982**—
American Worker.

Five blacks and a Chicano, the Bus Boys appeared on the
Los Angeles club circuit with pointed, satirical songs and
a stage show that parodied black stereotypes and white
rock styles. The O'Neal brothers had played in Top Forty
and disco bands since 1974; Brian O'Neal began writing
his own material in the late Seventies, but only new wave
venues were receptive to the band's songs and routines.
Lines like "I am bigger than a nigger/Wanna be an all-
American man/Wanna join the Ku Klux Klan/Play in a
rock & roll band" caught journalists' and record companies' attention, although their first album made little
impact. They appeared in the film and on the soundtrack
of *48 HRS.* in 1982.

KATE BUSH

Born July 30, 1958, Plumstead, England
1978—*The Kick Inside* (Capitol) *On Stage* (EMI)
Lionheart **1980**—*Never For Ever* **1982**—*The Dreaming*.

British singer/songwriter Kate Bush's debut single,
"Wuthering Heights," hit #1 in the U.K. a month after its
release in January 1978 and went on to become the year's
best-selling single there and in Australia (only Abba was
more popular in Western Europe). The daughter of a
British physician, Bush began playing piano at the age of
11. She had been writing songs for two years when family
friends told Dave Gilmour of Pink Floyd about the 16-
year-old's four-octave range and interest in the supernatural. Gilmour financed the demo tape that got her signed to
EMI. Because of her age and developing talent, she spent
the next two years studying music, dance and mime and
writing the songs for her first album, recorded in 1977
under the supervision of Gilmour and producer Andrew
Powell (Pink Floyd, Alan Parsons, Cockney Rebel). The
album was preceded by the release of "Wuthering
Heights." The song's runaway success also spurred sales
of the Emily Brontë novel. It was covered by Pat Benatar
on *Crimes of Passion*.

  The Kick Inside was a Top Ten album in the U.K., and
two singles—"Man with the Child in His Eyes" and
"Wow"—made Top Twenty. Bush's double EP of concert
recordings made the Top Ten. She sang on Peter Gabriel's
eponymous 1980 album, and her elaborately theatrical *The
Dreaming* shows his influence.

THE BUSH TETRAS

Formed 1979, New York City
Pat Place (b. 1954, Chicago), gtr.; Laura Kennedy (b.
1955, Cleveland), bass; Dee Pop (b. Dimitri Papado-
poulous, 1956, Forest Hills, N.Y.), drums; Cynthia Sley
(b. 1956, Cleveland), voc., percussion.
1980—*Too Many Creeps* (99) (EP) **1981**—*Rituals*
(Stiff) **1982**—(– Dee Pop) **1983**—*Wild Things*
(ROIR).

Emerging from Cleveland's "new wave" and New York's
"no wave" scenes, the Bush Tetras mix funk, noise and
no-nonsense urban-jungle lyrics. Pat Place moved to New
York in 1975, and in 1977 James Chance invited her to join
his incipient Contortions. Although she had no musical
experience, she joined first as a bassist, then switched to
slide guitar (as a Contortion and sometime member of
James White and the Blacks) and developed her atonal
slide style. Laura Kennedy and Cynthia Sley, classmates
at the Cleveland Institute of Art, were in a performing art
group, Johnny and the Dicks, associated with Pere Ubu.
Kennedy moved to New York in 1977 to make films.
Through a Cleveland acquaintance, Contortion Adele
Bertei, she also worked as a roadie for the Contortions.
When the Contortions broke up in 1979, she joined rehearsals with Bertei, Place, Pop and guitarist Jimmy Uliano.
Bertei and Uliano dropped out after several months (Bertei went on to form the Bloods) and were replaced by
lyricist and intoner Sley, who had been in New York since
1978 designing clothes for Lydia Lunch and Judy Nylon.

  The Bush Tetras debuted in New York in early 1980.
Concentrating on New York and its environs, they attracted both the art/anti-art community and dance enthusi-
asts. Their first record, a three-song EP, was followed by a
four-song EP, *Rituals*, produced by Topper Headon of the
Clash; it appeared on national disco charts early in 1982.

JERRY BUTLER

Born December 8, 1939, Sunflower County, Mississippi
1967—*Mr. Dream Merchant* (Mercury) **1968**—*Golden
Hits Live* **1969**—*The Ice Man Cometh; Ice on Ice*
1970—*You and Me* **1971**—*Sagittarius Movement*
1972—*The Spice of Life; The Best of Jerry Butler*
1973—*The Power of Love* **1974**—*Sweet Sixteen*
1976—*Love's on the Menu* (Motown) **1977**—*Suite for
the Single Girl; Thelma and Jerry; It All Comes Out
in My Song* **1978**—*The Soul Goes On* (Mercury)
1979—*Nothing Says I Love You Like I Love You* (Philadelphia International) **1980**—*The Best Love I Ever
Had* **1982**—*Ice and Hot* (Fountain).

A distinctive soul singer for two decades, Jerry Butler and
childhood friend Curtis Mayfield defined Chicago soul
with the Impressions. Butler, who had a gospel background, moved with his family from Mississippi to Chicago in 1942; by the time he and Mayfield put together
Jerry Butler and the Impressions in 1957, Butler was
perfecting a delicate, hesitant delivery. The Impressions
had their first hit with "For Your Precious Love" (#11,

1959), cowritten by Butler. Butler went solo shortly thereafter but worked with Mayfield as songwriter and producer for several more years. The team scored their first post-Impressions hit in 1960 with Mayfield's "He Will Break Your Heart" (#7). Specializing in mellow ballads, Butler continued to score occasional hits until he moved to Philadelphia in 1967 and shifted gears with Gamble and Huff.

Butler's two albums with that production team, *The Ice Man Cometh* and *Ice on Ice*, were among the most highly acclaimed soul works of the early Seventies. Hits of this collaboration include "Never Give You Up" (#20, 1968), "Hey, Western Union Man" (#16, 1968) and "Only the Strong Survive" (#4, 1969). In 1971, Butler and Gene Chandler recorded together, and later in the decade he teamed up with Thelma Houston. Butler remained active on the lounge circuit, and in 1979, he reunited with Gamble and Huff for *Nothing Says I Love You Like I Love You* and its followup, *The Best Love I Ever Had*. In 1980, he founded Fountain Records.

PAUL BUTTERFIELD
Born December 17, 1942, Chicago
1965—*The Paul Butterfield Blues Band* (Elektra)
1966—*East-West* **1967**—*The Resurrection of Pigboy Crabshaw* **1968**—*In My Own Dream* **1969**—*Keep on Moving* **1971**—*Sometimes I Just Feel Like Smilin';* *Live* **1972**—*Golden Butter—The Best of the Paul Butterfield Blues Band; Offer You Can't Refuse* (Red Lightnin') **1973**—*Better Days* (Bearsville) **1974**—*It All Comes Back* **1976**—*Put It in Your Ear* **1981**—*North-South.*

Paul Butterfield, a white singer and harmonica player who apprenticed with black bluesmen, helped spur the American blues revival of the Sixties. The teenage Butterfield ventured into Chicago's South Side clubs, eventually working his way into onstage jams with Howlin' Wolf, Buddy Guy, Otis Rush, Little Walter and Magic Sam and other blues legends. In 1963, after attending the University of Chicago, he formed the Paul Butterfield Blues Band with two former members of Howlin' Wolf's band, bassist Jerome Arnold and drummer Sam Lay, later adding his U. of C. classmate guitarist Elvin Bishop, second guitarist Mike Bloomfield and keyboardist Mark Naftalin. The group built a strong local following, and its debut album was released in 1965. At that year's Newport Folk Festival, after playing their own set, they backed Bob Dylan for his controversial premiere electric performance.

East-West, their second album and Bloomfield's last with the band, featured extended jams and showed the influences of jazz and Indian music. By 1967, Butterfield began the first of many experiments, adding a brass section and changing his orientation from blues to R&B. He played on Muddy Waters' 1969 album *Fathers and Sons* and, after disbanding the Blues Band in 1972, moved to Woodstock, New York, where he formed Butterfield's Better Days with Amos Garrett, Geoff Muldaur and Ronnie Barron.

Butterfield made an appearance at the Band's *Last Waltz* concert in 1976, and during the late Seventies he toured with Levon Helm's RCO All Stars and with ex-Band bassist Rick Danko in the Danko-Butterfield Band. In early 1980, while recording *North-South* in Memphis, Butterfield was stricken with a perforated intestine and peritonitis. He underwent two major operations before he could return to performing in late 1981.

THE BUZZCOCKS
Formed 1975, Manchester, England
Howard Devoto (b. Howard Trafford), voc.; Steve Diggles, gtr., bass; John Maher, drums; Pete Shelley, voc., gtr.
1977—(− Devoto; + Garth, bass.) *Another Music in a Different Kitchen* (IRS) **1978**—(− Garth; + Steve Garvey, bass) *Love Bites* **1979**—*Singles Going Steady* **1980**—(− Shelley) *A Different Kind of Tension.*

The Buzzcocks were a successful U.K. new wave singles band during the late Seventies. They came together at Manchester University in 1975 and made frequent London club appearances the following year. Their first recordings, including an independent EP called *Spiral Scratch*, were made with visionary early group leader Howard Devoto. When Devoto left the group in 1977 to form Magazine, Pete Shelley (who himself left the group in 1980) became chief vocalist and songwriter. During their second U.S. tour in 1980, they picked up an enthusiastic coterie of followers, but their record sales were disappointing. In mid-1980, displeased with their lack of international success, the group announced an indefinite disbandment. Shelley had a British hit on his own with "Homosapiens."

THE BYRDS
Formed 1964, Los Angeles
Roger McGuinn (b. July 13, 1942, Chicago), gtr., voc.; Chris Hillman (b. Dec. 4, 1942, Los Angeles), bass, voc.; Gene Clark (b. Nov. 17, 1941, Tipton, Mo.), voc., tambourine, gtr.; David Crosby (b. David Van Cortland, Aug. 14, 1941, Los Angeles), gtr., voc.; Michael Clarke (b. June 3, 1943, New York City), drums.
1965—*Mr. Tambourine Man* (Columbia) **1966**—*Turn! Turn! Turn!* (− Clark) *Fifth Dimension* **1967**—*Younger Than Yesterday* (− Crosby; − Clarke; + Kevin Kelley [b. 1945, Calif.], drums) **1968**—*Notorious Byrd Brothers* (+ Gram Parsons [b. Cecil Connor, Nov. 5, 1946, Winterhaven, Fla.; d. Sept. 19, 1973, Calif.], gtr., voc.) *Sweetheart of the Rodeo*

(− Hillman; − Gram Parsons; + Clarence White [b. June 6, 1944], drums, voc.) **1969**—(− York; + Skip Battin [b. Feb. 2, 1934, Gallipolis, Oh.], bass, voc.) **1970**—*Untitled* **1971**—*Byrdmaniax* **1972**—*Farther Along; Best of the Byrds—Greatest Hits, volume 2* (− Gene Parsons; + John Guerin) **1973**—(− Guerin; + Denis Dragon or Jim Moon, drums; − Dragon; − Moon; + Hillman; + Joe Lala, drums; original group reunited for one-shot album in 1973) *The Byrds* (Asylum) **1980**—*Singles 1965-67.*
Roger (Jim) McGuinn: **1973**—*Roger McGuinn* (Columbia) **1974**—*Peace on You* **1975**—*Roger McGuinn and Band* **1976**—*Cardiff Rose* **1977**—*Thunderbyrd.*
McGuinn, Clark and Hillman: **1979**—*McGuinn, Clark and Hillman* (Capitol). **McGuinn and Hillman:** **1980**—*City.*

The Byrds, led by Roger McGuinn, pioneered folk rock and later country rock. With their high harmonies, ringing guitars (especially McGuinn's electric Rickenbacker 12-string) and obsession with studio technique, they also became the sonic model for many rock bands including the Eagles, Tom Petty and the latter-day Fleetwood Mac.

The band was formed in summer 1964 as the Jet Set (McGuinn was fascinated by airplanes) and toyed with the name Beefeaters before settling on the Byrds, misspelled à la the Beatles. McGuinn had been a member of the Limeliters, the Chad Mitchell Trio, and had worked backing Judy Collins until he went solo in 1964. Hillman had worked in the Hillmen and the Green Grass Group. Gene Clark was a member of the New Christy Minstrels. He and Crosby met at L.A.'s Troubadour on a hootenanny night. A few months after their formation, with Beatles publicist Derek Taylor on the payroll, the Byrds were touted as "L.A.'s answer to London." After signing with Columbia in September 1964, they recorded demos released years later as *Preflyte.* In January 1965, they met Bob Dylan, who publicly endorsed them and, more importantly, provided their first hit, "Mr. Tambourine Man." The single, cut by studio musicians, with McGuinn on guitar and the group singing, had Dylan's lyrics, a guitar hook, chorus harmonies and a rock rhythm section: folk rock. *Mr. Tambourine Man,* released in August 1965, went to #1.

In 1966, the Byrds had a major hit with the anthemic "Turn! Turn! Turn!"—a Bible passage set to music by Pete Seeger. But the album of the same name suffered a dearth of new material, and the Byrds were less commercial for the rest of their existence. By the time *Fifth Dimension* was released in late 1966, Gene Clark had left. He had frequently argued with McGuinn, and he suffered from a fear of flying that made touring difficult. His departure, plus their somewhat avant-garde LP, marked the start of the Byrds "space rock" phase. The hit single "Eight Miles

High" from *Fifth Dimension* solidified their new style, sporting a thunderous bass line, free-form guitar lines and a corps of otherworldly harmonies. It was also one of the first records to be widely banned because of supposedly drug-oriented lyrics.

As McGuinn's technocratic grip on the Byrds began to tighten, internal tensions increased and occasionally erupted into onstage fisticuffs. After 1967's *Younger Than Yesterday,* Crosby was gone, bound for superstardom with Stills, Nash and Young. McGuinn and the two remaining Byrds—bassist Hillman and drummer Michael Clarke—added studio players for 1968's countryish *The Notorious Byrd Brothers.* Praised by some critics as a conceptual masterpiece, it fared less well with the record-buying public. By late 1968's *Sweetheart of the Rodeo,* Clarke had left to join the Dillard and Clark group. *Sweetheart,* recorded in Nashville with newcomer Gram Parsons, mixed country and rock as they had mixed folk and rock, anticipating groups from the Eagles to Firefall.

By 1969, McGuinn was the only original Byrd left (Parsons and Hillman left to continue their country experiments with the Flying Burrito Brothers). He kept the patchwork Byrds alive through 1973 with a series of partners who were occasionally brilliant (like former bluegrass guitarist Clarence White) but more often merely functional. The various combos toured steadily and put out a series of mildly successful albums, including *Untitled,* which contained McGuinn's "Chestnut Mare" (co-written with Jacques Levy, a later collaborator with Dylan), one of his signature tunes. Despite the regrouping of the original lineup for a one-shot album in 1973 (which, despite dubious quality—Hillman later called the disc "embarrassing"—reached the Top Twenty), the Byrds were finally put to rest.

McGuinn subsequently embarked on a low-key solo career, recording three Byrds-sounding albums for Columbia: *Roger McGuinn, Peace on You* and, in late 1974, after assembling a band to tour, *Roger McGuinn and Band.* Commercial results were lackluster. In late 1975 and early 1976, he was prominently featured in Dylan's Rolling Thunder Revue. With fellow Revue trouper Mick Ronson producing, he recorded *Cardiff Rose.* In early 1977, he assembled a new band, wryly dubbed Thunderbyrd, and recorded an album of the same name. By late in the year, he was playing occasional dates in tandem with Clark, and the alliance was soon expanded to include Hillman as well. After some well-received dates in early 1978 opening for Eric Clapton on his Canadian tour, the three went into the studio and recorded their self-titled debut disc. They enjoyed some pop success with "Surrender to Me" and "Don't You Write Her Off" (#11, 1979). In 1980, the three returned with *City,* before the band gradually fragmented and McGuinn took up his solo career again.

C

ROY C
Born Roy Charles Hammond, 1943, New York City
1973—*Sex and Soul* (Mercury) **1975**—*Something
Nice* **1977**—*More Sex and More Soul*

Roy C's songs about love and infidelity were rarely real
hits—he made the R&B Top Twenty only once—but their
consistency earned him respect within his profession.
After changing his name from Roy Charles Hammond to
avoid being mistaken for either Ray Charles or Roy
Hamilton, he joined the Genies as lead singer in the early
Sixties. In 1965, the Genies broke up and C began his solo
career with his biggest success: a Black Hawk single,
"Shotgun Wedding," (#14 R&B, 1965). Subsequent recordings for Black Hawk and Shout (where he was produced by Bert Berns) fared less well.

In 1969, he formed his own record company, Alaga, and
returned to the charts in 1971 with "Got to Get Enough."
After writing and producing the Mark IV's 1972 hit "Honey I Still Love You," C signed with that label. Mercury
repackaged his early singles in album form and released a
series of modestly successful new singles, including
"Don't Blame the Man" (1973), "Loneliness Had Got a
Hold of Me" (1974) and "Love Me Till Tomorrow Comes"
(1975).

THE CADETS
Formed mid-1950s, Los Angeles
Ted Taylor, tenor voc.; William "Dub" Jones, bass
voc.; Aaron Collins, voc.; Willie Davis, voc.; Lloyd
McCraw, voc.
N.A.—*The Cadets* (Crown) *Rockin' and Reelin' The
Cadets Greatest Hits* (Relic).

This Los Angeles vocal quintet was actually two groups in
one. As the Jacks, they sang soul ballads for RPM, scoring
their biggest hit with a cover of the Feathers' "Why Don't
You Write Me" (#4 R&B) in 1955. As the Cadets, they
sang rock & roll and R&B jump songs for the Modern
label. Their cover of the Jayhawks' "Stranded in the
Jungle" reached #4 on the R&B charts and #15 pop in
1956.

When they broke up in the late Fifties, their individual
voices were sought by the most prominent of the L.A.
vocal groups. Willie Davis and Aaron Collins joined the
Flairs, and William Jones replaced Bobby Nunn as bass in
the Coasters. With his gospel-style wail, Ted Taylor opted
for a solo career, which began to pay off in 1965 with "Stay
Away from My Baby" (#14), followed by "It's Too Late"

(#30, 1969), "Something Strange Is Goin' On in My
House" (#26, 1970) and "How's Your Love Life, Baby"
(#44, 1971).

THE CADILLACS
Formed New York City, 1953.
Earl Carroll (b. Nov. 2, 1937, New York), lead voc.;
Robert Phillips (b. 1935, New York), voc.; Laverne
Drake (b. 1938, New York), voc.; Gus Willingham (b.
1937, New York), voc.
N.A.—*The Crazy Cadillacs* (Jubilee) *Cruisin' with the
Cadillacs* (Harlem Hitparade) *The Fabulous Cadillacs*
(Jubilee) *Twisting with the Cadillacs.*

A distinguished Fifties R&B group whose legend has
grown appreciably over the years, the Cadillacs considered uptempo numbers like "Speedoo" (#17 pop, 1956,
#3 R&B, 1955) their forte, although latter-day fans often
prefer their slow ballads. Originally called the Carnations,
the Cadillacs came together in 1953 after a series of
informal singalong sessions in Harlem. A short time later,
they met manager Esther Navaroo, who persuaded them
to change their name to the Cadillacs and helped them
record "Gloria," a song she had written. (Navaroo received writer's credit for many of the group's releases,
although it was later revealed that some songs had been
written by the group members.) Their stage show included
flamboyant attire and tight choreography, a precursor of
the Motown style.

In late 1955, they released "Speedoo," a song about the
group's happy-go-lucky vocalist Earl Carroll. The record
employed fast scat harmonies and became one of their few
hits, along with "Peek-a-Boo" (#28, 1959) and "What
You Bet" (#30 R&B, 1961). Other releases included
"Zoom," "Woe Is Me," "Rudolph the Red-Nosed Reindeer" (1956); "My Girlfriend" (1957); and "Jay Walker"
and "Please Mr. Johnson" (1959).

In 1959, Earl Carroll left to join the Coasters, and he
was replaced by Bobby Spencer, who had written "My
Boy Lollipop," a hit for Millie Small in 1964. Following
Carroll's departure, the Cadillacs quickly lost prominence
despite subsequent recordings in the Sixties for such
labels as Smash, Capitol, Mercury and Polydor.

J. J. CALE
Born December 5, 1938, Oklahoma City
1972—*Naturally* (Shelter) *Really* **1974**—*Okie*
1976—*Troubadour* **1979**—*Number 5* **1981**—*Shades.*

While J. J. Cale remained a happy recluse in 1982 in his mobile home outside Los Angeles, the essentials of his style—sinuous, bluesy guitar lines and mumbly, near-whispered vocals—have been popularized by Eric Clapton and Dire Straits. Cale's songs, including "After Midnight" and "Cocaine," have been hits for Clapton and others.

Cale took up guitar at age ten. After playing in a succession of high school bands (one group included Leon Russell), he went on the road in 1959 and played with the Grand Ole Opry road company. By the early Sixties, he was back in Tulsa playing with Russell, and in 1964 the two moved to Los Angeles with fellow Oklahoma native Carl Radle (later of Derek and the Dominos). Cale hooked up with Delaney and Bonnie, and by 1965 he was recording on his own, including the first release of "After Midnight." He left Delaney and Bonnie and returned to Tulsa.

Radle passed on some of Cale's homemade demo tapes to Denny Cordell, and Cale became one of the first signings of Cordell and Russell's Shelter Records in 1969. Following Clapton's 1970 success with "After Midnight" (#18), Cale recorded *Naturally* in 1972, from which "Crazy Mama" went to #22. "Magnolia," also on that album, was later covered by Poco and José Feliciano. Throughout the Seventies, Cale recorded and, less often, toured at a leisurely pace. Although he toured in 1981, he spent most of that year in Nashville, where he could park his trailer next to his 16-track recording studio, Crazy Mama's.

JOHN CALE
Born 1942, Wales
1969—*Vintage Violence* (Columbia)   1971—*Church of Anthrax*   1972—*The Academy in Peril* (Reprise)
1973—*Paris 1919*   1974—*Fear* (Island)   *June 1, 1974*
1975—*Slow Dazzle; Helen of Troy*   1977—*Guts*
1980—*Sabotage/Live* (IRS)   1981—*Honi Soit* (A&M)
1982—*Music for a New Society* (Ze/Passport).

John Cale has brought an avant-garde ear to rock & roll ever since he founded the Velvet Underground with Lou Reed in 1966. His work shows a continuing fascination with diametrical opposites: lyricism and noise, subtlety and bluntness, hypnotic repetition and sudden change. Even as a student of classical music he was an extremist: during a recital at the Guildhall School of Music, London, where he was studying theory and composition, he demolished a grand piano. Cale studied in Britain with composer Humphrey Searle, came to America in 1963 to work with Iannis Xenakis and Aaron Copland under the auspices of a Leonard Bernstein Fellowship, then settled in New York to work with more radical composers like La Monte Young. Through his asssociation with the lower Manhattan art community, Cale met Reed, who directed him toward electric instruments and rock & roll and helped conceive the Velvet Underground, for whom Cale played keyboards, bass and electric viola.

After two Velvets albums, Cale left in 1968 to begin a multifarious solo career. In the early Seventies, he worked in the record business as an A&R man for Warner Bros. and Elektra, and as a consultant for Columbia, remixing albums by Barbra Streisand, and Paul Revere and the Raiders in quadraphonic sound. On his solo albums, he has used lyrical pop *(Paris 1919)*, hard rock *(Fear)*, Phil Spector/Brian Wilson gloss *(Slow Dazzle)*, minimalism *(Church of Anthrax,* with fellow La Monte Young pupil Terry Riley), full classical orchestra *(The Academy in Peril)* and punk *(Sabotage)*.

Cale has performed or recorded with Brian Eno, Kevin Ayers, and Kate and Anna McGarrigle, and scored soundtracks for Andy Warhol's *Heat* and Roger Corman's *Caged Heat*. He has also produced some of the groups that, along with the Velvets, fostered punk in America: the Stooges *(The Stooges)*, the Modern Lovers *(The Modern Lovers)*, Patti Smith *(Horses,* her debut), as well as Squeeze. Cale performs solo and with an everchanging band and continues to make unpredictable albums.

GLEN CAMPBELL
Born April 22, 1938, Delight, Arkansas
1967—*Gentle on My Mind* (Capitol)   *By the Time I Get to Phoenix*   1968—*Hey Little One; Bobbie Gentry and Glen Campbell; Wichita Lineman*   1969—*Glen Campbell Live*   1970—*Try a Little Kindness*   1971—*Glen Campbell's Greatest Hits*   1975—*Rhinestone Cowboy*   1977—*Southern Nights*   1978—*Basic*
1979—*Highwayman*   1980—*Somethin' 'Bout You Baby I Like*   1981—*It's the World Gone Crazy*.

Glen Campbell has been a mainstream country-pop star for more than a decade and made twelve gold and seven platinum albums.

Campbell was one of twelve children in a family where everyone played guitar and sang. He got his first guitar at age 4 and he left home as a teenager to tour with an uncle, a musician named Dick Bill. In 1960, Campbell moved to Los Angeles, where he became known in country and rock circles and supported himself with session work for Frank Sinatra, Johnny Cash, Dean Martin, the Mamas and the Papas, Gene Clark and several of Phil Spector's groups. In 1965, he played bass with the Beach Boys for several months following Brian Wilson's decision not to appear with the band.

Campbell signed with Capitol in 1962 and recorded with occasional and minor success; his 1965 cover of Donovan's "Universal Soldier" entered the Top Fifty. In 1967, he hit with John Hartford's "Gentle on My Mind," and became a regular guest on the Smothers Brothers' variety program. His other Sixties hits included the Jimmy Webb compositions "By the Time I Get to Phoenix" (#11,

1967), "Wichita Lineman" (#3, 1968) and "Galveston" (#4, 1969). Beginning in the late Sixties, Campbell hosted his own variety show for four and a half years. His later hits include "Rhinestone Cowboy" (#1, 1975), Allen Toussaint's "Southern Nights" (#1, 1977) and "Country Boy (You Got Your Feet in L.A.)" (#11, 1976).

Over the years, he has also worked in movies (*True Grit* with John Wayne; *Norwood*) and has made countless appearances on television. He also hosts the Glen Campbell Los Angeles Open Golf Tournament.

CAN

Formed 1968, Cologne, West Germany
Irmin Schmidt, kybds., voc.; Michael Karoli, gtr., violin, voc.; Holger Czukay, bass, voc., electonics; Jaki Liebezeit, drums, reeds, voc.; Malcolm Mooney, voc.; David Johnson, flute, electronics.
1970—*Monster Movie* (United Artists) (– Mooney; – Johnson; + Damo Suzuki, voc.) **1971**—*Tago Mago* **1972**—*Ege Bamyasi* **1973**—*Soundtracks; Future Days* (– Suzuki) **1974**—*Soon over Babaluma* **1975**—*Landed* (Virgin) **1976**—*Unlimited Edition* (reissue of the 1974 British release *Limited Edition* with new material) *Flow Motion; Opener* **1977**—(+ Rosko Gee, bass; + Reebop Kwaku Baah, percussion) *Saw Delight* **1978**—*Cannibalisms* (United Artists) *Out of Reach* (Lightning).

The European art-rock band Can was one of the first groups to use electronic "treatments" of instruments, and they pioneered an exploratory postpsychedelic rock style that would later influence Amon Duul, Ash Ra Temple and a wave of technopop bands. Can's sound was based on repetitive, trance-inducing rhythms overlaid with atmospheric noise and sudden bursts of distorted electronic effects, with instruments often unrecognizable in the mix. *Monster Movie* finds the approach still rather primitive.

But with Malcolm Mooney taken ill and replaced by Damo Suzuki—discovered by the band singing on the streets of Munich—Irmin Schmidt and Holger Czukay made fuller use of their studies with German avant-garde composer Karlheinz Stockhausen. The band expanded frontiers and sounded more assured on *Tago Mago, Ege Bamyasi, Future Days* and *Babaluma*. Can music was a natural for film soundtracks, and they scored part of Jerzy Skolimowski's *Deep End;* their film scores are collected on *Soundtracks*.

Can enjoyed a couple of hit singles abroad with "I Want More" and a version of "Silent Night" in 1976. With the addition of ex-Traffic members Rosko Gee and Reebop Kwaku Baah, Can's sound got funkier on the well-received *Saw Delight*. But then the band entered a limbo status, with various members splitting off for solo and collaboration LPs, of which Czukay's *Movies*, a Brian Eno–style tape-loop and *musique concrète* montage, was most successful.

CANNED HEAT

Formed 1966, Los Angeles
Bob "Bear" Hite (b. Feb. 26, 1945, Torrance, Calif.; d. Apr. 5, 1981, Venice, Calif.), voc., harmonica; Alan "Blind Owl" Wilson (b. July 4, 1943, Boston; d. Sep. 3, 1970, Torrance, Calif.), gtr., harmonica, voc.; Henry Vestine (b. Dec. 24, 1944, Washington, D.C.), gtr.; Larry Taylor (b. June 26, 1942, Brooklyn), bass; Frank Cook, drums.
1967—*Canned Heat* (Liberty) **1968**—(– Cook; + Adolpho "Fito" de la Parra [b. Feb. 8, 1946, Mexico City], drums) *Boogie with Canned Heat; Living the Blues* **1969**—(– Vestine; + Harvey Mandel [b. 1946, Detroit], gtr.) *Hallelujah* **1970**—*Vintage Heat* (Janus) *Canned Heat Live in Europe* (Liberty) *Future Blues; Cookbook* **1971**—*Live at the Topanga Corral* (Wand) **1972**—*Historical Figures and Ancient Heads* (United Artists) **1973**—*New Age* **1974**—*One More River to Cross* (Atlantic).

Blues-rockers Canned Heat evolved out of a jug band that was formed in 1965. Blues fanatics Alan Wilson and Bob Hite (nicknamed the "Bear" because of his 300-pound frame) changed the group's focus to electric boogie. In 1967, they signed with Liberty Records. Though their debut, *Canned Heat*, sold respectably, their appearance at the Monterey Pop Festival that year attracted more attention. Their second album spawned a #16 hit, Wilson's "On the Road Again," and they toured Europe. "Going Up the Country" gave them a #11 hit in 1969, and they played the Woodstock Festival in August.

The following year was a watershed, with a worldwide hit of Wilbert Harrison's "Let's Work Together" and an appearance at the Isle of Wight Festival in England. But the drug overdose death of Wilson (who was partly blind and subject to severe depression) in late 1970 proved to be a setback from which the band never recovered. They backed bluesman John Lee Hooker on *Hooker 'n' Heat* that year. By the early Eighties, Canned Heat was playing the California bar circuit. With the death of Hite in early 1981, Canned Heat became nothing more than a name.

FREDDY CANNON

Born Frederick Anthony Picariello, December 4, 1940, Lynn, Massachusetts
1961—*The Explosive Freddy Cannon* (Swan) **1962**—*Freddy Cannon Sings Happy Shades of Blue; Freddy Cannon's Solid Gold Hits; Freddy Cannon at Palisades Park* **1964**—*Freddy Cannon Steps Out* **1965**—*Freddy Cannon* (Warner Bros.) **1966**—*Freddy Cannon's Greatest Hits; Action!*

A major star in the early Sixties, singer/guitarist/songwriter Freddy Cannon broke big with two million-sellers: "Tallahassie Lassie" (#6, 1959) and an updated version of a 1922 jazz hit "Way Down Yonder in New Orleans" (#3,

1960). Cannon was discovered in 1957 by a Boston disc jockey; two years later he recorded "Tallahassie Lassie," a song his mother had written.

He toured internationally during the mid-Sixties, scoring minor hits regularly. His only other big hit, the Chuck Barris–penned "Palisades Park," was #3 in 1962. That same year, he was featured in the British film *Just for Fun.* In 1965, he had a minor hit with the theme song from the TV series "Where the Action Is." He remained a major performer in the U.K. years after his star had faded in America. In the Seventies he became a promotion man for Buddah Records, but he returned to the charts in 1981 with "Let's Put the Fun Back in Rock 'n' Roll."

THE CAPRIS
Formed 1957, New York City
Nick Santo (b. Nick Santamaria, 1941), voc.; Mike Miniceli (b. 1941), voc.; Frank Reina (b. 1940), voc.; John Cassese (b. 1941), voc.; Vin Naccarato (b. 1941), voc.
1980—(− Naccarato; − Cassese; + Tommy Ferrara, voc.; + Tony Danno, voc.) 1981—*There's a Moon Out Again* (Ambient Sound/Epic).

The Capris were a one-hit vocal group of the late Fifties who were rediscovered and revived in 1980 on the Ambient Sound label. The five original members had been singing in subway stations and on streetcorners in Queens, New York, before they were discovered by independent record producers. A song by Santamaria, "There's a Moon Out Again," was recorded in 1958 but went nowhere, and the group soon disbanded. Two years later, WINS disc jockey Murray the K used the song in a contest, and soon afterwards "There's a Moon Out Again" hit #3 (1961). The group re-formed and has continued to perform ever since. In 1980, three original Capris (Santamaria, Miniceli and Reina), former Del-Satin Tommy Ferrara and ex-Emotion Tony Danno came together to record an Ambient Sound LP that was released in 1981.

CAPTAIN AND TENNILLE
Daryl Dragon (a.k.a. the "Captain," b. Aug. 27, 1942, Los Angeles), kybds.; Toni Tennille (b. May 8, 1943, Montgomery, Ala.), voc.
1975—*Love Will Keep Us Together* (A&M) *Por Amor Viviremos* 1976—*Song of Joy* 1977—*Come in from the Rain; The Captain and Tennille's Greatest Hits*
1978—*Dream* 1979—*Make Your Move* (Casablanca)
1980—*Keeping Our Love Warm.*

The Captain and Tennille are a husband-and-wife pop duo who debuted on the pop charts with the top-selling single of 1975, a bouncy version of Neil Sedaka's "Love Will Keep Us Together." The single sold over 2½ million

copies and was awarded a Grammy for Record of the Year.

Toni Tennille began singing with her three sisters in their hometown of Montgomery. She studied classical piano for nine years. In 1964, Tennille moved with her family to Los Angeles, where she joined the South Coast Repertory Theater. She and Ron Thronson cowrote a rock musical entitled *Mother Earth,* and during the play's run she met Daryl Dragon, a keyboard player in the house band. The son of conductor Carmen Dragon, Daryl plays clarinet, keyboards, guitar, and bass. Before he met Tennille, he had also worked with the Beach Boys, and when Tennille's play closed in 1971, he invited her to come with him on a Beach Boys tour.

Three years later, the two financed and produced a single, "The Way I Want to Touch You." Shortly after A&M released the song in 1974, the two were wed (on Valentine's Day); the song became a regional hit. "Love Will Keep Us Together" followed; and upon its re-release in 1975, "The Way I Want to Touch You" went to #4. Other hit singles included "Lonely Night (Angel Face)" (#3, 1976), "Muskrat Love" (#4, 1976), a cover version of Smokey Robinson's "Shop Around" (#4, 1976), "Can't Stop Dancin'" (#13, 1977), "You Never Done It Like That" (#10, 1978) and "Do That to Me One More Time" (#1, 1979).

Although the Captain and Tennille tour regularly, their primary exposure has been via television; they hosted their own prime-time series on ABC in 1976, and in the early Eighties Tennille was hosting a daytime variety show (with Daryl as musical director). Of their hit singles, all are gold except "Dancin' " and "You Never" and the platinum "Love Will Keep Us Together." Similarly, all of their LPs (except *Viviremos, Keeping Our Love Warm* and *Dream*) are gold; *Love Will Keep Us Together* and *Song of Joy* are platinum.

CAPTAIN BEEFHEART AND THE MAGIC BAND
Formed 1964, California
Captain Beefheart (b. Don Van Vliet, Jan. 15, 1941, Glendale, Calif.), voc., saxes, harmonicas, bass clarinet, Chinese gongs; The Magic Band: Ry Cooder (b. March 15, 1947, Los Angeles), gtr.; Alex St. Claire Snuffy, gtr.; Jerry Handley, bass; John French, drums.
1967—*Safe As Milk* (Buddah) (− Cooder; + Jeff Cotton, gtr.) 1968—*Mirror Man; Strictly Personal* (Blue Thumb) (− St. Claire Snuffy; − Handley; + Drumbo [John French], drums; + Antennae Jimmy Semens [Jeff Cotton], gtr.; + Zoot Horn Rollo [Bill Harkleroad], gtr., + Rockette Morton [Mark Boston], bass; + the Mascara Snake [Van Vliet's unidentified cousin], bass clarinet; + Doug Moon, gtr. on "China Pig") 1969—*Trout Mask Replica* (Straight)

(− Cotton; − Moon; + Art Tripp [Ed Marimba],
drums and marimbas) **1970**—*Lick My Decals Off,
Baby* (Reprise) (− French; + Orejon [Roy Estrada],
drums) **1972**—*Clear Spot* (− Orejon; + John
French, drums; + Winged Eel Fingerling [Eliot Ingber],
gtr.) *The Spotlight Kid* (− French; − Ingber; +
Alex St. Claire, gtr.; + Mark Marcellino, kybds.)
1974—*Unconditionally Guaranteed* (Mercury) (all
new lineup: + Dean Smith, gtr.; + Ira Ingber, bass;
+ Gene Pello, drums; +Ty Grimes, percussion; + Jim
Caravan, kybds.; +Mike Smotherman, kybds.)
Bluejeans and Moonbeams (all new lineup: + Bruce
Lambourne Fowler, trombone; + Richard Redus, gtr.,
bass; + Robert Arthur Williams, drums; + Jeff Moris
Tepper, gtr.; + Erick Drew Feldman, kybds., bass)
1978—*Shiny Beast (Bat Chain Puller)* (Warner Bros.)
(− Redus; + Gary Lucas, French horn, gtr.; + John
French, drums) **1980**—*Doc at the Radar Station*
(Virgin) (−French; − Williams; + Cliff Martinez,
drums) **1982**—*Ice Cream for Crow* (Virgin/Epic).

The irregular rhythms, grating harmonies and earthy,
surreal lyrics of Captain Beefheart's songs and his blues-
inflected 7½-octave vocals suggest a near-chaotic improvised blend of Delta blues, avant-garde jazz, 20th-century
classical music and rock & roll. Actually, Beefheart's
repertoire is a sort of modern chamber music for rock
band, since he plans every note and teaches the band their
parts by ear. Because it breaks so many of rock's conventions at once, Beefheart's music has been more influential
than popular, leaving its mark on Devo, Pere Ubu, Public
Image Ltd., the Contortions and the Clash.

A child-prodigy sculptor, Don Van Vliet was noticed at
age four by Portuguese sculptor Augustinio Rodriguez,
who featured Van Vliet and his clay animals on his weekly
television show for the next eight years. When Van Vliet
was 13, his parents turned down their son's scholarship to
study art in Europe and moved the family to Lancaster,
California, in the Mojave Desert, where Van Vliet met the
young Frank Zappa. Van Vliet taught himself to play
harmonica and saxophone and played with local R&B
bands the Omens and the Blackouts before enrolling in
Antelope Valley College in 1959. After one semester, he
dropped out and went to Cucamonga, California, with
Zappa, intending to form a band, the Soots, and make a
film, *Captain Beefheart Meets the Grunt People*. Both
projects fell through, and while Zappa went to Los
Angeles to found the Mothers of Invention, Van Vliet
returned to Lancaster and formed the first Magic Band in
1964.

A&M signed the group in 1964 and released its version
of "Diddy Wah Diddy," which sold enough locally for
A&M to commission an album. Label president Jerry
Moss rejected the tapes of Van Vliet originals as "too
negative," and the band broke up. With a new band,

Captain Beefheart

Beefheart redid the songs for *Safe As Milk,* which attracted enough interest for the band to tour Europe in
1966. Shortly before a scheduled appearance at the 1967
Monterey Pop Festival, guitarist Ry Cooder's abrupt departure forced the group to cancel.

Mirror Man was recorded in late 1968, but Buddah
didn't release it until 1970, after Beefheart had left the
label. *Strictly Personal* was recorded in 1968, but radically
remixed by producer Bob Krasnow and released on his
own Blue Thumb label as the band toured Europe. Van
Vliet, disgusted, retired to the San Fernando Valley until
Zappa, now in charge of his own Straight Records, promised him complete artistic control of his next recordings.
After composing 28 songs in 8½ hours, Beefheart formed
a new Magic Band and recorded *Trout Mask Replica* over
the next year. That album and 1970's *Lick My Decals Off,
Baby* brought Beefheart critical acclaim and, along with
his appearance on Zappa's *Hot Rats* (1969), enough interest for a national tour. The next two albums, marginally
more commercial-sounding, reached the lower echelons of
the pop charts.

After a two-year hiatus, Van Vliet signed with Mercury
and released two openly conventional pop-blues albums
and toured and dissolved another Magic Band. For a short
time, he appeared as a vocalist with Zappa and the
Mothers of Invention, including songs on 1975's *Bongo
Fury*. In 1978, Warner Bros. re-signed him and released
Shiny Beast (Bat Chain Puller), and Beefheart toured a
somewhat more receptive new wave circuit. Virgin sued
to keep Beefheart on its roster (it had British rights to

Beefheart since his Mercury period) and won ownership of *Doc at the Radar Station* and *Ice Cream for Crow*. Beefheart's 1980 American and European tours, including a November 1980 appearance on "Saturday Night Live," were his most successful to date. Between tours, Beefheart is a painter, and his artwork is on one of the covers of his most recent albums. He and his wife, Jan, live in a trailer in the Mojave Desert.

CARAVAN

Formed 1967, England
Pye Hastings (b. 1947, Banffshire, Scot.), gtr., voc.;
David Sinclair (b. 1947, Herne Bay, Eng.), kybds.;
Richard Coughlan (b. 1947, Herne Bay, Eng.), drums;
Richard Sinclair, bass, voc.
1968—*Caravan* (MGM) **1970**—*If I Could Do It All Over Again, I'd Do It All Over You* (London) **1971**—*In the Land of Grey and Pink* (− D. Sinclair; + Steve Miller, kybds.) **1972**—*Waterloo Lily* (− Miller; + D. Sinclair; − R. Sinclair; + John G. Perry [b. 1947, Auburn, N. Y.], bass, voc.; + Geoffrey Richardson [b. 1950, Hinckley, Eng.], violin, viola, flute) **1973**—*For Girls Who Grow Plump in the Night* **1974**—*Recorded Live at the Theatre Royal, Drury Lane, On the 28th of October, 1973* (with the New Symphonia) (− Perry; + Mike Wedgwood, bass, voc.) **1975**—*Cunning Stunts* (− D. Sinclair, + Jan Schelhaas, kybds.) **1976**—*Canterbury Tales* (Decca) *Blind Dog at St. Dunstans* (Arista) **1977**—(− Wedgwood; + Dek Messecar, bass) *Better by Far* **1980**—*The Album* (Kingdom).

Caravan grew out of the mid-to-late-Sixties Canterbury psychedelic underground that bred many of England's rock experimentalists. All four original members had played at various times in the seminal Canterbury band, the Wilde Flowers, formed in 1963 by Kevin Ayers and Robert Wyatt. When Ayers and Wyatt left to form Soft Machine in 1966, Pye Hastings, Richard Coughlan and David Sinclair led the Wilde Flowers through their most successful period before turning the group into Caravan in 1967.

Initially, Caravan's music drew on classical and English folk traditions to arrive at a dreamy rock fusion. But jazz became a more pronounced influence when David Sinclair left to join Wyatt's Matching Mole and was replaced by Steve Miller, a pianist formerly with Delivery (not to be confused with the American rock guitarist/singer of the same name). After recording *Waterloo Lily*, however, Richard Sinclair joined his cousin David in Hatfield and the North, and Pye and Coughlan looked for new members. They found violinist Geoffrey Richardson, keyboardist Derek Austin and bassist Stuart Evans, but this lineup never recorded. David Sinclair returned and John Perry left his group, Spreadeagle, to record *For Girls* and the

1973 live set with the New Symphonia orchestra and chorus, after which Perry formed Quantum Jump and was replaced by Mike Wedgwood, ex–Curved Air.

Caravan first toured the United States at the end of 1974. *Cunning Stunts* was Caravan's first album to appear on the American charts (#124). But David Sinclair's second departure left the group in Hastings' command and they continued as a cult progressive band.

CARL CARLTON

Born 1952, Detroit
N.A.—*You Can't Stop a Man in Love* (Backbeat)
1974—*Everlasting Love* (ABC) **1975**—*I Wanna Be with You* **1981**—*Carl Carlton* (20th Century–Fox).

Carl Carlton's career, modeled on that of fellow Detroit native Little Stevie Wonder, began when he was 14. He had been singing since he was nine, first in churches, then for local talent shows, where he was discovered by scouts from Lando Records, a gospel label. When his contract was bought by Back Beat in 1968, he became a child star. Billed as Little Carl Carlton, he had a hit with "Competition Ain't Nothin' "(#36 R&B, 1968). His followup, "Forty-six Drums, One Guitar," made the R&B Top Twenty in 1968). He sustained his career after his voice matured, placing such singles on the charts as "Don't Walk Away" (#38, 1969) and "Drop by My Place" (#12, 1970).

He recorded "Everlasting Love" (a 1967 hit for Robert Knight) in 1972, just before Duke-Peacock was incorporated into ABC Records. ABC shelved the master and forgot about it until 1974, by which time Carlton was contemplating a factory job. It was released and rose to #11 R&B, and by the end of 1974 had crossed over to the pop market and reached #6. After he acquired a band, Mixed Company, "Smokin' Room" (#13 R&B, 1975) kept him on the charts. After that, though, Carlton's career waned. ABC dropped him, and he didn't find a new label until 1980. He returned on 20th Century–Fox with racier material: "This Feeling's Rated X-Tra" (#57 R&B, 1980). Then "She's a Bad Mama Jama (She's Built, She's Stacked)" gave him the biggest hit of his career (#22, 1981).

ERIC CARMEN

Born August 11, 1949, Cleveland
1975—*Eric Carmen* (Arista) **1977**—*Boats Against the Current* **1978**—*Change of Heart* **1980**—*Tonight You're Mine*.

After leaving the pop-rock Raspberries in the early Seventies, Eric Carmen sustained an intermittently successful solo career. He studied at the Cleveland Institute of Music from age two through his mid-teens, taking piano, violin, viola and music theory. This classical training would show up in his pop songs (like "My Girl," "Never Gonna Fall in

Love Again" and "All By Myself," all of which incorporated Rachmaninoff melodies). At 15, Carmen saw the Beatles, dropped his formal studies and took up electric guitar. He formed the Raspberries with some Cleveland friends in 1970; they released four albums of Beach Boys/Beatles/Who–flavored pop through 1974, when Carmen left. In 1975, his solo debut, *Eric Carmen*, went to #21 as "All By Myself" went to #2 and "Never Gonna Fall in Love Again" reached #11. Other hits include "Sunrise" (#34, 1976), "She Did It" (#23, 1977) and "Change of Heart" (#19, 1978). Carmen's later albums, leaning heavily on ballads, have sold only modestly.

KIM CARNES
Born 1948, Southern California
1972—*Rest on Me* (A&M)   1975—*Kim Carnes*   1976—
Sailin'   1979—*St. Vincent's Court* (EMI America)
1980—*Romance Dance*   1981—*Mistaken Identity*
1982—*Voyeur;   The Best of* (A&M).

Singer/songwriter Kim Carnes recorded the top-selling single of 1981, "Bette Davis Eyes." Carnes grew up in suburban Los Angeles. By her early twenties, she was working the city's nightclubs, singing mainly ballads. Such fare composed the bulk of her several albums (including *Sailin'*, which was produced by Jerry Wexler) through the Seventies. Her songs, some of which were co-written with her husband, Dave Ellingson (who is also a member of her backup band), have been covered by Frank Sinatra, Rita Coolidge, Anne Murray and Barbra Streisand. The couple's biggest break came in 1978, when Kenny Rogers recorded their songs on *Gideon*. Carnes duetted with Rogers on his hit "Don't Fall in Love with a Dreamer" (#4, 1980).

In 1978, she signed with Rogers' label and gradually began recording rock-oriented material. She had a #10 hit in 1980 with a cover of Smokey Robinson's "More Love." But album sales remained sluggish (her biggest seller was *Romance Dance*, which included "More Love," #10, 1980) until 1981's *Mistaken Identity* and its single, a Donna Weiss/Jackie DeShannon composition, "Bette Davis Eyes" (#1, 1981), which won a Grammy for Record of the Year.

THE CARPENTERS
Richard Carpenter (b. Oct. 15, 1946, New Haven), voc., kybds.; Karen Carpenter (b. Mar. 2, 1950, New Haven, d. Feb. 4, 1983, Los Angeles), voc., drums.
1969—*Ticket to Ride* (A&M)   1970—*Close to You*
1971—*Carpenters*   1972—*A Song for You*   1973—*Now and Then;   The Singles 1969–1973*   1975—*Horizon*
1976—*Kind of Hush*   1977—*Passage*   1978—*Christmas Portrait*   1980—*Made in America*.

A popular brother-and-sister team, the Carpenters sold millions of hit records in the early Seventies. Richard

started piano lessons at age 12 and studied classical piano at Yale before the family relocated to Downey, California, in 1963. Richard studied at USC and Cal State at Long Beach. He formed his first group in 1965, a jazz-pop instrumental trio which included younger sister Karen on drums and their friend Wes Jacobs (who later abandoned pop for a seat in the Detroit Symphony) on bass and tuba. The group won a battle of the bands at the Hollywood Bowl, thereby landing a contract with RCA. The resulting two LPs (deemed "too soft" by RCA execs) were never released. In late 1966, the trio broke up. Richard and Karen recruited four Cal State students into the vocal harmony-oriented band Spectrum. They played various Southern California venues to less than ecstatic response and disbanded.

The Carpenter siblings' densely layered, pop-oriented demo tapes eventually caught the attention of Herb Alpert, who signed them to A&M in 1970. They released their first album that November. Originally titled *Offering*, it was ignored until repackaged as *Ticket to Ride*, on the strength of the moderate success of their Beatles cover single. *Close to You*'s title track, a Burt Bacharach tune, sold more than a million copies and went to #1 in the U.S. and several other countries.

Their hits continued: "We've Only Just Begun" (#2, 1970); "For All We Know" (#3, 1971; it won an Oscar as Best Song of the Year in 1970); "Rainy Days and Mondays" (#2, 1971); "Superstar" (#2, 1971, written by Leon Russell); "It's Going to Take Some Time" (#12, 1972); "Hurting Each Other" (#2, 1972); "Goodbye to Love" (#7, 1972); "Sing" (#3, 1973); "Yesterday Once More" (#2, 1973); "Top of the World" (#1, 1973); "Won't Last a Day Without You" (#11, 1974); "Please Mr. Postman" (#1, 1975); and "Only Yesterday" (#4, 1975).

The 1973 LP *The Singles 1969–73* was a best seller, and the Carpenters were three-time Grammy winners. They hosted a short-lived variety series on NBC, "Make Your Own Kind of Music," in 1971. At the request of President Nixon, they performed at a White House state dinner honoring West German Chancellor Willy Brandt, May 1, 1974. They toured internationally through the mid-Seventies. Their 1976 tour of Japan was, at the time, the biggest-grossing concert ever in that country. Through the late Seventies, the pair was noticeably absent from the charts.

In early February 1983, Karen Carpenter died in her parents' home of cardiac arrest, believed to be the result of anorexia nervosa.

JOE "KING" CARRASCO AND THE CROWNS
Formed 1979, Texas
Joe "King" Carrasco (b. Joseph Teutsch, Dumas, Tex.), gtr., voc.; Kris Cummings, organ; Mike Navarro, drums; Brad Kizer, bass.

1980—*Joe "King" Carrasco and the Crowns* (Hannibal) **1981**—*Party Safari* (− Navarro; + Dick Ross, drums) **1982**—*Synapse Gap (Mundo Total)* (MCA) **1983**—*Party Weekend.*

Calling his music "nuevo wavo," Joe Carrasco blends garage rock (Sam the Sham), Tex-Mex (Doug Sahm), Chicano polkas and new-wavish intensity into speedy, good-humored party music. Carrasco started playing in West Texas rock & roll bands before he was a teenager. By 1973, when he settled in Austin, he had played with bands such as Salaman, a mariachi outfit, and Shorty y los Corvettes, who had a couple of local Spanish hits. His Chicano colleagues dubbed him "King" Carrasco.

In 1976, he formed his own band, El Molino, with local trumpeter Charlie McBurney and saxophonist Rocky Morales. El Molino was popular in Austin and San Antonio, where they recorded *Tex-Mex Rock-Roll* on Carrasco's Lisa label in 1978. The album found a cult audience in New York and London (Elvis Costello was an early admirer). Carrasco had no takers when he took the album to L.A. in search of a distribution deal, but he moved to the city's Mexican barrio and wrote songs with Sir Douglas Quintet drummer Johnny Perez.

Returning to Austin in 1979, he met Kris Cummings, Mike Navarro and Brad Kizer. Cummings had studied piano in New Orleans with Huey "Piano" Smith and Professor Longhair, but Carrasco gave her the Farfisa organ that defined the Crowns' trashy sound. They went to New York in late 1979, where their partylike shows, bolstered by Carrasco's antics (cape and crown, leaping from the stage during guitar solos and wandering as far as his sixty-foot cord allowed), won the enthusiastic support of clubgoers and the music press. They returned to Austin as heroes in the spring of 1980. In July, Stiff Records of England signed them to a contract, with American distribution going to Hannibal. Later that year, the band toured Europe and Canada.

JIM CARROLL
Born 1950, New York City
1980—*Catholic Boy* (Atco) **1982**—*Dry Dreams.*

Poet, novelist and former heroin addict Jim Carroll followed his friend Patti Smith into rock & roll. His first collection of poetry was published when he was 16, followed in 1970 by *The Basketball Diaries,* his teenage journal of high school, hustling and heroin. A later poetry collection, *Living at the Movies,* was rumored to have been nominated for a Pulitzer (it was not); his writings have also appeared in the *Paris Review.* In 1974, Carroll moved to northern California, where he kicked the drug habit and, along with a San Francisco band, began performing his version of rock & roll in area clubs.

On a visit to New York, he played his demo tape for Earl McGrath (then president of Rolling Stone Records), who arranged a record deal with Atco and produced *Catholic Boy.* The album featured "People Who Died," a minor hit. Carroll's band for his *Dry Dreams* consisted of drummer Wayne Woods, bassist Steve Linsley, guitarist Lenny Kaye (formerly of the Patti Smith group) and guitarist Paul Sanchez.

THE CARS
Formed 1976, Massachusetts
Ric Ocasek (b. Baltimore), voc., gtr.; Ben Orr (b. Benjamin Orzechowski), bass, voc.; Elliot Easton (b. Elliot Shapiro), gtr.; Greg Hawkes, kybds.; David Robinson, drums.
1978—*The Cars* (Elektra) **1979**—*Candy-O* **1980**—*Panorama* **1981**—*Shake It Up.* **Ric Ocasek solo: 1983**—*Beatitude* (Geffen).

Ric Ocasek's artful pop songs made the Cars into the new wave's fastest, most consistent success. Their debut and second albums sold more than six million copies worldwide, and each album since has sold over a million. While Ocasek's lyrics are more detached and alienated than those of his main influences, the Velvet Underground and Roxy Music, the Cars' arrangements, laced with keyboard and guitar hooks, have made the songs popular with both Top Forty and AOR audiences. Each Cars album has incorporated more avant-garde elements—especially minimalist repetition—yet they have maintained a vast audience.

Ocasek and Ben Orr had been partners for nearly a decade before starting the Cars. Ocasek took up guitar at ten and immediately began to write songs; he began working as a musician after he'd dropped out of Antioch College and Bowling Green State University. He met Orr—who as a teenager had fronted the house band on a TV rock show, "Upbeat"—in Cleveland, where Orr worked in a studio as a producer and session musician. After working together in various bands in Cleveland, New York City, Woodstock and Ann Arbor, they settled in Cambridge, Massachusetts, in the late Seventies.

As part of a folk trio, Milkwood, they released an album on Paramount in 1972, with Hawkes as session keyboardist. Ocasek and Orr continued to form bands, while Hawkes worked with Martin Mull and Boston country-rockers Orphan, and wrote music with progressive rockers Happy the Man. In 1974, Easton joined Cap'n Swing, Ocasek and Orr's current band, which became popular in Boston but broke up when no recording contract was forthcoming. Hawkes rejoined, and Robinson, formerly of Jonathan Richman's Modern Lovers, DMZ and Los Angeles' the Pop, completed the Cars in late 1976.

After intensive rehearsals in Ocasek's basement, the Cars made some demo tapes, including "Just What I Needed," which became a top requested song on Boston radio station WBCN. With Roy Thomas Baker, who has

The Cars: Greg Hawkes, Elliot Easton, Ben Orr, Ric Ocasek, David Robinson

produced all Cars albums, they made their first album in London in two weeks. *The Cars* yielded three chart singles—"Just What I Needed" (#27, 1978), "My Best Friend's Girl" (#35, 1978) and "Good Times Roll" (#41, 1979)—and went platinum, staying on the charts so persistently that the release of *Candy-O,* recorded early in 1979, was delayed.

By 1979, the Cars were on the arena circuit; with "Let's Go" (#14, 1979) and "It's All I Can Do" (#41, 1979), *Candy-O* went platinum in two months. The Cars hosted a "Midnight Special" segment on which they chose other acts, including Suicide, whom Ocasek later produced. On *Panorama,* the Cars toyed with dissonance and odd meters; it went platinum with "Touch and Go" (#37, 1980), while *Candy-O* also went platinum and *The Cars* remained on the charts.

In 1981, Ocasek produced Suicide's *Alan Vega and Martin Rev,* a single for Boston's New Models, and EPs for the Peter Dayton Band, Bebe Buell and Romeo Void. Robinson produced singles for the Vinny Band and Boy's Life; Easton produced the Dawgs. The Cars also bought Intermedia Studios in Boston and remodeled it as Syncro Sound, where they recorded parts of *Shake It Up.* That album, with singles "Shake It Up" (#4, 1981) and "Victim of Love," also went platinum. Ocasek, Orr and Hawkes started solo albums in 1982; Robinson sat in on percussion with the Boston band Ooh Ah Ah, and Easton produced Peter Bond Set and Jules Shear. Ocasek also did production for Bad Brains, and the whole band contributed to the soundtrack of the thirty-minute film *Chapter-X.* Ocasek's solo debut, *Beatitude,* was released in 1983, and he announced plans to make a Cars album and a solo album each year.

CLARENCE CARTER
Born January 1936, Montgomery, Alabama
1968—*This Is* (Atlantic) *The Dynamic* **1969**—*Testifyin'* **1970**—*Patches* **1974**—*Sixty Minutes* (Fame)
Real (ABC) **1975**—*Loneliness and Temptation* **1976**—*Heart Full of Song; The Best of* (Atlantic) **1981**—*Let's Burn* (Venture).

Blind singer/guitarist Clarence Carter is best known for his late-Sixties hit singles. His career began as part of Calvin and Clarence and the C and C Boys on the Duke label. In 1965, they joined Rick Hall's Fame Records. Calvin Thomas had a car accident shortly afterward and retired, but Carter stayed with Fame, recording solo and playing on sessions. In 1968, he met Candi Staton, whom he later married. Staton had hits as a soul ballad singer in the early Seventies and as a disco star in the late Seventies. (They are now divorced.)

Carter's hits began in 1968 with "Slip Away" (#6 pop, #2 R&B) and "Too Weak to Fight" (#13 pop, #3 R&B). He followed up in 1969 with "Snatching It Back" (#4 R&B), "The Feeling Is Right" (#9 R&B) and "Doin' Our Thing" (#9 R&B). His story song "Patches" (#4 pop, #2 R&B) in 1970 was hailed as an instant classic. Carter signed with ABC in the mid-Seventies but the hits stopped coming until he reappeared in 1981 with *Let's Burn.*

THE CARTER FAMILY
Formed 1926, Virginia
Alvin Pleasant Carter (b. Apr. 15, 1891, Maces, Va.; d. Nov. 7, 1960, Maces, Va.), voc.; Sara Dougherty Carter (b. July 21, 1898, Wise County, Va.; d. Jan. 9, 1979), voc., gtr., autoharp, banjo; Maybelle Addington Carter

(b. May 10, 1909, Nickelsville, Va.; d. Oct. 23, 1978), voc., gtr., autoharp, banjo.
1961—*The Famous Carter Family* (Harmony)
1963—*Great Original Recordings by the Carter Family*
1964—*Keep on the Sunny Side* (Columbia)   **1965**—*The Best of the Carter Family*   **1967**—*An Historic Reunion.*

The Carter Family pioneered modern country music by setting folk songs to string-band backup, and were one of the most popular groups in America from 1926 until they disbanded in 1943. After that, Maybelle and A. P. continued to perform separately with their children through the Fifties and Sixties. Their songs, which included such standards as "Wildwood Flower," "Wabash Cannonball," "I'm Thinking Tonight of My Blue Eyes," "Will the Circle Be Unbroken," and their radio program theme song, "Keep on the Sunny Side," were immensely popular; the 78 rpm version of "Wildwood Flower" sold over a million copies.

The group formed in 1926 when A. P. Carter and his wife, Sara Dougherty, were joined by A. P.'s brother Ezra's wife (and Sara's cousin), Maybelle. Each had performed with friends and neighbors and as a group for about a year before A. P. had them record for Ralph Peer, who had been sent by RCA Victor to record local musicians (Jimmie Rodgers was recorded on the same day). The Carter Family was soon recording quite frequently, although it wasn't until they had left Virginia some years later that any of them could stop working day jobs. In 1928, they recorded their biggest hit, "Wildwood Flower." Their success was considerable despite the fact that the group never ventured more than a few hundred miles from home to perform.

In 1936, A. P. and Sara were divorced, but the group continued to perform and record, and in 1938 moved to Del Rio, Texas, where for the next three years they were regulars on radio station XERA. They next moved to Charlotte, North Carolina, to work for WBT, but shortly after their arrival, A. P. and Sara decided to retire. The original Carter Family had their last radio shows around 1939. The next year, Maybelle began working with her daughters June, Helen and Anita as Maybelle Carter and the Carter Sisters. Meanwhile A. P. and several of his children had formed another group, with whom he performed until his death in 1960. After A. P. died, Maybelle and her daughters adopted the Carter Family name.

The family's influence on latter-day singers and songwriters derives not only from their songs and recordings but also from Maybelle Carter's unique acoustic guitar–strumming techniques, particularly what has become known as the "Carter" style, which is widely imitated by folksingers. Maybelle and Sara reunited at the 1967 Newport Folk Festival to record *An Historic Reunion.* Throughout the Sixties, Maybelle performed with her daughters in her son-in-law Johnny Cash's revue and later on his television program. She sang the title track on the Nitty Gritty Dirt Band's *Will the Circle Be Unbroken* in 1971. With the exception of Maybelle's three daughters and of June's daughter, Carlene Carter, none of the second- and third-generation Carters have achieved wide recognition, although many of them are active in country music as performers and session musicians.

JOHNNY CASH
Born February 26, 1932, Kingsland, Ark.
1957—*With His Hot and Blue Guitar* (Sun)   **1958**—*Songs That Made Him Famous*   **1959**—*Fabulous Johnny Cash* (Columbia)   **1960**—*Ride This Train*
1962—*Sound of Johnny Cash*   **1963**—*Ring of Fire*
1964—*Keep on the Sunny Side;   I Walk the Line*
1965—*Orange Blossom Special*   **1967**—*Greatest Hits*
1968—*The Holy Land;   At Folsom Prison*
1969—*Jackson;   At San Quentin*   **1970**—*Johnny Cash Show*   **1971**—*A Man in Black*   **1973**—*Gospel Road; Sunday Morning Coming Down;   America*   **1974**—*Five Feet High and Rising;   Ragged Old Flag*   **1975**—*Look at Them Beans*   **1977**—*Last Gunfighter Ballad*
1980—*Rockabilly Blues*   **1981**—*Encore (Greatest Hits), volume 4*   **1982**—*The Survivors* (with Jerry Lee Lewis, Carl Perkins).

Country music patriarch Johnny Cash, the "Man in Black," has been on the border of rock and country since his early days as a rockabilly singer. His songs' characteristic marching bass lines have influenced Waylon Jennings and others, while his deep, quavery baritone growl has become a trademark.

Johnny Cash

The son of Southern Baptist sharecroppers, Cash began playing guitar and writing songs at age 12. During high school, he performed frequently on radio station KLCN in Blytheville, Arkansas. Cash moved to Detroit in his late teens and worked there until he joined the Air Force as a radio operator in Germany. He left the Air Force and married Vivian Liberto in 1954; the couple settled in Memphis, where Cash worked as an appliance salesman and attended radio announcers' school.

With the Tennessee Two—guitarist Luther Perkins and bassist Marshall Grant—he began recording for Sam Phillips' Sun Records. The trio recorded "Cry, Cry, Cry" (#14 C&W, 1955), and followed it with "Folsom Prison Blues" (#5 C&W, 1956). Later in 1956 came Cash's most enduring hit, the million-seller "I Walk the Line" (#17, 1956). At Sun, he was also part of an impromptu gospel singalong with labelmates Elvis Presley, Carl Perkins and Jerry Lee Lewis that was widely bootlegged as *The Million Dollar Quartet*.

Cash moved near Ventura, California, in 1958, signed with Columbia and began a nine-year period of alcohol and drug abuse. He churned out records, among them "Ring of Fire" (#1 pop, #1 C&W, 1963), written by June Carter of the Carter Family and Merle Kilgore. By then, he had left his family and moved to New York's Greenwich Village. Late in 1965, Cash was arrested by Customs officials for trying to smuggle amphetamines in his guitar case across the Mexican border. He got a suspended sentence and was fined. After a serious auto accident and a near fatal overdose, his wife divorced him. By then Cash had moved to Nashville, where he became friends with Waylon Jennings. Together they spent what both have described as a drug-crazed year and a half.

But in Nashville, Cash began a liaison with June Carter, who helped him get rid of his drug habit by 1967 and reconverted him to fundamentalist Christianity. By the time Cash and Carter married in early 1968, they had been working together regularly. They had hit duets with "Jackson" (#2 C&W, 1967) and a version of Tim Hardin's "If I Were a Carpenter" (#2 C&W, 1970).

Cash's 1968 live album, *At Folsom Prison,* became a million-seller in 1968. Bob Dylan invited him to sing a duet ("Girl from the North Country") and write liner notes for *Nashville Skyline,* and Dylan appeared in the first segment of ABC-TV's "The Johnny Cash Show" in June 1969. The series lasted two years. Cash had a 1969 hit with Shel Silverstein's "A Boy Named Sue" (#1), recorded live at San Quentin.

In 1970, Cash performed at the Nixon White House. He and June Carter traveled to Israel in 1971 to make a documentary, *Gospel Road.* Cash continued to tour and make hits through the Seventies, including "A Thing Called Love" (#2 C&W, 1972) and "One Piece at a Time" (#1 C&W, 1976). He has won six Grammy Awards and is a member of the Nashville Songwriters' Hall of Fame, with over 400 songs to his credit. Cash has been active in benefit work, particularly for prisoners, Native American rights, and evangelist Billy Graham's organization.

Cash has also taken his place in the Carter Family music dynasty. His daughter by his first wife, Rosanne Cash, has emerged as a country hitmaker after starting out as a backup singer for Cash's road show; she is married to songwriter Rodney Crowell. June Carter's daughter by a previous marriage, Carlene Carter, also has a solo career and is married to Nick Lowe, who produced Johnny Cash's 1980 *Rockabilly Blues.* Cash and fellow surviving Million Dollar Quartet members Carl Perkins and Jerry Lee Lewis regrouped in 1982, five years after Elvis Presley's death, to record *The Survivors.*

ROSANNE CASH
Born May 24, 1955, Memphis
1980—*Right or Wrong* (Columbia)   **1981**—*Seven Year Ache*   **1982**—*Somewhere in the Stars.*

Daughter of country music star Johnny Cash and Vivian Liberto, and spouse since 1979 of singer/songwriter Rodney Crowell, Rosanne Cash blends Nashville and California country rock. Born in Memphis, Cash was raised in Ventura, California, where her mother moved after divorcing Cash in 1966. The day after graduating from high school, she joined her father's touring revue as a wardrobe assistant and later became a backup singer. After three years with the Johnny Cash show, she moved to London in 1976, returning home in 1977 to attend Vanderbilt University in Nashville. Then she moved to Hollywood and enrolled in the Lee Strasberg Theater Institute the next year. She took time off in January 1978 to record a demo (produced by Crowell), which attracted the attention of the German-based Ariola label. She went to Munich to record an album, and although it was never released in the U.S. it persuaded the Nashville branch of Columbia Records to sign her. For a while she played with Crowell's band, the Cherry Bombs, before Columbia released her debut U.S. album, *Right or Wrong,* which sold surprisingly well despite her inability to tour; she was pregnant. Her 1981 followup, *Seven Year Ache,* drew critical raves, solid sales, and yielded a country hit with the title tune.

DAVID CASSIDY
Born April 12, 1950, New York City or Englewood, New Jersey
N.A.—*David Cassidy*   **1972**—*Cherish* (Bell)   **1974**—*Cassidy Live*   **1975**—*The Higher They Climb* (RCA)   **1976**—*Home Is Where the Heart Is.*

Early-Seventies teen idol David Cassidy is the son of actor Jack Cassidy and actress Evelyn Ward. He moved to Hollywood in 1957 with his mother when his parents divorced. (His father then married actress Shirley Jones, who played Cassidy's mother in "The Partridge Family.") During his teens, Cassidy was expelled from two public schools before completing high school at the private Rexford School. He played guitar and drums, wrote songs and acted with the Los Angeles Theater Group. He appeared in Allan Sherman's Broadway production *Fig Leaves Are Falling*, and on television episodes of "Bonanza" and "Marcus Welby, M.D."

In fall 1970, he began a three-year run as Keith Partridge on the weekly TV series "The Partridge Family" (inspired by the Cowsills). The Partridge Family's premiere single, "I Think I Love You" (released before the TV series debuted), sold nearly six million copies. Several hits followed. Cassidy received royalties from the sales of Partridge Family coloring books, lunch boxes, dolls, comic books, postcards, clothes, books, records and the show itself.

His solo recording career began in 1971 with a remake of the Association's "Cherish." His several world tours inspired mass hysteria; Cassidy began to tone down the teen idol role after a 14-year-old fan named Bernadette Wheeler suffered a fatal heart attack at a London show in May 1974. That year, he quit the TV series. He signed a long-term contract with RCA in February 1975.

Cassidy's subsequent efforts did little to establish credibility with more mature fans. He later returned to TV with his own dramatic cop series. In 1976, Cassidy and Mick Ronson cut a single entitled "Gettin' It On in the Streets" and were supposed to record an album and form a band. None of it ever came to pass. In 1982, he was reportedly recording a country-influenced album in Nashville.

SHAUN CASSIDY

Born September 27, 1958, Hollywood
1977—*Shaun Cassidy* (Warner Bros./Curb) *Born Late* 1978—*Under Wraps* 1979—*Room Service; That's Rock 'n' Roll—Shaun Cassidy Live* 1980—*Wasp.*

Following in the footsteps of his half-brother David Cassidy, Shaun Cassidy was a teen idol in the late Seventies. The son of actor Jack Cassidy and actress Shirley Jones, he grew up in Beverly Hills and formed his first rock band at age 11, just after he began writing his own songs. Signed by Mike Curb to the Warner/Curb label in 1975, Cassidy had his first success in Europe, where his photos saturated the teen magazines. His debut single—"Morning Girl," released in January 1976—went Top Twenty in most of Europe. His second single, a cover of Eric Carmen's "That's Rock 'n' Roll," expanded his appeal to Australia, and went gold in the U.S. in a later release.

He starred in "The Hardy Boys" TV series from 1977 to 1978. His first U.S. single, a cover of the Crystals' 1963 hit "Da Doo Ron Ron," was released in May 1977 and went gold; his simultaneously released debut album, *Shaun Cassidy*, went platinum. Success followed him into the early Eighties with singles ("Hey Deanie," his own "Holi-

day") and with platinum albums and television work (a made-for-TV movie, *Like Normal People*, in 1979; the 1980 series "Breaking Away"). Like brother David before him, Shaun tried with little success to make the transition to a more serious rock style; his 1980 *Wasp* was produced by Todd Rundgren and featured versions of songs by David Bowie, Ian Hunter, Peter Townshend (the Who) and David Byrne (Talking Heads).

JIMMY CASTOR

Born June 22, 1943, New York City
N.A.—*Hey LeRoy* (Smash) 1973—*Dimension 3* (RCA) 1974—*The Everything Man* (Atlantic) 1975—*Super Sound* (Atco) *Butt of Course* 1976—*E Man Groovin'.*

Singer/songwriter/saxophonist Jimmy Castor is best known for "Troglodyte (Cave Man)," a 1972 funk novelty hit, but his career stretches back to the Fifties. He assembled his first group, Jimmy Castor and the Juniors (Johnny Williams, Orton Graves, Al Casey, Jr.), around 1955. Their "I Promise to Remember" (a Castor original) was a modest New York hit in 1956, but later that year Frankie Lymon and the Teenagers' cover version was a national hit. When Lymon left the Teenagers for a solo career in 1957, Castor was one of several singers who took his place fronting the group. He also sang with the Teenchords.

After graduating from New York's High School of Music and Art, Castor dropped out of the music business to study accounting at City College of New York. He reentered the music business in 1962, when he played the sax on Dave "Baby" Cortez's Top Ten hit, "Rinky Dink." He then recorded solo for the Winley, Clown, Jet-Set and Decca labels before forming the Jimmy Castor Bunch (percussionist Leonard Fridie, Jr., bassist Douglas Gibson, guitarist Harry Jensen, drummer Robert Manigault and keyboardist Gerry Thomas) in the mid-Sixties. The Bunch recorded for Compass and Capitol before "Hey, Leroy, Your Mama's Callin' You" (#31 pop, 1967; #16 R&B, 1966) hit on Smash. "Troglodyte" (RCA) hit #4 on the R&B charts and #6 on the pop charts in 1972. Castor left RCA for Atlantic and returned to the Top Twenty in 1975 with a sequel to "Troglodyte," "The Bertha Butt Boogie" (#16 pop, #22 R&B). His other hits on Atlantic were "Potential" (#25 R&B, 1975), "King Kong, Part 1" (#23 R&B, 1975) and "Space Age" (#28 R&B, 1977). By 1980, he was recording for Long Distance Records.

CERRONE

Born 1952, St. Michel, France
1976—*Love in C Minor* (Cotillion) 1977—*Cerrone's Paradise; Cerrone 3: Supernature* 1978—*Cerrone IV: The Golden Touch; Brigade Mondaine* (Malligator) 1979—*Cerrone V: Angelina* (Atlantic) 1982—*Back Track* (Pavillion).

Composer/producer/drummer Jean-Marc Cerrone was one of the principal architects of the late-Seventies synthesizer-dominated "Euro-disco" sound. After training to be a hairdresser, he began his musical career in the early Seventies working as a session drummer until he was able to open a chain of record stores in the suburbs of Paris. In 1976, he went to London, where he tried and failed to get a recording contract. He financed the production of his first album himself, recording *Love in C Minor* with English session musicians and singers Stephanie de Sykes and Madeline Bell. The album was rejected by every major French company, so Cerrone formed his own Malligator label and marketed it himself. As soon as it was given disco play in France, a commercial demand arose and the album was on the way to gold sales in France. The LP-side-long title track was edited to single-side length, and as such became a stateside disco hit (#36 pop, #29 R&B, 1977).

After that, Cerrone had little impact in this country. In Europe, however, he was a major star of the late Seventies, selling over ten million records. He continues to base his operations in France, where in 1982 he was completing work on a movie he had written, directed, scored and produced.

CHAD AND JEREMY

Formed circa 1963, London
Chad Stuart (b. Dec. 10, circa 1945, Eng.), voc., gtr., piano, sitar, tamboura, tablas, banjo, flute; Jeremy Clyde (b. Mar. 22, circa 1945, Eng.), voc., gtr.
N.A.—*The Ark* (Columbia) *Before and After* **1966**—*The Best of Chad and Jeremy* (Capitol) **1967**—*Of Cabbages and Kings* (Columbia) *Yesterday's Gone* (World Artists).

Chad and Jeremy's soft-rock hits kept them on the charts from 1964 through 1966. Sons of affluent British families, both were well educated (Eton, the Sorbonne). They met while studying at the Central School of Drama in London, where they began singing folk-based material. In 1964, one of their first singles, "Yesterday's Gone," went to #21 in the U.S.

The pair soon moved to Hollywood and began to rival Peter and Gordon as the world's top folk-rock duo. Chart hits like "A Summer Song" (#7, 1964) and "Distant Shores" (#30, 1966) combined with frequent television appearances ("Hullabaloo," "The Hollywood Palace") kept them in the public eye. They broke up in late 1966, when Jeremy departed to act in a London stage musical.

Clubs

Clubs have served as incubators for various rock styles, just as they have for jazz. They are social centers and fashion laboratories, and a good club or two can define a whole scene.

In the Fifties, Elvis Presley used to visit blues clubs on Beale Street in Memphis, where he learned some of his phrasing and his moves. The Sixties folk-music revival germinated at the Cambridge, Massachusetts, Club 47 (with Tom Rush and the Jim Kweskin Jug Band) and in New York's Greenwich Village, where Bob Dylan, Phil Ochs, Eric Andersen and others traded ideas at Gerde's Folk City, the Gaslight and Cafe Wha?

Swinging London in the early Sixties harbored numerous blues and R&B clubs; countless bands grew out of jams at the Marquee and the Crawdaddy Club, including the Rolling Stones, the Yardbirds, John Mayall's Bluesbreakers, Chicken Shack and Ten Years After.

The late Sixties saw the first wave of high-fashion discotheques, with multimedia environments at the Electric Circus and the Peppermint Lounge, while major rock acts moved into theaters like the Fillmores East and West (and black performers continued to play at the Apollo Theater).

In the late Sixties in Los Angeles, self-conscious singer/songwriters like Joni Mitchell, Neil Young and, in the Seventies, Karla Bonoff emerged from Hoot Night at the Troubadour, a sort of open audition.

New York in the mid-Seventies boasted the ratty Bowery bar CBGB & OMFUG (Country, Bluegrass, Blues and Other Music for Urban Gourmets), which hosted the burgeoning punk rock of the Ramones, the Talking Heads, Patti Smith and Television. (Los Angeles' later punk scene grew out of the Masque, a club in the basement of a pornography theater, where X and other bands first played.) At the same time, New York was the center of disco, with gay clubs like the Paradise Garage and tonier joints like Studio 54 turning records into underground hits. Rock disco, usually featuring live known-only-to-cognoscenti acts, back to back with recorded music, premiered at New York's Hurrah.

A modern, up-to-the-minute rock club is now often equipped with video projectors, multiple turntables for disco mixing, strobe lights and a sound system worthy of a good live band. Drinks are generally overpriced; some things never change.

The two later regrouped and recorded *Of Cabbages and Kings*, one of the first "concept albums," and *The Ark*. They ended their partnership in November 1967. Thereafter, Clyde resumed his acting career, and Stuart, after a try as a duet with his wife, Jill, worked as a musical-comedy composer.

CHAIRMEN OF THE BOARD
Formed 1969
General Norman Johnson (b. May 23, 1943), voc.; Danny Woods (b. Apr. 10, 1944), voc.; Harrison Kennedy (b. Ontario, Can.), voc.; Eddie Custis, voc. 1973—*Greatest Hits* (Invictus)   (current lineup: − Kennedy; − Custis; + Ken Knox [b. Dec. 15, 1951], voc.).

The Chairmen of the Board is a soul vocal group whose biggest hit was the Holland/Dozier/Holland–produced "Give Me Just a Little More Time" (#3, 1970). The group's leader and main songwriter, General Norman Johnson, grew up in Norfolk, Virginia, where he sang in church choirs as a child. By age 12, he had formed his first group, the Humdingers. During his senior year of high school (1961), Johnson and his group, the Showmen, recorded his salute to rock & roll, "It Will Stand," for Minit Records.

After several more singles for Minit and later Swan, Johnson left the group to sign with ex-Motown producers Holland/Dozier/Holland's Invictus label. There the Chairmen of the Board was formed, with Johnson; another Showman, Danny Woods; Harrison Kennedy of the Canadian group Stoned Soul Children; and Eddie Custis, an alumnus of Lee Andrews and the Hearts and Huey Smith and the Clowns. Their debut single, "Give Me Just a Little More Time," was followed by several minor hits and "Pay to the Piper" (#13) in 1970. They briefly disbanded the next year but regrouped in 1972. They continue to tour and have had local hits in the Southeast.

Several of Johnson's songs have been hits for other performers, including Honey Cone ("Want Ads," "Stick Up," "One Monkey Don't Stop No Show"), Freda Payne ("Bring the Boys Home") and 1968 Grammy Award winner Clarence Carter ("Patches").

THE CHAMBERS BROTHERS
Formed circa 1961, Los Angeles
George E. Chambers (b. Sep. 26, 1931, Flora, Miss.), voc., bass; Willie Chambers (b. Mar. 3, 1938, Miss.), voc., gtr.; Lester Chambers (b. Apr. 13, 1940, Miss.), voc., harmonica; Joe Chambers (b. Aug. 24, 1942, Scott County, Miss.), voc., gtr.
1965—(+ Brian Keenan [b. Jan. 28, circa 1944, N.Y.C.], drums) *People Get Ready* (Vault)   1966—*Chambers Brothers Now*   1968—*Shout!; The Time Has Come* (Columbia)   *A New Time, a New Day*   1969—*Love,*

Peace and Happiness   1970—*Chambers Brothers Live at Fillmore East;   Feelin' the Blues* (Vault)   1971—*A New Generation* (Columbia)   1972—*Oh My God!*   1974—*Unbonded* (Avco)   1975—*Right Move.*

Black gospel/funk/psychedelic innovators, the Chambers Brothers had an enthusiastic following in the late Sixties. The four brothers grew up in a poverty-stricken Mississippi sharecropping family and first sang together at the Mount Calvary Baptist Church in Lee County. George, the eldest, was drafted into the Army in 1952. Once discharged, he gravitated to south Los Angeles and was eventually joined by his brothers. They began performing around Southern California as a gospel and folk quartet in 1961.

After their first New York dates in 1965, they became an interracial group with the addition of drummer Brian Keenan, and moved toward rock. They attracted national attention at the 1965 Newport Folk Festival, and worked both the psychedelic ballrooms (the Fillmores, Electric Circus) and soul venues like New York's Apollo Theater. They signed with Columbia in 1967, and the title track from their first album, "Time Has Come Today," became a major hit (#11, 1968). They charted with several more singles, including "I Can't Turn You Loose" (#37, 1968), and LPs (*A New Time, a New Day* and *Love, Peace and Happiness*) over the next few years.

By the start of the Seventies, they had toured Europe twice and had played many domestic rock festivals. The original group broke up in early 1972, with drummer Keenan joining Genya Ravan's band. The Chambers Brothers reunited in 1974 for an album called *Unbonded* on Avco Records. They continue an on-again, off-again career. In 1980, they supported Maria Muldaur on her album for Takoma Records.

THE CHAMPS
Formed 1957, Los Angeles
Original personnel: Dave Burgess (b. Lancaster, Calif.), gtr.; Dale Norris (b. Springfield, Mass.), gtr.; Chuck Rio (b. Rankin, Tex.), sax; Gen Alden (b. Cisco, Tex.), drums; Bobby Morris (b. Tulsa, Okla.), bass. 1960—*Everybody's Rockin'* (Challenge).

The Champs were West Coast sessionmen whose first single, the instrumental "Tequila" (written by Rio), stayed on the charts 19 weeks, reached #1, eventually sold more than six million worldwide and won a Grammy Award for the best R&B record of 1958. Subsequent hits—"Too Much Tequila" (#30, 1960), "Limbo Rock" (#40, 1962) and "Tequila Twist" (#99, 1962)—failed to match the success of "Tequila." Over the years, the group underwent numerous personnel changes, including a brief membership by guitarist/vocalist Delaney Bramlett (later of Delaney and Bonnie), before disbanding in 1965. Two other ex-Champs, Jimmy Seals and Dash Crofts, went on to form the Dawnbreakers before they reemerged in 1970 as Seals and Crofts.

JAMES CHANCE

Born James Siegfried, 1953, Milwaukee
1978—*No New York* (Antilles) 1979—*Buy Contortions* (Ze) *Grutzi Elvis; Off-White* 1980—*Live Aux Bains Douches* (Invisible) 1981—*Second Chance* (Ze) *Live in New York* (Reachout) 1982—*Sax Maniac* (Skull).

James Chance's music is an edgy, atonal fusion incorporating funk, free-form jazz and punk aggression. His "punk funk" has been a pervasive influence in New York City dance music, and former bandmates show up in many New York groups.

Growing up in suburban Milwaukee, Siegfried started studying the piano in the first grade. In high school, he became interested in jazz and at age 19 took up the alto sax. He attended the Wisconsin Conservatory of Music but dropped out less than a semester short of receiving his degree. He went to New York in 1976 and studied for a short time with avant-garde saxophonist David Murray.

In 1977, Chance formed the original Contortions with organist Adele Bertei, guitarist Jody Harris, bassist George Scott III, slide guitarist Pat Place and drummer Don Christensen. Like Captain Beefheart, he planned and demonstrated to his musicians each of the instrumental parts of every song. Contortions concerts—the first of which were given in the fall of 1977—could be violent experiences: Chance was notorious for diving from the stage into spectators.

The first Contortions recordings were the four tracks they contributed to the Brian Eno–produced *No New York* anthology. In 1979, Chance dissolved the Contortions and regrouped as James White and the Blacks. At the recording of *Off-White,* the Blacks included all the original Contortions except Bertei, who performed with them as a guest, along with Lydia Lunch and Robert Quine. That group was also dissolved; Bertei formed the Bloods and Place the Bush Tetras, while Scott joined Lunch in Eight-Eyed Spy, later reuniting with Harris and Christensen in the Raybeats. Chance collaborated with Arto Lindsay (DNA, Lounge Lizards), Bradley Field (Teenage Jesus and the Jerks) and George Scott on a Diego Cortez film soundtrack, *Grutzi Elvis;* and he continued to perform in New York, backed by pickup musicians. *Second Chance* was compiled from *Buy* and *Off.*

In May 1980, Chance went to Paris, and from there toured Western Europe with pickup musicians. The reception and respect accorded him far exceeded what he received in America, and he made Paris his home. He returns periodically to New York, where he plays with musicians like trombonist Joseph Bowie (of the Black Arts Group, later founder of Defunkt), reedman Henry Threadgill (of the experimental jazz group Air) and guitarists Bern Nix (Ornette Coleman) and Tomas Doncker (the Dance).

GENE CHANDLER

Born Eugene Dixon, July 6, 1940
1962—*Duke of Earl* (Vee Jay) 1964—*Just Be True* (Constellation) Greatest Hits 1965—*Live! On Stage* 1966—*The Duke of Soul* (Checker) 1967—*The Girl Don't Care* (Brunswick) 1968—*There Was a Time* 1969—*The Two Sides of Gene Chandler* 1970—*The Gene Chandler Situation* (Mercury) 1971—*One and One* (with Jerry Butler) 1978—*Get Down* (Chi-Sound) 1979—*When You're #1* 1981—*Here's to Love* 1982—*I'll Make the Living If You Make the Loving Worthwhile.*

A fixture in Chicago soul for over twenty years, balladeer Gene Chandler was raised on the tough South Side and sang doo-wop in streetcorner groups before joining the Army in 1957. After his discharge in 1960 he joined Chicago's Dukays, who had a minor hit late in 1961 with "The Girl Is a Devil." A&R man Carl Davis, who had discovered the Dukays, renamed Eugene Dixon after Davis' favorite actor, Jeff Chandler, and produced his solo debut, a backward glance at doo-wop style called "Duke of Earl" (#1 pop, #1 R&B, 1962). The single sold a million copies within a month of its November 1961 release.

Chandler's string of hits lasted until the early Seventies. The best of them were written and arranged by Curtis Mayfield, including "Just Be True" (#19, 1964), "You Can't Hurt Me No More" (#92, 1965), "Nothing Can Stop Me" (#18, 1965) and "Good Times" (#92, 1965). After their partnership ended, Chandler did not have a Top Sixty hit for over a decade, except for his 1968 collaboration with Barbara Acklin, "From the Teacher to the Preacher" (#57).

Chandler gave up touring to concentrate on songwriting and production, bought Bamboo Records and moved it to Chicago. There he produced hits, including Mel and Tim's 1969 "Backfield in Motion," and continued to record throughout the Seventies, including a soul hit with Jerry Butler. He also founded Mr. Chand Records and worked for A&M as a producer from 1974 to 1977. In 1976 Chandler was convicted of selling 388 grams of heroin; he served a four-month sentence. A #53 disco hit, "Get Down," returned Chandler to the pop charts in 1979. Since that year, he has worked as executive vice-president of Chi-Sound Records.

THE CHANTELS

Formed 1956, New York City
Arlene Smith, voc.; Lois Harris, voc.; Sonia Goring, voc.; Jackie Landry, voc.; Rene Minus, voc.
N.A.—*The Chantels* (End) *The Chantels Sing Their Favorites* (Forum) 1959—(– Smith).

The Chantels were one of the first and most popular of the girl groups. The five girls (all between 13 and 16) were singing backstage at a Frankie Lymon concert when Richard Barrett, a member of the Valentines, heard them. Led by Arlene Smith, the group was named after Saint Francis de Chantelle School, the rival school of their own alma mater, Saint Anthony of Padua. Barrett produced their first singles ("He's Gone," "The Plea"), both Smith compositions that failed to hit. However, in 1958 the Chantels had their biggest success with a Barrett song, "Maybe" (#15), which sold over a million copies. After two flop singles, they moved to Carlton Records, but by then Smith had quit to pursue a solo career, and the following Chantels records were often recorded using other singers. Nonetheless, "Look into My Eyes" (#14, 1961) and "Well I Told You" (#29, 1961) were hits before the group disbanded. Smith later attended the Juilliard School.

HARRY CHAPIN

Born December 7, 1942, New York City; died July 16, 1981, Jericho, New York
1972—*Heads and Tales* (Elektra)   *Sniper and Other Love Songs*   **1973**—*Short Stories*   **1974**—*Verities and Balderdash*   **1975**—*Portrait Gallery*   **1976**—*On the Road to Kingdom Come;   Harry Chapin's Greatest Stories Live*   **1977**—*Dance Band on the Titanic* **1978**—*Living Room Suite*   **1979**—*Legends of the Lost and Found*   **1980**—*Sequel* (Boardwalk).

After establishing his popularity in the early Seventies with folk-rock story songs, Harry Chapin devoted his efforts to various humanitarian projects, notably the World Hunger Year. The son of a jazz drummer, Chapin sang in the Brooklyn Heights Boys Choir, and in his teens he played guitar, banjo and trumpet in a band with his brothers. After a stint at the Air Force Academy, Chapin spent a semester at Cornell University.

He and his brothers began working in Greenwich Village clubs and making documentary films. (A documentary he made with Jim Jacobs in the late Sixties called *Legendary Champions* was nominated for an Academy Award.) His brothers left the country in 1964 to escape the draft, and Chapin continued in filmmaking.

He formed his own band, including a cello player, in 1971. Chapin's debut album, *Heads and Tales*, was released in February 1972 and stayed on the charts for over half a year, peaking at #60, when "Taxi" became a Top Twenty single. His 1973 album, *Short Stories*, produced another solid hit with "W.O.L.D." (#36). *Verities and Balderdash* became Chapin's first gold album in 1974 on the strength of his #1 "Cat's in the Cradle." His subsequent albums sold respectably through the end of the Seventies.

Chapin's later backup band included his brother Steve (piano and vocals), who also produced Harry's 1977 LP *Dance Band on the Titanic*. Another Chapin brother, Tom, has carried on a career of his own in recent years. Besides frequent appearances with Harry, Tom released an album on Fantasy Records in 1976 and hosted the children's television series "Make a Wish" (for which Harry wrote the music) for five years.

Harry Chapin averaged more than 200 concerts per year between 1972 and 1980, more than half of them for various charity organizations, for which he raised literally millions of dollars. He was also an active lobbyist for various causes and a benefactor of Long Island arts organizations. He was killed in a car crash on the Long Island Expressway while driving to a benefit performance.

MARSHALL CHAPMAN

Born January 7, 1949, Spartanburg, South Carolina
1977—*Me, I'm Feeling Free* (Epic)   **1978**—*Jaded Virgin* **1979**—*Marshall*   **1982**—*Take It on Home* (Rounder).

Singer/songwriter/guitarist Marshall Chapman, of an aristocratic Southern family, was schooled at Nashville's Vanderbilt University, where she studied French and fine arts and started jamming with country, blues and rock musicians. Around 1973, after living in France and Boston, she moved back to Nashville. There she waited tables and wrote songs, waiting for the opportunity to sing in local bars. She won the admiration of country stars like Tompall Glaser, Linda Hargrove, Jessi Colter and Waylon Jennings.

In 1976, she went to Los Angeles, where she was signed by Columbia. Her debut album consisted predominantly of country-flavored songs. "Somewhere South of Macon" got airplay on country stations before it was decided that some of its lines were suggestive. Other songs—most often "A Woman's Heart (Is a Handy Place to Be)"—were covered by performers like Colter, Crystal Gayle, Glaser, Olivia Newton-John and the Earl Scruggs Revue. In concert, however, she fronted a rock & roll trio and drew rock crowds.

Despite critical praise, Chapman's records did not sell, and once her third one was released, Epic dropped her. She took the next year off from music, but began writing songs again in 1981.

THE CHARLATANS

Formed 1965, San Francisco
George Hunter, voc.; Mike Wilhelm, gtr.; Richard Olson, bass; Michael Ferguson, piano; Dan Hicks (b. Dec. 9, 1941, Little Rock, Ark.), drums.
1967—(− Ferguson; + Patrick Gogerty, piano; + Terry Wilson, drums; Hicks switched to gtr.)   **1968**—(− Hicks; − Hunter; − Gogerty; + Darrel DeVore, piano)   **1969**—*The Charlatans* (Philips).

As the original Haight-Ashbury band, the Charlatans remained true to the area's bohemian ethic. They were an amateur group, conceived by draftsman/designer George Hunter, whose main talent was a sense of rock's visual possibilities. Outfitted in Victorian and Old West costumes, they first played for three months at the Red Dog Saloon in Virginia City, Nevada, in the summer of 1965, before returning to the Haight. Soon they were sharing bills with the Jefferson Airplane and the Grateful Dead (then called the Warlocks) at the Fillmore, Avalon and other Bay Area venues.

The Charlatans' repertoire remained essentially unchanged throughout their brief career: folk, blues, ballads and jug-band tunes. MGM signed them, then sold the group to Kama Sutra. They recorded one unreleased album for that label (Kama Sutra did release an unsuccessful single over the group's objections). Reduced to a quartet (Hunter departed in early 1968, as did Dan Hicks to form his Hot Licks), the Charlatans finally released their first album in 1969, on Philips Records. They disbanded soon afterwards.

BOBBY CHARLES

Born 1938, Louisiana
1972—*Bobby Charles* (Bearsville).

Bobby Charles was discovered by Leonard Chess during a mid-Fifties talent search. He recorded several sides in New Orleans that garnered some attention when Chess released them in the late Fifties. Their impact with other artists was more substantial. Several of the songs ("See You Later Alligator," "Walkin' to New Orleans," "I Don't Know Why I Love You but I Do") were covered by Bill Haley, Fats Domino and Clarence "Frogman" Henry.

Charles toured with the Platters, Little Richard, Chuck Berry and B. B. King before retiring from personal appearances in the early Sixties. Throughout the Sixties, he recorded for several labels and did promotional work for Chess Records. By the early Seventies, he was living in Woodstock, New York, where he was signed by Albert Grossman to Bearsville Records. His much-ballyhooed comeback album *Bobby Charles* included guest appearances by the Band, Dr. John and other notables; but despite an excellent single release—"Small Town Talk" (later covered by Rick Danko of the Band)—the LP stiffed and Charles was soon dropped. He made a rare live appearance at the Band's *Last Waltz* concert, Thanksgiving Day 1976. That same year, two of his compositions were covered on Joe Cocker's *Sting Ray* album.

RAY CHARLES

Born Ray Charles Robinson, September 23, 1930, Albany, Georgia
1957—*Ray Charles* (Atlantic) 1958—*The Great Ray Charles* 1959—*What'd I Say; Genius of Ray Charles* 1962—*Story, volume 1; Story, volume 2; Modern Sounds in Country and Western Music* (ABC) *Modern Sounds in Country and Western Music 2* 1963—*Story, volume 3* (Atlantic) *The Greatest Ray Charles* 1964—*Have a Smile with Me* (HMV) *Great Hits* (Atlantic) 1973—*Ray Charles Live* (Atlantic) 1977—*True to Life* 1983—*Wish You Were Here Tonight* (Columbia).

Singer/composer/pianist Ray Charles virtually invented soul music by bringing together the fervor of gospel, the secular lyrics and narratives of blues and country, the big-band arrangements of jazz, and rhythms and improvisational possibilities from all of them, making music that was both sophisticated and spontaneous.

He was raised in Greenville, Florida, and started playing piano before he was five; at six, he contracted glaucoma, which went untreated and eventually left him blind. He studied composition (writing music in Braille) and learned to play alto saxophone, clarinet, trumpet and organ while attending the St. Augustine School for the Deaf and the Blind from 1937 to 1945. His father died when he was ten, his mother five years later, and he left school to work in dance bands around Florida, dropping his last name to avoid confusion with boxer Sugar Ray Robinson. In 1947, with $600 worth of savings, he moved to Seattle and worked as a Nat "King" Cole–style crooner.

Charles made his first single, "Confession Blues," in Los Angeles and recorded for several independent West Coast labels until he scored a Top Ten R&B hit in 1951 with "Baby Let Me Hold Your Hand" and began a national tour with blues singer Lowell Fulson.

Late in 1953, he went to New Orleans and became pianist and arranger for Guitar Slim (Eddie Jones). Guitar Slim's "The Things That I Used to Do," arranged by Charles, sold a million copies, and when Charles returned to recording—leading and arranging for his own band—the earthier style carried over to his own work. Atlantic signed him in 1954, and he made a few conventional recordings in New York; he also assembled a band for labelmate Ruth Brown.

"I've Got a Woman," with a seven-piece band fronted by Charles's pounding gospel piano and a new raspy, exuberant vocal sound, became his first national hit (#2 R&B, 1955). Through the decade, he appeared regularly on the charts as he synthesized more and more styles and was nicknamed the "Genius." He recorded with Milt Jackson of the Modern Jazz Quartet, sang standards with strings and expanded his band to a full-scale revue, complete with horns and gospel-style backup singers, the Raelettes.

"What'd I Say" (#6 pop, #1 R&B, 1959), a wild blues/gospel/Latin mix, became Charles's first million-seller. In late 1959, he signed to ABC Records and moved into the

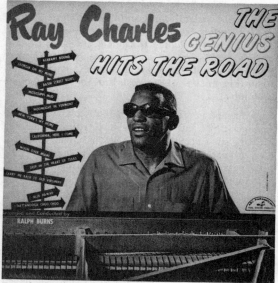

Ray Charles

pop market with "Georgia on My Mind" (#1, 1960) and "Hit the Road, Jack" (#1, 1961). *Modern Sounds in Country and Western* (1962), which included Charles's versions of songs by Hank Williams, Floyd Tillman and other country songwriters, sold over a million copies, as did its single, "I Can't Stop Loving You" (#1, 1962).

In 1965, Charles was arrested for possession of heroin, and revealed that he had been using it since he was 16. He cleaned up in a California sanatorium and spent a year away from performing. While his singing remained influential through the Sixties (especially on Steve Winwood and Joe Cocker) and he kept making hits—including Ashford and Simpson's "Let's Go Get Stoned" (#31, 1966)—his taste was moving away from rock, although he did appear on Aretha Franklin's *Live at Fillmore West* (1971).

His albums from the mid-Sixties onward have downplayed gospel and blues in favor of jazz standards, pop songs and show tunes, although his singing is still distinctive. Charles made custom label deals with ABC (Tangerine Records) and later Atlantic (Crossover), for whom he recorded an album a year. He appeared in the movie *The Blues Brothers* (1980) and continues to tour internationally. In 1982, he recorded another country album, *Wish You Were Here Tonight*.

CHASE
Formed 1970, Las Vegas
Bill Chase (b. 1935, Chicago; d. Aug. 9, 1974, Jackson, Minn.), trumpet; Alan Ware, trumpet; Jerry Van Blair, trumpet; Ted Piercefield, trumpet; Jay Burrid (b. Jay

Mitthauer), drums; Terry Richards, voc.; Angel South, gtr.; Dennis Johnson, bass.
1971—*Chase* (Epic) (− Burrid; − South) **1972**—*Ennea* (+ John Emma [b. 1952, Geneva, Ill.], gtr.; + Wallace Yohn [b. 1947, Scottsville, Ariz.], kybds.; + Walter Clark [b. 1949], drums) **1974**—*Pure Music* (entire group disbands and re-forms: Tom Gordon, drums; Dartanyan Brown, bass, voc.; Joe Morrissey, trumpet; Jay Sollenberger, trumpet; Jim Oatts, trumpet; Jim Peterik, voc.; Tom Gordon, drums) *Get It On.*

Inspired by the success of horn bands like Blood, Sweat and Tears and Chicago, big band trumpeter Bill Chase (who had worked with Woody Herman, Maynard Ferguson and Stan Kenton) assembled this jazz-rock group in 1970. Unlike other brass rock groups, Chase used four trumpets. Their debut album spawned the hit single "Get It On" (1971) and was voted the #1 LP in that year's *downbeat* readers' poll. The group toured internationally and released two more LPs and then disbanded. Chase had just reorganized an almost entirely new group and was on a comeback tour when the small airplane he was traveling in crashed near Jackson, Minnesota, killing him and three other band members (Walter Clark, John Emma, Wallace Yohn).

CHEAP TRICK
Formed 1974, Rockford, Illinois
Robin Zander (b. Jan. 23, 1952, Loves Park, Ill.), voc.; Tom Petersson (b. 1950, Rockford, Ill.), bass; Rick Nielsen (b. ca. 1946, Rockford, Ill.), gtr.; Bun E. Carlos (b. Brad Carlson, Rockford, Ill.), drums.
1977—*Cheap Trick* (Epic) *In Color* **1978**—*Heaven Tonight; Live at Budokan* **1979**—*Dream Police* **1980**—*All Shook Up* (− Petersson; + Pete Comita [b. Italy], bass) **1981**—(− Comita; + Jon Brant, bass) **1982**—*One on One.*

The aggressively marketed, hard-touring, self-caricaturing rock group Cheap Trick worked its way up to platinum sales with a blend of Beatles-style pop and a cartoonish stage act, which played Rick Nielsen's exaggerated mugging and guitar gymnastics against Robin Zander's good looks.

In 1961, Nielsen, then in his teens, began playing locally in Rockford, Illinois, utilizing his ever-increasing collection of rare and valuable guitars (now numbering nearly 100, estimated at $100,000 in value). His band, the Phaetons, became the Boyz, then the Grim Reapers and finally Fuse in 1967, with the addition of bassist Tom Petersson. One album for Epic in early 1969 was generally ignored. Frustrated, Fuse, which by then included college dropout Bun E. Carlos on drums, moved to Philadelphia in 1971. As Sick Man of Europe, they enlisted ex-Nazz vocalist Robert "Stewkey" Antoni, but the group soon disbanded.

After a year in Europe, Nielsen and Petersson returned to Rockford, reunited with Carlos, and a few months later asked folkie vocalist Zander to join the group they named Cheap Trick. Midwestern booking agent (and former member of one of Steve Miller's high school bands) Ken Adamany became their manager. Adamany encouraged them to develop their stage show, and Cheap Trick toured incessantly over the next several years, playing an average of 250 shows a year, opening for Kiss, the Kinks, Santana, Boston and others.

Cheap Trick's early releases were only moderately successful in the U.S.; their 1977 debut sold 150,000 copies, *In Color* and *Heaven Tonight* barely reached the Top Forty. In Japan, however, all three had gone gold, and their initial tour there in early 1978 was met with hysteria reminiscent of Beatlemania. During that visit, they recorded *Live at Budokan,* which went platinum in the States largely on the strength of their single "I Want You to Want Me" (#7, 1979). Their subsequent hit singles included "Dream Police" (#26, 1979).

By the time *Dream Police* was released in the fall of 1979, they were headlining at arena and stadium concerts. *All Shook Up* went gold in late 1980. The band contributed "Everything Works If You Let It" to the *Roadie* soundtrack that year, and Nielsen, Zander and Carlos played at John Lennon and Yoko Ono's recording sessions for *Double Fantasy.* Since they are not credited, it is unclear whether those tracks have been or will be released.

As the Eighties began, the group's activities slowed considerably. In 1981, Epic rejected an LP, and after a flurry of lawsuits and countersuits, the group began recording *One on One.* Original bassist Petersson departed in 1980 to form a group with his wife, Dagmar, as vocalist. He recorded an LP in 1982, but Epic refused to release it. Pete Comita replaced him, but was himself replaced by Jon Brant before the recording of *One on One,* which included two minor hits, "If You Want My Love" and "She's Tight."

CHUBBY CHECKER

Born Ernest Evans, October 3, 1941, Philadelphia
1962—*Twist* (Columbia) *Let's Twist Again* (Parkway) *Twistin' around the World* **1963**—*All the Hits* **1982**—*The Change Has Come* (MCA).

Although Chubby Checker didn't invent the Twist, the dance craze was his ticket to stardom. Written and recorded as a B side by R&B singer Hank Ballard, Checker's version of "The Twist" went to #1 in September 1960, stayed on the charts for four months, dropped off and returned to #1 early in 1962.

The young Ernest Evans worked as a chicken plucker in a local poultry shop while in high school. On the job he would frequently entertain customers by singing songs and telling jokes. Evans' boss put him in touch with Philly's Cameo-Parkway label, with whom he signed a contract in 1959. Shortly thereafter, he became "Chubby Checker" (in emulation of the similarly built Fats Domino). His first single, "The Class," released in the summer of 1959, featured Checker doing vocal impersonations, but it was only a minor hit and subsequent singles were even less successful.

Then "The Twist" hit. After it, Checker promoted several less successful dance crazes: the Hucklebuck, the Fly, the Pony, the Limbo. His Top Ten hits included "Pony Time" (#1, 1961), "Let's Twist Again" (#8, 1961), "The Fly" (#7, 1961), "Slow Twistin'" (#3, 1962), "Limbo Rock" (#2, 1962) and "Popeye the Hitchhiker" (#10, 1962). In December 1963, Checker married Dutch-born Catharina Lodders, who had been named Miss World the year before. His hits ended in 1965, and he became a mainstay on the nightclub circuit. He recorded for Buddah in 1969 and for Chalmac in 1971, with regular appearances as part of rock revival shows and a featured spot in the film *Let the Good Times Roll.* His recent recorded work has moved toward disco with some success for MCA in the early Eighties.

CLIFTON CHENIER

Born June 25, 1925, Opelousas, Louisiana
1965—*Louisiana Blues and Zydeco* (Arhoolie) **1966**—*Bon Ton Roulet* **1967**—*Black Snake Blues* **1970**—*King of the Bayous* **1972**—*Live* **1974**—*Out West* **1976**—*Bogalusa Boogie* **1977**—*And His Red Hot Louisiana Band; Cajun Swamp Music Live* (Tomato) **1980**—*Classic Clifton* (Arhoolie) **1982**—*I'm Here!* (Alligator).

Clifton Chenier is the king of zydeco music, the rousing black Cajun party music that mixes blues, French folk tunes, country, New Orleans R&B and rock & roll. Wearing a jeweled crown and flashing his gold tooth onstage, Chenier pumps his chrome-studded accordion and sings in French patois; he also plays harmonica, piano and organ.

He grew up as a sugar cane cutter and weekend musician in such places as New Iberia, Louisiana, where he met his wife, Margaret, in 1945. In 1946, he followed his brother Cleveland to Lake Charles, Louisiana, for a job at an oil refinery, where he worked until 1954. The brothers began playing at parties as a duet, with Clifton on accordion and Cleveland on "rub board," a piece of corrugated steel played with beer-can openers like a washboard. In 1954, Chenier made his first recordings at radio station KAOK in Lake Charles for Elko Records, and a year later recorded his more R&B-style material at Specialty, including "Eh 'Tite Fille" and "Boppin' the Rock."

Chenier became a full-time musician, performed on both coasts and in 1958 moved to Houston. In the early

Sixties, he began to record for the folk-oriented Arhoolie label, and had a number of regional Gulf Coast hits, including "Louisiana Blues" and "Black Gal." He appeared in 1966 at the Berkeley Blues Festival, and continues to appear regularly on the West Coast and more infrequently in the East. He was featured in the 1974 documentary *Hot Pepper* by Les Blank.

CHER (see Sonny and Cher)

CHIC
Formed 1976, Bronx, New York
Bernard Edwards (b. Oct. 31, 1952), bass; Nile Rodgers (b. Sep. 19, 1952), gtr.; Norma Jean Wright, voc.; Tony Thompson, drums; Alfa Anderson (b. Sep. 7, 1946), voc.
1977—*Chic* (Atlantic) (− Wright; + Luci Martin [b. Jan. 10, 1955], voc.) **1978**—*C'est Chic* **1979**—*Risqué; Greatest Hits* **1980**—*Real People* **1981**—*Take It Off* **1982**—*Tongue in Chic.*

Boasting a series of gold and platinum hit singles that began with 1977's #1 "Dance, Dance, Dance (Yowsah, Yowsah, Yowsah)," Chic's stripped-down, not-quite-mechanical groove made them the premier black disco group of the late Seventies. In addition, the group's cofounders, Nile Rodgers and Bernard Edwards, have produced, written or played on dance records by many other performers and become two of the most influential contemporary black writers and producers.

Edwards and Rodgers met in the Bronx while working at various gigs around New York in 1970. Over the next six years, they worked in various soul and R&B groups; Rodgers played for the Apollo Theater's house band. Soon after meeting drummer Tony Thompson, they formed a rock-fusion power trio called the Big Apple Band, but changed their name to Chic in the wake of Walter Murphy and the Big Apple Band's disco hit "A Fifth of Beethoven."

Frustrated by their inability to land a record deal, the band teamed with vocalists Alfa Anderson and Norma Jean Wright to record disco records. Their original demo tape of "Dance, Dance, Dance" was rejected by several record companies before Atlantic took it in late 1977. In less than a month, the single sold a million copies. Their second LP, *C'est Chic* (with the five-million-selling #1 single "Le Freak"), and its followup, *Risqué,* have both been certified platinum. "Dance, Dance, Dance" (#1, 1977), "I Want Your Love" (#7, 1979) and "Good Times" (#1, 1979) are gold singles. "Good Times" inspired two hits: the Sugar Hill Gang's "Rapper's Delight," based on the instrumental track, and Queen's "Another One Bites the Dust."

Edwards and Rodgers' outside productions include Sister Sledge's *We Are Family,* "He's the Greatest Dancer"

and *Love Somebody Today;* Diana Ross's "Upside Down" and "I'm Coming Out"; and Debbie Harry's *KooKoo.* The pair also made the *Soup for One* soundtrack including one cut sung by Carly Simon. In 1983 Rodgers released a solo album, *Adventures in the Land of the Good Groove,* and produced David Bowie's *Let's Dance.*

CHICAGO
Formed 1967, Chicago
Walt Perry (b. 1945, Chicago), brass; Terry Kath (b. Jan. 31, 1946, Chicago; d. Jan. 23, 1978, Los Angeles), gtr., voc.; Pete Cetera (b. Sep. 13, 1944, Chicago), bass, voc.; Robert Lamm (b. Oct. 13, 1944, Brooklyn), kybds., voc.; Walter Parazaider (b. Mar. 14, 1945, Chicago), saxes, clarinet; Danny Seraphine (b. Aug. 28, 1948, Chicago), drums; James Pankow (b. Aug. 20, 1947, Chicago), trombone; Lee Loughnane (b. Oct. 21, 1946, Chicago), trumpet.
1969—*Chicago Transit Authority* (Columbia) (− Perry) **1970**—*Chicago II* **1971**—*Chicago III; Chicago at Carnegie Hall* **1972**—*Chicago V* **1973**—*Chicago VI* **1974**—*Chicago VII* (+ Laudir De Oliveira [b. Brazil], percussion) **1975**—*Chicago VIII; Chicago IX* **1976**—*Chicago X* **1977**—*Chicago XI* **1978**—(− Donnie Dacus, gtr.) *Hot Streets* **1979**—*Chicago XIII* (− Dacus; + Chris Pinnick, gtr.) **1980**—*Chicago XIV* **1981**—*Chicago's Greatest Hits, volume 2* (− Pinnick; + Bill Champlin, kybds., gtr.) **1982**—*Chicago 16.*

Chicago followed the lead of Blood, Sweat and Tears and the Electric Flag by grafting a horn section onto a rock band. School friends Terry Kath and Walter Parazaider formed the band in 1967 and named it the Big Thing. After they were joined by James William Guercio, who had worked with the Buckinghams and Blood, Sweat and Tears as a Columbia staff producer, they changed their name to the Chicago Transit Authority. The band's 1969 debut, *Chicago Transit Authority,* like BS&T's, was an ambitious jumble of jazz and rock, including protesters' chants from the 1968 Chicago Democratic convention.

Under Guercio's guidance, Chicago shortened its name and moved toward MOR pop with a string of hits ("Does Anybody Really Know What Time It Is?" #7, 1970; "Color My World," #75, 1971; "Saturday in the Park," #3, 1972; "Feeling Stronger Every Day," #10, 1973; "Wishing You Were Here," #11, 1974, and many others) that made them a constant presence on AM radio and kept their albums in the gold and platinum range. Several band members made cameo appearances in the Guercio-produced-and-directed 1973 film *Electra Glide in Blue.*

In 1974, the group's unofficial leader, keyboardist Robert Lamm, made a solo album, *Skinny Boy.* Despite their moniker, Chicago worked out of Los Angeles (Guercio's base) from the late Sixties on. In the later Seventies, their appeal began to flag. In 1977, they left Guercio, who had founded his own Caribou studio. Kath died of an accidental self-inflicted gun wound in 1978; he was replaced by Donnie Dacus, formerly with Stephen Stills and Boz Scaggs. In 1979, Chicago played several benefits for presidential candidate Jerry Brown. Columbia, which had sold millions of Chicago records, dropped the group from its roster in 1981; Cetera released a solo album in 1981 entitled *Full Moon*. In 1982, *16* was a Top Twenty LP and "Hard to Say I'm Sorry" was a #1 hit.

CHICKEN SHACK
Formed 1967, London
Stan Webb, gtr., voc.; Andy Sylvester, bass; Christine Perfect (b. July 12, 1943, Birmingham, Eng.), piano, voc.; Dave Bidwell, drums.
1968—*Forty Blue Fingers, Freshly Packed and Ready to Serve* (Blue Horizon) *OK, Ken?* **1969**—(− Perfect; + Paul Raymond, kybds.) *Hundred Ton Chicken; Accept* **1970**—(− Sylvester; − Bidwell; − Raymond; + Hughie Flint, drums; + John Glascock, bass) **1971**—(− Flint; + Paul Hancox, drums) **1972**—*Imagination Lady* (London) (− Glascock; + Bob Daisley, bass; + Chris Mercer, reeds; + Tony Ashton, piano) **1973**—*Unlucky Boy* (disbanded) **1974**—*Goodbye* (Nova) **1978**—(− Webb; + Robbie Blunt, gtr.; + Ed Spevock, drums; + Dave Winthrop, sax; + Paul Martinez, bass) *The Creeper* (Ariola).

Chicken Shack was a leading band of the late-Sixties British blues revival but is best remembered for pianist/ singer Christine Perfect, who later became better known as Christine McVie of Fleetwood Mac. Stan Webb, Andy Sylvester and Perfect played together in a Birmingham band, the Shades of Blue, in 1965. That band broke up when Perfect completed art college and moved to London. She later met up with Webb and Sylvester, and they regrouped as Chicken Shack, adding Bidwell. They were signed to Mike Vernon's Blue Horizon label and, after a month of club dates in Hamburg, made their U.K. debut at the Windsor Blues Festival in August 1967 (where Perfect met her future husband, John McVie of Fleetwood Mac).

Chicken Shack's rendition of the Etta James blues "I'd Rather Go Blind" reached the U.K. Top Twenty in May 1969, but in August Perfect left the group. A year later, after recording a solo album, she joined Fleetwood Mac. Chicken Shack had a U.K. Top Thirty hit with "Tears in the Wind" before Sylvester, Dave Bidwell and Paul Raymond dropped out, later to join Savoy Brown.

Subsequent personnel under Webb's leadership included Hughie Flint (cofounder of McGuinness Flint), Paul Hancox (formerly of Wayne Fontana and the Mindbenders), Chris Mercer (veteran of numerous British blues sessions), Tony Ashton (of Family and Paice, Ashton and Lord) and Bob Daisley (who later joined Ritchie Black-

more's Rainbow). Webb disbanded Chicken Shack in 1973. After brief stints with Savoy Brown and his own Broken Glass (which cut one album for Capitol in 1975), he revived Chicken Shack with Robbie Blunt, who went on to play with Robert Plant after the demise of Led Zeppelin.

THE CHIFFONS
Formed 1960, Bronx, New York
Barbara Lee (b. May 16, 1947, Bronx), voc.; Patricia Bennett (b. Apr. 7, 1947, Bronx), voc.; Sylvia Peterson (b. Sep. 30, 1946, Bronx), voc.; Judy Craig (b. 1946, Bronx), lead voc.
N.A.—*The Chiffons* (Laurie) *One Fine Day; Sweet Talkin' Guy; Everything You Always Wanted.*

A black female vocal group, the Chiffons had several international hits in the early Sixties. They met and began singing together in high school. In 1960, manager/songwriter Ronald Mack got them a contract with Big Deal Records. After one small hit that year, "Tonight's the Night," they were not heard from again until they began a three-year string of hits including the Mack-penned "He's So Fine" (#1, 1963), which George Harrison was later found to have plagiarized with his early-Seventies hit "My Sweet Lord." Other hits for the Chiffons included "One Fine Day" (#5, 1963), "Nobody Knows What's Going On" (#49, 1965) and "Sweet Talkin' Guy" (#10, 1966). In 1963, the group also recorded two songs as the Four Pennies ("My Block" and "When the Boy's Happy"). After 1966, the group ceased to appear on the charts but continued to perform in New York clubs into the early Seventies.

THE CHI-LITES
Formed 1960, Chicago
Marshall Thompson, voc.; Creadel Jones, voc.; Eugene Record, voc.; Robert Lester, voc.
1968—*Give It Away* (Brunswick) **1971**—*Give More Power to the People* **1972**—*A Lonely Man* **1973**—*A Letter to Myself* **1974**—*The Chi-Lites; Toby* **1975**—*Half a Love* (− Jones; − Record; + David Scott, voc.; + Danny Johnson, voc.) *Chi-Lites Greatest Hits, volume 2* **1976**—*Happy Being Lonely* **1977**—*The Fantastic Chi-Lites* (Mercury) **1981**—*Me and You* (20th Century–Fox).

The Chi-Lites' yearning ballads, featuring falsetto vocals and close harmonies, made them a leading soul vocal group of the early Seventies. Formed as a vocal trio, Marshall and the Hi-Lites (later Chi-Lites), they performed around Chicago and recorded for local labels. In the late Sixties, cabdriver Eugene Record joined the band as lead singer and eventually became their songwriter and producer as well. The Chi-Lites signed with Chicago-based, nationally distributed Brunswick in 1968, and had a few soul hits before Record's "Have You Seen Her" (#3, 1971), cowritten with Barbara Acklin, became a pop hit. "Oh Girl" (#1, 1972) also sold in the millions. The Chi-Lites had 11 Top Twenty R&B hits between 1969 and 1974. In 1976, they were embroiled in the Brunswick label's tax evasion problems. Record went solo, recording for Warner Bros., while the Chi-Lites switched to Mercury, with meager results. Once signed to 20th Century–Fox, the group returned to the soul Top Thirty with "Hot on a Thing" in 1982.

CHILLIWACK

Formed 1969, Vancouver
Bill Henderson (b. Nov. 6, 1944, Vancouver), voc., gtr., synth.; Ross Turney, drums; Claire Lawrence, voc.; Glenn Miller, bass.
1969—*Chilliwack* (London) (– Miller) **1970**—*Chilliwack* (A&M) (– Lawrence; + Miller) **1972**—*All Over You* (+ Howard Froese [b. 1953], voc., gtr., kybds.) **1974**—*Riding High* (Sire) **1975**—*Rocker Box* **1977**—*Dreams Dreams Dreams* (– Froese; + Brian MacLeod [b. June 25, 1952, Halifax], gtrs., voc., kybds.; + Eddie Tuduri, drums) **1978**—*Lights from the Valley* (Mushroom) (– Turney; – Miller; – Tuduri; + Ab Bryant [b. Nov. 15, 1954, Vancouver], bass; + John Roles, gtr., voc.; + Bucky Berger, drums) **1979**—*Breakdown in Paradise* (Mushroom, Canada) (– Berger; – Roles) **1981**—*Wanna Be a Star* (Millennium) **1982**—*Opus X.*

Chilliwack is a Canadian hard-rock band that, despite great success in its homeland, only cracked the U.S. market in 1981, when "My Girl" from *Wanna Be a Star* was a moderate hit single. The group was formed by leader Bill Henderson (who by 1978 was the only remaining original member) and recorded for several labels, including the Canadian independent Mushroom, with varying degrees of success. They've had several hit singles in Canada, and several of their LPs (*Dreams Dreams Dreams*, *Lights from the Valley* and *Wanna Be a Star*) are Canadian platinum (100,000 copies sold).

THE CHIPMUNKS

Alvin Chipmunk, lead voc., harmonica; Simon Chipmunk, voc., percussion; Theodore Chipmunk, voc., kybds.
N.A.—*The Alvin Show* (Liberty) *The Chipmunk Songbook; The Chipmunks A-Go-Go; The Chipmunks Sing the Beatles; The Chipmunks Sing with Children; Christmas with the Chipmunks; Doctor Doolittle* (Sunset) *Let's All Sing with the Chipmunks* (Liberty) *Sing Along with the Chipmunks; The Very Best of the Chipmunks* (United Artists) **1980**—*Chipmunk Punk* (RCA) **1981**—*Urban Chipmunk;*

Christmas with the Chipmunks **1982**—*Chipmunk Rock; The Chipmunks Go Hollywood.*

The Chipmunks were one of the very biggest acts of the Golden Era of rock & roll; they sold over 30 million records before retreating into obscurity in the face of the British Invasion. In 1980, they revived their careers with a comeback album that was more successful than anything attempted by their peers like Bill Haley and Pat Boone— more successful, in fact, than most of the punk albums that precipitated their triumphant return.

The Chipmunk brothers began singing together at home, imitating the popular harmony groups of the time—the Drifters, the Clovers and especially the Coasters, with their penchant for novelty songs. They performed at high school dances and nut-gathering parties, but probably would never have gone professional had they not been discovered by songwriter/producer Ross Bagdasarian, a.k.a. David Seville (born January 27, 1919, Fresno, California). With his cousin William Saroyan, Bagdasarian had written "Come on a My House," a hit for Rosemary Clooney in 1951, and on his own had written and produced "Witch Doctor," a 1½-million-seller for David Seville and His Orchestra in 1958. With "Witch Doctor" he had devised a studio technique that involved synchronizing tracks recorded at different speeds. It was a technique that suited the Chipmunks' high-pitched voices and rodent vitality as perfectly as Sam Phillips' reverb suited Elvis Presley and Phil Spector's Wall of Sound suited the Ronettes.

Their first collaboration was "The Chipmunk Song"— released just before Christmas 1958, it hit #1 before the end of the year, sold 3½ million copies in five weeks (setting a new record for fast-selling discs) and eventually sold seven million. It also won three Grammys. While they never equaled that success, they followed it with a string of hits: "Alvin's Harmonica" (#3, 1959, another gold record), "Ragtime Cowboy Joe" (#16, 1959, gold), "Alvin's Orchestra" (#33, 1960), "Rudolph the Red-Nosed Reindeer" (#21, 1960) and "The Alvin Twist" (#40, 1962). All these records, singles as well as albums, were among the first stereo releases.

In the 1961–62 TV season, the Chipmunks starred in their own CBS series, "The Alvin Show," which Bagdasarian wrote and produced, but their recording career was already declining. They continued to make records through the mid-Sixties but were overshadowed first by the Beatles and their countrymen, then by American acts like the Monkees, the Archies, the Banana Splits and Josie and the Pussycats. When Bagdasarian died in 1972, the Chipmunks' career seemed over forever.

Their names appeared occasionally in the news: Simon was arrested in 1974 and charged with possession of poppy seeds, Theodore was hit with a paternity suit in 1976, and later that year Alvin, with much attendant publicity, was converted to a fundamentalist Christian sect, only to renounce it several months later. They hibernated through the peak of the disco years, although their former cohort Mickey Mouse got a hit.

The new wave shook them out of their idleness. In 1980, they cut their first album in over a decade, *Chipmunk Punk*, produced by Ross Bagdasarian, Jr., and covering songs by Blondie, the Cars, Tom Petty and the Knack. Without singles, it sold over 750,000 copies. It was followed by *Urban Chipmunk* and *Chipmunk Rock*. Expectations are high for their long-rumored reggae album.

CHARLIE CHRISTIAN
Born 1919, Dallas; died February 1942, New York City
N.A.—*Solo Flight—The Genius of Charlie Christian* (Columbia).

As the musician who took the guitar out of the rhythm section and made it a lead instrument, Charlie Christian had a profound influence on both jazz and rock & roll.

Christian's recording career spanned only three years. He was discovered playing in a jazz band in Oklahoma City by John Hammond in 1939. Benny Goodman brought him to New York to play with his sextet and his orchestra, and it was with Goodman that he revolutionized jazz guitar. The newly introduced electrified guitar gave the instrument an authoritative volume and tonal range it had never had, and Christian's innovative single-string picking technique made the guitar a solo voice equal to the trumpet and the saxophone. Additionally, as one of the participants in after-hours jam sessions with Thelonious Monk, Dizzy Gillespie and Kenny Clarke, he was one of the originators of be-bop, which became the dominant force in jazz after his death. Christian developed tuberculosis in 1940. He was hospitalized in the summer of 1941 and spent the last six months of his life in the hospital.

LOU CHRISTIE
Born Lugee Geno Saco, February 19, 1943, Glen Willard, Pennsylvania
1966—*Lou Christie Painter of Hits* (MGM)   *Lou Christie Strikes Again* (Colpix)   *Lou Christie Strikes Again* (Roulette)   *Lightnin' Strikes* (MGM)   **1969**—*I'm Gonna Make You Mine* (Buddah)   *This Is Lou Christie* (Marble Arch)   **1971**—*Paint America Love* (Buddah)   **1974**—*Lou Christie* (Three Brothers).

Singer Lou Christie had two big hits in 1963—"The Gypsy Cried" (#24) and "Two Faces Have I" (#6)—in the quavery falsetto style popularized by Del Shannon and Frankie Valli. Three years later, he returned to the charts with the Motown-influenced "Lightnin' Strikes" (#1, 1966).

In Pennsylvania, Lugee Saco had won a scholarship to Moon Township High School, where he studied classical music and vocal technique and also sang with a group called the Classics. From 1959 to 1962, he recorded with various local acts for several small Pittsburgh labels, adopted the stage name of Lou Christie and in October 1962 recorded "The Gypsy Cried" for C&C Records. The first of several songs cowritten with Twyla Herbert (a mystic twenty years Christie's senior who claimed she could foresee his future and predict his hits), it was a big local hit and was subsequently picked up for national distribution by Roulette Records. By then, Christie had moved to New York, where he found frequent session work as a background vocalist. Shortly after the release of "Two Faces Have I," he served two years in the Army. After his discharge in 1966, he signed with MGM and returned with the lushly produced "Lightnin' Strikes," which sold over two million copies.

His followups included "Rhapsody in the Rain" (#16, 1966), a fairly sexually explicit song for its time. Christie subsequently recorded for Colpix and Columbia before signing to Buddah in 1969. "I'm Gonna Make You Mine" (#10, 1969) was a hit in the U.S., Europe and the U.K. He has since recorded for Three Brothers, Midsong and Lifesong with little luck and has performed on the nightclub and nostalgia circuits.

ERIC CLAPTON
Born March 30, 1945, Ripley, England
1970—*Eric Clapton* (Polydor)   **1972**—*History of Eric Clapton* (Atco)   *Eric Clapton at His Best* (Polydor)   **1973**—*Eric Clapton's Rainbow Concert* (RSO)   **1974**—*461 Ocean Boulevard*   **1975**—*There's One in Every Crowd;   E. C. Was Here;   The Best of E. C.* (Polydor)   **1976**—*No Reason to Cry* (RSO)   **1977**—*Slowhand*   **1978**—*Backless*   **1980**—*Just One Night*   **1981**—*Another Ticket* (RSO)   **1982**—*Time Pieces*   **1983**—*Money and Cigarettes* (Duck/Warner Bros.).

In the Yardbirds, Cream, Derek and the Dominos and his own bands, guitarist Eric Clapton has continually redefined his own version of the blues. Raised by a foster family after his parents abandoned him at an early age, Clapton grew up a self-confessed "nasty kid." He studied stained-glass design at Kingston Art School and started playing guitar at 17. He stayed with his first band, the early British R&B outfit the Roosters (which included Tom McGuinness, later of Manfred Mann and McGuinness Flint), from January to August 1963 and frequently jammed in London clubs with, among others, future members of the Rolling Stones. He put in a seven-gig stint with a Top Forty band, Casey Jones and the Engineers, in September 1963. He joined the Yardbirds in late 1963 and stayed with them until March 1965, when they began to leave behind power blues for psychedelic pop.

Upon leaving the Yardbirds, Clapton did construction work until John Mayall asked him to join his Blues-

Eric Clapton

breakers in spring 1965. While with Mayall, he contributed to several LPs while perfecting the blues runs that drew a cult of worshipers (the slogan "Clapton is God" became a popular graffito in London). Also with Mayall, he participated in a studio band called Powerhouse (which included Jack Bruce and Steve Winwood), and they contributed three cuts to a 1966 Elektra anthology, *What's Shakin'*. Clapton left the Bluesbreakers in July 1966 and cut a few tracks with Jimmy Page, then with bassist Jack Bruce and drummer Ginger Baker he formed Cream.

Clapton perfected his virtuoso style, and Cream's concerts featured lengthy solo excursions, which Clapton often performed with his back to the crowd. During his tenure with Cream, Clapton contributed lead fills to the Beatles' "While My Guitar Gently Weeps" and appeared on Frank Zappa's *We're Only in It for the Money*.

When Cream broke up in November 1968, Clapton formed the short-lived supergroup Blind Faith with Baker, Winwood and Rick Grech. During their only U.S. tour, Clapton embraced Christianity, which he has given up and reaffirmed periodically ever since. As a corrective to Blind Faith's fan worship, Clapton began jamming with tour openers Delaney and Bonnie, then joined their band as an unbilled (but hardly unnoticed) sideman. Clapton's 1969

activities also included a brief fling with John Lennon's Plastic Ono Band (*Live Peace in Toronto*).

He moved to New York in late 1969 and continued to work with Delaney and Bonnie through early 1970. With several members of the Bramletts' band, and friends like Leon Russell and Stephen Stills, whose solo albums Clapton played on, he recorded his first solo album, *Eric Clapton,* which yielded a U.S. #18 hit, the J. J. Cale song "After Midnight."

The album marked Clapton's emergence as a strong lead vocalist, a role he continued to fill after forming Derek and the Dominos with bassist Carl Radle, drummer Jim Gordon and keyboardist Bobby Whitlock, all former Delaney and Bonnie sidemen. The Dominos' only studio album, the two-record *Layla,* was a guitar tour de force sparked by the contributions of guest artist Duane Allman. The title track, an instant FM standard, was a tale of unrequited love inspired by Patti Boyd Harrison (wife of ex-Beatle George), whom Clapton married in 1979. Clapton toured on and off with the Dominos through late 1971, and sat in on albums by Dr. John and Harrison, who enticed Clapton to play at the benefit concert for Bangladesh in August 1971.

Depressed and burdened by a heroin habit, Clapton retreated to the isolation of his Surrey home for most of 1971 and 1972. With the aid of Pete Townshend, he began his comeback with a concert at London's Rainbow Theatre in January 1973. Supported by Townshend, Winwood, Ron Wood, Jim Capaldi and others, Clapton released tapes from the ragged concert in a September 1973 LP. By the time *461 Ocean Boulevard* was released, he had kicked heroin for good.

In the Seventies, Clapton became a dependable hitmaker with the easygoing, more commercial style he introduced on *461*—a relaxed shuffle that, like J. J. Cale's, hinted at gospel, honky-tonk and reggae, retaining a blues feeling but not necessarily the blues structure. Playing fewer and shorter guitar solos, he emphasized his vocals—often paired with harmonies by Yvonne Elliman or Marcy Levy—over his virtuosity. He had hits with his cover of Bob Marley's "I Shot the Sheriff" (#1, 1974) and originals "Lay Down Sally" (#3, 1978) and "Promises" (#9, 1979). His albums regularly sell in gold quantities; *Slowhand* and *Backless* were certified platinum. He had a Top Ten hit in 1981 with "I Can't Stand It."

THE DAVE CLARK FIVE
Formed circa 1962, Tottenham, England
Dave Clark (b. Dec. 15, 1942, Tottenham), drums, voc.;
Mike Smith (b. Dec. 6, 1943, London), piano, voc.;
Rick Huxley (b. Aug. 5, 1942, Dartford, Eng.), gtr.;
Lenny Davidson (b. May 30, 1944, Enfield, Eng.), gtr.;
Dennis Payton (b. Aug. 11, 1943, London, Eng.), sax.
1963—*A Session with the Dave Clark Five* (Columbia)

1964—*Glad All Over* (Epic)   *American Tour;   The Dave Clark Five Return*   **1965**—*Coast to Coast;   Having a Wild Weekend*   **1966**—*I Like It Like That;   The Dave Clark Five's Greatest Hits;   Try Too Hard;   Satisfied with You;   More Greatest Hits*   **1967**—*5 By 5;   You Got What It Takes*   **1968**—*Everybody Knows* (Columbia)   *Weekend in London* (Epic)   **1971**—*Good Old Rock 'n' Roll.*

The Dave Clark Five, a British Invasion phenomenon, was formed in 1962 by members of the Tottenham Hotspurs soccer team in suburban London because they needed to raise funds to travel to Holland for a match. Leader Dave Clark had never played drums, but quickly adapted; he soon became the group's chief songwriter and manager as well. They played London clubs and a command performance at Buckingham Palace in 1965. Following the success of "Glad All Over" (#6, 1964), the group toured Europe and the U.S. for the next two years. They became the second British group after the Beatles to appear on the "Ed Sullivan Show."

Their string of mid-decade hits included "Can't You See That She's Mine" (#4, 1964), "Bits and Pieces" (#4, 1964), "Because" (#3, 1964) and "Catch Us If You Can" (#4, 1965), and they appeared in several low-budget films modeled on *A Hard Day's Night,* including *Get Yourself a College Girl* and *Having a Wild Weekend.* By late 1965, Clark and Smith's songwriting had dried up, and they made less successful covers of U.S. rock oldies. Although they broke up in 1970, the DC5 regrouped briefly for some nostalgia circuit concerts in 1973.

In 1978, a compilation of their hits, *25 Thumping Great Hits,* made a strong showing on the British charts. Clark appeared on Peter Noone's (formerly Herman of the Hermits) 1980 debut with the Tremblers. By then, Mike Smith was an established producer and session player. Dennis Payton went on to run a successful real estate office in Devon, Huxley took up electronics and Lenny Davidson became an antique dealer.

DICK CLARK
Born November 30, 1929, Mount Vernon, New York

Host of TV's longest-lived pop music series "American Bandstand," Dick Clark has been a major business figure in rock for three decades. "Bandstand" began broadcasting locally out of WFIL-TV in Philadelphia in 1952 and premiered nationally on ABC August 5, 1957. For the next five years it was a showcase for pop singers, particularly Philadelphia-based teen idols like Fabian and Frankie Avalon, in whose careers Clark had a stake, since he owned substantial interests in music publishing and record companies. Such apparent conflicts of interest inspired charges against Clark in the Congressional payola investigations in early 1960. He signed an affidavit denying any

wrongdoing, and his testimony eventually led to his escaping the inquiry virtually unscathed. But he quietly divested himself of interests in 33 businesses.

In his autobiography, *Rock, Roll and Remember,* Clark claims he was a millionaire by age thirty. As of 1983, "Bandstand" is still a Saturday morning fixture. Virtually every important pop act has played Clark's stage at one point or another, dutifully lip-synching its latest hit. In 1965, Clark hosted a spinoff daytime series, "Where the Action Is," featuring Paul Revere and the Raiders, Steve Alaimo and Tommy Roe among its regulars. Through his Dick Clark Teleshows, Inc., he continues to act as an independent TV producer of such made-for-TV movies as *Elvis* (with Kurt Russell) and *The Early Beatles.* In the Seventies, Clark branched out into game shows, hosting "The $20,000 Pyramid." He owns a dinner theater in Westchester, New York.

PETULA CLARK
Born November 15, 1932 or 1933, Epsom, England
1965—*Downtown* (Warner Bros.)   *Greatest Hits, volume 1.*

British pop singer Petula Clark is best known in America for her mid-Sixties hits "Downtown" and "Don't Sleep in the Subway," but has also carried on a varied career in Europe. She began singing professionally at age seven; by nine she was a regular on radio shows. During World War II she played more than 500 shows for British troops. She began appearing in films as a teenager, and by the early Fifties was a major star in the U.K. She has over twenty movie credits, including *A Medal for a General.*

In 1954, "The Little Shoemaker" (#12, U.K.) became her first hit, followed by "Majorca" and others. She got her first #1 in the U.K. with 1961's "Sailor," followed by her first million-seller, "Romeo" (#3, 1961, U.K.). That same year she married Vogue Records publicity director Claud Wolff, who became her manager. They moved to France and she became popular there with such hits as "Chariot" and "Monsieur," also a big seller in Germany. Her string of English hits continued throughout the early Sixties—"My Friend the Sea," "Ya Ya Twist," "Casanova"—and she cracked the American market with "Downtown" (#1, 1965), which won a Grammy Award in 1965.

She toured U.S. nightclubs for the next few years and managed follow-up hits like "I Know a Place" (#3, 1965), "My Love" (#1, 1966) and "I Couldn't Live without Your Love" (#9, 1966). Although she cut down her personal appearances to raise her family, there were a few more hits, like "Don't Sleep in the Subway" (#5, 1967), "The Other Man's Grass Is Always Greener" (#31, 1967) and "Kiss Me Goodbye" (#15, 1968). She also revived her film career in the late Sixties, starring in *Goodbye, Mr. Chips* and *Finian's Rainbow.* In the early Seventies, she began touring widely again—in England, Europe and America—and by 1977 she was in semi-retirement.

STANLEY CLARKE

Born June 30, 1951, Philadelphia
1973—*Children of Forever* (Polydor) 1974—*Stanley Clarke* (Nemperor) 1975—*Journey to Love* 1976—*School Days* 1978—*Modern Man* 1979—*I Wanna Play for You* (Epic) 1980—*Rock, Pebbles and Sand* 1981—*The Clarke/Duke Project* (with George Duke).

Stanley Clarke earned a considerable reputation as a jazz bassist before entering the rock market with Return to Forever and switching to electric bass. His trademark on acoustic bass is precise upper-register vamping; on the electric, a metallic plunk.

Clarke studied at the Philadelphia Musical Academy before moving to New York in 1970. He soon worked with Art Blakey, Gil Evans, the Thad Jones–Mel Lewis Orchestra and Chick Corea, a pianist/composer, whom he met in Philadelphia in 1971. Clarke also played in a group led by saxophonist Stan Getz; the vaguely Brazilian-style material Corea furnished for Getz became the repertoire for a Corea quintet with Clarke, reedman Joe Farrell, singer Flora Purim and percussionist Airto Moreira on a Corea album called *Return to Forever* (1972).

Corea and Clarke, both Scientologists, kept the name for the group and, following the example of the Mahavishnu Orchestra, formed an electrified band with drummer Lenny White and guitarist Al DiMeola, which grew increasingly bombastic and popular until it disbanded in 1976. Clarke had already begun releasing his own fusion albums, including 1975's *Journey to Love* with guest Jeff Beck.

In spring 1979, he joined Rolling Stones guitarists Ron Wood and Keith Richards for a North American tour as the New Barbarians, and followed the tour with a half-studio, half-live double album, *I Wanna Play for You*. He teamed up with keyboardist George Duke (who had appeared on previous Clarke LPs) as the Clarke/Duke Project in 1981, and had a hit with a ballad, "Sweet Baby." He also recorded with Corea, White and Chaka Khan on the acoustic jazz session *Echoes of an Era*.

Clarke has produced albums by Roy Buchanan (*Loading Zone*, 1977) and singer Dee Dee Bridgewater (*Just Family*, 1978). He has also played on albums by Santana, Aretha Franklin, Quincy Jones and others, and he appeared on Paul McCartney's *Tug of War*.

THE CLASH

Formed 1976, London
Mick Jones (b. 1956, London), gtr., voc.; Paul Simonon (b. 1956, London), bass; Tory Crimes (b. Terry Chimes, London), drums; Joe Strummer (b. John Mellor, 1953, Ankara, Turkey), voc., gtr.

1977—*The Clash* (Columbia) (− Crimes; + Nicky "Topper" Headon [b. 1956, Dover], drums) 1978—*Give 'Em Enough Rope* 1979—*The Clash; London Calling* 1980—*Black Market Clash* (EP) *Sandinista!* 1982—*Combat Rock* (− Headon; + Terry Chimes, drums).

Political rockers the Clash see the stakes of their music as "death or glory," and their fervent righteousness and increasingly eclectic pop have made them the most influential band to arise from England's late-Seventies punk movement.

Joe Strummer, the son of a British diplomat, grew up in a boarding school. He quit school while still in his teens and in 1974 formed the 101'ers, a pub-rock band named either for the address of the building where they squatted or the number of the torture room in the George Orwell novel *1984*.

The Sex Pistols inspired the formation of the Clash. Simonon was attending art school when he met Jones. He had never played an instrument until he heard the Pistols; he then acquired a bass and joined Jones's band, the London SS, which in its eleven-month existence included Tory Crimes and Topper Headon. Seeing the Pistols induced Strummer (a name he got when he strummed "Johnny B. Goode" on a ukulele as a busker in London subway stations) to leave the 101'ers, which included Keith Levene, soon after they recorded a single, "Keys to Your Heart." Strummer and Levene then joined Jones, Simonon and Crimes in their new group, named the Clash by Jones because that was the word that seemed to appear most often in newspaper headlines.

The Clash played their first gigs opening for the Sex Pistols in summer 1976 as a quintet. They opened for the Sex Pistols on their "Anarchy in the U.K." tour after Levene quit. (He eventually joined Public Image Ltd.)

Where the Pistols were nihilists, the Clash were protesters, with songs about racism, police brutality and disenfranchisement; most of them were Strummer's lyrics set to Jones's music. They mixed rock with reggae, the music of Britain's oppressed Jamaicans; one of their early singles was a cover of Junior Murvin's "Police and Thieves."

In February 1977, British CBS Records signed the Clash for a reported $200,000 advance. A month later, their debut album was released and entered the British charts at #12. Columbia considered the album too crude for American release (although the import sold 100,000 copies, making it the biggest-selling import album of all time). In response, the Clash recorded "Complete Control" with Jamaican producer Lee "Scratch" Perry.

Crimes quit the group in late 1976. Headon, who had been drumming with Pat Travers in Europe since his stint in the London SS, accompanied the group on its first national headlining tour. The "White Riot" tour, named after the current Clash single, ended at a London concert

The Clash: Mick Jones, Paul Simonon, Topper Headon, Joe Strummer

where the audience ripped the seats out of the floor. It was the first in a series of confrontations between the Clash and the police, especially in Britain, where the group members were arrested on charges ranging from petty theft to illegal possession of firearms (for shooting prize pigeons).

One of the four songs on an EP entitled *Cost of Living*, a cover of the Bobby Fuller–Sonny Curtis "I Fought the Law," was the first Clash record released in the U.S. At Columbia's behest, American producer Sandy Pearlman, best known for his work with Blue Öyster Cult, produced *Give 'Em Enough Rope*, which reached #2 on the British charts, but failed to reach the American Top 200.

The Clash launched their "Pearl Harbour" tour of America in February 1979. They persuaded Columbia to release their first album, which in its American version contained only ten of the original fourteen tracks. A bonus 45 and EP selections dating as far back as two years made up the rest. The American version sold considerably fewer copies than had the British import.

London Calling was both an artistic and commercial breakthrough. Produced by Guy Stevens (who had worked with Mott the Hoople) and supplemented by a brass section and the keyboards of Mickey Gallagher (Ian Dury and the Blockheads), it outsold the group's combined previous releases several times over and broke into the American Top Thirty thanks to a hit single, "Train in Vain." Their second American tour in February 1980 was a decided success. Beginning with *London Calling*, the Clash insisted that their records sell at lower than standard prices. *Sandinista!*, a triple-LP package, sold for less than most double albums, and Columbia took the lost profits out of the group's royalties and tour support funds. *San-*

dinista! was the first Clash album to sell more copies in the U.S. than in the U.K.

Over the years, the Clash has been active in several political causes and has performed benefit concerts for Rock Against Racism. The group was also the subject of a 1980 semi-documentary film, *Rude Boy*. In 1982, Headon left the group because of "political differences" and Crimes rejoined. *Combat Rock* hit the Top Ten in 1982 and went platinum; the single "Should I Stay or Should I Go" was a Top Fifty hit that summer and "Rock the Casbah" later hit the Top Ten.

THE CLASSICS IV

Formed mid-1960s, Atlanta
J. R. Cobb, gtr.; Dennis Yost, voc.; Kim Venable, drums; Joe Wilson, bass; Wally Eaton, gtr.
1975—*The Very Best of Classics IV* (United Artists).

The Classics IV made several major soft-pop hits, including "Stormy" and "Traces," featuring lead vocalist Dennis Yost. J. R. Cobb and producer/writer Buddy Buie went on to studio work and later anchored the Southern rockers Atlanta Rhythm Section in the Seventies.

THE REVEREND JAMES CLEVELAND

Born December 23, 1932, Chicago
N.A.—*Rev. James Cleveland with the Gospel All-Stars: Out on a Hill* (Savoy) **1982**—*It's a New Day; 20th Anniversary Album; Where Is Your Faith.*

The Reverend Cleveland is a dominant force in gospel music today. As the leader of the Southern California Community Choir, Cleveland has been a leader in expanding the musical base of gospel music and integrating jazz and pop rhythms and arrangements into spiritual material. The pop gospel of Andrae Crouch and Edwin Hawkins are offshoots of Cleveland's pioneering efforts. His vocal style, ridiculed by some when he started singing in the Fifties, earned Cleveland the title "Gospel's Louis Armstrong."

His recordings of "Peace Be Still," "Lord Remember Me," "Father, I Stretch My Hands to Thee" and "The Love of God" are gospel standards. His gold album with Aretha Franklin, *Amazing Grace,* is interesting not just because of the music, but for the fact that Franklin's father, the Reverend C. L. Franklin, gave the Reverend Cleveland the opportunity to arrange for Detroit's New Bethel Baptist Church choir when Cleveland was only 26. Cleveland also appeared on Elton John's *Blue Moves* LP in 1976.

In 1968, Cleveland organized the interdenominational Gospel Singers Workshop Convention, which brings together top gospel musicians with churchgoers annually. In the early Eighties the organization boasted over 25,000 members and 250 chapters. The GSW has played an important role in gaining exposure for gospel music outside churches.

JIMMY CLIFF
Born James Chambers, 1948, St. Catherine, Jamaica
1967—*Hard Road to Travel* (Island, U.K.) **1968**—*Jimmy Cliff* **1970**—*Wonderful World, Beautiful People* (A&M) **1971**—*Another Cycle* (Island, U.K.) **1972**—

Jimmy Cliff

The Harder They Come (with various artists) (Mango) **1973**—*Unlimited* (Warner Bros.) **1974**—*Struggling Man* (Island) *House of Exile* (EMI, U.K.) *Music Maker* (Warner Bros.) **1975**—*Brave Warrior* (EMI, U.K.) *Follow My Mind* (Warner Bros.) **1976**—*In Concert—The Best of Jimmy Cliff* **1978**—*Give Thanx* **1980**—*I Am the Living* **1981**—*Give the People What They Want* **1982**—*Special* (Columbia).

As the star of the film *The Harder They Come* and its soundtrack album, reggae star Jimmy Cliff helped popularize reggae outside of Jamaica. Like Ivan, the character he played in the film, he left his country home for the city when he was barely a teenager. He arrived in Kingston in 1962; within the year he had recorded his first record, a single called "Daisy Got Me Crazy." In the following months he cut a half-dozen tracks for various disc jockeys to play over their "sound systems" (mobile discos). In 1962, he had a hit produced by Leslie Kong, "Dearest Beverley." Cliff's second collaboration with Kong, "Hurricane Hattie," went to #1 on the island, followed by "My Lucky Day," "King of Kings" and "Miss Jamaica." As a vocalist for Byron Lee's Dragonaires, he toured the Americas in 1964; at the New York World's Fair, Cliff met Chris Blackwell of Island Records, who signed him and enticed him to move to London in 1965.

Cliff worked at first as a backup singer. By divesting himself of his Jamaican patois, assuming the style of a cosmopolitan and the repertoire of a jet-setting troubadour, he developed a following in France and Scandinavia, and in 1967, "Give and Take" hit the British charts. The following year, he traveled to Brazil as Jamaica's representative at an international music festival. His song "Waterfall" won a festival prize and became a South American hit. "Wonderful World, Beautiful People" was an international best seller in 1969, a Top Ten hit in the U.K. and one of the first reggae tunes heard widely outside of Jamaica.

In 1969, Desmond Dekker recorded Cliff's "The Song We Used to Sing." Cliff was best known at this time as a songwriter. (Bob Dylan described his "Vietnam" as "the best protest song ever written.") He wrote "You Can Get It If You Really Want" for Dekker, and the Pioneers had a hit with his "Let Your Yeah Be Yeah." Cliff returned to Jamaica at the end of 1969 and recorded "Many Rivers to Cross," which inspired Jamaican filmmaker Perry Henzell to offer him the lead role in *The Harder They Come.*

After the film, Cliff became a major star in Europe, Africa and Latin America. "Under the Sun, Moon and Stars," "Struggling Man" and "House of Exile" were international hits between 1973 and 1975. In the attempt to expand his following, he left Island in 1973, signing on with EMI in the U.K. and Warner Bros. in the U.S. But far from reaching new fans, he almost lost those he had. In

Jamaica, he was denounced for abandoning his musical, religious and national roots.

A Muslim—Cliff converted from Rastafarianism in 1973—he is welcomed in Africa and the Middle East. African religion, culture, history and music have become recurrent themes in his songs, and they were one focus of a film he made in 1980, *Bongo Man*.

He continues to make regular American tours, singing anthems from *The Harder They Come*, and he occasionally enjoys a modest advance into the mainstream—as when his single "Gone Clear" was given some disco play in 1981.

CLIMAX BLUES BAND
Formed 1968, Stafford, England
Original lineup: Colin Richard Francis Cooper (b. Oct. 7, 1939, Stafford), sax, harmonica, clarinet, gtr., voc.; Peter John Haycock (b. Apr. 4, 1952, Stafford), gtr., voc.; Arthur Wood (b. Stafford), kybds.; Derek Holt (b. Jan. 26, 1949, Stafford), bass, gtr., kybds., voc.; George Newsome (b. Aug. 14, 1947, Stafford), drums, harmonica.
1968—*Climax Chicago Blues Band* (Sire, U.K.) *Plays On* **1970**—*A Lot of Bottle* (Sire) **1972**—*Tightly Knit* **1973**—*Rich Man* **1974**—*FM Live; Sense of Direction* **1975**—*Stamp Album* **1976**—*Gold Plated* **1978**—*Shine On* **1979**—*Real to Reel* **1980**—*Flying the Flag* (Warner Bros.) **1981**—*Lucky for Some* **1983**—*Sample and Hold* (Virgin/Epic).

While its name reveals its British blues revival beginnings, the Climax Blues Band is by now a dependable AOR outfit that reaches the AM charts every few years, with a sound trademarked by shared lead vocals from Peter Haycock and Colin Cooper and Cooper's saxophone playing. They tour Europe and America frequently, taking time off to cut their annual album.

They recorded each of their first two albums in less than three days. At first, they were a derivative blues band distinguished mainly by their youthful lineup; Haycock was only 16 when the band got started. By 1973, when they first reached the U.S. charts with "Rich Man," they had already moved toward pop songwriting and production. Their first U.S. tour that same year yielded *FM Live*, recorded in New York during a simulcast Academy of Music concert. Their first self-produced album, *Gold Plated*, became their biggest seller on the strength of "Couldn't Get It Right" (#3, 1977), and 1980's *Flying the Flag* featured the MOR ballad "I Love You" (#12, 1981). By the time 1983's *Sample and Hold* was made, the group's name was carried by Haycock, Cooper and keyboardist George Glover, along with studio musicians.

Through its lengthy tenure, the group has kept a low profile and a reputation for professionalism. They all still live in their native Stafford area.

PATSY CLINE
Born Virginia Patterson Hensley, September 8, 1932, Winchester, Virginia; died March 5, 1963, Camden, Tennessee
N.A.—*Patsy Cline* (MCA) *Greatest Hits; The Patsy Cline Story.*

Country singer Patsy Cline's career was in full swing, with pop Top Forty hits and national concert tours, when she was killed in a plane crash at the age of thirty. Her honeyed soprano has been emulated not only by country singers like Loretta Lynn and Dolly Parton, but also by pop singers like Linda Ronstadt and Emmylou Harris.

Cline took up piano at age eight, but didn't begin singing until her teens. In 1948, she won a trip to Nashville through an audition; nine years later she appeared on TV on "Arthur Godfrey's Talent Scouts" and was spotted by Owen Bradley of Decca Records. Her first record, "Walkin' after Midnight," was both a country hit (#3) and a pop hit (#12) in 1957.

She was soon one of country music's biggest stars. Despite her numerous country hits, she sought a broader audience and refused to be saddled with a hillbilly or cowgirl image. Under Bradley's direction, she came to embody the smooth, sophisticated new Nashville sound. "I Fall to Pieces" was a pop hit (#12) in 1961, followed later that year by "Crazy" (#2 country, #9 pop), a song written by then-little-known writer Willie Nelson. She had another pop Top Twenty hit with "She's Got You" (#14) in 1962. In 1973 Cline was elected to the Country Music Hall of Fame.

CLOVER
Formed 1968, Muir Beach, California
John McFee, gtr., pedal steel; Sean Hopper, kybds.; Alex Call, voc., gtr.; Huey Lewis, voc., harmonica; John Ciambotti, bass; Michael Shine, drums.
1970—*Clover* (Mercury) **1971**—*Forty-Niner* (Fantasy) **1977**—*Love on the Wire* (Mercury) **1979**—*Chronicle* (Fantasy).

Clover was a promising West Coast country-rock group that released four albums but is best known for its backup work on Elvis Costello's debut LP, *My Aim Is True* (1977). The group was founded by John McFee and Alex Call and labored through the years as a cult band before moving to London to work with Costello. (Only the group's vocalist, Huey Lewis, does not appear on *My Aim.*) Clover worked in London until they disbanded in 1979. McFee joined the Doobie Brothers, and Lewis and Hopper formed Huey Lewis and the News, whose "Do You Believe in Love" was a hit in 1982. *Chronicle* is a repackage of Clover's first and second LPs.

THE CLOVERS
Formed late 1940s, Washington, D.C.

Charlie White (b. ca. 1930, Washington, D.C.), voc.; John "Buddy" Bailey (b. ca. 1930, Washington, D.C.), voc.; Matthew McQuater, voc.; Harold "Hal" Lucas, Jr., voc.; Harold Winley, voc.; Bill Harris, gtr. **1953**—(+ Billy Mitchell, voc.) **N.A.**—*The Clovers* (Atlantic) *In Clover* (United Artists) *Dance Party* (Atlantic)) *Love Potion No. 9* (United Artists) *The Original Love Potion No. 9* (Grand Prix) *Their Greatest Recordings* (Atco).

Emerging out of the Washington, D.C., area, the Clovers were one of the more popular of the early-Fifties R&B groups. They were an important force in the fusion of big-beat R&B with gospel-style vocals which laid the ground-work for soul music a decade later. With the Top Thirty success of "Love Love Love" in 1956, the Clovers became one of the first black vocal groups to chart on the pop Hot 100.

The group came together in a Washington, D.C., high school in the late Forties. They were singing at a local nightspot, the Rose Club, when they were discovered by Lou Krefetz, who became their manager and got them a contract with Atlantic Records in 1950.

Label president Ahmet Ertegun wrote their first of many R&B hits in 1951, "Don't You Know I Love You." That same year, they enjoyed substantial success with "Fool, Fool, Fool," as well. In 1952, they placed four songs in the R&B Top Ten ("One Mint Julep," "Ting a Ling," "Hey Miss Fannie," "I Played the Fool") and became a top draw at black nightclubs.

Their string of R&B hits continued through the early Fifties with "Crawlin'," "Good Lovin' " (1953), "Lovey Dovey," "I've Got My Eyes on You," "Your Cash Ain't Nothing but Trash" (1954), "Blue Velvet" (later covered by Bobby Vinton), "Devil or Angel" (later covered by Bobby Vee) and "Nip Jip" (1955). In 1956, they had another R&B hit with "From the Bottom of My Heart" and in 1959 with "Love Potion No. 9." Their releases were eclipsed commercially by competing cover versions by white acts.

THE COASTERS
Formed 1955, Los Angeles
Carl Gardner (b. Apr. 29, 1928, Tex.), tenor; Leon Hughes, tenor; Billy Guy (b. June 20, 1936, Los Angeles), baritone; Bobby Nunn, bass.
1956—*The Coasters* (Atco) (– Hughes; + Young Jessie, tenor; – Nunn; + Will "Dub" Jones, bass) **1957**—(– Jessie; + Cornelius Gunter, tenor) **1958**—*Greatest Hits* **1959**—*One by One* **1960**—*Coast Along* **1961**—(– Gunter; + Earl "Speedoo" Carroll [b. Nov. 2, 1937, New York], tenor) **1962**—*Greatest Recordings* **1964**—(– Jones; + Ronnie Bright [b. Oct. 18, 1938]; – Guy; + Jimmy Norman, baritone) **1974**—*On Broadway* (King) **1978**—*20 Great Originals* (Atlantic).

The Coasters' comic vocals plus the writing and produc-tion of Jerry Leiber and Mike Stoller resulted in a string of wisecracking doo-wop hits in the late Fifties. The group originated in the late Forties as a Los Angeles vocal quartet, the Robins. Protégés of Johnny Otis, they re-corded for Savoy Records, hitting #1 on the R&B charts in 1950 with "Double Crossing Blues," which featured Little Esther Phillips. They began their association with Leiber and Stoller when they moved from Crown Records to RCA in 1953. When Leiber and Stoller founded Spark Records in 1954, the Robins became the label's most successful act, hitting on the West Coast with "Riot in Cell Block No. 9," "Framed," "The Hatchet Man" and "Smokey Joe's Cafe." The last-named song attracted Atlantic Records, which bought the Robins' catalogue in 1955 and contracted Leiber and Stoller as independent producers.

At that point the Robins split into two groups, Carl Gardner and Bobby Nunn staying with Leiber and Stoller, while the other Robins went on to record for Whippet Records. Billy Guy and Leon Hughes joined Gardner and Nunn to become the Coasters (so named because of their West Coast origins).

Their first single as the Coasters, "Down in Mexico," made the R&B Top Ten in 1956. Its double-sided followup, "Searchin' " b/w "Young Blood," went to #1 on the R&B charts and #3 on the pop charts in 1957; it was the first of the Coasters' four gold records. The group, together with Leiber and Stoller, moved to New York and—after making several personnel changes (bringing in Cornelius Gunter from the Flairs)—returned to the charts with "Yakety Yak" (#1, 1958), "Charlie Brown" (#2, 1959), "Along Came Jones" (#9, 1959) and "Poison Ivy" (#7, 1959). Their backup group often featured King Curtis on sax and Mickey Baker or Adolph Jacobs on guitar. In the last years of the decade, the Coasters were the most popular black rock & roll group in America.

Four more Coasters records made the Top Forty in 1960 and 1961, and (joined by Earl Carroll, formerly of the Cadillacs, and Ronnie Bright, the featured vocalist on Johnny Cymbal's "Mr. Bass Man") they continued to record for Atco until 1966. Their last chart appearance was in 1971 ("Love Potion No. 9," #76), and they last worked with Leiber and Stoller in 1973. In recent years, Nunn, Gardner and Hughes individually, and Guy and Jones together, have led groups billed as the Coasters.

BILLY COBHAM
Born May 16, 1944, Panama
1973—*Spectrum* (Atlantic) **1974**—*Crosswinds; Total Eclipse* **1975**—*Shabazz; A Funky Thide of Sings* **1976**—*Life and Times; Live in Europe* **1978**—*Inner Conflicts; Simplicity of Expression* (Columbia) *A Live Mutha for Ya* **1979**—*B.C.* **1980**—*The Best of* **1982**—*Observations* (Elektra) **1983**—*Smokin'*.

Cobham is a jazz-rock drummer who has worked in numerous groups and as a solo artist. He learned to play the timbales by age three. When he was about seven, he and his mother moved from Panama to New York to join his father, a pianist. In 1959, he enrolled at the High School of Music and Art. After serving in the armed forces, he worked his way into New York jazz circles, playing regularly with the Billy Taylor Trio in 1967 and 1968.

That same year, he earned his first session credit, George Benson's *Giblet Gravy,* followed by two albums with Horace Silver. He has since played on more than 75 albums, backing James Brown, Carla Thomas, Quincy Jones, Roberta Flack, Mose Allison, Carlos Santana, Carly Simon, Sam and Dave, and Larry Coryell. In 1969, after stints with Stanley Turrentine and Kenny Burrell, he joined the Miles Davis band that virtually invented jazz rock, and played on five Davis albums. Concurrently, he cofounded the jazz-rock group Dreams, which lasted through 1970, disbanding after two albums for Columbia.

In 1971, Cobham joined fellow Davis alumnus John McLaughlin in his Mahavishnu Orchestra, staying with the group until the end of 1973. He then began his solo career, recording *Spectrum* with guest musicians like bassist Ron Carter, guitarist Tommy Bolin and saxophonist Joe Farrell. The album and its two successors made the pop Top Forty. In 1974, Cobham assembled a band called Spectrum, including keyboardist George Duke, guitarist John Scofield (who later joined Miles Davis) and ex-Santana bassist Doug Rauch (who was later replaced by Alphonso Johnson), which toured Europe that year. By 1976, the band had become the Billy Cobham–George Duke Band. In 1979 and 1980, he worked extensively as part of Jack Bruce's band. In 1980 and 1981, he played with Grateful Dead guitarist Bob Weir's Bobby and the Midnites. Cobham produced Airto's *Virgin Land* (1974) and pianist David Sancious' *Forest of Feelings* (1975).

EDDIE COCHRAN
Born October 3, 1938, Oklahoma City; died April 17, 1960, London
1960—*Eddie Cochran* (Liberty)   **1962**—*Cherished Memories;   Memorial Album;   Singing to My Baby*
1963—*Never to Be Forgotten*   **1964**—*My Way*   **1970**—*C'mon Everybody* (Sunset)   *10th Anniversary Album* (Liberty)   **1972**—*Legendary Masters* (United Artists).

In his brief career Eddie Cochran made a lasting imprint on rock with songs like "Summertime Blues." Born in Oklahoma, he was raised in Minnesota until 1949, when he moved with his family to Bell Gardens, California. By then he had taught himself to play the guitar in a blues style. He met songwriter Jerry Capehart, and together they released an unsuccessful single before moving to Nashville, where Cochran released another unsuccessful record in 1955. Capehart got Cochran a contract with

Liberty Records in 1956, and by mid-1957 his record sales justified his first national tours and a role in the film *Untamed Youth* (he also performed in *The Girl Can't Help It*). In March, 1958, Cochran and Capehart cowrote "Summertime Blues," an international hit a few months later. It has since revisited the charts in cover versions by the Who and Blue Cheer. Two hits—"C'mon Everybody" (#35, 1958) and "Somethin' Else" (#58, 1959)— established him as a star, especially in England.

Cochran toured steadily, backed by the Kelly Four (bassist Connie Smith, who was later replaced by Dave Schrieber; drummer Gene Ridgio and a series of pianists and saxophonists). He was an exceptionally talented guitarist, an energetic stage performer and an early master of studio overdubbing (he played and sang all the parts on both "C'mon Everybody" and "Summertime Blues"). Cochran was twenty-one when he died on April 17, 1960, in an auto accident en route to the London airport. His hit single at the time was "Three Steps to Heaven."

BRUCE COCKBURN
Born 1945, Ottawa
1970—*Bruce Cockburn* (Epic)   **1972**—*Sunwheel Dance*   **1973**—*Night Vision* (True North)   **1974**—*Salt Sun and Time*   **1975**—*Joy Will Find a Way*   **1976**—*In the Falling Dark* (Island)   **1977**—*Circles in the Storm*   **1978**—*Further Adventures*   **1979**—*Dancing in the Dragon's Jaw* (Millennium)   **1980**—*Humans*   **1981**—*Resume;   Inner City Front.*

Songwriter Bruce Cockburn is well known in Canada, but he has had only one U.S. hit. A virtuoso guitarist, he has progressed from folk-style songs to his own blend of jazz, reggae and rock, while his lyrics have moved from hippie-ish mysticism to openly fundamentalist Christianity. In his late teens, Cockburn traveled through Europe as a street musician, then studied at Boston's Berklee School of Music for three years before returning to Ottawa to play organ in a Top Forty cover band and harmonica in a blues band.

He made his recording debut in 1970 as a soloist; his first two albums, *Bruce Cockburn* and *Sunwheel Dance*, were released by American Epic, but his next four appeared only in Canada, where he began to win wide acclaim, including Juno Awards (Canadian Grammys). In 1976, he signed with Island and made forays into the U.S.; his first Millennium album included his first U.S. hit, "Wondering Where the Lions Are" (#21, 1980). *Resume* summed up his first ten albums.

JOE COCKER
Born John Robert Cocker, May 20, 1944, Sheffield, England
1969—*With a Little Help from My Friends* (A&M)
1970—*Joe Cocker!*   **1971**—*Mad Dogs and Englishmen*   **1972**—*Joe Cocker*   **1974**—*I Can Stand a*

Little Rain 1975—*Jamaica Say You Will* 1976—*Sting Ray* 1977—*Greatest Hits* 1978—*Luxury You Can Afford* 1982—*Sheffield Steel* (Island).

British white soul singer Joe Cocker parlayed Ray Charles-ish vocals and a spastic stage presence into a string of late-Sixties hits. By the mid-Seventies, Cocker's excesses in drugs and alcohol had earned him a reputation for vomiting onstage and made every tour a comeback.

Cocker attended Sheffield Central Technical School and worked as a gas fitter for the East Midlands Gas Board. In 1959, he joined his first group, the Cavaliers, playing drums and harmonica. He moved to lead vocals in 1961, and the band changed its name to Vance Arnold and the Avengers. They released regional singles and toured locally with the Hollies and the Rolling Stones. Decca offered Cocker a contract in 1964, and he took a six-month leave of absence from the gas company. Cocker's version of the Beatles' "I'll Cry Instead" and an English tour opening for Manfred Mann were ignored, and Cocker went back to his day job.

In the mid-Sixties, Cocker assembled the Grease Band, including guitarist Henry McCullough and keyboardist Chris Stainton, who stayed on as Cocker's musical director until 1972. They played Motown covers in northern England pubs until 1967, when producer Denny Cordell became Cocker's manager and persuaded him and the band to move to London. A Cocker-Stainton song, "Marjorine," became a minor British hit, and after some exposure in London, Cocker and the Grease Band, with guests Jimmy Page (Led Zeppelin), Steve Winwood and others recorded *With a Little Help from My Friends* in 1969. The title track went to #1 in England and #68 in the U.S., where Cocker's tour included an appearance at the Woodstock Festival.

During the U.S. tour, Cocker met Leon Russell, who wrote "Delta Lady" and coproduced *Joe Cocker!* Russell also pulled together the assemblage of musicians, animals and hangers-on for the boisterous "Mad Dogs and Englishmen" tour Cocker made in 1970, resulting in a double live album and a film. But the tour left Cocker broke and ill. On a 1972 tour, with Stainton again leading the band, Cocker was often too drunk to remember lyrics and hold down food, although material from that tour was released in 1976 as *Live in L.A.* Cocker toured Britain and then Australia, where he was arrested for possession of marijuana. He recorded intermittently through the Seventies, and in 1981 he recorded with the Crusaders. In 1982, his duet with Jennifer Warnes, "Up Where We Belong," from the movie *An Officer and a Gentleman*, hit #1.

DAVID ALLAN COE

Born September 6, 1939, Akron
1974—*Mysterious Rhinestone Cowboy* (Columbia)
Mysterious Rhinestone Cowboy Rides Again **1976**—

Once upon a Rhyme; Long-Haired Redneck **1977**—*David Allan Coe Rides Again; Tattoo* **1978**—*The Family Album* **1979**—*Human Emotions* **1980**—*I've Got Something to Say* **1981**—*Invictus Means Unconquered* **1982**—*DAC* **1983**—*Castles in the Sand.*

Singer/songwriter David Allan Coe is the composer of country hits like Tanya Tucker's "Would You Lay with Me (in a Field of Stone)" and Johnny Paycheck's "Take This Job and Shove It." Coe's life is the stuff of outlaw legends. Orphaned at age nine, he was arrested the next year for stealing a car. After spending several years in an Ohio reformatory, he was released on parole, only to be arrested again for possession of obscene material (a comic book). He was sentenced to the Ohio State Correctional Facility, where he claims to have fatally stabbed a fellow convict who made homosexual advances toward him. According to Coe, he was convicted of murder and spent three months on death row before Ohio's abolition of the death penalty. By the time he was finally released in 1967, he had been writing songs for 14 years.

Encouraged by fellow prisoner Screamin' Jay Hawkins, Coe pursued his music career and with singer Hugh X. Lewis' help met music publisher Audie Ashworth and producer Shelby Singleton, who helped get Coe a contract with his Plantation label; Coe later signed with Columbia. Coe's albums have sold respectably over the years, though his greatest success has been as a songwriter of hits for other artists. In 1976, he was featured in a PBS documentary, *The Mysterious Rhinestone Cowboy.*

LEONARD COHEN

Born September 21, 1934, Montreal
1968—*Songs of Leonard Cohen* (Columbia) *Songs from a Room* **1970**—*Songs of Love and Hate* **1973**—*Live Songs* **1974**—*New Skin for Old Ceremony* **1975**—*Greatest Hits* **1977**—*Death of a Ladies' Man* **1979**—*Recent Songs.*

Singer/songwriter Leonard Cohen was a noted poet and novelist before turning to music in the Sixties. His songs have been widely covered, by Judy Collins ("Suzanne," "Famous Blue Raincoat") and Tim Hardin ("Bird on a Wire"), among others, and in Europe his aura of quasi-suicidal romantic despair has won him acclaim as an heir of Jacques Brel.

Cohen studied English literature at Montreal's McGill University and later at Columbia University in New York, and published his first book of poems, *Let Us Compare Mythologies*, in 1956. In 1957, he recited his poetry to jazz piano backup, beat-style. Cohen tried and failed to sell songs in the late Fifties, and continued to write poems as well as two novels, *The Favorite Game* (1963) and *Beautiful Losers* (1966).

He set some poems from his 1966 collection, *Parasites*

of Heaven, to simple chord progressions; Judy Collins recorded one of them, "Suzanne," for her album *In My Life,* and she brought Cohen onstage at a 1967 Central Park concert. Cohen performed at the 1967 Newport Folk Festival, and his debut album came out early in 1968. Songs from that album later appeared on the soundtrack of Robert Altman's *McCabe and Mrs. Miller.*

After his second album, Cohen began extensive touring of the U.S. and Europe and appeared in 1970 at the Isle of Wight Festival. But he cut back on touring after *Songs of Love and Hate;* although he entertained Israeli troops in 1973, his *Live Songs* was recorded around 1970.

Cohen lived on a Greek island in the mid-Seventies and continued to write poems, prose and songs. In 1976, he resumed touring, and in 1977 he collaborated with Sixties pop producer Phil Spector on *Death of a Ladies Man,* which also included backing vocals by Bob Dylan. He pronounced the finished album mix a "castastrophe," and on *Recent Songs* he returned to a more conventional folk-pop style.

NATALIE COLE
Born February 6, 1950, Los Angeles
1975—*Inseparable* (Capitol)   1976—*Natalie*   1977—*Thankful*   1978—*Natalie . . . Live!*   1980—*Don't Look Back.*

Nat "King" Cole's daughter Natalie was a major star in the second half of the Seventies, although she never lived up to her original billing as the next Aretha Franklin. While attending the University of Massachusetts at Amherst, she began singing in local clubs and had secured professional management by the early Seventies. Her string of gold and platinum records began in 1975 with *Inseparable* and its single, "This Will Be" (#6, 1975).

She subsequently released a top-selling album nearly every year throughout the Seventies and made consistent appearances on the singles charts: "Sophisticated Lady" (#25, 1976), "I've Got Love on My Mind" (#5, 1977), "Our Love" (#10, 1978). In 1978, she hosted "The Natalie Cole Special" on prime-time TV. She has won several Grammys, including two in 1976 for "This Will Be." As of early 1982, she had left Capitol and was looking for a new label.

ORNETTE COLEMAN
Born March 19, 1930, Fort Worth
1958—*Something Else* (Contemporary)   *Tomorrow Is the Question*   1959—*The Shape of Jazz to Come* (Atlantic)   1960—*The Change of the Century;   This Is Our Music;   Free Jazz*   1965—*At the Golden Circle, vols. 1 and 2* (Blue Note)   *Crisis* (Impulse)   1971—*Science Fiction* (Columbia)   1972—*Skies of America* 1977—*Dancing in Your Head* (Horizon)   1979—*Body Meta* (Artists' House)   1980—*Soapsuds, Soapsuds*

1982—*Of Human Feelings* (Antilles)   *Broken Shadows* (Columbia).

Ornette Coleman's bluesy, playful music revolutionized jazz in the Sixties by ignoring regular harmonies and rhythms. In the Seventies he formalized his "harmolodic" theory and applied it to rock instrumentation with his group Prime Time, pioneering a powerful and increasingly influential jazz-rock-funk-ethnic-music fusion.

Coleman taught himself to play alto sax in his early teens. At age 16, he switched to tenor sax and began playing in R&B and jazz bands around the South. His unorthodox notions of music were already meeting resistance (he switched back to alto sax when three members of the audience in Baton Rouge threw his tenor sax over a cliff), and he got used to getting fired. In 1950, he wrote an unpublished book in which he theorized that melody "has nothing to do with harmony or chords or key centers."

He went to Los Angeles in 1952 with the Pee Wee Crayton Band. He returned to Fort Worth after Crayton fired him, then returned to Los Angeles in 1954. The L.A. jazz community ignored him for most of the decade. In 1958, he formed his first band with trumpeter Don Cherry, bassist Charlie Haden and drummer Billy Higgins, and established a mode of playing in which, as he explained, "no one player has the lead; anyone can come out with it at any time."

In 1959, the Coleman quartet went to New York, where their engagements and Atlantic recordings developed the concept of "free jazz." For *Free Jazz,* a collective improvisation, Coleman employed a "double quartet" (drummers Higgins and Eddie Blackwell, trumpeters Cherry and Freddie Hubbard, bassists Haden and Scott LaFaro and reedmen Coleman and Eric Dolphy).

Coleman withdrew from public performance from 1962 to 1965 and taught himself to play trumpet and violin. When he resumed performing, he introduced compositions for these instruments and for wind quintets, larger chamber ensembles and vocalists. He rarely performed with a regular band, although he continued to collaborate with Haden, Cherry, Higgins, Blackwell and tenor saxophonist Dewey Redman. (In the late Seventies, Cherry, Haden, Redman and Blackwell formed Old and New Dreams, playing their own music and occasional new Coleman tunes.) He also played with saxophonist Pharoah Sanders, drummer Elvin Jones and Yoko Ono (in 1970 on *Yoko Ono/Plastic Ono Band*).

A Guggenheim fellowship allowed him to compose *Skies of America,* a long work for orchestra which he debuted at 1972's Newport in New York Festival and recorded later that year with the London Symphony Orchestra. *Skies of America* introduced his theory of "harmelody," in which harmonies, rhythms and melodies function independently.

Coleman went to Morocco in 1973 to record with the

Master Musicians of Joujouka (a short selection was included on *Dancing in Your Head*), and in New York and Paris he turned to electric guitar, teaching himself to play the instrument and working with guitarist James "Blood" Ulmer. He rehearsed a new band, Prime Time (electric guitarists Bern Nix and Charles Ellerbee, electric bassist Rudy MacDaniel and drummers Ronald Shannon Jackson and his son Ornette Denardo Coleman), for two years before recording *Dancing in Your Head* in Paris and introducing them at the 1977 Newport in New York Festival.

Prime Time's music incorporates rock and funk rhythms and melodic fragments that recall Joujouka and R&B among its harmolodic possibilities; Coleman considers it dance music. The band's instrumentation—especially in more recent lineups—suggests a double rock band version of Coleman's double quintets. In the early Eighties, ex–Prime Time members Ulmer and Jackson started their own harmolodic rock-funk bands, and Coleman returned to public performance, touring the U.S. and Europe in 1982.

ALBERT COLLINS

Born October 1, 1932, Leona, Texas

N.A.—*Truckin' with Albert Collins* (Blue Thumb) *The Cool Sound of Albert Collins* (TCF Hall) *Love Can Be Found Anywhere (Even in a Guitar)* (Imperial) *The Compleat Albert Collins* 1971—*There's Gotta Be a Change* (Tumbleweed) 1978—*Ice Pickin'* (Alligator) 1980—*Frostbite; Alive and Cool* (Red Lightnin').

Guitarist/singer/songwriter Albert Collins' hard-rocking Texas shuffle blues and his gregarious showmanship have made him one of the most popular contemporary bluesmen.

The son of sharecroppers, he grew up in rural Texas before moving to Houston's Third Ward ghetto at age nine. He studied piano in school, and a cousin gave him a cheap electric guitar and taught him the unusual minor-key tuning that remains a distinctive aspect of his sound. Another cousin, Sam "Lightnin' " Hopkins, was a primary influence on his single-string guitar technique.

Collins began working the Houston blues-club circuit in 1948, playing with Clarence "Gatemouth" Brown. The following year, he formed his own band, the Rhythm Rockers, and fronted them until 1951, when he joined Piney Brown's band. After leaving Brown in 1954, he became a pickup guitarist, performing and occasionally recording with Johnny "Guitar" Watson, Little Richard and Willie Mae Thornton, among others. A 1958 session resulted in his first record, "The Freeze," an instrumental that introduced Collins' "cool sound"—the highly amplified, sustained treble notes of his guitar set against the three horns, keyboard (piano or, more often, organ), bass and drums. Over the next five years, he recorded more

than a dozen such instrumentals, including "Defrost," "Thaw-Out," "Sno-Cone" and "Hot 'n' Cold." Several were regional hits. "Frosty" reportedly sold a million copies in 1962 without placing on national charts.

In 1969, Collins moved to Los Angeles. Bob Hite of Canned Heat got him a contract with Imperial Records and members of Canned Heat produced three of his albums—his first recordings as a vocalist. The Canned Heat connection attracted young, white blues fans, and Collins frequently played West Coast rock venues, including the Fillmore West.

In 1971, Collins was the first artist signed to Bill Szymczyk's Tumbleweed label, but Tumbleweed folded two years later, and he did not record again until 1978. With his band the Icebreakers, he recorded *Ice Pickin'*, which was named Best Blues Album of 1979 by several American and European journals and nominated for a Grammy Award. He has since recorded regularly, toured the U.S. several times and performed at jazz and blues festivals in this country and abroad.

BOOTSY COLLINS

Born William Collins, October 26, 1951, Cincinnati

1976—*Stretchin' Out in Bootsy's Rubber Band* (Warner Bros.) 1977—*Ahh . . . the Name Is Bootsy, Baby!* 1978—*Bootsy? Player of the Year* 1979—*This Boot Is Made for Fonk-N* 1980—*Ultra Wave* 1982—*The One Giveth and the Count Taketh Away.*

As Parliament-Funkadelic bassist and songwriter, Collins has attracted a personal following to challenge George Clinton's. Already given to spontaneous reproduction, it was natural for P-Funk to spawn Bootsy's Rubber Band. While Bootsy's records have sold better than the parent group's, Collins continues to play with P-Funk.

Collins worked as a session musician for King Records in his hometown of Cincinnati until James Brown recruited the 16-year-old and his group, the Pacemakers, into his J.B.s in 1969. Two years later, Collins left Brown, and after doing sessions with the Spinners and Johnnie Taylor and turning down the Spinners' invitation to join them, he joined P-Funk. He became Clinton's right-hand man, contributing music and lyrics to many of P-Funk's best-known songs and helping to formulate the band's doctrine of "silly seriousness." When Clinton negotiated Funkadelic's contract with Warner Bros. in 1976, a solo contract for Collins was part of the deal.

Collins put together Bootsy's Rubber Band from musicians outside the P-Funk family. Guitarist Phelps "Catfish" Collins (Bootsy's elder brother) and drummer Frankie "Kash" Waddy had been Pacemakers and J.B.s; saxophonist Maceo Parker and trombonist Fred Wesley had been J.B. stalwarts until Collins lured them to the Rubber Band; others had been members of the Complete Strangers, a Cincinnati band Collins had sponsored—

Bootsy Collins

singers Gary "Mudbone" Cooper, Leslyn Bailey and Robert "Peanuts" Johnson; keyboardist Frederick "Flintstone" Allen (later replaced by Joel "Razor Sharp" Johnson); and trumpeters Rick Gardner and Richard "Kush" Griffith. The Rubber Band became part of P-Funk; its horn section, the Horny Horns, became an integral part of every P-Funk session; and Clinton brainchildren like the Brides of Funkenstein sang with the Rubber Band.

With Clinton collaborating with Collins on material and production, Bootsy's albums were very much in the P-Funk mold: irrepressibly rhythmic, ironic, at once earthy and spacy. The ostensible difference was in their intended audiences. While P-Funk was aimed at teenaged older American youth, Bootsy wrote for the "geepies"—kids six to 12 years old who could respond to songs of Collins' alter egos like Caspar the Friendly Ghost and Bootzilla. He advocated abstinence from drugs and liquor (if not prepubertal sex) and projected an aura of childlike optimism.

His first three albums went gold (*Player of the Year* went to #1 R&B), and he had eight R&B Top Thirty singles in five years: "Stretchin' Out" (#18, 1976), "I'd Rather Be with You" (#25, 1976), "The Pinocchio Theory" (#6, 1977), "Can't Stay Away" (#19, 1977), "Bootzilla" (#1, 1978), "Hollywood Squares" (#17, 1978), "Jam Fan (Hot)" (#13, 1979) and "Mug Push" (#25, 1980).

Aside from his work with the Rubber Band and P-Funk, Collins has produced, arranged and written songs for other acts. He arranged Johnnie Taylor's 1976 gold hit, "Disco Lady." He produced albums by Zapp and the Sweat Band in 1980 and by Godmoma in 1981. He has also collaborated on songs with Sly Stewart and James Brown.

JUDY COLLINS

Born May 1, 1939, Seattle
1961—*A Maid of Constant Sorrow* (Elektra) **1962**—*Golden Apples of the Sun* **1964**—*Judy Collins #3; The Judy Collins Concert* **1965**—*Judy Collins' Fifth Album* **1966**—*In My Life* **1967**—*Wildflowers* **1968**—*Who Knows Where the Time Goes* **1969**—*Recollections* **1970**—*Whales and Nightingales* **1971**—*Both Sides Now; Living* **1972**—*Colors of the Day/The Best of Judy Collins* **1973**—*True Stories and Other Dreams* **1975**—*Judith* **1976**—*Bread and Roses* **1977**—*So Early in Spring* **1979**—*The Most Beautiful Songs of Judy Collins; Hard Times for Lovers* **1980**—*Running for My Life* (Columbia).

Judy Collins, who describes herself as an "interpretive singer," was a major force in Sixties folk rock, and her cover versions provided exposure for then-unknown songwriters, including Joni Mitchell, Leonard Cohen, Sandy Denny and Randy Newman. Her later repertoire incorporated show tunes, pop standards and cabaret material. Collins' clear, unwavering soprano has been equally effective on "Both Sides Now" (#8, 1968) and "Send in the Clowns" (#19, 1975).

Inspired by her blind father, Chuck Collins, a bandleader and radio personality in the Rocky Mountain area, she began classical piano training at five and made her public debut at 13 with the Denver Symphony. Collins attended college in Jacksonville, Illinois, and then the University of Colorado. She had become interested in traditional folk music and began playing regularly in local coffee houses before moving to Chicago around 1960. By then she had married college lecturer Peter Taylor (they were divorced in 1966). Shortly after moving to Chicago, her debut album, *A Maid of Constant Sorrow*, was released.

She began steady club work and met politically conscious folksinger/songwriters with whom she frequently performed at civil rights rallies. Her later political concerns would include ecology, endangered species and abortion rights. *Judy Collins #3* and *The Judy Collins Concert* found her moving away from traditional ballads and focusing on protest material by Bob Dylan, Tom Paxton and Phil Ochs.

With *In My Life,* she abandoned the sparse production of her early folk-oriented efforts for the often idiosyncratic experiments of producer Joshua Rifkin, who later spurred the Scott Joplin revival with his piano rag recordings. On her first gold LP, *Wildflowers,* she debuted as a songwriter. Her gold string continued with *Who Knows Where the Time Goes,* on which her backing ensemble included Stephen Stills on guitar. The alliance prompted a short affair, which Stills later documented in the Crosby, Stills and Nash hit "Suite: Judy Blue Eyes."

In 1969, she played Solveig in the New York Shakespeare Festival's production of Ibsen's *Peer Gynt.* Two years later, *Whales and Nightingales* went gold with a hit single: an unaccompanied choral version of "Amazing Grace." In 1974 Collins codirected the documentary *Anto-*

nia: A Portrait of the Woman, about a former music teacher turned conductor; it was nominated for an Academy Award.

In 1975, she released one of her best-selling LPs, *Judith,* which produced a major European hit, "Send in the Clowns" (from Stephen Sondheim's *A Little Night Music).* Despite the help of veteran producer Jerry Wexler, *Bread and Roses* was her first album in nine years that did not go gold, and she maintained a very low profile for the next 2½ years. By 1980, she had switched from Elektra to Columbia.

Grammy Awards

Glen Campbell
1967 Best Vocal Performance, Male; Best Contemporary Male Solo Vocal Performance: "By the Time I Get to Phoenix"
Best Country and Western Recording; Best Country and Western Solo Vocal Performance, Male: "Gentle on My Mind"
1968 Album of the Year: *By the Time I Get to Phoenix*

Captain and Tennille
1975 Record of the Year: "Love Will Keep Us Together"

Kim Carnes
1981 Record of the Year: "Bette Davis Eyes"

The Carpenters
1970 Best New Artist of the Year; Best Contemporary Vocal Performance by a Group: "Close to You"
1971 Best Pop Vocal Performance by a Group: *Carpenters*

Johnny Cash
1967 Best Country and Western Performance Duet, Trio or Group, Vocal or Instrumental: "Jackson" (with June Carter Cash)
1968 Best Country Vocal Performance, Male: "Folsom Prison Blues"

1969 Best Country Vocal Performance, Male: "A Boy Named Sue"
1970 Best Country Performance by a Duo or Group: "If I Were a Carpenter" (with June Carter Cash)

The Champs
1958 Best R&B Performance: "Tequila"

Ray Charles
1960 Best Vocal Performance Single Record or Track; Best Performance by a Pop Single Artist: "Georgia on My Mind"
Best Vocal Performance, Album, Male: *Genius of Ray Charles*
Best R&B Performance: "Let the Good Times Roll"
1961 Best R&B Recording: "Hit the Road Jack"
1962 Best R&B Recording: "I Can't Stop Loving You"
1963 Best R&B Recording: "Busted"
1966 Best R&B Recording; Best R&B Solo Vocal Performance, Male: "Crying Time"
1975 Best R&B Vocal Performance, Male: "Living for the City"

Chubby Checker
1961 Best Rock & Roll Recording: "Let's Twist Again"

Chicago
1976 Best Pop Vocal Performance by a Duo, Group or Chorus: "If You Leave Me Now"

The Chipmunks (Ross Bagdasarian)
1958 Best Comedy Performance; Best Recording for Children: "The Chipmunk Song"
1960 Best Album Created for Children: *Let's All Sing with the Chipmunks*

Eric Clapton
1972 Album of the Year: *The Concert for Bangla Desh* (with others)

Petula Clark
1964 Best Rock & Roll Recording: "Downtown"
1965 Best Contemporary Rock & Roll Vocal Performance, Female: "I Know a Place"

Reverend James Cleveland
1974 Best Soul Gospel Performance: *In the Ghetto*
1977 Best Soul Gospel Performance, Traditional: *James Cleveland Live at Carnegie Hall*
1980 Best Soul Gospel Performance, Traditional: *Lord, Let Me Be an Instrument* (with the Charles Fold Singers)

Joe Cocker and Jennifer Warnes
1982 Best Pop Vocal Performance
by a Duo or Group with
Vocal: "Up Where We
Belong"

Natalie Cole
1975 Best New Artist of the Year;
Best R&B Vocal Performance,
Female:
"This Will Be"
1976 Best R&B Vocal Performance,
Female:
"Sophisticated Lady (She's a
Different Lady)"

Judy Collins
1968 Best Folk Performance:
"Both Sides Now"

Rita Coolidge
1973 Best Country Vocal Performance by a Duo or Group:
"From the Bottle to the
Bottom" (with Kris Kristofferson)

1975 Best Country Vocal Perform-
ance by a Duo or Group:
"Lover Please" (with Kris
Kristofferson)

Chick Corea
1975 Best Jazz Performance by a
Group:
No Mystery (with Return to
Forever)
1976 Best Jazz Performance by a
Group:
The Leprechaun
1978 Best Jazz Instrumental
Performance, Group:
Friends
1979 Best Jazz Instrumental
Performance, Group:
Duet (with Gary Burton)
1981 Best Jazz Instrumental
Performance, Group:
*Chick Corea and Gary Burton
in Concert, Zurich, October
28, 1979* (with Gary Burton)

John Cougar
1982 Best Rock Vocal Performance,
Male:
"Hurts So Good"

Steve Cropper
1968 Best R&B Song:
"(Sittin' on) The Dock of the
Bay" (with Otis Redding)

Crosby, Stills and Nash
1969 Best New Artist

Christopher Cross
1980 Best New Artist; Record of
the Year; Song of the Year:
"Sailing"
Album of the Year:
Christopher Cross

King Curtis
1969 Best R&B Instrumental
Performance:
"Games People Play"

COLOSSEUM AND COLOSSEUM II

Formed 1968, England
Jon Hiseman (b. June 21, 1944, London), drums; Dick
Heckstall-Smith (b. Sep. 26, 1934, Ludlow, Eng.), saxes;
Tony Reeves (b. Apr. 18, 1943, London), bass; Jimmy
Litherland (b. Sep. 6, 1949, Manchester, Eng.), gtr.,
voc.; Dave Greenslade (b. Jan. 18, 1943, Woking, Eng.),
kybds.
1969—*Those Who Are About to Die Salute You*
(Dunhill) *Valentyne Suite* (Bronze) (– Litherland;
+ Dave "Clem" Clempson [b. Sep. 5, 1949], gtr;
– Reeves) *The Grass Is Greener* (Dunhill) **1970**—
(+ Chris Farlowe [b. Oct. 13, 1940, Essex, Eng.], voc.;
+ Mike Clarke [b. July 25, 1950, Liverpool], bass)
Daughter of Time **1971**—*Live* (Warner Bros.)
Collectors' Colosseum (Bronze) (group disbanded;
Colosseum II formed summer 1975: Hiseman; Gary
Moore [b. Ire.], gtr.; Mike Starrs, voc.; Neil Murray,
bass; Don Airey, kybds.) **1976**—*Strange New Flesh*
(Warner Bros.) (– Murray; + John Mole, bass;
– Starrs) **1977**—*Electric Savage* (MCA) *Wardance*
1978—(– Moore; + Keith Airey, gtr.).

Drummer/composer Jon Hiseman's Colosseum, an early
British jazz-rock fusion band, turned out to be a training
ground for hard-rock and fusion musicians. Hiseman and
Dick Heckstall-Smith first played together in one of Gra-
ham Bond's early-Sixties R&B bands, then with John
Mayall. After Mayall's 1968 LP *Bare Wires*, they and ex-
Mayall bassist Tony Reeves started Colosseum to try
more complex music.

In 1969, Colosseum released two LPs and toured England and the U.S. Hiseman reorganized the band with
himself more clearly in charge, and the second lineup
recorded four albums before officially disbanding in 1971.
With Mike Clarke (later of Uriah Heep), Hiseman formed
the short-lived Tempest; Clempson replaced Peter Frampton in Humble Pie; Chris Farlowe joined Atomic Rooster;
and Dave Greenslade started his own band, Greenslade.
Hiseman and sometime Thin Lizzy guitarist Gary Moore
started Colosseum II in 1975, but after three LPs the group
disbanded in 1978.

JESSI COLTER

Born Miriam Johnson, Phoenix, Arizona
1970—*A Country Star Is Born* (RCA) **1975**—*I'm Jessi Colter* (Capitol) **1976**—*Jessi; Diamond in the Rough* **1977**—*Mirriam* **1978**—*That's the Way a Cowboy Rocks and Rolls* **1980**—*Leather and Lace* (with Waylon Jennings) **1981**—*Ridin' Shotgun.*

Country-pop singer Jessi Colter adopted her stage name from one of Jesse James's gang of outlaw rogues. At age 16 she married guitarist Duane Eddy. They divorced in 1968, and in 1969 she married Waylon Jennings. She first gained prominence by writing songs for Dottie West, Don Gibson, Nancy Sinatra and others. *I'm Jessi Colter* gave her a pop hit with "I'm Not Lisa" (#4, 1975). She has since released several more country-pop albums and appeared on the *Outlaws* compilation with her husband and Willie Nelson. She tours frequently with Jennings, who usually contributes background vocals and guitar to her albums.

COMMANDER CODY AND HIS LOST PLANET AIRMEN

Formed 1968, Ann Arbor, Michigan
Original personnel: Commander Cody (b. George Frayne, Boise, Id.), voc., piano; John Tichy (b. St. Louis), gtr., voc.; Andy Stein (b. New York City), fiddle, sax, trombone; Billy C. Farlow (b. Decatur, Ala.), voc., gtr.; Rick Higginbotham, gtr.; Stan Davis, pedal steel gtr.; Bill Kirchen (b. Ann Arbor), gtr., voc.
1971—*Lost in the Ozone* (Paramount) **1972**—*Hot Licks, Cold Steel and Trucker's Favorites* **1973**—*Country Casanova* **1974**—*Live from Deep in the Heart of Texas* **1975**—*Commander Cody and His Lost Planet Airmen* (Warner Bros.) *Tales from the Ozone* **1976**—*We Got a Live One Here!; Midnight Man* (Arista) **1977**—*Rock 'n' Roll Again.*

Behind their hard-drinking, deep-toking image, Commander Cody's various bands have always played a virtuosic, revved-up assortment of boogie-woogie, Western swing, country and rockabilly. Frayne grew up in Brooklyn and studied sculpture and painting at the University of Michigan; during summers, he was a lifeguard at Long Island's Jones Beach, where he performed with an all-lifeguard band, Lorenzo Lightfoot A. C. and Blues Band. After graduating, Frayne and some college friends formed the Lost Planet Airmen, which played around the Michigan and Wisconsin area while Frayne taught art for a year at Wisconsin State University.

When the band lineup stabilized, they moved to San Francisco in 1968 and earned a local following. Their debut album, *Lost in the Ozone,* mixed originals like "Seeds and Stems" and oldies, notably a hit remake of Tex Ritter's "Hot Rod Lincoln" (#9, 1972). The followup, *Hot Licks, Cold Steel and Trucker's Favorites,* was re-corded on four tracks for a mere $5000. They toured through the early Seventies and had two more novelty hits—"Beat Me Daddy Eight to the Bar" (#81, 1972), and Ritter's "Smoke Smoke Smoke" (#94, 1973)—before leaving Paramount to sign with Warner Bros.

The making of the band's Warner debut album was chronicled in Geoffrey Stokes's book *Starmaking Machinery.* The album included Cody's last U.S. hit, "Don't Let Go." After a 1976 European tour, the Airmen disbanded. Lance Dickerson and Bruce Barlow joined Roger McGuinn in his Thunderbyrd. Frayne has toured sporadically and recorded as Cody with various "New Commander Cody" bands that have included Nicolette Larson and ex-Wings drummer Joe English. He published some of his paintings in the 1979 book *StarArt.* Although he was without a U.S. label in the early Eighties, he scored a major hit in Europe with 1980's "Two Triple Cheese (Side Order of Fries)."

THE COMMODORES

Formed 1968, Tuskegee, Alabama
Lionel Richie, Jr. (b. 1950, Ala.), voc., sax; Milan Williams (b. 1949, Miss.), kybds., trombone, gtr.; Ronald LaPread (b. 1950, Ala.), bass, trumpet; Walter "Clyde" Orange (b. 1947, Fla.), drums; William King (b. 1949, Ala.), horns; Thomas McClary (b. 1950, Fla.), gtr.
1974—*Machine Gun* (Motown) **1975**—*Caught in the Act; Movin' On* **1976**—*Hot on the Tracks* **1977**—*Commodores; Commodores Live* **1978**—*Natural High; Greatest Hits* **1979**—*Midnight Magic; 1978 Platinum Tour* **1980**—*Heroes* **1981**—*In the Pocket.*

The Commodores are a pop-and-funk sextet whose record sales now total over 30 million. In their early years, they were a funky party band, whose music was heavily influenced by Sly and the Family Stone and the Bar-Kays. But during their second, more successful phase, the Commodores became a popular ballad group led by singer/songwriter Lionel Richie.

The six group members met at a Tuskegee Institute talent show when they were all freshmen. With drummer Walter Orange, the only one with prior professional experience, handling vocals, the group began performing as the Jays. They later picked the name Commodores out of a dictionary by placing a finger on the page. In the summer of 1969, they traveled via van to New York City, specifically to Harlem, where they sought summer employment. Soon after their arrival, their equipment was stolen, then sold back to them. Undaunted, they landed a gig at Small's Paradise, where they met a local businessman they knew, Benny Ashburn, who became their manager. They signed to Atlantic Records and released one single produced by Jerry "Swamp Dogg" Williams, which did not chart.

The Commodores: Thomas McClary, Walter Orange, Ronald LaPread, Milan Williams, William King, Lionel Richie

In 1971, the group signed to Motown, and for the first two years worked as the opening act for the Jackson 5. Refusing to conform to the established Motown style, they did not record until 1974, when they were teamed up with producer/arranger James Carmichael, who has produced all their albums.

On their first three albums, the Commodores' sound was dominated by a hard funk, which inspired one reviewer to describe them as "black music's answer to heavy metal." The group had several early hits, including "Machine Gun" (#22, 1974), "I Feel Sanctified" (#75, 1974), "Slippery When Wet" (#19, 1975) and "Fancy Dancer" (#39, 1977).

Although each of the group members writes, Richie eventually became the Commodores' main songwriter, and by 1977 his ballads were taking center stage; "Just to Be Close to You," "Sweet Love" and "Easy" were hits.

By 1978, when the group appeared in the disco movie *Thank God It's Friday,* the Commodores were moving swiftly toward crossover pop stardom, largely on the strength of Richie tunes like "Three Times a Lady" (#1, 1978), a platinum single that firmly established the Commodores as the premier black pop group. "Sail On" and "Still" were Top Five ballads in 1979.

Richie has since pursued outside projects. He wrote the #1 "Lady" and produced "Share Your Love" for Kenny Rogers. He also wrote and performed a duet with Diana Ross on another #1 hit, the title theme song from the movie *Endless Love.* In 1982 Richie released his solo debut, *Lionel Richie* (Motown), featuring his Top Five hit "Truly." Earlier that year Ashburn died of a heart attack in New Jersey. The Commodores' first three LPs are gold; all subsequent releases are platinum.

CON FUNK SHUN
Formed 1968, Vallejo, California
Michael Cooper, gtr., percussion, voc.; Karl Fuller, trumpet, voc.; Paul Harrell, saxes, flute, voc.; Cedric Martin, bass, voc.; Louis McCall, drums, voc.; Felton Pilate, trombone, trumpet, voc.; Danny Thomas, kybds., voc.
1976—*Con Funk Shun* (Mercury) 1977—*Secrets* 1978— *Loveshine* 1979—*Candy* 1980—*Spirit of Love; Touch* 1982—*Con Funk Shun 7.*

This Memphis soul band had been together almost ten years when they placed "Ffun" at the top of the national soul charts in 1977. In 1968, high school classmates Michael Cooper and Louis McCall formed the group, calling it Project Soul, and established its current lineup within a year. In the early Seventies, Project Soul backed the Stax Records group the Soul Children (and in that capacity appeared in the 1973 movie *Wattstax*). In 1972, they moved to Memphis and changed their name to Con Funk Shun. After several local hits on Memphis labels, Mercury signed them in 1976. Con Funk Shun made their first appearance on national charts with "Sho Feels Good to Me" the following year.

The success of "Ffun" (#23 on pop charts, it made *Secrets* the first of an as-yet-unbroken line of gold albums) has been followed up by "Confunkshunizeya" (#31, 1978), "Shake and Dance with Me" (#5, 1978), "So Easy" (#28, 1978), "Chase Me" (#4, 1979), "Love on Your Mind" (#24, 1979), "Got to Be Enough" (#8, 1980), "By Your Side" (#27, 1980) and "Too Tight" (#8, 1980).

ARTHUR CONLEY
Born April 1, 1946, Atlanta
1967—*Sweet Soul Music* (Atco) 1969—*More Sweet Soul.*

Arthur Conley was a minor soul star when his "Sweet Soul Music" hit #2 in 1967. Conley had been discovered by Otis Redding around 1965. He became Redding's protégé and was signed to Stax-Volt, later touring internationally with that label's revue. With Redding as producer, Conley recorded "Sweet Soul Music," a Conley-Cooke-Redding litany of praise for the black male soul stars of the era that used the melody of a Sam Cooke tune entitled "Yeah Man." As the Sixties closed, Conley had several minor hits, including a cover of the Beatles' "Ob-la-di, Ob-la-da" (#51, 1969). By the Seventies, he had faded from sight.

THE CONTOURS

Formed 1958, Detroit
Billy Gordon, voc.; Billy Hoggs, voc.; Joe Billingslea, voc.; Sylvester Potts, voc.; Hubert Johnson, voc.; Huey Davis, voc., gtr.
1981—*Do You Love Me?* (Motown).

Hoarse screams over feverish dance beats characterized the Contours' string of hits in the mid-Sixties. Originally a quartet formed in 1958 by Billy Gordon, Billy Hoggs, Joe Billingslea and Sylvester Potts, the Contours were unknown even in their hometown of Detroit until joined by Hubert Johnson. Johnson had them sing for his cousin Jackie Wilson, and in turn Wilson presented them to Motown owner Berry Gordy, Jr. They cut their first record, "Whole Lotta Woman," in 1961; when it flopped, Gordy prepared to drop them. Wilson persuaded Gordy to give them another chance. That chance was a Gordy composition, "Do You Love Me?," which the Contours took to the top of the charts in 1962 (#1 R&B, #3 pop). (The song was later covered many times, notably by the Dave Clark Five.)

While they never repeated the success of the million-selling "Do You Love Me?" they did follow it with five more clear-the-floor-'cause-I-gotta-dance numbers: "Shake Sherry" (#21 R&B, 1963), "Can You Jerk Like Me?" (#15, 1965), "The Day When She Needed Me" (#37, 1965), "First I Look at the Purse" (#12, 1965) and "Just a Little Misunderstanding" (#18, 1966). Their last chart hit, "It's So Hard Being a Loser" (#35, 1967), was a ballad. One later member of the Contours was future Temptation Dennis Edwards.

RY COODER

Born March 15, 1947, Los Angeles
1970—*Ry Cooder* (Reprise) **1972**—*Into the Purple Valley; Boomer's Story* **1974**—*Paradise and Lunch* **1976**—*Chicken Skin Music* **1977**—*Showtime* (Warner Bros.) **1978**—*Jazz* **1979**—*Bop till You Drop* **1980**—*Long Riders* (soundtrack) **1981**—*Borderline* **1982**—*The Border* (soundtrack) *The Slide Area.*

Ry Cooder is a virtuoso on fretted instruments—slide guitar, mandolin, Mexican tiple, banjo, Middle Eastern saz—who crossbreeds his own sense of syncopation with vernacular musics. As a fan/musicologist, he has sought out local styles such as calypso, Hawaiian "slack-key" guitar, Tex-Mex, gospel, country and vaudeville "coon songs." He records with L.A. session players and various "ethnic" musicians in and out of their own contexts.

Cooder began playing guitar when he was three years old. He has had a glass eye since he was four, when he accidentally stuck a knife in his left eye. In the early Sixties, Cooder became active in Southern California blues and folk circles, and in 1963 he played in an unsuc-

cessful group with vocalist Jackie DeShannon. With Taj Mahal, another musical archivist, he started the Rising Sons in 1966. He also appears on Mahal's debut album. Cooder was a busy session player in the late Sixties, working for Gordon Lightfoot and on numerous commercials. He was a member of Captain Beefheart's Magic Band and appeared on Beefheart's *Safe as Milk*, although he quit just before Beefheart was scheduled to play the Monterey Pop Festival. He also sat in on Little Feat's 1971 debut LP.

Cooder appeared on the soundtracks of *Candy* and *Performance* (with Mick Jagger), and claims to have recorded extensively on the Rolling Stones' *Let It Bleed*. Although he is credited only for the mandolin on "Love in Vain," he claims to have provided the main riff for the Stones' "Honky Tonk Women."

Since 1969, when he got a solo contract, Cooder has cut down on session work to concentrate on his yearly albums. His general strategy is to rework obscure songs (mostly pre-Sixties) in his own lunging, syncopated style laced with elements from outside rock. He has championed the music of Bahamian guitarist Joseph Spence (a major influence), and he later produced an album by the Gabby Pahinui Hawaiian Band. On *Paradise and Lunch* (1974), he recorded a duet with jazz pianist Earl "Fatha" Hines, and following *Chicken Skin Music* (1976), he toured with a band that included Mexican accordionist Flaco Jimenez and a Tex-Mex rhythm section alongside gospel-style singers Bobby King, Eldridge King and Terry Evans, which appears on the live *Showtime* (1977).

Jazz (1978) actually contained early-jazz ragtime and vaudeville songs. Cooder played a one-time concert at Carnegie Hall with an orchestral group and tap dancers for its unveiling. *Bop till You Drop* (1979), *Borderline* (1981) and *The Slide Area* (1982) turned toward Fifties and Sixties R&B. *Bop* was the first major-label digitally recorded album; the next two albums (and attendant tours) featured songwriter John Hiatt. Cooder also provided soundtracks for Walter Hill's 1980 *The Long Riders* and 1981 *Southern Comfort*.

Cooder played only a few session dates in the Seventies, behind Randy Newman (*Good Old Boys* and *Sail Away*), Arlo Guthrie and Van Dyke Parks.

SAM COOKE

Born January 22, 1935, Chicago; died December 11, 1964, Los Angeles
1960—*Cookes Tour* (RCA) *Hits of the 50's; Sam Cooke* **1961**—*My Kind of Blues; Twistin' the Night Away* **1962**—*Best of Sam Cooke, volume 1; Mr. Soul* **1963**—*Night Beat* **1964**—*Soul Stirrers* (London) *Ain't That Good News* (RCA) *At the Copa* **1965**—*Shake; Best of Sam Cooke, volume 2; Try a Little Love* **1966**—*Unforgettable Sam Cooke* **1968**—*Man Who Invented Soul* **1976**—*Forever.*

Sam Cooke

"Wonderful World" (#12, 1960), "Twistin' the Night Away" (#9, 1962), "Bring It on Home to Me" (#13, 1962), "Another Saturday Night" (#10, 1963) and "Shake" (#7, 1965).

His image was tarnished when the woman who shot him to death in a Los Angeles motel on December 11, 1964, claimed that Cooke had attacked her after another woman had fled. The posthumously released "A Change Is Gonna Come" hit #31 and placed Cooke back in the spiritual setting from which he had emerged. Cooke's hits have been covered widely by rock & soul singers.

Cooke was also a groundbreaking independent black music capitalist. He owned his own record label (Sar/Derby), music publishing concern (Kags Music) and management firm. His influence can be heard in the work of artists as varied as Michael Jackson and the Heptones, but is most profoundly felt in the singing of Otis Redding, Al Green and Rod Stewart.

RITA COOLIDGE
Born 1944, Nashville
1971—*Rita Coolidge* (A&M)   *Nice Feelin'*   1972—*Lady's Not for Sale*   1974—*Fall into Spring*   1975—*It's Only Love*   1977—*Anytime . . . Anywhere*   1978—*Love Me Again*   1979—*Satisfied*   1981—*Heartbreak Radio* (with Kris Kristofferson)   *Greatest Hits.*

Former backup singer Rita Coolidge became a hitmaking soloist in the late Seventies. The daughter of a Baptist minister and a Cherokee Indian, she sang in church choirs as a child. In her late teens, she briefly attended Florida State University before moving to Memphis, where she did radio jingles. She cut a locally successful hit single, then moved to Los Angeles.

By 1969, she was recording and touring regularly as part of Delaney and Bonnie and Friends, and she joined much of that same troupe on Joe Cocker's "Mad Dogs and Englishmen" tour, where her featured rendition of "Superstar" was a highlight. (Leon Russell wrote Cocker's "Delta Lady" about Coolidge.) She continued backup work in the early Seventies for Eric Clapton, Stephen Stills, Boz Scaggs, Graham Nash, Marc Benno (who later joined Coolidge's backup band, the Dixie Flyers) and Dave Mason.

(Her sister Priscilla recorded with her husband and producer, Booker T. Jones of Booker T. and the MGs.)

In 1971, Coolidge met Kris Kristofferson, whom she married two years later. By then, her first solo albums had been released to little response. In 1977, *Anytime . . . Anywhere* went platinum on the strength of three hit singles: Jackie Wilson's "Higher and Higher" (#22, 1977), Boz Scaggs's "We're All Alone" (#7, 1977) and the Temptations' "The Way You Do the Things You Do" (#20, 1978). She frequently toured with Kristofferson,

Songwriter and performer Sam Cooke merged gospel music and secular themes and provided the early foundation of soul music. Cooke's pure, clear vocals were widely imitated, and his suave, sophisticated image set the style of soul crooners for the next decades.

One of eight sons of a Baptist minister, Cooke grew up in Chicago and was a top gospel artist by 1951. As a teenager, he became lead vocalist of the Soul Stirrers (which later included Johnnie Taylor), with whom he toured and recorded for nearly six years. Cooke's phrasing and urban enunciation were distinctive from the start.

Hoping not to offend his gospel fans, he released his pop debut, "Lovable" (1956), as Dale Cooke, but Specialty dropped him for deserting the Soul Stirrers. He released his own "You Send Me" the following year, and the 1.7-million-selling #1 song was the first of many hits. In the next two years, his several hits—"Only Sixteen" (#28, 1959), "Everybody Likes to Cha Cha" (#31, 1959)—concentrated on light ballads and novelty items. He signed to RCA in 1960 and began writing bluesier, gospel-inflected tunes.

Beginning with his reworking of "Chain Gang" (#2) in August 1960, Cooke was a mainstay in the Top Forty charts through 1965, with "Sad Mood" (#29, 1961), whose growing movie career provided her cameo roles in *Pat Garrett and Billy the Kid, Convoy* and *A Star Is Born.* They also collaborated on 1979's *Natural Act,* released shortly before their divorce.

ALICE COOPER
Born Vincent Furnier, December 25, 1945, Detroit
The group that was formed in the mid-Sixties in Phoenix: Glen Buxton (b. Nov. 10, 1947, Akron), gtr.; Michael Bruce (b. Mar. 16, 1948), gtr., kybds.; Dennis Dunaway (b. Dec. 9, 1948, Cottage Grove, Ore.), bass; Neal Smith (b. Sep. 23, 1947, Akron), drums.
1969—*Pretties for You* (Straight) **1970**—*Easy Action* **1971**—*Love It to Death* (Warner Bros.) *Killer* **1972**—*School's Out* **1973**—*Billion Dollar Babies* **1974**—*Muscle of Love; Alice Cooper's Greatest Hits* (Cooper disbanded group and went solo with various backing musicians) **1975**—*Welcome to My Nightmare* **1976**—*Alice Cooper Goes to Hell* **1977**—*Lace and Whiskey; The Alice Cooper Show* **1978**—*From the Inside* **1980**—*Flush the Fashion* **1981**—*Special Forces* **1982**—*Zipper Catches Skin.*

Alice Cooper's shock-rock theatrics (which included simulated executions, the chopping up of baby dolls and Alice draping himself with a live boa constrictor) and explicit lyrics were hugely popular in the early and mid-Seventies. Vincent Furnier, son of a preacher, assembled his hardrocking band in Phoenix. They were first known as the Earwigs, then the Spiders, and finally the Nazz (not to be confused with Todd Rundgren's band). They moved en masse to Los Angeles in 1968. Billing themselves as Alice Cooper (who, according to a Ouija board, was a 17th-century witch reincarnated as Furnier), they established themselves on the Southern California bar circuit with a bizarre stage show and a reputation as the worst band in Los Angeles. Frank Zappa's Straight Records released their first two albums, which sold poorly and, with tour costs, left them $100,000 in debt.

The band moved to Detroit, where they lived for several months in a single hotel room. After seeing their live show, producer Bob Ezrin signed them for their breakthrough album, *Love It to Death,* which joined Cooper's taboo-defying lyrics to powerful hard rock. "Eighteen" (#21, 1971) was the first of a string of gold and platinum singles and albums. Cooper's later hit singles included "School's Out" (#7, 1972), "Elected" (#26, 1972), "Hello, Hooray" (#35, 1973) and "No More Mr. Nice Guy" (#25, 1973). Meanwhile, his stage show became even more notorious for his macabre makeup and bizarre theatrics.

After *Billion Dollar Babies,* Cooper's novelty began to wear off. He formed a new band in 1974, featuring ex–Lou Reed guitarists Dick Wagner and Steve Hunter. In 1977, former band members Bruce, Dunaway and Smith formed

Alice Cooper

Billion Dollar Babies and recorded two unsuccessful albums. An April 1975 prime-time TV special, "Alice Cooper—the Nightmare," seemed to mark Cooper's acceptance as a mainstream entertainer. He began performing regularly in Las Vegas and was frequently a member of the celebrity panel on "The Hollywood Squares" game show. His then-current hit was a ballad, "Only Women Bleed" (#12, 1975), as were two subsequent hits: "I Never Cry" (#12, 1976) and "You and Me" (#9, 1977).

In 1978, Cooper committed himself to a psychiatric hospital for treatment of alcoholism, an experience chronicled on *From the Inside,* which includes some lyrics by Elton John's partner Bernie Taupin, and the hit "How You Gonna See Me Now" (#12, 1978). As punk rock became commercially acceptable, Cooper released the hard-rocking *Flush the Fashion* and *Special Forces,* neither of which returned him to his former position at the top of the hard-rock heap. Cooper appeared in the 1980 film *Roadie* and contributed two songs to the soundtrack.

CHICK COREA
Born Armando Anthony Corea, June 12, 1941, Chelsea, Massachusetts
1966—*Tones for Joan's Bones* (Vortex) **1968**—*Now He*

Sings, Now He Sobs (Solid State) **1969**—*Is* **1970**—
Song of Singing (Blue Note) *Piano Improvisations,
volume 1* (Polydor) *Piano Improvisations, volume
2; Circling In* (Blue Note) **1971**—*A.R.C.* (ECM)
Circle, Paris Concert **1972**—*Inner Space* (Atlantic)
Crystal Silence (ECM) *Return to Forever* **1973**—*Light
As a Feather* (Polydor) *Hymn to the Seventh Galaxy*
1974—*Where Have I Known You Before* **1975**—*Chick
Corea* (Blue Note) *No Mystery* (Polydor) **1976**—*The
Romantic Warrior* (Columbia) *The Leprechaun* (Poly-
dor) *My Spanish Heart* **1977**—*Musicmagic* (Colum-
bia) **1978**—*Mad Hatter* (Polydor) *Friends; Circulus*
(Blue Note) *Secret Agent* (Polydor) **1979**—*Delphi 1*
(Blue Note) **1980**—*Top Step* (Warner Bros.) **1981**—
Three Quartets **1982**—*Trio Music* (ECM).

Chick Corea established himself as a major jazz keyboardist, including a three-year stint with Miles Davis, before
turning to rock fusion with Return to Forever. In the late
Seventies, he returned to acoustic piano. Corea's tone on
piano is distinctively brittle and precise and has been
widely imitated.

The son of a musician, Corea began studying classical
piano at four and played with his father's band. As a
teenager, he also played with a Latin band. He briefly
attended Columbia University and the Juilliard School,
but quit to go professional. Corea's first major job was
with Mongo Santamaria in 1962, followed by work with
Blue Mitchell, Stan Getz (for two years), Herbie Mann
and Sarah Vaughan. In 1968, Miles Davis Quintet drummer Tony Williams invited him to sit in for an ailing Herbie
Hancock, and Corea wound up playing with Davis for
three years; he played on *Filles de Kilimanjaro,* Davis'
last acoustic album, and began to experiment (at Davis'
behest) with electric Fender Rhodes piano on the landmark jazz-rock albums *In a Silent Way* and *Bitches Brew*
in 1969.

Corea formed the avant-gardist Circle with bassist
David Holland, drummer Barry Altschul and reedman
Anthony Braxton in 1971. Circle recorded three albums in
Europe while Corea recorded two solo sessions. Corea
was introduced to Scientology, which led him to adopt the
idea of "communication"—in practice, playing simpler
music. He returned to the U.S. to form Return to Forever
in 1972.

Fellow Scientologist Stanley Clarke, whom Corea met
during a brief stint with saxophonist Joe Henderson,
cofounded Return to Forever. Corea had written some of
the group's initial material for a Stan Getz band (on Getz's
Captain Marvel) including Clarke, percussionist Airto
Moreira and Tony Williams. When Corea recorded the
material on his own, Joe Farrell replaced Getz, Moreira
played both drums and percussion, and Moreira's wife,
Flora Purim, sang. The result was a Corea album called
Return to Forever, followed by *Light As a Feather.* The
two albums contained melodic pop jazz, full of buoyant
melodies and quasi-Latin rhythms.

When Moreira and Purim left to start their own group,
Fingers, in 1973, Farrell went back to session work and
Corea and Clarke revamped Return to Forever with drummer Lenny White and guitarist Bill Connors. Openly
modeled on the Mahavishnu Orchestra (Corea had performed with Mahavishnu John McLaughlin in Davis'
band and on Larry Coryell's *Spaces*), the new group made
bombastic use of electric instruments, including Corea's
synthesizer. After guitarist Al DiMeola replaced Connors,
Return to Forever reached a peak of popularity on the
rock circuit. Clarke and DiMeola went solo in 1976, and
Corea briefly expanded Return to Forever to a 13-piece
ensemble before retiring the band name. Corea, Clarke,
White and DiMeola did a reunion tour in 1983.

Since 1976, Corea has played mostly acoustic piano as
half of a duet with fellow pop refugee Herbie Hancock and
with various acoustic groups that have included drummer
Steve Gadd, bassist Eddie Gomez, Henderson, Farrell,
Moran, ex–Weather Report bassist Miroslav Vitous and
others. He has also recorded solo albums and duets with
vibraharpist Gary Burton. He continues to write a
monthly column for *Contemporary Keyboard.*

THE CORNELIUS BROTHERS AND SISTER ROSE

Formed circa 1970, Miami
Eddie Cornelius (b. 1943), voc.; Carter Cornelius (b.
1948), voc.; Rose Cornelius (b. 1947), voc.
1972—*Cornelius Brothers and Sister Rose* (United
Artists) **1973**—*Big Time Lover* **1976**—*Greatest Hits.*

The Cornelius family enjoyed a major pop hit in 1971 with
"Treat Her Like a Lady," which featured brother Eddie's
lead vocals. The two brothers and sister Rose began
working in the Sixties as a gospel act called the Split
Tones. Just after they hit with their first secular release,
"Lady," the group suffered a car crash that put them out
of action for several months. They came back with the Top
Five "Too Late to Turn Back Now" (#2, 1972) and
followed up with lesser hits like "Don't Ever Be Lonely."
By 1974, they were no longer a pop chart presence.

LARRY CORYELL

Born April 2, 1943, Galveston
1967—*Free Spirit* (ABC) **1969**—*Coryell* (Vanguard)
Lady Coryell **1970**—*Spaces; Coryell; Larry Coryell
at the Village Gate; Offering* **1973**—*The Real Great
Escape* **1974**—*Introducing the Eleventh House with
Larry Coryell* **1975**—*Essential; Restful Mind* **1976**—
Planet End; Level One (Arista) **1977**—*Lion and the
Ram; Twin House* (with Philip Catherine) (Elektra)

Back Together Again (with Philip Catherine) **1978—** *Two for the Road* (Arista) *Splendid* (with Philip Catherine) (Elektra/Asylum) *At Montreux* (Vanguard) **1979—***Free Smile* (Arista).

Guitarist Larry Coryell's penchant for high volume and fast fingerwork led him to jazz rock early. Coryell played piano as a child, switching to guitar in his teens. After studying journalism at the University of Washington, he moved to New York City in 1965, where he worked with drummer Chico Hamilton in 1966 and cofounded an early jazz-rock band, the Free Spirits. In 1967, he joined vibraharpist Gary Burton's band; two years later, he recorded "Memphis Underground" with flutist Herbie Mann.

Coryell began leading his own bands in 1969. He toured Europe and the U.S. that year with a band that included ex-Cream bassist Jack Bruce, ex–Jimi Hendrix Experience drummer Mitch Mitchell and Coryell's longtime keyboardist, Mike Mandel. In 1970, he joined John McLaughlin, Billy Cobham, Chick Corea and future Weather Report bassist Miroslav Vitous on *Spaces*. 1971's *Barefoot Boy* was a virtual tribute to Hendrix.

Coryell formed a variety of bands in the Seventies, including the Mahavishnu Orchestra–styled Eleventh House, and later toured playing solo acoustic guitar and in a duo with ex-Focus guitarist Philip Catherine or studio guitarist Steve Kahn. He teaches part-time, writes a column for *Guitar Player* magazine and continues to tour regularly.

ELVIS COSTELLO

Born Declan McManus, 1955, Liverpool
1977—*My Aim Is True* (Columbia) **1978—***This Year's Model* **1979—***Armed Forces* **1980—***Get Happy; Taking Liberties* **1981—***Trust; Almost Blue* **1982—** *Imperial Bedroom.*

Since his 1977 debut, Elvis Costello has emerged as one of the most distinctive writer/performers of the new wave. Early in his career, he listed "revenge and guilt" as his primary motivations, but what really counted was the construction of his songs, which set densely layered wordplays in an ever-expanding repertoire of styles. His wounded, clipped delivery became one of the definitive new wave vocal styles.

Costello purposely clouded his past, but it is known that he was born in England in 1955 and is the son of a dance band leader. Costello began to write songs in his early teens. He left home at 16 and programmed computers at an Elizabeth Arden factory. He continued to write songs, record demos and occasionally perform solo in London country & western pubs like the Nashville Room. In 1975, he quit his factory job, became a roadie for Brinsley Schwarz and got friendly with their bass player, Nick Lowe. Stiff Records signed him in 1976 on the advice of staff producer Lowe. One of the label's owners, Jake

Elvis Costello

Riviera, became his manager and rechristened him Elvis Costello.

Costello's debut single, "Less than Zero," was released in April 1977 and is included on *My Aim Is True*, which was produced by Lowe with backing by the Marin County country-rock band Clover. Soon Top Twenty in England, *Aim* made Costello a major British cult star and attracted critical kudos in the U.S. Costello then assembled the Attractions (Steve "Naive" Nason, keyboards; Pete Thomas, drums; Bruce Thomas, bass). Bolstered by his new cohorts on *This Year's Model*, he rocked harder, while his image was amplified by his punkish habits of onstage rudeness, brief sets and an aversion to the press. In late 1978, Costello left his wife and young son; a year later, he returned to his wife. His next release, *Armed Forces* (originally entitled *Emotional Fascism*), repeatedly equated love affairs with military maneuvers. By then, Costello's style encompassed lush, Beatles-style arrangements and other influences.

Touring the U.S. to support *Armed Forces* in early 1979, Costello's onstage contrariness and dark moods (sometimes the result of drinking) reached alarming peaks. In Columbus, Ohio, that March, Costello had a minor but much publicized conflict with American singers Bonnie Bramlett and Stephen Stills in a hotel bar after Costello reportedly referred to Ray Charles as a "blind, ignorant nigger." Besides tainting his work with the Rock Against Racism organization, his outburst brought the wrath of the previously supportive U.S. rock press, which hounded him long after a press conference in which he justified more than apologized. He lay low for a while, producing the Specials' 1979 debut and appearing at the Concert for Kampuchea. His next two albums consisted of previously released English material and studio out-takes. In 1980, he performed before 50,000 fans at the Canadian Heat Wave Festival and also played at the Montreux Jazz Festival.

Trust brought Costello back to front-line duty, and his subsequent U.S. tour found him displaying an uncharac-teristically polite and reserved stage manner. (Squeeze opened the tour, and Costello produced their break-through *East Side Story* LP). In late 1981 he released *Almost Blue*, an album of country & western covers recorded in Nashville, then returned to ever-more-eclec-tic rock with *Imperial Bedroom*. A C&W aficionado, Costello has re-covered a version of his "Stranger in the House" with George Jones. His songs have been covered by Dave Edmunds ("Girls Talk") and Linda Ronstadt ("Party Girl," "Alison" and "Girls Talk").

JAMES COTTON

Born July 1, 1935, Tunica, Mississippi
1967—*James Cotton Blues Band* (Verve) 1968—*Pure Cotton; Cotton in Your Ears; Cut You Loose* (Van-guard) 1974—*100% Cotton* (Buddah) 1976—*Live and on the Move.*

A blues harmonica player, Cotton has played for years with Muddy Waters and frequently contributed to the records of rockers like Johnny Winter. He has also led his own band for the past few years, supporting himself on club dates and recording sporadically.

Comedy

Rock is pretty funny all by itself, but that hasn't stopped comedians from taking it on. The most time-honored form of rock comedy is the parody record. They include answer records, like the Deter-gents' "Leader of the Laundromat" (à la the Shangri-Las' "Leader of the Pack"); Miss Chuckle Cherry's "My Pussycat" (after Chuck Berry's "My Ding-a-Ling"); and Geraldine Stevens' "Billy, I've Got to Go to Town" (vs. Kenny Rogers' "Ruby, Don't Take Your Love to Town").

There are also "cover versions" rearranged for maximum incongru-ity, like the pseudonymous Senator Bobby imitating Robert Kennedy singing "Wild Thing," or the Temple City Kazoo Orchestra's all-kazoo rendition of Led Zeppelin's "Whole Lotta Love," or Martin Mull's "2001 Polkas" and "Dueling Tubas."

Other rock comedy efforts parody whole styles, from Allan Sherman's phony folk efforts in the Sixties, to Frank Zappa's revamped doo-wop on *Ruben and the Jets,* to the National Lampoon's *Lemmings* and *Goodbye Pop* revue, with accurate impressions of James Taylor, Joe Cocker, Neil Young and others. The Tubes hovered between parody and pop in the Zappa tradition. Members of Monty Python did a meticulously researched pseudo-Beatles documentary, *The Rutles (All You Need Is Cash).* Various club acts, notably Mark Volman and Howard Kaylan as Flo and Eddie, mock current icons. And Elvis Presley has been aped, with varying degrees of affection, by the Bonzo Dog Band, Andy Kaufman and numerous others.

There have also been novelty records from the beginning of pop, from bawdy songs to the likes of "They're Coming to Take Me Away, Ha-Haaaa" by Napoleon XIV. A minor but persistent novelty genre, "flying saucers," ties together bits of current hits as answers to pseudo-reportorial questions; the idea was popularized by Dickie Goodman.

A more amorphous zone is comedy informed by a rock sensibility. Since rock dominates pop culture along with television and movies, it is rare for standard comedians to ignore it entirely. In the late Sixties, however, a few comedy troupes seemed to model themselves on rock bands rather than vaudeville acts; the best of them was Firesign Theater, a quartet of talkers who started out doing radio comedy in Los Angeles. Firesign Theater's complexly layered recordings free-associated through high and pop culture in a sort of verbal analogue to psychedelic rock. Another troupe, the Credibility Gap, used rock as subject matter for more standard skits; they redid Abbott and Costello's "Who's on First?" routine as a rock-festival lineup. But the most long-lived of the "rock" comedy troupes is Cheech and Chong, who do traditional slapstick on subjects ranging from drugs to sex to drugs. Younger comedians, such as those on television programs like "Saturday Night Live," "Fridays" and "Second City TV," simply take rock for granted.

But the funniest moments in rock are still unintentional—they usually occur when performers start to take themselves most seriously.

Cotton began playing blues harmonica after meeting Sonny Boy Williamson (Aleck "Rice" Miller). He left home at nine to seek out Williamson, whom he had heard on radio station KFFA in West Helena, Arkansas; he spent the next six years playing with him. For two years after that he was with Howlin' Wolf and then formed his own band with Willie Nix before joining Muddy Waters, with whom he worked for 12 years. In 1966, he left Waters to form his own band. Over the next few years, he worked with several rock acts, including Paul Butterfield, Janis Joplin, Steve Miller, Boz Scaggs, Johnny Winter, Edgar Winter, Elvin Bishop and the J. Geils Band's Peter Wolf.

JOHN COUGAR

Born John Mellencamp, October 7, 1951, Seymour, Indiana
1976—*Chestnut Street Incident* (Mainman/MCA)
1978—*A Biography* (Riva) **1979**—*John Cougar*
1980—*Nothing Matters and What If It Did* **1982**—
American Fool.

Singer/songwriter/hard-rock belter John Cougar became one of 1982's biggest stars when his fifth LP, *American Fool*, went to #1, sold over three million copies and yielded two hit singles, "Hurt So Good" (#2) and "Jack and Diane" (#1).

At age 14, Mellencamp started his first band, but didn't seriously pursue a career in music until nearly ten years later. In 1975, he moved to New York City, where he met David Bowie's manager, Tony DeFries, who christened Mellencamp Johnny Cougar, helped him get what has been reported as a $1-million deal with Mainman and oversaw the recording of his debut, *Chestnut Street Incident*. The LP, which consisted of cover tunes, failed to hit, and MCA dropped Cougar.

Four years later he signed with Riva Records and, working with Rod Stewart's manager, Billy Gaff, recorded two more LPs, the latter of which, *John Cougar*, contained "I Need a Lover," a hit for Pat Benatar. *Nothing Matters*, produced by Steve Cropper, sold half a million copies. In late 1982, Cougar began producing Mitch Ryder's *Never Kick a Sleeping Dog*.

THE COUNT FIVE

Formed circa 1965, San Jose, California
Ken Ellner (b. 1948, Brooklyn), voc.; John Michalski (b. 1948, Cleveland), gtr.; Sean Byrne (b. 1947, Dublin), gtr.; Roy Chaney (b. 1948, Indianapolis), bass; Craig Atkinson, drums.
1966—*Psychotic Reaction* (Double Shot).

A psychedelic garage band, the Count Five scored one major hit, "Psychotic Reaction" (#5, 1966). They emerged from the same California Bay Area bar circuit that spawned the Syndicate of Sound ("Little Girl") and

the Golliwogs (later Creedence Clearwater Revival). In 1966, they signed with the Los Angeles–based Double Shot label. Followups to "Psychotic Reaction" failed to make national impact, although the band remained popular for a while regionally.

COUNTRY

Country, the music of America's heartland, can be traced back to British immigrants who brought with them a tradition of storytelling Celtic ballads and string-instrument playing, especially fiddling. The tradition survived in isolated rural communities, but developed an American accent as music for square dances and hoedowns.

By the early 1900s, "mountain music" had separated into string-band music—the beginnings of bluegrass—and vocal-harmony music derived from church music; but as recordings and radio began to disseminate pop, other influences crept in. Nashville, Tennessee, with its weekly Grand Ole Opry broadcasts, became the center of country music by the Thirties, and has been a battleground between traditionalists and modernizers ever since.

In the late Thirties, Roy Acuff and others began to shift toward a pop-like solo singer-plus-band setup, while Western swing bands in Texas began to borrow from blues, jazz, even polkas. In the Forties and Fifties, country came to accept some improvisational elements, and became country & western music; but long after blues and rock & roll had appeared, drums were barred from the Opry stage.

The "honky-tonk" of the Fifties and Sixties—the music of Hank Williams, George Jones, Loretta Lynn and Merle Haggard—is now seen as classic country, although it was considered a dangerous hybrid in its time. In the Sixties, while rockabilly singers like Jerry Lee Lewis and Johnny Cash were returning to country roots, rockers like Bob Dylan and the Byrds rediscovered country and brought it to a younger audience. Meanwhile, young country musicians like Kris Kristofferson and widely ignored veterans like Willie Nelson and Waylon Jennings began to forge non-Nashville alliances with rockers.

By the Seventies, country rock (played by rock musicians) and outlaw country (played by country musicians) were becoming virtually indistinguishable. But although country has borrowed numerous pop trappings and recording techniques, there is still a strain of mainstream country music that tells simple stories with unobtrusive backing, with the twang of Southern accents echoed by the twang of steel guitars.

COUNTRY JOE AND THE FISH

Formed 1965, San Francisco
Country Joe McDonald (b. Jan. 1, 1942, El Monte, Calif.), voc., gtr.; Chicken Hirsch (b. 1940, Calif.),

drums; Bruce Barthol (b. 1947, Berkeley), bass; Barry Melton (b. 1947, Brooklyn), gtr.; David Cohen (b. 1942, Brooklyn), gtr., kybds.
1967—*Electric Music for the Mind and Body*(Vanguard) *I-Feel-Like-I'm-Fixin'-to-Die* 1968—*Together* 1969—*Greatest Hits* 1971—*Life and Times of Country Joe and the Fish (From Haight-Ashbury to Woodstock)* 1973—*The Best of Country Joe McDonald and the Fish* 1976—*The Essential Country Joe McDonald* 1977—*Reunion* (Fantasy).

Country Joe and the Fish were one of the most overtly political bands to emerge from San Francisco's late-Sixties folk-turned-psychedelic scene. Joe McDonald (named after Stalin by left-leaning parents) wrote his first song, "I Seen a Rocket," as a campaign song for a friend's high school class presidency attempt. At age 17, he joined the Navy for three years. After a year at Los Angeles City College, he moved to Berkeley and wrote protest songs while occasionally publishing a magazine, *Et Tu, Brute*.

McDonald made his first record, *The Goodbye Blues*, in 1964 with Blair Hardman. He then joined the Berkeley String Quartet and the Instant Action Jug Band, which included Barry Melton. The two started Country Joe and the Fish in 1965 to make a series of political EPs for Takoma, including the first appearance of the notorious "F-U-C-K" cheer ("Gimme an F!" etc.).

The group started as a loose-knit jug band, but switched to electric instruments late in 1966, and as the Summer of Love loomed, they were signed to Vanguard and settled into a stable lineup for two years. The "Feel-Like-I'm Fixin'-to-Die Rag," a black-humored electric shuffle about Vietnam, brought them notoriety with their second album; the "F-U-C-K" cheer was changed to "F-I-S-H."

The band appeared at the Monterey Pop Festival (and in the film of it), and at Woodstock, McDonald, solo, led nearly 500,000 people in the cheer. The band continued to tour and record, but by 1969 they were getting fewer bookings after their arrest in Worcester, Massachusetts, for inciting an audience to lewd behavior (the cheer). The group began to unravel, although McDonald and Melton (who also had a 1969 marijuana bust) kept a lineup together to appear in the 1971 film *Zachariah*. The Fish disbanded in 1970.

McDonald tried some film scores (including a Dutch version of Henry Miller's *Quiet Days in Clichy* and a Chilean political film, *Què Hacer*, in which he also appeared) and continued his solo career, sometimes in tandem with Melton, who released his own solo album in 1971, *Bright Sun Is Shining*. McDonald continued to tour (he has a strong European following). He joined Jane Fonda and Donald Sutherland in the FTA (Free/Fuck the Army) Revue, a non-USO show, and has been active in the cause of Vietnam veterans and saving whales.

While on tour in Europe in 1973, McDonald sat on a stove and had to be hospitalized for three months. His second wife, actress Robin Menken, filed for divorce and got an injunction to prevent him from visiting their daughter, Seven. With his debts mounting, he signed with Fantasy in late 1975 and recorded *Paradise with an Ocean View*. He married a third wife, Janice, and logged over 100,000 miles touring the U.S. The Fish regrouped for 1977's *Reunion*, but McDonald was solo again for *Music from the Planet Earth*.

JAYNE COUNTY
Born Wayne County, Georgia
1976—*Max's Kansas City* (Ram) 1978—*The Electric Chairs* (Safari) 1980—*Rock 'n' Roll Resurrection* (Attic).

Rock & roll's most famous transsexual, Jayne County, started out as rock & roll's most famous transvestite, Wayne County. His life in the spotlight began when he moved to New York from his native Georgia in the late Sixties. County appeared playing a female role opposite Patti Smith in an Off Broadway production of *Femme Fatale* before tackling the role of Florence Nightingale in *World—Birth of a Nation*. In 1970, Andy Warhol cast County in his show *Pork,* with which County traveled to England. David Bowie was impressed and signed County to his Mainman management company.

On returning to New York, County's first band, Queen Elizabeth, began performing in Lower Manhattan clubs like Max's Kansas City, where groups like the New York Dolls were forging a new union between camp and rock & roll. (Queen Elizabeth's drummer, Jerry Nolan, was a late addition to the Dolls' lineup and later a member of the Heartbreakers.) County's stage wardrobe consisted of skimpy pink dresses, fishnet stockings, heavy makeup and a platinum-blond wig, but in spite of the sexual spoofs, County's performances were more rock & roll show than drag show.

In 1975, after being dropped by Mainman, County cut an album for ESP-Disk; it was never released. His vinyl debut was three tracks on the double-album compilation *Max's Kansas City.* He formed the Electric Chairs in 1977 and toured Britain that year. In 1978, the Electric Chairs were signed up by a German label, Safari, and released their first album. County disappeared for some time after that, reemerging in 1980 after a sex-change operation. *Rock 'n' Roll Resurrection* was a live set that included "Cream in My Jeans," "If You Don't Want to Fuck, Fuck Off" and "Bad in Bed."

DON COVAY
Born March 1938, Orangeburg, South Carolina
1964—*Mercy* (Atlantic) 1966—*Seesaw* 1969—*The House of Blue Lights* (with the Jefferson Lemon Blues

Band) **1970**—*Different Strokes for Different Folks* (Janus)(with the Jefferson Lemon Blues Band) **1973**— *Super Dude I* (Mercury) **1974**—*Hot Blood* **1976**— *Travelin' in Heavy Traffic* (Philadelphia International).

As a soul singer with high gospel-inspired voice, Covay had a handful of hits in the Sixties and Seventies, but is best known for a songwriting catalog that includes Aretha Franklin's "Seesaw" and "Chain of Fools." The son of a Baptist minister who moved the family to Washington when Covay was a child, he sang with the family gospel quartet, the Cherry-Keys. When he was 17, he joined the Rainbows, who had already had a local hit, "Mary Lee." His solo career got under way two years later when he opened a Washington concert for Little Richard, who named him Pretty Boy and took him to Atlantic Records. Atlantic issued his first Pretty Boy disc, "Bip Bop Bip," in 1957.

Covay recorded under his own name and with his group, the Goodtimers, for Sue, Columbia, Epic, RCA, Arnold, Cameo, Parkway, Landa and Rosemart, placing two singles in the pop charts—"Pony Time" (1961) and "Mercy Mercy" (1964)—before Atlantic reacquired him in 1965.

With Atlantic he scored his first soul hit, "Please Do Something" (#21, 1965). "Seesaw" was both a soul hit (#5, 1965) and a pop hit (#44). Covay continued to record for Atlantic until 1971, when he signed with Janus. In 1972, he joined Mercury, both as an artist and A&R director. He returned to the charts in 1973 with "I Was Checkin' Out, She Was Checkin' In" (#29 pop, #6 R&B) and followed it the next year with "It's Better to Have (And Don't Need)" (#21 R&B). In 1972, he moved to Mercury. In 1981, he toured with Wilson Pickett and Solomon Burke in a package called the Soul Clan.

COVER

The term "cover" refers to the second version, and all subsequent versions, of a song, performed by either another act than the one that originally recorded it or by anyone except its writer. In the early days of rock & roll, white vocal groups often rushed to cover black doo-wop hits, and because they had more access to airplay, cover versions outsold original recordings. In the Sixties, as singer/songwriters came into their own, an established cover singer like Judy Collins or Linda Ronstadt would give unknown songwriters exposure by covering new songs; although they were the first recordings, they were cover versions.

THE COWSILLS

Formed mid-1960s, Rhode Island
Barbara Cowsill (b. 1929), Bill Cowsill (b. Jan. 9, 1948), Bob Cowsill (b. Aug. 26, 1950), Dick Cowsill (b. Aug. 26, 1950), Paul Cowsill (b. Nov. 11, 1952), Barry Cowsill (b. Sep. 14, 1954), John Cowsill (b. Mar. 2, 1956), Sue

Cowsill (b. May 20, 1960). (All born in Newport, R.I.)
1969—*The Best of the Cowsills* (MGM).

This musical family from Rhode Island provided the inspiration for TV's "The Partridge Family" (see David Cassidy). Under father William "Bud" Cowsill's direction, the Cowsill kids and mom played the New York City clubs regularly in the mid-Sixties, attracting the attention of MGM, which released their debut album in November 1967. By early 1967 they had had their first hit single, "The Rain, the Park, and Other Things" (#2). Lots of touring, network TV appearances and a few more hits, including the theme from the rock musical *Hair*, preceded their disbandment in early 1970.

KEVIN COYNE

Born January 27, 1944, Derby, England
1972—*Case History* (Dandelion, U.K.) **1973**—*Marjory Razorblade* (Virgin) **1974**—*Blame It on the Night* **1975**—*Matching Head and Feet* **1976**—*Heartburn; In Living Black and White* **1978**—*Dynamite Daze; Millionaires and Teddy Bears; Beautiful Extremes* **1979**—*Babble*.

British songwriter Kevin Coyne released several albums in the Seventies, but his unconventional song formats and abrasive vocal style have proven commercially unsuccessful. Born and raised in England, he attended art school in the early Sixties. In 1965, he began working as a social therapist in a psychiatric hospital in Preston, England, and his experiences were the subject of several of his songs. After appearing sporadically in the clubs in Preston, he moved to London in 1969.

In 1972, Coyne abandoned social work for a musical career. He was already known as lead vocalist with the group Siren, which recorded two albums for Dandelion. His first solo effort, *Case History*, was released on Dandelion in the U.K. and has since become a collector's item. He signed with Virgin in 1973 and drew critical kudos for his double set *Marjory Razorblade*, which was reduced to a single disc for U.S. release. Throughout the mid-Seventies, he continued to record regularly and generally kept his own band together. His strongest backing aggregation played on 1976's *Heartburn* and the following year's double live set, *In Living Black and White*. Group personnel were Zoot Money (keyboards and vocals), Steve Thompson (bass), Peter Woolf (drums) and Andy Summers (guitar), who joined the Police shortly thereafter. Coyne has also written and appeared in several theatrical productions.

FLOYD CRAMER

Born November 27, 1933, Shreveport, Louisiana
1965—*Hits from the Country Hall of Fame* (RCA) **1968**—*The Best of Floyd Cramer, volume 2* **1970**—*This Is Floyd Cramer* **1971**—*Sounds of Sunday* **1979**— *Super Hits*.

A Nashville session veteran, Cramer is credited with inventing the limpid, delicately ornamented style of piano playing that characterized the Nashville sound. In the late Fifties and early Sixties, he backed the Everly Brothers and Elvis Presley, among others, often in tandem with guitarist Chet Atkins. He has since had country hits on his own, along with several instrumental pop hits in the early Sixties on RCA, including "Last Date" (#2, 1960), "On the Rebound" (#4, 1961), "San Antonio Rose" (#8, 1961) and "Chattanooga Choo Choo" (#36, 1962).

CREAM

Formed 1966, England
Eric Clapton (b. Mar. 30, 1945, Ripley, Eng.), gtr., voc.; Jack Bruce (b. John Symon Asher Bruce, May 14, 1943, Lanarkshire, Scot.), bass, harmonica, voc.; Ginger Baker (b. Peter Baker, Aug. 19, 1939, Lewisham, Eng.), drums.
1966—*Fresh Cream* (Atco) **1967**—*Disraeli Gears* **1968**—*Wheels of Fire* **1969**—*Goodbye; The Best of Cream* **1970**—*Live Cream* **1972**—*Live Cream, volume 2; Off the Top* (Polydor) **1973**—*Heavy Cream* **1975**—*The Best of Cream Live* **1978**—*Early Cream* (Springboard).

Cream was the prototypical blues-rock power trio. In a mere three years they sold 15 million records, played to SRO crowds throughout the U.S. and Europe, and redefined the instrumentalist's role in rock. Cream formed in mid-1966 when drummer Ginger Baker left the Graham Bond Organisation, bassist Jack Bruce (formerly of Bond's band) left Manfred Mann, and Eric Clapton, already a famous guitarist in the U.K., left John Mayall's Bluesbreakers.

Debuting at the 1966 Windsor Festival, Cream established their enduring legend on the high-volume blues jamming and extended solos of their live shows. Their studio work, however, tended toward more sophisticated original rock material, most of it written by Bruce with lyricist Pete Brown. Their U.S. hit singles included "Sunshine of Your Love" (#5, 1968), "White Room" (#6, 1968) and a live version of the Robert Johnson country blues "Crossroads" (#28, 1969). *Wheels of Fire*, made up of a live LP and a studio LP (both recorded in the U.S.), was the first certified platinum album.

Tension within the band led to a quick breakup. Cream gave its farewell concert, which was filmed as *Goodbye Cream*, on November 26, 1968, at the Royal Albert Hall in London. After patching together the *Goodbye* LP—which featured "Badge," cowritten by Clapton and George Harrison—Clapton and Baker subsequently formed Blind Faith, and Bruce went solo; Clapton and Baker also went on to solo careers. (See also: individual member entries, Blind Faith.)

CREEDENCE CLEARWATER REVIVAL

Formed 1959, El Cerrito, California
John Fogerty (b. May 28, 1945, Berkeley, Calif.), gtr., voc., harmonica, sax, piano; Tom Fogerty (b. Nov. 9, 1941, Berkeley), gtr.; Stu Cook (b. Apr. 25, 1945, Oakland, Calif.), bass; Doug "Cosmo" Clifford (b. Apr. 24, 1945, Palo Alto, Calif.), drums.
1968—*Creedence Clearwater Revival* (Fantasy) **1969**— *Bayou Country; Green River* **1970**—*Willie and the Poor Boys; Cosmo's Factory* **1971**—*Pendulum* (− Tom Fogerty) **1972**—*Mardi Gras* **1973**—*Creedence Gold; More Creedence Gold* **1974**—*Live in Europe* **1976**—*Chronicle* (Fantasy) **1981**—*Live at Albert Hall* (later retitled *The Concert*).

John Fogerty's fervent vocals and modernized rockabilly songs built on his classic guitar riffs made Creedence Clearwater Revival the preeminent American singles band of the late Sixties. The Fogerty brothers were raised in Berkeley, where John studied piano and at the age of 12 got his first guitar. He met Cook and Clifford at the El Cerrito junior high school they all attended. They began playing together, and by 1959 were performing at local dances as the Blue Velvets. As the Golliwogs they were signed to San Francisco–based Fantasy Records in 1964 and began putting out singles. "Brown-Eyed Girl" sold 10,000 copies in 1965, but the followups were flops. Greater success came after they adopted the CCR moniker in 1967.

Several Fogerty compositions appeared on *Creedence*

Cream: Ginger Baker, Eric Clapton, Jack Bruce

Creedence Clearwater Revival: Tom Fogerty, Doug Clifford, Stu Cook, John Fogerty

Clearwater Revival, but cover versions of Dale Hawkins' "Suzie Q" and Screamin' Jay Hawkins' "I Put a Spell on You" were the group's first hit singles. With the release of *Bayou Country*, they became the most popular rock band in America. Beginning with the two-sided gold hit "Proud Mary" b/w "Born on the Bayou" (#2, 1969), Creedence dominated Top Forty radio for two years without disappointing the anticommercial element of the rock audience.

Their rough-hewn rockers often dealt with political and cultural issues, and they appeared at the Woodstock Festival. Creedence had seven major hit singles in 1969 and 1970, including "Bad Moon Rising" (#2, 1969), "Green River" (#2, 1969), "Fortunate Son" (#14, 1969), "Down on the Corner" (#3, 1969), "Travelin' Band" (#2, 1970), "Up Around the Bend" (#4, 1970) and "Lookin' Out My Back Door" (#2, 1970).

Although Creedence's success continued after *Cosmo's Factory*, it was their artistic peak. Internal dissension, primarily the result of John Fogerty's dominant role, began to pull the band apart in the early Seventies. Tom left in January 1971, one month after the release of the pivotal *Pendulum*, which became the group's fifth platinum album. They carried on as a trio, touring worldwide; *Live in Europe* was the recorded result. Their final album, *Mardi Gras*, gave all three members an equal share of the spotlight (songwriting, vocals). They disbanded in October 1972, and Fantasy has subsequently released a few albums, including a live recording of a 1970 Oakland concert, which upon original release was erroneously titled *Live at Albert Hall* (it was later retitled *The Concert*).

Tom Fogerty has since released several solo albums and worked occasionally in the early Seventies with organist Merl Saunders and Grateful Dead guitarist Jerry Garcia. Clifford released a solo album in 1972 of Fifties-style rock & roll. Thereafter, Clifford and Cook provided the rhythm

sections for Doug Sahm on his 1974 LP and the Don Harrison Band after 1976. Calling his one-man act the Blue Ridge Rangers, John Fogerty released an eponymously titled LP in 1972. In 1975, he released *John Fogerty* on Asylum; "Rockin' All Over the World" was a #27 hit. Since 1976, he has been living with his family on a farm in Oregon. He practices music for several hours a day, and has long been rumored to be making another solo album. In 1980, the group played at Tom Fogerty's wedding, but no reunion is planned.

THE CRESTS
Formed circa mid-1950s, Brooklyn
Johnny Maestro (b. John Mastrangelo), voc.; Tommy Gough, voc.; Jay Carter, voc.; Harold Torres, voc.

A male vocal quartet, the Crests had several hits on Coed Records between 1958 and 1960, including "Sixteen Candles" (#2, 1959) and "Step by Step" (#14, 1960). When the group's popularity waned in the early Sixties, leader Johnny Maestro moved on to success with the Del-Satins, which later evolved into the Brooklyn Bridge.

THE CRITTERS
Formed circa early 1960s, New Jersey
James Ryan (b. 1947, Plainfield, N.J.), gtr.; Don Ciccone (b. 1947, Plainfield, N.J.), gtr., voc.; Kenneth Gorka (b. 1947, East Orange, N.J.), bass; Christopher Daraway (b. 1947, Brooklyn), organ; Jack Decker (b. 1947, Newark, N.J.), drums.
1966—*The Critters* (Project 3) *Younger Girl* (Kapp) *Touch 'n' Go with the Critters* (Project 3).

With a mellow pop style similar to the Association's, the Critters had three minor pop hits in 1966 on Kapp Records, including a cover of the Lovin' Spoonful's "Younger Girl" and their only Top Twenty entry, the gentle "Mr. Dieingly Sad." They had one minor followup in 1967, "Don't Let the Rain Fall Down on Me." Originally called the Vibratones, they were formed by guitarist/vocalist Don Ciccone, who later joined the Four Seasons and was instrumental in the latter's substantial mid-Seventies comeback.

JIM CROCE
Born January 10, 1943, Philadelphia; died September 20, 1973, Natchitoches, Louisiana
1969—*Approaching Day* (Capitol) *Croce* **1972**—*You Don't Mess Around with Jim* (ABC) **1973**—*Life and Times; I Got a Name; Time in a Bottle* **1975**—*Photographs and Memories; The Faces I've Been* (Lifesong).

Singer/songwriter Croce had several early-Seventies hits before he died in a plane crash. Croce began playing guitar professionally at 18, when he entered Villanova University, where he hosted a folk and blues show on campus radio and played in local bands. After graduation, he did construction work and had to alter his guitar technique after breaking a finger with a sledge hammer. By 1967, he was living in New York City and playing the coffeehouse circuit. He signed with Capitol in 1969 and released the unsuccessful *Approaching Day*, produced with his wife, Ingrid. He returned to club work and drove trucks.

In 1971, he submitted some songs to producer Tommy West, an old college chum. With partner Terry Cashman, West helped Croce cut *You Don't Mess Around with Jim*. Released in early 1972, it produced two hit singles, "Operator" (#17, 1972) and the title track (#8, 1972). *Life and Times* and "Bad, Bad Leroy Brown" (#1, 1973) followed. He was killed when his chartered plane crashed into a tree soon after takeoff on September 20, 1973, in Louisiana. Among the five other victims of the crash was his longtime guitarist Maury Muehleisen. (Croce, in fact, had supported Muehleisen on his own Capitol album, *Gingerbread*.)

I Got a Name, completed before Croce's death and released in late 1973, went gold, as did its title track (which was included on the soundtrack of the movie *The Last American Hero*) and "Time in a Bottle" (#1, 1973). Within months of Croce's death, three of his LPs were in the Top Twenty: *Life and Times* (#7, 1973), *I Got a Name* and *You Don't Mess Around with Jim*, both of which went to #1.

STEVE CROPPER
Born October 21, 1941, Willow Springs, Missouri
1969—*Jammed Together* (Stax) **1970**—*With a Little Help from My Friends* (Volt) **1982**—*Night after Night* (MCA).

Guitarist/songwriter/producer Steve Cropper helped create an R&B guitar style that served as the foundation of many of the Stax-Volt hits of the Sixties. Raised in the backwoods of the Ozark Mountains, he moved to Memphis when he was nine. At 16, he began playing guitar, and in 1957 he became a cofounder of the Mar-Keys, one of the first house bands for the Satellite-Stax-Volt labels in Memphis. With the Mar-Keys he earned a gold record for the instrumental hit "Last Night" in 1961.

Cropper also played with other Stax-Volt house bands, including the Triumphs, the Van-Dells and the best-known of them, Booker T. and the MGs, who had instrumental hits and backed many of the leading soul singers. Along with much of the MGs material, Cropper has writing credits on Wilson Pickett's "In the Midnight Hour," Eddie Floyd's "Knock on Wood," Sam and Dave's "Soul Man," Otis Redding's "(Sittin' on) The Dock of the Bay" and at least twenty other Stax-Volt hits.

After producing records for Redding, Cropper opened his own Memphis studio, TMI, in 1969, and began producing for Jeff Beck, the Temptations, Joe Cocker, John Prine, Poco, the Tower of Power, José Feliciano and others. He recorded *Jammed Together* with Albert King and Roebuck Staples, and a solo album, *With a Little Help from My Friends*, with Leon Russell, Buddy Miles, Jim Keltner, Carl Radle, the Bar-Kays, the Memphis Horns and the MGs.

In 1975, with the MGs disbanded, Cropper moved to Los Angeles, where he resumed his session career by playing with Rod Stewart, Art Garfunkel and Sammy Hagar. Between 1978 and 1981, he was part of the Blues Brothers troupe, playing some of the riffs he had created for Sam and Dave.

CROSBY, STILLS, NASH AND YOUNG
Formed 1968, Los Angeles
David Crosby (b. David Van Cortland, Aug. 14, 1941, Los Angeles), gtr., voc.; Stephen Stills (b. Jan. 3, 1945, Dallas), gtr., kybds., bass, voc.; Graham Nash (b. 1942, Blackpool, Eng.), gtr., kybds., voc.; Neil Young (b. Nov. 12, 1945, Toronto), gtr., voc.
Crosby, Stills and Nash: 1969—*Crosby, Stills and Nash* (Atlantic) **1977**—*CSN* **1982**—*Daylight Again* **1983**—*Allies*. **Crosby, Stills, Nash and Young: 1970**—*Déjà Vu* (Atlantic) **1971**—*Four Way Street* **1974**—*So Far*. **Crosby and Nash: 1972**—*Crosby and Nash* (Atlantic) **1975**—*Wind on the Water* (ABC) **1976**—*Whistling Down the Wire* **1977**—*Live*. **David Crosby: 1971**—*If Only I Could Remember My Name* (Atlantic). **Graham Nash: 1971**—*Songs for Beginners* (Atlantic) **1973**—*Wild Tales* **1980**—*Earth and Sky* (EMI). **Stephen Stills: 1970**—*Stephen Stills* (Atlantic) **1971**—*Stephen Stills 2* **1972**—*Manassas* **1973**—*Down the Road* **1975**—*Stills* (Columbia) *Stills Live* (Atlantic) **1976**—*Illegal Stills* (Columbia) *The Best of* (Atlantic) **1978**—*Thoroughfare Gap* (Columbia). **Stills and Young: 1976**—*Long May You Run* (Reprise).

The close high harmonies and soft-rock songs of David Crosby, Stephen Stills and Graham Nash, sometimes joined by Neil Young, sold millions of albums and were widely imitated throughout the Seventies. The members were as volatile as their songs were dulcet, and continually split up and regrouped between 1970 and 1982. All four singer/songwriter/guitarists had already recorded before their debut LP, *Crosby Stills and Nash*, was released in 1969: Crosby with the Byrds, Stills and Young with Buffalo Springfield, and Nash with the Hollies.

Crosby had worked as a solo performer before joining the Byrds in 1964. In 1967, he quit because of differences with leader Roger McGuinn, among them McGuinn's refusal to record Crosby's "Triad," a song about a *ménage à trois* that the Jefferson Airplane recorded on *Crown of Creation;* Crosby sang it on *Four Way Street*. After leaving the Byrds, Crosby began preparation for a solo album, which eventually appeared in 1971 as *If I Could Only Remember My Name*. He also produced Joni Mitchell's debut album in 1968; Mitchell's "Woodstock" later became a hit for Crosby, Stills, Nash and Young.

Young had quit Buffalo Springfield on the eve of the 1967 Monterey Pop Festival, and Crosby sat in for him at that concert. After Buffalo Springfield broke up in May 1968, Stills and Crosby began jamming together and were soon joined by Nash. Nash, who had been dissatisfied with the Hollies—they had refused to record "Marrakesh Express" and "Lady of the Island"—joined Crosby and Stills.

Recorded early in 1969, *Crosby, Stills and Nash* was an immediate hit, with singles "Marrakesh Express" (#28) and Stills's "Suite: Judy Blue Eyes" (#21) (after Judy Collins); it sold two million copies within the year, and the trio won a Best New Artist Grammy. Although their harmonies were less than perfect outside the recording studio, Crosby, Stills, Nash and Young (who joined them in summer 1969) began touring in mid-year. Their second live appearance was before half a million people at the Woodstock Festival in August 1969.

The quartet's second album, *Déjà Vu*, took two months to make, but had advance orders for two million copies and included three hit singles: "Woodstock" (#11, 1970), "Teach Your Children" (#16, 1970) and "Our House" (#30, 1970). A few weeks after *Déjà Vu* was released, the National Guard shot and killed four students in an antiwar demonstration at Kent State University, and Young wrote "Ohio," which the group recorded and released as a single (#14, 1970). They toured that summer, but by the time the live album *Four Way Street* was released, they had disbanded.

Crosby and Nash released solo and duo albums in the early Seventies and toured together, while Young returned to his solo career and Stills started his. Stills's solo debut, which included "Love the One You're With" (#4, 1971), featured guest guitarists Eric Clapton and Jimi Hendrix. In 1974, the quartet toured together for the last time; Young traveled separately. Stills and Young made a duet album, *Long May You Run,* in 1976, but Young suddenly left Stills mid-tour and has not worked with the others since.

In 1977, Crosby, Stills and Nash regrouped for *CSN,* which included "Just a Song Before I Go" (#7, 1977). The next summer they toured as an acoustic trio, and in the fall of 1979 they performed at the antinuclear benefit concerts sponsored by Musicians United for Safe Energy. In 1982, the trio released *Daylight Again,* for which Stills wrote most of the songs, and toured arenas once more. *Daylight* was a Top Ten LP and boasted a Top Ten single, "Wasted on the Way."

CHRISTOPHER CROSS

Born Christopher Geppert, circa 1951, San Antonio, Texas
1980—*Christopher Cross* (Warner Bros.) **1983**—*Another Page.*

Christopher Cross was reared an Army brat in Texas. By his late teens, he was fronting a copy band in Texas clubs that, in 1972, was ranked Austin's leading cover band. Cross kept writing his own songs as well, and was finally signed by Warner Bros. in fall 1978. When his debut LP was released two years later, it went platinum and yielded a Top Five hit single in "Ride Like the Wind," which featured backing vocals by Michael McDonald of the Doobie Brothers. The album also featured backing vocals by Nicolette Larson and Valerie Carter.

In 1981, Cross won five Grammy Awards, including Best Record, Best Album and Best Song. His debut LP was still going strong in the charts in late 1981. In the fall of that year, Cross had another massive hit with "Arthur's Theme" (from the hit film *Arthur*), a song cowritten by Cross, Peter Allen, Burt Bacharach and Carole Bayer Sager, which received an Academy Award for Best Original Song.

RODNEY CROWELL

Born August 7, 1950, Houston
1978—*Ain't Living Long Like This* (Warner Bros.)
1980—*But What Will the Neighbors Think* **1981**—*Rodney Crowell.*

Rodney Crowell is a country-rock singer/songwriter best known for his compositions performed by other singers. He began drumming in his father's Houston rockabilly band when he was 11 years old, and he played with garage rock & roll bands in his high school and college years before moving to Nashville in the early Seventies. Jerry Reed got him a staff songwriting job and recorded several of his songs.

In 1976, Crowell joined Emmylou Harris' Hot Band as backup singer and guitarist, and Harris subsequently recorded almost a dozen Crowell originals ("Leaving Louisiana in the Broad Daylight," "Amarillo"). Waylon Jennings cut his "Till I Gain Control Again." In 1978, Crowell left the Hot Band to make his recording debut, produced by Harris' husband, Brian Ahern; guest musicians included Willie Nelson, Ry Cooder and Mac Rebennack (Dr. John). The album sold fewer than 20,000 copies, but two years later the title song hit #1 on the country charts twice, in versions by Waylon Jennings and the Oak Ridge Boys.

Other Crowell interpreters include Carlene Carter ("Never Together but Close Sometimes"), Willie Nelson ("Till I Gain Control Again"), the Dirt Band ("American Dream"), Bob Seger ("Shame on the Moon") and Crowell's wife, Rosanne Cash ("I Can't Resist"). In 1980, Crowell had a hit of his own with "Ashes by Now," which made the pop Top Forty. In addition to his own albums, he has produced Guy Clark's *South Coast of Texas,* Bobby Bare's *As Is,* Rosanne Cash's *Seven Year Ache* and Albert Lee's self-titled 1983 LP.

THE CROWS

Formed circa 1948, New York City
Sonny Norton, lead voc.; William Davis, baritone;
Harold Major, tenor; Mark Jackson, tenor; Gerald
Hamilton, bass.

The Crows' 1954 pop hit "Gee" (#14 pop, #6 R&B) was
one of the first records by a black group to cross over into
the pop market. The group was originally formed as a
quartet in the late Forties on the streetcorners of Harlem;
guitarist Mark Jackson joined later. They were playing a
talent show at the Apollo Theater when a talent scout
signed them to the newly formed Rama Records in 1954.
Under the guidance of label head George Goldner they
tailored their sound for the white audience. Although
William Davis' "Gee" proved to be the Crows' only pop
hit, its success prompted Goldner to launch a Gee subsidiary label in 1956 (whose roster included Frankie Lymon
and the Cleftones). The flip side of "Gee," "I Love You
So," was a Top Fifty hit for the Chantels in 1958. By then
the Crows had disbanded. In the late Fifties, the group
members retired to Harlem and two of them, Norton and
Hamilton, have since died.

ARTHUR "BIG BOY" CRUDUP

Born 1905, Forrest, Mississippi; died March 28, 1974,
Nassawadox, Virginia
1968—*Look on Yonder's Wall* (Delmark)   **1969**—*Mean
Ole Frisco* (Trip)   **1970**—*Crudup's Mood* (Delmark)
1971—*Father of Rock 'n' Roll* (RCA)   **1974**—*Roebuck
Man* (Liberty).

Bluesman Arthur "Big Boy" Crudup wrote "That's All
Right, Mama"—one of the first songs Elvis Presley recorded and his first hit—and other rock standards, including "My Baby Left Me" and "Rock Me Mama." Crudup
grew up in the Deep South, where he sang in church as a
child. In the late Thirties, he joined a gospel group called
the Harmonizing Four and moved with them to Chicago.
In 1939, he began playing the guitar and the blues. A year
later, he was discovered by Okeh and Bluebird Records
talent scout Lester Melrose, who helped Crudup get a
record deal, but also took advantage of his client's naiveté
and never paid him royalties. Crudup stayed with Melrose
until 1947, when he realized that he was being cheated.
Melrose sold Crudup's contract to RCA, but Crudup
recorded only sporadically, and often on other labels
under the name Elmore Jones or Percy Crudup (his son's
name).

Crudup recorded through the mid-Fifties until he quit in
disgust. "I just give it up," he said later. He was retired
from music, digging and selling sweet potatoes, when
during the Sixties, Philadelphia blues promoter Dick Waterman took an interest in him and his business problems.
Waterman began working with the American Guild of
Artists and Composers in an attempt to collect some of the

royalties Melrose (by then deceased) had withheld from
Crudup. Waterman eventually collected $60,000 from
BMI and reached a settlement with the music publisher
Hill and Range.

Crudup resumed his music career in 1968 and toured the
U.S. and Europe until his death from a heart attack in
1974. During his lifetime, he had supported a family of
thirteen children, only four of whom were actually his.

THE CRUSADERS

Formed 1958, Texas
Wilton Felder (b. 1940, Houston), tenor sax, bass; Joe
Sample (b. 1939, Houston), kybds.; Nesbert "Stix"
Hooper (b. ca. 1939, Houston), drums; Wayne Hender-
son (b. 1939, Houston), trombone.
1971—*Pass the Plate* (Chisa)   *Crusaders 1* (Blue
Thumb)   **1973**—*The 2nd Crusade; Unsung Heroes*
1974—*Scratch*   (+ Larry Carlton, gtr.)   *Southern
Comfort*   **1975**—*Chain Reaction*   **1976**—(+ Robert
"Pops" Popwell [b. Atlanta], bass)   *Those Southern
Knights*   **1977**—(– Henderson)   *Free As the Wind*
(– Carlton)   **1978**—*Images*   (– Popwell)   **1979**—
Street Life (MCA)   **1980**—*Rhapsody and Blues*   **1981**—
Standing Tall.

After ten years of playing under the name of the Jazz
Crusaders and being overlooked by pop, jazz and soul
audiences, the Crusaders became one of popular music's
hottest instrumental bands.

Wilton Felder, Joe Sample and Nesbert Hooper first
played together in their high school marching band in
Houston. They then formed the Swingsters, a be-bop jazz
and Texas-style R&B group. While attending Texas Southern University, they met Wayne Henderson and, with two
other students, formed the Modern Jazz Sextet (a tux-
edoed outfit modeled on the Modern Jazz Quartet). In
1958, the four future Crusaders dropped out of college and
moved to Los Angeles. As the Nighthawks, they backed
Jackie DeShannon at one point and played dance clubs
and ballrooms as far away as Las Vegas until 1961, when
they returned to jazz. As the Jazz Crusaders, they landed
a record contract from World Pacific Jazz, and during the
next decade built a modest following. But by 1969, frustrated by lack of recognition, the quartet took a year off.

When they reemerged as the Crusaders, their music had
changed to a blend of funk vamps and riffs, terse solos and
dance rhythms. Their singles began placing in the R&B
Top Forty—"Put It Where You Want It" (#39, 1972),
"Don't Let It Get You Down" (#31, 1973), "Keep That
Same Old Feeling" (#21, 1976) and "Street Life" (#17,
1979), sung by Randy Crawford—and the pop Top 100.
Most of their Seventies albums are gold. They have
worked as sidemen for Steely Dan, Curtis Mayfield, Joni
Mitchell, Ray Charles, Van Morrison, Joan Baez, B. B.
King and Barry White.

In 1974, Carlton became the first new full-fledged member in almost twenty years. Felder played both bass and sax in recording sessions until Popwell's induction in 1976. The next year both Henderson and Carlton left the band, Henderson to go into production work, Carlton to begin his successful solo career. With Popwell's departure, the band was back to the three who had met in their high school band room. All three have released solo albums.

THE CRYSTALS

Formed 1961, Brooklyn
Dee Dee Kennibrew (b. Delores Henry, 1945, Brooklyn), voc.; Dolores "La La" Brooks (b. 1946, Brooklyn), voc.; Mary Thomas (b. 1946, Brooklyn), voc.; Barbara Alston (b. 1945, Brooklyn), voc.; Pat Wright (b. 1945, Brooklyn), voc.
1962—(− Thomas) 1963—(− Wright; + Frances Collins, lead voc. on some hits, ca. 1962; + Darlene Love) N.A.—*Greatest Hits* (Philles).

One of producer Phil Spector's first successful groups, the Crystals used a rather sultry image and borrowed the vocal talents of Darlene Love for several hits in the early Sixties. The group was formed by Brooklyn schoolgirls. In 1961, they met Spector while auditioning in New York, and they became the first act signed to his Philles Records. Their first two releases—"There's No Other (Like My Baby)" (#20, 1961) (the B side of "Oh Yeah Maybe Baby") and Barry Mann and Cynthia Weil's "Uptown" (#13, 1962)—were hits, but their third, "He Hit Me (And It Felt Like a Kiss)," was denied airplay when radio programmers objected to the violent implications of its title and lyrics ("He hit me and I was glad . . .").

The group's only #1 hit, Gene Pitney's "He's a Rebel," was not recorded by the real Crystals but by a group of L.A. session singers, the Blossoms, fronted by Darlene Love, who also sang on the followup, "He's Sure the Boy I Love" (#11, 1963). The original Crystals were featured on the 1963 hits "Da Doo Ron Ron" (#3) and "Then He Kissed Me" (#6). But their 1964 releases—"Little Boy" and "All Grown Up"—were unsuccessful, and Spector lost interest in them. They bought their contract back from him and signed with United Artists, but their Motown-influenced singles also failed to hit. By the early Seventies, the group members were occasionally appearing on rock revival show bills.

MIKE CURB

Born December 24, 1944, Savannah, Georgia
1972—*Song for a Young Love* (MGM) 1977—*The Mike Curb Generation* (Warner/Curb).

Mike Curb is an unlikely combination of pop music mogul, MOR producer and conservative California politician. He was a college student in 1964 when he wrote the commercial jingle "You Meet the Nicest People on a Honda." He quickly wrote a pop song, "Little Honda," for the group that recorded the jingle, the Hondells. It made the Top Ten in 1964 and was later covered by the Beach Boys. Curb then quit college to start his own Los Angeles–based music publishing and marketing company, Sidewalk Productions. American International Pictures hired him to score "youth market" films like *The Wild Angels* (1966) and *Wild in the Streets* (1968). In 1968, he sold Sidewalk to the Transcontinental Investment Corporation and became a 23-year-old millionaire. TIC made him president of the entertainment subsidiary, and he moved the firm into records, TV, movies and talent management.

In 1969, he left to assume the presidency of MGM Records. He immediately fired 250 employees. In 1970, he purged 18 acts alleged to be "drug-oriented," although Connie Francis and the Cowsills were among them, and Eric Burdon (who happened to be making hits and using drugs) was not. In their place he signed MOR acts, including the Osmonds. He also returned to the charts as songwriter, producer and occasional performer for the Mike Curb Congregation, whose "Burning Bridges" reached #34 in 1971. The Mike Curb Congregation also performed at a number of Republican functions. President Nixon cited them as his "favorite act," although his daughter Tricia was quoted as saying, "If I have to hear them one more time, I'm going to vomit."

In 1973, Curb resigned from MGM and joined Warner Communications, for whom he set up Warner/Curb Records and signed acts like the Four Seasons and Jim Stafford. His ambitions, however, had grown beyond music. A member of the Republican National Committee, he became increasingly involved in politics. In 1978, he was elected the lieutenant-governor of California.

TIM CURRY

Born 1946, Cheshire, England
1978—*Read My Lips* (A&M) 1979—*Fearless* 1981—*Simplicity*.

Tim Curry's performance as Dr. Frank N. Furter in *The Rocky Horror Picture Show* (1975) brought him to the rock audience. The son of a Navy Methodist chaplain, Curry attended Cambridge and Birmingham universities, where he studied drama and English. He appeared for 15 months in the London production of *Hair* from 1968 to 1970 before continuing his studies with the Royal Court and Glasgow Civic Repertory companies.

In 1973, he got the Frank N. Furter role in the original London production of *The Rocky Horror Show* after singing "Tutti-Frutti" at an audition. He re-created his role onstage in L.A. and on Broadway before making the movie and appears on both the stage and movie soundtracks. While most of Curry's repertoire is made up of cover tunes, his own "I Do the Rock" (from his second LP) was a club hit (#91) in 1979. He tours infrequently (last in 1979).

In 1981, Curry received a Tony Award nomination for his portrayal of Mozart in the play *Amadeus*. He played the title role in the BBC's miniseries "The Life of Shakespeare," a Victorian aristocrat in *Three Men in a Boat* and appeared in Tom Stoppard's play *Travesties*. He also appeared in the movies *Times Square* (1980) and *Annie* (1982).

CURVED AIR

Formed 1970, England
Sonja Kristina, voc.; Darryl Way, violin, kybds.; Florian Pilkington-Miksa, drums; Ian Eyre, bass; Francis Monkman, synthesizers.
1970—*Air Conditioning* (Warner Bros.) **1971**—*Second Album* (− Eyre; + Mike Wedgwood, bass) **1972**—*Phantasmagoria* (− Way; − Pilkington-Miksa; − Monkman; + Jim Russell, drums; + Kirby, gtr.; + Eddie Jobson [b. Apr. 28, 1955, Billingham, Eng.], violin, synth.) **1973**—*Air Cut* (disbanded) **1974**—(+ Kristina; + Way; + Pilkington-Miksa; + Monkman; + Phil Kohn, bass) **1975**—*Live* (London) (− Pilkington-Miksa; − Monkman; − Kohn; + Tony Reeves, bass; + Mick Jacques, gtr.; + Stewart Copeland [b. July 16, 1952, Va.], drums) *Midnight Wire* (RCA) **1976**—*Airborne* (BTM).

Curved Air appeared in 1970 with a female vocalist, classically trained musicians playing electric violins and synthesizers, novel record packaging (their debut was pressed on colored vinyl and enclosed in a transparent cover) and much record company promotion. They attracted an ardent though limited British following that put "Back Street Luv" (from *Second Album*) into the U.K. Top Five.

The group broke up once in mid-career when Eddie Jobson accepted an invitation to replace Brian Eno in Roxy Music, Mike Wedgwood joined Caravan and Kirby was recruited to play with an ersatz Fleetwood Mac. Sonja Kristina, who was by that time the only remaining original member, attempted a solo career before rejoining the London cast of *Hair*, of which she had been a part in the late Sixties. Curved Air was reunited several months later by the original members (Kohn substituting for Eyre) for a once-only tour of Britain in the fall of 1974. That tour resulted in a live album, but prior commitments precluded a permanent regrouping. With new members (most notable of them, Stewart Copeland, later of the Police), Kristina and Way maintained the group until its final breakup in 1977.

JOHNNY CYMBAL

Born Cleveland

Johnny Cymbal had two hits: one under his own name, one under the pseudonym of Derek. The first was "Hey Mr. Bassman" (#16, 1963), a tribute to the bass vocalists on doo-wop records; the prominent bass part was sung by Ronald Bright, who had also appeared on recordings by the Valentines and the Coasters. Cymbal's followups, "Teenage Heaven" and "Dum Dum De Dum," failed to crack the Top Forty. As Derek, he hit #11 in 1968 with "Cinnamon." After an unsuccessful followup, "Back Door Man," he returned to his original name and has worked as a producer in the Seventies.

CYRKLE

Formed 1962, Easton, Pennsylvania
Don Dannemann (b. May 9, 1944, Brooklyn), gtr.; Tom Dawes (b. July 25, 1944, Albany, N.Y.), bass; Marty Fried (b. 1944, Wayside, N.J.), drums.
1966—*Red Rubber Ball* (Columbia) (+ Mike Losekamp [b. 1947, Dayton, Oh.], organ, bass, harmonica) **1967**—*Neon*.

Cyrkle had some pop-rock hits in the mid-Sixties, including Paul Simon's "Red Rubber Ball." Don Dannemann, Tom Dawes and Marty Fried met at Lafayette College in Easton in the early Sixties and formed a trio to play at frat parties. By 1963, they were regulars at Eastern Seaboard clubs. In early 1966, Beatles manager Brian Epstein signed them, got them a contract with Columbia and let them open on the Beatles' U.S. tour in summer 1966. The exposure sent their debut single, "Red Rubber Ball," to gold status. They followed up with "Turndown Day," toured steadily through 1967 (including Europe), then broke up in the late Sixties.

D

MICHAEL D'ABO

Born March 1, 1944, Bethworth, Surrey, England
1970—*D'Abo* (MCA) 1972—*Down at Rachel's Place*
(A&M) 1974—*Broken Rainbows* 1976—*Smith and
d'Abo* (Columbia).

A veteran of the English music scene, singer and songwriter Michael d'Abo was most visible during his several
years as lead vocalist with Manfred Mann in the Sixties.
Born to a wealthy English family, d'Abo was taught jazz
piano by his mother. He formed his first pop group, the
Band of Angels, at 16. After d'Abo had left to attend
Cambridge University, the group had a moderate English
hit with one of his compositions, "Invitation." His professional career began in 1966, when he joined the Manfred
Mann group and sang lead on their 1968 hit "Mighty Quinn
(Quinn the Eskimo)."

By the time he left Mann in the late Sixties, his songs
were often hits for others ("Build Me Up Buttercup," the
Foundations; "Handbags and Gladrags," Rod Stewart).
He briefly pursued an acting career, and then released
several solo LPs. *Broken Rainbows* featured Mike Bloomfield and Graham Nash. *Smith and d'Abo* was a collaborative effort between d'Abo and former Dave Clark Five
lead vocalist Mike Smith.

DICK DALE AND THE DEL-TONES

Formed circa 1960, Southern California
N.A.—*Greatest Hits* (Crescendo).

Guitarist Dick Dale's 1961 West Coast hit "Let's Go
Trippin' " is considered the beginning of the Sixties surf
music craze. Billed as the "King of Surf Guitar," Dale
pioneered a style that Beach Boy Brian Wilson and others
would later bring to fruition. His guitar work on "Trippin' "
and "Misirlou" (both of which were covered on early
Beach Boys LPs), featuring a twangy, heavily reverbed
tone, influenced Beach Boy Carl Wilson and many other
California guitarists. Dale's only other appearance on the
charts came in 1963 with "The Scavenger." Into the
Eighties, his work was still available on greatest hits
repackages and surf music anthologies.

THE DAMNED

Formed 1976, England
Brian James (b. Brian Robertson), gtr.; Captain Sensible (Ray Burns), bass; Rat Scabies (Chris Miller),
drums; Dave Vanian, voc.
1977—*Damned, Damned, Damned* (Stiff) (+ Lu

[Robert Edmunds], gtr.) *Music for Pleasure* 1979—
(− James; − Lu; + Alistair Ward, bass) *Machine Gun
Etiquette* (Chiswick) 1980—(− Ward; + Paul Grey,
bass) *The Black Album* (IRS) 1982—*Strawberries*
(Bronze).

The Damned were the first British punk band to record, to
chart and to tour America. Their history goes back to
early 1975, when Brian James joined Mick Jones in the
London S.S., a punk group whose members included Paul
Simonon and Terry Chimes (a.k.a. Tory Crimes), who
later formed the Clash with Jones; Tony James, who went
on to Chelsea and Generation X; and Rat Scabies, with
whom Brian James joined Nick Kent's Subterraneans.
When Kent returned to writing for the *New Musical
Express,* James, Sensible and Scabies stayed together as
the Master of the Backside. They were managed by
Malcolm McLaren (who later managed the Sex Pistols),
and their singer was Chrissie Hynde, who later formed the
Pretenders. Scabies enlisted Vanian, a gravedigger, into
the group after overhearing him sing "I Love the Dead" at
his sister's funeral.

The group first performed in London in July 1976. They
were notorious for their stage act, with Sensible dressed in
a tutu and prodding front-row spectators with his bass,
Scabies bounding from behind his drums to exchange
blows with onlookers and Vanian as Dracula in a black
cape. Stiff Records signed them in September, and in
October they released a single, "New Rose," one month
before the Sex Pistols' first record. Early in 1977, they
released their first album (produced by Nick Lowe, as was
"New Rose") and played clubs in New York, Los Angeles
and San Francisco.

Their second album (produced by Nick Mason of Pink
Floyd) got a poor reception. Scabies left to form a group
with Patti Smith, pianist Richard Sohl and former Clash/
future Public Image Ltd guitarist Keith Levene. He was
replaced by John Moss for a tour of Britain with the Dead
Boys, but by April 1978 the Damned had fallen apart.
James formed Tanz der Youth, Moss and second guitarist
Lu went to the Edge, and Sensible formed King.

In early 1979, Scabies, Sensible and Vanian got together
again. With bassist Henry Badowski of King they toured
Britain as the Doomed—James owned the name "the
Damned" and only later relinquished it. Their new records
were the most popular of their four years: "Love Song"
hit #20 on U.K. singles charts, and "Smash It Up" made
the Top Forty. Later in the year, they returned to the
U.S., and in 1980, after Ward had been replaced by Paul

Grey, formerly of Eddie and the Hot Rods, they cut their first American-released album. In 1982, Captain Sensible released a solo album in the U.K., *Women and Captains First* (A&M), and James and Dead Boys vocalist Stiv Bators formed the Lords of the New Church.

THE CHARLIE DANIELS BAND

Charlie Daniels, born 1937, Wilmington, North Carolina

1970—*Charlie Daniels* (Capitol)   *Te John, Grease, and Wolfman* (Kama Sutra) (reissued on Epic, 1978)   *Honey in the Rock* (reissued on Epic, 1976)   **1974**—*Way Down Yonder* (reissued as *Whiskey* on Epic, 1977)   *Fire on the Mountain*   **1975**—*Nightrider*   **1976**—*Saddle Tramp*

(Epic)   *Volunteer Jam* (Capricorn) (reissued on Epic, 1978)   **1977**—*High and Lonesome;   Midnight Wind* (Epic)   **1978**—*Volunteer Jam III and IV*   **1979**—*Million Mile Reflections*   **1980**—*Full Moon;   Volunteer Jam VI*   **1981**—*Volunteer Jam VII*   **1982**—*Windows.*

Sessionman-turned-bandleader Charlie Daniels worked his way up to platinum sales with heavy touring, an instinct for quasi-political novelty singles and an eclectic repertoire that touched on boogie, bluegrass, country, blues, hard rock and a touch of Tex-Mex music. The son of a North Carolina lumberman, guitarist/fiddler Daniels turned pro at 21 when he formed the Jaguars. For the next decade (except for five weeks when he worked in a Denver

Dances

Rock & roll started as dance music, and every time it gets too far away from a good beat, some kind of rebellion begins. The first rock fans danced like their parents, only wilder, bopping athletic, intricate versions of the Lindy and the Jitterbug. But whereas their parents had seen dances in the movies, young rock fans soon picked theirs up on television on shows like "American Bandstand," and the lifespan of dances grew shorter and more concentrated. A song like "The Loco-motion" would come out, with instructions in the lyrics, and rock fans would learn the step while the single was popular, then forget it and go on to the next one.

The definitive rock dance craze was the Twist in the early Sixties, which gave Chubby Checker ("The Twist") and later Joey Dee ("The Peppermint Twist," after New York's Peppermint Lounge discotheque) the hits they would capitalize on for years afterward. Both teenagers and youth-seeking adults learned the Twist, but what made it different was that it was done solo, involving no physical contact with a partner.

Freed of the burden of coordination, rock dances flourished: the Stroll, the Watusi, the Mashed Potato, the Jerk, the Climb, the Monkey, the Swim, the Funky Chicken, the Pony, the Boogaloo, the Hitch Hike, the Frug, Walking the Dog and countless regional variations, all involving some distinctive hip motion and/or an appropriate hand gesture. Go-go girls danced them on "Hullabaloo" and "Shindig"; high school girls tried to drag gawky boys onto the dance floor; Arthur Murray studios gave lessons.

The late Sixties ushered in free-form boogying, in which any motion passed for dancing among hip white teenagers; some imitated Mick Jagger's strut, itself borrowed from James Brown's routines. And in the progressive-jam heavy-metal trough of the early Seventies, the basic rock dance generally consisted of slumping in a corner and mouthing, "Oh, wow . . ."

But black music never lost touch with a kinetic beat—Sly and the Family Stone demanded that listeners "Dance to the Music"—and in the mid-Seventies black dance music was rediscovered and reclaimed by white gays, who brought it back into mainstream culture as disco, music designed exclusively for dancing. Disco

revived couple dancing, more or less, with the Bump, the Hustle (a variation on a more intricate Latin step) and the Spank. The Robot, the Freestyle and the Rock also came and went, as both whites and blacks watched the syndicated "Soul Train" and "Dance Fever" to check out the latest variations.

Not to be outdone, punk-rock patrons developed the Pogo, virtually the only dance possible in a packed club: jumping up and down in one place. When new wave revived Fifties and Sixties fashions, the dances made a tentative comeback, and rock disco brought in its own funky but alienated combinations. In the early Eighties, punks came up with slam dancing, an idea probably premiered by Iggy Pop in the late Sixties: diving from the stage directly toward a mass of bodies.

The most astonishing dancing of the early Eighties, however, was break dancing, the correlative of rap. "Crews" of black teenagers would vie with each other in robotic acrobatics, including contortions, mimelike one-muscle-at-a-time crawls and, literally, spinning on their heads.

junkyard), he played in Southern bars and roadhouses. In 1963, a song he cowrote became the B side of an Elvis Presley single ("It Hurts Me").

Daniels disbanded the Jaguars and settled in Nashville in 1967, where he became a session musician, playing guitar, fiddle, bass and banjo on albums by Bob Dylan, Ringo Starr, Leonard Cohen, Pete Seeger and numerous country sessions. His songs were covered by Tammy Wynette, Gary Stewart and others. He also worked as a producer, most notably on four albums by the Youngbloods.

In 1971, he started the Charlie Daniels Band, modeled after the Allman Brothers Band, with two drummers and twin lead guitars. *Honey in the Rock* included the talking-bluegrass novelty "Uneasy Rider." The band played nearly 200 shows a year and built a loyal following in the South and West. *Nightrider* included the definitive rebel rouser, "The South's Gonna Do It." Daniels began his annual Volunteer Jam concerts in 1974 in Nashville, and several have been recorded for live albums.

In 1975, Daniels moved to Epic for a reported $3 million contract, recorded *Saddle Tramp*, then realigned his band with three new members. He continued a grueling tour schedule (including benefits in 1976 for presidential candidate Jimmy Carter; he later performed at Carter's inaugural ball) and recorded albums, including his multimillion-selling breakthrough *Million Mile Reflections*, which yielded "Devil Went Down to Georgia" (#3, 1979), for which Daniels received the Best Country Vocal Grammy Award. During the 1980 Iran crisis, he had a hit with "In America"; the following year his version of Dan Daley's "Still in Saigon" was a hit. When he's not on the road, Daniels lives in Mount Juliet, Tennessee.

DANNY AND THE JUNIORS
Formed circa 1955, Philadelphia
Danny Rapp (b. May 10, 1941; d. Apr. 1983, Ariz.), lead voc.; Joe Terranova (b. Jan. 30, 1941), baritone; Frank Mattei, second tenor; Dave White (b. David White Tricker), first tenor.
1958—*Rock and Roll Is Here to Stay* (Singular) *Twistin' All Night Long* (Swan).

A harmony group all Philadelphia-born, Danny and the Juniors are best remembered for their 1958 #1 hit, "At the Hop." They came together in high school and were subsequently discovered by music entrepreneur Artie Singer, who became their manager in 1957. Together they wrote "At the Hop" and recorded it for the local Singular label (Leon Huff helped with the production). ABC-Paramount picked it up, and it went gold on both sides of the Atlantic. The group toured frequently over the next few years (often as part of disc jockey Alan Freed's revue) and scored a few minor hits, notably the Top Twenty followup "Rock and Roll Is Here to Stay" (1958). By the beginning of the Sixties they switched to the Swan label, where they last

charted in early 1963. David White Tricker released a solo album on Bell Records in 1971 under his full name. The Juniors' saxophonist, Lenny Baker, cofounded Sha Na Na in the late Sixties. Rapp committed suicide in 1983.

DANTE AND THE EVERGREENS
Formed late 1950s, Los Angeles
Dante Drowty (b. Sep. 8, 1941), lead voc.; Tony Moon (b. Sep. 21, 1941), first tenor; Frank Rosenthal (b. Nov. 12, 1941), bass; Bill Young (b. May 25, 1942), second tenor.

A short-lived novelty act of the early Sixties, Dante and the Evergreens had a big hit with the lighthearted "Alley Oop" (#13, 1960). A competing version by the Hollywood Argyles hit the top of the charts that year. The Evergreens were supposedly formed by high school friends in the Los Angeles area. They cut a demo that struggling producers Lou Adler and Herb Alpert liked, leading to their production of "Alley Oop" and the group's only other chart single, "Time Machine" (1960). Years later, Herb Alpert claimed that Dante and the Evergreens were actually himself and Adler.

BOBBY DARIN
Born Walden Robert Cassotto, May 14, 1936, Bronx, New York; died December 20, 1973, Los Angeles
N.A.—*The Best of Bobby Darin* (Capitol) *The Bobby Darin Story* (Atco) *Darin 1936–1973* (Motown) *If I Were a Carpenter* (Atlantic).

Bobby Darin, one of the most popular Fifties teen idols, briefly attended Manhattan's Hunter College before dropping out to pursue a career in music. He wrote some songs for Don Kirshner's Aldon Music and landed an Atco recording contract in 1957.

His records met with little success until label president Ahmet Ertegun produced "Splish Splash" (a song that Darin had written in 12 minutes). Reaching #3 in 1958, it sold over 100,000 copies in less than a month. Three more gold singles followed: "Queen of the Hop" (#9, 1958), "Dream Lover" (#2, 1959) and "Mack the Knife" (#15, 1959), for which Darin won two Grammy Awards. Brash, outspoken and ambitious (he said he wanted to be "bigger than Sinatra"), he went to Hollywood and made several movies, beginning in 1960 with *Come September* (he later married his leading lady, Sandra Dee) and *Capt. Newman, M.D.*, for which he received an Oscar nomination.

Darin later scored hits with "Things" and "You're the Reason I'm Living." In 1965, he recorded folk-rock material by writers like Randy Newman and Tim Hardin, whose "If I Were a Carpenter" (#8, 1966) provided Darin with his last major hit. In 1966, he divorced Dee. He continued to appear in Las Vegas and on TV through the mid-Sixties and worked extensively for Robert Kennedy during his 1968 presidential campaign. Darin claimed to have had a mystical-religious experience at Kennedy's funeral services that prompted him to stop working, sell his possessions and retreat to a mobile home at Big Sur, California. After more than a year of contemplation he reemerged, blue-jeaned and mustachioed, to start his own short-lived label, Direction Records.

Working in a soft-rock vein, he cut an unsuccessful politically oriented album called *Born Walden Robert Cassotto*. The early Seventies found Darin signed to Motown and playing Las Vegas again. He married legal secretary Andrea Joy Yeager in June 1972. He died during heart surgery in 1973.

CYRIL DAVIES

Born 1932, England; died January 7, 1964, England
1970—*The Legendary Cyril Davies* (Folklore, U.K.).

Cyril Davies was a catalyst of the early-Sixties British R&B scene. He began his professional career in the early Fifties as a banjoist in traditional jazz bands and later moved into skiffle, which led him to blues and R&B in the late Fifties. By then, Davies was concentrating on singing and playing blues harmonica. He and Alexis Korner opened a series of Soho (London) blues clubs and jammed with visiting blues performers like Sonny Terry, Brownie McGhee, Memphis Slim and Muddy Waters.

In the early Sixties, Korner and Davies went electric and in 1961 cofounded Blues Incorporated, which proved an important breeding ground for future stars like Mick Jagger, Charlie Watts and Brian Jones (Rolling Stones), and Jack Bruce and Ginger Baker (Cream). Blues Incorporated were the house favorites at London's Marquee Club by the end of 1962, but Davies left the group to form his Cyril Davies All-Stars. Guitarist Jeff Beck, keyboard player Nicky Hopkins and drummer Mickey Waller were all, at some time, members of the All-Stars, and the group's live performances and recordings inspired a cult following. When Davies died of leukemia in 1964, All-Stars vocalist Long John Baldry shaped his Hoochie Coochie Men from the remains of Davies' band.

THE REVEREND GARY DAVIS

Born April 30, 1896, Laurens, South Carolina; died May 5, 1972, Hammonton, New Jersey
N.A.—*Pure Religion* (Prestige, recorded 1960) *The Guitar and Banjo of Rev. Gary Davis* (recorded 1964)
1972—*When I Die I'll Live Again* (Fantasy) **1973**—*O, Glory* (Adelphi) *A Little More Faith* (Prestige).

Influential in both blues and folk, the Reverend Gary Davis' percussive finger-picked guitar style lives through the work of Ry Cooder, Taj Mahal and Jorma Kaukonen. Davis was born into a poor family. He suffered from ulcerated eyes, was partially blind throughout his youth and totally blind by age thirty. When he was five, he taught himself to play the harmonica, and during the next two

years he learned banjo and guitar. At 19, Davis enrolled in a school for the blind in Spartanburg, South Carolina.

Davis jammed the blues with Sonny Terry, Blind Boy Fuller, Big Red and others, spending the Twenties as an itinerant musician in the Carolinas. By the close of that decade, though, Davis had decided the blues was the "devil's music." He was ordained in 1933 at the Free Baptist Connection Church in Washington, North Carolina, and soon became a popular gospel singer on the revival circuit. In 1935, he was discovered by a talent scout for the New York "race" label Perfect Records, for whom he recorded religious songs. He lived as a street singer for the next three decades in Harlem, recording occasionally (the most noteworthy sessions in 1956 and 1957), and subsisting off his small royalties, music lessons and passing the plate whenever he had a congregation. He emerged in 1959 at the Newport Folk Festival, then toured America and England and moved his family to Jamaica, Queens. Davis died of a heart attack in 1972.

MAC DAVIS

Born 1941, Lubbock, Texas
1971—*I Believe in Music* (Columbia) **1972**—*Baby Don't Get Hooked on Me* **1973**—*Mac Davis* **1974**—*Song Painter; Stop and Smell the Roses* **1975**—*All the Love in the World; Burnin' Thing* **1976**—*Forever Lovers* **1977**—*Thunder in the Afternoon* **1978**—*Fantasy* **1979**—*Greatest Hits* **1981**—*Midnight Crazy* (Casablanca).

Mac Davis is a country-pop singer/songwriter whose songs, recorded by himself and by others, have sold millions of records. His father bought him his first guitar at age nine, but it wasn't until after a year at Emory University in Atlanta and after working in Atlanta's probation department that he formed his first rock band.

In the early Sixties, Davis became Vee Jay Records' Southern regional sales manager; four and a half years later he worked for Liberty Records. Liberty later sent him to Hollywood to work in their music publishing division. There he sold several of his tunes to major artists: "In the Ghetto," "Memories" and "Don't Cry Daddy" (Elvis Presley); "Friend, Lover, Woman, Wife" (O. C. Smith); "Watching Scotty Grow" (Bobby Goldsboro); "Something's Burning" (Kenny Rogers and the First Edition).

Since he first recorded it, "I Believe in Music" has sold millions of copies in cover versions by over fifty artists. In 1972, a #1 hit, "Baby Don't Get Hooked on Me," started a streak that continued through the mid-Seventies with "Rock and Roll (I Gave You the Best Years of My Life)" (#15, 1975), "One Hell of a Woman" (#11, 1974) and "Stop and Smell the Roses" (#9, 1974). In December 1974, he began hosting his own television variety program, the "Mac Davis Show."

Later recordings—"Burnin' Thing" (1975), "Forever

Lovers" (1976), "It's Hard to Be Humble," "Texas in My Rear View Mirror" (1980)—have been less successful.

Davis made his film debut in 1979, costarring with Nick Nolte as a quarterback in *North Dallas Forty*. He later starred in the romantic comedy *Cheaper to Keep Her*. In 1981, he signed a personal performance contract at the MGM Grand Hotel in Las Vegas.

MILES DAVIS

Born May 25, 1926, Alton, Illinois
1968—*Miles in the Sky* (Columbia)   *Filles de Kilimanjaro*   **1969**—*In a Silent Way*   **1970**—*Bitches Brew; Live at the Fillmore*   **1971**—*Jack Johnson;   Live/Evil*   **1972**—*On the Corner*   **1974**—*Big Fun;   Get Up with It*   **1975**—*Agharta*   **1978**—*Water Babies*   **1981**—*The Man with the Horn*   **1982**—*We Want Miles*   **1983**—*Star People*.

Miles Davis has played a crucial and inevitably controversial role in every major development in jazz since the mid-Forties, and no other jazz musician has had as much effect on rock.

In 1941, he began playing semi-professionally with St. Louis jazz bands. Four years later, his father sent him to study at New York's Juilliard School. Immediately upon arriving in New York, Davis sought out alto saxophonist Charlie Parker, whom he had met the year before in St. Louis. He became Parker's roommate and protégé, playing in his quintet on the 1945 Savoy sessions, the definitive recordings of the be-bop movement. He dropped out of Juilliard and played with Benny Carter, Billy Eckstine, Charles Mingus and Oscar Pettiford as well as with Parker.

As a trumpeter he was far from virtuosic, but he more than made up for his limitations by emphasizing his strengths: his ear for ensemble sound, his unique phrasing and a distinctive haunted tone. He started moving away from speedy bop toward something more introspective. His direction was defined by his collaboration with Gil Evans on the *Birth of the Cool* sessions in 1949 and early '50, playing with a nine-piece band that included Max Roach, John Lewis, Lee Konitz and Gerry Mulligan using meticulous arrangements by Evans, Mulligan, Lewis, Davis and Johnny Carisi.

By 1949, Davis had become a heroin addict. He continued to perform and record over the next four years, but his addiction kept his career in low gear until he cleaned up in 1954. The following year, he formed a group with drummer Philly Joe Jones, bassist Paul Chambers, pianist Red Garland and, in his first major exposure, tenor saxophonist John Coltrane. The Miles Davis Quintet quickly established itself as the premier jazz group of the decade.

Between 1958 and 1963, the personnel in Davis' groups—quintets, sextets and small orchestras—shifted constantly and included pianists Bill Evans and Wynton Kelly, saxophonists Cannonball Adderley, Sonny Stitt and Hank Mobley, and drummer Jimmy Cobb. Continuing the experiments begun with *Birth of the Cool*, Davis' work moved toward greater complexity—as on his orchestral collaborations with Gil Evans (*Miles Ahead*, 1957; *Porgy and Bess*, 1958; *Sketches of Spain*, 1959; *Quiet Nights*, 1962)—and greater simplicity, as on *Kind of Blue* (1959), where he dispensed with chords as the basis for improvisation in favor of modal scales and tone centers.

In 1963 Davis formed a quintet with bassist Ron Carter, pianist Herbie Hancock, drummer Tony Williams and saxophonist George Coleman, who was replaced by Wayne Shorter in 1965. This group stayed together until 1968. In that time, it exerted as much influence on the jazz of the Sixties as the first Davis quintet had on the jazz of the Fifties. Davis and his sidemen—especially Shorter—wrote a body of original material for the quintet.

In 1968, Davis began the process that eventually brought him to a fusion of jazz and rock. With *Miles in the Sky*, the quintet introduced electric instruments (piano, bass and George Benson's guitar on one piece) and the steady beat of rock drumming to their sound. With *Filles de Kilimanjaro*, on which Chick Corea substituted on some tracks for Hancock and Dave Holland replaced Carter, the rock influence became more pronounced. *In a Silent Way* featured three keyboardists—Hancock, Corea and composer Joe Zawinul, on electric pianos and organs—and guitarist John McLaughlin in addition to Williams, Shorter, Holland and Davis. For his next recording sessions he put together what he called "the best damn rock & roll band in the world"—Shorter, McLaughlin, Holland, Corea and Zawinul, plus organist Larry Young, bassist Harvey Brooks, bass clarinetist Bennie Maupin and percussionists Jack DeJohnette, Lenny White, Charles Alias and Jim Riley—and, with no rehearsals and virtually no instructions, let them jam. The result was the historic *Bitches Brew*, a two-LP set that sold over 400,000 copies.

In the three years following *Brew*'s release, Davis amassed a rock-star-level following and performed in packed concert halls in America, Europe and Japan. As his sidemen (who in the early Seventies included pianist Keith Jarrett and percussionists Billy Cobham and Airto Moreira) ventured out on their own, in such bands as Weather Report and the Mahavishnu Orchestra, jazz-rock fusion became one of the dominant new forms.

A car crash that broke both his legs in 1972 put a temporary stop to Davis' activity and marked the beginning of his growing reclusiveness. The recordings he made between 1972 and 1975 advanced the ideas presented on *Bitches Brew*, extracting the percussive qualities of tuned instruments, making greater use of electronics and high-powered amplification and deemphasizing solos in favor of ensemble funk. His sidemen in the mid-Seventies included bassist Michael Henderson, guitarists Reggie Lucas and

Pete Cosey, drummers Al Foster and Mtume, and saxophonists Sonny Fortune and Dave Liebman. *Agharta,* recorded live in Japan in 1975, was his last album of new material for five years. He spent much of that time recuperating from a hip ailment. With the encouragement of his new wife, actress Cicely Tyson, he reemerged in 1981 with a new album and concert appearances. While many old supporters were disappointed by his newly acquired pop clichés (including some vocals), *The Man with the Horn* was his most popular release since *Bitches Brew* and marked his return to live concerts. *We Want Miles* was a live set; *Star People* re-enlisted Gil Evans as arranger along with Davis' Eighties sextet: Mike Stern or John Scofield on guitar, Marcus Miller or Tom Barney on electric bass, Bill Evans on saxophone, Al Foster on drums and Mino Cinelu on percussion.

SPENCER DAVIS GROUP

Formed 1963, Birmingham, England
Original lineup: Spencer Davis (b. July 17, 1942, Wales), voc., gtr., harmonica; Pete York (b. Aug. 15, 1942, Eng.), drums; Steve Winwood (b. May 12, 1948, Birmingham), voc., gtr., kybds.; Muff Winwood (b. June 14, 1943, Birmingham), bass.
1965—*1st Album* (Sonet, U.K.)   *Every Little Bit Hurts* (Wing)   **1966**—*Second Album* (Fontana, U.K.)   *Autumn '66*   **1967**—*Gimme Some Lovin'* (United Artists)   *I'm a Man*   **1968**—*The Very Best of the Spencer Davis Group;   Spencer Davis Greatest Hits;   With Their New Face On*   **1969**—*Heavies*   **1972**—*Mousetrap* (Davis solo)   **1973**—*Gluggo* (Vertigo)   **1974**—*Living on a Back Street* (Mercury).

The Spencer Davis group was an R&B-influenced rock band best known for introducing Stevie Winwood to the pop audience with "Gimme Some Lovin' " and "I'm a Man." Various Spencer Davis groups continued to record into the Seventies.

Davis was a lecturer on German at the University of Birmingham who moonlighted as a musician. In 1963, he met drummer Pete York and persuaded brothers Steve and Muff Winwood to leave their trad-jazz band. They toured England and parts of the Continent, then moved to London and released "Keep On Running" in 1965. "Gimme Some Lovin' " went to #7; two months later, "I'm a Man" went to #10. Both were driving, repetitive Steve Winwood songs that featured his lead vocals. By 1967, Winwood had left to form Traffic. From 1969 to 1972, Davis performed in acoustic duos with Alun Davies (later with Cat Stevens) and Peter Jameson, with whom he recorded two bluegrass-influenced albums.

He re-formed the Spencer Davis Group with York in 1972, but their albums were ignored. By the late Seventies, Davis was working as an independent producer and as a publicist for Island Records. He occasionally played with the Los Angeles Rhythm Kings.

Later members Dee Murray and Nigel Olsson both quit to join Elton John's band. Muff Winwood, who left with Steve, became an executive and in-house producer for Island Records, where he produced LPs by Sparks and Dire Straits.

TYRONE DAVIS

Born 1938, Greenville, Mississippi
N.A.—*Turn Back the Hands of Time* (Columbia)   *Without You in My Life* (Davis)   *Homewreckers* (Columbia)   *Turning Point*   **1972**—*It's All in the Game* (Dakar)   *Tyrone Davis' Greatest Hits*   **1976**—*Love and Touch*   **1977**—*Let's Be Closer Together* (Columbia)   **1978**—*I Can't Go On This Way*   **1979**—*In the Mood with Tyrone Davis*   **1980**—*I Just Can't Keep On Going*   **1981**—*Everything in Place*   **1982**—*The Best of Tyrone Davis.*

Romantic mid-tempo ballads like 1968's "Can I Change My Mind" made Davis one of the top black singers of the early Seventies. As a child in Mississippi, Davis sometimes sang as Tyrone the Wonder Boy, and he recorded his first singles in the mid-Sixties after he had relocated in Chicago. By the time he hooked up with Dakar Records, however, he had smoothed out his delivery. A reworked version of a song he originally recorded for Tangerine Records, "Can I Change My Mind," was released late in 1968 and hit #5 on the pop charts. Its brassy flourishes, relaxed rhythms and aggressive horns perfectly complemented Davis' style. More hits followed: "Is It Something You've Got" in the spring of 1969, and his biggest song, "Turn Back the Hands of Time" (#3, 1970), which inspired comparisons between Davis and everyone from Al Green to Barry White. Davis' later releases ("I'll Be Right Here," "Let Me Back In," "Could I Forget You") were essentially MOR soul. By the mid-Seventies he had left Dakar for Columbia Records.

BOBBY DAY

Born Robert Byrd, 1934, Fort Worth, Texas
N.A.—*Rockin' with Robin* (Class).

Singer Bobby Day is best known for recording bright, driving pop like "Rockin' Robin." As a child, Day moved to L.A. with his family and later met and worked with Johnny Otis. He recorded his own "Little Bitty Pretty One" in late 1957, but Thurston Harris' more rousing version became the hit. Between solo sides, Day was lead vocalist with the Day Birds and then with the Hollywood Flames, whose "Buzz Buzz Buzz" made the Top Twenty in 1957. He released more singles for Class Records, peaking at #2 in 1958 with "Rockin' Robin," replete with bird sounds. Despite stints at several labels (RCA, Rendezvous, Sureshot), Day never again cracked the Top Ten, although "Over and Over," the "Robin" B side, was a #1 hit for the Dave Clark Five in 1965.

THE dB's

Formed 1978, New York City
Will Rigby (b. Mar. 17, 1956, Winston-Salem, N.C.),
drums, voc.; Peter Holsapple (b. Feb. 19, 1956,
Greenwich, Conn.), gtr., organ, voc.; Gene Holder (b.
July 10, 1954, Philadelphia), bass, gtr.; Chris Stamey (b.
Dec. 6, 1954, Chapel Hill, N.C.), gtr., organ, voc.
1981—*Stands for Decibels* (Albion, U.K.) *Repercussions.*

Ironic pop-rockers, the dB's met at elementary school in
Winston-Salem, North Carolina. Peter Holsapple and
Chris Stamey brought their first group together in 1972,
and as members of Rittenhouse Square they recorded an
album for an independent label the next year. In 1975, Will
Rigby joined a group that Stamey formed at the University
of North Carolina, Chapel Hill, called Sneakers. They
traveled to New York to play Max's Kansas City before
breaking up in 1977.

Stamey soon returned to New York, where he played
with the Erasers, Alex Chilton and Television guitarist
Richard Lloyd. He recorded a Chilton-produced single for
Ork records and set up his own label, Car Records. Rigby
and Gene Holder moved to New York, and as Chris
Stamey and the dB's, the trio began playing locally and
released a single, "If and When," on Car in 1978. Holsapple joined the group in 1978.

The dB's were favorites of the New York club scene and
rock press, but U.S. record companies shied away. A
Shake single, "Black and White," and a few tracks on
compilation albums (Planet's *Sharp Cuts* and Stiff's *Start
Swimming*) make up the group's American releases as of
mid-1982. Albion has released a handful of singles (including 1980's "Dynamite"). The group also appears on the
Shake compilation LP *Shake to Date*. The dB's toured
Britain and the Continent in the spring of 1981 and recorded their second album in London. A third album is
planned for 1983, as well as solo projects for all four
members, who have worked separately as producers and
sidemen in New York.

THE DEAD BOYS

Formed 1976, Cleveland
Cheetah Chrome (b. Gene Connor), gtr.; Stiv Bators,
voc.; Jimmy Zero, gtr.; Jeff Magnum, bass; Johnny
Blitz, drums.
1977—*Young, Loud and Snotty* (Sire) **1978**—*We Have
Come for Your Children.*

The Dead Boys, Cleveland natives (Chrome and Blitz had
played in the seminal Rocket from the Tombs), emigrated
to New York when the Bowery scene first gained national
attention in 1976. Managed by CBGB's owner, Hilly
Kristal, they were adopted by scenemakers for their
raucous, impish brand of punk, fully captured by the title
of their debut album if not exactly by the music on it. The
production by Genya Ravan couldn't hide the fact that, for
all their high jinks, the Boys had little to offer musically,

Death Rock

Death rock—songs about grisly,
melodramatic teen fatalities—
flourished when Elvis was in the
Army and the Beatles were still
playing the Star Club in Hamburg.
It remains one of pop's most
curious trends.

The heroine of "Teen Angel"
(Mark Dinning, 1959) was crushed
by a train after returning to the car
stalled on the tracks in search of
her steady's high school ring; the
hero of "Tell Laura I Love Her" (Ray
Peterson, 1960) was killed in an
auto race accident; and in a horrific
chorus of squealing tires and
shattering glass, the easy rider of
"Leader of the Pack" (Shangri-Las,
1964) was broadsided by a truck as
his teary-eyed girlfriend watched.

A recurrent theme was the angst
of modern Romeos and Juliets. In
Dickey Lee's "Patches," the couple
had to part because she came from
"old shanty town." The song ended
with Patches floating down the
river that divided the two sides of
town—face down. (In general,
teens in these songs took rejection
poorly.)

Lee's other death-rock entry,
"Laurie (Strange Things Happen in
This World)," was ghoulish enough
to make Edgar Allan Poe shudder,
with a story line right out of a
supermarket checkout paperback.
The plot: Boy meets Laurie. Lends
her his sweater. Kisses her
goodnight at her door.
Realizes he forgot the sweater and

backtracks to her house. Man tells
him, "You're wrong son, you
weren't with my daughter . . . she
died a year ago today." Boy walks
to graveyard, and finds his sweater
lying upon her grave. (Note:
"Laurie" was written before the
widespread use of drugs.)

Perhaps songs about death made
listeners feel more alive. Or
perhaps they were a manifestation
of the A-bomb generation's
anxieties. By the late Sixties,
songwriters focused on more
weighty matters, and although
similarly grisly tunes occasionally
surface (David Geddes' "Run Joey
Run," 1975), death rock is essentially extinct.

making them the American counterparts to England's the Damned.

After Johnny Blitz was seriously injured in a mugging, the band regrouped for the Felix Pappalardi–produced *We Have Come for Your Children*, then dissolved. Only Bators, who released several solo singles on Bomp and whose Lords of the New Church (including Brian James of the Damned) released a record in 1982, has been heard from since.

THE DEAD KENNEDYS

Formed 1978, San Francisco
Jello Biafra, voc.; East Bay Ray, gtr.; Klaus Fluoride, bass; J. H. Pelligro, drums.
1980—*Fresh Fruit for Rotting Vegetables* (IRS) **1981**— *In God We Trust, Inc.* (Alternative Tentacles) (EP)
1982—*Plastic Surgery Disasters*.

Emerging from a volatile San Francisco punk scene, the Dead Kennedys became one of the West Coast's most visible punk bands. Fueled by a cutting political preoccupation, lead singer Jello Biafra's vocals conveyed the excess that marked such songs as "Drug Me" and "California Uber Alles." They directed diatribes against the Moral Majority, creeping U.S. imperialism and fascism and their perceptions of a plastic suburban lifestyle, and the band's instrumental overkill defined the hard-core punk term "thrashing." They even matched the Sex Pistols on their home turf, going Top Five in England with the airplay-banned "Too Drunk to Fuck." Biafra ran for mayor of San Francisco; one of his campaign planks was that businessmen wear clown suits downtown. The Dead Kennedys formed their own record label, Alternative Tentacles, which in 1982 released a compilation album, *Let Them Eat Jellybeans*, consisting of tracks by various unsigned American bands.

JOEY DEE AND THE STARLIGHTERS

Formed 1958, Passaic, New Jersey
Joey Dee (b. Joseph Dinicola, June 11, 1940, Passaic), voc.; Carlton Latimor, organ; Willie Davis, drums; Larry Vernieri, voc., dancer; David Brigati, voc., dancer.
N.A.—*The Peppermint Twisters* (Scepter) *Doin' the Twist* (Roulette) *Hey, Let's Twist*. **Joey Dee solo:** *Joey Dee* (Roulette) *Dance, Dance, Dance*.

In 1960, Joey Dee and the Starlighters were the house band at New York's famed Peppermint Lounge. When Dee noticed that everyone there was gyrating to Chubby Checker's "The Twist," he and R&B producer Henry Glover decided to personalize the dance fad and they came up with the "Peppermint Twist." Released in late 1961, the song was a #1 smash and landed the group cameo roles in two quickie fad films, *Hey Let's Twist* and *Vive le Twist*. The group scored a few more hits ("Hey Let's Twist," "Shout," "What Kind of Love Is This," "Hot Pastrami with Mashed Potatoes") before sinking back into lounge-band anonymity in late 1963.

By then, however, the Starlighters featured three of the four future Young Rascals—Felix Cavaliere, Gene Cornish and Eddie Brigati (whose brother David had been with Dee from the beginning). A psychedelic twist—in 1966 the group included Jimi Hendrix. Dee continues to perform.

DEEP PURPLE

Formed 1968, Hertford, England
Rod Evans (b. 1945, Eng.), voc.; Nick Semper (b. 1946, Norwood Green, Eng.), bass; Jon Lord (b. June 9, 1941, Leicester, Eng.), kybds.; Ritchie Blackmore (b. Apr. 14, 1945, Weston-super-Mare, Eng.), gtr.; Ian Paice (b. June 29, 1948, Nottingham, Eng.), drums.
1968—*Shades of Deep Purple* (Tetragrammaton) *Book of Taliesyn* **1969**—*Deep Purple* (– Evans; + Ian Gillan [b. Aug. 19, 1945, Hounslow, Eng.], voc.; – Semper; + Roger Glover [b. Nov. 30, 1945, Brecon, S. Wales], bass) *Powerhouse* (released 1978) (Purple, Europe) **1970**—*Concerto for Group and Orchestra* (Warner Bros.) *Deep Purple in Rock* **1971**—*Fireball* **1972**—*Machine Head; Made in Japan; Purple Passages* **1973**—*Who Do We Think We Are* (– Glover; + Glenn Hughes [b. Penkridge, Eng.], bass; – Gillan; + David Coverdale [b. Sep. 21, 1951, Saltburn, Eng.], voc.) **1974**—*Burn; Stormbringer; Made in Europe* **1975**—(– Blackmore; + Tommy Bolin [b. 1951, Sioux City, Ia.; d. Dec. 4, 1976, Miami], gtr.) *Come Taste the Band* (– Bolin) *24 Carat Purple* **1978**—*When We Rock, We Rock and When We Roll, We Roll* **1980**—*Deepest Purple* **1982**—*In Concert* (Portrait).

Deep Purple shifted halfway through their career from rock with pseudoclassical keyboard flourishes to guitar-dominated heavy metal; in the latter, vastly popular phase, they were listed as loudest rock band by the *Guinness Book of World Records*. After woodshedding in Hertfordshire, England, Deep Purple had its first success with an American hit, a version of Joe South's "Hush" (#4, 1968), followed by Neil Diamond's "Kentucky Woman"(#38, 1968). Deep Purple's popularity couldn't keep their label, Tetragrammaton, from going under after the band's 1968 tour.

In 1969, with a new lineup including Ian Gillan, who had sung in *Jesus Christ Superstar*, Deep Purple recorded Lord's *Concerto for Group and Orchestra*, but after it failed to sell, Ritchie Blackmore began to dominate the band. His simple repeated guitar riffs helped make Deep Purple one of the most successful groups of the early Seventies.

In Rock and *Fireball* attracted attention, and *Machine*

Head made the U.S. Top Ten (#7), thus adding to the band's success in England, Europe, Japan and Australia. One year after *Machine Head* was released, "Smoke on the Water"—about the band's near-disastrous Montreux concert with Frank Zappa—became a #4 hit single, and the album returned to the Top Ten, eventually selling over four million copies. With two more U.S. Top Ten LPs (*Made in Japan* and *Burn)* by late 1974, Deep Purple had sold nearly 15 million albums. But the band was beginning to fall apart. Gillan left for a solo career in 1973; in 1975 he formed the Ian Gillan Band. After he left, Roger Glover departed for session and production work (for Judas Priest, Elf, Nazareth, Ian Gillan, Spencer Davis, Michael Schenker of UFO, Barbi Benton and Blackmore's Rainbow). Jon Lord recorded a solo album, *Gemini Suite* (1974). Blackmore left in 1975 to form Ritchie Blackmore's Rainbow. He was replaced by Tommy Bolin, with whom the group recorded one LP before retiring in 1976. Albums with subsequent release dates are repackages and greatest-hits compilations.

In 1980, a bogus reincarnation of Deep Purple led by original vocalist Evans popped up on the West Coast bar circuit. Blackmore and Glover took legal action to prohibit Evans from using the name.

DEF LEPPARD
Formed 1977, Sheffield, England
Joe Elliott (b. Eng.), voc.; Pete Willis (b. Eng.), gtr.; Rick Savage (b. Eng.), bass; Rick Allen (b. Eng.), drums; Steve Clark (b. Eng.), gtr.
1980—*On through the Night* (Polygram) **1981**—*High 'n' Dry* (− Willis; + Phil Collen, gtr.) **1983**—*Pyromania.*

A chartbreaking debut album and tours with more established heavy-metal bands made Def Leppard one of 1980's leaders of the British heavy-metal new wave. Unlike most heavy-metal rockers, the members of Def Leppard, all born in Sheffield, were as young as their teenaged following.

Pete Willis and Rick Savage started the group. Joe Elliott had coined the name Deaf Leopard before joining them; Willis and Savage changed the spelling. As a quartet with a since-forgotten drummer, they built a local pub following, and in 1978, after being joined by Steve Clark and hiring a temporary drummer, they produced their first record, an EP called *Getcha Rocks Off.* The record got airplay from BBC and sold 24,000 copies.

Their self-made success and precociousness (Elliott, the group's eldest member, was 19, and Rick Allen, who became their permanent drummer after playing with several professional Sheffield bands, was 15) brought them the attention of the British rock press. AC/DC manager Peter Mensch added them to his roster and got them a contract with Polygram. Their first album was a hit in the U.K. and reached #51 in the U.S. The group toured

Britain with Sammy Hagar and AC/DC, played the 1980 Reading Festival, and first toured the U.S. opening for Ted Nugent. A second U.S. tour, this time co-headlining with Blackfoot, indicated a growing American audience. In late 1982, Willis was replaced by Phil Collen, formerly of Girl. By mid-1983 *Pyromania* had sold over 2 million copies in the U.S. and its single "Photograph" was a Top Ten hit.

THE DeFRANCO FAMILY
Formed 1973, Port Colborne, Canada
Benny DeFranco (b. July 11, 1954, Port Colborne), Nino DeFranco (b. Oct. 19, 1956, Port Colborne), Marisa DeFranco (b. July 23, 1955, Port Colborne), Merlina DeFranco (b. July 20, 1957, Port Colborne), Tony DeFranco (b. Aug. 31, 1959, Port Colborne).
1973—*Heartbeat—It's a Lovebeat* (20th Century–Fox).

Modeled after wholesome family acts like the Osmonds, the Cowsills, the Jackson 5 and TV's Partridge Family (David Cassidy), the Canadian-born DeFranco Family were sponsored by Laufer Publications (publishers of *Tiger Beat* and *Fave* magazines), which managed the group and distributed fan-club material featuring ten-year-old Tony DeFranco. "Heartbeat—It's a Lovebeat" sold 2½ million copies in 1974, becoming the year's top single, but the DeFrancos' career was ultimately distinguished by its brevity.

DESMOND DEKKER
Born July 16, 1942, Jamaica
N.A.—*The Israelites* (Uni) *Double Dekker* (Trojan) *You Can Get It* **1978**—*Sweet 16 Hits* **1980**—*Black and Dekker* (Stiff) **1981**—*Compass Point.*

Desmond Dekker was one of the pioneers of reggae and the creator of one of the genre's best-known songs, "The Israelites." As a teenager in Jamaica, he worked in the same welding shop as Bob Marley, who encouraged him to audition for producer Leslie Kong. Kong helped Dekker put together a group, the Aces, and produced their first record, "Honour Thy Father and Mother," in 1963. Eventually a #1 hit in Jamaica, it was followed by a score of Caribbean hits that won Dekker the title "King of the Bluebeat" and the annual Golden Trophy (awarded to Jamaica's top singer) five times between 1963 and 1969.

In 1964, Chris Blackwell released "Honour Thy Father and Mother" in Britain on his Island label. Dekker's first U.K. Top Twenty hit was a 1967 single on Pyramid, "007 (Shanty Town)," later featured on the soundtrack of the 1972 film *The Harder They Come.* "The Israelites," which personalized imagery from the Biblical Exodus story, sold over a million copies worldwide, reaching #1 in Britain in 1969 and garnering Dekker his only hit in the U.S.

A handful of British hits, including "It Mek" (Top Ten in 1969) and "You Can Get It If You Really Want," written for him by Jimmy Cliff (#2 in 1970) followed. A reissue of

"The Israelites" returned him to the British Top Ten in 1975. "Sing a Little Song" made the Top Twenty later that year. Dekker didn't record again until 1980, when Stiff Records signed him at the height of the ska and rock-steady revival. His comeback album, *Black and Dekker*, featured one of the original rock-steady groups, the Pioneers, and the Rumour in supporting roles. Its followup, *Compass Point*, was produced by singer Robert Palmer.

DELANEY AND BONNIE
Bonnie Bramlett, born November 8, 1944, Acton, Illinois; Delaney Bramlett, born July 1, 1939, Pontotoc County, Mississippi
1969—*The Original Delaney and Bonnie* (Elektra) *Home* (Stax) **1970**—*On Tour (with Eric Clapton)* (Atco) *To Delaney from Bonnie* **1971**—*Motel Shot; Genesis* (GNP-Crescendo) **1972**—*D and B Together* (Columbia) **1973**—*The Best of Delaney and Bonnie* (Atco). **Bonnie Bramlett solo: 1973**—*Sweet Bonnie Bramlett* (Columbia) **1975**—*It's Time* (Capricorn) **1976**—*Lady's Choice* **1978**—*Memories.* **Delaney Bramlett solo: 1972**—*Something's Coming* (Columbia) **1977**—*Delaney and Friends—Class Reunion* (Prodigal) *Mobius Strip* (Columbia) *Giving Birth to a Song* (MGM).

The best songs of the Delaney and Bonnie husband-and-wife duo fused gospel, country, funk and rock, but they were overshadowed by their Friends, a backup crew that occasionally included Eric Clapton, Leon Russell, Dave Mason and George Harrison. The couple met in Los Angeles in 1967. Bonnie Lynn had worked as a bewigged, blackfaced Ikette with Ike and Tina Turner in the mid-Sixties; Delaney had fallen in with a group of Southwestern musicians including Russell and J. J. Cale, contacts that netted him a brief stint with the Champs and then a steady job with the Shindogs, house band for ABC's "Shindig." The Shindogs were moonlighting at a Los Angeles bowling alley when Bramlett met Lynn; a week later they were married.

Although the group's first three albums went largely unnoticed, Blind Faith offered Delaney and Bonnie an opening slot on their 1969 tour. Clapton began riding in the couple's tour bus, which turned into a rolling jam session. After Blind Faith disbanded, Clapton began to perform regularly with the duo, assuming a low-key, sideman-only stance.

Clapton brought them to England, where Harrison, Mason and others came onstage for shows that resulted in Delaney and Bonnie's best-selling album, *On Tour (with Eric Clapton)*. The entourage briefly participated in John Lennon's Plastic Ono Band in late 1969 and toured Europe with Clapton. They returned to America as headliners in 1970, but their drawing power plummeted when Clapton left, and Leon Russell then hired most of the Friends to tour with Joe Cocker's Mad Dogs and Englishmen. The Bramletts canceled their tour.

They appeared on Clapton's solo debut in 1970, produced by Delaney, and continued to record their own albums, which included two major hits, "Never Ending Song of Love" (#13, 1971), and Dave Mason's "Only You Know and I Know" (#20, 1971).

In 1972, they signed with Columbia and made their last album, *Together*, before their marriage dissolved. Delaney made two solo LPs for Columbia to fulfill contractual obligations (*Something's Coming* and *Mobius Strip*) as well as 1977's *Giving Birth to a Song* on MGM and *Class Reunion* for Motown's Prodigal label. Bonnie, backed by the uncredited Average White Band, made one album for Columbia (*Sweet Bonnie Bramlett*) before signing with Capricorn. While touring with Stephen Stills in 1979, she punched Elvis Costello in a Columbus, Ohio, bar when he called Ray Charles "a blind, ignorant nigger."

THE DELFONICS
Formed 1964, Philadelphia
William Hart (b. Jan. 17, 1945, Washington, D.C.), voc.; Wilbert Hart (b. Oct. 19, 1947, Philadelphia), voc.; Randy Cain (b. May 2, 1945, Philadelphia), voc.; Ritchie Daniels, voc.
1968—*La La Means I Love You* (Philly Groove) **1969**—*The Sound of Sexy Soul* **1971**—*The Delfonics; The Delfonics Super Hits* (− Cain; + Major Harris [b. Richmond, Va.], voc.) **1973**—*Tell Me This Is a Dream* (− Harris; + Bruce Peterson [b. Chicago], voc.) **1974**—*Alive and Kicking* **1975**—*Let It Be Me* (Sounds Superb).

The Delfonics' late-Sixties MOR soul hits were among producer Thom Bell's earliest works and set standards for elegant black pop. Originally the Four Guys, the group formed in the mid-Sixties around chief songwriter William Hart in a Philadelphia high school. Their high-pitched harmony style shone on medium-tempo ballads like "He Don't Really Love You," a local hit in 1967, shortly after they'd signed with manager Stan Watson, who persuaded them to call themselves the Delfonics. They worked East Coast clubs until early 1968, when Watson formed the Philly Groove label and brought in budding producer Thom Bell.

Their first collaboration with Bell, "La La Means I Love You" (a phrase Hart picked up from his young son), was an instant #4 smash in spring 1968. Bell also worked on subsequent Delfonics hits ("I'm Sorry," "Break Your Promise," "Ready or Not, Here I Come," "You Get Yours and I'll Get Mine" and their 1970 Top Ten landmark "Didn't I [Blow Your Mind This Time]"). R&B veteran Major Harris ("One Monkey Don't Stop No Show") joined the group in 1971, but failed to revitalize them.

THE DELLS

Formed 1953, Harvey, Illinois

Marvin Junior, first tenor; Mickey McGill, baritone; Johnny Funches, lead; Chuck Barksdale, bass; Vern Allison, tenor.

1958—(− McGill; − Funches; + Johnny Carter)
N.A.—*There Is* (Cadet)   *The Dells Greatest Hits* (Trip)
1973—*Best of the Dells* (Checker)   1974—*The Mighty Mighty Dells* (Cadet)   1975—*We Got to Get Our Thing Together* (Mercury)   *The Dells Greatest Hits, volume 2* (Cadet)   1976—*No Way Back* (Mercury)   1977—*Cornered* (DJM)   1979—*Face to Face* (ABC)   1980—*I Touched a Dream* (20th Century–Fox)   1981—*Whatever Turns You On* 1982—*The Dells* (Chess).   **The Dells and the Dramatics:** 1974—*The Dells vs. The Dramatics* (Cadet, U.K.).

The Dells are a black vocal group who have been together more than a quarter of a century. The original members of the group began singing together as early-fifties freshmen at Thornton Township High School in the Chicago suburb of Harvey. A streetcorner a cappella doo-wop group, they called themselves the El Rays and picked up their style from records by the Clovers and the Dominoes. Harvey Fuqua of the Moonglows took them as protégés, and within months the El Rays were including Mickey McGill's and Marvin Junior's originals in their club sets.

In late 1953, they recorded their first single for Chess, the a cappella "Darling Dear, I Know" b/w "Christine." The group's $36 in royalties sent them back to the streetcorners. They continued to record for Chess until 1955, when, billing themselves as the Dells, they switched to Vee Jay Records. Their second release for that label, "Oh What a Night," became a Top Ten R&B hit. En route to a gig in 1958, the group had an auto accident that left McGill in the hospital for six months, forced Funches to retire and put the band out of commission for a year. (Funches was replaced by ex-Flamingo falsetto Johnny Carter, who still sings with the core lineup.)

The early Sixties found them slowly regrouping and label-hopping between Vee Jay and Chess. By mid-decade, they had become a contemporary soul group à la the Temptations and the Impressions; they hit the pop charts in 1968 with three Top Twenty hits ("There Is" [#20], "Always Together" [#18] and their biggest hit, "Stay in My Corner"), and in 1969 with a medley of "I Can Sing a Rainbow"/"Love Is Blue" (#22) and a Top Ten remake of "Oh What a Night." They hit occasionally in the early Seventies ("Give Your Baby a Standing Ovation," "The Love We Had [Stays on My Mind]"). In 1974 they cut an album with the Dramatics called *The Dells vs. the Dramatics*. The group continues to perform and record.

THE DEL-VIKINGS

Formed 1955, Pittsburgh

Clarence Quick (b. Brooklyn), voc.; Dave Lerchey (b. New Albany, Ind.), voc.; Norman Wright (b. Oct. 21, 1937, Philadelphia), voc.; Donald "Gus" Backus (b. Southampton, N.Y.), voc.

1957—(+ Kripps Johnson [b. Cambridge, Md.], voc; later personnel changes frequent, included + Chuck Jackson [b. July 22, 1937, Latta, S.C.], voc.)   N.A.—*Come Go with Me* (Dot)   *Newies and Oldies* (Fee Bee)   *Swinging, Singing Del-Vikings Record Sessions* (Mercury)   *They Sing—They Swing;   Come Go with the Del-Vikings* (Luniverse)   *The Del-Vikings and the Sonnets* (Crown).

One of rock's first racially integrated groups, the Del-Vikings were a vocal quintet that came together at a Pittsburgh Air Force base and scored two Top Ten hits in 1957, "Come Go with Me" (#5) and "Whispering Bells" (#9). The group first recorded for Luniverse in 1956 with little success. The following year, after adding Kripps Johnson, they recorded the R&B-tinged million-seller "Come Go with Me" for the tiny Pittsburgh label Fee Bee. The group toured widely, and in mid-1957 scored again with "Whispering Bells," but after one minor hit ("Cool Shake") they disappeared. Chuck Jackson later had soul hits in the Sixties ("I Don't Want to Cry," "Any Day Now," "Tell Him I'm Not Home") and Seventies ("Needing You").

SANDY DENNY

Born January 6, 1941, Wimbledon, England; died April 21, 1978, London.

1968—*All Our Own Work* (Pickwick)   1970—*Fotheringay* (A&M)   *Sandy Denny* (Saga)   1971—*The Northstar Grassman and the Ravens* (A&M)   1972—*Sandy; Rock On*   1973—*Like an Old Fashioned Waltz* (Island)   1977—*Sandy Denny* (Nova)   *Rendezvous* (Island).

Sandy Denny's smoky alto made her one of England's most popular singer/songwriters of the early Seventies, both as a member of the electric folk group Fairport Convention and on her own. She studied classical piano, and while working as a nurse after graduating high school she learned guitar. She later enrolled in Kensington Art School (classmates included Jimmy Page [Led Zeppelin], Eric Clapton and John Renbourn) and began frequenting London's folk pubs and coffeehouses. Denny jammed with the then-struggling Simon and Garfunkel, who encouraged her to start performing regularly.

By the mid-Sixties, she was playing London folk clubs and had recorded one privately distributed LP. During 1967, she belonged to the nascent Strawbs (later an art-rock aggregate but then a country-folk group) for six months, recording one unreleased album. She also wrote "Who Knows Where the Time Goes?," later the title track of a gold album by Judy Collins. In May 1968, Denny joined Fairport Convention, with whom she recorded three albums. She quit the group in December 1969, following the release of their landmark *Leige and Lief*.

Denny hesitantly announced a solo career and formed Fotheringay (named after a song on *Fairport Convention*) with American guitarist Jerry Donahue, bassist Pat Donaldson, guitarist Trevor Lucas (whom she married in 1973), and drummer Gerry Conway. Though *Fotheringay* was moderately successful, the group disbanded late in 1970 before completing a second album.

Denny, voted top British female vocalist in the 1970 and 1971 *Melody Maker* polls, started her solo career in earnest, touring Europe, the U.S. and Britain frequently over the next few years, usually backed by Fairport and Fotheringay alumni. In 1972, she joined the Bunch, a casual aggregation of electrified folkies (including Richard Thompson and Fairport percussionist Dave Mattacks), and recorded an album of rock oldies, *Rock On*. She also contributed vocals to Led Zeppelin's "The Battle of Evermore."

Around the time of *Like an Old Fashioned Waltz*, Denny rejoined Fairport Convention, although she had already played a low-key support role in the group's 1973 tour. (She had been preceded into the group by Lucas and Donahue.) Though she contributed to 1975's *Rising for the Moon*, the reunion never quite clicked, and she and Lucas left Fairport in February 1976. She released *Rendezvous* in May 1977 and died the next year from head injuries sustained in a fall down a flight of stairs in her home.

JOHN DENVER
Born John Henry Deutschendorf, December 31, 1943, Roswell, New Mexico
1969—*Rhymes and Reasons* (RCA) **1970**—*Whose Garden Was This; Take Me to Tomorrow* **1971**— *Poems, Prayers and Promises; Aerie* **1972**—*Rocky Mountain High; Spirit* **1973**—*John Denver's Greatest Hits; Farewell Andromeda* **1974**—*Back Home Again; A John Denver Songbook; Beginnings with the Mitchell Trio* (Mercury) **1975**—*An Evening with John Denver* (RCA) *Windsong; Rocky Mountain Christmas* **1977**—*I Want to Live; John Denver's Greatest Hits, volume 2* **1979**—*John Denver; John Denver and The Muppets: A Christmas Together* **1980**—*Autograph* **1981**—*Some Days Are Diamonds* **1982**—*Seasons of the Heart.*

Through the Seventies, country-pop singer/songwriter John Denver was one of the most successful recording artists in the world. Of his 21 albums, all are gold and four are platinum, and in the mid-Seventies he had a string of gold singles.

Denver was raised in an Air Force family and lived in various Southern and Southwestern towns. In his early teens, his grandmother gave him a 1910 Gibson acoustic guitar. He enrolled at Texas Tech in 1961, majoring in architecture and playing in local clubs.

In 1964, he dropped out of college and moved to Los Angeles, and after he adopted Denver as his stage name he replaced Chad Mitchell in the Chad Mitchell Trio in 1965. The Trio, a major draw on the early-Sixties hootenanny circuit, was $40,000 in debt upon Denver's arrival, which he later helped them pay back. They recorded for Mercury (which later repackaged the results under Denver's name as *Beginnings*) and toured widely. At a 1966 Trio concert at the Gustavus Adolphus College in Minnesota, Denver met sophomore Ann Martell (born 1946), who married him the next year.

Rhymes and Reasons included "Leaving on a Jet Plane," which became a #1 hit for Peter, Paul and Mary; Denver shared their producer, Milt Okun. His own rise began with the million-selling "Take Me Home, Country Roads" (#2, 1970). After he had moved to Aspen, Colorado, *Rocky Mountain High* went platinum in 1972. "Annie's Song" (for his wife), "Sweet Surrender" (for the soundtrack of Walt Disney's *The Bears and I*) and "Sunshine on My Shoulder" made Denver the best-selling pop musician of 1974. *Greatest Hits*, including "Sunshine," sold over ten million copies and stayed in the Top 100 for two years. The Governor of Colorado proclaimed John Denver the state's poet laureate.

While the hits continued—"Thank God I'm a Country Boy" (#1, 1975), "Back Home Again" (#5, 1974), "I'm Sorry" (#1, 1975)—Denver tried TV and film appearances, with variety specials, dramatic roles and a screen debut in 1977's *Oh, God!* He started Windsong Records (distributed by RCA) in 1976, and signed the Starland Vocal Band, whose Bill and Taffy Danoff had written "Take Me Home . . .".

Denver has done volunteer work for ecological causes, ERA and space exploration (he's a board member of the National Space Institute) and against nuclear power.

RICK DERRINGER
Born Rick Zehringer, 1949, Union City, Indiana
With the McCoys: 1965—*Hang on Sloopy* (Bang) **1966**—*You Make Me Feel So Good* **1968**—*Infinite McCoys* (Mercury) *Human Ball.* **Solo: 1973**—*All American Boy* (Blue Sky) **1974**—*Outside Stuff, Rick Derringer and the McCoys* (Mercury) **1975**—*Spring Fever* (Blue Sky) **1976**—*Derringer* **1977**—*Sweet Evil; Live* **1978**—*If I Weren't So Romantic, I'd Shoot You* **1979**—*Guitars and Women* **1980**—*Face to Face.*

A teen star with the Sixties prototype garage band, the McCoys ("Hang on Sloopy"), singer/guitarist Rick Derringer joined Johnny and Edgar Winter for several successful albums in the early Seventies. He has conducted an uneven solo career since. Rick Zehringer formed the McCoys at age 13 after he and his younger brother, drummer Randy, persuaded the kid next door to buy a bass. Producer/songwriter Bert Berns brought them to New York, where they recorded "Hang on Sloopy." In mid-1965, that song became the McCoys' only #1 hit. "Fever" hit #7 later that year.

A few minor hits followed, and in the late Sixties Zehringer produced a couple of psychedelic blues-rock albums for the group. By 1969, the McCoys were the house band at Steve Paul's club, the Scene, in New York. Paul soon became their manager and introduced them to Johnny Winter. After changing his name to Derringer, Rick produced and played on several Winter albums (including *Johnny Winter And* and the gold *Johnny Winter And Live*). When Johnny quit touring to kick a heroin habit in late 1971, Derringer joined Johnny's brother Edgar Winter and his band White Trash for a seven-month tour (he appears on *Roadwork*). Derringer then produced Edgar's *They Only Come Out at Night* and the #1 single "Frankenstein." By December 1973, he was back on the road with Edgar and co-billed as a feature attraction.

Derringer's first solo album, *All American Boy,* featured his best-known composition, "Rock and Roll Hoochie Coo" (previously recorded by both Winters), which went to #15 as a single. In 1973, he produced Johnny Winter's "comeback" LP, *Still Alive and Well.* He continued studio work with Johnny (*Saints and Sinners*) and Edgar throughout the Seventies. In addition, he played guitar on sessions with Steely Dan, Alice Cooper, Bette Midler, Todd Rundgren and many others.

Derringer's unsuccessful second solo album prompted the 1976 formation of a group called Derringer, featuring second guitarist Danny Johnson and a rhythm section consisting of Carmine Appice's brother Vinnie on drums and bassist Kenny Aaronson. The group produced four albums (*Derringer, Sweet Evil, If I Weren't So Romantic, I'd Shoot You* and *Derringer Live*) and toured constantly through the late Seventies, opening for Blue Öyster Cult, Aerosmith and Foghat. But the group never clicked, and Rick ended the decade playing East Coast clubs with makeshift pickup bands that for a while included guitarist Neil Geraldo and drummer Myron Grombacher, who later joined Pat Benatar's band. As the Eighties dawned, Derringer was without a recording contract. Derringer is married to journalist Liz Derringer.

JACKIE DeSHANNON

Born August 21, 1944, Hazel, Kentucky
1972—*Jackie* (Atlantic)   1974—*Your Baby Is a Lady*
1975—*New Arrangement* (Columbia)   1978—*You're the Only Dancer* (Amherst)   *Songs* (Capitol).

Singer/songwriter Jackie DeShannon's career has spanned more than twenty years. Born into a musical Kentucky

family, she had her own local radio show by age eleven and scored a regional hit when she moved with her family to Chicago. She landed on the West Coast in 1960. There she sang backed by a group called the Nighthawks, which eventually evolved into the Crusaders.

DeShannon's first songwriting success came in the early Sixties with hits for Brenda Lee (including "Dum Dum"); the Fashionettes ("Day Dreamin' of You"); Evie Sands ("I Was Moved"); and the Searchers ("When You Walk in the Room"—a minor hit for DeShannon as well). In 1965, the Byrds included her "Don't Doubt Yourself, Babe" on *Mr. Tambourine Man.*

DeShannon began recording in 1960 as part of the Nomads. In 1963, she and Ry Cooder formed a short-lived and unrecorded band. In late 1964, she met Jimmy Page in England, and they wrote several songs in early 1965 that were recorded by Marianne Faithfull (for whom Jackie penned the British hit "Come Stay with Me"). DeShannon's single of Burt Bacharach's "What the World Needs Now Is Love" was a hit (#7, 1965) that earned four Grammy nominations. Her next hit was the two-million-selling "Put a Little Love in Your Heart" in 1969.

In the early Seventies, DeShannon recorded *Your Baby Is a Lady* and *Jackie* in a slick country-soul style; but neither LP sold well. In the early Seventies she also sang background vocals on some Van Morrison sessions; Morrison later produced some of her own sessions. She switched to Columbia in 1975 for *New Arrangement,* which also sold poorly. In 1977, she released an album on the small Amherst label. Her songwriting prowess is still recognized: Bruce Springsteen frequently performs "When You Walk in the Room"; and DeShannon and Donna Weiss cowrote Kim Carnes's 1981 international hit, "Bette Davis Eyes."

WILLIE DeVILLE (see Mink DeVille)

DEVO

Formed 1972, Akron, Ohio
Jerry Casale, bass, voc.; Mark Mothersbaugh, voc., kybds., gtr.; Bob "Bob I" Mothersbaugh, gtr., voc.; Bob "Bob II" Casale, gtr., voc.; Alan Myers, drums.
1978—*Q: Are We Not Men? A: We Are Devo!* (Warner Bros.)   1979—*Duty Now for the Future*   1980—*Freedom of Choice*   1981—*New Traditionalists*
1982—*Oh No! It's Devo.*

Spouting an original tongue-in-cheek world view proclaiming man to be in a state of genetic and cultural "de-evolution," Devo made the unlikely step from novelty act to real contender—an ironic new wave version of Kiss, whose marketing was as important as their music. They have exploited film and video from the beginning of their career.

The details of the group's pre-Devo existence have been intentionally obscured as part of their automatonlike im-

Devo

age (they always perform in uniform, favoring futuristic-yet-sturdy ensembles that have featured upturned red flowerpots for hats and roller derby–style gear). Mark Mothersbaugh and Jerry Casale met while studying art at Kent State University. Neither was musical. To build their band, Mothersbaugh and Casale recruited their "Bob I" and "Bob II" brothers and drummer Alan Myers and produced a ten-minute video clip entitled *The Truth about De-Evolution,* which won a prize at the Ann Arbor Film Festival in 1975. They followed up with club dates. In 1976, they independently released their first single, "Jocko Homo" b/w "Mongoloid" on their own Booji Boy Records (the infantile robot Booji is their corporate mascot and is often featured in their videos and concerts). In 1977, their follow-up single, a syncopated version of the Rolling Stones' "Satisfaction," increased the band's growing cult.

Q: Are We Not Men? A: We Are Devo!, produced by Brian Eno, was released in the fall of 1978, and the group hit the road in earnest. Their third LP, *Freedom of Choice,* provided their 1980 commercial breakthrough by going gold with a million-selling single, "Whip It."

Devo continue to revive rock chestnuts with noteworthy success. Besides "Satisfaction," they covered Johnny Rivers' "Secret Agent Man" in 1980 and received substantial airplay in mid-1981 with a hiccupy rendition of Lee Dorsey's "Working in a Coal Mine." The group also changes its identity. Clad in leisure suits and crooning born-again lounge music, they occasionally open their own concerts as "Dove, the Band of Love."

NEIL DIAMOND

Born January 24, 1941, Brooklyn, New York
1968—*Velvet Gloves and Spit* (MCA) *Greatest Hits* (Bang) **1969**—*Touching You, Touching Me* (MCA) *Sweet Caroline* **1970**—*Neil Diamond Gold; Tap Root*

Manuscript **1971**—*Stones* **1972**—*Hot August Night; Moods* **1973**—*Double Gold* (Bang) *Rainbow* (MCA) *Jonathan Livingston Seagull* (Columbia) **1974**—*His Twelve Greatest Hits* (MCA) *Serenade* (Columbia) **1976**—*Beautiful Noise; And the Singer Sings His Song* (MCA) **1977**—*Love at the Greek* (Columbia) *I'm Glad You're Here with Me Tonight* **1978**—*You Don't Bring Me Flowers* **1980**—*September Morning; The Jazz Singer* (soundtrack) (Capitol) **1981**—*On the Way to the Sky* (Columbia) *Yesterday's Songs* **1982**—*12 Greatest Hits, volume 2.*

Pop songwriter Neil Diamond, a veteran of the Brill Building song factories, became one of the best-selling MOR performers of the Seventies. Singing his own melodramatic quasi-gospel songs in a portentous baritone, he has amassed over thirty Top Forty singles.

Diamond recorded his first single soon after graduating from Brooklyn's Erasmus High School. He attended NYU as a premedical student on a fencing scholarship until 1962, when he dropped out and began hawking songs to Broadway publishers, one of whom soon hired him as a $50-a-week staff songwriter.

Diamond worked for various publishers, including Don Kirshner's Aldon Music, where he wrote the Monkees' 1966 hit "I'm a Believer." Fellow songwriters Jeff Barry and Ellie Greenwich helped him sign with Bang Records in 1965, for whom he recorded a string of Top Twenty hits ("Cherry, Cherry," #6, 1966; "You Got to Me," #18, 1967; "Girl, You'll Be a Woman Soon," #10, 1967; "I Thank the Lord for the Night Time," #13, 1967; "Kentucky Woman," #22, 1967). Bang was less interested when Diamond began looking for significance with songs like "Shiloh," and he moved to California in 1966, where Uni Records promised him full artistic control.

His Uni debut, *Velvet Gloves and Spit,* sold poorly, but subsequent singles—"Brother Love's Traveling Salvation Show," #22, 1969; "Sweet Caroline," #4, 1969; "Song Sung Blue," #1, 1972—established Diamond as a major star. He toured the U.S., Europe and Australia in 1972 and placed two albums in the U.S. Top Five—*Moods* and the live *Hot August Night* (which also became Australia's best-selling album, three million sales in a country of 14 million people). He also played a twenty-performance one-man show on Broadway in 1972.

In 1973, Diamond signed with Columbia for a record-breaking $5 million; his first Columbia album, the soundtrack to *Jonathan Livingston Seagull,* grossed more money than the film itself. He returned to touring in February 1976 and appeared in the Band's *Last Waltz* concert on Thanksgiving Day. Band guitarist Robbie Robertson produced Diamond's *Beautiful Noise,* a tribute to Diamond's Sixties songwriting days, his eleventh album in a row to go gold.

A TV special of Diamond in concert was aired on NBC on February 24, 1977, and in 1980 he starred in a remake of

The Jazz Singer. His soundtrack LP for that film went platinum. Meanwhile, Diamond continues to collect royalties for the many cover versions of his songs, including Deep Purple's "Kentucky Woman," the Hollies' "He Ain't Heavy, He's My Brother," Lulu's "The Boat That I Row" and Cliff Richard's "Girl, You'll Be a Woman Soon."

THE DIAMONDS
Formed circa 1955, Toronto
Dave Somerville, Mike Douglas, Ted Kowalski, Bill Reed, all vocalists.
1956—(− Kowalski; − Reed; + John Felton; + Evan Fisher) **N.A.**—*Pop Hits* (Wing) *America's #1 Singing Stylists* (Mercury).

The Diamonds were a clean-cut white vocal group that had sixteen hits between 1956 and 1961, ten of which were covers of songs recorded by black R&B artists. Their first was a rendition of Frankie Lymon and the Teenagers' "Why Do Fools Fall in Love?" The Teenagers' version was the bigger hit (#7 as compared to #16 for the Diamonds). From that point on, however, the Diamonds' copies outsold and sometimes totally eclipsed the originals.

Their biggest hit, "Little Darlin' " (originally by the Gladiolas), was #2 in the U.S. in 1957 and became a big hit in the U.K. and Europe as well. Later that year, they had a Top Five smash with Chuck Willis' "The Stroll," which briefly popularized the dance of the same name. The Diamonds played many package tours in the late Fifties and appeared frequently on TV variety shows. After several minor hits as the decade closed ("High Sign," "Kathy-O," "Walking Along," "She Say [Oom Dooby Doom]"), the Diamonds, by then plagued by frequent personnel changes, were reduced to a lounge act. Their last hit was 1961's "One Summer Night."

MANU DIBANGO
Born 1934, Douala, Cameroon
1972—*Soul Makossa* (Atlantic) **1973**—*Makossa Man; O Boso* (London) **1975**—*Makossa Music* (Creole) **1976**—*Manu '76* (Decca) *Super Kumba* **1978**—*Afrovision* (Island) *Sin Explosion* (Decca) **1980**—*Gone Clear* (Island) *Reggae Makossa* **1981**—*Ambassador*.

Manu Dibango's "Soul Makossa" was one of the few African pop songs to catch on in America.

Dibango moved from Cameroon to Europe at age 15 and studied piano and music theory in Paris and Brussels. At age twenty, he took up the saxophone, and over the next 15 years maintained a career as a jazz and R&B musician in Europe. In the late Sixties, he returned to Africa, settling in Kinshasa, Zaire. He assembled a band composed of African, European and Caribbean musicians to play an array of Western instruments (horns, keyboards, electric guitars and basses) and traditional African instruments on music that drew on jazz, R&B, calypso, Cuban, rock, and traditional and modern African forms.

Beginning in the early Seventies, he and his bands toured and recorded in Europe and Africa. "Soul Makossa," recorded in France by La Société Française du Son in 1972 and released in the U.S. the following year, reached #35 pop and #21 soul on American singles charts. In 1974, Dibango toured the U.S., but since then his activities have been restricted to Europe, Africa and the West Indies (where he recorded his 1980 and 1981 Island albums with Jamaican reggae musicians like Sly Dunbar and Robbie Shakespeare). He has used his reputation in Europe to secure recording contracts for musicians from all over Africa, and as head of Makossa Productions has spread recorded popular music throughout Africa and abroad.

DICK AND DEEDEE
Formed 1961, Santa Monica, California
Dick St. John Gosting, b. 1944, Santa Monica; Deedee Sperling, b. 1945, Santa Monica.
N.A.—*Songs We've Sung on Shindig* (Warner Bros.) *Tell Me the Mountain's High* (Liberty) *Thou Shalt Not Steal* (Warner Bros.) *Turn Around; Young and in Love*.

One of the more popular pop acts of the early Sixties, Dick and Deedee dressed the part of clean-cut preppies—he in conservative dark suits and she in chiffon. Friends since grammar school, they were both students at Santa Monica High School when they got a contract to cut a single in 1961 from Liberty (for whom Dick had previously recorded on his own). Their first release was "I Want Someone," backed by "The Mountain's High." The B side got such good response that Liberty reissued the disc with the songs transposed, and "The Mountain's High" became the duo's biggest hit, peaking at #2 in mid-1961.

In 1962, they left Liberty to go to Warner Bros., where they had a few successful chart records beginning with "Young and in Love," continuing through "Turn Around" and the Top Fifteen lesson in morality, "Thou Shalt Not Steal," in late 1964. They toured on and off, but continued to devote the bulk of their time to school, even at the height of their career. By the mid-Sixties they had retired from pop music.

THE DICTATORS
Formed 1974, Bronx, New York
Handsome Dick Manitoba (b. Richard Blum, Jan. 29, 1954), voc.; Ross the Boss (b. Jan. 3, 1954, Bronx), gtr., voc.; Scott "Top Ten" Kempner (b. Feb. 6, 1954, Bronx), gtr., voc.; Adny Shernoff (b. Apr. 19, 1952, Bronx), kybds., voc.; Mark Mendoza, bass; Ritchie Teeter (b. Mar. 16, 1951, Long Island, N.Y.), drums.

1975—*Go Girl Crazy* (Epic) **1977**—*Manifest Destiny* (Elektra) (– Mendoza) **1978**—*Bloodbrothers* (Asylum).

Loved by some, hated by many more and misunderstood and/or ignored by the rest, the Dictators straddled heavy metal and punk rock with a slapstick sense of humor. In the early Seventies Adny Shernoff was editing a mimeographed rock fanzine, *Teenage Wasteland Gazette,* an influence on *Creem* and a forerunner of *Punk* magazine. With virtually no musical experience, he gave up writing to form the Dictators with Scott Kempner and Ross the Boss; the latter had been in a unit called Total Crud. Manitoba, who began as their roadie, soon became their vocalist and frontman.

Though their music was much closer to brazenly amateurish heavy metal than punk, they were mainstays in the early days at Manhattan's CBGB. In 1976, Manitoba was nearly killed when, after heckling transvestite rocker (now transsexual) Wayne/Jayne County at CBGB, County hit him over the head with a microphone stand. Despite, or because of, such antics, their debut was a critical success, but sold only 6,000 copies.

They broke up in late 1978, Teeter resurfacing in a New York band called VHF a year later. Ross the Boss went to San Francisco in 1979 and formed Shakin' Street, which released one LP for Columbia in 1980; in 1982, he formed a heavy-metal band called Manowar. Shernoff has been involved in Off Broadway theatrical productions and has produced many records for New York bands. Handsome Dick and Top Ten began working with the New York group del-Lords in 1982. The Dictators played several reunion shows in 1981.

BO DIDDLEY
Born Ellas Bates, December 30, 1928, McComb, Mississippi
1963—*Is a Gunslinger* (Checker) *Bo Diddley Rides Again* (Pye) *Beach Party* **1964**—*Two Great Guitars; Hey Good Looking* (Chess) **1965**—*Let Me Pass* **1968**—*Super Blues Band* (Checker) **1973**—*Golden Decade* (Chess) **1974**—*Big Bad Bo* (Checker) **1975**— *Another Dimension* **1976**—*20th Anniversary* (RCA).

Bo Diddley's syncopated "hambone" beat—CHINK-a-CHINK-a-CHINK, a-CHINK-CHINK—is a cornerstone of rock & roll songs, from Diddley's own "Who Do You Love," "Mona," "Bo Diddley" and "I'm a Man" to the Who's "Magic Bus" and Bruce Springsteen's "She's the One." Dressed in black and sporting a low-slung rectangular-shaped guitar and thick horn-rimmed glasses, the 300-pound Diddley has been on the road for thirty years.

Adopted by a Mississippi sharecropping family, he moved with them to the South Side of Chicago. As a child, he began studying violin under Professor O. W. Frederick at the Ebenezer Baptist Church. By the time he entered Foster Vocational School in his early teens, he had switched to the guitar and regularly played on Chicago's Maxwell Street when he wasn't in school or training to be a Golden Gloves boxer at the local gym, where he acquired his Bo Diddley nickname (a "bo diddley" is a one-stringed African guitar). At 18, he married a young woman from his neighborhood, Louise (they were later divorced). After several years of performing on streetcorners, he played at the 708 Club in 1951 and became a regular South Side performer for the next four years.

In July 1955, Leonard Chess signed him to his Checker label. Diddley subsequently played on several recordings by fellow Chess artist Chuck Berry, including "Memphis" and "Sweet Little Rock 'n' Roller." Diddley's first single, "Bo Diddley," was an immediate R&B success. "I'm a Man" (1955, later recorded by the Yardbirds and others) also fared well on the R&B charts. His biggest pop success came in 1959, when "Say Man" hit the Top Twenty late in the year. He had a lesser hit in 1962 with the rollicking "You Can't Judge a Book by the Cover."

Diddley toured steadily through the late Fifties and early Sixties, playing rock package tours and one-nighters at R&B venues. The band that recorded with him in the mid-Fifties included drummer Frank Kirkland, pianist Otis Spann, harmonica player Billy Boy Arnold, Bo's half-sister "The Duchess" on guitar and vocals, and Diddley's eternal sidekick, bassist and maracas shaker Jerome Arnold (who also provided call-and-response repartee on "Hey Bo Diddley" and "Bring It to Jerome").

Diddley's legacy was enhanced considerably during the mid-Sixties, when many of his songs were covered by British Invasion groups like the Rolling Stones. Through the years, his material has also been recorded by the Doors, Tom Rush, Quicksilver Messenger Service and Ronnie Hawkins, among many others.

Diddley has recorded erratically over the past two decades. In the early Sixties, he even recorded surfing albums (*Surfin' with Bo Diddley*). In the mid-Sixties, he recorded traditional blues with Little Walter and Muddy Waters on *Super Blue*. In the early Seventies, Diddley continued to tour frequently (sometimes backed by Elephant's Memory), concentrating on Europe. One such outing was documented in *Let the Good Times Roll*. Around the same time, he also appeared in D. A. Pennebaker's *Keep On Rockin'*. In 1976, RCA released *20th Anniversary of Rock 'n' Roll*, a tribute to Bo Diddley featuring over twenty artists. Diddley opened several dates for the Clash on their 1979 U.S. tour. He made cameo appearances in George Thorogood's video "Bad to the Bone" (1982) and the Dan Aykroyd–Eddie Murphy movie, *Trading Places*.

THE DILLARDS
Formed circa 1960, Salem, Missouri
Rodney Dillard (b. May 18, 1942, Salem), voc., gtr., synth., dobro; Doug Dillard (b. Mar. 6, 1937, Salem),

banjo; Mitchell Jayne (b. May 7, 1930, Salem), bass; Dean Webb (b. Mar. 28, 1937, Independence, Mo.), mandolin; Byron Berline (b. July 6, 1944, Caldwell, Kan.), fiddle.

1963—*Back Porch Bluegrass* (Elektra) **1964**—*Live Almost* **1965**—*Pickin' and Fiddlin'* **1968**—*Wheatstraw Suite* (– Doug Dillard; – Berline) **1969**—(+ Herb Pedersen, banjo) **1970**—(+ Paul York, drums) *Copperfields* **1972**—*Roots and Branches* (Anthem) **1973**—*Tribute to the American Duck* (Poppy) **1976**—*Best of the Dillards* **1977**—*The Incredible LA Time Machine* (Flying Fish) **1979**—*Decade Waltz*.

A bluegrass band from the Ozarks that went electric, the Dillards paved the way for country rock. The original quartet left Missouri for Hollywood in 1962. They were cast to play a hillbilly band on the "Andy Griffith Show" and were signed by Elektra. Their 1964 debut, *Back Porch Bluegrass*, included "Duelin' Banjos," later popularized in the film *Deliverance*, where it was performed by Eric Weissberg. Their repertoire grew to include Bob Dylan's songs as well as traditional bluegrass, and on a 1965 tour with the Byrds, the Dillards reportedly helped Roger McGuinn arrange vocal harmonies on *Mr. Tambourine Man*. Their lineup included national fiddling champion Byron Berline from 1965 to 1968.

In 1967, Doug Dillard played on *Gene Clark with the Gosdin Brothers*, and he left the Dillards in 1968 to form the Dillard-Clark Expedition with ex-Byrd Clark. The Expedition's first album lineup included Bernie Leadon, later of the Flying Burrito Brothers and the Eagles; they toured with another ex-Byrd, drummer Michael Clarke, who then joined the Burrito Brothers. Berline joined the group for its second album, but the Expedition disbanded in 1969. Doug Dillard recorded solo albums in the early Seventies and has continued to work as a studio musician. Meanwhile, Rodney maintained the Dillards band name, and continued to record increasingly electric albums with a shifting band through the Seventies.

DINO, DESI AND BILLY
Formed circa 1964, Los Angeles
Dino Martin, Jr. (b. Nov. 17, 1953, Los Angeles), bass; Desi Arnaz, Jr. (b. Jan. 19, 1953, Los Angeles), drums; Billy Hinsche (b. June 29, 1953), gtr.

1965—*I'm a Fool* (Reprise).

Teenybopper favorites Dino, Desi and Billy were Dean Martin's son, Desi Arnaz, Jr., and the son of a real-estate broker who'd sold houses to both Martin and Arnaz, Sr. Frank Sinatra heard them playing at Dino Sr.'s home and helped them get a contract with Reprise. The trio hit the Top Twenty in mid-1965 with "I'm a Fool" and "Not the Lovin' Kind." Though presented as basically cuddly and cute, DD&B were also hip, and later tackled heavier fare like Dylan's "Chimes of Freedom." By 1966, they were

eclipsed by psychedelia. Hinsche later became a regular in the Beach Boys' touring troupe. Martin is a moderately successful tennis professional and is married to skating star Dorothy Hamill. And Arnaz has pursued an acting career.

DION AND THE BELMONTS
Formed 1958, Bronx, New York
Dion (b. Dion DiMucci, July 18, 1939, Bronx), lead voc.; Fred Milano (b. Aug. 22, 1939, Bronx), second tenor; Carlo Mastangelo (b. Oct. 5, 1938, Bronx), baritone; Angelo D'Aleo (b. Feb. 3, 1940, Bronx), first tenor.

1959—(– D'Aleo) **ca. 1960**—(+ Frank Lyndon, tenor) **N.A.**—*Presenting Dion and the Belmonts* (Laurie) *Runaround Sue; Lovers Who Wonder; Greatest Hits; 15 Million Sellers; More Greatest Hits; Wonder Where I'm Bound* (Columbia) *Dion* (Laurie) **1969**—*Sit Down Old Friend* (Warner Bros.) **1971**—*You're Not Alone; Sanctuary* **1972**—*Suite for Late Summer* **1973**—*Reunion* **1976**—*Streetheart* **1977**—*Dion's Greatest Hits* (Columbia).

Dion DiMucci was perhaps the suavest of New York City's late-Fifties teen idols. He started singing at age five and picked up a guitar a few years later. As a teenager, he began singing on streetcorners. He also began dabbling in drugs and eventually acquired a heroin habit that he didn't kick until 1968. Shortly after dropping out of high school, Dion recorded a demo as a Valentine's Day present for his mother. It reached the producers of the "Teen Club" TV show out of Philadelphia, where Dion made his performing debut in 1954.

Along with a backing group of buddies called the Timberlanes, he released "The Chosen Few," and in early 1958, Dion rounded up some neighborhood friends and dubbed them the Belmonts after a neighborhood Bronx thoroughfare, Belmont Avenue. Their second single, "I Wonder Why," skirted the Top Twenty. "No One Knows" and "Don't Pity Me" followed, but the big break came in the spring of 1959, when "A Teenager in Love" became an international hit. The next year, "Where or When" climbed to #3.

The group toured frequently, often on package tours with other stars; in February 1959, Dion passed up a ride on the chartered plane that later crashed, killing Buddy Holly and the Big Bopper. But soon Dion felt confined, and his drug dependency worsened. (When "Where or When" peaked he was in a hospital detoxifying.)

By the end of 1960, Dion was recording solo, backed by the uncredited Del-Satins. He hit the Top Ten with "Runaround Sue" (#1), "The Wanderer" (#2), "Lovers Who Wander" (#3) and "Little Diane" (#8) in 1962; and "Ruby Baby" (#2), "Drip Drop" (#6) and "Donna the Prima Donna" (#6) in 1963. By then he was recording for

Columbia, where staff producer John Hammond introduced him to country-blues recordings.

In 1964, Dion went into near seclusion, releasing a string of unsuccessful covers ("Johnny B. Goode," "Spoonful"). He reappeared in 1967 for another round with the Belmonts (who'd remained active after 1960, achieving moderate success with "Tell Me Why" and "Come on Little Angel"). Together they released "Mr. Movin' Man" and "Berimbau" and an album for ABC. In early 1968, he moved with his wife and their three daughters to Miami, where, with his father-in-law's help, he finally kicked heroin. Later that year, he recorded "Abraham, Martin and John," a #4 hit ballad tribute to Lincoln, King and Kennedy; the flop followup was a cover of Jimi Hendrix's "Purple Haze."

Dion spent the next few years on the coffeehouse circuit; and his Warner Bros. debut, *Sit Down Old Friend,* featured just his voice and acoustic guitar on eight songs, including the anti-drug "Clean Up Your Own Backyard." Both that folky album and the lusher *Suite for Lovers* failed to sell, and Warners persuaded Dion to reunite with the Belmonts. The group played Madison Square Garden in late 1973, as documented on the successful *Reunion* LP. Dion then briefly reentered the show-biz mainstream, frequently guesting on TV variety shows like "Cher." The transfusion also helped the Belmonts, whose *Cigars Acapella Candy* sold respectably, and they continued to team up with Dion for special shows. In the mid-seventies, Dion recorded with Phil Spector, but their collaboration, "Born to Be with You," was a commercial failure. Dion attempted to update with *Streetheart* in 1976.

DIRE STRAITS

Formed 1977, London
Mark Knopfler (b. Aug. 12, 1949), gtr., voc.; David Knopfler, gtr.; John Illsley, bass; Pick Withers, drums.
1978—*Dire Straits* (Warner Bros.) **1979**—*Communiqué* **1980**—(− D. Knopfler; + Hal Lindes, gtr.; + Alan Clark, kybds.) *Making Movies* (− Withers; + Tommy Mandel, kybds; + Terry Williams, drums) **1982**—*Love over Gold* **1983**—*Twisting by the Pool* (EP).

British songwriter/vocalist/guitarist Mark Knopfler led Dire Straits to international success in the late Seventies. Their debut album introduced Knopfler's minor-key Dylanesque songs and his limpid mixture of J. J. Cale's and Albert King's guitar styles; the Dire Straits trademark is a dialogue between Knopfler's vocals and guitar lines.

Mark and David Knopfler, sons of an architect, both learned guitar in their teens. Mark became a rock critic at the *Yorkshire Evening Post* while working for an English degree. He then taught problem students at Loughton College and an adult extension course, worked in South London pub bands and wrote some songs.

By early 1977, Mark was teaching literature part-time and jamming with David (then a social worker) and David's roommate, John Illsley, a timber broker who was working on a sociology degree at the University of London. In July 1977, after rehearsing with studio drummer Pick Withers, the group made a 5-track demo tape that included "Sultans of Swing." Critic and DJ Charlie Gillett played "Sultans" on his BBC radio show, "Honky Tonkin'," and listeners and record companies responded.

After opening for Talking Heads on a 1978 European tour, the group spent 12 days and about $25,000 to record *Dire Straits,* which eventually sold over a million copies worldwide as "Sultans of Swing" became a hit (#4, 1979). Jerry Wexler and Barry Beckett produced the three-million-selling *Communiqué.*

During sessions for *Making Movies* in July 1980, David Knopfler left, and Bruce Springsteen's E Street Band pianist Roy Bittan sat in. For the ensuing tour, Dire Straits added Lindes and Alan Clark to play the longer selections from *Making Movies,* which also went platinum. Later, Withers departed and was replaced by ex-Rockpile drummer Terry Williams. Tommy Mandel also joined. *Love over Gold,* with no singles-length cuts, sold over two million copies in six weeks.

DISCO

Disco reigned as the most popular dance music of the Seventies. It is music geared for just one purpose—to get people on a dance floor moving—and it exists primarily on records rather than in live performances. Almost all disco features the genre's characteristic rhythm, with a solid thump on each beat, and its vocals are often simple exhortations to dance, party or boogie. But the many variations within the style—from the plush orchestrations of Kenny Gamble and Leon Huff to the skeletal *charanga*-derived groove of Chic and the loping beat of the Bee Gees to the mechanical synthesizer patterns of Eurodisco—assure its continuing vitality.

Although discotheques, clubs where the main entertainment was dancing to recorded music, had existed since the Sixties—and before them, juke joints served the same purpose more informally—the disco beat arose in the mid-Seventies. Like punk, which followed soon thereafter, disco was a reaction to the extended dance-resistant FM rock of the early Seventies. It first surfaced from New York's gay male subculture, whose disc jockeys searched among obscure black pop records for the most danceable cuts.

Word of mouth made some of those songs into underground hits—such as Manu Dibango's "Soul Makossa" and Shirley and Co.'s "Honeybee"—and within a short time record companies began to look toward the disco scene as an incubator for hits, and to make records with instrumental breaks and novelty effects that disc jockeys could mix and match on their own. By the late Seventies, disco records were often marked with bpm—beats per minute—to make segues easier.

Disco became a fad in the mid-Seventies as pop practitioners of all sorts rushed to apply the latest beat to their own material. Because disco depended more on its instrumental groove than its vocals, and because recorded performances were far more important than live ones, disco became a producer's music. There were numerous one-shots, and a specific producer or studio—like the T.K. studio in Florida, home of George McCrae and KC & the Sunshine Band, or Giorgio Moroder in Munich, who produced Donna Summer's first hits—would be hot for a while before the vogue moved on. But disco was still stigmatized as music for blacks and gays until 1977, when the soundtrack for *Saturday Night Fever*, featuring the Bee Gees, the Trammps and other groups, sold 20 million copies. The movie convinced a mass audience that disco was theirs to enjoy, and the album provided a handle on the proliferation of anonymous disco acts; along with new material by the Bee Gees, it featured a selection of established disco hits.

After *Saturday Night Fever*, the pop market was flooded with disco; even the Rolling Stones ("Miss You") and Rod Stewart ("Da Ya Think I'm Sexy?") tried the beat. All-disco radio stations began earning top ratings in urban areas, and disco-derived fashions (spandex, lamé) were everywhere. But disco peaked as a commercial force by 1980; sales declined as consumers realized it was easier to listen to this week's disco hit on the radio than to buy it, and they made no long-term identification with disco's ephemeral "stars."

Musicians, however, were still intrigued. By the early Eighties, disco rhythms had filtered into new wave, and there was a subgenre of abrasive but danceable rock-disco records. Meanwhile, pure disco had returned to independent labels and reverted to its hard-core subculture of fans—still going regularly to clubs and still dancing.

THE DIXIE CUPS

Formed 1963, New Orleans
1964—*Chapel of Love* (Red Bird)   *Iko Iko;   Riding High* (ABC-Paramount).
Barbara Ann Hawkins (b. 1943, New Orleans), voc.; Rosa Lee Hawkins (b. 1946, New Orleans), voc.; Joan Marie Johnson (b. 1945, New Orleans), voc.

The Dixie Cups were a black girl group that hit the top of the charts in 1964 with "Chapel of Love," a song that producer Phil Spector (with Jeff Barry and Ellie Greenwich) had originally written for the Ronettes.

The trio first sang together in the grade school chorus. By 1963, the three had decided to pursue a career in music, and they began singing locally. Within a year, Joe Jones, a successful singer in his own right (notably, the Top Five 1960 release "You Talk Too Much"), became

their manager. He groomed them for five months and then took them to New York, where producer/songwriters Jerry Leiber and Mike Stoller signed them to their fledgling Red Bird Records.

Their initial release, "Chapel of Love," proved to be their biggest hit, although they enjoyed subsequent success with such efforts as "People Say" (#12, 1964), "You Should Have Seen the Way He Looked at Me" (#39, 1964), "Iko Iko" (#20, 1965, later a minor hit by Dr. John) and "Little Bell" (#51, 1965), the last of their hits. Red Bird Records went under in 1966; the Dixie Cups then switched to ABC-Paramount and have since retired from show business.

THE DIXIE HUMMINGBIRDS

Formed 1928, Greenville, South Carolina
James L. Davis, tenor; Paul Owens, baritone; Ira Tucker, tenor; William Bobo, bass; James Walker, baritone; Beechie Thompson, tenor; Howard Carroll, gtr.
N.A.—*Best of the Dixie Hummingbirds* (MCA) **1979**— *Golden Flight;   Gospel at Its Best;   We Love You Like a Rock*.

The Dixie Hummingbirds have been the leading Southern black gospel quartet for over fifty years, a seminal force in the development of that genre and in the parallel development of soul music. Clyde McPhatter, Bobby Bland and Jackie Wilson are only some of the singers influenced by lead Hummingbird Ira Tucker. Even James Brown's sex-machine calisthenics have some precedent in the Hummingbirds' fervid performances.

The quartet was founded by James Davis and became prominent in the Carolinas during the Thirties, making its first record for Decca in 1939. That same year, they were joined by two singers from Spartanburg, South Carolina—Tucker, formerly of the Gospel Carriers, and William Bobo, a member of the Heavenly Gospel Singers—when the Hummingbirds bettered the Carriers and the Heavenlies in a singing competition.

In 1942, the quartet moved to Philadelphia and began broadcasting regularly on radio and touring the Northeast gospel circuit. John Hammond began to book them into New York cafes and nightclubs beginning in 1942. In 1945, they began recording for the Apollo and Gotham labels, and in 1952, they signed with Peacock, recording such gospel classics as "Jesus Walked the Water," "In the Morning" and "I Just Can't Help It."

Original member Paul Owens left the Hummingbirds in the early Fifties to join the Dixie Nightingales and later the Swan Silvertones; he was replaced by James Walker. Several singers, including the great Claude Jeter of the Swan Silvertones, joined the group briefly during the Fifties. While the Hummingbirds remained essentially a vocal quartet, they added guitarist Howard Carroll in the early Fifties.

The Dixie Hummingbirds

The Dixie Hummingbirds performed at the Newport Folk Festival in 1966. The Seventies found them embracing contemporary pop styles—with mixed results. They backed Paul Simon in the studio, and on their *We Love You Like a Rock* covered Simon's "Loves Me Like a Rock" and Stevie Wonder's "Jesus Children of America" (which featured Wonder's keyboards). "Loves Me Like a Rock" was awarded a Grammy for Best Gospel Performance in 1973.

WILLIE DIXON
Born July 1, 1915, Vicksburg, Mississippi
1973—*Willie Dixon—Catalyst* (Ovation) **1975**—*I Am the Blues* (Columbia).

Willie Dixon was an important link between the blues and rock & roll and he wrote scores of blues classics in the Fifties. Growing up in Mississippi, he composed poetry and sang in church before moving with his family to Chicago in 1937. A big man (often weighing 250 pounds), the young Dixon won the city's Golden Gloves championship for his weight class in 1938, but soon after, when he was introduced to the washtub bass, his interest switched to music. He soon graduated to a four-string upright and later to a Fender electric. His walking bass lines played a major role in defining the postwar urban blues.

By the early Fifties, Dixon was selling his songs for $30 apiece and was thus cheated out of thousands of dollars in royalties. He is a prolific composer, and his catalogue includes "You Shook Me," "Little Red Rooster," "Back Door Man," "Bring It On Home," "I'm Your Hoochie Coochie Man," "The Seventh Son," "I Just Wanna Make Love to You," "Wang Dang Doodle," "You Can't Judge a Book by Its Cover," "I Can't Quit You Baby" and others.

Dixon's own recording career, which began in the early Fifties, has been relatively unsuccessful. For a while he was the bass player in the house band at Chess Records and regularly backed Chuck Berry, Bo Diddley, Muddy Waters and others, arranging and later producing the tunes as well. In between takes, he'd sell his own songs and act as the business intermediary between black artists and the Polish-born Chess brothers.

Dixon has remained sporadically active, touring Europe (where he is revered) almost annually since 1960. He played some U.S. dates in 1975 and '76 with his tour band, the Chicago Blues All-Stars. "Time makes everything change," he once said, "but the blues are basically about the facts of life. This is why they hang around so long, because everybody practically faces the same things in life sooner or later anyway."

DNA
Formed 1977, New York City
Arto Lindsay (b. May 28, 1953, Richmond, Va.), gtr., voc.; Ikue Ile Mori (b. Dec. 17, 1953, Tokyo), drums; Robin Crutchfield, kybds.
1978—(− Crutchfield; + Tim Wright, bass, gtr.)
1980—*A Taste of DNA* (American Clave).

DNA was a leading band in New York's "no wave." In a radical challenge to rock conventions, DNA's tightly structured songs, some of them under thirty seconds long, used neither fixed rhythms nor standard harmonies and its three instrumental parts were usually independent and clashing. Although Arto Lindsay started playing guitar in 1977, he has never learned a standard chord.

Chief writer Lindsay arrived in New York in 1975, having spent most of his life in a tiny village in Brazil, where his missionary father had built a school. While working as a messenger at the *Village Voice*, he played guitar for the first time when he jammed with James Chance and other founders of "no wave" in 1977. Out of those sessions emerged the Contortions (Chance's group), Teenage Jesus and the Jerks (Lydia Lunch) and Mars. Lindsay wrote lyrics for Mars and would have joined them as drummer had he not decided to form his own group with Ikue Ile Mori and Robin Crutchfield. Mori had just that year arrived in New York from Tokyo, accompanied by future Jerks bassist Rek. Through Jesus she met Lindsay, whose unorthodox guitar playing inspired her to try the drums.

DNA cut their first vinyl with a single, "Little Ants" b/w "You and You," on the Lust/Unlust label in 1978, shortly before contributing four tracks to the "no wave" compilation *No New York* produced by Brian Eno. At the end of 1978, Crutchfield left DNA to form Dark Day. Wright had been a founder of the Cleveland avant-garde rock group Pere Ubu in 1975 before he moved to New York. Under his influence, DNA's music became even more turbulent and concise. The group broke up in 1981.

In addition to playing with DNA, who toured the West Coast and South in 1980 (their first performances outside the New York area), each member has played with other musicians. Lindsay was a founding member of the "fake jazz" group the Lounge Lizards in 1979 and played with them until 1981. He has also recorded with James Chance, Kip Hanrahan and Seth Tillet, and since the breakup of DNA has worked with the Toykillers and Ambitious Lovers. Mori played violin, viola and cello on Mars's *John Gavanti*, an inversion of Mozart's *Don Giovanni*. Wright played bass on David Byrne and Brian Eno's 1981 album, *My Life in the Bush of Ghosts*.

DR. BUZZARD'S ORIGINAL SAVANNAH BAND/KID CREOLE AND THE COCONUTS

Formed 1974, Bronx, New York
Stony Browder, Jr. (b. 1949, Bronx), gtr., piano; August Darnell (b. Thomas August Darnell Browder, 1951, Montreal), bass, voc.; Cory Daye (b. Apr. 25, 1952, Bronx), voc.; "Sugar-Coated" Andy Hernandez (b. 1950, New York City), vibraphone; Mickey Sevilla (b. 1953, Puerto Rico), drums.
1976—*Dr. Buzzard's Original Savannah Band (RCA)*
1978—*Dr. Buzzard's Original Savannah Band Meets King Pennett* **1980**—*James Monroe H. S. Presents Dr. Buzzard's Original Savannah Band Goes to Washington* (Elektra).

Kid Creole and the Coconuts

Formed 1980, New York City
August Darnell, voc., bass, gtr.; "Sugar-Coated" Andy Hernandez, vibraphone, voc.; Fonda Rae, voc.; Lordes Cotto, voc.; Brooksie Wells, voc.; Franz Krauns, gtr.; Andrew Lloyd, perc.; Winston Grennan, drums; Peter Schott, piano.
1980—*Off the Coast of Me* (Ze) (− Rae; − Cotto; − Wells; + Adriana Kaegi, voc.; + Lori Eastside [b. Lori Smith], voc.; + Cheryl Poirier, voc.; − Krauns; + Mark Mazur, gtr.; + Carol Coleman, bass; + Yogi Horton, drums) **1981**—*Fresh Fruit in Foreign Places* (+ Taryn Haegy, voc.; + Jimmy Rippetoe, gtr.)
1982—*Wise Guy* (− Eastside; − Rippetoe; − Lloyd; + Eddie Magic, percussion; − Grennan; − Horton; + Al Mack, drums; + Charles Lagond, sax; + Lee Robinson, trumpet; + Ken Fradley, trombone).

Dr. Buzzard's Original Savannah Band was the most eccentric dance band of the Seventies.

Brothers Stony Browder and August Darnell (their father was Dominican, their mother French-Canadian) had played music together since they were teenagers, when they led a Bronx rock group called the In-Laws. In 1974, they hit on the idea of making what they called "mulatto music." Browder's arrangements combined pop, soul, big-band swing, disco and every imaginable Latin and West Indian style. Darnell—who held a master's degree in English literature and for three years taught junior high school in Hempstead, Long Island—wrote lyrics that set the urban underclasses of blacks, Hispanics, gays, showgirls, street musicians and dreamers against an ironic backdrop of theatrical glamour and nostalgia. The Original Savannah Band came together with Andy Hernandez, a vibes player since 1967 who had earned a degree in business management and worked with juvenile delinquents in East Harlem while playing in pop and jazz bands; Mickey Sevilla, who had grown up in Puerto Rico, the Virgin Islands, New Jersey, Chicago and New York, and studied and taught percussion at the Manhattan School of Music; and Cory Daye, Browder's girlfriend.

In 1976, "Cherchez la Femme," a single from their first album, broke in New York discos and eventually reached #31 on the R&B chart and #27 pop. The album went gold. But subsequent releases fell between radio formats and were picked up only by Dr. Buzzard cultists. RCA dropped the group, and the band was at the point of collapse—a rift had formed between Browder and Darnell, Daye had cut a solo album *(Cory and Me)*—when a deal with Elektra resulted in a third album. A commercial failure, it only delayed the band's breakup.

By that time, Darnell had also written songs for and produced albums by Machine and Gichy Dan's Beechwood #9. After signing with Ze Records in 1980, he produced James White and the Blacks (James Chance), Cristina and other avant-disco acts, and two Savannah Band offshoots, Don Armando's Second Avenue Rhumba Band (Armando Bonilla had played percussion on Savannah Band albums) and Coati Mundi (Hernandez' solo act). With Hernandez—now co-composer and arranger—he raised Kid Creole and the Coconuts from Dr. Buzzard's ashes. Darnell gave the band a mythology: Kid Creole represented the modern American who embodies all races and cultures. Onstage, bandmembers assumed fictitious characters, sported costumes, incorporated choreography into their show and linked songs with rhyming raps. (Adriana Kaegi, Darnell's Swiss-born wife, was costume designer and choreographer as well as a singing, dancing Coconut.) *Fresh Fruit in Foreign Places* was conceived as a modern epic along the lines of *The Odyssey* and *The Aeneid*. *Fresh Fruit* was staged in New York in 1981, with Gichy Dan providing narrative raps, and plans are still in the works to bring "the first rap musical" to Broadway under the aegis of impresario Joseph Papp.

Signs of fractures within the group surfaced with *Wise Guy*, which was first recorded as a Darnell solo album and then—at the request of Ze and Warner Bros. executives— made over as a Kid Creole and the Coconuts effort and sequel to *Fresh Fruit*, after which Darnell revamped the band. Former Coconut Rae scored a solo hit with "Over Like a Fat Rat," while Eastside joined the Rockaholics, Coati Mundi's backup vocal trio on his Spanish-rap "Me No Pop I" (a hit in Argentina and elsewhere). Meanwhile, Browder sporadically revived the Savannah Band with Daye and Sevilla, joined on stage infrequently by Darnell and Hernandez.

DR. FEELGOOD
Formed 1971, England
Lee Brilleaux, voc., harmonica, slide gtr.; John B. Sparks, bass; Wilko Johnson, gtr.; John "the Figure" Martin, drums.
1975—*Down by the Jetty* (United Artists)   *Malpractice*   **1976**—*Stupidity*   **1977**—*Sneakin' Suspicion* (− Johnson; + John Mayo, gtr.)   *Be Seeing You*   **1978**—*Private Practice*   **1979**—*As It Happens;   Let It Roll*   **1980**—*Case of Shakes.*

British R&B revivalists Dr. Feelgood were one of the leading bands of the British back-to-basics movement of the mid-Seventies. Lee Brilleaux, John B. Sparks and Wilko Johnson hailed from Canvey Island. They drifted around England and made the rounds of pub bands together and separately before forming Dr. Feelgood in 1971. Johnson brought in John Martin, previously a member of Finian's Rainbow. They took their name from a minor early Sixties British hit by Johnny Kidd and the Pirates (*not* from the Aretha Franklin song of the same title) and assembled a repertoire of Johnson originals and standards by Willie Dixon, Bo Diddley, Huey "Piano" Smith, Leiber and Stoller and other (mostly black) R&B and rock & roll patriarchs.
They signed a United Artists (U.K.) contract in 1974. Their debut album was recorded in mono, most of it in one take, with piano and saxes courtesy of Brinsley Schwarz and Bob Andrews of the Schwarz group. A growing concert following and enthusiastic support from people like Pete Townshend boosted their second album into the U.K. Top Twenty and a single, "She's a Wind Up," into the Top Forty. They toured the United States in 1976, but never found a foothold.
In 1977, Johnson left to form the Solid Senders; he later joined Ian Dury and the Blockheads. Henry McCullough stepped in for him on Dr. Feelgood's 1977 tour of Britain, but Mayo had replaced him by the time they recorded *Be Seeing You* with producer Nick Lowe. "Milk and Alcohol" hit #9 in 1979, and "As Long as the Price Is Right"

reached #40 later in the year. Their later albums were not released in the U.S. In 1982, the group disbanded.

DR. FEELGOOD AND THE INTERNS
Formed 1962, Atlanta

Dr. Feelgood and the Interns was not really a group but a nom-de-disc for noted bluesman Willie Perryman. Dr. Feelgood and the Interns had two moderate pop hits in 1962: "Dr. Feel-Good" and "Right String but the Wrong Yo Yo." The latter was recorded in 1930 by Perryman's brother Rufus under his alias Speckled Red. It had been revived in the Fifties by Perryman when he recorded under the alias of Piano Red ("Rockin' with Red," "Red's Boogie") for such labels as RCA, Jax, Checker and Arhoolie. He was with Okeh when he enjoyed his biggest pop success in 1962 as Dr. Feelgood. The flip side of the Interns' "Dr. Feelgood," "Mr. Moonlight," was covered by the Beatles on *Beatles '65.*

DR. HOOK (AND THE MEDICINE SHOW)
Formed 1968, Union City, New Jersey
Ray Sawyer (b. Feb. 1, 1937, Chickasaw, Ala.), voc., gtr.; Dennis Locorriere (b. June 13, 1949, Union City), voc., gtr.; William Francis (b. Jan. 16, 1942, Mobile, Ala.), kybds., perc.; George Cummings (b. July 28, 1938, Meridian, Miss.), pedal steel gtr.; John "Jay" David (b. Aug. 8, 1942, Union City), drums.
1971—*Dr. Hook and the Medicine Show* (Columbia) (+ Richard Elswit [b. July 6, 1945, New York City], gtr.; + Jance Garfat [b. Mar. 3, 1944, Calif.], bass)   **1972**— *Sloppy Seconds*   **1973**—*Belly Up*   (− David; + John Wolters, drums)   **1974**—*Fried Face*   **1975**—*Ballad of Lucy Jordan;   Bankrupt* (Capitol)   (− Cummings) **1976**—*A Little Bit More*   (+ Bob "Willard" Henke, gtr.)   **1977**—*Makin' Love and Music;   Street People* (Columbia)   *Revisited*   **1978**—*Pleasure and Pain* (Capitol)   **1979**—*Sometimes You Win*   **1980**—*Greatest Hits;   Rising* (Casablanca)   **1982**—*Players in the Dark.*

Dr. Hook and the Medicine Show are slapstick purveyors of parody rock, whose "Sylvia's Mother" was taken straight by Top Forty listeners and became the first of several Seventies hits. The group began performing professionally in New Jersey, doing cover versions. During those years, the two frontmen—ex-Jersey folkie Dennis Locorriere and Ray Sawyer, a man who has worn an eyepatch (hence, Dr. Hook) since he lost an eye after a car crash in Portland, Oregon, in the mid-Sixties—developed a repertoire spiced with off-color material.
Their manager, Ron Haffkine, discovered them while looking for backup musicians to perform *Playboy* cartoonist humorist/songwriter Shel Silverstein's material in the movie *Who Is Harry Kellerman and Why Is He Saying All*

Those Terrible Things About Me? (1970). The group played "Last Morning" on the soundtrack and also appeared in the movie. After several months of rehearsal, they went to California to record another batch of Silverstein's tunes. Their debut LP featured "Sylvia's Mother," which sold 3½ million copies worldwide but proved to be a mixed blessing. Its lilting style, a too-subtle parody of pop, left the public ill-prepared for the manic, unkempt group behind it. *Sloppy Seconds* was also written by Silverstein, and gave the group another Top Ten hit, "The Cover of *Rolling Stone*," which took a satirical look at the rock culture—and landed Dr. Hook on the cover of *Rolling Stone*. By the time of *Belly Up*, the band members were writing their own material, but with less success. By 1974, they had filed for bankruptcy and switched to Capitol. They had a hit with Sam Cooke's "Only Sixteen" (#6, 1976). The title track of *A Little Bit More* was a minor hit and made country Top Twenty, and in 1977 Sawyer released a self-titled solo album. By late 1979, Dr. Hook had amassed 35 gold and platinum albums in Australia and Scandinavia, where they have toured for years.

DR. JOHN

Born Malcolm "Mac" Rebennack, 1941, New Orleans
1968—*Gris-Gris* (Atco)   **1969**—*Babylon*   **1970**—
Remedies   **1971**—*The Sun, Moon & Herbs*   **1972**—*Dr. John's Gumbo*   **1973**—*In the Right Place*   **1974**—
Desitively Bonaroo   **1975**—*Cut Me While I'm Hot* (DJM)   *Hollywood Be Thy Name* (United Artists)
1978—*City Lights* (Horizon)   **1979**—*Tango Palace*
1981—*Dr. John Plays Mac Rebennack* (Clean Cuts).

Combining New Orleans funk, glitter and voodoo charm, pianist Dr. John was an energetic frontman in the early Seventies ("Right Place, Wrong Time") and a behind-the-scenes mover before and since.

Rebennack got his first taste of show biz through his mother, a model who got young Malcolm's face on Ivory Soap boxes; his father ran a record store. By his early teens, he was an accomplished pianist and guitarist, and hanging around at his dad's store and Cosimo Matassa's studio, he got to know local musicians.

By the mid-Fifties, he was doing session work with Professor Longhair, Frankie Ford and Joe Tex. He also helped form the black artists' cooperative AFO (All for One) Records, and he was the first white man on the roster. At the start of the Sixties, he had graduated to producing and arranging sessions for others (Lee Allen, Red Tyler, Earl Palmer) and recording some on his own (notably "Storm Warning" on Rex Records). Rebennack's reputation was based on his guitar and keyboard playing, but a hand wound suffered in a 1961 barroom gunfight forced him to take up bass with a Dixieland band.

In the mid-Sixties, Rebennack moved to L.A. and became a session regular, notably for producer Phil Spec-

tor. He played in various unsuccessful, wildly named bands like the Zu Zu Band (with Jessie Hill) and Morgus and the Three Ghouls. He also developed an interest in voodoo, to which he had been introduced by a mystical voodoo artist named Prince Lala in the Fifties at AFO.

In 1968, Rebennack unveiled his new public persona of Dr. John Creaux the Night Tripper (quickly shortened to Dr. John) after a New Orleans crony, Ronnie Barron, decided not to front the act. With New Orleans associates (Hill as Dr. Poo Pah Doo and Harold Battiste as Dr. Battiste of Scorpio of bass clef), he recorded *Gris-Gris* for Atlantic in 1968. As indicated by the song titles—"I Walk on Gilded Splinters," "Gris Gris Gumbo Ya Ya," "Croker Courtbouillion"—it was a brew of traditional Creole chants, mystical imagery and traces of psychedelia, an influence underscored by Rebennack's onstage wardrobe (brightly colored robes, feathered headdresses and a Mardi Gras–style retinue of dancers and singers).

Dr. John slowly acquired a loyal cult following, including Eric Clapton and Mick Jagger, who played on *The Sun, Moon & Herbs*. He moved to the more accessible regions of funk (backed by the Meters) on *In the Right Place*. Produced by Allen Toussaint (who also played in Dr. John's band in a 1973 tour and who produced *Desitively Bonaroo*) "Right Place, Wrong Time" was his biggest hit, followed a few months later by "Such a Night." In 1973, Dr. John also worked in Triumvirate, a short-lived trio with Mike Bloomfield and John Hammond, Jr. (John Paul Hammond). He appeared in the Band's 1978 farewell concert film, *The Last Waltz*. In 1981, he released a solo-piano LP, *Dr. John Plays Mac Rebennack*.

CLEMENT "COXSONE" DODD

Born circa 1932, Jamaica

One of Jamaica's first record producers, Clement Dodd—best known by his professional name, Sir Coxsone—was a seminal figure in the development of ska, rock steady and reggae. He got into the record business in the Fifties as owner/operator of the Downbeat Sound System, a sort of mobile discotheque that was—with other sound systems—a primary means by which American rhythm & blues and rock & roll records reached Jamaican listeners. At the end of the decade, Dodd became a producer in Jamaica's fledgling record industry. In 1964, he opened his own studio and record factory, the Jamaican Recording and Publishing Studio, Ltd., and began producing local talent for his Studio One, Coxsone and World Disc labels. His roster included the Maytals, the Wailers, the Heptones, Ken Boothe and Prince Buster (who had started his career as a Downbeat Sound System disc jockey). Another Dodd protégé was producer King Tubby, who began as an engineer at Dodd's studio.

In 1967, Dodd moved to England and set up his sound system at the Ram Jam Club in London, where he attracted English rock-steady fans as well as West Indian immigrants. Over the next three years, he helped Desmond Dekker, Derrick Morgan and the Pioneers place their records on the U.K. charts. He returned to Jamaica in 1969 and resumed producing records, including the first efforts by Burning Spear. In the Seventies, he worked with the Wailing Souls, Sugar Minott, Freddie McGregor and the Lone Ranger. Since 1981, he has been living in Brooklyn while his sons tend to business in Jamaica.

BILL DOGGETT

Born February 6, 1916, Philadelphia
N.A—*Everybody Dance to the Honky Tonk* (King)   *Hot Doggett; A Salute to Ellington.*

Pianist/organist Bill Doggett had a #2 hit in 1956 with the instrumental "Honky Tonk." He recorded for King beginning in 1952 and toured roadhouses throughout the decade with a band (including guitarist Billy Butler and saxophonist Clifford Scott, who later enjoyed moderate success as a solo act) that was renowned for its boogie-woogie groove.

Doggett had worked with several jazz bands in the Thirties and Forties, including a stint with Louis Jordan's Tympani 5. He followed up "Honky Tonk" with "Slow Walk," which nearly cracked the Top Twenty in late 1956 after Doggett's appearance on "American Bandstand." Doggett continued to place singles on both the pop and R&B charts over the next five years.

FATS DOMINO

Born Antoine Domino, May 10, 1929, New Orleans
N.A.—*The Fats Domino Story, volumes 1–6* (United Artists, U.K.)   **1956**—*This Is Fats Domino* (Imperial) **1957**—*Here Stands Fats Domino*   **1958**—*Fabulous Mr. D*   **1959**—*Let's Play Fats Domino*   **1960**—*Fats Domino Sings*   **1961**—*I Miss You So*   **1962**—*Twistin' the Stomp*   **1963**—*Just Domino*   **1966**—*Getaway with Fats Domino* (ABC)   **1968**—*Fats Is Back* (Reprise) **1970**—*Fats*   **1972**—*Legendary Masters Series* (United Artists).

With 65 million record sales to his credit, New Orleans singer and pianist Fats Domino outsold every Fifties rock & roll pioneer except Elvis Presley.

Born into a musical family, Antoine Domino began playing piano at nine and a year later was playing for pennies in honky-tonks like the Hideaway Club, where bandleader Bill Diamond accurately nicknamed him Fats. At fourteen, Domino quit school to work in a bedspring factory so he could play the bars at night. Soon he was playing alongside such New Orleans legends as Professor Longhair and Amos Milburn. He also heard the stride and boogie-woogie piano techniques of Fats Waller and Albert Ammons. He mastered the classic New Orleans R&B piano style—easy rolling left-hand patterns anchoring

Fats Domino

right-hand arpeggios. By the age of twenty, he was married and a father, had survived a near-fatal car crash and had almost lost his hand in a factory accident.

In the mid-Forties, he joined trumpeter Dave Bartholomew's band. It was soon apparent, however, that Domino was more than a sideman, and Bartholomew helped arrange his contract with Imperial and became his producer. Their first session in 1949 produced "The Fat Man," which eventually sold a million and whetted the national appetite for the "New Orleans sound." Domino and Bartholomew cowrote most of Domino's material.

By the time the rock & roll boom began in the mid-Fifties, Fats was already an established R&B hitmaker ("Goin' Home," 1952; "Going to the River," 1953), his records regularly selling between half a million and a million copies apiece. His pounding piano style was easily adapted to the nascent rock sound, although he proved less personally magnetic than contemporaries like Presley, Chuck Berry, Jerry Lee Lewis or Little Richard, all of whom recorded Domino material. Domino's big breakthrough came in mid-1955, when "Ain't That a Shame" (quickly covered by Pat Boone and revived in the late Seventies by Cheap Trick) established his identity with white teenagers. For the next five years, Domino struck solid gold with "I'm in Love Again" (#3), "Blueberry Hill" (#2), and "Blue Monday" (#5) in 1956; "I'm Walkin'" (#4, 1957); "Whole Lotta Loving" (#6, 1958); and others. He eventually collected 23 gold singles. His last million-seller came in 1960 with "Walkin' to New Orleans." He left Imperial for ABC in 1963 and subsequently switched to Mercury, Warner Bros., Atlantic and Broadmoor, all with less success.

In 1968, Domino revived public interest in his ongoing career with his rollicking cover of the Beatles' "Lady Madonna." (The Beatles consistently sang the Fat Man's praises, noting that "Birthday" on *The Beatles* was little more than a sampling from the old Domino-Bartholomew bag of riffs and tricks.) Through the mid-Seventies, Fats played six to eight months a year. In 1980, he performed at the Montreux Jazz Festival. Domino continues to record and tour periodically. He has lived for many years in a palatial home in New Orleans with his wife and eight children.

DON AND DEWEY (see Don "Sugarcane" Harris)

LONNIE DONEGAN

Born Anthony Donegan, April 29, 1931, Glasgow
1961—*More Tops with Lonnie* (Pye) **1962**—*Golden Age of Donegan* (Golden Guinea) **1968**—*Showcase* (Marble Arch) **1969**—*Lonnie Donegan Rides Again* **1978**—*Puttin' on the Style* (United Artists).

Banjoist Lonnie Donegan was one of the first British artists to enter the American Top Twenty, and his 1956 success with "Rock Island Line" inspired a generation of young Britons in the late-Fifties English skiffle craze.

Anthony Donegan's father was a violinist in the National Scottish Orchestra, and by the age of 13 Donegan was playing the drums. At 17, he became a Dixieland jazz convert, switched to the guitar and played in an amateur jazz band before entering Britain's National Service. He picked up the banjo while working as a drummer with the Wolverines Jazz Band. Once discharged, he moved to London and became banjoist and guitarist with the Ken Colyer Jazz Band, which in 1952 recorded one of the first jazz discs cut in England. By then, Donegan had adopted the name Lonnie, in honor of his idol Lonnie Johnson.

In 1953, Colyer's band was renamed Chris Barber's band; and in 1954, they recorded *New Orleans Joys*, which contained a version of "Rock Island Line" featuring Donegan's vocals. It became an international sensation, selling three million and launching Donegan's solo career as the "King of Skiffle" and one of England's top entertainers of the late Fifties. Donegan's followup, "Lost John," didn't crack the American Top Twenty; his only other U.S. hit was "Does Your Chewing Gum Lose Its Flavor (on the Bedpost Overnight)" in 1961.

"Lost John" went to #2 on the U.K. charts, beginning Donegan's six-year domination of the English hit parade,

Grammy Awards

Charlie Daniels Band
1979 Best Country Vocal Performance by a Duo or Group: "The Devil Went Down to Georgia"

Bobby Darin
1959 Best New Artist; Record of the Year: "Mack the Knife"

Billy Davis, Jr. (see also: the Fifth Dimension)
1976 Best R&B Performance by a Duo, Group or Chorus: "You Don't Have to Be a Star (to Be in My Show)" (with Marilyn McCoo)

Miles Davis
1960 Best Jazz Composition of More Than Five Minutes: "Sketches of Spain" (with Gil Evans)
1970 Best Jazz Performance, Large Group or Soloist with Large Group: *Bitches Brew*
1982 Best Jazz Instrumental Performance, Soloist: *We Want Miles*

Dazz Band
1982 Best R&B Performance by a Duo or Group with Vocal: "Let It Whip"

The Delfonics
1970 Best R&B Vocal Performance by a Duo or Group: "Didn't I (Blow Your Mind This Time)"

Neil Diamond
1973 Album of Best Original Score Written for a Motion Picture: *Jonathan Livingston Seagull*

The Dixie Hummingbirds
1973 Best Soul Gospel Performance: "Loves Me Like a Rock"

The Doobie Brothers
1979 Record of the Year: "What a Fool Believes" Best Pop Vocal Performance by a Duo, Group or Chorus: *Minute by Minute*

Bob Dylan
1972 Album of the Year: *The Concert for Bangla Desh* (with others)
1979 Best Rock Vocal Performance, Male: "Gotta Serve Somebody"

during which he enjoyed 17 Top Ten hits. In lieu of a fan club he formed a folk music appreciation society. Adam Faith (who later produced some of Donegan's sessions) and the nascent Beatles played at one of the society's 1958 membership drives in Liverpool. By 1963, Beatlemania eclipsed skiffle, although Donegan continued to tour.

In 1974, Donegan toured the U.S. as an opening act for Tom Jones. He settled in Lake Tahoe and began hanging out on the fringe of the rock crowd. At a backstage party following a Wings concert, an impromptu jam with Faith, Elton John, Ringo Starr and Leo Sayer led to the idea of an all-star Donegan reunion LP—*Puttin' on the Style*—which also featured Ron Wood, Rory Gallagher, Brian May of Queen, Albert Lee, Gary Brooker (Procol Harum), Mick Ralphs (Mott the Hoople, Bad Company) and other Donegan fans.

RAL DONNER

Born February 10, 1943, Chicago
N.A.—*Takin' Care of Business* (Gone) *Takin' Care of Business, volume 2* (Rondo) **1977**—*Elvis Scrapbook* (Gone) **1978**—*You Don't Know What You've Got* (Pye, U.K.) *Ral Donner, Ray Smith and Bobby Dale* (Crown).

After Elvis Presley came out of the Army, Ral Donner became the most successful imitator of Presley's earlier style. Donner cut his first sides for Scotty Records in 1958, then moved to New York and signed with Gone. In mid-1961, "Girl of My Best Friend" (previously recorded by Elvis on *Elvis Is Back*) became the first of four Donner singles ("Please Don't Go," "She's Everything," and his biggest hit, "You Don't Know What You've Got") to reach the Top Forty. Donner recorded extensively but unsuccessfully through the early Seventies for a plethora of labels—Tau (1960), Reprise (1963), Fontana (1965), Red Bird (1966), Rising Sons (produced by Billy Swan), Mid-Eagle and M.J. (1971) and Chicago Fire and Sunlight (1972).

DONOVAN

Born Donovan Leitch, May 10, 1946, Glasgow
1965—*Catch the Wind* (Hickory) **1966**—*Sunshine Superman* (Epic) **1967**—*Mellow Yellow; For Little Ones; Wear Your Love Like Heaven* **1968**—*Donovan in Concert; Barabajagal; The Hurdy Gurdy Man; A Gift from a Flower to a Garden* **1969**—*Donovan's Greatest Hits; The World of Donovan* **1970**—*Open Road* **1973**—*Cosmic Wheels* (Epic) *Essence to Essence* **1974**—*7-Tease* **1976**—*Slow Down World* **1977**—*Donovan* (Arista).

Though Donovan's flowery philosophy is now considered passé, his compositions ("Catch the Wind," "Sunshine Superman," "Season of the Witch," "Mellow Yellow")

Donovan

were novel in the way they linked folk rock to hippie mysticism.

Donovan Leitch grew up in the Gorbals section of Glasgow. His family moved to the outskirts of London when he was ten; at 15, he completed the British equivalent of secondary school and enrolled in college, but stayed only a year. At age 18, he began recording his songs. Talent scouts from the British rock TV program "Ready Steady Go" heard the demos, and in early 1965 Donovan became a regular on the show. His debut single, "Catch the Wind," hit the Top Twenty in mid-1965; like its followups—"Colours" and "Universal Soldier"—the song was almost entirely acoustic. Donovan's U.S. performing debut was at the 1965 Newport Folk Festival.

With producer Mickie Most (with whom he worked until 1969), he left Pye for Epic. Folklike refrains and exotic instrumentation (sitars, flutes, cellos, harps) kept Donovan's singles in the Top Forty. His biggest hit, "Sunshine Superman," hit #1 in 1966 on both sides of the Atlantic. "Mellow Yellow" quickly reached #2. Some claimed its lyrics referred to smoking banana peels, but Donovan later claimed the song's subject was an electric dildo. Subsequent hits included 1967's "Epistle to Dippy" (#19) and "There Is a Mountain" (#11). By the time of 1968's "Wear Your Love Like Heaven" (#23, later the ad jingle for Love cosmetics) and "Jennifer Juniper" (#26), Leitch's wardrobe had changed to love beads and flowing robes.

In 1967, Donovan traveled to India to study with the Maharishi Mahesh Yogi. Shortly thereafter, he publicly renounced all drug use and requested that his followers substitute meditation for getting stoned. A few more hits followed—"Hurdy Gurdy Man" (#5), "Atlantis" (#7), and "Goo Goo Barabajagal (Love Is Hot)" with the Jeff Beck Group in 1969 (#36)—but after 1970 no one paid much attention.

After a period of seclusion in Ireland, Donovan starred in and wrote the music for the 1972 German film *The Pied Piper*. He also scored *If It's Tuesday This Must Be Belgium*, then a full-length animation feature, *Tangled Details*, and Franco Zeffirelli's *Brother Sun, Sister Moon* in 1973. Following his sparsely attended 1971 U.S. tour, Donovan didn't perform in public until 1974, when he completed *7-Tease*, a conceptual LP about a young hippie and his search for inner peace.

The next year, *7-Tease* toured as a theatrical stage revue. In 1976, Donovan toured U.S. clubs in support of *Slow Down World*. He has published one book of poetry, *Dry Songs and Scribbles*.

THE DOOBIE BROTHERS
Formed in 1970, San Jose, California
Tom Johnston (b. Visalia, Calif.), gtr., voc.; John Hartman (b. Falls Church, Va.), drums; Patrick Simmons (b. San Jose), gtr., voc.; Dave Shogren (b. San Francisco), bass.
1971—*The Doobie Brothers* (Warner Bros.)
(— Shogren, + Tiran Porter [b. Los Angeles], bass; + Michael Hossack [b. Paterson, N.J.], drums) 1972—
Toulouse Street 1973—*The Captain and Me*
(— Hossack; + Keith Knudsen [b. Ames, Ia.], drums) 1974—*What Once Were Vices Are Now Habits* (+ Jeff "Skunk" Baxter [b. Dec. 13, 1948, Washington, D.C.], gtr.) 1975—*Stampede* (+ Michael McDonald [b. St. Louis, Mo.], kybds., voc.) 1976—
Takin' It to the Streets; The Best of the Doobie Brothers 1977—*Livin' on the Fault Line*

(— Johnston) 1978—*Minute by Minute*
(— Hartman; — Baxter; + John McFee [b. Santa Cruz, Calif.], gtr.; + Chet McCracken [b. Seattle, Wash.], drums; + Cornelius Bumpus, sax, kybds.) 1980—
One Step Closer.

Fans of the Doobie Brothers' first incarnation—as a California country-boogie band—have no use for the band's second, even more popular sound: an intricate jazz-inflected white funk. Tom Johnston, who fronted the early Doobies, met John Hartman through Skip Spence of Moby Grape, a group Johnston and Hartman hoped to emulate. They first played together in the short-lived group Pud with bassist Gregg Murphy. When Pud disbanded in 1969, Hartman and Johnston began jamming with local semi-pro musician Dave Shogren and later with Pat Simmons. They built up an avid following among California Hell's Angels by playing open jam sessions on Sunday afternoons, and dubbed themselves the Doobie Brothers ("doobie" is California slang for a marijuana cigarette).

Warner Bros. A&R man Ted Templeman signed them and produced all of their albums. Their debut LP failed to expand their audience much beyond their local following. With the addition of Michael Hossack and Tiran Porter, the group recorded *Toulouse Street*, which established the formula for the band's first hits: a strong beat, high harmonies and repetition of a single phrase like "Listen to the music." The second and third Doobies albums were both million-sellers.

The transformation of Steely Dan into a studio-based duo sent Jeff "Skunk" Baxter, who'd done session work on *What Were Once Vices*, into the Doobies full-time. Johnston quit touring because of a stomach ailment and was replaced by another Steely Dan alumnus, Michael

The Doobie Brothers: Cornelius Bumpus, Patrick Simmons, Tiran Porter, Michael McDonald, John McFee, Keith Knudsen, Chet McCracken

McDonald. Baxter and McDonald revamped the Doobies' old songs in concert, and McDonald wrote most of the group's new material, shifting the band toward its later amalgam of funk and pop. McDonald's burry tenor replaced high harmonies as the band's trademark. Johnston rejoined in 1976, but left permanently the next year to try a solo career; he has made two solo albums, *Everything You've Heard Is True* and *Still Feels Good.*.

The multimillion sales of *Minute by Minute* established McDonald as the clear leader of the band. After a 1978 tour of Japan, Baxter left to do session work; he has also produced albums by Livingston Taylor and Carla Thomas. Hartman quit the music business. More than a year of auditions enlisted ex-Clover guitarist John McFee and former session drummer (America, Hank Williams, Jr., Helen Reddy) Hugh McCracken. Cornelius Bumpus, who'd been in a late version of Moby Grape, joined in 1979. For a 1980 tour, the Doobies were clearly McDonald's backup band; the lineup included session drummer Andy Newmark. The group disbanded in fall 1982 after a farewell tour. Soon afterwards solo albums by McDonald (*If That's What It Takes*) and Simmons (*Arcade*) were released.

THE DOORS

Formed 1965, Los Angeles
Jim Morrison (b. Dec. 8, 1943, Melbourne, Fla.; d. July 3, 1971, Paris), voc.; Ray Manzarek (b. Feb. 12, 1935, Chicago), kybds.; Robby Krieger (b. Jan. 8, 1946, Los Angeles), gtr.; John Densmore (b. Dec. 1, 1945, Los Angeles), drums.
1967—*The Doors* (Elektra) *Strange Days* 1968—
Waiting for the Sun 1969—*The Soft Parade* 1970—
13; Morrison Hotel/Hard Rock Cafe; Absolutely Live 1971—*L.A. Woman* 1972—*Weird Scenes Inside the Gold Mine* 1978—*An American Prayer* 1980—
Greatest Hits.
Without Morrison: 1971—*Other Voices* 1972—*Full Circle.*

Sex, death, reptiles, charisma and a unique variant of the electric blues gave the Doors an aura of profundity that has survived the band by a decade. By themselves, Jim Morrison's lyrics come across as adolescent posturings, but with Ray Manzarek's dry organ and Robby Krieger's jazzy guitar, they became eerie invocations whose power has been envied and imitated by any number of bands.

Morrison and Manzarek, acquaintances from the UCLA Graduate School of Film, conceived the group at a 1965 meeting on a Southern California beach. After Morrison recited one of his poems, "Moonlight Drive," Manzarek—who had studied classical piano as a child and played in Rick and the Ravens, a UCLA blues band—suggested they collaborate on songs. Manzarek's brothers, Rick and Jim, served as guitarists until Manzarek met

Krieger, who brought in John Densmore; both had been members of the Psychedelic Rangers. Morrison christened the band the Doors, from William Blake via Aldous Huxley's book on mescaline, *The Doors of Perception.*

The Doors soon recorded a demo tape, and in the summer of 1966 they began working as the house band at the Whisky-a-Go-Go, a gig that ended four months later when they were fired for performing the explicitly Oedipal "The End," one of Morrison's many songs that included dramatic recitations. By then, Jac Holzman of Elektra Records had signed the band.

An edited version of Krieger's "Light My Fire" from the Doors' debut album became a #1 hit, as did the album, while "progressive" radio played (and analyzed) "The End." Morrison's image as the embodiment of dark psychological impulses was established quickly.

Strange Days (#3, 1967) and *Waiting for the Sun* (#1, 1968) both included hit singles and became best-selling albums. *Waiting for the Sun* also marked the first appearance of Morrison's mythic alter ego, the Lizard King, in a poem printed inside the record jacket entitled "The Celebration of the Lizard King." Though part of the poem was used as lyrics for "Not to Touch the Earth," a complete "Celebration" didn't appear on record until *Absolutely Live* (#8, 1970).

It was impossible to tell whether Morrison's Lizard King persona was a parody of a pop star or simply inspired exhibitionism, but it earned him considerable notoriety. In December 1967, he was arrested for public obscenity at a concert in New Haven, and in August 1968, he was arrested for disorderly conduct aboard an airplane en route to Phoenix. Not until his March 1969 arrest in Miami for exhibiting "lewd and lascivious behavior by exposing his private parts and by simulating masturbation and oral copulation" onstage, did Morrison's behavior adversely affect the band. Court proceedings kept Morrison in Miami most of the year, although the prosecution could produce neither eyewitnesses nor photos of Morrison performing the acts. Charges were dropped, but public furor (which inspired a short-lived Rally for Decency movement), concert promoters' fear of similar incidents and Morrison's own mixed feelings about celebrity resulted in erratic concert schedules thereafter.

The Soft Parade (#6, 1969), far more elaborately produced than the Doors' other albums, met with a mixed reception from fans, although it too had a #3 hit single, "Touch Me." Morrison began to devote more attention to projects outside the band: writing poetry, collaborating on a screenplay with poet Michael McClure, directing a film, *A Feast of Friends* (he had also made films to accompany "Break on Through" and the 1968 single "The Unknown Soldier"). Simon and Schuster published *The Lords and the New Creatures* in 1971; an earlier book, *An American Prayer,* was privately printed in 1970 but not made widely available until 1978, when the surviving Doors regrouped and set Morrison's recitation of the poem to music.

The Doors: John Densmore, Robby Krieger, Ray Manzarek, Jim Morrison

Soon after *L.A. Woman* (#9, 1971) was recorded, Morrison took an extended leave of absence from the group. With wife Pamela Courson Morrison, he moved to Paris, where he lived in seclusion until he died of heart failure in his bathtub in 1971. Partly because news of his death was not made public until days after his burial in Paris' Père Lachaise cemetery, some refuse to believe Morrison is dead. His wife, one of the few people who saw Morrison's corpse, died in Hollywood of a heroin overdose on April 25, 1974.

The Doors continued to record throughout 1973 as a trio, but after two albums it seemed they had exhausted the possibilities of a band without a commanding lead singer. Manzarek had hoped to reconstitute the group with Iggy Pop, whose avowed chief influence was Morrison, but plans fell through. After the Doors broke up, Manzarek recorded two solo albums, and one with a short-lived group called Nite City; he produced the first three albums by Los Angeles' X, and in 1983 he collaborated with composer Philip Glass on a rock version of Carl Orff's modern cantata, *Carmina Burana*. Krieger and Densmore formed the Butts Band, which lasted three years and recorded two albums. In 1972, a Doors greatest-hits collection, *Weird Scenes Inside the Gold Mine* was released, but only hit #55. Krieger released an instrumental album and toured in 1982.

Ironically, the group's best year was 1980, nine years after Morrison's death. With the release of the Danny Sugerman/Jerry Hopkins biography of Morrison, *No One Here Gets Out Alive,* sales of the Doors' music and the already large Jim Morrison cult—spurred by his many admirers and imitators in new wave bands—grew even more. Record sales for 1980 alone topped all previous figures. Of the twelve Doors albums, ten are either gold or platinum, and interest in the Doors shows no sign of subsiding.

DOO-WOP

A form of R&B-based harmony vocalizing using phonetic or nonsense syllables (like a repeated "doo-wop") for rhythm and intricate harmonic arrangements. Doo-wop began with black urban vocal groups, but was soon picked up by white hopefuls in New York and Philadelphia. The ornate vocal arrangements of doo-wop were based in a cappella vocalizing; their musical accompaniment was often muted and softly swinging for maximum moody romantic effect, with Latin rhythms very popular.

Classic doo-wop singles include "Sh-Boom" by the Chords, "Earth Angel" by the Penguins, and two of the few hard-rocking examples of the genre, "Book of Love" by the Monotones and "Get a Job" by the Silhouettes. Though now considered a nostalgic form, doo-wop had a burgeoning revival with the launching in 1982 of the Ambient Sound label, which released new recordings by the Harptones, the Moonglows and the Capris.

LEE DORSEY

Born December 24, 1924, New Orleans
N.A.—*New Lee Dorsey* (Amy)   *Ride Your Pony—Get Out of My Life; Working in the Coal Mine; Ya Ya* (Fury)   **1966**—*Lee Dorsey* (Amy)   **1970**—*Yes We Can* (Polydor)   **1978**—*Night People* (ABC).

New Orleans singer Lee Dorsey's dry voice fronted Allen Toussaint's songs ("Working in a Coal Mine," "Holy Cow") for over a decade. Dorsey had been a boxer and a Marine before signing with the Fury label at the start of the Sixties. In late 1961, "Ya Ya" (later covered by John Lennon and others) hit #7. "Do Re Mi" did well three months later, but Dorsey's promising start was cut short by the collapse of his record company.

He met Toussaint, who put him back on the charts in late 1965 with "Ride Your Pony," a moderate hit. The next year marked the zenith of Dorsey's career. His Amy Records releases included "Get Out of My Life Woman"; the loping Top Ten smash "Working in a Coal Mine" (a minor hit for Devo in 1981); and "Holy Cow" (later covered by the Band on *Moondog Matinee*), which rose to #23. Dorsey had two minor hits in 1967 ("My Old Car," "Go Go Girl"), then faded from view.

In 1969, he had another minor hit, "Everything I Do Gonna Be Funky." The following year, Dorsey and Toussaint recorded *Yes We Can* for Polydor Records. Dorsey remained active—mostly in New Orleans—throughout the Seventies and made a guest appearance on the debut album by Southside Johnny and the Asbury Jukes. He signed with ABC Records in December 1977, and Toussaint wrote and produced all the songs on 1978's *Night People*. But ABC was sold, and Dorsey again found himself professionally adrift.

CARL DOUGLAS
Born Jamaica
1974—*Kung Fu Fighting* (20th Century–Fox).

A 4,000-year-old Chinese martial art and a reggae-tinged disco beat provided Carl Douglas the inspiration for his gold hit record, "Kung Fu Fighting." Douglas, a Jamaican raised in the United States and England, got into the record business while studying engineering in London in the early Sixties.

His British-based career as a singer and composer was undistinguished (the soundtrack to the 1972 movie *Embassy* was his major accomplishment) until he cut "Kung Fu Fighting." The song hit first in England, where it made #1 in August 1974. By October, it had reached that position on American soul charts, and in December it reached #1 on the pop charts too. It inspired a dance step, the Kung Fu. Douglas appeared only once more on American charts—with a followup, "Dance the Kung Fu," in 1975 (#48 pop, #8 R&B), but he continued to have hits in England, where "Run Back" made the Top Thirty in 1977.

THE DOVELLS
Formed circa 1960, Philadelphia
Len Barry (b. Leonard Borisoff, Dec. 6, 1942), lead voc.; Arnie Satin (b. May 11, 1943), baritone; Jerry Summers (b. Dec. 29, 1942), first tenor; Mike Dennis (b. June 3, 1943), second tenor; Danny Brooks (b. Apr. 1, 1942), bass.
1961—*Bristol Stomp* (Parkway) **1962**—*All the Hits for Your Hully Gully Party; You Can't Sit Down; Biggest Hits* (Wyncote).

The Dovells were an early-Sixties white doo-wop group, all born in Philadelphia. The group's string of dance hits began in late 1961 with the #2 hit, "Bristol Stomp." Their other hits that year included "Do the New Continental" (#37), "Bristol Twistin' Annie" (#27) and "Hully Gully Baby" (#25). They reached #3 in 1963 with "You Can't Sit Down." But subsequent releases on Cameo Parkway went nowhere. The group's lead vocalist, Len Barry, later had solo hits ("1-2-3"). In their heyday, the Dovells frequently toured as part of Dick Clark's road revue.

NICK DRAKE
Born June 18, 1948, Burma; died November 25, 1974, Birmingham, England
1969—*Five Leaves Left* (Island) **1970**—*Bryter Layter* **1972**—*Pink Moon* **1979**—*Fruit Tree–The Complete Works of Nick Drake.*

Since Nick Drake's death, his eerie, jazz-tinged folk music has had an ever-growing cult following. Born to British parents, Drake spent his first six years on the Indian subcontinent before moving to the English village of Tamworth-in-Arden. He played saxophone and clarinet in school but turned to the guitar at age 16. Two years later, he began writing his own songs. He was a student at Cambridge University in 1968, when Ashley Hutchings of Fairport Convention heard him performing at London's Roundhouse. Hutchings introduced him to Joe Boyd, who managed Fairport, John Martyn and other leaders of the British folk revival. Boyd immediately signed Drake to Island Records and put him on Witchseason concert bills.

Drake was a shy, awkward performer and remained aloof from the public and press. By the end of 1970, he had stopped doing concerts. He lived for a short while in Paris at the behest of Françoise Hardy (who never released the recordings she made of his songs) and then settled in Hampstead, where he became increasingly reclusive, allowing the company of only his close friends John and Beverly Martyn. He recorded *Pink Moon* totally unaccompanied, submitted the tapes to Island by mail, and entered a psychiatric rest home. When he left the home months later, vowing never to sing another song, he got a job as a computer programmer. In 1973 he began writing songs again. He had recorded four when he died in bed at his parents' home in 1974, the victim of an overdose of antidepressant medication; suicide was considered probable by the coroner, but Drake's friends and family disagreed. *Fruit Tree* is a boxed set containing his three albums plus the four songs recorded in 1973.

THE DRIFTERS
Formed 1953, New York City
Clyde McPhatter (b. Nov. 15, 1933, Durham, N.C.; d. June 13, 1972, Bronx), lead voc.; Billy Pinkney (b. Aug. 15, 1925, Sumter, S.C.), voc.; Andrew Thrasher (b. Wetumpka, Ala.), voc.; Gerhart Thrasher (b. Wetumpka, Ala.), voc.
1955—(– McPhatter; through 1958 replacement lead vocalists included Dave Baughn [b. New York City]; Johnny Moore [b. 1934, Selma, Ala.]; Bobby Hendricks [b. 1937, Columbus, Oh.]) **1958**—(group disbanded) **1959**—(re-formed lineup included Ben E. King [b. Sep. 28, 1938, Henderson, N.C.], lead voc.; Charlie Thomas; Elsbeary Hobbs) **N.A.**—*The Drifters' Golden Hits* (Atlantic).

The Drifters helped create soul music by bringing gospel-styled vocals to secular material. Literally scores of singers (like Clyde McPhatter and Ben E. King) worked with this durable institution. According to an early press release, their name came from the fact that the original members had done a lot of drifting from one group to another. Their first lead vocalist, Clyde McPhatter (previously with the Dominoes and later successful on his own), propelled the group to immediate success but left after only six records—"Money Honey" (1953), later covered by Elvis Presley; "Such a Night" (1954); "Honey Love" (1954); "White Christmas" (1954, 1955); "Whatcha Gonna Do" (1955), all Top Ten R&B—before being drafted into the army in late 1954.

Following McPhatter's departure, the group filtered several vocalists through the lineup until disbanding in 1958. Manager George Treadwell (Sarah Vaughan's husband) retained rights to the group's name, however, and the following year took a group from Harlem called the Five Crowns and rechristened them the new Drifters.

This lineup, including Ben E. King, proved even more successful than the original group. They were assigned to producer/writers Mike Leiber and Jerry Stoller, and their first release, "There Goes My Baby," was a #2 hit in 1959. Often cited as the first R&B record to use strings, it was a lushly produced song whose style became a Drifters trademark. King was featured on several 1960 hits ("This Magic Moment," #16), but shortly after the group's biggest smash—the #1 "Save the Last Dance for Me" in October 1960—he left for a solo career. With his replacement, Rudy Lewis (from the Clara Ward Singers), several memorable hits followed—"Sweets for My Sweet" (#16, 1961), "On Broadway" (#9, 1963) and "Up on the Roof" (#5, 1962).

Through this peak period the Drifters worked with arrangers Phil Spector, Burt Bacharach and Bert Berns, among others. Following Lewis' death in 1964, mid-Fifties member Johnny Moore rejoined; he sang "Under the Boardwalk," the group's last big hit, in 1964. The Drifters managed to churn out steady R&B chart hits ("I've Got Sand in My Shoes," "Saturday Night at the Movies") through the Sixties while playing the club circuit.

When their Atlantic contract ended in 1972, they went to England and scored hits such as "Like Sister and Brother" (1973), "Kissin' in the Back Row of the Movies" (1974) and "Down on the Beach Tonight" (1974) for Bell Records under the guidance of writer/producers Roger Cook and Roger Greenaway. At the same time in America, any number of tenuously derived "New Drifters" could be found performing in nightclubs. McPhatter died in 1972 of complications from heart, liver and kidney disease.

DUCKS DELUXE
Formed 1972, London
Sean Tyla, gtr., kybds., voc.; Martin Belmont, gtr., voc.; Nick Garvey, bass, voc.; Tim Roper, drums.
1974—*Ducks Deluxe* (RCA) (− Roper; + Tim Rivoli, drums; + Andy McMasters, organ) *Taxi to the Terminal Zone* **1975**—(− Garvey; − McMasters) **1978**—*Don't Mind Rockin' Tonite*.

Ducks Deluxe were part of Britain's back-to-the-roots pub-rock movement in the early Seventies, attracting a cult following before they disbanded and went on to more successful projects. They played London pubs, including the Music Bar in Kensington and the Tally Ho in Kentish Town, with a repertoire of Fifties songs (by Eddie Cochran, Chuck Berry, Little Richard) and originals by Tyla, Belmont and Garvey. Their second album, *Taxi to the Terminal Zone* (produced by Dave Edmunds), wasn't released in America. After their last performance on July 1, 1975 (joined by Nick Lowe and Brinsley Schwarz), Tyla formed the Tyla Gang, Belmont eventually joined the Rumour and Nick Garvey founded the Motors.

DURAN DURAN
Formed 1978, Birmingham, England
Simon LeBon (b. Oct. 27, 1958, Bushey, Eng.), voc.; Andy Taylor (b. Feb. 16, 1961, Dolver-Hampton, Eng.), gtr., synth.; Nick Rhodes (b. June 8, 1962, Eng.), kybds.; John Taylor (b. June 20, 1960, Birmingham), bass; Roger Taylor (b. Apr. 26, 1960, Birmingham), drums.
1981—*Duran Duran* (Harvest) **1982**—*Rio; Carnival* (EP).

Duran Duran were one of several British New Romantic bands—that being a fashion-conscious merger of new wave and disco. Named after a character in Roger Vadim's sex-kitten sci-fi movie *Barbarella*, Duran Duran began as Nick Rhodes and John Taylor. Andy Taylor, answering an ad in *Melody Maker*, joined later. Simon LeBon met the group through a friend of his who worked at the Rum Runner, a club the group frequented and at which Rhodes had been a deejay. They had hit singles in Europe in 1981 with "Planet Earth" and in the U.S. in 1982 with "Hungry Like the Wolf." Lead singer Simon LeBon became a popular pin-up boy among British teens, and the group achieved some notoriety for its videos, particularly "Girls on Film," which featured female models in various stages of undress and was banned by BBC-TV and, in the U.S., by MTV.

IAN DURY
Born May 12, 1942, Billericay, England
1975—*Handsome* (Dawn) **1977**—*New Boots and Panties!!* (Stiff) *The Best of Kilburn and the High Roads* (Bonaparte) **1978**—*Wotabunch* (Warner Bros.) **1979**—*Do It Yourself* (Stiff) **1981**—*Laughter Lord Upminster* (Polydor) *Juke Box Dury* (Stiff).

While his Cockney accent eludes American audiences, Ian Dury has become a superstar in Great Britain with a good-natured mix of pop, funk, reggae, music hall and general boisterousness.

Stricken by polio at the age of seven, Dury spent two years in the hospital and several more in a school for the physically handicapped. He studied at the Royal College of Art and taught painting at the Canterbury Art College. In 1970, he formed his first group, Kilburn and the High Roads, a band specializing in Fifties rock & roll spiced with be-bop jazz. The High Roads established themselves on the pub circuit, and in 1973 Dury quit teaching.

The group's songs won the support of some influential British critics, among them Charlie Gillett, who became their manager. They cut an album for Raft Records, a subsidiary of Warner Bros., but Warner blocked its release until 1978. They released an album on Dawn, a Pye label, before disbanding in 1975.

Dury and High Roads pianist/guitarist Chaz Jankel continued to write songs together. Under Dury's name they recorded *New Boots and Panties!!*, with session musicians and former High Roaders like saxophonist Davey Payne. Then, invited to join the Live Stiffs package tour of Britain in the fall of 1977, Dury and Jankel assembled the Blockheads: Payne, bassist Norman Watt-Roy, drummer Charley Charles, pianist Mickey Gallagher and guitarist John Turnbull. *New Boots* stayed on the British charts for almost two years, eventually selling over a million copies worldwide. "What a Waste," a single from the album, reached #9 in 1978, and a later single, "Hit Me with Your Rhythm Stick," hit #1.

In 1978, Arista bought American distribution rights to Dury's Stiff catalogue and released *New Boots*. Sales were unimpressive, and Arista dropped the contract. Back home, *Do It Yourself* entered the charts at #2 on its mid-1979 release, and "Reasons to Be Cheerful (Part 3)" went to #3.

The Blockheads' 1979 tour of Britain included an appearance at the Concerts for Kampuchea. When the tour ended, Jankel left the band; he was replaced by Wilko Johnson, formerly of Dr. Feelgood. After signing with Polydor, Dury reunited with Jankel, who traveled with him to the Bahamas to record *Lord Upminster* with Sly Dunbar and Robbie Shakespeare. Included on that album was a single, "Spasticus Autisticus," written for the United Nations Year of the Disabled, but rejected.

BOB DYLAN
Born Robert Allen Zimmerman, May 24, 1941, Duluth, Minnesota
1962—*Bob Dylan* (Columbia) 1963—*The Freewheelin' Bob Dylan* 1964—*The Times They Are a-Changin'; Another Side of Bob Dylan* 1965—*Bringing It All Back Home; Highway 61 Revisited* 1966—*Blonde on Blonde* 1967—*Bob Dylan's Greatest Hits* 1968—*John Wesley Harding* 1969—*Nashville Skyline* 1970—*Self-Portrait; New Morning* 1971—*Bob Dylan's Greatest Hits, volume 2* 1972—*More Greatest Hits* 1973—*Pat Garrett and Billy the Kid; Dylan* 1974—*Planet Waves* (Asylum) *Before the Flood; Blood on the Tracks* (Columbia) 1975—*Basement Tapes; Desire* 1976—

Hard Rain 1978—*Street Legal* 1979—*Dylan at Budokan; Slow Train Coming* 1980—*Saved* 1981—*Shot of Love.*

Constantly changing, deliberately elusive and often prophetic, Bob Dylan was the most influential American pop musician of the Sixties in both his stance and his music—the repercussions of his many styles are still widespread. Dylan was deified and denounced for every shift of interest, while whole schools of musicians took up his ideas, and his lyrics became so well known that Jimmy Carter quoted them in his presidential inaugural speech. By personalizing folk songs, Dylan invented the singer/songwriter genre; by performing his allusive, poetic songs in his nasal, spontaneous vocal style with an electric band, he enlarged pop's range and vocabulary while creating a widely imitated sound. By recording with Nashville veterans, he reconnected rock and country, hinting at the country rock of the Seventies. The effect of his conversion to Christianity and his proselytizing songs of the late Seventies has yet to be seen.

Robert Zimmerman's family moved to Hibbing, Minnesota, from Duluth when he was six. After taking up guitar and harmonica, he formed the Golden Chords while he was a freshman in high school. He enrolled at the arts college of the University of Minnesota in 1959; during his three semesters there, he began to perform solo at coffeehouses as Bob Dylan (after Dylan Thomas; he legally changed his name in August 1962).

Dylan moved to New York City in January 1961, saying he wanted to meet Woody Guthrie, whom he then frequently visited at the hospital in East Orange, New Jersey. In April 1961, Dylan played New York's Gerdes' Folk City as the opener for John Lee Hooker, with a set of Guthrie-style ballads and his own lyrics to traditional tunes. A *New York Times* review by Robert Shelton alerted A&R man John Hammond, who signed Dylan to Columbia and produced his first album.

Although *Bob Dylan* included only two originals, "Talking New York" and "Song to Woody," Dylan stirred up the Greenwich Village folk scene with his caustic humor and gift for giving topical songs deep resonances. *The Freewheelin' Bob Dylan* included "Blowin' in the Wind" (a hit for Peter, Paul and Mary), "A Hard Rain's A-Gonna Fall" and "Masters of War," protest songs on a par with Guthrie's and Pete Seeger's. Joan Baez, already established as a "protest singer," recorded Dylan's songs and brought him on tour; in summer 1963 they became lovers as Dylan's fame grew.

By 1964, Dylan was playing 200 concerts a year. *The Times They Are a-Changin'* mixed protest songs ("With God on Our Side") and more personal lyrics ("One Too Many Mornings"). He met the Beatles at Kennedy Airport and reportedly introduced them to marijuana. *Another Side of Bob Dylan*, recorded in summer 1964,

Bob Dylan

concentrated on personal songs and imagistic free associations such as ''Chimes of Freedom''; Dylan repudiated his protest phase with ''My Back Pages.'' In late 1964, Columbia A&R man Jim Dickson introduced Dylan to Jim (later Roger) McGuinn, to whom Dylan gave ''Mr. Tambourine Man,'' which became the Byrds' first hit in 1965, kicking off folk rock. Meanwhile, the Dylan-Baez liaison fell apart, and Dylan met 25-year-old Shirley Noznisky, an ex-model a.k.a. Sara Lowndes, whom he married in 1965.

With *Bringing It All Back Home,* released early in 1965, Dylan turned his back on folk purism; for half the album he was backed by a rock & roll band. On July 25, 1965, he played the Newport Folk Festival (where two years earlier he had been the cynosure of the folksingers) backed by the Paul Butterfield Blues Band, and was booed. The next month, he played the Forest Hills tennis stadium with a band that included Levon Helm and Robbie Robertson, which accompanied him on a tour and later became the Band. ''Like a Rolling Stone'' (#2, 1965) became Dylan's first major hit.

The music Dylan made in 1965 and 1966 revolutionized rock. The intensity of his performances and his live-in-the-studio albums *(Highway 61 Revisited, Blonde on Blonde)* were a revelation, and his lyrics were analyzed, debated and quoted like no pop before them. With rage and slangy playfulness, Dylan chewed up and spat out literary and folk traditions in a wild, inspired doggerel. He

didn't explain; he gave off-the-wall interviews and press conferences in which he'd spin contradictory fables about his background and intentions. D. A. Pennebaker's documentary of Dylan's British tour, *Don't Look Back,* shows some of the hysteria. As ''Rainy Day Women #12 & 35'' went to #2 in April 1966, Dylan's worldwide record sales topped ten million, and more than 150 other groups or artists had recorded at least one of his songs.

On July 29, 1966, Dylan smashed up his Triumph 55 motorcycle while riding near his Woodstock, New York, home. With several broken neck vertebrae, a concussion and lacerations of the face and scalp, he was in critical condition for a week and bedridden for a month; after-effects included amnesia and mild paralysis, and he spent nine months in seclusion. As he recovered, he and the Band recorded the songs that were widely bootlegged—and legitimately released in 1975—as *The Basement Tapes,* whose droll, enigmatic, steeped-in-Americana sound would be continued by the Band on their own.

In 1968, Dylan made his public reentry with the quiet *John Wesley Harding,* which ignored the baroque psychedelia in vogue since the Beatles' 1967 *Sgt. Pepper;* Dylan wrote new enigmas into such folkish ballads as ''All Along the Watchtower.'' On January 20, 1968, he returned to the stage, performing three songs at a Woody Guthrie memorial concert, and in May 1969 he released the overtly countryish *Nashville Skyline,* featuring ''Lay Lady Lay'' (#7, 1969) and ''Girl from the North Country,'' with a guest vocal by Johnny Cash and a new, more mellow voice.

Dylan's early Seventies acts seemed less portentous. His 1970 *Self-Portrait* included songs by other writers and live takes from a 1969 Isle of Wight concert with the Band. By mid-1970, Dylan had moved to 94 MacDougal Street in Greenwich Village; on June 9, he received an honorary doctorate in music from Princeton.

George Harrison, with whom Dylan cowrote ''I'd Have You Anytime,'' ''If Not for You'' and a few other songs that summer, persuaded Dylan to appear at the Concert for Bangladesh; Leon Russell, who also performed, produced Dylan's single ''Watching the River Flow.'' Dylan sang at the Band concert that resulted in *Rock of Ages* (1972) but didn't appear on the album. In 1971, *Tarantula,* a collection of writings from the mid-Sixties, was published to an unenthusiastic reception.

After 1970's *New Morning* and a single, ''George Jackson'' (Dylan's first protest song since the mid-Sixties), he sat in on albums by Doug Sahm, Steve Goodman, McGuinn and others. Late in 1972, he played Alias and wrote a score for Sam Peckinpah's *Pat Garrett and Billy the Kid,* including ''Knockin' on Heaven's Door'' (#12, 1973). *Writings and Drawings by Bob Dylan,* a collection of lyrics and liner notes up to *New Morning,* was published in 1973. Between Columbia contracts, Dylan moved to Malibu in 1973 and made a handshake deal with David

Geffen's Asylum label, which released *Planet Waves;* Columbia retaliated with *Dylan,* embarrassing outtakes from *Self-Portrait.* Dylan and the Band played 39 shows in 21 cities, selling out 651,000 seats for a 1974 tour; the last three dates in L.A. were recorded for *Before the Flood.*

Dylan scrapped an early version of *Blood on the Tracks* and recut the songs with studio players in Minneapolis. He cowrote some of the songs on *Desire* with producer Jacques Levy; before making that LP, Dylan had returned to some Greenwich Village hangouts. A series of jams at the Other End led to the notion of a communal tour, and in October bassist Rob Stoner began rehearsing the large, shifting entourage (including Baez and such Village regulars as Ramblin' Jack Elliott and Bobby Neuwirth) that became the Rolling Thunder Revue, which toured on and off—with guests including Allen Ginsberg, Joni Mitchell, Mick Ronson, McGuinn and Arlo Guthrie—until spring 1976. The Revue started with surprise concerts at small halls (the first in Plymouth, Massachusetts, for an audience of 200) and worked up to outdoor stadiums like the one in Fort Collins, Colorado, where NBC-TV filmed *Hard Rain.* The troupe played two benefits for convicted murderer Rubin "Hurricane" Carter (subject of Dylan's "Hurricane"), which, after expenses, raised no money. Dylan's efforts helped Carter get a retrial, but he was convicted and one of the witnesses, Patty Valentine, sued Dylan over his use of her name in "Hurricane."

In 1976, Dylan appeared in the Band's *The Last Waltz.* His wife, Sara Lowndes, filed for divorce in March 1977. She received custody of their five children (Maria [Sara's daughter by a previous marriage whom Dylan had adopted], Jesse, Anna, Samuel and Jacob). Dylan took a $2 million loss on *Renaldo and Clara,* a four-hour film released early in 1978 including footage of the Rolling Thunder tour and starring himself and Joan Baez. He embarked on his most extensive tour (New Zealand, Australia, Europe, the U.S. and Japan, where he recorded *Live at Budokan*), redoing his old songs with some of the trappings of a Las Vegas lounge act.

Dylan announced in 1979 that he was a born-again Christian. McGuinn, the Alpha Band (an outgrowth of Rolling Thunder) and Debby Boone had introduced him to fundamentalist teachings. *Slow Train Coming,* overtly God-fearing, rose to #3; "You Gotta Serve Somebody" netted Dylan his first Grammy (for Best Rock Vocal Performance, Male). His West Coast tour late in 1979 featured only his born-again material; *Saved* and *Shot of Love* continued that message. In late 1981, he embarked on a 22-city U.S. tour; in 1982 there were rumors that his born-again phase was ending.

THE EAGLES

Formed 1971, Los Angeles
Don Henley (b. July 22, 1947, Gilmer, Tex.), drums, voc.; Glenn Frey (b. Nov. 6, 1948, Detroit), gtr., piano, voc.; Bernie Leadon (b. July 19, 1947, Minneapolis), gtr., banjo, mandolin, voc.; Randy Meisner (b. Mar. 8, 1946, Scottsbluff, Neb.), bass, gtr., voc.
1972—*Eagles* (Elektra) 1973—*Desperado* 1974— (+ Don Felder [b. Gainesville, Fla.], gtr., voc.) *On the Border* 1975—*One of These Nights; Eagles: Their Greatest Hits, 1971–1975* 1976—(− Leadon; + Joe Walsh [b. Nov. 20, 1947, Cleveland], gtr., voc.) *Hotel California* 1977—(− Meisner, + Timothy B. Schmit [b. Oct. 30, 1947, Sacramento], bass, voc.) **1979**—*The Long Run* **1980**—*Live.*

The Eagles epitomized California rock in the Seventies. Their songs incorporated vocal harmonies from country, hard rock guitar dynamics, studio perfectionism and lyrics that were alternately yearning and jaded. The Eagles also captured the pseudo-outlaw image of the Hollywood hustler in songs like "Life in the Fast Lane" and "Hotel California." During the band's hugely successful career, they had an increasingly indolent recording schedule until their breakup in 1981.

The band coalesced from Los Angeles' country-rock community. Before producer John Boylan assembled them as Linda Ronstadt's backup band on her *Silk Purse* album, the four original Eagles were already experienced professionals. Leadon had played in the Dillard and Clark Expedition and the Flying Burrito Brothers, Meisner with Poco and Rick Nelson's Stone Canyon Band. Frey had played with various Detroit rock bands (including Bob Seger's) and Longbranch Pennywhistle (with J. D. Souther, a sometime songwriting partner), and Henley had been with a transplanted Texas group, Shiloh. After working with Ronstadt, they decided to stay together.

The Eagles intended to take the country rock of the Byrds and Burritos a step further toward hard rock, and they recorded their first album with producer Glyn Johns in England. "Take It Easy," written by Frey and Jackson Browne, went gold shortly after its release, as did their debut album. *Desperado* was a concept album with two more hits, the title track and "Tequila Sunrise," and enough of a plot line to encourage rumors of a movie version. With *On the Border*, the Eagles changed producers, bringing in Bill Szymczyk (who worked on all subsequent albums) and adding Felder, who had recorded with Flow in Gainesville, Florida, then became a session

The Eagles: Glenn Frey, Don Henley, Timothy B. Schmit, Don Felder, Joe Walsh

guitarist and studio engineer in New York, Boston and Los Angeles (David Blue, Crosby and Nash). The increased emphasis on rock attracted more listeners but alienated Leadon. After *One of These Nights*, Leadon left to form the Bernie Leadon–Michael Georgiades Band, which released *Natural Progressions* in 1977.

Leadon was replaced by Joe Walsh, who had established himself with the James Gang and on his own. His Eagles debut, *Hotel California*, was their third consecutive #1 album; the title cut (#1, 1977) and "Life in the Fast Lane" (#11, 1977) spurred sales of 11 million copies worldwide.

Meisner left in 1977, replaced by Schmit, who had similarly replaced him in Poco. Meisner has released two solo albums, *Randy Meisner* (1978) and *One More Song* (1980), and he toured in 1981 with a group called the Silveradoes. Henley and Frey sang backup on his *One More Song*, and in the late Seventies they also appeared on albums by Bob Seger and Randy Newman.

Between outside projects, legal entanglements and perfectionism in the studio, it took the Eagles two years and $1 million to make the platinum LP *The Long Run*, their last album of new material; they also did some studio tinkering with their live double set.

Walsh has continued to release solo albums (including his self-mocking hit "Life's Been Good"), and in 1981 the rest of the Eagles announced solo projects. Felder's first solo work was a song on the *Heavy Metal* soundtrack. In 1982, Frey released *No Fun Aloud* and Henley released *I Can't Stand Still*, their solo debuts, which gave Henley a hit with "Johnny Can't Read."

EARTH QUAKE

Formed 1967, Berkeley, California
John Doukas (b. Richmond, Calif.), voc., gtr.; Robbie Dunbar (b. Levittown, N.Y.), gtr., voc.; Stan Miller (b. San Francisco), bass, voc.; Steve Nelson (b. Berkeley), drums, voc.
1971—*Earth Quake* (A&M) **1972**—*Why Don't You Try Me* **1973**—(+ Gary Phillips, gtr.) **1975**—*Earth Quake Live* (United Artists) *Rockin' the World* (Beserkley) **1976**—*8.5* **1977**—*Leveled* **1980**—*Two Years in a Padded Cell* (− Dunbar; + Rick Le Bleu, gtr., voc.; + Jan Hjorth, gtr., voc.).

Berkeley favorites and one of San Francisco's first hard-rock bands, the Anglo-influenced Earth Quake never attained more than regional hits ("Tickler," 1971; "I Get the Sweetest Feeling," 1972). But, along with Mathew King Kaufman and Steve Levine, they started their own label, Beserkley Records, in 1973. They received some national attention in 1974 when Beserkley licensed their cover of the Easybeats' "Friday on my Mind." Earth Quake released a live album in 1975 and have since concentrated primarily on running their small pop-rock label, whose roster includes Jonathan Richman and the Modern Lovers and Greg Kihn.

EARTH, WIND AND FIRE

Formed 1969, Chicago
Maurice White (b. Dec. 19, 1941, Memphis), voc., kalimba, drums; Verdine White (b. July 25, 1951), bass; Donald Whitehead, kybds.; Wade Flemons, electric piano; Michael Beale, gtr.; Phillard Williams, perc.; Chester Washington, horns; Leslie Drayton, horns; Alex Thomas, horns; Sherry Scott, voc.
1970—*Earth, Wind and Fire* (Warner Bros.) **1972**—*The Need of Love* (group disbands; new group: Maurice White and Verdine White; Philip Bailey [b. May 8, 1951, Denver], voc., perc.; Larry Dunn [b. June 19, 1953, Colo.], kybds., synth.; Jessica Cleaves [b. 1943], voc.; Roland Bautista, gtr.; Roland Laws, reeds) *Last Days and Time* (Columbia) (− Laws; − Bautista; − Cleaves; + Johnny Graham [b. Aug. 3, 1951, Ky.], gtr.; + Al McKay [b. Feb. 2, 1948, La.], gtr., perc.; + Andrew Woolfolk [b. Oct. 11, 1950, Tex.], sax, flute; + Ralph Johnson [b. July 4, 1951, Calif.], drums)

1973—*Head to the Sky* **1974**—*Another Time* (Warner Bros.) *Open Our Eyes* (Columbia) (+ Freddie White [b. Jan. 13, 1955, Chicago], drums) **1975**—*That's the Way of the World; Gratitude* **1976**—*Spirit* **1977**—*All 'n All* **1978**—*Best of, volume 1* **1979**—*I Am* **1981**—*Faces* (− McKay; + Bautista) *Raise* **1983**—*Powerlight.*

Innovative yet popular, precise yet sensual, calculated yet galvanizing, Earth, Wind and Fire changed the sound of black pop in the Seventies. Their music is encyclopedic, topping Latin-funk rhythms with gospel harmonies, unerring horns, Philip Bailey's sweet falsetto and various exotic ingredients chosen by leader and producer Maurice White. Unlike their ideological rivals, the down-and-dirty but equally eclectic Parliament/Funkadelic, EW&F have always preached clean, uplifting messages.

Maurice White is the son of a doctor and the grandson of a New Orleans honky-tonk pianist. After attending the Chicago Conservatory, he became a studio drummer at Chess Records in the early Sixties, where he recorded with the Impressions and Muddy Waters among others. From 1967 to 1969, he worked with the Ramsey Lewis Trio ("The In Crowd"); he later wrote and produced Lewis' 1975 hit "Sun Goddess." While with the trio, he took up kalimba, the African thumb piano, which became an EW&F trademark. White moved to Los Angeles in late 1969 and formed the first Earth, Wind and Fire (White's astrological chart has no water signs), who recorded for Capitol as the Salty Peppers. Warner signed the group for two moderately successful albums, but after 18 months, White hired a new, younger band, retaining only his brother, Verdine, on bass.

The new band's first Columbia LP, *Open Your Eyes*, went to #15 in 1974; in 1975, *That's the Way of the World*

Earth, Wind & Fire: Larry Dunn, Ralph Johnson, Philip Bailey, Maurice White, Al McKay, Fred White, Verdine White, Johnny Graham, Andrew Woolfolk

(a soundtrack) began a string of gold and, later, platinum albums, thanks to the Grammy-winning "Shining Star." The band moved up to the arena circuit with elaborate stage shows that included such mystical trappings as pyramids and disappearing acts. (Effects for their 1978 national tour were designed by magician Doug Henning.) Although White's longtime coproducer Charles Stepney died in 1976, EW&F continued to sell. *All 'n All* became their second platinum album, and they won two Grammies in 1978. They were a high point of Robert Stigwood's 1978 movie, *Sgt. Pepper's Lonely Hearts Club Band,* and their version of the Beatles' "Got to Get You into My Life" went to #9.

White began to do outside production in 1975 and worked on albums by the Emotions (*Rejoice,* 1977), Ramsey Lewis (*Sun Goddess,* 1975) and Deniece Williams (*This Is Niecy,* 1976). He did composing and production work on Valerie Carter's *Just a Stone's Throw Away* (1977). EW&F's 1979 album, *I Am,* featured the Emotions on "Boogie Wonderland" (#6, 1979). In 1980, the group toured Europe and South America; 1981's *Raise* featured the hit "Let's Groove." Since their inception, Earth, Wind and Fire have sold over 19 million albums. According to White, "We came out here to try to render a service to mankind, not to be stars. We are actually being used as tools by the Creator."

SHEENA EASTON
Born April 27, 1959, Glasgow
1981—*Sheena Easton* (EMI) **1982**—*You Could Have Been with Me* **1982**—*Madness, Money and Music.*

Sheena Easton became a pop star in 1981 with a vocal style and image suggesting a new-wave version of easy-rock singers Marie Osmond and Olivia Newton-John.

Easton attended the Royal Scottish Academy of Drama and Art and graduated in June 1979, qualified to teach, but instead began a singing career. (While in school, she had frequently moonlighted in local nightclubs and pubs.) She successfully auditioned for EMI Records in May 1979 and received national exposure when the BBC-TV show "Big Time" documented her grooming for stardom. Her first single, "Modern Girl," was released in February 1980 and hit the Top Ten in England; that November she performed for Queen Elizabeth at the Royal Variety Show.

Easton's American breakthrough came in the summer of 1981, when "Morning Train" stayed at #1 on the U.S. charts for two weeks. Its success propelled the reissued "Modern Girl" up the charts as well, and at one point she had the distinction of having two singles in the Top Ten. Her hits continued with "When He Shines" from her second album, *You Could Have Been with Me,* and the theme song from the James Bond film *For Your Eyes Only.* She has also received gold records in Japan and Canada, and a Grammy in 1982 for Best New Artist.

THE EASYBEATS
Formed early 1960s, Australia
George Young (b. Nov. 6, 1947), gtr.; Gordon Fleet (b. Aug. 16, 1945), drums; Dick Diamonde (b. Dec. 28, 1947), bass; Harry Vanda (b. Harry Wandan, Mar. 22, 1947), gtr.; Stevie Wright (b. Dec. 20, 1948), voc. (All apparently born in England and emigrated to Australia with their parents.)
1967—*Friday on My Mind* (United Artists) *Good Friday* **1968**—*Falling off the Edge of the World; Vigil* **1970**—*Friends.*

The Easybeats were the Sixties Australian rock band that launched producer/songwriters Harry Vanda and George Young. The group established themselves as Australia's leading pop band by 1965. In 1966, they returned to England and began recording with producer Shel Talmy (who also worked with the Kinks and the Who), an association that resulted in the worldwide hit "Friday on My Mind" (#16, 1967). After their initial success, Vanda and Young kept the Easybeats name for a few years and had some moderately successful U.K. hits before officially disbanding in 1970 and forming a production company back in Australia. As Happy's Whiskey Sour, they had a British hit with "Shot in the Head," and as the Marcus Hook Roll Band they recorded "Natural Man" in 1972. They produced Stevie Wright's solo debut, *Hard Road,* and oversaw the career of Young's brothers Angus and Malcolm's band, AC/DC. Vanda and Young also concocted three studio albums that enjoyed some European success as Flash and the Pan.

DUANE EDDY
Born April 26, 1938, Corning, New York
1958—*Have Twangy Guitar Will Travel* (Jamie) *Especially for You* **1959**—*Twang's the Thing* **1961**—*1,000,000 Dollars of Twang* **1962**—*1,000,000 Dollars of Twang 2; Twistin' and Twangin'* (RCA) **1965**—*Best of* **1970**—*Twangy Guitar* (London).

Guitarist Duane Eddy had a string of instrumental hits ("Rebel Rouser," #6, 1958; "Peter Gunn," #27, 1960) that invariably featured a staccato signature riff labeled the "twangy" guitar sound. His work has influenced numerous guitarists (the Ventures, Shadows, George Harrison), especially in England.

Eddy began playing the guitar at age five. In 1951, he moved with his family to Phoenix. Shortly after dropping out of Coolidge High School at 16, he got a series of steady jobs working with local dance groups, and he acquired the custom-made Chet Atkins–model Gretsch guitar he still plays. In 1957, Phoenix DJ/producer/entrepreneur Lee Hazlewood became his mentor, and Eddy started touring with Dick Clark's Caravan of Stars. The Hazlewood-produced "Rebel Rouser" (on Clark's Jamie label) in 1958 began a six-year streak of nearly twenty hits ("Ramrod,"

#27, 1958; "Cannonball," #15, 1958; "Forty Miles of Bad Road," #9, 1959). Though Eddy and Hazlewood parted company in 1961, they have gotten back together for comeback attempts.

Eddy switched to RCA in 1962 and had a hit with "Dance with the Guitar Man" (#12, 1962), followed by "Deep in the Heart of Texas" and "The Ballad of Paladin" (#33, 1962). He signed with Colpix in 1965 and released LPs like *Duane Does Dylan* and *Duane a Go-Go*. The various back-to-the-roots movements of the Seventies (especially the rockabilly revival) rekindled interest in Eddy, who occasionally performs at oldies shows in the U.S. but concentrates primarily on the U.K. (where he had a #9 hit in 1975 with "Play Me Like You Play Your Guitar").

Eddy's early backup group, the Rebels, included guitarist Al Casey, saxophonist Steve Douglas and pianist Larry Knechtel, later with Bread. At the height of his success, Eddy made his film debut in *Because They're Young* (1960), scoring a #4 hit with the theme song. He occasionally worked as a producer in the Seventies, including a solo LP by Phil Everly (*Star Spangled Springer,* 1973). Eddy moved to California in the late Sixties and then to Lake Tahoe, Nevada, in 1976. His comeback single on Asylum in 1977, "You Are My Sunshine," was produced by Hazlewood and included vocals by Willie Nelson and Waylon Jennings. Jennings' wife, Jessi Colter, was married to Eddy from 1966 to 1969.

DAVE EDMUNDS

Born April 15, 1944, Cardiff, Wales
1972—*Rockpile* (Mam) 1975—*Subtle as a Flying Mallet* (RCA) 1977—*Get It* (Swansong) 1978—*Tracks on Wax 4* 1979—*Repeat When Necessary* 1981— *Twangin'* 1982—*D.E. 7th.* 1983—*Information.*

Guitarist/singer/producer/songwriter Dave Edmunds, an active fan of American rockabilly, spurred Britain's pub-rock movement, cofounded Rockpile and has sustained a solo career for a decade. During the early Sixties, he played in several British blues-rock bands before forming Love Sculpture in 1967 with bassist John Williams and drummer Bob Jones (the group included Terry Williams, also of Rockpile and later with Dire Straits). They played rocked-up versions of light-classical pieces by Bizet and Khachaturian, whose "Sabre Dance" gave them a Top Five U.K. hit in 1968. They toured the U.S. for six weeks before disbanding the next year. (Some of Love Sculpture's efforts were compiled in the Seventies.)

Back in his native Wales, Edmunds built the eight-track Rockfield Studio in Monmouthshire and taught himself how to re-create Sam Phillips' Sun Records slap echo and Phil Spector's Wall of Sound. He spent the early Seventies in the studio producing himself (including a 1970 hit remake of Smiley Lewis' 1955 hit "I Hear You Knockin'" and an album called *Rockpile*) and others, including the

Flamin' Groovies, Del Shannon and pub-rockers Deke Leonard, Ducks Deluxe, and, later, Brinsley Schwarz and Graham Parker. When he produced Brinsley Schwarz's last LP in 1974, he met bassist Nick Lowe, later of Rockpile.

In 1975, Edmunds costarred in and scored most of the film *Stardust,* and he also released *Subtle as a Flying Mallet,* for which Lowe wrote songs and played bass. After 1977's *Get It,* Edmunds toured regularly with Rockpile. Most of his albums have consisted primarily of covers. *Repeat When Necessary* premiered songs by Elvis Costello ("Girls Talk") and Graham Parker ("Crawling from the Wreckage"). His 1981 LP *Twangin'* produced a minor hit single with a cover of John Fogerty's "Almost Saturday Night," and in "The Race Is On" introduced the Stray Cats, a Long Island neo-rockabilly group for whom Edmunds later produced multimillion-selling albums. After Rockpile's 1981 demise, Edmunds resumed his solo career. In 1982, *D.E. 7th* included a song written for Edmunds by Bruce Springsteen, "From Small Things (Big Things One Day Come)." *Information* featured a song written and produced for Edmunds by the Electric Light Orchestra's Jeff Lynne, "Slipping Away."

EFFECTS

This term refers to the electronic modification of an electric instrument's tone, almost always involving electric guitars. Basic effects, which in various combinations define the tone of every distinctive electric guitarist, include reverb (which extends a note), echo (a more percussive reverb, which repeats the note), tremolo (rapidly fluctuating volume) and vibrato (rapidly fluctuating pitch).

There are also all sorts of distortion effects, notably fuzz tone (which makes notes rougher) and phase-shifting or flanging (two different electronic techniques of producing a whooshing sound). Some effects change the attack on notes, such as wah-wah pedals (which filter certain frequencies and make a crying, speechlike sound) and volume pedals (which can completely remove the sound of a pick or fingers striking strings for a sighing, violinlike attack). More recent inventions include harmonizers and chorus effects, which add mathematically proportioned overtones of a note for a richer tone.

The first fuzz-tone effect was created by rockabilly guitarist Link Wray, who for his hit "Rumble" punched holes in his amplifier's speaker with a pencil. Wah-wah was popularized in the psychedelic era and used with most finesse by Jimi Hendrix. Phase-shifting first appeared on record with the Small Faces' "Itchykoo Park" in 1967, and volume pedals were essential to the sound of British art-rock guitarists such as King Crimson's Robert Fripp and Yes's Steve Howe.

Integrated circuits and microchips have made most effects available in miniature mass-produced form, usually as pedal-activated boxes.

THE ELECTRIC FLAG
Formed 1967, San Francisco
Michael Bloomfield (b. July 28, 1944, Chicago, d. February 15, 1981, San Francisco), gtr.; Buddy Miles, drums, voc.; Barry Goldberg, kybds.; Nick Gravenites (b. Chicago), voc.; Harvey Brooks, bass; Peter Strazza, tenor sax; Marcus Doubleday, trumpet; Herbie Rich, baritone sax.
1968—*A Long Time Comin'* (Columbia) (− Bloomfield) **1969**—*The Electric Flag* **1974**—(Bloomfield, Miles, Goldberg, Gravenites and Roger "Jellyroll" Troy, bass, voc.) *The Band Kept Playing* (Atlantic).

The short-lived Electric Flag intended to combine blues, rock, soul, jazz and country; they ended up sparking the rock-with-brass trend of Blood, Sweat and Tears and Chicago. Bloomfield started the band in 1967 after leaving the Paul Butterfield Blues Band, and he brought Nick Gravenites with him. Goldberg had played with Mitch Ryder and came to the Flag after the breakup of the Goldberg-Miller Blues Band (with Steve Miller), bringing Strazza with him. The rest had session background: Buddy Miles in R&B, drumming for Otis Redding and Wilson Pickett; Harvey Brooks as the folk-rockers' bassist with Bob Dylan, Judy Collins, Phil Ochs, Eric Andersen, as well as the Doors; Marcus Doubleday from early-Sixties work with the Drifters, Jan and Dean and Bobby Vinton.

Based in San Francisco, the Electric Flag debuted at the Monterey Pop Festival in June 1967, and their first album made the Top Forty. But ego conflicts among the members soon undermined them, and the band lasted only eighteen months. Bloomfield quit after the debut album, leaving Miles as leader for the Flag's remaining months. Before the breakup, they'd recorded enough material for a second album. The Buddy Miles Express was modeled after the Flag, but Miles left it to join Jimi Hendrix's Band of Gypsies. Gravenites turned to songwriting, then joined Big Brother and the Holding Company. The rest returned to work as sidemen.

In 1974, Bloomfield, Miles, Gravenites and Goldberg (joined by Roger "Jellyroll" Troy) reunited for a two-album deal. The first, produced by Jerry Wexler, recreated the old sound with Dr. John's Bonaroo Brass and the Muscle Shoals Horns. But the band's third incarnation broke up before recording a second album.

THE ELECTRIC LIGHT ORCHESTRA
Formed 1971, Birmingham, England
Roy Wood (b. Nov. 8, 1946), gtr., voc.; Jeff Lynne (b. Dec. 30, 1947), gtr., voc., synth.; Bev Bevan (b. Nov. 25, 1946), drums; Rick Price, bass. (All born in Birmingham.)
1972—*No Answer/ELO* (United Artists) (− Wood; − Price; + Richard Tandy [b. Mar. 26, 1948, Birmingham], kybds., gtr.; + Michael de Albuquerque, bass; + Mike Edwards, cello; + Colin Walker, cello; + Wilf Gibson, violin) **1973**—*ELO II* (− Walker; − Gibson; + Hugh McDowell [b. July 31, 1953, London], cello; + Mik Kaminsky [b. Sep. 2, 1951, Harrogate, Eng.], violin) **1974**—*On the Third Day* (− de Albuquerque; − Edwards; + Kelly Groucutt [b. Sep. 8, 1945, Coseley, Eng.], bass, voc.; + Melvyn Gale [b. Jan. 15, 1952, London], cello; − Groucutt; − Gale; + de Albuquerque; + Edwards) *Eldorado* **1975**—*Face the Music* **1976**—*Olé ELO; A New World Record* (Jet) **1977**—*Out of the Blue* (− Gale;

Grammy Awards

The Eagles
1975 Best Pop Vocal Performance by a Duo, Group or Chorus: "Lyin' Eyes"
1977 Record of the Year: *Hotel California*
1979 Best Rock Vocal Performance by a Duo or Group: "Heartache Tonight"

Earth, Wind and Fire
1975 Best R&B Vocal Performance by a Duo, Group or Chorus: "Shining Star"

1978 Best R&B Vocal Performance by a Duo, Group or Chorus: *All 'n All*
Best R&B Instrumental Performance: "Runnin' "
1979 Best R&B Vocal Performance by a Duo, Group or Chorus: "After the Love Has Gone"
Best R&B Instrumental Performance: "Boogie Wonderland"

1982 Best R&B Performance by a Duo or Group with Vocal: "Wanna Be With You"

Yvonne Elliman
1978 Album of the Year: *Saturday Night Fever* (with others)

Emotions
1977 Best R&B Vocal Performance by a Duo, Group or Chorus: "Best of My Love"

– Kaminski; – McDowell) **1979**—*Discovery;*
Greatest Hits **1981**—*Time.*

The Electric Light Orchestra became a major arena and stadium draw in the mid- and late Seventies on the strength of Beatles-like orchestral pop—"Can't Get It Out of My Head" (#9, 1975), "Telephone Line" (#7, 1977), "Evil Woman" (#10, 1976)—and elaborate staging. Formed in 1971 as an offshoot of the Move by leader Roy Wood (who left after ELO's first LP to form Wizzard), drummer Bev Bevan and guitarist/songwriter Jeff Lynne, ELO initially sought to explore classically tinged orchestral rock. The band has fashioned a series of multimillion-selling LPs and radio hits by sweetening futuristic electronic effects with rich strings, synthesizers, keyboards and occasional horns. They remain based in England, although their greatest success has been in America.

The Electric Light Orchestra has a history of facelessness—even the most ardent fans generally can't name more than one or two band members (original members Lynne and Bevan remain the backbone, with studio assistance from longtime member and multi-instrumentalist Richard Tandy). Their first hit was Chuck Berry's "Roll over Beethoven" with their chugging cellos sending up the opening strains of the Fifth Symphony (they occasionally use fragments of Grieg and others as well).

After Wood quit, Lynne brought the band to the U.S. in 1973 for a forty-date debut tour that was marred by technical problems in miking the cellos (a radical addition to the live rock format). *On the Third Day* produced a moderate hit with "Showdown" (#53, 1974). *Eldorado*, a pseudo-concept album, gave ELO a major hit with "Can't Get It Out of My Head." *Face the Music* went gold on the strength of "Evil Woman" (#10, 1976) and "Strange Magic" (#14, 1976). Every album after that went at least platinum. In 1977, ELO's records and tours grossed over $10 million, and *A New World Record* eventually sold five million copies worldwide.

By the late Seventies ELO were recording for their own label, Jet, whose distribution switch to CBS led ELO to sue the old distributor, United Artists, claiming they had flooded the market with millions of defective copies of the platinum double LP *Out of the Blue.*

ELO's most elaborate tour was in 1978, when they traveled with a laser-equipped "spaceship" (some said it looked like a giant glowing hamburger) that opened with the group playing inside. The Orchestra's live shows were also enhanced by taped backing tracks, and they were accused on more than one occasion of lip-synching the supposed "live parts." In 1979, they stayed off the road completely (the first time they hadn't toured since 1972). *Discovery* went platinum nonetheless, yielding two hits with "Don't Bring Me Down" (#15) and "Shine a Little Love" (#15). In 1980, Lynne contributed several songs to the Olivia Newton-John movie *Xanadu.* Ticket sales were

reportedly slow as ELO toured the U.S. in late 1981 to promote their latest album, *Time.*

THE ELECTRIC PRUNES
Formed 1965, Los Angeles
James Lowe, autoharp, harmonica, voc.; Mark Tulin, bass, kybds.; Ken Williams, gtr.; Preston Ritter, drums; Weasel Spagnola, gtr., voc.
1967—*Electric Prunes* (Reprise) (– Ritter; + Quint, drums) *Underground* (group disbands; new group: John Herren [b. Elk City, Okla.], kybds.; Mark Kincaid [b. Topeka, Kan.], gtr., voc.; Ron Morgan, gtr.; Brett Wade [b. Vancouver], bass, flute, voc.; Richard Whetstone [b. Hutchinson, Kan.], drums, voc.) *Mass in F Minor* **1968**—*Release of an Oath: The Kol Nidre* (– Herren) **1969**—*Just Good Old Rock 'n' Roll.*

The Electric Prunes were actually two separate groups. The original was one of the first psychedelic bands from Los Angeles. They signed to Reprise in 1966 and had a national hit with the reverb-heavy "I Had Too Much to Dream (Last Night)" (#11, 1966). They followed up with "Get Me to the World on Time" (#27) in 1967. For reasons unknown, the group disbanded and a totally new band calling itself the Electric Prunes emerged in 1967 with *Mass in F Minor* and with *Release of an Oath* in 1968, both the creations of writer/arranger David Axelrod. Their fifth LP, *Just Good Old Rock 'n' Roll*, was an attempt to return to roots music but was unsuccessful. The Electric Prunes again disbanded.

ELEPHANT'S MEMORY
Formed 1967, Massachusetts
Rick Frank (b. Feb. 12, 1942, New York City), drums; Stan Bronstein (b. July 17, 1938, Brooklyn), voc., sax, clarinet.
1969—(+ Richard Sussman [b. Mar. 28, 1946, Philadelphia], kybds.; + Myron Yules [b. Mar. 6, 1935, Brooklyn], bass, trombone; + John Ward [b. Feb. 12, 1949, Philadelphia], gtr.; + "Chester" Ayres [b.Richard Ayres, Sep. 5, 1942, Neptune, N.J.], gtr.; + "Michal" [b. Apr. 20, 1949, Israel], voc.) *Elephant's Memory* (Buddah) (+ Chris Robison, gtr., kybds., voc.; – Robison; – Sussman; – Yules; – Ward; – Ayres; – "Michal"; + Wayne "Tex" Gabriel, gtr.; + Adam Ippolito, kybds., voc.; + Gary Van Scyoc, bass, voc.) **1970**—*Take It to the Streets* (Metromedia) **1972**—*Elephant's Memory* (Apple) **1973**—(– Ippolito; – Gabriel; + Robison; + John Sachs, gtr., voc.) **1974**—*Angels Forever* (RCA).

Elephant's Memory, remembered for its street-band reputation and association with John Lennon, was formed in New York City's East Village by drummer Rick Frank and Stan Bronstein, a veteran of the strip-tease circuit. They started out as an eclectic seven-piece outfit playing brassy jazz-flavored rock and funk and earned a reputation for outrageous live spectacles featuring bizarre costumes, light shows and the destruction of plastic sculptures.

Around the time they got a contract with Buddah, Carly Simon was briefly a member but left the group when her boyfriend was pushed down some stairs after an argument with other bandmembers. She was replaced by an Israeli woman identified only as "Michal." Buddah pigeonholed them as a bubblegum act and, after working on the soundtrack for the film *Midnight Cowboy*, the group changed labels. In 1970, they dropped the horns, and Bronstein and Frank added new hard-rocking sidemen. They had a minor hit, "Mongoose," in 1970. Their LP *Take It to the Streets* added to their cult following.

When John Lennon was looking for a band in 1972, Jerry Rubin suggested Elephant's Memory. After a jam at Max's Kansas City, Lennon signed them up. Over the next two years, the group recorded with Lennon and his wife, Yoko Ono (*Some Time in New York City*, 1972; Ono's *Approximately Infinite Universe*, 1973). During the same period, they also released an LP on Apple and backed Chuck Berry and Bo Diddley. *Angels Forever* was recorded in Wales. In early 1981, ex-Elephant guitarist Tex Gabriel was active on the New York club scene with his band, Limozine.

RAMBLIN' JACK ELLIOTT

Born Elliott Charles Adnopoz, Aug. 1, 1931, Brooklyn
1968—*Young Brigham* (Reprise)   **1976**—*The Essential Ramblin' Jack Elliott* (Vanguard)   *Ramblin' Jack Elliott Sings Woody Guthrie and Jimmie Rodgers* (Monitor).

A Jew from Brooklyn, Ramblin' Jack Elliott is one of the last roaming cowboy-troubadours, a distinction he earned by wandering in the West with Woody Guthrie shortly before the latter was hospitalized with terminal Huntington's chorea.

Elliott left home in 1946 to join the rodeo in Chicago, beginning years of traveling that provided the stories he told on stage. As early as 1953, Elliott was performing regularly in Greenwich Village's Washington Square Park, helping to lay groundwork for the early-Sixties folk boom. In the late Fifties, he settled on the moniker "Ramblin' Jack" (after calling himself Buck Elliott for a while). He toured England and Europe for several years, jamming with traditional folk artists like Peggy Seeger and Ewan McColl and with British R&B stalwart Long John Baldry. He often performed Guthrie compositions ("Pretty Boy Floyd") and such flat-picking showcases as "Black Snake Moan."

Upon returning to the U.S. in 1961, Elliott found himself an old hand in the burgeoning folk renaissance, and his Vanguard debut album was received enthusiastically. Bob Dylan, also a Guthrie fan, was heavily influenced by

Elliott, who recorded several Dylan songs in the Sixties (claiming once that Dylan wrote "Don't Think Twice, It's All Right" for him). He was also part of Dylan's 1975 Rolling Thunder entourage.

Elliott has recorded consistently for the past two decades. In 1968, he performed at a star-studded memorial concert for Guthrie at Carnegie Hall. His best work can be found on compilations like Vanguard's *Essential Jack Elliott* and Folkways' *Songs to Grow On* (all Guthrie material).

SHIRLEY ELLIS

Born 1941, Bronx, New York
N.A.—*The Name Game* (Congress)   *Sugar, Let's Shing a Ling* (Columbia).

Soul singer Shirley Ellis had three Top Ten novelty hits in the early Sixties: "The Nitty Gritty" (#8, 1964), "The Clapping Song" (#8, 1965) and her signature song, "The Name Game" (#3, 1965). In the Fifties, Ellis wrote "One, Two, I Love You" for the Heartbreakers. She started working with writer Lincoln Chase, whom she later married.

Chase's previous hits included "Such a Night" for the Drifters and "Jim Dandy" for LaVern Baker. Before marrying Ellis, Chase had recorded for several labels (Decca, Liberty, Splash, Dawn, Columbia, RCA Victor, Swan) with minimal success. Chase wrote all of Ellis' hits, including lesser successes like "That's What the Nitty Gritty Is" (1964) and "The Puzzle Song" (1965). Ellis' pop success was fleeting. As the Sixties progressed, she switched to Columbia, had one minor hit—"Soul Time" (1967)—then retired.

JOE ELY

Born 1947, Amarillo, Texas
1977—*Joe Ely* (MCA)   **1978**—*Honky Tonk Masquerade*   **1979**—*Down on the Drag*   **1981**—*Must Notta Gotta Lotta* (Southcoast/MCA)   *Live Shots*.

Joe Ely's band and his songs are rooted in the traditions of his native West Texas—honky-tonk, country & western, R&B, rockabilly, Western swing and Tex-Mex. He has incorrectly been taken to be a "progressive country" singer. Outside of Lubbock, Texas, most of his support came from the rock press until the Clash introduced him to their fans in 1980.

Ely left Lubbock at age 16, dropping out to wander from Texas to California, Tennessee, New York, Europe, New Mexico and back to Texas. He worked as a fruit picker, a circus hand, a janitor, a dishwasher and an itinerant musician. Back in Lubbock in 1974, he decided to stay and form a band with guitarist Jesse Taylor, steel guitarist Lloyd Manes, bassist Gregg Wright and drummer Steve Keeton. They became local favorites, then began traveling the state honky-tonk circuit.

In 1977, MCA signed Ely, and producer Chip Young took him and his band to Nashville to cut his first album. By that time, he had assembled a repertoire of 300 songs, most of them his own or written by his Texas buddy Butch Hancock.

His second album, with accordionist Ponty Bone joining the band, was even more multifarious than the first. The third, produced by Bob Johnston (Bob Dylan, Aretha Franklin, Johnny Cash), focused his image as a tough-skinned-but-gentle-hearted singer/songwriter, but made him no more appealing to radio programers.

Ely picked up some valuable fans among musicians. Merle Haggard took him on a tour of Britain in 1979, and the next year the Clash asked him to open their Texas shows. The Clash's Joe Strummer invited him along for the rest of their American tour and back to England with them; *Live Shots* was recorded at Clash concerts in England.

Ely continues to forge his own sound from Texan raw materials. When, for example, steel guitarist Manes left his band, he replaced him with another Lubbocker, saxophonist Smokey Joe "Out of Chicago" Miller.

EMERSON, LAKE and PALMER

Formed 1970, England
Keith Emerson (b. Nov. 1, 1944, Todmorden, Eng.), kybds.; Greg Lake (b. Nov. 10, 1948, Bournemouth, Eng.), bass, gtr., voc.; Carl Palmer (b. Mar. 20, 1951, Birmingham, Eng.), drums, percussion.
1970—*Emerson, Lake and Palmer* (Cotillion)   1971— *Tarkus;   Pictures at an Exhibition* (Manticore)   1972— *Trilogy* (Cotillion)   1973—*Brain Salad Surgery* (Manticore)   1974—*Welcome Back, My Friends, to the Show That Never Ends—Ladies and Gentlemen, Emerson, Lake and Palmer*   1977—*Works, volume 1* (Atlantic) *Works, volume 2*   1978—*Love Beach*   1979—*Emerson, Lake and Palmer in Concert*   1980—*Best of Emerson, Lake and Palmer.*

Emerson, Lake and Palmer ushered in the classical-flavored progressive rock of the early Seventies. With Greg Lake's predominantly acoustic ballads becoming hit singles and Keith Emerson's keyboard excesses supplying pretensions, the trio was enormously popular in the early Seventies, although it never regained its full momentum after a 1975–77 hiatus.

The group was formed after Emerson, then leading the Nice, and Lake, formerly of King Crimson, jammed at the Fillmore West in 1969 while both were touring. Emerson had studied classical piano and later dabbled in jazz; he made his professional debut at 19 with British R&B singer Gary Farr and the T-Bones. Two years later, he joined the VIPs, some of whose members later surfaced in Spooky Tooth; and in early 1967 he joined American soul singer P. P. Arnold's band, then headquartered in Europe. Emer-

son formed the Nice in 1967, and broke up the band to work with Lake and Palmer. Lake's background included work with various local bands from the age of 12 (the Shame, the Gods and, later, King Crimson).

After plans to work with Jimi Hendrix Experience drummer Mitch Mitchell fell through, Palmer joined Emerson and Lake in early 1970. He had already played with Chris Farlowe, Arthur Brown and Atomic Rooster.

ELP made their debut at the 1970 Isle of Wight Festival, playing Emerson's transcription of Moussorgsky's *Pictures at an Exhibition,* which later became their third album. Their debut album, recorded in October 1970, went gold on the strength of Lake's "Lucky Man" (#48, 1971). A few months later, Lake's "From the Beginning" (#39, 1972) became the group's most successful single. FM radio play and flamboyantly bombastic concerts— with Emerson's electric keyboards flashing lights and whirling around; Palmer's $25,000 percussion set including xylophone, timpani and gong as well as an elevator platform, and the usual lights and smoke—cemented the group's following.

Each of their first five albums went gold, and *Trilogy* and the debut went platinum as ELP toured arenas. In 1973, they formed their own Manticore Records, which released albums by Italy's Premiata Forneria Marconi (P.F.M.) and sometime Lake lyricist Pete Sinfield, along with ELP's album *Brain Salad Surgery.* ELP's 1973–74 world tour called for 36 tons of equipment, including a quadraphonic sound system, lasers and other paraphernalia, and was documented on the triple live set *Welcome Back, My Friends, to the Show That Never Ends.*

With six million in sales behind them, ELP took a two-year break, ending it in 1977 with the release of *Works,* volume 1 in March, their worst seller to date. A 1977 world tour called for an entourage of 115 people, including full orchestra and choir, but had to be drastically reduced when ticket sales didn't materialize. After the late-1978 *Love Beach* sold poorly, the group announced its breakup in December 1979.

Emerson has been sporadically active; he released a single of the boogie-woogie standard "Honky-Tonk Train Blues" and scored the 1981 thriller film *Nighthawks.* Lake revived a solo career begun during the group's hiatus, when his "I Believe in Father Christmas" hit the Top Ten in England. He released a solo album in late 1981 on Chrysalis and did some touring in the U.S. In 1981, Palmer helped found the hugely successful Asia.

THE EMOTIONS

Formed 1968, Chicago
Wanda Hutchinson (b. Dec. 17, 1951, Chicago), voc.; Sheila Hutchinson (b. Jan. 17, 1953, voc.); Jeanette Hutchinson (b. 1951, Chicago), voc.
1970—(– Jeanette Hutchinson; + Teresa Davis

[b. Aug. 22, 1950, Chicago], voc.) *Untouched* (Stax) *So I Can Love You* **1976**—*Flowers* (Columbia) **1977**—(− Davis; + Pamela Hutchinson [b. 1958, Chicago], voc.) *Sunshine* (Stax) *Rejoice* **1979**—*Come into Our World* **1981**—*New Affair.*

A gospel-turned-soul family group in the Staples tradition, the Emotions have been entertaining black audiences since they could walk. Their biggest successes (like "Best of My Love") came in the late Seventies under the guidance of Maurice White of Earth, Wind and Fire (with whom they recorded EW&F's 1979 hit "Boogie Wonderland").

Father/manager (and occasional guitarist and vocalist) Joe had his three oldest daughters performing in church as tots. Beginning in 1961, they traveled the gospel circuit as the Hutchinson Sun Beams and occasionally toured with Mahalia Jackson. While attending Chicago's Parker High School in the mid-Sixties, they became the Three Ribbons and a Bow (Papa Joe was the "beau") and began concentrating on more secular material, cutting an unsuccessful series of singles for such Midwestern labels as One-Der-Ful, Vee Jay and Twinstacks. While touring, they met the Staples, who helped them acquire a contract (as the Emotions) with Stax-Volt in 1968.

The group enjoyed substantial R&B success and made occasional modest pop inroads—"So I Can Love You" (#39), "Show Me How" (#52)—through the early Seventies. They appeared in the 1973 film *Wattstax* and toured with the Jackson 5, Sly and the Family Stone, B. B. King, Stevie Wonder, Bobby "Blue" Bland and others.

When Stax folded in 1975, they signed with Maurice White's Kalimba Productions and thus got on the Columbia roster. White wrote the title track and produced their gold debut for the label, *Flowers* (which prominently featured Wanda's material and lead vocals), as well as the followup, *Rejoice.* They enjoyed hit singles with "Don't Wanna Lose Your Love" and the disco favorite "Best of My Love" and toured with Earth, Wind and Fire in 1976. By the late Seventies, they were writing the bulk of their material themselves.

THE ENGLISH BEAT

Formed 1978, Birmingham, England
Dave Wakeling (b. Feb. 19, 1956, Birmingham), gtr., voc.; Andy Cox (b. Jan. 25, 1956, Birmingham), gtr.; David Steele (b. Sep. 8, 1960, Isle of Wight), bass; Everett Morton (b. Apr. 5, 1951, St. Kitts, West Indies), drums.
1979—(+ Ranking Roger [b. Feb. 21, 1961, Birmingham], voc.; + Saxa [b. ca. 1930, Jamaica], sax)
1980—*I Just Can't Stop It* (Sire) **1981**—*Wha'ppen*
1982—*Special Beat Service* (I.R.S.).

The English Beat (known simply as the Beat everywhere except the U.S.) originated in the British ska revival of the late Seventies. While most of the other revivalist groups foundered when the craze had passed, the Beat were able to parlay their bright melodies, bouncy rhythms and politically incisive lyrics into an enduring career.

The three white members, Wakeling, Cox and Steele, began playing together in 1978. Reggae and other Jamaican rhythms tempered their punk-rock repertoire when they were joined by Morton, a black West Indian who had drummed for Joan Armatrading.

The quartet played its first gig at a Birmingham club in March 1979, opening for a punk group whose black drummer was Ranking Roger; soon after, Roger began "toasting" (chanting over the songs) at its gigs and later joined the Beat as second vocalist.

The Specials released the Beat's debut record, a cover of Smokey Robinson's "Tears of a Clown," on their 2-Tone label in late 1979. For that recording session, they enlisted Saxa, a fifty-year-old Jamaican saxophonist who had played with the Beatles in their Liverpool years and with ska stars like Prince Buster, Desmond Dekker and Laurel Aitken. When the single went to #6 on the U.K. pop charts, Saxa joined the Beat.

The group formed its own label, Go Feet; its first two releases, "Hands Off. . . She's Mine" and "Mirror in the Bathroom," made the U.K. Top Ten, and the third, "Best Friend," made the Top Thirty. After recording their debut album, the Beat toured Europe accompanied by David "Blockhead" Wright, who has been an unofficial member of the group ever since. They returned to Birmingham to find their album at #3, U.K. They toured the U.S. in the fall of 1980, opening for the Pretenders and Talking Heads as the English Beat (to avoid confusion with the L.A. power-pop group the Beat), and returned to tour as headliners in 1981 and '82. In Britain *Wha'ppen* went to #2, and "Too Nice to Talk To" hit #7, while "Drowning" and "Doors of Your Heart" made the Top Forty.

After making *Special Beat Service,* Saxa announced that he would no longer tour with the group, although he would continue to record with them. His stage replacement, Wesley Magoogan, had been a London session reedman and member of Helen O'Connor's band before joining the Beat.

BRIAN ENO

Born Brian Peter George St. John de Baptiste de la Salle Eno, May 15, 1948, Woodbridge, England
1973—*No Pussyfooting* (with Robert Fripp) (Island, U.K.; reissued in the U.S. by Editions EG, 1981) *Here Come the Warm Jets* **1974**—*June 1st, 1974* (with Nico, John Cale, Kevin Ayers) **1975**—*Taking Tiger Mountain by Strategy; Another Green World; Evening Star* (with Robert Fripp) (Island, U.K.; reissued in the U.S. by Editions EG, 1981) *Discreet Music* (Obscure)
1977—*Before and after Science* (Island) *Cluster and Eno* **1978**—*Music for Films* (Polydor, U.K.; reissued in

the U.S. by Editions EG, 1981) *After the Heat* (with Moebius and Rodelius) (Sky) **1979**—*Music for Airports* (Editions EG) **1980**—*Possible Music* (with John Hassell) *The Plateaux of Mirrors* (with Harold Budd) **1981**—*My Life in the Bush of Ghosts* (with David Byrne) (Sire) *Music for Airplay* (Editions EG) **1982**—*On Land* (Editions EG).

Self-described "non-musician" and studio experimentalist Brian Eno has been an important conduit between the conceptualism of art rock and the amateurism of punk. A founding member of Roxy Music, Eno went on to work as a solo artist and a producer/collaborator with Talking Heads, David Bowie, Robert Fripp, Devo, Ultravox, DNA, the Contortions and others. Recent projects have included a series of Ambient Music records (by himself and composers Jon Hassell, Harold Budd and Laraaji) and producing the Ghanaian pop group Edikanfo.

Eno attended the Convent of Jesus and Mary at St. Joseph's College and Winchester and Ipswich art schools. He was influenced by contemporary composers John Tilbury and Cornelius Cardew and occasionally participated in a rock band called Maxwell's Demon. In 1971, he helped start Roxy Music, for whom he played synthesizer and electronically "treated" the other instruments in the band. After working on *Roxy Music* and *For Your Pleasure*, friction with songwriter Bryan Ferry led to his departure in 1973.

Eno put out two albums of free-associative, noisily inventive songs—*Here Come the Warm Jets* and *Taking Tiger Mountain by Strategy*—and produced the Portsmouth Symphonia, an orchestra of quasi-competent musicians playing discordant versions of light classics. His only solo tour, backed by pub band the Winkies in 1974, ended when he was hospitalized for a collapsed lung, although he appears on two concert albums, *June 1st 1974* (with Kevin Ayers, John Cale and Nico) and *801 Live* (801 is the group led by Roxy Music guitarist Phil Manzanera).

Eno has since given up live performance. Although he dabbles on all sorts of instruments, he is most virtuosic on tape recorder, of which he owns dozens, and he is fascinated by the happy accidents of the recording process. He has created a deck of tarotlike cards called Oblique Strategies ("Honor your mistakes as hidden intention"; "Use another color"), and often uses them to make artistic decisions.

In 1975, Eno started his own Obscure Records to release some of his own tapes and works by other composers. He also worked in rock, including two collaborations with Robert Fripp, *No Pussyfooting* (for which he devised the tape echo/delay system known as Frippertronics) and *Evening Star*; a solo album by Robert Calvert of Hawkwind; a trilogy of David Bowie albums (*Low* and *"Heroes,"* 1977; *Lodger,* 1979); albums with the German synthesizer group Cluster; producing three albums with the Talking Heads (*More Songs about Buildings and Food,* 1978; *Fear of Music,* 1979; *Remain in Light,* 1980); debut albums for Ultravox (*Ultravox!,* 1977) and Devo (*Q: Are We Not Men? A: We Are Devo!,* 1978); and a compilation of no-wave bands DNA, the Contortions, Mars and Teenage Jesus and the Jerks (Lydia Lunch) called *No New York* (1978).

Billed under his own name, he has recorded Ambient Music albums (*Discreet Music, Music for Films, Music for Airports*), an album of songs (*Before and After Science*) and an assemblage of found voices and studio backup in collaboration with the Talking Heads' David Byrne (*My Life in the Bush of Ghosts*). Eno moved to New York in the late Seventies and has made some videotapes of the Manhattan skyline that have been shown publicly. In 1980, he was invited to visit Ghana by the Ministry of Culture after expressing his recent interest in African and Arabian music. Eno used ambient music from *On Land* as soundtracks to more recent videotapes.

ESQUERITA
Born New Orleans

Something of a Little Richard imitator, Esquerita (a.k.a. "Eskew Reeder" and "S.Q. Reeder") recorded a series of screamingly raucous singles: "Oh Baby," "Rockin' the Joint," "I Need You" and "Batty Over Hattie." The material did not sell. His biggest success was as the author of Jim Lowe's #1 hit in 1956, "The Green Door," which Esquerita later released as an organ instrumental on Minit Records out of New Orleans. He also recorded, with minimal success, for the Okeh and Instant labels. Esquerita records are currently of great interest to record collectors.

DAVID ESSEX
Born David Cook, July 23, 1947, London
1973—*Rock On* (Columbia) **1974**—*David Essex* **1975**—*All the Fun of the Fair* **1976**—*Out on the Street* **1979**—*Imperial Wizard* (Mercury) **1980**—*Hot Love* **1981**—*Be-Bop the Future.*

In the mid-Seventies, English pop star David Essex inspired teenybopper hysteria in his homeland. However, with the exception of his 1974 gold single, "Rock On," he enjoyed only nominal success in America. He grew up in London's East End, and at 14 he started playing the drums with a succession of amateur bands; by the time he graduated from high school he had become a lead singer.

In the late Sixties, theater columnist Derek Bowman put Essex through voice and dance training and then helped him land a role in the London production of *The Fantasticks.* He moved on to rave reviews as Jesus Christ in *Godspell,* which opened in November 1971 in London. Soon he was a teen pop idol. Essex had a hand in writing most of his U.K. hits ("Lamplight," "Gonna Make You a

Star," "Hold Me Close" and "Rock On"). Most were produced by former commercial jingles writer Jeff Wayne.

In late 1974, Essex toured Britain, where young fans greeted him with hysteria. Essex made two films based on the rags-to-riches-to-rags theme of rock stardom: *That'll Be the Day* (1973), in which he costarred with Ringo Starr and Keith Moon of the Who, and *Stardust* (1975), in which he shared billing with Ringo Starr and Dave Edmunds. He sang Paul McCartney's "Yesterday" in *All This and World War II*, but was forced to turn down a 1974 role in the Who's *Tommy* because of shooting conflicts with *Stardust*. None of these films had much impact in the U.S., but "Rock On" garnered a Grammy nomination.

His reputation as a teenybopper singer proved unshakable in the late Seventies despite attempts (i.e., *Out on the Street*) to attract a more mature audience. He played Che Guevara in the British stage production of *Evita* in 1978 and has since had several more hit singles in Britain.

"SLEEPY" JOHN ESTES

Born January 25, 1903, Ripley, Tennessee; died June 5, 1977, Brownsville, Tennessee
1963—*Legend of* (Delmark)   **1974**—*Down South Blues* (MCA)   *1929–1940* (Folkways).

An important first-generation bluesman, "Sleepy" John Estes lost the sight of one eye as a child and became completely blind by 1950. When Estes was 12, his sharecropper father gave him his first guitar. By the time he was twenty, he was playing local house parties. Shortly thereafter, he moved to Memphis, where he performed on Beale Street with mandolinist Yank Rachell. He supported himself by working the late shift at a trainyard, where his tendency to doze off (later discovered to be a result of blood-pressure problems) earned him his nickname. In the Thirties, Estes moved to Chicago with harmonica player Hammie Nixon. Over the next few years, he worked as a street musician and, occasionally, as a medicine-show barker, hawking swamp root for Dr. Grimm's Traveling Menagerie.

In 1941, Estes and Nixon recorded blues for Bluebird: "Someday, Baby" and "Drop Down, Mama." He subsequently returned to Brownsville, Tennessee, and remained an obscure performer until the late Fifties, when filmmaker Ralph Blumenthal (who was doing a documentary on black migration to the North) rediscovered him. The new attention got Estes a contract with the Chicago-based Delmark label. By 1964, he had gone on his first European tour and appeared at the Newport Folk Festival. Estes' LP *Broke and Hungry* included a guest spot by guitarist Mike Bloomfield, and Estes later played and sang on Ry Cooder's LP *Boomer's Story*. Around the same time, Joy of Cooking had a minor pop hit with the Estes-penned "Going to Brownsville" (1971). Estes died of a stroke in 1977 while preparing to embark on a European tour.

BETTY EVERETT

Born 1939, Mississippi
1974—*Love Rhymes* (Fantasy)   *There'll Come a Time* (MCA)   **1975**—*Happy Endings* (Fantasy)   **1976**—*It's in His Kiss* (DJM).

Soul vocalist Betty Everett had a decade's worth of hits in the Sixties and Seventies. She played piano and sang in church as a child before moving with her family to Chicago at the age of 17. Everett's career peaked with the pop novelty "The Shoop Shoop Song (It's in His Kiss)" (#6, 1964) and "Let It Be Me" (#5, 1964). Lesser hits included "You're No Good," "I Can't Hear You" and "Getting Mighty Crowded." A minor 1964 hit, "Smile," was a duet with Jerry Butler.

Vee Jay's mid-Sixties collapse brought her to a change in labels. After a hitless tenure with ABC-Paramount, Everett made a modest early 1969 comeback on Uni with "There'll Come a Time," "I Can't Say No to You" and "It's Been a Long Time." By 1970, she was recording for Fantasy ("I Got to Tell Somebody," 1971) and achieving respectable soul sales over the next couple of years with albums like *Love Rhymes* and *Happy Endings*. By then, she was taking advantage of her prestigious standing in Europe with regular Continental tours.

EVERLY BROTHERS

Don Everly (b. Feb. I, 1937, Brownie, Ky.), gtr., voc.;
Phil Everly (b. Jan. 19, 1939, Brownie, Ky.), gtr., voc.
1958—*The Everly Brothers* (Cadence)   *Songs Our Daddy Taught Us*   **1960**—*Fabulous Style of the Everly Brothers; It's Everly Time* (Warner Bros.)   **1961**—*A Date with the Everly Brothers*   **1962**—*Golden Hits*   **1963**—*Sing Great Country Hits*   **1965**—*Very Best of*   **1967**—*The Everly Brothers Sing*   **1968**—*Roots*   **1972**—*Stories We Could Tell* (RCA)   **1973**—*Pass the Chicken and Listen*.
Don Everly Solo: **1971**—*Don Everly* (Ode)   **1974**—*Sunset Towers*   **1977**—*Brother Juke Box* (Hickory).
Phil Everly Solo: **1973**—*Star Spangled Springer* (RCA)   **1974**—*Nothing's Too Good for My Baby* (Pye)   *Phil's Diner*   **1975**—*Mystic Line*   **1979**—*Phil Everly* (Elektra).

The Everly Brothers were the children of Midwestern country stars Ike and Margaret Everly. They toured with their parents around the South and Midwest and performed on the family radio show (a taped sample of which appears on *Roots*) throughout their childhoods. In the summer of 1955, still teenagers, they left for Nashville, where they were soon hired by Roy Acuff's publishing company as songwriters. Don had a minor success when his "Thou Shalt Not Steal" became a hit for Kitty Wells. The brothers also recorded a country single entitled "Keep On Loving Me" for Columbia before signing with Cadence in 1957.

Songwriters Felice and Boudleaux Bryant gave them "Bye Bye Love" (previously rejected by thirty acts). It was an international hit, topped the country charts in 1957 and established an Everly style with close country harmonies over a rocking beat.

The Everlys toured internationally with a small combo over the next few years, sporting matching suits and haircuts and leaving fans to identify each brother by the color of his hair (Don's was darker). Their heyday lasted through 1962, by which time they were at Warner Bros., with cumulative record sales of $35 million. In their three years with Cadence (whom they left in a dispute over royalties) they averaged a Top Ten hit every four months, including four #1 country hits: "Bye Bye Love," "Wake Up Little Susie," "All I Have to Do Is Dream" and "Bird Dog."

Some of their most successful records ("Till I Kissed You," "When Will I Be Loved") were written by Don or Phil Everly. Their best-selling single, "Cathy's Clown" (sales of which exceeded two million), came after their switch to Warner Bros., but their success with the new label was short-lived. In June 1962, their string of hits ended with "That's Old-Fashioned" (#9, 1962). They remained major stars in England, but their careers slowed markedly in the U.S. despite continued releases on Warner Bros. ("Bowling Green") and, beginning in 1972, RCA (where they moved shortly after hosting a summer TV series on CBS). Their latter-day backup band was led by keyboardist Warren Zevon and included future Los Angeles studio guitarist Waddy Wachtel.

By then, the brothers' personal lives had gone through serious upheavals (both were addicted to speed for a while, and Don was hospitalized for a nervous breakdown) and their relationship became increasingly acrimonious until it blew up at the John Wayne Theater at Knott's Berry Farm in Hollywood, July 14, 1973. Phil smashed his guitar to the stage and stalked off, leaving Don to announce the duo's obvious breakup. Subsequent solo attempts by both were largely unsuccessful. A reunion concert was planned in 1983.

F

FABIAN
Born Fabian Forte, February 6, 1943, Philadelphia
N.A.—*16 Greatest Hits* (ABC)   *The Very Best of Fabian* (United Artists).

Fabian was marketed alongside several other late-Fifties Philadelphia teen idols, including Frankie Avalon and Bobby Rydell. From 1959 to 1960, his several Chancellor Records Top Ten hits included "Turn Me Loose" (#9, 1959), his signature song, "Tiger" (#3, 1959) and an Elvis Presley imitation, "Hound Dog Man" (#9, 1959), the theme from his first feature film in 1959.

He then turned to acting. In 1960, he starred with John Wayne in *North To Alaska* and in 1966 was featured in *Fireball 500*. In the early Seventies, Fabian occasionally appeared on TV sitcoms, and in 1974 he posed nude for a woman's magazine, a move that he publicly regretted; he claimed he looked "fat and stupid." In 1977, he was involved in a program under the auspices of California Governor Jerry Brown to encourage citizen volunteers to work with mental patients.

TOMMY "BUBBA" FACENDA
Born November 10, 1939, Portsmouth, Virginia

Tommy Facenda came from the same Virginia axis that produced Gary (Anderson) "U.S." Bonds and Gene Vincent. A teenaged acquaintance of Vincent's, Facenda was a clapper boy in the Blue Caps from March to December 1957. In 1958, Norfolk record-company owner and producer Frank Guida attempted to help Facenda launch a solo career. The next year, they recorded "High School U.S.A." in 28 different versions, one for each major urban center. Every version mentioned the area's prominent high schools. It was leased to Atlantic for national distribution and became a Top Thirty hit in 1959. Facenda's followup failed to hit, and in 1960 his not yet successful career was ended by the draft.

THE FACES
Formed 1969, London
Rod Stewart (b. Jan. 10, 1945, London), voc.; Ron Wood (b. June 1, 1947, Eng.), gtr., voc.; Ronnie Lane (b. Apr. 1, 1948, London), bass; Ian McLagan (b. May 12, 1946, Eng.), kybds.; Kenney Jones (b. Sep. 16, 1948, Eng.), drums.
1970—*First Step* (Warner Bros.)   **1971**—*Long Player; A Nod's as Good as a Wink to a Blind Horse*   **1973**—*Ooh La La*   (− Lane; + Tetsu Yamauchi [b. Oct. 21, 1947, Japan], bass)   **1974**—*Overture/Coast to Coast* (Mercury)   **1976**—*Snakes and Ladders: The Best of the Faces* (Warner Bros.).

When Steve Marriott left the Small Faces to start Humble Pie in 1969, the band recruited ex–Jeff Beck Group members Ron Wood and Rod Stewart, who stood a head taller than the original members. From 1969 to 1975, they worked in the lucrative shadow of Stewart's solo career. Loose and boozy onstage and good-timey on record, the Faces made several arena-circuit U.S. tours playing material from Stewart's solo albums as well as the hits he sang with the group—"(I Know) I'm Losing You" (#24, 1971), "Stay with Me" (#17, 1972) and "Cindy Incidentally" (#48, 1973)—while enjoying as wild a lifestyle as possible.

In 1973, Ronnie Lane, an original Small Face, quit and was replaced by ex-Free bassist Tetsu Yamauchi. Lane then started a traveling rock circus, complete with jugglers and fire eaters, called the Passing Show, and recorded four albums with Slim Chance; he also made *Rough Mix* with Pete Townshend of the Who. In the late Seventies, Lane was debilitated by multiple sclerosis.

Meanwhile, the Faces were slowly dissolving. Wood joined the Rolling Stones in 1976, and McLagan regularly participates in Stones tours and such projects as the New Barbarians; he also records solo albums. Jones, who reunited with the original Small Faces in 1977–78, replaced Keith Moon in the Who in 1978.

FAIRPORT CONVENTION/FAIRPORT
Formed 1967, London
Judy Dyble, piano, voc.; Richard Thompson (b. Apr. 3, 1949, London), gtr., voc.; Simon Nicol (b. London), gtr., banjo, dulcimer, bass, viola, voc.; Ashley "Tyger" Hutchings, bass, voc., gtr.; Martin Lamble (b. 1950, Eng.; d. Aug. 1969, London), drums; Ian Matthews (b. Ian MacDonald, 1946, Eng.), voc., perc., gtr.
1968—*Fairport Convention* (Polydor)   (− Dyble; + Sandy Denny [b. Jan. 6, 1947, London; d. Apr. 21, 1978, London], gtr., voc., kybds.)   **1969**—*What We Did on Our Holiday* (Island)   (− Matthews; − Lamble; + Dave Swarbrick [b. Apr. 5, 1947, London], voc., violin, mandolin)   *Unhalfbricking*   (+ Dave Mattacks [b. 1948, London], drums, voc., kybds.)   *Liege and Lief*   (− Denny; − Hutchings; + Dave Pegg [b. Nov. 2, 1947, Eng.], gtr., viola, voc.)   **1970**—*Full House*   **1971**—*Angel Delight*   (− Thompson; − Nicol; + Roger Hill [b. Eng.], gtr., mandolin);   *Babbacombe*

Lee (− Hill; − Mattacks; + Tom Farnell, drums; + David Rea, gtr.; − Farnell; − Rea; + Trevor Lucas [b. Dec. 25, 1943, Australia], gtr.; + Jerry Donahue [b. Sep. 24, 1946, New York City], gtr., voc.; + Mattacks) **1972**—*The History of Fairport Convention* **1973**—*Rosie; Nine* (+ Denny) **1974**—*Live Convention (A Moveable Feast)* (− Mattacks; + Paul Warren, drums; − Warren; + Bruce Rowland [b. Eng.], drums) **1975**—*Rising for the Moon* **1976**—(− Denny; − Lucas; − Donahue; − Mattacks) **1977**— *Live at the L.A. Troubadour.*

Fairport Convention seeded Britain's folk-rock movement, and most British musicians who've tried to play Celtic folk material on modern instruments have some connection with Fairport or its many offshoots. The group's repertoire included traditional British songs rearranged for electric instruments, songs by Bob Dylan and other current songwriters, and originals by Richard Thompson and Ian Matthews (both founders) and Sandy Denny. As the Bunch, Fairport and friends also recorded an album of Fifties and Sixties rock classics entitled *Rock On.* Their eclecticism inspired their imitators and descendants.

The original Fairport Convention—at first called the Ethnic Shuffle Orchestra—included folk-club veterans who were also Byrds fans, and was named after Simon Nicol's house in Muswell Hill, London. From the beginning, the lineup was unstable. Judy Dyble left in 1968 to form Trader Horne and later Penguin Dust; her replacement, Sandy Denny, had sung with the Strawbs before their first album. Matthews left after *What We Did on Our Holidays* (in the U.S., *Fairport Convention*) to form the country-pop band Matthews Southern Comfort ("Woodstock," 1971) and to record solo and with the short-lived Plainsong. Lamble was killed in an equipment-van crash right before *Unhalfbricking* was released.

Fairport had its first European hit with *Unhalfbricking's* "Si Tu Dois Partir," a French translation of Dylan's "If You Gotta Go, Go Now." Denny, whose song "Who Knows Where the Time Goes" was covered by Judy Collins, left to form Fotheringay with husband Trevor Lucas and Jerry Donahue; but in 1973, Denny, Lucas and Donahue rejoined Fairport. *A Moveable Feast* was a live set from Denny's second stint with the band.

By then, Thompson had started a solo career, and fiddler Dave Swarbrick had joined Fairport. Swarbrick led the group in its later years, and it toured internationally. By 1976, the band had dropped "Convention" from its name; and by 1979, Fairport had given up. Pegg joined Jethro Tull; Swarbrick recorded solo albums. Nicol and Mattacks toured with Richard and Linda Thompson (who had sung with the Bunch as Linda Peters) in 1982. Most of Fairport's tangled career is documented on *Fairport Chronicles.*

ADAM FAITH
Born Terry Nelhams, June 23, 1940, London
1974—*I Survive* (Warner Bros.).

A pop idol in pre-Beatlemania England, Adam Faith had over a dozen major hits there in the early Sixties. He formed a teenage skiffle group called the Worried Men with fellow messenger boys at Rank Screen Services. By 1958, he was recording solo as Adam Faith. In 1959, he recorded "What Do You Want," which climbed to #1 and became Britain's best-selling record in 1960. More U.K. hits followed: "Poor Me" (#1, 1960, U.K.), "Someone Else's Baby" (#2, 1960, U.K.) and "Lonely Pup" (#4, 1960, U.K.).

Faith became interested in acting during the Sixties, appearing in *Beat Girl* (1962) and several other English films, as well as TV series like "Drumbeat" (1959) and "Budgie" in the early Seventies. In 1972, at the urging of David Courtney, the drummer from his backup band of the Sixties (another stalwart in that band was guitarist Russ Ballard, later of Argent), he eased back into music by becoming Leo Sayer's manager and producer (along with Courtney). He and Courtney also teamed up to produce Roger Daltrey's debut solo LP, *Daltrey.*

The early Seventies also found Faith filming *Stardust* with David Essex. After recovering from a severe car accident in 1973, Faith released an unsuccessful comeback record, *I Survive.* In 1977, he produced a star-studded comeback LP for British skiffle king Lonnie Donegan.

MARIANNE FAITHFULL
Born circa 1947, London
1965—*Come My Way* (Decca) **1966**—*Faithful Forever* (London) **1977**—*Faithless* (NEMS) **1979**—*Broken English* (Island) **1981**—*Dangerous Acquaintances* **1983**—*A Child's Adventure.*

Marianne Faithfull first appeared on the British pop scene as the angel-faced, sweet-voiced singer of "As Tears Go By" (#9 U.K.) in 1964, when she was 18. The song was written for her by Rolling Stones Mick Jagger and Keith Richards, and although she had three more hits independently of the Stones—"Come and Stay with Me" (#4 U.K.), "This Little Bird" (#6 U.K.) and "Summer Nights" (#10 U.K.), all in 1965—she became better known as Jagger's girlfriend than as a singer.

Faithfull is the daughter of a London University lecturer in Renaissance studies and an Austrian baroness descended from Leopold von Sacher-Masoch (from whose name "masochism" is derived). She attended St. Joseph's Convent School in Reading until she was 17. At 18, she married London art dealer John Dunbar, through whom she met Jagger. She and Dunbar were separated after the birth of their son, Nicholas, in 1965, and divorced in 1970.

During the late Sixties, Faithfull became pregnant by

Marianne Faithfull

Jagger (she miscarried) and was later heavily involved in drug use (she was hospitalized following an overdose on the Australian movie set of *Ned Kelly*, in which she was to costar with Jagger). Although she abandoned her recording career after 1966, she contributed lyrics (uncredited) to the Rolling Stones' "Sister Morphine." However, her major activity after 1966 was acting: with Alain Delon in a French film, *The Girl on the Motorcycle*, in 1968; in Chekhov's *Three Sisters* at the Royal Court Theatre, London, in 1969; and as Ophelia opposite Nicol Williamson in a film production of *Hamlet* in 1970.

Following her breakup with Jagger in 1970 and her widely publicized eight-month commitment to a hospital to cure her heroin addiction, Faithfull withdrew from public life, reappearing only briefly in 1974 on a David Bowie television special. In 1977, she recorded her first album in over ten years, and although it received little notice, it led to her signing with Island Records in 1979. Her Island debut, *Broken English*—marked by stark instrumentation, venomous lyrics and Faithfull's raspy vocals—was barely recognizable as the work of the woman who sang "As Tears Go By." A platinum album, it was followed by two other well-received albums for Island.

GEORGIE FAME

Born Clive Powell, June 26, 1943, Leigh, England
1966—*Yeh, Yeh* (Imperial) *Get Away* **1968**—*The Ballad of Bonnie and Clyde* (Epic) **1974**—*Georgie Fame* (Island, U.K.) **1979**—*Georgie Fame Right Now!* (Pye, U.K.).

Georgie Fame is best known in the U.S. for his 1968 novelty hit "The Ballad of Bonnie and Clyde," and as an R&B/jazz singer in Britain. Fame played keyboards in Eddie Cochran's band during his last tour, before English impresario Larry Parnes steered him to a 1960 job with Billy Fury's band, the Blue Flames. Parnes also suggested the name change.

In 1962, Fame left Fury and took along the Blue Flames. By the mid-Sixties Fame was playing jazzy R&B; guitarist John McLaughlin was in the band for a short time. In late 1963, his expanded group (including Cream's Ginger Baker) released two instrumental singles followed by their influential 1964 set, *Rhythm and Blues at the Flamingo*.

In 1965, Fame had a #1 U.K. hit, "Yeh Yeh," which also slipped into the U.S. Top Thirty. He had another U.K. #1 in 1966 with "Get Away." When Fame disbanded the Blue Flames in September 1966, the lineup included future Jimi Hendrix Experience drummer Mitch Mitchell.

Fame's first solo LP, *Sound Venture* (Columbia), was MOR jazz; the next year he played an Albert Hall concert with Count Basie. His ragtime novelty hit, 1968's "Bonnie and Clyde," hit #7 in the U.S. From 1971 to 1973, he teamed up with former Animals keyboardist Alan Price. He also recorded an LP, *Shorty*, in the early Seventies with his group. In 1974, Fame reincarnated the Blue Flames (including Colin Green) and released an album of R&B ballads, *Georgie Fame*. He continued to tour, including U.S. club dates in early 1982.

FAMILY

Formed 1966, Leicester, England
Roger Chapman (b. Apr. 8, 1944, Leicester), voc.; Rob Townsend (b. July 7, 1947, Leicester), drums; Rick Grech (b. Nov. 1, 1946, Bordeaux, France), bass, violin, voc.; Jim King (b. ca. 1945, Eng.), sax, flute; Charlie Whitney (b. June 4, 1944, Eng.), gtr., voc.
1968—*Music in a Doll's House* (Reprise) **1969**—*Family Entertainment* (− Grech; − King; + John "Poli" Palmer [b. May 25, 1943, Eng.], percussion, flute, piano; + John Weider [b. Apr. 21, 1947, Eng.], bass, violin) **1970**—*A Song for Me; Anyway* (United Artists) (− Weider; + John Wetton, bass, voc.) **1971**—*Fearless* (− Wetton; + Jim Cregan, bass, gtr.) **1972**—*Bandstand* (− Palmer; + Tony Ashton, kybds., voc.) **1973**—*It's Only a Movie* **1974**—*Best of Family* (Reprise).

Although Family's wildly eclectic progressive rock made them hitmakers in England, they remained relatively unknown in the U.S. The band featured the often grating, goatish vibrato singing of Roger Chapman and a repertoire by Chapman and Charlie Whitney, tempered in later years by the jazzy flute and vibraphone of John "Poli" Palmer. The group started in Leicester as the Farinas, then turned into the pinstripe-suited Roaring Sixties and finally settled on the Family name.

Traffic's Dave Mason (with Jimmy Miller) coproduced their debut. Their harder-rocking followup, *Family Entertainment,* prompted a U.S. tour. Unfortunately, Rick Grech quit the day before it was to start in order to join Blind Faith, and Family's debut performance at the Fillmore East ended in a fistfight between Chapman and promoter Bill Graham. A few days later, Chapman lost both his voice and his visa, and Family returned to England. The group's reputation continued to grow at home, with singles hits "In My Own Time" (from *Anyway*) and "Burlesque" (from *Bandstand*). Family's appearance at the 1970 Rotterdam Festival was filmed in *Stomping Ground,* and they were featured in Jenny Fabian's novel *Groupie.*

Family made further U.S. tours in 1970, and opened for Elton John in 1972, but never found a U.S. audience despite FM airplay for *Fearless* and *Bandstand. It's Only a Movie,* their final album, was released in Britain on their own Raft label in 1973. That fall, they played a farewell tour of England, including a final gig in Leicester. Chapman and Whitney founded Streetwalkers. Cregan and Palmer appear on Linda Lewis' 1973 *Fathoms Deep.* Cregan later joined Rod Stewart's band, and Palmer went into session work, appearing on albums by Pete Townshend of the Who.

FANNY
Formed 1970, California
June Millington (b. 1949, Manila), gtr., voc.; Alice de Buhr (b. 1950, Mason City, Ia.), drums; Nicoel Barclay (b. Apr. 21, 1951, Washington, D.C.), kybds.; Jean Millington (b. 1950, Manila), bass, voc.
1970—*Fanny* (Reprise) 1971—*Charity Ball* 1972— *Fanny Hill* 1973—*Mother's Pride* 1974—(− Jean Millington; − de Buhr; + Patti Quatro [b. Detroit], bass; + Brie Brandt-Howard, drums) 1975—*Rock and Roll Survivors* (Casablanca) (− Barclay; − Brandt-Howard).

Fanny was one of the first all-female hard-rock groups. The band's nucleus was the Philippine-born Millington sisters, who moved to Sacramento when their father, a Navy man, was transferred. They formed their first quartet, the Sveltes, with girlfriends in high school. In 1968, they bought an old Greyhound bus and toured West Coast clubs as Wild Honey.

Producer Richard Perry saw them and helped them get a contract with Warner Bros. in 1969. They changed their name to Fanny at George Harrison's suggestion, and Perry produced their first three albums. (The group also backed up Barbra Streisand on her 1970 LP, *Stoney End.*) Their second LP, *Charity Ball,* yielded their only chart single with its title cut. Perhaps their most fully realized effort was *Fanny Hill,* recorded at the Beatles' Apple studios in London. Their late 1973 release, *Mother's*

Pride, featuring their hardest rock, was produced by Todd Rundgren.

Around the same time, they toured extensively (including several dates with Jethro Tull) performing their rock opera, *Rock and Roll Survivors.* Bassist Patti Quatro, Suzy Quatro's elder sister, replaced Jean Millington. By mid-decade, the group had broken up. Keyboardist and chief songwriter Nickey Barclay, who had been included in Joe Cocker's Mad Dogs and Englishmen, went on to form her own group called Good News in 1976 and released an Ariola-American LP, *Diamond in a Junk Yard.* By 1979, Fanny founder Jean Millington was married to ex–David Bowie guitarist Earl Slick, playing club dates, and recording and producing for Olivia Records.

RICHARD AND MIMI FARIÑA
Richard Fariña (b. 1937, N.Y.; d. Apr. 30, 1966, Carmel, Calif.), dulcimer, voc.; Mimi Fariña (b. Mimi Baez, Apr. 30, 1945), gtr., voc.
1965—*Celebrations for a Grey Day* (Vanguard) 1966— *Reflections in a Crystal Wind* 1968—*Richard Fariña; Memories* 1971—*The Best of Richard and Mimi Fariña; Mimi Fariña and Tom Jans* (A&M).

The Fariñas were an American husband-and-wife folk duo whose promising career ended with Richard's death in 1966.

Richard was born to Irish and Cuban parents. Although his parents had emigrated to the United States in the Twenties, Fariña spent extended periods during his youth in Cuba as well as in Brooklyn and Northern Ireland. While living in Northern Ireland in the mid-Fifties, he became actively involved with the IRA, and the British government had him deported. He later moved to Cuba and supported Castro. In 1959, he moved to Greenwich Village and began performing; he was briefly married to folksinger Carolyn Hester.

In 1963, he wed Joan Baez's younger sister, Mimi, in Paris. The couple moved to California, where they began working as a duo. They recorded three albums for Vanguard in the mid-Sixties: *Celebrations for a Grey Day, Reflections in a Crystal Wind* (one of the earliest fusions of folk material with a rock rhythm section) and *Memories.* Material from all three was later included on Vanguard's *Best of Richard and Mimi Fariña.* Throughout, Fariña maintained his literary career, writing plays, magazine articles and *Been Down So Long It Looks Like Up to Me,* a novel concerned with the cultural transition from the beatniks to the hippies. He was returning home from a promotional party for the book when he died in a motorcycle crash in 1966—on his wife's twenty-first birthday. In 1983, the book was reprinted.

Mimi withdrew from public for a few years, but has subsequently worked as both a singer and an actress (notably as a member of the Committee). As the Sixties closed, she performed and recorded occasionally, often with other partners (including Tom Jans) and occasionally shared the stage with her sister, Joan. In the early Seventies, she helped establish Bread and Roses, a charitable organization that provides entertainment for prisoners, hospital patients and other institutionalized people.

CHRIS FARLOWE
Born John Henry Deighton, October 13, 1940, Essex, England
1970—*From Here to Mama Rosa* (with the Hill) (Polydor) *Fabulous Chris Farlowe and the Thunderbirds* (CBS) *Paint It Farlowe* (Immediate).

A minor English R&B figure in the early Sixties, vocalist Farlowe's records sold poorly until mid-decade, when Mick Jagger gave him his first major U.K. hit with a Jagger-Richards composition, "Out of Time."
John Deighton began playing the guitar at age 13 and soon formed the John Henry Skiffle Goup, which won the All-English Skiffle Championship. By 1962, he was calling himself Chris Farlowe and singing R&B at London's Flamingo Club with his Thunderbirds. Their early recordings included "Buzz with the Fuzz" and "Stormy Monday Blues" (which Farlowe released under the alias Little Joe Cook).
But it was only after Jagger (who sang occasional backup vocals on Farlowe's records) became his patron that the Thunderbirds sustained any serious impact. Farlowe disbanded the Thunderbirds in late 1966, but reformed them again the next year (with Carl Palmer on drums). In 1970, Farlowe sang with Colosseum, leaving in November 1971 to join Atomic Rooster for two LPs.
Concurrently, he worked on various solo projects, including a 1970 stint with a band called the Hill. In 1972, Farlowe retired from music to run his Nazi war memorabilia shop in North London. In 1975, he attempted a last-ditch comeback by reissuing "Out of Time" and an LP, *The Chris Farlowe Band Live*. He has since retired from the music business.

WES FARRELL
Born 1940, New York City

Pop songwriter Wes Farrell was responsible for late-Fifties and early-Sixties soul-rock hits like "Come a Little Bit Closer" (Jay and the Americans), "Hang On Sloopy" (McCoys) and "Goodbye Baby" (Solomon Burke), the last two collaborations with Bert Berns. He started his career with R&B producer Luther Dixon and joined Roosevelt Music in 1961 as a staff writer and talent scout (he signed Neil Diamond as a writer). By 1963, his tunes were regularly represented on the pop and soul charts. In 1967, he steered his publishing company into the bubble-gum market, concentrating on MGM acts like the Cowsills, Brooklyn Bridge and Every Mother's Son. He cre-

ated the made-for-TV band the Partridge Family and started the Chelsea and Roxbury record labels in the early Seventies.

THE FEELIES
Formed 1976, Haledon, New Jersey
Bill Million (b. William Clayton, Haledon), gtrs., voc.; Glenn Mercer (b. Haledon), gtr., voc.; Vinny DeNunzio (b. Aug. 15, 1956), drums; Keith DeNunzio (a.k.a. Keith Clayton) (b. Apr. 27, 1958, Reading, Penn.), bass.
1978—(− Vinny DeNunzio, + Anton Fier, drums)
1980—*Crazy Rhythms* (Stiff) 1981—(− Fier, + Stanley Demeski, drums; + Dave Weckerman, percussion).

With their quirky rhythms, frantically strummed "treated" guitars, pop melodies and nonsensical lyrics, the Feelies epitomized New York's post-punk bands. By performing only occasionally (usually on national holidays like the Fourth of July or Arbor Day) and recording even less often, however, they remained a cult band.
Glenn Mercer and Bill Million, the group's songwriters, met at high school in Haledon, New Jersey, in the late Sixties. They formed the Feelies with brothers Keith and Vinny DeNunzio in 1976. Their live debut at Max's Kansas City early the next year and subsequent appearances at other New York new wave venues placed them in the vanguard of that city's rock experimentalists. In the fall of 1978, Vinny DeNunzio left the group to play with Richard Lloyd (Television) and was replaced by Anton Fier.
Adamant about producing their own records, the Feelies did not sign a long-term recording contract until 1980, although they did record a single, "Fa Ce La," for the English independent label Rough Trade in 1979. After they recorded *Crazy Rhythms*, Mercer and Million did some work in films as soundtrack composers and as performers.
In 1982, Keith DeNunzio left the band and formed the World, which later broke up. Million and Mercer renamed their band the Willies and performed occasionally, with their ex-drummer Fier sometimes sitting in; Fier has also drummed for Pere Ubu. Other band members formed Young Wu and the Trypes, and in early 1983 the three bands were planning to share an album.

JOSÉ FELICIANO
Born September 10, 1945, Lares, Puerto Rico
1968—*Feliciano!* (RCA) 1969—*Feliciano/10 to 23; Alive, Alive-O!* 1970—*Fireworks* 1971—*Encore! José Feliciano's Finest Performances; José Feliciano* 1972—*José Feliciano Sings* 1973—*Compartments* 1974—*And the Feeling's Good* 1975—*Just Wanna Rock 'n' Roll* 1976—*Sweet Soul Music* (Private Stock) 1981—*José Feliciano* (Motown).

José Feliciano reached worldwide popularity with his obsessive flamenco-flavored versions of pop hits such as

"Light My Fire" (#3, 1968). Born blind, Feliciano was the second of 12 children of a poor Puerto Rican farmer; he grew up in New York's Spanish Harlem. Feliciano was introduced to the accordion and the guitar as a child. He first performed at the Bronx's El Teatro Puerto Rico. At 17, he dropped out of high school and began playing Greenwich Village clubs and coffeehouses like the Cafe Id (where he met his wife/manager, Hilda Perez) and Gerde's Folk City (where he was discovered).

The next year, he released his first single, "Everybody Do the Click," and album, *The Voice and Guitar of José Feliciano*, and appeared at the Newport Folk Festival. Initially, most of his releases were in Spanish, intended for the Latin market (in 1966, he played before 100,000 in Buenos Aires). In 1968, his cover of the Doors' "Light My Fire" hit the Top Five, nearly equaling the success of the original version. It went gold, as did *Feliciano!* He followed up with minor hits ("Hi Heel Sneakers") and

Festivals

Rock festivals tend to verge on disaster. The combination of huge crowds, various stimulants, vague seating arrangements, inadequate sanitation and, usually, bad weather has somehow been no deterrent to festivalgoers who expect a communal experience while seeing a slew of musicians at a bargain price. There had been jazz and folk festivals at least since the Fifties, notably the Newport Jazz and Folk festivals. Following is a chronological list of past major rock festivals.

Monterey International Pop Festival, Monterey, California, January 16–18, 1967; attendance: 50,000; tickets: $3.50–$6.50.

Performers included Janis Joplin, Otis Redding, Jimi Hendrix, the Who, the Grateful Dead, the Byrds, the Jefferson Airplane, the Association, the Electric Flag, the Paul Butterfield Blues Band, Canned Heat, the Blues Project, Laura Nyro, Hugh Masekela, Buffalo Springfield, Country Joe and the Fish, Booker T. and the MGs, the Mamas and the Papas, Quicksilver Messenger Service and Ravi Shankar.

As the first major rock festival, Monterey spawned a movie (D. A. Pennebaker's *Monterey Pop*), songs (Eric Burdon's "Monterey"), albums and good vibes galore. The performers played for free.

Newport Pop Festival, Costa Mesa, California, August 4–5, 1968; attendance: 100,000.

Performers included Tiny Tim, Iron Butterfly, the Paul Butterfield Blues Band, the Jefferson Airplane, the Byrds, Illinois Speed Press, Steppenwolf, Quicksilver Messenger Service, the Chambers Brothers and the James Cotton Blues Band.

Miami Pop Festival, Miami, Florida, December 28–30, 1968; attendance: 99,000; tickets: $7, $6 in advance.

Performers included Chuck Berry, Fleetwood Mac, Buffy Sainte-Marie, Flatt and Scruggs, Steppenwolf, Richie Havens, Sweetwater, Terry Reid, the McCoys, Pacific Gas and Electric, Marvin Gaye, Joni Mitchell, the Box Tops, Iron Butterfly, Jr. Walker and the All Stars, Joe Tex, the Grateful Dead, the Turtles, Ian and Sylvia, others.

Newport '69, Devonshire Downs, Northridge, California, June 20–22, 1969; attendance: 150,000.

Performers included Jimi Hendrix, Taj Mahal, Creedence Clearwater Revival, Jethro Tull, Spirit, Joe Cocker, Ike and Tina Turner, the Rascals, Johnny Winter, the Byrds, Booker T. and the MGs, Eric Burdon.

Presaging Altamont, there were violent gate-crashing incidents. A motorcycle gang, the Street Racers, had been hired for security.

Newport Jazz Festival, Newport, Rhode Island, July 3–6, 1969; attendance: 78,000.

The only edition of the jazz festival to include rock groups, the festival booked Jeff Beck, Led Zeppelin, Ten Years After, Blood, Sweat and Tears, James Brown and Jethro Tull.

Atlanta Pop Festival, Atlanta, Georgia, July 4–5, 1969; attendance: 140,000.

Performers included Ten Wheel Drive, Delaney and Bonnie, Canned Heat, Ian and Sylvia, Johnny Winter, Led Zeppelin, the Staple Singers, Chicago, Spirit, Joe Cocker, Creedence Clearwater Revival, others.

Atlantic City Pop Festival, Atlantic City, New Jersey, August 1–3, 1969; attendance: 110,000; tickets: $6 each day, $13 for all three.

Performers included the Jefferson Airplane, B. B. King, Booker T. and the MGs, Joni Mitchell, the Chambers Brothers, Dr. John, Iron Butterfly, Procol Harum, Janis Joplin, Arthur Brown, Three Dog Night, Canned Heat, Little Richard, Santana, others.

Woodstock Music and Arts Festival, Bethel, New York, August 15–17,

1969; attendance: over 400,000.

Performers included Santana, Ravi Shankar, Richie Havens, the Incredible String Band, Canned Heat, Sly and the Family Stone, the Jefferson Airplane, the Grateful Dead, Jimi Hendrix, the Who, Blood, Sweat and Tears, Joan Baez, Creedence Clearwater Revival, the Band, Arlo Guthrie, Bert Sommer, Quill, Melanie, Johnny Winter, Ten Years After, Country Joe and the Fish, Mountain, Tim Hardin, Sweetwater, Joe Cocker, John Sebastian, Keef Hartley, Sha Na Na, the Paul Butterfield Blues Band, Crosby, Stills, Nash and Young.

Woodstock was a quantum leap for festivals; its huge attendance quickly broke down all security, turning it into a free festival. The country roads in upstate New York had twenty-mile-long traffic jams, and the rain turned Max Yasgur's 600-acre farm into mud. In hindsight, it became a symbol for a communal, peaceful event, a model for the "Woodstock Nation."

There were three deaths, two births, and four miscarriages. Songs about it include Joni Mitchell's "Woodstock" and Eric Burdon's "Up in Woodstock." A film, *Woodstock,* was made by Michael Wadleigh; two albums of its music, *Woodstock* and *Woodstock II,* appeared. As the Woodstock myth spread, promoters began to scout sites for hitherto undreamed-of crowds.

Texas International Pop Festival, Lewisville, Texas, August 30– September 1, 1969; attendance: 120,000.

Performers included Johnny Winter, Janis Joplin, Rotary Connection, Sam and Dave, Grand Funk Railroad, Led Zeppelin, Delaney and Bonnie, the Incredible String Band, Nazz, Santana, Spirit, Sweetwater, Tony Joe White, Chicago, others.

Altamont, Livermore, California, December 6, 1969; attendance: 300,000; free.

Performers included the Rolling Stones, the Jefferson Airplane, the Flying Burrito Brothers, Santana, Crosby, Stills, Nash and Young.

What began as a free concert by the Rolling Stones at the Altamont Speedway was an all-day "festival" that turned sour when 18-year-old Meredith Hunter was stabbed to death in front of the stage. A suspect, Hell's Angel Alan Passaro, was identified from footage shot for the Rolling Stones documentary *Gimme Shelter,* but he was acquitted for "justifiable homicide." There were three other deaths.

Altamont was the subject of "The New Speedway Boogie" by the Grateful Dead, as well as the Maysles Brothers' *Gimme Shelter.* After Altamont, local politicking and public outcry put a damper on such festivals as Louisiana's Celebration of Life, Connecticut's Powder Ridge Rock Festival and San Francisco's Wild West in 1970– 71.

Atlanta Pop Festival, Byron, Georgia, July 3–5, 1970; attendance: over 200,000.

Performers included Jimi Hendrix, Johnny Winter, Jethro Tull, Rare Earth, Mountain, Procol Harum, the Chambers Brothers, the Allman Brothers, Lee Michaels, others.

Mar y Sol, Vega Baja, Puerto Rico, April 1–3, 1972; attendance: 30,000.

Performers included the Allman Brothers Band, the Mahavishnu Orchestra, Rod Stewart, Osibisa, Dave Brubeck, Emerson, Lake and Palmer, the J. Geils Band, Dr. John, Alice Cooper, others.

Mar y Sol solved security problems by holding the festival on an island accessible only to ticket holders. It yielded an album, *Mar y Sol.*

Mount Pocono Festival, Long Pond, Pennsylvania, July 8, 1972; attendance: 200,000.

Performers included Emerson, Lake and Palmer, Three Dog Night, the J. Geils Band, Humble Pie, Rod Stewart, others.

A far less eclectic bill than the earlier festivals, it concentrated on hard rock.

Watkins Glen Summer Jam, Watkins Glen, New York, July 28, 1973; attendance: 600,000.

Performers included the Band, the Grateful Dead and the Allman Brothers Band.

California Jam I, Ontario, California, April 6, 1974; attendance: 200,000.

Performers included Emerson, Lake and Palmer, Black Sabbath, Deep Purple, Black Oak Arkansas, Seals and Crofts, Rare Earth, the Eagles, Earth, Wind and Fire.

This festival and California Jam II were staged by ABC-TV and filmed for later broadcast.

California Jam II, Ontario, California, March 18, 1978; attendance: 250,000.

Performers included Santana, Dave Mason, Bob Welch, Ted Nugent, Aerosmith, Heart, Mahogany Rush, Rubicon.

Heatwave, Toronto, Canada, August 23, 1980; attendance: 50,000; tickets: $20 advance, $30 on-site.

Performers included Talking Heads, Elvis Costello, the Pretenders, the B-52's, Rockpile, the Rumour, Teenage Head.

Intended as a "new wave Woodstock," Heatwave lost $1 million.

The US Festival, San Bernardino, California, September 3–5, 1982; attendance: 400,000; tickets: $17.50 per day, $37.50 all three.

Performers included Fleetwood Mac, Tom Petty, the Police, Jackson

Browne, Pat Benatar, the Cars, Talking Heads, the Grateful Dead, the Kinks, the B-52's, Dave Edmunds, Santana, Eddie Money, Gang of Four, the Ramones, English Beat, Jerry Jeff Walker.

Bankrolled by Apple Computers founder Steven Wozniak, it lost a considerable amount of money, but by all reports was a technical masterpiece, including video blowups of the performers.

The US Festival '83, Southern California, May 28, 29, 30 and June 4 (country music day), 1983; attendance: 725,000.

Performers included the Clash, the Stray Cats, Men at Work, Judas Priest, Ozzy Osbourne, Scorpions, Missing Persons, U2, the Pretenders, Stevie Nicks, Van Halen and David Bowie.

Like 1982's US festival, this was underwritten by Steve Wozniak and

his Unuson corporation, and featured video blowups of the performers onstage. Although the attendance figures far surpassed 1982's, so did the performers' fees. David Bowie and Van Halen each received over $1 million. As a result, US '83 lost millions; Wozniak vowed he would not produce another. There were two deaths at the site, one a murder.

---

released a controversial rendition of "The Star-Spangled Banner" recorded live at the fifth game of the 1968 World Series.

Subsequent U.S. success has been meager, although in the early Seventies he recorded with Joni Mitchell ("Free Man in Paris"). Nevertheless, he has over thirty gold records in various countries and occasional U.S. hits like the 1974 theme song to the television series "Chico and the Man."

One of the first Western singers to appear behind the Iron Curtain, he has toured frequently each year for almost two decades. Besides guitar, Feliciano also plays bass, banjo, keyboards, timbales, mandolin and harmonica. His occasional compositions ("Rain," "Destiny") have been covered by Anne Murray and Blue Swede. He frequently appears on television shows, including dramatic roles on "Kung Fu" and "McMillan and Wife." Feliciano contributed to the soundtrack of the early-Seventies film *MacKenna's Gold*. He signed with Motown in 1980, and his label debut, *José Feliciano*, was produced by Berry Gordy, Jr., and Suzee Ikeda.

FREDDY FENDER
Born Baldemar Huerta, 1937, San Benito, Texas
1977—*Best of Freddy Fender* (Dot)   **1978**—*Swamp Gold* (ABC).

Freddy Fender is a Tex-Mex country rocker who specializes in a polka-waltz style called *conjunto* and is known for his tearful, choked up singing in Spanish and English. Fender began playing the guitar as a child, and started performing professionally in the late Fifties. At one Corpus Christi nightclub, he was the victim of an after-hours fight that left his nose permanently crooked and a deep knife scar in his neck.

An early recording, a Spanish version of Elvis Presley's "Don't Be Cruel," was the first of a string of local hits. In 1959, he cut "Holy One" and the original version of "Wasted Days and Wasted Nights," which sold 100,000 copies. On Friday, May 13, 1960, shortly after the release

of yet another moderate hit, "Crazy, Crazy, Baby," Fender was arrested for possession of one marijuana cigarette in Baton Rouge, Louisiana. He subsequently served three years in the Angola State Prison.

Upon his release, he played bars in New Orleans and in San Benito, Texas, from 1963 until 1968. By 1975, he had released more than 100 records on regional labels, and in early 1974 he met producer Huey Meaux, who masterminded Fender's 1975 national pop breakthrough, "Before the Next Teardrop Falls." Fender's subsequent releases have kept him before country audiences.

LEO FENDER
Born August 10, 1909, Buena Park, California

Striking a chord heard around the world, Leo Fender perfected the electric guitar and was essential to the history of rock & roll. Fender was not a guitarist, yet he began experimenting with an electrically amplified guitar in the Forties. In 1948, the Fender Broadcaster became the first mass-produced solid-body electric guitar, followed three years later by the first solid-body bass, the Fender Precision. In 1950, Fender had to change the trade name from Broadcaster to Telecaster, but the design has changed very little over the past thirty years.

Fender's Stratocaster was introduced in 1954 and was the favorite model of Buddy Holly, Hank Marvin (the Shadows) and Jimi Hendrix. The Fender company was sold to CBS in 1965. Rivaled only by Gibson (whose Les Paul model is the most widely played electric) for international prominence in guitars, Fender also produces a popular line of amplifiers. He founded G&L Musical Products in 1980 and continues to supervise operations.

THE FIFTH DIMENSION
Formed circa 1967, Los Angeles
Original lineup: LaMonte McLemore (b. Sep. 17, 1940, St. Louis), voc.; Marilyn McCoo (b. Sep. 30, 1943, Jersey City), voc.; Ron Townson (b. Jan. 20, 1941, St. Louis), voc.; Florence LaRue Gordon (b. Feb. 4, 1944,

Penn.), voc.; Billy Davis, Jr. (b. June 26, 1940, St. Louis), voc.

1967—*Up, Up and Away* (Soul City) 1968—*The Magic Garden; Stoned Soul Picnic* 1969—*The Age of Aquarius* 1970—*Greatest Hits; The July 5th Album Portrait* (Bell) 1971—*Love's Lines, Angles and Rhymes; The Fifth Dimension Live; Reflections* 1972—*Individually and Collectively; Greatest Hits on Earth* 1975—*Earthbound* (ABC) 1978—*Star Dancing* (Motown).

The Fifth Dimension had a string of pop-soul hits in the late Sixties (eight gold LPs, six gold singles), and they introduced songs by Laura Nyro and Jim Webb. Both the Fifth Dimension and the Friends of Distinction were offshoots of a vocal group, the Hi-Fi's, formed by Marilyn McCoo and LaMonte McLemore. McCoo, who had won the Grand Talent Award in the Miss Bronze California pageant, was working as a fashion model, and McLemore was photographing her when they decided to start the Hi-Fi's with Floyd Butler and Harry Elston, who later formed the Friends of Distinction. The Hi-Fi's toured with Ray Charles' revue before breaking up. McCoo then recruited Florence LaRue, who had also won a Grand Talent Award, and they brought in McLemore's fellow St. Louis–born Angeleno, Ron Townson. Billy Davis, Jr., was singing with a gospel group when McLemore, his cousin, invited him to join.

As the Versatiles, they signed with Johnny Rivers' Soul City label. After a minor West Coast hit, "I'll Be Loving You Forever," Rivers persuaded them to change their name. Their manager suggested the Fifth Dimension. Their first hit was a cover of the Mamas and the Papas' "Go Where You Wanna Go" (#16, 1967), but their pop dominance began with their first Jim Webb song, "Up, Up and Away" (#7, 1967), which received four Grammies. In 1968, they had hits with Laura Nyro's "Stoned Soul Picnic" (#3) and "Sweet Blindness" (#13); in 1969, they had their biggest seller with a medley from *Hair*, "Aquarius/Let the Sunshine In" (#1, 1969), which sold nearly two million copies. Their next #1 was Nyro's "Wedding Bell Blues," released the same year that LaRue married manager Marc Gordon and McCoo wed Davis.

In the early Seventies, the Fifth Dimension moved toward easy-listening ballads, with occasional hits, including "(Last Night) I Didn't Get to Sleep at All" (#8, 1972), as they moved toward the nightclub and television circuits; they also appeared at the Nixon White House. McCoo and Davis left to work as a duo in late 1975; their 1976 album *I Hope We Get to Love in Time* included the hit "You Don't Have to Be a Star" (#1). By 1980, McCoo and Davis had split up, and she was cohosting the TV show "Solid Gold." The remains of the Fifth Dimension, meanwhile, reunited with Webb in 1975 for the unsuccessful *Earthbound;* they continue to tour clubs.

Film Documentaries

There are lots of "rock movies"—movies with rock soundtracks, movies about people who like rock, movies with rebellious heroes that seem somehow inspired by rock. But the best-known and most important rock movies are the rock documentaries.

ABBA: The Movie (1977)
AC/DC: Let There Be Rock (1980)
The Big TNT Show (1966)
    With Joan Baez, the Byrds, Petula Clark, Bo Diddley, the Ronettes.
Black and Blue (1980)
    Black Sabbath, Blue Öyster Cult.
Bongo Man (1982)
    Jimmy Cliff, Mutabaruka.
Celebration at Big Sur (1971)
    With Joan Baez, Crosby, Stills, Nash and Young, Joni Mitchell, John Sebastian, the Edwin

Hawkins Singers, Mimi Fariña, others.
Cocksucker Blues (1976)
    The Rolling Stones.
The Concert for Bangla Desh (1972)
    With Eric Clapton, Bob Dylan, George Harrison, Billy Preston, Ringo Starr, Leon Russell, Badfinger, Ravi Shankar, Klaus Voormann.
Cream's Farewell Concert (1968)
The Decline of Western Civilization (1980)
    With Black Flag, Fear, Germs, X, Circle Jerks, Alice Bag Band, Catholic Discipline.
D.O.A. (1980)
    With the Sex Pistols, X-Ray Spex, the Dead Boys, the Clash, Iggy Pop, Generation X, Sham 69, Augustus Pablo.
Eat the Document (1972)
    Bob Dylan.

Elvis on Tour (1972)
    Elvis Presley.
Elvis: That's the Way It Is (1970)
    Elvis Presley.
Eric Clapton and His Rolling Hotel (1980)
    With George Harrison, Elton John and Muddy Waters.
Festival (1970)
    Footage from Newport Folk Festivals, with Judy Collins, Bob Dylan, the Paul Butterfield Blues Band, Donovan, Joan Baez, Howlin' Wolf.
Fillmore (1972)
    With It's a Beautiful Day, Hot Tuna, the Grateful Dead, the Jefferson Airplane, Santana, Tower of Power, others.
Gimme Shelter (1971)
    The 1969 Rolling Stones tour and the Altamont Festival, with the Rolling Stones, Ike and Tina

Turner, the Jefferson Airplane.

The Grateful Dead Movie (1977)

The Great Rock and Roll Swindle (1980)
The Sex Pistols.

Heartland Reggae (1980)
With the I-Threes, Bob Marley and the Wailers, Peter Tosh, U-Roy, others.

Janis (1975)
Janis Joplin.

Jimi Hendrix (1973)

Jimi Plays Berkeley (1971)
Jimi Hendrix.

Journey through the Past (1973)
Directed by Neil Young (a.k.a. Bernard Shakey), with Buffalo Springfield, Crosby, Stills, Nash and Young.

Keep On Rockin' (1972)
Originally *Toronto Pop*, with Bo Diddley, Jimi Hendrix, Janis Joplin, Jerry Lee Lewis, Chuck Berry, Little Richard, Big Brother and the Holding Company.

The Kids Are Alright (1979)
The Who.

The Kids Are United (1980)
Reading (England) Festival, 1978, with the Jam, the Pirates, Sham 69, Ultravox, Penetration.

Ladies and Gentlemen, the Rolling Stones (1974)

The Last Waltz (1978)
The Band's Thanksgiving Day, 1976, farewell concert, with Neil Diamond, Bob Dylan, Emmylou Harris, Ronnie Hawkins, Joni Mitchell, Van Morrison, Neil Young, Eric Clapton, Ringo Starr, others.

Let the Good Times Roll (1973)
With Chuck Berry, Chubby Checker, Fats Domino, the Five Satins, Bill Haley and His Comets, Little Richard, the Shirelles, Bo Diddley, the Coasters, Danny and the Juniors.

Let It Be (1970)
The Beatles.

Let's Spend the Night Together (1983)
The Rolling Stones' 1981 tour.

London Rock and Roll Show (1973)
With Chuck Berry, Jerry Lee Lewis, Little Richard, Bill Haley and His Comets, Bo Diddley, Lord Sutch, Heinz, the Houseshakers.

Mad Dogs and Englishmen (1971)
Joe Cocker, Leon Russell, the Grease Band.

The Medicine Ball Caravan (1971)
With Alice Cooper, Delaney and Bonnie, B. B. King, David Peel, the Youngbloods, Stoneground, Sal Valentino, Doug Kershaw.

Monterey Pop (1968)
The 1967 Monterey International Pop Festival, with the Animals, Canned Heat, Jimi Hendrix, Janis Joplin, the Mamas and the Papas, Otis Redding, Ravi Shankar, the Who, Simon and Garfunkel, others.

No Nukes (1980)
The MUSE (Musicians United for Safe Energy) benefit concerts, with Crosby, Stills and Nash, the Doobie Brothers, John Hall, Jackson Browne, Bonnie Raitt, Carly Simon, Bruce Springsteen, James Taylor, others.

Pink Floyd (1971) (a.k.a. *Les Pink Floyd à Pompeii*)

Punk in London (1979)
With the Clash, the Jam, the Stranglers, Boomtown Rats, X-Ray Spex, others.

Punk Rock Movie (1978)
With the Clash, Generation X, the Sex Pistols, the Slits, others.

Rock City (1973) (Originally *Sound of the City*)
With the Animals, Cream, Pink Floyd, Otis Redding, Rod Stewart, the Rolling Stones, Pete Townshend, Ike and Tina Turner, Cat Stevens, Jimi Hendrix, others.

Rockshow (1980)
Paul McCartney and Wings.

Roots Rock Reggae (1977)
With Jimmy Cliff, the Heptones, Bob Marley and the Wailers, others.

Rust Never Sleeps (1979) Neil Young.

Save the Children (1973)
With Marvin Gaye, Isaac Hayes, the Jackson 5, the O'Jays, the Temptations, Roberta Flack, others.

The Secret Policeman's Ball (1979)
With Pete Townshend, Neil Innes, Tom Robinson, others.

The Secret Policeman's Other Ball (1982)
With Pete Townshend, Sting, Jeff Beck, Eric Clapton, John Williams, others.

Sing Sing Thanksgiving (1974)
Joan Baez.

Son of Stiff Tour Movie (1981)
With Joe "King" Carrasco, Dirty Looks, Any Trouble, Ten Pole Tudor, the Equators, the Crowns.

The Song Remains the Same (1976)
Led Zeppelin.

Stamping Ground (1971) (Originally *Love and Music*)
With the Byrds, Dr. John, Pink Floyd, Santana, others.

The T.A.M.I. Show (1965)
Perhaps the best rock documentary of the Sixties, with the Barbarians, Chuck Berry, James Brown, Marvin Gaye, the Beach Boys, Smokey Robinson and the Miracles, Jan and Dean, the Rolling Stones, the Supremes, others.

This Is Elvis (1981)
Contains a few "docudrama"-style setup scenes, but vintage Presley clips are excellent.

To Russia . . . with Elton (1979)
Elton John in the U.S.S.R.

Urgh!—A Music War (1981)
With Dead Kennedys, Devo, the Go-Go's, Oingo Boingo, Pere Ubu, the Police, others.

Van Morrison in Ireland (1980)

Velvet Underground and Nico (1966)

Wattstax (1973)
1972 benefit concert for Watts, Los Angeles, with the Dramatics, Isaac Hayes, Luther Ingram, the Staple Singers, Johnnie Taylor, other Stax acts.

Welcome to My Nightmare (1975)
Alice Cooper.

Woodstock (1970)
The 1969 festival, with Joe Cocker, Crosby, Stills, Nash and Young, Richie Havens, Jimi Hendrix, Santana, Ten Years After, the Who, others.

Yessongs (1973) Yes.

FIREFALL

Formed circa 1974, Boulder, Colorado
Original lineup: Rick Roberts (b. 1950, Fla.), gtr., voc.;
Jock Bartley (b. Kan.), gtr., voc.; Mark Andes
(b. Feb. 19, 1948, Philadelphia), bass; Larry Burnett (b.
Washington, D.C.), gtr., voc.; Michael Clarke (b. June
3, 1944, New York City), drums.
1976—*Firefall* (Atlantic) 1977—*Luna Sea* 1978—
Élan 1980—*Undertow; Clouds across the Sun*
1982—*Break of Dawn.*

With their lightweight blend of acoustic guitars, high
harmonies and pop-flavored country rock, Firefall jumped
onto the national scene with one of 1976's biggest hits,
"You Are the Woman" (#9, 1976). The band's chief writer
and leader, guitarist Rick Roberts, sang on the Byrds'
Untitled before joining the Burrito Brothers (which included another ex-Byrd, drummer Michael Clarke), where
he stayed until 1972. Roberts then released a couple of
solo albums (*Windmills*, 1972, and *She Is a Song*, 1973)
while trying to establish himself in L.A. music circles.

He eventually retreated to Boulder, where he formed
Firefall in mid-decade, recruiting ex-Spirit and Jo Jo
Gunne bassist Mark Andes. With Washington, D.C.,
singer/songwriter Larry Burnett, he wrote most of the
material for their 1976 Atlantic debut, *Firefall*. Their
second LP contained "Just Remember I Love You" (#11,
1977). October 1978's *Élan* continued their platinum
streak, thanks to Roberts' "Strange Way" (#11, 1978).

THE FIRST EDITION (See Kenny Rogers)

WILD MAN FISCHER

Born 1945, Los Angeles
1969—*An Evening with Wild Man Fischer* (Bizarre)
1977—*Wildmania* (Rhino).

A man who got his start on streetcorners singing made-to-
order compositions for a dime, Larry "Wild Man" Fischer
was a well-known eccentric on the Los Angeles rock
fringe in the late Sixties. A former mental patient, he met
Frank Zappa, who produced *An Evening with Wild Man
Fischer* for Bizarre Records in 1969. Fischer spent a good
deal of the early Seventies roaming the country, singing
for his widely scattered band of cult followers. In 1975, he
released his first record in six years, a single promoting a
record store. His 1977 LP reconfirmed his out-to-lunch
status.

THE "5" ROYALES

Formed late 1940s, Winston-Salem, North Carolina
Johnny Taylor, voc.; Lowman Pauling, voc., gtr.;
Obediah Carter, voc.; Otto Jeffries, voc.; Johnny
Moore, voc.
N.A.—*All Time Hits* (King).

The "5" Royales were originally a gospel group called the
Royal Sons Quintet. They emerged in 1953 with two R&B
#1 hits on the Apollo label, "Help Me Somebody" and
"Baby Don't Do It," both of which were written by lead
guitarist Lowman Pauling.

They enjoyed their first pop success in 1957, when
"Think" skirted the lower rungs of the Hot 100, a feat
equaled in 1961 by the original "Dedicated to the One I
Love," another Pauling original, later recorded by the
Shirelles and the Mamas and the Papas. Later releases
(with little mass-market impact) came on ABC, Home of
the Blues, Vee Jay and Smash.

THE FIVE SATINS

Formed 1956, New Haven, Connecticut
Original lineup: Fred Parris (b. Mar. 26, 1936), lead
voc.; Rich Freeman (b. Dec. 1940), voc.; Al Denby,
voc.; Ed Martin, voc.; Jessie Murphy, piano.
1981—(new name Freddie Parris and the Satins:
Freddie Parris, lead voc.; Dennis Ray; Bernard Jones;
Larry DeSalvi).
N.A.—*The Best of the Five Satins* (Celebrity Show-
case) *The Five Satins' Greatest Hits, volumes 1, 2, 3*
(Relic) *The Five Satins Sing* (Ember) *The Five Satins
Encore, volume 2.*

The Five Satins were one of the best-known doo-wop
vocal groups of the Fifties. They evolved from a high
school group called the Scarlets. By 1956, they had
changed their name to the Five Satins and recorded lead
singer Parris' "In the Still of the Night" in the basement of
an East Haven Catholic church on a two-track machine.
Released in 1956 on the Standard label, it was later leased
to Ember Records and became a #24 hit in 1956. (The
song had some chart success when reissued in 1960 and
1961 and has become an R&B ballad standard. It has been
estimated to have sold 15 to 20 million copies.)

Soon after the single's release, Parris returned to the
Army in Japan (the Satins had recorded while he was on
leave), and the group continued to record with sporadic
success. "To the Aisle" (with Bill Baker on lead vocals)
hit #25 in 1957. Out of the Satins' many releases, only
"Shadows" and "I'll Be Seeing You" reached the lower
rungs of the Hot 100 as 1960 began. They re-created the
latter tune a cappella in the 1973 film *Let the Good Times
Roll.* Upon his discharge in 1958, Parris re-formed the
group.

They were featured on Dick Clark's "American Band-
stand" and many of his road revues in the late Fifties.
They also toured Europe, where they built up a following.
In 1970, the group appeared in the film *Been Down So
Long It Looks Like Up to Me.* By the early Seventies, they
were a staple item on rock revival shows. In 1974, with
Parris still underpinning the harmonies, they signed with
Kirshner Records and released "Two Different Worlds."

The group had an R&B Top Forty hit, "Everybody Stand Up and Clap Your Hands," in 1976 under the name Black Satin.

Onetime member Willie Wright went on to become a successful disc jockey in Connecticut. The many labels for which the Five Satins have recorded include Red Bird, Cub, Chancellor, Warner Bros., Roulette and Mama Sadie. By 1982, the group was recording for Elektra and experiencing limited success on the pop charts with "Memories of Days Gone By," as well as performing occasionally in East Coast clubs.

ROBERTA FLACK
Born February 10, 1939, Asheville, North Carolina
1969—*First Take* (Atlantic)   1970—*Chapter Two*
1971—*Quiet Fire*   1972—*Roberta Flack and Donny Hathaway*   1973—*Killing Me Softly*   1975—*Feel Like Makin' Love*   1977—*Blue Lights in the Basement*
1978—*Roberta Flack*   1980—*Featuring Donny Hathaway; Live and More* (with Peabo Bryson).

Roberta Flack's clear, reserved vocals have given her a string of ballad hits. The daughter of an organist, she attended Howard University in Washington, D.C., on a music scholarship, and in the early Sixties taught in a segregated high school in Farmville, North Carolina. Eventually she returned to Washington and began singing in local clubs. Her first album appeared in 1969 and sold well; by 1971, Flack had toured Europe and Ghana, as well as the U.S.

Her first hit single was a duet with Donny Hathaway, "You've Got a Friend" (#29, 1971), which she followed with a Carole King-Gerry Goffin composition, "Will You Love Me Tomorrow." Meanwhile, the movie *Play Misty for Me* was released with a song from Flack's debut album, "The First Time Ever I Saw Your Face," on the soundtrack. It became a #1 hit in 1972, followed by another Flack-Hathaway duet, "Where Is the Love" (#5, 1972). After two more major hits, "Killing Me Softly with His Song" (#1, 1973) and "Feel Like Makin' Love" (#1, 1974), Flack cut back her performing to concentrate on recording and to pursue outside interests, including educational programs for disadvantaged youth.

She reemerged in late 1977 with *Blue Lights in the Basement* and "25th of Last December"; by then she had been awarded four gold records in three years. Hathaway's death in 1979 interrupted the recording of *Roberta Flack Featuring Donny Hathaway;* the album included "You Are My Heaven" and "Back Together Again." In 1980, Flack toured and recorded a live album with vocalist Peabo Bryson. She continues to tour, and in 1981 recorded a Kentucky Fried Chicken commercial.

THE FLAMINGOS
Formed 1952, Chicago
Original lineup: Earl Lewis, voc.; Zeke Carey, voc.; Jake Carey, voc.; Johnny Carter, voc.; Sollie McElroy, voc.; Paul Wilson, voc.
N.A.—*Color Them Beautiful* (Ronze)   *The Flamingos* (Checker)   *Flamingo Favorites* (End)   *The Flamingos' Greatest Hits* (Meka).

The Flamingos' lengthy personnel-changing history has been characterized by one major pop success ("I Only Have Eyes for You") and contributions of talent to other noted black acts. The group began singing in 1952 on Chicago's South Side. Their cool and dramatic vocal style first appeared on the Chance label in 1953, and revealed influences ranging from gospel to the clean harmonies of the Four Freshmen on such releases as "Golden Teardrops," with lead vocals by Sollie McElroy, who soon left the group and was replaced by Nate Nelson, who subsequently joined the Platters.

The Flamingos followed with a variety of sentimental songs aimed at the white market. They remained also-rans until 1956, when the Fats Washington ballad "I'll Be Home" hit the R&B Top Ten (Pat Boone's version was the pop hit). After a variety of personnel changes, their crossover break came in 1959 on the languid "I Only Have Eyes for You" (#11), which became a standard.

For the next two years, the Flamingos had several hits on the End label, including "Lover Never Say Goodbye" and "Love Walked In" in 1959; "I Was Such a Fool" and "Nobody Loves Me Like You" in 1960; and "Time Was" in 1961.

They scored occasional soul hits through the early Seventies with such releases as "Boogaloo Party" (Philips, 1966), "Dealin' " (Julma, 1969) and "Buffalo Soldier" (Polydor, 1970). Other labels with which the group has been associated include Parrot, Decca and, beginning in 1972, Ronze. Onetime member Johnny Carter joined the Dells, while another, Tommy Hunt, became a minor soul star in the Sixties.

THE FLAMIN' GROOVIES
Formed 1965, San Francisco
Cyril Jordan (b. 1948, San Francisco), gtr., mellotron, voc.; Roy Loney (b. Apr. 13, 1946, San Francisco), voc., gtr.; George Alexander (b. May 18, 1946, San Mateo, Calif.), bass, voc., harmonica; Tim Lynch (b. July 18, 1946, San Francisco), gtr.
1966—(+ Ron Greco, drums; − Greco; + Danny Mihm [b. San Francisco], drums)   1969—*Supersnazz* (Epic)   1970—*Flamingo* (Kama Sutra)   1971—*Teenage Head* (− Tim Lynch; + James Farrell, gtr.; − Roy Loney; + Chris Wilson, voc., gtr., harmonica)   1973—(− Mihm; + Terry Rae, drums; − Rae; + David Wright, drums)   1976—*Shake Some Action* (Sire)   *Still Shakin'* (Buddah)   (− Farrell; + Mike Wilhelm, gtr.)   1978—*The Flamin' Groovies Now* (Sire)   1979—*Jumping in the Night.*

While the three-minute pop-rock song has gone in and out of fashion, the Flamin' Groovies have stuck to the form since the mid-Sixties despite marginal commercial success. They formed in the Bay Area during the tail end of the British Invasion, but were overshadowed by psychedelic jam bands on the San Francisco scene. The band was briefly known as the Chosen Few and then the Lost and Found before becoming the Flamin' Groovies.

In 1969, the group made its own album, *Sneakers*, which sold 2,000 copies and was bought by Epic. Re-released as *Supersnazz*, it was popular only in the Midwest. The Groovies toured the Midwest, then returned to San Francisco, where they booked concerts at what had been Bill Graham's Fillmore West. That venture ended when their business manager disappeared with the receipts.

The band moved to New York and made *Flamingo* and *Teenage Head,* but in 1971 founding member Tim Lynch was arrested for drug offenses and draft evasion. Roy Loney, the group's main songwriter, quit the group; he reemerged in the late Seventies with his own group, the Phantom Movers. The group moved to England in 1972, released two singles and returned to San Francisco.

Greg Shaw, editor of *Bomp* magazine, helped finance a single, "You Tore Me Down," and in 1976 pop revivalist Dave Edmunds (whom the band had met in Britain) produced the Groovies' major-label comeback, *Shake Some Action.* While the band toured Europe with the Ramones, Buddah released old tapes as *Still Shakin'.* Edmunds also produced *Now,* and the band continued to tour as the Eighties began.

FLEETWOOD MAC
Formed 1967, England
Peter Green (b. Oct. 29, 1946, London), gtr., voc.; Mick Fleetwood (b. June 24, 1942, London), drums; John McVie (b. Nov. 26, 1945, London), bass; Jeremy Spencer (b. July 4, 1948, West Hartlepool, Eng.), gtr., voc.
1968—*Fleetwood Mac* (Blue Horizon) *The Original Fleetwood Mac* (Polydor) (+ Danny Kirwan [b. May 13, 1950, London], gtr., voc.) **1969**—*Mr. Wonderful* (Blue Horizon, U.K.) *English Rose* (Warner Bros.) *Then Play On* **1970**—*Kiln House* (− Green; − Spencer; + Christine Perfect / McVie [b. July 12, 1943, Birmingham, Eng.], kybds., voc.) **1971**—*Future Games* (+ Bob Welch [b. July 31, 1946, Calif.], gtr., voc.) **1972**—*Bare Trees* (− Kirwan; + Bob Weston, gtr.; + Dave Walker, gtr.) **1973**—*Penguin* (− Walker) *Mystery to Me* (− Weston) **1974**—*Heros Are Hard to Find* (− Welch; + Lindsey Buckingham [b. Oct. 3, 1947, Palo Alto, Calif.], gtr., voc.; + Stevie Nicks [b. May 26, 1948, Phoenix, Ariz.], voc.) **1975**—*Fleetwood Mac* **1977**—*Rumours* **1979**—*Tusk* **1980**—*Live* **1982**—*Mirage.*

Fleetwood Mac: Lindsey Buckingham, John McVie, Christine McVie, Stevie Nicks, Mick Fleetwood

Whoever named Fleetwood Mac was either lucky or prescient. The only thing about the group that hasn't changed since the band formed in 1967 is the rhythm section of Mick Fleetwood and John McVie. Through the Seventies, the group's personnel and style shifted with nearly every recording as the band metamorphosed from a traditionalist British blues band to the makers of one of the best-selling pop albums ever, *Rumours.*

Peter Green's Fleetwood Mac was formed by ex-John Mayall's Bluesbreakers Green, McVie and Fleetwood along with Elmore James enthusiast Jeremy Spencer. McVie had been a charter member of the Bluesbreakers in 1963, Fleetwood had joined in 1965 and Green had replaced Eric Clapton in 1966. With its repertoire of blues classics and Green's blues-style originals, the group's debut at the British Jazz and Blues Festival in August 1967 netted them a record contract. They were popular in Britain immediately, and their debut album stayed near the top of the British charts for 13 months. They had hits in the U.K. through 1970, including "Black Magic Woman" and the instrumental "Albatross" (which was #1 in 1968 and reached #4 when rereleased in 1973). In America, however, they were largely ignored; their first U.S. tour had them third-billed behind Jethro Tull and Joe Cocker, neither of whom was as popular as Fleetwood Mac in Britain.

Green and Spencer recorded *Fleetwood Mac in Chicago* with Willie Dixon, Otis Spann and other blues patriarchs in 1969, yet the group was already moving away from the all-blues format. In May 1970, Green abruptly left the group to follow his ascetic religious beliefs. (He stayed out of the music business until the late Seventies, when he made two solo LPs.) His departure put an end to Fleetwood Mac's blues leanings; Danny Kirwan and Christine Perfect moved the band toward leaner, more melodic rock. Perfect, who had sung with Spencer Davis in folk and jazz outfits before joining British blues-rockers Chicken Shack in 1968, had performed uncredited on parts of *Then Play On*, but contractual obligations to Chicken Shack kept her from joining Fleetwood Mac officially until 1971; by then she had married McVie.

Early in 1971, Spencer disappeared in Los Angeles and turned up as a member of a religious cult, the Children of God (later the title of a Spencer solo effort). Fleetwood Mac went through a confused period. First Welch joined, supplementing Kirwan's and Christine McVie's songwriting. Next Kirwan was fired and replaced by Bob Weston and Dave Walker, both of whom soon departed. Manager Clifford Davis then formed a group around Weston and Walker, called it Fleetwood Mac, and sent it on a U.S. tour. An injunction filed by the real Fleetwood Mac forced the bogus band to desist (they then formed the group Stretch), but protracted legal complications kept Fleetwood Mac from touring for most of 1974. Since then, the band has managed itself, with Mick Fleetwood taking most of the responsibility.

The group relocated to California in 1974. After Welch left to form the power trio Paris in 1975, Fleetwood Mac finally found its best-selling lineup. Producer Keith Olsen played an album he'd engineered, *Buckingham-Nicks* (Polydor), for Fleetwood and the McVies as a demo for his studio; Fleetwood Mac hired not only Olsen but the duo of Lindsey Buckingham and Stevie Nicks, who had played together in the Bay Area acid-rock group Fritz from 1968 until 1972, before recording with Olsen.

Fleetwood Mac now had three songwriters, Buckingham's studio craft and an onstage focal point in Nicks, who became a late-Seventies sex symbol as *Fleetwood Mac* began to rack up its four million in sales. The McVies divorced in 1976, Buckingham and Nicks separated soon after—but the tensions of the two years between albums helped shape the songs on *Rumours*, which sold over fifteen million copies.

After touring the biggest venues around the world—with Nicks, who was prone to throat nodes, always in danger of losing her voice—Fleetwood Mac took another two years and approximately $1 million to make *Tusk*, an ambitious, frequently experimental project that couldn't match its predecessors' popularity, although it still turned a modest profit. Buckingham and Mac engineer Richard Dashut also produced hit singles for John Stewart and Bob Welch. Like many bands who've overspent in the studio, Fleetwood Mac's next effort was a live double album.

In 1980, Fleetwood and Dashut visited Ghana to record *The Visitor* with African musicians, and Nicks began work on her first solo LP, *Belladonna*, which hit #1 and went platinum with two Top Ten singles. Late 1981 saw the release of Buckingham's solo LP, *Law and Order*. Fleetwood Mac's first collection of new material in three years, *Mirage*, was less overtly experimental and featured the 1982 hit single "Hold Me."

THE FLEETWOODS
Formed 1958, Olympia, Washington
Gary Troxel (b. Nov 28, 1939, Centralia, Wash.), voc.; Barbara Laine Ellis (b. Feb. 20, 1940, Olympia), voc.; Gretchen Diane Christopher (b. Feb. 29, 1940, Olympia), voc.
N.A.—*The Fleetwoods' Greatest Hits* (Dolton)   *The Very Best of the Fleetwoods* (United Artists).

The Fleetwoods were three high school friends whose first single, "Come Softly to Me," was a #1 hit in 1959. Originally known as Two Girls and a Guy, the trio had several other hits, including "Tragedy" (#12, 1959), and a second #1 hit, the DeWayne Blackwell composition "Mr. Blue," in 1959.

FLO AND EDDIE
Mark Volman (Flo) (b. Apr. 19, 1944, Calif.), voc., gtr.; Howard Kaylan (Eddie) (b. June 22, 1945, Calif.), voc.
1972—*Phlorescent Leech and Eddie* (Reprise)   **1973**—*Flo and Eddie*   **1975**—*Illegal, Immoral and Fattening* (Columbia)   **1976**—*Moving Targets*   **1982**—*Rock Steady with Flo and Eddie* (Epiphany).

The Flo and Eddie mix of rock & roll satire with straight rock & roll has been popular with their fans for over a decade. After fronting the Turtles through the late Sixties, Mark Volman and Howard Kaylan joined Frank Zappa. They contributed to *Chunga's Revenge, Live at the Fillmore East, Just Another Band From L.A.* (which included the Turtles' "Happy Together") and the *200 Motels* album and film.

After leaving Zappa in 1972, the pair began working and recording as the Phlorescent Leech and Eddie, at first a group that included ex–Leaves and Turtles bassist Jim Pons and another Zappa alumnus, drummer Aynsley Dunbar. Although they originally used the Phlorescent moniker to avoid contractual problems, the name stuck. Their shows and albums combine straight songs with sendups of rock personalities, genres and events.

They briefly gave up touring in 1976 following the suicide of their guitarist, Philip Reed, and the accidental death of another close friend, Marc Bolan (T. Rex).

Besides several LPs (the second produced by Bob Ezrin), they scored and contributed dialogue to an X-rated animation film called *Cheap*. They have also written columns for *Teen Beat, Creem, Phonograph Record* and the *L.A. Free Press*, as well as hosting a syndicated radio show in the mid-Seventies and a short-lived late-night TV talk show in 1982. The pair has provided background vocals for Marc Bolan and T. Rex, Stephen Stills and Bruce Springsteen ("Hungry Heart").

THE FLOCK

Formed 1966, Chicago
Original lineup: Jerry Goodman, electric violin; Rick Canoff, sax; Fred Glickstein, gtr., voc.; Jerry Smith, bass; Ron Karpman, drums; Tom Webb, sax; Frank Posa, trumpet.
1969—*Flock* (Columbia) **1971**—*Dinosaur Swamps* (− Goodman; − Webb; − Posa; − Canoff; + Mike Zydowsky, electric violin) **1975**—*Inside Out* (Mercury) (+ Jim Hirsen, kybds.).

Progressive rockers, the Flock inserted jazz and classical interludes in pop songs, resulting in an eclectic hodgepodge that seemed impressive in the late Sixties. Formed by high school friends, the group moved up the rock circuit, including appearances at the Fillmore East and West and the Denver Pop Festival. Their debut album included a version of the Kinks' "Tired of Waiting for You" featuring violinist Jerry Goodman, originally the band's roadie. Goodman left in 1971 to join the Mahavishnu Orchestra, although the Flock continued to tour and record for some years afterward.

EDDIE FLOYD

Born June 25, 1935, Montgomery, Alabama
1967—*Knock on Wood* (Stax) **1968**—*I've Never Found a Girl* **1970**—*California Girl* **1973**—*Baby Lay Your Head Down (Gently on My Bed)* **1974**—*Soul Street* **1977**—*Experience* (Malaco).

R&B singer and songwriter Eddie Floyd had spent an extended period in a reform school before he moved to Detroit. A 1956 founding member of the gospel group the Falcons, he stayed with them as they slowly evolved into a soul group. (Wilson Pickett replaced him in the Falcons when Floyd left in 1962.) Over the next few years, Floyd released singles on Lupine, Atlantic and Safice, which he partly owned.

At Stax, his first hit was "Knock on Wood" (#28, 1966).

Grammy Awards

José Feliciano
1968 Best New Artist; Best Contemporary Pop Vocal Performance, Male: "Light My Fire"

The Fifth Dimension
1967 Record of the Year; Best Performance by a Vocal Group; Best Contemporary Single; Best Contemporary Group Performance, Vocal or Instrumental: "Up, Up and Away"
1969 Record of the Year; Best Contemporary Vocal Performance by a Group: "Aquarius/Let The Sunshine In"

Roberta Flack
1972 Record of the Year: "The First Time Ever I Saw Your Face"
Best Pop or Vocal Performance by a Duo, Group or Chorus:

"Where Is the Love" (with Donny Hathaway)
1973 Record of the Year; Best Pop Vocal Performance, Female: "Killing Me Softly With His Song"

Fleetwood Mac
1977 Album of the Year: *Rumours*

A Flock of Seagulls
1982 Best Rock Instrumental Performance: "D.N.A."

Aretha Franklin
1967 Best R&B Recording; Best R&B Solo Vocal Performance, Female: "Respect"
1968 Best R&B Vocal Performance, Female: "Chain of Fools"
1969 Best R&B Vocal Performance, Female: "Share Your Love with Me"

1970 Best R&B Vocal Performance, Female: "Don't Play That Song"
1971 Best R&B Vocal Performance, Female: "Bridge over Troubled Water"
1972 Best R&B Vocal Performance, Female: *Young, Gifted and Black*
Best Soul Gospel Performance: *Amazing Grace*
1973 Best R&B Vocal Performance, Female: "Master of Eyes"
1974 Best R&B Vocal Performance, Female: "Ain't Nothing Like the Real Thing"
1981 Best R&B Vocal Performance, Female: "Hold On, I'm Comin' "

Later hits included 1967's "Raise Your Hand," 1968's "I've Never Found a Girl" and "Bring It on Home to Me" (#17) and "California Girl" in 1970. He also wrote for others, including "Comfort Me" for Carla Thomas, whom he also produced; "Don't Mess with Cupid" for Otis Redding; "Someone's Watching Over You" for Solomon Burke; and "634-5789" for Wilson Pickett.

Floyd occasionally toured the U.S. and Europe as part of the Stax Revue, but the financially beleaguered label took his career under with it. In 1977, he put out a disco record on Malaco called *Experience*.

THE FLYING BURRITO BROTHERS
Formed 1968, Los Angeles
Gram Parsons (b. Cecil Connor, Nov. 5, 1946, Winterhaven, Fla.; d. Sep. 19, 1973, Joshua Tree, Calif.), gtr., voc., kybds.; Chris Hillman (b. Dec. 4, 1942, Los Angeles), bass, gtr., voc.; Sneaky Pete Kleinow (b. ca. 1935, South Bend, Ind.), pedal steel gtr.; Jon Corneal, drums; Chris Ethridge, bass.
1969—*The Gilded Palace of Sin* (A&M) (– Corneal; + Michael Clarke [b. June 3, 1944, Spokane, Wash.], drums, harmonica; – Ethridge [Hillman moves to bass]; + Bernie Leadon [b. July 19, 1947, Minneapolis], gtr., voc., banjo, dobro) **1970**—*Burrito Deluxe* (– Parsons; + Rick Roberts, gtr., voc.) **1971**—*Flying Burrito Brothers* (– Kleinow; + Al Perkins, pedal steel gtr.; – Leadon) *Last of the Red Hot Burritos* (+ Byron Berline, fiddle; + Roger Bush, bass; + Kenny Wertz, gtr.) **1972**—(– Hillman; – Perkins; – Clarke; + Alan Munde, banjo, gtr.; + Don Beck, pedal steel gtr.; + Erik Dalton, drums) **1974**—*Close Up the Honky Tonks* (re-formed group: + Kleinow; + Ethridge; + Floyd "Gib" Guilbeau, voc., gtr., fiddle; + Joel Scott Hill, bass, voc.; + Gene Parsons, drums) **1975**—*Hot Burrito* (Arista) *Flying Again* (Columbia) (– Ethridge; + Skip Battin) **1976**—*Sleepless Nights* (A&M) *Airborne* (Columbia).

When Gram Parsons led the Flying Burrito Brothers, his haunted songs and the band's bluegrass-based virtuosity set the standard for California country rock. After he left, the band quickly devolved into uninspired followers of the style they'd started, although a Flying Burrito Brothers band continued to perform on the honky-tonk circuit. Meanwhile, ex-Burritos went on to greater commercial success in Firefall and the Eagles.

Parsons and Chris Hillman had been Byrds for *Sweetheart of the Rodeo* before starting the Burritos. As the lineup shifted, they later recruited ex-Byrd Michael Clarke and Rick Roberts. The Rolling Stones were early Burritos fans and arranged for the group to play at Altamont. In 1970, Parsons left the band for a solo career, and leadership eventually fell to Rick Roberts. Leadon joined the nascent Eagles, while Hillman and Al Perkins joined Stephen Stills and Manassas. Roberts recruited members from bluegrass-rockers Country Gazette for a 1973 European tour (when *Live in Amsterdam* was made), but disbanded the Burritos late in 1973. Roberts went on to found Firefall.

In 1975, Kleinow and Ethridge revived the name with ex–Canned Heat bassist Joel Scott Hill and fiddler "Gib" Guilbeau, but Ethridge left in 1976. The current Burritos have only tenuous connections with the band's beginnings.

THE FLYING LIZARDS
Formed 1978, Ireland
1980—*Flying Lizards* (Virgin).

As the Flying Lizards, conceptual artist David Cunningham and session vocalist Deborah Evans enjoyed novelty hits with their radically rearranged, disinterested versions of Barrett Strong's "Money" and Eddie Cochran's "Summertime Blues."

Cunningham attended art school in Ireland, and while in school performed with a 13-piece band, Les Cochons Chic. He made a minimalist solo album, *Grey Scale*, in the late Seventies.

In 1978, he conceived the Flying Lizards and put out "Summertime Blues," which attracted some attention in Britain. The followup, "Money," had its signature riff played on an upright piano with rubber toys, sheet music, cassettes and telephone directories inside. The song was recorded for approximately $14 in a home studio. "Money" picked up substantial U.S. airplay in 1979 and prompted Virgin to ask for an album, which also included a Brecht-Weill song and more Cunningham instrumentals. Cunningham later worked with the Pop Group, the Modettes, the Electric Chairs and This Heat. He returned to experimental music and work in theater and film.

FOCUS
Formed 1969, Amsterdam
Thijs Van Leer (b. Mar. 31, 1948, Amsterdam), organ, flute, voc.; Martin Dresden, bass; Hans Cleuver, drums.
1970—(+ Jan Akkerman [b. Dec. 24, 1946, Amsterdam], gtr.) **1971**—*In and Out of Focus* (Sire) (– Cleuver; + Pierre Van der Linden [b. Feb. 19, 1946, Netherlands], drums) *Moving Waves* (– Havermans; + Bert Ruiter [b. Nov. 26, 1946], bass) **1972**—*Focus Three* **1973**—*Live at Rainbow* (– Van der Linden; + Colin Allen; – Havermans) **1974**—*Hamburger Concerto* (Atco) *Ship of Memories* (Harvest) **1975**—*Mother Focus* (– Allen) *Dutch Masters* **1976**—(+ Van der Linden, drums; – Akkerman; – Van der Linden; + Philip Catherine [b. London], gtr.; + Steve Smith, drums; + Eef Albers, gtr.) **1978**—*Focus Con Proby* (with P. J. Proby) (Harvest).

The progressive-rock band Focus became a major draw in Europe playing extended songs with tinges of classical melody from flutist Thijs Van Leer and pyrotechnical solos by guitarist Jan Akkerman. In the U.S., Focus is remembered for a yodeling novelty single, "Hocus Pocus" (# 9, 1973).

Classically trained Jan Akkerman became known in the Netherlands as a member of Brainbox, which also included drummer Pierre Van der Linden. Meanwhile, Thijs Van Leer, a classically trained keyboardist and flutist, formed Focus in 1969 as a trio; its first gig was as a pit band for the Dutch production of *Hair*. In 1970, Akkerman joined Van Leer in order to try making more complex music than Brainbox's. Focus' debut album was modestly successful in Europe, and the followup included "Hocus Pocus," which became an international hit. The band considered it a joke, but they were stuck with it as a signature song.

Focus had their second and last U.S. chart showing with "Sylvia" (1973), then returned to more ambitious compositions on *Focus III*, which went gold. In the early Seventies, Focus was a headlining band in the U.S. and Europe. After 1974's *Hamburger Concerto*, the group turned to more concise four-minute pop songs on 1975's *Mother Focus*. Akkerman left in 1976 to continue his concurrent solo career; he was replaced by guitarist Philip Catherine in the group's waning years. *Focus Con Proby* featured British pop star P. J. Proby. After Focus' peak, Akkerman released a string of solo albums and Van Leer released the three-volume *Introspection*, *Nice to Have Met You* and *O My Love*.

DAN FOGELBERG

Born August 13, 1951, Peoria, Illinois
1972—*Home Free* (Columbia) **1974**—*Souvenirs*
(Epic) **1975**—*Captured Angel* **1977**—*Netherlands*
1978—*Twin Sons of Different Mothers* (with Tim
Weisberg) **1979**—*Phoenix* **1981**—*The Innocent Age*
(Epic/Full Moon).

Singer/songwriter Dan Fogelberg studied piano for a few years, began playing the guitar and was composing at age 14. During the two years he studied art at the University of Illinois in Champaign, he also played campus coffee-houses, where he met Irving Azoff, ex-student and manager of local bands like REO Speedwagon. In 1971, Fogelberg dropped out of school, moved to Los Angeles and signed with Columbia. *Home Free* went largely unnoticed, but his second album, *Souvenirs,* went gold on the strength of "Part of the Plan" (# 31).

In the early Seventies, Fogelberg was very active in West Coast music circles, guesting on LPs by Jackson Browne, Roger McGuinn, Randy Newman and Michael Stanley. Uncomfortable with the starmaker lifestyle, he left California in late 1974. That same year, his backup group, Fool's Gold, released a self-titled LP on Arista that featured their own single, "Rain, Oh Rain."

Eventually settling in Boulder, Colorado, Fogelberg held his commercial ground but didn't break the platinum barrier until his fifth album, *Twin Sons of Different Mothers,* his 1978 collaboration with jazz-pop flutist Tim Weisberg. *Phoenix* eventually sold over two million copies. Nervous about live appearances, Fogelberg has canceled major engagements (including opening for Elton John at Dodger Stadium). He appeared on the soundtrack of *Urban Cowboy* in 1980, the same year he made his first live TV appearance. Although the singer/songwriter genre was in noticeable decline, Fogelberg bucked the trend with 1981's *The Innocent Age* (a 16-part song cycle lamenting the passage of childhood), which spent more than three months in the Top Ten.

FOGHAT

Formed 1971, London
"Lonesome" Dave Peverett (b. 1950, Eng.), gtr., voc.;
Roger Earl (b. 1949, Eng.), drums; Rod Price (b. Eng.),
gtr.; Tony Stevens (b. Sept. 12, 1949, Eng.), bass.
1972—*Foghat* (Bearsville) **1973**—*Rock and Roll*
1974—*Energized; Rock and Roll Outlaws*
(– Stevens; + Nick Jameson [b. Mo.], bass, kybds.,
synth.) **1975**—*Fool for the City* (– Jameson; +
Craig MacGregor [b. Conn.], bass) **1977**—*Night
Shift; Live* **1978**—*Stone Blue* **1979**—*Boogie Motel* **1980**—*Tight Shoes* (– Price; + Erik Cartwright,
gtr.) **1981**—*Girls to Chat and Boys to Bounce* **1982**—
In the Mood for Something Rude.

Foghat's basic blues-based boogie and extensive U.S. touring brought them a loyal audience and gold and platinum albums (*Rock and Roll Outlaws, Fool for the City, Night Shift*) in the mid-Seventies. "Lonesome" Dave Peverett founded Foghat along the lines of Savoy Brown, his previous band. After three years of heavy touring—throughout the Seventies, the group averaged eight months per year on the road—cofounder Tony Stevens was replaced by Nick Jameson, who had helped mix Foghat's first albums. While he was in the band, Jameson was also producer, and he oversaw their first hit single, "Slow Ride" (#20, 1976).

Jameson left in 1976 for a solo career and other production work. By then, the band was based on Long Island, and recruited replacements in the U.S. In 1977, Foghat hosted a benefit concert for the New York Public Library's blues collection, with guests Muddy Waters and John Lee Hooker. Their late-Seventies albums yielded two hits: "Stone Blue" (#36, 1978) and "Third-Time Lucky" (#23, 1979).

FOLK REVIVAL

As the Fifties ended and the Sixties began, students and city-dwellers became interested in folk music—authentic rural performers like Leadbelly and Woody Guthrie and collectors and re-creators like the Weavers, the Kingston

Trio, Josh White and Burl Ives. Guthrie had spread the idea of the topical protest song, and during the McCarthy era it was taken up by the American left. The Weavers' Pete Seeger had an international repertoire that included children's songs, spirituals, organizing songs and foreign pop. As McCarthyism wound down, folk music and pop for acoustic guitars spread in mainstream popularity, and the folk revival encouraged amateur strummers to try it themselves.

FOLK ROCK

Folk rock contained very little of either folk or rock. The idea was to set the "folk" songs of the hootenanny era, especially of Bob Dylan and his many disciples (which were newly composed, although some used folk melodies) to a "rock" beat, which was generally closer to the pop of the mid-Sixties than to rock. In practice, it generally meant that strumming guitars were augmented by a rhythm section, as in Simon and Garfunkel's "The Sounds of Silence," whose hit version simply replaced the acoustic guitars of their original recording with electric guitars, bass and drums.

But since the hootenanny singers had considered their lyrics important, so did the folk-rockers, and in so doing they gave rock songwriters the impetus to try unconventional lyrics. Only in the hands of someone like Bob Dylan, who tapped into rock's blues base when he decided to go electric, did folk rock really rock, although the meticulous pop of the Byrds laid part of the groundwork for the California rock of the Seventies.

WAYNE FONTANA AND THE MINDBENDERS

Formed 1963, England
Wayne Fontana (b. Glyn Geoffrey Ellis, Oct. 28, 1945, Manchester, Eng.), voc.; Bob Lang (b. Jan. 10, 1946, Manchester), bass; Eric Stewart (b. Jan. 20, 1945, Manchester), gtr.; Ric Rothwell (b. Mar. 11, 1944, Manchester), drums; Graham Gouldman (b. May 10, 1946, Manchester), bass.
1965—*Wayne Fontana and the Mindbenders* (Fontana) 1966—*Eric, Rick, Wayne, Bob; Wayne One* (solo record) *The Mindbenders* 1967—*With Woman in Mind; A Groovy Kind of Love.*

Wayne Fontana and the Mindbenders' contribution to the British Invasion was "Game of Love" (#1, 1965), and the Mindbenders minus Fontana followed up with "A Groovy Kind of Love" (#2, 1966).

Glyn Ellis started out in a school skiffle group, the Velfins. By 1963, he was playing in a Manchester pub band, the Jets, while working as an apprentice telephone engineer. Ellis arranged to have the Jets play for a Fontana Records talent scout at Manchester's Oasis Club, but only Ellis and bassist Bob Lang showed up for the audition.

They recruited some musician friends from the audience and landed a contract, with Ellis becoming Wayne Fontana at a Philips/Fontana Records executive's behest. They started recording R&B covers in 1963 and began to score British hits in 1964 with a version of Major Lance's "Um, Um, Um, Um, Um, Um."

In 1965, "Game of Love" became an international hit, but after one more hit, "It's Just a Little Bit Too Late" (#45, 1965), Fontana decided on a solo career. He had a few U.K. hits—"Pamela, Pamela" and "Come on Home"—before moving into cabaret and nostalgia-rock revues, including a major English tour in 1979.

The Mindbenders had two U.S. hits on their own, "A Groovy Kind of Love" and "Ashes to Ashes," and they appeared in *To Sir with Love* before they broke up in the late Sixties. Gouldman—whose songs were British Invasion hits for Herman's Hermits, the Yardbirds and others—and Stewart founded 10cc in the Seventies.

STEVE FORBERT

Born 1955, Meridian, Mississippi
1978—*Alive on Arrival* (Nemperor) 1979—*Jackrabbit Slim* 1980—*Little Stevie Orbit* 1982—*Steve Forbert.*

Folk-rock singer/songwriter Steve Forbert learned guitar at age 11 and later played in a variety of semi-pro rock bands on through college. At age 21, he quit his job as a truckdriver and moved to New York, where he began singing for spare change in Grand Central Station. Forbert worked his way up through the Manhattan clubs before landing a contract with Nemperor in 1978. His debut album, *Alive on Arrival*, was well received, and its followup, *Jackrabbit Slim*, yielded a #11 single, "Romeo's Tune." He continues to record and tour with his band, the Flying Squirrels.

EMILE FORD

Born Emile Sweetnam, 1937, Nassau, Bahamas

This shy Bahamian became the first nonwhite to hit the British charts when "What Do You Want to Make Those Eyes at Me For?" sold a million copies in 1959. Ford, who was discovered singing in London coffeehouses, was heavily influenced by Fats Domino. He was backed by a group called the Checkmates, whose original members included his brother George, John Cuffley and Ken Street. After his gold disc in 1959, Ford's followups flopped. He moved into record production and then relocated to the Continent, where he played on and off for the next several years, sometimes returning to Britain in rock revival shows.

FRANKIE FORD

Born August 4, 1940, Gretna, Louisiana
N.A.—*Best of Frankie Ford* (Ace).

Frankie Ford was a white singer who performed "Sea Cruise" (#14, 1959), one of the best New Orleans rockers.

Ford was marketed in the late Fifties as Ace Records' attempt at a teen idol. The "Sea Cruise" track was made by Huey "Piano" Smith and the Clowns; Smith's vocals were erased and Ford's overdubbed, as was the case with the less popular followup, "Alimony." Ford had minor hits in 1960 ("You Talk Too Much" and "Time After Time") and 1961 ("Seventeen"). He was drafted in 1962. After his discharge, he returned to recording, but supported himself primarily by performing in his own nightclub in New Orleans' French Quarter.

FOREIGNER

Formed 1976, New York City
Mick Jones (b. Eng.), gtr., voc.; Ian McDonald (b. Eng.), flute, kybds., reeds, gtr., voc.; Al Greenwood (b. New York City), kybds., synth.; Lou Gramm (b. Rochester, N.Y.), voc.; Ed Gagliardi, bass; Dennis Elliott (b. Eng.), drums.
1977—*Foreigner* (Atlantic) **1978**—*Double Vision*
1979— (− Gagliardi; + Rick Wills, bass) *Head Games* **1980**—(− McDonald; − Greenwood)
1981— *4*.

Despite accusations of formulaic commercialism, Foreigner's heavy metal with keyboard flourishes had racked up sales of over 21 million records worldwide by the early Eighties. On an international tour in 1978, they played to crowds of over 200,000 on some dates.

The band is led by British journeyman rocker Mick Jones, who played in the Sixties with Nero and the Gladiators, a Shadows-like group that had several hits in England, including "Hall of the Mountain King." He worked with French rock singer Johnny Halliday, then with a latter-day version of Spooky Tooth. Jones had worked as an A&R man in New York before joining the Leslie West Band. A year later, he decided to form his own band. In early 1976, he met ex–King Crimson multiinstrumentalist Ian McDonald at recording sessions for Ian Lloyd, former lead singer of Stories. A few months later, Jones and McDonald formed Foreigner with four unknown musicians, including lead vocalist Lou Gramm, founder and lead singer of Black Sheep, a Free and Bad Company cover band in upstate New York.

Their March 1977 debut sold more than three million copies in the U.S. It stayed in the Top Twenty for a year, on the strength of "Feels Like the First Time" (#4, 1977), "Cold as Ice" (#6, 1977) and "Long, Long Way From Home" (#20, 1978). *Double Vision* spawned "Hot Blooded" (#3, 1978) and a #2 hit with the title track. Late in the year they headlined the Reading, England, music festival. "Dirty White Boy" (#12) and "Head Games" (#14) hit in 1979. Several personnel changes occurred, including the addition of ex–Small Face and Roxy Music bassist Rick Wills. The group's LPs continued to sell. By 1981, their debut had sold five million; *Double Vision* seven million; and *Head Games* three million.

Foreigner: (top) Lou Gramm, Mick Jones, (bottom) Rick Wills, Dennis Elliott

Internal friction caused McDonald and Greenwood to quit the group in September 1980, leaving Jones the only original member. Continuing as a quartet for *4*, the group rebounded as the LP moved straight to #1 in 1981, providing two hit singles: a rare ballad, "Waiting for a Girl Like You," and "Urgent," which featured Junior Walker on saxophone.

THE FOUNDATIONS

Formed 1967, London
Peter Macbeth (b. Feb. 2, 1943, London), bass; Alan Warner (b. Apr. 21, 1947, London), gtr.; Clem Curtis (b. Nov. 28, 1940, Trinidad), voc.; Eric Allan Dale (b. Mar. 4, 1936, West Indies), trombone; Tony Gomez (b. Dec. 13, 1948, Ceylon), organ; Pat Burke (b. Oct. 9, 1937, Jamaica), sax, flute; Mike Elliot (b. Aug. 6, 1929, Jamaica), sax; Tim Harris (b. Jan. 14, 1948, London), drums; Colin Young (b. Sep. 12, 1944, Barbados), voc.
1967—*Baby Now That I've Found You* (Uni) *Build Me Up Buttercup* **1969**—*Digging the Foundations*.

The Foundations were a mid-Sixties pop band that had two major hits: the Motown-ish "Baby Now That I've Found You" and "Build Me Up Buttercup." In London, the group became the house band at the Butterfly Club in Westbourne Grove. Record store owner Barry Class became their manager and introduced them to songwriter Tony Macauley, who got them a record deal and then wrote and produced their hits.

Their debut single, "Baby Now That I've Found You" (#11, 1968), went gold. A minor hit, "Back on My Feet

Again," followed before "Build Me Up Buttercup" (co-written by Macauley and former Manfred Mann vocalist Mike d'Abo) hit #3 in early 1969. Followups like "In the Bad, Bad Old Days" and "My Little Chickadee" failed to hit, and the group split up in 1970, although the name was used by a British cabaret act (with little relation to the original group) for several years in the early Seventies.

THE FOUR SEASONS
Formed 1956, Newark, New Jersey
Original lineup: Frankie Valli (b. Francis Casteluccio, May 3, 1937, Newark), voc.; Tommy DeVito (b. June 19, 1936, Belleville, N.J.), gtr.; Nick DeVito, gtr.; Hank Majewski (d. 1969), bass.
1960—(− Nick DeVito; + Bob Gaudio [b. Nov. 17, 1942, Bronx, N.Y.], kybds.; − Majewski; + Nick Massi [b. Sep. 19, 1935, Newark], bass) **1963**—*Sherry* (Vee Jay) *Greetings; Big Girls Don't Cry; Ain't That a Shame* **1964**—*Stay; Dawn* (Philips) *Rag Doll* **1965**—(− Massi; + Joey Long, bass; and after this point numerous personnel changes) *Entertain You; Gold Vault Hits; Working My Way Back to You* **1966**—*Second Vault; Looking Back* **1968**—*Seasoned Hits* (Fontana) **1969**—*Genuine Imitation Life Gazette; Big Ones* **1972**—*Chameleon* (Mowest) **1975**—*Who Loves You* (Warner Bros.) **1977**—*Helicon* **1980**—(group re-forms: Valli; Gaudio; Gerry Polci [b. 1954, Passaic, N.J.], drums, voc.; + Don Ciccone [b. Feb. 28, 1946, New York], gtr.; + Jerry Corbetta [b. Sep. 23, 1947, Denver, Col.] kybds.; + Larry Lingle [b. Apr. 4, 1949, Kan.], gtr.) **1981**—*Reunited Live.*
Frankie Valli solo: **1975**—*Inside You* (Motown) *Close Up* (Private Stock) **1976**—*Story* **1978**—*Frankie Valli Is the Word* (Warner Bros.) **1979**—*Very Best of Frankie Valli* (MCA) **1981**—*Heaven Above Me; The Very Best of Franki Valli* (Warner Bros.).

During their twenty-year career, Frankie Valli and the Four Seasons have sold over 80 million records, making them the most long-lived and successful white doo-wop group. Lead singer Valli (whose three-octave range and falsetto are the group's trademark) has also maintained a successful solo career.

Valli, sometimes billed under his real name and later as Valley, began singing in his mid-teens with the Newark vocal groups the Romans and the Varietones. The Varietones, which included Hank Majewski and the DeVito brothers, eventually became the Four Lovers. The Lovers' "You're the Apple of My Eye," a tune songwriter Otis Blackwell gave them in exchange for their not recording his "Don't Be Cruel" (which he then gave to Elvis Presley), was a hit in 1956, and they appeared on the Ed Sullivan show.

The Four Lovers became the Four Seasons (named after a Jersey cocktail lounge) with the addition of Bob Gaudio, formerly of the Royal Teens and composer of their hit "Short Shorts." As the group's chief songwriter, Gaudio changed their repertoire and sound, which were later refined by producer Bob Crewe. After a single, "Bermuda," flopped, they again became the Four Lovers and returned to the clubs. They also served as Crewe's production group, arranging, performing and providing instrumental and vocal backing in singles Crewe produced for other singers. This arrangement continued until 1962, when Valli, desperate over the group's lack of success, nearly quit the band. Then they recorded a song by Gaudio, "Sherry." After the song was featured on "American Bandstand," the Four Lovers became the Four Seasons once again, and within months "Sherry" hit #1.

The followup, "Big Girls Don't Cry," also went to #1, and over the next five years (until Valli's first solo hit, "I Can't Take My Eyes Off of You" in 1967), the Four Seasons had fifty hits, including "Santa Claus Is Coming to Town" (in an arrangement later imitated by Bruce Springsteen) (#23, 1962); "Walk Like a Man" (#1), "Ain't That a Shame" (#22) and "Candy Girl" (#3) in 1963; "Dawn" (#3), "Stay" (#16), "Ronnie" (#6), "Alone" (#28), "Rag Doll" (#1), "Save It for Me" (#10) and "Big Man in Town" (#20) in 1964; "Bye Bye Baby" (#13), "Girl Come Running" (#30), "Let's Hang On" (#3) and "Working My Way Back to You" (#9) in 1965; "Opus 17 (Don't Worry 'bout Me)" (#12), "I've Got You Under My Skin" (#9) and "Tell It to the Rain" (#10) in 1966; "Beggin'" (#16), "C'mon Marianne" (#9) and "Watch the Flowers Grow" (#30) in 1967.

The group left Vee Jay over a royalty dispute in 1964, and by 1965 were recording for Philips, continuing their string of hits, which ended abruptly with their excursion into psychedelia, *Genuine Imitation Life Gazette.* (They had also recorded several singles, including a cover of Dylan's "Don't Think Twice" in 1965 under the pseudonym the Wonder Who.) As the Sixties closed, the group's popularity waned. By the time they signed to Motown's Mowest subsidiary, in 1971, Valli and Gaudio were the only original members left, and a $1.4 million debt had taken its toll.

In 1972, Crewe, whose independent label had folded, joined the group at Mowest. But even with the Crewe-Gaudio-Valli team intact, none of their singles hit. The release of a 1972 LP, *The Night,* was canceled, and the group toured supporting the Four Tops and the Vandellas. Valli's ten-year-old hearing problem (diagnosed as otosclerosis, excessive calcium deposits in the ear) became critical. (Faced with the possibility of going deaf, Valli underwent surgery in 1976.) Meanwhile, Gaudio retired from performing to concentrate on writing and producing. In 1973, one Gerald Zelmanowitz testified before a Senate subcommittee that the Four Seasons had ties to organized crime, a charge he later retracted.

Valli signed a solo contract with Private Stock in 1974 and soon had several hits, including "My Eyes Adored

You" (#1, 1975), "Swearin' to God" (#6, 1975) and "Our Day Will Come" (#11, 1975). The Four Seasons had almost ceased to exist, but in 1975 they made a comeback with one of their biggest-selling singles, "Who Loves You" (#3), followed the next year by "December 1963 (Oh What a Night)" (#1, 1976). Shortly before a 1977 tour, Valli announced—with some bitterness—that he would never work with the Four Seasons again, although he and Gaudio have retained co-ownership of the group and its name. But despite Valli's solo success ("Grease" hit #1 and sold over seven million copies), the Four Seasons reformed in 1980 with Gaudio, Valli, guitarist Don Ciccone (former lead singer of the Critters and a Season since 1974), keyboardist Jerry Corbetta (ex–lead singer of Sugarloaf), guitarist Larry Lingle and drummer Gerry Polci (who had been doing vocals with the group since 1973).

THE FOUR TOPS

Formed circa 1953, Detroit
Levi Stubbs (b. Detroit), voc.; Renaldo Benson (b. Detroit), voc.; Lawrence Payton (b. Detroit), voc.; Abdul Fakir (b. Detroit), voc.
1965—*Four Tops* (Tamla/Motown) **1966**—*Second Album; On Top* **1967**—*Live; Reach Out; On Broadway; Greatest Hits* **1968**—*Yesterday's Dreams* **1969**—*Four Tops Now; Soul Spin* **1970**—*Still Waters Run Deep; Changing Times* **1971**—*Greatest Hits, volume 2* **1972**—*Dynamite* (with the Supremes) *Nature Planned It; Keeper of the Castle* (Dunhill) **1973**—*Four Tops Story* (Tamla/Motown) *Main Street People* (Dunhill) **1981**—*Tonight* (Casablanca).

One of Motown's most consistent hitmakers, the Four Tops have charted with scores of upbeat love songs featuring Levi Stubbs' rough-hewn lead vocals. With 1981's "When She Was My Girl," the original lineup had been intact nearly thirty years. The four members met at a party in Detroit and soon began calling themselves the Four Aims. They were signed to Chess Records in 1956 and soon changed their name to the Four Tops. The single "Kiss Me Baby" was the first of a string of supper-club-style flops that lasted for seven years on a series of labels (Red Top, Riverside and Columbia).

By 1964, they had joined up with old friend Berry Gordy, Jr., the founder of Motown Records. Gordy had them cut *Breaking Through* for his experimental workshop subsidiary; it went nowhere. Later that year, they were finally directed toward contemporary soul. Under the wing of Motown's top production and writing team—Holland-Dozier-Holland—they were launched with "Baby I Need Your Loving," which went to #11 in 1964. Over the next eight years, they made almost thirty appearances on the charts, and Levi Stubbs (whose brother Joe sang in the Falcons with Wilson Pickett) became an

The Four Tops: (top) Lawrence Payton, Renaldo Benson, (bottom) Levi Stubbs, Abdul Fakir

international star and a major influence on other singers in the Sixties.

The group's 1965 hits included "Ask the Lonely" (#24), "Same Old Song" (#5) and "I Can't Help Myself (Sugar Pie, Honey Bunch)," which was #1. "Reach Out I'll Be There" hit the top of the pop charts in October 1966. They followed up with "Standing in the Shadows of Love" (#6, 1967).

Following the Motown game plan, the Tops solidified their success with extensive nightclub work that earned them a reputation as one of soul's best-choreographed teams. In 1967, they scaled the charts with "Bernadette" (#4) and "Seven Rooms of Gloom" (#14); but when Holland-Dozier-Holland left Motown in 1967 to form their own label, the group's successes dwindled. In fact, two of their bigger hits from 1968 were covers: the Left Banke's "Walk Away Renee" (#14) and Tim Hardin's "If I Were a Carpenter" (#20).

In 1972, the group left Motown for ABC/Dunhill, where they quickly recorded a couple of million-sellers: "Keeper of the Castle" (#10) and in 1973 "Ain't No Woman Like the One I've Got" (#4). But it proved to be only a brief resurgence, and the Tops spent most of the Seventies grinding out the oldies in Vegas and supper clubs until their 1981 comeback hit, "When She Was My Girl" (#11).

KIM FOWLEY

Born July 21, 1942, Manila
1967—*Love Is Alive and Well* (Tower/Capital) **1968**—*Born to Be Wild* (Imperial) **1969**—*Outrageous; Good*

Clean Fun 1972—*I'm Bad* (Capitol) 1973—*International Heroes* 1979—*Animal God of the Streets; Snake Document Masquerade* (Island).

Los Angeles–based songwriter/producer/manager and general scenemaker Kim Fowley is the son of actor Douglas Fowley (Doc on "Wyatt Earp") and grandson of composer Rudolf Friml. He claims he attended six colleges before settling in Los Angeles, where he worked as a street singer, shoe designer, dancer and fortune-teller; he also served briefly in the Air Force. In 1957, he made local news by singing with three members of a black vocal group, the Jayhawks. He then joined the Sleepwalkers, who included Sandy Nelson and, for a few shows, guitarist Phil Spector. Since then, Fowley has demonstrated an ear for new talent and a knack for gimmicky novelty singles.

In 1959, working as a disc jockey in Boise, Idaho, he produced the first sessions for Paul Revere and the Raiders ("Like, Long Hair" on Gardena). In the early Sixties, he assembled the Murmaids and produced their version of David Gates's "Popsicles and Icicles" (#3, 1964). He also produced the Hollywood Argyles' "Alley Oop" (#1, 1960); "Nutrocker," based on Tchaikovsky tunes, for B. Bumble and the Stingers (#23, 1962) and the Rivingtons' "Papa-Oom-Mow-Mow" (#48, 1962).

Fowley also spent time in London in the mid-Sixties. He worked with P. J. Proby (primarily as choreographer) and appeared on the TV show "Ready, Steady, Go" in 1966. He also produced sessions for Slade, Family, Dave Mason and Jim Capaldi of Traffic, and Soft Machine. Back in Los Angeles, he sang on the Mothers of Invention's *Freak Out*. He also produced records by the Seeds, Johnny Winter (*Progressive Blues Experiment*) and the Fraternity of Man ("Don't Bogart that Joint"). Fowler then produced Gene Vincent's 1969 comeback, *I'm Back and I'm Proud;* part of Warren Zevon's 1969 *Wanted Dead or Alive;* the Fifties parody band Flash Cadillac and the Continental Kids; and Jonathan Richman and the Modern Lovers.

Fowley also wrote or cowrote songs recorded by the Beach Boys, the Byrds, Doug Sahm's Sir Douglas Quintet, Them, Leo Kottke and Cat Stevens. He has also recorded sporadically on his own, both under his own name and as "groups" including the Renegades ("Charge!"). In the late Seventies, Fowley got in on the burgeoning punk movement by advertising for an all-female hard-rock band which became the Runaways, who included Joan Jett. He has had two books of poetry published: *The Earth Is Really Flat* and *The Oblong Tiger*.

INEZ AND CHARLIE FOXX
Inez Foxx, born September 9, 1942, Greensboro, North Carolina; Charlie Foxx, born October 23, 1939, Greensboro, North Carolina
1964—*Mockingbird* (Sue) 1973—*Inez at Memphis* (Volt).

Inez and Charlie Foxx were a brother-and-sister vocal duo who are best known for such novelty hits as "Mockingbird" (#7, 1963). The pair started recording around 1957 on the Sue label. Their sporadic success throughout the early Sixties peaked with "Mockingbird" (later covered by James Taylor and Carly Simon). The Foxxes tried to repeat that hit with several subsequent releases (some credited only to Inez, although Charlie usually supplied background vocals), like "Hi Diddle Diddle" (1963), "Hurt by Love" (1964), "I Stand Accused—Guilty" (1967) and "(1-2-3-4-5-6-7) Count the Days" (1968). By the late Sixties, they were recording for Musicor/Dynamo; in 1969 Inez began releasing solo records on Stax-Volt.

PETER FRAMPTON
Born April 22, 1950, Beckenham, England
1972—*Wind of Change* (A&M) 1973—*Frampton's Camel* 1974—*Something's Happening* 1975—*Frampton; Frampton Comes Alive!* 1977—*I'm in You* 1979—*Where I Should Be* 1981—*Breaking All the Rules* 1982—*The Art of Control*.

After years as the moderately successful lead guitarist and singer in a string of British bands—the Herd, Humble Pie and his own Frampton's Camel—Peter Frampton's nearly continuous U.S. touring paid off in 1976 when his live set *Frampton Comes Alive!* sold over ten million copies and was briefly ranked among the ten best-selling albums ever.

Frampton made his professional debut at age nine and joined the Herd at 16. The band had several U.K. teenybopper hits, including "From the Underworld" in 1967

Peter Frampton

and "Paradise Lost" and "I Don't Want Our Loving to Die." Frampton was named "Face of 1968" by several British magazines. He left the Herd in 1969 to establish a reputation as a more serious musician, and formed Humble Pie with ex–Small Faces Steve Marriott and ex–Spooky Tooth bassist Greg Ridley. He wrote and sang part of Humble Pie's early repertoire, but left in 1971 to pursue his own career.

After a stint of session work (George Harrison's *All Things Must Pass,* Harry Nilsson's *Son of Schmilsson*), Frampton recorded a solo debut with assistance from Ringo Starr, Billy Preston and others. He formed Frampton's Camel with ex–Spooky Tooth Mike Kellie, Rick Wills (later of Roxy Music, the reunited Small Faces and Foreigner) and Mike Gallagher in 1973 in order to tour the U.S. Frampton released an album a year and continued touring, making some inroads on FM radio, until 1975's *Frampton Comes Alive!,* recorded at Winterland in San Francisco with a band that included Bob Mayo (guitar and keyboards), Stanley Sheldon (bass) and John Siomos (drums). The album included the best of Frampton's solo compositions and yielded three 1976 hit singles: "Show Me the Way" (#6), "Baby I Love Your Way" (#12) and "Do You Feel Like We Do" (#10). By the end of 1976, Frampton had grossed nearly $70 million in concert fees and royalties.

The follow-up album, *I'm in You,* had a #2 hit with the title cut, although its other singles didn't reach the Top Ten. Frampton made his movie debut in Robert Stigwood's 1978 debacle, *Sgt. Pepper's Lonely Hearts Club Band,* but even before the movie was released there were rumors that he had succumbed to depression and heavy drinking. In June 1978 he suffered a car crash in the Bahamas that left him with a concussion, muscle damage and broken bones. Late in 1978, his relationship with longtime girlfriend Penny McCall ended. By the late Seventies, Frampton had returned to touring 10,000-seaters, although *Where I Should Be* included "I Can't Stand It No More" (#14, 1979). He currently lives in New York's Westchester County and continues to tour and record.

CONNIE FRANCIS
Born Concetta Franconero, December 12, 1938, Newark, New Jersey
1963—*Very Best of Connie Francis* (MGM).

During the period between the first rock & roll explosion in the mid-Fifties and the emergence of the Beatles, singer Francis had several hits, including "Stupid Cupid" (#14, 1958). Popular in Italy and Spain, where she records in the native languages, Francis has had over fifty chart singles in her career, more hits than any other female vocalist except Aretha Franklin.

She debuted at age five singing "O Sole Mio" at school. By 11 she had appeared on Arthur Godfrey's TV talent show, and Godfrey suggested that she change her name. Following high school, she turned semi-professional and falsified her age to sing in cocktail lounges. She began recording for MGM in 1955 while studying radio and television at New York University. Her father, a former dock worker, suggested she record an up-tempo version of one of his favorites, a 1923 tune called "Who's Sorry Now." It was a hit in early 1958, and she later had hits with other oldies like "Among My Souvenirs" (#7, 1960) and "Together" (#6, 1961), both of which were written in 1928.

Over the next five years, Francis had 25 records in the Top 100. Some of her best sellers included "My Happiness" (#2), "If I Didn't Care" (#22), "Lipstick on Your Collar" (#5) and "Frankie" (#9) in 1959; "Mama" (#8) and "Everybody's Somebody's Fool" (#1) in 1960. Francis appeared in the films *Where the Boys Are* and *When the Boys Meet the Girls.* She also sang the theme for *Where the Boys Are* and appeared in Brylcreem commercials: "A little dab'll do ya!"

Francis' big hits ended with the beginning of Beatlemania, though she had several minor successes through the end of the decade and continued to perform in nightclubs. Following a 1974 appearance at the Westbury Theater outside New York, she was raped in her motel room. (She later sued the motel for negligence and was awarded $3,055,000 in damages.) She stopped performing and underwent 2½ years of psychiatric treatment. In 1981, Francis made a well-publicized return appearance at Westbury.

ARETHA FRANKLIN
Born March 25, 1942, Memphis
1961—*Aretha* (Columbia)   1962—*The Electrifying Aretha Franklin*   1963—*Laughing on the Outside; The Tender, the Moving, the Swinging Aretha Franklin*   1964—*Running Out of Fools*   1964—*The Gospel Sound of Aretha Franklin* (Checker) (reissue 1972)   1965—*Yeah! Aretha Franklin in Person* (Columbia)   1966—*Soul Sister*   1967—*Greatest Hits; I Never Loved a Man the Way I Love You* (Atlantic)   *Aretha Arrives*   1968—*Lady Soul; Aretha Now; Aretha in Paris*   1969—*Soul '69; Aretha's Gold*   1970—*This Girl's in Love with You; Spirit in the Dark*   1971—*Live at Fillmore West; Greatest Hits*   1972—*Young, Gifted and Black; Amazing Grace*   1973—*Hey Now Hey (The Other Side of the Sky); The First Twelve Sides* (Columbia)   *The Best of Aretha Franklin* (Atlantic)   1974—*Let Me in Your Life; With Everything I Feel in Me*   1975—*You*   1976—*Sparkle; Ten Years of Gold*   1977—*Sweet Passion*   1978—*Almighty Fire*   1979—*La Diva*   1980—*Aretha* (Arista)   1981—*Love All the Hurt Away*   1982—*Jump to It*   1983—*Get It Right.*

Aretha Franklin was the definitive soul singer of the Sixties. She fused the unpredictable leaps and swoops of

Aretha Franklin

the gospel music she grew up on with the sensuality of R&B and the precision of pop, and when she hit her stride in 1967, she made over a dozen million-selling records. She moved toward the pop mainstream with fitful success in the Seventies and has continued to score hits into the Eighties with a less ecstatic, arguably more mature style.

Franklin's father, the Reverend C. L. Franklin, was the pastor of Detroit's 4,500-member New Bethel Baptist Church and a nationally known gospel singer. Her mother, also a gospel singer, deserted the family when Aretha was six and died four years later. Aretha and her sisters, Carolyn and Erma, sang regularly at her father's church, and Aretha's first recordings were made there when she was 14. The teenaged Aretha toured the gospel circuit with her father, and she was befriended by Clara Ward, Mahalia Jackson, James Cleveland and Sam Cooke.

By 1960, Aretha Franklin had crossed into secular music. She moved to New York City and was signed to Columbia Records by John Hammond. She found early acceptance in the R&B market with "Today I Sing the Blues" (#10 R&B, 1960), "Won't Be Long" (#7 R&B, 1961) and "Operation Heartbreak" (#6 R&B, 1961), but in six years and ten albums, she had only one pop hit: "Rock-a-bye Your Baby with a Dixie Melody" (#37 pop, 1961). In 1966, she left Columbia for Atlantic and—with the help of producer Jerry Wexler, arranger Arif Mardin and engineer Tom Dowd—began to make the records that would reshape soul music.

Her first session yielded "I Never Loved a Man (the Way I Love You)" (#1 R&B, #9 pop, 1967) and heralded a phenomenal two years in which she sold in the millions with "Respect" (#1 pop and R&B, 1967), "Baby I Love You" (#1 R&B, #4 pop, 1967), "Chain of Fools" (#1 R&B, #2 pop 1968), "Since You've Been Gone" (#1 R&B, #5 pop, 1968), "Think" (#1 R&B, #7 pop, 1968), "The House That Jack Built" (#2 R&B, #6 pop, 1968), "I Say a Little Prayer" (#3 R&B, #10 pop, 1968) and "See Saw (#9 R&B, #14 pop, 1968).

Franklin's material ranged from R&B numbers by Otis Redding, Don Covay and Ronnie Shannon to pop fare by Carole King and Gerry Goffin, and Burt Bacharach and Hal David, and included her own songs, cowritten with her husband and manager, Ted White. Most of her Sixties sessions were recorded with the Muscle Shoals Sound Rhythm Section in Alabama or with a New York band led by King Curtis; Franklin herself was responsible for the vocal arrangements, whose gospel-styled call-and-response choruses often featured the Sweet Inspirations, who included her sister Carolyn.

By 1968, Franklin reigned throughout America and Europe as "Lady Soul"—a symbol of black pride (she was presented an award by Martin Luther King and appeared on the cover of *Time*). But her personal life was turbulent. Her marriage to White broke up after he struck her in public on one occasion and shot her new production manager on another; she was arrested for drunken driving and disorderly conduct; and her father was arrested for possession of marijuana.

The hits continued (giving her more million-sellers than any other woman in recording history)—"Don't Play That Song" (#1 R&B, #11 pop, 1970), "Bridge over Troubled Water" (#1 R&B, #6 pop, 1971), "Spanish Harlem" (#1 R&B, #2 pop, 1971), "Rock Steady" (#2 R&B, #9 pop, 1971), "Day Dreaming" (#1 R&B, #5 pop, 1972) and "Until You Come Back to Me (That's What I'm Gonna Do)" (#1 R&B, 1973, #3 pop, 1974)—but the Seventies found her searching, sometimes aimlessly, for direction.

Her last burst of pure gospel, *Amazing Grace* (recorded live in Los Angeles with her father officiating and the Reverend James Cleveland playing piano and conducting the choir), was also her last album produced by Wexler. Thereafter, she moved from producer to producer: Quincy Jones (*Hey Now Hey*), Curtis Mayfield (*Sparkle*), Lamont Dozier (*Sweet Passion*), Van McCoy (*La Diva*). Her concerts became Las Vegas-style costume extravaganzas.

In 1980, Franklin left Atlantic, signed with Arista and positioned herself as the *grande dame* of pop, although she sang "Respect" and "Think" in *The Blues Brothers* movie that year. Her first two Arista albums were produced by Arif Mardin, and each included an old soul standard as well as glossier MOR material. "Love All the Hurt Away," a collaboration with George Benson, went to #6 on the R&B charts in 1981, and with *Jump to It,*

Franklin reestablished herself as a hitmaker when the title tune hit R&B #1 and pop #25 in 1982.

Erma Franklin (born 1939) and Carolyn Franklin (born 1945) have been professional singers as long as their better-known sister. After many years on the gospel circuit, Erma began recording soul and pop material in the mid-Sixties. Her 1967 Shout release, "Piece of My Heart" (#10, R&B), preceded Janis Joplin's version by several months. She recorded for the Brunswick label in the late Sixties and early Seventies. As a member of the Sweet Inspirations, Carolyn sang backup for many of Atlantic's stars in the Sixties and made the charts with "Sweet Inspiration" (#5 R&B, #18 pop, 1968). She later recorded as a solo act for RCA.

MICHAEL FRANKS

Born September 18, 1944, La Jolla, California
1973—*Michael Franks* (Brut, reissued in 1983, John Hammond) **1976**—*The Art of Tea* (Reprise) **1977**—*Sleeping Gypsy* (Warner Bros.) **1978**—*Birchfield Nines* **1979**—*Tiger in the Rain* **1980**—*One Bad Habit* **1982**—*Objects of Desire*.

Songwriter Michael Franks has been recording his own pop-jazz tunes since 1973, with occasional pop recognition; his songs have been covered by Melissa Manchester, Manhattan Transfer and the Carpenters.

Franks played folk and rock in high school in La Jolla, and he majored in contemporary literature at UCLA while working part-time as a musician. In the late Sixties, he completed a master's in contemporary culture at the University of Montreal. While in Canada, he opened shows for Gordon Lightfoot and worked with Carnival, later Lighthouse.

In the early Seventies, Franks taught undergraduate music courses and worked toward a Ph.D. at UCLA and Berkeley. His doctoral dissertation was entitled "Contemporary Songwriting and How It Relates to Society." He scored two films in 1971, *Count Your Bullets* and *Zandy's Bride*. In 1972, Sonny Terry and Brownie McGhee recorded three of his songs, with Franks backing them on mandolin and banjo. Buddah/Brut signed him in 1972, and his "Can't Seem to Shake This Rock 'n' Roll" received some airplay. He toured the U.S. opening for comedian Robert Klein in 1973.

After scoring another film in England, Franks returned to California and took on a research project for Warner Brothers pictures that led to his Reprise signing. His yearly albums have featured well-known backing musicians—the Crusaders on *The Art of Tea*, which included the minor hit "Popsicle Toes" (1976); Brazilian musicians on *Sleeping Gypsy*—and have earned him a cult following.

JOHN FRED AND HIS PLAYBOY BAND

Formed late 1950s, Baton Rouge, Louisiana
John Fred (b. May 8, 1941, Baton Rouge), voc., har-

monica; Charlie Spinosa (b. Dec. 29, 1948, Baton Rouge), trumpet; Ronnie Goodson (b. Feb. 2, 1945, Miami), trumpet; Andrew Bernard (b. 1945, New Orleans), sax; James O'Rourke (b. Mar. 14, 1947, Fall River, Mass.), gtr.; Harold Cowart (b. June 12, 1944, Baton Rouge), bass; Joe Micelli (b. July 9, 1946, Baton Rouge), drums; Tommy Dee (b. Thomas De Generes, Nov. 3, 1946, Baton Rouge), organ.
1965—*John Fred and His Playboys* (Paula) **1966**—*34:40 of John Fred and His Playboys* **1967**—*Agnes English* **1969**—*Permanently Stated* **1970**—*Love in My Soul* (Uni).

John Fred and His Playboy Band were an R&B-inspired rock band best known for their 1968 hit, the three-million-seller "Judy in Disguise (with Glasses)." Led by John Fred, a former all-American basketball player at Louisiana State University, who began recording in 1958 with "Shirley" on Montel Records, the group established itself in Louisiana and Texas clubs in the early Sixties. Its lone hit (which was also the group's sixteenth single), "Judy in Disguise" (a wordplay on the Beatles' "Lucy in the Sky"), went gold in early 1968; and the 45's success propelled *Agnes English* to the lower rungs of the album charts. But followups like "Hey Hey Bunny" (1968) didn't come close to matching "Judy," and the group broke up the next year. Between 1975 and 1977, Fred formed another Playboy Band before going to work for R.C.S. Records in Baton Rouge, where he coproduced a 1979 LP for Irma Thomas.

FREDDIE AND THE DREAMERS

Formed 1960, Manchester, England
Freddie Garrity (b. Nov. 14, 1940), voc., gtr.; Derek Quinn (b. May 24, 1942), gtr., harmonica; Roy Crewsdon (b. May 29, 1941), gtr., piano, drums; Pete Birrell (b. May 9, 1941), bass; Bennie Dwyer (b. Sep. 11, 1940), drums
1963—*Freddie and the Dreamers* (Columbia) **1964**—*You Were Made for Me* **1966**—*Freddie and the Dreamers* (Mercury).

Freddie and the Dreamers, all born in Manchester, were the buffoons of the British Invasion. The group was formed by ex-milkman Freddie Garrity, who had previously worked in a Fifties skiffle band. A bespectacled young man with a slight resemblance to Buddy Holly, Freddie looked silly while the rest of the group tried to act tough. In 1962, after successfully auditioning for the BBC, they rose to prominence in England and signed with Columbia. Their first single, a cover of James Ray's "If You've Gotta Make a Fool of Somebody," hit the British Top Five. Over the next few years, they enjoyed a half-dozen U.K. hits, including "You Were Made for Me" (#3, U.K.) and "I Understand" (#5, U.K.).

"I'm Telling You Now," originally released in England

in 1963, went to #1 in the U.S. in mid 1965, spurred by the group's touring and appearances on the "Shindig!" and "Hulabaloo" television shows. Another American hit, "Do the Freddie" (#18), sparked a momentary dance craze in emulation of Freddie's arm and leg waving. The group was featured in the 1963 film *What a Crazy World*. In 1965, they switched to Mercury, but their U.S. hits ended the next year. The band played cabarets and clubs until breaking up in the early Seventies. Garrity and Pete Birrell thereafter hosted their own children's TV series in England called "The Little Big Time." The Dreamers reformed in 1976, with only Garrity remaining from the original lineup, and they remain active in supper clubs and cabarets.

FREE

Formed 1968, London
Original lineup: Paul Rodgers (b. Dec. 17, 1949, Middleborough, Eng.), voc.; Paul Kossoff (b. Sep. 14, 1950, London; d. March 19, 1976, New York City), gtr.; Andy Fraser (b. Aug. 7, 1952, London), bass; Simon Kirke (b. July 28, 1949, Wales), drums.
1969—*Tons of Sobs* (A&M) *Free* **1970**—*Fire and Water; Highway; Free Live* **1972**—*Free at Last* (− Kossoff; − Fraser; + Tetsu Yamauchi [b. 1946, Fukuoka, Japan], bass; + John "Rabbit" Bundrick, kybds.) **1973**—*Heartbreaker* **1975**—*Best of Free*.

Free distilled British blues down to riffs, silences and Paul Rodgers' ornately anguished vocals—most memorably in "All Right Now" (#4, 1970). The style they established was made more ponderous and commercially successful by Bad Company, Foreigner and other Seventies hardrock bands. Free started in the London pubs when Simon Kirke and Paul Kossoff, then in the blues band Black Cat Bones, heard Rodgers singing with Brown Sugar. The three enlisted 16-year-old Andy Fraser from John Mayall's Bluesbreakers, and they got the name Free from Alexis Korner. Neither their first two albums nor a U.S. tour opening for Blind Faith in 1969 made inroads for them, but *Fire and Water,* including "All Right Now," signaled that they had honed their approach.

After 1970's *Highway,* the group split up. Kossoff and Kirke joined bassist Tetsu Yamauchi (later with the Faces) and session keyboardist John "Rabbit" Bundrick for one album; Rodgers formed a group called Peace; and Fraser started Toby. By 1972, the original Free had re-formed for *Free at Last.* Personal problems and drug use—especially Kossoff's—took a toll on the band, and they broke up again. Fraser joined guitarist Chris Spedding in Sharks for one album; Kossoff started Back Street Crawler (later Crawler), but died of a heart ailment in 1976 on an airplane en route to New York. Rodgers and Kirke rejoined Yamauchi and Bundrick for 1973's *Heartbreaker,* then retired the Free name to start Bad Company.

ALAN FREED

Born December 15, 1922, Johnstown, Pennsylvania; died January 20, 1965, Palm Springs, California

By playing "race" records for white teenagers, disc jockey Alan Freed helped disseminate early rock & roll, and he was an effective behind-the-scenes businessman. At one point, he claimed to have coined the term rock & roll and tried to copyright it. But when the antirock backlash of the early Sixties and the payola scandals began, Freed was their prime victim.

Raised in Salem, Ohio, Freed played trombone in high school and fronted a jazz band, the Sultans of Swing. He was drafted, and in the Army he developed an ear infection that led to a partial hearing loss. After his discharge, he earned a master's in engineering from Ohio State University in the early Forties, moved into radio work at WKST (New Castle, Pennsylvania), then as sportscaster/program director for WKBN (Youngstown, Ohio), WIBE (Philadelphia) and, finally, disc jockey at WAKR (Akron, Ohio). In 1950 he moved to Cleveland to work at WKEL and then in 1951 he moved to WJW, where he began hosting the late-night "Moondog Rock 'n' Roll Party." With a whiskey bottle within reach, Freed played R&B records from independent labels, bringing black music to a large new audience. He pioneered integrated concert bills with his Moondog Balls in Cleveland, where one 1952 show drew a crowd of 25,000 to a hall half that size; the resulting pandemonium caused the show to be canceled. (In May 1958, Freed was arrested for anarchy and incitement to riot after fighting broke out at a Freed-hosted show in Boston.)

New York's WINS recruited Freed in 1954 for $75,000 a year, and the station moved to the top of the ratings. Once in New York, Freed began staging live shows at the Paramount Theater in Brooklyn. He also picked up writing credits on hits by Chuck Berry and by the Moonglows, although it is not clear whether Freed simply received part interest in the songs in return for promotional favors. (Congressional payola investigations later established that Freed had accepted certain favors.) By the time ugly allegations first surfaced, Freed was working for WABC, New York, which fired him in 1959 after he refused to sign—"on principle"—an affidavit stating participation in bribes. He was by then America's top disc jockey.

From early in his career, Freed's taste in records had led him to be labeled a "nigger lover," and in 1957 a Freed-hosted TV show was summarily canceled when Frankie Lymon was shown dancing with a white girl. Freed's continuing practice of playing black originals rather than white acts' cover versions resulted in his having few defenders in the established music business. While Dick Clark, whose empire was built on white teen idols, escaped the payola investigations unscathed, Freed was blackballed within the music business. He was a broken man by the time he came to trial in December 1962, when he pleaded guilty to two counts of commercial bribery, for which he was fined $300 and given a suspended sentence. By March 1964, he was living in Palm Springs—an unemployed borderline alcoholic—when he was indicted on new charges of tax evasion. Before proceedings began, he was hospitalized with uremia and died in January 1965. It had only been a decade since he'd announced, "Anyone who says rock & roll is a passing fad or a flash in the pan has rocks in his head, dad!"

BOBBY FREEMAN

Born June 13, 1940, San Francisco
1958—*Do You Wanna Dance* (Jubilee) **1959**—*Get in the Swim* (Josie) **1960**—*Loveable Style of Bobby Freeman* (King) **1964**—*C'mon and Swim* (Autumn).

A journeyman R&B singer, Bobby Freeman is best known for "Do You Wanna Dance," which became a #5 hit for him in 1958 and was later covered by several artists, including the Beach Boys (1965) and the Ramones (1978). A pianist as well as a singer, by the age of 14 Freeman was working with a San Francisco group called the Romancers who recorded briefly for the Dootone label. He was 17 when he recorded his "Do You Wanna Dance." He followed up with lesser hits ("Betty Lou Got a New Pair of Shoes" and "Need Your Love") and made sporadic appearances on the pop charts through the late Fifties and mid-Sixties with "Mary Ann Thomas" (1959), "Ebb Tide" (1959), "(I Do the) Shimmy Shimmy" (1960) and "The Mess Around" (1961).

In 1964 Freeman enjoyed a brief resurgence with some Sly Stone-produced sides on Autumn Records, most notably the dance-craze-inspired "C'mon and Swim," which hit the Top Five. He tried to milk the brief dance craze with the followup "S-W-I-M," but by then the public had cooled, although he continued to tour widely over the next couple of years. By the late Sixties, he was supporting himself primarily as a singer in strip bars. In 1974, he was signed by Touch Records, a small Los Angeles–based label that released a single, "Everything's Love," with little success.

KINKY FRIEDMAN

Born Richard Friedman, October 31, 1944, Palestine, Texas
1973—*Sold American* (Vanguard) **1975**—*Kinky Friedman* (ABC) **1976**—*Lasso from El Paso* (Epic).

Country songwriter and sometime leader of the Texas Jewboys, Kinky Friedman drawls his way through tunes like "High on Jesus," "Ride 'em Jewboy" and "Get Your Biscuits in the Oven and Your Buns in Bed." Richard Friedman studied psychology at the University of Texas, then joined the Peace Corps, for which he claims to have instructed natives in Borneo in throwing the Frisbee. Back in Texas, at a farm called Rio Duckworth, he started King

Arthur and the Carrots, whose songs like "Beach Party Boo Boo," and Friedman's penchant for gaudy stage outfits, attracted the attention of Austin patrons like Kris Kristofferson and Commander Cody.

Friedman has been making albums since 1972, with the support over the years of Waylon Jennings (who produced "Carryin' the Torch"), Ringo Starr, Billy Swan and Bob Dylan, who invited Kinky to appear with the Rolling Thunder Revue, which provided some live cuts for Friedman's *Lasso from El Paso*. Friedman has appeared at Nashville's Grand Ole Opry, but is apparently too vulgar for the mainstream country audience. In 1981, advice columnist Abigail van Buren unsuccessfully sued over his "Dear Abbie," which he claims he wrote for Abbie Hoffman. Friedman moved to New York City in 1979 and is a frequent headliner at the Lone Star Cafe. As of late 1982, he was working on a Broadway musical.

THE FRIENDS OF DISTINCTION

Formed 1967, Los Angeles
Harry Elston (b. Nov. 4, 1938, Dallas); Floyd Butler (b. June 5, 1941, San Diego); Jessica Cleaves (b. Dec. 10, 1948, Beverly Hills); Barbara Love (b. July 24, 1941, Los Angeles).
1969—*Grazin'* (RCA).

Black MOR pop vocal group the Friends of Distinction are best remembered for their 1969 "Grazin' in the Grass" (#3). The group was formed around chief composer Harry Elston, who had worked with Ray Charles, as did Floyd Butler. Ex-football-star-turned-Hollywood-actor Jim Brown became the group's financial backer, and they signed with RCA in 1968.

By early 1969, "Grazin' " had hit the Top Five. Lesser hits—"Going in Circles" (#15, 1969) and "Let Yourself Go" (#63, 1969)—followed. "Love or Let Me Be Lonely" was their last big hit (#6, 1970). In 1971, Barbara Love (daughter of West Coast disc jockey Reuben Brown) left the group, which soon disbanded. Jessica Cleaves went on to join Earth, Wind and Fire.

ROBERT FRIPP (see King Crimson)

THE FUGS

Formed 1965, New York City
Ed Sanders (b. Kansas City), voc., gtr.; Tuli Kupferberg (b. New York City), voc.; Ken Weaver (b. Galveston), voc., drums.
1965—*First Album* (ESP) **1966**—*Virgin Fugs* **1968**—*Tenderness Junction* (Reprise) *It Crawled into My Hand, Honest* **1969**—*The Belle of Avenue A* **1970**—*Golden Filth* **1983**—*Proto-punk* (PVC).

These perverse post-Beatnik poets were too pointedly topical and obscene for mass consumption, but the Fugs were the most relentless comic satirists of the hippie era.

Their targets included sexual repression, rock, politics and the foibles of humanity in general.

Ed Sanders had graduated from NYU in 1960 with a BA in ancient Greek; in 1961, he marched on the Pentagon. He was a published poet who briefly ran the Peace Eye bookstore and published the literary magazine *Fuck You*. Tuli Kupferberg, a lanky, hirsute, perenially bedraggled-looking figure whom Beat poet Allen Ginsberg immortalized in *Howl* as "the person who jumped off the Brooklyn Bridge and survived," was also a published poet, a graduate of Brooklyn College.

With Weaver and an ever-changing roster of backing musicians—including Peter Stampfel and Steve Weber of the Holy Modal Rounders, guitarists Vinny Leary, Pete Kearney and Ken Pine, bassists John Anderson and Charles Larkey and drummer Bob Mason—they became a long-running Off Off Broadway rock-theater phenomenon in Greenwich Village, with audiences often walking out on their scathingly profane, put-down-riddled theater-of-outrageous-absurdity performances.

After more than 900 performances at the Players Theater and the Bridge Theater, they embarked on a cross-country tour in a borrowed Volkswagen van. In late 1968, they toured Europe, at one point trying unsuccessfully to get into then-troubled Czechoslovakia in order to masturbate in front of invading Russian tanks.

In the late Sixties, Sanders released solo albums on Reprise, *Sanders' Truckstop*, and *Beer Cans on the Moon*, and reported on the Charles Manson trial for the underground press; he later wrote a book about the murder case and the trial, *The Family*, which became a best seller. In mid-1979 Sanders presented a two-hour rock-theater extravaganza in Woodstock. Kupferberg went on to publish books like *1001 Ways to Make Love* and to publish cartoons in the underground press. From the mid-Seventies to 1982, he worked as a production assistant for the now-defunct *SoHo Weekly News*. He became the Director of Revolting Theater and continues to perform at colleges and at New York venues.

THE BOBBY FULLER FOUR
Formed mid 1960s, El Paso, Texas
Bobby Fuller (b. Oct. 22, 1943, Baytown, Tex.; d. July 18, 1966, Los Angeles), gtr., voc.; Randy Fuller, bass; DeWayne Quirico, drums; Jim Reese, gtr.
1965—*I Fought the Law* (Mustang) 1966—*KRLA King of the Wheels* 1981—*The Best of the Bobby Fuller Four* (Rhino).

"I Fought the Law" established the Bobby Fuller Four for a half-year of stardom in 1966. The group, all Texans, established a reputation in El Paso, then moved to Los Angeles. "Let Her Dance" became popular in the Southwest in 1965, and "I Fought the Law"—written by a member of Buddy Holly's Crickets, Sonny Curtis—

reached #9 in 1966 nationally. A Buddy Holly cover, "Love's Made a Fool of You" (#26, 1966), was a follow-up hit, and Bobby Fuller costarred in *Bikini Party in a Haunted House*.

In July 1966, Bobby Fuller died under mysterious circumstances in his car parked in front of his Hollywood home. The fact that he had been beaten up and had ingested gasoline was not released to the public. Although the police ruled his death a suicide, friends speculated that he was murdered, possibly by mobsters. Afterwards, the Randy Fuller Four continued, but without success.

JESSE "LONE CAT" FULLER
Born March 12, 1896, Jonesboro, Georgia; died January 29, 1976, Oakland, California
1963—*San Francisco Bay Blues* (Prestige).

Jesse Fuller was a country-bluesman, a one-man band and the composer of "San Francisco Bay Blues." Fuller never knew his father, and the man his mother lived with often brutally mistreated him. By age five, Fuller had learned to play a homemade stringed mouth bow. After living with his mother's relatives a few years, he left home at ten and began traveling around the South and Midwest, working odd jobs and playing the blues.

In the early Twenties, Fuller was discovered outside Universal Film Studios shining shoes. He was given bit parts in *The Thief of Bagdad, East of Suez* and other movies, for which he was paid $7.50 a day. During his middle age, he worked a succession of jobs including cowherding, broom making and car washing. He remained committed to music, however, and in the late Thirties debuted on radio station KNX (Oakland) singing "John Henry."

In 1951, Fuller decided to devote himself entirely to his music, and over the next decade he built a small cult following. He often used a one-man band setup he had devised that allowed him to play guitar, harmonica, hi-hat with castanets, and his own invention, the footdella (a piano-string bass operated with a foot pedal). He wrote "San Francisco Bay Blues" in 1954, and five years later appeared at the Monterey Jazz Festival.

Fuller became popular in Europe and England, and toured the U.S. regularly throughout the Sixties. It wasn't until the mid-Fifties that he began recording, cutting his early tracks for Prestige (later reissued on Fantasy). In 1976, he died of heart disease.

LOWELL FULSON
Born 1921, Tulsa, Oklahoma
1975—*Lowell Fulson* (Arhoolie) *The Ol' Blues Singer* (Jet).

A journeyman R&B performer whose recording career spans three decades, Fulson hit the pop charts in the mid-Sixties. A singer and guitarist, Fulson (a.k.a. Fulsom) began recording in Oakland, California, in 1946, concentrating on dance hall blues numbers he had learned during a lengthy alliance with Texas Alexander. His R&B hits began in 1949 with "Three O'Clock Blues," "You Know That I Love You" and "Come Back Baby" for Downbeat. They continued on the Swingtime label in 1950 and 1951 with "Every Day I Have the Blues" (#5 R&B, 1950), "Blue Shadows" (#1 R&B, 1950) and "Lonesome Christmas" (#7 R&B, 1950).

By the mid-Fifties Fulson was recording for Chess/Checker, notably "Reconsider Baby" (#3 R&B, 1954), now a blues standard. His brief pop success began in 1965, when "Black Nights" (#11 R&B, 1965), on the Kent label, became a minor hit, followed two years later by "Make a Little Love" (#20 R&B, 1967) and his most successful release, "Tramp" (#5 R&B, 1967), which almost cracked the pop Top Fifty. Throughout the Seventies and into the Eighties, Fulson continued to tour and perform on the nightclub and college circuits.

FUNK

In its narrowest sense, funk is percussive, polyrhythmic black dance music, with minimal melody and maximum syncopation; it has a clear lineage from James Brown's one-chord workouts of the Sixties on through Booker T. and the MGs, Sly and the Family Stone, the Ohio Players, Parliament/Funkadelic and various other bands. With some simplification of its rhythms, funk provided the basis for disco.

In the late Seventies funk became a much-abused term of praise, along with "funky." Originally, "funky" meant dirty and sexy, as in "funky drawers," and before it was stretched entirely out of shape, as a description of music it implied something more urgent and repetitive than "swinging."

RICHIE FURAY

Born May 9, 1944, Yellow Springs, Ohio
1976—*I've Got a Reason* (Asylum)   1978—*Dance a Little Light*   1979—*Satisfied*.

A country-rock veteran of Buffalo Springfield, Poco and the Souther-Hillman-Furay Band, singer/songwriter Furay launched a mildly successful solo career after becoming a born-again Christian. He started playing the guitar at age eight. He dropped out of Otterbein College in Westerville, Ohio, to go to New York, where he soon joined the Au Go Go Singers, which included Stephen Stills. They made TV appearances and recorded one LP for Roulette. When the group broke up, Furay got a job in an aircraft factory.

Six months later, he met Stills again in California. They formed the original Buffalo Springfield in April 1966, together with Neil Young, Bruce Palmer and Dewey Martin. The Springfield disbanded 25 months after its forma-

tion, leaving behind three LPs. Furay composed some of the group's material, including "Kind Woman," generally considered the first rock number to feature pedal steel guitar. Pedal steel guitarist Rusty Young and another Springfield expatriate, Jim Messina, were included in the original 1968 lineup of Poco, Furay's next band.

Furay was Poco's chief vocalist and songwriter—*Pickin' Up the Pieces* (1969), *Crazy Eyes* (1973), *Good Feelin' to Know* (1972)—during the five years and six LPs he was with the group. In 1974, he was part of a "superstar" aggregate assembled by Asylum Records president David Geffen, with John David Souther and ex–Byrd Chris Hillman. Souther-Hillman-Furay had one hit, "Fallin' in Love" (#27, 1974) and recorded two LPs. The group broke up in 1976, and Furay began a solo career.

BILLY FURY

Born Ronald Wycherly, April 17, 1941, Liverpool, England; died January 28, 1983, London
1960—*The Sound of Fury* (Decca, U.K.)   *Billy Fury* (Ace of Clubs, U.K.)   **1961**—*Halfway to Paradise* **1963**—*Billy* (Decca, U.K.)   *We Want Billy* **1967**—*Best of* (Ace of Clubs, U.K.)   **1977**—*The Billy Fury Story* (Decca, U.K.).

Billy Fury was one of England's major pre-Beatles pop stars. In late 1958, he was writing songs while working on a Mersey tugboat. Impresario Larry Parnes, impressed by the young singer, gave him his stage name and sent him touring through the U.K.

Fury's first British hit came in the spring of 1959 with "Maybe Tomorrow" (#18, U.K.), followed in 1960 by two of his own songs: "Colette" (#9, U.K.) and "That's Love" (#19, U.K.). Around the same time, he released a rockabilly album, *The Sound of Fury*. Shortly thereafter, keyboardist Georgie Fame led a defection of Fury's entire band (including guitarist Colin Green, bassist Tony Makins and drummer Red Reece) in 1962. They then backed Fame on his own successful solo career.

Fury gradually abandoned rock & roll for MOR covers of American hits, which provided mid-decade successes like "Halfway to Paradise" (#3, U.K.), "Jealousy" (#2, U.K.) and "I'd Never Find Another You" (#5, U.K.). By the time his chart records ended in 1965, he had nearly twenty English hits. He was featured in David Essex's film *That'll Be the Day* in 1973. Ill health had been a persistent problem, and Fury worked when he could while retaining hopes of someday retiring to open a bird sanctuary. He died of heart disease in 1983.

FUSION

Almost any genre that merges two or more musical forms can be considered "fusion"—for instance, British progressive rock, which fused rock instrumentation with classical motifs. But most bands categorized as fusion groups derive from jazz-rock fusion, pioneered by jazz trumpeter Miles Davis, who in the mid-Sixties used electric instruments and rock rhythms in extended improvisatory jazz suites.

Various Davis alumni—John McLaughlin and Billy Cobham with the Mahavishnu Orchestra, Chick Corea with Return to Forever, Josef Zawinul and Wayne Shorter with Weather Report, Tony Williams (and McLaughlin) with Lifetime—codified jazz-rock fusion into a commercially successful format, featuring complicated riffs and flashy virtuoso solos in bands led by Jean-Luc Ponty, Stanley Clarke, Al DiMeola and others.

The term "jazz-rock" has also been applied to such brass-dominated pop bands as Chicago and Blood, Sweat and Tears, but in these cases both "jazz" and "rock" seem incidental at best. Since the first jazz-rock fusions, other kinds of fusion have sprung up: in the late Seventies, free-jazz saxophonist Ornette Coleman revolutionized jazz-rock fusion with the more dense, inventive and challenging "harmolodic fusion."

G

PETER GABRIEL

Born May 13, 1950, England
1977—*Peter Gabriel* (Atco) **1978**—*Peter Gabriel*
(Atlantic) **1980**—*Peter Gabriel* (Mercury) **1982**—*Peter
Gabriel (Security)* (Geffen).

As the vocalist for British progressive-rock band Genesis,
Peter Gabriel cowrote, sang and acted out elaborate story
songs, wearing masks and costumes. He left Genesis in
1975 for a solo career and has released four solo albums,
each entitled *Peter Gabriel* (like issues of a magazine, he
has explained). While his songs still create characters, his
stage shows have downplayed costumes to leave Gabriel's
image more open-ended and enigmatic.

Gabriel cofounded Genesis with classmates at the Charterhouse School in 1966 as a "songwriters' collective"
originally called the Garden Wall. After graduation, Genesis began performing and recording, and by the early
Seventies the group was known for elaborate stage spectacles, culminating in *The Lamb Lies Down on Broadway*.
Gabriel left in 1975, as Genesis became one of the most
popular bands of the late Seventies.

Peter Gabriel

Gabriel released his first solo album in 1977 and had a
minor hit with "Solsbury Hill." His second solo LP was
produced by King Crimson guitarist Robert Fripp and
yielded another minor hit, "D.I.Y." Atlantic considered
his third solo album, produced by Steve Lillywhite, to be
too uncommercial; Mercury released it, and it became a
worldwide hit, with "Games Without Frontiers" reaching
#11 in the U.S. Gabriel resumed touring with a band that
included bassist Tony Levin (later to join King Crimson)
and studio drummer Jerry Marotta.

In July 1982, Gabriel financed the World of Music, Arts
and Dance Festival, designed to bring Third World music
(from Africa and the Far East) to British ears; those
influences had been showing up in his music. To offset part
of the festival's debt, he played a one-time reunion concert with Genesis and released a WOMAD album featuring cuts by himself, Fripp and Peter Townshend alongside
ethnic-music sources.

Gabriel's fourth solo album was packaged with a sticker
identifying it as *Security*; once out of its package, the
album was the fourth *Peter Gabriel*, including the hit
single "Shock the Monkey."

RORY GALLAGHER

Born March 2, 1949, Ballyshannon, Ireland
1971—*Rory Gallagher* (Atco) **1972**—*Deuce* (Poly-
dor) *Live!* **1973**—*Blueprint; Tattoo* **1974**—*Irish
Tour '74; In the Beginning* (Emerald Gem) **1975**—
Against the Grain (Chrysalis) *Sinner . . . and Saint*
(Polydor) **1976**—*The Story So Far; Calling Card*
(Chrysalis) *The Best Years* (Polydor) **1978**—*Photo
Finish* (Chrysalis) **1979**—*Top Priority* **1980**—*Stage
Struck* **1982**—*Jinx*.

Blues guitarist Rory Gallagher grew up in Cork,
Southwest Eire, and got his first guitar at age nine. He
played in pickup bands until leaving school at age 15 and
toured in the early Sixties with the Fontana Showband. By
the time the group broke up in 1965, they were called the
Impact. Gallagher then began working regularly in Hamburg, Germany, and in Ireland with bassist Charlie Mc-
Cracken and drummer John Wilson in a power trio he
called Taste. They moved to London in 1969 and released
the first of several guitar showcase LPs, which were met
with some enthusiasm in the U.K. and Europe. Taste
specialized in heavy-metal versions of blues and country
chestnuts like "Sugar Mama." The group broke up in
1971, and Gallagher began leading small bands under his
own name.

He has since conducted a moderately successful solo career, with increasing emphasis on his own material. Gallagher played in 1972 on Muddy Waters' *London Session* and in 1977 on the star-studded comeback LP by English skiffle star Lonnie Donegan. He regularly tours in the U.S., Britain and Europe; a 1974 Irish tour was the subject of a documentary by director Tony Palmer.

GAMBLE AND HUFF
Kenny Gamble and Leon Huff

Producers Gamble and Huff, along with protégé-turned-rival Thom Bell, reestablished Philadelphia as a soul capital in the mid-Seventies. Their records, particularly those on their own Philadelphia International label, feature lush orchestrations, with each instrument precisely etched atop a propulsive rhythm section—a nostalgia-free combination of big-band arranging and a disco beat that was perfected by their house orchestra, MFSB. Philadelphia International's roster included Harold Melvin and the Blue Notes, the Intruders, the O'Jays and the Three Degrees.

Gamble and Huff were both active during Philadelphia's initial pop heyday. Gamble met his future wife, singer Dee Dee Sharp, during the early Sixties when he led a band called Kenny Gamble and the Romeos, which included keyboardist Thom Bell and guitarist Roland Chambers, later a mainstay of MFSB. Huff made an early-Sixties name for himself as an R&B session pianist in New York, notably for Leiber and Stoller productions. He also produced, lending a hand to Danny and the Juniors' "At the Hop" and Len Barry's "1-2-3."

Back in Philadelphia, Huff masterminded Patti and the Emblems' 1964 soul hit "Mixed Up Shook Up Girl." He was hired to add piano to Candy and the Kisses' "81," a song written by Gamble, who subsequently asked Huff to join the Romeos. The pair formed Excel Records in 1966 and had a regional hit with the Intruders. In 1967, Gamble and Huff produced the Top Ten "Expressway to Your Heart" by the Soul Survivors. As the Sixties closed, the pair worked as independent producers for Archie Bell and the Drells, Dusty Springfield, Wilson Pickett, Jerry Butler, Joe Simon and others. They started calling their label Gamble Records, then Neptune after they hooked up with Chess for national distribution. When Chess failed in the late Sixties, they formed Philadelphia International, distributed by CBS.

Gamble and Huff's trademark style had its genesis with the Intruders, for whom they fashioned a series of R&B novelty hits like "Cowboys to Girls" and "(Love Is Like a) Baseball Game" (1968). Their productions started racking up regular gold singles in 1972 with the O'Jays and Billy Paul. In 1975, they were indicted by a government payola probe that charged Philadelphia International with influence peddling. Huff was cleared the next year, and Gamble paid a $2,500 fine. They remain active (producing

the Jacksons in 1977 and the O'Jays' 1978 comeback hit "Use ta Be My Girl"), although their arranging and production have been delegated more frequently to the Philadelphia International stable.

GANG OF FOUR
Formed 1977, Leeds, England
Jon King, voc.; Hugo Burnham, drums; Andy Gill, gtr.; Dave Allen, bass.
1980—*Entertainment!* (Warner Bros.) **1981**—*Solid Gold* (− Dave Allen; + Sara Lee) **1982**—*Songs of the Free.*

The English-born Gang of Four play atonal funk with political lyrics. They have been extremely influential in the U.K. and a solid concert draw in the U.S. The group started at art school in Leeds in 1977 and released an EP, *Damaged Goods,* on the independent Fast Product label. Touring and the record, which became a hit at rock discos, brought them a contract with EMI in Britain and, after a self-financed tour, with Warner Bros. in the U.S., which began a jumbled release schedule. *Entertainment!* was released in Britain in October 1979 and in the U.S. in May 1980; Warner released an EP that included selections from *Damaged Goods* in late 1980; *Solid Gold* was released in the U.S. in March 1981.

In the middle of the U.S. tour supporting *Solid Gold,* bassist Dave Allen quit; he was replaced on tour by Busta Jones, who had performed with Talking Heads and Chris Spedding. Later in 1981, bassist Sara Lee, who had been a member of the League of Gentlemen with Robert Fripp, joined the Gang of Four as a fulltime member. On their 1982 tour, the Gang of Four appeared as a five-piece group with vocalist Edi Reader. Although their music has apparently been too raw for U.S. radio, they have received extensive play in clubs; their British hits include "At Home, He's a Tourist," "Damaged Goods" and "Man in Uniform."

THE GAP BAND
Formed early 1970s, Los Angeles
Ronnie Wilson, trumpet, kybds.; Charles Wilson, lead voc., kybds.; Robert Wilson, bass.
1974—*Magician's Holiday* (Shelter) **1977**—*Gap Band* (Tattoo) **1979**—*Gap Band II* (Mercury) **1981**—*Gap Band III* **1982**—*Gap Band IV.*

As the Gap Band, the three Wilson brothers, natives of Tulsa, Oklahoma, became one of the most popular funk bands of the Eighties. Their father is a preacher and their mother a pianist, and every Sunday the boys sang prior to their father's sermon. When they started the band in the early Seventies, they named themselves using the first initials of three neighborhood streets—Greenwood, Archer and Pine—to form Gap.

By 1974, they had met Leon Russell, who signed them

to his Shelter Records, where they cut one album. They also performed as Russell's backup band for several years. In the mid-Seventies, the Wilsons moved to Los Angeles, where they recorded one gospel-styled single, "This Place Called Heaven," for A&M. They then moved to RCA-distributed Tattoo Records and cut a self-titled album that attracted some attention.

After the Gap Band signed to Mercury Records, "Shake," "Open Up Your Mind (Wide)" and "Steppin' (Out)," all R&B Top Ten hits, brought them to national prominence. Then "Burn Rubber on Me" (#1 R&B) and "Yearning for Your Love" (#5 R&B) from the platinum *III* in 1981 established them as a major act. *Gap Band IV* contained two popular singles: "Early in the Morning" (#1, R&B) and "You Dropped a Bomb on Me" (#1, R&B) in 1982.

ART GARFUNKEL
Born October 13, 1941, New York City
1973—*Angel Clare* (Columbia)   1975—*Breakaway*
1977—*Watermark*   1979—*Fate for Breakfast*   1981—
Scissors Cut.

Art Garfunkel contributed high harmonies and arranging ideas to Simon and Garfunkel's string of folk pop hits in the late Sixties. When that duo disbanded in 1970, part of the reason was Garfunkel's growing interest in film, although he has released occasional solo albums since. The two reunited to sing for half a million fans at a September 1981 concert in New York's Central Park.

Garfunkel met Paul Simon in grade school in Queens. The two had a teenybopper hit record, "Hey Schoolgirl" (#49, 1958), as Tom and Jerry. Garfunkel also recorded a few unsuccessful sides on his own as "Arty Garr" for the Octavia and Warwick labels in the early Sixties. But he had been seriously studying architecture and mathematics at Columbia University before deciding to join Simon in a professional music career.

Garfunkel's first film, *Catch-22,* was shot in 1969 as he and Simon drifted apart, and Garfunkel appeared in *Carnal Knowledge* (1971) and in Nicolas Roeg's *Bad Timing/A Sensual Obsession.* He didn't revive his recording career until 1973, with the lavishly orchestrated *Angel Clare,* which included the first of his solo hit singles, "All I Know" (#9, 1973). His other appearances in the Top Forty in the Seventies included "I Only Have Eyes for You" (#18, 1975) and "Breakaway" (#39, 1976). All Garfunkel's releases have been covers, and he is particularly fond of moody, romantic ballads. His 1975 LP, *Breakaway,* included a studio reunion with Simon for "My Little Town," which became a substantial hit.

Late in the Seventies, Garfunkel teamed with Simon and James Taylor for a version of Sam Cooke's "(What a) Wonderful World," which hit the Top Twenty. In 1978, he undertook his first U.S. tour since splitting with Simon.

LEIF GARRETT
Born November 8, 1961, Hollywood
1977—*Leif Garrett* (Atlantic)   1978—*Feel the Need* (Scotti Brothers)   1979—*Same Goes for You*   1980—
Can't Explain   1981—*My Movie of You.*

Leif Garrett was a mid-Seventies television teen idol. He began his recording career at age 16 with a self-titled collection of rock oldies that included "Surfin' U.S.A." It became the first of several moderate hits, followed by remakes of "Runaround Sue" and "The Wanderer." He has released one album each year since.

Despite his recording career, Garrett remains primarily a television phenomenon. In 1979, he hosted a special with Bob Hope and Brooke Shields and has appeared on several prime-time TV programs. His film debut was as Elliott Gould and Dyan Cannon's son in *Bob and Carol and Ted and Alice* (1969). He also appeared in *Macon County Line* and all three of the *Walking Tall* films.

MARVIN GAYE
Born April 2, 1939, Washington, D.C.
1961—*Soulful Mood* (Tamla)   1963—*That Stubborn Kinda Fellow*   1964—*Together* (with Mary Wells)
1965—*How Sweet It Is*   1966—*Greatest Hits; United* (with Tammi Terrell)   1967—*Greatest Hits, volume 2*
1968—*You're All I Need to Get By; Marvin Gaye and His Girls* (Terrell, Wells, Kim Weston)   1970—*Superhits*   1971—*What's Going On*   1972—*Hits of Marvin Gaye*   1973—*Let's Get It On*   1974—*Anthology; Live*   1976—*The Best of Marvin Gaye*   1978—
Here, My Dear   1981—*In Our Lifetime*   1982—
Midnight Love (Columbia).

Marvin Gaye is one of the most consistent and enigmatic of the Motown hitmakers. A mellifluous tenor with a three-octave vocal range, he was nominated for eight Grammys before winning one in 1983. Gaye has avoided TV and rarely performs live, sometimes not showing up for the few concerts he schedules.

The son of a Washington, D.C., Apostolic preacher, Gaye started singing at age three in church and was soon playing the organ as well. After a stint in the Air Force, he returned to D.C. and started singing in streetcorner doowop groups, including a top local group, the Rainbows. He formed his own group, the Marquees, in 1957. Under the auspices of supporter Bo Diddley, they cut "Wyatt Earp" for the Okeh label. In 1958, Harvey Fuqua heard the group and enlisted them to become the latest version of his ever-changing backing ensemble, the Moonglows. As such, Gaye was heard on "Mama Loocie" and other songs for the Chess label in 1959.

By the early Sixties, the group was touring widely. While playing a club in Detroit, they were heard by local impresario Berry Gordy, Jr., who quickly signed Gaye to

Marvin Gaye

his fledgling Motown organization in 1961. Soon after, Gaye married Gordy's sister Anna. Gaye's first duties with the label were as a session drummer (he played on all the early hits by Smokey Robinson and the Miracles).

Gaye got his first hit with his fourth release, "Stubborn Kind of Fellow," in 1962. Over the next ten years, working with nearly every producer at Motown (including Holland-Dozier-Holland, Smokey Robinson and Norman Whitfield), he enjoyed over twenty big hits. Although he specialized in mid-tempo ballads, he also had dance hits: "Hitch Hike" (#30, 1963), the 12-bar blues "Can I Get a Witness" (#22, 1963, which became a virtual anthem among the British mods) and "Baby Don't You Do It" (#27, 1964).

But by and large he favored romantic, sometimes sensual ballads. His Top Ten hits included "Pride and Joy" (#10, 1963), "I'll Be Doggone" (#8, 1965), "Ain't That Peculiar" (#8, 1965) and "How Sweet It Is to Be Loved by You" (#6, 1965). Additionally, in 1964 Gaye was teamed with Mary Wells for a couple of hits, "Once Upon a Time" (#19, 1964) and "What's the Matter with You" (#17, 1964), and with Kim Weston for "It Takes Two" (#17, 1967). But his greatest duets were with the late Tammi Terrell: "Ain't No Mountain High Enough" (#19, 1967), "Your Precious Love" (#5, 1967), "Ain't Nothing Like the Real Thing" (#8, 1968) and "You're All I Need to Get By" (#7, 1968). In a 1967 concert Tammi Terrell collapsed into his arms onstage, the first sign of the brain tumor that killed her three years later. Gaye had his biggest solo hit of the Sixties with "I Heard It through the Grapevine" (#1, 1968).

The second, quite distinct phase of Gaye's career began in 1971 with *What's Going On*. Along with Stevie Wonder, Gaye was one of the first Motown artists to gain complete artistic control of his records. *What's Going On* was a self-composed-and-produced song cycle that could rightfully be called a concept album. Songs like "What's Going On" (#2, 1971) and "Mercy Mercy Me (the Ecology)" (#4, 1971) were impassioned statements on Vietnam and pollution. In 1972, Gaye scored the 20th Century–Fox film *Trouble Man*, and the title track gave him yet another Top Ten hit (#7, 1973). By 1973, he had shifted his attention to pure eroticism with *Let's Get It On*, whose title track went to #1 in 1973. His late-1973 album with Diana Ross produced three fairly successful singles: "You're a Special Part of Me" (#12, 1973), "Don't Knock My Love" (#46, 1974) and "My Mistake (Was to Love You)" (#19, 1974).

Gaye's rocky marriage of fourteen years to Anna Gordy Gaye was the subject of *Here, My Dear* as the Seventies closed with Gaye still reeling from the divorce settlement; he filed for bankruptcy and his ex-wife later considered suing him for invasion of privacy over the content of *Here, My Dear*. (The album had been precipitated by court hearings in 1976, when a judge instructed Gaye to make good on overdue alimony payments by recording an album and giving his wife $600,000 in royalties.) He married his second wife, Janice, in 1977 and that year had a #1 hit, "Got to Give It Up, Pt. 1."

Still with Motown in 1981, Gaye's release *In Our Lifetime* concentrated on his philosophies of love, art and death.

In 1982, Gaye left Motown for Columbia. His first album for the label, *Midnight Love*, included the hit "Sexual Healing," which won a Grammy for Best R&B Vocal Performance, Male. He sang live on the Grammy broadcast and, in 1983, in concert at Radio City Music Hall.

CRYSTAL GAYLE
Born Brenda Gail Webb, circa 1953, Paintsville, Kentucky
1975—*Crystal Gayle* (United Artists)   *Somebody Loves You* **1976**—*Crystal*   **1977**—*We Must Believe in Magic*   **1978**—*When I Dream*   **1981**—*Hollywood, Tennessee* (Columbia)   **1982**—*True Love* (Elektra).

Loretta Lynn's younger sister, Crystal Gayle became a country-pop singer in the late Seventies with hits like "Don't It Make My Brown Eyes Blue." Sixteen years younger than Loretta, Crystal was the eighth and last child of the family, the only one born in a hospital. When she was four, her family moved to Wabash, Indiana, where Gayle sang in church and at civic organizations. Upon graduation from high school, she toured with Conway Twitty and Loretta, who suggested her sister's stage name, after the Krystal hamburger chain. Crystal soon had a contract with Decca/MCA, and Loretta wrote her first country hit, "I've Cried (the Blue Right Out of My Eyes)," which became her first pop hit when re-released in 1977 as "Don't It Make My Brown Eyes Blue" (#2).

Gayle worked nightclubs, state fairs and TV talk shows dutifully through the Seventies, racking up consistent country chart success with singles like "Wrong Road Again" (#6, 1974), "This Is My Year for Mexico" (#15, 1975), "I'll Get Over You" (#1, 1976) and "I'd Do It All Over Again" (#2, 1977). Her crossover success began with her third United Artists album, *Crystal,* and peaked with her next release, *We Must Believe in Magic,* which besides staying on the country charts for nearly a year, went platinum. In June 1978, she released *When I Dream,* including "Talking in Your Sleep," which hit #18.

GLORIA GAYNOR
Born September 7, 1949, Newark, New Jersey
1975—*Never Can Say Goodbye* (MGM) *Experience Gloria Gaynor* 1976—*I've Got You* (Polydor) 1977—*Glorious* 1978—*Gloria Gaynor's Park Avenue Sound* 1979—*Love Tracks; I Have a Right* 1982—*Gloria Gaynor* (Atlantic).

Gloria Gaynor is a late-Seventies disco star. One of six children, she grew up listening to records by Nat "King" Cole and Sarah Vaughan. Following high school, she worked as an accountant but quit to join a band in Canada. She soon found herself back in Jersey, however, working day jobs until one night at a club a friend persuaded her to sing with the band. The group, the Soul Satisfiers, took her on tour for a year and a half. She then formed her own band and went to New York, where she was discovered by Columbia Records.

Gaynor's first single, "Honey Bee," was a disco hit in 1973, but Columbia soon lost interest. She signed to MGM, and *Never Can Say Goodbye* was a hit in late 1974. One of the first LPs specifically programed for dancing, the title cut (an earlier hit for Isaac Hayes and then the Jackson 5) hit #9. She followed up with a less successful cover of another Motown hit, the Four Tops' "Reach Out I'll Be There," before her career came to a standstill. But five years later, "I Will Survive" hit #1 on the pop charts; *Love Tracks* went platinum. Gaynor continues to tour.

THE J. GEILS BAND
Formed 1967, Boston
Jerome Geils (b. Feb. 20, 1946, New York City), gtr.; Peter Wolf (b. Peter Blankfield, Mar. 7, 1946, Bronx, N.Y.), voc.; Magic Dick (b. Dick Salwitz, May 13, 1945, New London, Conn.), harmonica; Danny Klein (b. May 13, 1946, New York City), bass; Stephen Jo Bladd (b. July 13, 1942, Boston), drums.
1968—(+ Seth Justman [b. Jan. 27, 1951, Washington, D.C.], kybds.) 1971—*The J. Geils Band* (Atlantic) 1972—*The Morning After; Full House* 1973—

Bloodshot; Ladies Invited 1974—*Nightmares (and Other Tales from the Vinyl Jungle)* 1975—*Hot Line* 1976—*Blow Your Face Out* 1977—*Monkey Island* 1978—*Sanctuary* (EMI) 1980—*Love Stinks* 1981—*Freeze-Frame* 1982—*Showtime!*

In over a decade without a personnel change, the J. Geils Band have merged their collectors' dedication to blues, doo-wop and R&B with enough pop know-how to keep them contemporary. The band was named after guitarist J. (Jerome) Geils, but its lyricist and onstage focus is singer Peter Wolf. A high school dropout who learned to jive-talk on Bronx streetcorners, Wolf moved to Boston before he was twenty and earned a passable reputation as a painter before becoming a disc jockey on Boston's WBCN-FM, where he called himself Woofuh Goofuh. He joined the Hallucinations, which included drummer and fellow doo-wop collector Stephen Jo Bladd, and by 1967 the group was playing covers of R&B, blues and Fifties rock & roll, from John Lee Hooker to the Miracles. Meanwhile, Geils, bassist Klein and harpist Magic Dick were working as an acoustic trio called the J. Geils Blues Band. After the Hallucinations broke up in 1967, Bladd and Wolf joined the J. Geils Band, which by then had gone electric.

While other fledgling bands were going psychedelic, this group acted like greasers, and their showmanship and taste in obscure covers earned them a following in New England. Justman, who has become the band's producer and composer, was an organist who had moved north from Atlantic City to attend Boston University; he joined in 1968.

The band toured almost constantly in the early Seventies, while occasionally reaching the Top Forty with such songs as "Looking for a Love" (#39, 1971), the reggae-style "Give It to Me" (#30, 1973, making its album, *Bloodshot,* gold) and "Must of Got Lost" (#12, 1974). In 1977, they briefly called themselves Geils and released *Monkey Island,* the group's first self-produced effort. In 1979, Wolf's five-year marriage to actress Faye Dunaway ended in divorce.

After nine LPs with Atlantic, the band switched to EMI in 1978 for *Sanctuary,* their first gold disc in five years. In 1980, they conducted their most extensive tour ever (U.S., Japan, Europe) to support *Love Stinks.* The album introduced Justman's synthesizer work and got them a hit single with "Come Back." *Freeze-Frame,* with the hits "Centerfold" and "Angel in Blue," was their best-selling album to date.

GENESIS
Formed 1966, England
Tony Banks (b. Mar. 27, 1950, Eng.), kybds.; Michael Rutherford (b. Oct. 2, 1950, Eng.), gtr., bass, voc.; Peter Gabriel (b. May 13, 1950, Eng.), voc.; Anthony Phillips, gtr.; Chris Stewart, drums.

1968—(– Stewart; + John Silver, drums; – Silver)
1969—*From Genesis to Revelation* (London) 1970—
(+ John Mayhew, drums) *Trespass* (Buddah)
(– Phillips; – Mayhew; + Phil Collins [b. Jan. 31,
1951, London], drums, voc.; + Steve Hackett [b. Feb.
12, 1950, Eng.], gtr.) 1971—*Nursery Cryme* 1972—
Foxtrot 1973—*Genesis Live; Selling England by the
Pound* (Atco) 1974—*The Lamb Lies Down on Broadway* (– Gabriel) 1976—*A Trick of the Tail* (for
Mar.–Nov. tour: + Bill Bruford, drums) *Wind and
Wuthering* 1977—(+ Chester Thompson, drums; –
Hackett; + Daryl Steurmer, gtr.) *Seconds Out*
1978—*. . . And Then There Were Three . . .* 1980—
Duke 1981—*Abacab* 1982—*Three Sides Live.*
Steve Hackett solo: 1976—*Voyage of the Acolyte*
(Chrysalis) 1978—*Please Don't Touch* 1979—
Spectral Mornings (Charisma, U.K.) 1980—*Defector*
1981—*Cured* (Virgin/Epic).
Phil Collins solo: 1982—*Face Value* (Duke) 1983—
Hello, I Must Be Going!

The majestic art rock of early Genesis set the style for
such acts as Kansas and Styx: story songs set to complex,
richly textured music with hints of classical pomp. Genesis started as a highly theatrical cult band when they were
fronted by Peter Gabriel; after he left the band and
drummer Phil Collins became lead singer, they moved on
to arenas and gave up costume drama in favor of laser light
shows.

The group was started as a "songwriters' collective"
called Garden Wall by Peter Gabriel, Tony Banks, Mike
Rutherford and Anthony Phillips while all four were students at Charterhouse, an exclusive British secondary
school. In late 1968, British record mogul Jonathan King
suggested the name Genesis and got them a contract that
resulted in the poppish 13-song *From Genesis to Revelation,* not released in the U.S. until 1974.

On graduation, the four members lived together in a
British country cottage and rehearsed for several months
before playing their first concerts in 1970. They developed
an elaborate stage show—Gabriel had a series of costume
changes, including a bat and a flower—and their songs
grew into extended suites on *Trespass, Foxtrot* and *Selling
England by the Pound.* They gained a large following in
Britain and a dedicated cult in the United States. In 1974,
Genesis' theatricality peaked with a two-LP set and attendant live show, *The Lamb Lies Down on Broadway,* in
which Gabriel played Rael, who suffered various metamorphoses in a surreal Manhattan.

Gabriel left Genesis after *Lamb* for a solo career, and
the group took 18 months to adjust. They auditioned over
400 singers before deciding Phil Collins could take over;
on tour, they employ a second drummer so that Collins
can roam the stage. Genesis dispensed with costumes but
continued to perform older material, which was credited
to the whole group. *Wind and Wuthering* and *A Trick of the*
Tail expanded their cult, and *. . . And Then There Were
Three . . . ,* with somewhat shorter songs, became their
first gold album in 1978. Hackett had earlier left for his
own solo career *(Voyage of the Acolyte, Spectral Mornings).*

Genesis began to score U.S. hit singles with "Follow
You, Follow Me" (#23, 1978) from *. . . And Then There
Were Three . . .* and "Misunderstanding" (#14, 1980)
from *Duke,* in which they turned their narrative skills to
love songs. Duke also became the name of their custom
label. For *Abacab,* they incorporated some new-wave
conciseness, and "No Reply At All" hit #29 in 1981. It
featured the horn section from Earth, Wind and Fire,
which had also appeared on Collins' 2-million selling solo
debut album, *Face Value,* a few months earlier. Collins'
second solo LP, *Hello, I Must Be Going!,* was a Top
Twenty hit in 1983.

GENTLE GIANT
Formed 1970, England
Derek Shulman (b. Feb. 2, 1947, Glasgow), voc., sax;
Ray Shulman (b. Dec. 8, 1949, Glasgow), voc., bass,
violin, percussion; Phil Shulman (b. Aug. 27, 1937,
Glasgow), sax; Kerry Minnear (b. Apr. 2, 1948), voc.,
kybds.; Gary Green (b. Nov. 20, 1950), voc., gtr.;
Martin Smith, drums; Malcolm Mortimer, drums.
1970—*Gentle Giant* (Vertigo) 1971—(– Mortimer)
Acquiring the Taste 1972—(– Smith; + John
Weathers, drums, voc.) *Three Friends* (Columbia)
1973—*Octopus* (– P. Shulman) *In a Glass House*
(WWA, U.K.) 1974—*The Power and the Glory* (Capitol) 1975—*Free Hand; A Giant Step* (Vertigo, U.K.)
1976—*Interview* (Capitol) *Playing the Fool* 1977—
The Missing Piece; Pretentious 1978—*Giant for a
Day* 1980—*Civilian* (Columbia).

Merging medieval madrigals and Béla Bartók's dissonances with rock dynamics, Gentle Giant was one of the
most dauntingly complex of Seventies British progressive-rock bands. They'd been formed from the remains of
obscure late-Sixties British pop band Simon Dupree and
the Big Sound, which included all three Shulman brothers
(Derek was Simon Dupree). The Big Sound had had one
hit single in 1967, "Kites," which made the U.K. Top Ten.

Weathers had been with Graham Bond and the Grease
Band before joining the Shulmans; Green had played with
blues and jazz bands; Minnear had studied at the Royal
Academy of Music.

With Gentle Giant, the Shulmans moved in the direction
of King Crimson and Jethro Tull, though they often used
dissonant counterpoint far more intricate than either of
them. At first, they had only a small European cult. The
political concept album *The Power and the Glory* finally
saw them breaking through in America. *The Missing Piece*
flirted with shorter, harder-rocking song structures, and

the group simplified its music, to little commercial avail, in the late Seventies. For a short time, the group was managed by radio consultant Lee Abrams, who produced their final LP, *Civilian*.

BOBBIE GENTRY
Born Bobbie Lee Street, July 27, 1944, Chickasaw County, Mississippi
1967—*Ode to Billy Joe* (Capitol)   *Bobbie Gentry's Greatest.*

Bobbie Gentry came to national prominence in 1967 with the first—and biggest—hit of her career, the enigmatic ballad "Ode to Billy Joe." From childhood, Gentry was determined to be a music star, and she wrote her first song at age seven on a piano. By her teens, she had moved to California, where she attended UCLA (majoring in philosophy) and the L.A. Conservatory of Music. She worked as a secretary, occasionally performing in clubs at night, and then briefly as a Las Vegas showgirl before cutting her debut disc in 1967. "Ode to Billy Joe" went gold, as did the album of the same name that year. A triple Grammy winner, "Ode" went on to sell three million copies internationally. The ballad provided the groundwork for a movie in 1976.

Gentry's later career never matched the success of her debut, although she was a star in England and hosted a British TV series in the early Seventies. In America, her late-Sixties releases generally stalled in the middle rungs of the pop charts, except for a 1970 duet with Glen Campbell on "All I Have to Do Is Dream" (#27). By the mid-Seventies, she was a staple on the Vegas-Reno circuits, with a multimillion-dollar contract with the Hughes hotels and a thirty-room mansion in Hollywood.

THE GENTRYS
Formed 1963, Memphis
Larry Raspberry, gtr., voc.; Larry Wall, drums; Jimmy Johnson, trumpet, organ; Bobby Fisher, sax, piano; Pat Neal, bass; Bruce Bowles, voc.; Jimmy Hart, voc.
1965—*Keep On Dancing* (MGM)   **1970**—*The Gentrys* (Sun Records).

The Gentrys were a Memphis garage band whose biggest hit was 1965's "Keep On Dancing." They formed in 1963 to play sock hops and were soon winning local talent contests and battles of the bands. In 1965, they were signed to the local Youngstown label, and their first release, "Sometimes," was a regional hit. Their followup, "Keep On Dancing," was leased to MGM and hit #4 on the charts in October 1965. Their 1966 releases, "Spread It On Thick" and "Everyday I Have to Cry," failed to crack the Top Forty. Four years later, they had a modest comeback with minor hits like "Why Should I Cry," "Cinnamon Girl" and "Wild World" on Sun. In 1973, group leader Larry Raspberry started the Highsteppers,

who recorded for Stax. The rest of the Gentrys continued to record as such for Capitol. In the early Seventies, the Bay City Rollers revived "Keep On Dancing."

GERRY AND THE PACEMAKERS
Formed 1959, Liverpool, England
Gerry Marsden (b. Sep. 24, 1942, Liverpool, Eng.), voc., gtr.; Les Maguire (b. Dec. 27, 1941, Wallasey, Eng.), piano; John Chadwick (b. May 11, 1943, Liverpool), bass; Freddie Marsden (b. Nov. 23, 1940, Liverpool), drums.
1963—*How Do You Do It* (Columbia)   *Gerry and the Pacemakers' Second Album* (Laurie)   **1964**—*Ferry Cross the Mersey* (Columbia)   *Gerry and the Pacemakers' Greatest Hits* (Laurie).

Gerry and the Pacemakers were on the pop end of Liverpool's mid-Sixties Merseybeat trend. They built up a following in Liverpool clubs like the Cavern and in the Hamburg, Germany, clubs. In 1962, they became the second group (after the Beatles) to be signed by manager Brian Epstein. Produced by George Martin, their first three records hit #1 on the British charts—"How Do You Do It?", "I Like It" and "You'll Never Walk Alone." "How Do You Do It?" was one of their biggest U.S. hits in 1964. They scored Top Ten successes in the U.S. that year with the ballad "Don't Let the Sun Catch You Crying" and in 1965 with "Ferry Cross the Mersey." That year, they starred in a movie of the same name, which featured nine original songs by leader Gerry Marsden.

By 1966, however, their releases ceased having much impact on U.S. charts, and the group disbanded a few years later. Marsden began a marginally successful cabaret career, scoring minor U.K. hits like "Please Let Them Be" and "Gilbert Green" and acting on stage and TV, where he hosted a children's show for several years. In 1973, he re-formed the Pacemakers for a nostalgia tour of America.

ANDY GIBB
Born March 5, 1958, Brisbane, Australia
1977—*Flowing Rivers* (RSO)   **1978**—*Shadow Dancing*   **1980**—*Andy Gibbs' Greatest Hits;   After Dark.*

Pop singer Andy Gibb is the younger brother of the Bee Gees (who often contributed songs and harmonies to his albums). He began a successful solo career in the late Seventies with hits like "I Just Want to Be Your Everything" (#1, 1977) and "Shadow Dancing" (#1, 1978) from the album of the same name. By the time the elder Gibb brothers were getting their international career rolling in the late Sixties, young Andy was already playing in amateur bands of his own. Following his brothers, he first established himself in Australia in the mid-Seventies with tours and singles like "Words and Music." He then signed with Bee Gees manager Robert Stigwood, on whose RSO

Records his first album was recorded under the tutelage of brother Barry. Brother Maurice supervised *Shadow Dancing*, which continued Gibb's success with the teeny-bopper market. He continues to record regularly, although his discs have become less successful. From 1981 to mid-1982, he hosted the syndicated TV show "Solid Gold." In late 1982, he joined the cast of the Broadway musical *Joseph and the Amazing Technicolor Dreamcoat.*

JIMMY GILMER AND THE FIREBALLS
Formed circa 1963, Texas
Fireballs: Stan Lark, bass; Eric Budd, drums; George Tomsco, gtr.
1963—*Sugar Shack* (Dot).

Jimmy Gilmer and the Fireballs had the biggest hit of 1963 with "Sugar Shack."

Born in Illinois, Gilmer began singing as a youngster, and in 1951 he moved with his family to Amarillo, Texas, where he studied piano for four years at the Musical Arts Conservatory. While studying engineering at Amarillo College in 1957, he formed his first pop band. In the early Sixties, he met the Fireballs (who had already had hits with "Torquay" and "Bulldog") at the Clovis, New Mexico, studios of Buddy Holly's producer, Norman Petty. With Gilmer on piano and vocals, their first release, "Quite a Party," made the Top Thirty, and "Sugar Shack" held the #1 spot on the charts for over a month.

Tours at home and abroad followed, as did lesser hits like "Daisy Petal Pickin' " and "Ain't Gonna Tell Anybody" in 1964. By mid-decade, however, Gilmer and the Fireballs had gone their separate ways. Gilmer had little subsequent success, while the Fireballs stormed back onto the charts in 1968 with "Bottle of Wine."

GIRL GROUPS

In the early Sixties, individually faceless and collectively appealing female vocal groups like the Shangri-Las, the Ronettes, the Crystals and the Shirelles produced one of rock's most charmingly "innocent" styles. The "girl group sound" was designed to capture a yearning adolescent romanticism, and it contained enough intrinsic moral tension to keep sociologists occupied for some time. With a highly theatrical style based partly on doo-wop vocalizing (e.g., the Crystals' "Da Doo Ron Ron"), the girl groups were hugely successful for several years before being swept away by the British Invasion and psychedelic rock.

They provided platforms for such auteur producers as Phil Spector and Shadow Morton, who created dense, ornate "walls of sound" around the pristine adolescent harmonizing of the vocal groups and crafted girl group records as mini-melodramas or, as Spector put it, "little symphonies for the kids." The first girl group hit was probably the Shirelles' 1961 "Will You Love Me Tomorrow."

Girl groups provided a top-selling forum for the best of New York's Brill Building songwriting teams, such as Carole King and Gerry Goffin, Doc Pomus and Mort Shuman, and Barry Mann and Cynthia Weil. The girl group sound carried over into the Motown sound of the later Sixties via the Supremes and Martha Reeves and the Vandellas.

PHILIP GLASS
Born January 31, 1937, Baltimore
1972—*Music with Changing Parts* (Chatham Square)
Solo Music (Shandar)   1973—*Music in Similar Motion/Music in Fifths* (Chatham Square)   1974—*Music in 12 Parts—Parts I & II* (Virgin)   1977—*North Star*   1979—*Einstein on the Beach* (Tomato)   *Dance Nos. 1 & 3*
1982—*Glassworks* (Columbia)   1983—*The Photographer.*

Most of minimalist composer Philip Glass's music is written for an ensemble of reeds, electric organs and voices, an ensemble that has toured both rock clubs and classical venues. Glass, the son of a record store owner, studied flute as a child and took up piano at the University of Chicago, where he also studied philosophy and mathematics. In 1957, he began studying composition at New York's Juilliard School, where he earned a master's degree and won a variety of prizes. A Fulbright grant sent him to Paris in 1964 to study with Nadia Boulanger. But while in Paris, Glass got a job transcribing Indian music with Ravi Shankar, and his fascination with Eastern structures led him to repudiate his earlier work.

After hitchhiking through Africa and India, Glass returned to New York in 1967 and began composing music according to principles that would soon be termed minimalist; the music involved repeated rhythmic cycles of notes and, over the years, gradually incorporated counterpoint and harmony. To play it, Glass formed the Philip Glass Ensemble, which built a touring circuit of art galleries and, as early as 1974, rock clubs including Max's Kansas City. He supported himself as a carpenter, a furniture mover and a taxicab driver. Glass initially refused to publish his music so that the Ensemble could get more jobs playing it live, but in 1971 he formed his own Chatham Square Productions to record his works. He made a substantial impact overseas—David Bowie and Brian Eno attended his 1971 Royal College of Art concerts in Britain—and British rock label Virgin signed him in 1974.

Glass and scenarist Robert Wilson collaborated in 1976 on *Einstein on the Beach*, a 4½-hour "opera" that toured Europe and played the Metropolitan Opera House. After Virgin released an album of short pieces, *North Star*, in 1977, Glass began gigging at both Carnegie Hall and rock clubs with the Ensemble. He produced two albums for the new wave band Polyrock. Mike Oldfield did a disco version of Glass's "North Star."

From the late Seventies onward, however, most of Glass's efforts went into theater works—operas, more or less—including 1980's *Satyagraha* (based on the life of Mahatma Gandhi), 1983's *Akhenaton* (an Egyptian pharaoh). He also scored a documentary, *Koyaanisqatsi* (1982), and plays for the Mabou Mines company. In 1982, Glass signed the first exclusive composer's contract with CBS Masterworks since Igor Stravinsky, and released *Glassworks,* orchestral and ensemble pieces. *The Photographer,* a music-theater work, included a song with lyrics by David Byrne of Talking Heads. In 1983, Glass collaborated with ex-Doors keyboardist Ray Manzarek on a version of Carl Orff's cantata *Carmina Burana.*

GLITTER

Also known as "glam," glitter rock sprang out of an early-Seventies backlash against the late-Sixties sexual revolution, and revolved around a glorified sexual ambiguity and androgyny as practiced by performers like David Bowie, and Marc Bolan of T. Rex, and a fashion consciousness best expressed by British proto-art-rockers Roxy Music. Self-consciously decadent, glitter-rockers adorned themselves with foppish and/or futuristic clothing, lots of makeup and the glitter dust that gave the genre its name and that subsequently became a debased code that could even apply to such performers as Jobriath and British pop star Gary Glitter.

Glitter-rock music was usually a slicker form of hard rock, and included everything from British pop-rockers Sweet to New York "glitter punks" the New York Dolls, who in many senses apotheosized glitter even as they signaled its decline. The genre influenced contemporary rockers like Joan Jett and, to a limited extent, early Kiss.

GARY GLITTER

Born Paul Francis Gadd, May 8, 1944, Banbury, England
1973—*Glitter; Touch Me; Gary Glitter* **1981**—*Glitter and Gold* (EP) (Epic).

Gary Glitter was at the forefront of the English glam-rock phase, along with David Bowie, T. Rex and Slade. He had several hits in Britain (with a distinctive sound, later revived by Adam and the Ants, featuring heavy drumming, handclaps, echo guitar and football-cheer choruses) but only minor success in America.

Around the start of the Sixties, Paul Francis Gadd began releasing ballads on Decca and Parlophone as Paul Raven. He toured with Cliff Richard, Tommy Steele and Billy Fury. His "Paul Raven" rendition of Burt Bacharach's "Walk On By" became a big hit in the Middle East in 1961. He began working with writer/producer Mike Leander in 1965; the association continued into the Seventies.

Gadd performed in *Jesus Christ Superstar* in the late Sixties and, under the name Paul Monday, he worked clubs in Frankfurt and Hamburg, Germany. After considering such monikers as Terry Tinsel and Horace Hydrogen, he and Leander settled on the Gary Glitter identity late in 1971.

Unashamedly climbing onto the glitter-rock bandwagon, Gary Glitter burst onto the English scene in 1972 and by midyear was inspiring regular crowd hysteria. "Rock and Roll Part II" eventually hit #2 in England and became his only U.S. Top Ten entry. Over the next two years, he reeled off a string of hits, many of which topped the U.K. charts, like "I Didn't Know I Loved You (Till I Saw You Rock 'n' Roll)," "Do You Wanna Touch Me?" (later revived by Joan Jett), "Hello, Hello, I'm Back Again," "I'm the Leader of the Gang," "I Love You Love Me" (1973), "Always Yours," "Oh Yes You're Beautiful," "Love Like You and Me" and "Remember Me This Way" (1974).

As the decade progressed, Glitter moved further and further into self-parody. By the first of his highly publicized and short-lived "retirements" in 1976, he could boast of 13 consecutive English hits. Through his glory years he was perpetually backed by the Glitter Band wearing stacked heels and playing bejeweled, oddly shaped guitars. Led by Peter Oxendale (piano) and Gerry Shephard (guitar), the Glitter Band began making records on its own in the mid-Seventies, including some disco-ish U.K. hits and a 1979 Oxendale and Shephard album, *Put Your Money Where Your Mouth Is,* on Nemperor.

In October 1980, Glitter was in London bankruptcy court trying to work out a deal to pay off his nearly half-million pounds in back taxes. He tried to raise some of the money by auctioning off his extravagant stage wardrobe. Royalties from Glitter's 1981 U.S. compilation EP, *Glitter and Gold,* and from his performance of "Suspicious Minds" on the British Electric Foundation's 1982 compilation, *Music of Quality and Distinction, volume 1,* may help.

GERRY GOFFIN
Born February 11, 1939, Queens, New York

Gerry Goffin has been the lyricist for dozens of Top Twenty soul, pop and rock hits, many of them written with Carole King, for such acts as Aretha Franklin, Herman's Hermits and the Animals.

Goffin met King in 1958 while studying chemistry at Queens College. As husband and wife, they began working for Don Kirshner and Al Nevins' Aldon Music as part of the Brill Building stable of songwriters. Goffin and King's first chart entry as a team—the Shirelles' "Will

You Love Me Tomorrow?''—went to #1 in 1961. That same year, they had their second #1 hit with Bobby Vee's "Take Good Care of My Baby."

In 1962, Kirshner formed Dimension Records and asked Goffin and King to do most of the writing and producing for the label. Their first Dimension release, "The Locomotion," was sung by their babysitter at the time, Little Eva (Boyd), and became their third #1 single. Little Eva's followup, "Keep Your Hands Off My Baby" (#12, 1962), was also a Goffin-King composition. Other Goffin-King hits were recorded on Dimension by the Cookies— "Chains" (#17, 1962), and "Don't Say Nothin' Bad (About My Baby)" (#7, 1963)—and by King herself: "It Might As Well Rain until September" (#22, 1962).

Before the Brill Building era ended, Goffin and King wrote hits for the Drifters ("Up on the Roof," #5, 1963), the Chiffons ("One Fine Day," #5, 1963), Skeeter Davis ("I Can't Stay Mad at You," #7, 1963), Freddie Scott ("Hey, Girl," #10, 1963) and the Righteous Brothers ("Just Once in My Life," #9, 1965, cowritten by Goffin and producer Phil Spector).

During the British Invasion, they continued to score hits, now with British acts. Herman's Hermits' "I'm into Something Good" hit #13 in 1964; and in 1966 the Animals recorded their "Don't Bring Me Down" (#12). In 1967, they had two Top Ten entries with Aretha Franklin ("A Natural Woman" #8, cowritten with producer Jerry Wexler) and the Monkees ("Pleasant Valley Sunday," #3).

Since their divorce, Goffin's accomplishments have been overshadowed by those of King. While none of his solo recordings has been commercially successful, he has continued to write hits for others, notably "I've Got to Use My Imagination" (#4, 1974) for Gladys Knight and the Pips, cowritten with his primary latter-day songwriting partner, Barry Goldberg.

As a postscript, the baby that Little Eva was hired to look after was Louise Goffin (born in Brooklyn, March 23, 1960), who made her recording debut in 1979 with the LP *Kid Blue*.

THE GO-GO'S
Formed 1978, Hollywood
Belinda Carlisle (b. Aug. 17, 1958, Hollywood), voc.; Charlotte Caffey (b. Oct. 21, 1953, Santa Monica, Calif.), gtr.; Jane Wiedlin (b. May 20, 1958, Oconomowoc, Wisc.), gtr.; Margot Olaverra, bass; Elissa Bello, drums.
1979—(− Bello; + Gina Schock [b. Aug. 31, 1957, Baltimore], drums) **1980**—(− Olaverra; + Kathy Valentine [b. Jan. 7, 1959, Austin, Tex.], bass) **1981**— *Beauty and the Beat* (I.R.S.) **1982**—*Vacation*.

The Go-Go's began as a comically inept all-girl punk novelty act, but within a few years they had made a #1 debut album that yielded two Top Twenty hit singles ("Our

Lips Are Sealed" and the gold "We Got the Beat") and were selling out arenas on tour.

Belinda Carlisle, who had been a cheerleader in high school, nearly became a member of seminal L.A. punk band the Germs. With Jane Wiedlin, another L.A. punk-scene regular, she began playing guitar. They were soon joined by a more experienced guitarist, Charlotte Caffey, and they recruited a rhythm section in the inexperienced Olaverra and Bello.

The group debuted as the Go-Go's at Hollywood's punk club, the Masque, with a 1½-song set. Though onlookers considered them another hilariously daring bunch of amateurs, they began rehearsing in earnest and soon recruited Gina Schock, a serious and adept drummer who'd toured briefly with cult film star Edie Massey and her Eggs. By that time, the Go-Go's had been playing the punk circuit for nearly a year, their sound gradually growing from punk to a Blondie-ish bouncy pop rock.

They went to England, where they attracted the attention of British ska-rockers Madness, who had the Go-Go's open a tour there. The British independent label Stiff recorded a Go-Go's single, and "We Got the Beat" became a minor hit in new wave dance clubs in Britain and America. In early 1980, Olaverra became ill and was eventually replaced by Kathy Valentine. Valentine had played briefly with British all-female heavy-metal band Girlschool on a trip to England, later joined L.A. punk band the Textones, and joined the Go-Go's after a four-day crash course in bass and the band's repertoire.

The first Go-Go's album was produced by girl-group veteran Richard Gottehrer, who'd also produced Blondie's first albums. By spring 1982, *Beauty and the Beat* was #1, and "We Got the Beat" and "Our Lips Are Sealed" (the latter cowritten with Terry Hall of Britain's Specials and Fun Boy Three) were long-running hits. *Vacation* was slightly less popular, but yielded a summer-of-'82 hit single in the title cut.

ANDREW GOLD
Born August 2, 1951, Burbank, California
1975—*Andrew Gold* (Asylum) **1976**—*What's Wrong with This Picture?* (Elektra/Asylum) **1978**—*All This and Heaven Too* **1980**—*Whirlwind*.

A studio musician who was instrumental in Linda Ronstadt's pop breakthrough, Andrew Gold went solo and had a hit of his own with "Lonely Boy" (#7, 1977). Gold is the son of soundtrack composer Ernest Gold *(Exodus)* and singer Marni Nixon, who dubbed vocals for nonsinging stars in *West Side Story*, *My Fair Lady* and other Hollywood musicals. In the late Sixties, Andrew cofounded Bryndle with Karla Bonoff, Wendy Waldman and ex-Stone Poney Kenny Edwards, and met his producer-to-be, Chuck Plotkin. The group recorded one unreleased album for A&M.

When Bryndle broke up, Gold and Edwards started the Rangers; a demo tape reached Edwards' former employer Linda Ronstadt, who hired them both for her backing band. Gold became her arranger through 1977 and worked on albums including *Heart Like a Wheel* and its hit single, "You're No Good," on which Gold played most of the instruments. He made his first solo album in 1975 and opened shows for Ronstadt while continuing to play in her backup band. In 1977, *What's Wrong with This Picture?* yielded "Lonely Boy"; *All This and Heaven Too* included "Thank You for Being a Friend" (#25, 1978).

Gold's songs have been covered by Leo Sayer, Judy Collins, the James Gang, Cliff Richard and Ronstadt; he has played sessions for Wendy Waldman, Carly Simon, Art Garfunkel, Loudon Wainwright III, James Taylor, Maria Muldaur, Karla Bonoff, John David Souther and Eric Carmen.

GOLDEN EARRING

Formed 1960s, Netherlands
George Kooymans (b. Mar. 11, 1948, The Hague), gtr., voc.; Rinus Gerritsen (b. Aug. 9, 1946, The Hague), bass, kybds., harmonica; Barry Hay (b. Aug. 16, 1948, Saizabad, Neth.), voc., flute, sax; Cesar Zuiderwijk (b. July 18, 1950, The Hague), drums.
1964—*Just Earring* (Polydor) **1972**—*Together* **1973**—*Hearing Earring* (Track) **1974**—*Moontan* (MCA) **1975**—*Switch* **1976**—*To the Hilt* **1977**—*Golden Earring Live* **1979**—*Grab It for a Second*; *No Promises, No Debts* (Polydor) **1980**—*Long Blond Animal* **1982**—*Cut*.

A Dutch heavy-metal group, Golden Earring were superstars in their homeland and a minor act every place else until "Radar Love" hit #13 in 1974.

The group's original lineup in the mid-Sixties included longtime mainstays George Kooymans and Rinus Gerritsen. As schoolboys, they had their first hit in 1964 with the bubblegum-ish "Please Go." It was the first of nearly twenty Dutch hits. By 1968, the maturing band had tired of the pop format and shifted to hard rock. Attempts to break into the U.S. and U.K. markets were largely unsuccessful, and their first U.S. tour in 1968 went unnoticed. In 1972, shortly after they enjoyed a big hit in Europe with

Gold and Platinum Records

Gold and platinum records certify record sales that have been audited by the Recording Industry Association of America. Although music-business types like to call them awards, they connote no artistic merit, reflecting only the ability to please vast numbers of record buyers. Some record companies have chosen not to be audited by the RIAA (including Motown in the Sixties), so their records never "went gold," although they may have sold millions of copies.

When the first gold record was given for Perry Como's "Catch a Falling Star" in 1958—the year that certifications began—the requirement was that a record, either a single or an LP, have sold at least $1 million worth at wholesale, which was taken as one-third of list price. But as record sales rose precipitously through the Sixties and the value of the

dollar fell, the gold certification began to lose some of its impact. On January 1, 1976, new standards were established, with separate categories for albums and singles.

For an album released after 1976 to be certified gold, it must sell at least 500,000 copies (cassettes and multiple-LP sets count as single copies, or units) and the manufacturer's dollar volume must be at least $1 million. Gold singles must have sold one million copies; 12-inch disco singles count as two copies each.

A platinum category was also introduced in 1976. Platinum albums have sold at least one million units with a dollar volume of at least $2 million. Platinum singles must sell at least two million copies. The first platinum album was the Eagles' *Their Greatest Hits,* and the first platinum single was Johnnie Taylor's "Disco Lady."

For all records released after January 3, 1980, the RIAA adopted a 60-day waiting period after release, so that manufacturers could not ship huge quantities of records upon release and receive certification before record stores returned unsold discs. A record company must apply for certification for each record.

The gold and platinum records themselves, framed by the RIAA, are made from the metal stampers used to press vinyl copies of albums, electroplated with gold or silver alloy. They are intrinsically worthless and are not necessarily copies of the record certified.

The RIAA does not certify quantities above platinum; claims above sales of one million ("double platinum," for example) are made by record company sales departments.

"Back Home," the Who (whose live histrionics the group openly imitated during their concerts) hired them to open for a European tour and signed them to their Track label. 1973's *Hearing Earring* was a compilation of previous Dutch releases and preceded their breakthrough tour of British college campuses.

Moontan spawned "Radar Love," and they briefly became widely known in the U.S., where they opened stadium shows for the Doobie Brothers and Santana. But follow-up success to "Radar" proved elusive, and later LPs never reached the U.S. Top 100, although the group continues to score European hits. In addition to his activities with Earring, Kooymans produced the 1979 European hit remake of "Come On" by the young Dutch group New Adventures. In 1982, they returned to the U.S. charts with the hit single and video "Twilight Zone" from *Cut*.

BOBBY GOLDSBORO

Born January 18, 1941, Marianna, Florida
N.A.—*Bobby Goldsboro's Greatest Hits* (United Artists) **1976**—*A Butterfly for Bucky* **1977**—*Bobby Goldsboro's 10th Anniversary Album* **1978**—*Brand New Kind of Love; We Gotta Start Lovin'.*

Singer/songwriter Bobby Goldsboro had over 25 hit singles between 1962 and 1973. Two of his biggest, "Honey" and "Watching Scotty Grow," were sentimental MOR million-sellers. Goldsboro moved to Dothan, Alabama, with his family in his teens. He later studied at Auburn University, but left after two years and began playing the guitar with various local groups before joining Roy Orbison, with whom he cowrote some songs. He worked in Orbison's backup band until 1962, when he started on a solo career.

His first major hit was "See the Funny Little Clown" (#9, 1964), but his solo career hit full stride by the mid-Sixties, when singles like "Little Things" (1965) and "It's Too Late" (1966) regularly went gold. With "Honey," an international blockbuster in 1968 about the death of a young bride, Goldsboro became a major star. He became a regular on TV talk shows and in supper-club venues. Subsequent hits included "Autumn of My Life" (#19, 1968) and "Watching Scotty Grow" (#11, 1971).

GONG

Formed 1970, Paris
Original lineup: Daevid Allen (b. Australia), gtr.; Gillie Smyth (b. France), voc.; Christian Tritsch, bass, gtr.; Didier Malherbe, saxes, flute; Pip Pyle, drums.
1973—*The Flying Teapot* (Virgin) *Angel's Egg* **1974**—*Continental Circus* (Philips) *Camembert Electrique* (Caroline) *You* (Virgin) **1976**—*Shamal* **1977**—*Gazeuse; Live; Magick Brother* (Affinity) *Gong Est Mort* (Tapioca) *Expresso* (Virgin) **1978**—*Expresso II* (Arista) **1979**—*Downwind; Time Is the Key; Pierre Moerlen's Gong Live.*

Gong started out as a European post-hippie band with its own mythology of Pothead Pixies and UFOs and an unpredictable, punning mixture of rock and folk and jazz and synthesizers. Eventually, after numerous personnel changes and offshoots (some called Gong), the band moved into more conventional jazz rock.

The group's founder and leader was Daevid Allen, an Australian beatnik who had arrived in England in 1961. While attending Canterbury College of Art in 1966, he joined the original Soft Machine, part of a floating group of Canterbury musicians who were later associated with such bands as Hatfield and the North, National Health, Matching Mole and Caravan. Following the group's first European tour, Allen was refused reentry to the U.K. He then returned to France, where he lived and wrote poetry through 1969. By then, he was playing regularly with vocalist Gillie Smyth, with whom he cut two LPs in 1969, *Magick Brother, Mystic Sister* and *Banana Moon*.

By 1970, the duo had expanded into the group Gong. Allen began dropping in and out of the group in 1972, but before his departure in 1974 he contributed to *You*, which, coupled with earlier releases *Flying Teapot* and *Angel's Egg*, completed his trilogy about the imaginary planet Gong. Allen later recorded several LPs for Virgin and occasionally performed (sometimes billed as Gong), but has generally kept a low profile. His 1976 LP, *Good Morning,* featured backup from the Spanish group Euterpe. By 1977, he was working with a punkish group dubbed Material (previously the Zu Band) for *About Time*. (Material—synthesizer player Michael Beinhorn and bassist Bill Laswell—went on to make progressive dance music in the early Eighties, producing Nona Hendryx and making their own albums with guests from New York's funk, jazz, salsa and progressive rock circles.) In 1979, he released *N'existe Pas* and then led the first Gong-related group to play the United States. During the late Seventies, Allen lived in Woodstock, New York, and did solo tours (backed by tape collages), billed as the Divided Alien Clockwork Band.

Following Allen's exit from Gong proper, the leadership was assumed by percussionist Pierre Moerlen, who had joined the group in 1973 for *Angel's Egg*. Moerlen was born in Colmar, France. His father was the Strasbourg Cathedral organist and taught at the Strasbourg Conservatory, where Pierre studied from 1967 until 1972. Under Moerlen's influence, the group began to specialize in percussion-heavy jazz rock. His rotating cast of sidemen included such guitarists as Steve Hillage (who had departed by 1976 for a fairly successful solo career including an album produced by Todd Rundgren) and ex–Rolling Stone Mick Taylor (on whose 1979 solo debut Moerlen guested), as well as keyboardists Mike Oldfield and Moerlen's brother Benoit. Of the original group, Didier Malherbe remained.

In 1977, Moerlen's group reunited with Allen to record

Gong Est Mort. That same year the group released *Ga-zeuse* (released in the U.S. as *Expresso*), which featured guitarist Allan Holdsworth, also known for his work with Tony Williams' Lifetime and his own solo ventures. In the late Seventies the group moved to Arista, who released the group's live LP in America but passed on the studio effort *Leave It Open*, which did fairly well in Europe. In 1980, Moerlen finally led his version of Gong stateside for some little-noticed U.S. concerts. In recent years, he has had to compete with other Gong incarnations led by numerous band alumni.

STEVE GOODMAN

Born July 25, 1948, Chicago
1971—*Steve Goodman* (Buddah)   **1973**—*Somebody Else's Troubles*   **1975**—*Jessie's Jig and Other Favorites* (Asylum)   **1976**—*Words We Can Dance To*   **1978**—*Say It in Private*   **1979**—*High and Outside*   **1980**—*Hot Spot*   **1983**—*Artistic Hair* (Red Pajamas).

Singer/songwriter Steve Goodman is best known as the author of Arlo Guthrie's 1972 hit "The City of New Orleans," a modern train song. Through the Seventies he released a series of folk albums.

Goodman enrolled in 1964 at the University of Illinois to study political science; in the summer of 1967, he went to New York City and played in the parks for spare change for several months until he moved back to Chicago, where he began attending Lake Forest College. In the summer of 1969, he gave up academics for music and started performing in Chicago folk clubs.

Despite critical acclaim, Goodman's recordings never sold particularly well, and by 1973 he was still living in a $145-a-month apartment several blocks from Wrigley Field. *Somebody Else's Troubles* featured Bob Dylan (as Robert Milkwood Thomas) on piano on the title track. Goodman toured through the early Seventies, but was ultimately best remembered for "City of New Orleans," which he wrote about his experiences while campaigning for Edmund Muskie. His songs have since been covered by David Allan Coe, John Denver, Joan Baez and others.

THE GOOD RATS

Formed 1965, Long Island, New York
1969—*Good Rats* (Kapp)   **1974**—*Tasty* (Warner Bros.)   **1976**—*Rat City in Blue* (Rat City)   **1978**—*From Rats to Riches* (Passport)   *Birth Comes to Us All* **1981**—*Great American Music* (Great American).

The Good Rats have been regulars on the Long Island bar circuit since 1965. Founded by brothers Peppi and Mickey Marchello, the group originally played crude garage rock. Peppi Marchello was known to pelt the audience with rubber rats.

They cut their self-titled debut for Kapp Records in 1969, but little came of it. In August 1972, they temporarily disbanded. Mickey pumped gas, while Peppi worked as a dishwasher, a truck driver and a garbageman, all the while planning their comeback. In January 1973, the brothers re-formed the group with new musicians recruited from New York area bar bands. In 1974, Warner Bros. signed them, but their label debut, *Tasty,* sold poorly.

By the mid-Seventies, the group was still toiling in the bars. In 1976, they released *Rat City in Blue* on their own Rat City Records, and in late 1978, they signed with Passport. *From Rats to Riches* was produced by anarchic kindred spirits Flo and Eddie. *Birth Comes to Us All* was recorded at the Who's Ramport studio in England and included guest appearances by Manfred Mann and Max Middleton (a Jeff Beck alumnus).

ROBERT GORDON

Born 1947, Washington, D.C.
1977—*Robert Gordon with Link Wray* (Private Stock)   **1978**—*Fresh Fish Special*   **1979**—*Rockabilly Boogie* (RCA)   **1980**—*Bad Boy*   **1981**—*Are You Gonna Be the One.*

Singer Robert Gordon emerged from the New York new wave scene in 1976 looking and sounding every bit the rockabilly revivalist he has always claimed not to be.

Gordon grew up in the D.C. suburb of Bethesda, Maryland, where he began playing guitar at age 15 with his groups, the Newports and the Confidentials. In the mid-Sixties, he enrolled in college to avoid the draft. By 1970, he had moved to New York and dropped out of music for several years while he worked various jobs to support his wife and two children. With his marriage falling apart mid-decade, he became involved with the new wave band Tuff Darts, with whom he appeared on *Live at CBGB's.* While Gordon has since denounced his work with Tuff Darts, it nonetheless brought him to the attention of producer Richard Gottehrer.

Gordon's debut, *Robert Gordon with Link Wray,* featured his childhood hero Link Wray on guitar. "Red Hot" was a minor hit in 1977, and Gordon and Wray toured Europe and the U.S. that year. *Fresh Fish Special* featured Bruce Springsteen's "Fire," which was written especially for Gordon and later became a hit for the Pointer Sisters.

In December 1978, Gordon signed with RCA and in 1979 released *Rockabilly Boogie.* In 1980, Gordon's fifth album, featuring three songs by Marshall Crenshaw, was released. With its emphasis on a more contemporary pop sound, the LP was a decisive change from the rockabilly of his previous albums. Gordon had a minor hit with Crenshaw's "Someday, Someway" in 1981.

BERRY GORDY, JR.

Born November 28, 1929, Detroit

As the owner of Motown Records, Berry Gordy, Jr., is a pivotal figure in the development of pop. He ran his

Motown empire like a Detroit assembly line, grinding out classic records designed for both black and white teenagers: "The Sound of Young America."

In the early Fifties, after a stint as a pro boxer, Gordy opened a jazz record shop that went bankrupt, spurring his shift in interest to R&B. He worked at various day jobs mid-decade while supplying local acts with original songs.

Gordy's first national success came in 1957, when Jackie Wilson recorded his "Reet Petite." Wilson's recording of another Gordy tune, "Lonely Teardrops," sold a million copies in 1959. Gordy penned another gold disc in 1959, "You Got What It Takes," for Marv Johnson. Yet Gordy was still working on the Ford assembly line in the late Fifties, while dreaming of starting his own independent production company and record label. He got started in 1959, when he borrowed $700 from his sister Anna (who married Motown star Marvin Gaye in 1961). Beginning with the sister labels Tamla and Motown (for Motortown), which he later expanded into a number of subsidiaries like Soul and Gordy, working out of a two-story building at 2648 West Grand Boulevard, Gordy shaped a roster of young performers drawn from the Detroit ghetto through regular talent hunts. Those singers would be matched to material from in-house songwriters, producers, managers and musicians.

Gordy groomed Smokey Robinson and the Miracles, the Temptations, Stevie Wonder, Diana Ross and the Supremes, Mary Wells, Martha and the Vandellas and many others. Motown used top-flight in-house producers and songwriters, particularly Robinson, Marvin Gaye, Nick Ashford, Valerie Simpson and the prolific team of Holland-Dozier-Holland. The Motown sound had a pounding beat, insistent bass lines, hooks on keyboards and guitars, and vocals stripped of ghetto inflections. Gordy also packaged his acts into professional road shows as the Motown Revue.

Through the Sixties, Motown dominated the soul market with over 120 Top Twenty hits. In 1971, Gordy shifted his operations from Detroit to Los Angeles. While the trademark Motown sound faded with the Sixties, the label continued to hold its own with consistent sales from such superstar acts as Wonder and Gaye, who had both demanded and gotten artistic control. Gordy produced Diana Ross's 1972 movie, *Lady Sings the Blues,* and the label's biggest contemporary act, the Commodores. By 1977, Tamla-Motown was the largest black-owned conglomerate in the United States and still selling millions of albums by Rick James and others, although many of its most successful acts, like the Jackson 5, Diana Ross and Marvin Gaye, were moving to other labels.

LESLEY GORE

Born May 2, 1946, New York City
1965—*The Golden Hits of Lesley Gore* (Mercury)
1968—*Golden Hits of Lesley Gore, volume 2* **1972**—

Someplace Else Now (Mowest) **1978**—*Love Me by Name* (A&M).

As a teenager, Lesley Gore wrote and sang a series of pop weepers; after her hits ended, she moved into acting and songwriting. Gore's father was a swimsuit manufacturer who sent her to the Dwight Preparatory School for Girls in Englewood, New Jersey. In her senior year, she was discovered by Quincy Jones, who got her a deal with Mercury and produced her recordings through 1967. As she turned 17, they released her song "It's My Party," which went to #1.

At year's end, she had three more Top Five smashes— "Judy's Turn to Cry," "She's a Fool" and the ballad she performed in the filmed *T.A.M.I. Show,* "You Don't Own Me." She had two more hits, "That's the Way Boys Are" (#12, 1964) and "Maybe I Know" (#12, 1964), before moving away from rock with 1965's "Sunshine, Lollipops and Rainbows" and 1967's "California Nights."

Throughout her peak years, Gore studied at least part-time at Sarah Lawrence College, and she graduated in 1968 after her hits had stopped in 1967 (her last chart record was 1967's "Brink of Disaster"). After moving to California, she worked with independent producer Bob Crewe on a series of unsuccessful releases. She tried acting—in films like *Girls on the Beach* and *Ski Party* and TV fare like "Batman."

Largely out of sight for several years, Gore made some club appearances in 1970 and 1971, and in 1972 she signed with Motown subsidiary Mowest, but *Someplace Else Now* sold poorly. In late 1974, she switched to A&M and was reunited with Quincy Jones for *Love Me by Name.* Again, sales were disappointing. In 1980, Gore contributed lyrics ("Out Here on My Own") to the *Fame* soundtrack, which featured music by her brother, Michael.

GOSPEL

The term "gospel music" was probably coined in the Twenties by Thomas A. Dorsey, a Georgia blues singer who was converted and began composing religious songs in popular styles. The music was initially denounced, but it caught on in the black sanctified church, and has since evolved alongside black secular music, although it is somewhat more conservative and serves different functions. Gospel singing is rooted in the ornate vocal style of old spirituals and in the impassioned "testifying" declamation of Baptist preachers.

The close-harmony group vocals of late Forties and Fifties gospel—with the group responding to and urging on a soaring, improvising lead singer—had many links to the a cappella and doo-wop pop of the Fifties; and such church-trained singers as Sam Cooke and Clyde McPhatter moved from gospel groups into pop. In the Sixties, soul music was spearheaded by gospel-turned-pop singers like Aretha Franklin, Wilson Pickett and Solomon Burke.

The characteristic gospel sound—shouted responses from the congregation and bluesy rolling keyboard riffs (on piano or church organ) that could be repeated rhythmically to build excitement—has shown up in the music of everyone from Ray Charles to Keith Jarrett to Randy Newman.

LARRY GRAHAM/GRAHAM CENTRAL STATION

Born August 14, 1946, Beaumont, Texas
1974—*Graham Central Station* (Warner Bros.) *Release Yourself* 1975—*Ain't No Bout-A-Doubt It* 1976—*Mirror* 1977—*Now Do U Wanta Dance* 1978—*My Radio Sure Sounds Good to Me* 1979—*Star Walk*.
Larry Graham solo: 1980—*One in a Million You* (Warner Bros.) 1981—*Just Be My Lady* 1982—*Sooner or Later*.

As bassist for Sly and the Family Stone, Larry Graham updated the percussive bass lines of James Brown into a style that set the groove for the progressive funk of the Seventies. After leaving Sly, he led Graham Central Station and developed a new image as a ballad singer.

Graham moved with his family to Oakland, California, at age two. By his teens, he could play guitar, bass, harmonica and drums; he also had a three-octave-plus vocal range. At 15, he began playing guitar with his cocktail lounge singer/pianist mother in her Dell Graham Trio. When they were reduced to a duo, Graham switched to bass. After four years, he quit to attend college for a year and a half, while working as a backup musician for John Lee Hooker, Jimmy Reed, the Drifters and Jackie Wilson.

In 1967, Graham joined Sly and the Family Stone and stayed with the group until late 1972. He then took a local group called Hot Chocolate and, with the addition of ex-Billy Preston keyboardist Robert Sam, formed the original Graham Central Station. They released their debut album in December 1973 and soon had a contract with Warner Bros. *Graham Central Station* sold over a quarter-million copies and yielded a minor pop hit, "Can You Handle It," in 1974. September 1974's *Release Yourself* featured another small hit, "Feel the Need." Their third LP, *Ain't No Bout-A-Doubt It* ("Your Love") went gold four months after its release.

Graham wrote every selection on the group's fourth release, *Mirror*, a progressive funk outing. In early 1977, the group released *Now Do U Wanta Dance*, but neither it nor *My Radio Sure Sounds Good to Me* (which marked the addition of Graham's wife, Tina, as vocalist) attracted the hoped-for pop crossover success. *Star Walk* was the last group effort. By the end of 1980, Graham was billed on his own and singing ballads. *One in a Million You* hit #26 on the pop charts, and the title track was a #9 single. In 1981, Graham produced and played nearly all the instruments on *Just Be My Lady*. He attributes his success to divine guidance: "God has a lot to do with it. He's like directing me and I'm just following His orders. I just lay back and wait for Him to tell me what to do next."

GRAND FUNK RAILROAD

Formed 1969, Flint, Michigan
Mark Farner (b. Sep. 29, 1948, Flint), gtr., voc.; Mel Schacher (b. Apr. 3, 1951, Owosso, Mich.), bass; Don Brewer (b. Sep. 3, 1948, Flint, Mich.), drums.
1969—*On Time* (Capitol) 1970—*Grand Funk; Closer to Home* 1971—*Survival; E Pluribus Funk* 1972—

Grammy Awards

Gale Garnett
1964 Best Folk Recording: "We'll Sing in the Sunshine"

Marvin Gaye
1982 Best R&B Vocal Performance, Male; Best R&B Instrumental Performance: "Sexual Healing"

Crystal Gayle
1977 Best Country Vocal Performance, Female: "Don't It Make My Brown Eyes Blue"

Gloria Gaynor
1979 Best Disco Recording: "I Will Survive"

Bobbie Gentry
1967 Best New Artist; Best Vocal Performance, Female; Best Contemporary Female Solo Vocal Performance: *Ode to Billie Joe*

Barry Gibb (see also: Bee Gees)
1980 Best Pop Performance by a Duo or Group with Vocal: "Guilty" (with Barbra Streisand)

Al Green
1981 Best Soul Gospel Performer, Traditional: *The Lord Will Make a Way*
1982 Best Soul Gospel Performance, Contemporary: *Higher Plane* Best Soul Gospel Performance, Traditional: *Precious Lord*

Mark, Don and Mel, 1969–1971 (+ Craig Frost [b. Apr. 20, 1948, Flint], kybds.) *Phoenix* **1973**—*We're an American Band* **1974**—*Shinin' On; All the Girls in the World Beware!!* **1975**—*Caught in the Act; Born to Die* **1976**—*Good Singin', Good Playin'* (MCA) (disbanded) **1977**—*Hits* (Capitol) **1981**—(re-formed: Farner; Brewer; Dennis Bellinger [b. Flint], bass) *Grand Funk Lives* (Full Moon/Warner Bros.) **1983**— *What's Funk.*
Mark Farner solo: 1977—*Mark Farner* (Atlantic) **1978**—*No Frills.*

Grand Funk Railroad: Mel Schacher, Don Brewer, Mark Farner, Craig Frost

Grand Funk Railroad, the most commercially successful American heavy-metal band from 1970 until they disbanded in 1976, established the Seventies success formula: continuous touring. Unanimously reviled or ignored by critics and initially by radio programers, Grand Funk (Railroad) nonetheless became the first group to be awarded ten consecutive platinum LPs; they sold over 20 million albums and regularly set attendance records at arenas and stadiums. A prototypical "people's band," Grand Funk was a simplified model of blues-rock power trios like Cream and the Jimi Hendrix Experience. The members were all millionaires within two years of their debut.

Mark Farner began playing guitar at age 15 after a broken finger and bad knees ended his football career. After he was expelled in his senior year of high school, he started playing full-time in semi-pro bands and, briefly, with Terry Knight and the Pack, a group that had a hit with "I (Who Have Nothing)" in 1966. The group also included drummer Don Brewer.

In late 1968, Farner and Brewer hooked up with bassist Mel Schacher, ex-? and the Mysterians; they made Knight their manager and gave him complete business and artistic control. Their first date was in Buffalo, New York, in March 1969; the following July they played (for free) for 125,000 people at the Atlanta Pop Festival. While the music consisted mostly of power chords, the group's onstage writhing and sweating made up in energy what it lacked in finesse. With Knight producing, Grand Funk released their debut album late in 1969. Two years later, they had five gold LPs. Farner wrote and sang most of the early material, though subsequently Brewer was the group's lead vocalist on a few tunes. In their best year, 1970, they supposedly sold more than any other group in America. The next year, they broke the Beatles' ticket sales record at Shea Stadium, selling out their two-day stand in 48 hours and grossing over $300,000.

An undeniably triumphant moment, it marked the end of the honeymoon between Knight and the band. On March 27, 1972, Grand Funk terminated their relationship with Knight; he responded with $60 million in lawsuits. The band lost momentum while courts straightened the mess out, but with attorney John Eastman (Linda McCart-

ney's father) handling their affairs, the group eventually broke their contract with Knight.

Their first popular post-Knight LP was *Phoenix*, which introduced a fourth member, organist Craig Frost (who later joined Bob Seger's Silver Bullet Band). In 1973, Todd Rundgren produced *We're an American Band*, the title track of which was their first big AM hit (#1). Rundgren also produced their tenth LP, *Shinin' On*, which yielded another gold single, a remake of Little Eva's "The Locomotion" (#1). They continued to tour in 1975, as documented in *Caught in the Act*, but interest within the group was lagging. They scored two more pop hits that year: "Some Kind of Wonderful" (#3) and "Bad Time" (#4). Their 1976 LP, *Born to Die*, was to be their last, but when Frank Zappa agreed to produce, they stayed together for *Good Singin', Good Playin'*.

The group broke up soon thereafter and returned to Michigan. Brewer and Schacher formed Flint, which released one album locally before disbanding. By the late Seventies, Don Brewer had moved to Boca Raton, Florida. Farner spent his time with his wife and two children on his 1,500-acre farm in upstate Michigan and opened an alternative energy store. He released two solo LPs—*Mark Farner* in 1977 and *No Frills* in 1978—and toured on occasion. In January 1981, Farner and Brewer, with a new bassist, re-formed the band under the guidance of David Geffen for *Grand Funk Lives*, which picked up some AOR airplay with a remake of the Animals' "We Gotta Get Out of This Place." The group was included on the soundtrack of *Heavy Metal* around the same time but broke up again. Brewer joined Bob Seger's Silver Bullet Band in 1983.

GRANDMASTER FLASH AND THE FURIOUS FIVE

Formed 1977, Bronx, New York
Grandmaster Flash (b. Joseph Saddler, 1957, Bronx), turntables; Cowboy (b. Keith Wiggins), voc.; Melly Mel (b. Melvin Glover), voc.; Kid Creole (b. Danny Glover), voc.; Mr. Ness (b. Eddie Morris), voc.; Rahiem (b. Guy Williams), voc.
1982—*The Message* (Sugarhill).

Disco DJ Grandmaster Flash and his rap group, the Furious Five, were the premier DJ-rap team of the early Eighties. Flash began spinning records at Bronx block parties, gym dances and parks when he was 18. Within a year, he was working at local discos while studying electronics at technical school by day. He developed an idiosyncratic style that involved "cutting" (segueing between tracks precisely on the beat), "back-spinning" (turning records manually to make the needle repeat brief lengths of groove) and "phasing" (manipulating turntable speeds) to create aural montages. Strictly a spinner, he began working with rappers around 1977, first with Kurtis Blow and then with the Furious Five, who had mastered a routine of trading and blending lines and had introduced choreography to their act.

Flash and the Five were popular throughout New York by 1978, but they did not record until the Sugar Hill Gang showed that rap records could be hits in 1979. Flash and the Five recorded "Superrappin'" for Harlem-based Enjoy Records before signing with Sugarhill Records in 1980. Their first Sugarhill release, "Freedom" (#19 R&B, 1980), sold over 50,000 copies; it was followed by "Birthday Party" (#36 R&B, 1981).

These records' appeal was not limited to New York, and in 1980 Flash and the Five toured the nation. "The Adventures of Grandmaster Flash on the Wheels of Steel" (#55 R&B, 1981) was the first record to capture the urban "cutting" technique pioneered by Flash; it incorporated snatches of Chic's "Good Times," Blondie's "Rapture" and Queen's "Another One Bites the Dust." "The Message" (#4 R&B, 1982), which raps about the grim reality of ghetto life in terms that are very rarely heard in popular music, was one of the most controversial songs of 1982.

THE GRASS ROOTS

Formed 1967, Los Angeles
Warren Entner (b. July 7, ca. 1944, Boston), gtr., voc., kybds.; Creed Bratton (b. Feb. 8, 1943, Sacramento, Calif.), gtr., banjo, sitar; Ricky Coonce (b. Aug. 1, 1947, Los Angeles), drums; Rob Grill (b. Nov. 5, 1944, Los Angeles), bass, voc.
1968—(− Bratton; + Dennis Provisor [b. Nov. 5, ca. 1950, Los Angeles], organ) *Golden Grass* (Dunhill)
1969—*Lovin' Things* **1970**—*More Golden Grass*
1971—*Their 16 Greatest Hits* **1975**—*The Grass Roots*
(Haven) **1982**—*Powers of the Night* (MCA).

The Grass Roots were a major American singles band during the late Sixties. The group was formed when pop producer/writers P. F. Sloan and Steve Barri, who had recorded the 1966 hit "Where Were You When I Needed You" (#28) under the name the Grassroots, decided to continue recording and drafted a Los Angeles bar band, the 13th Floor, to play on the records. Barri and Sloan continued to work together. The group that recorded the 1967 hits "Let's Live for Today" (#12) (a remake of an Italian hit by the Rokes) and "Things I Should Have Said" (#23) became the Grass Roots.

The group had several major hits, including "Midnight Confessions" (#5, 1968), "I'd Wait a Million Years" (#15, 1969), "Heaven Knows" (#24, 1969), "The River Is Wide" (#31, 1969), "Temptation Eyes" (#15, 1971), "Sooner or Later" (#9, 1971) and "Two Divided by Love" (#16, 1971).

By 1972, the hits ended and they returned to small clubs. Their biggest-selling LP was a greatest-hits package, *Golden Grass*. By the mid-Seventies, the band was recording for the small Haven Records, where they managed one moderate comeback hit, "Mamacita" (#71, 1975).

Grill's 1980 solo LP, *Uprooted*, featured John McVie, Mick Fleetwood and Lindsey Buckingham of Fleetwood Mac, and he toured as Rob Grill and the Grass Roots in 1981 before releasing *Powers of the Night* in 1982. Ex-Grass Root Warren Entner was the executive producer of the *Pirates of Penzance* film in 1983.

THE GRATEFUL DEAD

Formed 1965, San Francisco
Jerry Garcia (b. Jerome John Garcia, Aug. 1, 1942, San Francisco), gtr., voc.; Bob Weir (b. Robert Hall, Oct. 16, 1947, San Francisco), gtr., voc.; Ron "Pigpen" McKernan (b. Sep. 8, 1945, San Bruno, Calif.; d. Mar. 8, 1973, San Francisco), kybds., harmonica, voc.; Phil Lesh (b. Philip Chapman, Mar. 15, 1940, Berkeley, Calif.), bass, voc.; Bill Kreutzmann, a.k.a. Bill Sommers (b. Apr. 7, 1946, Palo Alto, Calif.), drums.
1967—*The Grateful Dead* (Warner Bros.) (+ Mickey Hart [b. circa 1950, New York City], perc.) **1968**—*Anthem of the Sun* (+ Tom Constanten, kybds.)
1969—*Aoxomoxoa* **1970**—*Live Dead* (− Constanten) *Workingman's Dead; American Beauty* (− Hart) **1971**—*Grateful Dead* (+ Keith Godchaux [b. July 14, 1948, San Francisco; d. July 23, 1980, Marin County, Calif.], kybds.; + Donna Godchaux [b. Aug. 22, 1947, San Francisco], voc.) **1972**—*Europe '72*
1973—*History of the Grateful Dead, volume 1* (MGM) *Wake of the Flood* (Grateful Dead) **1974**—*From the Mars Hotel; Skeletons from the Closet* (Warner Bros.) (+ Hart) **1975**—*Blues for Allah* (Grateful Dead) **1976**—*Steal Your Face* **1977**—*Terrapin Station* (Arista) **1978**—*What a Long Strange Trip It's Been: The Best of the Grateful Dead* (Warner

Bros.) *Shakedown Street* (Arista) **1979**—(− Keith and Donna Godchaux; + Brent Mydland [b. 1953], kybds.) **1980**—*Go to Heaven* **1981**—*Reckoning; Dead Set.*
Jerry Garcia solo: 1972—*Garcia* (Warner Bros.) *Hooteroll* (Douglas) **1973**—*Live at the Keystone* (Fantasy) **1974**—*Garcia* (Round) **1976**—*Reflections* **1978**—*Cats Under the Stars* (Arista) **1982**—*Run for the Roses.*

The Grateful Dead are the only surviving psychedelic band, and probably the most improvisatory major rock group. As they have for more than 15 years, they play long, free-form concerts that touch down on their own country-, blues- and folk-tinged rock songs, usually for audiences largely composed of Dead Heads, their mailing list/fan club/cult. Although Grateful Dead albums sell a dependable 250,000 copies, the group has never had a Top Ten single. They concentrate on live shows rather than the recording process. In true psychedelic style, they prefer the moment to the artifact.

Lead guitarist Jerry Garcia took up guitar at 15, spent nine months in the Army in 1959, then moved to Palo Alto, where he began his long-standing friendship with Robert Hunter, later the Dead's lyricist. In 1962, he bought a banjo and began playing in folk and bluegrass bands, and by 1964 he was a member of Mother McCree's Uptown Jug Champions, along with Bob Weir, Pigpen and longtime associates Bob Matthews (who engineered Grateful Dead albums and formed Alembic Electronics, an electronic equipment company) and John Dawson (later of New Riders of the Purple Sage).

In 1965, the band became the Warlocks: Garcia, Weir, Pigpen, Bill Kreutzmann and Phil Lesh, a former electronic-music composer. With electric instruments, the Warlocks debuted in July 1965 and soon became the house band at Ken Kesey's Acid Tests, a series of public LSD parties and multimedia events held before the drug had been outlawed. LSD chemist Owsley Stanley bankrolled the Grateful Dead—a name from an Egyptian prayer that Garcia spotted in a dictionary—and later supervised construction of the band's state-of-the-art sound system. The Dead lived communally at 710 Ashbury Street in San Francisco in 1966–67 and played numerous free concerts; by 1967's Summer of Love, they were regulars at the Avalon and Carousel ballrooms and the Fillmore West.

MGM signed the band in 1966, and they made some mediocre recordings that were eventually released in 1971. Their legitimate recording career began when Warner Bros. signed them. While their 1967 debut album featured zippy three-minute songs, *Anthem of the Sun* and *Aoxomoxoa* included extended suites and studio experiments that left the band $100,000 in debt to Warner Bros., mostly for studio time, by the end of the Sixties. Meanwhile, the Dead's reputation had spread, and they appeared at the Monterey Pop Festival in 1967 and Woodstock in 1969.

As the Seventies began, the Dead recouped their Warner debt with three comparatively inexpensive albums—*Live Dead* (recorded in concert), *Workingman's Dead* and *American Beauty*—for which they wrote concise countryish songs and worked out clear-cut, well-rehearsed arrangements. *Workingman's Dead* (including "Uncle John's Band") and *American Beauty* (including "Truckin," "Ripple" and "Box of Rain") received considerable FM airplay, sold respectably and have provided much of the Dead's concert repertoire ever since.

With a nationwide following, the Dead expanded their touring schedule and started various solo projects, detailed below. They worked their way up to a 23-ton sound system and a large traveling entourage of road crew, family, friends and hangers-on, and they finished out their Warner contract with a string of live albums including 1971's *Grateful Dead,* their first gold album. In 1973, they played for over half a million people in Watkins Glen, New York, on a bill with the Band and the Allman Brothers. By then, they had formed Grateful Dead Records and a subsidiary, Round, for non-band efforts.

Europe '72 was the last album to include Pigpen, a heavy drinker who died in 1973 of a liver disease. Keith Godchaux, who had played piano with Dave Mason, joined the band and brought along his wife, Donna, as background vocalist. The pair toured and recorded with the Dead until 1979, when they were asked to leave and were replaced by pianist Brent Mydland. The following year, Keith Godchaux was killed in a car crash in Marin County.

In 1974, the Dead temporarily disbanded while members pursued outside projects, but they resumed touring in 1976. After signing with Arista, they began to use non-Dead producers for the first time: Keith Olsen for *Terrapin Station* and Little Feat's Lowell George for *Shakedown*

The Grateful Dead: Mickey Hart, Phil Lesh, Jerry Garcia, Brent Mydland, Bill Kreutzmann, Bob Weir

Street. In 1978, the band played three concerts at the foot of the Great Pyramid in Egypt, which were recorded but not released. *Go to Heaven* yielded "Alabama Getaway." The Dead's main support continues to be their touring six months each year. They celebrated their 15th anniversary with the release of two more live albums, including the mostly acoustic *Reckoning.*

Garcia's outside projects include session work with Jefferson Airplane and Crosby, Stills, Nash and Young. He produced the debut album for New Riders of the Purple Sage in 1970 and sat in on pedal steel guitar. From 1970 to 1973, he played occasional gigs with Bay Area keyboardist Merl Saunders, and he also kept up his bluegrass banjo skills with Old and In the Way, which also featured Peter Rowan (Seatrain), Vassar Clements and David Grisman. Garcia recorded his first solo album, *Garcia,* in 1971; the cover shows his right hand, which has been missing its third finger since a childhood accident. Garcia joined organist Howard Wales on *Hooteroll,* and he toured and recorded with various Jerry Garcia bands in the Seventies and early Eighties.

Weir's first solo effort was 1972's *Ace.* During the Dead's sabbatical he formed Kingfish with ex–New Rider Dave Torbert; Kingfish released a debut album in 1976. The Bob Weir Band released *Heaven Help the Fool* in 1978, and in the early Eighties Weir toured and recorded with Bobby and the Midnites, including Billy Cobham (Mahavishnu Orchestra), Bobby Cochran (Steppenwolf, Flying Burrito Brothers) and Alphonso Johnson (Weather Report).

Phil Lesh teamed with electronic music composer Ned Lagin to record *Seastones.* The Godchauxs recorded as a duo, backed by Garcia and friends, while the Dead's other drummer, Mickey Hart, experimented with world music as part of the Diga Rhythm Band. Hart released a solo album, *Rolling Thunder,* in 1972, and with Kreutzmann composed incidental music for *Apocalypse Now,* released as *Play River Music,* by their band, the Rhythm Devils, in 1980.

DOBIE GRAY
Born Leonard Victor Ainsworth, 1942, Brookshire, Texas
1973—*Drift Away* (MCA) 1975—*New Ray of Sunshine* (Capricorn) 1978—*Midnight Diamond* (Infinity).

Following a brief but successful mid-Sixties pop career, singer Dobie Gray turned to country soul. Gray was born to sharecroppers with eight children. By the early Sixties, he had moved to the West Coast to become a singer. Through a radio ad, he met Sonny Bono, who helped him get started. Gray had a minor hit, "Look at Me" (1963), but his next single, "The 'In' Crowd," was the biggest hit of his early period (#13, 1965), and a gold record. "See You at the 'Go-Go,' " which followed, stalled on the lower rungs of the charts.

By the late Sixties, Gray had enrolled in pre-law classes and started acting. He appeared in a New York production of *The Beard,* Jean Genet's *The Balcony* and the L.A. production of *Hair.* Despite his success in theater, Gray returned to music and through 1969 and 1970 he worked with the group Pollution. While cutting demos for songwriter Paul Williams, he met Williams' brother, Mentor, with whom he worked as staff writer for A&M Records.

In 1973 Gray released *Drift Away,* the first of three MCA albums produced by Mentor Williams. The title track (written by Williams and later covered by Rod Stewart, among others) sold 1½ million copies and hit #5. Late in the summer of 1973, Gray followed up with "Loving Arms," which sold over 600,000 copies. In 1975 (the same year he signed with Capricorn for the disco-tinged *New Ray of Sunshine*), Gray began playing benefit concerts for presidential candidate Jimmy Carter; in January 1977, he sang at Carter's inaugural eve ceremonies. By the late Seventies, Gray's MCA LPs were no longer in print, and recent country-rock efforts were unsuccessful. Gray is a regular guest at the Charlie Daniels Band's annual Volunteer Jam in Nashville.

AL GREEN
Born April 13, 1946, Forrest City, Arkansas
N.A.—*Back Up Train* (Action) 1970—*Green Is Blues* (Hi) (reissued in 1972) *Gets Next to You* 1972—*Let's Stay Together; I'm Still in Love with You* 1973—*Call Me* 1974—*Living for You; Explores Your Mind* 1975—*Al Green Is Love; Greatest Hits* 1976—*Full of Fire; Have a Good Time* 1977—*The Belle Album; Greatest Hits, volume 2* 1978—*Love Ritual* 1979—*Truth and Time* 1980—*Cream of* (Cream) 1981—*The Lord Will Make a Way* (Myrrh) 1981—*Tokyo . . . Live* (Motown) 1982—*Higher Plane.*

To a greater extent than even his predecessors Sam Cooke and Otis Redding, Al Green embodies both the sacred and the profane in soul music. He was one of the most popular vocalists in the Seventies, selling over 20 million records. His wildly improvisational, ecstatic cries and moans came directly from gospel music, and in the late Seventies he returned to the Baptist church as a preacher. He continues to record albums in a pop-gospel style with close ties to the Memphis soul music that made him famous.

Green was born to a large family of sharecroppers. When he was nine, he and his brothers formed a gospel quartet, the Green Brothers. They toured the gospel circuits in the South and—after the family moved to Grand Rapids, Michigan, three years later—in the Midwest. Green's father dismissed him from the quartet after he caught him listening to the "profane music" of Jackie Wilson. At 16, he formed a pop group, Al Green and the Creations, with high school friends. Two members of the Creations, Palmer James and Curtis Rogers, founded a record company, Hot Line Music Journal, for which the

Al Green

group—renamed Al Green and the Soul Mates—cut "Back Up Train" in 1967. The single went to #5 on the national soul charts. Followups failed, however, and the group broke up.

Green met Willie Mitchell in Midland, Texas, in 1969. Mitchell was a bandleader, a producer and a vice-president of Hi Records of Memphis, to which he signed Green. He also became Green's producer and songwriting partner for the next eight years. Mitchell rounded up a band that included drummers Al Jackson (of Booker T. and the MGs) and Howard Grimes, keyboardists Archie Turner and Charles Hodges, bassist Leroy Hodges, guitarist Teenie Hodges, trumpeter Wayne Jackson (of the Mar-Keys and the Memphis Horns), baritone saxophonist James Mitchell and trombonist Jack Hale. With the exception of Al Jackson, who died in 1975, this band played on every Green record until 1978.

Green Is Blues introduced the sound that would distinguish all the records Green made with Mitchell: simple but emphatic backbeats riding subdued horns and strings, Green's voice floating untethered over the instruments.

His second album contained Green's first solo hits—"You Say It" (#28 R&B, 1970), "Right Now, Right Now" (#23 R&B, 1970) and "I Can't Get Next to You" (#11 R&B, 1970)—and his first gold single, "Tired of Being Alone" (#7 R&B, #11 pop, 1971), which he wrote. That began a five-year string of gold singles, most of them written by Green, Mitchell and Jackson: "Let's Stay Together" (#1 R&B, 1971, #1 pop, 1972), "Look What You Done for Me" (#2 R&B, #4 pop, 1972), "I'm Still in Love with You" (#1 R&B, #3 pop, 1972), "You Ought to

Be with Me" (#1 R&B, #3 pop, 1972), "Call Me (Come Back Home)" (#2 R&B, #10 pop, 1973), "Here I Am (Come and Take Me)" (#2 R&B, #10 pop, 1973), "Sha La La (Make Me Happy)" (#2 R&B, #7 pop, 1974), "L-O-V-E" (#1 R&B, #13 pop, 1975).

In October 1974, Green was hospitalized with second-degree burns on his back, arm and stomach. A former girlfriend, Mrs. Mary Woodson of New Jersey, had poured boiling grits on him while he was bathing in his Memphis home and then killed herself with his gun. The incident apparently triggered a spiritual crisis in Green, and he announced his intention to go into the ministry. In 1976, he purchased a church building in Memphis and was ordained pastor of the Full Gospel Tabernacle.

He did not, however, give up his pop career, and he preached at his church only when he was not on tour. His records continued to place regularly on the soul charts and occasionally on the pop charts. In 1977, he built himself a studio and, with *Belle,* began producing his own records, maintaining the style and standards he had set with Mitchell. But during a 1979 concert in Cincinnati, he fell off the stage and narrowly escaped serious injury. He considered the incident a warning from God, and since then he has devoted himself to the ministry. His public appearances have been limited to religious services in churches around the country, where he both sings and preaches.

His records, now distributed by Myrrh, a gospel label, contain only religious songs, both standard hymns and Green's originals, in a style that mixes Memphis soul with gospel. In 1982, he did a stint on Broadway, costarring with Patti LaBelle in Vinnette Carroll's gospel musical *Your Arms Too Short to Box with God.*

NORMAN GREENBAUM
Born November 20, 1942, Malden, Massachusetts
1969—*Spirit in the Sky* (Reprise)   **1970**—*Back Home Again*   **1972**—*Petaluma.*

In 1970, folksinger/songwriter Norman Greenbaum's electrified jug-band stomp "Spirit in the Sky" sold two million copies. After playing local coffeehouses while attending Boston University, he had moved to the West Coast in the mid-Sixties and formed Dr. West's Medicine Show and Junk Band, a psychedelic jug band that had a minor hit, "The Eggplant That Ate Chicago" (#52, 1966) before disbanding in 1967. Greenbaum then formed several other unsuccessful groups before embarking on his solo career in 1968. Working with producer and cowriter Eric Jacobson, he released a couple of unsuccessful singles from his Reprise debut, *Spirit in the Sky,* before the title track hit #3 on the American charts. Greenbaum's followups ("Canned Ham," 1970; "California Earthquake," 1971) never hit. When *Petaluma* was released in 1972, he was largely out of the public eye, spending most of his time breeding goats on his farm near Petaluma, California.

ELLIE GREENWICH

Born 1940, Long Island, New York
1973—*Let It Be Written, Let It Be Sung* (Verve)
Composes, Produces and Sings (United Artists).

Ellie Greenwich and her then-husband Jeff Barry wrote the lyrics and music for a catalogue of Sixties hits—including "Hanky Panky," "Leader of the Pack" and many Phil Spector productions—that have sold over 20 million records.

Greenwich started recording for RCA in the late Fifties as Ellie Gay. She went to college, majored in English and taught for a while before cowriting songs for Jay and the Americans ("This Is It") and the Exciters ("He's Got the Power"). She met Barry and married him in 1962, and collaborated with him even after the marriage ended in 1965. Working with Phil Spector, they churned out teen epics for the Crystals ("Then He Kissed Me," "Da Doo Ron Ron") and the Ronettes ("Be My Baby"), and in 1966 their "River Deep, Mountain High" was a European hit for Ike and Tina Turner. They were staff songwriters at Leiber and Stoller's Red Bird Records from 1964 to 1966, where they wrote and produced "Chapel of Love" for the Dixie Cups (#1, 1964) and "Good Night Baby" for the Butterflys. From 1965 to 1967, they worked for Bert Berns's Bang label, where they discovered Neil Diamond.

Greenwich has recorded sporadically on her own. As the Raindrops, a studio concoction, she sang a few minor hits in 1963 and 1964, including "The Kind of Boy You Can't Forget" (#17, 1963). In the wake of Carole King's *Tapestry*, Greenwich released *Let It Be Written, Let It Be Sung* under her own name a few months after she had opened her own commercial-writing company, Jingle Habitat. In 1983, she wrote two songs for an album by Ellen Foley.

STEFAN GROSSMAN

Born April 16, 1945, New York City
1975—*Yazoo Basin Boogie* (Kicking Mule) 1976—*Acoustic Music for Body and Soul* 1978—*Stefan Grossman and John Renbourn.*

A patron and champion of country blues, Stefan Grossman has been a peripheral figure on the international music scene for nearly two decades. He first gathered attention in 1965 and 1966 in New York when he played with the Even Dozen Jug Band and on occasion with the anarchic Fugs. He attempted to spread the word about such stalwart genuine articles as the Reverend Gary Davis, one of Grossman's heroes. By 1968, he had moved to England and was prominent in the blues revival there. By the start of the Seventies, he had relocated to Rome and issued a number of instructional books and records (mostly on the Transatlantic label) on blues guitar technique. In 1972, he formed his own Kicking Mule label to gain a wider hearing for budding folk and blues talent. He has toured and recorded with John Renbourn, formerly of Pentangle.

THE GROUNDHOGS

Formed 1963, England
1976 lineup: T. S. "Tony" McPhee (b. March 22, 1944, Lincolnshire, Eng.), gtr., voc.; David Wellbelove, gtr.; Martin Kentin, bass; Mark Cook, drums.
1968—*Scratching the Surface* (Liberty) 1969—*Blues Obituary* (Imperial) 1970—*Thank Christ for the Bomb* (Liberty) 1971—*Split* (United Artists) 1972—*Who Will Save the World?* 1973—*Hogwash; The Groundhogs with John Lee Hooker and John Mayall* (Cleveland) 1974—*Solid* (WWA, U.K.) *Best of Groundhogs 1969–1972* (United Artists) 1976—*Black Diamond; Crosscut Saw.*

Tony McPhee's Groundhogs shifted slowly from blues to heavy metal and established a sizable cult following in Britain by the early Seventies. McPhee, who had worked for the post office, established the first Groundhogs in 1963, and they backed up visiting U.S. blues musicians including Little Walter and John Lee Hooker. They recorded a single ("Shake It") and an album with Hooker for Britain's Xtra label. The initial group disbanded in 1965, but McPhee re-formed the group in 1968, and they put out blues albums through the late Sixties.

In 1970, they moved into heavy metal with *Thank Christ for the Bomb*, their first substantial British success, and played that year's Isle of Wight Festival. *Split* hit the British Top Ten in 1971, as did 1972's *Who Will Save the World?* The Groundhogs continued to tour the U.K. extensively. Their only U.S. tour ended prematurely in 1972, when McPhee was injured while horseback riding in the Pocono Mountains.

The Groundhogs recorded *Hogwash* and *Solid* in 1973 and 1974, but McPhee had begun solo activities, including a 1973 album, *The Two Sides of T. S. McPhee*, and collaborations with blues-folksinger Jo Ann Kelly. McPhee also produced an album for blues singer Big Joe Williams, and in early 1976 he revived the Groundhogs once more.

THE GUESS WHO

Formed 1963, Winnipeg, Canada
Chad Allan (b. ca. 1945), voc.; Bob Ashley, bass; Randy Bachman (b. Sep. 27, 1943), gtr., voc.; Garry Peterson (b. May 26, 1945), drums.
1965—(− Allan; − Ashley; + Burton Cummings [b. Dec. 31, 1947, Winnipeg], kybds., voc.; + Bruce Decker, bass) 1966—(− Decker; + Jim Kale [b. Aug. 11, 1943], bass) 1968—*Shakin' All Over* (Scepter) *Guess Who* (MGM) 1969—*Wheatfield Soul* (RCA) *Canned Wheat Packed by the Guess Who* 1970—*American Woman* (− Bachman; + Greg Leskiw [b.

Aug. 5, 1947], gtr.; + Kurt Winter [b. Apr. 2, 1946], gtr.) *Share the Land* **1971**—*So Long, Bannatyne* **1972**—*Best of; Rockin'* (− Leskiw; + Don McDougall [b. Nov. 5, 1947], gtr.) *Live at the Paramount* (− Kale; + Bill Wallace [b. May 18, 1949], bass, voc.) **1973**—*#10; Best of, volume 2* **1974**—*Artificial Paradise; Road Food* (− Winter; − McDougall; + Domenic Troiano [b. ca. 1945, Mondugno, Italy], gtr., voc.) *Flavours* **1975**—*Power in the Music; Born in Canada* **1976**—(disbanded) **1977**—*The Greatest of the Guess Who* (RCA) (re-formed: Kale; McDougall; Peterson; Winter) **1978**—(− Winter; − Peterson; + Vance Masters, drums; + David Inglish, gtr.; + Ralph Watts, gtr., kybds.) **1979**—*All This for a Song* (Hilltak).

The Guess Who were Canada's premier singles band through the early Seventies. The group, all born in Winnipeg, dates back to the early Sixties, when buddies Chad Allan and Randy Bachman formed Allan and the Silvertones, later the Reflections and then (to avoid confusion with a Detroit group) Chad Allan and the Expressions. Shortly before Allan left to continue his studies, the group changed its name to the Guess Who and had a surprise hit with a cover of Johnny Kidd and the Pirates' "Shakin' All Over" (#22, 1965). The band toured the United States through 1965 as part of Dick Clark's Caravan of Stars Road Revue. Allan was replaced by Burton Cummings.

In 1967, they landed a regular spot on the CBC-TV show "Where It's At," hosted by ex-leader Allan. They had minor success in Canada, but were unable to crack the U.S. market until producer Jack Richardson mortgaged his house to pay for the group to record in New York in September 1968. Richardson produced the first gold Guess Who single in the U.S., "These Eyes" (#6, 1969). Their second RCA LP, *Canned Wheat*, boasted two hits— "Laughing" (#10, 1969) and "Undun" (#22, 1969).

In 1970, their record sales totaled $5 million, largely on the strength of their third album, *American Woman*, whose fuzz guitar-propelled title track and "No Time" (#5, 1970) were U.S. hits. But Cummings and Bachman (who, having recently converted to the Mormon faith, found the band's hedonistic lifestyle offensive) feuded bitterly. By 1970, Bachman had departed (first for a brief collaboration with Allan as Brave Belt, and then without Allan as Bachman-Turner Overdrive). The group replaced Bachman with two guitarists and continued their singles success with "Share the Land" (#10, 1970) and "Hand Me Down World" (#17, 1970). But with Bachman's departure came a series of personnel changes, and the group's hits waned. They continued to tour, and even appeared at the White House in 1970 with Prince Charles and Princess Anne in attendance; Pat Nixon requested that they delete "American Woman" from their set.

The group carried on with *So Long, Bannatyne*, which produced the minor hits "Rain Dance" (#19, 1971) and "Albert Flasher" (#29, 1971); but their sales lagged. In 1974, they had a hit with a novelty tribute to disc jockey Wolfman Jack, "Clap for the Wolfman" (#6). The group's work was enhanced in 1974 with the addition of ex-James Gang guitarist Domenic Troiano for *Flavours*. But despite new blood, the group disbanded in 1976.

Cummings had a hit on his first solo album with "Stand Tall" (#10, 1976) and has continued to record solo into the early Eighties with such albums as *Sweet Sweet* on Alfa Records in early 1981.

In 1977, a string of Guess Who re-formations began when CBC-TV enticed some of the band's alumni (except Cummings and Bachman) to regroup for a television special. With many personnel changes over the next few years (including some stints during which the group had not one original or early-era member), the band became a club-circuit fixture in western North America and, with notable impetus from longtime associate Jim Kale, released several marginal albums on small labels like Hilltak and El Mocambo.

GUITAR SLIM

Born Eddie Jones, December 10, 1926, Greenwood, Mississippi; died February 7, 1959, New York City
1954—*Things That I Used to Do* (Specialty).

Blues guitarist/singer Eddie "Guitar Slim" Jones's "Things That I Used to Do" was one of the top R&B records of 1954, selling a million copies. The song (now a blues standard) fused gospel and the blues, and featured Jones's electric guitar as well as the piano of a then largely unknown Ray Charles.

Jones began singing in church choirs as a child. While still in his teens, he formed a trio with pianist Huey "Piano" Smith and later began working solo. He recorded for Imperial and JB between 1951 and 1952. He may have served in the U.S. Army in Korea in the early Fifties. An electric guitar pioneer, Jones was also a flashy dresser and a famed showman, known for playing hot in-concert solos while wandering as far as his 200-foot extension cord would allow. He died of pneumonia at the age of 32 and is buried in Thibodaux, Louisiana. His son has performed under the name Guitar Slim, Jr.

The first known "Guitar Slim," incidentally, was a blues musician from Texas, Norman Green (born July 25, 1907; died September 28, 1975), who had minor hits including "Fifth Street Alley Blues" and "Old Folks Boogie."

ARLO GUTHRIE

Born July 10, 1947, Coney Island, New York
1967—*Alice's Restaurant* (Reprise) **1968**—*Arlo* **1969**—*Running Down the Road* **1970**—*Washington County; Alice's Restaurant* (soundtrack) (United Artists) **1972**—*Hobo's Lullaby* (Reprise) **1973**—*Last of the Brooklyn Cowboys* **1974**—*Arlo Guthrie* **1975**—*Pete Seeger/Arlo Guthrie Together in Concert* **1976**—*Amigo* **1977**—*The Best of* (Warner Bros.)

1978—*One Night*   **1979**—*Outlasting the Blues*
1981—*Power of Love.*

Folksinger Arlo Guthrie became popular in the late Sixties when his tall-tale "Alice's Restaurant" became an underground favorite and later a movie in which he appeared. His biggest pop hit was Steve Goodman's "City of New Orleans," and he is still a regular attraction on the folk circuit.

One of several children born to folksinger Woody and Marjorie Guthrie, Arlo grew up among musicians. At age three, he danced and played the harmonica for Leadbelly. Pete Seeger was also a frequent guest. His mother taught him guitar at age six. He attended private schools in Brooklyn and then in Stockbridge, Massachusetts, the setting of "Alice's Restaurant." He attended college in Billings, Montana, but soon returned to New York to pursue a music career.

By late 1965, Guthrie was a regular on the East Coast coffeehouse circuit, and in 1967 he toured Japan with Judy Collins. His debut LP was released shortly after his appearance at the Newport Folk Festival, which included the 15-minute-plus "Alice's Restaurant." As the Sixties closed, he continued to build a following, and he appeared at Woodstock in August 1969.

Guthrie's career picked up noticeably in the early Seventies with *Washington County* and *Hobo's Lullaby,* which included the #18 hit, "The City of New Orleans" (1972). Subsequent LPs have been well received, although his record sales have dropped off; he has been less interested in elaborate pop productions.

In 1977, Guthrie converted to Catholicism. During the late Seventies, he regularly toured the U.S. and Europe backed by Shenandoah, with whom he also recorded. Throughout the Seventies, he often performed and recorded with Pete Seeger (*Together in Concert*), and he was an activist for numerous causes, including the antinuclear and ecological movements.

WOODY GUTHRIE

Born Woodrow Wilson Guthrie, July 14, 1912, Okemah, Oklahoma; died October 3, 1967, Queens, New York
1967—*This Land Is Your Land* (Folkways)   **1977**—*A Legendary Performer* (RCA).

In the Thirties and Forties, Woody Guthrie reinvented the American folk ballad as a vehicle for social comment and protest, laying the groundwork for Bob Dylan and numerous other rock singer/songwriters with such neotraditional songs as "This Land Is Your Land," "Pastures of Plenty," "So Long, It's Been Good to Know You" and nearly a thousand others.

Guthrie's father was a singer, banjo player and sometime professional boxer. Woody left home at 16 and roamed through Texas and Louisiana, working as a news-

Woody Guthrie

boy, sign painter, spittoon washer, farm laborer and other menial jobs; he also sang in the streets. While visiting his uncle Jeff Guthrie in Pampa, Texas, in 1929, he learned to play guitar. During the Depression, Guthrie rode the rails as a hobo until around 1937, when he settled in Los Angeles and hosted a radio show on KFVD for a dollar a day.

Guthrie's politics moved leftward, and at the start of World War II he relocated to New York, where he met the Weavers and Pete Seeger. He briefly embraced communism, although he was denied membership in the U.S. Communist Party because he refused to renounce his religion, but he did write a column for a communist newspaper, *The People's Daily World.*

Although these leanings did not endear Guthrie to the U.S. government, his anti-Hitler songs did; his guitar had a sign on it saying, "This Machine Kills Fascists." From 1943 to 1945, Guthrie was with the U.S. merchant marine in the U.K., Italy and Africa.

Although Guthrie's songs traveled widely, he didn't record until 1940, when Alan Lomax taped several hours of talking and singing for the Library of Congress. Those sessions were later released on commercial labels including RCA (*Woody Guthrie—A Legendary Performer* and *Dust Bowl Ballads*) and Elektra. He also recorded with Leadbelly and Sonny Terry, but his recordings had little impact by themselves.

During his years of riding the rails, Guthrie developed a drinking problem. In 1952, he was diagnosed as alcoholic and confined to a mental institution before his problem was correctly diagnosed as Huntington's chorea, a genetically transmitted degenerative disorder of the nervous system from which Guthrie's mother had died. The disease kept him largely inactive and hospitalized during the last decade of his life.

Guthrie's fame has steadily increased over the years. Bob Dylan, who had traveled to New York to visit Guthrie in the hospital, sang his idol's praises early on, and Guthrie's son, Arlo, has also carried on the family name as a singer/songwriter.

Pete Seeger, whose relationship with Woody dates back to the Thirties, organized a series of memorial concerts for the singer in the late Sixties. Two of those concerts—at Carnegie Hall in 1968 and the Hollywood Bowl in 1970—were recorded and released as albums featuring Dylan, Tom Paxton, Joan Baez, Judy Collins, Richie Havens and Country Joe McDonald. In 1976, Guthrie's autobiography, *Bound for Glory* (published in 1943), was made into a motion picture with David Carradine playing Guthrie. That same year, Guthrie's previously unpublished prose work, *Seeds of Man,* was published.

H

SAMMY HAGAR

Born circa 1949, Monterey, California
1976—*Nine on a Ten Scale* (Capitol)   1977—*Sammy Hagar*   1978—*Musical Chairs;   All Night Long*   1979—*Street Machine;   Danger Zone*   1980—*Loud and Clear*   1982—*Standing Hampton* (Geffen)   *Three Lock Box.*

Sammy Hagar entered the rock market as lead vocalist with Montrose, and he went solo in 1975. Years of touring as an arena show opening act made him a middle-level star, and in certain areas—St. Louis, Washington, Detroit—he is a headliner.

As a teenager, Hagar considered following his father into the boxing ring, but by age 19, he was supporting himself as a musician in Southern California bar bands. After seven years of beer-joint one-nighters, he was invited to join Montrose in 1973, and went solo two years later. His first solo disc picked up some AOR airplay with a cover of Van Morrison's "Flamingos Fly," but it wasn't until 1977, when he formed his own band, that his career picked up momentum.

Hagar gathered three Montrose alumni—bassist Bill Church, keyboardist Alan Fitzgerald and drummer Dennis Carmasi (who replaced original drummer Scott Matthews and was later replaced by Chuck Ruff)—and guitarist David Lewark (later replaced by Gary Pihl). The Sammy Hagar Band began touring widely in the late Seventies, opening for Boston, Electric Light Orchestra, Kansas, Foghat, Kiss and other high-volume bands. His late-Seventies releases all sold in the 100,000 to 200,000 range. Hagar had a hit with "Your Love Is Driving Me Crazy" from *Three Lock Box.*

MERLE HAGGARD

Born April 6, 1937, Bakersfield, California
1969—*Okie from Muskogee* (Capitol)   1970—*The Fightin' Side of Me*   1972—*The Best of Merle Haggard*   1976—*Songs I'll Always Sing*   1977—*A Working Man Can't Get Anywhere Today*   1981—*Songs for the Mama Who Tried* (MCA)   1982—*Big City* (Epic)   1983—*Poncho and Lefty* (with Willie Nelson);   *Going Where the Lonely Go.*

In his songs, Merle Haggard is country music's symbol of the American workingman—dignified, downtrodden and not unlikely to frequent the neighborhood bar. He is also a staunch upholder of musical traditions, particularly Western swing, and he leads one of the country's most improvisatory bands.

Haggard was born to a family of transplanted Oklahomans who were living in a converted boxcar in California. When he was nine, his father died of a brain tumor. He quit school in the eighth grade and hopped a freight train at age 14. Through the end of his teens, he mostly roamed the Southwest. Haggard had been in reformatories by the age of 14 for petty crime (car theft, bad checks). Later, he was arrested for holding up a cafe and spent nearly three years in San Quentin. He was paroled in 1960. (In 1972, then-California Governor Ronald Reagan expunged Haggard's criminal record, granting him a full pardon.)

After prison, Haggard went back to Bakersfield and worked for his brother digging ditches. He started playing lead guitar in a local country band, and by 1962, when he went to Las Vegas to back singer Wynn Stewart, Haggard had decided to make music his career.

In 1963, he formed an enduring partnership with Lewis Talley and Fuzzy Owens, the owners of Tally Records, an independent label in the Bakersfield area for whom Haggard made his early recordings. In 1963, Haggard's first release sold only 200 copies, but his second, "Sing Me a Sad Song," made #19 on the *Billboard* country charts. He recorded with Tally through 1965, and Owens remains one of Haggard's close associates. But after Haggard's third single "(All My Friends Are Gonna Be) Strangers" hit the country Top Ten he was signed by Capitol.

Haggard formed his own backing group, the Strangers, with whom he has toured an average of about 200 nights a year ever since (the Strangers released their first album of instrumentals in 1970). Around this time, Haggard married Buck Owens' ex-wife, Bonnie Owens. He had previously recorded with her for Tally, but their duet career began in earnest with their first joint Capitol LP, *Just between the Two of Us* in 1965. They shared hit records, tours and awards until their divorce.

In 1966, "Swinging Doors" and "The Bottle Let Me Down" hit the Top Five on the country charts, and later in the year "The Fugitive" became his first country #1 as he was voted the Academy of Country Music's Top Male Vocalist of the Year. He has amassed more than fifty country chart singles since—including 27 #1 hits—and has had at least one Top Five country hit every year since 1966 through early 1982's success, "Big City." Among his biggest hits are "Mama Tried," "Sing Me Back Home," "Hungry Eyes," "It's Not Love (But It's Not Bad)," "Everybody's Had the Blues," "If We Make It through December" and "It's All in the Movies."

He has written hundreds of songs, many of which have become country standards (his "Today I Started Loving

234

You Again" has been recorded by over 400 singers). Haggard may be best known to rock fans for his late-Sixties songs extolling the virtues of patriotism, like "The Fightin' Side of Me" and "Okie from Muskogee."

But Haggard was more a traditionalist than a hard-line conservative. His many recordings—nearly fifty albums since 1963—include a tribute to Western swing pioneer Bob Wills (*A Tribute to the Best Damn Fiddle Player in the World*); a gospel tribute, *A Land of Many Churches,* which included backing from the Carter Family; and a 1974 tribute to Dixieland jazz recorded in New Orleans. He played at the White House in 1973 for President Nixon and his family.

In the late Seventies, Haggard's 11-year marriage to Bonnie Owens fell apart, although she continued to tour and record with him for a couple of years after the separation. In 1978, he married one of his backup singers, Leona Williams. In May 1980, he became the first country artist ever featured on the cover of *Downbeat.* Haggard published an autobiography (cowritten by Peggy Russell) in 1981, *Sing Me Back Home.*

An occasional actor as well as singer, he has appeared on TV in "The Waltons" and "Centennial." He made his movie debut in 1968's *Killers Three* and was featured the next year in *From Nashville with Music.* In 1980, he made a cameo appearance in *Bronco Billy,* singing a duet with Clint Eastwood. In 1982, he recorded a duet album with Willie Nelson, *Poncho and Lefty.*

BILL HALEY
Born July 6, 1925, Highland Park, Michigan; died February 9, 1981, Harlingen, Texas
1956—*Rock Around the Clock* (Decca)   **1968**—*Greatest Hits* (MCA)   **1974**—*Golden Hits.*

Bill Haley emerged from country music with "Rock Around the Clock," a rockabilly song that made him a teen idol. He cut his first record, "Candy Kisses," when he was 18, then hit the road for four years as a singer and guitarist with various country & western bands. In 1949, he became a disc jockey at WPWA in Chester, Pennsylvania. Calling himself the Ramblin' Yodeler, he put together a band, the Four Aces of Western Swing, to perform regularly on his radio show. With another group—first called the Down Homers, then the Saddlemen—he recorded country songs that quickly disappeared into obscurity. In 1950, they were signed to a Philadelphia label, Essex, and recorded a handful of country sides before covering Jackie Brenston's 1951 R&B hit, "Rocket 88." That record sold only 10,000 copies, but the song convinced Haley that high-energy music which kids could sing along to, clap to and dance to—something like black R&B—would prove popular. In 1952, he dropped his cowboy image altogether, changed the group's name to Bill Haley and His Comets, and covered another R&B hit,

"Rock the Joint," which sold 75,000 copies. A Haley original, "Crazy Man Crazy," was covered by one Ralph Marterie and given extensive airplay, but Haley's own more rambunctious version was the one sought in record shops, and in 1953 it became the first rock & roll record to make the *Billboard* pop charts.

In 1954, Haley left Essex and signed with Decca under producer Milt Gabler. His first record for his new label was a song written by Jimmy DeKnight and his manager, Dave Myers, and originally recorded in 1952 by Sunny Dae—"Rock Around the Clock." It sold only moderately well when it was first released in the spring of 1954, but its followup, a cover of Joe Turner's "Shake, Rattle and Roll," hit the Top Ten both in the U.K. and in the U.S., eventually selling a million copies. When "Rock Around the Clock" was re-released in 1955 it rose to #1. The song was included in the soundtrack of *Blackboard Jungle,* a 1955 movie about juvenile delinquents, and it led viewers to identify the balding Haley as a young rebel. Throughout 1955 and 1956, he was the most popular rock & roll performer in the world, and within those two years he had 12 U.S. Top Forty records, including "See You Later Alligator," "Burn That Candle," "Dim, Dim the Lights," "Razzle-Dazzle" and "R-O-C-K."

In Britain, where authentic rock & rollers were scarcer than in America, he was even more popular: his visit there in February 1957 was met with wild enthusiasm. But by that time his star was descending in America. High exposure (he starred in two Hollywood movies, *Rock Around the Clock* and *Don't Knock the Rock*) revealed him to be a pudgy, rather stiff, hardly rebellious family man. His last Top Forty hit was "Skinny Minnie" in May 1958. While he never attempted to modernize his sound or his image, he continued to work as a nostalgia act, especially in Britain and Germany, where he was always treated as a star ("Rock Around the Clock" reentered the U.K. pop charts seven times, most recently in 1974). In 1969 and through the early seventies, Bill Haley and His Comets traveled with the Rock 'n' Roll Revival Shows promoted by Richard Nader and documented in a movie, *Let the Good Times Roll.* By the time of Haley's death, he had sold an estimated 60 million records.

HALL AND OATES
Formed 1969, Philadelphia
Daryl Hall (b. Oct. 11, 1949, Pottstown, Penn.); John Oates (b. Apr. 7, 1949, New York City).
1972—*Whole Oates* (Atlantic)   **1973**—*Abandoned Luncheonette*   **1974**—*War Babies*   **1975**—*Daryl Hall/ John Oates* (RCA)   **1976**—*Bigger Than Both of Us* **1977**—*No Goodbyes* (Atlantic)   *Beauty on a Back Street* (RCA)   **1978**—*Along the Red Ledge;   Live Time*   **1979**—*X-Static*   **1980**—*Voices*   **1981**—*Private Eyes*   **1982**—*H₂O.*
Daryl Hall solo: 1980—*Sacred Songs* (RCA).

Daryl Hall and John Oates

Daryl Hall and John Oates's blend of rock and R&B has kept them on the singles charts since 1976. Both were raised in Philadelphia suburbs. Oates had moved there at age four from New York City, and he began playing guitar at age eight. Hall studied voice and piano. As teens, the two frequented Philadelphia ghettos, where they joined doo-wop groups. In 1967, Hall recorded a single with Kenny Gamble and the Romeos (which included future producers Gamble, Leon Huff and Thom Bell). He met Oates later that year when his group, the Temptones, and Oates's group, the Masters, competed in a battle of the bands at Philadelphia's Adelphi Ballroom; they shared a freight elevator while escaping a gang fight. At Temple University Oates earned a degree in journalism and Hall studied music but dropped out in his senior term.

Hall formed Gulliver, a group that recorded one LP on Elektra in 1969, and Oates joined before it disbanded. Oates then traveled to Europe, and Hall became a studio musician, singing backup for the Delfonics, the Stylistics and the Intruders. Upon Oates's return, the two decided to team up. In 1972, they signed with Atlantic Records and released their Arif Mardin–produced debut, *Whole Oates,* a folky album that attracted little attention. Their next LP, the R&B-oriented *Abandoned Luncheonette* (also produced by Mardin), yielded "She's Gone," a flop for Hall and Oates but a #1 R&B hit for Tavares six months later. In 1974, the two recorded *War Babies,* a concept LP, with producer Todd Rundgren. A drastic departure from their earlier efforts, the LP sold 100,000 copies in the New York area. Citing a lack of hit singles and stylistic inconsistency, Atlantic dropped them, but in 1976 the rereleased version of "She's Gone" made #7.

Their RCA debut *(Daryl Hall/John Oates)* contained

"Sara Smile," a #4 hit cowritten by Hall for his frequent collaborator/girlfriend Sara Allen (whose sister Janna Allen cowrote "Kiss on My List"). With the release of 1976's *Bigger Than Both of Us,* the two previous albums went gold. *Bigger* eventually became their first platinum LP and contained their first #1 single, "Rich Girl."

Hall, the more prolific writer of the two, began working with Robert Fripp on a solo LP, *Sacred Songs* (which RCA refused to release until 1980). Hall also sang on Fripp's *Exposure.* Yet apart from the Top Twenty "It's a Laugh" on *Along the Red Ledge, Live Time, Beauty on a Back Street* and *X-Static* all failed to deliver hits. Hall and Oates retrenched and decided to produce their next LP themselves. The result, *Voices,* returned the duo to the singles charts. Boasting four hit singles—"How Does It Feel to Be Back" (#30), "Kiss on My List" (#1), a cover of the Righteous Brothers' "You've Lost That Loving Feeling" (#12) and "You Make My Dreams" (#5)— *Voices* went platinum. In 1981, *Private Eyes* was similarly successful; the title cut and "I Can't Go for That (No Can Do)" were both #1. "Did It in a Minute" went Top Ten, and *H₂0* yielded a hit with "Maneater." According to *Billboard* magazine, Hall and Oates are the most successful recording duo in the history of the charts.

JOHNNY HALLIDAY
Born Jean-Phillippe Smet, June 15, 1943, Paris
1962—*Johnny Halliday Sings America's Rockin' Hits* (Philips).

A major rock star in Europe in the early and mid-Sixties, Johnny Halliday made his career covering the American and British hits of the day for Continental rock fans. Billed as the French Elvis but closer to Cliff Richard, Halliday reached his zenith in the pre-Beatlemania era, when his stage shows caused riots in France. His biggest hit was a multilingual reading of "Let's Twist Again" ("Viens Danser le Twist") which sold a million copies in 1961. The following year saw the release of his most successful album, *Johnny Halliday Sings America's Rockin' Hits,* which helped institutionalize cover versions as a marketing strategy overseas.

As the decade progressed, Halliday traveled to London and Memphis to record, searching for authentic backing tracks for his revamps of hits by others. With the advent of the Beatles, Halliday's career lost most of its momentum, but he remained a star in his homeland for several more years. By the late Sixties, young rock talent was often shipped over from England to play on Halliday's sessions, among them Jimmy Page, Humble Pie's Steve Marriott, Peter Frampton and Mick Jones, later of Foreigner (who wrote some songs for Halliday). Halliday's wife, Sylvie Vartan, was also a popular singer in France in the Sixties. In 1964, she opened concerts for the Beatles at the Olympic Theatre in Paris.

ROY HAMILTON

Born April 16, 1929, Leesburg, Georgia; died July 20, 1969

Roy Hamilton's late-Fifties work was characterized by a blend of R&B and gospel strains that influenced Jerry Butler and the Righteous Brothers. Hamilton grew up in Jersey City, where he sang with the Searchlight Gospel Singers in 1948. Impressed by his powerful baritone, local disc jockey Bill Cook became his manager and in the early Fifties got him a contract with Epic.

Hamilton's career took off in 1954 with "You'll Never Walk Alone," which topped the R&B charts but didn't dent the pop Hot 100. He became a major attraction in black nightclubs, and by 1955 he was enjoying limited crossover success with "Everybody's Got a Home" (#42) and "Without a Song" (#77). Additionally, Hamilton released "Unchained Melody." It was the best-selling R&B record of 1955, but competing cover versions by mainstream pop artists Les Baxter and Al Hibbler kept Hamilton's version from the pop charts. Hamilton had pop hits with "Don't Let Go" (#13, 1958), "Pledging My Love" (#45, 1958), "I Need Your Lovin' " (#62, 1959), "Time Marches On" (#84, 1959) and "You Can Have Her" (#12, 1961). Hamilton's career nosedived after his success early in the Sixties, despite recordings for MGM, RCA and AGP. He died from a heart attack in 1969.

JOHN HAMMOND, SR.

Born December 10, 1910, New York City

Producer and talent scout Hammond has discovered some of the best-known jazz and rock musicians over the past four decades. Born into an upper-middle-class family, he studied classical music at both Yale and Juilliard. Before the Thirties were over, he had written for music publications like *Melody Maker* and *The Gramophone* in Britain and *Downbeat* in the U.S. He also published articles on racial topics for nonmusic magazines and served as vice-president of the National Association for the Advancement of Colored People (NAACP).

Hammond maintained the courage of his convictions in his budding career as a music executive. He began a longtime association with Columbia Records in the Thirties (although he has worked concurrently for other labels since), using his influence to champion mainstream jazz. He organized racially integrated recording sessions and tours long before such were commonplace or even acceptable. His landmark concerts at Carnegie Hall in 1938 and 1939, "From Spirituals to Swing," were among the first to present black talent in a formal concert setting.

But Hammond's main contribution to popular music has been the talent he has discovered. While working as a jazz producer for Columbia in the Thirties, he signed Billie Holiday, Count Basie, Teddy Wilson, Lester Young, Char-lie Christian and Meade Lux Lewis. Hammond also took an active interest in budding blues talent. He invited Robert Johnson to perform at one of his Carnegie Hall concerts, but Johnson was killed just weeks before the event. Many years later, Hammond was a key figure in packaging the retrospective Columbia release *Robert Johnson, King of the Delta Blues Singers*. Around the same time in the early Sixties Hammond also produced a latter-day effort by Delta bluesman Son House. He signed Pete Seeger, a courageous act, since Seeger was at the time under indictment for contempt of Congress. A few months later, Hammond signed both Aretha Franklin and the Four Tops to Columbia.

Perhaps Hammond's most famous protégé was Bob Dylan, whom he signed in 1961 and whose debut album he produced the next year. (For the first several months of Dylan's association with Columbia, he was referred to in-house as "Hammond's folly.") It was Hammond who signed Bruce Springsteen in 1973.

JOHN PAUL HAMMOND

Born November 13, 1943, New York City
1963—*John Hammond* (Vanguard)   **1964**—*Big City Blues*   **1965**—*So Many Roads;   Country Blues*
1968—*Mirrors;   I Can Tell* (Atlantic)   *Sooner or Later*
1970—*Southern Fried*   **1971**—*Source Point* (Columbia)   **1972**—*I'm Satisfied*   **1973**—*When I Need;   Triumvirate* (with Michael Bloomfield and Dr. John)
Spirituals to Swing (Vanguard)   **1975**—*Can't Beat the Kid* (Capricorn)   *My Spanish Album* (Coytronics)
1976—*John Hammond: Solo* (Vanguard)   **1978**—*Factwork;   Hot Tracks*   **1980**—*Mileage* (Sonet)
1982—*Frogs for Snakes* (Rounder).

John Paul Hammond is a white blues singer and the son of talent scout/producer John Hammond. He studied art and sculpture in his youth and he became interested in country and Delta blues. While attending Antioch College in Yellow Springs, Ohio, Hammond learned guitar and harmonica and started singing.

His professional career began in New York in 1963, when he recorded an acoustic blues album for Vanguard. He continued to record regularly for Vanguard in the early Sixties. In late 1963, he met some musicians who were backing rockabilly singer Ronnie Hawkins in a Toronto bar. Hammond enticed the group, the Hawks (who would later become the Band), to come with him to New York. They backed Hammond until they were lured away by Bob Dylan (a discovery of Hammond's father). In the mid-Sixties, his backing band included, briefly, Jimi Hendrix.

Hammond played clubs regularly in the late Sixties and many small concert venues (the Fillmores, Matrix Ballroom) as well. In 1970, he performed on the soundtrack of the Dustin Hoffman film *Little Big Man*. The following year he recorded an album with bluesman Larry Johnson for the Biograph label. In 1973, he recorded for Columbia as part of a short-lived supergroup called Triumvirate, which also included Dr. John and Mike Bloomfield. By the late Seventies, he was still playing clubs.

HERBIE HANCOCK
Born April 12, 1940, Chicago
1963—*Takin' Off* (Blue Note; reissued 1979 by Columbia) 1964—*Empyrean Isles* (Blue Note) *Herbie Hancock* 1965—*Inventions and Dimensions* 1966—*My Point of View* 1968—*Maiden Voyage; Blow Up* (soundtrack) (MGM) 1969—*Speak Like a Child* (Blue Note) 1971—*Mwandishi* (Warner Bros.) 1972—*Crossing; Sextant* (Columbia) 1973—*Headhunters* 1974—*Thrust; Fat Albert Rotunda* (Warner Bros.) 1974—*Succotash* (Blue Note) *The Prisoner; Best of* 1975—*Death Wish* (soundtrack) (Columbia) *Manchild; Live in Japan* (Columbia, Sony import) *Hancock* (Blue Note) 1976—*Secrets* (Columbia) *Kawaida* (DJM/import) 1977—*Flood* (Columbia) *Herbie Hancock Trio; Live under the Sky* (Columbia, Sony import) *V.S.O.P.* (Columbia) 1978—*Sunlight; Quintet* (Columbia, U.K.) *Tempest in the Colosseum* (Columbia, Sony import) 1979—*An Evening with* (Columbia, U.K.) *Corea/Hancock* (Polydor) *Feets Don't Fail Me Now* (Columbia) 1980—*Monster* 1981—*Mr. Hands* 1982—*Magic Windows; Light Me Up* 1983—*The Quartet.*

Keyboardist Herbie Hancock first came to prominence as the pianist in Miles Davis' landmark mid-Sixties quintet, a unit that went from refined postbop chamber jazz to pioneering electric fusion. The latter spurred Hancock on to a funk-fusion direction of his own. Once he established himself commercially, however, Hancock divided his time between funk and his harmonically adventurous, impressionistic acoustic jazz.

Before joining Davis' band, Hancock had played jazz piano with saxophonist Hank Mobley and trumpeter Lee Morgan while working toward a BA in engineering at Grinnell College. In 1963, he worked with jazz trumpeter Donald Byrd, at whose instigation Hancock recorded his first solo LP. His "Watermelon Man" was a pop-jazz crossover hit for Mongo Santamaria. From 1963–68, Hancock worked with Miles Davis; he also played on many sessions for Blue Note Records. After scoring Michelangelo Antonioni's film *Blow-Up*, he left Davis and began pursuing fusion with *Mwandishi.*

His breakthrough came with *Headhunters,* for which Hancock formed the band of the same name, later explaining, "Rather than work with jazz musicians who could play funk, I worked with funk musicians who could play jazz." That album yielded the huge crossover hit "Chameleon." *Thrust, Manchild* and the *Death Wish* film soundtrack also sold well, as did *Fat Albert Rotunda,* his soundtrack to a Bill Cosby TV-cartoon special. In 1976,

Hancock briefly diverged from his electric-funk course to form V.S.O.P. (Very Special Onetime Performance), an acoustic jazz group with Tony Williams, Weather Report's Wayne Shorter, bassist Ron Carter and trumpeter Freddie Hubbard, playing in the early Blue Note–Miles Davis mode. They conducted a successful tour and recorded an album, and have since reconvened frequently.

Shortly thereafter, Hancock converted to Nicheran Shoshu Buddhism and two years later undertook an acoustic-piano duo tour with Chick Corea. In 1979, *Feets* was another commercial success, as was *Monster* in 1980. In 1981, V.S.O.P. toured and recorded as a quartet, minus Shorter and with trumpeter Wynton Marsalis replacing Hubbard.

TIM HARDIN
Born December 23, 1941, Eugene, Oregon; died December 29, 1980, Los Angeles
1966—*Tim Hardin I* (MGM) 1967—*Tim Hardin II; This Is Tim Hardin* (Atco) 1968—*Tim Hardin III Live in Concert* (Verve) 1969—*Tim Hardin IV* 1970—*Suite for Susan Moore and Damian* (Columbia) *The Best of Tim Hardin* (Verve) 1971—*Bird on a Wire* (Columbia) 1973—*Painted Head; Archetypes* (MGM) *Nine* (Antilles).

Singer/songwriter Tim Hardin came to prominence during the folk-blues revival in the early Sixties. He enjoyed critical acclaim for his smoky voice but had little commercial success on his own; others recorded his songs "If I Were a Carpenter" and "Reason to Believe."

Hardin traced his lineage back to the 19th-century Western outlaw John Wesley Hardin. He dropped out of high school in 1959 and joined the Marines for two years, then enrolled in the American Academy of Dramatic Art in New York, but dropped out after a week. He moved to Cambridge, Massachusetts, and began performing in the folk clubs around Harvard.

Hardin's first tapes were recorded in 1962, but they were not released until 1967, as his third album. He returned to New York in 1963 and became an influential figure in Greenwich Village folk circles, blending strains of folk, blues and jazz and playing with a group when most folkies were strictly soloists. He began to receive national attention in 1966, when he performed at the Newport Folk Festival and *Tim Hardin* picked up critical accolades. About this time, Bob Dylan named him the country's greatest living songwriter.

His songs included "If I Were a Carpenter" (covered by Johnny Cash and June Carter, Bobby Darin, the Four Tops and Bob Seger among others), "Reason to Believe" (covered by Peter, Paul and Mary and Rod Stewart) and "Misty Roses." In the mid-Sixties, he was a regular attraction on the college campus circuits both in the U.S. and in Europe. By the late Sixties, he had settled into the rural artists' community in Woodstock, New York, and curtailed his performances. In 1969, he enjoyed his only Top Fifty single with Bobby Darin's "Simple Song of Freedom." Hardin's *Bird on a Wire* LP used other writers' material; its studio band included future members of East-West folk-fusion band Oregon and jazz-rockers Weather Report.

In 1974, Hardin moved from the U.S. to southern England with his family and played regularly in English clubs. After a year in England, he moved back to Los Angeles. His death in his Los Angeles apartment at age 39 was attributed to an overdose of heroin.

ROY HARPER
Born June 12, 1941, Manchester, England
1967—*Come Out Fighting, Genghis Smith* (Columbia) 1970—*Flat Baroque and Berserk* (Harvest)
1971—*Stormcock* 1973—*Life Mask* 1974—*Valentine;   Flashes from the Archives of Oblivion*
1977—*Commercial Break;   The Early Years* (Embassy)
1978—*Roy Harper 1970–75* (Chrysalis)
1980—*Unknown Soldier* (Harvest).

Folksinger/songwriter/guitarist Roy Harper is best known to rock fans as the subject of Led Zeppelin's "Hats Off to Harper," from their third LP. But in folk circles, and particularly in England, Harper is well known for his eccentric songs.

At age 15 he quit school and after a while joined the Royal Air Force. In an attempt to obtain a discharge, Harper pretended to be mentally ill; following his 1959 discharge he was committed to a mental institution. After his release 15 weeks later, he wrote poems and songs in the streets of Blackpool. In 1964, he moved to London, and a year later began performing in clubs, part of a circle that included Jimmy Page, John Paul Jones and Ronnie Lane. He also performed frequently in London's Hyde Park.

Beginning in 1971 with *Stormcock*, Jimmy Page began appearing on Harper's LPs. Among other musicians who have backed Harper are Henry McCullough, Bill Bruford and Chris Spedding. In 1972, Harper made his film debut in the British *Made*. Harper sang lead on Pink Floyd's "Have a Cigar" (*Wish You Were Here*). In 1977, Harper was hospitalized with a strange illness he claims to have contracted while giving a lamb mouth-to-mouth resuscitation. He continues to tour and record in Europe.

HARPER'S BIZARRE
Formed 1963, San Francisco
Ted Templeman (b. Oct. 24, 1944), lead voc.; Dick Scoppettone (b. July 5, 1945), voc., gtr.; Eddie James (b. Santa Cruz, Calif.), voc., gtr.; Dick Yount (b. Jan. 9, 1943, Santa Cruz, Calif.), voc., bass, gtr., drums.
1966—(+ John Peterson [b. Jan. 8, 1945, San Fran-

cisco], voc., drums) 1967—*Feelin' Groovy* (Warner Bros.) *Anything Goes* 1968—*The Secret Life of Harper's Bizarre* 1969—*Harper's Bizarre 4* 1974—*Best of Harper's Bizarre* 1976—*As Time Goes By* (Forest Bay).

A pop-rock group from prepsychedelic San Francisco, Harper's Bizarre had one big hit with Paul Simon's "The 59th Street Bridge Song" on *Feelin' Groovy* (#13, 1967). The group began by playing surf music in local bars, calling themselves the Tikis. As such, they made their first records in the mid-Sixties for the San Francisco–based Autumn Records. When Autumn went under, the Tikis became Harper's Bizarre, picked up John Peterson from another Autumn band, the Beau Brummels, and got signed to Warner Bros. Having by this time abandoned surf music for pop rock, they cut *Feelin' Groovy* with arrangements by Leon Russell. Specializing in five-part harmonies, the group revived several standards like Cole Porter's "Anything Goes" (#43, 1967), Glenn Miller's "Chattanooga Choo Choo" (#45, 1967) and Johnny Horton's "Battle of New Orleans" (#95, 1968).

They disbanded in 1970 after recording four albums for Warner Bros. Lead singer Ted Templeman stayed on with Warner Bros. and became one of their top in-house A&R men and producers (Van Morrison, the Doobie Brothers, Van Halen, among others). Templeman also produced an album in 1974 by the re-formed Beau Brummels, which included his old Harper's Bizarre mate, John Peterson.

SLIM HARPO
Born James Moore, January 11, 1924, Lobdell, Louisiana; died January 31, 1970, Baton Rouge
1965—*A Long Drink of the Blues* (Stateside) 1976—*Blues Hangover* (Flyright) 1980—*Got Love If You Want It;   The Best of Slim Harpo* (Excello).

Slim Harpo was a blues singer/songwriter/guitarist/harp player who wrote "I'm a King Bee," an early Rolling Stones showpiece.

One of at least four children, Harpo grew up in Port Allen, Louisiana. His parents died while he was still a child, and he quit school to support his siblings. At age 18, he moved to New Orleans to work as a longshoreman, and later went to Baton Rouge to work as a contractor. In the early Forties, he played bars and clubs as Harmonica Slim.

Harpo met guitarist Lightnin' Slim, with whom he toured and performed (Lightnin' appears on "Rainin' in My Heart" and "I'm a King Bee") over the next twenty years. He eventually owned his own trucking business but continued to work in clubs, often with Lightnin' Slim. He had a hit in 1961 with "Rainin' in My Heart" (#17) and in 1966 with "Baby, Scratch My Back" (#1 R&B). He toured rock clubs through the late Sixties. He died of a heart attack.

THE HARPTONES
Formed 1953, New York City
William Winfield (b. Aug. 24, 1929), lead tenor; William James (b. 1946), first tenor; William Galloway, second tenor; Bill Brown (b. 1936; d. 1956), bass; Nicky Clark (b. 1943), tenor; Raoul Cita (b. Feb. 11, 1928), piano.
1954—(− Galloway; + Jimmie Beckum, second tenor) **late 1950s**—(numerous changes) **1982**—*Love Needs* (Ambient/Epic).

A New York doo-wop group that enjoyed limited success in the Fifties and early Sixties, the Harptones only cracked the pop market with "What Will I Tell My Heart" (#96, 1961).

Formed on the streetcorners of Harlem as the Harps, they changed their name to avoid conflicts with another group. In 1953, they were first featured on one of Alan Freed's revues in Cleveland, and they began recording for the New York–based Bruce label. Led by Raoul Cita, the group's organizer, arranger, composer and pianist, they specialized in slow, romantic songs. Their first R&B hit for Bruce was "A Sunday Kind of Love." By 1954, a year after their first record, they had changed both lineup and label with "Life Is But a Dream" on Paradise. Among the labels the group recorded for in the next decade were Rama Records ("The Masquerade Is Over"), Old Town, Andrea, Tip Top, Gee, Warwick, Coed, Cub, Companion ("What Will I Tell My Heart") and KT.

The group disbanded in 1964. Willie Winfield became a funeral director, occasionally reviving the name with new associates for local club work. In 1982, Winfield and Cita regrouped the Harptones for *Love Needs;* the liner notes claimed that the group had rehearsed weekly for 28 years.

DON "SUGARCANE" HARRIS/DON AND DEWEY
Born June 18, 1938, Pasadena, California
N.A.—*Keep on Driving* (Musidisc) **1970**—*Fiddler on the Rock* (Polydor) *Sugarcane* (Epic) **1973**—*Cup Full of Dreams; Sugarcane's Got the Blues* (BASF).
Don and Dewey LPs: N.A.—*Don & Dewey* (Specialty) *They're Rockin' Till Midnight.*

He plays guitar, harmonica and piano, but R&B veteran Don "Sugarcane" Harris is best known for his blues-rock electric violin. As half of the Fifties duo Don and Dewey, Harris cowrote "I'm Leaving It Up to You," "Farmer John" and "Big Boy Pete." He then went on to play with Johnny Otis, Little Richard, Frank Zappa and John Mayall. The son of carnival performers, Harris studied classical violin with L. C. Robinson from 1944 to 1954. In the mid-Fifties, he graduated from Manual Arts High School in Los Angeles. He formed the Squires in 1956, and they played local bars for many months until Harris teamed with Dewey Terry to form Don and Dewey.

They recorded for Specialty Records in the late Fifties and toured the West Coast as part of the Johnny Otis show. Otis nicknamed Harris "Sugarcane," reportedly in reference to his reputation as a ladies' man. Harris later recorded with Otis' band for Epic in 1969 *(Cuttin' Up)* and toured with his show before he and Dewey tried a comeback in the early Seventies. (They toured the U.S. and Europe together and recorded for MPS.) After his original pairing with Dewey had disintegrated in the early Sixties, Harris then worked with Little Richard, touring the U.S. and Europe and recording with him.

In 1970, Harris hooked up with Frank Zappa, with whom he recorded, most notably on *Hot Rats* and *Weasels Ripped My Flesh,* which featured Harris' vocals as well as his violin playing. Zappa has said that Don and Dewey's single "Soul Motion" b/w "Stretchin' Out" on Rush Records was one of the all-time great R&B records. Both sides featured Harris' kinetic electric violin work.

Harris also toured and recorded with John Mayall in 1970 and 1971, working concurrently throughout as an occasional solo act in L.A. clubs. In 1970, he began his solo recording career.

EMMYLOU HARRIS
Born 1947, Birmingham, Alabama
1970—*Gliding Bird* (Jubilee) **1975**—*Pieces of the Sky* (Reprise) **1976**—*Elite Hotel* **1977**—*Luxury Liner* (Warner Bros.) **1978**—*Quarter Moon in a Ten-Cent Town; Profile/The Best of Emmylou Harris* **1979**—*Blue Kentucky Girl* **1980**—*Roses in the Snow; Light of the Stable* **1981**—*Evangeline* **1982**—*Cimarron.*

Emmylou Harris began the Seventies as a backup vocalist and ended the decade as a country hitmaker, with her clear soprano fronting husband Brian Ahern's neotraditionalist arrangements.

Harris grew up in a Virginia suburb of Washington. In high school she was a cheerleader, beauty pageant queen and class valedictorian. She played alto sax in the marching band. In 1965, she enrolled at the University of North Carolina in Greensboro and played there with a folk duo, but moved to Greenwich Village a year and a half later, where she played clubs and sat in with Jerry Jeff Walker and David Bromberg. She also recorded an unsuccessful album for the small Jubilee label. In 1970 she returned to her parents' house in Washington, D.C., after a short time in Nashville, and eventually found a band and began gigging around D.C. clubs.

At a Washington club, Harris met the Flying Burrito Brothers and later began a liaison with Gram Parsons; when he went solo, she recorded and toured with him until his sudden death in 1973. (She later wrote a song about Parsons, "Boulder to Birmingham," which was covered by Dolly Parton.)

After a few months, Harris formed a new band (Angel

Emmylou Harris

Band) and signed with Warner Bros. On 1975's *Pieces of the Sky* she was backed by Elvis Presley's former sidemen Ron Tutt, James Burton and Glen D. Hardin. Since then, her Hot Band has included guitarists Albert Lee and Rodney Crowell, bassist Emory Gordy, Jr., and pedal steel guitarist Hank DeVito.

In 1975, her remake of the Louvin Brothers' "If I Could Only Win Your Love" topped the country charts; subsequent country hits include "Together Again" (#1, 1976), "One of These Days" (#3, 1976), "Sweet Dreams" (#1, 1976), "(You Never Can Tell) C'est la Vie" (#6, 1977), "Making Believe" (#8, 1977) and "To Daddy" (#3, 1977). While 1976's *Elite Hotel* and 1977's *Luxury Liner* won her some rock fans, she has yet to crack the pop singles market, flirting with Top Forty success on such releases as "If I Could Only Win Your Love" (#58, 1975), the Beatles' "Here, There and Everywhere" (#65, 1976) and her duet with Roy Orbison, "That Lovin' You Feelin' Again" (#55, 1980), which was included on the soundtrack of the film *Roadie*.

Harris married producer Brian Ahern (whose other credits include Anne Murray and Crowell) in 1977 in Halifax. In 1979 she began to concentrate on pure country material. Her sixth album, *Blue Kentucky Girl,* won her a Grammy for Best LP by a Female Country Singer.

By 1982, *Elite Hotel, Luxury Liner, Blue Kentucky Girl, Profile, Roses in the Snow* and *Evangeline* were all gold LPs. During that year, *Cimarron* was still holding its own in the *Billboard* Top Fifty while the single "Tennessee Rose" was in the country Top Fifteen. In addition to the Gram Parsons records, she has also sung on recordings by Dolly Parton, Linda Ronstadt, the Band (with whom she appears in the studio footage of their 1976 documentary, *The Last Waltz,* singing Robbie Robertson's "Evangeline"), Neil Young, Little Feat, John Sebastian, Jesse Winchester (the bulk of *Nothing But a Breeze*) and Bob Dylan *(Desire)*.

WYNONIE HARRIS
Born August 24, 1915, Omaha, Nebraska; died June 14, 1969, Los Angeles
N.A.—*Good Rockin' Blues* (King)   *Good Rockin' Tonight;   Party After Hours* (Aladdin).

Wynonie Harris was a big-band blues shouter whose style was a major influence on early rock & roll.

Harris dropped out of Creighton University in Omaha and began working as a comedian and dancer in the Thirties. After teaching himself to play the drums, in the late Thirties and early Forties he led his own local combo. When he moved to Los Angeles in the early Forties, he quit drumming and worked as a club emcee for a while; he also appeared as a dancer in the film *Hit Parade of 1943*.

In 1944, Harris became a vocalist with Lucky Millinder's band, with whom he cut his first records that year for Decca (and, a few years later, for King Records) and toured major ballrooms throughout America. He continued recording with jazz bands in the mid-Forties (Jack McVea, Oscar Pettiford, Illinois Jacquet and others). He also worked with Johnny Otis, who influenced him toward a pop-tinged R&B style. While recording for King Records, he had his biggest successes with "Good Morning Judge," "Lovin' Machine," "All She Wants to Do Is Rock" and his mid-Fifties British hit, "Bloodshot Eyes." Harris also covered Roy Brown's "Good Rockin' Tonight," later an Elvis Presley hit. He toured widely throughout the late Forties with such traveling bands as the Lionel Hampton orchestra, Dud Bascomb and Big Joe Turner.

Harris continued club work, often as part of package shows, into the early Fifties, cutting records for Cincinnati-based King Records and New York's Apollo label. In the mid-Fifties, he opened a cafe in Brooklyn and in 1963 went to Los Angeles and did the same. He was working as a bartender when he died of cancer at the age of 54. Harris had attempted several comebacks in the interim. In the early Sixties, he recorded for Atco and Roulette in New York and for Chicago-based Cadet. For one of his last public performances, in 1967, he played Harlem's venerable Apollo Theater.

GEORGE HARRISON
Born February 25, 1943, Liverpool, England
1968—*Wonderwall Music* (Apple)   **1969**—*Electronic Sounds* (Zapple)   **1971**—*All Things Must Pass* (Apple)   **1972**—*Concert for Bangladesh*   **1973**—*Living in*

the Material World   1974—Dark Horse   1975—Extra Texture (Read All About It)   1976—33⅓ (Dark Horse) The Best of George Harrison (Capitol)   1979—George Harrison (Dark Horse)   1981—Somewhere in England (Warner Bros.)   1982—Gone Troppo.

George Harrison played lead guitar and wrote occasional songs for the Beatles; he also was the group's only convert to Eastern religion. Since the Beatles broke up, he has had an uneven solo career.

Born into a working-class family, Harrison attended Dovedale Primary School, three years behind John Lennon. In 1954, he entered Liverpool Institute, a grade behind Paul McCartney.

In 1956, at the height of Britain's skiffle craze, Harrison formed his first group, the Rebels. He started jamming occasionally with his new acquaintance Paul McCartney, and in 1958 McCartney introduced him to John Lennon; soon all three were playing in the Quarrymen, who later became the Silver Beatles and then the Beatles.

Harrison played lead guitar and sang backup vocals and an occasional lead in the Beatles. In the mid-Sixties, he was one of the first rock musicians to experiment with Indian and Far Eastern instruments; he studied with Bengali master sitarist Ravi Shankar. Harrison first played sitar on 1965's "Norwegian Wood" and later on "Within You, Without You," "The Inner Light" and others.

Harrison wrote songs as early as 1963 ("Don't Bother Me"), but it was difficult for him to get the group to record his material, one of the problems that led to the Beatles' breakup. Harrison's compositions include "I Need You," "You Like Me Too Much," "Taxman," "Love You To," "Piggies," "Savoy Truffle," "While My Guitar Gently Weeps," "Here Comes the Sun" and "Something," the only Harrison song to become a hit single for the Beatles.

After the Beatles officially disbanded in early 1970, Harrison then continued his solo career, which he'd begun in November 1968 with the electronic sound collage soundtrack Wonderwall Music. In November 1970, he released his three-record set All Things Must Pass, produced by Phil Spector, which included the #1 hit single "My Sweet Lord." (A 1976 lawsuit successfully established that Harrison "unknowingly" plagiarized the song's melodic structure from the early-Sixties hit by the Chiffons, "He's So Fine.") In late summer 1971, Harrison sponsored and hosted two benefit concerts at Madison Square Garden for the people of Bangladesh. With guests including Ringo Starr, Eric Clapton, Leon Russell and Bob Dylan, the concerts, the documentary film and the Grammy-winning three-record set, Concert for Bangladesh, were a resounding success, although funds raised by the proceedings were impounded during a nine-year audit of Apple by the IRS. (In 1981, a check for $8.8 million was finally sent through UNICEF; $2 million had been sent in 1972 before the audit began.) Harrison's song about the plight of the refugees, "Bangladesh," hit the pop Top 25 in

late 1971. Living in the Material World produced a second #1 hit in 1973, "Give Me Love (Give Me Peace on Earth)."

In 1974, Harrison formed his own Dark Horse Records (with distribution via A&M), releasing a gold album of the same name late in the year (the title track of which hit #15 as a single) and touring America to support it. The sales of Extra Texture (Read All About It), were disappointing, a trend that continued unabated with 33⅓ and George Harrison. A tribute to the slain Lennon, "All Those Years Ago," went #2 in 1981. Starr and Paul and Linda McCartney also appear on the record.

Harrison began producing albums in the late Sixties by Apple Records protégés Jackie Lomax, Billy Preston and Badfinger; he also participated in sessions by artists signed to his Dark Horse label in the mid-Seventies. He has been regularly involved with members of the Monty Python comedy group axis as executive producer of film projects, including The Life of Brian and Time Bandits. Harrison also appeared in the Python Beatles parody film, All You Need Is Cash. In 1979, he privately published an autobiography, I Me Mine (mass market edition out in 1982).

He met his first wife, model Patti Boyd (born March 17, 1945), in early 1964 on the set of the Beatles film A Hard Day's Night (in which she briefly appeared). They were married on January 21, 1966, but their marriage began coming apart a few years later and they separated and eventually divorced in 1977. Boyd later married guitarist Eric Clapton and was the subject of Clapton's "Layla." Harrison married Olivia Arias in England in September 1978, a month after their son, Dhani, was born.

WILBERT HARRISON
Born January 6, 1929, Charlotte, North Carolina
1962—Battle of the Giants (Joy)   Kansas City (Sphere)   1969—Let's Work Together (Sue)   1971—Wilbert Harrison (Buddah).

Jump-blues singer Wilbert Harrison had two major pop hits a decade apart: "Kansas City" in 1959 and "Let's Work Together" in 1969. Harrison began recording in the early Fifties with "This Woman of Mine" on Rockin. He recorded for DeLuxe and Savoy without notable success. In 1959, Fury Records released "Kansas City," a version of Leiber and Stoller's "K.C. Lovin' " (written in 1952) that went to #1.

Harrison recorded through the Sixties for numerous labels (Seahorn, Neptune, Doc, Port, Vest) until "Let's Work Together," on Sue, went to #32; it was later covered by Canned Heat and Roxy Music's Bryan Ferry. "My Heart Is Yours," on SSS International, went to #98 in 1971, and he recorded through the Seventies for Buddah, Hotline, Brunswick and Wet Soul. For much of his career, Harrison—unable to afford sidemen—has performed live as a one-man band.

JOHN HARTFORD

Born December 30, 1937, New York City
1967—Looks at Life (RCA)   Earthwords and Music
1968—The Love Album;   Housing Project;   Gentle on
My Mind and Other Originals   1969—John Hartford
1970—Iron Mountain Depot   1971—Aero-Plain
(Warner Bros.)   1972—Morning Bugle   1975—
Tennessee Jubilee (Flying Fish)   1976—Mark Twang;
Nobody Knows What You Do   1977—Dillard, Hartford,
Dillard;   All in the Name of Love   1978—Heading
Down into the Mystery Below   1979—Slumberin' on
the Cumberland.

Singer/songwriter/banjoist Hartford wrote "Gentle on My Mind" for Glen Campbell and has recorded many folk-oriented solo albums.

Best known for his banjo work but also adept at guitar and fiddle, Hartford was raised in St. Louis, where his father was a doctor and his mother a painter. He studied art at Washington University in St. Louis, and before moving to Nashville in the mid-Sixties he worked as a sign painter, a commercial artist, a riverboat deckhand and a disc jockey. His session work slowly picked up, and by the end of the Sixties he had participated in the Byrds' *Sweetheart of the Rodeo*. Hartford continued studio gigs through the early Seventies. In 1966, he signed with RCA, for whom he eventually recorded eight albums.

But his biggest success came as a writer, notably "Gentle on My Mind," which, in addition to Campbell's Grammy-winning hit, has been covered more than 200 times and has sold 15 million copies internationally. It was originally a minor country hit for Hartford in 1967. Among his other compositions are "California Earthquake" and "Natural to Be Gone."

Hartford had his most extensive exposure in the late Sixties as a regular on the "Smothers Brothers Comedy Hour," which was followed by a stint on Glen Campbell's show. At the start of the Seventies, he hosted his own syndicated show, "Something Else." He switched from RCA to Warner Bros. in mid-1971, releasing his debut for the label, the David Bromberg–produced *Aero-Plain* (featuring guitarist Norman Blake, dobro player Tut Taylor and fiddler Vassar Clements). Then he switched to the small Flying Fish label, and 1976's *Mark Twang* won a Grammy in the ethnic-traditional category.

DAN HARTMAN

Born Harrisburg, Pennsylvania
1976—Images (Blue Sky)   1978—Instant Replay
1979—Relight My Fire.

After playing bass with Edgar Winter during his peak years in the mid-Seventies, multiinstrumentalist Dan Hartman embarked upon a modestly successful solo career highlighted by dance-oriented singles like "Instant Replay" (#29, 1978). Hartman joined Winter as bassist in early 1972 and stayed with him until 1976. He wrote Winter's platinum single, "Free Ride."

Following his stint with Winter, Hartman began a solo career for Blue Sky. He records regularly but rarely tours, preferring to operate his custom recording studio, the Schoolhouse, in Connecticut. The studio has been the site of sessions by Foghat, .38 Special, Muddy Waters, Rick Derringer and both the Winter brothers, among others. Hartman continues to contribute songs to Edgar Winter albums and occasionally to produce them.

DONNY HATHAWAY

Born October 1, 1945, Chicago; died January 13, 1979, New York City
1970—Everything Is Everything (Atco)   1971—Donny
Hathaway   1972—Donny Hathaway Live;   Roberta
Flack and Donny Hathaway (Atlantic)   1973—Extension
of a Man   1978—The Best of Donny Hathaway
(Atco)   1979—Roberta Flack Featuring Donny Hathaway (Atlantic)   1980—Donny Hathaway in Performance.

A singer/songwriter/keyboardist best known for his duets with Roberta Flack, Donny Hathaway fused R&B, gospel, jazz, classical and rock strains in a modestly successful solo career. He was raised in St. Louis by his grandmother, Martha Pitts, a professional gospel singer. From the age of three Hathaway accompanied her on tours, billed as the Nation's Youngest Gospel Singer. He attended Howard University in Washington, D.C., on a fine arts scholarship.

One classmate was Roberta Flack, and in the early Seventies, shortly after Flack started her solo career, the two began singing together. Their hits included Carole King's "You've Got a Friend" (#29, 1971), the Righteous Brothers' "You've Lost That Lovin' Feelin' " (#71, 1971) and "Where Is the Love" (#5, 1972), which established them as a duo. *Roberta Flack and Donny Hathaway* was a gold album, but due to personal problems both the partnership and Hathaway's solo career were put on hold for several years. When they reunited in 1978, they had their biggest hit, the gold single "The Closer I Get to You" (#2, 1978). Hathaway was working on *Roberta Flack Featuring Donny Hathaway* when he died after falling from his fifteenth-floor hotel room of the Essex House. (The police called it suicide; close friends refused to believe it.)

At the time of his death, Hathaway had released four solo albums in addition to his discs with Flack. He had recorded briefly for Curtom Records with June Conquest as June and Donnie, and got his first solo contract with Atlantic in 1970 under the patronage of King Curtis. Hathaway enjoyed some chart success in the early Seventies with singles like "The Ghetto, Part I" (#23 R&B, 1970), "Little Ghetto Boy" (#25 R&B, 1972), "Giving Up" (#21 R&B, 1972), "I Love You More Than You'll

Ever Know" (#20 R&B, 1972) and "Love, Love, Love" (#16 R&B, 1973).

Concurrently, Hathaway worked as a producer and composer for others, including Aretha Franklin, Jerry Butler and the Staple Singers. He also did freelance production work for Chess, Uni, Kapp and Stax. By the mid-Seventies, he had formed his own independent production company and scored the film *Come Back Charleston Blue*. He also sang the theme song for the television series "Maude."

RICHIE HAVENS

Born January 21, 1941, Brooklyn, New York
1965—*Richie Havens Record* (Douglas) **1966**—*Electric Havens* **1967**—*Mixed Bag* (Verve) **1968**—*Something Else Again* **1969**—*Richard D. Havens 1983* **1970**—*Stonehenge* (Stormy Forest) **1971**—*Alarm Clock; "The Great Blind Degree"* **1972**—*Richie Havens on Stage* **1973**—*Richie Havens Portfolio* **1974**—*Mixed Bag II* (Polydor) **1976**—*The End of the Beginning* (A&M) **1977**—*Mirage* **1979**—*Connections* (Elektra/ Asylum).

Richie Havens, a black folksinger with a percussive, strummed guitar style, enjoyed his greatest popularity during the late Sixties. He was born and raised in the Bedford-Stuyvesant ghetto, the eldest of nine children in a family headed by a pianist father. As a youth, he sang for spare change on streetcorners. By age 14, he was singing with the McCrea Gospel Singers in Brooklyn, and three years later he dropped out of high school to pursue a music career. He worked his way into Greenwich Village folk circles in the early Sixties.

After recording two albums for the Douglas International–Transatlantic label, Havens started touring clubs throughout the U.S. in 1967, and he became a familiar act on the outdoor festival circuit, playing at the Newport Folk Festival (1966), the Monterey Jazz Festival (1967), the Miami Pop Festival (1968), the Isle of Wight Festival (1969) and Woodstock (1969). Despite such massive exposure, Havens never really transformed his concert audiences into record consumers. Signed to Verve in 1966, he jumped from there to MGM, A&M, Elektra and others.

His repertoire has featured songs by Lennon-McCartney, Van Morrison, Bob Dylan and James Taylor. His only chart success was with his cover of George Harrison's "Here Comes the Sun" (#16, 1971). He continued to be a reliable club and concert performer throughout the Seventies. In the late Seventies, he conducted extensive tours of the Middle East and Europe, around the same time he released his fifteenth album, and first for Elektra, *Connections*, in 1979. As an actor, his film credits include *Catch My Soul* (1974) and Richard Pryor's *Greased Lightning* (1977). He was also featured in the 1972 stage presentation of the Who's *Tommy*.

DALE HAWKINS

Born August 22, 1938, Goldmine, Louisiana
N.A.—*Dale Hawkins* (Chess) **1958**—*Susie Q* **N.A.**— *L.A., Memphis and Tyler, Texas* (Bell).

A rockabilly original, singer/guitarist/bandleader Dale Hawkins was an important influence on such later rockers as John Fogerty, whose Creedence Clearwater Revival had a #11 hit in 1968 with Hawkins' "Suzie Q."

Hawkins signed with Chess in the mid-Fifties and recorded for their Checker subsidiary for the next several years. He enjoyed his most rewarding year in 1957, when "Suzie Q" climbed to #27 on the pop charts. Hawkins followed up with more modest releases like "La Do-Dada" (#32, 1958), "A House, a Car and a Wedding Ring" (#88, 1958), "Class Cutter Yeah Yeah" (#52, 1959) and uncharted singles like "My Babe" and "Liza Jane." James Burton (who claims to have been coauthor of "Suzie Q"), Scotty Moore (of Elvis Presley's band) and Toy Buchanan were among the guitarists in Hawkins' band.

After touring the U.S. several times, Hawkins left Chess in 1961 and in the next few years recorded, with little impact on the market, for such labels as Tilt, Zonk, Atlantic, Roulette and ABC-Paramount. By the mid-Sixties, he was living in Tyler, Texas, and was working as a producer on pop hits by the Five Americans ("Western Union," "Do It Again a Little Bit Slower") and Bruce Channel ("Hey Baby"). At the close of the Sixties, Hawkins revitalized his recording career with an album recorded in Nashville with Box Tops producer Dan Penn.

EDWIN HAWKINS SINGERS

Formed 1967, Oakland, California
1970—*Oh Happy Day* (Buddah) *More Happy Days* **1971**—*Children (Get Together)* **1972**—*I'd Like to Teach the World to Sing* **1973**—*New World* **1974**— *Live*.

The Edwin Hawkins Singers had one of the most successful gospel pop hits ever in 1969 with "Oh Happy Day" (#4) and returned to the Top Ten the following year backing Melanie on "Lay Down (Candles in the Rain)" (#6, 1970). The group's arranger/director/pianist, Edwin Hawkins (born August 1943, Oakland), was a student at Berkeley in 1967 when he and an associate, Betty Watson, organized the large choir to represent their Oakland church, the Ephesian Church of God in Christ, at a Pentecostal Youth Congress in Washington, D.C. The group was originally called the Northern California State Youth Choir.

By 1969, the group was 46 members strong and backed by keyboards, drums and electric bass. To help raise money to finance a trip to the National Youth Congress in Cleveland that year, they recorded an album in a San Francisco church on an old two-track stereo machine. The album included a fiery reading of the gospel standard "Oh Happy Day," which a local disc jockey started airing. By the spring of 1969, the single was a Top Ten hit; Buddah picked up the LP, *Let Us Go into the House of the Lord,* for national distribution.

Featured on the album was vocalist Dorothy Morrison who was born in Longview, Texas, in 1945 and who went on to some prominence as a solo gospel artist in her own right, including an appearance at the 1969 Big Sur Folk Festival. Other featured soloists in the Hawkins group included Elaine Kelly ("To My Father's House") and Margarette Branch ("I'm Going Through").

After contributing to Melanie's hit and touring Europe in 1970, the group quickly faded from prominence, partly because the personnel kept changing, and keeping such a large retinue active proved prohibitively expensive. But they remained a respected gospel force, especially in the Bay Area, for several years. Edwin Hawkins remains active as a gospel musician.

RONNIE HAWKINS

Born January 10, 1935, Fayetteville, Arkansas
1963—*The Best of Ronnie Hawkins* (Roulette)   **1970**—*Ronnie Hawkins* (Cotillion)   **1971**—*The Hawk*   **1972**—*Rock and Roll Resurrection* (Monument)   **1974**—*The Giant of Rock 'n' Roll.*

A thirty-year veteran of roadhouse rock & roll, Ronnie Hawkins is best known as the man who assembled the Band. He formed his first group in 1952 while attending the University of Arkansas and shortly thereafter cut his first record, a cover of an Eddy Arnold tune for a local label. In the mid-Fifties, before moving to Memphis, he played piano behind Carl Perkins and Conway Twitty.

After a stint in the Army, Hawkins went to Canada for the first time in 1958. For the next four years, he alternated between club work there and one-nighter tours of Southern honky-tonks. In that period, he met the four Canadians and one American who later became known as the Band (Levon Helm, like Hawkins, was a transplanted Arkansan). They joined his band, the Hawks, and accompanied him on his auto tours through the South before leaving him to back John Hammond, Jr., in 1964. (A year later they became Bob Dylan's backing band, and by 1968 they were on their own.) Among other onetime Hawks were guitarists Roy Buchanan, Duane Allman and Dominic Troiano.

Hawkins recorded extensively for the Roulette label in the late Fifties and early Sixties. In 1959, he enjoyed two American chart hits, "Mary Lou" (#26) and "Forty Days" (#45). But rockabilly was on its way out by the time Hawkins got his recording career under way. In 1962, he settled in Toronto and became proprietor and featured attraction at the Hawk's Nest Bar. His records were hits in Canada, especially his 1963 recording of Bo Diddley's "Who Do You Love."

By the mid-Sixties, Hawkins was recording for his own Hawk label in Canada. He performed regularly on the rock ballroom circuit in the late Sixties, and in 1969 he signed with Atlantic/Cotillion. *Ronnie Hawkins* was recorded in Alabama with the Muscle Shoals Rhythm Section, and it produced his last American chart single, "Down in the Alley" (#75, 1970).

In 1976, Hawkins appeared at the Band's farewell concert, documented in Martin Scorsese's film *The Last Waltz.* He continues to perform in clubs, and had a cameo role in Michael Cimino's 1981 film *Heaven's Gate.*

SCREAMIN' JAY HAWKINS

Born Jalacy Hawkins, July 18, 1929, Cleveland, Ohio
1957—*At Home with* (Epic)   **1969**—*I Put a Spell on You*   **1970**—*Screamin' Jay Hawkins* (Philips).

A show-biz eccentric, Screamin' Jay Hawkins was known more for his flamboyant dress and onstage shenanigans than for his singing or piano and sax playing.

Hawkins was orphaned in infancy and raised by a foster family. He took piano lessons as a child and by his early teen years was performing for tips in neighborhood bars. He was a Golden Gloves champion by 1943, continued boxing through the close of the decade, and in 1949 he won the middleweight championship of Alaska. He began his music career in 1952, working as a pianist and singer with a band led by guitarist Tiny Grimes, with whom he toured and recorded in the early Fifties, and he recorded with the Leroy Kirkland Band in 1954. He also toured U.S. clubs that year with Fats Domino's revue.

In 1955, Hawkins began his solo career. Adopting the "Screamin' " moniker to fit his unrestrained rocking R&B, he started working clubs, earning a reputation for energetic showmanship that bordered on lunacy; as part of Alan Freed's package tours, Hawkins would be carried offstage in a flaming coffin.

His recorded efforts had far less of an impact. Aside from a few exceptional recordings like "I Put a Spell on You" (1956), "Alligator Wine" (1958) and "Feast of the Mau Mau" (1967), his records have virtually been ignored. Nonetheless, he has recorded extensively over the years for numerous labels, including Okeh, Mercury, Roulette, Decca and RCA.

In the early Sixties, Hawkins lived, performed and recorded mainly in Hawaii and England, returning to the continental U.S. in mid-decade to play the club circuit. In the early Seventies, he worked out of New York City, frequently performing at the Apollo Theater in Harlem. He made his most recent recordings in 1974. In the mid-Seventies, he toured Europe extensively with the Rhythm and Blues Roots of Rock and Roll troupe. Hawkins remains active playing club dates. He has appeared in rock films, notably *Mister Rock 'n' Roll* in 1957 and *American Hot Wax* in 1978.

HAWKWIND/HAWKLORDS
Formed 1969, London
Original members (as Group X/Hawkwind Zoo): Terry Ollis, drums; Nik Turner, sax, voc., flute; Dave Brock, gtr., voc., synth.; Dik Mik, electronics, kybds.; John Harrison, bass; Mick Slattery, gtr. Over thirty personnel changes followed.
1971—*Hawkwind* (United Artists)   **1972**—*In Search of Space; Doremi Fasol Latido*   **1973**—*Space Ritual, Alive in Liverpool and London*   **1974**—*Hall of the Mountain Grill*   **1975**—*Warrior on the Edge of Time* (Atco)   **1976**—*Road Hawks* (United Artists, U.K.) *Astounding Sounds* (Charisma, U.K.)   *Masters of the Universe* (United Artists, U.K.)   **1977**—*Quark, Strangeness and Charm* (Sire)   **1978**—*"25 Years On"* (Charisma)   **1980**—*Repeat Performance* (U.K.)   *Live '79* (Bronze, U.K.)   *Levitation* (U.K.).

An English psychedelic rock band, Hawkwind (later Hawklords) has been a cult act since its inception, touring and often playing for free (one of their most memorable appearances was outside the gates of the Isle of Wight Festival in 1970). They were originally called Group X, then Hawkwind Zoo, then Hawkwind, and their first public performance—a ten-minute set at All Saints Hall in Notting Hill Gate—attracted a booking agent. They were signed to United Artists in November 1969.

With the 1972 addition of South African–born lyricist (and sometimes vocalist) Robert Calvert, the group's material improved. That year the quasi-psychedelic *In Search of Space* sold over 100,000 copies in Britain alone. Part of a live 1972 concert was taped, and from it sprang the pre-punk heavy-metal "Silver Machine," a #3 hit. Their most successful album ever was the double LP *Space Ritual*, which cracked the English Top Ten in 1973. That year, their hit-bound single "Urban Guerilla" was pulled from distribution by UA because of a coincidental outbreak of terrorist bombings in London.

The group toured the U.S. for the first time in late 1973, with a revue including a semi-nude dancer, Stacia. They made a couple of subsequent trips to the States in 1974 to support *Hall of the Mountain Grill*, but late in the year police in Indiana, claiming the group owed $8,000 in back taxes, impounded all its equipment and the band returned to England.

By spring 1975, undaunted, they were back in America for their fourth tour, to support *Warrior on the Edge of Time*. Bassist Ian "Lemmy" Kilminster was arrested by Canadian customs officials for possession of amphetamine sulphate and was jailed. Not wishing to jeopardize yet another U.S. tour, the band fired him; he later formed Motorhead, a heavy-metal band.

Hawkwind played to much acclaim at the Reading Festival in August 1975; soon thereafter, longtime collaborator science-fiction author Michael Moorcock released *New World's Fair* with instrumental backing from the band. Moorcock and coauthor Michael Butterworth featured the group in their 1976 novel, *The Time of the Hawklords* (which inspired the group's name change a few years later).

With lyricist Calvert back in the fold (during his mid-decade absence he released two solo albums: *Captain Lockheed and the Starfighters* [1974] and *Lucky Lief and the Longships* [1975], the latter produced by Brian Eno), the group reshuffled their lineup once again and by 1978 (after a brief tenure as the Sonic Assassins) had changed names to Hawklords, around the same time that Simon House (with Hawkwind since April 1974) left to join David Bowie's band. With longtime linchpin Brock (who by the late Seventies had a ten-acre farm in Devon) still dominating the band, they continued with moderate English success through the end of the Seventies.

ISAAC HAYES
Born August 6, 1938, Covington, Tennessee
1967—*Presenting Isaac Hayes* (Enterprise)   **1969**—*Hot Buttered Soul*   **1970**—*The Isaac Hayes Movement*   **1971**—*Shaft;   Black Moses*   **1973**—*Joy;   Live at the Sahara Tahoe*   **1975**—*Disco Connection* (Hot Buttered Soul)   **1976**—*Juicy Fruit (Disco Freak)* (ABC)   **1977**—*New Horizon* (Polydor)   **1978**—*Hotbed* (Stax)   **1979**—*Don't Let Go* (Polydor)   *Royal Rappin's* (with Millie Jackson)   **1980**—*And Once Again.*

As a songwriter, arranger, producer and vocalist for Stax-Volt Records in the Sixties, Isaac Hayes played an essential part in the making of Memphis soul, and in the early Seventies he laid the groundwork for disco.

Hayes was raised by his sharecropper grandparents, and by the age of five was singing in church. By his teens, he and his grandparents had moved to Memphis, where he learned to play sax and piano. He began singing in local clubs with his own band, Sir Isaac and the Doo-Dads, and cut his first records for local labels in 1962. Around the same time, he started playing sax with the Mar-Keys, and his association with the group led to studio work with Stax Records that turned into a formal relationship in 1964, when he was hired to play on Otis Redding sessions.

In the mid-Sixties, Hayes became more active as keyboardist in the Stax house band, and at Stax he developed a songwriting partnership with lyricist David Porter. Among their more than 200 collaborations were such hits as "Soul Man" and "Hold on, I'm Coming" for Sam and Dave; "B-A-B-Y" for Carla Thomas; "I Had a Dream" for Johnnie Taylor; and many others.

Hayes began making his own Stax records in 1967, but made his reputation as a performer in 1969, when he recorded *Hot Buttered Soul*. With long songs (there were only four cuts on the whole album) and elaborate arrangements, the album hit #8 on the pop charts and went platinum. (Barry White, for one, is indebted to Hayes for his plush-carpeted bedroom style.)

Hayes's biggest commercial triumph came in 1971, when he scored the Gordon Parks film *Shaft*. The double album soundtrack won an Academy Award as it yielded "The Theme from *Shaft*," which, with its insistent hi-hats, wah-wah guitars and intoned monologue, hit #1 on the pop charts in 1971, went platinum, won a Grammy and made Hayes an international superstar. His other pop hits include covers of Burt Bacharach's "Walk on By" (#13 R&B, #30 pop, 1969) and Jimmy Webb's "By the Time I Get to Phoenix" (#37 R&B and pop, 1969) and "Never Can Say Goodbye" (#5 R&B, #22 pop, 1971), all on Stax's Enterprise subsidiary.

Hayes's early-Seventies concerts featured a twenty-piece orchestra, the Isaac Hayes Connection, and Hayes himself, wearing tights, cape, gold chains around his bare chest, and dark glasses fronting his shaved head. One performance was documented in the film *Wattstax* (1973). He scored "blaxploitation" movies like *Tough Guys* and *Truck Turner* (1974), in which he also acted.

In 1975, after fighting with Stax over royalties, he signed with ABC Records, setting up his own Hot Buttered Soul subsidiary. His first ABC album went gold, but subsequent efforts were ignored in the disco market. In 1976, the bottom fell out of Hayes's career and, $6 million in debt, he moved from Memphis to Atlanta. In 1978, Wallace Johnson, cofounder of the Holiday Inn chain, became his manager, but by 1980 he was suing Hayes for breach of contract.

In the meantime, however, Hayes was taking steps toward a comeback. In 1977, he recorded a double set, *A Man and a Woman*, with Dionne Warwick, and he co-wrote Warwick's 1979 Top Twenty pop hit "Déjà Vu." On his own on the Polydor label, he returned to the charts with "Zeke the Freak" (#19 R&B, 1978), "Don't Let Go" (#11 R&B, #21 pop, 1979) and "Do You Wanna Make Love" (#30 R&B, 1979). His duet album with Millie Jackson, *Royal Rappin's* (1979), was popular on the soul charts. He acted in John Carpenter's *Escape from New York*.

LEE HAZLEWOOD

Born July 9, 1929, Mannford, Oklahoma
N.A.—*Friday's Child* (Reprise) *Nancy and Lee; Nancy and Lee Again* (RCA) *Poet, Fool or Bum* (Capitol).

Lee Hazlewood's long career includes work as a songwriter, a record producer and a singer (most notably in duets with Nancy Sinatra). He was raised in Port Arthur, Texas, and attended Southern Methodist University before being drafted to fight in Korea. Upon his discharge in 1953, he became a country disc jockey in Phoenix. By 1955, he was writing songs and producing an occasional recording session. His major success of the period was

Sanford Clark's 1956 hit "The Fool," which he wrote and produced and which sold 800,000 copies. (The song was also a modest hit when covered by the Gallahads that year.)

In 1957, Hazlewood moved to Philadelphia and co-founded Jamie Records (Dick Clark was one of the partners), which he used to launch the career of guitarist Duane Eddy. In a 3½-year period, he produced, among others, "Rebel Rouser," "Yep!" and "Forty Miles of Bad Road," which collectively sold about 20 million copies. In the early Sixties, Hazlewood had a hand in running such minor labels as Trey, East-West and Gregmark, and in 1965, he produced several hits for Dino, Desi and Billy.

Hazlewood is best known for his work with Nancy Sinatra. Besides producing her hits "These Boots Are Made for Walkin' " (#1, 1966) and "Sugar Town" (#5, 1966), Hazlewood dueted with her on "Jackson" (#14, 1967), "Summer Wine" (#49, 1967), "Lady Bird" (#20, 1967) and "Some Velvet Morning" (#26, 1968). By the close of the Sixties, Hazlewood was living in Stockholm, Sweden, and alternating between periods of virtual retirement and occasional solo activity in Europe. He released his first solo album in the U.S. in the early Seventies, *Poet, Fool or Bum*.

HEAD, HANDS AND FEET

Formed 1969, England
Albert Lee (b. Dec. 21, 1943, Leominster, Eng.), gtr., kybds.; Tony Colton (b. Feb. 11, 1942, Tunbridge Wells, Eng.), voc.; Ray Smith (b. July 9, 1943, London), gtr.; Chas Hodges (b. Nov. 11, 1943, London), bass; Pete Gavin (b. Sep. 9, 1946, London), drums; Mike O'Neill, kybds.
1971—(– O'Neill) *Head, Hands and Feet* (Capitol)
1972—*Tracks* **1973**—*Old Soldiers Never Die* (Atco).

Head, Hands and Feet was a conglomeration of British rock studio veterans. Most notable among their ranks was guitarist Albert Lee, who went on to play in Emmylou Harris' Hot Band and Eric Clapton's backup band, and to record solo.

The group was cofounded by Tony Colton (who had previously written U.K. hits for such groups as the Merseybeats and the Tremeloes) and Ray Smith in 1969, after the two had played together informally for about nine years. Originally called Poet and the One Man Band, they adopted the name Head, Hands and Feet in late 1969 and stayed together till 1973. Tony Colton had previous experience as a producer, with credits including Atomic Rooster, Yes and Richard Harris.

Their initial efforts were impaired by management and record company problems. Their first U.S. disc, the two-record set *Head, Hands and Feet*, was released in early 1971, at which time they played just one West Coast performance. Neither it nor the Capitol followup, *Tracks*, aroused much more than idle curiosity, however. By 1973, they had hooked up with Atlantic for *Old Soldiers Never Die,* perhaps their most consistent effort. That album might have established them as a major act, but the members were quickly losing interest in their band as studio work beckoned.

HEART

Formed 1972, Seattle, Washington
Ann Wilson (b. June 19, 1951, San Diego), voc., gtr., flute; Nancy Wilson (b. Mar. 16, 1954, San Francisco), voc., gtr., mandolin; Roger Fisher (b. 1950), gtr.; Howard Leese (b. 1952), kybds., synth., gtr.; Michael Derosier, drums; Steve Fossen, bass.
1976—*Dreamboat Annie* (Mushroom) **1977**—*Little Queen* (Portrait) **1978**—*Magazine* (Mushroom) *Dog and Butterfly* (Portrait) **1980**—*Bebe le Strange* (Epic) *Greatest Hits Live* (− Derosier; − Fossen; + Mark Andes [b. Feb. 19, 1948, Philadelphia], bass; + Denny Carmassi, drums) **1982**—*Private Audition.*

Heavy-metal band Heart, led by singer Ann Wilson and featuring her sister Nancy on guitar, have sold several million records.

The Wilson sisters grew up in southern California and Taiwan before their Marine Corps captain father retired to the Seattle suburbs. After attending college, they returned to Seattle, with Nancy working as a folksinger and Ann joining an all-male local group in 1970 called Heart. (The group was formed in 1963 by Steve Fossen and Roger and Mike Fisher as the Army. They later changed the name to White Heart, shortened to Heart in 1974.) Upon joining, Ann became lead guitarist Roger Fisher's girlfriend, and when Nancy joined in 1974, she became involved with Fisher's brother Mike, who by then had retired from the stage to become the group's soundman.

Heart: Mark Andes, Ann Wilson, Nancy Wilson, Denny Carmassi, Howard Leese

After many one-nighters in the Vancouver area, in 1975 they attracted the attention of Canada's Mushroom label, run by Shelly Siegel. He had them cut *Dreamboat Annie,* which upon release in Canada sold 30,000 copies. In the U.S., Siegel released it first in Seattle, where it quickly sold another 25,000. With two hit singles—"Crazy on You" (#35, 1976) and "Magic Man" (#9, 1976)—the album eventually sold 2½ million copies.

By early 1977, the Wilson sisters switched to CBS's subsidiary Portrait, a move that resulted in a prolonged legal fight with Siegel. In retaliation, he released the partly completed *Magazine* at the same time Portrait released *Little Queen.* A Seattle court ruled that Mushroom had to recall *Magazine* so that the Wilsons could remix several tracks and redo vocals before rereleasing the disc. (The Wilsons had wanted the album to be taken off the market completely.)

Little Queen, with the hit "Barracuda" (#11, 1977), became Heart's second million-seller. During sessions for *Bebe,* the Wilson-Fisher liaisons ended. Roger Fisher has since formed his own band in the Seattle area. Howard Leese and Nancy took up the guitar slack, and Nancy Wilson's childhood friend Sue Ennis helped out on song collaborations. The group hit the road for a 77-city tour to support *Bebe,* then returned to make *Private Audition.* Both *Dog and Butterfly* and *Bebe le Strange* have gone platinum.

HEAVY METAL

This heavily amplified, bombastic electric-guitar-dominated rock, which was introduced by bands like Led Zeppelin, Black Sabbath, Deep Purple, Grand Funk Railroad and Blue Cheer, has become hugely popular, despite the fact that there are hardly any heavy-metal hit singles (Deep Purple's "Smoke on the Water" is one rare example). Although it is generally less melodic than AOR, heavy metal shares AOR's primarily white, adolescent audience. The electric guitar is heavy metal's primary icon, though more recently the genre has also wallowed heavily in the trappings of devil worship and related exotic cult mythologies both real (as in the case of Led Zeppelin's Jimmy Page) and put on (as typified by Blue Öyster Cult, Black Sabbath and Judas Priest).

The term heavy metal was originally coined by Beat novelist William Burroughs in his *Naked Lunch,* reintroduced into the pop vocabulary by Steppenwolf in their hit "Born to Be Wild" ("heavy metal thunder") and subsequently redefined by rock critic Lester Bangs in the heavy-metal fan magazine *Creem.*

Although heavy metal was generally regarded as a limited form, the late Seventies saw an international revival led by new groups like Britain's Def Leppard and Iron Maiden, Sweden's Krokus, Australia's AC/DC, Germany's Scorpions and America's Van Halen.

BOBBY HEBB

Born July 26, 1941, Nashville

Singer/songwriter Bobby Hebb is best known for "Sunny" (#2, 1966). He was one of seven children of blind parents who taught him to play the guitar. At age 12, Roy Acuff invited him to perform at the Grand Ole Opry, Hebb becoming one of the first blacks to do so. In the early Sixties, he moved to Chicago, graduated from a dental technician's course and took music classes while occasionally accompanying Bo Diddley on the spoons. He studied guitar with Chet Atkins, who helped him break into show business. Hebb eventually met Sylvia Shemwell, with whom he worked as Bobby and Sylvia. He later cut such tunes as "Night Train to Memphis" and "You Broke My Heart and I Broke Your Jaw."

In 1963, Hebb's brother Hal (a member of the Marigolds) was killed in a mugging. Hebb responded with "Sunny." He was unable to sell it to publishers, but in 1966, while recording an album, he cut the song at the end of a session to use up some extra time, and it became a hit. By the end of the year, Hebb had appeared on several major network television shows and had toured the U.S. with the Beatles. Follow-up hits proved elusive. His last two chart appearances came before the year was out, with "A Satisfied Mind" (#39) and "Love Me" (#84).

Hebb had isolated U.K. hits like "Love Love Love" in the early Seventies on GRT Records. As the decade progressed, he made occasional club appearances in America but mostly lived a quiet life in a colonial mansion in Salem, Massachusetts.

Hebb claims to have written over 3,000 songs, a third of them published—including material for Percy Sledge, Mary Wells, Marvin Gaye, Billy Preston, Herb Alpert and Lou Rawls, whose recording of Hebb's "A Natural Man" won a Grammy in 1971. "Sunny" was widely covered as well, showing up on discs by Cher, Georgie Fame and Gloria Lynne, among others.

RICHARD HELL AND THE VOIDOIDS

Formed September 1976, New York City
Richard Hell (b. Richard Myers, Oct. 2, 1949, Lexington, Ky.), bass, voc.; Marc Bell (b. New York City), drums; Robert Quine (b. Dec. 30, 1942, Akron, Oh.), gtr., voc.; Ivan Julian (b. June 26, 1955, Washington, D.C.), gtr., voc.
1976—*Blank Generation* (EP) (Stiff) 1977—*Blank Generation* (Sire) 1978—(− Bell; + Jerry Antonius, bass, kybd.; + Frank Mauro, drums) 1980—(− Antonius; − Mauro; + Naux [b. July 20, 1951, San Jose, Calif.], gtr.; + Fred Maher, drums) 1982—*Destiny Street* (Red Star).

Richard Hell led one of the most harshly uncompromising bands on New York's late-Seventies punk scene, playing songs with dissonant, jagged guitar lines and dark free-association imagery that owed something to both Captain Beefheart and the Velvet Underground. Hell had played with Johnny Thunders' Heartbreakers and with the Neon Boys, who later became Television; then he formed the Voidoids to perform his own songs. They were regular attractions at punk showcase CBGB, along with Blondie, the Ramones and the Talking Heads.

Hell's 1977 debut album, *Blank Generation,* provided two anthems for the scene, the title cut and "Love Comes in Spurts." But although Hell performed frequently, he remained obscure outside New York and London. In 1979, Nick Lowe produced a single, "The Kid with the Replaceable Head," that was released in England. In 1982, Hell resurfaced with a new band and an album, *Destiny Street.* (Original Voidoids guitarist Robert Quine, meanwhile, had joined Lou Reed's band for *The Blue Mask.*) Hell also began an acting career, appearing in the 1982 film *Smithereens* as a punk-rock musician.

JIMI HENDRIX

Born November 27, 1942, Seattle, Washington; died September 18, 1970, London
1967—*Are You Experienced?* (Reprise) 1968—*Axis: Bold as Love; Electric Ladyland* 1969—*Smash Hits* 1970—*Band of Gypsies* (Capitol) 1971—*The Cry of Love* (Reprise) *Rainbow Bridge* 1972—*Hendrix in the West* 1973—*Soundtrack Recordings from the Film, Jimi Hendrix* 1978—*The Essential Jimi Hendrix* 1979—*The Essential Jimi Hendrix, volume 2* 1982—*The Jimi Hendrix Concerts.*

Jimi Hendrix was one of the most innovative and influential rock guitarists of the late Sixties and perhaps the most important electric guitarist after Charlie Christian. Hendrix pioneered the use of the instrument as an electronic sound source. Rockers before him had experimented with feedback and distortion, but he turned those effects and others into a controlled, fluid vocabulary every bit as personal as the blues he began with. Hendrix's studio craft and his virtuosity with both conventional and unconventional guitar sounds have been widely imitated, and his image—as the psychedelic voodoo child conjuring uncontrollable forces—is a rock archetype.

As a teenager, Hendrix taught himself to play guitar by listening to records by blues guitarists Muddy Waters and B. B. King and rockers such as Chuck Berry and Eddie Cochran. He played in high school bands before enlisting in the U.S. Army in 1959. Discharged after parachuting injuries in 1961, Hendrix began working under the pseudonym Jimmy James as a pickup guitarist. By 1964, when he moved to New York City, he had played behind Sam Cooke, B. B. King, Little Richard, Jackie Wilson, Ike and Tina Turner and Wilson Pickett. In New York, he played the club circuit with King Curtis, the Isley Brothers, John Paul Hammond and Curtis Knight.

Jimi Hendrix

In 1965, Hendrix formed his own band, Jimmy James and the Blue Flames, to play Greenwich Village coffeehouses. Chas Chandler of the Animals took him to London in the autumn of 1966 and arranged for the creation of the Jimi Hendrix Experience, with Noel Redding on bass and Mitch Mitchell on drums.

The Experience's first single, "Hey Joe," reached #6 on the U.K. charts early in 1967, followed shortly by "Purple Haze" and their debut album. Hendrix fast became the rage of London's pop society. Though word of the Hendrix phenomenon spread through the U.S., he was not seen in America (and no records were released) until June 1967, when, at Paul McCartney's insistence, the Experience appeared at the Monterey Pop Festival. The performance, which Hendrix climaxed by burning his guitar, was filmed for *Monterey Pop*.

Hendrix quickly became a superstar. Stories such as one reporting that the Experience were dropped from the bill of a Monkees tour at the insistence of the Daughters of the American Revolution became part of the Hendrix myth, but he considered himself a musician more than a star. Soon after the start of his second American tour, early in 1968, he renounced the extravagances of his stage act and simply performed his music. A hostile reception led him to conclude that his best music came out in the informal settings of studios and clubs, and he began construction of Electric Lady, his own studio in New York.

Hendrix was eager to experiment with musical ideas, and he jammed with John McLaughlin, Larry Coryell and members of Traffic, among others. Miles Davis admired his inventiveness (and, in fact, planned to record with him), and Bob Dylan—whose "Like a Rolling Stone," "All Along the Watchtower" and "Drifter's Escape" Hendrix recorded—later returned the tribute by performing "All Along the Watchtower" in the Hendrix mode.

As 1968 came to a close, disagreements arose between manager Chas Chandler and comanager Michael Jeffrey; Jeffrey, who opposed Hendrix's avant-garde leanings, got the upper hand. Hendrix was also under pressure from black-power advocates to form an all-black group and play to black audiences. These problems exacerbated already existing tensions within the Experience, and early in 1969 Redding left the group to form Fat Mattress. Hendrix replaced him with an Army buddy, Billy Cox. Mitchell stayed on briefly, but by August the Experience was defunct.

Hendrix appeared at the Woodstock Festival with a large informal ensemble called the Electric Sky Church, and later that year he put together the all-black Band of Gypsies with Cox and drummer Buddy Miles (Electric Flag), with whom he had played behind Wilson Pickett. The Band of Gypsies' debut concert at New York's Fillmore East on New Year's Eve 1969 provided the recordings for the group's only album. Hendrix walked offstage in the middle of their Madison Square Garden gig; when he performed again some months later it was with Mitchell and Cox, the group that recorded *Cry of Love*, Hendrix's last self-authorized album, and played at the Isle of Wight Festival, his last concert, in August 1970. A month later he was dead. The cause of death was given in the coroner's report as inhalation of vomit following barbiturate intoxication. Suicide was not ruled out, but evidence pointed to an accident.

In the years since his death, virtually every note Hendrix ever allowed to be recorded has been marketed on approximately 100 albums. Of these—recordings dredged up from his years as a pickup guitarist, live concerts and jam sessions, both bootleg and legitimate, even interviews and conversations—most attention has been given to a series produced by Alan Douglas, who recorded over 1,000 hours of Hendrix alone at the Electric Lady studio in the last year of his life. With the consent of the Hendrix estate, Douglas edited the tapes, erased some tracks and dubbed in others, with mixed results.

CLARENCE "FROGMAN" HENRY
Born March 19, 1937, Algiers, Louisiana
1961—*You Always Hurt the One You Love* (Argo)
1970—*Bourbon Street, Canal Street* (Roulette).

"I can sing like a man . . . I can sing like a girl . . . I can sing like a frog," claimed Clarence Henry in his rollicking 1956 Top Ten R&B hit "Ain't Got No Home." And he did—a piercing falsetto shriek and the guttural inhaled style that earned him his nickname.

Henry, who'd learned piano and trombone as a child, went on to sing and play piano with Bobby Mitchell's New Orleans R&B band in 1955 and remained a Crescent City favorite after his first hit. In 1961, he scored national pop and R&B hits with the Allen Toussaint–produced ballads "I Don't Know Why I Love You but I Do" (by Bobby Charles) and "You Always Hurt the One You Love." His other chartmaking singles included "Lonely Street" and "On Bended Knee" (1961) and "A Little Too Much" (1962). In the late Sixties, Henry appeared in a number of rock & roll revival shows, and in the early Seventies he was still a popular act in New Orleans clubs.

HENRY COW

Formed 1968, Cambridge, England
Original lineup: Fred Frith, gtr., violin, piano; Tim Hodgkinson, kybds., reeds; Chris Cutler, drums, tape effects; John Greaves, bass, piano, voc.; Geoff Leigh, reeds.
1973—*Legend* (Virgin, U.K.) **1974**—*Unrest* (reissued 1979 by Red) **1975**—*Desperate Straights; In Praise of Learning* (reissued 1979 by Red) (Henry Cow merged with Slapp Happy) **1976**—*Concerts* (Caroline, U.K.; reissued 1978 by Fidardo/Compendium) **1978**—*Western Culture* (Broadcast).
Art Bears: 1978—*Hopes and Fears* (Random Radar) **1979**—*Winter Songs* (Recommended).
John Greaves/Peter Blegvad: 1977—*Kew. Rhone.* (Virgin).
Fred Frith: 1974—*Guitar Solos* (Caroline) **1976**—*Guitar Solos 2* **1979**—*Guitar Solos 3* (Rift) **1980**—*Gravity* (Ralph) **1982**—*Speechless* (with Massacre).

Henry Cow's determined, uncompromising eclecticism— their music spans rock, fusion, free improvisation, medieval chamber music, modern-classical and avant-garde *musique concrète*—and committed socialist politics have limited their following to a small, dedicated cult. Initially, their anticommercial leanings (they were formed in the year of the Paris student riots) even kept them from a recording contract. In 1971, they played the semi-legendary Glastonbury Fayre (a sort of British Woodstock) on their way to London to record their critically acclaimed debut LP. In 1973, they scored an avant-garde British production of Shakespeare's *Tempest,* toured with the German progressive group Faust and appeared on one side of the out-of-print *Greasy Truckers Live at Dingwall's Dance Hall* LP.

They opened for Captain Beefheart on a European tour in 1974 and released their second LP, which included "Bittern Storm Over Ulm," a radical refraction of the Yardbirds' "Got to Hurry." Henry Cow merged in 1975 with the mutant cabaret outfit Slapp Happy (Dagmar Krause, Anthony Moore and Peter Blegvad) for *Desperate Straights,* a collection of shorter songs, and for *In*

Praise of Learning, where political lyrics were accompanied by noisy modern-classical music.

In 1978, just before *Western Culture* was released, Fred Frith, Chris Cutler and Peter Blegvad made their first U.S. appearances at Giorgio Gomelsky's Zu Manifestival of Progressive Music in New York City.

Since the mid-Seventies, Henry Cow have worked only fitfully as a group. Fred Frith's various projects include the Art Bears with Cutler and Krause, recording dissonant art songs; Massacre, a trio with bassist Bill Laswell of Material and drummer Fred Maher, who joined Lou Reed's band in 1983; and solo work, including free improvisations on disassembled guitars and various homemade electric instruments. Now headquartered in New York, Frith has released solo albums since 1974, some shared with fellow avant-garde guitarists such as Hans Reichel, Henry Kaiser and Derek Bailey.

Blegvad performed in New York in the early Eighties with Carla Bley, John Greaves of Henry Cow and Arto Lindsay of DNA. Moore recorded two poppish solo albums as A. More; the first of them, *Flying Doesn't Help,* yielded a minor hit, "Judy Get Down."

THE HEPTONES

Formed 1965, Kingston, Jamaica
Earl Morgan (b. 1945); Leroy Sibbles (b. 1949).
1970—*Heptones on Top* (Studio One) *Black Is Black* **1971**—*Freedom Line; Heptones and Friends, Volume 1* (Joe Gibbs) **1976**—*Cool Rasta* (Trojan) *Night Food* (Island) **1977**—*Party Time* **1978**—*In Love with You* (United Artists) *Better Days* (Third World) **1979**—*The Good Life* (Greensleeves) (– Sibbles; + Naggu Morris [b. ca. 1951]) **1981**—*Street of Gold* (Park Heights) **1982**—*One Step Ahead* (Sonic).

With their lilting rhythms and American-style soul harmony singing, the Heptones were the archetypical rocksteady group. Like the "rude boys" who were their first fans, the band members came from the Kingston slum called Trenchtown. Morgan had led a previous group called the Heptones (whose other members subsequently recorded as the Cables), and he formed the new vocal trio with Sibbles, formerly a welder, and Llewelyn, an auto mechanic, in 1965.

After five unsuccessful singles for Ken Lack's label, Coxsone Dodd released the Heptones' "Fatty Fatty" on his Studio One label in 1966; although it was banned from Jamaican radio because of its sexual innuendos, "Fatty Fatty" was a huge hit. In Britain, it was credited to Ken Boothe (a Studio One singer who had already built a small following in the U.K.); none of the Heptones' early British releases carried their name. The Heptones were one of Jamaica's most popular groups of the late Sixties, hitting with Sibbles songs like "Baby (Be True)," "Why Must I," "Why Did You Leave" and "Cry Baby Cry."

They stayed with Dodd's label until 1970, by which time

rock steady was hardening into reggae. Their songs showed reggae's influence mostly in their increasingly political lyrics. Among their hits for producers Joe Gibbs, Geoffrey Chung and Harry J. were "Young, Gifted and Black" (1970), "Hypocrites" (1971), "Freedom to the People" (1972—used as an anthem by the Jamaican People's National Party in their successful election campaign), a cover of Harold Melvin and the Blue Notes' "I Miss You" (1972) and "Book of Rules" (1973—featured in the 1979 film *Rockers*).

In 1973 the Heptones moved to Canada for two years, making Toronto their base for tours in the U.S. and Great Britain. They celebrated their return to Jamaica in 1975 with the chart-topping "Country Boy," and the following year they signed their first multinational contract. Their first American-released album, *Night Food*, contained new versions of "Fatty Fatty" and "Book of Rules." *Party Time*, produced by Lee Perry, had a more reggaefied sound than previous recordings.

In 1979, Sibbles left the group to begin a solo career. Morgan and Llewelyn maintained the Heptones with the addition of Morris. They toured the U.S. in 1982, while Sibbles toured with his own Heptones.

HERMAN'S HERMITS
Formed 1963, Manchester, England
1964 lineup: Peter "Herman" Noone (b. Nov. 5, 1947, Manchester), voc., piano, gtr.; Karl Greene (b. July 31, 1947, Salford, Eng.), gtr., harmonica; Keith Hopwood (b. Oct. 26, 1946, Manchester), gtr.; Derek "Lek" Leckenby (b. May 14, 1945, Leeds, Eng.), gtr.; Barry Whitham (b. July 21, 1946, Manchester), drums.
1965—*The Best of Herman's Hermits* (MGM) **1966**— *Best of, Volume 2* **1968**—*Best of, Volume 3.*

Major stars from the pop side of the British Invasion, Herman's Hermits had ten Top Ten hits from 1964 to 1966. By the time changing musical trends had reduced the group to curiosities, they had already sold over 40 million singles and albums worldwide.

Peter Noone studied singing and acting at the Manchester School of Music, and was featured in the early Sixties in several plays and on the BBC-TV. By 1963, he was playing with a local Manchester group called the Heartbeats. Members of the band claimed that Noone resembled Sherman of the "Rocky and Bullwinkle" television cartoon series; then they shortened the nickname to Herman.

In early 1964, they attracted the attention of U.K. producer Mickie Most, who released the group's first single, "I'm into Something Good" (#13), late in 1964. It spent three weeks at the top of the British charts and sold over a million copies worldwide. The Hermits sold over 17 million records worldwide between 1964 and 1967. In 1965, they dominated the U.S. charts.

The group appeared on U.S. television in the film *Where the Boys Meet the Girls*. Their Top Ten hits included "Mrs. Brown You've Got a Lovely Daughter" (#1), "I'm Henry the Eighth, I Am" (#1) (originally written in 1911 for a Cockney comedian), "Can't You Hear My Heartbeat" (#2), "Wonderful World" (#4), "Silhouettes" (#5) (originally recorded by the Rays), "Just a Little Bit Better" (#7) (all in 1965); "Listen People" (#3), "Dandy" (#5) (written by Ray Davies of the Kinks), "A Must to Avoid" (#8), "Leaning on the Lamp Post" (#9) (all 1966). *The Best of Herman's Hermits* stayed on the album charts 105 weeks. Their last big hit was "There's a Kind of Hush" (#4) in early 1967.

By 1971, the group had disbanded amid legal battles for royalties. The Hermits surfaced a few years later, sans Herman, for an abortive attempt at a comeback with Buddah Records. (Noone rejoined the others briefly in 1973 for some British Invasion Revival shows.)

Initially Noone returned to acting. In 1970, he met David Bowie, who supplied him with his first British solo hit, "Oh You Pretty Things," and played piano on the sessions. Their subsequent collaborations failed however, as did Noone's other early-Seventies releases for Rak Records. Mid-decade, Noone spent three years hosting a mainstream British television series but quit to avoid being pigeonholed as a cabaret performer. He moved to the south of France and cut a few singles that were moderate hits there and in Belgium.

By the late Seventies, Noone had taken up part-time residence in Los Angeles, where the thriving club scene induced him to try a comeback with a contemporary rock band, the Tremblers (including guitarist and keyboardist Gregg Inhofer, drummer Robert Williams, guitarist Geo. Conner and bassist Mark Browne), who had variously played with the Pop, Tonio K., Barbra Streisand and Olivia Newton-John. Their debut album in 1980, *Twice Nightly*, was the first of his records Noone had ever produced. In 1982, he released an LP entitled *One of the Glory Boys* and appeared as Frederic in the Broadway production of *The Pirates of Penzance*.

JOHN HIATT
Born 1952, Indianapolis, Indiana
1974—*Hangin' Around the Observatory* (Epic) **1975**— *Overcoats* **1979**—*Slug Line* (MCA) **1980**—*Two Bit Monsters* **1982**—*All of a Sudden* (Geffen).

Singer/songwriter John Hiatt has had his songs covered by Rick Nelson, Dave Edmunds, the Searchers, Three Dog Night and others, although his solo career has been only moderately successful.

Hiatt played in various garage bands before leaving his hometown at age 18 in 1970. He was discovered in Nashville by an Epic talent scout and made two quirky albums for the label—*Hangin' Around the Observatory* and *Overcoats*—that drew critical kudos but no sales.

Without a record contract, Hiatt spent the next few years touring folk clubs as a solo act, until signing with MCA. He released two more records, the more new-wavish *Slug Line* and *Two Bit Monsters,* and received more critical nods, but despite some touring, they failed in the marketplace. Hiatt played and sang on sessions and toured with Ry Cooder, and he appears with Cooder (singing two songs) on the soundtrack to 1982's *The Border.*

DAN HICKS AND HIS HOT LICKS

Formed 1968, San Francisco
Original lineup: Dan Hicks (b. Dec. 9, 1941, Little Rock, Ark.), gtr., voc., harmonica, drums; David LaFlamme, violin; Bill Douglas, bass; Mitzy Douglas, voc.; Patti Urban, voc.

Shortly after formation, Hicks put together a new lineup: Sherry Snow, voc.; Tina Natural (b. Christina Gancher, 1945), voc., celeste, percussion; Jimmie Bassoon, bass; Jon Weber (b. 1947), gtr.; Gary Pozzi, violin.
1969—(− Bassoon; + Jaime Leopold [b. 1947, Portland, Ore.], fiddle, bass; − Pozzi; + Sid Page [b. 1947, Portland, Ore.], violin, mandolin) *Original Recordings* (Epic) (− Snow; − Gancher; − Weber; +Nicole Dukes, voc.; + Naomi Eisenberg [b. Brooklyn], voc., violin; + Maryanne Price [b. Providence, R.I.], voc., cornet; + Bob Scott [b. Ozarks], drums; − Dukes; − Eisenberg) **1971**—*Where's the Money* (Blue Thumb) (+ John Girton [b. Burbank, Calif.], gtr.) **1972**—*Strikin' It Rich* **1973**—*Last Train to Hicksville . . . the home of happy feet* **1978**—*It Happened One Bite* (Warner Bros.).

Dan Hicks writes wry, jazzy, ironic pseudo-nostalgia songs, and in the late Sixties and early Seventies he performed them with the Hot Licks, a group modeled on Django Reinhardt's quintet, and a pair of female vocalists, the Lickettes.

Hicks grew up in Santa Rosa, California, started playing drums at age 11 and switched to the guitar at age 20. In his teens, he played in various local folk and jazz bands, and while attending San Francisco State College he continued to drum on the side. Eventually he landed in the original Charlatans, a self-confessed amateur band, with whom he played from 1965 to 1968. During his last six months with the Charlatans, he began playing with his own group, including violinist David LaFlamme, who later formed It's a Beautiful Day.

By early 1968, Hicks's drummerless group, the Hot Licks, were signed to Epic; their only album for the label, *Original Recordings,* flopped. After a series of personnel changes, the group was signed to Blue Thumb in 1971. Their three albums for that label—*Where's the Money* (recorded live at L.A.'s Troubadour), *Strikin' It Rich* and *Last Train to Hicksville* (their first with a drummer)—

blended the Andrews Sisters, Western swing, ragtime and jazz.

Hicks became known for compositions like "How Can I Miss You (When You Won't Go Away)" and "Walkin' One and Only," which was covered by Maria Muldaur. Violinist Sid Page (who later played with Sly and the Family Stone) departed after *Last Train,* and by 1974 the Hot Licks were no more.

Following the group's breakup, Hicks has been sporadically active in the Bay Area as a solo artist, sometimes billed as Lonesome Dan Hicks. In early 1978, he reemerged with *It Happened One Bite.*

JESSIE HILL

Born December 9, 1932, New Orleans
N.A.—*Naturally* (Blue Thumb).

New Orleans pianist Jessie Hill's moment of national glory came with "Ooh Poo Pah Doo—Parts I & II" (#28, 1960, Minit), the first national hit produced by Allen Toussaint. Hill wrote the song, which Toussaint orchestrated with a call-and-response format recalling Ray Charles' "What'd I Say." But Hill was unable to come up with a follow-up hit while recording for Minit through 1963. The closest he came was "Whip It on Me" (#91, 1960). He then moved to Los Angeles and fell in with other New Orleans expatriates like Dr. John (who covered Hill's "Qualify" on one of his solo albums). He recorded sporadically throughout the decade, culminating in a 1970 album for Blue Thumb. In the early Seventies, Hill returned to New Orleans, where he continues to write and perform in nightclubs.

HOLLAND-DOZIER-HOLLAND

Brian Holland (born February 15, 1941, Detroit); Lamont Dozier (born June 16, 1941, Detroit); Eddie Holland (born October 30, 1939, Detroit).

The songwriting and production team of Holland-Dozier-Holland was responsible for many of Motown's (see also: Berry Gordy, Jr.) hits during the mid-Sixties. Between 1963 and 1966 alone, the three were responsible for 28 Top Ten hits.

Lamont Dozier sang in a church choir as a youth and started his recording career at age 15 in a short-lived local group called the Romeos. In 1958, a friend introduced him to Berry Gordy, Jr., who was laying the groundwork for Motown. Gordy signed Dozier as a solo artist to his Anna and Melody labels, and Dozier recorded, to no avail, as Lamont Anthony. He began to concentrate on his songwriting and in 1961 was teamed with Brian Holland, who'd already worked on the Marvelettes' "Please Mr. Postman."

Brian's brother Eddie was enjoying some success as a solo singer for the label, notably "Jamie" (#30, 1962), in a style similar to Jackie Wilson's (for whom he'd sung on demos). Subsequent releases—"Just Ain't Enough Love" (#54, 1964), "Candy to Me" (#58, 1964), "Leaving Here" (#76, 1964)—failed, but by that time Eddie had joined his brother and Dozier.

They worked with virtually every Motown artist, including the Supremes, the Temptations, the Four Tops, Marvin Gaye, Martha and the Vandellas, the Isley Brothers and others during the mid-Sixties peak years. The trio was responsible for "Heat Wave," "Stop! In the Name of Love," "Where Did Our Love Go," "Baby Love," "I Hear a Symphony," "Baby, I Need Your Loving," "It's the Same Old Song," "I Can't Help Myself," "You Keep Me Hangin' On" and "Reach Out, I'll Be There."

By 1968, after frequent royalty battles with Gordy, the trio left Motown and formed their own label, Invictus/Hot Wax. While their operations were slowed by legal problems with Motown, by the early Seventies they had managed hits by the Chairmen of the Board, Freda Payne and Honey Cone, whose "Want Ads" became the company's first #1 in 1971. Both Dozier and Brian Holland reactivated their recording careers in the early part of the decade.

Holland had his greatest solo success with "Don't Leave Me Starving for Your Love (Part 1)" (#52, 1973). Dozier signed with ABC (having already released one solo album on Invictus), for whom he released two solo albums before joining Warner Bros. in 1975, then Columbia; he continues to record and occasionally plays live dates. Like the others, Dozier remains sporadically active as an independent producer (including Aretha Franklin's *Sweet Passion*).

THE HOLLIES
Formed 1962, Manchester, England
Graham Nash (b. Feb. 2, 1942, Blackpool, Eng.), gtr., voc.; Allan Clarke (b. April 15, 1942, Salford, Eng.), voc.; Anthony Hicks (b. Dec. 16, 1943, Nelson, Eng.), gtr.; Donald Rathbone (b. Eng.), drums; Eric Haydock (b. Eng.), bass.
1963—(− Rathbone; + Robert Elliott [b. Dec. 8, 1943, Burnley, Eng.], drums) 1965—*Here I Go* (Imperial) *Hear Here; The Hollies* 1966—(− Haydock; + Bernard Calvert [b. Sep. 16, 1943, Burnley, Eng.], bass) *Bus Stop* 1967—*Stop, Stop, Stop; Evolution* (Epic) 1968—*Hollies Greatest* (− Nash; + Terry Sylvester [b. Jan. 8, 1945, Liverpool], gtr., voc.)
1969—*Words and Music by Bob Dylan* 1970—*He Ain't Heavy, He's My Brother* 1971—(− Clarke; + Mikael Rikfors [b. Sweden], voc.) 1972—*Distant Light; Romany* 1974—(− Rickfors; + Clarke) *Hollies* 1975—*Another Night; History of the Hollies* 1976— *Write On* (Polydor) *Russian Roulette* 1977—*The Hollies/Clarke, Hicks, Sylvester, Calvert, Elliot* (Epic) (− Clarke) 1978—*A Crazy Steal* 1979—*Double Seven O Four* 1980—*Buddy Holly* 1983—(Nash,

The Hollies: Bernie Calvert, Graham Nash, Tony Hicks, Allan Clarke, Bobby Elliott

Elliott, Hicks, Clarke regroup) *What Goes Around . . .* (Atlantic).

After the Beatles, the Hollies were the most consistently successful singles band in Britain, and their string of hits extended into the Seventies.

The group was formed by childhood friends Allan Clarke and Graham Nash, who had worked together as the Two Teens, Ricky and Dane, and the Guytones. They became the Deltas with the addition of Rathbone and Haydock, then the Hollies after Tony Hicks joined them. Sources disagree as to whether the group was named after the plant or Buddy Holly. By late 1963, they had British Top Twenty hits with covers of the Coasters' "Searchin'" and Maurice Williams and the Zodiacs' "Stay." Around this time, they wrote a book, *How to Run a Beat Group*.

With Clarke on lead vocals, and Nash leading the harmonies, the Hollies had a string of U.K. hits that included "Just One Look," "Here I Go Again," "We're Through" (1964), "Yes I Will," "I'm Alive" (their first British #1) and "Look through Any Window" (1965). The latter was one of the several singles that entered the U.S. charts, but it wasn't until "Bus Stop" (#5) in 1966 that the group cracked the U.S. Top Ten. Over the next several months, their U.S. hits included "Stop Stop Stop" (#7, 1966), "Carrie-Anne" (#9, 1967), "On a Carousel" (#11, 1967) and "Pay You Back with Interest" (#28, 1967).

In the late Sixties, the Hollies shifted to more experimental rock. The results—*For Certain Because, Evolution* and *Butterfly*—didn't establish them as an album group. Nash, one of the group's main writers, quit in late 1968. He was reportedly upset that the band was recording an entire LP of Dylan covers (*Words and Music by Bob Dylan*) and yet had refused to record several of his own songs, including "Marrakesh Express," a hit for his next band, Crosby, Stills and Nash.

The Hollies advertised in British trade papers for Nash's replacement and found Terry Sylvester, who stayed with the group until 1981. In 1970, "He Ain't Heavy, He's My Brother" hit #7, but within a year, Clarke was forced out because of personality clashes with other band members. This left Hicks the only original member. Clarke briefly pursued a solo career (*My Real Name Is 'Arold* and *Headroom*), only to rejoin the group in 1973 after his replacement, Swedish vocalist Mikael Rikfors, was fired because his thickly accented lead vocals sounded strange onstage.

The Hollies had their biggest U.S. hit with "Long Cool Woman (in a Black Dress)" and hit a second peak with "The Air That I Breathe" (#6, 1974). In 1977, Clarke again quit the band and released another solo LP (*I Wasn't Born Yesterday*), yet returned to the group for *A Crazy Steal*. Epic dropped the Hollies in 1979. Their last group effort was a British LP entitled *Buddy Holly*, released in conjunction with Paul McCartney's Buddy Holly Week. In 1982, Nash, Clarke, Elliott and Hicks re-formed to record.

BUDDY HOLLY AND THE CRICKETS
Born Charles Hardin Holley, September 7, 1938, Lubbock, Texas; died February 3, 1959, near Clear Lake, Iowa
Crickets: (Note: The Crickets were Buddy Holly's backup group until late 1958, when they went their separate ways. See text. The Crickets remained active following Holly's death as well.)
Formed circa 1955, Lubbock, Texas
Sonny Curtis (b. May 9, 1937, Meadow, Tex.), gtr.; Don Guess, bass; Jerry Allison (b. Aug. 31, 1939, Hillsboro, Tex.), drums.
The Crickets also included, at various times: Niki Sullivan, gtr.; Larry Welborn, bass; Joe Mauldin, bass; Tommy Allsup, gtr.; Glen Hardin (b. Apr. 18, 1939, Wellington, Tex.) piano; Jerry Naylor (b. Mar. 6, 1939, Stephenville, Tex.); Waylon Jennings (b. 1937, Littlefield, Tex.), gtr.
1957—*Chirpin' Crickets* (Brunswick) (reissued as *Buddy Holly and the Crickets* by Coral, 1962) 1963—*Reminiscing* (Coral) 1964—*Showcase* 1966—*Best of*

1978—*The Buddy Holly Story* (soundtrack) (Epic)
1981—*The Complete Buddy Holly* (MCA) 1982—*For the First Time . . . Anywhere.*

Buddy Holly was a rock pioneer. He wrote his own material; used the recording studio for double-tracking and other advanced techniques; popularized the two guitars, bass and drums lineup; and recorded a catalogue of songs that continue to be covered: "Not Fade Away," "Rave On," "That'll Be the Day" and others. His playful, mock-ingenuous singing, with slides between falsetto and regular voice and a trademark "hiccup," has been a major influence on Bob Dylan, Paul McCartney and numerous imitators. When he died in an airplane crash at 21, he had been recording rock & roll for less than two years.

Holly learned to play the piano, fiddle and guitar at an early age. He was five when he won five dollars for singing "Down the River of Memories" at a local talent show.

In the early Fifties, he formed the country-oriented Western and Bop Band with high school friends Bob Montgomery and Larry Welborn. Between late 1953 and 1955, they performed on local radio station KDAV and recorded demos and garage tapes, several of which were posthumously released as *Holly in the Hills*. By 1956 (after Holly had dropped the *e* from his last name), the group's reputation on the Southwestern country circuit led to a contract to cut country singles in Nashville for Decca (bassist Don Guess was now in the backup band, by then called the Three Tunes).

Buddy Holly

Holly's first release was "Blue Days, Black Nights" b/w "Love Me," and, like subsequent pure country releases ("Modern Don Juan," "Midnight Shift" and "Girl On My Mind"), it went unnoticed. One of his last recordings for the label (which Decca refused to release) was "That'll Be the Day," a song that in a later rock version became one of Holly's first hits. During this period, Holly began writing prolifically. Typical of his romantic fare was a song that began as "Cindy Lou" but was changed to "Peggy Sue" at Cricket Jerry Allison's suggestion ("Peggy Sue" was the future Mrs. Allison; they've since divorced), and eventually became one of Holly's biggest hits.

Following the failed sessions with Decca, Holly and his friends returned to Lubbock. In 1956–57, Holly and drummer Allison played as a duo at the Lubbock Youth Center and shared bills with well-known stars as they passed through the area. Once they opened for a young Elvis Presley (Holly later said, "We owe it all to Elvis"), who influenced Holly's move into rock & roll.

On February 25, 1957, Holly and the newly named Crickets drove ninety miles west to producer Norman Petty's studio in Clovis, New Mexico, to cut a demo. Their rocking version of "That'll Be the Day" attracted a contract from the New York–based Coral/Brunswick label, and it rose to #3 by the end of 1957. As with many of Holly's early hits, producer Petty picked up a cowriter's credit. The song's success prompted the Crickets' first national tour in late 1957. Several promoters (including those at the Apollo Theater in New York, where Holly and his group became one of the first white acts to appear) were surprised that the group was white.

Under a contractual arrangement worked out by Petty (who quickly became Holly's manager), some discs were credited to the Crickets, while some releases bore only Holly's name. His first hit under the latter arrangement was "Peggy Sue" (#3, 1957), which also became one of several big hits in England, where he toured to much acclaim in 1958. "Oh, Boy!" which was released late in 1957 by the Crickets hit #10. By 1958, Holly had reached the charts with "Maybe Baby" (#17), "Think It Over" (#27), "Early in the Morning" (#32), "Rave On" (#37) and "Fool's Paradise" (#58).

In October 1958, Holly left Petty and the Crickets (who continued on their own), moved to Greenwich Village and married Puerto Rico–born Maria Elena Santiago after having proposed to her on their first date. His split from Petty led to legal problems, which tied up his finances and prompted Holly to reluctantly join the Winter Dance Party Tour of the Midwest in early 1959. He also did some recording in New York; many of the tapes were later overdubbed and released posthumously. During that last tour, Holly was supported by ex-Cricket guitarist Tommy Allsup and future country superstar Waylon Jennings (whose first record, "Jolé Blon," was produced by Holly).

Tired of riding the bus, and in order to get his laundry done, Holly, along with a couple of the tour's other featured performers, the Big Bopper and Ritchie Valens, chartered a private plane after their Clear Lake, Iowa, show to take them to Moorhead, Minnesota. Piloted by Roger Peterson, the small Beechcraft Bonanza took off from the Mason City, Iowa, airport at about 2 A.M. on February 3, 1959, and crashed a few minutes later, killing all on board.

Holly's death was marked by the release of "It Doesn't Matter Anymore" (#13, 1959), which topped the English charts for six consecutive weeks. In his wake, Holly left behind enough old demos and uncompleted recordings to fill several posthumous collections, of which the most extensive is *The Complete Buddy Holly Story*, a nine-record set. A 1978 feature film, *The Buddy Holly Story,* revived interest in Holly's life and career.

The Crickets continued on as a group into the Sixties, with a variety of personnel revolving around Allison, Curtis and Glen D. Hardin. With this lineup, they had some minor U.S. success but, like Holly, were most popular in England, where they had three early-Sixties hits—"Love's Made a Fool of You," "Don't Ever Change" and "My Little Girl"—the latter of which was included in the British film *Just for Fun.* The Crickets later costarred with Lesley Gore in *The Girls on the Beach.* As the Sixties progressed, the Crickets' activities became more sporadic and included a Holly tribute album recorded with Bobby Vee.

In 1973, Hardin left to join Elvis Presley's band (he would later join Emmylou Harris' Hot Band). Around this time, the Crickets' last album was recorded with a lineup that included Allison, Curtis and English musicians Rick Grech and Albert Lee. Curtis and Mauldin regrouped the original Crickets in 1977 to perform in England for Buddy Holly Week (sponsored by Paul McCartney, who had just purchased the entire Holly song catalogue).

Some of the Crickets have had solo careers. In 1958, Allison released "Real Wild Child" for Coral Records (with Holly on lead guitar) under the nom de disc of Ivan. Curtis, who wrote Holly's "Rock Around with Ollie Vee," went on to write "I Fought the Law" (covered by the Bobby Fuller Four and the Clash), "Walk Right Back" (for the Everly Brothers, for whom Curtis played lead guitar off and on throughout the Sixties) and the theme song of "The Mary Tyler Moore Show." He has made solo albums since 1958 for A&M, Mercury, Coral, Liberty, Imperial and other labels. By the early Eighties, he was still active with Elektra/Asylum, for whom he released the single "The Real Buddy Holly Story" as a response to the film. Curtis maintained that the film's facts were not correct.

EDDIE HOLMAN
Born 1946, Norfolk, Virginia

R&B/soul vocalist Eddie Holman's intermittently successful career has spanned nearly two decades. He attended the Victoria School of Music and Art in New York and studied music at Cheyney State College in Pennsylvania. His debut single was the regionally successful "Crossroads" in 1963, and he first cracked the national pop charts with "This Can't Be True" (#57) in 1966.

As the Sixties closed, Holman left Cameo for Bell Records before signing with ABC in 1969. His remake of Ruby and the Romantics "Hey There Lonely Boy," retitled "Hey There Lonely Girl," hit #2 in 1970. Two lesser hits—"Don't Stop Now" (#48, 1970) and "Since I Don't Have You" (#95, 1970)—followed, but he did not reappear on the charts again until "This Will Be a Night to Remember" charted in 1977 (#90).

HOLY MODAL ROUNDERS
Formed 1963
Peter Stampfel (b. Oct. 29, 1938, Milwaukee), banjo, fiddle, voc.; Steve Weber (b. June 22, 1942, Philadelphia), gtr., voc.
1967—*Indian War Whoop* (ESP)   **1968**—*Holy Modal Rounders, Volume 1* (Prestige)   *Holy Modal Rounders, Volume 2*   **1969**—*Moray Eels Eat the Holy Modal Rounders* (Elektra)   *Good Taste Is Timeless* (Metromedia)   **1972**—*Stampfel and Weber* (Fantasy)   **1976**—*Alleged in Their Own Time* (Rounder)   **1979**—*Last Round* (Adelphi)   **1981**—*Goin' Nowhere Fast* (Rounder).

The Holy Modal Rounders, a loose group centering on Peter Stampfel and Steve Weber, are gonzo traditionalists who mix old folk and bluegrass tunes with their own bouncy, absurdist free associations. The Rounders' closest brush with commercial success came when their "If You Wanna Be a Bird" appeared on the *Easy Rider* soundtrack, but such songs as "Boobs a Lot" and "My Mind Capsized" kept folk rock from taking itself too seriously.

Stampfel was previously with folk groups like MacGrundy's Old Timey Wool Thumpers. He and Weber met in 1963 on the East Coast. They recorded albums for Prestige and then began working with the Fugs and contributed to the Fugs' first record on the Broadside label.

In 1965, the groups went their separate ways; Stampfel formed the Moray Eels, and Weber revived the Rounders moniker and added other musicians for the first time (including playwright Sam Shepard, who played drums and wrote songs) for *Indian War Whoop* on ESP. They also scored Shepard's play *Operation Sidewinder*. Around the same time, the group's free-flowing lineup also briefly included Jeff "Skunk" Baxter, later with Steely Dan and the Doobie Brothers.

In the early Seventies, their *Good Taste Is Timeless*, featuring "Boobs a Lot," got some FM airplay. Shortly thereafter, Fantasy Records released *Stampfel and Weber*, followed in 1976 by a reunion LP, *Alleged in Their Own Time*, on Rounder Records (named in their honor). In

late 1981, still folk-cult favorites, Stampfel and Weber did some East Coast dates as a duo to support *Goin' Nowhere Fast*, and Stampfel continued to appear around New York City with his group, the Bottle Caps.

THE HONEYCOMBS
Formed 1963, London
Martin Murray (b. Oct. 7, 1941, London), gtr.; Alan Ward (b. Dec. 12, 1945, Nottingham, Eng.), gtr., piano, organ; Denis Dalziel (b. Oct. 10, 1943, London), piano, gtr., harmonica, jew's harp, voc.; John Lantree (b. Aug. 20, 1940, Newbury, Eng.), bass; Ann "Honey" Lantree (b. Aug. 28, 1943, Hayes, Eng.), drums.
N.A.—*Here Are the Honeycombs* (Vee Jay).

A British Invasion band, the Honeycombs were one of the first rock groups to have a female drummer. The band was formed in 1963 by ex-skiffle guitarist Martin Murray and began playing London pubs. In the wake of the Beatles' international success, their 1964 debut, "Have I the Right?," was leased to Vee Jay/Interphon in the U.S. and hit the Top Five. It was #1 for two weeks in Britain, and its international combined sales topped one million.

The group quickly became media staples in the U.K. and also toured France, Australia and New Zealand. They had only one more chart entry in the U.S.—"I Can't Stop" (#48, 1965)—although they continued to have success in England until 1966, when producer Joe Meek died.

HONEY CONE
Formed 1969, Los Angeles
Carolyn Willis (b. 1946, Los Angeles), voc.; Edna Wright (b. 1944, Los Angeles), voc.; Shellie Clark (b. 1943, Brooklyn), voc.

The Honey Cone was a black female vocal group composed of veteran R&B singers whose biggest hit was "Want Ads" (#1, 1971).

The best-known member of the original group was Carolyn Willis, formerly of the Girlfriends. Edna Wright was a Raelette in several Ray Charles roadshows, a backup vocalist on hits by the Righteous Brothers and Johnny Rivers and a solo performer with a minor 1964 hit, "A Touch of Venus." Clark had worked as an Ikette with Ike and Tina Turner and toured with Little Richard and Dusty Springfield.

The trio first sang together in 1969 as backup vocalists for Burt Bacharach on an Andy Williams TV special. Eddie Holland of Motown's Holland-Dozier-Holland signed them to the new Hot Wax label and named them. They had two minor hits that year ("While You're Out Looking for Sugar" and "Girls It Ain't Easy") before perfecting an upbeat pop-soul style similar to that of Martha and the Vandellas. In 1971, "Want Ads" (cowritten by General Johnson, a member of the Showmen and then the Chairmen of the Board), went gold and stayed at the #1 spot for two weeks.

Honey Cone followed up with two more tunes cowritten by Johnson—"Stick Up" (#11, 1971) and "One Monkey Don't Stop No Show, Part 1" (#15, 1971). In 1972, they had their last Hot 100 entries with "The Day I Found Myself" (#23) and "Sittin' on a Time Bomb (Waitin' for the Hurt to Come)" (#96). By 1973, the group had disbanded and returned to independent studio work. A few years later, Carolyn Willis was prominently featured on Seals and Crofts' "Get Closer."

JOHN LEE HOOKER

Born August 22, 1917, Clarksdale, Mississippi
1962—*Folklore of John L. Hooker* (Vee Jay) **1966**—*It Serves You Right* (Impulse) **1968**—*Urban Blues* (Stateside) **1970**—*No Friend Around* (Red Lightnin') **1971**—*Coast to Coast* (United Artists) *Endless Boogie* **1972**—*Boogie Chillun* (Fantasy) *Never Get Out of These Blues Alive* **1974**—*Best of* (Crescendo) *Don't Turn Me from Your Door* (Atco) **1975**—*John Lee Hooker* (New World) **1976**—*Blues before Sunrise* (Bulldog) **1978**—*Live* (Lynarz) *The Cream* (Tomato) **1980**—*This Is Hip* (Charly) **1981**—*Hooker Alone, Volume 1* (Labor) **1982**—*Hooker Alone, Volume 2*.

Blues musician John Lee Hooker helped define the post–World War II electric blues with his one-chord boogie compositions and his rhythmic electric guitar work, although his deep voice is inimitable. Hooker was one of the links between the blues and rock & roll.

Hooker was one of eleven children in a family. He sang at church in Clarksdale, and his first musical instrument was an inner tube stretched across a barn door. In his adolescence he was taught some rudimentary guitar technique by his stepfather, William Moore, with whom Hooker often performed at local fish fries, dances and other social occasions in the late Twenties; another early influence was Blind Lemon Jefferson. In 1931, he went to Memphis, where he worked odd jobs on Beale Street, moonlighting in blues clubs. He moved to Cincinnati in 1933 and sang with gospel groups like the Big Six, the Delta Big Four and the Fairfield Four.

Hooker moved in 1943 to Detroit, where his career eventually took root. He began recording in the late Forties. He was exclusively a singles artist for his first few very prolific years, and his first release was the eventually gold "Boogie Chillun" on the Modern label. "I'm in the Mood" sold a million in 1951, and the blues-record market was soon laden with Hooker material on myriad labels, often released under such pseudonyms as Birmingham Sam, John Lee Booker, Boogie Man, John Lee Cooker, Delta John, Johnny Lee, Texas Slim, Johnny Williams and others. His only pop chart entry was with "Boom Boom" (#60, 1962).

In 1959, he cut his first album for Riverside Records,

and made his debut performance at the Newport Folk Festival. British and American rockers, including the Animals, the Spencer Davis Group, the J. Geils Band, Canned Heat and George Thorogood covered his songs. He toured England and Europe widely in the early Sixties and recorded and toured extensively with Britain's Groundhogs in the mid-Sixties.

By 1970, Hooker was living in Oakland, California, when he wasn't touring, and that year he teamed up with Canned Heat for *Hooker 'n' Heat* (Liberty), which made inroads on the charts in the U.S. and abroad. He was joined by Charlie Musselwhite and Van Morrison in 1972 for *Never Get Out of These Blues Alive*, which was released at about the same time Fantasy put out some previously unreleased tapes and a Galaxy release (both from 1962) on the double LP *Boogie Chillun*. Hooker continued to tour in the Seventies and Eighties, often opening for rock acts like Canned Heat and Foghat. In 1980, he appeared in *The Blues Brothers* film, and in the early Eighties he recorded solo albums.

MARY HOPKIN

Born May 3, 1950, Pontardawe, South Wales
1969—*Postcard* (Apple) **1971**—*Earth Song* **1972**—*Those Were the Days* **1979**—*Welsh World of* (Decca) *Kidnapped*.

Welsh singer Mary Hopkin was briefly an international star in the late Sixties. She began singing at age four and was soon taking voice lessons and singing in the Congregational Tabernacle Choir. Hopkin studied music, art and English at the local grammar school and continued at Cardiff College of Music and Drama. While a student there, she earned extra money by singing in pubs. When she appeared on the BBC-TV variety show "Opportunity Knocks" in 1968, she was spotted by Twiggy, who told Paul McCartney about her. McCartney signed her to Apple and supervised her first sessions, which produced "Those Were the Days" (#2, 1968). The song had already been recorded by the Limeliters, who adapted it from a Russian folk song called "Darogoi Dlimmoya" (Dear for Me), first recorded in the Twenties.

Hopkin was 18 years old when her debut album, *Postcard,* was released. McCartney wrote and produced her second single, "Goodbye" (#13, 1969), which hit #2 on the British charts. She then moved on to work with producer Mickie Most. She enjoyed lesser hits in the early Seventies—including "Temma Harbour," "Que Sera, Sera (Whatever Will Be, Will Be)," "Think About Your Children" (1970) and "Knock Knock Who's There" (1972)—and toured a bit.

As an actress, in 1970 she costarred with Tommy Steele in a pantomime production of *Dick Whittington* at the London Palladium and in 1971 appeared with David Essex in *Cinderella* in Manchester. Around the same time, she married British record producer Tony Visconti and began raising a family. Through the mid-Seventies, her singing career was limited to occasional backup vocals (as Mary Visconti) for Ralph McTell, David Bowie and Thin Lizzy. In 1976, "If You Loved Me" hit the English charts. She starred in a Christmas production in 1980 of *Rock Nativity* at the Hexagon Theatre in Reading.

LIGHTNIN' HOPKINS

Born March 15, 1912, Centerville, Texas; died January 30, 1982, Houston

1965—*Down Home Blues* (Prestige) **1968**—*Texas Blues Man* (Arhoolie) **1970**—*Lightnin', Volume 1* (Poppy) **1972**—*Double Blues* (Fantasy) *Lonesome Lightnin'* (Carnival) **1976**—*All Them Blues* (DJM).

The most frequently recorded traditional blues artist in history (who, paradoxically, did the bulk of his performing as an impoverished street singer), Sam "Lightnin' " Hopkins was a country blues stylist whose career spanned more than three decades, even though he did not begin in earnest until he was nearing middle age. His solo style, with its irregular verses and its call-and-response between voice and guitar, has roots in the earliest blues.

Born in a small farming community, Hopkins lived virtually his entire life in the Houston area. He was one of six children (his sister and four brothers were also musicians), and at age eight he debuted on a guitarlike instrument fashioned from a cigar box and chicken wire. Subsequently his brother Joel "John Henry" Hopkins (later a well-known bluesman in his own right) taught him to play guitar. Hopkins dropped out of school to hobo through Texas, playing informally in the streets and jamming with folk legends like Blind Lemon Jefferson, whom he met in the summer of 1920. As the Thirties progressed, he supported himself primarily as a farmworker, while playing for tips in Texas bars and nightspots. More than once, Hopkins found himself working the Houston County Prison Farm's road gang. After drifting for several years, he settled in Houston's Third Ward ghetto after World War II and then rarely left.

In 1946, Hopkins and pianist Wilson "Thunder" Smith went to Los Angeles and cut some sides for the Aladdin label. While there, he gained his Lightnin' moniker. When little came of the Aladdin sessions, he returned to Houston and, backed only by his own guitar, cut "Short Haired Woman" b/w "Big Mama Jump" in 1947 for Gold Star Records. It sold 40,000 copies; and the followup, "Baby Please Don't Go," doubled that figure, beginning two years of local success.

Over the next few years Hopkins recorded prolifically for several companies based in Houston, Los Angeles and New York. He insisted upon being paid in cash for each studio take, thereby relinquishing his rights to his material (he rarely received royalties on his massive catalogue of work) and causing confusion in his recording legacy. (A complete Hopkins discography would include efforts for over twenty record companies.) His style and stance are represented on reissues and compilation/anthologies like Tradition's *Autobiography* and *Best*, Arhoolie's *Early Recordings*, Prestige's *Greatest Hits* and others compiled from his hundreds of sides. Among his many compositions were "December 7, 1941," "Don't Embarrass Me, Baby," "Ball of Twine," "I'm Gonna Meet My Baby Somewhere" and "Little Antoinette."

When Texas blues fell from national favor by the mid-Fifties, Hopkins' career nosedived. Reduced once again to Houston street singing (perennially working the Dowling Street area), he was saved by the later folk and blues revival and was rediscovered by musicologist and author Sam Charters (*The Country Blues*), who recorded him for Folkways in 1959. That same year, he played the University of California Folk Festival and in 1960 appeared at Carnegie Hall in a show featuring Joan Baez and Pete Seeger. In 1961, Hopkins toured with Clifton Chenier's band and continued to play regularly at Houston nightspots like Irene's and the Sputnik Bar. In the Sixties, he was also featured in two short documentary films by Les Blank and performed at folk festivals and in rock venues. (In the late Fifties he had recorded and toured in Europe, usually solo, occasionally with a backing ensemble.)

As the blues boom died down, Hopkins was slowed by an auto crackup in 1970 that put his neck in a protective brace and impeded his touring, although he continued his club work on and off through the Seventies. In the early Seventies, he recorded for the Denver-based Tumbleweed Records. Meanwhile, tapes continued to surface on a variety of labels, and in 1972 he contributed to the soundtrack of the feature film *Sounder*. He remained sporadically active for the rest of the decade, capping his lengthy career with an appearance at Carnegie Hall in spring 1979. He did little recording in his final years but could be seen prowling the Houston streets in his black Cadillac Coupe de Ville. In the summer of 1981, he underwent surgery for cancer of the esophagus, which later proved terminal.

NICKY HOPKINS

Born February 24, 1944, London

1966—*Revolutionary Piano* (Columbia, U.K.) **1973**—*The Tin Man Was a Dreamer* **1975**—*No More Changes* (Mercury).

Studio keyboardist Nicky Hopkins has been in and out of groups in Britain and the U.S. since the Sixties; Ray Davies wrote the Kinks' "Session Man" in his honor.

Hopkins began playing the piano at age three and studied at the Royal Academy of Music from 1956 to 1960. He joined Screamin' Lord Sutch's Savages in 1960 and two years later moved to the Cyril Davies R&B All-Stars;

the two groups included many musicians who would make their names in the British Invasion and its aftermath. Hopkins left Davies in May 1963 because of illness and began work as a session keyboardist after he emerged from the hospital nineteen months later. He recorded with the Rolling Stones, the Beatles, the Who, the Small Faces, the Kinks and other bands, and in 1968 he joined the Jeff Beck Group along with Rod Stewart and Ron Wood.

In the late Sixties, he also recorded with his own short-lived group, Sweet Thursday, which included future Cat Stevens guitarist Alun Davies and Jon Mark of Mark-Almond. But after nine months in the Jeff Beck Group, Hopkins joined the Quicksilver Messenger Service in San Francisco and recorded with them on *Shady Grove*. He also recorded with Steve Miller and the Jefferson Airplane and appeared with the Airplane at the Woodstock Festival.

In the Seventies, Hopkins returned to work as a sideman, touring with the Rolling Stones in 1972 and sporadically with the Jerry Garcia Band, and backing Graham Parker and others on records. His attempt at a solo career in the mid-Seventies was widely ignored. In 1979 he joined the group Night, which had a hit single in 1979, "Hot Summer Nights."

JOHNNY HORTON
Born April 30, 1927, Tyler, Texas, or November 30, 1929, Los Angeles; died November 5, 1960, Milano, Texas
1959—*The Spectacular Johnny Horton* (Columbia)
1960—*Johnny Horton Makes History; Johnny Horton's Greatest Hits* **1971**—*The World of Johnny Horton.*

Johnny Horton was one of the first country & western singers to cross over onto the pop charts. His "The Battle of New Orleans" was a #1 hit in 1959.

Sources disagree as to where and when Horton was born. His mother taught him to play guitar at an early age, and he later attended Seattle University, where he majored in petroleum engineering and dabbled in songwriting. After traveling around Alaska and Louisiana, he started performing in clubs and on Pasadena's radio station KXLA, billed as the Singing Fisherman.

In 1951, Horton moved to Shreveport, Louisiana, where for eight years he was a star attraction on the "Louisiana Hayride" radio show. He began recording in 1951 for the Cormac and Abbott labels, moved to Mercury in 1952, but had little success until his move to Columbia.

Grammy Awards

Emmylou Harris
1976 Best Country Vocal Performance, Female:
Elite Hotel
1979 Best Country Vocal Performance, Female:
Blue Kentucky Girl
1980 Best Country Performance by a Duo or Group with Vocal:
"That Lovin' You Feelin' Again" (with Roy Orbison)

George Harrison (see also: The Beatles)
1970 Best Original Score Written for a Motion Picture or TV Special:
Let It Be
1972 Album of the Year:
The Concert for Bangla Desh

John Hartford
1967 Best Folk Performance; Best Country & Western Song:
"Gentle on My Mind"

1976 Best Ethnic or Traditional Recording:
Mark Twang

Donny Hathaway
1972 Best Pop Vocal Performance by a Duo, Group or Chorus:
"Where Is the Love" (with Roberta Flack)

Edwin Hawkins Singers
1969 Best Soul Gospel:
"Oh Happy Day"
1970 Best Soul Gospel Performance:
"Every Man Wants to Be Free"
1977 Best Soul Gospel Performance, Contemporary:
Wonderful!

Isaac Hayes
1971 Best Instrumental Arrangement:
"Theme from *Shaft*"

Best Original Score Written for a Motion Picture:
Shaft
1972 Best Pop Instrumental Performance by an Arranger, Composer, Orchestra and/or Choral Leader:
Black Moses

Jennifer Holliday
1982 Best R&B Vocal Performance, Female:
"And I Am Telling You I'm Not Going"

Johnny Horton
1959 Best Country & Western Performance:
"The Battle of New Orleans"

Thelma Houston
1977 Best R&B Vocal Performance, Female:
"Don't Leave Me This Way"

There his version of Jimmie Driftwood's "Battle of New Orleans" hit in 1959; it was also a hit for Lonnie Donegan in England (#2, 1959). Horton's subsequent hits included "Johnny Reb" (#54, 1959), "Sink the Bismarck" (#3, 1960) and "North to Alaska" (#4, 1960). Around 1960, Horton, an avid believer in the occult, became convinced that his death would soon occur. He rescheduled engagements frequently, but perhaps not often enough, for while returning home from a performance at the Skyline in Austin he was killed in a car accident. By strange coincidence, the Skyline was the last place Hank Williams had played before his death, and Horton's widow, Billy Joe, had been married to Hank Williams as well.

HOT CHOCOLATE
Formed 1970, London
Errol Brown (b. Jamaica), voc.; Patrick Olive (b. Grenada), gtr., percussion, bass; Larry Ferguson (b. Nassau), kybds.; Harvey Hinsley (b. Mitcham, Eng.), gtr.; Ian King, drums; Tony Wilson (b. Trinidad), bass, voc.
1973—(− King; + Tony Connor [b. Romford, Eng.], drums) 1974—Cicero Park (Big Tree) 1975—Hot Chocolate (− Wilson) 1976—Man to Man 1977—10 Greatest Hits 1978—Every 1's a Winner (Infinity) 1979—Going Through the Motions 1983—Mystery (EMI-America).

This Caribbean British interracial soul band had Seventies hits with social-comment dance tunes. Their biggest one in America was "You Sexy Thing" (#3, 1976), and their "Brother Louie" (a Top Ten hit for them in England in 1973) became a #1 hit for Stories in America the same year. The London-based band got its first contract with the Beatles' Apple label, for whom it released a reggae-style version of John Lennon's "Give Peace a Chance" (1970). They then worked with producer Mickie Most of RAK Records in Britain. Concentrating on singles, they established themselves in the U.K. in the early Seventies with moderately successful releases like "Love Is Life" and "I Believe in Love." A single, "Emma" (#8, 1975), finally broke them stateside in early 1975, followed by "Disco Queen" (#28, 1975) and "You Sexy Thing."

Errol Brown and Tony Wilson wrote most of Hot Chocolate's songs, and in the early Seventies their compositions were covered by Mary Hopkin, Peter Noone (Herman's Hermits), April Wine and Suzi Quatro. But in 1975, Wilson left the group for a solo career (his solo debut, I Like Your Style, came out in 1976). Hot Chocolate persevered with the mid-1976 Man to Man, which expanded their considerable following in Europe. They continued to enjoy moderate U.S. singles success with "Don't Stop It Now" (#42, 1976) and "So You Win Again" (#31, 1977); and in early 1979 they cracked the U.S. Top Ten again with "Every 1's a Winner" (#6).

HOT TUNA
Officially split from Jefferson Airplane, 1972
Jorma Kaukonen (b. Dec. 23, 1940, Washington, D.C.), gtr.; Jack Casady (b. Apr. 13, 1944, Washington, D.C.), bass; Will Scarlett, harmonica.
1970—Hot Tuna (RCA) 1971—First Pull Up—Then Down (+ Papa John Creach [b. May 28, 1917, Beaver Falls, Penn.], elec. violin; + Sammy Piazza, drums) 1972—Burgers (Grunt) 1973—(− Papa John Creach) 1974—Phosphorescent Rat (− Piazza; + Bob Steeler, drums) 1975—America's Choice; Yellow Fever 1976—Hoppkorv 1977—Double Dose 1979—Final Vinyl.

Jack Casady and Jorma Kaukonen were original recording members of the Jefferson Airplane. They grew up together in the Chevy Chase section of northwestern Washington D.C. After high school, Kaukonen headed for the Philippines to join his relocated government-service parents and traveled in the Orient before moving to San Francisco and working as a folkie. He soon fell in with the Airplane and called his old friend Casady, then teaching guitar in Washington, D.C. The two stayed with the Airplane until 1972.

By then, they had already started Hot Tuna (they originally called the group Hot Shit, but RCA balked), which was intended to operate as a satellite. (Early on, other members of the Airplane played with Tuna, including vocalist Marty Balin and drummers Spencer Dryden and Joey Covington.) Their low-key debut was recorded live at San Francisco's New Orleans House with harmonica player Will Scarlett and Kaukonen on acoustic guitar. Their music eventually became loud and electric.

First Pull Up—Then Down marked the arrival of the middle-aged black electric violinist Papa John Creach. Born in Pennsylvania in the early part of the century, Creach was 18 when his family moved to Chicago, where he received some classical training and was briefly affiliated with the Illinois Symphony Orchestra. By the late Thirties, he had begun two decades of touring the cocktail lounge circuit. After settling in San Francisco in the Sixties, he became friends with drummer Joey Covington, who recommended that Tuna get in touch with Creach. Creach was with Hot Tuna from 1971 until 1973. He played concurrently with the Airplane and launched a solo career with his 1971 self-titled Grunt/RCA debut. By the time of 1972's Filthy, Creach had formed his own band, Zulu, with whom he continued after leaving Tuna.

Hot Tuna's first album as a completely autonomous entity was their fourth, Phosphorescent Rat. The group was a commercial oddity; despite the fact that its mid-Seventies releases weren't big sellers, it insisted on playing concerts of at least two hours, which necessitated headliner status. In early 1978, the group disbanded, and the Tuna legacy was laid to rest with Double Dose (1977) and Final Vinyl (1979).

Casady continues to work on occasion with the new wave band SVT. Kaukonen had released his first solo album, the acoustic-oriented *Quah*, in 1974 with Casady producing; and following Tuna's breakup, he resumed his solo work with 1979's *Jorma*, the 21st album that he'd played on. He continues to tour as a solo act, and is known for his ever-changing hair color and affection for tattoos (his back is now completely covered).

SON HOUSE

Born Eddie House, March 21, 1902, Riverton, Mississippi
N.A.—*Delta Blues; Father of the Folk Blues* (Columbia).

Blues vocalist and guitarist Son House—often cited as a major influence by Muddy Waters, Robert Johnson, Bob Dylan and Bonnie Raitt—was one of the Mississippi Delta bluesmen who laid the groundwork for rock & roll in the years prior to World War II. House was one of the instigators of the regional tendency toward biting guitar sounds, dramatic vocal deliveries and full-tilt rhythm sections.

House was born on a plantation and by age 15 was delivering sermons in churches in Louisiana and Tennessee. In the early Twenties, he became pastor of a Baptist church in Lyon, Mississippi. In 1927, he taught himself to play guitar, and from then on he was a fixture on the Delta house-party circuit. Around 1928, he worked as part of Dr. McFadden's Medicine Show, but that career was quickly ended by a stint in the state prison at Parchman, Mississippi. Released in 1929, he moved to Lula, Mississippi, where he came under the tutelage of Delta legend Charley Patton. Through Patton, he recorded his first sides for the Paramount label in 1930. He did not record again for ten years, but he was an active performer, in partnership with Willie Brown, in the rural South. In the early Forties, musicologist Alan Lomax recorded House for the Library of Congress (in sessions later released commercially on Arhoolie). House moved to Rochester, New York, in 1943, and from then until 1964 he played only occasionally and only locally.

Spurred by the folk-blues revival of the early Sixties, House reemerged to much acclaim, attracting a large white audience for the first time in his life. He began recording in earnest, touring the campus and coffeehouse circuits, appearing at folk and blues festivals in the U.S., Canada and Europe, and performing at rock venues. House was the subject of a 1969 film short, and he appeared in several documentaries and on television.

While living in Buffalo, New York, he was largely inactive because of poor health in the early Seventies. He moved to Detroit in 1976 and continued a more limited concert schedule.

CISSY HOUSTON

Born circa 1932, Newark, New Jersey
1971—*Cissy Houston (Janus)* **1977**—*Cissy Houston* (Private Stock) **1979**—*Warning—Danger* (Columbia) **1980**—*Step Aside for a Lady.*

Gospel-soul singer Cissy Houston was a member of the Sixties soul group the Sweet Inspirations and has since pursued a sporadic solo career (abetted by occasional session work) as she splits her time between music and raising a family. She first sang with a family gospel group, the Drinkard Singers, which sometimes included her nieces Dionne and Dee Dee Warwick. The group was well known on the East Coast gospel circuit and recorded for RCA and Savoy.

After quitting the Drinkards, Houston established herself as a pop backup singer in New York. By 1967, she had become lead vocalist in the Sweet Inspirations. "Sweet Inspiration," a gospel-pop single, cracked the Top Twenty for the group in early 1968, and they established further credentials with their backup work for Aretha Franklin and Elvis Presley. Houston quit the group in 1970 and began recording solo with *Cissy Houston,* which included "Be My Baby" (#92, 1971). Houston was the first to record "Midnight Train to Georgia," which later became a hit single for Gladys Knight. She devoted the next several years primarily to raising her three children, so her second solo disc was not released until 1977.

She has continued to be a popular backup vocalist, notably on Chaka Khan's *Chaka* (1978), Aretha Franklin's *Aretha* and *Love All the Hurt Away* (1981) and Luther Vandross' *Never Too Much* (1981) and *Forever, For Always, For Love* (1982). She now hosts a weekly radio broadcast from the New Hope Baptist Church in Newark and plays occasional New York club dates featuring her daughter, Whitney.

THELMA HOUSTON

Born Mississippi
1977—*The Devil in Me* (Tamla) **1981**—*Superstar Series, Volume 20* (Motown) *Never Gonna Be Another One* (RCA) **1983**—*Thelma Houston* (MCA).

Thelma Houston's dramatic quavering gospel-based delivery made her one of disco's most distinctive voices.

She sang in churches as a youngster in Mississippi before her family moved to California. By the late Sixties, she was working Southern California clubs, thereby attracting the attention of the Fifth Dimension's manager, Marc Gordon, who landed her a contract with ABC/Dunhill. Over the next few years, she made pop records (now out of print) with such producers as Jimmy Webb and Joe Porter.

Houston's most successful effort from this period was "Save the Country" (#74, 1970). Her breakthrough came via Tamla/Motown and the Gamble-Huff disco hit "Don't Leave Me This Way" (#1, 1977). Other efforts for Motown included an appearance on the soundtrack of the Motown-produced film *The Bingo Long Traveling All Stars & Motor Kings* (1976). In 1977, she joined Jerry Butler for *Thelma and Jerry*. "Saturday Night, Sunday Morning" (#19 R&B, 1979) returned her to the charts as the disco era came to a close. Since then she's had modest success on RCA and MCA.

HOWLIN' WOLF

Born Chester Arthur Burnett, June 10, 1910, West Point, Mississippi; died, January 10, 1976, Hines, Illinois
1964—*Moaning in the Moonlight* (Chess) **1965**—*Poor Boy* **1966**—*Real Folk Blues* **1967**—*More Real Blues; Evil; Live and Cookin' at Alice's Revisited* **1972**—*The London Sessions* (Chess).

Delta bluesman Howlin' Wolf was one of the most influential musicians of the post–World War II era, and his electric Chicago blues—featuring his deep, lupine voice—shaped rock & roll.

He was raised on a cotton plantation in Mississippi and learned guitar as a child. In the Mississippi Delta area, he began studying with the rural masters, notably guitarist and vocalist Charley Patton, his biggest single influence, and harmonica player Sonny Boy Williamson (Rice Miller).

Wolf played his first gig in the South on January 15, 1928, and throughout the Thirties frequently performed on streetcorners. He formed his first band (whose personnel later included at various times harmonica players James Cotton and Little Junior Parker, pianist Ike Turner and guitarist Willie Johnson) in Memphis in the late Forties.

In the early Fifties, Turner, a freelance talent scout, had Wolf record for Sam Phillips' Memphis-based Sun Records. Those masters were then leased to Chess Records, and in 1957 one of them, "Moanin' at Midnight," became his first R&B hit. In 1952, Wolf moved to Chicago, where his music was well received. Some consider the recordings he made for Chess during the Fifties and Sixties his best. Among them were the 1957 R&B hit "Sitting on Top of the World," "Spoonful," "Smokestack Lightnin'," "Little Red Rooster," "I Ain't Superstitious," "Back Door Man," "Killing Floor" and "How Many More Years." His songs, many of them written by Willie Dixon, have been covered by American and English rock acts like the Rolling Stones (with whom Wolf appeared on the "Shindig" TV show in 1965), the Grateful Dead, the Yardbirds, Jeff Beck, the Doors, Cream, the Electric Flag, Little Feat and Led Zeppelin.

Wolf frequently appeared at blues and rock festivals in the late Sixties and early Seventies. His 1972 album *The London Sessions* featured backup support by Eric Clapton, Ringo Starr, Steve Winwood and Charlie Watts and Bill Wyman of the Rolling Stones. That same year, Wolf received an honorary doctorate from Columbia College in Chicago. He lived the last years of his life in Chicago's crumbling South Side ghetto. He suffered several heart attacks and received kidney dialysis treatment, but he continued to play occasionally; one of his last concerts was in November 1975 at the Chicago Amphitheatre with B. B. King. He entered a hospital in mid-December and died at age 65 of complications from kidney disease.

THE HUES CORPORATION

Formed 1969, Los Angeles
H. Ann Kelly (b. Apr. 24, 1947, Fairchild, Ala.), voc.; St. Clair Lee (b. Bernard St. Clair Lee Calhoun Henderson, Apr. 24, 1944, San Francisco), voc.; Karl Russell (b. Apr. 10, 1947, Columbus, Oh.), voc.
1973—(+ Fleming Williams [b. Flint, Mich.], voc.) **1974**—*Freedom for the Stallion* (RCA) (– Williams; + Tommy Brown [b. Birmingham, Ala.], voc.) *Rockin' Soul* **1975**—*Love Corporation* (– Brown; – Russell) **1977**—*I Caught Your Act* (Warner/Curb) *Best of the Hues Corporation* (RCA) **1978**—*Your Place or Mine* (Warner Bros.).

Disco-soul group Hues Corporation had its one big hit with "Rock the Boat" (#1, 1974), which sold over two million copies. A black vocal trio featuring two men and a woman, the Hues took its name from Howard Hughes (changing the spelling to avoid legal problems).

After working the lounge circuit, they signed with RCA in 1973 and had a minor pop hit with the title track of their debut album, *Freedom for the Stallion*. Their big success came in late 1974, when member Tommy Brown sang lead on "Rock the Boat." Brown left soon after for a solo career. Followups like "Rockin' Soul" (#18, 1974) and "Love Corporation" (#62, 1975) were modest in comparison.

The group made frequent TV appearances in the mid-Seventies and also appeared in the film *Blacula*. Tours took them to Europe, South America, the Far East and Australia. Their longtime vocal arranger and producer, Wally Holmes, was still on board after the group switched to Warner/Curb Records in 1977 for *I Caught Your Act*, whose title track (#92, 1977) was their last chart appearance. Thereafter, the Hues Corporation slipped back into the nightclub anonymity from which they had emerged.

HUGO AND LUIGI

Hugo Peretti and Luigi Creatore, born New York City

This duo had some success in the mid- and late Fifties and early Sixties as recording artists, but they had their biggest impact as producers, songwriters and label executives. Their first national recognition came in 1955 with their vocal rendition of "Young Abe Lincoln" (#90, 1955) for Mercury Records. After buying Roulette Records in 1957, they devoted themselves to writing (often publishing their efforts under the pseudonym Mark Markwell) and producing. Their first big success was Jimmie Rodgers' 1957 gold single "Falling in Love Again."

After giving up their interest in the Roulette company in 1959, they moved to RCA and continued producing (notably much of the Sam Cooke catalogue and recordings by Della Reese and the Isley Brothers). They reactivated their recording careers as well with such releases as "La Plume de Ma Tante" (#86, 1959) and "Just Come Home" (#35, 1960). At the start of the Seventies, they took executive positions with the Avco/Embassy label, occasionally involving themselves in studio work, notably as producers and writers for the Stylistics.

THE HUMAN LEAGUE
Formed 1977, Sheffield, England
Phil Oakey (b. Oct. 2, 1955), voc., synth.; Martyn Ware (b. ca. 1955), synth.; Ian Craig (b. ca. 1955), synth.; Philip Wright (b. June 30, ca. 1955), slides, synth.
1979—*Reproduction* (Virgin) **1980**—*Travelogue* (– Ware; – Craig; + Ian Burden [b. Dec. 24, ca. 1955], synth.; + Jo Callis [b. May, ca. 1955], synth.; + Susanne Sulley [b. Mar. 26, 1963], voc.; + Joanne Catherall [b. Sep. 18, 1963], voc.) **1982**—*Dare* (A&M) **1983**—*Love and Dancing*.

Armed with synthesizers and electronic percussion devices, the Human League became the undisputed leaders of the British electro-pop movement in 1982. The League topped the American charts with the #1 million-selling "Don't You Want Me," taken from *Dare,* the group's third British album and first American release.

Led by Philip Oakey, the League had released its debut album, *Reproduction,* in 1979, followed by *Travelogue*—two critically acclaimed works featuring synthesizer textures reminiscent of Kraftwerk as well as a dark lyrical approach. Because Oakey felt the band's heavy reliance on pre-recorded tapes in live shows was dishonest, he broke the group up in 1980.

Shortly thereafter, Philip Oakey, along with original League member Philip Wright, recruited bassist/synthesizer player Ian Burden, two female backing singers and synthesizer player Jo Callis, former leader of Scotland's punk-kitsch rockers the Rezillos. Allying themselves with producer Martin Rushent (the Stranglers, Buzzcocks), the Human League recorded *Dare,* which quickly brought them fame in England. Coinciding with their subsequent American success, the League toured the States, where audiences got a good taste of electro-pop: a drum computer kept the beat. *Love and Dancing* reprised the instrumental tracks from *Dare.*

HUMBLE PIE
Formed 1969, Essex, England
Steve Marriott (b. Jan. 30, 1947, London), gtr., voc., kybds., harmonica; Peter Frampton (b. Apr. 22, 1950, Beckenham, Eng.), gtr., voc.; Greg Ridley (b. Oct. 23, 1947, Eng.), bass, voc.; Jerry Shirley (b. Feb. 4, 1952, Eng.), drums.
1969—*As Safe as Yesterday Is* (Immediate) *Town and Country* **1970**—*Humble Pie* (A&M) **1971**—*Rock On; Performance—Rockin' the Fillmore* (– Frampton; + David "Clem" Clempson [b. Sep. 5, 1949, Eng.], gtr., voc.) **1972**—*Smokin'* **1973**—*Eat It; Lost and Found* (reissue of first two LPs) **1974**—*Thunderbox* **1975**—*Street Rats* (disbanded) **1980**—(reformed: Shirley; Marriott; Bobby Tench, voc., gtr.; Anthony Jones, bass) *On to Victory* (Atco) **1981**—*Go for the Throat* **1982**—*The Best.*
Steve Marriott solo: 1976—*Marriott* (A&M) **1981**—*Steve Marriott.*

Early-Seventies hard-rock band Humble Pie was formed and fronted by the raspy-voiced Steve Marriott, who had left the Small Faces in 1968. He hooked up with ex-Herd guitarist Peter Frampton (whose boyish good looks had already elicited teenybopper acclaim), ex–Spooky Tooth bassist Greg Ridley and drummer Jerry Shirley. In late 1968, the group retired to Marriott's Essex cottage for months of rehearsal. Their first single, "Natural Born Boogie," hit the Top Five on the U.K. charts. Neither their debut album, *As Safe as Yesterday Is,* nor the acoustic-oriented *Town and Country* made much of an impact in the U.S. until repackaged as *Lost and Found.*

Humble Pie toured the U.S. for the first time in late 1969 but returned home to find that the Immediate label had gone under. They found a new manager (Dee Anthony) and label (A&M), and their next LP, *Humble Pie,* featured Frampton's melodic acoustic rock. But neither it nor the gutsier *Rock On* provided an American breakthrough. Anthony sent them to America on a frenzied tour that produced *Performance—Rockin' the Fillmore,* recorded live at New York's Fillmore East in May 1971. Loud and raucous, it sold well. Frampton left the group in late 1971.

The loss of Frampton, combined with the outstanding sales of the rock-and-blues-oriented *Fillmore* album, prompted the group to concentrate on boogie material, but with decreasing success for the next few years. *Eat It* found them recording and then touring with a three-member female chorus, the Blackberries (Clydie King, Venetta Fields and Billie Barnum). The group broke up in 1975.

Shirley formed an L.A. group, Natural Gas, with ex-Badfinger member Joey Molland. Frampton's replacement, Clem Clempson (previously with Colosseum), joined Greenslade before he and Pie bassist Ridley teamed up with former Jeff Beck drummer Cozy Powell to form the short-lived Strange Brew. Clempson has since played with Jack Bruce, among others.

Marriott, meanwhile, led Steve Marriott's All-Stars before participating in a Small Faces reunion in 1977. By 1980, Marriott and Shirley had re-formed Humble Pie with ex–Jeff Beck vocalist Bobby Tench. Their two albums—1980's *On to Victory* and 1981's *Go for the Throat*—met with limited success. In mid-1981, the group's tour of the U.S. was interrupted when Marriott's hand was smashed in a hotel door. In June, having recovered, he had to halt the tour again when he was hospitalized in Dallas with an ulcer.

ALBERTA HUNTER
Born April 1, 1895, Memphis
1961—*Songs We Taught Your Mother* (Prestige/Bluesville)   **1978**—*Remember My Name*   **1980**—*Amtrak Blues* (Columbia).

Alberta Hunter (a.k.a. May Alix, Josephine Beatty, Helen Roberts) has been singing the blues for over seventy years, and was one of the first black American musicians to tour the world. She began singing professionally as a teenager in Chicago. In 1921, she performed and recorded with the Fletcher Henderson orchestra and made her first solo recordings. Upon moving to New York that year, she began recording regularly for Paramount, Okeh, Victor and Columbia; she recorded in 1924 with Louis Armstrong's Red Onion Jazz Babies for the Gennett label.

Hunter first performed on Broadway when she replaced Bessie Smith in the musical comedy *How Come* in 1923 and then toured the U.S. with the road company. By 1925, she was leading her own trio in club work and took them on subsequent national tours. In 1927, billed as "America's Foremost Brown Blues Singer," she played in England, France and Monaco. She visited Scotland, Egypt, Greece and the Scandinavian countries in the Thirties. Back home, Hunter appeared with Paul Robeson in a 1928 Broadway production of *Showboat* and, beginning in the early Thirties, expanded her audience through a featured spot on WABC radio's "Negro Achievement Hour." By the end of the decade, she was regularly featured on several East Coast stations. In the mid-Thirties she had one of her most active club periods, playing Harlem's Cotton Club and appearing at Connie's Inn with Louis Armstrong.

Hunter's recording career revitalized alongside the Depression economy, and in the mid-Thirties she recorded with the Jack Jackson Orchestra on HMV. She recorded in 1939 with the Charlie Shavers Quartet for Decca and in 1940 with the Eddie Heywood orchestra for Bluebird. She spent most of World War II with the USO touring China, Burma, India, Egypt and Africa, including a 1945 command performance for General Eisenhower at Frankfurt, Germany. She was given a meritorious service award for her contributions to the war effort.

Hunter returned to New York club work after the war and by the early Fifties was recording again, notably for the Juke Box/Regal label. In 1953, she worked engagements in Toronto and Montreal, but in 1957 decided to retire from music to work as a nurse, which she did for two decades, with only infrequent returns to performing: some sessions in 1961 and 1962 for the Prestige/Bluesville, Riverside and Folkways labels, and a 1971 Scandinavian TV documentary, "Faces in Jazz."

In 1977, at the age of 82, Hunter reemerged to establish residency at the Cookery in New York's Greenwich Village. The attendant publicity prompted television exposure (NBC's "Today Show," Mike Douglas, Dick Cavett, "60 Minutes" and a widely aired 1978 commercial for Clairol hair products) and a Columbia contract. Her songs were used in the soundtrack of *Remember My Name* in 1978. Hunter continues to perform at the Cookery.

IAN HUNTER
Born June 3, 1946, Shrewsbury, England
1975—*Ian Hunter* (Columbia)   **1976**—*All American Alien Boy*   **1977**—*Overnight Angels* (Columbia, U.K.)   *Shades of Ian Hunter* (Columbia)   **1979**—*You're Never Alone with a Schizophrenic* (Chrysalis)   **1980**—*Welcome to the Club*   **1981**—*Short Back n' Sides*   **1983**—*All of the Good Ones Are Taken* (Columbia).

The former leader of Mott the Hoople, singer/songwriter Ian Hunter has pursued a moderately successful solo career. His family settled in Blackpool but moved frequently, as Hunter's father, who worked for MI5, the British CIA, was regularly transferred. By the time Hunter was 11, he had attended 17 different schools. His family finally settled in Shrewsbury, where he played with a band called Silence that recorded an unsuccessful album. In 1962, he played harmonica in another amateur band, but continued to work day jobs until 1968, when he started playing bass in Germany with Freddie "Fingers" Lee. A few months later he helped launch Mott the Hoople in England.

With their debut album in 1969, Mott the Hoople established themselves as Dylan-influenced hard-rockers with "Rock and Roll Queen" and, under the tutelage of David Bowie, became glitter-rock favorites with *All the Young Dudes* and its title single. During his last days with the group, Hunter wrote the autobiographical *Reflections of a Rock Star* (it was published in 1976). In late 1974, he left after being hospitalized in New Jersey for physical exhaustion.

Hunter moved to New York, where he made his self-titled solo debut, which featured ex-Bowie guitarist Mick Ronson, who had played in a late version of Mott. The album produced a British hit single, "Once Bitten, Twice Shy." Hunter toured America and England in late 1975.

His next two albums were *All American Alien Boy* ("You Nearly Did Me In") and *Overnight Angels* (which Hunter later called "disgusting" and which wasn't issued in the U.S. until Columbia included it on the retrospective *Shades of Ian Hunter*).

You're Never Alone with a Schizophrenic, his Chrysalis debut, found Mick Ronson once again producing, arranging and touring with Hunter. By 1980, Hunter had formed his own band, including Ronson, guitarist Tom Morringello and keyboardists George Meyer and Tom Mandell. In 1980, he toured to promote his live *Welcome to the Club*, one of his most popular records in years. Mick Jones of the Clash produced *Short Back n' Sides* in 1981. Hunter has produced records, including Ellen Foley's debut album and Generation X's second LP, *Valley of the Dolls*. Hunter also wrote Barry Manilow's hit "Ships."

IVORY JOE HUNTER
Born October 10, 1914, Kirbyville, Texas; died November 8, 1974, Memphis
1971—*The Return of Ivory Joe Hunter* (Epic)   *16 of His Greatest Hits* (King)   *Ivory Joe Hunter* (Everest).

A pop-blues singer, pianist and songwriter, Ivory Joe Hunter was a popular R&B figure in the Forties and Fifties, and one of the first R&B singers to interpret country songs. He started playing the piano in grade school and eventually developed a style influenced by Fats Waller. He worked as program director at KFDM radio in Beaumont, Texas, and made his first recordings in 1933 for the Library of Congress, via musicologist Alan Lomax.

Hunter recorded briefly with Johnny Moore's Three Blazers for the Exclusive label. He soon started his own Ivory Records, and scored his first regional hit with "Blues at Sunrise." He then left Texas in 1942 for California, where he helped form and recorded for Pacific Records ("Pretty Mama Blues"). With King Records from 1947 to 1950, his R&B hits included "Landlord Blues," "Guess Who" (1949) and "I Quit My Pretty Mama" (1950). By 1950, Hunter had signed with MGM and released "I Almost Lost My Mind," which hit #1 on the R&B charts and had sold a million copies by the time Pat Boone covered it in 1956. He spent most of the Fifties on the R&B charts, first with such MGM releases as "I Almost Lost . . ." and "I Need You So" (#2, 1950), and then, after signing with Atlantic in 1954, alongside Ray Charles and Chuck Willis.

Hunter finally reached white listeners with "Since I Met You Baby" (#12, 1956), which got him exposure on the Ed Sullivan TV show. After "Empty Arms" (1957), "Yes I Want You" (1958) and "City Lights" (1959), Hunter's popularity declined, although he continued to record. In the late Sixties, he sang country as a revue member of the Grand Ole Opry in Nashville, and he tried a comeback in

1970 when he released *The Return of Ivory Joe Hunter* (Epic). In late 1974, Hunter died of cancer in a Memphis hospital. His songs have been covered by Nat "King" Cole, the Five Keys and Elvis Presley, who cut "My Wish Came True" and "Ain't That Loving You, Baby."

MISSISSIPPI JOHN HURT
Born July 3, 1893, Teoc, Mississippi; died November 2, 1966, Grenada, Mississippi
1965—*The Best of Mississippi John Hurt* (Vanguard)
1966—*Mississippi John Hurt Today*   **1968**—*The Immortal Mississippi John Hurt*   **1972**—*Last Sessions*.

Blues singer Mississippi John Hurt was renowned for his fingerpicking and restrained phrasing. He was one of sharecroppers Isom and Mary Hurt's three children, and he lived as a sharecropper most of his life. A frequent singer in local churches, Hurt dropped out of school at age ten and by 1903 he had taught himself to play a three-finger-picking style of guitar.

Most of Mississippi John Hurt's performances were for audiences in the Avalon, Mississippi, area. Heavily influenced, as were many bluesmen of the era, by Jimmie Rodgers, he slowly developed an original country/Delta blues style. In 1928, he was taken to New York and Memphis to cut a few sides for Okeh Records, among them a rendition of the blues standard "Stack-O-Lee." But during the Great Depression, Hurt faded back into rural anonymity until he was rediscovered, at age 71, during the early-Sixties folk-blues revival by blues enthusiast Tom Hoskins.

Hurt played at the Newport Folk Festival in 1963, 1964 and 1965, at Carnegie Hall, at rock clubs like the Cafe Au Go Go in New York, on TV's "Tonight Show" in 1963, and in the Canadian Broadcasting documentary, *This Hour Has Seven Days,* in 1965. He also reactivated his recording career, cutting several albums, including *Today, The Immortal Mississippi John Hurt* and *Last Sessions,* which was recorded in a Manhattan hotel in 1966, shortly before his death from a heart attack. Hurt helped popularize such traditional material as "Candy Man Blues" and "C. C. Rider" as well as his own "Coffee Blues" and "Chicken." He was survived by his widow, Jessie, and their fourteen children.

BRIAN HYLAND
Born November 12, 1943, Woodhaven, New York
N.A.—*Sealed with a Kiss* (ABC/Paramount)   *The Joker Went Wild* (Philips).

Brian Hyland began his lengthy and sporadically successful pop career with 1960's biggest novelty hit, "Itsy Bitsy Teenie Weenie Yellow Polkadot Bikini," which hit the top of the charts while Hyland was still in high school. More novelty fare followed ("Lop-Sided, Overloaded and It Wiggled When I Rode It") before Hyland switched labels to ABC/Paramount, dropped his adjectival schtick in favor of pop love songs and scored with "Let Me Belong to You" (#20, 1961).

He hit off and on through the early Sixties, his best year coming in 1962, when he released "Sealed with a Kiss" (#3), "Ginny Come Lately" (#21) and "Warmed Over Kisses (Left Over Love)" (#25). After a dry spell, he returned to the charts in 1966 with "Run, Run, Look and See" (#25) and "The Joker Went Wild" (#20). In the late Sixties, he recorded with slight success, jumping from label to label (Philips, Dot, Uni). He had a surprise hit in 1970 with a Del Shannon–produced remake of Curtis Mayfield's "Gypsy Woman" (#3), which found Hyland working in an uncharacteristic folk-rock mode. Subsequent attempts to revive rock and country chestnuts, like "Lonely Teardrops" (#54, 1971), proved less fruitful.

JANIS IAN

Born Janis Eddy Fink, May 7, 1951, New York City
1967—*Janis Ian* (Verve Forecast) **1968**—*. . . For All the
Seasons of Your Mind; The Secret Life of J. Eddy
Fink* **1969**—*Who Really Cares* **1971**—*Present Company* (Capitol) **1974**—*Stars* (Columbia) **1975**—*Between the Lines; Aftertones* **1977**—*Miracle Row*
1978—*Janis Ian* **1979**—*Night Rains* **1980**—*Best of
Janis Ian* **1981**—*Restless Eyes.*

Singer/songwriter Janis Ian began her career at 15 with a
hit about interracial romance entitled "Society's Child" in
1967. After an eight-year slump, Ian returned to pop radio
in 1975 with a platinum LP and Grammy Award–winning
single, "At Seventeen."

The daughter of a music teacher, Ian studied piano as a
child and began writing songs when she enrolled in Manhattan's High School of Music and Art. There, she
changed her surname from Fink to Ian (her brother's
middle name). The folk journal *Broadside* published her
"Hair of Spun Gold" and invited her to perform at a
hootenanny at the Village Gate. Ian soon had a contract
with Elektra, but was dropped when she insisted upon
recording her own material; she then signed to Verve.

Janis Ian

In 1966, she recorded a song she had written while
waiting to see her guidance counselor, "Society's Child
(Baby I've Been Thinking)." It was banned by several
stations and ignored by the rest until conductor Leonard
Bernstein featured Ian on his CBS-TV special "Inside
Pop: The Rock Revolution," where she performed the
song accompanied by the New York Philharmonic. "Society's Child" became a #14 hit in 1967.

Ian dropped out of high school in her junior year and
released her first album. She recorded two more albums
for Verve but never produced a follow-up hit single. She
gave away most of her earnings to friends and charities;
management and taxes took the rest. Ian retired before she
was twenty.

She moved to Philadelphia and married photojournalist
Peter Cunningham. Her marriage lasted only a short
while, and Ian returned to recording with the unsuccessful
Present Company. She moved to California, where she
lived alone and continued writing. Her next album, *Stars*,
included "Jesse," a #30 hit for Robert Flack, later covered by Joan Baez on *Diamonds and Rust*.

Ian's most commercially successful year was 1975,
when she sold over $5 million worth of records. She
released the platinum *Between the Lines*, which included
"Watercolors" and "At Seventeen" (#3), the latter of
which got her a Grammy for Best Female Vocal. Followups like *Aftertones, Miracle Row, Janis Ian* and *Night
Rains* were less popular.

IAN AND SYLVIA

Formed 1959, Toronto
Ian Tyson (b. Sep. 25, 1933, Victoria, British Columbia,
Canada); Sylvia Tyson (b. Sylvia Fricker, Sep. 19, 1940,
Chatham, Ontario, Canada).
1962—*Ian and Sylvia* (Vanguard) **1964**—*Four Strong
Winds; Northern Journey* **1965**—*Early Morning
Rain* **1966**—*Play One More* **1967**—*So Much for
Dreaming; Ian and Sylvia* (Columbia) **1968**—*Nashville* (Vanguard) *Full Circle; The Best of Ian and
Sylvia* **1970**—*Greatest Hits, Volume 1* **1971**—*Greatest
Hits, Volume 2* **1972**—*You Were on My Mind* (with the
Great Speckled Bird) (Columbia) **1973**—*The Best of
Ian and Sylvia.*
Ian solo: 1975—*Ol' Eon* (A&M) **1979**—*One Jump
Ahead of the Devil* (Boot).
Sylvia solo: 1975—*Woman's World* (Capitol).

Canadian folksingers/songwriters Ian and Sylvia were
active in the folk revival of the early Sixties as performers

and composers. By the late Sixties, they had turned to country music.

Ian Tyson was raised on a Canadian farm and he traveled much of western Canada working various jobs, including performing in the rodeo, until he was seriously injured at age 19. Shortly after turning 21 and enrolling in the Vancouver School of Art he started singing in clubs, sometimes as part of a group called the Sensational Stripes. Tyson graduated from art school and moved to Toronto, where he worked days as a commercial artist, and with a partner, Don Francks, played blues and traditional folk material. He was well known in Canadian music circles by the time he met Sylvia Fricker in 1959.

Fricker's mother was a music teacher, organist and choir director at their church, and Fricker became involved in the Toronto folk scene after graduating from high school. She met Tyson in 1959 while in a Toronto club, and within a year they were performing regularly as a duo.

They moved to New York in the early Sixties and began working on the club-and-campus folk circuit. Their first album, recorded in a Masonic temple in Brooklyn, featured traditional songs; their second contained Ian Tyson's best-known song, "Four Strong Winds." Sylvia's "You Were on My Mind" (later a hit for We Five) was on the duo's fourth album, *Northern Journey*, which was released around the time they were married in 1964.

As the Sixties ended, the Tysons moved toward country music and briefly toured and recorded with a C&W band called Great Speckled Bird. Tyson began a solo career with a country single, "Love Can Bless the Soul of Anyone," and has since become the host of a music-variety show on Canadian television. He produced Sylvia's solo debut, *Woman's World*, and she began hosting a folk-music show, "Touch the Earth," on CBC radio.

IDES OF MARCH

Formed circa 1964, Berwyn, Illinois
James Peterik, lead voc., gtr., kybds., sax; Ray Herr, voc., gtr., bass; Larry Millas, gtr., organ, voc.; Bob Bergland, bass, sax; John Larson, trumpet; Chuck Somar, horn; Michael Borch, drums.
1970—*Vehicle* (Warner Bros.)   N.A.—*Common Bond*;   *World Woven* (RCA)   1973—*Midnight Oil*.

A seven-piece group (with horns) from the suburbs of Chicago, the Ides of March were often accused of being Blood, Sweat and Tears imitators. Their one big hit— "Vehicle" (#2, 1970)—sounded like BS&T, but the Ides of March had actually formed before Blood, Sweat and Tears (or the Ides' local contemporaries Chicago).

The group members met in elementary school, and they formed the band while in high school. In the next few years, they all remained enrolled in the same college, thereby greatly inhibiting their tour schedule.

They scored two minor 1966 hits—"You Wouldn't Listen" and "Roller Coaster"—and faded until 1970, when Peterik's "Vehicle" was released. The record had been certified gold by November 1972, but the Ides proved unable to find a follow-up hit.

The group left Warner Bros. for RCA, to little avail, then disbanded. A mid-Seventies attempt to regroup never got off the ground. Peterik returned to the charts over a decade later as a member of Survivor, whose single "Eye of the Tiger" hit #1 in the summer of 1982.

THE IMPRESSIONS

Formed 1957, Chicago
Curtis Mayfield (b. June 3, 1942, Chicago); Jerry Butler (b. Dec. 8, 1939, Sunflower, Miss.); Arthur Brooks (b. Chattanooga, Tenn.); Richard Brooks (b. Chattanooga, Tenn.); Sam Gooden (b. Sep. 2, 1939, Chattanooga, Tenn.).
1958–59—(– Butler; + Fred Cash [b. Oct. 8, 1940, Chattanooga])   1961—(– Arthur and Richard Brooks)   1964—*The Impressions* (ABC)   1965—*People Get Ready*;   *Greatest Hits*   1968—*Best of the Impressions*   1974—*Finally Got Myself Together* (Curtom)   1976—*For Your Precious Love* (Vee Jay)   *Originals* (ABC)   *The Vintage Years* (Sire)   1979—*Come to My Party* (20th Century–Fox)   1981—*Fan the Fire*.

The Impressions' close vocal harmonies and big band–style horn arrangements were a major influence on Sixties soul. The group's original members—Sam Gooden, Fred Cash and Richard and Arthur Brooks—were in a Tennessee group, the Roosters, and made their way to Chicago, where they hooked up with a team of songwriter/producers, Jerry Butler and Curtis Mayfield. Both Butler and Mayfield went on to successful solo careers.

The Impressions' first hit, "For Your Precious Love" (#11, 1958), featured Butler's lead vocals, but within the year he left the group for a solo career (although he continued to work with Mayfield). Cash, who had not been in the initial lineup, replaced Butler; after the group's next major hit, "Gypsy Woman" in 1961, the Brooks brothers dropped out.

Mayfield became the Impressions' leader and lead vocalist, and made them one of the most popular vocal groups of the Sixties. Their trio vocals were also a major influence on Jamaican pop. Through the Sixties, the group had hits with Mayfield's love songs, such as "Talking About My Baby" (#14, 1964), and his message songs, including "Keep on Pushin' " (#10, 1964), "People Get Ready" (#14, 1965) and "Amen" (#7, 1965). Mayfield also kept up an active career as producer, arranger and songwriter; he left the Impressions in 1970.

Howard University graduate Leroy Hutson took over the group in the early Seventies and kept them on the soul charts with "Check Out Your Mind," "(Baby) Turn On to Me" and "Ain't Got Time," among others, before going solo in 1973. Cash and Gooden regrouped with Reggie Torian and Ralph Johnson, and had a Top Twenty pop hit

(#1 R&B) in 1974 with "Finally Got Myself Together," and they did the soundtrack for the blaxploitation film *Three the Hard Way*. They have continued to record for various labels into the Eighties, with middling success. In 1983, Butler and Mayfield rejoined the group for a reunion tour.

THE INCREDIBLE STRING BAND
Formed 1965, Glasgow
Mike Heron (b. Dec. 12, 1942), voc., gtr., assorted instruments; Robin Williamson (b. Nov. 24, 1943), voc., gtr., assorted instruments.
1966—*The Incredible String Band* (Elektra) **1967**—*The 5000 Spirits or the Layers of the Onion* **1968**—*The Hangman's Beautiful Daughter* (+ Christina "Licorice" McKenzie, violin, assorted instruments; + Rose Simpson, bass) *Wee Tam and the Big Huge* **1969**—*Changing Horses* **1970**—*I Looked Up; U; Be Glad for the Song Has No Ending* (Reprise) **1971**—(− Simpson; + Malcolm Le Maistre, bass, voc.) **1972**—*Liquid Acrobat as Regards the Air* (Elektra) *Earth Span* (Island) **1973**—(− McKenzie) *No Ruinous Feud* (+ Gerard [or Gerald] Dott, kybds., reeds) **1974**—*Hard Rope and Silken Twine* (+ John Gilston, drums; + Graham Forbes, gtr.) **1976**—*Seasons They Change*.

The Incredible String Band was a highly eclectic Scottish folk group that started in the mid-Sixties playing original songs derived not just from British traditional ballads and U.S. Appalachian tunes and blues, but from Indian ragas, Ethiopian oud music, calypso, Gilbert and Sullivan and an international assortment of folk styles. Though there were other shifting members of the band, ISB was essentially just two Glasgow-born songwriters, Robin Williamson and Mike Heron, who between them played a wide assortment of instruments.

Heron first played in the Edinburgh rock group Rock Bottom and the Deadbeats. Williamson played in a jugband duo in 1965 at the Incredible Folk Club in Glasgow with Clive Palmer, who owned the club. Heron joined soon after, and the trio took their name from Palmer's club. They released their eponymous debut on Elektra in 1966. Afterwards, Williamson and Palmer traveled in North Africa. Upon their return in late 1966, Palmer left the group but the other two kept performing in local clubs. In November, they made their first concert appearance outside Scotland, at London's Royal Albert Hall, with Tom Paxton and Judy Collins on the bill. The two American artists helped spread ISB's reputation in the U.S. (Collins later recorded Williamson's "First Girl I Loved"), and in 1967 their second LP, *The 5000 Spirits or the Layers of the Onion*, was acclaimed on both sides of the Atlantic.

A cult audience developed in the U.S., but in England they were a mainstay of the hippie movement. In 1968, the virtuoso multiinstrumentalist duo version of ISB recorded one more LP, *The Hangman's Beautiful Daughter*. They then added two women—Christina McKenzie on violin, kazoo and other instruments, plus Rose Simpson on bass. Their first double album together, *Wee Tam and the Big Huge*, was seen by some as indulgent and disappointing, and their reputation declined as the Sixties ended, though their music became increasingly ambitious. The album *U* was conceived as a loose stage show that played with a mime troupe.

In 1971, Simpson left, replaced by Malcolm Le Maistre in 1972. Gerard Dott, another multiinstrumentalist, replaced McKenzie in 1973. He knew Heron from childhood and had played in a skiffle band with Williamson and Heron. In 1971, Heron put out the solo LP *Smiling Men with Bad Reputations*, and the next year Williamson issued his own LP, *Myrrh*. The band members were drifting apart. By the time of their last show together, in 1974, they had become harder-rocking after adding drummer Gilston and guitarist Forbes; both Heron and Williamson had become Scientologists. Heron did some session work and later formed Mike Heron's Reputation with ex-ISB's Gilston, Forbes and Le Maistre. Williamson moved to L.A., formed Robin Williamson's Merry Band and released three LPs of poetry and music and a 1981 solo album on Flying Fish Records.

THE INK SPOTS
Formed 1934, New York City
Members have included Jerry Daniels, gtr., voc.; Orville "Hoppy" Jones (b. Feb. 17, 1905, Chicago; d. Oct. 18, 1944, Chicago), voc.; Charles Fuqua, gtr., voc.; Ivory Watson; Bill Kenny (b. 1915; d. Mar. 23, 1978); and Herb Jones.
N.A.—*The Ink Spots' Greatest Hits* (Grand) *The Ink Spots' Greatest Hits, Volume 2*.

Though the Ink Spots enjoyed their greatest popularity years before rock & roll came into being, their vocal style was a precursor to the smooth doo-wop vocal groups of the Fifties, including the Ravens, the Marcels, the Flamingos, the Platters and others.

The original group was formed when the four were working as porters at New York's Paramount Theater. By 1935, they were recording for Victor. They later switched to Decca, and soon thereafter lead singer Jerry Daniels left the group. He was replaced by Bill Kenny. In February 1939, the Ink Spots released "If I Didn't Care," their first million-selling record. Subsequent hits included "My Prayer." Jones died on October 18, 1944, from what was discovered to have been brain hemorrhages. By that time, however, internal dissension among members had cast the group's future in some doubt. However, Jones was replaced by his brother Herb. The Ink Spots had a final #1 hit with "To Each His Own" in 1946.

THE INTRUDERS

Formed Philadelphia
Phil Terry, Robert Edwards, Samuel Brown, Eugene Daughtry.
1973—*Intruders Super Hits* (Gamble).

This vocal quartet was an early project for the production team of Kenny Gamble and Leon Huff. The group's members sang around Philadelphia in the early Sixties and recorded one single for the local Gowen Records. In 1964, they met Leon Huff, who produced their single "All the Time" on Musicor Records. By 1966, Huff had teamed with Kenny Gamble to form Gamble Records, and the Intruders became the company's first signing.

The Intruders' first charted single, "(We'll Be) United" (#14 R&B), started a hot streak in 1966. "Devil with Angel's Smile" hit #26 R&B, also in 1966. "Together" (#9 R&B; later a huge hit for Tierra), "Baby, I'm Lonely" (#9 R&B) and "A Love That's Real" (#35 R&B), in 1967, built the Intruders' and the Gamble and Huff team's national reputation.

The next year was the Intruders' peak, with the million-selling "Cowboys to Girls" (#6 pop, #1 R&B). "Love Is Like a Baseball Game" (#26 pop, #4 R&B) and "Slow Drag" (#12 R&B) followed in 1969. Gamble and Huff gave them "Sad Girl" (#14 R&B) in 1970 and "When We Get Married" (#8 R&B) and "(Win, Place or Show) She's a Winner" (#12 R&B) in 1972. The Intruders' "I'll Always Love My Mama" (#6 R&B, 1975) was a disco mainstay and a perennial Mother's Day favorite.

THE IRON BUTTERFLY

Formed 1966, San Diego
Doug Ingle (b. Sep. 9, 1946, Omaha, Neb.), kybds., voc.; Ron Bushy (b. Sep. 23, 1945, Washington, D.C.), drums, voc.; Jerry Penrod (b. San Diego), bass; Darryl DeLoach (b. San Diego), voc.; Danny Weis (b. San Diego), gtr.
1968—*Heavy* (Atco) (− Penrod; − DeLoach; − Weiss; + Lee Dorman [b. Sep. 19, 1945, St. Louis], bass, gtr., piano; + Erik Braunn [b. Aug. 11, 1950, Boston], gtr., voc.) *In-A-Gadda-Da-Vida* 1969—*Ball* 1970—*Live* (− Braunn; + Mike Pinera [b. Sep. 29, 1948, Tampa, Fla.], gtr., voc.; + Larry "Rhino" Reinhardt [b. July 7, 1948, Fla.], gtr.) 1971—*Evolution; Metamorphosis* (group broke up) 1974— (group re-formed: Braunn; Bushy; + Phil Kramer [b. July 12, 1952, Youngstown, Oh.], bass; + Howard Reitzes [b. Mar. 22, 1951, Southgate, Calif.], kybds., gtr.) 1975—*Sun and Steel* (MCA) *Scorching Beauty*.

Now remembered as an oddity of the acid-rock era, at their peak the Iron Butterfly were considered a leading hard-rock band. During their relatively brief lifetime, the Iron Butterfly sold about seven million albums; *In-A-Gadda-Da-Vida* sold three million copies alone. The album's focal point was the 17-minute title track (featuring a 2½-minute drum solo), which was also something of a catalyst in establishing "progressive" FM radio programing.

"In-A-Gadda-Da-Vida" was written by group leader, organist and chief vocalist Doug Ingle, whose father was a church organist. Ingle formed his first group at age 16 in San Diego, where he met drummer Ron Bushy, one of four San Diegans to accompany Ingle to Los Angeles in late 1966.

In Los Angeles, Iron Butterfly worked Bido Lito's and eventually moved to the Galaxy and to Whisky-a-Go-Go. By early 1967, they had a recording contract. Their debut disc stayed on the charts for nearly fifty weeks, partly because of the national exposure they got as an opening act for the Doors and the Jefferson Airplane. Shortly after the LP was released, three of the original members left, among them Danny Weis, later in Rhinoceros.

With new bassist Lee Dorman and guitarist Erik Braunn, Iron Butterfly recorded *In-A-Gadda-Da-Vida* ("In a Garden of Eden," some suggested), which became Atlantic's biggest seller (although the record's sales have since been eclipsed by Led Zeppelin, among others). The album stayed on the charts for 140 weeks, 81 of them in the Top Ten. An edited version of the title track hit #30. *Ball* hit #3 and went gold, but subsequent efforts failed.

In late 1969, Braunn left (and later formed Flintwhistle with Penrod and DeLoach of the original lineup; he also discovered Black Oak Arkansas). He was replaced by two guitarists, Mike Pinera (formerly of the Blues Image) and Larry "Rhino" Reinhardt (who had been living with Gregg and Duane Allman). *Metamorphosis* followed, and the group broke up after its farewell performance on May 23, 1971.

During their career, all six of their albums charted; they toured the U.S. eight times and Europe as well. They were featured in the film *Savage Seven* (along with Cream), whence came the first of several singles ("Possession"/ "Unconscious Power"). Yet another, "Easy Rider," was featured in the film of the same name. Pinera went on to play with Cactus. In the mid-Seventies, the group was revived by Braunn and Bushy with the inconsequential *Scorching Beauty* and *Sun and Steel* on the MCA label.

IRON MAIDEN

Formed 1977, England
Paul Di'anno, voc.; Steve Harris, voc.; Dave Murray, gtr.; Doug Samson, drums; Clive Burr, drums; Dennis Stratton, gtr., voc.
1980—*Iron Maiden* (Harvest/Capitol) (− Stratton; + Adrian Smith, gtr.) 1981—*Killers; Maid in Japan* (− Di'anno; + Bruce Dickinson, voc.) 1982—*The Number of the Beast* (− Burr; + Nicko McBrain, drums) 1983—*Piece of Mind.*

Taking its name from the medieval torture device, Iron Maiden is part of England's new crop of heavy-metal bands that avoid the stylistic diversity of the new wave in favor of exactly what put Led Zeppelin and Black Sabbath on the map in the Seventies: simple guitar riffs, bone-crunching chording and shrieking vocals. Formed in 1977 by Steve Harris, the first incarnation of Iron Maiden was inspired by the do-it-yourself punk ethos, and released an EP, *The Soundhouse Tapes,* on its own label, Rock Hard Records. *Iron Maiden,* the band's 1980 Capitol debut album, was pure, unadulterated screaming heavy metal. Although the denim- and leather-clad group hasn't scored any gold albums in America as it has in England, Iron Maiden remains a popular concert attraction, competing with other young British metal bands like Def Leppard and Saxon. Typical of the genre's fascination with violence and destruction, Iron Maiden's lead singer, Bruce Dickinson, is nicknamed the Air Raid Siren.

THE ISLEY BROTHERS
Formed Cincinnati, Ohio
Rudolph Isley (b. Apr. 1, 1939), voc.; Ronald Isley (b. May 21, 1941), lead voc.; O'Kelly Isley (b. Dec. 25, 1937), voc. New members added in 1969: Ernie Isley, bass, percussion, gtr.; Marvin Isley, bass, percussion; Chris Jasper, kybds., synth.; Everett Collins, drums.
1959—*Shout* (RCA)   **1962**—*Twist and Shout* (Wand)
1964—*Twisting and Shouting* (United Artists)   **1966**—*This Old Heart of Mine* (Tamla)   **1969**—*It's Our Thing* (T-Neck)   **1971**—*In the Beginning . . . with Jimi Hendrix;   Greatest Hits   1973*—*3 + 3   1976*—*Best of* (Buddah)   **1977**—*Forever Gold* (T-Neck)   *Go for Your Guns   1978*—*Showdown;   Timeless   1979*—*Winner Take All   1980*—*Go All the Way   1981*—*Grand Slam   1983*—*Between the Sheets.*

A Cincinnati-born family group, which by now has included two generations of Isleys, the Isley Brothers started out on the black R&B circuit and had occasional pop and AOR successes. The original members (including a fourth brother, Vernon, who died in the early Fifties in a bicycle accident) were encouraged to sing by their father, a professional singer. Tenor Ronnie Isley was soon designated lead vocalist.

While still in their teens, Ronald, Rudolph and O'Kelly (who later dropped the O') went to New York in 1957 and over the next year recorded several unsuccessful neodoo-wop tunes ("Angels Cried"). While performing at the Howard Theater in Washington, D.C., in the summer of 1959, the group was spotted by an RCA executive, who signed the Isleys. Their debut single for the label was "Shout," written in the call-and-response gospel vocal style; it was the first and most successful of the RCA recordings produced for them by Hugo and Luigi. "Shout" only reached #47 on the pop charts but became an R&B standard (since covered by such diverse artists as Lulu, Joey Dee and the Starliters, Tom Petty, and the Blues Brothers). It eventually sold over a million copies, and the group earned enough to move the entire family from Cincinnati to New Jersey.

Although they toured widely, it wasn't until they'd left RCA in 1962 and recorded "Twist and Shout" (#17) on Wand Records (originally recorded by the Topnotes, later covered by the Beatles) that they had their next hit. Subsequent releases on Wand and United Artists failed to hit, and the brothers toured on the R&B circuit with their backup band, which included Jimmy James (a.k.a. Jimi Hendrix). Hendrix was with the Isleys for most of 1964 and made his first recordings with them, including several sides for Atlantic and one for the Isleys' T-Neck label ("Testify"). Some of his work with the group was released in 1971 as *In the Beginning.*

In 1965, the Isleys signed to the Motown subsidiary Tamla, but although they worked with Motown's top writing and production team, Holland-Dozier-Holland, only their first single, "This Old Heart of Mine" (#12, 1966) became a pop hit. The song hit #3 in England two years later, after the Isleys had moved there to sustain their career. In 1969, they returned home from England and began recording for their own label, T-Neck Records. Named after their adopted hometown of Teaneck, New Jersey, the label was a revival of a company started in the early Sixties and then abandoned. Their first release, "It's Your Thing" (#2, 1969), became their biggest pop hit, eventually selling over two million copies; it won a Grammy for Best R&B Vocal Performance. "It's Your Thing" was written and produced by the Isleys them-

Grammy Awards

Janis Ian
1975 Best Pop Vocal Performance, Female:
  "At Seventeen"

Isley Brothers
1969 Best R&B Vocal Performance by a Group or Duo:
  "It's Your Thing"

selves, as were "I Turned You On" (#23, 1969) and "Pop That Thang" (#24, 1972).

In 1969, the Isleys added a second generation: brothers Ernest and Marvin, as well as brother-in-law Chris Jasper and non-relative drummer Everett Collins. With Ernie's Hendrix-like guitar lines, the group often covered material by rock writers like Stephen Stills—whose "Love the One You're With" was a #18 hit in 1971 for the Isleys—Eric Burdon and War's "Spill the Wine" (#49, 1971) and Bob Dylan's "Lay Lady Lay" (#71, 1971).

"That Lady (Part I)" (#6, 1973), a two-million-selling single, made *3 + 3* a platinum album. The Isleys' next big pop hit—the gold "Fight the Power (Part I)" (#4, 1975)—came from *The Heat Is On*. While the following year's *Harvest for the World* didn't produce any gold singles, it still sold over half a million copies in three days.

In the latter part of the Seventies, the Isleys adapted to the disco market. Though their pop hits ended, albums (*Go for Your Guns, Showdown, Winner Take All, Go All the Way* and others) continued to sell platinum. The early Eighties found the Isleys still active both in concert and on record. Early 1981's *Grand Slam* went gold.

IT'S A BEAUTIFUL DAY

Formed 1967, San Francisco
Original lineup: David LaFlamme (b. Apr. 5, 1941, Salt Lake City), electric violin, voc.; Linda LaFlamme, kybds.; Val Fuentes (b. Nov. 25, 1947, Chicago), drums; Pattie Santos (b. Nov. 16, 1949, San Francisco), voc., percussion; Bill Gregory, gtr.; Tom Fowler, bass. Subsequent personnel changes: − Linda LaFlamme; − Gregory; − Fowler; + Hal Wagenet (b. Willits, Calif.), gtr.; + Michael Holman (b. Denver, Colo.), bass; + Fred Webb (b. Santa Rosa, Calif.), kybds.

1969—*It's a Beautiful Day* (Columbia) **1970**—*Marrying Maiden* **1971**—*Choice Quality Stuff* **1972**—*Live at Carnegie Hall* **1973**—*It's a Beautiful Day . . . Today* **1974**—*1001 Nights* **1979**—*It's a Beautiful Day* (compilation).

It's a Beautiful Day came to national prominence with their FM standard, "White Bird." The group was led by David LaFlamme, who started playing violin at age five, and later played as soloist with the Utah Symphony. After serving in the Army, he moved to California in 1962. Through the Sixties, he performed several styles of music, including jazz with the John Handy Concert Ensemble. LaFlamme often jammed with several future members of Big Brother and the Holding Company and was part of an early version of Dan Hicks and His Hot Licks.

By the time he formed It's a Beautiful Day on a summer afternoon (hence the group name), LaFlamme was playing jazz, classical, folk and rock. He played on a specially adapted amplified solid-body five-string violin (the fifth string was a low C, so the instrument's range was as wide as that of a violin and viola combined), and LaFlamme's soloing established the group as a top local draw. Three of the songs on their self-titled 1969 debut, including "White Bird," were penned by LaFlamme and his wife, Linda, who left the group shortly thereafter and formed the communal San Francisco band Titus' Mother.

In 1970, the group toured England. After several personnel changes, they released *Marrying Maiden*. The LP included "Don and Dewey," a tribute to the Fifties duo of the same name and featured the eponymous Don "Sugarcane" Harris. The group disbanded in 1974 after its sixth LP, *1001 Nights*, went largely unnoticed. LaFlamme later recorded two solo LPs, *White Bird* (1977) and *Inside Out* (1978).

J

JOE JACKSON
Born Aug. 11, 1955, Burton-on-Trent, England
1979—*Look Sharp; I'm the Man* **1980**—*Beat Crazy*
1981—*Jumpin' Jive* **1982**—*Night and Day*.

When singer Joe Jackson first emerged at the height of 1979's pop-new wave explosion, he was frequently compared to Elvis Costello and Graham Parker. He has since experimented with reggae, big band jazz and more exotic hybrids.

Jackson began studying violin at age 11, but after a few years persuaded his parents to buy him a piano so that he could write songs. He studied composition at London's Royal Academy of Music from 1971 to 1974. After graduation, he formed a band called Arms and Legs. While working as musical director at the Portsmouth Playboy Club, Jackson produced an LP-length demo of his songs that got him a publishing contract with Albion Music. Soon afterwards, A&M producer David Kershenbaum got Jackson a recording contract with his label.

Look Sharp was recorded in a week and a half. The single "Is She Really Going Out with Him?" hit #15, and the album went to #20. *I'm the Man,* released six months later, hit #22. Jackson was quickly labeled a power-pop performer, an image that was changed with the release of *Beat Crazy,* an ominous reggae-inflected LP. Jackson himself produced it, and his group was billed for the first time as the Joe Jackson Band. The LP was less commercially successful, and a three-song EP that included Jackson singing Jimmy Cliff's "The Harder They Come" (available only on British import) got considerably more U.S. airplay.

Within months of the LP's release, Jackson was back in the studio working on *Jumpin' Jive,* a collection of Forties swing tunes, including some songs by Louis Jordan. A novel idea, *Jumpin' Jive* was fairly popular but yielded no hit singles, although Jackson toured the U.S. with a big band. In 1982, Jackson moved to New York to record *Night and Day,* which incorporated hints of salsa, funk and minimalism; "Steppin' Out" sold 250,000 copies and the album went gold. In 1983, Jackson appeared on the soundtrack for *Mike's Murder.*

MAHALIA JACKSON
Born October 26, 1911, New Orleans; died January 27, 1972, Chicago
N.A.— *World's Greatest Gospel Singer* (Kenwood)
Mahalia Jackson: Greatest Hits (Columbia) *The Great Mahalia Jackson.*

Mahalia Jackson is generally regarded as one of the best and certainly the most popular gospel singer ever. Her forceful bluesy style was greatly influenced by Ma Rainey and Bessie Smith, though Jackson never sang secular music. Aretha Franklin cites Jackson as her favorite singer.

Jackson and family regularly attended New Orleans' Mount Moriah Baptist Church. Despite her strict religious training, she heard and enjoyed New Orleans' wealth of jazz and blues. She often listened to the music of Smith and Rainey on record. In 1927, she moved to Chicago, where she worked as a domestic and a nurse.

In 1935, Jackson made her recording debut after scouts for Decca Records had heard her sing at a funeral. From Decca, Jackson moved to the small Apollo label, where she became a gospel legend. Her recording of "Move On Up" sold more than two million copies. In concert, Jackson was known to extend it to as long as 25 minutes. Crucial to her popularity was her accompanist, pianist Mildred Falls, whom record executive John Hammond called "the greatest gospel accompanist that ever lived."

In 1954, Jackson signed to Columbia Records, where A&R director Mitch Miller used strings and choirs to back her, increasing her popularity with whites, but inhibiting much of her earlier fire. At the time of her death, she had a larger white than black following.

MICHAEL JACKSON (See the Jackson 5)

MILLIE JACKSON
Born 1943, Thompson, Georgia
1972—*Millie Jackson* (Spring) *It Hurts So Good*
1974—*Caught Up* **1976**—*Best of Millie Jackson*
(Polydor) *Lovingly Yours* (Spring) **1977**—*Feelin' Bitchy* (Polydor) **1978**—*Get It Out Cha System*
1979—*Royal Rappin's; A Moment's Pleasure; Live and Uncensored* (Spring) **1980**—*For Men Only; I Had to Say It* **1981**—*Just a Lil' Bit Country* **1982**—*Live and Outrageous (Rated XXXX).*

Soul singer and songwriter Millie Jackson has been internationally popular for a decade, thanks to live shows that interweave gritty deep-soul singing and raunchy raps.

Jackson grew up in Georgia and lived with her grandfather, a preacher, until she ran away at age 14. She came to New York and worked as a model (mostly for confession magazines). In 1964, on a bet, she jumped onstage and sang at the Palm Cafe in Harlem. For the rest of the Sixties, she worked as a singer around New York. She cut a single in 1969 for MGM, but kept her day job until she signed with Spring Records in 1971.

Jackson had her first soul hit in 1972 with "A Child of God" (#22 R&B), followed by "Ask Me What You Want" (#14 R&B) and "It Hurts So Good" (#3 R&B, 1973), which was included on the soundtrack of *Cleopatra Jones*.

Her breakthrough was the 1974 album *Caught Up*, the first recording of her live act. It was a concept album in which Jackson played a wife on one side and the Other Woman on the other; it yielded a hit single, "(If Loving You Is Wrong) I Don't Want to Be Right," and went gold. Since 1975, most of Jackson's albums have gone gold, although her language is often so blunt that she gets no airplay. *Feelin' Bitchy* was a platinum album. Jackson recorded a duet album, *Royal Rappin's*, with Isaac Hayes in 1979 and continues to play large halls and record regularly. She is also her own manager and coproducer, through her own publishing company, Double Ak-Shun Music.

WANDA JACKSON

Born October 20, 1937, Maud, Oklahoma
1960—*Rockin' with Wanda* (Capitol) **1966**—*Wanda Jackson Sings Country Blues* **1972**—*Praise the Lord* **1974**—*Country Gospel* (Word) **1979**—*Greatest Hits* (Capitol).

Although Jackson is known for her mid- to late-Fifties recordings as the "Queen of Rockabilly," she has since worked as a country singer and a born-again Christian gospel singer. Her father was an amateur musician, and both parents encouraged her to sing. At age 15 she had her own radio program on KLPR in Oklahoma City; the next year she began recording for Decca. She soon joined Hank Thompson's swing band and in 1956 was signed by Capitol.

None of her hits reached the Top Twenty ("Let's Have a Party," #37, 1960; "Right or Wrong," #29, 1961; and "In the Middle of Heartache," #27, 1961), but Jackson became known for her aggressive approach, which was considered unique for the time. She has recorded in German, Dutch and Japanese (phonetically), and frequently tours internationally. Her first hit, "Let's Have a Party," featured backing by Gene Vincent's Blue Caps.

THE JACKSON 5/THE JACKSONS

Formed 1967, Gary, Indiana
Sigmund Esco (Jackie) Jackson (b. May 4, 1951);
Toriano Adaryll (Tito) Jackson (b. Oct. 15, 1953), gtr.;
Marlon David Jackson (b. Mar. 12, 1957); Jermaine La Jaune Jackson (b. Dec. 11, 1954), bass; Michael Joe Jackson (b. Aug. 29, 1958); Steven Randall (Randy) Jackson (b. Oct. 29, 1961).

1969—*I Want You Back* (also known as *Diana Ross Presents the Jackson 5*) (Motown) **1970**—*ABC; Third Album; Christmas Album* **1971**—*Maybe Tomorrow* **1972**—*The Jackson 5's Greatest Hits* **1973**—*Get It Together* **1974**—*Dancing Machine* **1976**—*The Jacksons* (Epic) **1977**—*Motown Special* (Motown) *Anthology; Goin' Places* (Epic) **1978**—*Destiny* **1979**—*20 Golden Greats* (Motown, U.K.) **1981**— *Triumph* (Epic) **1982**—*Live*.
Michael Jackson solo: 1972—*Got to Be There* (Motown) **1975**—*Forever, Michael; The Best of Michael Jackson* **1979**—*Off the Wall* (Epic) **1982**—*Thriller*.
Jermaine Jackson solo: 1976—*My Name Is Jermaine* (Motown) **1977**—*Feel the Fire* **1978**—*Frontiers* **1980**—*Jermaine; Let's Get Serious* **1981**—*I Like Your Style* **1982**—*Let Me Tickle Your Fancy*.
Jackie Jackson solo: 1973—*Jackie Jackson* (Motown).

Since their national debut in 1969 with "I Want You Back," the Jackson family has been the most successful black pop soul vocal group, selling over 100 million records worldwide.

The group's father and manager had been a guitarist for the Falcons; he worked as a crane operator, but maintained an interest in music. In the late Sixties, Tito, Jermaine and Jackie performed around Gary, Indiana, as the Jackson Family; in 1969, Michael and Marlon joined and the group became the Jackson 5. Popular in their hometown, they cut one unsuccessful single, "Big Boy," before being brought to Motown's attention by Bobby Taylor of the Vancouvers, a Motown group touring through Gary.

Within months, the Jackson 5 were on the Motown roster. Diana Ross, often mistakenly credited with their discovery, took them under her wing. In January of 1970, "I Want You Back" hit #1 and sold over two million copies, becoming the first of a string of 13 Top Twenty singles, which included "ABC" (#1, 1970), "The Love You Save" (#1, 1970), "I'll Be There" (#1, 1970, their biggest seller), "Mama's Pearl" (#2, 1971), "Never Can Say Goodbye" (#2, 1971), "Maybe Tomorrow" (#20, 1971), "Sugar Daddy" (#10, 1971), "Little Bitty Pretty One" (#13, 1972), "Lookin' through the Windows" (#16, 1972), "Corner of the Sky" (#18, 1972), "Dancing Machine" (#2, 1974) and "I Am Love" (#15, 1975). Many of the group's Motown hits were written by "The Corporation" (Freddie Perren, Fonso Mizell, Deke Richards and Berry Gordy). The Jackson 5 toured frequently, always tutored and supervised by the Motown staff, although their father remained their manager.

In 1972, the group received a commendation from Congress for its "contributions to American youth." Jermaine married Berry Gordy, Jr.'s daughter Hazel in 1973, and two years later, when the group left Motown, Jermaine stayed with his father-in-law's label. Like many other

The Jacksons: Michael Jackson, Tito Jackson, Randy Jackson, Jackie Jackson, Marlon Jackson

Motown artists, the Jackson 5 left the label over artistic control. When the group announced its departure, Motown sued for breach of contract. The $20-million suit was eventually settled in 1980, with the Jacksons paying $600,000 ($100,000 in cash and $500,000 in "other items") and the label retaining all rights to the name the Jackson 5.

They changed their name to the Jacksons and signed with Epic in March 1976. Kenny Gamble and Leon Huff produced their first two Epic LPs, *The Jacksons* and *Going Places,* and the Jackson brothers began writing their own material, beginning with *Destiny* (which contained "Shake Your Body (Down to the Ground)"); within a few years they were producing most of their own material as well. Except for four singles that failed to crack the Top Forty, the Jacksons picked up the streak where they'd left off and the hits kept coming: "Enjoy Yourself" (#6, 1976), "Show You the Way to Go" (#28, 1977), "Shake Your Body (Down to the Ground)" (#7, 1979), "Lovely One" (#2, 1980), "Heartbreak Hotel" (#22, 1980). They continued to appear regularly on television and in Las Vegas in addition to their tours. Two sisters, La Toya and Maureen, joined the group briefly in the mid-Seventies, but Maureen soon retired and La Toya launched a largely uneventful solo career.

Michael Jackson, the group's lead singer and focal point, became more popular than the Jacksons as the Eighties began. He had a string of solo hits in the early Seventies ("Got to Be There," #4, 1971; "Rockin' Robin," #2, 1972; "Ben," #1, 1972) and played the Scarecrow in *The Wiz* in 1978. But he had the biggest success of his career with two albums produced by Quincy Jones: *Off the Wall* and *Thriller. Off the Wall* included four

hit singles—"Don't Stop Till You Get Enough" (#1, 1979), "Rock with You" (#1, 1979), "Off the Wall" (#10, 1980) and "She's Out of My Life" (#10, 1980)—and Epic claims it has sold over six million copies. The Jacksons' *Triumph* sold a million copies in its wake and prompted a 39-city tour that grossed $5.5 million.

Michael Jackson's *Thriller* had yielded three hit singles by early 1983—"The Girl Is Mine" (#2, 1982) (a duet with Paul McCartney), "Billie Jean" (#1, 1983) and "Beat It" (#1, 1983) (which included a guitar solo by Eddie Van Halen)—and the album had gone platinum.

Although less spectacular than brother Michael's, Jermaine's solo career has been consistent. While a few of his singles have crossed over to the pop Top Forty ("Daddy's Home," #9, 1973; "Let's Get Serious," #9, 1980), most have hit the R&B charts.

THE JAGGERZ/DONNIE IRIS

Formed 1965, Pittsburgh
Ben Faiella (b. Beaver Falls, Penn.), gtr., bass; Donald Iris (b. 1943, Ellwood City, Penn.), gtr., voc.; Thom Davies (b. Duquesne, Penn.), kybds., trumpet; James Ross (b. Aliquippa, Penn.), bass, trombone; William Maybray, bass; James Pugliano, drums.
1969—*Introducing the Jaggerz* (Gamble) (− Iris; + Domenic Terrace, gtr., bass, trumpet) **1970**—*We Went to Different Schools Together* (Kama Sutra) **1971**—(− Ross).

Led by frontman/lead vocalist Donnie Iris (credited on the LPs as D. Ierace), the Jaggerz had a #2 single with the million-selling "The Rapper." Their debut single, "Baby I Love You" (Gamble Records), with Maybray on lead vocals, was a flop. The next year, they signed to Kama Sutra and recorded *We Went to Different Schools Together,* which contained "The Rapper." Two subsequent singles, "I Call My Baby Candy" and "What a Bummer," never even reached the Top Seventy. By then, Iris had left the band to pursue a solo career; the group continues to play club dates with different personnel.

Iris worked in a Pittsburgh recording studio and then joined Wild Cherry, who had a platinum single in 1976 with "Play That Funky Music." With ex–Wild Cherry keyboardist Mark Avsec, Iris began composing. Around 1979, he recorded *Back on the Streets* for a Cleveland label, Midwest National. He then formed his own band. MCA later released the LP nationally, and in 1980 Iris' "Ah! Leah!" went to #29. In 1981, Iris, with his band the Cruisers, released *King Cool.* It failed to break the Top Sixty, but Iris still continues to tour and often performs "The Rapper" in his shows.

THE JAM

Formed 1973, Woking, England
Paul Weller (b. 1958), gtr., voc.; Bruce Foxton (b. 1956), bass, voc.; Rick Buckler (b. 1956), drums, voc.

1977—*In the City* (Polydor)   1978—*This Is the Modern World*   1979—*All Mod Cons*   1980—*Setting Sons; Sound Affects*   1981—*Absolute Beginners*   1982— *The Gift.*

Though they first came to prominence in London's 1976 punk-rock explosion, the Jam shared only a high-speed, stripped-down approach with their contemporaries. Their clothes, haircuts and tunes reflected an obsession with the mid-Sixties mod style, and some termed the band the new Who. Although Paul Weller's gruffly accented vocals and his earnest songs never broke through to American audiences, the Jam became consistent hitmakers in Britain.

Weller, attending Sheerwater Secondary Modern School in Woking, had originally formed a folk duo with guitarist Steve Brooks in 1972. They later formed the Jam with guitarist Dave Waller and drummer Rick Buckler. Waller and Brooks quit in 1974, and bassist Bruce Foxton joined. With Weller's father as manager, they worked on Sixties R&B and mod-rock covers and some originals; in 1976 they made a successful London debut at the 100 Club's first punk extravaganza. Their debut album was a British hit, yielding a Top Forty U.K. single in the title tune (from which the Sex Pistols later used a riff for their "Holiday in the Sun"). *Modern World* followed the same format, but the album was so harshly criticized by the British music press that the highly sensitive Weller nearly broke the band up. That year the Jam also released soul covers of "Back in My Arms Again" and "Sweet Soul Music."

Just prior to the well-received *All Mod Cons*, they released three successful U.K. singles: "News of the World" (#27); a cover of the Kinks' "David Watts" (#25);

and "Down in the Tube Station at Midnight" (#15), which revealed a new political commitment. "Tube Station," a protest against Britain's anti-immigrant "Paki-bashing" phenomenon, was banned by the BBC. *Setting Sons* was a decline-of-the-Empire/class-conflict concept album and yielded the British hit "Eton Rifles" (#3, 1979); it also included "Heatwave." *Sound Affects* was their biggest commercial success to date, with a #1 British hit in "Start!" and another minor U.K. hit in the acoustic ballad "That's Entertainment."

The Jam continued making inroads on the American market with *The Gift*, which yielded the Motown-ish minor hit single "Town Called Malice." Both *Cons* and *Sons* went gold in England. In 1980, Weller appeared on Peter Gabriel's third solo LP. In October 1982, he announced that the group was breaking up: "It really dawned on me how secure the situation was, the fact that we could go on for the next ten years making records, getting bigger and bigger. . . . That frightened me because I realized we were going to end up . . . like the rest of them." He released his first post-Jam efforts as leader of Style Council in 1983.

ELMORE JAMES
Born Elmore Brooks, January 27, 1918, Richland, Mississippi; died May 24, 1963, Chicago
N.A.—*Whose Muddy Shoes* (Chess)   1966—*Blues Masters, Volume 1* (Blue Horizon)   1970—*Tough*   1971—*The Sky Is Crying* (Sphere Sound)   *I Need You; The Legend of* (Polydor, U.K.)   1973—*Street Talkin'* (Muse)   *All Them Blues* (DJM, U.K.)   1976— *Anthology of the Blues: Legend of Elmore James* (Kent)   *Anthology of the Blues: Resurrection of Elmore James.*

One of the most influential postwar urban blues guitarists, Elmore James was the one Chicago bluesman perhaps most responsible for shaping the styles of slide-guitar playing that translated from blues to rock. His anthems, like "It Hurts Me Too," "I Believe I'll Dust My Broom" (by Robert Johnson), "Shake Your Money Maker" and "The Sky Is Crying," have been covered by Eric Clapton, Fleetwood Mac, John Mayall, Savoy Brown, George Thorogood and others. His influence can most directly be heard in the slide-guitar work of Duane Allman and Brian Jones.

James began picking on a homemade lard-can guitar as a child. By the late Thirties he was working Mississippi taverns with blues legends Robert Johnson and Sonny Boy Williamson (Rice Miller). Between 1943 and 1945, he served in the Navy. He began recording in 1951 for the Trumpet label in Jackson, Mississippi. He later moved to Chicago but continued to perform in the South and parts of the Midwest.

It was when he began recording in Chicago that James

The Jam: Rick Buckler, Paul Weller, Bruce Foxton

became one of the first and foremost modernizers of the Delta blues tradition. In 1963, while visiting the home of his cousin Homesick James, a bluesman with whom he'd performed in the Forties, Elmore James suffered a fatal heart attack. Aside from Duane Allman, James's stylistic influence can be traced to bluesmen like J. B. Hutto, B. B. King, Freddie King, Jimmy Reed and Hound Dog Taylor, as well as rockers like Jimi Hendrix and Johnny Winter. His son, Elmore James, Jr., is also a musician.

ETTA JAMES
Born Etta James Hawkins, circa 1938, Los Angeles
1961—*At Last* (Cadet) *Second Time Around* **1963**— *Etta James; Top Ten* **1964**—*Rocks the House* **1965**—*Queen of Soul* **1967**—*Call My Name* **1968**— *Tell Mama* **1970**—*Sings Funk* **1971**—*Losers Weepers; Peaches* (Chess) **1972**—*Miss Etta James* (Crown) *Best of; Twist with; Golden Decade* (Chess) **1973**—*Etta James* **1974**—*Come a Little Closer* **1975**—*Etta Is Better Than Evah!* **1978**—*Deep in the Night* (Warner Bros.).

Soul singer Etta James survived a decade-long heroin addiction to forge a career that has seen her turn out well over a dozen hits, and she is still going strong with concert appearances. James was discovered by Johnny Otis while she was still in her early teens. When Otis' revue was playing the Fillmore Theater in San Francisco (at that time a ghetto theater like New York City's Apollo), she called him in his hotel room before a show and demanded to come up to his room and sing for him. Otis heard her and phoned her mother to say he was taking Etta on tour with him. At Otis' Los Angeles home, he and Etta cowrote her first hit, "Roll with Me, Henry," an answer to Hank Ballard and the Midnighters' off-color "Work with Me, Annie." Under the title "The Wallflower," "Henry" became a #2 R&B hit in 1955. That year Georgia Gibbs had a #1 pop hit with a mild cover of the tune called "Dance with Me, Henry." Later, James's version was retitled "Dance with Me, Henry."

Through the mid-Fifties, James became a mainstay of Otis' revue and scored another R&B hit with "Good Rockin' Daddy" (#12, 1955). In 1960, she moved from Modern to Chess Records' Argo subsidiary, and the R&B hits began coming again: "All I Could Do Was Cry" (#2), "My Dearest Darling" (#5) and a duet as Etta and Harvey (with Harvey Fuqua of Harvey and the Moonglows) entitled "If I Can't Have You" (#52 pop, #6 R&B).

James continued making R&B hits through the early Sixties. In 1961, she had more Top Ten R&B hits with "At Last" (#2) and "Trust in Me" (#4), and in 1962 with "Something's Got a Hold on Me" (#4) and "Stop the Wedding" (#6). In 1963, she hit the pop charts with "Pushover" (#25 pop, #7 R&B), as well as "Pay Back" (#78), "Two Sides to Every Story" (#63) and "Would It Make Any Difference to You" (#64); 1964 brought "Baby,

What You Want Me to Do?" (#82) and "Loving You More Every Day" (#65).

In the Sixties she developed a heroin addiction that lasted through 1974 and kept her much of the time in L.A.'s Tarzana Psychiatric Hospital. Still, she hit big with "Tell Mama" (#23 pop, #10 R&B, 1967), "Losers Weepers" (#26 R&B, 1970) and "I've Found a Love" (#31 R&B, 1972). Though she has not had any major hit records since ending her heroin addiction, she's remained a popular concert performer. She played the Montreux Jazz Festival in 1977 and opened some dates for the Rolling Stones' 1978 U.S. tour.

RICK JAMES AND THE STONE CITY BAND
Born James Johnson, February 1, 1952, Buffalo, New York
1978—*Come Get It* (Motown) **1979**—*Bustin' Out of L Seven; Fire It Up* **1980**—*Garden of Love* **1981**— *Street Songs* **1982**—*Throwin' Down.*

Singer/songwriter/keyboardist/guitarist Rick James emerged in the late Seventies with an energetic blend of blatant come-ons and dance music he calls "punk funk." James attended and was expelled from five different schools before leaving Buffalo at 15 to join the U.S. Naval Reserves. Soon after, he went AWOL and ended up in Toronto, where he formed and fronted a band called the Mynah Birds, which included Neil Young and Bruce Palmer (later of Buffalo Springfield) and Goldy McJohn (of Steppenwolf). They were signed to Motown and recorded, but nothing was released and the group soon disbanded. James then worked as a sideman, playing bass with several groups through the Seventies, with only minimal success.

In 1978, James re-signed with Motown, this time as a songwriter and producer. That year, his solo debut, *Come Get It,* sold two million copies and "You and I" was a hit (#13 pop, #1 R&B). Subsequent singles—"Mary Jane" (#41 pop, #3 R&B, 1978), "Bustin' Out" (#6 pop, #8 R&B, 1979), "High on Your Love Suite" (#12 R&B, 1979), "Love Gun" (#13 pop, #13 R&B, 1979), "Big Time" (#17 R&B, 1980), "Give It to Me Baby" (#40 pop, #1 R&B, 1981), "Super Freak (Part 1)" (#16 pop, #3 R&B, 1981)— have propelled each of his releases, including the uncharacteristically ballad-laden *Garden of Love* onto the pop charts.

James's stage image—long corn-rowed and beaded hair, elaborate sequined costumes and instruments—and his bass-heavy music have prompted comparisons with Sly Stone and George Clinton's Parliament-Funkadelic. James has also produced Teena Marie, the Temptations ("Standing on the Top") and Carl Carlton.

TOMMY JAMES AND THE SHONDELLS
Formed 1960, Niles, Michigan
Original Shondells unknown; lineup in 1966: Tommy

James (b. Thomas Gregory Jackson, Apr. 29, 1947, Dayton, Oh.), voc.; Joseph Kessler, gtr.; Ronald Rosman (b. Feb. 28, 1945), kybds.; Michael Vale (b. July 17, 1949), bass; Vincent Pietropaoli, drums; George Magura, sax, bass, organ. Subsequent pesonnel changes: − Pietropaoli; + Peter Lucia (b. Feb. 2, 1947), drums; − Magura; − Kessler; + Eddie Gray (b. Feb. 27, 1948).

1966—*Hanky Panky* (Roulette) 1968—*Mony Mony* 1969—*Crimson and Clover* 1970—*The Best of Tommy James.*
Tommy James solo: 1976—*In Touch* (Fantasy) 1977—*Midnight Rider* 1980—*Three Times in Love* (Millennium).

Tommy James and the Shondells were one of the most consistently successful American pop groups of the late Sixties, amassing 14 gold singles, and four gold and two million-selling LPs. Group leader and singer James taught himself to play guitar at age nine; four years later he formed the Shondells. The group played locally, and in 1962 recorded a Jeff Barry-Ellie Greenwich song, "Hanky Panky," as a favor for a local disc jockey. Four years later, a Pittsburgh DJ began playing it and more than 20,000 copies were sold within a few days. After its national release on Roulette in 1966, it hit #1 and sold a million copies.

Between 1966 and 1970 (when the Shondells disbanded), the group had 12 Top Thirty hits, including seven million-sellers: "Hanky Panky" (#1, 1966), "I Think We're Alone Now" (#3, 1967), "Mirage" (#10, 1967), "Mony, Mony" (#3, 1968), "Crimson and Clover" (#1, 1969), "Sweet Cherry Wine" (#7, 1969) and "Crystal Blue Persuasion" (#1, 1969). With "Crimson and Clover" (the group's biggest seller at 5½ million) the Shondells' sound became more psychedelic than bubblegum; James began producing as well. After the group disbanded, James returned to his home in upstate New York for several months (partially to recuperate from a drug problem) before reemerging in 1970 to produce Alive and Kickin's hit version of his "Tighter and Tighter," and in 1971 to record his #4 hit "Draggin' the Line."

James's subsequent singles failed to crack the Top Thirty, and solo LPs like *Midnight Rider* (produced by Jeff Barry) never hit. He returned to the charts in 1980 with "Three Times in Love" (#19). By that time, it was estimated James had sold over 30 million records.

THE JAMES GANG
Formed 1966, Cleveland
Jim Fox, drums; Tom Kriss, bass; Glen Schwartz, gtr.
1969—(− Schwartz; + Joe Walsh [b. Nov. 20, 1947, Wichita, Kan.], gtr., voc.) *Yer Album* (ABC) (− Kriss; + Dale Peters, bass) 1970—*James Gang Rides Again* 1971—*Thirds; Live in Concert* (− Walsh; + Domenic Troiano [b. Modugno, Italy], gtr.; + Roy

Kenner, voc.) 1972—*Straight Shooter; Passin' Through* 1973—*Best of* (− Troiano; + Tommy Bolin [b. 1951, Sioux City, Iowa; d. Dec. 4, 1976, Miami], gtr.) *Bang* (Atco) *Gold Record* (ABC) 1974—*Miami* (Atco) (− Bolin; − Kenner; group disbanded) 1975—(regrouped with Richard Shack, gtr., and Bubba Keith, gtr., voc.) *Newborn* 1976—*Jesse Come Home.*

The James Gang was a favorite American hard-rock band during the early Seventies. Founded by drummer Jim Fox, who had played in Cleveland bands since the age of 14, the group earned a word-of-mouth reputation throughout the Midwest. Glen Schwartz (who left to join Pacific Gas and Electric) was replaced by future Eagle Joe Walsh, perhaps the group's most famous member and, it could be argued, its best musician and star attraction. Pete Townshend, a friend of the Gang, arranged for them to open for the Who in Europe in 1971.

Despite a career-long lack of hit singles, their first four LPs were successful, and they continued to be a major concert draw around the world for a while after Walsh's departure to form Barnstorm. His replacement, Domenic Troiano, left in 1973 to join the Guess Who, and Walsh recommended Bolin for the part. But Bolin (who had worked with Billy Cobham) contributed to only two LPs—*Miami* and *Bang* (originally titled *James Gang Bang*)—before joining Deep Purple. Vocalist Roy Kenner soon left as well, and in 1974 the group temporarily disbanded only to re-form a year later with Bubba Keith and Richard Shack. The James Gang never recaptured their early momentum and disbanded for good in 1976.

JAN AND DEAN
Jan Berry, born April 3, 1941, Los Angeles; Dean Torrence, born March 10, 1941, Los Angeles
1962—*Golden Hits* (Liberty) 1965—*Golden Hits, Volume 2* 1966—*Golden Hits, Volume 3* 1971—*Legendary Masters* (United Artists) 1974—*Gotta Take That One Last Ride* 1982—*One Summer Night/Live* (Rhino).

Between their 1958 debut single, "Jennie Lee," and Jan Berry's near-fatal car crash in April 1966, Jan and Dean were the premier surf music duo, charting 13 Top Thirty singles and selling over ten million records worldwide.

The two were friends and football teammates at Emerson Junior High in Los Angeles. They jammed with neighbors Sandy Nelson and future Beach Boy Bruce Johnston. With a singer named Arnie Ginsberg, they recorded a #8 hit for Arwin Records entitled "Jennie Lee." Torrence was serving in the National Guard when the contracts were signed, and so the single was credited to Jan and Arnie.

Once Torrence returned, he and Berry resumed their partnership, Ginsberg joined the Army, and Arwin dropped them. Herb Alpert and Lou Adler produced "Baby Talk" (#10, 1959). Five Top 100 entries on the Dore and Challenge labels preceded their signing with Liberty. After three minor hits, they recorded their only gold single, "Surf City." Their friend Beach Boy Brian Wilson worked with them on their debut LP, *Linda Goes Surfin'*, and cowrote "Surf City" with Berry: Torrence, uncredited, sings the lead on the Beach Boys' "Barbara Ann." The Beach Boys and Jan and Dean often appeared on each others' records until their record companies objected.

Berry did the bulk of the duo's songwriting, including the soundtrack for a 1964 Fabian beach movie entitled *Ride the Wild Surf*. The pair hosted *The T.A.M.I. Show* in 1964. Both continued their education full-time (Torrence was a pre-med and then an architecture student at UCLA, Berry an art and design student at USC), until they were convinced of their musical success. Their hits included "Heart and Soul" (#25, 1961), "Linda" (#28, 1963), "Surf City" (#1, 1963), "Honolulu Lulu" (#11, 1963), "Drag City" (#10, 1964), "Dead Man's Curve" (#8, 1964), "The Little Old Lady (from Pasadena)" (#3, 1964), "Ride the Wild Surf" (#16, 1964), "Sidewalk Surfin'" (#25, 1964), "You Really Know How to Hurt a Guy" (#27, 1965), "I Found a Girl" (#30, 1965) and "Popsicle" (#21, 1966).

But by the mid-Sixties, their friendship became strained to the point that they considered breaking up. In April 1966, Berry hit a parked truck at 65 mph on L.A.'s Whittier Boulevard. His three passengers were killed and he sustained brain damage so severe that it wasn't until 1973 that he was able to remember an entire song lyric (he is still partially paralyzed and suffers speech difficulties). During the years of recovery, he regularly recorded demos for Lou Adler as therapy. Meanwhile, Torrence had recorded a solo album, *Save for a Rainy Day* (which Berry was furious about), and became head of Kitty Hawk Graphics in Hollywood. He has since won design awards for his album covers. The pair made a premature and unsuccessful comeback appearance in 1973, but by 1978 they were again performing live on occasion. A television movie account of their lives entitled *Dead Man's Curve* aired in 1978.

JAY AND THE AMERICANS
Formed 1961, Brooklyn, New York
John "Jay" Traynor, lead voc.; Kenny Vance (b. Dec. 9, 1943), voc.; Sandy Deane (b. Sandy Yaguda, Jan. 30, 1943), voc.; Marty Sanders (b. Feb. 28, 1941), gtr.; Howie Kane (b. June 6, 1942), voc.
1962—(− Traynor; + David "Jay" Black [b. Nov. 2, 1941], lead voc.) 1965—*Greatest Hits, Volume 1* (United Artists) 1967—*Greatest Hits, Volume 2*
1969—(− Kane) 1975—*The Very Best of Jay and the Americans.*

Jay and the Americans were a clean-cut vocal quintet whose Sixties hits included four Top Ten entries. The group's first hit, the Leiber and Stoller–produced "She Cried" (#5, 1962), featured the original Jay, John Traynor, on lead vocals. That year he left the group and guitarist Marty Sanders invited his songwriting partner, David Black, to audition. Black adopted the monicker Jay and the reconstituted group had its first hit with "Only in America" (#25, 1963), a song originally intended for the Drifters. The following year they hit #3 with "Come a Little Bit Closer," and in 1965 the grandiose "Cara Mia" hit #4. This, their best-remembered hit, was revived in the Netherlands in 1980 and reached #1.

In 1965, they released an uptempo cover of "Some Enchanted Evening" (#13) and Neil Diamond's first hit as a songwriter, "Sunday and Me" (#18). It was not until 1969 that they again hit the Top Ten, this time with the million-selling "This Magic Moment" (#6).

The group stopped recording in 1970 after hitting the Top Twenty for the last time with "Walking in the Rain" (#19). A contractual dispute with United Artists over publishing rights kept them from recording for a number of years. Jay Black kept the name alive by touring throughout the Seventies and into the Eighties with Richard Nader's rock nostalgia shows. As a solo artist, he recorded an album in 1975 and later had a minor European hit with "Love Is in the Air" (John Paul Young covered it in the U.S.). In 1982, K-Tel released *Jay Black of Jay and the Americans: This Magic Moment* in Canada while he awaited a new record deal in the U.S.

Future Steely Dan founders Donald Fagen and Walter Becker were part of the group's backup band in the early Seventies, and in 1970 Kenny Vance produced their soundtrack album for *You Got to Walk It Like You Talk It*. Vance also worked as a solo act, recording his solo debut album in 1975.

THE JAYNETTS
Formed 1956, Bronx, New York
Mary Sue Wells, Ethel Davis, Ada Ray, Yvonne Bushnell.

A female quartet from the Bronx, the Jaynetts began recording in 1956. In 1963, they recorded "Sally Go 'Round the Roses" (with then-unknown drummer Buddy Miles). The single hit #2 that year, but their followup, "Dear Abby," flopped and the group disbanded.

JAZZ

Jazz is music that depends primarily on improvisation and reflects a long tradition of changing ideas of structure, freedom and swing. The first music known as jazz was the New Orleans style (later called Dixieland), in which a small group would improvise collectively on a well-known tune. No one in particular carried melody or harmony, but everyone was aware of them. In the Twenties, Louis Armstrong and others began to separate soloists from accompaniment, each permitted different degrees of freedom—an idea that ruled jazz for the next few decades, through the harmonic and rhythmic revolutions of the big bands of the Thirties swing era (Duke Ellington, Count Basie, Fletcher Henderson, Benny Goodman), be-bop in the late Forties (Charlie Parker, Dizzy Gillespie), "cool" and hard-bop and modal playing in the Fifties (Miles Davis, Thelonious Monk).

In the Sixties, John Coltrane began to work on a fusion of Eastern and Western improvisation, while Ornette Coleman, Cecil Taylor and others reconsidered collective improvisation in the light of new ideas about rhythm and harmonic freedom. Rockers toyed with jazz in the late Sixties, and Miles Davis tried a version of jazz rock that spawned various Seventies bands. Pure jazz, meanwhile, grew ever more eclectic in terms of structure and style, with bands like the Art Ensemble of Chicago and Air drawing on music from ragtime to Indian raga. Jazz is a continuum, more respectful of tradition than rock, and in places like New York or Paris it is possible to hear musicians from every jazz era still working.

BLIND LEMON JEFFERSON
Born circa July 1897, Couchman, Texas; died circa December 1930, Chicago
1968—*Master of the Blues, Volume 1* (Biograph)
1969—*Blind Lemon Jefferson 1926-1929* **1971**—*Master of the Blues, Volume 2* **1971**—*Black Snake Moan* (Milestone) **1975**—*Blind Lemon Jefferson.*

One of the first country bluesmen of the Twenties, arguably the most influential, and surely the most commercially popular, singer/guitarist Blind Lemon Jefferson (Lemon was his given first name) influenced other bluesmen like Lightnin' Hopkins, Big Joe Williams, Robert Pete Williams, T-Bone Walker and B. B. King.

Blind from birth, Jefferson began performing in his early teens in streets and at parties and picnics. He was as much a "songster"—with a repertoire spanning blues, shouts, moans, field hollers, breakdowns, ballads, religious hymns, prison and work songs—as a bluesman. As a teenager, he worked throughout Texas, then hoboed through the South and Southwest, from Georgia to St. Louis, into the early Twenties, although Dallas was always his home base. Around 1925, he was signed to Paramount Records, for which he recorded his own distinctive, haunting country blues under his own name, and religious songs under the pseudonym Deacon L. J. Bates. His blues recordings were among the best-selling "race" records of the 1925–30 era.

Jefferson reportedly suffered a heart attack in 1930 in Chicago, and was left on the streets to die of exposure just before Christmas.

His best-remembered tunes include "Black Snake Moan," "See That My Grave Is Kept Clean," "Long Lonesome Blues," and "Booger Rooger Blues," in which he coined the term "booger rooger" (for a wild party), which later became "boogie-woogie." In 1970, a biography, *Blind Lemon Jefferson* by Bob Groom, was published by Blues World.

THE JEFFERSON AIRPLANE/JEFFERSON STARSHIP
Jefferson Airplane formed early 1965, San Francisco
Marty Balin (b. Jan. 30, 1942, Cincinnati), voc.; Paul Kantner (b. Mar. 12, 1942, San Francisco), gtr., voc.; Jorma Kaukonen (b. Dec. 23, 1940, Washington, D.C.), gtr., voc.; Signe Anderson, voc.; Bob Harvey, bass; Skip Spence, drums.
1965—(− Harvey; + Jack Casady [b. Apr. 13, 1944, Washington, D.C.], bass) **1966**—*Jefferson Airplane Takes Off* (RCA) (− Anderson; + Grace Slick [b. Grace Wing, Oct. 30, 1939, Chicago], kybds., voc.; − Spence; + Spencer Dryden [b. Apr. 7, 1943, New York City], drums) **1967**—*Surrealistic Pillow; After Bathing at Baxter's* **1968**—*Crown of Creation* **1969**—*Bless Its Pointed Little Head; Volunteers* **1970**—*Blows against the Empire* (credited to Jefferson Starship, featuring other guest musicians) *The Worst of the Jefferson Airplane* (− Dryden; + Joey Covington, drums) **1971**—(− Balin) *Bark* (Grunt) **1972**—(− Covington; + John Barbata, drums; + Papa John Creach [b. May 28, 1917, Beaver Falls, Penn.] fiddle) *Long John Silver* (+ David Freiberg, bass, gtr., kybds.; − Kaukonen; − Casady; − Covington) **1973**—*Thirty Seconds over Winterland* **1974**—*Early Flight.*
Jefferson Starship formed 1974, San Francisco
1974—(Slick; Barbata; Freiberg; Creach; Kantner; + Peter Kangaroo [b. Peter Kaukonen], bass; + Craig Chaquico [b. 1955], gtr.; − P. Kaukonen; + Pete Sears [b. Eng.], bass) *Dragon Fly* **1975**—(+ Balin) *Red Octopus* (− Creach) **1976**—*Spitfire* **1977**—*Flight Log* **1978**—*Earth* (− Slick; − Balin) **1979**—*Jefferson Starship Gold* (+ Mickey Thomas, voc.; − Barbata; + Aynsley Dunbar [b. 1946, Liverpool, Eng.], drums) *Freedom at Point Zero* **1981**—(+ Slick) *Modern Times* **1982**—*Winds of Change* (− Dunbar; + Don Baldwin, drums).
Paul Kantner solo (all with Grace Slick): **1971**—*Sunfighter* (Grunt) **1973**—*Baron Von Tollbooth and the Chrome Nun* (with Freiberg).
Grace Slick solo: 1974—*Manhole* (Grunt) **1980**—*Dreams* (RCA) **1981**—*Welcome to the Wrecking Ball.*
Marty Balin solo: 1973—*Bodacious DF* (RCA) **1981**—*Balin* (EMI) **1983**—*Lucky.*

At the start, the Jefferson Airplane not only epitomized the burgeoning Haight-Ashbury culture but also provided its soundtrack. The Airplane established a psychedelic unity with communal vocal harmonies and a synthesis of elements from folk, pop, jazz, blues and rock.

The band got started in 1965 when Marty Balin, formerly with the acoustic group the Town Criers, met Paul Kantner at the Drinking Gourd, a San Francisco club. They were first a folk-rock group, rounded out by Jorma Kaukonen, Skip Spence, Signe Anderson and Bob Harvey, though the latter was soon replaced by Jack Casady. Their first major show was on August 13, christening the Matrix Club, which later became *the* outlet for new S.F. bands. RCA signed them late in the year, and *Jefferson Airplane Takes Off* came out in September 1966 and went gold.

Just before the LP came out, in the summer of 1966, Signe Anderson left to have a baby and was replaced by former model Grace Slick. Slick had been a member of the Great Society, a group formed in 1965. The Great Society, which included Grace's husband of the time, Jerry Slick, and her brother-in-law Darby, had completed two LPs for Columbia, which weren't released until after Slick became a star with the Airplane. Spence left the Airplane to form Moby Grape, and was replaced by a former jazz drummer, Spencer Dryden, completing the Airplane's most inventive lineup.

Slick's vocals were stronger and more inventive than Anderson's; she later claimed that she always tried to imitate the yowl of the lead guitar. She contributed two former Great Society songs to *Surrealistic Pillow*—"Somebody to Love" (by Grace, Darby and Jerry Slick) and Darby's "White Rabbit" (which was banned in some areas as a drug song)—both of which became Top Ten singles, and the album sold a million copies.

After Bathing at Baxter's included a nine-minute psychedelic jam-collage, "Spayre Change," and occasioned the group's first battle with RCA over obscene language: the word "shit" was deleted from the lyric sheet. *Baxter's* had no hit singles, and didn't sell well, but the Airplane recouped with the gold *Crown of Creation*, which included Slick's "Lather" and David Crosby's "Triad," a song about a *ménage à trois* that had been rejected by Crosby's current group, the Byrds.

The band's ego battles were already beginning, however, as Slick stole media attention from Balin (the band's founder) and the songwriting became increasingly divergent. Live, Slick and Balin traded vocals in battles that became increasingly feverish, and the volatile sound of the band in concert was captured on *Bless Its Pointed Little Head.*

By the time they recorded 1969's *Volunteers,* the Airplane's contract allowed them total "artistic control," which meant that the "Up against the wall, motherfuckers" chorus of "We Can Be Together" appeared intact. The Airplane performed at the Woodstock and Altamont festivals, but then had its second major shakeup. Dryden

left in 1970 to join the New Riders of the Purple Sage (replaced by Joey Covington), and the band stopped touring when Slick became pregnant by Kantner. Anxious to perform, Kaukonen and Casady formed Hot Tuna (originally Hot Shit), which later seceded from the Airplane.

In the meantime, Kantner and the housebound Slick recorded *Blows against the Empire.* Billed as Paul Kantner and Jefferson Starship (the debut of the name), the LP featured Jerry Garcia, David Crosby, Graham Nash and other friends. The album became the first musical work nominated for the science-fiction writers' Hugo Award. At the same time, a greatest-hits package entitled *The Worst of the Jefferson Airplane* was released. On January 25, 1971, Slick and Kantner's baby girl, China, was born; and that spring, Balin, who had nothing to do with *Blows* and contributed only one cowritten composition to *Volunteers,* left. He formed a short-lived band, Bodacious D.F., and then tried to write a rock opera, which never got off the ground.

In August, the Airplane formed their own label, Grunt, distributed by RCA. The band's reunited effort, *Bark,* saw them with Covington and all of Hot Tuna, including violinist Papa John Creach, who had first performed with Hot Tuna at a Winterland show in 1970. The band had grown apart, though, and Hot Tuna and Kantner-Slick were each writing for their own offshoot projects. In December 1971, Slick and Kantner released *Sunfighter* under both their names, with China as cover girl.

In July of 1972, the Airplane recorded its last studio LP, *Long John Silver,* with some drumming from ex-Turtle John Barbata. In August 1972, at a free concert in New York's Central Park, the band introduced ex–Quicksilver Messenger Service bassist/vocalist David Freiberg to the ranks. The Airplane unofficially died at that point. By that September, Casady and Kaukonen decided to go full-time with Hot Tuna, though they appeared on the live LP *Thirty Seconds over Winterland,* which came out in April 1973. Slick, Kantner and Freiberg recorded *Baron Von Tollbooth and the Chrome Nun,* one of the band's least popular efforts. Slick's equally disappointing solo debut, *Manhole,* appeared in January 1974. Her drinking problem had become serious, and the band was hoping that the Tuna players would return. They did not.

Finally in February of 1974, Slick and Kantner formed the Jefferson Starship (no strict relation to the group on *Blows*), with Freiberg, Creach, Barbata and 19-year-old lead guitarist Craig Chaquico. Chaquico had played with the Grunt band Steelwind with his high school English teacher Jack Traylor and on Slick and Kantner collaborative LPs beginning with *Sunfighter.* The new group also included Peter Kangaroo (Jorma's brother), though in June he was replaced by Pete Sears, a British sessionman who played on Rod Stewart's records and had been a member of Copperhead. On *Dragon Fly,* Slick made a

Jefferson Airplane: Paul Kantner, Grace Slick, Spencer Dryden, Marty Balin, Jorma Kaukonen, Jack Casady

guest appearance with Marty Balin on his and Kantner's song "Caroline." The LP went gold.

Balin tentatively rejoined the band in January 1975, and things began to look up. *Red Octopus* was the real breakthrough. It was their first #1 LP, hitting that position several times during the year and selling over 2½ million copies. Balin's ballad "Miracles" was a #1 single. They were more popular than ever, but in Slick's opinion the music had become bland and corporate, and her rivalry with Balin had not diminished. Their follow-up LP, *Spitfire*, also went #1 platinum; but after the successful *Earth* (also platinum) in 1978, both Slick and Balin left.

Slick's alcoholism forced her to quit the band in the middle of a European tour, leading to a crowd riot in Germany when she did not appear. Her solo album was neither a great critical nor commercial success. Balin did a solo LP of MOR love songs. (In 1981 he had a hit single with "Hearts.") On Nov. 29, 1976, Slick married the band's 24-year-old lighting director, Skip Johnson. The group's future again seemed in question, but in 1979 singer Mickey Thomas, best known as lead vocalist on the Elvin Bishop hit "Fooled Around and Fell in Love," joined, and Barbata was replaced by Aynsley Dunbar, a former Frank Zappa and David Bowie sideman who had just left Journey. In 1980, Balin produced a rock opera entitled *Rock Justice* in San Francisco. That year, Kantner suffered a brain hemorrhage that, despite its severity, left no permanent damage. The band's *Freedom at Point Zero* went gold. Their equally commercial 1981 followup, *Modern Times*, featured Slick on one track; she rejoined the band in February 1981.

GARLAND JEFFREYS

Born circa 1944, Brooklyn, New York
1969—*Grinder's Switch Featuring Garland Jeffreys* (Vanguard) **1973**—*Garland Jeffreys* (Atlantic) **1977**—*Ghost Writer* (A&M) **1978**—*One Eyed Jack* **1979**—*American Boy and Girl* **1981**—*Escape Artist* (Epic) *Rock and Roll Adult* **1983**—*Guts for Love.*

Garland Jeffreys' urban-romantic lyrics and tough-edged rock & roll have gained him a large critical following, though little commercial success in the U.S. Jeffreys, who is part black, part white and part Puerto Rican, endured growing up mulatto in Sheepshead Bay, Brooklyn. He attended Syracuse University, in part because it was football hero Jim Brown's alma mater. There he befriended Lou Reed and upon graduating in 1965 spent a short while in Florence, Italy, studying Renaissance art. After briefly attending New York's Institute of Fine Arts, he began writing and singing songs.

By 1966, Jeffreys was performing solo in the lower Manhattan club the Balloon Farm, which also featured musicians like John Cale, Eric Burdon and Lou Reed. Jeffreys made his living waiting tables and playing in several small-time bands—Train, Mandoor Beekman and Romeo—before joining with the Buffalo area group Raven to form Grinder's Switch in 1969. The band cut only one LP, *Grinder's Switch Featuring Garland Jeffreys*, before breaking up in 1970. Jeffreys resumed his solo career, playing Manhattan clubs and signing with Atlantic in 1973. His self-titled debut, part of which was recorded in Jamaica, was released that March, and a nonalbum single entitled "Wild in the Streets" became an FM anthem. Critics applauded Jeffreys' emotive voice and tense music, but the single flopped. Frustrated, Jeffreys retired for a while, then returned in 1975 with a single on Arista, "The Disco Kid."

Following tours with Jimmy Cliff and Toots and the Maytals, Jeffreys re-signed with A&M in late 1976 and released *Ghost Writer* the next year. That album was praised for its romantic lyrics and Jeffreys' unique vocals, but neither it nor its two followups sold well. Jeffreys left A&M after 1979's *American Boy and Girl*. The samba "Matadoor" went Top Ten in several European countries, winning him a new U.S. deal with Epic, who released *Escape Artist* in 1981. The album, which included a cover of "96 Tears," was well received. Jeffreys toured, backed by the Rumour, resulting in a live LP out in late 1981 called *Rock and Roll Adult*.

WAYLON JENNINGS

Born June 15, 1937, Littlefield, Texas
1969—*Waylon Jennings* (Vocalion) **1970**—*The Best of Waylon Jennings* (RCA) *Singer of Sad Songs* **1971**—*The Taker/Tulsa* **1972**—*Good Hearted Woman; Ladies Love Outlaws; Lonesome, On'ry and Mean*

1973—*Honky Tonk Heroes* 1974—*This Time; Only Daddy That'll Walk the Line; The Ramblin' Man* 1975—*Dreamin' My Dreams* 1976—*Waylon Live; Are You Ready for the Country* 1977—*Ol' Waylon* 1978— *Waylon and Willie; I've Always Been Crazy* 1979— *What Goes Around Comes Around; Waylon Jennings' Greatest Hits* 1980—*Music Man* 1982—*Black on Black.*

Waylon Jennings, along with Willie Nelson, was one of the founding fathers of the so-called outlaw country movement in the early Seventies, reviving honky-tonk country rather than the string-laden Nashville style.

At age 12, Jennings became one of the youngest disc jockeys in radio, working at a Texas country station. At 22, he moved to Lubbock, where he continued to work as a DJ and then teamed up with early rocker Buddy Holly, who asked him to join the Crickets on bass. He toured with Holly in 1959, and Holly produced Jennings' first solo single, "Jolé Blon," on Brunswick Records. Jennings was booked on the charter plane flight in which Holly was killed, but gave his seat to the Big Bopper.

In 1963, Jennings formed his own group, the Waylors, and played a brand of folk country, recording for Trend, J.D.'s (part of Vocalion), Ramco and A&M. He was signed to RCA by Chet Atkins in 1965, began to play mainstream country and had a hit with his version of "MacArthur Park" in 1969. But in the early Seventies, with albums like 1972's *Ladies Love Outlaws,* Waylon began to develop a more rebellious style, with a rockier edge. He played in front of many rock crowds, performing with the Grateful Dead and Commander Cody, among others. By the mid-Seventies he had established himself. In 1976, the album *Wanted: The Outlaws,* featuring Waylon, Willie Nelson, Tompall Glaser and Jennings' wife, Jessi Colter, was the first country LP to be certified platinum. Jennings had solo hits like 1977's "Luckenbach, Texas" (#1 C&W) plus his duets with Willie Nelson, "Good Hearted Woman" and "Mamas Don't Let Your Babies Grow Up to Be Cowboys" (1978). Both "Luckenbach, Texas" and "Good Hearted Woman" crossed over to #25 on the pop charts. His *Greatest Hits* LP, released in March 1979, sold over three million copies and included the #1 country hit "Amanda." Jennings has five platinum LPs and four platinum and eight gold singles.

JETHRO TULL
Formed 1968, Blackpool, England
Ian Anderson (b. Aug. 10, 1947, Edinburgh), voc., flute, gtr.; Mick Abrahams (b. Apr. 7, 1943, Luton, Eng.), gtr.; Glenn Cornick (b. Apr. 24, 1947, Barrow-in-Furness, Eng.), bass; Clive Bunker (b. Dec. 12, 1946), drums.
1969—*This Was* (Reprise) (– Abrahams; + Martin Barre [b. Nov. 17, 1946], gtr.) *Stand Up* 1970—(+ John Evan [b. Mar. 28, 1948], kybds.) *Benefit* 1971— (– Cornick; + Jeffrey Hammond-Hammond [July 30,

1946], bass; *Aqualung* (– Bunker; + Barriemore Barlow [b. Sep. 10, 1949], drums) 1972—*Thick as a Brick* (Reprise) *Living in the Past* (Chrysalis) (compilation) 1973—*A Passion Play* (Chrysalis) 1974—*War Child* 1975—*Minstrel in the Gallery* 1976—*Best of (M.U.)* (– Hammond-Hammond; + John Glascock [b. 1953, d. Nov. 17, 1979, London], bass; + David Palmer, kybds.) *Too Old to Rock 'n' Roll* 1977— *Songs from the Wood; Repeat: Best of, Volume 2* 1978—*Heavy Horses; Bursting Out (Live)* (– Glascock; + Tony Williams, bass) 1979—(– Williams; – Evan; – Barlow; + Eddie Jobson [b. Apr. 28, 1955, Eng.], kybds., violin; + Dave Pegg [b. Nov. 2, 1947, Birmingham, Eng.], bass; + Mark Craney [b. Los Angeles], drums) *Stormwatch* 1980—*A* 1982—*The Broadsword and the Beast.*

Named for no apparent reason after an 18th-century British agronomist who invented the machine drill for sowing seed, Jethro Tull has been one of the most commercially successful and eccentric progressive-rock bands. They began as a blues-based band with some jazz and classical influences, and were initially proclaimed by the British press in 1968 as "the new Cream." By the early Seventies, they'd expanded into a full-blown classical-jazz-rock-progressive band, and in the late Seventies turned toward folkish, mostly acoustic rock, all the while selling millions of albums and selling out worldwide tours.

Jethro Tull's driving force is Ian Anderson. With his shaggy mane, full beard and penchant for traditional tartan-plaid attire, Anderson acquired a reputation as a mad Fagin-esque character with his Olde English imagery and stage antics like playing the flute while hopping up and down on one leg.

Anderson moved to Blackpool as a child and met the future members of Jethro Tull in school. He and members of both early and later Jethro Tull lineups formed the John Evan Band in the mid-Sixties, which played in northern England with middling success. In late 1967, the band regrouped as Jethro Tull, adding guitarist Mick Abrahams and drummer Clive Bunker, and Anderson took up the flute.

The band had its first big success at the 1968 Sunbury Jazz and Blues Festival in England. They recorded their debut, *This Was,* that summer, and by autumn it was high on the LP charts in England. The album was released in the U.S. in 1969, and though it sold only moderately, critics hailed the band. That year, the British music weekly *Melody Maker* made Jethro Tull its #2 Band of the Year, after the Beatles (the Rolling Stones were third).

Abrahams left after the first LP (Black Sabbath's Tony Iommi briefly replaced him) to form Blodwyn Pig and later the Mick Abrahams Band. Jethro Tull's first U.S. tour in 1969 paved the way for the chart success of *Stand Up,* on which Martin Barre replaced Abrahams. One of the more popular numbers on that album was an Anderson flute instrumental based on a Bach "Bouree" (*This Was* had featured Rahsaan Roland Kirk's "Serenade to a Cuckoo;" Anderson had acquired his trademark flute effects—singing through the flute, flutter-tonguing—from Kirk). Their next LP, *Benefit,* went gold in the U.S., and Tull began selling out 20,000-seat arenas. Cornick left to form Wild Turkey and was replaced by Jeffrey Hammond-Hammond, a childhood buddy of Anderson's who'd been mentioned in several Tull tunes ("A Song for Jeffrey," "Jeffrey Goes to Leicester Square," "For Michael Collins, Jeffrey and Me").

Aqualung was an anti-church/pro-God concept album, which eventually sold over two million, yielding FM standards like "Cross-Eyed Mary," "Hymn 43" and "Locomotive Breath." Then Bunker left to form the abortive Jude with ex–Procol Harum Robin Trower, ex–Stone the Crows Jim Dewar and Frankie Miller. His replacement was Barriemore Barlow, whose superlative technique was

put to good use on *Thick as a Brick,* another concept album in which one song stretched over two sides in a themes-and-variations suite, a vague protest against Life Itself. The album reached #1 in the U.S. and went gold. *A Passion Play* followed the same format but was even more elaborate and went to #1 as well; critics soundly thrashed Anderson for his indulgence, resulting in his permanent mistrust of the music press and a two-year touring layoff.

However, the heavily orchestrated *War Child* became Tull's next gold LP (the *Living in the Past* compilation, with a hit in its title tune, had also gone gold) and yielded a #12 hit single in "Bungle in the Jungle." *Minstrel in the Gallery,* Tull's first extended flirtation with Elizabethan folk ideas, went gold, and *M.U.* went platinum. Hammond-Hammond then left, replaced by John Glascock, who never toured with the band because of a chronic heart ailment that eventually killed him. In the title cut of *Too Old to Rock 'n' Roll,* Anderson turned ironic self-depreca-

Grammy Awards

Mahalia Jackson
1961 Best Gospel or Other Religious Recording: "Every Time I Feel the Spirit"
1962 Best Gospel or Other Religious Recording: *Great Songs of Love and Faith*
1976 Best Soul Gospel Performance: *How I Got Over*

Michael Jackson
1979 Best R&B Vocal Performance, Male: "Don't Stop Till You Get Enough"

Al Jarreau
1977 Best Jazz Vocal Performance: *Look to the Rainbow*
1978 Best Jazz Vocal Performance: *All Fly Home*
1981 Best Jazz Vocal Performance, Male: "Blue Rondo à la Turk"
Best Pop Vocal Performance, Male: *Breakin' Away*

Waylon Jennings
1969 Best Country Performance by a Duo or Group: "MacArthur Park" (with the Kimberleys)
1978 Best Country Vocal Performance by a Duo or Group: "Mamas Don't Let Your Babies Grow Up to Be Cowboys" (with Willie Nelson)

Billy Joel
1978 Record of the Year; Song of the Year: "Just the Way You Are"
1979 Album of the Year; Best Pop Vocal Performance, Male: *52nd Street*
1980 Best Rock Vocal Performance, Male: *Glass Houses*

Brothers Johnson
1977 Best R&B Instrumental Performance: *Q*

General Johnson
1970 Best R&B Song: "Patches" (with Ronald Dunbar)

Quincy Jones
1963 Best Instrumental Arrangement: "I Can't Stop Loving You"
1969 Best Instrumental Jazz Performance, Large Group or Soloist with Large Group: "Walking in Space"
1971 Best Pop Instrumental Performance: *Smackwater Jack*
1973 Best Instrumental Arrangement: "Summer in the City"
1978 Best Instrumental Arrangement: Main Title (*The Wiz,* original soundtrack with Robert Freedman)
1981 Best R&B Performance by a Duo or Group with Vocal: *The Dude* Producer of the Year, Non Classical

Rickie Lee Jones
1979 Best New Artist

tion into self-glorification. *Songs from the Wood,* with its minor hit single, "The Whistler," was Tull's deepest exploration into acoustic folk (Anderson had just produced an LP for Steeleye Span, too); since that time, their albums have merged the rustic with Anderson's tortuously intricate classical/jazz/rock thematics. Before *A,* Anderson revamped the band completely to include ex–Roxy Music Eddie Jobson and ex–Fairport Convention Dave Pegg. In 1981, Anderson starred in an ambitious album-length video production called *Slipstream.*

JOAN JETT
Born September 22, 1960, Philadelphia
1981—*Bad Reputation* (Boardwalk)   *I Love Rock 'n' Roll* **1983**—*Album* (MCA/Blackheart).

Singer/guitarist Joan Jett is one of the most surprising success stories of the early Eighties. The latter-day leader of the much maligned all-female teenage hard-rock group the Runaways, Jett could barely get a U.S. deal for her first solo album at the beginning of 1981. One year later, her second solo LP had a #1 single and went Top Five and platinum.

Jett's family moved to Baltimore when she was in grade school and to Southern California when she was 14. That Christmas she got her first guitar. Her initial and continuing inspiration was the British early-Seventies glitter-pop music of T. Rex, Gary Glitter, Slade, David Bowie and Suzi Quatro, whose tough stance Jett has most closely emulated. At 15, she met producer Kim Fowley at Hollywood's Starwood Club and became part of his group, the Runaways. The band gave its last show New Year's Eve 1978 in San Francisco. In the spring of 1979 Jett was in England trying to get a solo project going. While there, she cut three songs with ex–Sex Pistols Paul Cook and Steve Jones, two of which came out as a single in Holland only. Back in L.A., Jett produced the debut album by local punks the Germs and acted in a movie based on the Runaways (with actresses playing the rest of the band) called *We're All Crazy Now* (title taken from the Slade song). The movie was never released, but while working on it Jett met Kenny Laguna (producer of Jonathan Richman, Greg Kihn and the Steve Gibbons Band) and Ritchie Cordell (bubblegum legend who cowrote Tommy James and the Shondells' "I Think We're Alone Now" and "Money Money" and produced "Gimme Some Lovin' ").

Jett spent six weeks in the hospital suffering from pneumonia and a heart-valve infection. She then assembled a solo debut, with Laguna and Cordell producing, using the Jones-Cook British tracks plus guest musicians Sean Tyla and Blondie's Clem Burke and Frank Infante. As *Joan Jett,* the album came out in Europe only. It was rejected by every major and minor label in the U.S., and finally Laguna put out the LP himself. After much positive U.S. press, the album was picked up by Boardwalk in late January 1981 and renamed *Bad Reputation.* But it didn't sell.

After a year of touring with her band, the Blackhearts, Jett's second LP, even harder-rocking than the first, came out in December 1981, including a version of "Little Drummer Boy" on the pre-Christmas editions. It immediately bolted up the charts, aided by a remake of a B side by the Arrows, the pop-heavy-metal single "I Love Rock 'n' Roll," which hit #1 in early 1982.

THE JIVE FIVE
Formed 1959, Brooklyn, New York
Original lineup: Eugene Pitt, voc.; Billy Prophet, voc.; Richard Harris, voc.; Norma Johnson, voc.; Jerome Hanna, voc.
1971—(The Jyve Fyve: E. Pitt; Casey Spencer, voc.; Webster Harris, voc.; Johnny Watson, voc.) **1982**—(E. Pitt; Frank Pitt, voc.; Prophet; Beatrice Best, voc.) *Here We Are!* (Ambient Sound).

This doo-wop vocal group had a #1 R&B hit (#3 pop) in 1961 with the melodramatic saga of teen angst "My True Story," featuring the impassioned lead vocals of Eugene Pitt, who'd sung with the Genies (who hit in 1959 with "Who's That Knocking"). The Jive Five followed with the R&B Top Thirty "These Golden Rings" (1962), and later made the doo-wop/soul transition with "I'm a Happy Man," #26 R&B, 1965. Its followup, "Bench in the Park," sold poorly. Their only other successes were minor, with "Sugar" in 1968 and "I Want You to Be My Baby" in 1970. They then renamed themselves the Jyve Fyve, but had little success. In 1982, they regrouped again to record (along with other long-unrecorded New York–area doo-wop groups) for the Ambient Sound label.

JOBRIATH
Born Jobriath Boone, circa 1949, California
1973—*Jobriath* (Elektra)   *Creatures of the Street.*

Jobriath tried to cash in on the glitter-rock trend and turned out to be one of the most costly and least successful hypes in rock history. Elektra Records reportedly paid up to $500,000 (some say $300,000) to sign the unknown singer. Jobriath's manager, Jerry Brandt, claimed to have discovered him by overhearing a demo that Columbia Records was about to pass up. Brandt, who had previously run New York's Electric Circus and managed Carly Simon (he currently runs the Ritz in Manhattan), supposedly tracked down the 24-year-old Jobriath in L.A. The singer's only prior professional credit was starring as Woof in the L.A. and New York productions of *Hair.* Other facts about his past are vague.

After Jobriath and Brandt cinched the Elektra deal, they secured a 43 × 41-foot Times Square billboard of the star nearly nude (a reproduction of the LP jacket) and set up what they claimed was a $200,000 stage debut at the Paris

Jobriath

Opera House. The show featured the singer doing mime in an eight-foot-high Lucite cube, which later turned into a forty-foot phallic symbol/Empire State Building with which Jobriath played King Kong. All this got ample media attention, aided by the singer constantly referring to himself in interviews as "a true fairy"—at least giving him historical importance as one of the few openly gay rock "stars." But it didn't help sell any records; neither did Jobriath's Jaggeresque vocals. After a second album, he vanished.

BILLY JOEL

Born May 9, 1949, Long Island, New York.
1972—*Cold Spring Harbor* (Family/Philips) 1973— *Piano Man* (Columbia) 1974—*Street Life Serenade* 1976—*Turnstiles* 1977—*The Stranger* 1978—*52nd Street* 1980—*Glass Houses* 1981—*Songs in the Attic* 1982—*The Nylon Curtain* 1983—*An Innocent Man.*

Though he's taken his share of critical lumps, singer/ songwriter/pianist Billy Joel has also had enough commercial success to render critical objections irrelevant. His *Stranger* album is reputedly the biggest seller in the Columbia Records catalog, having gone beyond five million. The biggest of several hit singles from that LP, "Just the Way You Are" (written to his wife/manager, Elizabeth, an alumna of the UCLA Graduate School of Management who was once married to the drummer in one of Joel's early Long Island bands), has become a standard.

Joel grew up in a middle-class Levittown family and ran with a leather-jacketed street gang as a teenager. He also boxed for three years during his adolescence, breaking his nose in the process. By the late Sixties, he was a member of the Hassles, who recorded two meager-selling albums for United Artists. He then formed a hard-rock duo, Attila, with Hassles drummer Jonathan Small, and recorded one flop LP for Epic. Joel tried his hand at commercial songwriting and in 1971 signed with Artie Ripp's Family Productions. *Cold Spring Harbor* demonstrated both Joel's fondness for his native Long Island and the somber side of his singing/songwriting approach, but the tapes were sped up slightly when the album was made, making Joel's voice sound nasal and unnatural.

Legal and managerial problems kept Joel from recording a followup, and for two years he settled on the West Coast and performed in piano bars under the name Bill Martin. These experiences informed his first successful album, *Piano Man,* which yielded hits in the title track (which went Top Forty), "Worse Comes to Worst" and "Travelin' Prayer" (which went Top 100). His next LP included a #34 hit in "The Entertainer." Both albums sold respectably, but not spectacularly. When *Turnstiles* yielded only the minor hit "New York State of Mind," Joel's career appeared to be in a holding pattern. Then came *The Stranger,* and a string of hit singles: "Just the Way You Are" (#3), "Movin' Out (Anthony's Song) (#17), "Only the Good Die Young" (#24), "She's Always a Woman" (#17) and "My Life" (#3). "Just the Way You Are" won two Grammy Awards in 1979.

Joel had a few more hits—"Big Shot" (#14, 1979), "Honesty" (#24, 1979), "You May Be Right" (#7, 1980), and "It's Still Rock and Roll to Me" (#1, 1980)—and in 1979 he appeared at the Havana Jam Concert in Cuba. In 1981, he released *Attic,* a live collection of pre-*Stranger* songs; one of them, "Say Goodbye to Hollywood" (recorded earlier by Ronnie Spector), was a hit in late 1981. In 1982, Joel released the socially conscious *The Nylon Curtain,* featuring a song about a Vietnam veteran, "Goodnight Saigon," and an unemployment song, "Allentown."

DAVID JOHANSEN

Born Jan. 9, 1950, Staten Island, New York
1978—*David Johansen* (Blue Sky) 1979—*In Style* 1981—*Here Comes the Night* 1982—*Live It Up.*

David Johansen's solo career, like his time as frontman for the legendary pre-punk band the New York Dolls, has garnered him tremendous critical status but few commercial rewards. Growing up, Johansen played in many local bands (including the Vagabond Missionaries and the Electric Japs) before forming the Dolls in late 1971. He was the Dolls' rubber-faced, loose-jointed lead singer, a self-mocking showman.

Just as their tremendous influence on early punk was

being recognized, the Dolls fell apart in 1975, and Johansen didn't enter a recording studio again until late 1977, when he recorded his debut solo LP. Dolls guitarist Syl Sylvain toured with Johansen to support the LP, which included several songs written by Syl and Johansen in the old Dolls days. *David Johansen* attempted to bring the Dolls' spirit to the masses. The album bombed commercially (selling only about 48,000 copies) but critics raved.

Johansen's next two solo LPs saw him making some musical compromises to try and reach the mass audience. *In Style* (1979) had a thicker, more Motown-influenced sound (the Four Tops' Levi Stubbs is one of Johansen's early favorites). The record was again praised by critics, but sold only a bit better than the debut. *Here Comes the Night* tried a more overt commercial turn, but despite a tour opening for Pat Benatar, the album still didn't spark much consumer interest, and since all along Johansen had been known for his top-notch live shows, he tried to recoup in 1982 by releasing his first live record, *Live It Up*. The single, an Animals medley featuring "We Gotta Get Out of This Place," "It's My Life" and "Don't Bring Me Down," was a minor hit. That year, Johansen appeared at Shea Stadium, opening for the Clash and the Who. (See also: the New York Dolls.)

ELTON JOHN
Born Reginald Kenneth Dwight, March 25, 1947, Pinner, England

1969—*Empty Sky* (MCA) (released U.S. 1975) **1970**—*Elton John;   Tumbleweed Connection* **1971**—*Friends* (Paramount)   *11-17-70 (17-11-70 in U.K.)   Madman across the Water* (MCA) **1972**—*Honky Chateau* **1973**—*Don't Shoot Me, I'm Only the Piano Player; Goodbye Yellow Brick Road* **1974**—*Caribou; Greatest Hits* **1975**—*Captain Fantastic and the Brown Dirt Cowboy;   Rock of the Westies* **1976**—*Here and There;   Blue Moves* **1977**—*Greatest Hits, Volume 2* **1978**—*A Single Man* **1979**—*The Thom Bell Sessions;   Victim of Love* **1980**—*21 at 33* **1981**—*The Fox* (Geffen) **1982**—*Jump Up!* **1983**—*Too Low for Zero*.

For most of the Seventies, Elton John and lyricist Bernie Taupin were a virtual hit factory, with 23 singles in the Top Forty, 15 in the Top Ten, and five that reached #1; 15 of the 16 albums released in the United States during that time went gold. John's nasal tenor and gospel-chorded piano, boosted by aggressive string arrangements, established a musical formula, while he reveled in an extravagant public image.

As Reginald Dwight, John won a piano scholarship to the Royal Academy of Music at 11. Six years later, he left school for show business. By day, he ran errands for a music publishing company; he divided evenings between a group, Bluesology, and solo gigs at a London hotel bar. Bluesology was then working as a backup band for visiting American soul singers such as Major Lance, Patti LaBelle and the Bluebelles and Billy Stewart. In 1966, British R&B singer Long John Baldry hired Bluesology as his backup band. After Baldry scored a British #1 hit with "Let the Heartaches Begin" in 1967, he tried his luck as a solo cabaret act. (In 1971 Elton coproduced an album of Baldry's.)

Responding to an ad in a British music trade weekly, Dwight auditioned for Liberty Records with his hotel repertoire. The scouts liked his performance but not his material. (Liberty wasn't his only audition; he was also rejected by King Crimson and the fledgling Gentle Giant.) Lyricist Bernie Taupin (born May 22, 1950, Sleaford, England) had also replied to the Liberty ad, and one of the scouts gave Dwight a stack of Taupin lyrics. Six months later the two met. By then, Dwight was calling himself Elton John, after John Baldry and Bluesology saxophonist Elton Dean. (Some years later, he made Elton Hercules John his legal name; Hercules was a childhood nickname.) John and Taupin took their songs to music publisher Dick James, who hired them as house writers for £10 (about $25) a week, and whose Dick James Music owned all John-Taupin compositions until 1975.

Taupin would write lyrics all day, sometimes a song an hour, and deliver a bundle to John every few weeks. Without changing a word, and rarely consulting Taupin, John would fit his tunes to the phrases. Arrangements were left to studio producers. They worked this way throughout their partnership. For two years, they wrote easy-listening tunes for James to peddle to singers, and on the side John recorded current hits for budget labels like Music for Pleasure and Marble Arch.

On the advice of another music publisher, Steve Brown, John and Taupin started writing rockier songs for John to record. The first was a single, "I've Been Loving You" (1968), produced by Caleb Quaye, former Bluesology guitarist. With Quaye, drummer Roger Pope and bassist Tony Murray, John recorded another single, "Lady Samantha," and an album, *Empty Sky* (1969). The records didn't sell, and John and Taupin enlisted Gus Dudgeon to produce a followup with Paul Buckmaster as arranger. (Brown continued to advise John until 1976; Dudgeon produced his records through *Blue Moves*.) *Elton John* established the formula for subsequent albums: gospel-chorded rockers and achingly sincere ballads.

MCA released *Elton John* (withholding *Empty Sky* until 1975), and John made his American debut at the Troubadour in Los Angeles in August 1970, backed by drummer Nigel Olsson and bassist Dee Murray (both formerly of the Spencer Davis Group). Kicking over his piano bench Jerry Lee Lewis–style and performing handstands on the keyboards, John left the critics raving. "Your Song" carried the LP to the American Top Ten. *Tumbleweed Connection,* with extensive FM airplay, sold even faster. By the middle of 1971, two more albums had been released: a live set taped from a WPLJ-FM New York radio broadcast on November 17, 1970, and the soundtrack to *Friends,* which John and Taupin had written three years before. Despite John's public repudiation of it, *Friends* went gold. Elton John was the first act since the Beatles to have four albums in the American Top Ten simultaneously. *Madman across the Water* came out in October 1971, and before the year was over a Bernie Taupin recitation-and-music album, *Taupin,* was on the market.

Honky Chateau was the first album credited to the Elton John group—John, Olsson, Murray and guitarist Davey Johnstone. Del Newman took over as arranger on *Goodbye Yellow Brick Road.* With the 1972 release of "Rocket Man" (#6), John began to dominate the Top Ten. "Crocodile Rock" was his first #1; "Daniel" and "Goodbye Yellow Brick Road" reached #2. Then came the tidal wave: "Bennie and the Jets" (#1), "Don't Let the Sun Go Down on Me" (#2), "The Bitch Is Back" (#4), a cover of Lennon and McCartney's "Lucy in the Sky with Diamonds" (#1), "Philadelphia Freedom" (#1), "Someone Saved My Life Tonight" (#4) and "Island Girl" (#1). *Honky Chateau* was the first of seven consecutive #1 albums.

In the mid-Seventies, John's concerts filled arenas and stadiums worldwide. He was the hottest act in rock & roll. And somehow his extravagances, including a $40,000 collection of custom-designed and uniformly ridiculous eyeglasses, seemed positively charming.

In 1974, Elton John joined John Lennon in the studio on Lennon's "Whatever Gets You thru the Night," then recorded "Lucy in the Sky with Diamonds" with "Dr. Winston O'Boogie" (Lennon) on guitar. Dr. O'Boogie joined Elton John on the stage of Madison Square Garden, Thanksgiving Day 1974, to sing both tunes plus "I Saw Her Standing There." It was Lennon's last appearance on any stage, and came out on an EP released after Lennon's death.

In 1973, John formed his own MCA-distributed label and signed acts—notably Neil Sedaka and Kiki Dee—in which he took personal interest. Instead of releasing his own records on Rocket, he opted for $8 million offered by MCA. (When the contract was signed in 1974, MCA reportedly took out a $25-million insurance policy on John's life.)

After *Captain Fantastic,* John overhauled his band: Johnstone and Ray Cooper were retained, Quaye and Roger Pope returned, and the new bassist was Kenny Passarelli (formerly of Joe Walsh and Barnstorm). James Newton-Howard joined to arrange in the studio and to play keyboards. John introduced the new lineup before an intimate crowd of 75,000 in London's Wembley Stadium in the summer of 1975, then recorded *Rock of the Westies.* But John's frenetic recording pace had slowed markedly, and he performed less often. A live album, *Here and There,* had been recorded in 1974. John's biggest hit in

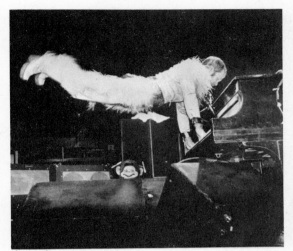

Elton John

1976 was a duet with Kiki Dee, "Don't Go Breaking My Heart" (#1). *Blue Moves* reeked of self-pity, but "Sorry Seems to be the Hardest Word" reached #6, and the album made #3.

In November 1977, John announced he was retiring from performing. After publishing a book of his poems—*The One Who Writes the Words for Elton John*—in 1976, Taupin began collaborating with others. John secluded himself in any of his three mansions, appearing publicly only to cheer the Watford Football Club, a perennially losing English soccer team he had followed since he was a child and eventually bought. He is also a director of the Los Angeles Aztecs. Some speculated that John's retreat from stardom was prompted by adverse reaction to his public admission in 1976 that he was bisexual.

A Single Man, 1978, used a new lyricist, Gary Osborne. The next year, accompanied by Ray Cooper, John became the first Western pop star to tour the Soviet Union, then mounted a two-man comeback tour of the U.S. in small halls. John returned to the singles charts with "Mama Can't Buy You Love" (#9, 1979), a song from an EP recorded in 1977 with Philadelphia soul producer Thom Bell. A new album, *Victim of Love,* failed to sustain the rally, in spite of the production of Pete Bellotte.

In 1980, John and Taupin reunited to write songs for *21 at 33* and *The Fox.* (Taupin put out a solo album, *He Who Rides the Tiger.*) A single, "Little Jeannie," reached #3. An estimated 400,000 fans turned out for a free concert in New York's Central Park in August, later broadcast on Home Box Office. Olsson and Murray were back in the band, and John had just signed a new recording contract. His second Geffen LP—*Jump Up!*—contained "Empty Garden," his tribute to John Lennon, which he performed at his sold-out Madison Square Garden show in August 1982. He was joined on stage by Yoko Ono and Sean Ono Lennon, Elton John's godchild. In 1983 he had a hit with "I'm Still Standing."

LITTLE WILLIE JOHN

Born William J. Woods, November 15, 1937, Camden, Arkansas; died May 27, 1968, Walla Walla, Washington
1977—*Little Willie John 1953–1962* (King).

Little Willie John was part of the same revolutionary generation of gospel-trained soul singers that yielded Sam Cooke, James Brown and Jackie Wilson. He was 18 when he had his first hit, "All Around the World," and only 23 when he made his biggest hit, "Sleep." John stood just over five feet (which, combined with his youthfulness, earned him his nickname) and had a voice that was stronger and rougher than Wilson's or Cooke's, and richer and more wide-ranging than Brown's. He was first discovered at a Detroit talent show in 1951 by Johnny Otis, though Otis' recommendation to King Records' Syd Nathan was ignored (Nathan instead signed Hank Ballard, who performed at the same show).

For the next few years John occasionally sang with the Duke Ellington and Count Basie orchestras and toured with R&B saxophonist Paul Williams' combo before King finally signed him. He first dented the R&B charts with the Joe Turner-ish big band rock of "All Around the World." John was the first artist to record the R&B standard "Fever," which he cowrote. His version hit the Top Thirty, but two years later Peggy Lee's version went to #8. Through the late Fifties, he scored other R&B hits with "Talk to Me, Talk to Me," "Let Them Talk" (both ballads) and the James Brown–inspired "Heartbreak." Only "Talk to Me, Talk to Me" and "Sleep" made the pop Top Twenty. Several years after his hits had run out, Little Willie John was convicted of manslaughter and sent to prison in Walla Walla, Washington, where he died of pneumonia. Though he is an overlooked figure, his significance is perhaps best indicated by the title of an album by fellow King Records artist James Brown: *Thinking of Little Willie John and a Few Nice Things*.

JOHNNY AND THE HURRICANES

Formed 1950s, Toledo, Ohio
Johnny Paris (b. 1941), sax; Paul Tesluk (b. 1941), organ; David Yorko (b. 1941), gtr.; Lionel "Butch" Mattice (b. 1941), bass; Don Staczek, drums.
1960—*Johnny and The Hurricanes* (Warwick) *Stormsville; Big Sound* (Big Top) **1965**—*Live at the Star Club, Hamburg* (Atila) **1973**—*Remember . . .* (United Artists).

Immortalized in the Kinks song "One of the Survivors" (on *Preservation Act I*), Johnny and the Hurricanes had two highly charged Top Forty instrumental hits featuring Johnny Paris' roaring tenor sax and Paul Tesluk's Hammond chord organ: "Crossfire" (#23, 1959) and the million-selling "Red River Rock" (based on the traditional "Red River Valley"), which made #5 the same year. At that time the Hurricanes were all in their teens and were playing at park bandstands in their hometown of Toledo. They toured America and Britain, where "Red River Rock" had reached #3. They had some follow-up hits, "Reveille Rock" (1959), "Beatnik Fly" and "Rocking Goose" (1960), but soon developed managerial problems with Irving Micahnik and Harry Balk (the same team that had managed Del Shannon). Their last hits were "Down Yonder" in 1960 and "Ja-Da" in 1961. The band underwent several personnel changes, leaving only Paris; in the meantime, Micahnik and Balk, under the names Tom King and Ira Mack, had taken credit for writing the band's hits.

The Hurricanes went to Hamburg in the early Sixties, where they played a short engagement, often appearing with the Beatles. In 1965, Paris formed his own label, Atila, and released the *Live at the Star Club* album, hoping to profit from the association with the by-now-famous Beatles. But by 1967, the band was popular only in Europe. As of the mid-Seventies, Paris and the Hurricanes were still playing Toledo bars with no recording contract.

LINTON KWESI JOHNSON

Born circa 1952, Jamaica
1978—*Dread Beat an' Blood* (Virgin Front Line import; reissued 1981 by Heartbeat) **1979**—*Forces of Victory* (Mango) **1980**—*Bass Culture* **1981**—*LKJ in Dub*.

A Jamaican-English intellectual and poet, Linton Kwesi Johnson has earned critical respect and cult-level sales by assaulting British racism with protest verses sung/spoken in Jamaican patois and in a distinctive, deep voice to rock-solid reggae accompaniment.

Living in England since 1963, Johnson has been inspired by the black American scholar W. E. B. Du Bois. He was associated with the British Black Panther Party, and while studying for a sociology degree he started to give poetry readings backed by a group of drummers called Rasta Love (he claims to write with a reggae bass line in his head).

His first album, *Dread Beat an' Blood*, is the soundtrack to an independent British film about Britain's Jamaican immigrants. *Forces of Victory* yielded minor underground hits in "Reality Poem" and "Sonny's Lettah," while *LKJ in Dub* is predominantly instrumental.

Despite his cult success as a recording artist, Johnson regards himself primarily as a political activist, working for Race Today, a black political organization, and writing on black affairs for academic and political publications.

ROBERT JOHNSON

Born May 8, 1911, Hazelhurst, Mississippi; died August 16, 1938, Greenwood, Mississippi

1961, 1970—*King of the Delta Blues Singers, Volumes 1 and 2* (Columbia).

Though reportedly a street singer whose repertoire was not limited to the blues, Robert Johnson has become known as one of the first and most influential Delta bluesmen. He is credited with writing blues standards like "Dust My Broom" (which Elmore James made into a postwar electric-blues anthem), "Sweet Home Chicago," "Ramblin' on My Mind," "Crossroads" (covered by Cream), "Love in Vain" and "Stop Breaking Down" (covered by the Rolling Stones), and "Terraplane Blues" (covered by Captain Beefheart and His Magic Band on *Mirror Man*).

Little is known of Johnson's life. He apparently was influenced by pioneering Delta bluesmen like Charley Patton and Willie Brown, as well as obscure bluesman Ike Zinneman, with whom Johnson reportedly studied guitar. He performed for several years but didn't record until 1936 (these recordings are the ones reissued by Columbia). A restless itinerant, moving from town to town and woman to woman, Johnson did marry in 1929 (in 1930 his wife, 17-year-old Virginia Travis, died in childbirth); he later remarried.

His life was beset by violence, reflected in his often harrowing music. Many of Johnson's peers claimed that he had made a pact with Satan, and he was supposedly murdered with a poisoned drink by a jealous husband whose wife Johnson had been romancing.

Despite his comparatively small number of recordings, Johnson has a paramount place in blues history, and, though he played acoustically, was a strong influence on such electric bluesmen as Muddy Waters, Elmore James, Johnny Shines, Robert Jr. Lockwood, Robert Nighthawk and others. There were rumors that Johnson had played electric guitar. Just after his death, producer/manager John Hammond, organizing his first landmark Spirituals to Swing concert, wanted Johnson to perform; unable to locate the late Delta bluesman, Hammond settled for Big Bill Broonzy.

JO JO GUNNE

Formed 1971, Los Angeles
Jay Ferguson (b. May 10, 1947, Burbank, Calif.), voc., kybds.; Mark Andes (b. Feb. 19, 1948, Philadelphia), bass; Matt Andes (b. Calif.), gtr.; Curley Smith (b. Jan. 31, 1952, Wolf Point, Mont.), drums.
1972—*Jo Jo Gunne* (Asylum) (− Mark Andes; + Jimmy Randell [b. Feb. 14, 1949, Dallas], bass) **1973**—*Bite Down Hard; Jumping the Gunne* (− Matt Andes) **1974**—(+ Star Donaldson, gtr.; − Donaldson; + John Staehely [b. Jan. 25, 1952, Austin, Tex.], gtr.) *So . . . Where's the Show*.

Jay Ferguson and Mark Andes, formerly members of Spirit, left that band in January 1971 to form the straight-ahead rock band Jo Jo Gunne. Rounded out with Mark's brother on guitar and Curley Smith, the band took its name from a song by Chuck Berry. Their debut gave them a #27 hit with "Run Run Run." Mark Andes soon left to go solo (leaving Ferguson as the main songwriter) and was replaced in November 1972 by Jimmy Randell, who'd previously played in various Texas bands.

The group recorded two more low-selling records before Matt Andes left in 1973, replaced by San Francisco guitarist Star Donaldson, who was soon replaced by John Staehely (who had played in a brief-lived post-Ferguson/Andes edition of Spirit, and also worked with Smith in a Texas band called Pumpkin). The new band lasted only one LP, *So . . . Where's the Show*. The Andes brothers joined yet another re-formed Spirit in 1976 (later in 1976, Mark hit it big with Firefall). Ferguson went on to become a solo artist with *All Alone in the End Zone* and the successful single "Thunder Island" (#9, 1978). Mark Andes joined Heart in 1982.

GRACE JONES

Born May 19, 1952, Spanishtown, Jamaica
1977—*Portfolio* (Island) **1978**—*Fame* **1979**—*Muse* **1980**—*Warm Leatherette* **1981**—*Nightclubbing* **1982**—*Living My Life*.

Grace Jones, the provocative six-foot model-turned-disco-singer, was first mainly a cult artist of the New York gay dance clubs. There she developed a reputation as much for her archly stylish look and S&M-tinged theatrical stage show (she'd enter on motorcycle and dance with body builders) as for her monotone singing. In 1980, when she followed the dance-club trend to emphasize *rock* disco, her music won more broad-based support and critical respect.

Jones grew up in Jamaica, where her father was a clergyman and influential in local politics (as was his father before him). She moved with her family to Syracuse when she was 12, and, after attending college, traveled to Manhattan to work for the Wilhelmina Modeling Agency. After a stint of acting, appearing in the film *Gordon's War*, she was far more successful as a model in Paris, posing for the covers of *Vogue, Der Stern* and *Elle*. Jones wanted to be a singer, and while in France did some recording.

In 1977, Jones landed a record deal with Island, with disco mixer Tom Moulton as her producer, and recorded "I Need a Man," a big dance hit that summer. She had other disco hits with "La Vie en Rose" and "Do Or Die." Her first three albums catered mainly to the urban dance crowd, receiving little critical attention, but that changed when she began to cover more rock-oriented material on *Warm Leatherette*. Produced by Chris Blackwell, the album included versions of the Pretenders' "Private Lives," Roxy Music's "Love Is the Drug" and Tom Petty's "Breakdown." The Sly Dunbar/Robbie Shake-

Grace Jones

speare–produced *Nightclubbing*, in 1981, with a David Bowie/Iggy Pop–penned title track, had her biggest R&B single (#5) with "Pull Up to the Bumper" and was voted album of the year by England's *New Musical Express*. "Nipple to the Bottle" helped *Living My Life* reach #96 in 1983.

QUINCY JONES
Born March 14, 1933, Chicago
1969—*Walking in Space* (A&M)   **1970**—*Gula Matari*
1972—*Smackwater Jack*   **1973**—*You've Got It Bad,
Girl*   **1974**—*Body Heat*   **1975**—*Mellow Madness*
1976—*I Heard That!*   **1977**—*Roots*   **1978**—*Sounds and
Stuff Like That*   **1981**—*The Dude*   **1982**—*Q.*

One of the most prolific and successful figures in contemporary pop, Quincy Jones began as a jazz and soul trumpeter, became a bandleader overseas and returned to America to carve out a long and still-prospering career as composer/arranger/producer. Jones has worked for hundreds of successful acts, including Herb Alpert, Louis Armstrong, LaVern Baker, Glen Campbell, Ray Charles, José Feliciano, Roberta Flack, Aretha Franklin, Herbie Hancock, B. B. King, Little Richard, Manhattan Transfer, Johnny Mathis, Frank Sinatra, Billy Preston, Paul Simon, Ringo Starr, George Benson, Bill Withers, James Ingram and the Jacksons, as well as Michael Jackson solo. Jones has also had a successful career recording under his own name, and has scored over 35 films and composed about a dozen TV-show themes. As of 1982, he had been nominated for 55 Grammy Awards and won 11. And, as one of the first blacks to score films and hold record company executive posts, Jones has helped advance the status of blacks in the music business.

Jones moved with his family at an early age to Seattle, where he began studying trumpet while in grade school. At 14, he met Ray Charles, and the two formed a band that began playing Seattle soul clubs. While working with Charles, he became an arranger. At age 15, he joined Lionel Hampton's big band and was all set to embark on a European tour when the vibraphonist's wife demanded he be kept off the tour so he could attend school.

Within a year, Jones had won a scholarship to Boston's Berklee School of Music, where he took ten classes a day and earned money by playing in strip joints at night. Word of the young trumpeter's skills got out through the jazz grapevine, and at 17 he was invited to New York by jazz bassist Oscar Pettiford to write two arrangements for an album. Jones received $17 per arrangement. He stayed in New York, relishing the opportunity to hang out with Charlie Parker, Thelonious Monk and Miles Davis. He began playing at recording sessions and at Manhattan jazz clubs, and eventually rejoined Hampton's orchestra for a European tour. Jones also toured Europe with Dizzy Gillespie. In the mid-Fifties he made Paris his home.

In Paris, he became music director for Barclay Records and was staff composer/arranger for Harry Arnold's Swedish All-Stars of Stockholm. He also studied classical composition with Nadia Boulanger, who had once taught Igor Stravinsky. Through the Fifties, Jones won awards in Europe for his arranging and composing. Toward the end of the decade, he began leading an 18-piece big band, which was a financial failure. He returned to the States in 1961 $100,000 in debt.

In New York, Jones became a vice-president at Mercury Records, one of the first blacks to hold such a post. There he produced, arranged and played on hundreds of sessions, as well as producing ten gold records for Lesley Gore, including "It's My Party," "Judy's Turn to Cry" and "You Don't Own Me." He stayed with Mercury from 1961 to 1968, and also recorded albums of his own.

In 1965, Jones scored his first film, Sidney Lumet's *The Pawnbroker*. He went on to score or write theme songs for *Mirage, The Slender Thread, Walk Don't Run, In the Heat of the Night, A Dandy in Aspic, In Cold Blood, Enter Laughing, For the Love of Ivy* and *Bob and Carol and Ted and Alice*. Jones received Oscar nominations for his *In Cold Blood* score and for "The Eyes of Love" from *Banning* (1967) and "For the Love of Ivy" (1969). He won an Academy Award for his score for *In the Heat of the Night*. He also composed theme music for TV shows including "Ironside," "The Bill Cosby Show" and "Sanford and Son," and most recently PBS's "Rebop," and has received several Emmy Awards.

In 1969, Jones signed with A&M Records. *Walking in Space, Gula Matari* and *Smackwater Jack* were best sellers, and the first and third won Grammys. In 1971, Jones scored the music for the Academy Awards show. By that time Jones had been married for several years to Peggy Lipton, star of TV's "The Mod Squad." In 1973, he collaborated on Aretha Franklin's *Hey Now Hey* LP and won a Grammy for his hit single "Summer in the City" from *You've Got It Bad, Girl.* In 1974, his *Body Heat* album made the pop Top Ten and went gold. Later that year, he was hospitalized for the first of two severe neural aneurisms.

Jones returned in 1976 with the first of his many protégés, the Brothers Johnson, who had performed on Jones's *Mellow Madness.* He produced and arranged their platinum debut LP, *Look Out for #1.* In 1977, Jones won an Emmy for his score for the TV miniseries *Roots,* and in the late Seventies he scored the film of *The Wiz.* In 1979, Jones produced and arranged Michael Jackson's multimillion-selling *Off the Wall.*

Jones continued his producing/arranging successes in the early Eighties with Chaka Khan and Rufus, George Benson and James Ingram. He released another of his own smash hit albums, *The Dude,* in 1981; it yielded a hit single in a version of Chaz Jankel's "Ai No Corrida" and stayed on the charts for a year. In 1982, Jones produced another Ingram hit, "One Hundred Ways" ("Just Once" had been the first), and won five Grammy Awards, including one for *The Dude.* A compilation album of his solo work, entitled *Q,* was also released to big sales, and Jones went on to produce Donna Summer's self-titled album that year, as well as Michael Jackson's *Thriller.*

RICKIE LEE JONES

Born November 8, 1954, Chicago
1979—*Rickie Lee Jones* (Warner Bros.) **1981**—*Pirates* **1983**—*Girl at Her Volcano* (EP).

Though Rickie Lee Jones's music is an eccentric mixture of R&B, beat jazz and folk, her debut album made her an instant star. Released in 1979, the LP quickly went platinum, bolstered by the single "Chuck E's in Love."

Jones grew up in Phoenix, Arizona, Olympia, Washington, and various cities in California. In 1973, at age 19, she went to Los Angeles, where she worked as a waitress and eventually began performing in small clubs, where much of her act consisted of rhythmic "spoken word" monologues. This Beat influence was also a crucial part of her later music and led to her friendship with singer/songwriter Tom Waits. (Jones is pictured on the back of Waits's 1978 *Blue Valentine* LP, and sang a Waits song on the *King of Comedy* soundtrack.) The two met at the Tropicana Motel on Santa Monica Boulevard in the fall of 1977, a time when she wrote many of the songs that later appeared on her debut.

Jones attracted the interest of Warner Bros. Records in late 1978, when her early manager Nick Mathe sent the company a four-song demo she had originally cut under the auspices of A&M. In addition, friend Ivan Ulz sang the song "Easy Money" over the phone to Lowell George, who, after visiting Jones, recorded her song for his *Thanks I'll Eat It Here* solo LP. All this intrigued Warner staff

producer Ted Templeman and A&R man Lenny Waronker, who signed her. The latter coproduced her debut with Russ Titleman.

In April 1979, "Chuck E's in Love" shot to #4. On the album, Jones's voice ranged from a faint moan to a sexy, full-throated roar. Some critics praised her unique song structures with their jazz and show-tune shadings, plus her lyrical "visions," filled with colorful low-down characters. Others saw her as a pseudo-bohemian. Her 1981 followup, *Pirates,* used longer and more complex songs about death and transfiguration; it went gold. *Girl at Her Volcano* was a 10-inch EP; all but one song were ballad covers.

TOM JONES

Born Thomas Jones Woodward, June 7, 1940, Pontypridd, Wales
1967—*Thirteen Smash Hits* (Decca/Parrot) **1969**—*This Is Tom Jones* **1970**—*I (Who Have Nothing)* **1972**—*Close Up* **1973**—*The Body and Soul of* **1976**—*Say You'll Stay Until Tomorrow* (Epic) **1977**—*What a Night.*

One rock writer perhaps summed it up best—and most diplomatically—when he called Tom Jones "the missing link between Elvis Presley and middle-class sex-symbol clones like Engelbert Humperdinck." With his long, lean, muscular frame, his dark, rough-hewn good looks and his pelvis-grinding moves, Jones is what his female fans like to call "a hunk," and the one to whom they often tossed home and hotel-room keys. As of the late Seventies, Tom Jones was one of the biggest-selling acts in Las Vegas.

Tom Woodward began singing as a child in church. The son of a coal miner, he grew up in a home that had no bath; as a teenager he had problems with drinking and delinquency. By the time he graduated from school at 16, he had married and was working odd jobs from carpentry and glove-cutting to construction. He worked occasionally as a pub singer, and later taught himself drums and played with various local bands. In the early Sixties, he adopted the stage name Tommy Scott and formed the Senators, who by 1963 had become a popular local attraction. In 1964, fellow Welshman Gordon Mills became his manager.

In 1964, Woodward changed his stage name to Jones, after the success of the film *Tom Jones,* and he and Mills went to London, where he got a contract with Decca in late 1964. After one flop single, Jones requested a new Mills number, "It's Not Unusual," which had originally been intended for a female singer. Jones's brassy version went #1 in Britain and Top Ten in America in 1965; later that year came the million-selling followup, the Bacharach-David theme from the film *What's New Pussycat?* Jones also had a minor hit with the theme song from *Thunderball.* With 1967 came another major international hit, Jones's version of Porter Wagoner's country tune, "Green, Green Grass of Home." He earned gold records for "Delilah" and "Love Me Tonight" (1968) and "I'll Never Fall in Love Again" (1969).

Jones's biggest year was 1969. Four of his LPs went gold, and that summer he debuted on his own highly rated American network TV show. The show remained a hit for a few seasons, and at one point featured the memorable sight of Jones and guest Janis Joplin gyrating together on one of many "Hullabaloo!"-styled go-go ministages. "Daughter of Darkness" and "She's a Lady" were Jones's last uptempo hits; from there, he moved right into MOR with "I (Who Have Nothing)" (1970), followed by "Till" and "I Can't Stop Loving You." Though the hit singles came with less frequency after that, Jones was already a guaranteed success.

JANIS JOPLIN
Born January 19, 1943, Port Arthur, Texas; died October 4, 1970, Hollywood
1967—*Big Brother and the Holding Company* (Mainstream) **1968**—*Cheap Thrills* (Columbia).
Joplin solo: 1969—*I Got Dem Ol' Kozmic Blues Again, Mama* (Columbia) **1971**—*Pearl* **1972**—*In Concert* **1973**—*Greatest Hits* **1974**—*Janis* (soundtrack) **1980**—*Anthology* **1982**—*Farewell Song.*

Singer Janis Joplin was perhaps the premier white blues singer of the Sixties. Even before her death, her tough blues-mama image only barely covered her vulnerability. The publicity concerning her sex life and drinking and drug problems had made her something of a legend.

Janis Joplin

Born into a comfortable middle-class family, Joplin was a loner by her early teens, developing a taste for blues and folk music; soon she retreated into poetry and painting. She ran away from home at age 17 and began singing in clubs in Houston and Austin, Texas, to earn money to finance a trip to California. By 1965, she was singing folk and blues in bars in San Francisco and Venice, California, had dropped out of several colleges, and was drawing unemployment checks. She returned to Austin in 1966 to sing in a country & western band, but within a few months a friend of San Francisco impresario Chet Helms told her about a new band, Big Brother and the Holding Company, that needed a singer in San Francisco. She returned to California and joined Big Brother.

Joplin and Big Brother stopped the show at the 1967 Monterey Pop Festival; Albert Grossman agreed to manage them, and Joplin was on her way to becoming a superstar. After a fairly successful first LP with Big Brother, Columbia Records signed the unit; and *Cheap Thrills*, with the hit single "Piece of My Heart," became a quick million-seller. Within a year, Joplin had come to overshadow her backing band, and she left Big Brother (though she appears, uncredited, on a few tracks on the group's 1971 *Be a Brother* LP), taking only Sam Andrew with her to form the Kozmic Blues Band.

Joplin toured constantly and made television appearances as a guest with Dick Cavett, Tom Jones and Ed Sullivan. Finally, the *Kozmic Blues* LP appeared, with gutsy blues-rock hits like "Try (Just a Little Bit Harder)." During this time she became increasingly involved with alcohol and drugs, eventually succumbing to heroin addiction. Yet her life seemed to be taking a turn for the better with the recording of *Pearl*. She was engaged to be married and was pleased with the Full Tilt Boogie Band she'd formed for the *Pearl* album (Pearl was her nickname). On October 4, 1970, her body was found in her room at Hollywood's Landmark Hotel, face down with fresh puncture marks in her arm. The death was ruled an accidental heroin overdose.

The posthumous *Pearl* LP yielded her #1 hit version of former lover Kris Kristofferson's "Me and Bobby McGee" and was released with one track, "Buried Alive in the Blues," missing the vocals Joplin didn't live to complete. Several more posthumous collections have been released, as well as the 1974 documentary, *Janis.* The 1979 film *The Rose*, starring Bette Midler, was a thinly veiled account of Joplin's career. See also: Big Brother and the Holding Company.

JOURNEY
Formed 1973, San Francisco
Neal Schon (b. 1955, San Mateo, Calif.), voc., gtr.; Ross Valory (b. 1950, San Francisco), bass; Gregg Rolie (b. 1948), voc., kybds.; Prairie Prince (b. May 7, 1950, Charlotte, N.C.), drums; George Tickner, gtr.
1974—(— Prince; + Aynsley Dunbar [b. 1946],

drums) **1975**—*Journey* (Columbia) (− Tickner)
1976—*Look into the Future* **1977**—*Next* (+ Robert
Fleischman, voc.) **1978**—(− Fleischman; + Steve
Perry [b. 1949, Hanford, Calif.], voc.) *Infinity* (−
Dunbar; + Steve Smith [b. Boston], drums) **1979**—
Evolution; In the Beginning **1980**—*Departure* (−
Rolie; + Jonathan Cain, kybds.) **1981**—*Captured;
Escape* **1983**—*Frontiers*.

Between their 1975 debut as a predominantly instrumental
progressive rock group and their first platinum LP in 1978,
Journey underwent format changes that led to their emergence as one of the top American hard-pop bands. Gregg
Rolie had cofounded Santana with Carlos Santana and had
sung lead on several Santana tunes, including "Evil
Ways" and "Black Magic Woman." Neal Schon joined
Santana after their second LP, *Abraxas;* he was 17. The
two left Santana in 1972. Rolie and his father opened a
restaurant in Seattle, while Schon jammed with other Bay
Area musicians.

Former Santana road manager Walter Herbert brought
Schon and Rolie together again with ex–Steve Miller
bassist Ross Valory, who, along with George Tickner, had
played in Frumious Bandersnatch (a Bay Area group
Herbert managed).

In an impromptu contest on San Francisco station
KSAN-FM, listeners were asked to name the band; the
winning name was Journey. The group played its first
shows with Prairie Prince, then drummer with the Tubes.
When he decided to stay with the Tubes, British journeyman Aynsley Dunbar, whose earlier associations included
John Mayall, Jeff Beck, Bonzo Dog Band, Mothers of
Invention, Lou Reed and David Bowie, joined. Within a
year of its 1974 New Year's Eve debut at San Francisco's
Winterland, the group had been signed to Columbia.
Following their debut LP, on which Rolie did most of the
singing, Tickner, tired of touring, left the band. The
group's next two albums sold moderately. Herbert, convinced the group needed a lead singer, hired Robert
Fleischman. Meanwhile, Steve Perry, a drummer/singer,
had contacted the group several times asking to join. Due
to a series of fortuitous events—Perry was recommended
to Herbert by a Columbia executive around the time
Herbert had decided to fire Fleischman—Perry was in.
With *Infinity*, their fourth LP and the first with Perry,
Journey became a top group, as moderately successful
singles ("Wheel in the Sky," "Lights") and constant
touring made *Infinity* the group's first platinum LP.

In September 1978, soon after *Infinity*'s success, Dunbar was dismissed from the group for what Herbert
termed "incompatibility of the first order." In April 1980,
Journey's Nightmare Productions charged that Dunbar
had been overpaid more than $60,000 in advances. In May
1980, Nightmare Productions (in which the band members
and Herbert owned stock) was sued for $3.25 million by
Dunbar, who claimed that he had been "squeezed out" of

Journey: Jonathan Cain, Steve Perry, Neal Schon, Ross
Valory, Steve Smith

the group just when the earnings were increasing and sued
for breach of contract, nonpayment of royalties and other
charges.

Meanwhile, Dunbar (who joined Jefferson Starship) was
replaced by Steve Smith, formerly Journey's drum roadie,
who had studied at the Berklee School of Music and
played with Focus, Jean-Luc Ponty and Montrose.
"Lovin', Touchin', Squeezin' " from *Evolution* was Journey's first Top Thirty hit; earlier that year, "Just the Same
Way" had been a moderate success.

In 1980, "Anyway You Want It" from *Departure* hit
#23. Columbia repackaged material from the first three
(pre-Perry) LPs as *In the Beginning*. After *Departure*,
Rolie tired of touring and left. He was replaced by ex-
Babys Jonathan Cain, who cowrote their 1981 #4 hit,
"Who's Crying Now." In 1981, Schon recorded a duo LP
entitled *Untold Passion* with Jan Hammer. *Escape* became the group's first #1 LP, its single "Open Arms" a #2
hit. All of the Perry LPs have been certified platinum, and
in late 1982 the group became the first rock band to inspire
a video game, *Journey—Escape*.

JOY OF COOKING
Formed 1967, Berkeley, California
Terry Garthwaite (b. July 11, 1938, Berkeley), gtr.; Toni
Brown (b. Nov. 16, 1938, Madison, Wis.), voc., piano;
Ron Wilson (b. Feb. 5, 1933, San Diego, Calif.), con-
gas; Fritz Kasten (b. Oct. 19, Des Moines, Ia.), drums;
David Garthwaite (b. Calif.), bass.
1970—*Joy of Cooking* (Capitol) (− D. Garthwaite;
+ Jeff Neighbor [b. Mar. 19, 1942, Grand Coulee,
Wash.], bass) *Closer to the Ground* **1972**—*Castles*
(− Brown).

Joy of Cooking was one of the first rock bands led by
women. Though the group lasted over five years, it had

only one hit, "Mockingbird," from its debut, and a small cult following. Terry Garthwaite began singing and playing guitar in junior high school and made her television debut at 14. A graduate of UC at Berkeley, she met Toni Brown, a creative writing graduate of Bennington, and together with Garthwaite's brother David and Ron Wilson and Fritz Kasten, they formed Joy of Cooking, a folk-rock group. Four years later, they signed a record deal with Capitol and "Mockingbird" became an FM hit. After their third LP, Brown left the group and Garthwaite formed a larger band, which toured and recorded an album that was never released because of contractual problems.

In 1973, Brown and Garthwaite recorded an album entitled *Cross Country*. They have each recorded solo albums and were reunited in 1977 for *The Joy*, which received positive critical reaction but garnered few sales. They have since disbanded; Garthwaite has toured solo and with Rosalie Sorrels.

JOY DIVISION/NEW ORDER

Formed 1977, Manchester, England
Ian Curtis (b. ca. 1957; d. May 18, 1980, Macclesfield, Eng.), voc.; Bernie Albrecht, gtr.; Peter Hooke, bass; Stephen Morris, drums.
1980—*Unknown Pleasures* (Factory, U.K.) *Closer*
1981—*Still* (New Order formed **1980**: Albrecht, Hooke, Lewis; + Gilliam Gilbert, gtr.) *Movement*
1983—*1981-1982* (Factory/Rough Trade) *Power, Corruption and Lies.*

One of Britain's most critically admired post-punk bands, Joy Division (named after Nazi military prostitutes) purveyed a doomy Velvet Underground–derived drone that adorned the morbid visions of lead singer Ian Curtis, who eerily bore out the gloom in his lyrics by hanging himself.

Joy Division had scored significant new wave club hits with "She's Lost Control," "Transmission" and "Love Will Tear Us Apart." After Curtis' suicide, the band's remaining members regrouped as New Order and had minor new wave hits with "Everything's Gone Green" in 1981 and "Temptation"—the first upbeat love song the band had ever recorded—in 1982, which appeared on the singles compilation *1981-1982.*

JUDAS PRIEST

Formed 1969, Birmingham, England
K. K. Downing, gtr.; Ian Hill, bass.
1971—(+ Rob Halford, voc.) **1974**—(+ Glenn Tipton, gtr.; + Alan Moore, drums) *Rocka Rolla* (Gull) **1976**—*Sad Wings of Destiny* **1977**—(− Moore; + Simon Phillips, drums) *Sin after Sin* (Columbia) **1978**—(− Phillips; + Les Binks, drums) *Stained Class* **1979**—*Hell Bent for Leather; Un-*

Judas Priest: Ian Hill, K. K. Downing, Rob Halford, Glenn Tipton, David Holland

leashed in the East (− Binks; + Dave Holland, drums) **1980**—*British Steel* **1981**—*Point of Entry* **1982**—*Screaming for Vengeance.*

Judas Priest, a leather-clad heavy-metal band, was formed by guitarist K. K. Downing and bassist Ian Hill. In 1971, frontman Rob Halford joined (he'd previously worked in theatrical lighting), having met Hill, whom his sister was then dating (and later married). The band didn't get a contract until 1974, just after Glenn Tipton joined. Its first LP was released that year, but both it and the 1976 followup, *Sad Wings of Destiny,* sold marginally.

The band began to develop a following in England, and in April 1977 they signed with Columbia, who released *Sin after Sin.* Produced by ex–Deep Purple bassist Roger Glover, *Sin* featured guest drummer Simon Phillips and an unlikely heavy-metal version of Joan Baez's "Diamonds and Rust" (similar in style to Nazareth's early-Seventies version of "This Flight Tonight"). Their songs, highlighted by a dual lead guitar attack, were catchier and shorter than most other early-Seventies heavy metal, anticipating late-decade bands like Def Leppard.

Stained Class featured new drummer Les Binks, replaced with ex-Trapeze member Dave Holland after their live-in-Japan *Unleashed in the East* record. The live LP included a version of Fleetwood Mac's "Green Manalishi." Over the years, Judas Priest became increasingly known for their live show, which featured Halford in his trademark S&M gear, thundering onstage on a Harley-Davidson motorcycle. Their seventh album, 1980's *British Steel,* was their first U.S. Top Forty entry. Though they've had considerable success in England and the Far East, it was not until October 1982 that they had their first U.S. gold LP, *Screaming for Vengeance.*

K

TONIO K.

Born Steve Krikorian, 1950, California
1979—*Life in the Foodchain* (Full Moon/Epic) **1980**—
Amerika (Arista) **1983**—*La Bomba* (Capitol).

Los Angeles singer/songwriter Tonio K. distinguished himself from his colleagues with his sardonic, self-consciously literate lyrics and high-velocity rock & roll. K. has purposely kept his background a mystery. In his first Arista press bio, he described himself as an "American Negro musician, born in New Orleans" in 1900, but in fact he was from a white middle-class San Joaquin Valley family. In 1972, he joined a latter-day version of Buddy Holly's group, the Crickets, and played bass with them for three years. When the Crickets disbanded for the last time, Krikorian turned to songwriting and a solo career, taking his pseudonym from the protagonist of Thomas Mann's short story "Tonio Kröger."

Eagles manager Irving Azoff hailed K. as a "brilliant lyricist," promoted him as a new Bob Dylan and signed him to Full Moon, a subsidiary of Epic. His debut album was well received by the music press but aroused little public interest. In 1979, he signed with Arista, but his first album for them lost him his support from the critics, who found his arrogance, intellectual conceit (lyrics in German and Greek) and belligerence too much to take. His 1983 LP featured an antinuclear remake of Richie Valens' "La Bamba" called "La Bomba."

KALEIDOSCOPE

Formed 1966, Berkeley, California
Fenrus Epp (a.k.a. Max Buda, Templeton Parceley, Connie Crill), violin, kybds.; John Vidican, percussion; Solomon Feldthouse (b. Turkey), gtr., voc., strings; David Lindley (b. 1944, San Marino, California), violin, gtr., voc.; Chris Darrow, gtr., voc., fiddle.
1967—*Side Trips* (Epic) **1968**—*A Beacon from Mars* (– Darrow; – Vidican; + Stuart Brotman, bass; + Paul Lagos, drums) **1969**—*Kaleidoscope* **1970**—*Bernice* (Columbia) **1976**—*When Scopes Collide* (Pacific Arts) *Brother Mary* (Polydor).

Kaleidoscope were known in the late Sixties for eclectic albums that drew from bluegrass, blues, Cajun music, Middle Eastern music and acid rock, using various exotic instruments (e.g., saz, oud). Today, they are remembered primarily as being the band David Lindley led before he hooked up with Jackson Browne. In the Eighties, Lindley also recorded solo LPs.

Despite a noteworthy appearance at the 1968 Newport Folk Festival and a live act that included flamenco and belly dancers, Kaleidoscope's early albums, *Sidetrips* and *Beacon from Mars*, were ignored. Vidican and Darrow were replaced by Paul Lagos and Stuart Brotman, with no resulting rise in popularity for subsequent LPs *Kaleidoscope* and *Bernice*. The band broke up in 1970, though it reunited in 1975 for *When Scopes Collide*, with only minor contributions from Lindley (under the name DeParis Letante).

Darrow recorded solo albums for United Artists and other labels after leaving Kaleidoscope, including one with members of British folk-rockers Fairport Convention. "Max Buda" made a guest appearance on Darrow's 1979 LP, *Fretless*.

KANSAS

Formed 1970, Topeka, Kansas
Kerry Livgren, gtr., kybds., synth.; Steve Walsh, kybds., synth., voc.; Robby Steinhardt, violin, voc.; Richard Williams, gtr.; Phil Ehart, drums; Dave Hope, bass.
1974—*Kansas* (Kirshner) **1975**—*Masque; Song for America* **1976**—*Leftoverture* **1977**—*Point of Know Return* **1978**—*Two for the Show* **1979**—*Monolith* **1980**—*Audio-Visions* **1982**—(– Walsh; + John Elefante [b. 1958, New York City], voc., kybds.) *Vinyl Confessions*.

Although Kansas' ornate and complex rock has been dismissed by critics as a pastiche of early-Seventies British progressive rock, some of their albums have sold in the millions.

For years, the band labored through the Midwest, playing clubs and bars, its odd mix of Anglophilia and boogie falling mostly on bewildered ears. The members met while attending high school in Topeka, and after playing in various local groups, Kerry Livgren, Phil Ehart and Dave Hope formed the first edition of Kansas in 1970. A year later, they changed their name to White Clover and added Robby Steinhardt, a classically trained violinist who had played with orchestras in Europe when his father, chairman of the music history department at the University of Kansas, was there on sabbatical. The group went through numerous personnel changes before Ehart, seeking new ideas, went to England in 1972. On his return four months later, he revived White Clover, with Hope, Steinhardt, Richard Williams and Steve Walsh; Livgren, who became the group's main songwriter, joined soon after, and they reverted to the name Kansas.

Their first album initially sold about 100,000 copies; but constant touring built the group's following, and its second and third LPs each sold about 250,000. *Leftoverture*, which featured "Carry On Wayward Son" (#11, 1977), sold over two million copies. *Point of Know Return*, released later that year, "shipped gold" and soon went platinum, garnering two hit singles—"Point of Know Return" (#28) and "Dust in the Wind" (#6). *Two for the Show*, a live album, is also platinum, and *Monolith* (their first self-produced venture) and *Audio-Visions* are gold.

In 1980, schisms began to form within the group. Livgren and then Hope became born-again Christians. Livgren cut a solo album, *Seeds of Change*, in 1980, as Walsh had the previous year with *Schemer-Dreamer*. Walsh also sang on ex-Genesis Steve Hackett's solo album, *Please Don't Touch*. By the end of 1981, Walsh had left the group and was replaced by John Elefante.

KASENETZ-KATZ

Jerry Kasenetz and Jeff Katz were the producers and occasionally the writers of virtually every bubblegum hit of the late Sixties on Buddah Records, notably those of the 1910 Fruitgum Company ("Simon Says," "May I Take a Giant Step," "1,2,3, Red Light") and the Ohio Express ("Yummy Yummy Yummy," "Chewy Chewy"). Those two groups, along with the members of six other Kasenetz-Katz bands, made up the 46-strong Kasenetz-Katz Singing Orchestral Circus, conceived as a publicity stunt for a Carnegie Hall date, but which actually scored a hit single in 1968, "Quick Joey Small" (#25). Before coming to Buddah in late 1967, Kasenetz and Katz worked at Cameo with Ohio Express on "Beg, Borrow and Steal" at Laurie, and on the Music Explosion's hit "Little Bit o' Soul" (#2, 1967).

ERIC KAZ

Born 1947, Brooklyn, New York
1972—*If You're Lonely* (Atlantic)   1974—*Cul-de-Sac*
1978—*Fuller/Kaz* (Columbia).

A sometime member of the Blues Magoos and American Flyer, Eric Kaz is best known as a songwriter. His morose, romantic heartbreak songs—including "Love Has No Pride," cowritten with Libby Titus—have been covered by Linda Ronstadt, Randy Meisner, Bonnie Raitt, Rita Coolidge, Tom Rush, Lynn Anderson, Tracy Nelson and Peter Yarrow.

Kaz grew up in a musical family but was unenthusiastic about music lessons. He left his Brooklyn home before graduating from high school and moved to Greenwich Village, where he played in numerous folk and rock groups in the mid-Sixties. He recorded an album with Happy and Artie Traum in a group called the Children of Paradise before joining the Blues Magoos in 1970. After two years, the Magoos broke up.

Kaz wrote and performed soundtracks for two early Brian DePalma movies (*Greetings*, 1968; *Hi Mom*, 1970) before signing a solo contract with Atlantic in 1972. But his singing was not as popular as his songs, and his albums served largely as demos for other singers. Tracy Nelson was one of the first to cover Kaz compositions extensively. Bonnie Raitt was the first to do "Love Has No Pride," but it was Linda Ronstadt's rendition that became a minor hit in 1973. (Kaz has accompanied both Raitt and Ronstadt in the studio.) In 1975, he joined the middleweight supergroup American Flyer (with ex–Blood, Sweat and Tears Steve Katz, ex–Velvet Underground Doug Yule and ex–Pure Prairie League Craig Fuller), who recorded two albums for United Artists before disbanding.

K.C. AND THE SUNSHINE BAND

Formed 1973, Florida
Harry Wayne Casey (b. Jan. 31, 1951, Hialeah, Fla.), voc., kybds.; Richard Finch (b. Jan. 25, 1954, Indianapolis), bass; Jerome Smith (b. June 18, 1953, Miami), gtr.; Robert Johnson (b. Mar. 21, 1953, Miami), drums; Fermin Goytisolo (b. Dec. 31, 1951, Havana, Cuba), congas; Ronnie Smith (b. 1952, Hialeah, Fla.), trumpet; Denvil Liptrot, sax; James Weaver, trumpet; Charles Williams (b. Nov. 18, 1954, Rockingham, N.C.), trombone.
1974—*Do It Good* (T.K.)   1975—*The Sound of Sunshine* (a.k.a. *The Sunshine Band*)   1976—*Part 3*;   *K.C. and the Sunshine Band*   1977—*I Like to Do It* (President)   1978—*Who Do Ya (Love)* (T.K.)   1979—*Do You Wanna Go Party?*   1980—*Greatest Hits*   1981—*The Painter* (Epic)   1982—*All in a Night's Work*.

K.C. and the Sunshine Band were the most successful promulgators of the boisterous, tropically funky dance music known as the Miami Sound. The Sunshine Band originated in the T.K. Studios in Hialeah, Florida, near Miami. H. W. Casey, a former record retailer, began working in 1973 for Tone Distributors, where he met Richard Finch, a Miami session bassist hired by T.K. as an engineer. The two formed a songwriting partnership and recorded as K.C. and the Sunshine Junkanoo Band. (Junkanoo is a percussion-oriented pop from the Bahama Islands, characterized by a liberal mix of horns, whistles and vocal chants.) Their first record, "Blow Your Whistle," reached #27 on R&B charts in 1973, and its followup (as K.C. and the Sunshine Band), "Sound Your Funky Horn," went to #21 early the next year, persuading T.K. to release an album.

Do It Good was a hit in Europe, and the single "Queen of Clubs" went to #7 on British charts in 1974 (not placing on American charts until its reissue two years later), when K.C. and the Sunshine Band toured the U.K. Casey and Finch wrote, arranged and produced "Rock Your Baby," a #1 hit for George McCrae (who had sung on *Do It Good*) on both pop and R&B charts in 1974, which sold a reported 11 million copies worldwide. The following year, K.C. and the Sunshine Band struck gold with "Get Down Tonight" (#1 pop and R&B).

K.C. and the Sunshine Band—now expanded to nine members, all black except for Casey and Finch—ruled the charts and the dance floors for the next three years. "That's the Way (I Like It)" and "(Shake, Shake, Shake) Shake Your Booty" reached #1 on the pop charts in 1975 and early 1976, respectively. The Sunshine Band became the first act to score three #1 pop singles in one year since the Beatles in 1964. Each song was #1 R&B as well. The band's string of hit singles continued with "I'm Your Boogie Man" (#1 pop, #3 R&B, 1977) and "Keep It Comin' Love" (#2 pop, #1 R&B, 1977).

It looked as if they had come to the end of the string in 1978 with the minor hits "Boogie Shoes" and "It's the Same Old Song," but in 1979 they returned with "Do You Wanna Go Party" (#8 R&B), "Please Don't Go" (#1 pop) and "Yes, I'm Ready"—featuring the vocals of Teri De Sario—(#2 pop, #20 R&B).

Casey and Finch were also involved in hitmaking—as songwriters, producers or both—for Betty Wright (her Grammy-winning "Where Is the Love"), Jimmy "Bo" Horne, Fire (the female vocal group that backed the Sunshine Band on "That's the Way") and Leif Garrett.

ERNIE K-DOE
Born Ernest Kador, Jr., February 22, 1936, New Orleans
N.A.—*Ernie K-Doe* (Janus)   *Mother-in-Law* (Minit).

With his national charttopper "Mother-in-Law," Ernie K-Doe was one of the young black singers whose jaunty beat and rollicking good humor popularized New Orleans R&B in the early Sixties.

Raised by an aunt in New Orleans, Kador was heavily influenced by gospel. By the time he was 15 he had become a member of the Golden Chain Jubilee Singers and the Zion Travellers. He made his first recording when he was in Chicago visiting his mother in 1953. It was never released. He went on to sing with the Moonglows and the Flamingos, and two years later, he returned to New Orleans, where he made a name for himself with a vocal group called the Blue Diamonds. By then he had legally changed his name to K-Doe (which he has since copyrighted).

An outgoing showman, K-Doe made the Blue Diamonds a favorite act in the Crescent City. After recording with them for Savoy, he cut his first solo record, "Do Baby Do," for Specialty in 1956. He also recorded for Herald before "Hello My Lover," a single for Minit, became a regional hit in 1959. His next hit was "Mother-in-Law," a novelty song produced by Allen Toussaint. The record went to #1 on both the pop and R&B charts in 1961.

He followed "Mother-in-Law" with a handful of singles

for Minit, the most successful of which were "Te-Ta-Te-Ta-Ta" (#53 pop, #21 R&B, 1961) and "I Cried My Last Tear" (#69, 1961). He later recorded for Duke, placing "Later for Tomorrow" at #37 on the R&B charts in 1967, and subsequently for Janus. Allen Toussaint produced a couple of K-Doe albums in the early Seventies, though K-Doe soon left Toussaint. He remains active on the New Orleans club circuit and appears regularly at Delta region music festivals.

KEITH
1967—*Keith;   Out of Crank* (Mercury)   **1969**—*The Adventures of Keith* (RCA)   *98.6/Ain't Gonna Lie* (Mercury).

Philadelphia-born James Barry Keefer changed his name to Keith and recorded the single "Ain't Gonna Lie," which failed to crack the Top Thirty. But his next 45, "98.6," made it all the way to #7 and spent 14 weeks on the charts in 1967. Five more singles and three albums went nowhere.

EDDIE KENDRICKS
Born December 17, 1939, Union Springs, Alabama
1971—*All By Myself* (Tamla)   **1972**—*People . . . Hold On*   **1973**—*Eddie Kendricks*   **1974**—*Boogie Down; For You*   **1975**—*The Hit Man*   **1976**—*He's a Friend; Goin' Up in Smoke*   **1977**—*Slick*   **1978**—*At His Best; Vintage '78* (Arista)   **1981**—*Love Keys* (Atlantic).

After 11 years as the Temptations' lead tenor, Eddie Kendricks left for what proved to be an intermittently successful solo career that peaked in 1973–74 with "Keep On Truckin' " and "Boogie Down."

Raised in Birmingham, he moved to Cleveland after high school, and from there to Detroit, where he formed his first vocal group, the Cavaliers. After several personnel changes, they became the Primes in 1959. In the early Sixties, Berry Gordy, Jr., signed them to Motown, changing their name to the Temptations. (Gordy also signed the Primes' sister act, a female group that Kendricks had named the Primettes and which Gordy renamed the Supremes.) Kendricks sang the lead on the Temptations' first hit, "The Way You Do the Things You Do," in 1964, and either lead or high harmony on more than twenty subsequent pop and soul hits between 1963 and 1971.

In the second half of the Sixties, when the Temps were at the height of their popularity, conflicts arose among members of the group and their Motown bosses, some over money, others over the stylistic changes wrought by producer Norman Whitfield, who directed the group toward funkier street-hip songs. Kendricks quit the group in 1971. He moved to the West Coast and began to build a solo career with Motown.

His early solo recordings—"It's So Hard for Me to Say Goodbye" and "Can I" (1971), "Eddie's Love" and "If

You Let Me" (1972), "Girl You Need a Change of Mind" and "Darling Come Back Home" (1973)—were R&B hits. His jump to the top of the R&B, soul and pop charts came in 1973 with the falsetto-topped "Keep On Truckin' " and in 1974 with "Boogie Down," both of which hit #1 on the R&B charts; the former made #1 on the pop charts, while the latter peaked at #2.

For the next three years Kendricks' songs were regularly in the R&B Top Ten: "Son of Sagittarius" (#28 pop, #5 R&B, 1974), "Tell Her Love Has Felt the Need" (#8 R&B, 1974), "One Tear" (#8 R&B, 1974), "Shoeshine Boy" (#18 pop, #1 R&B, 1975), "Get the Cream Off the Top" (#7 R&B, 1975), "Happy" (#8 R&B, 1975), "He's a Friend" (#36 pop, #2 R&B, 1976). In 1977 he signed with Arista. His last single hit for Motown was "Intimate Friends" (#24 R&B, 1978). The move proved to be not as smooth as expected. His only big hit for Arista was "Ain't No Smoke without Fire" (#13 R&B, 1978), and in 1980 he signed with Atlantic.

CHRIS KENNER

Born December 25, 1929, Kenner, Louisiana
1963—*Land of a Thousand Dances* (Atlantic).

New Orleans vocalist Chris Kenner had a hit single in 1961 with "I Like It Like That." But in the record business—and especially the New Orleans music community in which he has been active since the Fifties—he is known for writing hits for Fats Domino, Wilson Pickett and the Dave Clark Five.

Kenner started his career as a singer with a gospel quartet, the New Orleans Harmonizing Four, in the early Fifties and made his first records for the Baton and Imperial labels in 1957. His "Sick and Tired" on Imperial was cut that year, but Fats Domino's cover made #22 in 1958. Kenner remained a local figure, recording for labels like Pontchartrain, until he teamed up with Allen Toussaint, producer for Minit Records' Instant label. "I Like It Like That," their first collaboration, went to #2 on both the R&B and pop charts in 1961. The song returned to the Top Ten four years later in a cover version by the Dave Clark Five. Kenner's "Land of 1000 Dances"—which, in his rendition, made it to the Top 100—was a hit for Wilson Pickett and for Cannibal and the Headhunters, and a modest hit for the Three Midniters and for Electric Indian. Kenner's 1964 recording of "Something You Got" was a huge success in New Orleans. He continued to record with Instant until 1969.

DOUG KERSHAW

Born January 24, 1936, Tiel Ridge, Louisiana
1969—*The Cajun Way* (Warner Bros.) 1970—*Spanish Moss* 1971—*Doug Kershaw; Devil's Elbow* 1973— *Douglas James Kershaw* 1974—*Mama Kershaw's Boy* 1975—*Alive and Pickin'* 1976—*The Ragin'*

Cajun 1977—*Flip Flop Fly* 1978—*Louisiana Man* 1979—*Louisiana Cajun Country* (Starflite).

Doug Kershaw is America's best-known Cajun fiddler, though his traditional bayou sound has always been a bit too exotic to secure him a major country or rock audience.

Kershaw was born on a tiny island in the Gulf of Mexico in a poor French-speaking community and didn't learn English until after he turned eight. His father was an alligator hunter who shot himself through the head when Doug was just seven. The family soon relocated to Lake Arthur, Louisiana, where Doug went to school and practiced on his older brother's fiddle, which he'd first fooled with at age five; he has since taught himself 28 other instruments.

Kershaw played his first date at age eight, at a local bar called the Bucket of Blood, with his mother accompanying him on guitar. He graduated from McNeese State University with a degree in mathematics, and then with two of his brothers he formed the Continental Playboys.

Kershaw was writing by the time he left the bayou at age 18, to try to record in Nashville. Billed as Rusty and Doug (Rusty was his 16-year-old brother), the two recorded for Hickory Records and became regulars on the Grand Ole Opry by 1957. After a stint in the Army, Kershaw penned his best-known piece, "Louisiana Man," in 1960, which went to #10 on the country & western charts the next year and became a country standard. Also in 1961, the two hit the C&W list with "Diggy Liggy Lo" (#14), but he and his brother had no followup, and they soon broke up.

It wasn't until the later Sixties that Kershaw got beyond his regional reputation. With the help of producer Buddy Killen, he got a contract with Warner Bros., which led to *The Cajun Way*. His appearance on "The Johnny Cash Show" that summer (on the same program as Bob Dylan) attracted national attention and brought him to the rock circuit.

Kershaw was offered a cameo acting role in *Zachariah* and also appeared in *Medicine Ball Caravan* (a rock tour film), *We Have Come for Your Daughters* and 1978's *Days of Heaven*. He continues to tour and record.

CHAKA KHAN

Born Yvette Marie Stevens, March 23, 1953, Great Lakes, Illinois
1978—*Chaka* (Warner Bros.) 1980—*Naughty* 1981— *What 'Cha Gonna Do for Me* 1982—*Echoes of an Era* (Elektra-Musician) 1982—*Chaka Khan* (Warner Bros.).
Rufus albums:
1973—*Rufus* (ABC) 1974—*Rags to Rufus; Rufu-sized* 1975—*Rufus Featuring Chaka Khan* 1977—*Ask Rufus* 1978—*Street Player* 1979—*Numbers; Masterjam* (MCA).

Chaka Khan, lead singer for Rufus and later a solo act, grew up on Chicago's South Side. She formed her first band at age 11, the Crystalettes, who played the Chicago area. She was also very active at school and became president of the Black Students Union at age 16. At the time, she was also a member of the Afro-Arts Theater, which toured briefly with Mary Wells. A few years later, when Khan was working on the Black Panthers' breakfast program, she took her African name, Chaka, which means fire.

In 1969, Khan quit school and worked with a band called Lyfe and then the Babysitters, doing endless sets of dance music. In 1972, she teamed up with Kevin Murphy (who'd previously played in the American Breed) and Andre Fisher to form Rufus. The band went on to earn six gold or platinum LPs before Khan left to go solo in 1978. Her first album, *Chaka*, was produced by Arif Mardin and featured members of the Average White Band and Rufus guitarist Tony Maiden. It went gold and contained the hit "I'm Every Woman" (#21) written by Ashford and Simpson.

While under contract to do two more LPs with Rufus, with whom she traded barbs in the press, Khan continued to record solo LPs and tour with her own band. In 1979, she did some backup vocals on Ry Cooder's *Bop Till You Drop*, and in 1982 she recorded live with Rufus at New York's Savoy Theater. She also collaborated with Lenny White, Chick Corea, Freddie Hubbard, Joe Henderson and Stanley Clarke on an album of jazz standards, *Echoes of an Era*.

KID CREOLE AND THE COCONUTS (See Dr. Buzzard's Original Savannah Band)

JOHNNY KIDD AND THE PIRATES
Formed 1959, England
Johnny Kidd (b. Frederick Heath, Dec. 23, 1939, London; d. Oct. 7, 1966, Eng.), voc.; Mick Green, gtr.; Johnny Spencer, bass; Frank Farley, drums.
1971—*Shakin' All Over* (Starline) *Your Cheatin' Heart* (Pathe) *Memorial Album* **1978**—*Best of Johnny Kidd and the Pirates* (EMI) *Out of Their Skulls* (Warner Bros.) **1979**—*Skull Wars*.

Johnny Kidd is best remembered as coauthor of the rock classic "Shakin' All Over" (a tune covered by many bands, including the Who). But Kidd's band, the Pirates, was one of the first hard-rocking bands England produced before 1962 and a prototype for the heavy-metal guitar trios it predated by nearly a decade.

Kidd and the Pirates were primarily a singles and live concert act. On stage, vocalist Kidd wore black leather and an eyepatch. Their first hit was Kidd's 1959 "Please Don't Touch," which hit #25 on the U.K. singles charts. A year later "Shakin' All Over," epitomizing Kidd's intense hard-rockabilly approach, was a #1 hit. "You Got What It Takes" (#25) and "Restless" (#22) were other

1960 successes, but the band didn't hit again until 1963's "I'll Never Get Over You," which went to #4. "Hungry for Love," which got as high as #20 that year, was the band's last commercial gasp, as the Merseybeat explosion put it permanently out of the limelight. Kidd and the Pirates never gained a commercial foothold in America. Kidd was killed in a car crash in 1966; ten years later, Mick Green briefly re-formed the original Pirates.

GREG KIHN BAND
Formed 1975, Berkeley, California
Greg Kihn (b. 1952, Baltimore), voc., gtr.; Robbie Dunbar, gtr.; Larry Lynch, drums, voc.; Steve Wright, bass, voc.
1976—*Greg Kihn* (Beserkley) (− Dunbar; + Dave Carpender, lead gtr.) **1977**—*Greg Kihn Again* **1978**—*Next of Kihn* **1979**—*With the Naked Eye* **1980**—*Powerlines* (U.K.) *Glass House Rock* (Beserkley) (+ Gary Phillips, kybds.) **1981**—*Rockihnroll* **1982**—*Kihntinued* (− Carpender; + Greg Douglass, lead gtr.) **1983**—*Kihnspiracy*.

Greg Kihn's band—a power-pop outfit influenced by the Yardbirds, the Beau Brummels, Bruce Springsteen and others—began as one of the four original acts on the Beserkley label out of Berkeley. Kihn first came to Berkeley from Baltimore in late 1974 and wound up contributing two solo songs to 1975's anthology *Beserkley Chartbusters, Volume 1*. He also did backup vocals on Jonathan Richman's "Roadrunner."

At the time, Kihn used Earth Quake as his support band, and his first album in 1976 featured guitarist Robbie Dunbar from that band (Dunbar's brother Tommy was in the Rubinoos), plus bassist Steve Wright and drummer Larry Lynch. Kihn kept Wright and Lynch and added Dave Carpender to replace Dunbar in early 1976. The band's second album in 1977 was harder rocking than the first and included a re-working of Springsteen's "For You," whose arrangement Springsteen later adapted for his own live shows.

The band's next few albums began to sell (about 125,000 copies each), and it built a following in the Bay Area. But the group never developed more than a cult following until "The Breakup Song" reached the pop charts in 1981. Keyboardist Phillips, who joined after *Glass House Rock*, had previously worked in Earth Quake and Copperhead, with ex-Quicksilver guitarist John Cipollina. "Jeopardy" brought Kihn to the Top Five in 1983.

ALBERT KING
Born April 25, 1923, Indianola, Mississippi
1962—*The Big Blues* (King) **1967**—*Born Under a Bad Sign* (Stax) **1968**—*King of the Blues Guitar* (Atlantic) **1972**—*I'll Play the Blues for You* (Stax) **1975**—*Truckload of Lovin'* (Utopia) **1977**—*The Pinch* (Stax)

1979—*Chronicle; New Orleans Heat* (Tomato)
1982—*Albert King Masterworks* (Atlantic/Deluxe).

Albert King's mammoth physical presence—he weighs more than 250 pounds and stands six feet four—is reflected in his harsh, imposing vocals and biting, influential blues style.

He bought his first guitar for $1.25 sometime around 1939 (he now plays a left-handed Flying V), and his first inspiration was T-Bone Walker. For a long while he had to work non-music jobs to survive (including bulldozer operator and mechanic), but in the late Forties he settled in Osceola, Arkansas, and worked local gigs with the In the Groove Boys. He then migrated north, where he played drums for Jimmy Reed and also provided guitar and vocals on his own singles, including "Lonesome in My Bedroom" and "Bad Luck Blues" for the Parrot label in 1953.

King then moved to St. Louis and formed another band, but didn't record again until 1959, when he signed to the local Bobbin label. He worked for several small companies in the early Sixties, including King Records, which released his 1961 hit "Don't Throw Your Love on Me Too Strong" (#14 R&B). But his real break finally came in 1966, when he signed to Stax. Using the label's famed Memphis sidemen, he cut some of his best-known works, including "Laundromat Blues" (1966) and his album *Born Under a Bad Sign,* made with Booker T. and the MGs in 1967. King began to break through to white audiences. He appeared on the first Fillmore East show on March 8, 1968 (with Tim Buckley, Big Brother and Janis Joplin), and played at the closing concerts of the hall on June 27, 1971. (A live album, *Live Wire/Blues Power,* had been recorded at Fillmore West.)

In November 1969, King played with the St. Louis Symphony Orchestra, forming what was termed "an 87-piece blues band." Over the years, his songs have been covered by Free, John Mayall, the Electric Flag and others. He toured more than ever in the Seventies, though he left Stax in 1974. He signed to Utopia in 1976 and to Tomato in 1978, charting some minor R&B singles.

B. B. KING
Born Riley B. King, September 16, 1925, Indianola, Mississippi
1965—*Live at the Regal* (ABC)   **1968**—*B. B. King Story* (Blue Horizon)   **1969**—*B. B. King Story, Volume 2; Live and Well* (ABC/Dunhill)   **1970**—*Indianola Mississippi Seeds* (ABC)   **1973**—*The Best of B. B. King*   **1975**—*Lucille Talks Back*   **1976**—*B. B. King Anthology*   **1977**—*Kingsize; Lucille*   **1978**—*Midnight Believer*   **1979**—*Take It Home*   **1981**—*There Must Be a Better World Somewhere* (MCA)   **1983**—*Blues 'n' Jazz.*

B. B. King is universally recognized as the leading exponent of modern blues. Playing his trademark Gibson guitar, which he refers to affectionately as Lucille, King

influenced numerous rock guitarists, including Mike Bloomfield and Eric Clapton, with his voice-like string bends and left-hand vibrato.

King picked cotton as a youth, for which he earned as little as 35¢ per 100 pounds. In the Forties, he played on the streets of Indianola before moving on to perform professionally in Memphis around 1949. As a young musician he studied recordings by both blues and jazz guitarists, including T-Bone Walker, Charlie Christian and Django Reinhardt. During his first years in Memphis, he lived with his cousin, bluesman Bukka White.

In the early Fifties, King was a disc jockey on Memphis black station WDIA, where he was dubbed the "Beale Street Blues Boy." Eventually, Blues Boy was shortened to B. B. and the nickname stuck. The radio show and performances in Memphis with friends Johnny Ace and Bobby "Blue" Bland built King's strong local reputation.

One of his first recordings, "Three O'Clock Blues" (#1 R&B), for the RPM label was a national success in 1951, landing King bookings at major black venues like Harlem's Apollo and Washington, D.C.'s Howard theaters. During the Fifties, King was a consistent record seller and concert attraction. In 1956, he played 342 one-nighters. He had recorded for the small black-oriented labels Kent, Crown and Blue Horizon before signing with ABC Records in 1961.

King's *Live at the Regal* is considered one of the definitive blues albums. The mid-Sixties blues revival

B. B. King

introduced him to white audiences, and by 1966 he was appearing regularly on rock concert circuits and receiving airplay on progressive rock radio. He continued to have hits on the soul charts ("Paying the Cost to Be the Boss," #10 R&B, 1968) and always maintained a solid black following. *Live and Well*, produced by Bill Szymczyk (who later produced the Eagles), was a notable album featuring "Why I Sing the Blues" (#13 R&B, 1969) and King's only pop Top Twenty single, "The Thrill Is Gone" (#15 pop, #3 R&B).

In the Seventies King also recorded albums with longtime friend and onetime chauffeur Bobby Bland: *Together for the First Time . . . Live* (1974) and *Together Again . . . Live* (1976). Stevie Wonder produced King's "To Know You Is to Love You." In 1982, King recorded a live album with the Crusaders.

King's tours have taken him to the U.S.S.R. (1979), South America (1980) and to more than forty prisons. His concern for prisoners led him, along with attorney F. Lee Bailey, to establish the Foundation for the Advancement of Inmate Rehabilitation and Recreation in 1972. Nineteen-eighty marked the publication of Charles Sawyer's authorized biography, *The Arrival of B. B. King*. In 1981, *There Must Be a Better World Somewhere* won a Grammy award.

BEN E. KING
Born Benjamin Earl Soloman, September 28, 1938, Henderson, North Carolina
1961—*Spanish Harlem* (Atco)   1964—*Ben E. King's Greatest Hits* (Atlantic)   1975—*Supernatural Thing; Ben E. King Story*   1976—*I Had a Love*   1977—*Benny and Us* (with the Average White Band) (Atco)   1978—*Let Me Live in Your Life* (Atlantic)   1981—*Street Tough*.

Ben E. King's smooth tenor earned him a reputation as a romantic R&B singer for a career spanning more than twenty years. He hit a commercial peak as lead vocalist for the late-period Drifters, and as a solo artist in the early Sixties.

King sang in church choirs in North Carolina, and when his family moved to Harlem he formed his first group while attending James Fenimore Cooper Junior High. It was called the Four B's, as all members' names started with B.

In the mid-Fifties King tried out unsuccessfully for the Moonglows, but by 1956 he had joined a professional band, the Five Crowns, whose manager supposedly found the 18-year-old King through a chance meeting. King toured with the band, which included Bobby Hendricks, who left to become lead singer for the Drifters in early 1958.

The Five Crowns made 11 records between October 1952 and March 1958, none of them hits, but in 1959 the Drifters' manager, George Treadwell (who owned the name but was deserted by the original band), thought the Crowns were good enough to become his "new Drifters." The new group immediately hit it big with "There Goes My Baby" (#2 pop, #1 R&B), sung and cowritten by twenty-year-old King, and reputedly the first R&B hit to use strings. King sang lead on two other gold singles for the band (all produced by Leiber and Stoller), including their biggest pop smash—their only #1—"Save the Last Dance for Me" (1960). He also sang on the standard "This Magic Moment" (#16 pop, #4 R&B, 1960).

In midwinter 1960, King went solo and had a #10 pop, #15 R&B hit in 1961 (supervised by Phil Spector) with "Spanish Harlem," a song Spector wrote with Jerry Leiber. King followed it with another Top Ten the same year, the stark self-penned "Stand by Me" (#4 pop, #10 R&B). In 1962 he hit with "Don't Play That Song" (#11 pop, #2 R&B). After that King fared better on the soul than the pop charts, though his 1963 hit "I (Who Have Nothing)" (#29 pop, #16 R&B) became a top seller for Tom Jones in 1970. By the end of 1963, King's career slowed; and though he often played in Europe, he was largely out of the spotlight until 1975, when he re-signed with his old label, Atlantic, and had an immediate hit with "Supernatural Thing, Part 1" (#5). In 1977, he collaborated with longtime admirers the Average White Band on *Benny and Us*, while continuing with several solo hits, including 1980's "Music Trance" (#29 R&B).

CAROLE KING
Born Carole Klein, February 9, 1942, Brooklyn, New York
1969—*Now That Everything's Been Said* (Ode)   1970—*Carole King: Writer*   1971—*Tapestry; Music*   1972—*Rhymes and Reasons*   1973—*Fantasy*   1974—*Wrap Around Joy*   1975—*Really Rosie*   1976—*Thoroughbred*   1977—*Simple Things* (Capitol)   1978—*Welcome Home* (Avatar)   *Her Greatest Hits* (Ode)   1979—*Touch the Sky* (Capitol)   1980—*Pearls: Songs of Goffin and King*   1982—*One to One* (Atlantic).

Singer/songwriter Carole King has had two outstanding careers. Throughout the Sixties, she was one of pop's most prolific songwriters, writing the music to songs like "Will You Love Me Tomorrow?" and "Up on the Roof," with most lyrics by her first husband, Gerry Goffin. Then in 1971, with her multimillion-selling *Tapestry*, she helped inaugurate the Seventies' singer/songwriter style.

King began playing piano at age four; in high school she started her first band, the Co-sines. While attending Queens College in 1958, she met Gerry Goffin and the two became cowriters. King had written some early singles like "Goin' Wild" and "Baby Sittin,' " but they went nowhere. Neil Sedaka had a hit dedicated to her in October 1959 called "Oh! Carol," but her reply song, "Oh! Neil," stiffed.

In 1961, she and Goffin cowrote "Will You Love Me Tomorrow?", a #1 hit for the Shirelles, and the song has been covered countless times since. The two young writers, like Sedaka, Cynthia Weil and Barry Mann, wrote their songs for Don Kirshner and Al Nevins' Aldon Music in Brill Building cubicles. They wrote over 100 hits in countless styles, including "Wasn't Born to Follow" (for the Byrds), "Chains" (for the Cookies), "Don't Bring Me Down" (for the Animals) and "I'm into Something Good" (for Herman's Hermits). In 1962, the King-Goffin team wrote, arranged, conducted and produced the song "The Loco-Motion" for their 17-year-old babysitter, Little Eva (Boyd), and it went #1 that summer. That year, King made a brief foray into solo recording, but her only hit single at the time was "It Might As Well Rain Until September" (#22).

In the mid-Sixties, Goffin, King and columnist Al Aronowitz tried to launch their own label, Tomorrow Records. It failed, but one band they produced, the Myddle Class, included bass player Charles Larkey, who became King's second husband after she divorced Goffin and moved to L.A. with her two children, Sherry and Louise (who later launched a recording career of her own at age 19 in 1979 with *Kid Blue*).

In 1968, King formed a group called the City with Larkey and Danny Kortchmar, who had both previously played on three Fugs albums. They also knew each other from the New York club circuit, where the Myddle Class played with Kortchmar's band the Flying Machine, which also included vocalist James Taylor. The City never toured, because of King's stage fright, though they did make one unsuccessful LP on Ode records, *Now That Everything's Been Said.* The LP later yielded hits for Blood Sweat and Tears ("Hi-De-Ho") and James Taylor ("You've Got a Friend," which also appeared on King's *Tapestry*). Taylor encouraged King to write her own lyrics and finally record solo again, resulting in 1970's *Writer,* with a backup band including Kortchmar and others (who later recorded two Atlantic albums under the name Jo Mama). King toured with Jo Mama and Taylor, and they all worked on the 1971 critical and commercial windfall, *Tapestry,* which had four top singles, went #1, stayed 302 weeks on the charts (until January 1977) and sold over 13 million copies.

King's early-Seventies LPs went gold and Top Ten, and in late 1974 she had a #2 hit with "Jazzman" from the *Wrap Around Joy* album. In 1975, King wrote the music for a children's program, "Really Rosie," and began to write with Goffin again. She switched to Capitol Records in late 1976, and her first album for them, *Simple Things,* went gold. She began touring with a band called Navarro, introduced to her by Dan Fogelberg, and married her collaborator of the time, Rick Evers, who died of a heroin overdose in 1978.

By 1978, her albums were selling modestly, though she did better with her 1980 *Pearls* LP, which featured King's versions of some of her best-known Sixties collaborations with Goffin, such as "One Fine Day" (#12) and "Hey Girl."

EARL KING
Born Solomon Johnson, February 7, 1934, New Orleans
1978—*New Orleans Rock 'n' Roll* (Sonet)   *Earl King* (Vivid).

Along with Robert Parker, Irma Thomas and Lee Dorsey, Earl King is one of New Orleans' major R&B singers.

King started his career as a gospel singer around 1950 and learned to play guitar and sing the blues a few years later. He sang with pianist Huey "Piano" Smith until 1953, when he recorded his first solo work for Savoy under the name Earl Johnson. In 1954, King was signed by Art Rupe to Specialty Records and had a regional hit with "A Mother's Love" that year.

His touring group was then called Earl King and the Kings (they also recorded separately for Specialty), but in 1955 King signed with Johnny Vincent's new Ace label, where he immediately scored his biggest hit, "Those Lonely, Lonely Nights." It sold 250,000 copies without ever entering the national charts. The song, a two-chord slow ballad, was a major influence on all future Louisiana swamp rock, paving the way for people like Dr. John, who later covered King's "Let's Make a Better World" on *Desitively Bonnaroo.* Later that year, "Don't Take It So Hard" went to #13 on the R&B charts.

King had some local hits in 1958, like "Well-O Well-O Well-O Baby." He worked for Rex Records in 1959 with then staff sessionman Mac Rebennack (later Dr. John). That year he also sold 80,000 copies of "Everybody Has to Cry Sometime" under the pseudonym Handsome Earl. His first release for Imperial in 1960 was the savage "Come On," later covered by Jimi Hendrix, and his biggest hit for the label was a #17 R&B hit in 1962, "Always a First Time." His witty "Trick Bag" (an archetypal piece of New Orleans funk) was later redone by the Meters in 1976 with King sitting in. In 1963 and 1964, he played with Professor Longhair, cutting one of the Professor's best-known songs, "Big Chief." In the mid-Sixties, he worked as a session musician for Motown. King recorded for many obscure labels in the Sixties while also continuing on the New Orleans scene as a songwriter (for the Dixie Cups among others) and producer. During the Seventies and early Eighties he performed almost every year at the New Orleans Jazz and Heritage Festival.

EVELYN "CHAMPAGNE" KING
Born 1960, Bronx, New York
1977—*Smooth Talk* (RCA)   1979—*Music Box*   1980—*Call on Me*   1981—*I'm in Love*   1982—*Get Loose.*

Pop-soul singer Evelyn "Champagne" King was 17 when she hit it big with the single "Shame" (#9 pop, #7 R&B),

a sexy song which was part of disco's domination of the charts in 1978. The publicity fable goes that King, who grew up in Philadelphia, was working nights cleaning toilets at Philadelphia International Studios when staff producer T. Life overheard her quietly crooning Sam Cooke's "A Change Is Gonna Come." He immediately offered to produce her, resulting in 1977's *Smooth Talk* LP, which included "Shame" and "I Don't Know If It's Right" (#23 pop, #7 R&B). The album and both singles went gold by July 1978, as did her next album, *Music Box*. In 1981, she had her first #1 R&B hit with "I'm in Love," followed by a second R&B #1, "Love Come Down."

FREDDIE KING
Born September 3, 1934, Gilmer, Texas; died December 28, 1976, Dallas
1970—*My Feeling for the Blues* (Cotillion) 1971—*Getting Ready . . .* (Shelter) 1972—*Texas Cannonball* (A&M) 1973—*Woman across the River* 1974—*Burglar* (RSO) 1975—*The Best of Freddie King* (Shelter) *Larger Than Life* (RSO) 1976—*Best of Freddie King* (Island) 1977—*Original Hits* (Starday/King) *(1934–1976)* (RSO).

Freddie King, a pioneering modern blues guitarist, was a major influence on rock guitarists, especially in the British blues boom of the Sixties. Growing up in Texas, King heard the recordings of Arthur Crudup, Big Bill Broonzy, Blind Lemon Jefferson and Lightnin' Hopkins, but he later described his guitar style as a cross between Muddy Waters, T-Bone Walker and B. B. King (no relation)—a mixture of country and urban blues. When he was 16, his family moved to Chicago, where he would sneak into blues clubs to hear Muddy Waters' band, which he later jammed with. He also played with Memphis Slim, LaVern Baker, Willie Dixon and others before recording his first solo record in 1956.

In 1960, King joined the Federal label out of Cincinnati and had several big R&B hits, including "Hideaway" and "Have You Ever Loved a Woman?" (later covered on *Layla* by Eric Clapton, a longtime admirer). Federal released 77 songs by King, including thirty instrumentals, in the next six years. But by 1966 King was without a contract, living as a semi-obscure legend in Texas.

Meanwhile, his songs were being covered in England by bands like Chicken Shack and various John Mayall bands, and he eventually took advantage of the blues revival, playing some shows in England. In 1968, that led to a contract with Cotillion and two albums produced by King Curtis. He then signed to Leon Russell's Shelter label, released three albums and did enough full-time concert hall touring to earn him a more mainstream white rock audience—the largest following of his career. In 1974, King switched to RSO and cut an album in England with help from Eric Clapton, called *Burglar*, and followed it up

with *Larger Than Life* in 1975. The next year, three days after a Christmas night show in Dallas, he died of heart failure, a bloodclot and internal bleeding from ulcers.

JONATHAN KING
Born Kenneth King, December 6, 1948, London

As the Sixties ended, Jonathan King hit the British charts repeatedly with bubblegum ditties recorded under various jokey pseudonyms, like Weathermen (a name Phil Ochs suggested, despite the song's light touch), Bubblerock, 100 Ton and a Feather and Father Abraphart and the Smurps. One of his biggest U.K. hits was under the name Sakkarin, performing a heavy-metal version of the Archies' "Sugar, Sugar."

King first became known with his mock-psychedelic 1965 smash (under his own name) "Everyone's Gone to the Moon," which reached #17 in the U.S. and went gold. He had attended Cambridge University, and as his intentionally schlocky ultracommercial music hints, he's always had an interest in behind-the-scenes record company business. He became assistant to the head of Decca Records in London in the late Sixties and produced the first album by Genesis, a band he'd named. He later produced the Bay City Rollers' first English hit, "Keep on Dancing," and went on to form his own label in 1972, UK Records, which featured the debut of 10cc. After several more British hits in the mid- and late Seventies under his own name (notably his biggest seller, 1975's "Una Paloma Blanca"), his record company wound down here and in England in 1978. He went back to work for Decca (U.K.) in 1979 for one year and later did a radio talk show on WMCA in New York and wrote the novel *Bible Two*, published in England in 1982.

King does a regular program for BBC Radio entitled "A King in New York" (initiated in 1980) and is a regular feature on British television's "Top of the Pops." His 1979 British chart entry, "Gloria," became a disco hit in the summer of 1982 as covered by Laura Branigan.

KING CRIMSON
Formed 1969, England
Robert Fripp (b. May 1946, Dorset, Eng.), gtr.; Greg Lake (b. Nov. 10, 1948, Bournemouth, Eng.), bass, voc.; Ian McDonald (b. 1946, Eng.), kybds., sax, flute, voc.; Michael Giles (b. 1942, Bournemouth, Eng.), drums; Pete Sinfield (b. Eng.), lyrics, lightshow.
1969—*In the Court of the Crimson King* (Atlantic) (− McDonald; − Giles; − Lake) 1970—*In the Wake of Poseidon* (+ Gordon Haskell, voc., bass; + Andy McCulloch, drums; + Mel Collins, sax, flute) 1971—*Lizard* (− Haskell; − McCulloch; + Boz Burrell, bass, voc.; + Ian Wallace, drums; − Sinfield) 1972—*Islands* (− Boz Burrell; − Wallace; band regroups: + Bill Bruford [b. May 17, 1950, Eng.], drums; + Jamie

Muir, percussion; + John Wetton [b. 1950, Derby, Eng.], bass; + David Cross [b. 1948, Plymouth, Eng.], violin; Robert Palmer-Jones, lyrics) **1973**—*Larks' Tongues in Aspic* (− Muir) **1974**—*Starless and Bible Black; Red* (− Cross; group disbands) **1975**—*U.S.A.* **1976**—*A Young Person's Guide to King Crimson* **1981**—(Band re-forms: Fripp; Adrian Belew, gtr., voc.; Tony Levin, bass; Bruford) *Discipline* (Warner Bros.) **1982**—*Beat.*
Robert Fripp solo: **1972**—*No Pussyfooting* (with Eno) (Antilles) **1975**—*Evening Star* (with Eno) **1979**—*Exposure* (Polydor/EG) **1980**—*God Save the Queen/ Under Heavy Manners* **1981**—*The League of Gentlemen; Frippertronics/Let the Power Fall* **1982**—*I Advance Masked* (with Andy Summers) (A&M).

The eerie, portentous sound of early King Crimson set the tone of British art rock. But by the time the group's Mellotron-heavy sound and psychedelic lyrics had turned into lucrative clichés, leader Robert Fripp had long since shifted the group's style toward music that was far more eccentric, complex and dissonant.

The original Crimson's roots went back to 1967, when the Bournemouth trio Giles, Giles and Fripp began making whimsical pop, which resulted in one British-only album in 1968 called *The Cheerful Insanity of Giles, Giles and Fripp.* (For a short time Judy Dyble, early Fairport Convention vocalist, also sang with them.) The band broke up in November of 1968 and, while bassist Peter Giles went on to become a solicitor's clerk, Fripp and drummer Mike Giles formed Crimson with ex-Gods bassist Greg Lake and their old associate Ian McDonald, who introduced them to lyricist Pete Sinfield. Sinfield also worked the band's psychedelic light show.

Crimson made their debut at the London Speakeasy on April 9, 1969, and on July 5 they played to 650,000 people at the Rolling Stones' free Hyde Park concert. In October, *In the Court of the Crimson King,* with music by McDonald and Fripp, was released, and endorsed by Pete Townshend as "an uncanny masterpiece." But the group soon began an endless series of personnel changes (only Fripp remained through it all). On their debut U.S. tour Giles and McDonald left (the latter in a band-control squabble). The two recorded a Crimson soundalike album, *McDonald and Giles,* in 1970. During the sessions for Crimson's second album, Greg Lake also left, to form Emerson, Lake and Palmer. He'd met Emerson during Crimson's disastrous U.S. tour. Crimson might have ended there if Fripp had accepted offers to replace Pete Banks in Yes or to join Aynsley Dunbar in Blue Whale. Instead, he brought in Gordon Haskell to complete the vocals on the second album (Elton John had also tried out), got old friend Pete Giles for a brief stint on bass, persuaded brother Mike to do "guest drumming" and pulled in some other friends, including future member Mel

Collins to finish it up. Fripp's guitar style was already distinctive; he used classical-guitar technique to create angular, sustained, screaming phrases on his Gibson, and he usually performed seated.

In late 1970, Fripp formed a new Crimson with Collins, Haskell, Sinfield and drummer Andy McCulloch. Jon Anderson of Yes did a guest vocal on the resulting *Lizard.* Two days after the album was finished, the band fell apart.

One vocalist who tried out for the next Crimson was Roxy Music's Bryan Ferry, but Fripp opted for singer Boz Burrell, whom he taught to play bass. This band, rounded out by Collins and drummer Ian Wallace, recorded the subdued *Islands* in 1971 and, like the first group, fell apart on its U.S. tour. (Burrell later joined Bad Company.) Even the long-standing Pete Sinfield left this time; he recorded a solo LP and produced the debut Roxy Music album. The *Islands* period band did manage to release a poorly recorded live document of its U.S. tour, *Earthbound,* available only on import in America.

Fripp emerged in 1972 with his most forward-looking and brashest Crimson, including Bill Bruford (who left the far more successful Yes to join), John Wetton (of Family), new lyricist Robert Palmer-Jones, David Cross and Jamie Muir (who left for a Buddhist monastery after *Larks' Tongues in Aspic*). Cross also left, after the followup, *Starless and Bible Black,* but he did play with the band up through its last tour, culminating in a final show in New York's Central Park on July 1, 1974. A live LP from that date and *Red,* recorded with Cross as a "guest" member in late summer 1974, were both released after the disbanding. Ian McDonald was about to rejoin the band and did play on *Red* (he later joined Foreigner in 1976).

But as artistically successful as *Red* was, Fripp came to hate the entire art-rock movement (which was at its commercial peak) along with the mechanics of the music business itself, and so he officially ended the band on September 28. On October 18, 1974, Fripp stated, "King Crimson is completely over. For ever and ever."

Fripp decided to work as a "small, intelligent mobile unit." Using the echo-delay tape system devised by Brian Eno for *No Pussyfooting,* which he dubbed "Frippertronics," Fripp played solo concerts, slowly building minimalist chords with the notes on tape. He produced Daryl Hall's *Sacred Songs* and two albums by the Roches, and added guitar lines to albums by David Bowie, Peter Gabriel, Talking Heads and Blondie. In 1980, he returned to group performing with the short-lived League of Gentlemen (the name of one of Fripp's earliest amateur bands), which added a rock beat to his repeating guitar lines; bassist Sara Lee went on to join the Gang of Four.

In 1981, Fripp revived King Crimson as a quartet that he had been planning to call Discipline, including session bassist Tony Levin (who had toured with Peter Gabriel), guitarist Adrian Belew (ex-Zappa, ex-Bowie, ex–Talking Heads) and Bruford. The new band drew on minimalism,

African and Far Eastern polyrhythms and the angularity of the final Crimsons of the Seventies. The group toured the U.S. and Europe to wide acclaim.

KING CURTIS
Born Curtis Ousley, February 7, 1934, Fort Worth, Texas; died August 13, 1971, New York City
1967—*Live at Small's Paradise* (Atco)   **1968**—*Best of King Curtis;   Blues at Montreux* (Atlantic).

Saxophonist King Curtis, a definitive R&B session soloist and bandleader (of the Kingpins), was a favorite of pop, rock, soul and jazz performers, especially after his famous tenor sax solo on the Coasters' 1957 hit "Yakety-Yak." An adopted child, Curtis was first influenced by fellow South-westerners T-Bone Walker and Buster Smith, plus such jazz saxophonists as Lester Young and Louis Jordan. He got his first sax at age 12, played in several high school bands and turned down several college scholarships to tour with Lionel Hampton's band.

Curtis arrived in New York in 1952 and was discovered by a record company scout who found him session work. He went on to back more than 125 performers, including the Shirelles, Wilson Pickett, Sam and Dave, Eric Clapton, the Allman Brothers and Delaney and Bonnie. He'd begun making his own records in the late Fifties for small labels, including Enjoy Records, on which his "Soul Twist" went to #1 on the R&B charts. He later signed with Capitol and then in October 1965 with Atco. His first release for the label was an instrumental version of "Spanish Harlem." He was appointed Aretha Franklin's musical director just before he died. (He'd played on her earlier recordings, including "Bridge over Troubled Water.") Curtis also produced or coproduced albums by Roberta Flack, Delaney and Bonnie, Donny Hathaway, Freddie King and Sam Moore (of Sam and Dave). He was stabbed to death during an argument outside his home on New York's West 86th Street.

KING FLOYD
Born February 13, 1945, New Orleans
1971—*King Floyd* (Cotillion)   **1975**—*Well Done* (Chimneyville)   **1977**—*Body English*.

Soul-funk singer King Floyd began his career at age 12 in New Orleans. He began recording for the local Uptown label in 1964, and two years later he moved to Pulsar, where he enjoyed further regional success. By the time he released his biggest hit, the self-penned slow and sassy (with reggae overtones) "Groove Me" (#6, 1971), he was working under the guidance of another New Orleans veteran, Wardell Queezergue, at the Malaco studios in Jackson, Mississippi. He made other isolated appearances on the pop charts in the early Seventies with songs like "Baby Let Me Kiss You," "Don't Cry No More," "Think About It" and "Woman Don't Go Astray." Floyd remains active in New Orleans and does session work.

THE KINGSMEN
Formed 1960, Portland, Oregon
Lynn Easton, voc., sax; Gary Abbot, drums; Mike Mitchell, lead gtr.; Don Gallucci, organ; Norman Sundholm, gtr., bass.
N.A.—*The Kingsmen in Person—Featuring "Louie Louie"* (Wand)   *15 Great Hits; The Kingsmen, Volume 2; The Kingsmen, Volume 3*.

The Northwest was a particularly fertile breeding ground for raunchy rock & roll groups in the early Sixties. Paul Revere and the Raiders became the most successful, but the most famous song—indeed one of the best-known and most notorious songs in the history of rock & roll—was "Louie Louie." Though the Raiders cut their version, it was the Kingsmen who had the hit.

"Louie Louie" is marked by a three-chord progression simple enough to endear it to every last fratband. The Kingsmen's version stood out thanks to Easton, who garbled his words to the extent that no one knew exactly what he was singing; by educated guesses it was obscene enough to be banned by many radio stations. The Kingsmen, however, always maintained that they had said nothing lewd.

The band retired in 1968, and Mitchell formed another Kingsmen group. They signed a contract with Capitol in 1973, but nothing came of it.

KINGSTON TRIO
Formed 1957, San Francisco
Bob Shane (b. Feb. 1, 1934, Hilo, Hi.); Nick Reynolds (b. July 27, 1933, San Diego, Calif.); Dave Guard (b. Nov. 19, 1934, Honolulu).
1961—(– Guard; + John Stewart [b. Sep. 5, 1939, San Diego, Calif.])   **1962**—*Best of the Kingston Trio* (Capitol)   **1965**—*Best of the Kingston Trio, Volume 2*
1967—(– Stewart; – Reynolds)   **1973**—("New Kingston Trio": + Roger Gamble; + George Grove; + Bob Shand).

The Kingston Trio was a clean-cut, more commercial alternative to the left-tinged folksingers of the late Fifties. Inspired by Woody Guthrie and the Weavers, the trio scored their only #1 hit in 1958 with "Tom Dooley" and remained the preeminent folksingers until Peter, Paul and Mary started having hits.

The original lineup of Nick Reynolds, Bob Shane and Dave Guard lasted from 1957 until 1961, when John Stewart replaced Guard. The group attempted to broaden its repertoire from traditional American and English folk songs to include contemporary protest songs, such as their 1962 single, "Where Have All the Flowers Gone." Nevertheless, their popularity waned, and by 1967 both Reynolds and Stewart had left (the latter for a solo career). They were replaced by Roger Gamble and George Grove in 1973, when Shane re-formed the group and began touring again. A 1982 PBS TV special brought together all six Kingston Trio members for the first time.

THE KINKS

Formed 1962, England
Ray Davies (b. June 21, 1944, London), gtr., voc.; Dave Davies (b. Feb. 3, 1947, London), gtr., voc.; Mick Avory (b. Feb. 15, 1944, London), drums; Pete Quaife (b. Dec. 27, 1943, Tavistock, Eng.), bass.
1964—*Kinks* (Pye) *You Really Got Me* (Reprise)
1965—*Kinks-Size; Kinda Kinks* **1966**—*Kinks Kingdom; The Kinks Kontroversy; The Kinks Greatest Hits!; Face to Face* **1967**—*Live at the Kelvin Hall; Something Else*
1969—*(The Kinks Are) The Village Green Preservation Society* (− Quaife; + John Dalton, bass) *Arthur, or the Decline and Fall of the British Empire* **1970**—*Lola Versus Powerman and the Moneygoround, Part One* (+ John Gosling, kybds.) **1971**—*Muswell Hillbillies* (RCA) **1972**—*The Kinks Kronikles* (Reprise) *Everybody's in Show-Biz* (RCA) **1973**—*Preservation Act 1*
1974—*Preservation Act 2* **1975**—*Soap Opera; Schoolboys in Disgrace* **1977**—*Sleepwalker* (Arista) (− Dalton; + Andy Pyle, bass) **1978**—*Misfits* (− Pyle; − Gosling; + Jim Rodford [b. July 7, 1945, Eng.], bass, voc.; + Gordon Edwards, kybds.; − Edwards)
1979—*Low Budget* (+ Ian Gibbons, kybds., voc.)
1980—*One for the Road* **1981**—*Give the People What They Want* **1983**—*State of Confusion.*

The Kinks: (top) Dave Davies, Mick Avory, (bottom) Peter Quaife, Ray Davies

The Kinks were part of the British Invasion, and their early hits, "You Really Got Me" and "All Day and All of the Night," paved the way for the power chords of the next decade's hard rock. But most of leader Ray Davies' songs have been chronicles of the beleaguered British middle class, scenarios for rock theater and tales of show-business survival. After their first burst of popularity, the Kinks became a cult band in the mid-Seventies until, buoyed by the new wave's rediscovery of the Davies catalogue, they returned to arenas in the Eighties.

Ray Davies was attending art school in England when he joined his younger brother Dave's band, the Ravens. In short order, Ray had taken over the group—renamed the Kinks—retaining bassist Pete Quaife and recruiting Mick Avory to play drums. With this lineup they released a pair of unsuccessful singles before recording "You Really Got Me," a #1 hit in England that reached #7 in the U.S. in 1964. The following year, "All Day and All of the Night" and "Tired of Waiting for You" both reached the Top Ten in the U.S. and set a pattern for future releases of alternating tough rockers ("Who'll Be the Next in Line") and ballads ("Set Me Free").

In 1966, the Kinks released two singles of pointed satire, "A Well Respected Man" and "Dedicated Follower of Fashion," indicating the personal turn Ray Davies' songs were taking. Their next album, *The Kinks Kontroversy*, though containing another hard-rock 45, "Till the End of the Day," was increasingly introspective, with songs like "I'm on an Island." Also that year, an appearance on the American TV show "Hullabaloo" resulted in a problem with the American Federation of Musicians that wasn't resolved until 1969 and prevented the group from touring the U.S. for some time. "Sunny Afternoon" (#14, 1966) from *Face to Face* was their last hit of that period.

During their years of exile, Ray Davies became increasingly introspective; he later composed the first of many concept albums, *(The Kinks Are) The Village Green Preservation Society*, an LP of nostalgia for all the quaint English customs (such as virginity) that other bands were rebelling against. Dave Davies, who had been writing the occasional song for the Kinks almost from the beginning, had a "solo" hit in England with "Death of a Clown," actually a Kinks song that he wrote and sang. More of Dave's singles followed ("Susannah's Still Alive," "Lincoln County"), none of which repeated the success of "Clown." A planned solo album was recorded, but released in drips and drabs years later on collections. The Kinks' next LP, *Arthur, or the Decline and Fall of the British Empire*, was, with the Who's *Tommy*, an early rock opera, written for a British TV show that was never aired.

The Kinks' next concept album, *Lola Versus Powerman and the Moneygoround, Part One*, was built around the story of trying to get a hit record; the proposed hit, "Lola," actually reached #9. The group left Reprise for RCA, continuing to work on concept pieces, once again without hits. Nevertheless, they were acquiring a reputation as a cheerfully boozy live band, and their live performances were known for the group's messy musicianship and onstage arguments between Ray and Dave Davies, while Ray clowned with limp wrists. This was chronicled on *Everybody's in Show-Biz,* a double album split between Ray Davies' first road songs and a loose live set.

Concept albums became soundtracks for theatrical presentations starring the Kinks in the next years. *Preservation Acts 1* and *2, Soap Opera* and *Schoolboys in Disgrace* were all composed for the stage, complete with extra horn players and singers. For all of the elaborate shows, though, the albums weren't selling.

The Kinks left RCA and concept albums behind in 1976. They finally scored a hit in 1978 with "A Rock 'n' Roll Fantasy" (#30, 1978), off *Misfits. Low Budget,* aided by another successful 45, "(Wish I Could Fly Like) Superman" (#41, 1979), became the Kinks' first gold record since the Reprise greatest hits collection of their early singles.

In the meantime, new groups began rediscovering the Kinks' catalogue, notably Van Halen ("You Really Got Me") and the Pretenders ("Stop Your Sobbing"). The group, which had tightened up as a live band considerably since *Everybody's in Show-Biz,* responded with *One for the Road,* a double live album including both those songs, and accompanied by a full-length rock video (one of the first). It, too, went gold, and a live version of "Lola" was a chart single as well. Less successful was *Give the People What They Want* and its single "Better Things" (#91, 1981).

Over the years, Ray Davies has also produced two albums by Claire Hamill (for his ill-fated Konk Records), worked with Tom Robinson and scored the films *The Virgin Soldiers* and *Percy.* Dave Davies finally came out with a solo album on RCA, *AFL1-3603,* in 1980 and another in 1981, *Glamour,* both of which featured Dave on most of the instruments and achieved modest success.

DON KIRSHNER
Born April 17, 1934, Bronx, New York

Since the end of the Fifties, Don Kirshner has been active as a pop businessman, first by launching the songwriting careers of Neil Sedaka, Carole King and many others, later as the man behind the Monkees, the Archies and Kansas. More recently, he pioneered late-night television rock programing.

Kirshner had hoped to play pro baseball or basketball, but abandoned sports for songwriting (with Bobby Darin), management (Darin, Connie Francis), publishing and song plugging until 1958, when he and partner Al Nevins formed Aldon Music, located in the Brill Building (1619 Broadway). Aldon hired then-unknowns like Gerry Goffin

and Carole King, Barry Mann and Cynthia Weil, Howard Greenfield and Neil Sedaka, and Neil Diamond, and gave them tiny rooms equipped with pianos in which they churned out songs: "Will You Love Me Tomorrow," "Uptown," "On Broadway," "Up on the Roof" and hundreds of others. Kirshner had linked Tin Pan Alley–style professionalism with teenage pop.

In 1963, he sold Aldon Music, then at the peak of its success, and his Dimension Records (Little Eva, the Cookies) to Screen Gems, which promptly appointed him president of the music division. He continued to discover songwriters, Harry Nilsson and Tommy Boyce and Bobby Hart among them. The entire stable, especially Boyce and Hart, worked on Kirshner's next big project, the Monkees. On the group's first two albums, Kirshner limited the Monkees' contribution to lead vocals and one guitar. With the Archies, he did away with people altogether, realizing that cartoon characters would not complain (as the Monkees had) about stifled artistic drives. Dimension Records had evolved into Calendar for the Archies' 6-million-selling "Sugar Sugar" (1969) and into Kirshner Records for the followup, "Jingle Jangle."

In the Seventies, Kirshner fostered a series of successful, if critically reviled, television projects: the groundbreaking "In Concert" (simulcast over FM stations across the country), the "Rock Music Awards" and "Don Kirshner's Rock Concert." Kirshner Records continued to thrive, thanks partly to the success of Kansas.

KISS
Formed 1972, New York City
Peter Criss (b. Peter Crisscoula, Dec. 20, 1947, Brooklyn), drums, voc.; Ace Frehley (b. Apr. 22, Bronx), gtr.; Gene Simmons (b. Gene Klein, Aug. 25, Queens), bass, voc.; Paul Stanley (b. Paul Eisen, Jan. 20, Queens), gtr., voc.
1974—*Kiss* (Casablanca) *Hotter Than Hell* 1975—*Dressed to Kill; Alive* 1976—*Destroyer; Kiss—The Originals; Rock and Roll Over* 1977—*Love Gun; Alive 2* 1978—*Double Platinum* 1979—*Dynasty* 1980—*Unmasked* (− Criss; + Eric Carr [b. Brooklyn], drums) 1981—*Music from "The Elder"* 1982—*Creatures of the Night.*
Kiss solo LPs: 1978—*Gene Simmons* (Casablanca) *Ace Frehley; Peter Criss; Paul Stanley.*

Kiss may have been one of the biggest-selling acts of the Seventies, but they will always be known, above all else, as the band without a face. Supposedly, their faces have never been photographed (although pictures of them applying their makeup for an early photo session ran in *Creem* magazine in the early Eighties). Their theatrics and mystery image have been their main calling card. They formed in the heyday of glitter and rock theater and they set out to define, at first, evil cartoon-character personas,

Kiss: Gene Simmons, Paul Stanley, Peter Criss, Ace Frehley

highlighted by Gene Simmons' bass-playing, fire-breathing, blood-spewing ghoul.

The group was founded by Simmons and Stanley, who met in a band in 1970. They found Criss through his ad in *Rolling Stone.* After rehearsing as a trio, the group took out an ad in *The Village Voice* and discovered Ace Frehley. At the time, they were all working dead-end jobs, with the exception of Simmons, who was teaching at P.S. 75 in Manhattan. Their visual image and game plan were in place from the start. After a few New York City shows, they met independent television director Bill Aucoin, who helped them get a deal with Casablanca Records.

The critics hissed at the anonymous heavy-metal thud-rock on the band's first three albums and howled at its mock-threatening image. Nonetheless, the group hit it off with its fans (a.k.a. the Kiss Army) from the very start. After some hard financial times (an entire 1975 tour was reportedly financed on Aucoin's American Express card), the band took off with *Alive.* The LP eventually went platinum.

In 1976, the band's sound and image shifted toward not necessarily softer but certainly more commercial fare, beginning with Criss's "Beth" (#7, 1976), a million-seller that he wrote for his wife, Lydia. Accordingly, their audience grew from mostly male adolescent heavy-metal fans to include more teenyboppers. As they racked up more and more platinum records—hitting their peak between 1976 and 1978—they became increasingly less threatening. Young fans were frequently photographed wearing the makeup of their favorite Kiss member.

On June 28, 1977, Marvel Comics published a Kiss comic book. The red ink used supposedly contained a small amount of blood from the band members themselves. It sold over 400,000 copies. In the fall of 1978, NBC broadcast a feature-length animated cartoon entitled *Kiss Meets the Phantom of the Park,* and Marvel issued a

second Kiss comic. But the group's popularity was beginning to wane. Their four simultaneously released solo LPs sold poorly—Frehley's was most popular—although the group had several hit singles, including "I Was Made for Loving You" (#16, 1979). In May 1980, Criss left for a solo career. The group then temporarily changed its image, abandoning the comic-book characters for a New Romantic–influenced look. *The Elder,* a concept album, featured songs cowritten by Lou Reed and introduced drummer Eric Carr. It sold only modestly. By late 1982, they had reverted to their ghoul makeup and primitive hard-rock music.

KLAATU
Formed 1970s
John Waloschuk; Cary Draper; David Lang; Dino Tome.
1976—*Klaatu* (Capitol) **1977**—*Hope* **1978**—*Sir Army Suit* **1981**—*Endangered Species.*

Klaatu was a so-called mystery group which in 1977 briefly benefited from a record company–fueled rumor that its members were in fact the Beatles. Capitol (also the Beatles' label) claimed to be unaware of the band members' true identities, all the while stressing Klaatu's musical similarities to *Magical Mystery Tour* and *Sgt. Pepper* in press releases.

The band's debut LP came out in August 1976, but the real hype didn't begin until February 1977, when Steve Smith, a reporter for the *Providence Journal,* wrote an article citing the "Paul is dead"–style allusions to the Beatles, concluding that one or all of them were involved in Klaatu. Capitol sent the article all around, and soon after other newspapers and radio stations picked up on the pseudo-mystery and the band's album leapt into the Top Forty. Later, one of its songs, "Calling Occupants of Interplanetary Craft," was a hit for the Carpenters. Research by more skeptical reporters revealed that Klaatu was in fact four studio musicians from Toronto.

In September of 1977, the band released its second album; although a spokesman said they weren't (and hadn't meant to pretend they were) the Beatles, they still never formally revealed their identities. Their anonymity eventually backfired, though, and after another album in August of 1978 the band faded. A 1981 comeback album was released in Canada only.

THE KNACK
Formed 1978, Los Angeles
Doug Fieger (b. Aug. 20, Detroit), gtr., voc.; Berton Averre (b. Dec. 13, Van Nuys, Calif.), gtr.; Bruce Gary (b. Apr. 7, 1952, Burbank, Calif.), drums; Prescott Niles (b. May 2, New York City), bass.
1979—*Get the Knack* (Capitol) **1980**—*. . . but the Little Girls Understand* **1982**—*Round Trip.*

In the summer of 1979, while the Knack enjoyed one of the biggest commercial debuts in rock history (their first album, recorded in 11 days for a mere $18,000, went gold in 13 days, platinum in seven weeks and eventually sold a reported five million copies), they simultaneously suffered an equally intense backlash. With their Beatles-like packaging (the back cover of *Get the Knack* imitates *A Hard Day's Night*), plus what critics saw as their contrived pop innocence and sexist lyrics, the band members were labeled cynical fakes—an accusation heightened by their refusal to do interviews (which led people to believe they had something to hide). Many felt the band stole the thunder of the more adventurous punk new wave by offering itself as the acceptable face of a "new" power-pop wave, and in the wake of the Knack's success scores of "innocent pop" L.A. bands were signed. A "Knuke the Knack" movement arose in the more radical quarters of the very same L.A. club scene where the band began.

Though the group's publicity tried to present it as having no past, the two main songwriters, Doug Fieger and Berton Averre, knew each other for many years. Fieger met Averre in California when he moved there from Detroit in 1971 with his band Sky, who made two LPs for RCA. During the mid-Seventies, the two began writing together, and all four did backup and session work. After working abroad, Fieger moved back to L.A., where he, Averre and Bruce Gary teamed up with Prescott Niles to form the Knack in May 1978.

They played frequently on the Southern California club scene, and by December of that year they had 13 record companies bidding on them. Capitol won out, and the Knack's debut, produced by Mike Chapman (who did many of the successful pop new wave LPs of that year), was released by June of 1979 with the #1 single "My Sharona." The critical backlash and the lack of individual image caught up with them commercially, though, and their follow-up album sold disappointingly by comparison (600,000 copies). The band members began to argue constantly—they got a new manager and used producer Jack Douglas for their third LP, *Round Trip*, but despite a sudden availability to the press, they couldn't shake their hype reputation, and following an unsuccessful tour in 1982 they disbanded. Averre, Gary and Niles continued as the Game. Fieger founded Doug Fieger's Taking Chances.

THE KNICKERBOCKERS
Formed 1964, Bergenfield, New Jersey
Buddy Randell, voc., sax; Jimmy Walker, drums, voc.; John Charles, bass; Beau Charles, gtr.
N.A.—*Lies* (Challenge).

The Knickerbockers had their one and only major U.S. hit in 1966 with a Beatles-like raver called "Lies" (#20). The band formed in 1964 as the Castle Kings, featuring Buddy Randell from the Royal Teens (who cowrote the #1 novelty hit "Short Shorts.") After being discovered by pro-

Grammy Awards

K.C. and the Sunshine Band
1978 Album of the Year:
Saturday Night Fever (with others)

B. B. King
1970 Best R&B Vocal Performance, Male:
"The Thrill Is Gone"
1981 Best Ethnic or Traditional Recording:
There Must Be a Better World Somewhere

Carole King
1971 Record of the Year:
"It's Too Late"
Album of the Year; Best Pop Vocal Performance, Female:
Tapestry
Song of the Year:
"You've Got a Friend"

Kingston Trio
1958 Best Country & Western Performance:
"Tom Dooley"
1959 Best Performance, Folk:
The Kingston Trio at Large

Gladys Knight and the Pips
1973 Best Pop Vocal Performance by a Duo, Group or Chorus:
"Neither One of Us (Wants to Be the First to Say Goodbye)"
Best R&B Vocal Performance by a Duo, Group or Chorus:
"Midnight Train to Georgia"

Kool and the Gang
1978 Album of the Year:
Saturday Night Fever (with others)

Kris Kristofferson
1971 Best Country Song:
"Help Me Make It Through the Night"
1973 Best Country Vocal Performance by a Duo or Group:
"From the Bottle to the Bottom" (with Rita Coolidge)
1975 Best Country Vocal Performance by a Duo or Group:
"Lover Please" (with Rita Coolidge)

ducer Jerry Fuller (Union Gap, Ricky Nelson), they changed their name, inspired by Knickerbocker Avenue in their hometown of Bergenfield, New Jersey. The band tried to follow up "Lies" with "One Track Mind," but it only made it to #46 and the group soon fizzled. Thereafter Walker became one of the Righteous Brothers for a while, replacing Bill Medley. He then launched an unsuccessful solo career, as did Buddy Randell.

GLADYS KNIGHT AND THE PIPS
Formed 1952, Atlanta
Gladys Knight (b. May 28, 1944), voc.; Merald Knight (b. Sept. 4, 1942), voc.; Brenda Knight, voc.; William Guest (b. June 2, 1941), voc.; Elenor Guest, voc. 1957—(− Brenda; − Elenor; + Edward Patten [b. Aug. 2, 1939, Atlanta], voc.; + Langston George, voc.) **1960**—(− George) **1970**—*Greatest Hits* (Soul) **1971**—*If I Were Your Woman* **1972**—*Neither One of Us* **1974**—*Anthology* (Tamla) **1975**—*The Best of Gladys Knight and the Pips* (Buddah) **1976**—*Gladys Knight and the Pips' Greatest Hits* **1980**—*About Love* (Columbia) **1982**—*Touch* **1983**—*Visions*.

Gladys Knight and the Pips rose to prominence on the Motown label in the late Sixties, but their popularity peaked after they moved to Buddah in 1973.

Gladys Knight and the Pips are a family, all born in Atlanta, where Gladys' parents sang in church choirs. As a child, Gladys herself sang with the Mount Mariah Baptist Church choir, and toured Southern churches with the Morris Brown Choir before she was five. At seven, she won a grand prize on the "Ted Mack Amateur Hour," which led to several TV appearances. The Pips were formed in 1952 at Gladys' older brother Merald's birthday party, when, to entertain the family, Gladys arranged an impromptu singing group, including Merald, sister Brenda, and cousins William and Elenor Guest. Cousin James Woods urged them to go pro; they adopted his nickname, "Pip."

They toured nationally with Jackie Wilson and Sam Cooke before Gladys was 13, but their 1957 recording debut with Brunswick went nowhere; Elenor and Brenda left to get married and were replaced by cousin Edward Patten and Langston George. This configuration, with Gladys' grainy alto still up front, recorded its first R&B Top Twenty hit in 1961, the Johnny Otis–penned "Every Beat of My Heart." George left after two more singles ("Letter Full of Tears" went Top Five), and the band has been a quartet ever since.

The group faltered in the early Sixties. In 1962, Gladys had a baby and the Pips did studio backups; even after they reunited they were still known only to R&B fans. They had no connection to the mass audience until the mid-Sixties, when they were a guest act on the Motown touring revue. Signed to Motown, their cover of "Heard It Through the Grapevine" became a #2 smash in 1967.

Gladys Knight and the Pips: Edward Patten, Merald (Bubba) Knight, William Guest, Gladys Knight

They also scored with "The End of the Road," "Friendship Train" and "If I Were Your Woman."

The band decided to leave Motown in 1973 just as "Neither One of Us" was mounting the charts, citing lack of label support. Their first LP for Buddah, *Imagination*, made the move worthwhile. It was their biggest seller, going gold and yielding three gold singles: "Midnight Train to Georgia" (#1, 1973), "I've Got to Use My Imagination" (#4, 1974) and "Best Thing That Ever Happened to Me" (#3, 1974). Motown continued to release albums by the band after it had left; the group claims it has never received royalties from these or "Neither One of Us."

The hits continued with "The Way We Were," and they did the movie soundtrack to *Claudine* with Curtis Mayfield in 1974, which included the single "On and On." Gladys made her acting debut in 1976 in a film with the unlikely subject of love set among the Alaskan oil pipelines, called *Pipe Dreams*. The Pips did not appear in the film. In 1977, because of legal proceedings involving the band's attempted switch of labels to Columbia, plus an old unsettled suit by Motown, Gladys was not allowed to record with the Pips on LP for three years (though they did sing together live). In the meantime, the band's popularity waned. Gladys recorded a solo LP and the Pips did two albums for Casablanca, finally reuniting in 1980 on Columbia with *About Love*, produced by Ashford and Simpson, yielding the #3 R&B hit "Landlord." *Visions* also had a hit single, "Save the Overtime."

LESLIE KONG
Born 1933, Jamaica; died 1971, Jamaica

Producer Leslie Kong was a key figure in the growth of the Jamaican record business in the Sixties and in the development of Jamaican pop from ska to rock steady to reggae. A Chinese-Jamaican, he got into the record business when he expanded his ice cream shop, Beverley's, into a record store in 1960. In 1962, Jimmy Cliff—a teenager with a few unsuccessful singles behind him—persuaded Kong to try producing records. With popular singer Derrick Morgan supervising, Kong produced Cliff's "Dearest Beverley," Beverley's Records' first release. Distributing Beverley's through Island Records, he attracted many of Jamaica's best young musicians with his unusual reputation for paying fair royalties.

In the early Sixties, Kong produced hits for Cliff, Morgan, Eric Morris and Delroy Wilson. When rock steady supplanted ska as the prevalent beat of Jamaican music in 1966, he kept Beverley's on the charts with Desmond Dekker's "007 (Shanty Town)." In 1968, he produced some of the first records in the new reggae style—Dekker's "Israelites" and "It Mek" and the Pioneers' "Long Shot Kick de Bucket"—which, distributed overseas by Pyramid Records, were also the first Jamaican records to make the British charts. In 1969, he produced the Wailers' *Soul Captives* (five years earlier he had produced one unsuccessful single by the solo Bob Marley), and in 1970 he capped his career with "Monkey Man" by the Maytals, "Rivers of Babylon" by the Melodians, "Freedom Street" by Ken Boothe, and hits by John Holt and Tyrone Evans of the Paragons.

Kong died after a cardiac arrest the following year. His reputation was cemented in the U.S. when the soundtrack from *The Harder They Come*, featuring four Kong productions, opened America to reggae in 1972. In 1981, Island issued *The "King" Kong Collection*, a compilation of some of his most important work.

KOOL AND THE GANG
Formed 1964, Jersey City
Robert "Kool" Bell (b. Oct. 8, 1950, Youngstown, Oh.), voc., bass; Ronald Bell (b. Nov. 1, 1951, Youngstown, Oh.), tenor sax; Dennis "Dee Tee" Thomas (b. Feb. 9, 1951, Jersey City), sax, flute; Claydes Smith (b. Sept. 6, 1948, Jersey City), lead gtr.; Robert "Spike" Mickens (b. Jersey City), trumpet; Rickey West (b. Jersey City), kybds.; George "Funky" Brown (b. Jan. 5, 1949, Jersey City), drums.
N.A.—*The Best of Kool and the Gang* (De-Lite) *Live at PJs* 1972—*Good Times* 1973—*Wild and Peaceful* 1974—*Light of Worlds* 1975—*Kool and the Gang Greatest Hits; Spirit of the Boogie* (Polydor) 1976—*Love and Understanding; Behind the Eyes; Open Sesame;* 1977—*The Force* (− West) 1978—*Kool and the Gang Spin Their Top Hits* (+ James "JT" Taylor [b. Aug. 16, 1953, S.C.], voc.) 1979—*Ladies Night* 1980—*Celebrate* (+ Curtis Williams [b. Dec. 11, 1962, Buffalo], kybds.; + Cliff Adams [b. Oct. 8, 1952, N.J.], trombone; + Michael Ray [b. Dec. 24, 1962, N.J.]) 1981—*Something Special* 1982—*As One.*

In the Seventies and Eighties, Kool and the Gang enjoyed many platinum hits with their horn-driven funky dance and pop music, but they started out in the mid-Sixties playing jazz. They began as the Jazziacs, formed while they were all attending Lincoln High School in Jersey City (except guitarist Smith). Leader Robert "Kool" Bell's father used to room with Thelonious Monk, whose music, along with Miles Davis' and John Coltrane's, offered early influences, as did Pharoah Sanders and Leon Thomas, who sometimes showed up at the band's local jam sessions. The group went through several name changes, including the Soul Town Review and the New Dimensions, before becoming Kool and the Gang in 1968. They shifted to more accessible funk R&B, and their eponymous debut single in 1969 reached #19 on the R&B charts.

Their sound was highlighted by chunky guitar fills, staccato horn blasts and group "party" vocal chants. Several modest dance hits, like "Funky Man" (#16 R&B, 1970) and "Love the Life You Live" (#31 R&B, 1972), led to their massive breakthrough in 1973 with three top singles on one gold album, *Wild and Peaceful*, including "Funky Stuff" (#29 pop, #5 R&B, 1973), "Hollywood Swinging" (#6, 1974) and "Jungle Boogie" (#4 pop, 1974, #2 R&B, 1973). Their dance style anticipated disco, but they were temporarily shoved in the background by the trend, though they got a hit with "Open Sesame" in 1977, on the *Saturday Night Fever* soundtrack. Some of their music in the mid-Seventies reflected their "spiritual phase"—several members are devout Muslims.

In 1978, the band got new management and a full-fledged lead singer who could handle ballads. Tenor James Taylor (no relation to the pop-folk singer) fronted the band on 1979's *Ladies Night*, and with the help of coproducer Eumir Deodato (giving the band a more pop sound, focusing on Taylor), they hit the pop Top Ten (#1 R&B) with the title track. The single went gold, the album, platinum. Later in the year they released "Celebration," which went platinum #1 in 1980 and became a theme song for the return of the U.S. hostages from Iran. The *Celebration* LP also went platinum, as did *Something Special*, yielding the hits "Take My Heart" (#17 pop, #1 R&B, 1981), "Steppin' Out" (#12 R&B, 1982) and "Get Down On It" (#10 pop, #4 R&B, 1982).

AL KOOPER
Born February 5, 1944, Brooklyn, New York
1968—*Super Session* (Columbia) 1969—*I Stand Alone; You Never Know Who Your Friends . . .* 1970—*Kooper Session; Easy Does It* 1971—*Landlord* (United Artists) *New York City* (Columbia) 1972—*A Possible*

*Projection of the Future/Childhood's End; Naked
Songs* **1975**—*Unclaimed Freight—Al's Big Deal*
1976—*Act Like Nothing's Wrong* (United Artists) *Al
Kooper and Steve Katz* (Verve) **1982**—*Championship
Wrestling* (Columbia).
Kooper and Bloomfield LPs: 1968—*Super Session: Mike
Bloomfield, Al Kooper, Steve Stills* (Columbia) **1969**—
*The Live Adventures of Mike Bloomfield and Al
Kooper.*

Al Kooper played a major role in the blues-rock of the
Sixties. He originated what has become commonly known
as the "Dylanesque organ" with his work on *Highway 61;*
he helped popularize the blues with the Blues Project; and
he put together Blood, Sweat and Tears, who began the
Big Band "jazz-rock" trend that influenced bands like
Chicago. He also discovered Lynyrd Skynyrd and the
Tubes.

Kooper, who prefers to play piano or guitar, turned
professional at age 15 when he joined the Royal Teens
after they had a #3 hit in 1958 with "Short Shorts." He left
the band in the late Fifties, turned to writing and session
work, and he studied for a year at the University of
Bridgeport. In 1965, he cowrote a #1 hit for Gary Lewis
and the Playboys, "This Diamond Ring." That same year,
producer Tom Wilson gave Kooper a job playing organ on
Dylan's single "Like a Rolling Stone" and later on *Highway 61.* Kooper also backed Dylan at his 1965 Newport
Folk Festival appearance and worked on *Blonde on
Blonde* and *New Morning.*

Al Kooper

In 1965, Kooper and Steve Katz formed the Blues
Project, and in 1967 they founded Blood, Sweat and Tears.
Kooper picked the band members and produced their 1968
debut, *The Child Is Father to the Man,* but he left before
the band's big commercial success, to work as a Columbia
staff producer and record several collaborative LPs. The
first was 1968's *Super Session* with guitarists Mike Bloomfield (whom he met during the Dylan sessions) and
Stephen Stills. That album became one of the year's best
sellers. Kooper again collaborated with Bloomfield in 1969
for a live LP. He went on to record several solo albums,
which received less attention than his collaborations or
the albums he'd done session work on, which included the
Rolling Stones' *Let It Bleed* and Jimi Hendrix's *Electric
Ladyland.*

By the Seventies, Kooper had become known more as a
producer than as a musician. He produced the first three
Lynyrd Skynyrd records, the Tubes' 1975 debut and Nils
Lofgren's *Cry Tough.* In 1976, he cut his first solo LP in
three years and published an autobiography, *Backstage
Passes.* On St. Patrick's Day 1981, he performed in New
York City in a Blues Project reunion, and later that year he
toured with Bob Dylan.

ALEXIS KORNER
Born Alexis Koerner, April 19, 1928, Paris
1969—*Alexis Korner's All Stars Blues Incorporated*
(Transatlantic) **1970**—*The New Church* (Metro-
nome) **1972**—*Accidentally Born in New Orleans*
(Warner Bros.) **1974**—*Snape Live on Tour* (Brain)
1975—*Get Off My Cloud* (Columbia) **1978**—*Just Easy*
(Intercord) **1979**—*Me* (Jeton).

Alexis Korner is better known for the musicians he discovered than for the music they made in his bands. His
group Blues Inc., formed in 1961, was a major factor in the
Sixties blues revival in England and America.

Educated throughout Europe, Korner was already 34
years old and a veteran of a dozen years in jazz and skiffle
groups when he formed Blues Inc. with Charlie Watts
(later a Rolling Stone), Cyril Davies and Dick Heckstall-
Smith (later of John Mayall's Bluesbreakers and Colosseum). Among the dozens of musicians to woodshed with
Blues Inc. before Korner broke up the group in 1967 were
the Rolling Stones' Mick Jagger; Cream's Ginger Baker
and Jack Bruce; Hughie Flint (later with Mayall, then
McGuinness-Flint); Danny Thompson, John Renbourn
and Terry Cox (all future Pentangle); Graham Bond; and
Long John Baldry. Between Blues Inc. and his next band,
New Church, with Danish singer Peter Thorup, Korner
worked with pre–Led Zeppelin Robert Plant, Humble
Pie's Steve Marriott, and Andy Fraser, who later formed
Free with an assist from Korner that included suggesting
their name and arranging for their debut performance.
New Church had a sizable European following, but it

wasn't until 1970 and CCS (the Collective Consciousness Society), a 25-member-plus group assembled by noted British pop producer Mickie Most and fronted by Korner and Thorup, that he had his first hit, at the age of 42: "Whole Lotta Love." In 1971, Korner appeared on B. B. King's London LP, Korner's first American record. He and Thorup toured the U.S. the next year, opening for King Crimson. By the end of the tour, Mel Collins, Ian Wallace and Boz Burrell (later of Bad Company) had quit Crimson and formed Snape with Korner and Thorup. They recorded the album *Accidentally Born in New Orleans* around the same time that *Bootleg Him*, a retrospective of Korner's work, was finally released in America.

LEO KOTTKE
Born September 11, 1945, Athens, Georgia
1969—*Twelve String Blues* (Oblivion)   1970—*Circle 'Round the Sun* (Symposium)   1971—*Mudlark* (Capitol)   1972—*Six and Twelve-String Guitar* (Takoma) *Greenhouse* (Capitol)   1973—*My Feet Are Smiling; Ice Water*   1974—*Dreams and All That Stuff; Chewing Pine*   1976—*Leo Kottke* (Chrysalis)   1978—*Burnt Lips*   1979—*Balance*   1980—*Live in Europe*   1982— *Guitar Music*   1983—*Time Step*.

Leo Kottke's propulsive fingerpicked guitar instrumentals and (to a lesser extent) his gallows-humor lyrics have garnered him a solid cult following.

He grew up in 12 different states and tried playing violin and trombone. While living in Muskogee, Oklahoma, a cherry bomb planted by a neighborhood kid in a bush went off in his left ear, leaving his hearing impaired. Later, during a brief stint in the Naval Reserve, his right ear was damaged by firing practice. After the Navy, Kottke went to St. Cloud State College in Minnesota, but after three years he dropped out and began hitchhiking and practicing the guitar, which he'd been fooling with since he was 11.

Kottke's first LP, *Twelve String Blues*, was a 1969 set at the Scholar Coffee House in Minneapolis. He sent tapes to guitarist John Fahey, who signed him to his own Takoma label and introduced him to manager/producer Denny Bruce (who had played drums for the early Mothers of Invention). Kottke's one album for Takoma, *Six and Twelve-String Guitar*, was a collection of solo instrumentals that eventually sold 400,000 copies; in its liner notes, Kottke described his voice as "geese farts on a muggy day." He signed with Capitol and put out six albums, using bass and drums as studio backup and introducing his vocals, which weren't so bad. He appeared on the soundtrack of Terence Malick's 1978 film *Days of Heaven*. *Guitar Music* was his first all-instrumental LP since his Takoma album; *Time Step* was produced by T-Bone Burnett and included guest vocals by Emmylou Harris. Kottke continues to tour as a soloist.

KRAFTWERK
Formed 1970, Düsseldorf, West Germany
Ralf Hutter, voc., electronics; Florian Schneider, voc., electronics.
1971—*Kraftwerk 1* (Philips)   1972—*Kraftwerk 2* 1973—*Kraftwerk* (Vertigo)   *Ralf and Florian*   1974—(+ Klaus Roeder, violin, gtr.; + Wolfgang Flur, electronic percussion)   1974—*Autobahn*   (− Roeder; + Karl Bartos, electronic percussion)   *Radio-Activity* (Capitol)   *Exceller 9* (Vertigo)   1977—*Trans-Europe Express* (Capitol)   1978—*The Man-Machine*   1981—*Computer World* (Warner Bros.).

Kraftwerk's robotic, repetitive all-electronic music in the mid-Seventies influenced virtually every synthesizer band that came in their wake, with both their sound and their ironic man-machine imagery. In 1970, Ralf Hutter and Florian Schneider, who had met studying classical music at Düsseldorf Conservatory, founded Kling-Klang Studio, where they produced two German albums. The first, *Tone Float*, was recorded when the group was called Organization, and it was heavily influenced by Pink Floyd and Tangerine Dream. Hutter and Schneider left Organization and took the name Kraftwerk ("power plant") and began experimenting with integrating mechanized sounds from everyday life into music. After *Ralf and Florian* (1973, not released in the U.S. until 1975), they added Klaus Roeder and Wolfgang Flur.

The German band had immediate success with their first U.S. release—*Autobahn*, which went Top Five. The requisite hit was an edited version of the 22-minute minimalist title track. (Kraftwerk's follow-up albums were multi-intentional paeans to such other modern-world wonders as the radio and the train.) They toured the U.S. playing electronic instruments, including electronic "drums."

Roeder was replaced by Karl Bartos for 1975's more abstract *Radio-Activity*. David Bowie claimed the band was an influence for *Low* and *"Heroes."* The band confirmed its cold conceptualist image with "Trans-Europe Express" and "Showroom Dummies," both of which became late-Seventies disco hits. Around this time, the band threatened to tour by sending over electronic dummies of themselves while they rested at home. Their 1978 *Man-Machine* LP featured more accessible music, but after that the group disappeared for three years, not emerging until May 1981 with the pop-oriented *Computer World*. Meanwhile, their "Trans-Europe Express" melody made its way into rap, on Afrika Bambaataa's "Planet Rock."

BILLY J. KRAMER AND THE DAKOTAS
Formed 1963, Liverpool, England
Billy J. Kramer (b. William Howard Ashton, Aug. 19, 1943, Bootle, Eng.), voc.; Tony Mansfield (b. May 28, 1943, Salford, Eng.), drums; Mike Maxfield (b. Feb. 23,

1944, Manchester, Eng.), gtr.; Robin Macdonald (b. July 18, 1943, Nairn, Scot.), gtr.; Raymond Jones (b. Oct. 20, 1939, Oldham, Eng.), bass.
1963—*Listen to Billy J. Kramer and the Dakotas* (Parlophone) **N.A.**—*I'll Keep You Satisfied* (Imperial) *Little Children; Trains and Boats and Planes; The Best of Billy J. Kramer and the Dakotas* (Capitol).

Billy J. Kramer was the type of crooner that dominated the British pop charts until the Beatles changed the rules. But he owed his fleeting fame largely to the Beatles: he shared their manager, Brian Epstein; their label, EMI-Parlophone; and their producer, George Martin. And two of his biggest hits were written by John Lennon and Paul McCartney.

Liverpudlian William Ashton had already adopted his stage name, Billy J. Kramer, by 1963, when he and his group, the Coasters, were spotted by Brian Epstein. Epstein set Kramer up with a Manchester combo, the Dakotas, and the Beatles' songwriters, John Lennon and Paul McCartney. "Do You Want to Know a Secret" was his first success, in 1963, followed by "Bad to Me" (the success of which was due in part to George Martin double-tracking the vocal to make up for Kramer's deficiencies). Kramer's biggest non-Lennon/McCartney number was his 1964 record, "Little Children." His last hit came in 1965, with "Trains and Boats and Planes." Soon after, Brian Epstein began devoting his attentions to the Beatles, and the Dakotas split up. Kramer continued performing on the cabaret circuit until the mid-Seventies, when he unsuccessfully attempted a comeback. He resurfaced in 1980 with the New Dakotas and a new recording contract.

KRIS KRISTOFFERSON
Born June 22, 1937, Brownsville, Texas
1970—*Kristofferson* (Monument) **1971**—*Me and Bobby McGee; Cisco Pete* (Columbia) *The Silver-Tongued Devil and I* (Monument) **1972**—*Border Lord; Jesus Was a Capricorn* **1974**—*Spooky Lady's Sideshow* **1975**—*Who's to Bless and Who's to Blame* **1976**—*Surreal Thing; A Star Is Born* (Columbia) **1977**—*Songs of Kristofferson* **1978**—*Easter Island* **1979**—*Shake Hands with the Devil* **1980**—*Help Me Make It through the Night; To the Bone.*
Kris Kristofferson and Rita Coolidge: 1973—*Full Moon* (A&M) **1974**—*Breakaway* (Monument) **1978**—*Natural Act* (A&M).

Kris Kristofferson finished out the Seventies as a movie star, but several of his songs—"Sunday Morning Coming Down," "Me and Bobby McGee" and "Help Me Make It through the Night"—have become country-rock standards. In the early Seventies, their boozy romanticism helped define "outlaw" country.

After receiving a Ph.D. from Pomona College, Kristofferson went to Oxford University on a Rhodes scholarship in 1958. He first wanted to be a novelist, but he was also

writing songs; he changed his name to Kris Carson and was signed by Tommy Steele's manager. In 1960, he joined the Army, but five years later, when he was about to accept a job teaching English at West Point, he decided instead to invest all his time in songwriting once again, encouraged by a meeting with his idol, Johnny Cash. He moved to Nashville in 1965 and tried to pitch his songs while working as a night janitor at the Columbia studios, cleaning ashtrays at the same time Bob Dylan was recording *Blonde on Blonde* there. (Billy Swan, Kristofferson's future guitarist, later worked the same job.)

His break finally came in 1969, when Johnny Cash gave Kristofferson's song "Me and Bobby McGee" to Roger Miller, who made it a hit on the country charts. Kristofferson appeared on Cash's TV show, and Cash had a hit with "Sunday Morning" in 1969. In March 1971, Janis Joplin's version of "Bobby McGee" went to #1, and about the same time Sammi Smith topped the pop charts with "Help Me Make It through the Night." Kristofferson's own performing debut was released in June 1970. His commercial potential caught up to his critical success on 1971's *The Silver-Tongued Devil and I*, which went gold. His next LP, 1972's *Border Lord*, was panned, and from then on his recording career declined. Meanwhile, he made his film debut in 1972's *Cisco Pike* and two years later appeared in *Pat Garrett and Billy the Kid*, a film in which his second wife, Rita Coolidge, also appeared. They were married in 1973; they had met two years earlier. From there, Kristofferson established himself as an actor in *Alice Doesn't Live Here Anymore* and in *The Sailor Who Fell from Grace with the Sea, Semi-Tough, Convoy* and a remake of *A Star Is Born* with Barbra Streisand.

Kristofferson had a twenty-year drinking problem, which he finally kicked in the late Seventies. He continued to tour and record throughout it all, though with much less commercial success. He did some joint shows and records with Coolidge until their marriage dissolved in December 1979. In 1980, Kristofferson starred in *Heaven's Gate* and in 1981 played opposite Jane Fonda in *Rollover*.

FELA ANIKULAPO KUTI
Born Fela Ransome Kuti, 1941, Nigeria
1974—*Shakara* (Makossa) **1975**—*Question Jam Answer; Roforofo Fight* **1976**—*Kalakuta Show* **1977**—*Upside Down* (London, U.K.) *Zombie* (Mercury) **1981**—*Black-President* (Arista, U.K.) *Original Sufferhead; Expensive Shit* (Makossa) **1982**—*Unnecessary Begging; Alagbon Close.*

Fela Anikulapo Kuti is the leading exponent—and arguably the originator—of Afro-beat, an urban West African dance-while-you-protest style that modernized traditional Yoruba music (call-and-response chanting over polyrhythmic drumming) with repeated R&B-styled horn figures and funk-styled guitar chords. He is also one of the most politically outspoken figures in international pop.

Fela Kuti is the son of Funmilayo Kuti, a woman well known in Nigeria as a feminist and labor organizer; she exerted an early and lasting influence on Fela, although his youthful interests were more musical than political. In 1959, he went to England to study at the London School of Music, and he began playing piano in jazz, R&B and rock bands with African, British and American musicians, among them Ginger Baker of Cream. He also took up the alto saxophone.

Returning to Nigeria in the mid-Sixties, he formed a band that was successful enough to afford a move en masse to the U.S. in 1969. Alternating between New York and Los Angeles, Kuti and his band made virtually no impression on American audiences, but a deep impression was made on him by American black militants, and he returned to Nigeria in 1970 with new ideas about the role of the musician in political change.

He formed a new band, Africa 70 (also spelled Afrika 70), an ensemble of twenty instrumentalists, singers and dancers, and began making albums that showed the influences of James Brown and Sly and the Family Stone. He set up a communal estate for the band and their families on the outskirts of Lagos, eventually building a hospital and a recording studio on its grounds (the latter with the help of Ginger Baker, who lived in Nigeria for much of the Seventies). The site became a meeting place for West African radical artists, writers and activists and the object of harassment by Nigeria's military junta. Fela Kuti's songs were highly critical of governmental corruption, police brutality and the greed of foreign investors. Nigerian hits (most of his releases) such as "Zombie" and "Monkey Banana" openly mocked the authorities.

After Kuti and associates were jailed and beaten by police on a number of occasions, he declared his property the independent Kalakuta Republic. On February 18, 1977, presumably in reaction to that treason, a thousand armed soldiers attacked Kalakuta. In a full day of fighting, Kalakutans were raped, wounded or arrested. Kuti's mother was killed, and the settlement was burned. After being released from jail, Kuti and his followers exiled themselves to Ghana for a year. There he changed his middle name from Ransome to Anikulapo and, in a related ceremony, married his 27 female singers and dancers, giving him 28 wives.

On his return to Nigeria, Kuti rebuilt Kalakuta but was banned from giving concerts, which previously had drawn as many as 100,000 fans to a single performance. So, for the first time since 1970, he took his show abroad, and traveled through Germany, Italy and France with his entourage of seventy. Back in Nigeria in 1979, he formed a political party, the Movement of the People, and ran for the presidency of Nigeria that year until banned from the campaign by election authorities. (He has promised to run again in 1983.)

While Kuti has found an enthusiastic following in Europe, both for his records and for his occasional concerts, he remains unfamiliar to most Americans. Only one of his fifty-odd albums has been released by a major label in the U.S., and so far no American promoters have met his pay demands for a tour.

JIM KWESKIN JUG BAND

Jim Kweskin, gtr., voc.; Bill Keith, pedal steel gtr., banjo; Mel Lyman, harmonica; Fritz Richmond, jug, washtub bass; Richard Greene, fiddle; Maria D'Amato Muldaur (b. Sep. 12, 1943, New York City), voc., kazoo, tambourine; Geoff Muldaur, gtr., voc.
1968—*Best of* (Vanguard)   **1970**—*Greatest Hits.*

The Jim Kweskin Jug Band was a slaphappy answer to the earnestness of the "folk revival" as typified by Peter, Paul and Mary. The members rarely wrote their own material but specialized in uncovering folk, blues, jazz and novelty tunes of the past and remaking them in their raucous acoustic style. Kweskin was merely the nominal leader of the ever-shifting aggregation; Geoff Muldaur was more likely to be heard on lead vocal and guitar. Maria D'Amato, who would later wed Muldaur and have a successful duo and solo career under her married name, also sang and played fiddle, although the latter instrument would eventually be manned by future Blues Project/Seatrain virtuoso Richard Greene. Fritz Richmond blew jug and became a virtuoso on washtub bass.

One of the later additions to the band was harmonica player Mel Lyman. Lyman, a self-styled prophet and authoritarian religious leader, split up the group, with Kweskin becoming a disciple, and the others going on to either solo careers or oblivion.

LABELLE
Formed as Patti LaBelle and the Blue Belles, 1961, Philadelphia
Patti LaBelle (b. Patricia Louise Holt, Oct. 4, 1944, Philadelphia), voc.; Nona Hendryx (b. Aug. 18, 1945, Trenton, N.J.), voc.; Sarah Dash (b. May 24, 1942, Trenton, N.J.), voc.; Cindy Birdsong (b. Dec. 15, 1939, Camden, N.J.), voc.
1967—(− Birdsong) *Dreamer* (Atlantic) **1971**— (group was renamed Labelle) *Labelle* (Warner Bros.) *Gonna Take a Miracle* (with Laura Nyro) (Columbia) **1972**—*Moonshadow* (Warner Bros.) **1973**—*Pressure Cookin'* (RCA) **1974**—*Nightbirds* (Epic) **1975**— *Phoenix* **1976**—*Chameleon*.
Patti LaBelle solo: 1977—*Patti LaBelle* (Columbia) **1979**—*It's Alright with Me* **1980**—*Released* **1981**— *Best of*.

In their sixteen years together, Labelle developed from a fairly conventional Sixties girl group—replete with sequined gowns, bouffants and polished choreography—into a band with a unique space-queen look, an idealistic political consciousness and an individual gospel-tinged funky rock & roll sound. They began as Patti LaBelle and the Blue Belles, bringing together LaBelle and Cindy Birdsong from the Ordettes with Nona Hendryx and Sarah Dash from the Del Capris. Their 1962 single "I Sold My Heart to the Junkman" became a #15 hit, followed by versions of "Danny Boy" (#76, 1964) and "You'll Never Walk Alone" (#34, 1964).

The Blue Belles became a trio in 1967 when Birdsong left to replace Florence Ballard in the Supremes. Although they were hugely popular at the Apollo Theater and on the soul circuit, they were mismanaged. In 1970, Britisher Vicki Wickham (who knew them from their mid-Sixties appearance on the English TV show "Ready Steady Go," which she produced) became their manager, revamping their image and leading them toward more contemporary rock. She also encouraged Hendryx to contribute more of her own songs.

In 1971, after Wickham rechristened the band Labelle, they released an eponymous debut on Warner Bros. and toured the U.S. with the Who. That same year, they collaborated with Laura Nyro on *Gonna Take a Miracle*, a collection of Fifties and Sixties pop remakes. In 1973, Labelle, at a headline Bottom Line show, joined the glitter trend, debuting their soon-to-be-famous lamé space cadet suits. In 1974, they became the first black band ever to play New York's Metropolitan Opera House, where they

Labelle: Nona Hendryx, Patti Labelle, Sarah Dash

introduced what was to become their only million-selling hit, "Lady Marmalade" (#1, 1975), a shouter about a Creole hooker. The single, written by Bob Crewe, Allen Toussaint and Kenny Nolan, highlighted their *Nightbirds* LP, produced by Toussaint in New Orleans.

Since Hendryx and Patti LaBelle had basic musical differences, Labelle broke up in early 1977. Hendryx went on to record a hard-rock LP on Epic in 1977, and she later played with several New York bands—Material ("Bustin' Out" was a club hit in 1981) and then her own Propaganda. In 1983 Material coproduced *Nona* (RCA). Sarah Dash played small clubs and began recording solo albums in 1979, and Patti LaBelle (who still lives in Philadelphia with her high school house director husband and her three children) enjoyed the most solo success, with four LPs and several national concert hall tours. In 1982, she costarred with Al Green in the Broadway revival of *Your Arms Too Short to Box with God*.

MAJOR LANCE
Born April 4, 1941, Chicago
N.A.—*Rhythm of* (Okeh) **1973**—*Greatest Hits* (Contempo) **1976**—*Best of* (Epic) **1977**—*Live at the Torch* (Contempo) **1978**—*Now Arriving* (Tamla).

With Curtis Mayfield writing his material and Carl Davis producing, soul vocalist Major Lance enjoyed many hits in the early Sixties and helped establish what became known as the Chicago soul sound, along with the Impressions, Jerry Butler, Gene Chandler and others. Lance had spent some time as a professional boxer, and he recorded for Mercury before meeting Mayfield and signing with Okeh, Columbia's revitalized "race" label. After hearing the song "The Monkey Time," which Mayfield had written for Lance, Okeh president Carl Davis hired Mayfield as staff producer and Lance as a singer.

Mayfield and Lance's first release, "Delilah" (1962), was a flop. But the followup, "The Monkey Time," shot to #8 in September 1963 and helped kick off a dance trend called the Monkey. The song's orchestral sound (arranged by Johnny Pate) was adapted by Okeh as a "Chicago style" and can be heard on Mayfield's later recordings with the Impressions. Lance's highest-charted pop hit, "Um, Um, Um, Um, Um, Um," hit #5 in February 1964 (the song was also the first major English hit for Wayne Fontana and the Mindbenders the same year).

Although Lance's pop hits ceased soon after, he had several minor R&B chart successes through 1970. He switched to Carl Davis' Dakar Records in 1968 and then to Mayfield's Curtom label. In 1972, Lance recorded for Volt, and in 1974 he signed to Playboy Records, where he re-recorded "Um, Um, Um. . ." with little success. In 1982, eight of Lance's songs were included on the Epic compilation *Okeh Soul*.

STACY LATTISAW

Born November 25, 1966, Washington, D.C.
1979—*Young and in Love* (Cotillion) **1980**—*Let Me Be Your Angel* **1981**—*With You* **1982**—*Sneakin' Out*.

Singer Stacy Lattisaw was only 13 when she scored an international disco hit with "Dynamite" in 1980 (#8 R&B). Her mother encouraged her to go into singing, and she made her debut at ten at a high school homecoming. After many local appearances, she won a spot opening for Ramsey Lewis at a National Park Service show in Washington, D.C., for a crowd of 30,000. The show's organizer, Al Dale, sent a tape of her performance to Frederick Knight, head of T.K. Records, who offered Lattisaw a contract and wrote "Ring My Bell" for her. Lattisaw's family lawyer, acting as manager, rejected the contract, and the song wound up a #1 pop, #1 R&B hit for Anita Ward in 1979. But the lawyer introduced Lattisaw to Cotillion president Henry Allen, who signed her.

Shortly before his death, Van McCoy produced her debut LP, which went nowhere. Her second LP, *Let Me Be Your Angel*, produced by Narada Michael Walden, with songs by Walden and lyricist Bunny Hull, had two hits, "Dynamite" and the title track (#21 pop, #8 R&B). She supported it by playing shows with the Jacksons, the Spinners, Smokey Robinson and the Manhattans. In 1981, she released *With You*, again produced by Walden, yielding the remake of "Love on a Two Way Street" (#26 pop, #2 R&B, 1981), originally a hit for the Moments in 1970. In 1982 she had a Top Five R&B hit with "Attack of the Name Game."

LEADBELLY

Born Huddie Ledbetter, January 20, 1889, Mooringsport, Louisiana; died December 6, 1949, New York City
1950—*Leadbelly's Library of Congress Recordings* (Elektra) **1953**—*Leadbelly's Last Sessions, Volume 1* (Folkways) *Leadbelly's Last Sessions, Volume 2* **1968**—*Leadbelly Sings Folk Songs* **1969**—*Leadbelly* (Capitol) **1973**—*Leadbelly* (Fantasy).

Leadbelly, the self-styled "king of the 12-string guitar," was one of the modern world's prime links to rural traditions. He helped inspire the folk and blues revivals of the Fifties and Sixties.

Folklorists John A. and Alan Lomax discovered Leadbelly in 1933 while recording music for the Library of Congress. The Lomaxes first recorded Leadbelly at the Louisiana State Prison Farm at Angola, where he was serving time for attempted homicide. A song they recorded was addressed to Louisiana governor O. K. Allen, who upon hearing it commuted the singer's ten-year term.

Leadbelly grew up in Louisiana and Texas, where his family moved when he was five. He was eight when he started playing the Cajun accordion (windjammer). According to Leadbelly, at age seven he broke up arguments between his parents by hitting his father in the head with a poker and threatening him with a shotgun. Traveling around in his early teens, the singer picked up music that dated back to slave days, and by the time he was 17, he was playing guitar—first an eight- and then the 12-string. At 18, he was forced to leave his home after he impregnated the same girl twice without marrying her. He went to West Texas to pick cotton and did some playing with his friend and mentor Blind Lemon Jefferson in Dallas.

But Leadbelly's troubles followed him, and he spent a year in prison on the Harrison County chain gang for assaulting a woman. He escaped and adopted the name Walter Boyd. When he was 33, he shot a man through the forehead in an argument over a woman, and on December 13, 1917, he received a thirty-year sentence; legend has it he was later freed by charming the officials with his singing. Leadbelly's hollering style reflected his hard years in prison, and it wasn't long before he was back there, at Angola, where the Lomaxes discovered him.

Upon his release, the Lomaxes brought him to New York. They published a book about him in 1936, and he recorded his best-known songs: "The Rock Island Line," "The Midnight Special" and "Goodnight Irene." Whether Leadbelly wrote, adapted or simply remembered the songs and copyrighted them for himself is unknown, though it is certain that he was the first to bring them to the public. Leadbelly again landed in jail (Rikers Island in New York) and served two years for assault. But all of this only enhanced his legend. While in New York, he played with Pete Seeger, Woody Guthrie and Sonny Terry and later toured the East Coast.

Ironically, six months after the singer died of sclerosis in 1949, his "Goodnight Irene" became a folk hit for the Weavers. There were many repackagings of his work in the late Sixties to early Seventies, and in 1976 a film about his life, directed by Gordon Parks, was released.

LED ZEPPELIN
Formed 1968, England
Jimmy Page (b. Jan. 9, 1944, Heston, Eng.), gtr.; John Paul Jones (b. John Baldwin, June 3, 1946, Sidcup, Eng.), bass; Robert Plant (b. Aug. 20, 1948, Bromwich, Eng.), voc.; John "Bonzo" Bonham (b. May 31, 1948, Redditch, Eng.; d. Sep. 25, 1980, Windsor, Eng.), drums.
1969—*Led Zeppelin* (Atlantic) *Led Zeppelin II*
1970—*Led Zeppelin III* 1971—*Untitled* (known as the Runes album or *Zoso*) 1973—*Houses of the Holy*
1975—*Physical Graffiti* (Swan Song) 1976—*Presence; The Song Remains the Same* 1979—*In through the Out Door* 1982—*Coda*.

It wasn't just Led Zeppelin's thunderous volume, sledge-hammer beat and edge-of-mayhem arrangements that made them the most influential and successful heavy-metal pioneers—it was their finesse. Like their ancestors the Yardbirds, Led Zeppelin used a guitar style that drew heavily on the blues, and their early repertoire included remakes of songs by bluesmen Howlin' Wolf, Albert King and Willie Dixon. But what Jimmy Page brought to the band was a unique understanding of the guitar and the recording studio as electronic instruments, and of rock as sculptured noise; like Jimi Hendrix, Page had a reason for every bit of distortion, feedback, reverberation and out-and-out noise that he incorporated—and few of the bands that imitate Led Zeppelin can make the same claim. Page and Robert Plant were grounded also in British folk music and fascinated by mythology, Middle Earth fantasy and the occult, as became increasingly evident from the band's later albums (the fourth LP is entitled in Druidic runes). A song that builds from a folk-baroque acoustic setting to screaming heavy metal, "Stairway to Heaven" fittingly became the best-known Led Zeppelin song and a staple of FM airplay, although like most of their "hits," it was never released as a single.

When the Yardbirds fell apart in the summer of 1968, Page was left with rights to the group's name and a string of concert obligations. He enlisted John Paul Jones, who had done session work with the Rolling Stones, Herman's Hermits, Lulu, Dusty Springfield and Shirley Bassey. Page and Jones had first met, jammed together and discussed forming a group when both were hired to back Donovan on his *Hurdy Gurdy Man* LP. Page had hoped to complete the group with drummer B. J. Wilson of Procol Harum and singer Terry Reid. Neither was available, but Reid recommended Plant, who in turn suggested Bonham, drummer for his old Birmingham group, Band of Joy. The four first played together as the session group behind P. J. Proby on his *Three Week Hero*. In October 1968, they embarked on a tour of Scandinavia under the name the New Yardbirds. Upon their return to England they recorded their debut album in thirty hours.

Adopting the name Led Zeppelin (allegedly coined by Keith Moon), they toured the U.S. in early 1969 opening for Vanilla Fudge. Their first album was released in February; within two months it had reached *Billboard*'s Top Ten. Their second album reached #1 two months after its release, and since then every Led Zeppelin album has gone platinum. After touring almost incessantly during their first two years as a group, they began limiting their appearances to alternating years. Their 1973 U.S. tour broke box-office records throughout the country (many of which had been set by the Beatles), and by 1975 their immense ticket and album sales had made Led Zeppelin the most popular rock & roll group in the world. In 1974, they established their own label, Swan Song.

On August 4, 1975, Plant and his family were seriously injured in a car crash while vacationing on the Greek island of Rhodes. As a result, the group toured even less frequently. That and speculation among fans that super-natural forces may have come into play (Plant believed in psychic phenomena, and Page, whose interest in the occult was well known, resides in the former home of

Led Zeppelin: Jimmy Page, John Bonham, Robert Plant, John Paul Jones

infamous satanist Aleister Crowley) also heightened the Zeppelin mystique.

In 1976, Led Zeppelin released *Presence*, followed by 1979's *In through the Out Door*, the band's last group effort. In 1980, Bonham died at Page's home of what was described as asphyxiation; he had inhaled his own vomit after having consumed alcohol and fallen asleep. That December, Zeppelin released a cryptic statement to the effect that they could no longer continue as they were. Soon thereafter, it was rumored that Plant and Page were going to form a band called XYZ (ex-Yes and Zeppelin) with Alan White and Chris Squire of Yes; the group never materialized. In 1982, Page released a solo LP, the soundtrack to the movie *Death Wish II*. Plant's solo debut, *Pictures at Eleven*, released the same year, was a Top Five hit. That December, the group released *Coda*, a collection of early recordings and outtakes.

As of 1983, Led Zeppelin's concert movie *The Song Remains the Same* (originally released in 1976) is still a staple of midnight shows around the country, and Zeppelin tunes like "Stairway to Heaven," "Kashmir," "Communication Breakdown," "Whole Lotta Love" and "No Quarter" are still in heavy rotation on AOR radio playlists.

ALBERT LEE

Born December 21, 1943, Leominster, England
1979—*Hiding* (A&M) **1982**—*Albert Lee.*

British guitarist Albert Lee has earned a strong reputation as a sideman for Jackson Browne, Dave Edmunds, Joan Armatrading, Joe Cocker, Eric Clapton, Emmylou Harris, Rodney Crowell and others. Beyond his adaptability, he is one of the few English guitarists more interested in country music than in blues.

Lee began playing piano at age seven, emulating Jerry Lee Lewis. But by 16, he had switched to guitar. In 1964, he joined Chris Farlowe's backup group, the Thunderbirds, which also included Carl Palmer. The Thunderbirds were a popular R&B outfit in England, and Jimmy Page and Steve Howe have cited Lee's work as an early influence. In 1968 the band dissolved. Lee joined Country Fever and later formed the country-influenced Heads, Hands and Feet. After three albums, that band folded, and Lee went on to play on Jerry Lee Lewis' *The Session* LP.

In 1973, Lee joined Rick Grech with the Crickets, still singing Buddy Holly's tunes; a year later he was in Los Angeles doing session work, including a stint with Don Everly. He joined Joe Cocker for his 1974 tour of Australia and New Zealand, and A&M offered Lee a solo contract in 1975. Before he got around to finishing an album, though, Lee joined Emmylou Harris' Hot Band. He stayed in Harris' band for two years and left in 1978 to finally record his solo album but continued to play on Harris' records as well.

Instead of touring to support his own album, Lee took to the road in 1979 as part of Eric Clapton's band. He played on Clapton's live LP *Just One Night* (1980) and on his 1981 and 1983 studio albums, *Another Ticket* and *Money and Cigarettes*. Between tours with Clapton, he finished a second solo album.

BRENDA LEE

Born Brenda Mae Tarpley, December 11, 1944, Atlanta
1960—*Brenda Lee* (Decca) **1964**—*By Request; Merry Christmas* **1965**—*Top Teen Hits* **1966**—*10 Golden Years* (MCA) **1975**—*Brenda Lee Now* **1976**—*L.A. Sessions* **1980**—*Take Me Back; Even Better.*

Singer Brenda Lee's more than 25-year career began when she was only 11 and her single "Rockin' around the Christmas Tree" became an international hit.

By age seven, Lee was singing on radio and TV shows in Atlanta. Her father died when she was eight, and her income helped support the family. In 1956, she met Red Foley's manager, Dub Albritten. He booked her on shows with Foley, which led to national TV exposure. On July 30 of that year, she entered a Nashville studio with Owen Bradley (producer of Patsy Cline and later Loretta Lynn) and recorded "Rockin' around the Christmas Tree" (#14, 1960). Lee soon toured Europe, where, to appease French promoters who had thought she was an adult, Albritten spread the rumor that she was a 32-year-old midget.

Back in the U.S., Lee next recorded some of her biggest hits: "Sweet Nothings" (#4, 1960), "I'm Sorry" (#1, 1960), "I Want to Be Wanted" (#1, 1960) and many other early-Sixties Top Tens. She soon became known as "Little Miss Dynamite," and by the time she was 21 she had cut 256 sides for Decca Records.

In the Seventies, Lee's hits were on the country rather than the pop charts, scoring with "If This Is Our Last Time" (#30 C&W, 1971), "Nobody Wins" (#3 C&W, 1973) and three Top Tens in 1974. A set of her early tracks recorded between 1956 and 1964 was released in England in 1977. She continues to record country hits while also doing a syndicated Nashville interview show. Lee had a small acting role in *Smokey and the Bandit 2* and sang the title song of Neil Simon's *Only When I Laugh.*

DICKEY LEE

Born Dick Lipscomb, September 21, 1943, Memphis
N.A.—*Dickey Lee Sings Laurie and the Girl from Peyton Place* (TCF Hall) *The Tale of Patches* (Smash).

Perhaps best known for the melodramatic "Patches," Dickey Lee was also one of the very few Sun Records rockabilly artists to attend college *after* having released several records. Lee signed with Sun in 1957 and had a minor local hit with a version of "Good Lovin'." He attended Memphis State University, then in the early Sixties went on to write, produce and record with Jack Clement for Hallway Records in Beaumont, Alabama.

Lee moved to Nashville in 1962 and established himself

as a writer of country songs. He made a name for himself that year with "Patches," which hit #6 on the charts. Though primarily a songwriter, he continued to record, hitting with "I Saw Linda Yesterday" (#14, 1963) and "Laurie (Strange Things Happen)" (#14, 1965), and he later had a country hit with "Never Ending Song of Love." Lee cowrote "She Thinks I Still Care," a hit for Elvis Presley in 1977.

PEGGY LEE

Born Norma Deloris Egstrom, May 6, 1920, Jamestown, North Dakota
N.A.—*The Best of Peggy Lee* (Capitol).

Peggy Lee's subdued singing style, which embraces jazz, blues, Latin, swing and pop, first came to public attention in her work with the Benny Goodman orchestra, especially in 1943, when she recorded the enormous hit "Why Don't You Do Right?" Lee's mother died when she was four, and she began working on a farm by 11 and singing professionally as a teen, first at a Fargo, North Dakota, radio station and later at a Palm Springs hotel, where she met Goodman.

After her hit with Goodman's band, she married the group's guitarist, David Barbour, and retired for several years to have a child before she and Barbour began writing new material together, with Peggy usually providing the lyrics. Lee was one of the forerunners of the rock trend that encouraged singers to write their own material, and with Barbour she wrote "I Don't Know Enough About You," "Mañana" and "It's a Good Day." She has also collaborated with Sonny Burke, Duke Ellington, Quincy Jones and Dave Grusin. Lee's hit most covered by rock performers is "Fever" (1958), although it was written by Little Willie John.

She was one of the first old-guard performers to recognize the Beatles' talents, and as a "reward" Paul McCartney later wrote "Let's Love" for her, which became the title of her Atlantic debut in 1974. In 1969, she had one of her biggest hits with "Is That All There Is?," arranged by Randy Newman.

Lee appeared in three films, making her debut in 1951's *Mr. Music*, followed by a remake of *The Jazz Singer* with Danny Thomas (1953) and *Pete Kelly's Blues* (1955), for which she was nominated for an Academy Award.

THE LEFT BANKE

Formed 1966, New York City
Steve Martin, voc.; Tom Finn, bass; Rick Brand, banjo, gtr.; George Cameron, drums; Michael Brown (b. Apr. 25, 1949, Brooklyn), organ, piano, harpsichord.
1967—*Walk Away Renee/Pretty Ballerina* (Smash) (— Brown; + Jeff Winfield, kybds.) 1969—*The Left Banke Too*.

The Left Banke's leader Michael Brown began studying piano and harpsichord when he was eight. At 16, he wrote

"Walk Away Renee." Two years later, in 1966, his band, the Left Banke, released it as their first single and it became a #5 hit. The followup, "Pretty Ballerina," was similar to "Renee" in its classical-tinged melody, choirboy vocals and strings-and-harpsichord accompaniment (then dubbed baroque rock). It reached #15. After composing the bulk of the material for the Left Banke's debut LP and a second album, Brown left the group. The Left Banke continued unsuccessfully without him.

Brown's next band, Montage, was not particularly successful, and he then formed Stories with vocalist Ian Lloyd but left before their big hit, "Brother Louie" (written by members of Hot Chocolate). Brown then worked for a while as an A&R man for Mercury Records.

In 1976, he formed the Beckies; they lasted long enough to record a single LP for Sire. Since then, Brown has remained mostly out of sight, surfacing briefly as a sideman with New York singer Lisa Burns. "Walk Away Renee" was covered by the Four Tops in 1968 and was once again a smash. The Left Banke regrouped without Brown in 1980 for an independent single on Camerica, "Queen of Paradise" b/w "And One Day."

JERRY LEIBER AND MIKE STOLLER

Jerry Leiber, born April 25, 1933, Baltimore; Mike Stoller, born March 13, 1933, Belle Harbor, New York

"We didn't write songs, we wrote records," Jerry Leiber and Mike Stoller have said, and in the Fifties and early Sixties they were a hugely influential songwriting/production team, creating hits for Elvis Presley, the Drifters and the Coasters, among others.

Leiber grew up poor in Baltimore, living among black families. He moved to Los Angeles in the mid-Forties, and there he met Mike Stoller. Stoller shared Leiber's fondness for black music, but his original interest was composing "serious" music. That changed when he was so impressed by Leiber's lyrics that he volunteered to compose music for them. The result was a distinctive pop-blues, with an atypically well-defined melody, as heard on one of their earliest works, "K.C. Loving," later retitled "Kansas City," and a huge hit for Wilbert Harrison in 1959.

The pair's career took off in 1952, when they began producing records. They had written "Hound Dog" for Big Mama Thornton, and famed R&B bandleader Johnny Otis was to produce the session. But when it turned out that Otis was the only one present who could play the drum part, Leiber and Stoller became the producers. From then on, they not only wrote the songs but arranged and produced them as well, as would later rock producers (like one of their protégés, Phil Spector).

In 1953, Leiber and Stoller (with Lester Sill) formed Spark Records and began having regional hits with a group known as the Robins. Atlantic Records offered them national distribution two years later. Meanwhile, the Robins split, and the faction that stayed with Leiber and Stoller was renamed the Coasters. The Coasters' comedy-story songs, all written and produced by Leiber and Stoller, made them legends and include "Along Came Jones," "Framed," "Searchin'," "Yakety Yak," "Charlie Brown," "Riot in Cell Block #9" and "Young Blood," among others.

In the fall of 1957, Leiber and Stoller moved to New York City and began supervising sessions by the Drifters, who had already had two R&B hits with Leiber and Stoller compositions. Meanwhile, Elvis Presley had recorded his own version of "Hound Dog" (Leiber and Stoller didn't write the line "You ain't never caught a rabbit") and asked Leiber and Stoller to contribute material to his films. The pair wrote music—including the title songs—for *Love Me Tender, Loving You, King Creole* and *Jailhouse Rock.* With all their outside activity, they began using material by other songwriters, including Carole King and Doc Pomus, for the Drifters' records. But Leiber and Stoller left their mark with their creative productions, using Latin percussion and atmospheric strings on "Save the Last Dance for Me" and "There Goes My Baby."

They left Atlantic in 1964 and made a second attempt to start their own record company. This time the label was Red Bird, now noted mostly for the girl groups like the Shangri-Las ("Leader of the Pack") and the Dixie Cups ("Chapel of Love"). Two years later, they sold out of Red Bird and began a new, less teen-oriented phase with the Peggy Lee hit "Is That All There Is?" In the ensuing years, they have continued to work prodigiously, producing acts as diverse as Procol Harum and Leslie Uggams, as well as discovering Stealer's Wheel, who had a hit record in 1973 with "Stuck in the Middle with You."

Leiber and Stoller's songs have been covered by countless performers, including the Beatles, Joni Mitchell, the Rolling Stones, Genesis and the Monkees. Among their many well-known compositions are "(You're So Square) Baby, I Don't Care," "On Broadway," "I'm a Hog for You, Baby" and "Treat Me Nice."

THE LEMON PIPERS
Formed late 1960s
R. G. Nave (b. 1945), organ, tambourine; Ivan Browne (b. 1947), voc., gtr.; Bill Bartlett (b. 1946), lead gtr.; Steve Walmsley (b. 1949), bass; Bill Albaugh (b. 1948), drums.
1968—*Green Tambourine* (Buddah)   *Jungle Marmalade.*

The Lemon Pipers combined bubblegum and mild psychedelia for a #1 hit in early 1968, "Green Tambourine." Subsequent hits released later that year included "Rice Is Nice" (#46) and "Jelly Jungle (of Orange Marmalade)" (#51). By the end of the year, the group had disbanded.

JOHN LENNON AND YOKO ONO
John Lennon, born October 9, 1940, Liverpool, England; died December 8, 1980, New York City; Yoko Ono, born February 18, 1933, Tokyo
John Lennon and Yoko Ono: 1968—*Unfinished Music No. 1: Two Virgins* (Apple)   **1969**—*Unfinished Music No. 2: Life with the Lions* (Zapple)   *Wedding Album* (Apple)   *Live Peace in Toronto, 1969* (with the Plastic Ono Band)   **1972**—*Some Time in New York City* **1980**—*Double Fantasy* (Geffen).
John Lennon solo: 1970—*John Lennon/Plastic Ono Band* (Apple)   **1971**—*Imagine* **1973**—*Mind Games* **1974**—*Walls and Bridges* **1975**—*Rock 'n' Roll; Shaved Fish.*
Yoko Ono solo: 1970—*Yoko Ono/Plastic Ono Band*

Grammy Awards

Peggy Lee
1969 Best Contemporary Vocal Performance, Female: "Is That All There Is"

John Lennon (see also: the Beatles)
1966 Song of the Year: "Michelle" (with Paul McCartney)
1970 Best Original Score Written for a Motion Picture or TV Special: *Let It Be*

1981 Album of the Year: *Double Fantasy* (with Yoko Ono)

Kenny Loggins
1979 Song of the Year: "What a Fool Believes" (with Michael McDonald)
1980 Best Pop Vocal Performance, Male: "This Is It"

Loretta Lynn
1971 Best Country Vocal Performance by a Group: "After the Fire Is Gone" (with Conway Twitty)

(Apple) 1971—*Fly* 1973—*Approximately Infinite Universe; Feeling the Space* 1981—*Season of Glass* (Geffen) 1982—*It's Alright* (Polydor).

John Lennon was the Beatles' most committed rock & roller, their social conscience and their slyest verbal wit. After the breakup of the Beatles, he and his wife, Yoko Ono, carried on intertwined solo careers. Ono's early albums presaged the elastic, screechy vocal style of late-Seventies new-wavers like the B-52's and Lene Lovich; Lennon made efforts to break taboos and to be ruthlessly, publicly honest. When he was murdered on December 8, 1980, he and Ono seemed on the verge of a new, more optimistic phase.

Like the other three Beatles, Lennon was born to a working-class family in Liverpool. His parents, Julia and Fred, separated before he was two (Lennon saw his father only twice in the next twenty years), and Lennon went to live with his mother's sister, Mimi Smith; when Lennon was 17, his mother was killed by a bus. He attended Liverpool's Dovedale Primary School and later the Quarry Bank High School, which supplied the name for his first band, a skiffle group called the Quarrymen, which he started in 1955. In the summer of 1956, he met Paul McCartney, and they began writing songs together and forming groups, the last of which was the Beatles.

Just before the Beatles' official breakup in 1970 (Lennon had wanted to quit the band earlier), Lennon began his solo career, more than half of which consisted of collaborations with Ono.

Ono was raised in Tokyo by her wealthy Japanese banking family. She was an excellent student (in 1952, she became the first woman admitted to study philosophy at Japan's Gakushuin University) and moved to the U.S. in 1953 to study at Sarah Lawrence College. After dropping out, she became involved in the Fluxus movement, led by New York avant-garde conceptual artists including George Maciunas, La Monte Young, Diane Wakoski and Walter De Maria. During the early Sixties, Ono's works (many of which were conceptual pieces, some of which involved audience participation) were exhibited and/or performed at the Village Gate, Carnegie Recital Hall and numerous New York galleries. In the mid-Sixties, she lectured at Wesleyan College and had exhibitions in Japan and London, where she met Lennon in 1966 at the Indica Gallery.

The two began corresponding, and in September 1967 Lennon sponsored Ono's "Half Wind Show" at London's Lisson Gallery. In May 1968, Ono visited Lennon at his home in Weybridge, and that night they recorded the tapes that would later be released as *Two Virgins.* (The nude cover shots, taken by Lennon with an automatic camera, were photographed then as well.) Lennon soon separated from his wife, Cynthia (with whom he had one child, Julian, in 1964); they were divorced that November. Lennon and Ono became constant companions.

Frustrated by his role with the Beatles, Lennon, with Ono, got a chance to explore avant-garde art, music and film. While he regarded his relationship with Ono as the most important thing in his life, the couple's inseparability and Ono's influence over Lennon would be a source of great tension among the Beatles, then in their last days.

Three days after Lennon's divorce, he and Ono released *Two Virgins,* which, because of the full frontal nude photos of the couple on the jacket, was the subject of much controversy; the LP was shipped in a plain brown wrapper. On March 20, 1969, Lennon and Ono were married in Gibraltar; for their honeymoon, they held their first "Bed-in for Peace," in the presidential suite of the Amsterdam Hilton. The peace movement was the first of several political causes the couple would take up over the years, but it was the one that generated the most publicity. On April 22, Lennon changed his middle name from Winston to Ono. In May, they attempted to continue their bed-in in the United States, but when U.S. authorities forbade them to enter the country because of their arrest on drug charges in October 1968, the bed-in resumed in Montreal. That May, in their suite at the Queen Elizabeth Hotel, they recorded "Give Peace a Chance"; background chanters included Timothy Leary, Tommy Smothers and numerous Hare Krishnas. Soon afterward, "The Ballad of John and Yoko" (#8, 1969) was released under the Beatles name, though only Lennon and McCartney appear on the record.

In September, Lennon, Ono and the Plastic Ono Band (which included Eric Clapton, Alan White and Klaus Voormann) performed live in Toronto at a Rock 'n' Roll Revival show. The appearance, which was later released as *Live Peace in Toronto, 1969,* was Lennon's first performance before a live concert audience in three years. Less than a month later, he announced to the Beatles that he was quitting the group, but it was agreed among them that no public announcement would be made until after pending lawsuits involving Apple and manager Allen Klein were resolved. In October, the Plastic Ono Band released "Cold Turkey" (#30, 1969), which the Beatles had declined to record, and the next month Lennon returned his M.B.E. medal to the Queen. In a letter to the Queen, Lennon cited Britain's involvement in Biafra and support of the U.S. in Vietnam and—jokingly—"Cold Turkey" 's poor chart showing as reasons for the return.

The Lennons continued their peace campaign with speeches to the press; "War Is Over! If You Want It" billboards erected on December 15 in 12 cities around the world, including New York, Hollywood, London and Toronto, and plans for a peace festival in Toronto. While the festival plans deteriorated, Lennon turned his attention to recording "Instant Karma!", which was produced by Phil Spector, who was then also editing hours of tapes into the album that would be the Beatles' last official release, *Let It Be.* In late February 1970, Lennon disavowed any connection with the Peace Festival and the

Yoko Ono and John Lennon

event was abandoned. In April, McCartney—in a move that Lennon felt was an act of betrayal—announced his departure from the Beatles and released his solo LP. From this point on (if not earlier), Ono replaced McCartney as Lennon's main collaborator. The Beatles were no more.

In late 1970, Lennon and Ono released their Plastic Ono Band solo LPs. Generally, Ono's Seventies LPs were regarded as highly adventurous avant-garde works, and were thus never as popular as Lennon's. Lennon's contained "Mother," which, along with other songs, was his most personal and, some felt, disturbing work—the direct result of his and Ono's primal scream therapy with Dr. Arthur Janov. In March 1971, "Power to the People" hit #11, and that September Lennon's solo LP *Imagine* was released; it went to #1 a month later. By late 1971, Lennon and Ono had resumed their political activities, drawn to leftist political figures like Abbie Hoffman and Jerry Rubin. Their involvement was reflected on *Some Time in New York City* (recorded with Elephant's Memory), which included Lennon's most overtly political releases ("Woman Is the Nigger of the World," "Sisters, O Sisters").

Over the next two years Lennon released *Mind Games* (#9) and *Walls and Bridges* (#1), which yielded his only solo #1 hit, "Whatever Gets You thru the Night," recorded with Elton John. On November 28, 1974, Lennon made his last public appearance, at John's Madison Square Garden concert. The two performed three songs, "Whatever Gets You thru the Night," "I Saw Her Standing There" and "Lucy in the Sky with Diamonds," released on an EP after Lennon's death. Next came *Rock 'n' Roll*, a collection of Lennon's versions of Fifties and early-Sixties rock classics like "Be-Bop-a-Lula." The release was preceded by a bootleg copy, produced by Morris Levy, over which Lennon successfully sued Levy. *Rock*

'n' Roll would be Lennon's last solo release except for *Shaved Fish,* a greatest hits compilation.

Meanwhile, Lennon's energies were increasingly directed toward his legal battle with the U.S. Immigration Department, which sought his deportation on the grounds of his previous drug arrest and involvement with the American radical left. On October 7, 1975, the U.S. Court of Appeals overturned the deportation order; in 1976, Lennon received permanent resident status. On October 9, 1975, Lennon's 35th birthday, Ono gave birth to Sean Ono Lennon. Beginning in 1975, Lennon devoted his full attention to his new son and his marriage, which had survived an 18-month separation from October 1973 to March 1975. For the next five years, he lived at home in nearly total seclusion, taking care of Sean while Ono ran the couple's financial affairs. Not until the publication of a full-page newspaper ad explaining his and Ono's activities in May 1979 did Lennon even hint at a possible return to recording.

In September 1980, he and Ono signed a contract with the newly formed Geffen Records, and on November 15 they released *Double Fantasy* (#1, 1980, 1981). A series of revealing interviews were published, "(Just Like) Starting Over" hit #1, and there was talk of a possible world tour. But on December 8, 1980, Lennon, returning with Ono to their Dakota apartment on New York City's Upper West Side, was shot seven times by Mark David Chapman, a 25-year-old drifter and Beatles fan to whom Lennon had given an autograph a few hours earlier. Lennon was pronounced dead on arrival at Roosevelt Hospital. At Ono's request, on December 14, a ten-minute silent vigil was held at 2 P.M. EST in which millions around the world participated. Lennon's remains were cremated in Hartsdale, New York.

Three months later, Ono released *Season of Glass,* an LP that deals with Lennon's death (his cracked and bloodstained eyeglasses are shown on the front jacket), although many of the songs were written before his shooting. *Season of Glass* is the best known of Ono's solo LPs; it was the first to receive attention outside avant-garde and critical circles. In 1982, Ono left Geffen for Polydor, where she released *It's Alright. Double Fantasy* won a Grammy for Album of the Year (1981).

THE LETTERMEN
Formed 1960, Los Angeles
Original lineup: Tony Butala, Jim Pike, Bob Engemann.

The Lettermen have been harmonizing pop songs for more than 20 years. Personnel have changed, their repertoire has been revamped with the times and their hits are long behind them, but they continue.

Original members Tony Butala, Bob Engemann and Jim Pike all had a measure of music-business experience, in guises ranging from the Mitchell Boys Choir to Stan Kenton, when they formed the Lettermen in 1960. They were hired by George Burns and Jack Benny to open their shows. A brief tenure with Warner Bros. Records followed before the Lettermen signed with Capitol in 1961. Their first single for the label, "The Way You Look Tonight," went gold; in 1962, "When I Fall in Love" and "Come Back Silly Girl" were Top Twenty hits. Their albums always made the Top 100; nine of them earned gold records. They have grossed over $25 million in sales for Capitol Records. As tastes in music changed, the Lettermen adapted their smooth voices to the latest trend: folk revival when they started out, electric guitars in the mid-Sixties, even disco and new wave in later years.

In 1968, they went through their first shift in personnel. Engemann was replaced by Gary Pike without affecting their hitmaking abilities; they scored one of their biggest that year with a medley of "Goin' Out of My Head" and "Can't Take My Eyes Off of You." "Hurt So Bad" (#12, 1969) was their last gold record, though the band continued releasing records on Capitol throughout the Seventies. They also branched into commercials, earning a Golden Globe Award for a Pan-Am ad. In 1982, the Lettermen left Capitol for the Applause label.

BOBBY LEWIS
Born February 17, 1933, Indianapolis
N.A.—*The Best of Bobby Lewis* (United Artists).

With the booming cry "I didn't sleep at all last night!" singer Bobby Lewis opened "Tossin' and Turnin'," an R&B stomp that held the #1 position on U.S. singles charts for seven weeks in 1961. Despite another hit that year with "One Track Mind," "Tossin' " proved to be Lewis' finest moment.

Growing up in an orphanage, Lewis was playing the piano by age five. Adopted at age 12, he moved with his new family to Detroit, where he was soon featured on a morning radio show. He became a journeyman blues-boogie performer in small clubs and theaters throughout the Midwest. During the Fifties, he recorded a lot of jump blues and other such material in one-shot deals for a variety of labels; none of the records went anywhere. Beltone Records signed him in 1961, and then came the hits. He continued to perform in clubs and theaters through the first half of the Sixties. United Artists signed him and eventually released two volumes of *The Best of Bobby Lewis*.

FURRY LEWIS
Born March 6, 1893, Greenwood, Mississippi; died September 14, 1981, Memphis
1969—*Presenting the Country Blues* (Blue Horizon)
1970—*In Memphis* (Matchbox)   1971—*Furry Lewis* (Xtra)   *& Fred McDowell* (Biograph)   *Furry Lewis Band* (Folkways).

Legendary Memphis bluesman Walter "Furry" Lewis is thought by some to be the first guitarist to play with a bottleneck, a technique later used by Robert Johnson, Bukka White and Johnny Shines (earlier musicians had achieved a similar effect using a knife across the strings).

The son of a Mississippi sharecropper, Lewis moved from his birthplace to Memphis in 1899 and while still in school began playing guitar in local bands with W. C. Handy, Will Shade and the Memphis Jug Band. He was a teen when he began performing on Beale Street.

Lewis toured the country in medicine shows and also played the jukes with Memphis Minnie and Blind Lemon Jefferson as early as 1906 and straight through the Twenties. In 1917, he lost a leg in a railroad accident; it was replaced by a wooden stump. In 1927, he and Jim Jackson auditioned for the Vocalion label in Chicago. The next year his first recordings, including "Good Looking Girl Blues," "John Henry" and "Billy Lyons and Stack O'Lee," were released.

His singing style was a kind of talking blues, but the market for that music died in the Depression, and Furry spent the next 44 years supporting himself as a street cleaner. He did some performing by night, but he didn't record again until the late Fifties, when Sam Charters recorded him for Prestige. Later recordings for Biograph, Folkways, Adelphi and Rounder never earned enough for Lewis to quit the sanitation department. He did play many blues and folk festivals in the Sixties and Seventies and recorded with Bukka White, though his best shot at fame came in the early Seventies, when he toured with Don Nix and the Alabama State Troopers and appeared on a Leon Russell television special.

In 1975, the Rolling Stones invited him along as their opening act in Memphis, and after a meeting with him, Joni Mitchell wrote "Furry Sings the Blues." Lewis also appeared on "The Tonight Show" and in two films, Burt Reynolds' *W. W. and the Dixie Dance King*, and *This Is Elvis*. He died of heart failure at age 88.

GARY LEWIS AND THE PLAYBOYS
Formed 1964, Los Angeles
Gary Lewis (b. Gary Levitch, July 31, 1946, Los Angeles), drums, voc.; Al Ramsey (b. July 27, 1943, N.J.), gtr.; John R. West (b. July 31, 1939, Uhrichsville, Oh.), gtr.; David Walkes (b. May 12, 1943, Montgomery, Ala.), kybds.; David Costell (b. Mar. 15, 1944, Pittsburgh), bass.
1965—*This Diamond Ring* (Liberty)   1966—*Golden Greats*   1968—*More Golden Greats*.

With seven consecutive Top Ten singles in 1965 and 1966, and over 7½ million records sold, Gary Lewis was certainly the most successful Hollywood offspring turned rock-&-roller. Lewis was drafted in 1966, and since his 1968 Army discharge he has attempted several comebacks.

Son of comedian Jerry Lewis, Gary Lewis started playing drums at age 14, and four years later he formed the

Playboys. They became a regular fixture at Disneyland and producer Snuff Garrett signed them to Liberty in 1964. With Leon Russell's arrangements and Al Kooper as cowriter, the Playboys scored a #1 hit their first time out with "This Diamond Ring."

Russell also worked on the subsequent singles: "Count Me In" (#2, 1965), "Save Your Heart for Me" (#2, 1965), "Everybody Loves a Clown" (#4, 1965), "She's Just My Style" (#3, 1966), "Sure Gonna Miss Her" (#9, 1966), and "Green Grass" (#8, 1966).

The group appeared in *A Swingin' Summer* (1965) and *Out of Sight* (1966). The Playboys' popularity had waned just slightly when Lewis was drafted, and upon his discharge, he re-formed the group. Though Lewis would score two more chart singles, he would never again have a Top Ten hit, despite an attempt to update his image from teenage pop star to "sensitive" singer/songwriter. His career was further complicated by drug problems and a divorce. Lewis has attempted comebacks from time to time, veering between the oldies circuit (1973, for example) and eschewing old material completely (1981).

JERRY LEE LEWIS

Born September 29, 1935, Ferriday, Louisiana
1964—*Live at the Star Club Hamburg* (Philips)   **1968**—*Another Place, Another Time* (Smash)   **1970**—*Original Golden Hits* (Sun)   *Original Golden Hits, Volume 2; Memphis Country;   The Best of Jerry Lee Lewis* (Smash)   **1971**—*Original Golden Hits, Volume 3* (Sun)   **1973**—*The Session* (Mercury).

Though he had only three Top Ten hits in the first purely rock & roll phase of his career, many critics believe Jerry Lee Lewis was as talented a Fifties rocker as Sun labelmate Elvis Presley. Some also believe he could have made it just as big commercially if his piano-slamming musical style was not so relentlessly wild, his persona not so threateningly hard-edged.

Lewis' first musical influences were eclectic—his parents (who were poor) spun swing and Al Jolson records. But his earliest big influence was country star Jimmie Rodgers. In his early teens he absorbed both the softer country style of Gene Autry and the more rocking music of local black clubs, along with the gospel hymns of the local Assembly of God church. Lewis first played his aunt's piano at age eight and made his public debut in 1949 at age 14, sitting in with a local C&W band in a Ford dealership parking lot. When he was fifteen, Lewis went to a fundamentalist Bible school in Waxahachie, Texas, from which he was soon expelled. He has often said that rock & roll is the Devil's music.

In 1956, Lewis headed for Memphis (financed by his father) to audition for Sam Phillips' Sun Records. Phillips' assistant, Jack Clement, was impressed with Lewis' piano style but suggested he play more rock & roll, in a style similar to Elvis Presley's. (Presley had recently switched from Sun to RCA.) Lewis' debut single, "Crazy Arms" (previously a country hit for Ray Price), did well regionally, but it was the followup, 1957's "Whole Lotta Shakin' Going On," that finally broke through. The song first sold 100,000 copies in the South; after an appearance by Lewis on Steve Allen's TV show, it sold over six million copies nationally. "Great Balls of Fire" sold more than five million copies and was followed by more than a half-million in sales for "Breathless" and "High School Confidential," the title theme song of a movie in which Lewis also appeared. Both "Whole Lotta Shakin' " and "Great Balls" were #1 on the pop, country and R&B charts simultaneously. Lewis' high school nickname was the "Killer," and it stuck with him as he established a reputation as a tough, rowdy performer, with a flamboyant piano style that used careening glissandos, pounding chords and bench-toppling acrobatics.

Lewis' career slammed to a stop, though, after he married his 13-year-old third cousin, Myra Gale Brown, in December 1957. (She was his third wife; at age 16 he had wed a 17-year-old, and soon after that ended he had got caught in a shotgun marriage.) The marriage lasted 13 years, but at the time, Lewis was condemned by the church in the U.S. and hounded by the British press on a 1958 tour. His career ran dry for nearly a decade. He had a modest 1961 hit with "What'd I Say," but in 1963 he left Sun for Smash/Mercury. He toured relentlessly, playing clubs, billing his act "the greatest show on earth." On the way, he developed a drinking problem. In 1968, he played

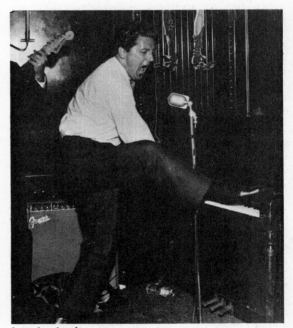

Jerry Lee Lewis

Iago in a rock musical version of Shakespeare's *Othello* called *Catch My Soul.*

Eventually, Lewis and his producer, Jerry Kennedy, decided to abandon rock & roll for country music. In 1968, Lewis had the first of many Top Ten country hits with "Another Place, Another Time," followed by "What Made Milwaukee Famous (Made a Loser Out of Me)." Between then and the early Eighties, he had more than thirty big country hits, including "To Make Love Sweeter for You" (#1 C&W, 1968), "There Must Be More to Love Than This" (#1 C&W, 1971), "Would You Take Another Chance on Me" (#1 C&W, 1971), "Chantilly Lace" (#1 C&W, 1972), "Middle Age Crazy" (#4 C&W, 1977) and "Thirty-nine and Holding" (#4 C&W, 1981).

Lewis' life has been marked by tragedy. In 1973, Jerry Lee Lewis, Jr., who played drums in his father's band, was killed in an automobile accident. (Lewis' brother had died when hit by a car when Jerry was two.) His other son, Steve, drowned in 1962. In September 1976, Lewis accidently shot his bassist in the chest, and in 1982 his estranged wife, Jaren Pate Lewis, also drowned in a pool.

In 1973, Lewis released *The Session,* a return-to-rock album recorded in London with a host of top British musicians, including Peter Frampton, Alvin Lee, Klaus Voormann and Rory Gallagher, redoing oldies, resulting in some pop chart success with "Drinkin' Wine Spo Dee O-dee"—an R&B song he'd performed at his public debut in 1949. In 1978, Lewis signed with Elektra and enjoyed some FM radio play with "Rockin' My Life Away." He also continued to tour, performing all the styles of his career—rock, country, gospel, blues, spirituals and more. In 1981, Lewis played a German concert with fellow Sun alumni Johnny Cash and Carl Perkins. The show was released as an album called *Survivors* in 1982. On June 30, 1981, Lewis was hospitalized in Memphis with hemorrhaging from a perforated stomach ulcer. After two operations, he was given a 50-50 chance of survival; four months later he was back on tour. He appeared on the 1982 Grammy Awards telecast with his cousin Mickey Gilley; another cousin is TV evangelist Jimmy Swaggart.

LINDA LEWIS
Born in London
1970—*Hacienda View* (Ariola, U.K.)   **1971**—*Say No More* (Reprise, U.K.)   **1972**—*Lark* (Reprise)   **1973**—*Fathoms Deep*   **1975**—*Not a Little Girl Anymore* (Arista)   **1977**—*Woman Overboard.*

Singer/songwriter Linda Lewis' career was grounded by the same problems Joan Armatrading later faced: how to get an American audience to accept a black female singer who isn't an R&B artist. Though Lewis' music shows some soul influence, it is more often a bubbly combination of English folk rock with reggae and pop.

Lewis was born to Jamaican parents in the Dockland area of London's East End, and her first influence was calypso. As a preteen, she had bit acting parts in *A Hard Day's Night* and *A Taste of Honey.* At age 14, her mother took her to see John Lee Hooker, and Lewis reportedly wound up taking the stage with the old bluesman for a version of Martha and the Vandellas' "Dancing in the Streets." She left acting and school to start playing in bands, first joining Herbie Goins and the Nightmares, then her own group, White Rabbit; in 1967, she achieved some recognition in Europe with Ferris Wheel.

After two years, she went solo with her own material. She toured Britain with Elton John and Family, all before releasing her 1971 album *Say No More.* Critics praised Lewis' flighty 3½-octave voice and pop-folky material, but the record was never released in the U.S. Her next LP, the first in America, *Lark,* was produced by Jim Cregan (who later left Family for Cockney Rebel and then Rod Stewart's band). It was followed by her first U.K. hit, "Rock-a-Doodle-Do" (#15, 1973).

In 1974, Lewis did a world tour with Cat Stevens, and in 1975 she was signed to Arista, where Clive Davis tried to improve her commercial potential by matching her with R&B producers Tony Sylvester and Bert DeCoteaux. *Not a Little Girl Anymore* yielded a #6 U.K. hit with Betty Everett's 1964 smash "It's in His Kiss (The Shoop Shoop Song)." She had another British score with "Baby I'm Yours" (#33, 1976), but she didn't release another LP until 1977's *Woman Overboard,* produced by Cregan, Allen Toussaint and Cat Stevens. The album didn't click in the U.S., and she soon lost her recording contract.

RAMSEY LEWIS
Born May 27, 1935, Chicago
1964—*Barefoot Sunday Blues* (Cadet)   **1965**—*The In Crowd*   **1966**—*Hang On Ramsey; Wade in the Water*   **1968**—*Ramsey Lewis Trio*   **1973**—*Greatest Hits* (Columbia) *Non-Stop Golden Hits*   **1975**—*Sun Goddess*   **1977**—*Tequila Mockingbird*   **1978**—*Legacy*   **1979**—*Ramsey*   **1980**—*Routes*   **1981**—*Three Piece Suite*   **1982**—*Live at the Savoy.*

Keyboardist Ramsey Lewis has had much commercial success with his pop-jazz instrumentals, particularly in the mid-Sixties with remakes of current hits. In 1965 the Ramsey Lewis Trio won a Grammy for Best Jazz Instrumental for their #5 gold hit "The 'In' Crowd" (originally recorded by Dobie Gray). Their version of the McCoys' "Hang On Sloopy" went to #11 and likewise went gold.

Lewis studied classical piano at the Chicago College of Music and De Paul University. He began playing professionally at age 16 with the Clefs, a group that included bassist Eldee Young and drummer Red Holt, with whom he formed the Ramsey Lewis Trio in 1956. Besides the Trio's own albums, Lewis also played with Max Roach, Sonny Stitt and Clark Terry. The Trio enjoyed a third Top Twenty hit, "Wade in the Water," in 1966, before breaking up that year. His two former sidemen founded Young-Holt

Unlimited, who had a #3 hit with "Soulful Strut" in 1969.

Lewis' new trio included bassist Cleveland Eaton and drummer Morris Jennings, who'd previously played with Donny Hathaway and Curtis Mayfield. Lewis enjoyed much success through the mid-Seventies on Columbia Records (whom he'd signed with in 1973). His *Sun Goddess* LP went gold; it was produced by Earth, Wind and Fire's Maurice White, who'd once played with Lewis. Lewis continues to tour and record.

SMILEY LEWIS
Born Overton Amos Lemons, July 5, 1920, Union, Louisiana; died October 7, 1966, New Orleans
1970—*Shame Shame Shame* (Liberty)   **1978**—*I Hear You Knocking* (United Artists)   *The Bells Are Ringing*.

Singer/guitarist/pianist Smiley Lewis was a major New Orleans R&B performer, though his best songs only became pop hits for other people.

His parents moved to New Orleans from his small-town birthplace when he was 11, and he began recording there in 1947 for Deluxe Records under the name Smiling Lewis. The best-loved work of this gravel-voiced singer came during his 1950–60 period, when he was produced by Dave Bartholomew, yielding such songs as "Shame Shame Shame" and two R&B hits, "The Bells Are Ringing" (#10, 1952) and "I Hear You Knocking" (#2, 1955), which featured a classic piano intro from Huey Smith. A few months later, Lewis' version of "Knocking" was eclipsed by Gale Storm's #2 pop hit cover. The song was revived fifteen years later by Dave Edmunds, who made it a hit again. Another of Lewis' tunes, "One Night (of Sin)," was cleaned up and changed to "One Night (of Love)" and became a hit for Elvis Presley in 1958.

Beginning in 1961, Lewis recorded for Okeh, then Dot and Loma Records (at the last, produced by Allen Toussaint), and he worked until his death in 1966 of stomach cancer.

GORDON LIGHTFOOT
Born November 17, 1938, Orillia, Ontario
1966—*Lightfoot* (United Artists)   **1968**—*The Way I Feel; Did She Mention My Name?*   **1969**—*Back Here on Earth; Early Lightfoot; Sunday Concert*   **1970**—*Sit Down Young Stranger* (Reprise)   *If You Could Read My Mind*   **1971**—*Summer Side of Life*   **1972**—*Don Quixote; Old Dan's Records*   **1973**—*Sundown*   **1975**—*Cold on the Shoulder; Gord's Gold; Very Best of* (United Artists)   **1976**—*Early Morning Rain; Summertime Dream* (Reprise)   **1978**—*Endless Wire* (Warner Bros.)   **1980**—*Dream Street Rose*   **1982**—*Shadows*.

One of the most successful Canadian singer/songwriters, baritone Gordon Lightfoot was inspired to write his own songs by writers like Bob Dylan, Tom Paxton and Phil Ochs in the early Sixties. Prior to that, he played piano,

worked summers in his father's laundry, and then emigrated to Los Angeles in 1958 to attend the now defunct Westlake College. There he studied orchestration but soon returned to Toronto, where he worked as an arranger and producer of commercial jingles until 1960, when, encouraged by Pete Seeger and friends Ian and Sylvia, he switched to guitar and, along with his studio work, began playing folk music at local coffeehouses.

Lightfoot soon developed his own identity with country-ish material, like his debut Canadian hit, "Remember Me." Ian and Sylvia added two of his folky numbers to their stage show, "For Lovin' Me" and "Early Morning Rain," and introduced Lightfoot to their manager, Albert Grossman, who promptly gave both songs to his other clients Peter, Paul and Mary. The trio made "For Lovin' Me" a #30 U.S. hit in 1965.

On his own, Lightfoot began releasing solo albums in 1966; the first six on United Artists. Each sold between 150,000 and 200,000 copies. In 1969, he switched to Reprise, and his label debut, *Sit Down Young Stranger*, sold 750,000 copies with the help of his first U.S. hit, "If You Could Read My Mind" (#5, 1971). Many other artists, including Bob Dylan, Jerry Lee Lewis, Johnny Cash, Elvis Presley, Barbra Streisand and Judy Collins, continued to cover his songs.

Lightfoot's popularity peaked in the mid-Seventies with a #1 gold LP and single in 1974, both called *Sundown*. He hit #2 with "The Wreck of the Edmund Fitzgerald" (about an ore vessel that sank on Lake Superior), released on the *Summertime Dream* LP in May 1976. He still has a large, loyal following.

LINDISFARNE
Formed 1969, England
Alan Hull (b. Feb. 20, 1945, Newcastle, Eng.), gtr., voc.; Rod Clements (b. Nov. 17, 1947, North Shields, Eng.), bass, violin; Ray Jackson (b. Dec. 12, 1948, Wallsend, Eng.), harp, mandolin; Simon Cowe (b. Apr. 1, 1948, Tynemouth, Eng.), gtr.; Ray Laidlaw (b. May 28, 1948, North Shields, Eng.), drums.
1970—*Nicely Out of Tune* (Elektra)   **1971**—*Fog on the Tyne*   **1972**—*Dingly Dell*   **1973**—(– Clements; – Cowe; – Laidlaw; + Kenny Craddock, voc., gtr., kybds.; + Charlie Harcourt, voc., gtr.; + Tommy Duffy, voc., bass; + Paul Nichols, drums)   *Lindisfarne Live* (Charisma)   *Roll On, Ruby* (Elektra)   **1974**—*Happy Daze*   **1975**—*Finest Hour* (Charisma)   (broke up)   **1978**—(re-formed with same original lineup)   *Back and Fourth* (Atco)   *Magic in the Air* (Mercury, U.K.)   **1979**—*The News*.
Alan Hull solo: 1974—*Pipedream* (Elektra)   **1975**—*Squire* (Warner Bros.)   **1979**—*Phantoms* (Rocket, U.K.).

Lindisfarne's pop folk rock was popular in England during the early Seventies, peaking in 1972 with their Top Ten U.K. album *Fog on the Tyne*.

The band goes back to the mid-Sixties, when various members were playing in local Newcastle groups, including Rod Clements and Ray Laidlaw in the Downtown Faction Blues Band. All the future Lindisfarne members, except Hull, worked together as Brethren in the summer of 1969. With the departure of guitarist Jeff Sandler in late 1969, the group switched to quieter folk pop, especially after taking on folksinger/songwriter Alan Hull, who became co–lead writer with Clements in the spring of 1970. The band was briefly known as Alan Hull and Brethren before choosing Lindisfarne (after a small island off the Northumberland coast).

Though their debut album, *Nicely Out of Tune,* was released in the U.S., most interest was in Europe, generated by their many college and festival shows. The big British breakthrough was *Fog on the Tyne,* which was produced by Bob Johnston (who'd previously worked with Bob Dylan) and yielded the lushly melodic #5 hit "Meet Me on the Corner" (1972). Around this time, Jackson played mandolin on Rod Stewart's *Every Picture Tells a Story.* Another single, "Lady Eleanor," hit #3 in England but only #82 in the U.S., and soon the band was having trouble in the U.K. as well. *Dingly Dell* was a critical and commercial disappointment, and in 1973 Clements, Cowe and Laidlaw left to form Jack the Lad. (Clements left Jack shortly after their mid-1974 debut.)

Hull and Jackson kept the band name, and the group became a sextet with the inclusion of Kenny Craddock (who in 1968 played with Yes drummer Alan White in Happy Magazine, and later Ginger Baker's Air Force and Mark-Almond) and Charlie Harcourt (formerly with Cat Mother and the All Night News Boys). Both *Roll On, Ruby* and *Happy Daze* were flops. Hull had released his first solo record, *Pipedream; Squire* came out around the time the band broke up in 1975.

Lindisfarne resurfaced in October 1978 on Atlantic with the album *Back and Fourth* (they had first reunited with all the original members at Christmastime 1977). At this late date, they had their first relatively successful U.S. hit, "Run for Home" (#33 U.S., #10 U.K.).

DAVID LINDLEY

Born 1944, San Marino, California
1981—*El Rayo-X* (Asylum) **1982**—*Win This Record.*

David Lindley is a Los Angeles session musician best known for his work as Jackson Browne's sideman and for his collection of "cheapo" guitars. He has also performed on records by Rod Stewart, James Taylor, Linda Ronstadt, Joe Walsh, Warren Zevon, David Crosby, Graham Nash and others.

At 14, Lindley picked up a baritone ukulele and later a flamenco guitar. By age 18, he'd won five consecutive Topanga Canyon Banjo and Fiddle competitions. Lindley's first band, the Mad Mountain Ramblers, used to play at Disneyland; his next group, called the Scat Band,

included Seatrain fiddler Richard Greene, leading to Kaleidoscope, which was formed in 1966 and released four albums.

His first major session credit was the haunting violin intro to the Youngbloods' "Darkness Darkness" in 1969. The next year, Kaleidoscope broke up and Lindley toured England with Terry Reid. In 1971, he joined Jackson Browne's band. Besides helping to shape Browne's bittersweet sound, Lindley played mandolin on Rod Stewart's *Atlantic Crossing* (1975) and collaborated with fellow multiinstrumentalist Ry Cooder on *The Long Riders* soundtrack (1980).

In 1980, Lindley signed a solo deal with Asylum; after spending a year and a half with a vocal coach, in mid-1981 he released a debut album, *El Rayo-X,* produced by Browne and Greg Ladanyi and recorded with ex–King Crimson drummer Ian Wallace and Little Feat keyboardist Bill Payne. On a solo tour, he played guitars rarely seen outside pawnshops.

MANCE LIPSCOMB

Born April 9, 1895, Navasota, Texas; died January 30, 1976, Navasota
1962—*Mance Lipscomb, Texas Songster* (Arhoolie)
1964—*Mance Lipscomb, Texas Songster, Volume 2*
1966—*Mance Lipscomb, Texas Songster, Volume 3*
1968—*Mance Lipscomb, Texas Songster, Volume 4*
1970—*Mance Lipscomb, Texas Songster, Volume 5; Trouble in Mind* (Reprise).

Discovered during the early-Sixties folk-blues boom, singer/guitarist/fiddler Mance Lipscomb is generally considered a Texas country blues great, an artistic descendant of Blind Lemon Jefferson and compatriot of Lightnin' Hopkins. Actually, though, Lipscomb was a bluesman and more—a songster and minstrel who performed ballads, reels, shouts and breakdowns as well as blues. Though he didn't record until age 65, his influence has been noted in the work of Bob Dylan, Janis Joplin and the Grateful Dead, among others.

Lipscomb learned to play fiddle from his father, an emancipated slave turned professional musician, and played with him around the Navasota-Brazos area until 1911. Between shows, Lipscomb taught himself guitar and worked the fields. Before 1956, he only played for small gatherings of friends and coworkers at picnics or dances. He moved to Houston in 1956, and in 1960 was discovered by Chris Strachwitz, a folk-music archivist and founder of Arhoolie Records, who brought tapes of his music to various members of the folk-blues community. Lipscomb played several folk festivals, and was recorded by Arhoolie. He continued recording and performing until 1974, when heart disease forced him to retire. Lipscomb also appeared in several documentary films: *The Blues* (1962), *The Blues Accordin' to Lightnin' Hopkins* (1968), *Blues Like Showers of Rain* (1970), Les Blank's *A Well-*

Spent Life (1971) and *Out of the Blacks into the Blues* (1972).

LITTLE ANTHONY AND THE IMPERIALS
Formed 1957, New York City
Anthony Gourdine (b. Jan. 8, 1941, New York City), lead voc.; Ernest Wright, Jr. (b. Aug. 24, 1941, Brooklyn, N.Y.), second tenor; Clarence Collins (b. Mar. 17, 1941, Brooklyn, N.Y.), bass; Tracy Lord, first tenor; Glouster Rogers, baritone.
1964—(− Lord; − Rogers; + Sammy Strain [b. Dec. 9, 1941], first tenor) **later**—(+ Kenny Seymour; − Wright; − Strain) *I'm on the Outside Lookin' In* (DCP) **1965**—*Goin' Out of My Head* (Veep) **1966**—*The Best of Little Anthony and the Imperials* **1974**—*On a New Street* (Avco) **1980**—*Daylight* (MCA/Songbird).

Little Anthony and the Imperials were a late-Fifties doo-wop group whose first and biggest hit was the million-selling "Tears on My Pillow" (#4, 1958). Lead singer Anthony Gourdine began his career with the Duponts, a band of Brooklyn singers who cut two singles in 1955 on the Winley and Royal Roost labels. He then formed the Chesters, who cut one song under that name in 1957 on Apollo and then were renamed the Imperials by their new label, End. The Little Anthony moniker for the five-foot-four singer was added by Alan Freed and first turned up on later pressings of "Tears on My Pillow." The band had another hit in 1960, "Shimmy, Shimmy, Ko-ko Bop" (#24), but then broke up. Little Anthony was idle until 1964, when the group re-formed minus Lord and Rogers, adding Sammy Strain. This band lineup had more consistent chart success on DCP Records with "Goin' Out of My Head" (#6, 1964), "Hurt So Bad" (#9, 1965) and "Take Me Back" (#16, 1965).

After that, the group had no more major chart action but continued recording on Veep from 1966 to 1968, United Artists (1969 to 1970) and on Avco in 1974, which yielded the #25 soul hit "I'm Falling in Love with You." Little Anthony played solo on the Las Vegas circuit in the early Seventies and, after a slow period later in the decade, became a born-again Christian. He signed a solo deal in 1980 with MCA/Songbird and released *Daylight*, produced by B. J. Thomas. He still tours. Strain later joined the O'Jays.

LITTLE EVA
Born Eva Narcissus Boyd, June 29, 1945, Bell Haven, North Carolina
1962—*Llllloco-motion* (Dimension).

Perhaps no baby-sitter in history ever got a bigger break than Eva Boyd, who, the story goes, at age 17 was baby-sitting for songwriters Carole King and Gerry Goffin. They asked her to record a tune they'd just written called "The Loco-Motion." The song borrowed its arrangement from the Marvelettes' "Please Mr. Postman." With the Cookies (who did "Chains") as backup singers plus the powerhouse voice of the newly named Little Eva, the record went #1 on the pop and R&B charts in 1962. Eva had another danceable followup with "Keep Your Hands Off My Baby" (#12 pop, #6 R&B, 1962) and in 1963 she scored a Top Twenty with "Let's Turkey Trot" (#20 pop, #16 R&B)—all recorded for Dimension. Eva also recorded "Swingin' on a Star" (#38, 1963), a duet with Big Dee Irwin, formerly of the Pastels.

Eva's sister Idalia also recorded with the label, earning only one minor hit, "Hoola Hooping." Eva cut a few more records for other labels, including Spring and Amy, but never re-created her original overnight success.

LITTLE FEAT
Formed 1969, Los Angeles
Lowell George (b. 1945; d. June 29, 1979, Arlington, Va.), voc., gtr., slide gtr., harmonica; Bill Payne (b. March 12, 1949, Waco, Tex.), kybds., voc.; Richard Hayward, drums; Roy Estrada, bass, voc.
1971—*Little Feat* (Warner Bros.) **1972**—*Sailin' Shoes* (− Estrada; + Kenny Gradney [b. New Orleans], bass; + Paul Barrère [b. July 3, 1948, Burbank, Calif.], gtr., voc.; + Sam Clayton, congas) **1973**—*Dixie Chicken* **1974**—*Feats Don't Fail Me Now* **1975**—*The Last Record Album* **1977**—*Time Loves a Hero* **1978**—*Waiting for Columbus* **1979**—*Down on the Farm* **1981**—*Hoy-Hoy!*
Lowell George solo: 1979—*Thanks I'll Eat It Here* (Warner Bros.).
Paul Barrère solo: 1983—*On My Own Two Feet* (Atlantic).

Little Feat mixed every strain of Southern music—blues, country, gospel, rockabilly, boogie, New Orleans R&B and Memphis funk—with surreal lyrics and a sense of absurdity and professionalism that could only have come from Southern California. They may have been too eclectic for their own commercial good, yet although they had only one gold album, the live *Waiting for Columbus*, they had a strong cult following and became one of California's most influential bands of the Seventies.

The band was formed by Lowell George and Roy Estrada, both former Mothers of Invention; Richie Hayward, ex–Fraternity of Man (of "Don't Bogart That Joint" on the *Easy Rider* soundtrack); and classically trained pianist Bill Payne.

George's bluesy vocals and slide guitar dominated the sound of the band, and his playful songwriting set its tone; although he could write conventional country-rock songs like "Willin' " (which appeared on the first two Feat albums and has been covered by Linda Ronstadt, Commander Cody and others), he reveled in wordplay and non sequiturs. As a child, George appeared on the Ted Mack Original Amateur Hour playing a harmonica duet with his brother Hampton; he played flute in the Hollywood High School orchestra and, later, oboe and baritone saxophone on Frank Sinatra recording sessions. In 1965, he started a folk-rock group, the Factory, which Hayward joined after answering an ad; the Factory recorded for Uni Records. When it broke up, George became rhythm guitarist in Frank Zappa's Mothers of Invention and was with a short-lived Standells reunion before starting Little Feat.

After "Easy to Slip" from *Sailin' Shoes* failed to hit, Little Feat went through one of its many breakups, the only one that resulted in personnel changes. Estrada went into computer programing, though he briefly rejoined Zappa a few years later. He was replaced by two New Orleans musicians, Kenny Gradney and Sam Clayton, along with guitarist Paul Barrère.

The Little Feat of *Dixie Chicken* was slightly less raucous and more funky; they toured with New Orleans songwriter Allen Toussaint, whose "On Your Way Down" appeared on *Dixie Chicken*. For the rest of the decade, Little Feat established itself as a touring band, particularly on the East Coast and in the South. They also became mainstays of the Los Angeles music community; Payne, especially, did a lot of session work. The band kept an erratic recording schedule, partly because it was frequently breaking up, and partly because George, who had become Feat's producer, had trouble making final decisions; song titles and lyrics would often appear on album covers but not on the LPs themselves.

Beginning with *The Last Record Album*, Barrère and Payne (usually as collaborators) began to take on a larger share of the songwriting, moving the band toward jazz rock. George produced an album by the Grateful Dead (*Shakedown Street*) and announced periodically that he was working on a solo album. When *Thanks I'll Eat It Here* (originally the projected title of *Sailin' Shoes*) finally appeared in 1979, George announced that Little Feat had broken up and he went on tour with his own band; in the middle of the tour, he died, apparently of a heart attack. Little Feat finished *Down on the Farm* and disbanded; *Hoy-Hoy!* compiled live tracks and alternate takes.

Since George's death, Hayward has toured with Joan Armatrading. Payne returned to studio work and occasional tours, including one with James Taylor. In 1983, Barrère released a solo album and toured with his own band.

LITTLE MILTON

Born Milton Campbell, September 17, 1934, Inverness, Mississippi
1972—*Little Milton Greatest Hits* (Chess) **1974**—*Golden Decade* (Phonogram) **1976**—*Blues Masters* (Chess) **1983**—*Age Ain't Nothin' But a Number* (MCA).

Veteran blues singer/guitarist Little Milton took up guitar at age 12 and a few years later left home to play with Eddie

Kusick and Willie Love. In 1953, he was signed to Sun Records, where he recorded with Ike Turner (later of Ike and Tina fame). Milton soon moved on to other labels, including Meteor in 1957 and St. Louis' Bobbin in 1958.

His single "I'm a Lonely Man" caught the attention of Leonard Chess, who signed him to Checker in 1961. There he had his first real success with "So Mean to Me" (#14 R&B, 1962). In 1965, he went all the way to #1 with "We're Gonna Make It." His gospel-soulful vocals were reminiscent of Bobby Bland, yet still distinctive, earning him another top hit that year with "Who's Cheating Who" (#4 R&B). Some of his Checker hits were arranged by Donny Hathaway. In 1967, he had a #7 R&B hit with "Feel So Bad."

Milton had many other Checker hits (five R&B Top Twenties in 1969) before going to Memphis in 1971 to sign with Stax. He enjoyed R&B hits with that label as well, including "That's What Love Will Make You Do" (#9, 1972). He also performed in the 1972 film *Wattstax*. After leaving Stax in 1976, Milton produced LPs for the Glades label in Miami. Milton continued to tour and record.

LITTLE RICHARD

Born Richard Penniman, December 25, 1932 or 1935, Macon, Georgia
N.A.—*Biggest Hits* (Specialty) *Greatest Hits* **1965**—*King of Gospel Songs* (Mercury) *Little Richard's Greatest Hits Recorded Live* (Okeh) **1975**—*The Very Best of Little Richard* (United Artists).

Pounding the piano and howling lyrics in a wild falsetto, Little Richard became a seminal figure in the birth of rock & roll. His no-holds-barred style, mascara-coated eyelashes and high—almost effeminate—pompadour were exotic and in many ways personified the new music's gleeful sexuality and spirit of rebellion.

One of 12 children, Penniman grew up in a devout Seventh Day Adventist family; his two uncles and a grandfather were preachers, though his father sold bootleg whiskey. The young Penniman sang gospel and learned piano at a local church. But his parents never encouraged his musical interests, and at age 13 Penniman was ejected (in a 1982 televised interview Penniman claimed it was because of his homosexuality) from their house. He moved in with a white family, Ann and Johnny Johnson, who ran Macon's Tick Tock Club, where Richard first performed.

In 1951, Penniman won a contract with RCA after playing at an Atlanta radio audition. His recordings during the next two years were fairly conventional jump blues, like "Every Hour" and "Get Rich Quick," neither of which made any commercial impression. In 1952, he moved to Houston, where he recorded for Don Robey's Peacock label. Initially he recorded with the backup groups the Deuces of Rhythm and the Tempo Toppers, though in 1955 he switched to fronting the Johnny Otis

Little Richard

orchestra for four sides. He toured small black nightclubs, performing mostly blues; his rock numbers were not well received.

Down on his luck, he sent a demo tape to Art Rupe of Specialty Records in L.A., who—as luck would have it—had been looking for a hard-edged voice like Penniman's to front some New Orleans musicians. Rupe signed on "Bumps" Blackwell as the producer and, with a Crescent City rhythm section, Little Richard entered the studio on September 14, 1955. One of the songs he cut was an old between-song filler piece called "Tutti Frutti" (with lyrics cleaned up by New Orleans writer Dorothy La Bostrie). Richard's whooping, shouting vocals, sexy-dumb lyrics and wild piano banging on "Tutti Frutti" set the style for his future hits. The single sold to both black and white fans—over three million copies by 1968—and its influence was incalculable. Out of Richard's approximately 36 sides for Specialty, seven were gold: "Tutti Frutti" (#17), "Long Tall Sally" (#6), "Rip It Up" (#17) in 1956; "Lucille" (#21), "Jenny, Jenny" (#10) and "Keep a Knockin' " (#8) in 1957; and "Good Golly, Miss Molly" (#10, 1958). Penniman also appeared in three early rock & roll movies: *Don't Knock the Rock, The Girl Can't Help It* (both 1956) and *Mister Rock 'n' Roll* (1957).

But in 1957, at the height of his success, Little Richard suddenly quit his rock career after a tour of Australia. He claimed that a vision of the apocalypse came to him in a dream, and that he saw his own damnation. He also tells a story of a plane flight during which one of the engines caught fire. He prayed to God and promised that if the plane landed safely he would change his ways. Soon after the airplane incident, Richard entered Oakwood College in Huntsville, Alabama, where he received a BA and was ordained a minister in The Seventh Day Adventist Church. Specialty tried to keep his conversion a secret, issuing the hit "Keep a Knockin'," pieced together from half-finished sessions.

Little Richard did not return to rock until 1964. After a failed attempt to gain a major audience on the evangelical circuit with his gospel recordings, he tried to resurrect his rock following with the anachronistic and unsuccessful "Bama Lama Bama Loo" on Specialty in 1964. The world was already switching its attention to the newer sounds of the Beatles. (Ironically, Little Richard was one of Paul McCartney's idols.) Through the years, Little Richard mounted many unsuccessful comeback attempts on Vee Jay, Modern, Okeh and Brunswick.

His best shot came in the early Seventies, when he got a contract with Reprise and recorded three R&B/rock LPs—*The Rill Thing, King of Rock 'n' Roll* and *Second Coming*—which garnered some fair critical notices and led to some recording sessions with Delaney and Bonnie and Canned Heat. He also performed at the Toronto Pop Festival, coverage of which is included in D. A. Pennebaker's documentary of the event, *Keep On Rockin'* (a.k.a. *Toronto Pop,* 1970) (1972). Richard did some late-night talk shows and club dates during the early Seventies, but by the decade's close he was again stressing his attachment to the church, preaching and singing gospel, and renouncing rock & roll, drugs and his own homosexuality (he has alluded to having reformed to heterosexuality). He appeared on the 1982 Grammy Awards telecast.

LITTLE RIVER BAND

Formed 1975, Melbourne, Australia
Beeb Birtles (b. Holland), gtr.; Graham Goble (b. 1944, Austral.), gtr.; Glenn Shorrock (b. Eng.), lead voc.; Roger McLachlan (b. New Zealand), bass; Derek Pellicci (b. Eng.), drums; Rick Formosa (b. Italy), gtr.
1975—*Little River Band* (Capitol) **1976**—(− Formosa; − McLachlan; + David Briggs, gtr., voc.; + George McArdale, bass) *After Hours* **1977**—*Diamantina Cocktail* **1978**—*Sleeper Catcher* **1979**—(− McArdale; + Barry Sullivan, bass; + Mal Logan [b. New Zealand], kybds.) *First under the Wire* **1980**—(− Briggs; + Wayne Nelson, voc., bass; + Steve Housden, gtr.) *Backstage Pass* **1982**—(− Shorrock; + John Farnham [b. Adelaide, Austral.], voc.).

Australia's Little River Band has enjoyed numerous hits in America with their vocal-harmony country-pop. The band began in 1975 from the ashes of a CSN&Y-type group called Mississippi. Though they were formed in Australia, only Graham Goble was born there. Glenn Shorrock, born in England, moved to Australia as a teenager and was part of one of the country's most successful Sixties teenybop bands, the Twilights (their big local competition was the Easybeats). At the same time, Beeb Birtles played in the successful Aussie band Zoot, who used to dress entirely in pink. Rick Formosa was invited to join the Edgar Winter band at 16, but his parents made him turn the offer down.

In 1972, Shorrock moved to England, joined the classical-rock band Esperanto and later did studio sessions with

Cliff Richard. There, in 1975, he met Birtles, Goble and Pellicci, who'd just broken up Mississippi, and the four agreed to form a new band (taking their name from a road sign) back in Melbourne, eventually with McLachlan (bass) and Formosa (guitar). They signed with Harvest and released their eponymous debut in 1976, which included the #28 U.S. hit "It's a Long Way There." Before the first U.S. tour in 1976, Formosa and McLachlan left.

The band's next American record was a "best of" from two Australian LPs. It was called *Diamantina Cocktail* and included the breakthrough hit "Help Is on the Way" (#14, 1977). They also scored big with "Lady" (#10, 1979), "Reminiscing" (#3, 1978) and in late 1979 with "Lonesome Loser" (#6), which made their fifth U.S. LP, *First under the Wire*, platinum. McArdale left after a January 1979 U.S. tour (he gave away all his money and moved into Australia's Blue Mountains for a three-year Bible study course).

In the spring of 1980, the band released a double live album and David Briggs was replaced by Wayne Nelson. In early 1982, Shorrock left to go solo. He was replaced by John Farnham, a pop singer from Adelaide. Shorrock began working on his first solo album for Capitol with former LRB producer John Boylan. The band scored another Top Ten single in late 1981 with "Take It Easy on Me" from *Time Exposure*, produced by George Martin.

LITTLE WALTER
Born Marion Walter Jacobs, May 1, 1930, Marksville, Louisiana; died February 15, 1968, Chicago
N.A.—*The Best of Little Walter* (Chess) *Little Walter and His Jukes* (Python) **1970**—*Quarter to Twelve* (Red Lightnin').

Whether or not Little Walter was actually the first person to amplify the harmonica, as has been claimed, he was a pioneer in using the microphone to bring out the moaning, echoing and hornlike sounds that are basic to modern blues harmonica.

Jacobs began playing the harmonica as a child in the South, and he attracted the attention of Muddy Waters, with whom he often recorded and toured in the late Fifties. When the blues scene centralized in Chicago and went electric in the Fifties, with Waters as one of its stars, Walter moved north. He joined Waters' band and started releasing his own records. The instrumental "Juke" was a #1 hit on the R&B charts in 1952, one of the biggest hits of any Delta-Chicago bluesman.

Throughout the Fifties, Little Walter placed records in the R&B Top Ten: "Sad Hours," "Blues with a Feeling," "Mean Old World," "You Better Watch Yourself," "You're So Fine," "Key to the Highway" and his other #1 record, "My Babe." He toured with the Aces, formerly Junior Wells's band, breaking out of the blues circuit to play Harlem's Apollo and other large venues. And though he never made the pop charts, his reputation and influence were widespread, especially in England,

where a generation of harmonica players learned from his records and from his disciple Cyril Davies. Walter was stabbed in a street fight in Chicago and died within hours of coronary thrombosis.

NILS LOFGREN
Born 1952, Chicago
1975—*Nils Lofgren* (A&M) **1976**—*Cry Tough; Back It Up!!* **1977**—*I Came to Dance; Night After Night* **1979**—*Nils* **1981**—*Night Fades Away* (Backstreet).

Pop-rock singer/songwriter/guitarist Nils Lofgren was the leader of Grin and later led his own bands. He moved with his parents to Maryland, near Washington, D.C., as a child, and there he began playing accordion at age five and studied jazz and classical music before turning to rock at 15.

He formed Grin in 1969 with bassist Bob Gordon and drummer Bob Berberich (later adding younger brother Tom on second guitar). The group's local reputation attracted Neil Young and Danny Whitten of Crazy Horse, whom Nils met while they were touring through Maryland. At age 17, Lofgren played piano and sang on Young's 1970 LP *After the Goldrush*, and the next year he did a guest spot on Crazy Horse's debut LP, to which he also contributed two songs.

Instead of staying with Young or Crazy Horse, though, Lofgren used the credits to help him get a record contract for Grin. They signed to Spindizzy (a Columbia subsidiary), and their 1971 debut was critically praised for its tuneful ballads and tight melodic rockers, as was the followup, *1+1*, which included "White Lies." The single never passed #75, though, and Grin's tours failed to attract large audiences. In 1973, Young again asked Lofgren to take time out from Grin to join him for the *Tonight's the Night* tour. Lofgren agreed and later played on the 1975 album of the same name. In 1973, Grin signed with A&M, but *Gone Crazy* was not well received. That and the group's financial problems caused them to disband in mid-1974. Later that year, when Mick Taylor left the Stones, it was rumored that Lofgren was considered as a replacement, but this has never been confirmed.

Lofgren signed with A&M and debuted in 1975 with the acclaimed *Nils Lofgren*. In 1976 he followed it with *Cry Tough*, produced by Al Kooper. He began to build a following, largely on the strength of live shows, captured on a promotional-only live LP entitled *Back It Up!!* and later on a less-well-received double live set, *Night After Night*. *Nils* included three songs Lofgren had cowritten with Lou Reed. (A different three written by the two appear on Reed's *The Bells* LP.) In 1980, Lofgren signed with Backstreet Records, who issued *Night Fades Away*.

LOGGINS AND MESSINA
Kenny Loggins, born January 7, 1948, Everett, Washington; Jim Messina, born December 5, 1947, Maywood, California

1972—*Kenny Loggins with Jim Messina Sittin' In* (Columbia) *Loggins and Messina* **1973**—*Full Sail* **1974**—*On Stage; Motherlode* **1975**—*So Fine* **1976**—*Native Sons; The Best of Friends* **1978**—*Finale* **1980**—*Best of.*

The highly successful Loggins and Messina partnership began by accident. Ex-Poco and Buffalo Springfield guitarist Jim Messina agreed to act as producer of Kenny Loggins' solo album, but during the recording sessions the two discovered their styles complemented one another and decided to form a band, which scored a string of country-pop hits.

Jim Messina was raised in Harlingen, Texas, and began playing guitar at age five. He was 12 when his parents moved back to California. After graduating high school in 1965, Messina began doing studio work at Harmony Recorders Audio Sound, Wally Heider and Sunset Sound, where in late 1967 he met the Buffalo Springfield while they were recording their second LP, *Buffalo Springfield Again.* He wound up producing and playing bass on their final LP, *Last Time Around,* and then he formed Poco with fellow ex-Springfield Richie Furay. After two years and three albums, he left Poco in November 1970 to become an independent producer for Columbia; his first project was to be Kenny Loggins.

Their live debut at the Troubadour in Los Angeles was billed as the Kenny Loggins Band with Jim Messina. On Loggins and Messina's 1972 debut album, Messina was billed as *Sittin' In.* The debut album took a slow climb up the charts but eventually went gold, aided by one of its tunes, "Danny's Song," which became a Top Ten hit for Anne Murray. It also included the light Caribbean FM hit "Vahevalla."

The duo's second LP was their first equal billing and gave them the hit single "Your Mama Don't Dance." The album went gold, as did the followup, *Full Sail.* Although generally dismissed by critics, Loggins and Messina continued to sell more gold records. Their reworking of Fifties hits, *So Fine,* sold disappointingly, and even though their final and seventh LP, *Native Sons,* went gold, they broke up in November 1976. Loggins, who went on to a hugely popular solo career, claims his and Messina's partnership was an informal union (each was contracted separately to Columbia), and they always thought each LP would be their last together.

KENNY LOGGINS

Born January 7, 1948, Everett, Washington
1977—*Celebrate Me Home* (Columbia) **1978**—*Nightwatch* **1979**—*Keep the Fire* **1980**—*Alive* **1982**—*High Adventure.*

Singer/songwriter Kenny Loggins has been successful both as half of the duo Loggins and Messina and later as a solo artist. He began playing guitar while in the seventh grade of a parochial school in California. His father was a traveling salesman, and the family had lived in Detroit and Seattle before settling in Alhambra, California. In college, Loggins joined a folk group, but by the late Sixties he had turned to rock, first in Gator Creek, who recorded for Mercury, and then in Second Helping, on Viva Records. In 1969, he left Second Helping and worked for $100 a week as a songwriter for ABC Records' publishing outlet, Wingate Music. Around this time, he toured with the remnants of the Electric Prunes.

Back in Los Angeles, Loggins met Jim Ibbotson of the Nitty Gritty Dirt Band. Ibbotson and the band decided to record four of Loggins' songs on their *Uncle Charlie and His Dog Teddy;* one of them, "House at Pooh Corner," was a minor hit. In 1971, Don Ellis, an A&R staffer at Columbia (who was also a close family friend), introduced Loggins to Jim Messina, who was looking for acts to produce. Clive Davis signed Loggins to the label, and the singer spent the year working up material with Messina, leading to their informal joint debut. Their union wound up lasting five years, yielding seven successful albums before the split in late 1976.

By 1977, Loggins had released his solo debut, *Celebrate Me Home.* His solo music continued in the same pop-rock style as Loggins and Messina's, and it netted him tremendous success on his second LP, 1978's platinum *Nightwatch,* which included the #5 single "Whenever I Call You 'Friend' " (cowritten with Melissa Manchester and featuring a vocal by Stevie Nicks). The first album eventually went platinum as well. Loggins' equally successful *Keep the Fire* boasted "This Is It" (#11, 1979). Loggins cowrote the Doobie Brothers' 1979 hit "What a Fool Believes." He had a hit in 1980 with "I'm Alright" (#7), the theme song from the film *Caddy Shack.*

JACKIE LOMAX

Born May 10, 1944, Liverpool, England
1969—*Is This What You Want?* (Apple) **1971**—*Home Is in My Head* (Warner Bros.) **1972**—*Three* **1976**—*Livin' for Lovin'* (Capitol) **1977**—*Did You Ever Have That Feeling?*

Jackie Lomax is a well-traveled British singer. He began playing blues-tinged rock at age 16 and his second group, the Undertakers, played Hamburg at the same time as the Beatles. Lomax signed with Beatles manager Brian Epstein, who formed a new band around him called the Lomax Alliance. After Epstein died, Lomax became the first to sign for the Beatles' Apple Records. A single, "Sour Milk Sea," written and produced by George Harrison, was released in 1968, and *Is This What You Want?* was produced by Harrison and featured Eric Clapton, Ringo Starr and Paul McCartney.

Because Apple's business accounts were not complete, no one knows how the album sold, although some say as many as 50,000 copies. After playing a short while with the band Heavy Jelly (who got started by planting a fake review in a London magazine for a show they'd never done), Lomax, disillusioned with life in England, moved to Woodstock, New York, in 1970.

After two more solo albums, *Home Is in My Head* and *Three*, Lomax returned to England in 1974 and joined Badger—previously a semi-progressive band headed by ex-Yes keyboardist Tony Kaye. Allen Toussaint produced one disappointing album, *White Lady*, and then, after a disastrous London debut, the band broke up.

Lomax then moved to Los Angeles, where he eventually got another solo contract with Capitol in 1975. His first LP for the label, *Livin' for Lovin'*, came out in late 1975. A 1977 followup, *Did You Ever Have That Feeling?*, also failed to click and he lost his contract.

LOS BRAVOS

Formed 1965, Spain
Michael Kogel (b. Apr. 25, 1945, Berlin), lead voc., gtr.; Manuel Fernandez (b. Sep. 29, 1943, Seville), kybds.; Miguel Vicens Danus (b. June 21, 1944, Palma de Mallorca), bass; Pablo Sanllehi, a.k.a. Pablo Gomez (b. Nov. 5, 1943, Barcelona), drums; Antonio Martinez (b. Oct. 3, 1945, Madrid), gtr.

Los Bravos became the first Spanish rock band to have an international hit single when "Black Is Black" reached #4 in 1966. A combination of local bands Mike and the Runaways (who had several hits in Spain during the early Sixties) and Los Sonor, they were signed to British Decca after Decca's Spanish representative sent one of the group's singles to producer Ivor Raymonde. Though Los Bravos were unable to ever match the sales of "Black Is Black," "Going Nowhere" and "Bring a Little Lovin' " were minor successes in 1966 and 1968 respectively, and "I Don't Care" climbed to #16 on the British charts in 1966. By the end of the decade, their popularity was confined to Spain. In 1972, Kogel had a minor hit single, "Louisiana," under the name Mike Kennedy.

JOHN D. LOUDERMILK

Born March 31, 1934, Durham, North Carolina
N.A.—*Language of Love* (RCA)   *Twelve Sides of Loudermilk*   **1966**—*John D. Loudermilk Sings a Bizarre Collection of the Most Unusual Songs*   **1967**—*Suburban Attitudes*   **1968**—*Country Love Songs*   **1969**—*The Open Mind of John Loudermilk*   **1971**—*Volume 1- Elloree* (Warner Bros.)   **1973**—*Best of John D. Loudermilk* (RCA)   **1975**—*Encores*   **1978**—*Just Passing Through* (MIM).

Though he's made recordings of his own, John D. Loudermilk is generally known as the writer of "Tobacco Road" and hits for George Hamilton IV, Eddie Cochran, Paul Revere and the Raiders, Anne Murray and many others.

Growing up in Durham, Loudermilk first played a multitude of instruments with a Salvation Army band. When he was 13, he already had his own local radio show (under the

name Johnny Dee). His big break came a few years later when, while working as a staff musician for local TV station WTVD, he performed his own "A Rose and a Baby Ruth" on the air. It was heard by a freshman at the University of North Carolina, George Hamilton IV, who recorded it and sold a million copies. (Hamilton also had a Top Ten country hit with Loudermilk's "Abilene" in 1963.) In 1957, Loudermilk's "Sittin' on the Balcony" became the first hit for Eddie Cochran (#18; Loudermilk's version hit #38 during the same period), and in 1959 a song he wrote with Marijohm Wilkin, "Waterloo," became a million-seller for Stonewall Jackson.

Most of Loudermilk's songs had a country feel, but he also had a solid rock and pop sense, as in his "Indian Reservation," a #1 hit for Paul Revere and the Raiders in 1971. Two more of his songs became standards, "Break My Mind" and "Bad News." Loudermilk himself recorded with only minor success for RCA in the early Sixties and for Warner Bros. in the Seventies.

LOVE

Formed 1965, Los Angeles
Arthur Lee (b. ca. 1944, Memphis), gtr., voc.; Bryan MacLean (b. ca. 1947, Los Angeles), gtr., voc.; John Echols (b. ca. 1945, Memphis), lead gtr.; Ken Forssi (b. ca. 1943, Cleveland), bass; Don Conka, drums; Alban "Snoopy" Pfisterer (b. ca. 1947, Switz.), drums.
1966—*Love* (Elektra)   (+ Michael Stuart, drums; + Tjay Cantrelli, horns; Pfisterer switches to kybds.) **1967**—*Da Capo*   (- Pfisterer; - Cantrelli)   **1968**— *Forever Changes*   (- MacLean; - Echols; - Forssi; - Stuart; + Frank Fayad, bass; + George Suranovitch, drums; + Jay Donnellan, gtr.)   **1969**—*Four Sail; Out Here* (Blue Thumb)   (- Donnellan; + Gary Rowles, gtr.)   **1970**—*False Start*   **1974**—(Band reforms: + Lee; + Melvan Whittington, lead gtr.; + John Sterling, rhythm gtr.; + Sherwood Akuna, bass; + Joe Blocker, drums; + Herman McCormick, congas)   *Reel to Real* (RSO)   **1975**—(Band breaks up again; periodic reunions in late 1970s).

Love, headed by singer/guitarist Arthur Lee, were a seminal Sixties L.A. band, emerging from the Sunset Strip at the same time as the Byrds, Buffalo Springfield, the Doors and the Mamas and the Papas. They started out playing a Byrds-influenced folk rock, but later covered many styles, including bluesy R&B, pop and hard rock. Arthur Lee still performs on the L.A. club circuit.

Lee moved from his Memphis birthplace to L.A. with his family when he was five. By age 17 he was playing in local bands, including Arthur Lee and the LAGs (styled after Booker T. and the MGs). The band, which included later Love member John Echols, cut one single for Capitol, an instrumental, "The Ninth Wave." Love was formed with all unknown musicians: MacLean had been a roadie for the Byrds, and Forssi had played with the Surfaris after their hits faded. Lee originally called the group the Grassroots, but changed it, since the name was already taken by another soon-to-be-well-known band.

Their first album was hailed by critics as a classic in the new folk-rock style and sold 150,000 copies. Their 1966 single "My Little Red Book" (penned by Burt Bacharach and Hal David) was a hit. The band's second album, *Da Capo,* featured some topically druggy lyrics, jazz touches and a few personnel changes. The album was another groundbreaker, featuring one of the first side-long cuts in rock, the twenty-minute-long "Revelation." The album also included the hit "Seven and Seven Is." *Forever Changes,* however, is considered by many to be Love's best, their answer to *Sgt. Pepper,* with orchestral touches, including horn and string arrangements, and a psychedelic feel that influenced many of the early-Eighties neo-psychedelic British bands like the Monochrome Set, the Teardrop Explodes and Echo and the Bunnymen.

In 1968 Lee reorganized the group and hired a new band of three, plus four sessionmen to help out in the studio on *Four Sail* and *Out Here;* he briefly renamed himself Arthurly. Love next toured England (they seldom left L.A.), and Lee recorded a full LP with Jimi Hendrix. The album was buried in legal problems, though one track, "The Everlasting First," turned up on *False Start* in 1970. In 1971, Lee dismissed his band.

Lee was supposed to have recorded a solo album for Columbia, but his debut wound up on A&M in 1972, the hard-rocking *Vindicator,* credited to Arthur Lee and Band Aid. Like later Love LPs, the record didn't sell well. In 1973, he planned to make another solo album with Paul Rothchild's new Buffalo Records, but the label folded before the LP was released. In 1974, Lee came back on RSO with an all-new Love, but the music disappointed many and included three remakes of old Love cuts. His next effort was a solo EP in 1977 on Da Capo Records. In 1979, he toured locally with MacLean and another incarnation of Love, and in 1980 Rhino Records put out *Best of Love,* a compilation of Sixties tunes. In 1981, the label issued a new Arthur Lee solo LP, his first in seven years.

DARLENE LOVE
Born Darlene Wright, 1938, Los Angeles

As one of Phil Spector's hand-picked early-Sixties girl-group singers, Darlene Love sang some lead vocals with the Crystals, Bob B. Soxx and the Blue Jeans, and also had hits under her own name.

Darlene Wright started singing in 1958 with a L.A. vocal group called the Blossoms. (Her sister Edna later sang with Honey Cone.) As a foursome, the Blossoms recorded without success for Capitol Records between 1958 and 1960, and then recorded as a trio for Challenge and Okeh. They also did backup singing on the L.A. session circuit,

supporting Bobby Darin, Nino Tempo and April Stevens, James Darren and others.

When Love came to the attention of Spector, he put her in front of the Crystals for their only #1 hit, "He's a Rebel" (1962). She also sang lead on their "He's Sure the Boy I Love" (#11, 1963) and in the short-lived vocal trio Bob B. Soxx and the Blue Jeans, who had a hit with "Zip-A-Dee Doo-Dah" (#8 pop, #7 R&B, 1963) from the Walt Disney movie *Song of the South.* All of these recordings were on Spector's Philles label. Darlene Love next went on to record six singles on that label under her own name, including "Wait till My Baby Gets Home" (#26, 1963), "(Today I Met) The Boy I'm Gonna Marry" (#39, 1963) and "A Fine Fine Boy" (#53, 1963). She also appears on Phil Spector's classic Christmas album. Love continued to sing with the Blossoms throughout the Sixties. They were regulars on "Shindig," and they toured with Elvis Presley in the early Seventies.

LOVERBOY
Formed 1979, Calgary, Canada
Paul Dean, gtr.; Mike Reno, voc.; Doug Johnson, kybds.; Matt Frenette, drums; Scott Smith, bass.
1980—*Loverboy* (Columbia)   **1981**—*Get Lucky*
1983—*Keep It Up.*

Paul Dean had been involved with 13 unsuccessful Canadian bands (including Streetheart) before meeting Mike Reno, himself a veteran of many groups, having recorded with Moxy. They teamed up originally to work as a studio-based duo à la Steely Dan. But when record-company interest hinged on their forming a band, they held auditions. Doug Johnson, Matt Frenette and Scott Smith were chosen, and the quintet was named Loverboy (Coverboy was also under consideration). Their modernized, new wave–tinged heavy metal became the surprise hit of 1981 as, buoyed by the group's incessant touring, their self-titled debut album went gold and hatched two hit singles: "Turn Me Loose" (#35, 1981) and "The Kid Is Hot Tonite" (#55, 1981). Their second album, *Get Lucky,* featured the hit single "Working for the Weekend" (#29, 1981). Both LPs have gone platinum.

LENE LOVICH
Born Detroit
1979—*Stateless* (Stiff/Epic)   *Flex*   **1981**—*New Toy* (EP)   **1983**—*No Man's Land.*

Though she has had hit singles in England and Europe, Lene Lovich has yet to reach the American singles charts. Her Slavic-milkmaid getup and ululating vocals are distinctive, to say the least, and they fit the oddball lyrics and pop hooks devised by Lovich and cowriter Les Chappell.

Lovich was born in Detroit and moved to England when she was 13. After studying sculpture at London's Central School of Art, she took part in experimental theater, worked as a go-go dancer, played all manner of music and became interested in dream images (inspiring her to visit Salvador Dali). She and Chappell joined the soul-funk band the Diversions in 1975, with whom she made five singles, the last of which featured the Lovich-Chappell composition "Happy Christmas." In 1978, author and disc jockey Charlie Gillett introduced Lovich to Stiff Records' president, Dave Robinson. A few months later, Stiff issued her version of Tommy James and the Shondells' "I Think We're Alone Now" and put her on the "Be Stiff Tour '78" with Rachel Sweet, the Records, Wreckless Eric, Mickey Jupp and Jona Lewie.

After American record companies refused her debut LP (as well as those by most other "Be Stiff" artists), the tour came to New York. Epic Records got interested, and in the summer of 1979, almost a year after its release in the U.K., *Stateless* came out in the U.S. In England, "Lucky Number" and "Say When" (written by James O'Neill of Fingerprintz) had become hit records, as did "Bird Song," the first single off *Flex*, released in 1980. "New Toy," the title track of Lovich's six-song mini-LP of 1981, was another British success that failed to crack the U.S. charts, although it was a rock-disco favorite; its writer, Thomas Dolby, subsequently started a successful solo career. In addition to her records, Lovich also costarred with Herman Brood and Nina Hagen in the 1979 film *Cha-Cha* and in the title role of the 1983 film *Mata Hari*.

LOVIN' SPOONFUL

Formed 1965, New York City
John Sebastian (b. Mar. 17, 1944, New York City), gtr., autoharp, harmonica, lead voc.; Steve Boone (b. Sep. 23, 1943, Camp Lejeune, N.C.), bass; Zal Yanovsky (b. Dec. 19, 1944, Toronto), lead gtr., voc.; Joe Butler (b. Jan. 19, 1943, N.Y.), drums.
1967—(− Yanovsky; + Jerry Yester, gtr.) *Best of, Volume 1* (Kama Sutra) 1968—*Best of, Volume 2* 1970—*Greatest Hits*.

Electrified jug band the Lovin' Spoonful had two years as New York's leading folk-rockers. Their sound was dubbed "good time music," and when the good times stopped in 1967 after publicity about the arrest of Steve Boone and Zal Yanovsky for drugs, so did their hits.

John Sebastian and Yanovsky founded the Spoonful; they had been members of the Mugwumps with future Mamas and Papas Cass Elliot and Denny Doherty (as immortalized on the Mamas and Papas' "Creeque Alley"). Their first single, Sebastian's "Do You Believe in Magic," went Top Ten in 1965, as did its followup, "You Didn't Have to Be So Nice," in early 1966. More hits followed in 1966 and 1967: "Daydream," "Summer in the City" (their lone #1), "Rain on the Roof" and "Nashville Cats." During their peak period, the Spoonful made three albums and also provided the soundtracks to Francis Ford Coppola's *You're a Big Boy Now* and Woody Allen's *What's Up, Tiger Lily?*

But that ended after Boone and Yanovsky reportedly set up someone they knew in a drug bust in May 1966. Apparently, both Boone and Yanovsky were arrested in Berkeley for possession of marijuana and, in exchange for the police department *not* prosecuting, the two introduced an undercover narcotics agent to an acquaintance who purchased drugs, resulting in the acquaintance's arrest. The ensuing publicity created a public outcry calling for a boycott of their records and concerts. Yanovsky left the group. He was replaced by Jerry Yester, the former producer of the Association, which included his brother Jim Yester. Though the hits didn't stop altogether ("She Is Still a Mystery," for instance), the Spoonful's popularity was waning. After one LP without Yanovsky, *Everything Playing*, Sebastian, who wrote and sang most of the songs, left to start his solo career.

The group broke up in 1968. Butler formed a new Lovin' Spoonful and put out an album, *Revelation: Revolution '69*, with no success. Yester recorded *Farewell Aldebaran* with his wife, Judy Henske (coproduced by Yanovsky), and formed the band Rosebud, which made one album. He has continued to work as a producer, credited on Tom Waits's first album. The original Lovin' Spoonful reunited in 1980 to perform "Do You Believe in Magic" in Paul Simon's film *One Trick Pony*.

NICK LOWE

Born March 25, 1949, England
1978—*Pure Pop for Now People* (Columbia) 1979—*Labour of Lust* 1982—*Nick the Knife* 1983—*The Abominable Showman*.

After more than five years with pub-rockers Brinsley Schwarz, Nick Lowe began writing more openly sardonic pop songs while performing with Rockpile and producing. The son of a Royal Air Force officer, Lowe grew up in England and the Mideast. His first band, Kippington Lodge, eventually became Brinsley Schwarz, for which Lowe did much of the songwriting.

When Brinsley Schwarz broke up in 1975, Lowe began releasing singles under a variety of names, honing his broad ironic streak and his unapologetic talent for lifting other people's hooks. For "Bay City Rollers, We Love You" and "Rollers Show," Lowe recorded as the Tartan Horde ("Rollers Show" later turned up on *Pure Pop*). "Let's Go to the Disco" was supposedly by the Disco Bros. In 1976, Lowe launched Stiff Records with "So It Goes" b/w "Heart of the City"; he also recorded "I Love My Label." In the next year, working as staff producer, he oversaw records by Elvis Costello, Mickey Jupp (whose "Switchboard Susan" Lowe covered on *Labour of Lust*), the Damned, Wreckless Eric and Alberto y Los Trios Paranoias, as well as two records of his own. These included the EP *Bowi* (an "answer" to David Bowie's LP *Low*), which featured a version of Sandy Posey's "Born a Woman" and "Marie Provost," later on *Pure Pop*.

In late 1977, Lowe and Costello left Stiff to join label cofounder Jake Riviera's new venture, Radar Records. He had his first British hit with "I Love the Sound of Breaking Glass," which was included on that year's LP *Pure Pop* (*Jesus of Cool* in the U.K.). *Labour of Lust,* though billed as a solo album, was really the work of Rockpile. It yielded Lowe's only American Top Forty single, "Cruel to Be Kind."

Over the years, Lowe has remained an active producer, working on five of Costello's albums, several LPs by Graham Parker and the Rumour, one by Dr. Feelgood, and the Pretenders' debut single, in addition to his wife Carlene Carter's *Musical Shapes* and *Blue Nun* and a session with her father, Johnny Cash, who performed Lowe's "Without Love" (off *Labour of Lust*).

In 1981, Rockpile disbanded and Lowe resumed his solo career, releasing *Nick the Knife* and returning to the road with a band alternately known as the Chaps and Noise to Go that included former Rumour guitarist Martin Belmont, ex-Ace/Squeeze pianist Paul Carrack (for whom Lowe produced a solo album) and Lowe playing rhythm guitar instead of bass.

LULU
Born Marie McDonald McLaughlin Lawrie, November 3, 1948, Lennox Castle, Scotland
1967—*To Sir with Love* (Epic) **1970**—*New Routes* (Atco) **1979**—*Don't Take Love for Granted* (Rocket) **1981**—*Lulu* (Alfa).

At age 19, Lulu recorded "To Sir with Love," the title theme from the movie in which she costarred with Sidney Poitier. It quickly went to #1 on the U.S. charts, becoming the first hit by an artist from the U.K. to hit the top of the U.S. charts without ever entering the British charts. This success led her to much work on TV and on the cabaret circuit. Before recording this pop ballad, however, she and her band, the Luvvers, had hit the British Top Ten with a cover of the Isley Brothers' hit "Shout." (Lulu's version hit #94 in the U.S. Top 100 in 1964 and #96 as a reissue in 1967 at the height of her U.S. popularity.)

Marie Lawrie made her show-business debut at age nine singing at Bridgeton Public Hall and soon began appearing regularly with a local accordion band. At age 14, she began singing weekend gigs in Glasgow clubs and by 15 was a regular in that area with her group the Glen Eagles. In 1964, her group was renamed Lulu and the Luvvers and hit the charts with "Shout."

In 1966, Lulu went solo (and became the first British female act to perform behind the Iron Curtain—in Poland), and in 1967 she hit the British Top Ten again with Neil Diamond's "The Boat That I Row." That year, her performance in *To Sir with Love* garnered raves as her version of the theme song hit #1 in the U.S.

In the late Sixties, Lulu worked as both TV personality and recording artist, and in 1969 she married Bee Gee Maurice Gibb (they divorced in 1973). With the production team of Jerry Wexler, Tom Dowd and Arif Mardin she recorded *New Routes* at Muscle Shoals in 1970, from which sprang the U.S. Top Thirty hit "Oh Me, Oh My, I'm a Fool for You, Baby."

In the early Seventies, she toured throughout the world, headlining in such places as Las Vegas and Berlin, and had her own prime-time BBC-TV weekly music series. She was absent until 1974, when she again hit the Top Ten with the David Bowie–arranged cover of his "The Man Who Sold the World," and from the U.S. charts until 1981, when she hit with "I Could Never Miss You (More Than I Do)" (#18) and "If I Were You" (#44).

LYDIA LUNCH
Born 1959
1980—*Queen of Siam* (Ze) **1981**—*Eight-Eyed Spy* (Fetish) *Pre-Teenage Jesus* (EP) (Ze) *13.13* (Ruby).

At 17, Lydia Lunch was one of New York's first "no wave" artists with her band Teenage Jesus and the Jerks. Working with a variety of bassists, Lunch (vocals and guitar)—alternately shrieking and chanting in a monotone—and Bradly Field (drum [*sic*]) recorded two singles (later collected on a 12-inch), four cuts for Brian Eno's *No New York* compilation, and an EP (pre–Teenage Jesus) featuring original member James Chance (then Siegfried) on saxophone before he left the band to form the Contortions. A side project of the period was Beirut Slump, whose lone 45 included sometime-Jerk Jim Sclavunos on bass and filmmaker Vivienne Dick on violin. Lunch also starred in three of Dick's super 8mm movies, as well as in Beth and Scott B's *Black Box, The Offenders* and, in 1982, *Vortex* (which debuted at the New York Film Festival).

In 1980, Lunch left "no wave" behind and recorded *Queen of Siam* with the aid of ex–Contortions/John Cale bassist George Scott (a.k.a. Jack Ruby), saxophonist Pat Irwin, ex-Voidoid and Teenage Jesus producer Robert Quine on guitar and big-band arranger Billy Ver Planck, the composer of the theme to *The Flintstones*. Concurrently, Lunch, Scott, Irwin, Sclavunos (on drums) and guitarist Michael Paumgardhen started the bluesy Eight-Eyed Spy. Scott's death in 1980 kept Eight-Eyed Spy from making a full studio LP, though a combination of live performances and studio work with Irwin on bass filled a posthumous cassette and an album.

With the end of Eight-Eyed Spy, Irwin concentrated on his instrumental group, the Raybeats, while Sclavunos and Paumgardhen joined Lunch's Devil Dogs. But turnover in personnel and a repertoire of cover songs kept that group from recording. Instead, Lunch moved to California and started 13.13. The lineup of the group has been typically fluid (one version included three members of early L.A. punk rockers the Weirdos). In 1981, Lunch appeared on an EP with members of the English avant-punk group Birthday Party. Lunch has also collaborated with X's Exene on a book of poetry entitled *Adulterers Anonymous*, which was issued by Grove Press on Halloween 1982.

FRANKIE LYMON AND THE TEENAGERS

Formed 1954, New York City

Frankie Lymon (b. Sep. 30, 1942, New York City; d. Feb. 28, 1968), lead voc.; Sherman Garnes (b. June 8, 1940, New York City; d. 1978), bass; Joe Negroni (b. Sep. 9, 1940, New York City; d. 1977), baritone; Herman Santiago (b. Feb. 18, 1941, New York City), first tenor; Jimmy Merchant (b. Feb. 10, 1940, New York City), second tenor.

1956—*Why Do Fools Fall in Love* (Gee).

When he was 13, Frankie Lymon had a #1 R&B (#6 pop) record with "Why Do Fools Fall in Love?" At 18, his career was over; eight years later, he died of a heroin overdose. The rags-to-riches-to-rags story began in New York, where Lymon and the Teenagers were school friends who sang on street corners. In 1955, Richard Barrett of the Valentines heard them and arranged for the group to be signed by his record label, Gee. At this time, they were known as the Premieres, but were soon renamed by Gee executives. "Why Do Fools Fall in Love?", credited to Lymon and producer George Goldner, was their first record. Originally, Santiago was to sing the tune, but when he begged off with a sore throat, Lymon took lead, and his boy soprano became the group's trademark.

"Fools" was one of four Top Twenty R&B songs off the Teenagers' debut album; the others were "I Promise to Remember" (#10, 1956), "I Want You to Be My Girl" (#3, 1956) and "The ABC's of Love" (#14, 1956). The LP also included "I'm Not a Juvenile Delinquent," which the group sang in the film *Rock, Rock, Rock* in 1956. A year later, after appearing in another movie, *Mr. Rock and Roll*, Lymon left the group for a solo career.

The Teenagers continued without him, but were unsuccessful. Lymon, too, fell on hard times, mostly due to his worsening drug addiction. His first 45, "Goody Goody," was a modest hit (#20 pop, 1957); subsequent records were outright flops. A comeback attempt in 1960 with Bobby Day's "Little Bitty Pretty One" hit #58. In 1980, Santiago and Merchant recruited Pearl McKinnon and, in 1981, Derek Ventura, and started performing once more as the Teenagers. "Why Do Fools Fall in Love?" has proven its durability, becoming a hit record again for the Happenings in 1967 and for Diana Ross in 1981.

BARBARA LYNN

Born Barbara Lynn Ozen, January 16, 1942, Beaumont, Texas

1976—*Here Is Barbara Lynn* (Oval).

Barbara Lynn is a New Orleans R&B singer (and left-handed guitar player) with a bluesy voice and a casual, low-key style. Her first and biggest hit, the New Orleans standard "You'll Lose a Good Thing" (#8 pop, #1 R&B, 1962), was written by the 16-year-old Lynn as a poem. She was discovered singing blues in Louisiana clubs by New Orleans musician/arranger Huey P. Meaux, who subsequently produced all her records. Most of her early hits—including "You're Gonna Need Me" (#13 R&B, 1963) and "It's Better to Have It" (#26 R&B, 1965)—were recorded in Cosimo Matassa's New Orleans studio but were released by Philadelphia-based Jamie Records.

In 1966, Lynn signed to Meaux's Tribe label, but recorded no hits. In 1968, she went to Atlantic, hitting with "This Is the Thanks I Get" (#39 R&B, 1968) and "(Until Then) I'll Suffer" (#31 R&B, 1971). The Rolling Stones covered her "Oh! Baby (We Got a Good Thing Goin')" on *Rolling Stones Now!*

LORETTA LYNN

Born Loretta Webb, April 14, 1935, Butcher Hollow, Kentucky

N.A.—*Loretta Lynn Sings 'Em and Writes 'Em; Coal Miner's Daughter* (Decca)   *Loretta Lynn* (MCA)
1974—*Loretta Lynn's Greatest Hits*   **1976**—*When the Tingle Becomes a Chill*   **1977**—*I Remember Patsy*.
Loretta Lynn and Conway Twitty: 1979—*The Very Best of Loretta and Conway* (MCA).

Country singer and songwriter Loretta Lynn grew up in the remote, poverty-stricken town of Butcher Hollow, Kentucky. (Her sister is the more pop-oriented Crystal Gayle.) Named after Loretta Young, Lynn didn't do much singing in her early youth. Instead, after one month of dating, she was married at age 13 to Moony (Moonshine) Lynn (he was 19), who took her 3,000 miles away to Custer, Washington, where he worked in logging camps. Lynn became a mother at 14 and had four children in her first four years of marriage. (She was a grandmother at 32.) Besides taking care of the kids, taking in other people's laundry and occasionally making extra money by picking strawberries with migrant workers, Lynn began writing songs on her Sears Roebuck guitar. Her husband encouraged her to go public and became her manager, lining up shows at local bars and clubs. At age 18, Lynn cut a record for the California Zero label, "I'm A Honky Tonk Girl," which she and Moony promoted themselves by visiting radio stations around the country. They worked their way to Nashville, and the song eventually became a #14 hit on the national country & western charts.

Once in Nashville, Lynn persuaded Ott Devine, manager of the Grand Ole Opry, to book her, and she first appeared there in October 1960. An appearance with Buck Owens led to a contract with Decca (now MCA), for whom she's made over thirty records over a period of twenty years. Her first Decca hit, produced by Owen Bradley in 1962, was called "Success." Since then, she has had many #1 country hits, including the standard "Don't Come Home Drinkin' (With Lovin' on Your Mind)" (1966), "Fist City" (1968), "Woman of the World" (1969) and the autobiographical "Coal Miner's Daughter" (1970). Also in 1970 she began touring regularly with Conway Twitty, releasing many joint hits like "As Soon As I Hang Up the Phone" and "You're the Reason Our Kids Are Ugly." Lynn was the first woman ever to win the Entertainer of the Year Award from the Country Music Association, in 1972. Her self-penned controversial hit "The Pill" in 1975 was seen by some as a down-home feminist classic.

In 1976, Lynn (with *New York Times* reporter George Vecsey) wrote her autobiography, *Coal Miner's Daughter,* and it became one of the ten biggest-selling books of that year. In 1980, a movie based on the book came out starring Sissy Spacek, to much acclaim. (Spacek, who sang Lynn's songs in the film, won the Best Actress Oscar for her performance.) Loretta Lynn today is still recording for MCA and remains one of the most popular country stars.

LYNYRD SKYNYRD

Formed 1966, Jacksonville, Florida
Ronnie Van Zant (b. 1949; d. Oct. 20, 1977, Gillsburg, Miss.), voc.; Gary Rossington, gtr.; Allen Collins, gtr.; Billy Powell, kybds.; Leon Wilkeson, bass; Bob Burns, drums.
1973—(+ Ed King, gtr.) *Pronounced Leh-Nerd Skin-Nerd* (MCA) **1974**—*Second Helping* **1975**—(- King; - Burns; + Artimus Pyle [b. Spartanburg, S.C.], drums) *Nuthin' Fancy* **1976**—*Gimme Back My Bullets* (+ Steven Gaines [b. Seneca, Mo.; d. Oct. 20, 1977, Gillsburg, Miss.], gtr.) *One More from the Road* **1977**—*Street Survivors* **1978**—*Skynyrd's First . . . And Last* **1979**—*Gold and Platinum.*

Lynyrd Skynyrd were the most critically lauded and commercially successful of the Allman Brothers–influenced Southern bands. When they first rose to prominence in 1973, they epitomized regional pride that stressed a cocky, boisterous hard rock, as opposed to the Allmans' open-ended blues. When the band broke up in 1977 after a plane crash killed Ronnie Van Zant and Steve and Cassie Gaines, Southern rock suffered irreparable damage.

The nucleus of what would become Lynyrd Skynyrd first met in high school in their hometown, Jacksonville, Florida. Van Zant, Allen Collins and Gary Rossington formed the band My Backyard in 1965, eventually joined by Leon Wilkeson and Billy Powell. Their later name

Lynyrd Skynyrd: Leon Wilkeson, Allen Collins, Ronnie Van Zant, Gary Rossington, Artimus Pyle, Steve Gaines, Billy Powell

immortalized a gym teacher, Leonard Skinner, who was known to punish students who had long hair.

The band, with original drummer Bob Burns, were playing in Atlanta at a bar called Funocchio's in 1972 when they were spotted by Al Kooper, who was on a tour with Badfinger and also scouting bands for MCA's new Sounds of the South label. Kooper signed Skynyrd and produced their 1973 debut, *Pronounced Leh-Nerd Skin-Nerd*, adding session guitarist Ed King (late of Strawberry Alarm Clock). The group's initial hook was its three-guitar attack, topping the Allmans' trademark two-guitar leads. They first got major FM airplay with the long "Freebird," written as a tribute to Duane Allman, which eventually became an anthem for Skynyrd fans and—when revived, without lyrics, by the Rossington Collins Band in 1980—a tribute to Van Zant.

The band hooked up with the Who's *Quadrophenia* tour in 1973 and began to acquire a reputation as a live band. Their 1974 follow-up LP, the platinum *Second Helping*, also produced by Kooper, reached #12. It included another instant Southern standard, "Sweet Home Alabama," a reply to Neil Young's "Alabama" and "Southern Man." But Van Zant often wore a Neil Young T-shirt, and Young later offered the band several songs to record, though they never made it to vinyl.

In late 1974, King left, leaving the band with just two guitars, and in early 1975 Artimus Pyle joined as replacement for Burns. The band's third record went to #9, but 1976's *Gimme Back My Bullets,* produced by Tom Dowd, sold somewhat less. They recouped in October 1976 with the double live *One More from the Road,* recorded at Atlanta's Fox Theater, which went to #9, sold platinum and featured new third guitarist Steven Gaines, plus a trio of female backup singers, including Gaines's sister Cassie. The band became one of the biggest U.S. concert draws.

Street Survivors, their sixth LP, was released three days

before the plane crash of October 20, 1977. The band was traveling in a privately chartered plane between shows at Greenville, South Carolina, and Baton Rouge, Louisiana, when it crashed just outside Gillsburg, Mississippi, killing (along with three others) Van Zant, Steven Gaines and his sister Cassie. The rest escaped with injuries. Fuel shortage was a possible cause of the crash, although by the next year a lawsuit filed against the airline company faulted the plane's personnel and its mechanical integrity. Ironically, the cover of the band's last LP pictured them standing in flames and included an order form for a "Lynyrd Skynyrd survival kit." There was also a Van Zant composition about death called "That Smell." The LP cover was changed shortly after the accident, and the album went on to become one of their biggest sellers. The next year *Skynyrd's First . . . And Last* was released, consisting of previously unavailable early band recordings from 1970–72 (the band had planned on releasing it before the accident). It went platinum, and in early 1980 MCA released a "best of" called *Gold and Platinum*.

A new band finally emerged from Lynyrd Skynyrd's ashes in mid-1980 called the Rossington Collins Band (see separate entry) featuring three of the surviving members plus female lead singer Dale Krantz. In March 1982, Artimus Pyle toured with the Artimus Pyle Band.

M

MADNESS
Formed 1976, England
Lee Thompson, sax; Chris Foreman, gtr.; Mike Barson, kybds.; Dan Woodgate, drums; Mark Bedford, bass; Graham "Suggs" McPherson, voc.; Chas Smash, emcee, steps.
1979—*One Step Beyond* (Stiff) **1980**—*Absolutely* **1981**—*7* **1982**—*Complete Madness* (Stiff U.K.) *Rise and Fall* **1983**—*Madness* (Geffen).

Madness first came to prominence in 1978, along with the Specials, in the forefront of Great Britain's ska revival. (Ska was a pre-reggae Jamaican dance rhythm popular in the Sixties.) In time, Madness became a vaudevillian pop group, matching their self-proclaimed "nutty sound" to soul, R&B and music-hall music as well as ska and becoming a top singles band in Britain.

Lee Thompson, Mike Barson and Chris Foreman had been together since 1976 in the band Morris and the Minors. As group membership varied, Chas Smash and future Madness manager John Hassler auditioned as replacements without success; by 1978, Graham McPherson, Dan Woodgate and Mark Bedford had all joined the group, now known as the Invaders. That year they changed their name to Madness, after a favorite Prince Buster ska song.

In 1979, the Specials' 2-Tone label released "The Prince," dedicated to Prince Buster. When it reached #16 on the British charts, Madness signed with Stiff. Chas Smash joined as emcee and dancer, and Madness recorded *One Step Beyond;* the title cut became a Top Ten British single, and the album stayed in the British Top 75 for most of a year, peaking at #2, U.K. *Absolutely,* with the single "Baggy Trousers" (a Madness trademark onstage) also peaked at #2, as Madness began to broaden its style, becoming spokesmen for Cockney youth.

In 1981, Madness made a film about starting a group, *Take It or Leave It,* playing themselves. The album *7* included two more hits, "It Must Be Love" and "Cardiac Arrest," and Madness' first #1 British single, "House of Fun," which brought the LP to #1 as well.

But U.S. response to Madness was confined to concert audiences. *Rise and Fall* and *Complete Madness,* the latter a greatest-hits collection released simultaneously with a videocassette, were not released on a U.S. label, although they were best sellers in Britain and Europe. *Madness* included a number of previous British hits from 1981–82. In 1983 the group had a Top Ten hit with "Our House."

MAGAZINE
Formed 1977, Manchester, England
Howard Devoto, voc.; John McGeoch, gtr., sax; Dave Formula, kybds.; Barry Adamson, bass; Martin Jackson, drums.
1978—*Real Life* (Virgin) (− Jackson; + John Doyle, drums) **1979**—*Secondhand Daylight* (− McGeoch; + Robin Simon, gtr.) **1980**—*The Correct Use of Soap; Play (Live)* **1981**—*Magic, Murder and the Weather* (IRS) **1982**—*After the Fact.*

Howard Devoto formed Magazine after leaving seminal Manchester punk band the Buzzcocks. The band first came to prominence with a critically acclaimed British hit single, "Shot by Both Sides," which shared its guitar line with a Buzzcocks tune, "Lipstick" (both tunes were cowritten by Devoto and Buzzcock Pete Shelley). From there, though, the band's sound became more chilly and ponderous, rounding off its punky edges with Formula's adept art-rockish keyboard hooks and fills. The second album was much smoother than the first, and *Soap* was an extremely polished bid for a wider commercial market, something the band might have actually earned had it not broken up after recording only one more LP. McGeogh went on to play with Siouxsie and the Banshees; Formula and Adamson went with Visage; and Devoto named his next band Howard Devoto.

MAGMA
Formed 1969, France
1970—*Magma* (Philips, France) **1971**—*1001 Degrees Centigrade* **1974**—*Kohntarkosz* (A&M) *Mekanik Destruktiw Kommandoh* **1975**—*Live* (Utopia) **1976**—*Udu Wudu* (Tomato) **1977**—*Edits* (Tapioca) *Attahk* (WEA).

Christian Vander's group Magma was a leading art-rock band in France, and is probably the only rock band anywhere to have invented its own language: Kobaian, from the mythical planet Kobaia. Vander created Kobaian for Magma's second album and continued to use it throughout the band's recordings. Advanced members of the band's international cult were said to be able to converse in Kobaian.

Vander, a percussionist, was a disciple of jazz drummer Elvin Jones and a devotee of both contemporary classical music (Stockhausen, Stravinsky, Bartok) and modern jazz (John Coltrane, Sun Ra). For Magma, he composed complex polyrhythmic song-suites and came up with concept albums about interplanetary communication, galactic warfare and the apocalypse. Magma earned a following in Europe by touring, along with Gong, under such low-budget circumstances that they often stayed in fans' homes. Considering the eccentricity of their music, they have had a surprising number of albums available in the U.S.

TAJ MAHAL

Born Henry Saint Clair Fredericks, May 17, 1942, New York City

1967—*Taj Mahal* (Columbia)   1969—*Giant Step/De Ole Folks at Home*   1971—*The Real Thing; Happy Just to Be Like I Am*   1973—*Recycling the Blues (and Other Related Stuff); Ooh So Good 'n' Blues*   1974—*Mo' Roots*   1975—*Music Keeps Me Together*   1976—*Satisfied 'n' Tickled Too; Music Fuh Ya' (Musica Para Tu)* (Warner Bros.)   1977—*Brothers*   1978—*Evolution (the Most Recent)*   1979—*Taj Mahal and International Rhythm Band Live* (Crystal Clear)   1980—*Taj Mahal and International Rhythm Band* (Magnet)   *Going Home* (Columbia)   1981—*Live* (Magnet).

Taj Mahal began developing his archival interest in the roots of black American and Caribbean music while studying at the University of Massachusetts in the early Sixties. His family had moved to Springfield from Brooklyn when he was young; although his parents were musical (his father is a noted jazz arranger and pianist), young Fredericks first sought a college degree in animal husbandry. At the same time, he became a member of the Pioneer Valley Folklore Society and studied the ethnomusicology of rural black styles.

After receiving his BA, he played blues at Boston folk clubs before moving to Santa Monica and, in 1965, forming a blues-rock band with Ry Cooder called the Rising Sons. They signed with Columbia but broke up before they recorded. Columbia offered Taj Mahal a solo deal, and his debut was released in early 1968. His first albums, including the doubles *Giant Step/De Ole Folks at Home* and *The Real Thing*, were blues records laced with ragtime. On later LPs he explored calypso and reggae. Live, he's worked solo, accompanying himself with piano, guitar, bass and harmonica, and he's also appeared with bigger bands—one included Jesse Ed Davis, another had four tubas and another included steel drums. The Pointer Sisters backed him on some recordings in their early days.

Mahal has done movie scores: for *Sounder* (in which he had a small acting role) and 1977's *Brothers*. In 1974, he played bass with the short-lived Great American Music Band, with David Grisman and violinist Richard Greene. His records have never sold more than about 100,000 copies each, although he continues to perform and record regularly.

MAHAVISHNU ORCHESTRA
Formed 1971

Original lineup: John McLaughlin (b. Jan. 4, 1942, Yorkshire, Eng.), gtr.; Rick Laird (b. Feb. 5, 1941, Dublin), bass; Jerry Goodman, violin; Billy Cobham (b. May 16, 1944, Panama), drums; Jan Hammer (b. Apr. 17, 1948, Prague), kybds.

1972—*The Inner Mounting Flame* (Columbia)   1973—*Birds of Fire; Between Nothingness and Eternity*   1974—*Apocalypse*   1975—*Visions of the Emerald Beyond*   1976—*Inner Worlds*   1980—*Best of the Mahavishnu Orchestra.*

John McLaughlin solo: 1970—*Devotion* (Douglas)   1972—*My Goal's Beyond; Extrapolation* (Polydor)   1973—*Love, Devotion, Surrender* (with Carlos Santana) (Columbia)   1978—*Johnny McLaughlin, Electric Guitarist*   1979—*One Truth Band*   1980—*Best of John McLaughlin*   1981—*Belo Horizonte* (Warner Bros.)   1982—*Music Spoken Here.*

The original Mahavishnu Orchestra was the apotheosis of the career of guitar virtuoso John McLaughlin. Prior to their formation in 1971, McLaughlin made his name in England with numerous local blues bands, notably Graham Bond's group (where he played with Jack Bruce, pre-Cream, for the first time) and Brian Auger's group. He moved to America in the late Sixties and became a guitarist in demand, recording six albums between 1969 and 1971, split between the early jazz-rock fusions of Miles Davis and Tony Williams' Lifetime.

In the meantime, having recorded *Extrapolation* with jazz musicians in England, McLaughlin cut his second solo LP, *Devotion,* with R&B drummer Buddy Miles. McLaughlin recruited rock studio drummer Billy Cobham (who had played with the progressive horn-laden band Dreams and with Davis) and violinist Jerry Goodman (a veteran of the classical-influenced Flock) for his third solo album, 1972's *My Goal's Beyond,* which also featured an Indian tabla player, Alla Rakha. Next he founded the Mahavishnu Orchestra by adding European jazz-oriented players Rick Laird (one-time bassist with Buddy Rich) and keyboardist Jan Hammer (who had played with Elvin Jones and Sarah Vaughan). Mahavishnu was a name given him by his guru, Sri Chinmoy, and for a time the guitarist billed himself as Mahavishnu John McLaughlin.

To Miles Davis' fusion of jazz and rock, McLaughlin added his own synthesis of East and West, mixing the stop-and-start melodies and rhythms of Indian ragas with the force of rock and the improvisational options of jazz. The Mahavishnu Orchestra was an immediate sensation, opening a whole new era of jazz-rock fusion, although even those players that could match McLaughlin's speed couldn't approach his lyricism. The Mahavishnu Orchestra's second album, *Birds of Fire,* reached the Top Twenty. But conflicts within the group—especially over composer credit, most of which was claimed by McLaughlin—broke up the first Mahavishnu Orchestra after their third album, a live recording.

McLaughlin recorded *Love, Devotion, Surrender*, a duet album, with fellow Sri Chinmoy disciple Devadip Carlos Santana, and retained the Mahavishnu Orchestra name for a variety of groups, including one with drummer Narada Michael Walden (later a hit R&B producer and songwriter) and keyboardist Gayle Moran (later of Return to Forever). *Apocalypse* involved the London Symphony Orchestra and former Beatles producer George Martin. None of the later Mahavishnu orchestras got the same commercial and critical response as the first one.

In 1976, McLaughlin renounced Sri Chinmoy and gave up both the name Mahavishnu and the group name Mahavishnu Orchestra. He formed an acoustic group, Shakti (a form of yoga involving worldly pleasures), with whom he recorded three albums that were even closer in style to Indian ragas than the Orchestra had been. After a collaboration with ex–Return to Forever guitarist Al DiMeola, he formed a new electric group, the One Truth Band, which recorded one album and toured. McLaughlin then moved from New York to Paris, and has continued to record with European musicians.

The other original Orchestra members have continued to record and perform. Laird has played around New York with numerous jazz and rock groups; after a 1974 collaboration with Hammer, *Like Children*, Goodman apparently dropped out of the music business. Hammer has recorded frequently on his own, with Jeff Beck, and in 1982 with Journey's Neal Schon; he has his own Red Gate Studio. And Cobham has recorded and performed with a new jazz-rock band nearly every year, also touring with Grateful Dead guitarist Bob Weir's Bobby and the Midnites.

MAHOGANY RUSH

Formed 1971, Montreal
Frank Marino (b. Aug. 22, 1954, Del Rio, Tex.), gtr., voc.; Paul Harwood (b. Feb. 30, 1939, Quebec), bass; Jimmy Ayoub (b. Dec. 7, 1941, Honolulu), drums.
1971—*Maxoom* (20th Century–Fox) 1973—*Child of the Novelty* 1975—*Strange Universe* 1976—*Mahogany Rush IV* (Columbia) 1977—*World Anthem; Mahogany Rush Live* 1979—*Tales of the Unexpected* 1980—*What's Next*.

Guitarist Frank Marino formed Mahogany Rush, a heavy-metal trio, with a supernatural alibi. Accounts vary, but the gist of the story is that a teenaged Marino was in a Montreal hospital recovering from either illness or an auto accident. He lapsed into a deep coma for several days, and upon awakening claimed he'd been visited by the spirit of Jimi Hendrix. Although a non-musician before he was hospitalized, Marino picked up the guitar and began playing a lot like Jerry Garcia and Hendrix. He found a bassist and drummer and Mahogany Rush was born.

The recorded evidence of *Maxoom* (first issued in 1971 on the tiny Montreal-based Kot'ai label) shows a competent heavy-metal guitarist with an intense Hendrix fetish. Marino slowed the pace a bit for *Novelty*, which concentrated more on actual songs, and has since diversified his guitar style a bit in a jazz-rock fusion direction. Critical acclaim has been next to nil and record sales moderate at best, although Marino tours steadily.

THE MAIN INGREDIENT

Formed 1960s, New York City
Enrique Antonio "Tony" Silvester (b. Oct. 7, 1941, Colon, Panama), voc.; Luther Simmons, Jr. (b. Sep. 9, 1942, New York City), voc.; Don McPherson (b. July 9, 1941, Indianapolis; d. July 4, 1971), voc.
1971—(– McPherson; + Cuba Gooding [b. Apr. 27, 1944, New York City], voc.) 1973—*Afrodisiac* (RCA) *Greatest Hits* (+ Carl Tompkins [b. Petersburg, Va.], voc.; – Silvester) 1974—*Euphrates River* 1975—*Shame on the World; Rolling Down a Mountainside* 1976—*Spinning Around* (group disbands) 1977—*Music Maximus* (regroup with Silvester, Simmons, Gooding) 1980—*Ready for Love* 1981—*I Only Have Eyes for You*.

In 1971, the Main Ingredient were a smooth black vocal trio on the rise. After years of struggle, they had placed three singles in a row on the R&B charts—"You've Been My Inspiration" (#25, 1970), "I'm So Proud" (#13, 1970) and "Spinning Around" (#7, 1971)—when lead singer Don McPherson died of leukemia. With his replacement, Cuba Gooding, they went on to their greatest success.

McPherson, Luther Simmons, Jr., and Tony Silvester formed the Poets in the early Sixties and were signed to Mike Stoller and Jerry Leiber's Red Bird label in 1965. Their one chart record came the next year, "She Blew a Good Thing," a #2 soul hit. In 1967, they left Red Bird for RCA, renaming themselves the Insiders. But their luck did not improve until they changed their name. "You've Been My Inspiration" followed soon after.

After McPherson's death, the Main Ingredient moved toward pop. "Black Seed Keep on Growing" was another soul hit, reaching #15 in 1971, after which they finally had their first pop hit, "Everybody Plays the Fool" (#3 pop, #2 R&B, 1972). More pop hits followed in 1974—"Just Don't Want to Be Lonely" (#10 pop, #8 R&B) and "Happiness Is Just Around the Bend" (#35 pop, #7 R&B)—as well as four more Top Forty R&B records before the Main Ingredient broke up in 1976: "You've Got to Take It" (#18) and "You Can Call Me Rover" (#34) in 1973, and "Rolling Down a Mountainside" (#7) and "Shame on the World" (#20) in 1975. In 1980, a reunion as the Main Ingredient featuring Cuba Gooding yielded one last R&B chart single, "Think Positive" (#69).

MALO

Formed 1971, San Francisco

Original lineup: Jorge Santana (b. June 13, 1954, Jalisco, Mex.), gtr.; Arcelio Garcia, Jr. (b. May 7, 1946, Manati, Puerto Rico), voc., percussion; Abel Zarate (b. Dec. 2, 1952, Manila, Philippines), gtr., voc.; Roy Murray, trumpet, trombone, flute, sax; Pablo Tellez (b. July 2, 1951, Granada, Nicaragua), bass; Rich Spremich (b. July 2, 1951, San Francisco), drums; Richard Kermode (b. Oct. 5, 1946, Lovell, Wyo.), kybds.; Luis Gasca (b. Mar. 23, 1940, Houston), trumpet, fluegelhorn.

1972—*Malo* (Warner Bros.) *Dos* **1973**—*Evolution* **1974**—*Ascensión*.

Like Carlos Santana, brother Jorge formed his own Latin-rock band, Malo (Spanish for bad). Reinforcing the Santana connection, two of Carlos' percussionists, Coke Escovedo and Victor Pontoja, guested on Malo's debut LP, which spent a number of weeks in the Top Fifteen and yielded the band's one hit, "Suavecito" (#18, 1972).

Many of Malo's members were veterans of the San Francisco scene, either with rock bands or with Latin bands from the Mission District. Kermode and Gasca had played together in Janis Joplin's Kozmic Blues Band; Gasca's jazz credentials include stints with Count Basie, Woody Herman and Mongo Santamaria. *Dos* and *Evolution* both had minor success in the album charts; *Ascensión* fared worse, and the band broke up. Gasca has recorded pop-jazz albums for Fantasy Records.

THE MAMAS AND THE PAPAS

Formed 1965, New York City

John Phillips (b. Aug. 30, 1935, Parris Island, S.C.), voc., gtr.; Dennis Doherty (b. Nov. 29, 1941, Halifax), voc.; Michelle Gilliam Phillips (b. Apr. 6, 1944, Long Beach, Calif.), voc.; Cass Elliot (b. Sep. 19, 1943, Baltimore; d. July 29, 1974, London), voc.

1966—*If You Can Believe Your Eyes and Ears* (Dunhill) *The Mamas and the Papas* **1967**—*Deliver* **1968**—*Farewell to the First Golden Era; The Papas and the Mamas* (group broke up) **1969**—*16 of Their Greatest Hits* **1970**—(re-formed briefly with same lineup) *A Gathering of Flowers* **1972**—*People Like Us; 20 Golden Hits* **1981**—(re-formed again: J. Phillips; Doherty; + Mackenzie Phillips, voc.; + Elaine "Spanky" McFarlane [b. June 19, 1942, Peoria, Ill.], voc.).

Although the Mamas and the Papas made their commercial impact with airy California folk-pop and were on the scene as Los Angeles went psychedelic, they were a product of the Greenwich Village folk community. John Phillips had been active in New York since 1957; he had previously attended George Washington University and, for three months, the U.S. Naval Academy. In 1962, he met and married Holly Michelle Gilliam, who had come to

New York to be a model; she began singing with his group, the Journeymen.

Denny Doherty had been a member of the Halifax Three, which, after two albums for Epic, included future Lovin' Spoonful member Zal Yanovsky. Doherty and Zanovsky joined Cass Elliot and her first husband, Jim Hendricks, to form Cass Elliot and the Big Three. The group changed its name to the Mugwumps and went electric, with Art Stokes on drums and John Sebastian on harmonica. The Mugwumps recorded one album—not released until 1967—and broke up. Sebastian and Yanovsky formed the Lovin' Spoonful; Elliot fronted a jazz trio; and Doherty joined John and Michelle Phillips as the New Journeymen.

To rehearse, the New Journeymen went to St. Thomas in the Virgin Islands; Elliot joined them and worked on the island as a waitress, then moved to California with her husband. The New Journeymen relocated to California, where they stayed with Elliot and Hendricks, and Elliot officially joined the group. They recorded backing vocals for a Barry McGuire record, then got their own contract as the Mamas and the Papas.

In 1966 and 1967, they had six Top Five hits—"California Dreamin' " (#4), "Monday, Monday" (#1), "I Saw Her Again" (#5), "Words of Love" (#5), "Dedicated to the One I Love" (#2) and the autobiographical "Creeque Alley" (#5, 1967)—and two million-selling albums, *If You Can Believe . . .* and *The Mamas and the Papas*. Phillips also wrote a signature song of the flower-power era, the gold "San Francisco (Be Sure to Wear Flowers in Your Hair)," which was recorded by Scott McKenzie, an ex-Journeyman. The band also appeared at the 1967 Monterey Pop Festival, which Phillips helped finance.

By 1968, though, the group was falling apart and decided to disband. John and Michelle Phillips had marriage problems; Phillips made a solo LP, *The Wolf King of L.A.*, and then coproduced (with Lou Adler) Robert Altman's 1970 film *Brewster McCloud*. Michelle Phillips appeared in *The Last Movie* with Dennis Hopper, to whom she was later married for eight days. In addition to the Phillipses' divorce (1970), the band had other legal problems. Dunhill and band members sued each other for breach of contract (excluding Elliot, who continued to record for the label on her own) and fraudulent withholding of royalties, respectively. In 1970, the group made what it later admitted was a poor reunion album, *People Like Us*. Cass Elliot continued her solo career until her death in 1974.

Doherty recorded two solo albums but with little success. Michelle Phillips' acting career began to pick up with films like *Dillinger* and Ken Russell's 1976 movie bio of Rudolph Valentino, in which she costarred with Rudolf Nureyev. In 1977, she recorded a solo LP for A&M, *Victim of Romance*.

John Phillips had become idle by the mid-Seventies, reportedly living off his $100,000-a-year royalties from songs like "California Dreamin'." By 1975, he had

The Mamas and the Papas: John Phillips, Cass Elliot, Denny Doherty, Michelle Phillips

stopped work altogether. He was arrested by federal narcotics agents on July 31, 1980. Phillips' eight-year, $15,000-fine sentence was reduced to thirty days. Phillips cleaned up, as did his daughter, actress Mackenzie Phillips. The two appeared on numerous television programs and lectured around the country. The pair also decided to revive the Mamas and the Papas. Phillips contacted Doherty (who by then was hosting a popular television show in Nova Scotia) and filled out the new foursome with Elaine "Spanky" McFarlane, from Spanky and Our Gang. The four toured in early 1982, doing oldies and new Phillips originals.

MELISSA MANCHESTER

Born February 15, 1951, Bronx, New York
1973—*Home to Myself* (Bell) *Bright Eyes* 1975—*Melissa* (Arista) 1976—*Help Is on the Way; Better Days and Happy Endings* 1977—*"Singin' . . ."* 1978—*Don't Cry Out Loud* 1979—*Melissa Manchester* 1980—*For the Working Girl* 1982—*Hey Ricky; Greatest Hits.*

Melissa Manchester is a singer and sometime songwriter in the Peter Allen/Carole Bayer Sager/Barry Manilow MOR axis.

Coming from a musical family (her father is a bassoonist

with the Metropolitan Opera), Manchester began singing jingles at age 15. She attended the High School of Performing Arts in the late Sixties while working as a staff writer at Chappell Music. Upon graduation, she entered New York University, where she enrolled in a songwriting seminar taught by Paul Simon. She then played clubs in Manhattan, where she was discovered by Bette Midler and her accompanist, Barry Manilow. They hired her as a backup singer (Harlette) in 1971.

Six months later, Manchester got a record contract of her own. Her 1973 debut, *Home to Myself*, featured many songs cowritten by Carole Bayer Sager. In 1975, her third LP, *Melissa*, yielded her first hit, "Midnight Blue." She didn't have a really big followup until her version of Peter Allen/Carole Bayer Sager's song "Don't Cry Out Loud," which went to #10 in 1979. She cowrote Kenny Loggins' smash duet with Stevie Nicks, "Whenever I Call You 'Friend.' "

In 1980, Manchester became the first performer to have recorded two of the movie themes nominated for an Academy Award, "Ice Castles" and "The Promise." In 1982, she had her biggest hit with "You Should Hear How She Talks About You" from *Hey Ricky*.

MANDRILL

Formed 1968, New York City
Original lineup: Lou Wilson (b. Panama), trumpet, congas, voc.; Ric Wilson (b. Panama), sax, voc.; Carlos Wilson (b. Panama), trombone, flute, gtr., percussion, voc.; Omar Mesa (b. Havana), gtr., voc.; Bundie Cenac (b. St. Lucia, W. Indies), bass, voc.; Claude Cave, kybds., vibraphone, voc.; Charlie Padro, drums, voc.
1971—*Mandrill* (Polydor) (− Cenac; + Fudgie Kae, bass) 1972—*Mandrill Is* (− Padro; + Neftali Santiago, drums) 1973—*Composite Truth; Just Outside of Town* (− Mesa; + Doug Rodrigues, gtr.) 1974—*Mandrilland* 1975—*Best of Mandrill* (− Kae; + Brian Allsop, bass, voc.; − Santiago; + Andre Locke [b. Brooklyn], drums, voc.; − Rodrigues; + Tommy Trujillo, gtr., voc.) *Solid* (United Artists) (+ Wilfredo Wilson [b. Panama], voc., percussion) *Beast from the East* 1977—(Wilfredo Wilson switches to bass; − Locke; + Santiago, returned as drummer; − Allsop; − Trujillo; + Juaquin Jessup, gtr., percussion, voc.) *We Are One* (Arista) 1978—(− Santiago; − Jessup) *New Worlds* 1980—*Getting in the Mood.*

Emerging from the tough Bedford-Stuyvesant area of Brooklyn, Mandrill played a mixed urban brew encompassing elements of Santana-tinged Latin rock, Chambers Brothers–style soul and early Chicago horn-driven rock.

The band was founded by the four Wilson brothers, all of whom spent their childhood in Panama. After spending various amounts of time at college (Ric got a medical degree from Harvard), Ric, Lou and Carlos began jamming together with other musicians, eventually settling on the seven-member lineup.

The fledgling band won a contract with Polydor in 1969, and their debut LP became a big breakout on rock FM radio as well as black stations, aided by the eponymous title song. The LP sold 150,000 copies in the New York area alone. The band's biggest hits were on the soul charts, peaking with 1973's "Fencewalk" at #19. Also that year, the band played with Duke Ellington at the Newport Jazz Festival. Altogether, Mandrill recorded five albums for Polydor, but in January 1975 they switched to United Artists, moved to L.A. and went through some major personnel changes, all the while retaining the three Wilsons and original member Cave.

For *Beast from the East*, the youngest and fourth Wilson brother, Wilfredo, joined the fold as singer/percussionist. The band did well on concert tours, but still did not break big, and in 1977 it switched to Arista after contributing to the soundtrack of Muhammad Ali's film biography, *The Greatest*. They recorded two albums for Arista, but their biggest hit was "Too Late" (#37 R&B, 1978).

CHUCK MANGIONE
Born November 29, 1940, Rochester, New York
1962—*Recuerdo* (Jazzland) **1970**—*Friends and Love . . . A Chuck Mangione Concert* **1971**—*Together* **1972**—*The Chuck Mangione Quartet; Alive!* **1973**—*Land of Make Believe* **1975**—*Chase the Clouds Away* (A&M) **1976**—*Bellavia; Main Squeeze* **1977**—*Feels*

Managers

Managers are supposed to make musicians profitable. To that end, they can serve as business agents, financial backers, artistic advisers, disciplinarians, coaches and surrogate parents. Managers might come from the music business—as former musicians, concert promoters, booking agents, record company executives—or from law, accounting or organized crime; they might be a musician's ex–best friend. And depending on the musician, their job might entail anything from deciding on a band's songs, wardrobe and equipment to simply holding a genius' hand. The ideal manager is a good judge of music, a creative career planner, a tough contract negotiator, a comfort and a fan. The ideal manager does not exist.

The archetypal rock manager is Colonel Tom Parker, who until 1983 earned 25 percent of Elvis Presley's millions. Parker decided Presley's every business move, from movies to memorial albums; but while he built up an empire, he also made some strange decisions: Presley appeared only in B movies, and he never did concerts overseas, where he would have been lionized. He also sang more than his share of

mediocre songs, although rock songwriters all over the world would have gladly supplied him with material. But Presley stayed with Parker, who gave up management of the Presley estate only in 1983, six years after Presley's death.

It is almost inevitable for musicians on the way up to have some sort of legal wrangle in order to escape their first management deal. Bruce Springsteen was legally barred from recording for three years while he fought it out with his original manager, Mike Appel. Fleetwood Mac have managed themselves ever since a manager, signing contracts in their name, sent a phony band on a concert tour as Fleetwood Mac. Those are extreme cases, but sooner or later every musician has some problem, small or large, with management.

Managers, meanwhile, tend to be empire builders. Bill Graham got started as a West Coast concert promoter, and in the Sixties he ran the two best-known rock theaters, the Fillmores East and West. When running theaters that size became financially unsound, he closed them and moved into bigger venues, a trend which culminated

when he booked the 1981 Rolling Stones tour and consulted for the US Festival in 1982. Meanwhile, he became manager of Van Morrison, Santana, Eddie Money and a handful of other acts, and started running his own custom label, Wolfgang Records, for Columbia. David Geffen, another management entrepreneur, became a booking agent and then a personal manager for some West Coast friends: Joni Mitchell, Jackson Browne, the Eagles and others. In 1971, he started Asylum Records as a low-pressure recording outlet for those friends, who turned out to sell millions of records. In 1976, two years after Asylum merged with Elektra Records, Geffen left the company, claiming it lacked the excitement of the early days; four years later he started Geffen Records with a roster including John Lennon, Elton John and Donna Summer. Other vertically integrated managers include Jerry Weintraub, who manages Frank Sinatra, John Denver and others and controls Concerts West; and Peter Asher, the producer who now manages Joni Mitchell, James Taylor and Linda Ronstadt.

So Good **1978**—*Children of Sanchez* **1979**—*Live at the Hollywood Bowl* **1980**—*Fun and Games* **1981**—*Tarantella* **1982**—*Love Notes* (Columbia) **1983**—*Journey to a Rainbow.*

Pop-jazz fluegelhornist Chuck Mangione emerged in the late Seventies with a million-selling instrumental, "Feels So Good."

Mangione grew up in a musical family, and big jazz names passing through Rochester were entertained and fed in the Mangione household. He took up piano at age eight, trumpet two years later. In the early Sixties, he performed with Art Blakey and the Jazz Messengers and in trumpeter Maynard Ferguson's band.

Recording on his own, Mangione moved away from jazz's complexities to write and arrange instrumentals for a small group, often backed by strings or full orchestra. He recorded *Friends and Love* with the Rochester Philharmonic, and his "Hill Where the Lord Hides" received the first of his many Grammy Award nominations, as Best Instrumental Composition. *Make Believe* and *Chase the Clouds Away* got two Grammy nominations each. He won his first Grammy (Best Instrumental Composition, 1976) for "Bellavia."

Feels So Good went gold in February 1978; by April of that year it was platinum, and eventually sold more than two million copies. "Chase the Clouds Away" was played as background music by ABC-TV during telecasts of the 1976 Olympic Games. In 1980, Mangione was commissioned by ABC Sports to write music for the Winter Olympics (which made up the *Fun and Games* LP), and he played his "Give It All You Got" at the closing ceremony; his Olympic music won an Emmy that year for Music Composition/Direction. Mangione won another Grammy (Best Pop Instrumental Performance, 1978) for *Children of Sanchez,* a score for a film based on the Oscar Lewis book. The year 1980 brought two more Grammy nominations: *Fun and Games* (Best Jazz Fusion Performance) and "Give It All You Got" (Best Instrumental Composition). In December 1980, Mangione held a massive benefit in his hometown for the earthquake victims in Italy; Dizzy Gillespie, Chick Corea and Steve Gadd were among those present. He continues to sell albums steadily, although he has not repeated the success of "Feels So Good."

THE MANHATTANS

Formed 1964, Jersey City
George "Smitty" Smith, lead voc.; Winfred "Blue" Lovett (b. Nov. 16, 1943, N.J.), bass voc.; Edward "Sonny" Bivins (b. Jan. 15, 1942, N.J.), tenor voc.; Kenneth Kelley (b. Jan. 9, 1943, N.J.), 2nd tenor voc.; Richard Taylor, baritone voc.
1966—*Dedicated* (Carnival) **1967**—*For You and Yours* **1968**—*With These Hands* (King/Deluxe) **1969**—*Million to One* **1970**—(− Smith; + Gerald Alston [b. Nov. 8, 1942], tenor voc.) **1972**—*There's No Me without You* (Columbia) **1974**—*That's How Much I Love You* **1976**—*The Manhattans* **1977**—*It Feels So Good* **1978**—*There's No Good in Goodbye* **1979**—*Love Talk* **1980**—*After Midnight* **1981**—*Black Tie; Follow Your Heart* (Solid Smoke).

Steadfast practitioners of a suave soul-ballad harmony style rooted in doo-wop, anchored by the recitations of "Blue" Lovett, the Manhattans have never maintained mass popularity despite a long string of hits.

Winfred Lovett and Kenneth Kelley had sung in rival Jersey City doo-wop groups; Richard Taylor met Edward Bivins during an Air Force hitch in Germany in the late Fifties. Returning to the New York area, Taylor and Bivins united with Lovett, Kelley and Smith to form Ronnie and the Manhattans, who recorded several unsuccessful singles, one for Bobby Robinson's Enjoy Records. The Manhattans finally got their break when Barbara Brown, a singer with Joe Evans' Newark-based Carnival Records, retired from recording; she recommended the Manhattans to Evans, who caught them at Harlem's Apollo Theater and signed them.

After several unsuccessful singles, the group hit big with Lovett's tune "I Wanna Be (Your Everything)," which sold 500,000 copies and made the R&B Top Twenty. (Bivins and Taylor also write songs for the group.) In the next two years the Manhattans followed with a string of transitional doo-wop/soul hits like "Searchin' for My Baby," "Follow Your Heart," "Baby I Need You" and "Can I," all of which made the R&B Top Thirty. In 1968, the group signed with King subsidiary Deluxe, for whom it had only minor successes like "If My Heart Could Speak" and "From Atlanta to Goodbye."

In 1970, the group was dealt a seemingly crushing blow when Smith died of spinal meningitis. However, a replacement, Gerald Alston, was discovered in North Carolina, and with a signing to Columbia in 1972 the Manhattans continued to release romantic soul hits. Among those that made the R&B Top Ten were "There's No Me without You" (1973), "Don't Take Your Love from Me" (1974), "Hurt" (1975), the R&B and pop #1 "Kiss and Say Goodbye" (1976), "I Kinda Miss You" (1976), "It Feels So Good (to Be Loved So Bad)" (1977), "Am I Losing You" (1978) (the only one that did not enter the pop charts) and "Shining Star," which went to R&B #4 and pop #5 in 1980, by which time the Manhattans had been together nearly twenty years. They still record and perform regularly.

THE MANHATTAN TRANSFER

Formed 1969, New York City
Tim Hauser (b. ca. 1940, Troy, N.Y.), voc., gtr., banjo; Pat Rosalia, tambourine, voc.; Erin Dickens, gtr., tambourine, voc.; Gene Pistilli, gtr., voc.; Marty Nelson, gtr., clarinet, piano.

Sometime after 1969—(– Rosalia; – Dickens; – Nelson; – Pistilli) **1972**—(+ Alan Paul [b. ca. 1949, Newark), voc.; + Janis Siegel [b. ca. 1953, Brooklyn], voc.; + Laurel Masse [b. ca. 1954], voc.) **1975**—*Jukin'* (Capitol, recorded before 1972) *The Manhattan Transfer* (Atlantic) **1976**—*Coming Out* **1978**—*Pastiche; Live* **1979**—(– Masse; + Cheryl Bentyne [b. Mount Vernon, Wash.], voc.) **1980**—*Extensions* **1981**—*Mecca for Moderns; The Best of the Manhattan Transfer.*
Janis Siegel solo: **1982**—*Experiment in White.*

The Manhattan Transfer is a four-part vocal harmony group that specializes in vocal-harmony material from the Twenties through the early Sixties, including swing, doo-wop, jazz scat and pop ballads.

The group first formed in 1969 as a Jim Kweskin Jug Band–style good-time group and signed to Capitol. They took their name from a novel by John Dos Passos about New York in the Twenties. They soon broke up, though, and the only remaining member was Tim Hauser. (Also in that early incarnation was Gene Pistilli, who had written "Sunday Will Never Be the Same" with Terry Cashman for Spanky and Our Gang.)

The new Manhattan Transfer formed in 1972, and soon became popular on New York's cabaret circuit. Hauser had sung in doo-wop groups as a youth, around 1958 with the Criterions in high school and later with the Viscounts, who had a hit with "Harlem Nocturne." Later he played in a folk band with Jim Croce. Alan Paul was a child actor who had appeared in road companies of *Oliver* and *Grease*, in movies *(The Pawnbroker)* and TV commercials. Janis Siegel had recorded with the Young Generation, a group produced by Leiber and Stoller and at one time groomed to be the next Shangri-Las. With fourth member Laurel Masse they released their Atlantic debut in 1975 (containing "Operator," a #12 hit) and immediately got a summer network TV replacement series, which lasted three weeks in August. But even with the nostalgia trend of the time, the band didn't sell in this country, though it had a #1 hit in England and France with "Chanson d'Amour."

In 1979 Masse left, replaced by Cheryl Bentyne, daughter of a swing musician. The band had begun to modernize its look—shifting from tuxedos to a new wave/Deco combination—and broadened its audience with the release of *Extensions*, from which "Twilight Zone/Twilight Tones" became a modest hit (#30, 1980). In mid-1981 they had a Top Ten hit with a remake of the old Ad Libs song "Boy from New York City."

BARRY MANILOW

Born June 17, 1946, Brooklyn, New York
1973—*Barry Manilow* (Arista) **1974**—*Barry Manilow II* **1975**—*Tryin' to Get the Feeling* **1977**—*This One's for You; Barry Manilow Live* **1978**—*Even Now* **1979**—*Barry Manilow's Greatest Hits; One Voice* **1980**—*Barry* **1981**—*If I Should Love Again.*

Pop singer/songwriter Barry Manilow has sold over 50 million records worldwide. In 1977, his unabashedly romantic (verging on mawkish) pop gave him five albums on the charts simultaneously, a record surpassed only by Frank Sinatra and Johnny Mathis.

When Manilow was seven, he picked up his first instrument, accordion. He later attended New York College of Music and the Juilliard School. He also worked in the CBS mailroom, and there, at 18, he met a director who encouraged him to do some musical arranging. Soon after, Manilow wrote an Off Broadway musical adaptation of *The Drunkard*, which had a long run. In 1967, he became musical director of the CBS-TV series "Callback" and later did conducting and arranging for Ed Sullivan productions. He also played in a cabaret act duo, and in the spring of 1972, while filling in as house pianist at New York's Continental Baths, he met Bette Midler and soon became her musical director, arranger and pianist. He coproduced and arranged her 1972 Grammy-winning debut and her 1973 followup. During this time he wrote commercial jingles for Dr Pepper, Band-Aids, State Farm Insurance, among others (contrary to popular opinion, he did not write, although he sang, McDonald's "You Deserve a Break Today").

Manilow landed a solo deal with Bell (later Arista) in 1973 but first toured with Midler as featured performer before releasing his debut LP and doing his own roadshow in 1974. His second LP came out later in the year, and in only nine weeks his cover of "Mandy" went to #1 in January of 1975. Hits like "Could It Be Magic" (#6, 1975), "It's a Miracle" (#12, 1975), Bruce Johnston's "I Write the Songs" (#1, 1976) and "Trying to Get the Feeling" (#10, 1976) followed. His debut album went platinum, as did the next seven, including the four-million-seller *Barry Manilow Live.* His regular coproducer was ex-Archie Ron Dante up until his tenth LP in 1981.

Manilow won an Emmy for one of his TV specials, a special Tony for a Broadway concert and a Grammy in 1979. In 1980, he produced Dionne Warwick's platinum comeback LP, which contains the hit "I'll Never Love This Way Again." In early 1982, he hit the Top Twenty with "The Old Songs" and later had a lesser hit with a remake of the Four Seasons' "Let's Hang On."

BARRY MANN AND CYNTHIA WEIL

Barry Mann, born February 9, 1939, Brooklyn, New York
Barry Mann: **1974**—*Survivor* (RCA) **1975**—*Joyride* (United Artists).

Barry Mann and Cynthia Weil are one of the most successful and stable songwriting teams that emerged in the late Fifties and early Sixties. In New York's Brill Building, they wrote such dramatic teen anthems as "You've Lost That Loving Feeling," and together and with others they have continued to write hits into the Eighties.

With various other collaborators, Mann had written a number of pop hits—The Diamonds' "She Say Oom Dooby Doom" (1959), Steve Lawrence's "Footsteps" (1960), The Paris Sisters' "I Love How You Love Me" (1961)—and had sung his own Top Ten hit, 1961's "Who Put the Bomp" (cowritten with Gerry Goffin), before meeting and marrying Cynthia Weil in 1961. She had been an aspiring actress and a lyricist for Frank Loesser's music-publishing house. Together they went to work for Al Nevins and Don Kirshner's Aldon Publishing, working in cubicles alongside Goffin and Carole King, Neil Sedaka and Howie Greenfield, and Doc Pomus and Mort Shuman.

Their first cowritten hit was Tony Orlando's "Bless You" in 1961, followed by the Crystals' "Uptown" in 1962, an example of their flair for strong but understated social protest. They also wrote hits for James Darren ("Conscience"), Shelley Fabares ("Johnny Loves Me") and Paul Petersen ("My Dad"), both of the Donna Reed TV show in 1962, before capping the year with another Crystals hit, "He's Sure the Boy I Love." In 1963, they wrote "Blame It on the Bossa Nova" for Eydie Gorme, "I'll Take You Home" for the Drifters and, with Phil Spector, "Walking in the Rain" for the Ronettes. They again collaborated with Spector in 1964 for the Righteous Brothers' "You've Lost That Loving Feeling," and they penned "Saturday Night at the Movies" for the Drifters.

The social-protest vein running through Mann/Weil's work became most pronounced in 1965, when they wrote "We Gotta Get Out of This Place," a Top Twenty hit for the Animals. That year they also wrote "Home of the Brave" for Jody Miller, and followed in 1966 with the anti-drug "Kicks" by Paul Revere and the Raiders, the Righteous Brothers' "Soul and Inspiration," the Vogues' "Magic Town" and Paul Revere's "Hungry."

Mann and Weil were the last of the Brill Building songwriting teams to leave New York City, finally moving to the West Coast in 1970. Shortly thereafter, Mann, in the wake of Carole King's solo success, tried to launch his own singing/songwriting career, but with little success. Still, he continued to write hit tunes, including "Sometimes When We Touch" (with Dan Hill) and "Here You Come Again" (for Dolly Parton).

MANFRED MANN

Formed 1964, England
Manfred Mann (b. Michael Lubowitz, Oct. 21, 1940, Johannesburg, S. Afr.), kybds.; Paul Jones (b. Paul Pond, Eng.), voc.; Mike Hugg (b. Aug. 11, 1942, Andover, Eng.), drums; Michael Vickers (b. Apr. 18, 1941, Southampton, Eng.), gtr.; Tom McGuiness (b. Dec. 2, 1941, London, Eng.), bass.
1964—*The Manfred Mann Album* (Ascot) *The Five*

Faces of Manfred Mann; Mann Made **1965**—*My Little Red Book of Winners* (− Vickers; + Jack Bruce [b. May 14, 1943, Bishopsbriggs, Scot.], bass) *Mann Made Hits* **1966**—*Pretty Flamingo* (United Artists) *Greatest Hits* (Capitol) (− Bruce; − Jones) **1967**—*Up the Junction* (Fontana) (+ Klaus Voormann [b. Apr. 29, 1942, Berlin], bass; + Michael D'Abo [b. 1944, Bethworth, Eng.], voc., gtr., flute) *The Mighty Quinn* (Mercury).
Manfred Mann's Earth Band: formed 1971, England; Mann; Mick Rogers, voc., gtr.; Colin Pattenden, bass; Chris Slade, drums.
1972—*Manfred Mann's Earth Band* (Polydor) *Glorified, Magnified* **1973**—*Get Your Rocks Off* (also known as *Messin'*) **1974**—*Solar Fire; The Good Earth* (Warner Bros.) **1975**—*Nightingales and Bombers* (+ Chris Thompson, gtr.; + Dave Flett, gtr.; + Pat King, bass; − Flett; + Steve Waller, gtr.; − Waller; + John Lingwood, drums) **1976**—*The Roaring Silence* **1978**—*Watch* **1979**—*Angel Station* **1980**—*Chance.*

Although led by two trained musicians who shared a measure of disdain for pop music, Manfred Mann scored an impressive 16 British hit singles during the Sixties, many of which were American successes as well, including the #1 record "Do Wah Diddy Diddy" in 1964. Mann himself later moved into jazz-rock and AOR.

Manfred Mann and Mike Hugg formed the eight-man Mann-Hugg Blues Brothers in 1962, playing blues and jazz. The following year, they pared the group down to a quintet with a new name, Manfred Mann. At this point, they turned to pop-oriented rock & roll.

Their first two singles ("Why Should We Not?" and "Cock-A-Hoop") were not especially successful, but their third, "5-4-3-2-1," became their first hit, its popularity aided by its adoption as the theme song of the British rock television program "Ready Steady Go" (Manfred Mann's "Hubble Bubble Toil and Trouble" became the show's theme song later on.) The hits came rapidly after that—"Do Wah Diddy Diddy" (#1, 1964), "Come Tomorrow" (#50, 1965) and "Pretty Flamingo" (#29, 1966).

Around this time, Vickers quit the band, and was replaced briefly by Jack Bruce, who left six months later to form Cream. Bruce was replaced by *Revolver* jacket artist Klaus Voormann. Later Paul Jones quit as well to concentrate on acting and a solo recording career. He had two British hits, "High Time" and "I've Been a Bad Bad Boy," from the 1967 film *Privilege*, in which he starred, playing a pop idol. He was replaced by Mike D'Abo.

Fluctuating personnel had less discernible effect on the group's continued chart success than its leader's growing ambivalence. British hits those years included "Semi-Detached Suburban Mr. James," "Ha! Ha! Said the Clown," "My Name Is Jack" and their international hit cover of Bob Dylan's "The Mighty Quinn" (#10, 1968). After scoring the film *Up the Junction* in 1967, Mann and

Hugg broke up the band, and formed the more ambitious Manfred Mann's Chapter Three, complete with a five-man horn section, while McGuinness joined ex–John Mayall drummer Hughie Flint to form McGuinness Flint. Chapter Three recorded a pair of albums (*Chapter Three*, 1969; *Chapter Three, Volume 2*, 1970) before Mann and Hugg parted company, Hugg to compose soundtracks (some believe he alone was responsible for *Up the Junction*) and Mann to launch Manfred Mann's Earth Band.

The Earth Band was designed to show off the group's virtuosity in a heavy-rock format. Upon their formation in 1971, they toured extensively, building their audience until in 1976 their version of Bruce Springsteen's "Blinded by the Light" became a hit single. In 1973, they had a British hit with "Joybringer," based on a tune from Gustav Holst's *The Planets*. In five more years of recording, they were not able to repeat the feat, even when they tried another Springsteen composition, "Spirit in the Night."

MARK-ALMOND BAND
Formed 1970, London
Johnny Almond (b. 1946, Eng.), voc., sax, flute, vibes, congas, oboe; Jon Mark (b. Cornwall, Eng.), gtrs., voc., percussion; Rodger Sutton (b. Eng.), bass, cello; Tommy Eyre (b. Sheffield, Eng.), piano, organ, gtr.
1971—*Mark Almond* (Blue Thumb) (+ Dannie Richmond, percussion) **1972**—*Mark Almond 2* (Columbia) (+ Ken Craddock, kybds.; + Colin Gibson, bass) *Rising* **1973**—(− Craddock; − Gibson) *Mark Almond 73* (− Sutton; − Eyre; + Geoff Condon, horns; + Alun Davies, gtr.; + Wolfgang Melz, bass; + Bobby Torres, percussion) (disbanded) **1975**—(Mark and Almond reunited) **1976**—*To the Heart* (ABC) **1978**—*Other People's Rooms* (A&M).

In 1970, Jon Mark and Johnny Almond, two longtime British sessionmen, left John Mayall's Bluesbreakers to form a band that combined mellow jazz and folk.

Before joining Mayall, Mark had coproduced Marianne Faithfull's early albums with Mick Jagger, and later spent two years writing for Faithfull and accompanying her on the road. He also toured with folksinger Alun Davies (later guitarist for Cat Stevens), and from there the two formed a short-lived band called Sweet Thursday, with Nicky Hopkins, Brian Odgers and Harvey Burns. Though their sole LP on Tetragrammaton was released the day the company folded, "Gilbert Street" became an FM hit in the U.S.

Almond had worked in Zoot Money's Big Roll Band, the Alan Price Set and his own Johnny Almond's Music Machine, who recorded two solo LPs for Deram in England. Both he and Mark joined Mayall in 1967 (they appear on *Turning Point*), but after a second LP with Mayall, *Empty Rooms*, the two formed the Mark-Almond Band with Tommy Eyre (who'd backed Joe Cocker, Juicy

Lucy and Aynsley Dunbar) and Roger Sutton, formerly of Jody Grind. The Mark-Almond Band's debut contained the FM hit "The City," an 11-minute jam. An audience began to grow, especially for their tours, which featured long instrumental forays. With their second LP, they added guest drummer Dannie Richmond, who'd long been associated with jazz bassist Charles Mingus. Mark-Almond was briefly a seven-piece band for their *73* album, before disbanding. Mark lost a finger in an accident that year, but came out with a solo LP, *Songs for a Friend*, in 1975.

Later that year they reunited to record *To the Heart*. They still hadn't found a major audience, but they got another deal on Horizon in 1978, resulting in *Other People's Rooms*, which included a new version of "The City." They really were no longer a group, though (the album was recorded with all studio musicians besides the two principals), and they called it quits for good soon after.

THE MAR-KEYS
Formed 1957, Memphis
Terry Johnson, drums; Steve Cropper (b. Oct. 21, 1941, Willow Springs, Mo.), gtr.; Donald "Duck" Dunn (b. Nov. 24, 1941, Memphis), bass; Jerry Lee "Smoochie" Smith, piano; Charles Axton, sax; Don Nix, sax; Wayne Jackson, trumpet.
1961—*Mar-Keys* (Atlantic) **1965**—*Great Memphis Sound*.

Though they had just one Top Ten single, the Mar-Keys were among those most responsible for the development of the Memphis sound of the Sixties, the hallmark of the influential Stax-Volt label. Guitarist Steve Cropper formed the band in 1957, when he was just 16, as a quartet. By the early Sixties, they had added horns and keyboards and were backing up Satellite Records (later Stax-Volt) soul stars Rufus and Carla Thomas. They also began releasing their own singles and albums of instrumentals, scoring a Top Ten hit and a gold record in 1961 with their first 45, "Last Night." In later years, after much shifting of personnel, the name Mar-Keys was quietly retired, but various bandmembers remained active. Cropper and Dunn had many hits as half of Booker T. and the MGs. Onetime Mar-Key Don Nix went on to a modestly successful solo career, while Jackson joined the Memphis Horns.

BOB MARLEY AND THE WAILERS
Formed 1963, Jamaica
The Wailers: Bob Marley (b. Apr. 6, 1945, Rhoden Hall, Jamaica; d. May 11, 1981, Miami), voc., gtr.; Peter Tosh (b. Winston Hubert MacIntosh, Oct. 19, 1944, Westmoreland, Jamaica), voc., gtr.; Bunny Livingston (b. Apr. 10, 1947, Kingston, Jamaica), voc., percussion.
1969—(+ Aston "Family Man" Barrett [b. Nov. 22, 1946, Kingston], bass; + Carlton Barrett [b. Dec. 17, 1950, Kingston], drums) *Soul Revolution* (Trojan)

1970—*African Herbsman; Rasta Revolution* **1973**—*Catch a Fire* (Island) (+ Earl "Wire" Lindo [b. Jan. 7, 1953, Kingston], kybds.) *Burnin'* (− Tosh; − Livingston) **1977**—*The Birth of a Legend* (Calla) *Early Music* (collected 1963–69 singles) **1981**—*Soul Captives* (ALA) (collected 1963–69 singles).

Bob Marley and the Wailers: **1974**—(+ Bernard "Touter" Harvey [b. Jamaica], kybds.; + Al Anderson [b. U.S.], gtr.; + the I-Threes [Rita Marley, Marcia Griffiths, Judy Mowatt, all b. Jamaica], voc.) *Natty Dread* (Island) **1975**—*Live* (− Harvey; − Lindo; + Tyrone Downie [b. Jamaica], kybds.; + Alvin "Seeco" Patterson [b. Jamaica], percussion; + Julian "Junior" Marvin [b. U.S.], gtr.) **1976**—*Rastaman Vibration* **1977**—*Exodus* **1978**—*Kaya* (+ Lindo) *Babylon by Bus* **1979**—*Survival* **1980**—*Uprising.*

Tremendously popular in their native Jamaica, where Bob Marley was regarded as a national hero, the Wailers were also reggae music's most effective international emissaries. Marley's songs of determination, rebellion and faith found an audience all over the world.

Marley left his rural home for the slums of Kingston at age 14. When he was 17, Jimmy Cliff introduced him to Leslie Kong, who produced Marley's first single, "Judge Not," and several other obscure sides. In 1963, with the guidance of Jamaican pop veteran Joe Higgs, Marley formed the Wailers, a vocal quintet, with Peter Tosh, Bunny Livingston, Junior Braithwaite and Beverly Kelso. Their first single for producer Coxsone Dodd, "Simmer Down," was one of the biggest Jamaican hits of 1964, and the Wailers remained on Dodd's Studio One and Coxsone labels for three years, hitting with "Love and Affection."

When Braithwaite and Kelso left the group around 1965, the Wailers continued as a trio, Marley, Tosh and Livingston trading leads. In spite of the popularity of singles like "Rude Boy," the artists received few or no royalties, and in 1966 they disbanded. Marley spent most of the following year working in a factory in Wilmington, Delaware (where his mother had moved in 1963). Upon his return to Jamaica, the Wailers reunited and recorded, with little success, for Dodd and other producers. During this period, the Wailers devoted themselves to the religious sect of Rastafari.

In 1969, they began their three-year association with Lee Perry, who directed them to play their own instruments and expanded their lineup to include Aston and Carlton Barrett, formerly the rhythm section of Perry's studio band, the Upsetters. Some of the records they made with Perry—like "Trenchtown Rock"—were locally very popular, but so precarious was the Jamaican record industry that the group seemed no closer than before to establishing steady careers. They formed an independent record company, Tuff Gong, in 1971, but the venture foundered when Livingston was jailed and Marley got caught in a contract commitment to American pop singer

Bob Marley

Johnny Nash, who took him to Sweden to write a film score (and later had moderate hits with two Marley compositions, "Guava Jelly" and "Stir It Up").

In 1972, Chris Blackwell—who had released "Judge Not" in England in 1963—signed the Wailers to Island Records and advanced them the money to record themselves in Jamaica. *Catch a Fire* was their first album marketed outside Jamaica. (They continued to release Jamaica-only singles on Tuff Gong.) Their recognition abroad was abetted by Eric Clapton's hit version of "I Shot the Sheriff," a song from their second Island album. They made their first overseas tour in 1973, but before the end of the year, Tosh and Livingston left for solo careers.

Marley expanded the instrumental section of the group and brought in a female vocal trio, the I-Threes, which included his wife, Rita. Now called Bob Marley and the Wailers, they toured Europe, Africa and the Americas (with their old mentor Higgs taking Livingston's part for a while), building especially strong followings in the U.K., Scandinavia and Africa. They had U.K. Top Forty hits with "No Woman No Cry" (1975), "Exodus" (1977), "Waiting in Vain" (1977) and "Satisfy My Soul" (1978); and British Top Ten hits with "Jamming" (1977), "Punky Reggae Party" (1977) and "Is This Love" (1978).

In the U.S., only "Roots, Rock, Reggae" made the pop charts (#51, 1976), while "Could You Be Loved" placed on the soul charts (#56, 1980), but the group attracted an ever-larger audience: *Rastaman Vibration* went to #35 and *Exodus* reached #20. In Jamaica, the Wailers reached unprecedented levels of popularity and influence, and Marley's pronouncements on public issues were accorded the attention usually reserved for political or religious leaders. In 1976, he was wounded in an assassination attempt.

A 1980 tour of the U.S. was canceled when Marley collapsed onstage during one of the first concerts. It was discovered that he had developed brain and lung cancer, which killed him seven months later. Rita Marley continues to record, tour and run the Tuff Gong studios and record company.

MARSHALL TUCKER BAND
Formed 1971, South Carolina
Toy Caldwell (b. 1948), lead gtr., steel gtr., voc.; George McCorkle, rhythm gtr.; Doug Gray, lead voc.; Paul Riddle, drums; Jerry Eubanks, alto sax, flute, organ, piano, voc.; Tommy Caldwell (b. 1950; d. Apr. 30, 1980, Spartanburg, S.C.), bass, voc.
1973—*The Marshall Tucker Band* (Capricorn) 1974—*A New Life; Where We All Belong* 1975—*Searchin' for a Rainbow* 1976—*Long Hard Ride* 1977—*Carolina Dreams* 1978—*Together Forever; Greatest Hits* 1979—*Running Like the Wind* (Warner Bros.) 1980—*Tenth* (− Tommy Caldwell; + Franklin Wilkie, bass) 1981—*Dedicated* 1982—*Tuckerized* 1983—*Just Us.*

The Marshall Tucker Band tempered Southern rock with pop, country, ballad and even a few MOR "jazz" influences.

The band centered on the Caldwell brothers, who like all the future bandmembers were born and grew up in Spartanburg, South Carolina, where they all continue to live. As a teen, Toy Caldwell first worked in a rock & roll outfit, the Rants, which included George McCorkle on rhythm guitar. At the same time, brother Tommy played with Doug Gray in the New Generation. Both groups toured the club circuit until 1966, when they were all drafted into the Army. After their discharge four years later, Toy wrote "Can't You See?," which later became the Marshall Tucker Band's first U.S. single and a Top Five country hit for Waylon Jennings in 1976. But first he formed the Toy Factory, with Gray and Eubanks, a band that lasted almost two years, until 1971, when McCorkle, Riddle and Tommy Caldwell joined to form the Marshall Tucker Band, named after the piano tuner who owned their rehearsal hall.

Their self-titled debut was released in March 1973, and they were openers on the Allman Brothers' tour; by 1974 they were headliners. The band's songs received much FM airplay, especially "Take the Highway," "24 Hours at a Time" and "Fire on the Mountain." Their debut went gold two years after its release, followed by six other gold records and two platinum—*Searchin' for a Rainbow* and *Carolina Dreams*—which included "Heard It in a Love Song" (#14, 1977). On January 20, 1977, the band, along with Sealevel, played at the inauguration of President Jimmy Carter. In 1979, the group signed to Warner Bros. for *Running Like the Wind.*

On April 28, 1980, Tommy Caldwell died from injuries sustained in an automobile accident six days earlier, and the band's LP in memory of him, released one year later, was called *Dedicated.* Tommy's replacement was Franklin Wilkie, who'd played with Toy and McCorkle in the Rants. He had also played in the Toy Factory, but instead of joining the initial Marshall Tucker, played for six years with Garfeel Ruff, who recorded two albums for Capitol.

MARTHA AND THE VANDELLAS
Formed 1962, Detroit
Martha Reeves (b. July 18, 1941, Detroit), lead voc.; Annette Sterling, voc.; Rosalind Ashford (b. Sep. 2, 1943, Detroit), voc.
1963—(− Sterling; + Betty Kelly [b. Sep. 16, 1944, Detroit], voc.) 1967—(− Kelly; + Lois Reeves, voc.) 1970—(− Ashford; + Sandra Tilley, voc.) 1974—*Anthology* (Motown) *Martha Reeves* (MCA) 1977—*The Rest of My Life* (Arista) 1978—*We Meet Again* (Fantasy) 1981—*Super Star Series, Volume 2* (Motown).

Martha Reeves and the Vandellas, Motown's earthier, more aggressive "girl group" alternative to the Supremes, made some of the most popular dance records of the Sixties.

Reeves, Sterling and Ashford sang as the Del-Phis in high school and cut one single on Check-Mate Records, a subsidiary of Chess. In 1960, Reeves got a job at Motown as a secretary in the A&R department. One day, Motown head Berry Gordy, Jr., needed background singers in short order for a session; Reeves and her friends were called in. They sang behind Marvin Gaye on "Stubborn Kind of Fellow" and "Hitch Hike" before recording "I'll Have to Let Him Go" as Martha and the Vandellas, taking their new name from Detroit's Van Dyke Street and Reeves's favorite singer, Della Reese. Another story has it that "Vandellas" came from the word "vandal," since many believed they stole the spotlight from anyone they backed.

Their first hit, a beat ballad called "Come and Get These Memories" (#29 pop, #6 R&B, 1963), was followed by two explosive Holland-Dozier-Holland dance records: "Heat Wave" (#4 pop, #1 R&B, 1964) and "Quicksand" (#8 pop, 1963). After being turned down by Kim Wells, Holland-Dozier-Holland's "Dancing in the Streets" was given to Martha and the Vandellas; they turned it into their biggest hit (#2 pop, 1964). Their other big hits were "Nowhere to Run" (#8 pop, #5 R&B, 1965) and "I'm Ready for Love" (#9 pop, #2 R&B, 1966). "Jimmy Mack" (#10 pop, #1 R&B, 1967) and "Honey Chile" (#11 pop, #5 R&B, 1967) were the last Holland-Dozier-Holland compositions they recorded, and were their last big hits.

In 1967, by which time the group was billed as Martha

Reeves and the Vandellas, Betty Kelly left and was replaced by Martha's younger sister Lois. The group broke up in 1973. They gave their farewell performance on December 21, 1972, in Detroit. Reeves signed with MCA as a solo act, moving to Arista in 1977, but she never attained the success she had enjoyed with the Vandellas.

MOON MARTIN

Born circa 1950, Oklahoma
1978—*Shots from a Cold Nightmare* (Capitol) **1979**—*Escape from Domination* **1980**—*Street Fever* **1982**—*Mystery Ticket.*

A Midwest power popper, Moon Martin is best known as the writer of Robert Palmer's 1979 hit "Bad Case of Loving You."

John "Moon" Martin was born and raised near the Texas-Oklahoma border, and in high school he played in a country band called the Disciples and then in a Beatles soundalike group. Upon graduation, he moved to Detroit; but he soon relocated to Los Angeles around 1968, where he joined Southwind. Martin played lead guitar on their three Blue Thumb records (*Southwind*, 1969; *Ready to Ride*, 1971; *What a Place to Land*, 1972). He also did some studio work on Linda Ronstadt's *Silk Purse* LP and Jesse Ed Davis' *Ululu* in 1972. Later that year, Southwind disbanded and Martin began concentrating on writing and selling his songs.

His work came to the attention of producer Jack Nitzsche, who used his "Cadillac Walk" on Mink DeVille's 1977 debut. Michelle Phillips recorded three Martin songs on *Victim of Romance*. Nitzsche wanted to produce Martin's debut, but he was working on Mink DeVille's *Return to Magenta*, which included Martin's "Rolene," and the songwriter made *Shots from a Cold Nightmare* with producer Craig Leon. Backing Martin up were Phil Seymour and original Blondie member Gary Valentine. *Escape from Domination* contained his own #30 hit with "Rolene." In 1980, Martin's "I've Got a Reason" was covered by Rachel Sweet on *Protect the Innocent*. *Mystery Ticket* was coproduced by Robert Palmer.

JOHN MARTYN

Born 1948, Glasgow
1968—*London Conversation* (Island) *The Tumbler* **1970**—*Stormbringer; The Road to Ruin* **1971**—*Bless the Weather* **1973**—*Solid Air; Inside Out* **1974**—*Sunday's Child* **1975**—*Live at Leeds* **1977**—*So Far, So Good* (compilation) *One World* **1980**—*Grace and Danger* (Antilles) **1982**—*Glorious Fool* (Duke).

Though never a great commercial success, John Martyn's eccentric brand of folk— elliptical songwriting, intimately bluesy singing, heavily jazz-flavored music—has held steady appeal for critics and cultists. As early as 1968's *The Tumbler*, Martyn was causing something of a stir in British folk circles by working with jazz reedman Harold McNair. *Bless the Weather* (now out of print, though some of its material can be found on the *So Far, So Good* compilation) fully extended the jazz tendencies, while *Solid Air* and *Inside Out* found Martyn using hypnotically repeated melodies and echo-plexed acoustic guitar.

One World introduced a new ethno-eclecticism; Martyn had spent time in Jamaica with reggae producers Lee Perry and Jack Ruby. *Grace and Danger* featured the percussion, vocals and production assistance of Genesis' Phil Collins, a longtime Martyn fan. Martyn has also recorded two albums with his wife, Beverley—1970's *Stormbringer* and *The Road to Ruin*.

THE MARVELETTES

Formed 1961, Inkster, Michigan
Gladys Horton (b. 1944); Katherine Anderson (b. 1944); Georgeanna Dobbins (b. 1944; d. Jan. 6, 1980, Detroit); Juanita Cowart (b. 1944); Wanda Young (b. 1944).
1961—(– Dobbins; – Cowart) **1966**—*Greatest Hits* (Tamla) **1967**—*Marvelettes* **1969**—(– Horton; + Anne Bogan; – Young).

Among Motown's female vocal groups, the Marvelettes were the only one whose sound closely resembled the Sixties girl-group style.

The original Marvelettes were founded by Gladys Horton, a 15-year-old high school student who, together with four girlfriends from Inkster High School, decided to enter a school talent contest. The acts who placed first through third were allowed to audition for Motown talent scouts; the Marvels, as they were then called, came in fourth. Nonetheless, they did audition for a Motown scout, who advised them to develop original material. Dobbins wrote "Please Mr. Postman," and after the group was signed by Berry Gordy, Jr., "Postman" became their debut recording and their first and biggest hit. The song stayed on the charts for almost six months and eventually hit #1. Soon after, health problems forced both Dobbins and Cowart to quit, and the group continued as a trio.

The next year proved their most successful, with: "Playboy" (#7 pop, #4 R&B), "Beechwood 4-5789" (#17 pop, #7 R&B), "Someday, Someway" (#9 R&B) and "Strange I Know" (#10 R&B). "Too Many Fish in the Sea" (#25 pop, #15 R&B), "I'll Keep Holding On" (#11 R&B) and "Danger Heartbreak Dead Ahead" (#11 R&B) were their 1965 hits. Around this time they were offered—and they refused—a Holland-Dozier-Holland song entitled "Baby Love." When recorded by the Supremes, "Baby Love" turned out to be one of the year's biggest hits and one of Motown's best sellers. However, over the next two years, the Marvelettes regained the pop charts with three Smokey Robinson tunes: "Don't Mess with

Bill" (#7 pop, #3 R&B, 1966), "The Hunter Gets Captured by the Game" (#13 pop, #2 R&B, 1967) and "My Baby Must Be a Magician" (#17 pop, 1968; #8 R&B, 1967).

"Here I Am Baby" (#14 R&B, 1968) and "Destination: Anywhere" (#28 R&B) marked the end of the Marvelettes' most lucrative years. By this time, Horton (who along with Young had been a lead singer) had left, and the numerous personnel changes that followed reduced the group to nothing more than a name. But perhaps most important, Gordy and Motown were busy developing the groups whose legacies would eventually eclipse the Marvelettes'. In 1980, Dobbins died in her mother's Detroit home of sickle cell anemia. Throughout the Seventies, various groups performed under the Marvelettes name, though none contained any of the original members.

DAVE MASON

Born May 10, 1947, Worcester, England
1970—*Alone Together* (Blue Thumb) **1971**—*Dave Mason and Cass Elliot* **1972**—*Headkeeper; Dave Mason Is Alive!* **1974**—*It's Like You Never Left* (Columbia) *The Best of Dave Mason* (Blue Thumb) *Dave Mason* (Columbia) *Split Coconut* **1976**—*Certified Live* **1977**—*Let It Flow* **1978**—*Mariposa de Oro* **1980**—*Old Crest on a New Wave.*

Singer/songwriter/guitarist Dave Mason has gone from being an integral early member of the acclaimed British jazz-pop band Traffic, to a top-selling solo act, to performing beer commercials when his solo albums were faltering.

Mason was working by the mid-Sixties in a band with drummer Jim Capaldi. In 1967 the pair met Steve Winwood and they formed Traffic. Mason's songwriting gave the band its first big commercial successes (until *Low Spark of High Heeled Boys,* at least) with "Hole in My Shoe," "You Can All Join In" and "Feelin' Alright." However, Mason's pop-rock sensibility clashed with Winwood's jazz/blues leanings, and Mason was in and out of the band frequently, finally leaving for good in late 1968. He coproduced (with Jim Miller) the debut LP by the British band Family, *Music in a Doll's House,* then formed a short-lived band with Capaldi, Traffic reedman Chris Wood and Wynder K. Frog.

Having met seminal country-rocker Gram Parsons while touring with Traffic, Mason went to Los Angeles. There, Parsons introduced him to Delaney and Bonnie Bramlett, and he joined their Friends tour of 1969, much of which was shared with Eric Clapton and Blind Faith (which included Winwood).

Back in L.A., Mason recorded *Alone Together* with Capaldi, Leon Russell, Rita Coolidge, Delaney and Bonnie, and others. The LP stayed in the album charts over six months and sold more than 100,000 copies. Mason toured the U.S. much of the year, taking time off in June to play a London show with Clapton's Derek and the Dominos at their Lyceum debut.

In the summer of 1970, Mason renewed his acquaintance with Mama Cass Elliot, forming a duo act that debuted at L.A.'s Hollywood Bowl that September, and recording a poorly received LP together. When the partnership dissolved, Mason briefly returned to England to guest with Traffic for a tour that resulted in the live LP *Welcome to the Canteen,* and he played on George Harrison's *All Things Must Pass.*

From that point on, Mason's solo career was erratic, though many of his subsequent LPs still sold well. *Headkeeper* was half new material, half live renditions of earlier material, and *Is Alive* was all of the latter. *Best of* furthered the apparent holding pattern, though *Never Left,* with support from Graham Nash and Stevie Wonder, and later albums saw Mason recoup somewhat. He had his biggest solo hit in 1977, when "We Just Disagree" reached #12. By late 1981, Mason could be heard singing radio commercials for Miller Beer.

JOHNNY MATHIS

Born September 30, 1935, San Francisco
1956—*Johnny Mathis* (Columbia) **1959**—*More Johnny's Greatest Hits* **1963**—*Johnny's Newest Hits* **1977**—*Johnny's Greatest Hits.*

Johnny Mathis' smooth ballad singing has made him, by some people's figures, the second most consistently charted album artist in popular music, just after Frank Sinatra. He is said to have become one of America's first black millionaires. His *Greatest Hits* spent 490 weeks—nine and a half years—on the charts.

Mathis' parents worked as domestics for a San Francisco millionaire. At 13, he took professional opera lessons, though his early goal was to become a physical education teacher. (In 1956, while attending San Francisco State College, he was invited to the Olympic trials held in Berkeley.) Singing in a jam session at San Francisco's 440 Club, Mathis was discovered by Columbia Records executive George Avakian, who sent him to New York to record. His first recordings were jazz-influenced, but Columbia A&R head Mitch Miller told him to switch to pop ballads.

His first hit came just one year later in July 1957, "Wonderful! Wonderful!" (#14), followed by "It's Not for Me to Say" (#5) and his big #1 in November, "Chances Are." Most of Mathis' big hits, including "The Twelfth of Never" (#9, 1957), "Misty" (#12, 1959) and "What Will Mary Say" (#9, 1963), were in the late Fifties and early Sixties, though his albums sold consistently well thereafter (always at least 250,000 copies, as he covered whatever MOR songs were hits at the time). His biggest score of recent years was his 1978 duet with Deniece Williams, "Too Much, Too Little, Too Late," which soared to #1 on both soul and pop charts.

IAN MATTHEWS

Born Ian Matthew MacDonald, 1946, Lincolnshire, England

1970—*Matthews Southern Comfort* (Uni; reissued 1974 by MCA) *Second Spring* (Decca; reissued 1974 by MCA) *Later That Same Year* (MCA) **1971**—*If You Saw Thro' My Eyes* (Vertigo) *Tigers Will Survive* **1973**—*Valley Hi* (Elektra) **1974**—*Some Days You Eat the Bear . . . and Some Days the Bear Eats You; Journeys from Gospel Oak* (Mooncrest; reissued 1979 by Boulevard) **1975**—*Best of Matthews Southern Comfort* (MCA) **1976**—*Go for Broke* (Columbia) **1977**—*Hit and Run* **1978**—*Stealin' Home* (Mushroom) **1979**—*Siamese Friends* (Rockburgh) **1980**—*Spot of Interference.*

A founding member of the seminal British folk-rock band Fairport Convention, Matthews (who used his middle name for a surname to avoid confusion with King Crimson's Ian McDonald) left that band in 1969 after its second LP to form his own group, Matthews Southern Comfort, which hit with a cover of Joni Mitchell's "Woodstock" (#1 U.K., #23 U.S., 1971). As well as Matthews' songwriting, vocals and guitar, Matthews Southern Comfort also featured the pedal steel guitar of Gordon Huntley, who went on to play on Rod Stewart's solo album, *Never a Dull Moment.* Matthews left Southern Comfort in late 1970 for a solo career; in 1972 he formed Plainsong, which recorded *In Search of Amelia Earhart* (Elektra) before disbanding. He moved to California and continued recording solo albums.

Although, despite the Fairport association, he has never considered himself a folkie (his first band, Pyramid, was a surf group) Matthews did record *Siamese Friends,* an album of traditional music. But most of Matthews' efforts have been country-flavored pop suited to his high tenor voice. He had a pop hit in 1979 with "Shake It" (#13). In the late Seventies, Matthews moved to Seattle, Washington, where he formed the band Hi-Fi with David Surkamp, former vocalist with St. Louis progressive-rockers Pavlov's Dog. Hi-Fi released a live EP *(Hi-Fi Demonstration Record)* for First American–SP&S.

JOHN MAYALL/JOHN MAYALL'S BLUESBREAKERS

John Mayall, born November 29, 1943, Manchester, England
The Bluesbreakers formed 1963, England

1963—(Davy Graham, gtr.; John McVie [b. Nov. 26, 1945, London], bass; Peter Ward, drums; − Graham; +Sammie Prosser, gtr.; − Prosser; + Bernie Watson, gtr.) **1964**—(− Watson; + John Gilbey, gtr.; − Gilbey; + Roger Dean, gtr.; − Ward; + Hughie Flint, drums) *John Mayall Plays John Mayall* (London) **1965**—(− Dean; + Jeff Kribbit, gtr.; − Kribbit; + Eric Clapton [b. Mar. 30, 1945, Ripley, Eng.], gtr.; − McVie; + Jack Bruce [b. May 14, 1943, Lanarkshire, Scot.], bass) **1966**—*Bluesbreakers—John Mayall with Eric Clapton* (+ McVie, bass; − Clapton; − Bruce; + Peter Green [b. Oct. 29, 1946, London], gtr.) *A Hard Road* (− Flint; + Mickey Waller, drums; − Waller; + Aynsley Dunbar, drums) **1967**—*The Blues Alone* (− Dunbar; + Mick Fleetwood (b. June 24, 1942, London), drums; − Green; + Mick Taylor [b. Jan. 17, 1948], gtr.; + Chris Mercer; + Rip Kant, horns) *Crusade* (− Fleetwood, + Keef Hartley, drums; − McVie; + Paul Williams, bass; − Williams; + Keith Tillman, bass; − Kant; + Dick Heckstall-Smith, horns) **1968**—*Diary of a Band, Volumes 1 and 2* (− Tillman; + Andy Fraser [b. Aug. 7, 1952, London], bass; − Fraser; + Tony Reeves, bass; − Hartley; + Jon Hiseman, drums) *Bare Wires* (− Reeves; + Steve Thompson, bass; − Hiseman; + Colin Allen, drums) *Blues from Laurel Canyon* **1969**—(− Taylor; + Jon Mark [b. Cornwall, Eng.]; + John Almond [b. 1946, Eng.]; − Allen) *The Turning Point* **1970**—(− Mark; − Almond; + Harvey Mandel, gtr.) *Empty Rooms* (− Thompson; + Larry Taylor, bass; + Don "Sugarcane" Harris [b. June 18, 1938, Pasadena, Calif.], violin) *USA Union* **1971**—(− Mandel; + Jimmy McCulloch [b. 1953, Glasgow; d. Sept. 27, 1979, London]; + Freddy Robinson; + Paul Lagos; − Lagos; + Hartley, drums) *Back to the Roots* (− Hartley; + Ron Selico, drums) *Jazz-Blues Fusion* (− Selico) **1972**—(− Taylor; + Victor Gaskin; + Hartley, drums) *Through the Years* **1973**—*Moving On* (Polydor) *Ten Years Are Gone* **1975**—*The Latest Edition; New Year, New Band, New Company* (ABC) **1976**—*Notice to Appear; John Mayall* (Polydor) *A Banquet in Blues* (ABC) **1977**—*The Hard Core Package* **1979**—*Bottom Line* (DJM) *No More Interviews.*

The father of the British blues movement, John Mayall has also been its hardiest perennial, taking the phrase "back to the roots" with more dogged seriousness than most. He's been one of the most famous talent scouts in rock music, having discovered many musicians—Eric Clapton, Mick Taylor, Jack Bruce, Keef Hartley, Aynsley Dunbar, Jon Mark, John Almond, Jon Hiseman, Peter Green, Mick Fleetwood and John McVie—who went on to significant careers of their own. He was also something of an iconoclast; he formed his first band when he was nearly thirty, and in the late Sixties, when hyperamplification was the rage, Mayall veered toward a subdued acoustic sound.

Mayall began playing guitar and ukulele at age 12; by 14 he was playing boogie-woogie piano as well. After graduating Manchester Junior School of Art in 1949, he worked briefly as a window dresser. In 1955, he formed his first group, the Powerhouse Four.

At age 18, Mayall entered the British Army; upon his discharge, he returned to art school. After graduating art school in 1959, he became a successful typographer and graphic artist (he later designed many of his album covers). He moved to London in 1962, and in 1963, he formed the Blues Syndicate.

By the time of the first Bluesbreakers LP (with Clapton and McVie), Mayall had been playing music for nearly twenty years. In 1965, Clapton was on guitar, and Jack Bruce had replaced McVie, who returned in 1966 to join Green on guitar and Hughie Flint (later with McGuinness-Flint) on drums. Green, McVie and Mick Fleetwood left after 1967 to form Fleetwood Mac, and Mick Taylor (later of the Rolling Stones) came in on guitar that year; at age 16, bassist Andy Fraser (later with Free) joined in 1968; in the early Seventies, guitarists Harvey Mandel (later with Canned Heat, among others) and Jimmy McCulloch (later with Paul McCartney's Wings) joined the band. Mayall never seemed perturbed by the many personnel changes; in fact he often encouraged his musicians to leave for greater fame and wealth.

Crusade introduced 18-year-old Mick Taylor, drummer Keef Hartley (who, like Mayall, had an intense interest in American Indian culture) and horn arrangements played by noted British jazz-rock sessionmen like Chris Mercer and Dick Heckstall-Smith. On *Blues Alone* Mayall played all the instruments except drums (handled again by Hartley). *Bare Wires* made a transition from blues to progressive jazz-rock; Heckstall-Smith and Hiseman left after this album to form the jazz-rock band Colosseum.

After he had become known in the U.S., Mayall bought a house in the Los Angeles area and recorded *Laurel Canyon,* a subdued record featuring local musicians like Canned Heat bassist Larry Taylor. *Turning Point* was all acoustic, with no drums; it featured Jon Mark's acoustic rhythm guitar and Johnny Almond's reed arsenal and included one of Mayall's most popular tunes, "Room to Move." *Jazz-Blues Fusion* featured jazz trumpeter Blue Mitchell and string bassist Victor Gaskin.

By the mid-Seventies, Mayall's star had faded somewhat, as had his falsetto voice—hence the addition of female singer Dee McKinnie on *New Year, New Band, New Company. Notice to Appear* was produced by New Orleans songwriter Allen Toussaint, but won little success commercially or critically. Still, Mayall kept recording through the Seventies. In early 1982, Mayall, McVie and Taylor staged a brief Bluesbreakers reunion, playing a short series of dates in America and Australia.

CURTIS MAYFIELD

Born June 3, 1942, Chicago
1972—*Superfly* (Curtom) **1973**—*His Early Years with the Impressions* (ABC) **1974**—*Sweet Exorcist* (Curtom) *Roots; Curtis* **1975**—*America Today* **1976**—*Give, Get, Take and Have* **1977**—*Never Say You Can't Survive* **1978**—*Do It All Night* **1979**—*Heartbeat* **1981**—*Love Is the Place* (Boardwalk).

Curtis Mayfield

Curtis Mayfield has been a driving force in black music since the early Sixties as a singer, writer, producer and label owner.

Mayfield began singing with gospel groups such as the Northern Jubilee Singers, who were part of his grandmother's Traveling Soul Spiritualist Church. He met lifelong friend and collaborator Jerry Butler at a gospel function, and they went on to form the Impressions, a rhythm & blues vocal group, in 1957. In 1958, they, along with Sam Gooden and Richard and Arthur Brooks, recorded "For Your Precious Love" on Vee Jay Records. Butler's cool baritone dominated the record, and he left to pursue a solo career. Mayfield and Butler teamed up again in 1960, with Butler singing and Mayfield writing and playing guitar on "He Will Break Your Heart" (#7 pop, #1 R&B). A re-formed Impressions with Mayfield, Gooden and Fred Cash signed with ABC-Paramount and scored with Mayfield's flamenco-sounding "Gypsy Woman" (#20 pop, #2 R&B).

Mayfield then entered a prolific period during which his writing and singing would come to define the Chicago sound, which rivaled Motown in the early and mid-Sixties. With the Impressions, Mayfield produced, wrote and sang lead on numerous hits; some included uplifting civil rights movement messages. "It's All Right" (#4 pop, #1 R&B) in 1963; "I'm So Proud" (#14 pop), "Keep On Pushing" (#10 pop) and "Amen" (#7 pop, #17 R&B) in 1964; "People Get Ready" (#14 pop, #3 R&B) in 1965; and "We're a Winner" (#14 pop, #1 R&B) in 1968 reflect the quality of Mayfield's work.

Meanwhile, as the staff producer for Columbia-distributed Okeh Records, Mayfield wrote memorable music for Major Lance—"The Monkey Time" (#8 pop, #4 R&B)

and "Um, Um, Um, Um, Um, Um" (#5 pop)—and for Gene Chandler, "Just Be True" (#19 pop) and "Nothing Can Stop Me" (#18 pop, #3 R&B). On his own Windy C and Mayfield labels, he produced hits with the Five Stairsteps and Cubie, "World of Fantasy" (#12 R&B), and the Fascinations, "Girls Are Out to Get You" (#13 R&B), respectively.

In the late Sixties, Mayfield started his third company, Curtom, this one distributed by Buddah Records. During the Seventies, Curtom moved from Buddah to Warner Bros. to RSO Records for distribution. In 1970, Mayfield also made a major career move, leaving the Impressions to go solo, though he continued to direct the group's career through the Seventies.

Solo albums—*Curtis* (#19 pop), *Curtis—Live* (#21 pop) and *Roots* (#40 pop)—all sold well, establishing Mayfield as a solo performer. But it was his soundtrack to the blaxploitation film *Superfly* that was generally considered his masterpiece—an eerie yet danceable blend of Mayfield's knowing falsetto with latin percussion and predisco rhythm guitars. The two-million selling album (#1 pop) included two gold singles, "Superfly" (#8 pop, #5 R&B) and "Freddie's Dead" (#4 pop, #2 R&B); it also sold a million copies as a tape. It foreshadowed Mayfield's continued involvement with film in the Seventies. He scored *Claudine,* writing the Gladys Knight and the Pips' single "On and On" in 1974; *Let's Do It Again,* which featured the Staple Singers on the title song in 1975; and *Sparkle* with Aretha Franklin in 1976. Two years later, Mayfield and Franklin would team again for *Almighty Fire.* In 1977, Mayfield would both score and act in the low-budget prison drama *Short Eyes,* a critical success.

In 1981, Mayfield signed with Boardwalk Records and enjoyed a popular album and singles with *Love Is the Place* and "Toot 'n' Toot 'n' Toot" (#2 R&B) and "She Don't Let Nobody (But Me)" (#15 R&B). Mayfield rejoined the Impressions for a 1983 reunion tour.

PAUL McCARTNEY

Born June 18, 1942, Liverpool, England
Solo: (McCartney on bass, gtr., kybds., drums, voc., usually alone): **1970**—*McCartney* (Apple/Capitol) **1971**—*Ram* (credited to Paul and Linda McCartney) **1980**—*McCartney II* (MPL/Columbia) **1982**—*Tug of War* (Columbia).
Wings: 1971—(+ Linda McCartney [b. Linda Louise Eastman, Sep. 24, 1942, Scarsdale, N.Y.], kybds., voc.; + Denny Laine [b. Brian Hines, Oct. 29, 1944, Eng.], gtr., kybds., voc.; + Denny Seiwell, drums) *Wild Life* (Apple/Capitol) **1972**—(+ Henry McCullough [b. Scotland], gtr.) **1973**—*Red Rose Speedway* (− McCullough; − Seiwell) *Band on the Run* **1974**— (+ Jimmy McCulloch [b. 1953, Glasgow; d. Sep. 27, 1979, London], gtr.; + Geoff Britton, drums; − Britton; + Joe English [b. Feb. 7, 1949, Rochester,

N.Y.], drums) **1975**—*Venus and Mars* (Capitol) **1976**—*At the Speed of Sound* **1977**—*Over America* (− English; − McCulloch) **1978**—*London Town; Greatest* (+ Steve Holly, drums; + Laurence Juber, gtr., voc.) *Back to the Egg* (Columbia).

Paul McCartney's gift for light pop songwriting has made him the most commercially successful ex-Beatle. He answered his critics in 1976 with the single "Silly Love Songs," one of many post-Beatles hits. If, as some critics maintain, his solo work hasn't measured up to the standards of his collaborations with Lennon, McCartney has still shown a consistent talent for writing songs that are tuneful and popular. McCartney was also the only ex-Beatle to form a permanent working band; by now, Wings has recorded for more years than the Beatles.

McCartney's father James led the Jim Mac Jazz Band in the Twenties; a few months after his mother Mary died in 1956, he bought his first guitar and learned to play. In June 1956, McCartney met Lennon and asked to join his band, the Quarrymen; McCartney's rendition of Eddie Cochran's "Twenty Flight Rock" at a subsequent audition won him entry. In 1963, McCartney met Jane Asher, to whom he addressed many of his best-known love songs, and on Christmas Day 1967, at a McCartney family party, he announced his engagement. But by July 1968, the engagement was off. Soon after, he met American photographer Linda Eastman, whom he married on March 12, 1969.

McCartney released his first solo album—a one-man-studio-band LP recorded in Campbelltown, England, in late 1969—in April 1970, only two weeks before the scheduled release of the Beatles' *Let It Be. McCartney* had a pronounced homemade quality; it was spare and sounded almost unfinished, but it also contained "Maybe I'm Amazed," which became an international hit and McCartney's first post-Beatles pop standard (the Beatles had only recently disbanded as the tune became a hit). The winsome homespun-ditty motif continued with *Ram,* credited to Paul and Linda McCartney. It also inspired Lennon's "How Do You Sleep?"—a vicious, thinly veiled attack on McCartney. Meanwhile *Ram* yielded two major hit singles in "Another Day" (#5, 1971) and "Uncle Albert/Admiral Halsey," which made #1 in America.

Later in 1971, McCartney formed Wings, which was intended as a recording and touring outfit. Along with Linda, Wings featured American session drummer Denny Seiwell and ex–Moody Blues guitarist Denny Laine. Wings' *Wild Life,* with Linda McCartney on keyboards and backup vocals, sold only moderately, failing to yield a hit single. In 1972, ex–Grease Band guitarist Henry McCullough joined. McCartney spent 1972 releasing several singles including "Give Ireland Back to the Irish" (#16 U.K.) (rush-released after the January 1972 "Bloody Sunday" incident in which British soldiers killed 13 Irish civilians in Londonderry, Ireland, and banned by the

Paul McCartney

BBC), "Mary Had a Little Lamb" (Top Ten, U.K., #28 U.S.) (yes, the nursery rhyme) and "Hi Hi Hi." Only the hard-rocking "Hi Hi Hi" was a U.S. hit.

Red Rose Speedway, the next Wings album, yielded a #1 hit single in the U.S. in the heavily orchestrated ballad "My Love." Also in 1973, McCartney was arrested and then released on a drug charge, and he did his own television special, which received mixed reviews in both the U.S. and the U.K. Later Wings made their first tour of Britain, and recorded the title theme song for the James Bond film *Live and Let Die*, which went to #2 in the U.S. Laine released a solo LP, *Ahh Laine.*

After Wings' U.K. tour, Seiwell and Henry McCullough left Wings. Denny Laine accompanied Paul and Linda on a trip to Nigeria to record *Band on the Run*. While each of the previous Wings albums had ended up going gold, *Band on the Run* went platinum in short order and yielded two Top Ten hit singles—"Helen Wheels" (#10, 1973) and "Jet" (#7, 1974)—and the bouncy mini-suite title track (#11, 1974). It also included McCartney's answer to Lennon's "How Do You Sleep?" in "Let Me Roll It," and featured a cover photo of McCartney accompanied by such celebrities as film actors James Coburn and Christopher Lee.

McCartney formed a new Wings, recruiting guitarist James McCulloch from Thunderclap Newman and Stone the Crows, and drummer Geoff Britton, a British karate expert. They recorded "Junior's Farm" in Nashville in 1974, and later that year went to New Orleans (where they found new drummer Joe English) to record *Venus and*

Mars, which yielded several hit singles (including "Listen to What the Man Said") and went platinum.

At the Speed of Sound found McCartney giving his bandmembers a chance to compose and sing much of the material, but McCartney's own contributions were almost all hits. Two went gold: "Silly Love Songs" (#1, 1976) and "Let Em In" (#3, 1976). Shortly after the album's release, Wings completed a world tour that had begun in Britain on September 9, 1975, and ended on October 21, 1976. The *Over America* triple-record live album was recorded on that tour.

In 1977, McCartney, under the pseudonym Percy Thrillington, recorded an obscure all-instrumental version of *Ram* and produced Denny Laine's *Holly Days,* a solo album of Buddy Holly songs. A live "Maybe I'm Amazed" hit #10 in 1977. That year saw the release of the McCartney-Laine "Mull of Kintyre," based on a Scottish folk song, which became the first single ever to sell two million copies in Britain, and was a minor hit in the U.S. as well. It was McCartney's first #1 single since he'd left the Beatles. Later that year, under the name Susie and the Red Stripes, McCartney and Wings had another minor hit single in the reggae-inflected "Seaside Woman."

After *London Town,* which yielded "With a Little Luck," Jimmy McCulloch departed for the re-formed Faces; he later died of undetermined causes. *Back to the Egg* failed to yield a hit and sold unspectacularly. In January 1980, McCartney was arrested for possession of marijuana in Tokyo at the beginning of a Japanese tour, jailed for ten days, then freed and not prosecuted. Soon after, he and Wings embarked on a British tour, after which drummer English left. McCartney then organized all-star benefit concerts for the people of Kampuchea and released *McCartney II,* his first one-man-band album since his solo debut. It contained the hit "Coming Up."

In April 1981, Denny Laine announced he was leaving Wings, the reason being McCartney's reluctance to tour because of the death threats he was receiving in the wake of John Lennon's murder. McCartney continued with the well-received *Tug of War,* a solo album featuring a host of guest performers (Laine, ex-Beatle Ringo Starr, Beatles producer George Martin), most notably Stevie Wonder, who sang with McCartney on the hit single "Ebony and Ivory." McCartney sang on Michael Jackson's "The Girl Is Mine," a Top Ten hit in 1983.

Over the years, McCartney has invested extensively in pop-song copyrights; among his holdings are the entire Buddy Holly catalogue, "On Wisconsin" and "Autumn Leaves."

DELBERT McCLINTON
Born November 4, 1940, Lubbock, Texas
1972—*Delbert and Glen* (Clean) **1973**—*Subject to Change* **1975**—*Victim of Life's Circumstances* (ABC)
1976—*Genuine Cowhide* **1977**—*Love Rustler* **1978**—*Second Wind* (Capricorn) *Very Early Delbert McClin-*

ton (Le Cam) **1979**—*Keeper of the Flame* (Capricorn) **1980**—*The Jealous Kind* (Capitol).

Delbert McClinton has been singing R&B, blues, rockabilly and country for 25 years, starting on the Texas honky-tonk circuit. In the late Fifties, McClinton's Straitjackets were the house band and one of the few white acts at Jacks, a Fort Worth club where they backed up Howlin' Wolf, Lightnin' Hopkins and Big Joe Turner. McClinton's first record, a cover of Sonny Boy Williamson's "Wake Up Baby," released in 1960, was the first white single played on Fort Worth's KNOK.

Inspired by bluesman Jimmy Reed, McClinton switched from guitar to harmonica, and in the early Sixties, when he toured England with Bruce Channel (with whom he played on "Hey Baby"), he taught some harp licks to John Lennon, who was playing in a then-unknown opening act, the Beatles. In 1964 and 1965, he had a group called the Ron Dels, who were shunted around to three labels, though one song ("If You Really Want Me To, I'll Go") did reach the national charts.

McClinton spent the late Sixties on the local Texas bar circuit, until he and Glen Clark formed Delbert and Glen, a duo that cut two LPs for Atlantic's Clean subsidiary in 1972 and 1973. He didn't get a solo contract until 1975, and his subsequent albums on ABC won critical kudos but sold poorly. In 1978, he recorded two discs for Capricorn just before the label folded; his composition "Two More Bottles of Wine" later became a #1 country hit for Emmylou Harris, and the Blues Brothers recorded his "B Movie Boxcar Blues." His next record, *The Jealous Kind* (1980), recorded for Capitol with some Muscle Shoals musicians, turned his luck around, earning him his own Top Forty hit, "Giving It Up for Your Love" (#8, 1980).

VAN McCOY
Born January 6, 1944, Washington, D.C.; died July 6, 1979
1975—*Disco Baby* (Avco) **1976**—*The Hustle* (H&L) **1978**—*My Favorite Fantasy* (MCA) **1979**—*Lonely Dancer; Sweet Rhythm* (H&L).

Throughout the Sixties and Seventies, Van McCoy was primarily a songwriter and producer for artists like Aretha Franklin, Gladys Knight and the Pips, Peaches and Herb, and Melba Moore. He had one of disco's biggest hits with his own 1975 instrumental single "The Hustle" (#1 pop, #1 R&B).

McCoy studied piano from age four, and a year later he and his older brother Norman, a violinist, began performing at Washington teas as the McCoy Brothers. He wrote his first song at age 12, and while studying psychology at Howard University he began singing with the Starlighters, a group that cut a few locally released records. During his second year at Howard, he moved to Philadelphia and started a record label with his uncle.

McCoy then began writing and producing hits for Ruby and the Romantics, Gladys Knight, Barbara Lewis and others. He recorded an album on Columbia, then in 1967 with Joe Cobb formed his own record production and music publishing company. In 1973, he and Charles Kipps established White House Productions, renamed McCoy-Kipps Productions in 1976. Other popular singles by McCoy include "Change with the Times" (#46 pop, #6 R&B, 1975) and "Party" (#69 pop, #20 R&B, 1976). He died of a heart attack.

MISSISSIPPI FRED McDOWELL
Born January 12, 1904, Rossville, Tennessee; died July 3, 1972, Memphis
1972—*Mississippi Fred McDowell 1904–1972* (Just Sunshine) **1973**—*Keep Your Lamp Trimmed and Burning* (Arhoolie).

Although Mississippi Fred McDowell didn't make his first recording until the age of 55, he proved to be among the most influential of blues singer/guitarists on rock & roll, particularly with singer/guitarist Bonnie Raitt, who brought him on her tours and recorded his songs. McDowell made dozens of records, but is probably best known as the composer of "You Got to Move," covered by the Rolling Stones on *Sticky Fingers*.

McDowell taught himself the guitar as a teenager and played locally in Tennessee while working as a farmer. In 1926, he moved to Memphis to become a professional musician, which he gave up for farming again in 1940, when he relocated to Como, Mississippi. His recording career began in 1959, at which point he began devoting more and more time to music. He made records, frequently with his wife, Annie Mae, and played at all the major folk and blues festivals of the Sixties. With the increased attention paid by rock & rollers to bluesmen, he appeared at a number of rock festivals as well. In addition to his many records, McDowell was captured in nearly a half-dozen films, including *The Blues Maker* (1968) and *Fred McDowell* (1969). He died of cancer.

McFADDEN AND WHITEHEAD
Gene McFadden, born circa 1948, Philadelphia; John Whitehead, born circa 1948, Philadelphia
1979—*McFadden and Whitehead* (Philadelphia International) **1980**—*I Heard It in a Love Song*.

Gene McFadden and John Whitehead are prolific songwriters who contributed greatly to the success of Kenny Gamble and Leon Huff's Philadelphia International Records.

The duo's career began when both belonged to a vocal group called the Epsilons. They worked with many of the Stax stars, including Otis Redding, and sang background vocals on Arthur Conley's "Sweet Soul Music." Later the group's name was changed to Talk of the Town.

Frustrated by their lack of success as performers, McFadden and Whitehead turned to songwriting. During their tenure as staff writers for PIR, they wrote "Bad Luck," "Where Are All My Friends" and "Wake Up Everybody" for Harold Melvin and the Blue Notes (all with arranger Vic Carstarphen); "Backstabbers" (Whitehead with Gamble and Huff) for the O'Jays; and "I'll Always Love My Mama" (Whitehead, Carstarphen, Huff) for the Intruders.

In 1979, they recorded one of that summer's most popular singles, "Ain't No Stoppin' Us Now" (#3 pop, #1 R&B). In the early Eighties, the duo produced records for Teddy Pendergrass, Melba Moore and others.

MC5

Formed 1967, Detroit
Rob Tyner, voc.; Wayne Kramer (b. Apr. 30, 1948, Detroit), gtr.; Fred "Sonic" Smith (b. W. Va.), gtr.; Michael Davis, bass; Dennis Thompson, drums.
1969—*Kick Out the Jams* (Elektra) **1970**—*Back in the USA* (Atlantic) **1971**—*High Time.*

Some called the MC5 (for "Motor City Five," after their home base) the first Seventies band of the Sixties. The MC5's loud, hard and fast sound and violently anti-establishment ideology almost precisely prefigured much of punk rock. There was, however, one crucial difference: the MC5 unironically believed in the power of rock & roll to change the world.

The band first formed in high school and came to prominence in 1967–68 as the figureheads (or "house band") of John Sinclair's radical White Panther Party. At concerts and happenings, they caused a sensation by wearing American flags and screaming revolutionary slogans laced with profanities. In 1968, they went with Sinclair to Chicago, to play at the Democratic Convention riots. Their debut LP, recorded live in 1968, captured the band in typical raw, revved-up, radical form, and embroiled Elektra Records in controversy over the title tune's loud-and-clear shout "Kick out the jams, motherfuckers!" Some stores refused to stock the album; in response, the MC5 took out strongly worded ads in underground papers and, to Elektra's further distress, plastered one offending store's windows with Elektra stationery on which was scrawled, "Fuck you." Elektra and the MC5 parted company shortly thereafter—but not before the band had cut another version of "Kick Out the Jams," with "brothers and sisters" substituted for the offending expletive (available as a single and on some subsequent issues of the album, against the band's wishes).

When Sinclair went to jail on a marijuana charge, the MC5 were left with neither a manager nor a label. Atlantic signed them then, and their debut was produced by rock critic Jon Landau. *Back in the USA* was hailed by critics as one of the greatest hard-rock albums of all time. Record sales were almost nil, however, and never improved. Dropped by Atlantic, the band went to England but soon fell apart, with Davis and Thompson the first to leave.

The MC5: Fred "Sonic" Smith, Michael Davis, Dennis Thompson, Wayne Kramer, Rob Tyner

Since then, Tyner has had modest success as a songwriter and photographer; Davis was last heard from in an Ann Arbor band called Destroy All Monsters, with ex-Stooge Ron Ashton; Thompson was struggling with abortive solo ventures; Smith formed a late-Seventies band, Sonics Rendezvous, that toured Europe with Iggy Pop and recorded one single. He married Patti Smith in 1980 in Detroit. Kramer, after pleading guilty to a cocaine-dealing charge and spending two years in prison, has returned to music. He formed a short partnership with ex–New York Doll and ex-Heartbreaker Johnny Thunders (Gang War), was featured guitarist with Motor City funksters Was (Not Was) (Kramer played the psychedelic guitar on their hit single "Wheel Me Out"), released two singles, and led his own band, Air Raid. The band's first two LPs were reissued in England to meet the popular demand of the first punk wave in 1977, and their debut album was quietly restored to Elektra's U.S. catalogue in the early Eighties.

KATE AND ANNA McGARRIGLE

Kate McGarrigle, born 1946, Montreal; Anna McGarrigle, born 1944, Montreal
1976—*Kate and Anna McGarrigle* (Warner Bros.)
1977—*Dancer with Bruised Knees* **1978**—*Pronto Monto* **1981**—*French Record* (Hannibal) **1983**—*Love Over and Over* (Polydor).

The McGarrigle sisters' songs bring together a wide range of folk and pop styles, from Stephen Foster parlor songs to Celtic traditional songs to Cajun fiddling to gospel to pop standards. Although their wry, generally unsentimental songs have been best-known in the U.S. as covers (by Linda Ronstadt, Maria Muldaur and others), they have had hits in Canada and Europe, especially with songs recorded in French.

The McGarrigles grew up in Montreal and are bilingual. In the mid-Sixties, they were half of the Mountain City

Four, whose other members (Chaim Tannenbaum and Dane Lanken) continue to perform and record with them. While Anna was studying at Montreal's École des Beaux Arts and Kate was attending McGill University, the National Film Board of Canada commissioned the Mountain City Four to score a film, *Helicopter Canada.*

Kate performed around New York in the Sixties, sometimes as a duo with Roma Baran (who later produced Laurie Anderson), and both sisters wrote songs. Anna's first effort, "Heart Like a Wheel," was used in the soundtrack of *Play It As It Lays,* and became the title tune of a multimillion-selling Linda Ronstadt album; Ronstadt has also covered Kate's "Mendocino" and "You Tell Me That I'm Falling Down." Maria Muldaur covered Kate's "The Work Song" and Anna's "Cool River."

Kate married New York singer/songwriter Loudon Wainwright III, and her song "Come a Long Way" appeared on Wainwright's *Attempted Moustache,* which also included Kate's backup vocals; Kate and Anna both sang on Wainwright's *Unrequited.* Shortly after the birth of their son, Rufus (*not* Loudon Wainwright IV), the marriage broke up.

The McGarrigles' songwriting brought them a contract on their own, but their high, reedy voices and homey arrangements were not well received by U.S. radio programers despite critics' raves. The McGarrigles toured infrequently; their U.S. tour after their debut LP consisted of two weeks of Massachusetts dates. After *Pronto Monto,* an attempt to make more conventional-sounding folk pop, the McGarrigles were dropped by Warner Bros. Kate appeared on an album by Albion Country Band, a Fairport Convention offshoot. The McGarrigles reemerged with a Canadian best seller, *French Record,* a compilation of material in French from previous albums and new French songs. *Love Over and Over,* a return to their original style, was the occasion for a U.S. tour.

MIKE McGEAR
Born Mike McCartney, January 7, 1944, Liverpool, England
1972—*Woman* (Island)   1974—*McGear* (Warner Bros.).

Other than being known as Paul McCartney's younger brother, Mike McGear has made little impact in the U.S., though he has had a modestly successful career in England.

Around the time that the Beatles were making a name for themselves, 18-year-old Mike McCartney was entering show business with a satirical theater group he met at the Merseyside Arts Festival. Members of that ensemble went on to perform as the Liverpool One Fat Lady All Electric Show, and then further refined the act into a trio: John Gorman, Roger McGough and Mike McCartney, now known as McGear (punning around with British slang), henceforth dubbed the Scaffold.

The group began writing, singing and recording novelty pop songs. "Thank U Very Much," a McGear composition, reached #4 in England in 1967, followed up by three more British chart hits, "Do You Remember" (#34, 1968), "Lily the Pink" (#1, 1968) and "Gin Can Coulie" (#38, 1969); "Lily the Pink" sold a million copies worldwide. In the Seventies, Scaffold expanded their ranks to include, among others, ex–Bonzo Dog Band coleaders Neil Innes and Viv Stanshall. The resultant Grimms released three albums mixing poetry and music, only one of which, *Rockin' Duck,* was released in America.

In 1974, McGear recorded the album *McGear,* which was a flop although it was produced by brother Paul with backup by Wings. That same year, the Scaffold had a final British hit, "Liverpool Lou" (#7). The group gave up for good in the late Seventies. McGear wrote and illustrated the children's book *Roger Bear* in 1974, and assembled a family album, *The Macs,* in 1981.

BARRY McGUIRE
Born October 15, 1937, Oklahoma City
1965—*Eve of Destruction* (Dunhill)   1966—*This Precious Time*   1968—*The World's Last Private Citizen.*

Singer/songwriter Barry McGuire's first and last hit was his debut solo record, the prototypical protest song "Eve of Destruction." The Bob Dylan–style folk-rock tune made #1 in 1965, although some stations banned it because of its pessimistic lyrics. It also inspired an answer record, "Dawn of Correction."

Before "Eve," McGuire had been with the New Christy Minstrels and had been the featured vocalist on their 1963 hit "Green Green." He was further credited with helping to launch the career of the Mamas and the Papas, for which he was thanked with a mention in "Creeque Alley." In the Seventies, McGuire had his own dawn of redemption: he became a born-again Christian and began recording for Myrrh, a label specializing in religious pop.

ELLEN McILWAINE
Born October 1, 1948, Nashville
1972—*Honky Tonk Angel* (Polydor)   1973—*We the People*   1974—*The Real Ellen McIlwaine* (Kot'ai)
1976—*Ellen McIlwaine* (United Artists)   1982—*Everybody Needs It* (Blind Pig).

One of the more accomplished white blueswomen, Ellen McIlwaine has a distinctive, powerful soprano voice. She is also, with Bonnie Raitt, one of very few white female slide guitarists.

At three weeks old, McIlwaine was adopted by a missionary couple who moved to Kobe, Japan, three months later; she stayed there until 1963, when she moved back to Nashville. She attended colleges in Tennessee and Georgia and began performing in 1969 in Atlanta clubs and coffeehouses. In Atlanta in 1970, she joined the folk-rock band Fear Itself, with whom she moved to New York City, where they recorded one album in 1971 for Dot Records before disbanding.

McIlwaine settled in Woodstock, New York, delving into the blues, folk and rock repertoires to find the blues and R&B chestnuts she would later rearrange. She toured with Lily Tomlin in 1972, then moved in 1973 to Montreal, where she recorded *The Real Ellen,* distributed in Canada only. She returned to Atlanta in 1976 and signed with New York independent production company Zembu, which licensed out the United Artists album. She then toured with Laura Nyro and left off recording until 1980, when she recorded *Everybody,* which featured vocal, bass and production assistance from a songwriter she had frequently covered, ex-Cream member Jack Bruce. That LP was released in 1982.

DON McLEAN

Born October 2, 1945, New Rochelle, New York
1970—*Tapestry* (United Artists)   **1971**—*American Pie*
1972—*Don McLean*   **1973**—*Playin' Favorites*   **1974**—
Homeless Brother   **1976**—*Solo*   **1977**—*Prime Time*
(Arista)   **1980**—*Chain Lightning* (Millennium)   **1981**—
Believers.

Though he continues to have occasional hits, singer/songwriter Don McLean is chiefly remembered for his #1 single of 1972, "American Pie," an 8½-minute saga inspired by the death of Buddy Holly. The song propelled his second album to #1, and obscured McLean's folksinging past and future for many years.

Before his sudden fame, McLean had earned a small following for his work with Pete Seeger on the sloop *Clearwater,* which sailed up and down the Hudson River on ecology campaigns. Perry Como turned one of the songs from McLean's debut album, "And I Love You So," into an international hit, and songwriters Charles Gimble and Norman Fox made McLean the subject of "Killing Me Softly with His Song," Roberta Flack's Grammy Award–winning single of 1973. But even as *American Pie* yielded a second hit, the ballad "Vincent" (#12) (played daily at Amsterdam's Van Gogh Museum), McLean's smash success proved unrepeatable, and he spent a period of several years refusing to play "American Pie" and letting his career wind down.

McLean's albums for his new label, Millennium, started selling, and in 1981 he had a few hits, a remake of Roy Orbison's "Crying" (#5), his own "Castles in the Air" (#36) and "Since I Don't Have You" (#23).

BIG JAY McNEELY

Born Cecil McNeely, April 29, 1928
N.A.—*Big Jay in 3D* (Federal)   *Big Jay McNeeley*
(Warner Bros.)   *Big Jay McNeely Selections* (Savoy).

One of the original honking and shouting rock & roll tenor saxophonists, Big Jay McNeely was famed for his playing-on-his-back acrobatics and his raw, hard-swinging play-

ing, both of which influenced subsequent rock guitarists. His best-known composition is "There Is Something on Your Mind," a #5 R&B hit (#44 pop) in 1959 when sung by his own band's vocalist, Little Sonny Warner (Aaron Willis), Part 2 becoming an even bigger hit (#1 R&B, #31 pop) a year later for New Orleans singer Bobby Marchan. McNeely now works for the post office in Los Angeles.

RALPH McTELL

Born Farnborough, England
1971—*You Well-Meaning Brought Me Here* (Paramount/ABC)   **1972**—*Not Till Tomorrow* (Reprise)
1973—*Easy* (Reprise)   **1975**—*Streets* (Warner Bros.)
1976—*Right Side Up*   **1977**—*Ralph, Albert, Sydney;
Maginot Waltz*   **1978**—*Ralph McTell* (Pickwick)
1979—*Live* (Fantasy)   *Slide Away the Screen* (Warner
Bros.).

British folkie McTell learned the guitar, went to street-sing in Europe, came back home, and a couple of years later wrote and recorded "Streets of London." "Streets" was a cult success upon its first release, only somewhat expanding his limited English audience. Warner Bros. added strings and a female chorus to it in 1975, and it went to #1 on the British charts.

McTell responded to the acclaim with his first concert tour and another first—a band that included Maddy Prior of Steeleye Span on backing vocals. The tune was never a real chart success in the U.S., though it was well enough known to give McTell something of a following. His *You Well-Meaning* was especially well received by critics.

In 1980, McTell appeared at a Christmas benefit show in London with Donovan. His name surfaced again in early 1982, when Scotland Yard raided British independent record label/store Rough Trade to seize several thousand copies of a single by British punk band Anti-Nowhere League, the B side of which was an obscene cover version of "Streets of London."

MEAT LOAF

Born Marvin Lee Aday, September 27, 1947, Dallas
1971—*Stoney and Meat Loaf* (Rare Earth) (re-released in 1979 as *Meat Loaf (Featuring Stoney)* (Prodigal/Motown)   **1977**—*Bat Out of Hell* (Cleveland International)   **1981**—*Dead Ringer*   **1983**—*Midnight at the Lost and Found.*

Bat Out of Hell made Meat Loaf rock's first 250-pound-plus superstar since Leslie West. One of the biggest-selling LPs of the Seventies, *Bat* eventually sold five million copies.

It's unclear exactly when and how Marvin Lee Aday became Meat Loaf, but by 1966, when he moved from his native Texas to California, he'd formed a band alternately known as Meat Loaf Soul and Popcorn Blizzard, which, until its breakup in 1969, had opened shows for the Who, Iggy and the Stooges, Johnny and Edgar Winter, and Ted

Nugent. He then auditioned for and got a part in a West Coast production of *Hair* and traveled with the show to the East Coast and then to Detroit, where he hooked up with a singer named Stoney to record the unsuccessful LP *Stoney and Meat Loaf.* Meat Loaf went to New York to appear in the Off Broadway gospel musical *Rainbow in New York* in 1973, and then successfully auditioned for *More Than You Deserve,* written by Jim Steinman.

Steinman, a New Yorker who'd spent his early teen years in California, had studied classical piano. At Amherst College he formed a band called The Clitoris That Thought It Was a Puppy. Later he wrote a play called *Dream Engine* in New York. Meanwhile, Meat Loaf had played Eddie in the hugely successful cult film *The Rocky Horror Picture Show* and sung lead vocals on one side of Ted Nugent's platinum LP *Free for All.*

After meeting at *More Than You Deserve* auditions, Meat Loaf and Steinman toured with the National Lampoon Road Show; then Steinman wrote a musical called *Never Land* (a Peter Pan update), from which would come much of the material for *Bat Out of Hell.* (*Never Land* was produced in 1977 at Washington's Kennedy Center.) Meat Loaf and Steinman rehearsed for a full year before Todd Rundgren, an early supporter of the project, agreed to produce them.

At first, *Bat,* with its highly theatrical, bombastically orchestrated teen drama, sold well only in New York and Cleveland. Then Meat Loaf hit the road with a seven-piece band including singer Karla DeVito in the role Ellen Foley had played on the LP's "Paradise by the Dashboard Light" (which also included a cameo by New York Yankees announcer Phil Rizzuto). The LP was platinum by the end of the year, with the hit singles "Paradise by the Dashboard Light" (#39), "Two Out of Three Ain't Bad" (#11) and "You Took the Words Right Out of My Mouth" (#39).

The *Stoney and Meat Loaf* LP was reissued with the order of the names of the principals switched accordingly. Meat Loaf appeared in the films *Americathon* (1979) and *Roadie* (1980). In 1981, Steinman released his own Rundgren-produced solo LP, *Bad for Good.* Still the world awaited *Bat*'s sequel. Stories circulated that Meat Loaf had been coaxed to sing *Bad for Good* but couldn't or wouldn't because of a variety of physical and emotional problems. Finally, toward the end of 1981, *Dead Ringer* was released to meager response. Meanwhile, Steinman initiated lawsuits against Epic and Meat Loaf. *Midnight at the Lost and Found* had no Steinman material and included a few songs cowritten by "M. Lee Aday."

MEL AND TIM
Formed mid-1960s, St. Louis
1970—*Good Guys Only Win in the Movies* (Bamboo) *Mel and Tim* (Stax) 1972—*Starting All Over Again.*

Cousins Mel Harden and Tim McPherson are best known for their three hit singles: "Backfield in Motion" (1969),

"Good Guys Only Win in the Movies" (1970) and "Starting All Over Again" (1972). "Backfield" (#10 pop, #3 R&B) was written by McPherson and produced by singer Gene Chandler for his own Bamboo Records. "Movies" (#17 R&B) was also on Chandler's label. After solving some contractual difficulties, Mel and Tim left Bamboo and recorded at the Muscle Shoals studio in Alabama. In 1972, they cut Phillip Mitchell's "Starting," which was leased to Memphis' Stax Records, becoming a #4 R&B hit.

MELANIE
Born Melanie Safka, February 3, 1947, Queens, New York
1969—*Born to Be* (Buddah) *Melanie* 1970—*Candles in the Rain; Leftover Wine* 1971—*The Good Book; Gather Me* (Neighborhood) 1972—*Four Sides of Melanie* (Buddah) *Stoneground Words* (Neighborhood) 1973—*At Carnegie Hall* 1974—*Mad Rugada; As I See It Now* 1975—*Sunset and Other Beginnings* 1976—*Photograph* (Atlantic) 1978—*Phonogenic—Not Just Another Pretty Face* (Midsong) 1979—*Ballroom Streets* (RCA).

Singer/songwriter Melanie caught the last upsurge of hippie innocence in songs like "Lay Down (Candles in the Rain)" and "Beautiful People." While she sold over 22 million records around the world, her childlike demeanor, cracked voice and naive lyrics made her a novelty act before her time.

Melanie Safka's family moved to Boston and then to Long Branch, New Jersey, when she was a teenager. After high school, she studied at the American Academy of Dramatic Arts. Soon after, she signed a song publishing agreement with her future producer and husband, Peter Schekeryk. In 1967, she won a recording contract with Columbia Records, which released her single "Beautiful People." When the record did not sell, Columbia dropped her and she returned to the local folk clubs until 1969, when a single from her *Born to Be,* "What Have They Done to My Song, Ma," hit in France and became a smash in the U.S. for the New Seekers.

In August 1969, she appeared at Woodstock, which inspired her to write "Lay Down (Candles in the Rain)." Released in spring 1970, it became a #6 single, and the *Candles in the Rain* LP went gold. From then on it became a ritual for her loyal fans to light candles at her shows. In the summer of 1970, "Peace Will Come (According to Plan)" hit #32, and she made a live album, *Leftover Wine.*

In 1971, Melanie and her husband formed their own record company, Neighborhood, and the singer immediately had her biggest success, the #1 "Brand New Key," which sold over three million copies. Another single off the LP, "Ring the Living Bell," hit the Top Forty. *Stoneground Words* also went gold. In 1971, she performed and toured the world as a spokesperson for UNICEF.

After that, her records stopped selling, and in 1975 Neighborhood folded. She was signed by Atlantic Records, and her label debut, *Photograph,* was coproduced by label president Ahmet Ertegun and Schekeryk. In 1978, she recorded for Midsong, and the next year released *Ballroom Streets* on RCA.

HAROLD MELVIN AND THE BLUE NOTES
Formed 1956, Philadelphia
Original lineup: Harold Melvin, John Atkins, Lawrence Brown, Bernard Wilson.
1970—(— Atkins; + Teddy Pendergrass; + Lloyd Parks) 1972—*Harold Melvin and the Blue Notes* (Philadelphia International) 1973—*I Miss You; Black and Blue* (— Parks; + Jerry Cummings) 1975—*To Be True; Wake Up Everybody* 1976—(— Pendergrass; + David Ebo) *All Their Greatest Hits* 1977—*Reaching for the World* (ABC) (+ Dwight Johnson; + Bill Spratley) 1980—*The Blue Album* (Source) 1981—*All Things Happen in Time* (MCA).

Although formed in 1956, this Philadelphia-based vocal group attained widespread popularity only during the mid-Seventies with Teddy Pendergrass as lead singer. Harold Melvin founded the Blue Notes as a doo-wop group with lead singer John Atkins and with Lawrence Brown and Bernard Wilson, who handled the group's choreography. Wilson also provided other local groups like the Delfonics, Brenda and the Tabulations and the O'Jays with stage movements.

The Blue Notes recorded their first single, "If You Love Me," for Josie, and after years in the Sixties on the chitlin' circuit they were signed to the William Morris Agency on the recommendation of Martha Reeves. They frequently appeared in supper clubs in Las Vegas, Lake Tahoe, Reno and Miami Beach and were known for their trademark "tie and tails" look.

In 1970, Pendergrass replaced Atkins as lead singer. (He had briefly been the group's drummer.) The next year, the group signed with Kenny Gamble and Leon Huff's Philadelphia International Records, and soon became one of the first groups associated with the Sound of Philadelphia. During this period, Lloyd Parks joined, making the group a quintet.

From 1972 until Pendergrass left in 1976 to pursue a solo career, Harold Melvin and the Blue Notes had three #1 soul singles: "If You Don't Know Me By Now" (#3 pop, 1972), "The Love I Lost" (#7 pop, 1973) and "Wake Up Everybody" (#12 pop, 1976). Other hits included "I Miss You" (#7 R&B, #58 pop, 1972), "Satisfaction Guaranteed" (#6 R&B, #58 pop, 1974), "Where Are All My Friends" (#8 R&B, 1974), "Bad Luck" (#4 R&B, #15 pop, 1975), "Tell the World How I Feel About 'Cha Baby" (#7 R&B, 1976) and "Hope That We Can Be Together Soon" (#42 pop) (featuring Sharon Paige) in 1975.

Following Pendergrass' departure for a hugely successful solo career, Melvin brought in lead singer David Ebo, and the group signed to ABC. Although their label debut, "Reaching for the World," hit #6 on the soul charts, subsequent releases failed to match their mid-Seventies success. In 1979, they switched to Source Records, where "Prayin' " was a moderate R&B hit (#18).

MEMPHIS SLIM
Born Peter Chatman, September 3, 1915, Memphis
1973—*Legacy of the Blues* (GNP/Crescendo) 1975—*Rock Me Baby* (Black Lion) 1976—*Chicago Boogie* 1978—*Boogie Woogie* (Festival).

Blues singer and barrelhouse pianist Memphis Slim was perhaps the first bluesman to leave America for Europe and become a star there. He is also the composer of "Every Day (I Have the Blues)," which became a Big Band standard when sung by Joe Williams with Count Basie's orchestra.

Having taught himself the piano, and having learned from such Memphis greats as Speckled Red and Roosevelt Sykes, Slim went to Chicago in 1939, where he met Big Bill Broonzy. Broonzy told Slim that he had talent but lacked an original style, but by 1940 Slim had become Broonzy's accompanist, a job he held until the late Forties. Slim led his own groups as a singer/pianist on the late-Forties blues circuit, and had a minor R&B hit in the early Fifties with his own "Beer Drinkin' Woman." With the folk boom of the late Fifties and early Sixties, Slim's popularity was renewed, and he played for large white audiences for the first time. His band at that time included the Chicago bassist/composer Willie Dixon. In 1959, Slim earned a standing ovation at the Newport Folk Festival, and then shared the bill at New York City's Village Gate with Pete Seeger. At this time, he recorded for Folkways; he now has dozens of albums out on many labels.

In 1960, Memphis Slim first toured Europe and was well enough received that he went back again in 1962, doing especially well at his French debut. After an Israeli tour in 1963, he made Paris his home. He became a celebrity, a star performer at major music halls in England and all over the Continent, and an often-seen face on French TV. Though his most recent recordings have failed to recapture the raw energy of his classic Fifties small-group recordings, Memphis Slim has recorded with a number of British, American and European jazz and rock musicians, including Alexis Korner (touring England in the early Sixties on occasion with Korner and Cyril Davies), Alex Harvey and others.

MEN AT WORK
Formed 1979, Melbourne, Australia
Colin Hay (b. Scot.) voc., gtr.; Ron Strykert (b. Austral.), gtr., voc.; Jerry Speiser (b. Austral.), drums,

voc.; Greg Ham (b. Austral.), sax, flute, voc., kybds.; John Rees (b. Austral.), bass, voc.
1982—*Business as Usual* (Columbia)   **1983**—*Cargo*.

Australia's Men at Work were one of the most successful rock groups of 1982. Their debut LP, *Business as Usual*, broke the Monkees' 1966 record for the longest run at #1 for a debut LP (15 weeks) and included two #1 singles, "Who Can It Be Now?" and "Down Under." They were awarded the 1982 Grammy for Best New Group.

Colin Hay, the group's lead singer and main songwriter, moved with his family to Australia from Scotland at age 14. The group, several of whose members had played together in other aggregations, became a regular Australian pub band, first gaining a following at the Cricketer's Arms Hotel bar. By the time they were signed by Australian Columbia, they had a national following and were the highest-paid unrecorded band in the country. Their debut LP, when released in their homeland, stayed at #1 for ten weeks, beating the record previously held by Split Enz's *True Colours*.

Cargo, released in April 1983, had been finished in the summer of 1982, but was held for release because of the debut's phenomenal success. As it was, *Cargo* debuted in the Top Thirty with *Business* still in the Top Five. Within weeks they were both in the Top Ten.

THE MERSEYBEATS
Formed 1963, Liverpool, England
Tony Crane, gtr., voc.; Aaron Williams, gtr., voc.; Bill Kinsley, bass, voc.; John Banks, drums.
1964—*The Merseybeats* (Fontana)   (− Kinsley; + John Gustafson, bass)   *England's Best Sellers* (Arc Int'l).

Taking their name from the label given to Liverpool's British Invasion bands, the Merseybeats first scored U.K. hits with ballads, starting with covers of the Shirelles' "It's Love That Really Counts" (#24, 1963) and Dusty Springfield's "Wishin' and Hopin' " (#13, 1964). Their next, and biggest, hit came with Peter Lee Stirling's "I Think of You" (#5, 1964), followed by "Don't Turn Around" (#13, 1964) and "Last Night" (#40, 1964).

In 1964, they were joined by bassist John Gustafson (later briefly with Roxy Music) from another local hitmaking unit, the Big Three. They broke up in 1966, but Tony Crane and Billy Kinsley continued as the Merseys, scoring their biggest hit with "Sorrow" (#4, 1966, U.K.), later covered by David Bowie. After a few more hits, "I Love You, Yes I Do" (#22, 1965) and "I Stand Accused" (#38, 1966), the Merseys broke up.

THE METERS
Formed 1967, New Orleans
Art Neville (b. 1938, New Orleans), kybds., voc.; Leo Nocentelli, gtr., voc.; Joseph "Zigaboo" Modeliste, drums, voc.; George Porter, bass, voc.

1971—*The Meters* (Josie)   **1972**—*Look-Ka Py Py; Chicken Strut; Cabbage Alley* (Reprise)   **1974**—*Rejuvenation; Cissy Strut* (Island)   **1975**—(+ Cyril Neville [b. 1950, New Orleans], percussion, voc.)   *Fire on the Bayou* (Reprise)   **1976**—*Trick Bag*   **1977**—*New Directions* (Warner Bros.)   **1980**—*Second Line Strut* (Charly).

The Meters were better known—and better paid—as New Orleans' finest backup band than as a self-contained feature act. Their lean, peppery R&B gave a funky flavor to recordings by out-of-towners like Paul McCartney and Labelle; but on their own, their rhythms were too tricky, their vocals too understated and their sound altogether too spare to reach a broad audience.

When Art Neville formed the group in 1967, he had been a prominent musician in New Orleans for almost 15 years. He was still in high school when, leading the Hawketts, he cut the 1954 Chess single "Mardi Gras Mambo," which made them a popular regional act, and which is still pressed every year for Mardi Gras. He had put out a handful of regional hits as a soloist—"Cha Dooky Doo" and "Ooh-Wee Baby" on Specialty in the late Fifties, and "All These Things" on Instant in 1962, before he formed Art Neville and the Sounds with his brothers Charles and Aaron as singers, along with guitarist Leo Nocentelli, bassist George Porter and drummer Ziggy Modeliste around 1966. They played local clubs until producer Allen Toussaint and his business partner Marshall Sehorn hired the group, minus Charles and Aaron, to be house rhythm section for their Sansu Enterprises in 1968. As such, they backed Lee Dorsey, Chris Kenner, Earl King, Betty Harris and Toussaint himself on stage and in the studio in the late Sixties and early Seventies.

Concurrently, the quartet performed on its own as the Meters. Their popularity was not limited to New Orleans, and their hits—mostly dance instrumentals—included "Sophisticated Cissy" (#34 pop, #7 R&B, 1969), "Cissy Strut" (#23 pop, #4 R&B, 1969), "Look-Ka Py Py" (#11 R&B, 1969) and "Chicken Strut" (#11 R&B, 1970).

In 1972, they signed with Reprise Records, retaining Toussaint as their producer and Sehorn as manager. The major label did not bring about a commercial breakthrough—in fact, the moderate hits gave way to minor hits—but the Meters were widely heard, if not recognized, on albums by Dr. John, Robert Palmer, Jess Roden, Labelle, King Biscuit Boy and Paul McCartney and Wings. They backed Dr. John on tours in 1973 and King Biscuit Boy in 1974, and opened shows for the Rolling Stones on their 1975 American and 1976 European tours.

In 1975, the Meters joined George and Amos Landry—members of a Mardi Gras ceremonial "black Indian tribe," the Wild Tchoupitoulas, and uncle and cousin to Neville—in recording *The Wild Tchoupitoulas* (Island, 1976). Aaron, Charles and Cyril Neville contributed vocals to the sessions, reuniting the Neville Sounds for the occasion. Cyril then joined the Meters. A year later, the group cut ties with Toussaint and Sehorn, complaining that they were denied artistic control. For *New Directions* they teamed with San Francisco producer Dave Rubinson, but that album was not to their satisfaction either, and in 1977, when Toussaint and Sehorn claimed the Meters name, they broke up. Art and Cyril joined Aaron and Charles as the Neville Brothers. The others found freelance work in New Orleans. Modeliste drummed for Keith Richards and Ron Wood on their New Barbarians tour in 1979.

MFSB

Formed early 1970s, Philadelphia
1973—*MFSB* (Philadelphia International) *MFSB: Love Is the Message* **1974**—*TSOP* (TSOP) **1975**—*Universal Love* (Philadelphia International) **1976**—*Philadelphia Freedom; Summertime* **1977**—*The End of Phase I* **1978**—*MFSB and Gamble Huff Orchestra* (TSOP) **1980**—*Mysteries of the World.*

MFSB (Mother, Father, Sister, Brother) was the nickname for the crew of studio musicians who played on most of the Sound of Philadelphia records released by Kenny Gamble and Leon Huff's Philadelphia International Records in the early Seventies. Many of these musicians appeared on Cliff Nobles' popular dance tune (#2 R&B and pop) "The Horse" in 1968. Under the MFSB title they had a #1 pop and soul single, "TSOP (The Sound of Philadelphia)," in 1974. For many years, that Kenny Gamble-Leon Huff composition was the theme for the syndicated music show "Soul Train." Many MFSB members also appeared on Salsoul Orchestra recordings. Although personnel changed frequently in the later years, musicians on their most popular early LPs included: Ron Kersey and Kenny Gamble (keyboards); Norman Harris, Roland Chambers, Bobby Eli (guitars); Lenny Pakula (organ); Zach Zachery (sax); Ronnie Baker (bass); Vince Montana (vibes); Earl Young (drums); Larry Washington (percussion); and Don Renaldo (conductor).

LEE MICHAELS

Born November 24, 1945, Los Angeles
1968—*Carnival of Life* (A&M) **1969**—*Recital; Lee Michaels* **1970**—*Barrel* **1971**—*5th* **1972**—*Life; Space and First Takes* **1973**—*Nice Day for Something* (Columbia) **1974**—*Tailface* **1975**—*Saturn Rings* (ABC).

Grammy Awards

The Mamas and the Papas
1966 Best Contemporary Rock & Roll Group Performance, Vocal or Instrumental: "Monday, Monday"

Melissa Manchester
1982 Best Pop Vocal Performance, Female: "You Should Hear How She Talks About You"

Chuck Mangione
1976 Best Instrumental Composition: "Bellavia"
1978 Best Pop Instrumental Performance: *The Children of Sanchez*

Manhattan Transfer
1980 Best Jazz Fusion Performance, Vocal or Instrumental: "Birdland"
1981 Best Pop Performance by a Duo or Group with Vocal: "Boy from New York City"

Best Jazz Vocal Performance, Duo or Group: "Until I Met You (Corner Pocket)"

Manhattans
1980 Best R&B Performance by a Duo or Group, with Vocal: "Shining Star"

Barry Manilow
1978 Best Pop Vocal Performance, Male: "Copacabana (at the Copa)"

Paul McCartney (see also: the Beatles, Wings)
1966 Song of the Year: "Michelle" (with John Lennon)
Best Contemporary Rock & Roll Solo Vocal Performance, Male or Female: "Eleanor Rigby"
1970 Best Original Score Written for a Motion Picture or TV Special: *Let It Be*

1971 Best Arrangement Accompanying Vocalist(s): "Uncle Albert/Admiral Halsey" (with Linda McCartney)
1974 Best Pop Vocal Performance by a Duo, Group or Chorus: "Band on the Run"

Marilyn McCoo (see also: the Fifth Dimension)
1976 Best R&B Vocal Performance by a Duo, Group or Chorus: "You Don't Have to Be a Star (to Be in My Show)" (with Billy Davis, Jr.)

Van McCoy
1975 Best Pop Instrumental Performance: "The Hustle" (with the Soul City Orchestra)

Michael McDonald (see also: the Doobie Brothers)
1979 Song of the Year; Best Arrangement Accompanying Vocalist(s):
"What a Fool Believes" (with Kenny Loggins)

Men at Work
1982 Best New Artist

Pat Metheny Group
1982 Best Jazz Fusion Performance, Vocal or Instrumental:
Offramp

MFSB
1974 Best R&B Instrumental Performance:

"TSOP (The Sound of Philadelphia)"
1978 Album of the Year:
Saturday Night Fever (with others)

Bette Midler
1973 Best New Artist of the Year
1980 Best Pop Vocal Performance:
"The Rose"

Mighty Clouds of Joy
1978 Best Soul Gospel Performance, Traditional:
Live and Direct
1979 Best Soul Gospel Performance, Traditional:
Changing Times

Joni Mitchell
1969 Best Folk Performance:
Clouds
1974 Best Arrangement Accompanying Vocalists:
"Down to You" (with Tom Scott)

Anne Murray
1974 Best Country Vocal Performance, Female:
Love Song
1978 Best Pop Vocal Performance, Female:
"You Needed Me"
1980 Best Country Vocal Performance, Female:
"Could I Have This Dance"

Screaming himself hoarse, pounding his overamped Hammond organ and backed only by an enormous drummer called Frosty, Lee Michaels made his name as one of the original hard-rockers—and surely the first, perhaps the only, to play hard rock on a keyboard rather than a guitar. His #6 single, "Do You Know What I Mean?" stands as the classic example of Michaels' unique sound.

Though he concentrated on this heavy-keyboard approach during much of his career, Michaels could also play sax, accordion, trombone and guitar. He'd started out as a lounge pianist in Fresno in the mid-Sixties, with aspirations to be a jazz/blues horn player. Instead he joined his first band, the Sentinels, in 1965 (John Barbata, later with Jefferson Starship, was the drummer). He and Barbata then joined a Bay Area band led by Joel Scott Hill, but Michaels left to pursue his own sound, inspired by a Jefferson Airplane show. He assembled a five-piece band named for himself, and recorded his debut LP.

After another change of heart—and much experimentation with organs and amplifiers—Michaels dismissed his band. Though the public responded favorably to his one-man-band debut, *Recital,* his greatest success resulted from collaborations with Frosty (Bartholomew Eugene Smith-Frost). About six and a half hours' worth of jamming resulted in *Lee Michaels,* his most successful LP until then. Michaels and Frosty toured as a duo, selling out major halls across the U.S. The third LP yielded "Heighty Hi" and a cover of the blues standard "Stormy Monday." Frosty then left to form his own band, Sweathog.

Michaels kept at it and had another pair of hits in 1971 with "Do You Know What I Mean?" (#6) and "Can I Get a Witness?" (#39); *5th* was a million-selling LP. *Space and First Takes* featured drummer Keith Knudsen, who later left Michaels to join the Doobie Brothers, at which

point Michaels retired for an extended holiday in Hawaii to "sit under a tree." He reunited with Frosty for *Tailface,* but with his successes apparently behind him, Michaels again retired after *Saturn Rings.* In 1982, he told *Rolling Stone* of a planned comeback with a new LP, *Absolute Lee,* to come out on his own Squish label.

MICKEY AND SYLVIA
Mickey Baker, born McHouston Baker, October 15, 1925, Louisville, Kentucky; Sylvia Robinson, born Sylvia Vanderpool, March 6, 1936, New York City
N.A.—*Love Is Strange* (Camden) *Mickey and Sylvia Do It Again* (RCA) *New Sounds* (Vik).

In 1954, Mickey Baker, a blues guitarist who had recorded as a solo act, met vocalist Sylvia Vanderpool. He gave her guitar lessons, and from this evolved a partnership that in 1956 produced the million-selling hit "Love Is Strange" (#11 pop, #2 R&B). The pair had two more hits—"There Oughta Be a Law" (#46 pop, #15 R&B, 1957) and "Baby You're So Fine" (#52 pop, #27 R&B, 1961)—before breaking up in 1961 when Mickey moved to Europe. (They came back together briefly in 1965 to perform a few gigs.) Later Mickey wrote several guitar instruction books, including the best seller *Jazz Guitar.*

In 1956, Sylvia had married Joe Robinson, and more than a decade later, the couple founded All Platinum Records and All Platinum Studios. As a producer, Sylvia's credits range from the 1961 Ike and Tina Turner hit "It's Gonna Work Out Fine" (on which she also played guitar), to the Moments' 1970 gold single "Love on a Two-Way Street" (which she cowrote) and Shirley (and Company)'s 1976 disco hit "Shame, Shame, Shame" (which she wrote).

In 1973, Sylvia returned to the charts with "Pillow Talk" (#3 pop, #1 R&B) on her own Vibration label and continued to hit the R&B charts through 1978, notably with "Sweet Stuff" (#16, 1974) and "Automatic Lover" (#43, 1978). In the late Seventies, Sylvia revived the ailing All Platinum label by renaming it Sugar Hill and putting together a group of rap vocalists, the Sugar Hill Gang, who had a smash hit with "Rapper's Delight" (#26 pop, #4 R&B, 1979). She went on to sign and produce other top rap acts like Grandmaster Flash and the Furious Five and Funky Four Plus One.

BETTE MIDLER
Born December 1, 1945, Paterson, New Jersey
1972—*The Divine Miss M* (Atlantic)   1973—*Bette Midler*   1976—*Songs for the New Depression*   1977—*Broken Blossom; Live at Last*   1979—*Thighs and Whispers; The Rose*   1980—*Divine Madness.*

Singer Bette Midler's sexpot camp image—trash with flash—has proven as important to her success as her singing.

Midler was born in New Jersey and raised in Hawaii. From an early age, she took an interest in acting (her mother named her after Bette Davis), and in high school Midler worked in theater and sang in a female folk trio called the Pieridine Three. In 1965, she had a bit part as a missionary's wife in the film *Hawaii*, after which she left for Los Angeles and then later moved to New York. There (in between odd jobs like go-go dancing in a New Jersey bar), Midler got parts in several Tom Eyen Off Broadway productions, followed by a three-year run in Broadway's *Fiddler on the Roof*, where she eventually moved from the chorus to the featured part of Tzeitel. In 1971, she played the double role of Mrs. Walker and the Acid Queen in the Seattle Opera Association's production of *Tommy*.

Around 1970, Midler decided to concentrate on singing and was soon performing at the Continental Baths, a gay men's club in New York City. She developed her campy comedy routines and a broad musical repertoire that included Andrews Sisters takeoffs, blues, show tunes and Sixties girl-group numbers. Her piano accompanist was Barry Manilow. She quickly became a cult item and soon an aboveground sensation on major TV talk shows. Her debut, *The Divine Miss M*, went gold and won her the Grammy for Best New Artist. She appeared on the cover of *Newsweek* and had a #8 hit with a remake of the Andrews Sisters' "Boogie Woogie Bugle Boy."

But sales after the second LP dropped off sharply, though she retains a loyal concert following. In 1979, she starred in *The Rose*, loosely based on the life of Janis Joplin. Midler was nominated for an Oscar. The soundtrack LP went platinum in 1980, aided by the Top Ten title song. Later in the year, a Midler concert film and soundtrack entitled *Divine Madness* were released. Her humorous memoirs of her first world tour, *A View from a Broad*, hit the best-seller lists that year. In 1982, *Jinxed*, directed by Don Siegel, was released.

MIGHTY CLOUDS OF JOY
Formed circa 1960, Los Angeles
Joe Ligon (b. Troy, Ala.); Johnny Martin (b. Los Angeles, Calif.); Paul Beasley; Elmeo Franklin (b. Fla.); Richard Wallace (b. Ga.).
1962—*Live at the Music Hall* (Peacock)   1964—*Presenting: The Untouchables*   1966—*Sing Songs of Rev. Julius Cheeks and the Nightingales*   1968—*Live! At the Apollo*   1970—*The Best of*   1972—*A Bright Side*   1973—*Best of*   1974—*It's Time* (ABC/Dunhill)   1975—*Kickin'* (ABC)   1977—*Truth Is the Power*   1978—*The Very Best of*   1980—*Cloudburst* (Myrrh).

One of the top young modern gospel vocal units, and one of the very few to attempt a pop/soul crossover, the Mighty Clouds of Joy first got together in high school in Los Angeles; later Paul Beasley joined them from the Gospel Keynotes. They have shared stages with Earth, Wind and Fire, the Rolling Stones, the Reverend James Cleveland and Andrae Crouch. Lead singer Joe Ligon was heavily influenced by the gritty, grunting style of the Reverend Julius Cheeks of the Sensational Nightingales, as was Wilson Pickett. Toward the end of their Peacock label days, critics began comparing the Clouds' high-harmony sound to that of Curtis Mayfield and the Impressions, and in the mid-Seventies the Clouds teamed with Philadelphia soul producers Gamble and Huff for a series of LPs, the first of which, *It's Time*, was most critically successful. In 1980, they moved to Earth, Wind and Fire's Myrrh label, and *Cloudburst* was produced by EWF's Al McKay.

THE MIGHTY DIAMONDS
Formed 1973, Kingston, Jamaica
Donald "Tabby" Shaw, lead voc.; Lloyd "Judge" Ferguson, harmony voc.; Fitzroy "Bunny" Simpson, harmony voc.
1976—*Right Time* (Virgin)   1977—*Ice on Fire*   1978—*Planet Earth; Stand Up* (Channel One)   1979—*Deeper Roots* (Front Line/Virgin Int'l)   1980—*Tell Me What's Wrong* (J&J)   1981—*Indestructible* (Alligator)   1982—*Reggae Street* (Shanachie).

One of the young reggae vocal trios modeled on the original Wailers, the Heptones and others of the late Sixties and early Seventies, the Mighty Diamonds became one of the most popular reggae groups of the second generation by setting their incisive, militant lyrics in close soft-toned harmonies and languorous rhythms.

They had their first hit in Jamaica in 1974 with "Shame and Pride." Two more hits that year showed the range of their material: "Jah Jah Bless the Dreadlocks" was based on Rastafarian chants, while "Let's Put It All Together" was a reggae version of the Stylistics' hit. (American soul music has been an essential element of virtually every Diamonds song.)

By the end of 1975, Jamaican hits like "Right Time," "Have Mercy" and "I Need a Roof" had been picked up by reggae fans in England, and in 1976 the group was signed to Virgin Records, who released their first album in the U.K. and in the U.S. later that year. The year 1976 also saw the Diamonds' first visit to America, when they toured with Toots and the Maytals. They made a name for themselves as entertaining showmen with their comic stage banter and occasional straight soul ballads.

But in spite of their Americanisms (*Ice on Fire* was produced by New Orleans R&B veterans Allen Toussaint and Marshall Sehorn), they were no more able to break into the American pop market than their Jamaican compatriots. In Jamaica, on the other hand, they continued to score big hits—"Tamarind Farm" in 1979 and "Wise Son" (#1) in 1980. "Pass the Kouchie," a hymn to marijuana, was banned by the Jamaican government, but when re-released as "Pass the Knowledge," it also went to #1 (1981). (Another version of the song, "Pass the Dutchie," was a hit for Musical Youth in late 1982.)

AMOS MILBURN

Born April 1, 1927, Houston; died January 3, 1980, Houston
N.A.—*Amos Milburn* (Blues Spectrum) *Return of the Blues Boss* (Motown).

Amos Milburn was one of rhythm & blues' most consistent-selling vocalists from the mid-Forties into the Fifties. He signed with Los Angeles–based Aladdin Records in 1946 and the next year had a million-seller with "Chicken Shack Boogie." Subsequently, Milburn would top the charts with songs about alcohol: "Bad Bad Whiskey" (#1 R&B, 1950), "One Scotch, One Bourbon, One Beer" (#2 R&B, 1953), "Thinking and Drinking" (#8, 1952) and "Let Me Go Home, Whiskey" (#3, 1953). "One Scotch" was revived by George Thorogood and the Destroyers in the late Seventies. Milburn recorded for various labels, including Motown and Ace, until a stroke in the late Sixties left him partially paralyzed.

BUDDY MILES

Born September 5, 1946, Omaha, Nebraska
1968—*Expressway to Your Skull* (Mercury) 1969—*Electric Church* 1970—*Them Changes; We Got to Live Together; Message to the People* 1971—*Live* 1972—*Carlos Santana and Buddy Miles Live* (Columbia) 1973—*Chapter VII; Booger Bear* 1974—*All the Faces of Buddy Miles* 1975—*More Miles Per Gallon* (Casablanca) 1976—*Bicentennial Gathering* 1981—*Sneak Attack* (Atlantic).

Though Buddy Miles's biggest break came when he joined Jimi Hendrix's Band of Gypsys, with whom he recorded "Them Changes," Miles had years of experience behind him.

By the time he was 15, he was drumming for the Ink Spots, and he also had played on the session that produced the Jaynetts' hit "Sally Go 'Round the Roses." He later played in Wilson Pickett's backup band in the mid-Sixties; and at a New York gig, guitarist Mike Bloomfield invited him to join Electric Flag.

In 1968, Miles formed his own band, the Buddy Miles Express, from the ruins of Electric Flag; the Express (which featured guitarist Jim McCarty, later with Cactus) peppered Miles's melange of hard rock and soul with brassy horn charts. Miles also played drums on an early John McLaughlin album, *Devotion.* The Express came to a halt when Miles joined Hendrix; after Hendrix's death, bassist Billy Cox from the Band of Gypsys joined the Buddy Miles Band.

"Them Changes" came out, and though Miles would remain prodigiously active for some time, it was his only real hit. In 1974, he joined the reunited Electric Flag for a comeback that dissolved before the end of the year. Beginning in 1978, he served a jail term for grand theft. He formed a band at the California Institution for Men at Chino.

FRANKIE MILLER

Born circa 1950, Glasgow
1972—*Once in a Blue Moon* (Chrysalis, U.K.) 1974—*Frankie Miller's High Life* (Chrysalis) 1975—*The Rock* 1977—*Full House; Jealous Guy* (EP) 1978—*Double Trouble* 1979—*Perfect Fit* 1980—*Easy Money* 1982—*Standing on the Edge* (Capitol).

Frankie Miller is a raspy-voiced British R&B/rock singer who writes most of his own material.

At 14, Miller played with his first Glasgow band, and then he joined the Stoics, moving with them to London in the late Sixties. After the Stoics disbanded, Miller was discovered singing in a London pub by guitarist Robin Trower, who had just left Procol Harum, and drummer Clive Bunker, who had just left Jethro Tull. Together with bassist Jim Dewar (fresh from Stone the Crows, later to join Trower's own power trio), they formed Jude, which never recorded.

Miller embarked on a solo career, backed on his first album by Brinsley Schwarz. He toured the U.K. with Schwarz and other pub-rockers, like Ducks Deluxe and Bees Make Honey. Miller then formed a short-lived band of his own with guitarists Neil Hubbard and Henry McCullough, bassist Alan Spenner and drummer Robbie McIntosh. Hubbard and Spenner, both veteran U.K. sessionmen, had come from Joe Cocker's Grease Band; McCullough would go on to join Paul McCartney's Wings;

and McIntosh, the Average White Band. Miller next recorded the well-received *High Life* LP in New Orleans and Atlanta, with Allen Toussaint producing and contributing seven songs. McCullough returned to back Miller (along with ex–Spooky Tooth bassist Chris Stewart) on *The Rock.*

Stewart remained in Miller's 1976 Full House band, whose album featured guest shots from Procol Harum's Gary Brooker. After disbanding Full House in 1978, Miller got together with, among others, drummer B. J. Wilson (ex–Procol Harum), reedman Chris Mercer (ex–John Mayall and Ginger Baker) and keyboardist Paul Carrack (formerly with Ace and later of Squeeze). Again, only bassist Stewart remained from his prior group. Despite little in the way of commercial success in America (he finally had a Top Five single in England with "Darlin' " from *Perfect Fit* in 1978), Miller has kept at it. In early 1982, he recorded a new LP at Muscle Shoals.

In 1980, Delbert McClinton recorded Miller's "Fool in Love" and "Heartbreak Hotel,"; Ray Charles covered his "I Can't Change It."

STEVE MILLER BAND
Formed 1966, San Francisco
Steve Miller (b. Oct. 5, 1943, Milwaukee, Wis.), gtr., voc.; Jim Peterman, kybds.; James Curly Cooke, gtr., voc.; Lonnie Turner, bass; Tim Davis, drums. **1967**—(+ Boz Scaggs, gtr., voc.; − Cooke) **1968**—*Children of the Future; Sailor* (Capitol) (− Scaggs; − Peterman; + Ben Sidran, kybds.) **1969**—*Brave New World; Your Saving Grace* (− Turner; − Sidran; + Bobby Winkelman, gtr., bass, voc.) *Number 5* **1971**—(− Davis; − Winkelman; + Ross Valory, bass; + Jack King, drums; + Dickie Thompson, kybds.; + Gerald Johnson, bass) *Rock Love* **1972**—(− Valory; + Sidran; + Roger Clark, percussion) *Recall the Beginning . . . A Journey from Eden; Anthology* (− Johnson) **1973**—(+ Turner; − Jack King; + John King, drums) *The Joker* (− King; − Sidran) **1976**—(+ Gary Mallaber, drums) *Fly Like an Eagle* **1977**—(+ Byron Allred, kybds.; + David Denny, gtr.; + Greg Douglas, gtr.) *Book of Dreams* **1978**—*Greatest Hits* **1981**—(− Denny; − Douglas; + Johnson) *Circle of Love* (+ Kenny Lee Lewis, gtr.; + John Massaro, gtr.) **1982**—*Abracadabra* **1983**—*Live.*

In his long career, Steve Miller has gone from being one of the first young white West Coast blues-rockers to one of the biggest-selling pop/rock artists of the late Seventies and early Eighties.

Miller's father was a music-loving pathologist who often brought home guests like Charles Mingus and T-Bone Walker. At age four, Steve met Les Paul, who taught him some chords and later let him sit in on some Les Paul–Mary Ford studio sessions. At age 12 Miller formed his first blues band, the Marksmen Combo. The band stayed together for five years, and included Boz Scaggs, who played off and on with Miller later on and had a prominent career of his own.

At the University of Wisconsin, Miller led one of the first blues-rock bands in town, the Ardells, which included Scaggs, pianist Ben Sidran and future Cheap Trick manager Ken Adamany. The group later evolved into the Fabulous Knight Trains. Miller left college to go to Denmark, where he studied literature at the University of Copenhagen. He soon grew disillusioned with academia and moved to Chicago, where his interest in blues was rekindled both by the classic black city-blues artists on the South Side and by the new generation of young white blues players that included Mike Bloomfield, Elvin Bishop and Paul Butterfield. He formed a short-lived band with Barry Goldberg (who went on to join Bloomfield in the Electric Flag), the Goldberg-Miller Blues Band.

In 1966, Miller moved to San Francisco, where he formed the Steve Miller Blues Band. The band became a local favorite, playing many free outdoor shows; they also backed Chuck Berry on a live album recorded in 1967 at the Fillmore, and contributed three tunes to the soundtrack of the film *Revolution.* After playing the Monterey Pop Festival in 1967, Miller was approached by Capitol Records. He helped change the economics of rock music by holding out for what was at the time a record-breaking advance payment for a debut LP, and a sizable royalty rate. The band's first LP was recorded in England, with Glyn Johns and the band coproducing. The band became an almost instant staple of progressive FM radio, although it failed to yield a hit single. The second LP contained "Livin' in the USA," which went Top Twenty. By that time, the band had dropped the Blues from its name.

In early 1972, Miller broke his neck in an auto accident, but it wasn't diagnosed until several weeks later. He then developed hepatitis, which sidelined him through early 1973. Meanwhile, the *Anthology* collection was selling well (it eventually went gold in 1977). Miller kept writing tunes while convalescing, and in 1973 *The Joker* revealed a new Steve Miller. The sound was slick and bouncy; the LP's title song was a #1 single in the U.S. and went gold, as did the album (which eventually went platinum as well). Miller's first platinum LP, *Fly Like an Eagle,* consolidated his newfound popular success. It stayed in the charts for 5½ months, going as high as #3; the title tune made #2 on the singles charts and also went gold; "Rock 'n Me" was a #1 single; and "Take the Money and Run" was a #11 single; the LP and its single even made the Top Twenty on the R&B chart.

Book of Dreams, like *Eagle,* passed the platinum mark (as of this writing *Dreams* has sold five million copies), stayed on the LP charts for over a year, going as high as

#2, and yielded three hit singles—Paul Pena's "Jet Air-liner" (#8, 1977), "Swingtown" (#17, 1977) and "Jungle Love" (#23, 1977). *Greatest Hits* became Miller's fourth platinum LP, staying on the charts 15 weeks.

In 1978, Miller took a break and moved to a farm in Oregon, where he built a 24-track studio. He did not release another record until *Circle of Love* in 1981, which contained "Heart like a Wheel" (#24, 1981) (not the Anna McGarrigle song popularized by Linda Ronstadt).

GARNET MIMMS AND THE ENCHANTERS
Formed 1963, Philadelphia
Garnet Mimms (b. Nov. 26, 1937, Ashland, W. Va.), voc.; Sam Bell (b. Philadelphia), voc.; Charles Boyer (b. N.C.), voc.; Zola Pearnell (b. Philadelphia), voc.
1963—*Cry Baby* (United Artists)   **1964**—*As Long as I Have You*   **1966**—*I'll Take Good Care of You*   **1973**—*Remember* (EP)   **1977**—*Garnet Mimms Has It All* (Arista).

In 1962, Garnet Mimms was a promising but unsuccessful singer with an R&B unit, the Gainors. The Philly vocal group the Enchanters were veteran gospel singers and songwriters. Philadelphia producer Jerry Ragavoy put the two together and in 1963 got a million-selling hit, "Cry Baby" (#4 pop, #1 R&B), a gritty James Brown–styled gospel-soul frenzy featuring Mimms screaming the title phrase over and over. The tune was written by Ragavoy (a.k.a. Norman Meade) and producer Bert Berns (a.k.a. Bert Russell), a co-owner of Bang.

Within a year, Mimms and the Enchanters had three more hits: "For Your Precious Love" (#26 pop, 1963), "Baby Don't You Weep" (#30 pop, 1963) and "A Quiet Place" (#78 pop, 1964). In 1964, Ragavoy split Mimms from the Enchanters. The latter went more or less ignored, but Mimms himself had hits with "Tell Me Baby" (#69), "One Girl" (#67) and "Look Away" (#73) in 1964; "A Little Bit of Soap" (#95, 1965) and "I'll Take Good Care of You" (#30 pop, #15 R&B) in 1966.

In 1977, Mimms, backed by his new group, the Truckin' Co., had a minor hit in both the U.S. and the U.K. with "What It Is" from the album *Garnet Mimms Has It All*.

MINK DEVILLE
Formed 1974, San Francisco
Willy DeVille (b. *ca.* 1953, New York City), voc., gtr., harp; Louis X. Erlanger, gtr., voc.; Bobby Leonards, kybds.; Ruben Siguenza, bass; T. R. "Manfred" Allen, drums.
1977—*Cabretta* (Capitol)   **1978**—*Return to Magenta* (− Leonards; − Siguenza; − Allen)   **1980**—*Le Chat Bleu*   (− Erlanger; + Rick Borgia, gtr.; + Kenny Margolis, accordion, kybds.; + Joey Vasta, bass; + Tommy Price, drums; + Louis Cortelezzi, horns)   **1981**—*Coup de Grâce* (Atlantic).

Although Mink DeVille emerged from New York's late-Seventies punk-rock scene, their music was romantic R&B. After the band appeared on the 1976 *Live from CBGB* compilation LP, it was signed by Capitol. The core of the band was formed in San Francisco, where leader Willy DeVille had traveled after a 1971 trip to London from his Lower East Side home. There he met Ruben Siguenza and Tom Allen, and the three began playing leather bars and lounges under names like Lazy Eights and Billy DeSade and the Marquis. After reading about the Ramones and CBGB in a music magazine, the three of them formed Mink DeVille.

The band's debut LP was produced by Jack Nitzsche and was a critical success, yielding a U.K. Top Twenty hit single in "Spanish Stroll." In 1979, Willy DeVille moved to Paris to record *Le Chat Bleu*, firing most of his band in the process. When Capitol heard the tapes of the new LP—replete with accordion-backed traditional-French and Cajun-style romantic ballads—they delayed the album's U.S. release for nearly a year, prompting DeVille to sign with Atlantic.

JONI MITCHELL
Born Roberta Joan Anderson, November 7, 1943, Alberta, Canada
1967—*Song to a Seagull* (Reprise)   **1968**—*Joni Mitchell*   **1969**—*Clouds*   **1970**—*Ladies of the Canyon*   **1971**—*Blue*   **1972**—*For the Roses* (Asylum)   **1974**—*Court and Spark; Miles of Aisles*   **1975**—*The Hissing of Summer Lawns*   **1976**—*Hejira*   **1977**—*Don Juan's Reckless Daughter*   **1979**—*Mingus*   **1980**—*Shadows and Light*   **1982**—*Wild Things Run Fast* (Geffen).

Joni Mitchell

Joni Mitchell is one of the most respected singer/songwriters. Her career has ranged from late-Sixties and early-Seventies popularity with confessional folk-pop songs to late-Seventies cult status with a series of jazz-inflected experiments. Some of Mitchell's early compositions became famous in versions recorded by others—"Both Sides Now" (Judy Collins), "The Circle Game" (Tom Rush) and "Woodstock" (Crosby, Stills and Nash, and Ian Matthews' Southern Comfort)—but her own ululating vocals and open-tuned guitar inspired numerous imitators.

As a young girl, Roberta Anderson studied art in Saskatoon and later enrolled at the Alberta College of Art in Calgary. She took a ukulele with her to college, began playing regularly and developed an interest in folk music. She soon moved to Toronto, where she began performing on the local folk scene, and in 1965 married folksinger Chuck Mitchell. They moved together to Detroit a year later, where they soon separated.

Mitchell became a critical sensation on Detroit's folk scene, and her notices led to a series of successful engagements in New York City, where in 1967 she was signed by Reprise Records. In late 1968, Judy Collins had a smash hit with Mitchell's "Both Sides Now." Collins also recorded Mitchell's "Michael from Mountains" on her *Wildflowers* album; the British folk-rock band Fairport Convention recorded Mitchell's "Eastern Rain"; and Tom Rush recorded "The Circle Game." Thanks to this indirect success, Mitchell's debut LP sold fairly well. *Clouds* sold better. *Ladies of the Canyon* went gold and yielded a minor hit single—"Big Yellow Taxi."

Mitchell's next album was the critically acclaimed *Blue,* which featured "Carey," "My Old Man" and "The Last Time I Saw Richard." *For the Roses* also went gold and contained another minor hit single, "You Turn Me On (I'm a Radio)." Mitchell's top-selling album was *Court and Spark,* with the hit single "Help Me" (#7, 1974). By this time, her sound had grown from simple, unadorned acoustic guitar and voice into a sophisticated Continental-pop blend. *Court and Spark* predicted Mitchell's future direction with its version of Annie Ross's jazz-jive "Twisted," Mitchell's first recorded cover.

For the live *Miles of Aisles* album, Mitchell was accompanied by the jazz-fusion band L.A. Express. *The Hissing of Summer Lawns* was a complex, esoteric avant-garde experiment that fared poorly critically and commercially; it was the first pop album to use Burundi drums, later central to Adam and the Ants. *Hejira,* though smoother and more spare instrumentally, met a similar commercial fate. In 1976, Mitchell appeared at the Band's San Francisco farewell concert and in the filmed documentary of that event, *The Last Waltz.*

Don Juan's Reckless Daughter continued Mitchell's mysterious, introverted experimentation. Her lyrics had grown more convoluted and less clearly confessional, while her melodies stretched to accommodate them. In 1978, Mitchell hooked up with jazz bassist/composer Charles Mingus, then dying of Lou Gehrig's disease. She set lyrics to some of the last melodies Mingus wrote, wrote the rest of the material herself and released *Mingus* not long after the bassist's death. It, too, sold poorly and received mixed reviews, as did the live album *Shadows and Light,* which featured a band including bassist Jaco Pastorius of Weather Report and jazz-rock guitarist Pat Metheny. In 1982, Mitchell released *Wild Things Run Fast,* a more pop-oriented album, and married her bassist, Larry Klein.

WILLIE MITCHELL
Born 1928, Ashland, Tennessee

Although he reached the Top Forty of the R&B charts repeatedly during the Sixties as a bandleader, Willie Mitchell really made his mark in the music business as vice-president of Hi Records, where he helped fashion modern Memphis soul.

Mitchell studied trumpet in high school and performed in dance bands before forming his first group in 1954. By the end of the decade, that group had become the house band at the Home of the Blues label, where they also began recording their own instrumentals. Mitchell signed with Hi in 1963, and started slowly with "20-75" and "Percolatin' " in 1964, before scoring his first R&B hit in 1965, "Buster Browne" (#29). It was followed by the R&B hits "Bad Eye" (#23, 1966), "Soul Serenade" (#10, 1968), "Prayer Meetin' " (#23, 1968), "30-60-90" (#31, 1969) and "My Babe" (#37, 1969). Mitchell began producing singers, including O. V. Wright, Syl Johnson, and Otis Clay.

After the death of Hi president Joe Cuoghi around 1964, Mitchell took on more production and administrative duties for the label, and in 1969 he abandoned what remained of his own recording career to produce his discovery, Al Green.

Mitchell's first two 1970 hits as a producer were Green's "I Can't Get Next to You" and Ann Peebles' "Part Time Love." Through the decade, his success was uninterrupted. He oversaw all the recordings that placed Al Green high among the most influential singers of the Seventies, and produced others in the soul style they pioneered.

MOBY GRAPE
Formed 1967, San Francisco
Skip Spence (b. Apr. 18, 1946, Windsor, Ont.), gtr.;
Peter Lewis (b. July 15, 1945, Los Angeles), gtr.; Jerry Miller (b. July 10, 1943, Tacoma, Wash.), gtr.; Bob Mosley (b. Dec. 4, 1942, Paradise Valley, Calif.), bass; Don Stevenson (b. Oct. 15, 1942, Seattle, Wash.), drums.
1967—*Moby Grape* (Columbia) **1968**—*Wow*

(– Spence) **1969**—*Moby Grape '69* **1970**—*Truly Fine Citizen* **1971**—*20 Granite Creek* (Reprise) *Great Grape* (Columbia).

Of the many groups to emerge from San Francisco in the late Sixties, Moby Grape stood out as the band that most preferred structured songs to free-form jamming, the ones who mixed L.A. folk rock with San Francisco's standard psychedelia. But they were never able to capitalize on their potential, partly because of hype from Columbia Records that threatened to bury their debut album.

Moby Grape grew out of a Northern California group, the Frantics, that included Jerry Miller, Bob Mosley and Don Stevenson. Mosley met Peter Lewis, who had recently abandoned Peter and the Wolves for solo work; Skip Spence was a guitarist who had played drums with the Jefferson Airplane. Their self-titled debut LP became infamous at once when Columbia chose to release 8 of its 13 cuts simultaneously on 45s (all of which were unsuccessful). The record also came with a poster of the band and a front cover photograph that featured Stevenson with his middle finger extended (later airbrushed). Amid the furor, the group's music was virtually ignored.

Their second album, *Wow*, was similarly derailed by gimmickry; it contained a track that could only be played at 78 rpm and a "bonus" LP, *Grape Jam*, that included Al Kooper and Mike Bloomfield. Moby Grape then disbanded.

They re-formed as a quartet soon after, without Spence, commemorating the event with *Moby Grape '69*, setting a pattern of breakup, re-formation, album, breakup that continued until 1972. A final attempt at a partial reunion was scotched in 1974 when Mosley, Lewis and Miller were informed by an old manager that they were legally forbidden to use the name Moby Grape. They settled on Maby Grope. Mosley recorded an eponymous solo LP in 1972. Spence released *Oar* in 1969.

MOLLY HATCHET

Formed 1975, Jacksonville, Florida
Dave Hlubek (b. 1952, Jacksonville), gtr.; Duane Roland (b. Dec. 3, 1952, Jeffersonville, Ind.), gtr.; Steve Holland (b. 1954, Dothan, Ala.), gtr.; Danny Joe Brown (b. 1951, Jacksonville), voc.; Banner Thomas, bass; Bruce Crump, drums.
1978—*Molly Hatchet* (Epic) **1979**—*Flirtin' with Disaster* **1980**—*Beatin' the Odds* (– Brown; + Jimmy Farrar [b. La Grange, Ga.], voc.) **1981**—*Take No Prisoners* (– Farrar; + Brown) **1982**—(– Thomas; – Crump; + Barry Borden [b. May 12, 1954, Atlanta], drums; + Riff West [b. Apr. 3, 1950, Orlando, Fla.], bass) **1983**—*No Guts . . . No Glory.*

Molly Hatchet is a guitar-heavy Southern-blues-boogie and heavy-metal band from Jacksonville, home of Lynyrd Skynyrd, Grinderswitch, Blackfoot and .38 Special. The

band formed in 1975 and toured the South until a 1977 Epic signing.

Their debut LP sold 900,000 copies, the second 1.4 million and the third over two million. All the while, Molly Hatchet—their name is from Hatchet Molly, a legendary Southern prostitute who allegedly lured men to her lair, where she castrated and mutilated them—were touring, as steadily as any working band, often playing more than 250 dates per year. They also established an image as gun-toting, hard-drinking rowdies. Vocalist Danny Joe Brown left in early 1980 because of diabetes, but in 1981 he released a solo LP, *Danny Joe Brown and the Danny Joe Brown Band*. Along with new vocalist Jimmy Farrar, the band added a horn section (from Tower of Power) for the first time on *Take No Prisoners*. Jimmy Farrar then left for a solo career; Brown rejoined.

THE MOMENTS

Formed mid-1960s, Hackensack, New Jersey
Al Goodman (b. Mar. 31, 1947, Jackson, Miss.); Harry Ray (b. Dec. 15, 1946, Hackensack); William Brown (b. June 30, 1946, Perth Amboy, N.J.).
1977—*The Moments' Greatest Hits* (Stang) **1980**—*Ray, Goodman and Brown* (Polydor).

This harmony group recorded numerous hits for New Jersey–based All Platinum Records' Stang label. The original Moments, featuring Mark Greene's falsetto, charted with "Not on the Outside" (#57 pop, #13 R&B) in 1968. Those Moments were replaced by Billy Brown, Al Goodman and Johnny Morgan. This trio had a million-selling single with "Love on a Two-Way Street" (#3 pop, #1 R&B) in 1970.

With Harry Ray replacing Morgan in the early Seventies, the group maintained its popularity with black audiences. The Moments had another big hit with 1974's "Sexy Mama" (#17 pop, #3 R&B). A legal battle with All Platinum in the mid-Seventies left them idle for 2½ years. They resurfaced as Ray, Goodman and Brown on the Polydor label in the late Seventies and had a hit with "Special Lady" (#5 pop, #1 R&B, 1980).

EDDIE MONEY

Born Edward Mahoney, *circa* 1949, New York City
1977—*Eddie Money* (Columbia) **1978**—*Life for the Taking* **1980**—*Playing for Keeps* **1982**—*No Control.*

Eddie Money is a rough-voiced rock singer who enjoyed his greatest success to date with his self-titled debut album in 1977. It contained two 1978 hit singles, "Baby, Hold On" (#11) and "Two Tickets to Paradise" (#22).

The son of a New York City policeman, Edward Mahoney seemed destined to follow in his father's footsteps, and he attended the New York Police Academy. But at night he moonlighted in a rock & roll band as Eddie Money. Deciding he loved rock more than police work, the singer quit the academy and moved to Berkeley, California, where he sang at Bay Area bars. Promoter Bill Graham signed on as Money's manager and negotiated his contract with Columbia Records. *Life for the Taking, Playing for Keeps* and 1982's *No Control* maintained the tough-guy image his debut initiated. *No Control* also boasted the hit singles "I Think I'm in Love" and "Take a Little Bit of My Love."

THE MONKEES

Formed 1965, Los Angeles
David Jones (b. Dec. 30, 1945, Manchester, Eng.), voc.; Michael Nesmith (b. Dec. 30, 1943, Tex.), gtr., voc.; Peter Tork (b. Feb. 13, 1944, Washington, D.C.), bass, voc.; Mickey Dolenz (b. Mar. 8, 1945, Los Angeles), drums, voc.
1966—*The Monkees* (Colgems)   1967—*More of the Monkees; Headquarters; Pisces, Aquarius, Capricorn and Jones*   1968—*The Birds, the Bees and the Monkees*   1969—*Instant Replay; Greatest Hits; Head* (soundtrack) *Changes*   1976—*Jones, Dolenz, Boyce and Hart* (Capitol)   1980—*Forty Timeless Hits* (EMI).

The Monkees were the first, and arguably the best, of the prefabricated Sixties pop groups (e.g., the Partridge Family, the Archies). Though as a group manufactured by TV executives to capitalize on the success of the Beatles they were hard to take seriously, the Monkees—thanks in large part to the songwriting of Neil Diamond, Tommy Boyce, Bobby Hart and their own Mike Nesmith—did make some exceptionally good pop records, like "I'm a Believer" and "I'm Not Your Stepping Stone."

Davy Jones had been a stage actor and a race-horse jockey in Britain; Mickey Dolenz, whose father had starred in several films, became a child actor at age ten in various TV shows under the name Mickey Braddock; Michael Nesmith and Peter Tork had worked as musicians before becoming Monkees.

The group was formed for a TV comedy series dreamed up by Columbia Pictures executives, specifically inspired by the Beatles' film *A Hard Day's Night*. Some 500 candidates auditioned for the show in the fall of 1965; among those rejected were Stephen Stills and Danny Hutton (who went on to Three Dog Night). The Monkees were chosen for their personalities and photogenic capacities, not for musical ability.

In the beginning, they sang but did not play any instruments (leaving that to L.A. studio players), and in the TV show they only went through the motions of playing as they lip-synched. The show was first aired in September 1966 and became an immediate success. That same year, their debut LP went gold and yielded three Top Twenty gold singles: "I'm a Believer" (by Neil Diamond), "Last Train to Clarksville" and "Stepping Stone."

The Monkees frantically learned instruments so they could go on tour and at least appear competent. They

The Monkees: Peter Tork, Mickey Dolenz, Davy Jones, Mike Nesmith

succeeded at this, though they certainly couldn't reproduce the studio sound live (with hordes of screaming teens attending every show, it may not have mattered that much anyway). This, combined with Colgems' (a Don Kirshner company) refusal to reveal the truth about the Monkees' lack of playing ability, rankled Nesmith in particular. After intergroup arguments about what to do, Nesmith told a 1967 New York press conference, "There comes a time when you have to draw the line as a man. We're being passed off as something we aren't. We all play instruments, but we didn't on any of our records. Furthermore, our record company doesn't want us to and won't let us." *Look* magazine ran the story, prompting a heated meeting between group members and Screen Gems, in which Nesmith nearly came to blows with an executive when told he could be legally suspended from the band. Eventually the band got its wish, and the hits kept on coming: Diamond's "Little Bit Me, Little Bit You" (#2), "Pleasant Valley Sunday" (#3) and John Stewart's "Daydream Believer" (#1) in 1967; "Valleri" (#3) in 1968. The LPs *Headquarters; Pisces, Aquarius;* and *Birds, Bees* went gold.

The group staged successful worldwide tours in 1967 and 1968. In 1968 in London, Dolenz brought Jimi Hendrix to the band's attention, and they invited him to tour America with them. Hendrix was usually booed as an opening act on that tour, and left the tour after a few shows.

The TV show was canceled in late 1968, after which Tork left, while the other three continued for a few years. The Monkees film *Head*—which took the playful surrealism of the TV show to new heights—was released in 1969 but flopped, and has since been occasionally revived as a cult film. Nesmith went on to have a fairly prolific and successful career as a country-rock songwriter ("Different Drum"), singer and producer and an early rock-video maker; Jones and Dolenz reunited with Boyce and Hart for a 1976 LP. Tork and his band the New Monks conducted small-scale tours in late 1981 and early 1982.

MONTROSE

Formed 1974, California
Ronnie Montrose (b. Colo.), gtr.; Sammy Hagar, voc.; Bill Church, bass; Denny Carmassi, drums.
1973—*Montrose* (Warner Bros.) 1974—(– Church; + Alan Fitzgerald, bass, kybds.) *Paper Money* 1975—(– Hagar; + Bob James, voc.; + Jim Alcivar, kybds.) *Warner Brothers Presents Montrose* 1976—(+ Randy Jo Hobbs, bass) *Jump on It* 1978—(– Hobbs; – Carmassi; – James; + Edgar Winter, kybds.; + Rick Schlosser, drums) *Open Fire*.

Ronnie Montrose's heavy-metal power band seems at odds with the delicate acoustic and restrained electric guitar he lent to Van Morrison's *Tupelo Honey* and *St. Dominic's Preview* LPs.

After playing in local bands in Colorado, Montrose went to California around 1970, where he played on sessions for Beaver and Krause, the Beau Brummels, Gary Wright, Kathi McDonald and Dan Hartman, as well as Morrison. In 1972, he played with Boz Scaggs before joining the Edgar Winter Band, and in 1973 turned down an offer to be Mott the Hoople's lead guitarist before forming his own band.

Lead vocalist Sammy Hagar left after Montrose's second LP for a solo career; by 1978, ex-Montrose members Church, Fitzgerald and Carmassi were with Hagar. In the early Eighties, Montrose was leading another band, Gamma, which to date has released three albums.

MOODY BLUES

Formed 1964, Birmingham, England
Denny Laine (b. Brian Hines, Oct. 29, 1944, Eng.), gtr., voc.; Mike Pinder (b. Dec. 12, 1942, Birmingham), kybds., voc.; Ray Thomas (b. Dec. 29, 1942, Stourport-on-Severn, Eng.), flute, voc.; Clint Warwick (b. Clinton Eccles, June 25, 1949, Birmingham), bass; Graeme Edge (b. Mar. 30, 1942, Staffordshire, Eng.), drums.
1965—*Go Now* (London) 1966—*The Magnificent Moodies* (Decca) 1967—(– Laine; – Warwick; + Justin Hayward [b. 1946, Swindon, Eng.], gtr., voc.; + John Lodge, bass, voc.) *Days of Future Passed* (Deram) 1968—*In Search of the Lost Chord* 1969—*On the Threshold of a Dream; To Our Children's Children's Children* (Threshold) 1970—*A Question of Balance* 1971—*Every Good Boy Deserves Favour* 1972—*Seventh Sojourn* 1974—*This Is the Moody Blues* 1975—*In the Beginning* (Deram) 1977—

Caught Live Plus Five (London) (– Pinder; + Patrick Moraz [b. Jan. 24, 1948], kybds.) **1978**—*Octave* **1981**—*Long Distance Voyager*.

Though their first hit single, "Go Now" (#1 U.K., 1965), was a classic Merseybeat ballad, the Moody Blues—named after a Slim Harpo blues song—are best known as one of rock's first classical-pomp groups.

All the band members had worked in various local blues and R&B bands: Ray Thomas with El Riot and the Rebels (who often opened for the Beatles in England in the mid-Sixties); Mike Pinder with the Crew Cats, popular in Hamburg, Germany, while the Beatles were there. After "Go Now" hit, Denny Laine and Clint Warwick left (Laine later joined Paul McCartney's Wings), and the band's popularity declined.

Were it not for their purchase of a Mellotron (a keyboard instrument that reproduces the sounds of violins, flutes, choirs, etc., through tapes) in 1967, the Moody Blues might never have been heard from again. But with the Mellotron (and, occasionally, actual orchestras) providing grandiose symphonic accompaniment, the Moodies' material changed to cosmic lyrics set to heavily orchestrated pop tunes and extended suites, beginning with *Days of Future Passed*. That LP went gold in 1970, and kept returning to album charts as late as 1973. *Every Good Boy Deserves Favour* also went gold, and *Seventh Sojourn* was a #1 U.S. LP in 1972.

Though primarily an album band, the Moody Blues still had occasional hit singles: "Question" (#21, 1970), "Story in Your Eyes" (#23, 1971), "Isn't Life Strange?" (#29, 1972). "Nights in White Satin" (re-released from *Future Passed*) was an English success at first, then it made #2 (1972) in the U.S., spurring its album's massive

The Moody Blues: Justin Hayward, Ray Thomas, Patrick Moraz, Graeme Edge, John Lodge

sales. In 1969, the band established their own Threshold label, a Decca subsidiary.

After 1972's *Seventh Sojourn*, the band ceased recording as a group to allow all the members to pursue solo and collaborative projects, all on Threshold until 1977. Graeme Edge recorded *Kick Off Your Muddy Boots* (1974) with Adrian Gurvitz; Lodge and Hayward became the Blue Jays, a sort of Moody Blues continuation, and released a self-titled LP in 1975; Thomas issued *From Mighty Oaks* that year; in 1976, Pinder followed with *The Promise.*

In 1977 the Blue Jays split so its principals could make their own solo LPs: Hayward's *Songwriter* and Lodge's *Natural Avenue.* In 1978, the Moody Blues regrouped for *Octave,* though on a subsequent U.S. tour Pinder was replaced by ex-Refugee, ex-Yes keyboardist Patrick Moraz. With Moraz, the band once again regrouped to record *Voyager,* which stayed on the U.S. album charts over thirty weeks (peaking at #1) and boasted the hit singles "The Voice" (#15) and "Gemini Dream" (#12).

GIORGIO MORODER
Born circa 1941, Italy

Producer and songwriter Giorgio Moroder has emerged as a leading proponent of the synthesizer in pop music and an architect of the Eurodisco style. He settled in Munich in the late Sixties, where he began working with producer/lyricist Pete Bellotte. Though Moroder's previous musical experience had been playing bass, he became fascinated with the synthesizer.

In 1976, he produced a massive international hit, "Love to Love You Baby," performed by a then-unknown vocalist named Donna Summer. Moroder produced seven of Summer's LPs. He also recorded four solo albums of synthesized music: *Battlestar Galactica, From Here to Eternity, Knights in White Satin* and $E = MC^2$, the last of which was the first LP to be recorded and mastered digitally.

Moroder's soundtrack for the 1978 film *Midnight Express* won an Academy Award, the first synthesizer film score so honored. He produced two cuts on Janis Ian's *Night Rains* in 1979. In 1980, Moroder moved to Los Angeles, and that year he produced and composed the score for *American Gigolo,* which featured Blondie's #1 single "Call Me." He continued his soundtrack work with the 1982 score for *Cat People;* the theme, with lyrics and vocals by David Bowie, became a hit single.

VAN MORRISON
Born August 31, 1945, Belfast

1965—*Them* (Parrot) *Them Again* **1967**—*Blowin' Your Mind* (Bang) **1968**—*Astral Weeks* (Warner Bros.) **1970**—*Moondance; His Band and the Street Choir* **1971**—*Tupelo Honey* **1972**—*St. Dominic's Preview* **1973**—*Hard Nose the Highway* **1974**—*It's Too Late to Stop Now; Veedon Fleece; T. B. Sheets* (Bang) (compilation of first Bang LP and unreleased material) **1977**—*This Is Where I Came In; A Period of Transition* (Warner Bros.) **1978**—*Wavelength* **1979**—*Into the Music* **1980**—*Common One* **1982**—*Beautiful Vision* **1983**—*Inarticulate Speech of the Heart.*

Part Celtic bard, part soul singer and part ecstatically scatting mystical visionary, Van Morrison is a painfully introverted figure who rarely gives interviews and is at a loss to explain his own lyrics. In the studio, he can sing like a soul man getting the spirit; onstage, he tends to baffle and alienate audiences by rushing through songs and remaining noncommunicative between them.

Morrison's mother was a singer, and his father collected classic blues and jazz records. He learned guitar, saxophone and harmonica while in school, and was playing with Belfast blues, jazz and rock bands by his mid-teens. At 15, he quit school, joined an R&B band called the Monarchs and toured Europe with them as saxophonist. While in Germany, a film director offered Morrison a role in a movie as a jazz saxophonist. The film project expired, and Morrison returned to Belfast and opened an R&B club in the Maritime Hotel. He recruited some friends to form Them, who became an immediate local sensation as the club's house band.

Them recorded two singles in late 1964: "Don't Start Crying Now" (a local hit) and Big Joe Williams' "Baby Please Don't Go" (which made the British Top Ten in early 1965). After the latter's success, they moved to London and hooked up with producer Bert Berns. They recorded Berns's "Here Comes the Night," which went to #2 in the U.K. and made Top Thirty in the U.S. Them's next two singles, "Gloria" (by Morrison) and "Mystic Eyes," were minor U.S. hits; "Gloria" has since been covered by the Shadows of Knight and by Patti Smith. Them's lineup underwent constant changes, and Berns brought in sessionmen like Jimmy Page for their albums. After a mostly unsuccessful U.S. tour in 1966, the group returned to England. Morrison disbanded Them, which soon reformed with Ken McDowell as vocalist.

Morrison, meanwhile, grew depressed at music-business manipulations (Them had wrongly been given a rough-kids image by their company), stopped performing and moved back to Belfast. Bert Berns (a.k.a. B. Russell) formed Bang Records in New York. He sent Morrison a plane ticket and an invitation to record four singles for Bang. One of them, "Brown Eyed Girl," went Top Ten in the U.S. in the summer of 1967. Morrison toured America, but was again disgruntled when Berns released the other singles-demos as *Blowin' Your Mind.*

After Berns died of a sudden heart attack in December 1967, Morrison undertook an East Coast tour and wrote material for his next album. Warner Bros. president Joe

Van Morrison

Smith signed him in early 1968, and Morrison went into a New York studio that summer with a bunch of jazz musicians. In 48 hours he cut one of rock's least classifiable and most enduring albums, *Astral Weeks,* the first (and possibly still the most intense and profound) manifestation of Morrison's Irish-romantic mysticism. Though most of its cuts were meandering and impressionistic, with folky guitars over jazzy rhythms, topped by Morrison's soul-styled vocals, critics raved, and it sold fairly well.

His next album, *Moondance,* traded the jazz-and-strings sound of *Astral Weeks* for a horn-section R&B bounce. The title tune and "Come Running" were chart singles, the latter in 1970 (#39), the former not until late 1977. The fittingly titled "Into the Mystic" became a minor hit for Johnny Rivers while "Caravan" became an FM radio favorite. *His Band and the Street Choir* yielded two uptempo R&B-flavored Top Forty hits in "Domino" (#9) and "Blue Money" (#23) and it sold quite respectably. By this time, Morrison had moved to Marin County, California, and married a woman who called herself Janet Planet.

Tupelo Honey reflected a new sense of domestic contentment. It yielded a hit in "Wild Night" (#28) and sold quite well, thanks to progressive FM radio, which latched on to the lyrical title tune (featuring Modern Jazz Quartet drummer Connie Kay). *St. Dominic's Preview* included the hit single "Jackie Wilson Said" (#61) and contained two extended journeys into the mystic: "Listen to the Lion" and "Almost Independence Day." In 1972, Morrison guested on the John Lee Hooker-Charlie Musselwhite album *Never Get Out of These Blues Alive.*

By the time of *Hard Nose the Highway,* Morrison had formed the 11-piece Caledonia Soul Orchestra, which was featured on the live LP *It's Too Late to Stop Now.*

Suddenly in 1973, Morrison was divorced from Janet Planet, disbanded the Caledonia Soul Orchestra and returned to Belfast for the first time since 1966. There he began writing material for *Veedon Fleece.*

Morrison took three years to produce a followup. He reportedly began four different album sessions (one with jazz-funk band the Crusaders), which were never completed. By 1976 he was living in California. In late 1976, he appeared in the Band's film *The Last Waltz.*

Finally in 1977 came *A Period of Transition,* which featured short jazz and R&B-oriented tunes and backup by pianist Mac "Dr. John" Rebennack. For *Wavelength,* Morrison took on concert promoter Bill Graham as manager (they split in 1981); the album sold well, with its title cut a Top 100 single. Still, Morrison's chronic stage fright continued to plague him. At a 1979 show at New York's Palladium, he stormed off the stage mid-set without a word and didn't return.

The more serene *Into the Music* signaled that Morrison had become a born-again Christian, and *Common One* delved more into extended mysticism. It included "Cleaning Windows," which contained references to such Morrison inspirations as Leadbelly, bluesmen Blind Lemon Jefferson, Sonny Terry, Brownie McGhee and Muddy Waters, as well as Beat author Jack Kerouac and country singer Jimmie Rodgers. *Beautiful Vision* was more varied and concise, and it received, as usual, sizable critical acclaim and respectable sales; *Inarticulate Speech of the Heart* had "special thanks" to L. Ron Hubbard, inventor of Scientology.

GEORGE "SHADOW" MORTON
Born 1942, Richmond, Virginia

Though his production career continued into the Seventies, George Morton is best known as one of the premier auteurs of early-Sixties pop, having written and/or produced a string of highly theatrical hit records for the Shangri-Las and others.

As a child, Morton moved with his family to Brooklyn, where he sang with a vocal group called the Gems. He also worked as a club bouncer, an ice cream vendor and a hairdresser before launching his record industry career in 1964 by forming Red Bird Records with Phil Spector, Jerry Leiber and Mike Stoller. With the company, Morton drew on the songwriting of Ellie Greenwich and Jeff Barry and wrote tunes himself.

Morton's production style utilized romantic teen-rebellion lyrics against a grand backdrop of New York pop and light R&B, featuring both white and black artists. His first hit was "Remember (Walking in the Sand)" (#5, 1964) by the Shangri-Las; legend has it Morton wrote the tune in 12 minutes. This was followed by more Shangri-Las hits, like "Leader of the Pack" (#1, 1964), "Give Him a Great Big Kiss" (#18, 1965), "Give Us Your Blessings" (#29, 1965) and "I Can Never Go Home Anymore" (#6, 1965). Morton also had big success with the Dixie Cups ("Chapel of Love"), the Jelly Beans ("I Wanna Love Him So Bad"), the Tradewinds ("New York's a Lonely Town") and the Ad Libs ("The Boy from New York City").

Throughout, Morton did most of his own arranging and engineering. He branched out into protest music with Janis Ian's debut single, "Society's Child" (#14, 1967), hard rock with the Vanilla Fudge's "You Keep Me Hanging On" (#6, 1968) and folk with Richie Havens' debut LP (1965). Morton's commercial heyday ended with the Sixties, but he went on to produce the New York Dolls' *Too Much Too Soon* in 1974, and an album by all-female rock band Isis.

THE MOTELS
Formed 1972, Los Angeles
Original lineup: Martha Davis, voc.; Dean Chamberlain, gtr.; Richard D'Andrea, bass.
1976—(− Chamberlain; − D'Andrea; + Michael Goodroe, bass; + Marty Jourard, sax., kybds.; + Brian Glascock, drums; + Jeff Jourard, gtr.) **1979**—*Motels* (Capitol) (− J. Jourard; + Tim McGovern, gtr.) **1980**—*Careful* (− McGovern; + Guy Perry, gtr.) **1982**—*All Four One*.

The Motels were one of Los Angeles' original new wave bands and one of its most respected, though it took them a long time to capitalize commercially on either point. After a number of personnel shakeups, the Motels had their first hit single, "Only the Lonely," and first hit album, *All Four One*, their third try.

Motels singer/songwriter Martha Davis started her first band in 1972. Over four years, they went from the name Warfield Foxes to the Motels, from a joke to a serious venture, and from Berkeley to Los Angeles. Early members Dean Chamberlain (now of Code Blue) and Richard D'Andrea (who later played with Gary Valentine's the Know) left the group. The next version, with current Motels Marty Jourard, Michael Goodroe, Brian Glascock, and Jourard's brother Jeff, was signed to Capitol and recorded *The Motels*. Tim McGovern, once of L.A. power-poppers the Pop, replaced Jourard for *Careful* and an early version of *All Four One*. Capitol rejected the LP, McGovern left the Motels (to reappear with the Burning Sensations), and the band re-recorded the songs with studio musicians. The gambit paid off with "Only the Lonely," as the band once again considered new members.

MOTHERS OF INVENTION (See Frank Zappa.)

MOTORHEAD
Formed 1975, England
Current lineup: Lemmy Kilmister, bass, voc.; Eddie Clark, gtr.; Phil Taylor, drums; Brian Robertson, bass.
1977—*Motorhead* (Chiswick, U.K.) **1979**—*Overkill* (Bronze) *Bomber* **1980**—*Ace of Spades* (Mercury) **1981**—*No Sleep Till Hammersmith* **1982**—*Iron Fist* (− Clark).

Known to produce no less than 126 decibels in its live shows, England's Motorhead is easily one of the loudest rock & roll bands. The heavy-metal trio's raunchy leather-biker image underlines its fascination with violence, as do its album titles: *Overkill, Bomber* and *Iron Fist*.

Bassist/vocalist Lemmy Kilmister, formerly with progressive British rockers Hawkwind, put together Motorhead in 1975, and the group released its self-titled debut album in 1977 in the middle of the punk boom. After establishing itself on the British charts with two subsequent albums, the band recorded *Ace of Spades*, its official American debut. Motorhead has yet to make a significant dent in the American charts, but is a huge concert draw in the U.K.

THE MOTORS
Formed 1977, England
Nick Garvey, voc., gtr., bass; Andy McMaster, voc., kybds., bass; Bram Tchaikovsky, gtr., voc.; Ricky Slaughter, drums, voc.
1977—*The Motors I* (Virgin) **1978**—*Approved by the Motors* (− Tchaikovsky; − Slaughter) **1980**—*Tenement Steps*.

The Motors' two songwriters, Nick Garvey and Andy McMaster, met in Ducks Deluxe, a British pub-rock band. Garvey joined Ducks in their early stages in December 1972, after working as road manager for the Flamin' Groovies. The Scottish McMaster had been involved in rock since the mid-Sixties, playing for a while with the Stoics, which included Frankie Miller. He'd also written a successful record of children's songs. McMaster joined Ducks just before their second and final record, *Taxi to the Terminal Zone*. After they broke up, Garvey switched from bass to guitar and formed the Snakes. McMaster worked for a music publisher.

In early 1977, the two began collaborating on songs, soon recruiting the rest of the band, ex-Snakes drummer Ricky Slaughter and guitarist Bram Tchaikovsky. Their debut, highlighted by Garvey and McMaster's dual lead vocals, boasted the British hit single "Dancing the Night Away."

After the British success of "Airport" (from *Approved by the Motors*), Garvey and McMaster decided to fire the rest of the band and go on as a studio twosome with revolving musicians. Tchaikovsky went on to a promising solo career; Garvey produced his debut album. The two Motors decided to forego touring, and they released *Tenement Steps* (produced by Jimmy Iovine) in 1980. The LP featured "Love and Loneliness," with Rockpile's Terry Williams on drums and ex–Man Martin Ace on bass.

MOTT THE HOOPLE
Formed 1969 Hereford, England
Stan Tippens (b. Eng.), lead voc.; Mick Ralphs (b. Mar. 31, 1948, Hereford), gtr., voc.; Overend Pete Watts (b. May 13, 1947, Birmingham), bass; Dale "Buffin" Griffin (b. Oct. 24, 1948, Ross-on-Wye), drums; Verden Allen (b. May 26, 1944, Hereford), organ.
1969—(– Tippens; + Ian Hunter [b. June 3, 1946, Shrewsbury, Eng.], piano, gtr., lead voc.) *Mott the Hoople* (Atlantic) **1970**—*Mad Shadows* **1971**— *Wildlife; Brain Capers* **1972**—*Rock 'n' Roll Queen; All the Young Dudes* (Columbia) **1973**—(– Allen) *Mott* (– Ralphs; + Morgan Fisher, kybds.; + Ariel Bender, a.k.a. Luther James Grosvenor [b. Dec. 23, 1949, Evesham, Eng.], gtr.) **1974**—*The Hoople; Mott the Hoople Live* (– Bender; + Mick Ronson [b. Hull, Eng.], gtr.; – Hunter; – Ronson) **1975**—(name changed to Mott; + Ray Major, gtr.; + Nigel Benjamin, voc.) *Drive On* **1976**—*Shouting and Pointing; Greatest Hits.*

Mott the Hoople started out as an uneven hard-rock Dylanesque curiosity, but ended as a glitter-age group. Mott also gave rise to the solo career of songwriter Ian Hunter.

The group began in the late Sixties, when Mick Ralphs, Verden Allen, Overend Pete Watts and Dale Griffin began playing around Hereford, England, in a group called Silence with Allen and Ralphs. They got a record contract in early 1969 and went to London with vocalist Stan Tippens to record, produced by Guy Stevens. They took the Mott name from a novel by Willard Manus. Tippens was replaced by Ian Hunter in July. (Tippens subsequently became the band's road manager and later worked for the Pretenders.)

The group recorded their eponymous debut album in August 1969, and it garnered much curious attention for Hunter's Dylan-like rasp and the odd choice of covers, such as Sonny Bono's "Laugh at Me." *Mad Shadows* was moodier and poorly received; and the country-oriented *Wildlife* was their worst seller yet. The latter also featured a cover of Melanie's "Lay Down" and nine minutes of a live Little Richard interpretation (included because they had spent $4,000 to tape a scrapped concert album).

Mott became a big live attraction in England, even though their records didn't sell. Around this time, they caused a mini-riot at London's Albert Hall, which was a factor in the hall management's decision to ban rock completely. After the release of *Brain Capers*, the group was ready to disband, when David Bowie stepped in to give them a focused glam-rock image and a breakthrough single.

He first offered "Suffragette City," but the band wanted "Drive In Saturday," which Bowie refused to give them. Luckily they accepted his offer of "All the Young Dudes." Bowie produced the LP of the same name, and Mott had a top British single with "Dudes." The song became a signature piece for glitter rock and a gay anthem (something it took the all-straight band a while to get used to). "All the Young Dudes" went to #37 in the U.S.

The group's followup, 1973's *Mott*, was their masterpiece—a self-produced effort, with the British hit singles "Honaloochie Boogie" and "All the Way from Memphis." It was also a concept album about the fight for, and mistrust of, success, highlighted by the autobiographical "Ballad of Mott the Hoople." Around this time, Hunter's *Diary of a Rock Star* was published in England.

Despite their success, the band began to fall apart. Allen left because the group rarely recorded his songs. Ralphs quit because he was upset by Allen's leaving and irked that one of his songs for *Mott*, "Can't Get Enough," was beyond the singing range of either himself or Hunter. (The song was the first hit for Ralphs's next band, Bad Company. Hunter and company filled the guitar gap with Luther Grosvenor—formerly with Spooky Tooth and Stealer's Wheel—who changed his name to Ariel Bender upon joining. The *Live* album was recorded during a week of shows at New York's Uris Theater in May 1974.

The band had just begun to sell well in the States when they had another falling out. Late in 1974, Mick Ronson (ex–Bowie Spider from Mars) replaced Bender. By the end of the year, Hunter and Ronson split together, and Mott the Hoople was no more. Hunter had a solo deal with Columbia; but his first tour, billed as the Hunter-Ronson Band, was a disaster, with half-filled houses and a disillusioned band. Meanwhile, Watts, Griffin and Fisher carried on as Mott, joined by Ray Major and Nigel Benjamin. They released two undistinguished albums, *Drive On* and *Shouting and Pointing*, after which Benjamin left and the band fell apart. After Allen had left Mott back in 1973, he formed Cheeks, with future Pretenders James Honeyman-Scott and Martin Chambers, who toured through 1976 but never recorded.

MOUNTAIN
Formed 1969, New York City
Felix Pappalardi (b. 1939, Bronx; d. April 17, 1983, New York City), bass; Leslie West (b. Leslie Weinstein, Oct. 22, 1945, Queens), gtr., voc.; N. D. Smart, drums; Steve Knight, organ.
1969—*Leslie West—Mountain* (Leslie West solo) (Windfall) **1970**—(– Smart; + Corky Laing [b. Jan. 28, 1948, Montreal], drums) *Mountain Climbing* **1971**—*Nantucket Sleighride; Flowers of Evil* **1972**— *Mountain Live; The Road Goes on Forever* **1973**— *Best of* (Columbia) **1974**—*Avalanche* (Epic) **1977**—*Twin Peaks* (Columbia).

Cream pioneered the power-trio format; Mountain capitalized on it. The trio was formed in 1969 by Cream's producer Felix Pappalardi and 250-pound ex-Vagrant Leslie West.

The Vagrants had been Long Island legends, but never could expand their appeal as had local predecessors the Young Rascals. Although the release of the Vagrants' single "Respect" preceded Aretha Franklin's, the group was buried when Franklin's rendition came out soon after. Atco turned to Pappalardi to record the group's fourth single, but it was another flop. When the fifth attempt proved no better, the band broke up.

West set to recording a solo album, produced by Pappalardi. The result, *Leslie West—Mountain,* inspired the two to form Mountain, with N. D. Smart held over from the Mountain LP, and the addition of Steve Knight. Mountain proved akin to a cruder, louder version of Cream; propelled by the momentum of West's solo album and Pappalardi's production credentials, success was nearly instantaneous. Their fourth live performance was at the Woodstock festival. Smart was then replaced by Corky Laing. Their debut album, *Mountain Climbing,* went gold in 1970 and yielded the #21 hit "Mississippi Queen."

Nantucket Sleighride earned the group another gold album in 1971. But the formula began to wear thin (in marked contrast to West's waistline; his 1975 solo LP is entitled *The Great Fatsby*), and after one more studio album and a live LP, Pappalardi decided to return to production. Knight disappeared along the way as well, and ex-Cream bassist Jack Bruce joined what was thereafter known as West, Bruce and Laing. The group recorded two LPs for Columbia, 1972's *Why Dontcha* and 1973's *Whatever Turns You On,* both of which were moderately successful. After the second LP, the group disbanded; a live LP followed.

In the ensuing years, West and Laing periodically resurrected the Mountain moniker, sometimes with Pappalardi, sometimes not. They have also appeared in the New York metropolitan area billed as the Leslie West Band or the New Mountain. In 1983, Pappalardi was shot dead by his wife and songwriting collaborator, Gail Collins.

THE MOVE
Formed 1966, Birmingham, England
Roy Wood (b. Nov. 8, 1946), gtr., voc.; Bev Bevan (b. Nov. 25, 1944), drums, voc.; Carl Wayne (b. Aug. 18, 1944), voc.; Trevor Burton (b. Mar. 9, 1944), gtr., voc.; Chris "Ace" Kefford (b. Dec. 10, 1946), bass, voc.
1968—The Move (Regal Zonophone, U.K.) (— Kefford) **1969**—(— Burton; + Rick Price [b. June 10, 1944], bass, voc.) **1970**—Shazam (A&M) (— Wayne; + Jeff Lynne [b. Dec. 30, 1947], gtr., kybds, voc.) *The Best of the Move* **1971**—Looking On (Capitol) *Message from the Country* **1972**—(disbanded) *Split Ends* (United Artists) *California Man* (Harvest) **1979**—Shines On.

The Move's half-ironic pop made them popular in Britain in the late Sixties. But they were virtually unknown in America until their final days, when their energies were concentrated on their transformation into the Electric Light Orchestra. With Roy Wood's songwriting, they were a remarkably versatile group, sending pop singles to the top of the English charts while their albums featured extended forays into all manners of folk rock, heavy-metal and psychedelia.

The Move started in 1966, when five of Birmingham's top musicians left their respective cover bands for a greater challenge: Wood from Mike Sheridan and the Nightriders; Trevor Burton from the Mayfair Set; Carl Wayne, Bev Bevan and Ace Kefford from Carl Wayne and the Vikings. With the aid of crafty management, the Move achieved almost instant notoriety. Their stage act climaxed with ax destruction of television sets and automobiles. Wood's compositions acknowledged British trends, notably the controversial psychedelic movement. A publicity mailing for an early 45, "Flowers in the Rain," depicted Prime Minister Harold Wilson in bed with his secretary, resulting in a lawsuit and the band's loss of royalties. The single reached #2 on the British charts.

Even within the group, the Move's image was divided. In Carl Wayne, the Move had an aspiring cabaret balladeer; Trevor Burton and Chris Kefford were rock & rollers. Kefford quit first, not to be heard from again. Burton followed, upset by the implications of the Move's first and only English #1, the lush "Blackberry Way." He has stayed active as a member of the Uglys (with future ELO member Richard Tandy), the Balls (with Moody Blue/Wings Denny Laine and Steve Gibbons) and most recently the Steve Gibbons Band.

With Rick Price on bass, the Move recorded *Shazam,* six cuts in six different styles interspersed with man-on-the-street interviews. The album was calculated to combat their British bubblegum image. Soon after, Wayne left for an unsuccessful solo career, his place taken by Jeff Lynne, who had replaced Wood in the Nightriders as they were renamed the Idle Race. The Idle Race enjoyed modest British popularity, due in part to the Wood composition "Here We Go Round the Lemon Tree." The Move then announced a planned metamorphosis into the Electric Light Orchestra, incorporating cello and violin.

But there were to be more Move records. In now-standard fashion, there was a series of commercial singles (collected on *Split Ends*) and an adventurous LP, *Message from the Country.* Meantime, Price had left the band, as he had become superfluous once the group abandoned the stage. While the Move put out their last contract-fulfilling singles (including Lynne's "Do Ya," a minor hit for the Move, later a much greater one for ELO), the recording of the first Electric Light Orchestra album was under way. On its release, the Move were finished.

MUD
Formed 1973, England
Les Gray, voc.; Rob Davis, gtr.; Roy Stiles, bass; Dave Mount, drums.

1974—*Mud Rock* (RAK) 1975—*Mud Rock, Volume 2; Greatest Hits; Use Your Imagination* (Private Stock) 1976—*It's Better Than Working* 1977—*Mud Pack* 1978—*Rock On* (RCA).

Like their RAK label contemporaries Sweet, Mud were a hard-rock/pop formula band playing a sort of heavy-metal bubblegum, protégés of the Nicky Chinn-Mike Chapman songwriting/production team. Though they had several U.K. hits, they never experienced even the minor success that Sweet had in the U.S.

Mud's U.K. hits included "Dyna-Mite" (#4, 1973), "Tiger Feet" (#1, 1974), "The Cat Crept In" (#2, 1974), "Rocket" (#6, 1974), "Lonely This Christmas" (#1, 1974), "The Secrets That You Keep" (#3, 1975), "Oh Boy" (#1, 1975) and "Moonshine Sally" (#10, 1975). In 1975 they left RAK and recorded more hits for Private Stock, including "L-L-Lucy" (#10, 1975), "Show Me You're a Woman" (#8, 1975) and "Lean on Me" (#7, 1976). When their 1978 RCA album failed to sell, they disbanded.

GEOFF AND MARIA MULDAUR
Geoff Muldaur, born circa 1945; Maria Muldaur, born Maria Grazia Rosa Domenica d'Amato, September 12, 1943, New York City
Geoff Muldaur: 1964—*Geoff Muldaur* (Prestige) 1965—*Sleepy Man Blues* 1975—*Is Having a Wonderful Time* (Reprise) 1976—*Motion* 1978—*Geoff Muldaur and Amos Garrett* (Flying Fish) 1979—*Blues Boy*.
Maria Muldaur: 1972—*Mud Acres* (Rounder) 1973—*Maria Muldaur* (Reprise) 1974—*Waitress in a Donut Shop* 1976—*Sweet Harmony* 1978—*Southern Winds* (Warner Bros.) 1979—*Open Your Eyes* 1980—*Gospel Nights* (Takoma).
Geoff and Maria Muldaur: 1969—*Pottery Pie* (Reprise) 1972—*Sweet Potatoes* (Warner Bros.).

The Muldaurs, who were married in the mid-Sixties and divorced in 1972, both graduated from the early-Sixties folk scene, Geoff with Jim Kweskin's Jug Band, Maria with the Even Dozen Jug Band (which included John Sebastian, Stefan Grossman, Steve Katz and Joshua Rifkin). They have recorded solo and together, and Maria's has been by far the most commercially successful career.

The two married while they were both with Kweskin's Jug Band. Geoff Muldaur had made a couple of rather obscure albums that demonstrated his attraction to folk blues, vintage jazz, gospel and country music. Maria D'Amato, in the meantime, had grown up listening to blues and Big Band music. In high school, she formed an all-girl Everly Brothers–inspired group, the Cameos, and then the Cashmeres, who were offered a recording contract that her mother forbade her to sign (Maria was still a minor). She gravitated to the Greenwich Village folk scene with the Even Dozen Jug Band; she left Even Dozen for

Kweskin—where she sang the blues and Leiber and Stoller—and married Geoff.

Their two duo LPs were eclectic and folksy to the point of sounding homemade ("Produced by Nobody" proclaimed the *Sweet Potatoes* sleeve), and both featured the guitar of Amos Garrett, with whom both Muldaurs would remain associated. In 1973, Geoff moved to Woodstock and worked with Paul Butterfield's Better Days band. Maria also took part in the soundtrack to *Steelyard Blues* with Butterfield, Nick Gravenites and Mike Bloomfield.

Maria began her own career in 1972 with her enormously successful debut LP, which featured a wide range of material by Dolly Parton, Dan Hicks, Dr. John, Kate McGarrigle and Wendy Waldman. "Midnight at the Oasis" was a Top Ten single from the album, and the LP eventually sold platinum. Her second album featured horn arrangements by Benny Carter. The failure of her third album to sell well, despite continuing critical acclaim, left her disillusioned. Geoff, in the meantime, released elaborately produced solo albums on Reprise and folksier ones on Flying Fish. Maria continued to record solo, albeit more and more sporadically. In 1978, she guested on Elvin Bishop's *Hog Heaven* LP. By 1980, she was a born-again Christian, and within a year had released a gospel album.

MARTIN MULL
Born August 18, 1943, Chicago
1971—*In the Soop* (Vanguard) 1972—*Martin Mull* (Capricorn) 1973—*Martin Mull and His Fabulous Furniture in Your Living Room* 1974—*Normal* 1975—*Days of Wine and Neuroses* 1976—*No Hits, Four Errors* 1977—*I'm Everyone I've Ever Loved* (ABC) 1978—*Sex and Violins* 1979—*Near Perfect/Perfect* (Elektra).

Musician/comedian Martin Mull was raised in Illinois, Ohio and Connecticut and earned an MA degree in painting at the Rhode Island School of Design. After graduating, he worked for a year as producer in a Boston recording studio, then signed on as staff writer at Warner Bros. Records, where he wrote "A Girl Named Johnny Cash" for singer Jane Morgan, an answer song to Cash's earlier hit "A Boy Named Sue." He left Warner Bros. in 1971, and began performing with his Magical Midget Band in Boston.

Mull has since maintained a cult following for his comedy songs—hit sendups like "Dueling Tubas" and original songs like "Noses Run in My Family." In the early Seventies, he wrote the theme music for two PBS series, "The Great American Dream Machine" and "51st State." In the mid-Seventies, he starred in two satirical late-night TV series that attracted large-scale cult followings: "Mary Hartman, Mary Hartman" and "Fernwood 2-Night."

MOON MULLICAN
Born Aubrey Mullican, March 29, 1909, Polk County, Texas; died January 1, 1967, Beaumont, Texas

N.A.—*Moon Mullican* (Starday) *Moon Mullican Sings and Plays 16 of His Favorite Tunes* (King) *Moon Mullican Sings His All-Time Greatest Hits.*

Although no rock & roller—his "Seven Nights to Rock" in 1957 was as close to a hit as he came and it wasn't that close—Moon Mullican earned his place in the music's history as a seminal influence on the piano style of Jerry Lee Lewis, among others.

Mullican learned to play guitar and organ as a child. At the age of 21, he moved to Houston, where he played piano in a house of prostitution at night, and so was nicknamed Moon. During the Thirties and Forties, he performed in clubs throughout Texas and Louisiana. He made his recording debut in 1939, and he had several country hits, including the million-seller "Jolé Blon" (1947) and "I'll Sail My Ship Alone" (1951), featuring Mullican's distinctive pumping left hand and two-fingered right, which secured his reputation as the "King of the Hillbilly Piano Players." He performed at the Grand Ole Opry from 1949 to 1955, and his last hit was "Ragged but Right" in 1961. He died of a heart attack.

MUNGO JERRY

Formed 1969, London
Ray Dorset (b. March 21, 1946, Ashford, Eng.), gtr., voc.; Colin Earl (b. May 6, 1942, Hampton Ct., Eng.), piano; Paul King (b. Jan. 9, 1948, Dagenham, Eng.), banjo, gtr., jug; Mike Cole, string bass.
1970—*Mungo Jerry* (Janus) *Memoirs of a Stockbroker; In the Summertime* (Pye) 1975—*Mungo Jerry* 1978—*Ray Dorset and Mungo Jerry* (Polydor).

Mungo Jerry were a British quartet of skiffle revivalists (skiffle was roughly the English equivalent of jug band music) who had a novelty hit in 1970 with "In the Summertime," a #3 single (#1 in England) that earned them a gold record in the U.S.

Prior to 1970, they had been known as the Good Earth, and if the name change helped them achieve their hit, it never did the trick again in the U.S., although they had an impressive list of Top Forty successes in Britain: "Baby Jump," "Alright, Alright," "You Don't Have to Be in the Army to Fight the War," "Lady Rose," "Open Up," "Wild Love" and "Longlegged Woman Dressed in Black."

MICHAEL MURPHEY

Born in Dallas
1972—*Geronimo's Cadillac* (A&M) 1973—*Cosmic Cowboy Souvenir* 1974—*Michael Murphey* (Epic) 1975—*Blue Sky Night Thunder; Swans against the Sun* 1976—*Flowing Free Forever* 1978—*Lone Wolf* 1979—*Peaks, Valleys, Honky-Tonks and Alleys* 1982—*Michael Martin Murphey* (EMI).

One of the original "cosmic cowboys" of country rock, Michael Murphey started out as one of the leaders of the late-Sixties to mid-Seventies Austin, Texas, "progressive country" music scene.

Before he became a musician, Murphey had been intent on joining the Southern Baptist ministry, and had studied Greek at North Texas State University and creative writing at UCLA. After working as a staff songwriter at Screen Gems for five years in the late Sixties and a brief stint with the Dillard and Clark Expedition, Murphey began performing solo. Producer Bob Johnston signed him to A&M and produced Murphey's debut LP in Nashville.

The title tune of his debut made #37 on the singles charts and was covered by Hoyt Axton, Cher, Claire Hamill and others. He smoothed out his style for his biggest hit, 1975's "Wildfire" (#3); others included "Carolina in the Pines" (#21, 1975) and "Renegade" (#39, 1976). In 1980, his "Cherokee Fiddle" was featured in the *Urban Cowboy* film soundtrack; he also appeared in the film *Take This Job and Shove It*. In 1982 he had a hit with "What's Forever For?"

ELLIOTT MURPHY

Born March 16, 1949, Garden City, New York
1973—*Aquashow* (Polydor) 1975—*Lost Generation* (RCA) 1976—*Night Lights* 1977—*Just a Story from America* (Columbia) 1981—*Affairs* (Courtesan) 1982—*Murph the Surf.*

Singer/songwriter Elliott Murphy's 1973 recording debut was hailed as "the best Dylan since 1968," and over the years Murphy has developed a following both in the U.S. and in Europe.

Murphy was born and raised in an upper-middle-class Long Island suburb. His father owned an Aquashow in Queens, near the World's Fair grounds, where Big Band acts like Duke Ellington would perform. He began playing guitar at age 12, and by age 13 he had formed his first band. In 1966, his group, the Rapscallions, won a New York State battle of the bands.

Murphy then moved to Europe, where he sang in the streets and, in 1971, had a bit part in Fellini's *Roma*. During the early Seventies, he was a regular in New York's Mercer Arts Center scene with the New York Dolls, Patti Smith and others. He was discovered by critic Paul Nelson, and though *Aquashow* was widely acclaimed, commercial success eluded him (only "Drive All Night" from *Just a Story from America* became a minor hit), and his only hits have been in Europe. In 1981, Murphy formed his own label, Courtesan, and is currently writing short stories and a novel. He continues to tour and record.

ANNE MURRAY

Born June 20, circa 1946, Springhill, Nova Scotia
1970—*Snowbird* (Capitol) 1973—*Danny's Song* 1974—*Country; Love Song* 1976—*Keeping in Touch* 1978—*Let's Keep It That Way* 1979—*New Kind of*

Feeling **1980**—*Anne Murray's Greatest Hits* **1981**—*Where Do You Go When You Dream.*

Anne Murray, the MOR country-pop singer, was the first female Canadian vocalist to earn a gold record in the U.S. (Joni Mitchell with *Ladies of the Canyon* was second).

Born and raised in a coal-mining village, Murray was always interested in singing. While attending the University of New Brunswick in the mid-Sixties, she auditioned unsuccessfully for the Halifax TV show "Sing Along Jubilee"; two years later, she was hired for the station's summer series. She taught physical education on Prince Edward Island, but also sang in small clubs and sometimes on another Canadian show, "Let's Go," spurred on by Brian Ahern (her first producer) and Bill Langstroth (who became her husband).

In the late Sixties, Murray recorded her first LP for Arc (a small Canadian label), which led to a deal with Capitol of Canada. She debuted in America in mid-1970 with the *Snowbird* LP and single (#8), which became the first Canadian female gold 45 later in the year. Murray began to appear regularly on Glen Campbell's U.S. TV show, and toured and recorded the LP *Anne Murray/Glen Campbell* with him in 1971. But she didn't have another major American hit until March 1973 and her Top Ten cover of Kenny Loggins' "Danny's Song." Other hit singles include a cover of Lennon and McCartney's "You Won't See Me" (#8, 1974) and "Love Song" (#12, 1975).

Murray came back in January 1978 (after three years' maternity leave) with *Let's Keep It That Way,* her biggest success ever, which went platinum in December, bolstered by the #1 pop, #4 country, gold ballad "You Needed Me" and the Top Five country hit "Walk Right Back." *New Kind of Feeling* went gold.

THE MUSCLE SHOALS SOUND RHYTHM SECTION

Formed 1967, Florence, Alabama
Jimmy Johnson (b. 1943, Sheffield, Ala.), gtr.; Roger Hawkins (b. 1945, Mishawaka, Ind.), drums; David Hood (b. 1943, Sheffield, Ala.), bass; Barry Beckett (b. 1943, Birmingham, Ala.), kybds.

The Muscle Shoals Sound Rhythm Section has provided studio band backing on more than 500 R&B, rock & roll, country and disco records. The quartet originated in the stable of session musicians at Rick Hall's Fame Studios in Florence, Alabama, home of the original Muscle Shoals Sound.

Jimmy Johnson began working for Hall as an engineer in 1962 and returned to the guitar he had played as a teenager three years later. Roger Hawkins had been in Johnson's group, the Del-Rays, and joined the Fame stable in 1965. David Hood started out at Fame as a trombonist, replacing Norbert Putnam as bassist when Putnam moved to Nashville in 1966. Barry Beckett took over the Fame keyboards from Spooner Oldham in 1967. As the Fame house band, their lineup was often expanded to include lead guitarists like Duane Allman, Chips Moman and Eddie Hinton. They made their reputation as musicians on hits by Aretha Franklin, Wilson Pickett, Percy Sledge, Arthur Conley, Clarence Carter, and James and Bobby Purify (most of them produced by Atlantic Records' Jerry Wexler).

In 1969, Johnson, Hawkins, Hood and Beckett left Fame to set up their own studio, Muscle Shoals Sound, in nearby Sheffield, Alabama. Since then, the band has played on records by Paul Simon, the Staple Singers, Dusty Springfield, Leon Russell, Sam and Dave, Cat Stevens, Cher, Bobby Womack, King Curtis, Johnny Taylor, Bob Seger, Eddie Rabbitt and Millie Jackson; in 1972 and 1973, Hawkins and Hood toured as part of the expanded lineup of Traffic. Rod Stewart, the Rolling Stones and Boz Scaggs are among those who have recorded at the Muscle Shoals Sound Studios, with Johnson engineering.

Each of the four has worked as a producer: Johnson for Lynyrd Skynyrd, the Amazing Rhythm Aces and Levon Helm; Hood for Wayne Perkins; Hawkins for Mel and Tim and Canned Heat; and Beckett for Bob Dylan, Dire Straits, Phoebe Snow, Southside Johnny and the Asbury Jukes, Joan Baez, John Prine and Delbert McClinton. The year 1979 saw the unveiling of Muscle Shoals Sound Records.

N

JOHNNY NASH

Born August 19, 1940, Houston
1972—*I Can See Clearly Now* (Epic)   1973—*My Merry-Go-Round*   1974—*Celebrate Life*   1979—*Let's Go Dancing.*

Johnny Nash was one of the first performers to bring reggae to the attention of the American public, with his #1 hit, the self-penned "I Can See Clearly Now," in 1972. He also recorded Bob Marley's first U.S. hit song in 1973 with a cover of Marley's "Stir It Up" (#12).

Nash, who many believed was Jamaican, grew up in Texas and had been recording since 1957. He began singing gospel in a Baptist church and by 13 was on the Houston TV show "Matinee," breaking the local television color bar of the time. He sang C&W as well as pop, easy-listening soul and calypso. In 1956, Arthur Godfrey gave him a spot on his TV show, where he performed for the next seven years.

Nash began his recording career in 1957 for ABC-Paramount with "A Teenager Sings the Blues." His first chart single was "A Very Special Love" (#23, 1958), followed by "The Teen Commandments," sung with Paul Anka and George Hamilton IV (#29, 1959). In the early Sixties, he recorded unsuccessfully for Warner Bros. (1962–63), Groove and Argo (1964). Still, his compositions did well for others, like "What Kind of Love Is This," a Top Twenty hit for Joey Dee in 1962.

In the late Sixties, Nash began recording at Byron Lee's studio in Jamaica and went on to build his own studio there. He formed his own labels, Joda and Jad, before hitting the charts again with the reggae "Hold Me Tight," a Top Five pop hit in 1968. Around this time he had more hits in England, including a reggae cover of Sam Cooke's "Cupid" in 1969. Nash also began to star in films, such as *Take a Giant Step*, Sweden's *Love Is Not a Game* (1974) and *Key Witness*. In 1971, living in England, he signed to Epic, leading to his "I Can See Clearly Now" peak in 1972. After 1973's "Stir It Up" (a hit in England back in 1971), he had no more big American hits, though he continued to be popular in England.

NAZARETH

Formed 1969, Scotland
Dan McCafferty, voc.; Manny Charlton, gtr.; Darrel Sweet, drums; Pete Agnew, bass.
1971—*Nazareth* (Warner Bros.)   1972—*Exercises*
1973—*Razamanaz* (A&M)   *Loud 'n' Proud*   1975—*Hair of the Dog;   Rampant*   1976—*Close Enough for Rock 'n' Roll; Play 'n' the Game*   1977—*Hot Tracks;   Expect No Mercy*   1978—(+ Zal Cleminson [b. May 4, 1949, Glasgow], gtr.)   *No Mean City*   1980—*Malice in Wonderland*   (− Cleminson)   1981—*Fool Circle*   (+ Billy Rankin, gtr.; + John Locke, kybds.)   1982—*2XS* (A&M).

Nazareth are a hard-rocking (sometimes heavy-metal) group from Scotland whose major distinguishing feature, besides their Rod Stewartish lead singer Dan McCafferty, has been their penchant for offering pile-driving versions of quieter songs by writers like Joni Mitchell, Woody Guthrie, Tim Rose and Bob Dylan.

All of the members were born in Scotland, where they met in Dunfermline in the semi-pro band the Shadettes, which included Pete Agnew, Dan McCafferty and Darrel Sweet. When Manny Charlton joined in 1969, they changed their name to Nazareth (inspired by the first line of the Band's "The Weight") and got their first record contract in 1971. Their first two LPs were generally ignored, but for 1973's *Razamanaz* they switched to A&M and got Roger Glover (ex–Deep Purple bassist) to produce. They had their first British hits that year: "Broken Down Angel" (#9) and "Bad Bad Boy" (#10). *Loud 'n' Proud* yielded a brutal version of Joni Mitchell's "This Flight Tonight," which hit big in the U.K. and got some FM airplay in the U.S. It also included a nine-minute metallic rendition of Dylan's "The Ballad of Hollis Brown." The LP established them in Europe and Canada, where the group has had many gold and platinum records.

They've been less successful in the U.S., where their only hit was off the gold *Hair of the Dog*, "Love Hurts" (#8, 1976), the song Boudleaux Bryant wrote for the Everly Brothers, and also a hit for Jim Capaldi in England. Also that year, the band hit #14 in England with "My White Bicycle," originally a psychedelia-period song from Tomorrow (a band that included future Yes guitarist Steve Howe). Vocalist McCafferty released a solo LP in 1975.

Nazareth kept their lineup intact until 1978, when they added second guitarist Zal Cleminson, who had spent five years with the Sensational Alex Harvey Band and also played on McCafferty's solo LP. He appeared only on *No Mean City* and *Malice in Wonderland*. By 1981, they were back to a foursome. *Malice in Wonderland* and *Fool Circle* were produced by ex–Steely Dan and Doobie Brother Jeff Baxter. (The previous five had been produced by Charlton, taking over for Glover, who had produced *Razamanaz, Loud 'n' Proud* and *Rampant*.) By 1982, Nazareth had added two new members, ex-Spirit keyboardist John Locke and guitarist Billy Rankin.

THE NAZZ

Formed 1967, Philadelphia

Todd Rundgren (b. June 22, 1948, Upper Darby, Penn.), gtr., voc.; Stewkey (b. Robert Antoni, Nov. 17, 1947, Newport, R.I.), kybds., lead voc.; Thom Mooney (b. Jan. 5, 1948, Altoona, Penn.), drums; Carson G. Van Osten (b. Sep. 24, 1946, Cinnaminson, N.J.), bass.
1968—*Nazz* (SGC)   **1969**—*Nazz Nazz;   Nazz 3.*

The Nazz, Todd Rundgren's first recording band, were a power-pop quartet from Philadelphia. Rundgren and Carson Van Osten came from Woody's Truck Stop (a Philly blues band), Thom Mooney was from the Munchkins and Stewkey had previously been with Elizabeth—all local groups. They made their live debut in July 1967 opening for the Doors at Philadelphia's Town Hall, and by February of the next year had a record contract.

Their debut LP, *Nazz*, had Rundgren as its chief writer, though Stewkey handled lead vocals. The material was Beatles- and early Who-influenced, like the hard-rocking "Open My Eyes" and "Hello It's Me," which later appeared on Todd's *Something/Anything* solo LP in 1972. The band got good press, and they began turning up in the teen magazines. But problems set in with their second LP, *Nazz Nazz*. There were ego conflicts (Rundgren and Mooney fought the most); and the band's second album, originally planned as a double LP called *Fungo Bat,* was split by management into 1969's *Nazz Nazz* and 1970's *Nazz 3*. The tracks on the latter LP originally featured Rundgren's lead vocals, which were erased, with Stewkey put on instead. Before it came out, Rundgren and Van Osten quit.

Stewkey and Mooney kept a version of the band going until mid-1970. Mooney then left for California and later played with the Curtis Brothers and Tattoo, with ex-Raspberry Wally Bryson. Van Osten became an animation

artist; Rundgren became a producer and then successful solo artist; Stewkey joined a band with Rick Nielsen (later of Cheap Trick) called Fuse, who recorded one LP for Epic. Mooney also joined Fuse for a while but left before they became Sick Man of Europe, which later included Tom Petersson (also a future member of Cheap Trick). One bootleg disc of theirs surfaced, *Retrospective Foresight*, which included, besides some originals, several Nazz outtakes from various incarnations.

FRED NEIL

Born 1937, St. Petersburg, Florida

1964—*Hootenanny Live at the Bitter End* (FM)   *World of Folk Music; Tear Down the Walls*   **1966**—*Fred Neil* (Capitol)   **1967**—*Bleecker and Macdougal* (Elektra)
1969—*Everybody's Talkin'* (Capitol)   **1970**—*Little Bit of Rain* (Elektra) *Other Side of This Life* (Capitol)   **1971**—*Sessions.*

Songwriter Fred Neil has stayed on the folk circuit while his songs have become pop hits for others. In the late Fifties, Buddy Holly recorded a number of his tunes; in the late Sixties, Harry Nilsson helped establish his own career with a hit cover of Neil's "Everybody's Talkin'," part of the *Midnight Cowboy* soundtrack.

While still in his teens, Neil performed at the Grand Ole Opry. He moved to New York and became part of the Greenwich Village folk scene, where his songwriting and his mastery of 12-string guitar made him a leading figure. His earliest recordings featured backing by John Sebastian and Felix Pappalardi, but none of his albums sold well, even after Nilsson's hit.

Neil moved to Coconut Grove, Florida, becoming a recluse once more. His songs have been covered by Frank Sinatra, Jefferson Airplane, José Feliciano, Tim Buckley, It's a Beautiful Day, Roy Orbison, the Youngbloods and Linda Ronstadt. It is generally thought that the Airplane's "Ballad of You and Me and Pooneil" is dedicated to him.

NEKTAR

Formed 1968, Germany

Derek "Mo" Moore, bass, voc.; Roy Albrighton, gtr., voc.; Alan "Taff" Freeman, kybds., voc.; Ron Howden, drums, voc.; Mick Brockett, lights and sound.
1972—*Journey to the Centre of the Eye* (Bellaphon)
1973—*Live at the Roundhouse; (Nektar) Sounds Like This*   **1974**—*Remember the Future*   **1975**—*Down to Earth* (Passport) *Recycled*   (– Albrighton; + Dave Nelson [b. U.S.], gtr.)   **1976**—*A Tab in the Ocean; Magic Is a Child* (Polydor).

Nektar began as a group of British expatriates living in Germany, where they developed a Hawkwind/Camel/ early Genesis style of melodic semi-psychedelic art rock which engendered cult interest in the U.S. during the mid-Seventies.

The band's members first came to Germany in 1965, as

The Nazz: Todd Rundgren, Thom Mooney, Stewkey, Carson Van Osten

did Deep Purple and Pink Floyd. Derek Moore and Ron Howden had met in 1964 in Tours, France, while playing in different bands. Howden joined Moore's group, the Upsetters, and the pair soon formed the Prophets. In Germany in 1965, they picked up Alan Freeman from the band MI5 and changed their name to Prophecy. Roy Albrighton (formerly with Rainbows) joined in 1968, and by late 1969 they had changed their name to Nektar. In 1970, they added Mick Brockett, officially dubbed "light musician," adding backdrop films and visual elements to complete the band's psychedelic image. Indeed, a 1977 press release warns that epileptics should avoid their shows lest a "psychic energizer" film trigger seizures.

Their first LP, *Journey to the Centre of the Eye* came out on the German Bellaphon label, in Europe only, as did the next three albums. Their U.S. debut was 1974's *Remember the Future,* a concept LP about an extraterrestrial bluebird who helps a child see the future. The group's music fit in well with art rock's commercial peak in mid-Seventies America, and the *Remember* LP became an FM staple and went gold. It was aided by their record company's risky decision to avoid presenting the group as an opening act by financing their U.S. headline tour. (This approach also proved successful for Genesis and Supertramp on their U.S. live debuts.)

Nektar had moved to America around 1976. Drummer Howden began to double as lead singer, and American guitarist Dave Nelson replaced Albrighton. The band's sales had declined steadily after *Remember the Future,* though, and they eventually broke up.

RICK NELSON

Born Eric Hilliard Nelson, May 8, 1940, Teaneck, New Jersey

1957—*Ricky* (Imperial)   **1959**—*Songs by Ricky*   **1960**—*More Songs by Ricky*   **1961**—*Ricky Is 21*   **1963**—*Best Sellers by Ricky Nelson*   **1967**—*Country Fever* (Decca)   **1968**—*Another Side of Rick*   **1969**—*Perspective*   **1971**—*Legendary Masters* (United Artists)   **1972**—*Garden Party* (Decca)   **1974**—*Windfall* (MCA)   **1981**—*Playing to Win* (Capitol).

Singer Ricky Nelson was the first rock teen idol to use television as a way to promote hit records. He later made a fairly successful transition to become a country-rock singer.

In 1952, he began playing himself on his parents' TV series, "The Adventures of Ozzie and Harriet." In the late Forties, "The Ozzie and Harriet Show" had been a radio show, and Ricky and his older brother, David, were added when they switched to television. Ricky didn't begin singing on the show until he was 17 in 1957. According to Nelson, he had no musical ambitions until after a girlfriend told him she was in love with Elvis Presley.

Nelson's first hit (on Verve) was 1957's "I'm Walking" (the Fats Domino song), which went to #4 and sold a

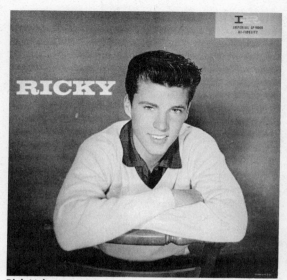

Rick Nelson

million records after Nelson performed it on TV. Between then and 1961, he had several rockabilly-flavored pop hits, including "Poor Little Fool" (#1, 1958), "Just A Little Too Much" (#9, 1959), "Travelin' Man," "Hello Mary Lou" (#1, 1961) and "Believe What You Say" (#4, 1958). Some of his early hits were penned by Dorsey and/or Johnny Burnette; his backup band featured James Burton, who later became Presley's lead guitarist.

By the mid-Sixties, Nelson's hits began to dry up, and in 1966, when his parents' show went off the air, he slid into obscurity. Though he continued to record for Decca (with whom he signed a twenty-year contract in 1963), his music was eclipsed by the British Invasion. During 1966 and 1967, though, on albums like *Country Fever* and *Bright Lights and Country Music,* he began to mix country and rock. He dropped the "y" from his first name when he turned twenty.

In 1969, Nelson formed the country-rock outfit the Stone Canyon Band and scored a minor commercial comeback with a cover of Dylan's "She Belongs to Me" (#33). His next success rose out of failure. In October 1971, when Nelson and his band appeared at a rock & roll revival at Madison Square Garden, the audience booed his long-hair look and new material. Out of the experience, he wrote "Garden Party," which hit #6 and went gold in 1972, his first million-seller in over a decade.

In various stages, the Stone Canyon Band included Randy Meisner (between Poco and the Eagles); Dennis Larden of Every Mother's Son; Richie Hayward, briefly on leave from Little Feat; Tom Brumley of Buck Owens' Buckaroos; and Steve Love, later with Roger McGuinn and the New Riders of the Purple Sage. Nelson's follow-up albums didn't catch on, and by the mid-Seventies he had lost his MCA contract. He came back in 1981 with an LP on Capitol called *Playin' to Win*, and he continues to tour and record.

SANDY NELSON
Born December 1, 1938, Santa Monica, California

Sandy Nelson scored several hits in the late Fifties and early Sixties with his rocking guitar and drum-based instrumentals, most notably 1959's "Teen Beat" (#4).

Nelson was friends with Jan and Dean, Nancy Sinatra and Phil Spector when they were all in high school. His first band was Kip Tyler and the Flips, which at one point included future Beach Boy Bruce Johnston on piano. That band recorded for Ebb and Challenge records. Nelson later played on the Teddy Bears' gold "To Know Him Is to Love Him" (he also toured with them), and also drummed on Gene Vincent's 1959 *Crazy Times* LP before recording "Teen Beat" for the small Original Sound label. It went gold and Nelson was quickly signed by Imperial Records, but his second hit didn't come until 1961, with "Let There Be Drums" (#7).

Just before he cut that record, Nelson lost his left foot in a car accident, but it didn't affect his drumming. He later hit with "Drums Are My Beat" in 1962 (#29) and a "Teen Beat" update inventively titled "Teen Beat '65" (#44, 1964). He continued to record, with only minor success, through the Sixties.

TRACY NELSON
Born December 27, 1944, Madison, Wisconsin
1965—*Deep Are the Roots* (Prestige)   1968—*Living with the Animals* (Mercury)   1969—*Make a Joyful Noise; Mother Earth Presents Tracy Nelson Country*   1970—*Satisfied*   1971—*Bring Me Home* (Reprise)   1973—*A Poor Man's Paradise* (Columbia)   1974—*Tracy Nelson* (Atlantic)   1975—*Sweet Soul Music* (MCA)   1976—*Time Is on My Side*   1978—*Homemade Songs* (Flying Fish)   1980—*Doin' It My Way* (Adelphi).

Tracy Nelson has long been considered one of the strongest female singers around—especially with Mother Earth during the late Sixties, when she was sometimes compared to Janis Joplin. But she soon edged away from Mother Earth's R&B gospel and began stressing country when the band moved to Nashville. One of her songs, "Down So Low," has been covered by Linda Ronstadt and many other singers.

Growing up in Wisconsin, Nelson began playing piano at age five, guitar at 13. She also sang in the church choir. She played coffeehouses while attending the University of Wisconsin and formed her first band, the Fabulous Imitations, followed by the White Trash Blues Band (no relation to Edgar Winter), which lasted two weeks. She recorded

her first solo LP around this time—the blues-influenced *Deep Are the Roots* on Prestige.

In 1966, Nelson moved to San Francisco and in July, formed Mother Earth (named after a Memphis Slim blues song). Their critically respected debut, *Living with the Animals*, included backup by Elvin Bishop and Mark Naftalin, of the Paul Butterfield Blues Band. In 1969, the group moved to a farm outside of Nashville, and their music became increasingly country-oriented (as evidenced on *Mother Earth Presents Tracy Nelson Country*). After *Bring Me Home*, the band went through many personnel changes; the only member to stick with Nelson through them was guitarist John "Toad" Andrews.

In 1973, the band (by now billed as Tracy Nelson/Mother Earth) released *A Poor Man's Paradise*, and in 1974 Nelson recorded her self-titled solo Atlantic debut. The album included a duet with Willie Nelson, "After the Fire Is Gone," which was nominated for a Grammy. In 1975, she signed with MCA, and in the late Seventies she recorded albums for the independent Flying Fish and Adelphi labels. *Homemade Songs* included a duet with Carlene Carter.

WILLIE NELSON
Born April 30, 1933, Abbott, Texas
1962—*. . . And Then I Wrote* (Liberty)   1963—*Here's Willie Nelson*   1967—*Make Way for . . .* (RCA)   *The Party's Over*   1968—*Texas in My Soul; Good Times*   1971—*Willie Nelson and Family;   Yesterday's Wine*   1972—*The Willie Way*   1974—*Phases and Stages* (Atlantic)   1975—*What Can You Do to Me* (RCA)   *Red Headed Stranger* (Columbia)   1976—*The Sound in Your Mind;   Troublemaker;   Wanted: The Outlaws* (with Waylon Jennings, Tompall Glaser, Jessi Colter) (RCA)   *Live*   1977—*To Lefty from Willie* (Columbia)   1978—*Waylon and Willie* (RCA)   *Stardust* (Columbia)   1979—*Willie and Family Live;   Pretty Paper; . . . Sings Kristofferson;   Sweet Memories* (RCA)   *One for the Road* (with Leon Russell) (Columbia)   1980—*San Antonio Rose* (with Ray Price)   *Honeysuckle Rose* (film soundtrack)   1981—*Somewhere over the Rainbow;   Willie Nelson's Greatest Hits and Some That Will Be*   1982—*Always on My Mind;   Poncho and Lefty* (with Merle Haggard)   *Waylon and Willie: WW II*.

One of country & western's most popular, prolific and distinctive singer/songwriters, Nelson started out as a songwriter without much of a solo singing career, and eventually became a star singer mostly covering pop and C&W standards. In the Seventies, he spearheaded "outlaw" country—the non-Nashville alliance between "redneck" country musicians and "hippie" rock musicians—and helped establish Austin, Texas, as a country-rock capital. His grizzled face brought him film roles in *Electric Horseman*, *Honeysuckle Rose* and *Barbarossa*.

Nelson was raised by his grandparents, and worked

Willie Nelson

cotton fields until he was ten, when he began playing guitar in local German and Czech polka bands. He joined the Air Force, and later attended Baylor University in Waco, Texas. Before dropping out, he sold Bibles and encyclopedias door-to-door, worked as a disc jockey and musician and taught Sunday school. While teaching Sunday school in Fort Worth, Willie was also playing honky-tonk clubs on Saturday nights; when his parishioners demanded he choose between the church and music, he chose the latter. He played bars around the country, taught guitar and wrote songs.

With the $50 he earned from his first published song, "Family Bible," Nelson went to Nashville, where songwriter Hank Cochran got him a publishing contract.

Nelson wrote pop and C&W hits for many artists: "Night Life" for Rusty Draper, "Funny How Time Slips Away" for Jimmy Elledge and Johnny Tillotson, "Crazy" for Patsy Cline, "Hello Walls" for Faron Young, "Wake Me When It's Over" for Andy Williams and "Pretty Paper" for Roy Orbison. Eventually he had a recording contract of his own, but his weathered tenor and his taste for sparse backup were considered uncommercial.

When his Nashville home burned down around 1970, Nelson moved back to Texas, continuing to record, write and perform. In 1972, he held his first annual Fourth of July picnic with young and old rock and country musicians in Dripping Springs, Texas—an event that would soon become a local institution, with the Fourth of July named "Willie Nelson Day" by the Texas Senate in 1975. In Austin, Nelson also began to clarify his own ideas on country music, simultaneously reclaiming traditions of honky-tonk, Western swing and early country music and

giving the songs a starker, more modern outlook. *Phases and Stages,* a concept album produced by Arif Mardin, introduced Nelson's mature style, and 1975's *Red Headed Stranger,* a "country opera," made his music a commercial success. With a hit remake of Fred Rose's "Blue Eyes Crying in the Rain" (originally recorded by Roy Acuff in the Forties), the album went gold. In 1976, Nelson shared the *Outlaws* compilation LP with Waylon Jennings, Tompall Glaser and Jessi Colter, three other country musicians ignored by the Nashville establishment; it was the first platinum country LP.

Nelson and his band, which included his older sister Bobbie on piano, toured constantly through the Seventies, and were a major concert attraction through the South and West before the rest of the country caught on. But by the end of the decade, he was an established star; 1979's *Willie and Family Live* went platinum, as did a 1978 duo album with Waylon Jennings.

Meanwhile, Nelson's songwriting tapered off; he did an album-length tribute to Kris Kristofferson and made duet albums with George Jones, Merle Haggard and Ray Price. *Stardust,* produced by Memphis veteran Booker T. Jones, was an album of old pop standards, and it, too, went platinum. For *Honeysuckle Rose,* Nelson wrote one new song, "On the Road Again," that became a #1 country single and a #20 pop hit. In the Eighties, Nelson had platinum albums with *Always on My Mind* and *Greatest Hits,* while maintaining his prolific output of albums and films.

Since the early Seventies, even while performing in Las Vegas (as he did in the late Seventies), Nelson has sported his standard attire: long hair and beard, headband, jeans, T-shirt and running shoes.

MIKE NESMITH
Born December 30, 1943, Texas
1968—*Wichita Train Whistle Sings* (Dot; reissued 1978 by Pacific Arts)   **1970**—*Magnetic South* (RCA)   *Loose Salute*   **1971**—*Nevada Fighter*   **1972**—*Tantamount to Treason;   And the Hits Just Keep on Coming* (reissued 1977 by Island/Pacific Arts)   **1973**—*Pretty Much Your Ranch Standard Stash* (reissued 1977 by Island/Pacific Arts)   **1975**—*The Prison* (Pacific Arts)   **1976**—*Best of* (RCA)   **1977**—*From a Radio Engine to a Photon Wing* (Island/Pacific Arts)   **1978**—*Live at the Palais* (Pacific Arts)   *Compilation*   **1979**—*Infinite Rider on the Big Dogma*   **1980**—*Elephant Parts.*

Michael Nesmith came to the Monkees as an experienced musician, and continued to prosper after the group dissolved in 1969.

Nesmith's mother, an ex-secretary, grew rich after inventing Liquid Paper. He grew up in Farmers Branch, Texas, just outside Dallas. When he was twenty, he got a guitar as a Christmas gift upon his discharge from the Air Force. Nesmith formed local folk-country bands and played club dates, venturing farther and farther afield during the Sixties. On the way home from a Rhode Island gig, he stopped off in Memphis to do some session work with Stax/Volt Records. He then moved to Los Angeles and played the folk circuit as a solo act, until he auditioned for—and became one of—the Monkees.

In 1967, Nesmith's "Different Drum" became Linda Ronstadt's first big hit. In 1968, before the Monkees broke up, he recorded an instrumental LP of his own compositions, *Wichita.* When the Monkees finally dissolved, Nesmith formed the First National Band—featuring steel guitarist Red Rhodes—and made *Magnetic South,* which yielded a hit single, "Joanne."

After *Loose Salute,* the First National Band broke up, and Nesmith—retaining Rhodes and adding bassist Johnny Meeks, who'd played with Gene Vincent's Blue Caps—formed the Second National Band. At this time, he announced plans for a trilogy of three-album sets, nine LPs in all, that would detail the past, present and future of country & western music. However, when Jac Holzman stepped down as president of Elektra Records—with whom Nesmith's Countryside label was affiliated—his replacement, David Geffen, was less receptive to the idea, which was shelved.

As time went on, Nesmith's projects tended to grow more ambitious. He formed the Pacific Arts Corporation and released the concept album *The Prison.* The book enclosed with the album was eventually worked into a stage play/ballet. By 1981, Nesmith had become something of a pioneer with *Elephant Parts,* a conceptual rock video that combined music, comedy and dance, received much critical acclaim and, in 1981, won the first Grammy ever awarded to a video.

THE NEVILLE BROTHERS

Formed 1977, New Orleans
Arthur Neville (b. 1938), kybds., voc.; Charles Neville (b. 1939), saxes, percussion, voc.; Aaron Neville (b. 1941), percussion, voc.; Cyril Neville (b. 1949), percussion, voc.
1978—*The Neville Brothers* (Capitol) **1981**—*Fiyo on the Bayou* (A&M).

By the time the four Neville brothers formed their own group in 1977, the family name had been prominent in New Orleans R&B for more than two decades. Art Neville's high school band, the Hawketts, had recorded the perennial Carnival hit "Mardi Gras Mambo" in 1954. Charles and Aaron Neville had joined the Hawketts briefly, and when Art went into the Navy in 1958, Aaron inherited the group's leadership.

In 1960, Aaron had his first solo hit, "Over You" (#21 R&B), on the Minit label; his second came with "Tell It Like It Is" (#2 pop, #1 R&B) for Parlo in 1966. Art and Aaron were reunited in the Sixties, when with a three-man rhythm section they gigged in New Orleans as the Neville

Sounds. In 1967, producer Allen Toussaint hired Art and the rhythm section—the future Meters—as his house band, and the Neville Sounds broke up.

Aaron resumed his solo career, recording intermittently for Instant, Safari and Bell, but also working as a dock hand. Charles went to New York to play sax in various jazz bands; he returned to New Orleans in the early Seventies and served a three-year sentence at Angola Prison Farm for possession of two joints of marijuana.

The Nevilles got together in the studio again, this time with youngest brother Cyril, in 1975, when they backed the Wild Tchoupitoulas, a "tribe" of Mardi Gras "black Indians" led by the Nevilles' uncle, George "Big Chief Jolly" Landry. *The Wild Tchoupitoulas* was released on Island Records in 1976, and the following year, after the Meters had disbanded, the Nevilles backed Landry on stage. Soon they were performing their own sets as the Neville Brothers, a vocal group specializing in four-part harmonies. Their first album, produced by Jack Nitzsche, presented them as something of a disco band, however, and Capitol dropped their contract.

It was three years before they recorded their second album, after Bette Midler persuaded producer Joel Dorn to work with them and the Nevilles secured the aid of R&B veteran arranger Wardell Quezergue. The result, which featured Aaron's delicate, quavering tenor on vocal warhorses like "Mona Lisa" and "The Ten Commandments of Love," as well as New Orleans "second-line" standards like "Iko Iko," was widely praised but rarely bought, and again the Neville Brothers lost their contract. In 1982, having opened some U.S. shows for the Rolling Stones the year before, they were expected to sign with Rolling Stones Records. They continued to tour, carrying the feathered costumes and additional singers that transformed them into the Wild Tchoupitoulas to climax their shows.

THE NEW CHRISTY MINSTRELS

Formed 1961

The New Christy Minstrels were an ultracommercial folk-based group that provided an early training ground for Kenny Rogers and the First Edition, John Denver, Larry Ramos and some of the Association, actress Karen Black, future Byrd Gene Clark and Barry McGuire, who had a solo hit with "Eve of Destruction" in 1965.

The group was formed by Randy Sparks in 1961. He'd taken the name from the Christy Minstrels formed back in 1842 by Edwin P. Christy. The original minstrels were a vaudeville act who popularized the work of Stephen Foster until 1921, and in the later stages included Al Jolson and Eddie Cantor. The "New" Minstrels were in no way related to the originals. They wrote their own material and first began to hit the charts in 1963 with "Green Green" (#14), cowritten by McGuire and Sparks, "Saturday Night" (#29) and "Today" in 1964 (#17). Clark was with the group at this time, when they began playing the White House and other archetypical "establishment" places.

In 1964, they hosted their own summer television show. In the mid-Sixties, their musical director at the time, Mike Settle, took three other band members, Thelma Camacho, Kenny Rogers and Terry Williams, and formed the First Edition. The Minstrels continued to record, with steadily declining sales, until their breakup in the early Seventies.

RANDY NEWMAN

Born November 28, 1944, New Orleans
1968—*Randy Newman* (Reprise) **1970**—*12 Songs*
1971—*Live* **1972**—*Sail Away* **1974**—*Good Old Boys* **1977**—*Little Criminals* (Warner Bros.) **1979**—*Born Again* **1983**—*Trouble in Paradise.*

Randy Newman writes mordant, ironic, concise songs with chromatic twists worthy of George Gershwin and Kurt Weill. He sings in a deep drawl and accompanies himself on piano (Fats Domino was an early hero) and often tours alone. Newman tends to write lyrics about characters usually bordering on the pathological: bigots, perverts, slaveship captains, ELO fans. While this practice tends to limit his pop appeal, a few of his songs have been widely covered, and he has a solid cult following. He has had hit singles with "Short People" (#2, 1978) and "The Blues" (#54, 1983).

Newman grew up in a musical family with Hollywood connections; his uncles Alfred and Lionel both scored numerous films. By age 17, Randy Newman was staff writer for a California publishing company. One semester short of a BA in music from UCLA, he dropped out of school. Lenny Waronker, son of Liberty Records' president, was a close friend and later, as a staff producer for Warner Bros., helped get Newman signed to the label.

Newman's early songs were recorded by a number of performers. His friend Harry Nilsson recorded an entire album with Newman on piano, *Nilsson Sings Newman,* in 1970; and Judy Collins ("I Think It's Going to Rain Today"), Peggy Lee ("Love Story") and Three Dog Night—for whom "Mama Told Me (Not to Come)" hit #1—all enjoyed success with Newman's music.

Newman became a popular campus attraction when touring with Nilsson. His status as a cult star was affirmed by his critically praised debut, *Randy Newman,* in 1968, which featured his own complex arrangements for full orchestra, and later by 1970's *12 Songs.* He also sang "Gone Dead Train" on the 1970 soundtrack of *Performance.* *Randy Newman/Live* and *Sail Away* were his first commercial successes. But his audience has been limited to some degree because his songs are often colored by his ironic, pointed sense of humor, which is rarely simple and frequently misunderstood.

Good Old Boys, for example, was a concept album about the South, with the lyrics expressing the viewpoint of white Southerners. Lyrics such as "We're rednecks and

Randy Newman

we don't know our ass from a hole in the ground" made people wonder whether Newman was being satirical or sympathetic. He toured (to Atlanta and elsewhere) with a full orchestra that played his arrangements and was conducted by his uncle Emil Newman.

Little Criminals in 1977 contained Newman's first hit single, "Short People," which mocked bigotry and was taken seriously by a small minority. "Baltimore" from that album was covered by Nina Simone. Following that album's release, Newman toured for the first time since 1974. In the interim, he claims he did nothing but look at television and play with his three sons. In 1979, his *Born Again* featured guest vocals by members of the Eagles. Newman composed the soundtrack for the film *Ragtime* and was nominated for two Oscars (Best Song, Best Score). His 1983 album, *Trouble in Paradise,* included guest appearances by Linda Ronstadt, members of Fleetwood Mac and Paul Simon, who sang a verse of "The Blues."

THE NEW ORLEANS SOUND

At the mouth of the Mississippi, New Orleans has stood at a crossroads where Amerindian, French, Spanish, English, African, Caribbean and Latin-American cultures have met and mixed for over two centuries. New Orleans has been a capital city of American music at least since the Civil War, and its culture has helped shape rhythm & blues, rock & roll and reggae no less than ragtime, jazz and Delta blues.

The barrelhouse piano styles of Kid Stormy Weather and Sullivan Rock, the crude but gentle vocal styles of Creole folksingers, and dances from Cuba and Trinidad were the raw materials from which Professor Longhair forged his prototypical rock & roll in the mid-Forties. In the same period, Dave Bartholomew put together a band that in the coming years featured many of the city's strongest and most inventive musicians and developed a sound that combined the loose cohesiveness of the best jazz ensembles with the "second line" syncopations and raucous brass work of Mardi Gras parade bands.

With the arrival of independent record companies such as De Luxe and Imperial in the last years of the decade, a recording industry began to flourish. Blues singer Roy Brown had the first New Orleans rock & roll hit with "Good Rockin' Tonight" in 1948, followed by Longhair admirer and Bartholomew frontman Fats Domino.

Attracted by Domino's success, independent labels like Specialty, Regal, Aladdin, Chess and Atlantic went scouting for talent in New Orleans throughout the Fifties and were rewarded with hits by Lloyd Price, Guitar Slim, Shirley and Lee, Clarence "Frogman" Henry and Bobby Charles. Virtually every Crescent City recording was cut at studio owner/engineer Cosimo Matassa's primitive facility in the French Quarter and with Lee Allen's Studio Band (composed of the stars of the Bartholomew band). Matassa's unadorned live-in-the-studio production and the Studio Band's fat rolling bottom and light rocking top defined the New Orleans sound—a sound that Ray Charles and Little Richard, among others, went to New Orleans to capture on some of their biggest hits.

Ace Records, founded in 1955, was the first New Orleans–based label, and with Huey Smith and the Clowns, Jimmy Clanton, Frankie Ford and Earl King, the company quickly challenged the out-of-towners' supremacy. By the end of the decade, as national tastes turned to milder fare, new local labels such as Ric, Instant, Red Bird, Minit and AFO followed Ace's lead. The most prominent young producers were Allen Toussaint and Wardell Quezergue (both protégés of Bartholomew), who updated the New Orleans sound by relaxing the beat without weakening the funk; Jessie Hill, Chris Kenner, Ernie K-Doe, Irma Thomas and the Dixie Cups kept the sound before the public in the early Sixties. During the mid and late Sixties, most of the local labels either folded or moved to Los Angeles. Nonetheless, local talent continued to be heard around the country via hits by Robert Parker, Aaron Neville, Lee Dorsey and the Meters.

By the Seventies, the New Orleans sound was still emulated by popular artists like Dr. John (a Californian transplanted from New Orleans), the Rolling Stones, the Band, Paul Simon, Labelle, Kool and the Gang, Paul McCartney, Parliament/Funkadelic and, later, the Clash—many of whom recorded in New Orleans. And within the city, music festivals, the Mardi Gras and an active club scene kept old traditions alive and fostered new ones. Professor Longhair recorded several highly acclaimed new albums and returned to the concert circuit a few years before his death in 1980; Mardi Gras "black Indian"

groups like the Wild Tchoupitoulas and the Wild Magnolias concocted a blend of ceremonial dances and R&B rhythms; and the Neville Brothers combined four-part vocal harmonies with electric funk.

NEW RIDERS OF THE PURPLE SAGE
Formed 1969, Marin County, California
John "Marmaduke" Dawson (b. 1945, San Francisco), gtr., voc.; David Nelson (b. San Francisco), gtr., voc.; Jerry Garcia (b. Aug. 1, 1942, San Francisco), pedal steel gtr.; Mickey Hart (b. ca. 1950, New York City), drums; Phil Lesh (b. Mar. 15, 1940, Berkeley, Calif.), bass.
1970–71—(− Hart; − Lesh; + Spencer Dryden [b. Apr. 7, 1943, New York City], drums; + Dave Torbert, bass) 1971—New Riders of the Purple Sage (Columbia) (− Garcia; + Buddy Cage [b. Toronto], pedal steel gtr.) 1972—Powerglide 1973—Gypsy Cowboy; Adventures of Panama Red 1974—Home Home on the Road (− Torbert; + Skip Battin [b. Feb. 2, 1934], bass) 1975—Brujo; Oh, What a Mighty Time 1976—Best of the New Riders of the Purple Sage (− Battin; + Stephen Love [b. Ind.], bass) New Riders (MCA) 1977—Who Are These Guys 1978—Marin County Line.

The New Riders of the Purple Sage began as a loosely constructed offshoot of the Grateful Dead. The group's history dates back to spring 1969, when Dead lead guitarist Jerry Garcia first bought a pedal steel guitar and was searching for a country band to use it in. Jams developed among Garcia and the core of the new band—David Nelson and main songwriter John Dawson—plus other Dead members, Mickey Hart and Phil Lesh, thus forming the first Riders band.

Nelson and Dawson had loose connections to Dead members dating back to 1962. Nelson first knew Garcia and lyricist Bob Hunter from his days in the Wildwood Boys back in art school. Nelson was also an early member of Big Brother and later the New Delhi River Band in Marin County, California, which included Dave Torbert and Dawson (who in 1964 had played in another Dead progenitor, Mother McCree's Uptown Jug Champions).

Hunter and Nelson named the Riders after a 1912 novel by Zane Grey, and they became the opening band for the Dead tours in 1970. By the time they got a contract with Columbia Records in 1971 (by then called New Riders of the Purple Sage), Spencer Dryden (former Jefferson Airplane drummer) had replaced Hart, and Torbert had taken over for Lesh. Garcia bowed out after the debut (the Dead took up too much of his time), and in late 1971 they added Buddy Cage on pedal steel. He'd previously played with Ian and Sylvia's Great Speckled Bird.

Like the Dead and Commander Cody, the Riders became associated with dope-smoking hippiedom, especially with their anthemic "Panama Red," written by non-member Peter Rowan. This made them a strong concert attraction, though their albums sold only moderately. The lineup was stable until February 1974, after the live LP *Home Home on the Road,* when Torbert left to form King-fish with Bob Weir. Ex-Byrd Skip Battin took his place for two LPs and then left in 1976 to join a new version of the Flying Burrito Brothers. The group then switched to MCA and added Steve Love on bass. He'd previously played with Roger McGuinn and Rick Nelson's Stone Canyon Band. They recorded two LPs for MCA before they lost their contract. They continued to tour, with Dawson still at the helm, playing small clubs across the U.S.

JUICE NEWTON
Born Virginia Beach, Virginia
1975—*Juice Newton and Silver Spur* (RCA) **1976**—*After the Dust Settles; Come to Me* (Capitol) **1978**—*Well Kept Secret* **1979**—*Take Heart* **1981**—*Juice* **1982**—*Quiet Lies.*

Country-pop singer Juice Newton recorded five mostly ignored albums before she suddenly hit it big in 1981 with a platinum LP and three Top Ten singles, starting with a remake of Merrilee Rush's 1968 hit "Angel of the Morning."

Newton grew up in a Virginia seaside community and taught herself acoustic guitar at 13. She moved to Los Gatos, California, in the late Sixties, and with Texas-born Otha Young formed Dixie Peach. A year later, in 1972, Newton and Young formed Silver Spur with bassist Tom Kealey. After years of doing cover-heavy bar gigs, the three began to concentrate on original material.

In 1975, they were signed to RCA (billed as Juice Newton and Silver Spur) and released an eponymous LP with heavy folk-rock leanings. They did one more unsuc-cessful album for RCA, *After the Dust Settles,* in 1976, and the next year signed to Capitol for *Come to Me,* produced by Elliot Mazer (who'd worked with Janis Joplin, Neil Young and the Band). The LP was closer to country rock this time, and included a song given to her by Bob Seger called "Good Luck Baby Jane." She also did backup vocals that year on Bob Welch's solo LP *French Kiss.* In 1978, Silver Spur disbanded and Newton went solo with *Well Kept Secret.* In 1979, she had her first country hit, "Sunshine," from *Take Heart.*

Juice was her breakthrough LP. Following the success of "Angel of the Morning" (#4), she hit with "Queen of Hearts" (#2), a rockabilly track recorded earlier by Dave Edmunds, both gold singles, and "The Sweetest Thing" (#1 country, #7 pop, 1981). The LP went platinum. "Love's Been a Little Bit Hard on Me" hit #7 pop, #2 country in 1982.

OLIVIA NEWTON-JOHN
Born September 26, 1948, Cambridge, England
1973—*Let Me Be There* (MCA) **1975**—*If You Love Me,*

Let Me Know **1977**—*Olivia Newton-John's Greatest Hits* **1978**—*Totally Hot* **1981**—*Physical.*

Olivia Newton-John's career has mirrored the Sandra Dee-to-leather-girl transformation of her role in *Grease*—from fresh-faced pop country singer to a sexier pop rock & roll singer. In both guises she has had great commercial success. By April of 1982, she had scored 11 Top Five singles over her career, beating Donna Summer's previous record.

Newton-John's grandfather was Nobel Prize–winning German physicist Max Born, and her father was headmas-ter of Ormond College in Melbourne, Australia. Newton-John grew up in Melbourne, where in high school she formed her first band with three other girls, the Sol Four. She quit school and at age 16 won a talent contest and was sent to England. For the next two years she worked there with fellow Australian Pat Carroll (who later married Newton-John's producer John Farrar). When Carroll's visa expired, she was sent back to Australia, and Newton-John joined Don Kirshner's attempt to make a British Monkees, a short-lived band called Tomorrow (no relation to Steve Howe's first band).

She began appearing regularly on the BBC series "It's Cliff Richard," which greatly boosted the British sales of her first single, Bob Dylan's "If Not for You" (1971), which was also a minor hit (#25) in America. She had other British hits with covers of George Harrison's "What Is Life" (1972) and John Denver's "Take Me Home Country Roads" (1973). Her U.S. breakthrough came in 1973 with her first American LP, *Let Me Be There,* which went gold, aided by the gold single title track (#6), which also won her a Grammy as Best Country Female Singer. Her next LP, *If You Love Me, Let Me Know,* went gold and included the title track gold single (#5) and a gold hit for her version of Peter Allen's "I Honestly Love You" (#1).

Newton-John moved to L.A., and her albums continued to go gold. But a number of country performers resented her presence on country charts—with hits like "Have You Never Been Mellow" (#1 pop, #3 C&W, 1975) and "Please Mr. Please" (#3 pop, #5 C&W, 1975)—and when she won the Best Female Singer award in 1976 from the Country Music Association, some members quit.

Until then, she had a girl-next-door image, but that all changed in 1978 with the release of *Grease.* The film went on to become the most profitable movie musical ever made, grossing over $150 million worldwide and yielding three singles for Newton-John—"You're the One That I Want," sung with John Travolta (#1), "Summer Nights" (#5) and "Hopelessly Devoted To You" (#3), all gold. Her sexier image was reinforced with *Totally Hot* and *Physical* (both platinum), the latter of which boasted three hit singles in 1982, including the #1 title single, "Physi-cal." In 1980 she and Cliff Richard hit with their duet "Suddenly" (#20). She also appeared in the August 1980 film fantasy *Xanadu,* which (most unusual for a Newton-John product) was a commercial flop. The album, however, went platinum.

NEW WAVE

A virtually meaningless term that arose shortly after punk rock in the late Seventies, new wave is variously pop with punkish trappings—such as faster tempos, stripped-down arrangements and alienated lyrics, like those of the Cars or Blondie—or a catch-all term for bands that emerged after 1976 and could not be categorized as pure punk, like the Talking Heads or Pere Ubu. It is also a marketing term for bands that dress in geometric clothes rather than heavy-metal leather and studs or less extreme pop wardrobes.

THE NEW YORK DOLLS

Formed 1971, New York City
Johnny Thunders (b. John Genzale), gtr.; Arthur Kane, bass; Billy Murcia (b. 1951, New York City; d. Nov. 6, 1972, London), drums; Rick Rivets, gtr.; David Johansen (b. Jan. 9, 1950, Staten Island, N.Y.), voc.
1972—(+ Sylvain Sylvain, gtr.; − Rivets; − Murcia; + Jerry Nolan, drums) **1973**—*New York Dolls* (Mercury) **1974**—*Too Much Too Soon.*

When the New York Dolls formed in late 1971, they were not only creating some of the most passionate music of the new glitter era (and in fact defining a new New York rock style) but setting the stage for the punk movement that followed five years later.

The band members were born and grew up in various boroughs of New York City and played in local bands; several had been in Actress. In late 1971, Johnny Thunders, Rick Rivets, Arthur Kane and Billy Murcia began jamming, and soon they were joined by singer David Johansen. After they had replaced Rivets with Syl Sylvain, they started playing the Mercer Arts Center in Lower Manhattan, where they opened for a group called Eric Emerson's Magic Tramps. A local glitter scene of sorts developed around the group. The Dolls' music was strongly influenced by the Rolling Stones, the MC5, the Stooges and the Velvet Underground, but deliberately more amateurish. And their look—outrageous clothing and women's makeup—captured the outrage and threat of glitter. Despite this, their music and attitude were down to earth, and their stardom-by-self-definition stance served to keep most record companies at a distance.

During their first tour of England, Murcia died after mixing alcohol with pills; the official cause of death was suffocation. The band replaced him with Jerry Nolan, who appeared on their Todd Rundgren–produced debut. Though both the debut and its followup (which was produced by George "Shadow" Morton) were critical successes, they were commercial disasters; the group's sound and image were just too weird. After they lost their

recording contract, the Dolls were briefly managed by Malcolm McLaren (later with the Sex Pistols), who suggested that they use a communist flag as a stage backdrop. When no new record contract developed, both Nolan and Thunders left the band and Johansen and Sylvain continued to tour with various backing musicians under the Dolls name through 1977.

Thunders and Nolan formed the Heartbreakers, and later Thunders created his own bands, one of which, Gang War, included MC5 guitarist Wayne Kramer. In the fall of 1978, Nolan and Kane played a few shows backing Sex Pistol Sid Vicious. Johansen began his solo career in 1978 (see separate entry), and Sylvain stayed with Johansen's band until he quit in 1979 to start his own solo career. To date he has released two albums on RCA, *Sylvain Sylvain* (1980) and *Syl Sylvain and the Teardrops* (1981). In November 1981 ROIR released the cassette-only *Lipstick Killers,* a formative Dolls studio tape from 1972.

NICE

Formed 1967, London
Keith Emerson (b. Nov. 1, 1942, Todmorden, Eng.), organ, piano, synthesizers, voc.; Lee Jackson (b. Jan. 8, 1943, Newcastle-upon-Tyne, Eng.), bass, gtr., voc.; Brian "Blinky" Davison (b. May 25, 1942, Leicester, Eng.), drums; David O'List (b. Eng.), gtr., voc.
1968—*The Thoughts of Emerlist Davjack* (Immediate) (− O'List) *Ars Longa Vita Brevis* **1969**—*Nice* **1970**—*Five Bridges* (Mercury) **1971**—*Elegy* **1975**—*Keith Emerson and Nice.*

Besides providing the blueprint for Emerson, Lake and Palmer, the Nice were a link between the early experimentalism of late-Sixties psychedelia and classical-influenced art rock. As Keith Emerson's initial platform, their snickering desecration of the classics along with their long instrumental interludes helped expand the form—and pretensions—of rock.

The band began in August 1967 as a backup for English black female soul vocalist P. P. Arnold. All the members had previously played in other British groups; Emerson and Lee Jackson knew each other from the R&B aggregation Gary Farr and the T-Bones. By October, the Nice had split from Arnold and released their debut single in England on manager Andrew Oldham's Immediate Records, "The Thoughts of Emerlist Davjack," also the title of their debut LP. The album's centerpiece was "Rondo," an organ raveup based on Mozart. Live, Emerson went wild on numbers like this (or on his jazzed-up version of Bob Dylan's "She Belongs to Me"), stabbing his keyboard with knives and pulling mock-masturbatory moves. Along with these antics (continued later in ELP), Emerson also wore flashy gold lamé clothes and performed stunts like burning a U.S. flag on stage at the Royal Albert Hall in London during a performance of Leonard Bernstein's "America" from *West Side Story.* The Nice was subsequently banned from the hall and Bernstein tried to stop the group from releasing their version of the song in the U.S. Partly because Emerson had become the star, guitarist David O'List left. For a few days in 1969 he replaced Mick Abrahams in Jethro Tull.

During most of Nice's 2½-year career, they were a three-piece power trio, with Emerson establishing himself as the Hendrix of the organ. The group was popular in Europe but never sold many records in the U.S. They were just beginning to draw some attention Stateside when Emerson, playing the Fillmore West with the band, met Greg Lake while the latter was touring with King Crimson on their 1969 U.S. debut. The Nice were frustrated by their lack of success and Emerson proposed a new band with Lake, trashed the Nice in early 1970 and formed ELP with third member Carl Palmer in mid-1970. The Nice's last LP, *Elegy,* was released shortly after ELP's debut in 1971.

Jackson formed Jackson Heights (which recorded five LPs between 1970 and 1973), and in 1974 he and Davison teamed up with keyboardist Patrick Moraz in an ELP-styled group called Refugee. But it didn't last, and Moraz went on to Yes and to the Moody Blues. Davison played briefly with Gong in the mid-Seventies.

NICO

Born 1944, Berlin
1968—*Chelsea Girl* (MGM)   *The Marble Index* (Elektra)   **1971**—*Desert Shore* (Reprise)   **1974**—*The End* (Island)   *June 1, 1974*   **1981**—*Drama of Exile* (ROIR)   **1983**—*Do or Die—Live.*

At one time she was billed as the Moon Goddess. Singer Nico's gloomy, romantic music and hypnotic monotone voice were first heard in the Velvet Underground, part of Andy Warhol's Sixties coterie the Exploding Plastic Inevitable.

Nico first worked as a model in Paris but got into music in the mid-Sixties through a friendship with Rolling Stone Brian Jones. He introduced her to Stones manager Andrew Loog Oldham, for whom she cut a British single, "The Last Mile," on his Immediate label in 1965. The song was produced, cowritten and arranged by Jimmy Page. The next year, Nico met Warhol in New York, socialized at the Factory and appeared in his *Chelsea Girls.* (She had played a small role in Fellini's *La Dolce Vita.*) Warhol later introduced her to Lou Reed and John Cale in the Velvet Underground. She got feature billing in the band ("the Velvet Underground and Nico"), but left after the first album.

Nico's connection with the old group remained strong, though, and on her 1968 solo debut she recorded songs by Cale and Reed, as well as some by a 16-year-old named Jackson Browne, who accompanied her during shows. Besides Browne, at some early shows she was accompanied by Tim Hardin and Tim Buckley. *The Marble Index* and *Desert Shore* were produced and arranged by Cale; on *The Marble Index* he played all the instruments except Nico's own droning harmonium, her trademark.

Nothing was heard from Nico for the next few years. She spent most of her time in Paris, but in early 1974 she signed with Island. She appeared in a special London concert at the Rainbow Theatre with Kevin Ayers, Cale

Grammy Awards

Willie Nelson
1975 Best Country Vocal Performance, Male:
"Blue Eyes Crying in the Rain"
1978 Best Country Vocal Performance, Male:
"Georgia on My Mind"
Best Country Vocal Performance by a Duo, Group or Chorus:
"Mamas Don't Let Your Babies Grow Up to Be Cowboys" (with Waylon Jennings)
1980 Best Country Song:
"On the Road Again"

1982 Best Country Vocal Performance, Male:
"Always on My Mind"

The New Christy Minstrels
1962 Best Performance by a Chorus:
Presenting the New Christy Minstrels

New Vaudeville Band
1966 Best Contemporary Rock & Roll Recording:
"Winchester Cathedral"

Juice Newton
1982 Best Country Vocal Performance, Female:
"Break It to Me Gently"

Olivia Newton-John
1973 Best Country Vocal Performance, Female:
"Let Me Be There"
1974 Record of the Year; Best Pop Vocal Performance, Female:
"I Honestly Love You"

Harry Nilsson
1969 Best Contemporary Vocal Performance, Male:
"Everybody's Talkin' "
1972 Best Pop Vocal Performance, Male:
"Without You"

and Brian Eno, resulting in an album named after the date of the event, *June 1, 1974,* with Nico doing a lengthy, especially morbid version of the Doors' "The End." That song title was the name of her solo return, out later in the year, again produced by Cale. She and Island allegedly had disputes during the recording (Eno kept them from dropping her), but in 1975 they let her go.

In the later Seventies and early Eighties, Nico did periodic solo shows on the club circuit. In 1981, she released her first LP in seven years, *Drama of Exile,* which includes versions of the Velvet's "Waiting for the Man" and Bowie's "Heroes."

WILLIE NILE
Born 1949, Buffalo, New York
1980—*Willie Nile* (Arista)   **1981**—*Golden Down.*

Singer/songwriter Willie Nile won much critical praise in 1980 for his Dylan-turned-early-Springsteenesque folk rock, with heavy accent on the rock part of the equation. He debuted late in the game by rock standards—at age 31—after spending seven years appearing sporadically on the Greenwich Village folk scene.

Nile's grandfather had played piano with Bill "Bojangles" Robinson and Eddie Cantor. In college, Nile studied and wrote poetry and got swept up in Bob Dylan's hyperverbal style of the Sixties. Late in the decade, he made some periodic forays to New York City to play the same clubs where Dylan began. In 1973, Nile finally moved to the Village, where he frequently played clubs like Kenny's Castaways on Bleecker Street, concentrating on folk mainly because he couldn't afford a backup band.

Tommy Flanders, ex–lead vocalist for the Blues Project, brought record company executives to Kenny's to see Nile. In 1978, with the help of a rave review from the *New York Times,* Nile got a contract with Arista. His debut, produced by Roy Halee, who had engineered the Yardbirds and Simon and Garfunkel in the Sixties, was praised for its Byrdsy guitars, its folk-melodiousness and rocking Buddy Holly influences, plus Nile's affecting, nervous vocals. But others found his lyrics disappointing.

Nile's live band featured ex-Television bassist Fred Smith and former Patti Smith drummer Jay Dee Daugherty. In July, the band did some stadium openers for the Who when Pete Townshend asked him on personally after hearing his debut. Nile's followup, *Golden Down,* again was much talked about in the press, but he has yet to break through commercially. In 1982, he signed to Geffen Records.

HARRY NILSSON
Born Harry Edward Nelson III, June 15, 1941, Brooklyn, New York
1967—*The Pandemonium Shadow Show* (RCA)
1968—*Aerial Ballet*   **1969**—*Harry; Skidoo*
(soundtrack)   **1970**—*Nilsson Sings Newman; The Point* (soundtrack)   **1971**—*Aerial Pandemonium Ballet* (compilation of first two LPs)   *Nilsson Schmilsson* **1972**—*Son of Schmilsson*   **1973**—*A Little Touch of Schmilsson in the Night*   **1974**—*Son of Dracula* (soundtrack, with Ringo Starr) (Rapple)   *Pussy Cats* (with John Lennon)   **1977**—*That's the Way It Goes* (RCA)   *Knnillssonn*   **1978**—*The World's Greatest Lover; Nilsson's Greatest Music.*

Singer/songwriter Harry Nilsson moved to California with his family, and after graduating from a Los Angeles parochial school became a processor at a Van Nuys, California, bank. In the meantime, he learned guitar and piano. By the mid-Sixties, using the Nilsson name for his musical persona, he was writing songs, trying to sell them during the day while working nights at the bank. He sold three tunes to Phil Spector; two were recorded by the Ronettes and one by the Modern Folk Quartet. Nilsson earned extra money by singing on demos and in radio commercials, and in 1967 he signed with RCA. While Nilsson was recording his debut LP, his "Cuddly Toy" became a hit for the Monkees, as his "One" would be for Three Dog Night in 1969.

Despite the success of "Cuddly Toy" and extravagant critical acclaim, *Shadow Show* sold poorly. However, it did bring a call from London one night: "It's John . . . John Lennon. Just want to tell you your album is great! You're great!" Later, Brian Epstein made an unsuccessful attempt to woo Nilsson from RCA to Apple.

Aerial Ballet fared better, as it included the smash hit "Everybody's Talkin'," a Fred Neil song that stayed in the U.S. Top Ten much of 1969 and was the theme song for the film *Midnight Cowboy.* Nilsson had written another song intended to be that film's theme, "I Guess the Lord Must Be in New York City"—a #34 hit in 1969. *Harry* sold fairly well, too, and Nilsson did scores for Otto Preminger's film *Skidoo* (1968) and the TV sitcom "The Courtship of Eddie's Father" (1969). Nilsson would later write and sing an original score for the animated TV movie *The Point,* which yielded the #34 hit "Me and My Arrow." Nilsson never performed a public concert, and only rarely made televised appearances.

In 1970, Nilsson recorded an album of his friend Randy Newman's compositions. Though critically acclaimed, it sold little. The next year, though, Nilsson achieved his commercial breakthrough with *Nilsson Schmilsson,* which, with the #1 hit version of Badfinger's "Without You," eventually went platinum. The "Schmilsson" persona, a sort of schmaltzy alter ego, returned on subsequent LPs, like the gold *Son of Schmilsson;* Nilsson proudly announced that he was recording with Frank Sinatra's arranger, Gordon Jenkins. As time went on, Nilsson never quite matched *Schmilsson's* success. Still, several hits followed: "Coconut" (#8, 1972), "Jump into the Fire" (#27, 1972) and "Space Man" (#23, 1972).

He made the *Son of Dracula* (1974) film with Ringo Starr, then became Lennon's companion during the ex-Beatle's separation from his wife, Yoko Ono. During this time the two recorded *Pussy Cats*, an album of old rock & roll songs.

1910 FRUITGUM COMPANY
Formed 1968

Joey Levine, voc.; Bruce Shay (b. 1948), voc., gtr., percussion; Frank Jeckell, voc., gtr.; Mark Gutkowski (b. 1948), gtr.; Larry Ripley (b. 1948), horns; Rusty Oppenheimer (b. 1948), drums; Pat Karwan, gtr., voc.; Floyd Marcus, drums, voc.; Chuck Travis (b. 1946), voc., gtr.

1968—*Simon Says* (Buddah)   *1, 2, 3 Red Light*   **1969**—*Indian Giver.*

The 1910 Fruitgum Company, like the Ohio Express (with whom it shared lead singer Joey Levine), was a faceless studio assemblage formed by the Kasenetz-Katz production team for Buddah Records to record bubblegum pop.

Their first hit, "Simon Says" (#4, 1968), pioneered the genre, and was followed by "1, 2, 3 Red Light" (#5, 1968—later covered in concert by the Talking Heads), "Goody Goody Gumdrops" (#37, 1968), "Indian Giver" (#5, 1969) and "Special Delivery" (#38, 1969). Their last chartmaking tune came in 1969 with "The Train" (#57). In 1968, Kasenetz and Katz merged them with another bubblegum group, the Kasenetz-Katz Singing Orchestral Circus, who hit with "Quick Joey Small (Run Joey Run)" (#25). The 1910 Fruitgum Company disbanded in 1970.

NITTY GRITTY DIRT BAND
Formed 1966, Long Beach, California

Jeff Hanna (b. July 11, 1947, Detroit), gtr., voc.; Jimmie Fadden (b. Mar. 9, 1948, Long Beach), gtr., harmonica, voc.; Jackson Browne (b. Oct. 9, 1948, Heidelberg, W. Ger.), gtr., voc.; Ralph Barr (b. Boston), gtr., voc.; John McEuen (b. Dec. 19, 1945, Long Beach), gtr., violin, voc.; Les Thompson (b. Long Beach), bass, gtr., voc.; Bruce Kunkel (b. *ca* 1948, Long Beach), gtr., violin, voc.

1967—*Nitty Gritty Dirt Band* (Liberty)   *Ricochet* (+ Chris Darrow, gtr.)   **1968**—*Rare Junk; Pure Dirt*   **1969**—*Alive* (− Darrow, − Kunkel, − Barr; band splits up for short time)   *Dead and Alive* (+ Jim Ibbotson [b. Jan. 21, 1947, Philadelphia], drums, kybds.)   **1970**—*Uncle Charlie and His Dog Teddy*   **1972**—*All the Good Times* (United Artists)   **1973**—*Will the Circle Be Unbroken*   **1974**—*Stars and Stripes Forever* (− Thompson)   **1975**—*Dream*   **1976**—*Dirt, Silver and Gold* (compilation)   (− Ibbotson; + Merle Bregante, drums; + Richard Hathaway, bass; + Al Garth, reeds, violin, voc.)   **1978**—*The Dirt Band*   **1979**—*American Dream.*

One of the few country-rock bands that moved *from* straight country folk *to* rock, rather than vice versa, the Nitty Gritty Dirt Band (or Dirt Band, as they have been known since 1976) have delved into all sorts of musical Americana. Through the years, their material has gone from jug-band and novelty-string-band modes, through bluegrass and hoedowns, to country swing and country rock.

They were originally the Illegitimate Jug Band; Jackson Browne's short stint with the group was around this time. They joined with John McEuen's producer brother Bill and made their first LP, which yielded a modest hit single, "Buy for Me the Rain." As the band was trying to decide whether to go with rock or stay traditional, they made an appearance in the 1968 film *Paint Your Wagon* and then temporarily disbanded, though all kept busy with various musical pursuits.

When they regrouped, they recorded *Uncle Charlie*, their breakthrough LP with the Top Ten cover of Jerry Jeff Walker's "Mr. Bojangles." Their next important project was a historic meeting with a bevy of oldtime country music stars like Roy Acuff, Earl Scruggs, Maybelle Carter, Doc Watson, Merle Travis and Vassar Clements to record *Will the Circle Be Unbroken*. This three-album set of traditional folk and country tunes sold well and received critical raves.

Though always popular for their lively concerts, in which band members traded myriad string and other instruments about, the Dirt Band didn't attract major attention again until 1977, when it became the first American rock group to tour the Soviet Union.

JACK NITZSCHE
Born Bernard Nitzsche, circa 1937, Michigan

Jack Nitzsche is a behind-the-scenes jack-of-all-trades—musician, producer, songwriter, movie soundtrack composer—but he is perhaps most lauded in rock circles as an arranger, especially for his work on many of Phil Spector's best-known Sixties hits.

Nitzsche had classical musical training as a child and attended Westlake College of Music. His first job in Hollywood was as a music copyist and then as arranger for Sonny Bono at Specialty Records. He then went on to Original Sound Records (working with Preston Epps, who had had the hit single "Bongo Rock") and later did arranging for songwriter/producer Lee Hazlewood.

Through a mutual friend, Nitzsche met Spector, who had at that time two previous hits recorded in New York ("Uptown" and "There's No Other [Like My Baby]," both by the Crystals). Spector wanted to produce records on the West Coast, and with Nitzsche as arranger the two first worked on the Crystals' "He's a Rebel." Over the next four years, the pair produced countless hits, until Spector's temporary retirement following Ike and Tina Turner's "River Deep, Mountain High" in 1966.

Nitzsche also worked with many artists outside the Spector stable: Tim Buckley, Jackie DeShannon, Frankie Laine, Bobby Darin and others. Over the years he has also recorded four solo albums for Reprise, including *The Lonely Surfer* (his first) and *St. Giles Cripplegate* (his last, in 1972, recorded with the London Symphony Orchestra).

After his time with Spector, Nitzsche began to work with the Rolling Stones (whom he had met on their debut U.S. tour). He played piano for them and arranged many of their records. He also was a member of Crazy Horse for a while, producing, playing piano and writing songs on their debut album. But after one tour with them (his first time playing on the road), he left. He wrote the string arrangements for Neil Young's *Harvest* and played piano on his *Time Fades Away*.

Nitzsche's extensive work in film scores began with *Performance* in 1970 and includes Robert Downey's *Greaser's Palace*, *The Exorcist* and *One Flew over the Cuckoo's Nest*. He also produced the first two Mink DeVille LPs.

NO WAVE

This movement, based in late-Seventies New York City, grew from the crossovers between Lower Manhattan's avant-garde art and music scenes—especially punk rock, which attracted the attention of artists looking for something radical.

No wave was certainly that: it was played mainly by untrained musicians who had become disenchanted with the doctrinaire conservatism of rock music; they even saw punk as something that was quickly becoming institutionalized. Still, the no-wavers made full use of punk's themes of nihilistic disgust, as the name indicates. The music was rough-hewn, minimal, often atonal, using noise for noise's sake. The atonal, deconstructivist tendencies were best represented by the trio DNA and the quartet Mars, while Lydia Lunch's trio Teenage Jesus and the Jerks (whose drummer played only a snare and one cymbal) perhaps best personified the genre's negativity.

On the other hand, the Contortions were the most "musicianly" of the lot, fusing noise, free jazz and Captain Beefheart–derived harsh guitar sonorities with a punk-paced funk rhythm. As the Contortions entered the Eighties, they evolved into the slicker, more conventional James White and the Blacks. Teenage Jesus and the Jerks broke up, with Lydia Lunch going on to form other units that remained gloomy, if less musically radical.

No wave was dying, in fact it seemed to have had its short lifespan built in from its inception. Glenn Branca, onetime member of the no wave band Theoretical Girls, has gone on to forge his own brand of mega-heavy-metal monumental minimalism with layered, hyper-amped guitar ensembles; and Manhattan's Lower East Side is still full of struggling "underground" bands (documented on the 1982 *Peripheral Vision* compilation on Zoar Records)

making noisy, adventurous, challenging music that owes obvious debts to no wave's "avant-punks."

NRBQ

Formed 1967, Miami, as the New Rhythm and Blues Quintet

Terry Adams (b. Aug. 14, Louisville, Ky.), kybds., voc., harmonica; Joey Spampinato (b. Aug. 16, New York City), bass, voc.; Steve Ferguson (b. Louisville, Ky.), gtr., voc.; Tom Staley (b. Ft. Lauderdale, Fla.), drums; Frank Gadler (b. New York City), voc.

1969—*NRBQ* (Columbia) **1970**—*Boppin' the Blues* (with Carl Perkins) **1971**—(+ Al Anderson [b. July 26, 1947, Windsor, Ct.], gtr.) **1972**—*Scraps* (Kama Sutra) **1973**—*Workshop* **1974**—(− Ferguson; − Gadler; + Donn Adams [b. Jan. 16, Fleming, Ky.], trombone; + Keith Spring [b. Dec. 28, Louisville, Ky.], sax; + Tom Ardolino [b. Jan. 12, Springfield, Mass.], drums) **1977**—*All Hopped Up* (Red Rooster) **1978**—*At Yankee Stadium* (Mercury) **1979**—*Kick Me Hard* (Rounder/Red Rooster) **1980**—*Tiddlywinks* (Rounder) **1983**—*Grooves in Orbit* (Bearsville).

Since the late Sixties, NRBQ have been playing their unique, often wacky mix of rockabilly, country, pop, jazz and every other style of popular music. Though they have never come close to having a hit record, their incessant touring and intermittent releases have garnered them a dedicated cult following.

The band formed when a couple of Kentucky natives, Terry Adams and Steve Ferguson, met Bronx-born Joey Spampinato in Miami. While playing in a New Jersey club, they were spotted by Slim Harpo, who encouraged Steve Paul to book them into his New York club, the Scene. Their performances there drew positive press, and within the year Columbia had signed them. The band's first album was nearly buried by a "new Beatles" hype, and their second, a collaboration with rockabilly Carl Perkins, was generally misunderstood. Al Anderson, onetime leader of the Wildweeds, a country-rock group from Connecticut, joined them in 1971.

After two LPs for Kama Sutra, NRBQ did not record for the next four years. During this period, Ferguson and Gadler quit the group and Tom Ardolino replaced Tom Staley on drums. The Whole Wheat Horns—Terry Adams' brother Donn on trombone and Gary Windo and Keith Spring on saxes—became semi-official members of the group. In 1977, they formed their own label, Red Rooster, and released *All Hopped Up*. It was followed by another unhappy stint with a major label, Mercury, recording *At Yankee Stadium*, after which they returned to Red Rooster, now distributed by Rounder. Two more LPs and a reissue of *All Hopped Up* later, NRBQ signed to Bearsville in 1982. Since 1977, they have produced themselves.

Through it all, their sound has not changed. Albums

have included covers of Chipmunks songs, requests from the group's fabled Magic Box (in which they play any song the audience demands) and originals that have been recorded by other artists, including the Box Tops, the Carpenters and Ian Matthews. In 1982 alone, Adams' "Me and the Boys" was covered by Bonnie Raitt and Dave Edmunds. Edmunds also covered Adams' "I Want You Bad." In addition, Adams compiled the Thelonious Monk LP *Always Know* in 1979, coordinated the reissue of the Shaggs' *Philosophy of the World* and toured with Carla Bley (1977) in Europe. NRBQ has also backed Windo and country singer Skeeter Davis.

TED NUGENT

Born December 13, 1948, Detroit
1975—*Ted Nugent* (Epic)   **1976**—*Free for All*   **1977**—*Cat Scratch Fever; Double Live Gonzo*   **1978**—*Weekend Warriors*   **1979**—*State of Shock*   **1980**—*Scream Dream*   **1981**—*Intensities in Ten Cities*   **1982**—*Ted Nugent*.

As the self-proclaimed Motor City Madman, guitarist Ted Nugent has fashioned a sharply defined, not-so-noble-savage persona, garnering him endless publicity and resulting in multiplatinum sales.

Growing up in Detroit, Nugent picked up guitar at age nine. His first band was called the Royal High Boys (1960–61), followed by the Lourdes (1962–64). By the time he was 14, he and the band played Cobo Hall, opening for the Supremes and the Beau Brummels. The band broke up in 1965 when his family moved to Chicago, where he immediately formed the Amboy Dukes, signing with Mainstream, who released their debut that year. Though they had a local hit with "Baby Please Don't Go" in 1967, the band's only sizable success was "Journey to the Center of the Mind" (#16, 1968). They continued in various forms until 1975, recording also for Polydor and Discreet.

When they signed with the last label in 1972, they became known as Ted Nugent and the Amboy Dukes. Nugent tried to boost album sales with his publicity savvy, staging guitar contests against Mike Pinera (of Iron Butterfly and Blues Image), Wayne Kramer (MC5) and Mahogany Rush's Frank Marino.

Things didn't begin to happen for Nugent until he signed a solo deal with Epic in 1975, got Tom Werman as producer and Leber-Krebs as managers. In his new band, he retained bassist Rob Grange from the old Amboy Dukes. (After this he went through periodic changes in personnel.) He continued to tour widely, and suddenly his music was getting airplay; the national press, amused by his cartoonish caveman image, began to write him up. Even if many found his music to be standard heavy-metal fare, his penchant for hunting his own food, his relatively conservative antidrug stance, his general sexism and his reactionary politics—including strongly supporting the National Rifle Association—made him good copy.

Free for All featured Meat Loaf on some vocals (Nugent rarely sings), but the real breakthrough was 1977's *Cat Scratch Fever*, whose platinum success boosted sales of the two previous LPs to a million each. Also out that year was *Double Live Gonzo* (near two million sales), followed by the platinum *Weekend Warriors*. Stern Electronics introduced a Ted Nugent pinball game. Nugent showed a slight softening of attack by covering the Beatles' "I Want to Tell You" on *State of Shock*. This LP ended his platinum streak. Also disappointing sales-wise was 1980's *Scream Dream*, though it contained "Wango Tango" with its cars-and-garages sexual imagery; but Nugent's LPs and concerts still sold respectably.

In the spring of 1981, Nugent was backed by the D.C. Hawks (which included three brother lead guitarists, Kurt, Rick and Verne Wagoner) for a four-axe attack. His first self-production, 1982's *Ted Nugent*, barely grazed the charts.

GARY NUMAN

Born Gary Webb, March 1958, Hammersmith, England
1979—*Tubeway Army* (Beggar's Banquet)   *Replicas* (Atco)   *The Pleasure Principle*   **1980**—*Telekon*   **1981**—*Dance*   **1982**—*I Assassin*.

Gary Numan's synthesizer-dominated music, heavily influenced by Kraftwerk, Ultravox and David Bowie, gave him much British success and some U.S. attention in the early Eighties.

Numan joined his first band in 1977 at age 19, but he soon quit. He auditioned to be guitarist for the British band the Lasers, and after Numan became frontman, they changed their name to Tubeway Army. They were signed by Beggars' Banquet (a WEA subsidiary) in early 1978. At that time, they were a standard post–Sex Pistols punk outfit, releasing two angry singles, "That's Not It" and "Bombers."

Once they entered the studio to cut their first LP, Numan discovered synthesizers; he decided to put down his guitar and make electronics the basis of Tubeway Army's sound. The rest of the band (except for bassist Paul Gardiner) hated the idea and regrouped as another punk group, Station Bombers. Numan completed the LP with Gardiner and Gary's uncle Jess Lidyard on drums. The resulting LP, *Tubeway Army*, was billed to Gary Numan and Tubeway Army as was the followup, *Replicas*, which came out in 1979, yielding the British #1 hit "Are 'Friends' Electric?" Besides its robot-loving lyrics, its "futurist" electronic sound had a solid dance beat, and it anticipated the electro-pop trend of 1981–82.

In 1979, Numan also played on and wrote songs for Robert Palmer's *Clues* album. Numan's *The Pleasure Principle* (now billed solo, without Tubeway Army) entered at #1 on the U.K. charts and provided the synthesized dance-rock hit "Cars," which broke Numan in the U.S., where it hit #9. He drew a lot of attention for his elaborate pyramid-shaped live stage setup, but Americans, after some initial curiosity, didn't really appreciate his stylized look and sound, and *Telekon* was only modestly successful (#64). Shortly after, Numan announced his retirement from performing, although he continued to record.

THE NUTMEGS

Formed 1954, New Haven, Connecticut
Leroy Griffin, James Griffin, William Emery, James Tyson, Leroy McNeil

Taking their name from Connecticut's state emblem, the a cappella vocal group the Nutmegs had their biggest hit in 1955 with the doo-wop/R&B ballad "Story Untold" (#2 R&B), which may have been the first a cappella hit. The followup, "Ship of Love," sold fairly well later that year, but that was the last of their hits. Still, they kept performing, even after Leroy Griffin was killed in a smelting furnace accident in 1969. He was replaced by his nephew, Harold Jaynes, when the group reunited in 1974 to record a remake of "Story Untold," which didn't sell nearly as well as the original.

LAURA NYRO

Born 1947, Bronx, New York
1966—*More Than a New Discovery* (Verve)   **1968**—*Eli and the Thirteenth Confession* (Columbia)   **1969**—*New York Tendaberry*   **1970**—*Christmas and the Beads of Sweat*   **1971**—*Gonna Take a Miracle*   **1973**—*The First Songs* (re-release of *More Than a New Discovery*)   **1975**—*Smile*   **1977**—*Season of Light*   **1978**—*Nested*.

Singer/songwriter Laura Nyro's dramatic gospel- and R&B-powered ballads received tremendous attention during her brief peak in the late Sixties to early Seventies. She was most commercially successful as a songwriter, but was also a critically acclaimed performer herself, although her own albums never sold over 400,000 copies. With her long black hair, black clothes and moody persona, she gained a reputation as an arty urban chanteuse, helping to start the trend toward self-absorbed, "sensitive" singer/songwriters.

Nyro began writing songs as a young girl. Her Italian-Jewish parents were both musical; her father was a jazz trumpeter. She went to the High School of Music and Art in Manhattan and concentrated on songwriting. In 1967, she got a spot at the Monterey Pop Festival. It was her second concert appearance ever, and the audience was loudly unappreciative of her costume (one gossamer angel wing) and her soul revue (which included two black backup singers).

After this trauma, Nyro rarely toured. Her debut, *More Than a New Discovery*, went nowhere, but young manager David Geffen got her a deal on Columbia, resulting in *Eli and the Thirteenth Confession,* produced by ex–Four Season Charlie Callello. The album and its followup, *New York Tendaberry,* were critical triumphs (especially *Eli*), lavishly praised for their poetic lyrics and gospel-soul fusion. Nyro became known for her strange, intense phrasing, unexpected rhythm changes and distinctive, wailing vocals.

Though these two albums encouraged a healthy cult audience, other performers had the real hits with her songs: "Stoned Soul Picnic," "Sweet Blindness" and "Wedding Bell Blues" for the Fifth Dimension; "Stoney End" for Barbra Streisand in 1971; "And When I Die" for Blood, Sweat and Tears in 1969; and "Eli's Coming" for Three Dog Night. *New York Tendaberry* also contained her own well-known songs "Time and Love" and "Save the Country."

Nyro released two more celebrated records, *Christmas and the Beads of Sweet* and *Gonna Take a Miracle* (the latter featured backup from Labelle and covers of old R&B tunes like "Jimmy Mack" and "Dancing in the Street"), before she retired at age 24. Columbia reissued her old Verve LP as *The First Songs* in 1973, but Nyro did not release any new material until after her marriage broke up. *Smile* received guarded praise but didn't sell, nor did *Season of Light* (produced by ex-Rascal Felix Cavaliere) or *Nested,* after which she disappeared once again. In 1983, Todd Rundgren was reportedly producing her latest album.

Laura Nyro

O

PHIL OCHS

Born December 19, 1940, El Paso, Texas; died April 9,
1976, Far Rockaway, New York
1964—*All the News That's Fit to Sing* (Elektra) **1965**—*I
Ain't Marchin' Anymore* **1966**—*In Concert* **1967**—
Pleasures of the Harbor (A&M) **1968**—*Tape from
California* **1969**—*Rehearsals for Retirement* **1970**—
Greatest Hits **1971**—*Gunfight at Carnegie Hall*
1976—*Chords of Fame; Phil Ochs Sings* (Folkways)
Interviews.

Phil Ochs

Folksinger/songwriter Phil Ochs was a man of contradic-
tions: a patriotic American who came to prominence as
one of the harshest establishment critics in the mid-Sixties
folk-protest boom; a renowned folkie who "went electric"
and rocked out some time after it had been newsworthy to
do so.

After moving to Queens with his family, Ochs followed
family tradition by attending military school in Virginia.
He later studied journalism at Ohio State University. He
had begun writing songs while serving 15 days in jail on a
vagrancy charge and his first musical venture was with a
late-fifties folk duo, the Singing Socialists, who became
the Sundowners. Ochs then went solo, performing in
Cleveland before moving to New York in 1961. Within a
few years, he'd moved into Greenwich Village and the
folk-protest circle that included Bob Dylan, to whom Ochs
was most frequently compared.

By the time he recorded *All the News* (which featured
guitar work by Danny Kalb, later of the Blues Project),
Ochs had merged his literary/journalistic background with
a songwriting style that was direct and abrasive. He hit his
stride on *I Ain't Marchin'*. The title tune and "Draft
Dodger Rag" became antiwar anthems, despite a ban that
prevented him from being broadcast on American radio
and TV. During and after the ban, Ochs remained active in
causes and protest movements. His "There But for Fortune" was a Top Fifty hit for Joan Baez in 1965.

Harbor yielded some of Ochs's most famous tunes,
such as "Outside of a Small Circle of Friends" and "The
Party." After that LP's release, Ochs moved from New
York to L.A., where, with some top sessionmen backing
him, and Van Dyke Parks producing, he recorded *Tape
from California*. That LP also contained some rock & roll
as well as more traditional folk tunes, such as "Joe Hill,"
and the antiwar anthem "War Is Over," as well as "When
in Rome," an answer of sorts to Dylan's "Desolation
Row." *Rehearsals* and *Greatest Hits* maintained the sessionmen backing, to fascinating, if not especially popular,

effect. The former was a bitter rocking examination of
Ochs's own role as a Sixties culture hero, and saw his
depression growing; the latter contained all-new material.

Gunfight saw Ochs dressed in gold lamé and backed by
his L.A. sessioneers, singing his own greatest hits, as well
as Merle Haggard's "Okie from Muskogee" and a medley
of Presley and Buddy Holly hits; it included the audience's
boos. The LP was released only in Canada. In 1973, while
traveling in Africa, Ochs was the victim of a mysterious
assault during which he was nearly strangled and his vocal
cords were severely damaged.

During the early Seventies, Ochs lived in Africa and
London; he continued to perform occasionally, even
though his voice had pretty much gone, and he wrote for
the London periodical *Time Out*. In 1974, he was reunited
with Dylan at a New York concert in Felt Forum protesting the military junta in Chile; just prior to that event,
Ochs had released the Watergate-era protest "Here's to
the State of Richard Nixon." It was the last Phil Ochs
record released in his lifetime. His last public appearance
was at New York's Folk City on October 23, 1975. Six
months later, Ochs hanged himself at his sister's home.
The posthumous *Chords of Fame* was compiled by his
brother Michael.

ODETTA

Born Odetta Holmes, December 31, 1930, Birmingham, Alabama

N.A.—*Odetta at the Gate of Horn* (Tradition) **1973**—*The Essential Odetta* (Vanguard).

As a folk-blues institution, Odetta's vocal power and clarity and rich, intense singing style have long set her apart. She has made numerous recordings for various labels—none, according to critics, capturing her live impact—but most are now out of print. Odetta, influenced by Bessie Smith, went on to influence a variety of singers, including Joan Armatrading and Janis Joplin.

Upon her father's death, young Odetta Holmes assumed her stepfather's surname, Felious, and moved with her family to Los Angeles at age six. She sang in her junior high school glee club and worked as an amateur at Hollywood's Turnabout Theater around 1945. She then studied music at L.A.'s City College. From 1949, she began playing West Coast folk clubs as a singing/guitar-playing solo act. She steadily built up a reputation and through the mid- to late Fifties was touring nationwide and in Canada.

Odetta first recorded for San Francisco's Tradition label in 1956. In 1959, she married Dan Gordon, and subsequently remarried twice, to Gary Shead in the late Sixties and bluesman Iverson "Louisiana Red" Minter in 1977. She played the Newport Jazz Folk Festival in 1959, 1960, 1964 and 1965, and the Montreux Music Festival in Switzerland in 1976. In the early Sixties, she made her first European tour, and stopped off in Nigeria on the way home. Since then, she's played Japan, Australia, New Zealand, the West Indies, Morocco and several Western European countries. Along the way, she performed with Count Basie, poet/playwright Langston Hughes, Pete Seeger, Sonny Terry, ex-Basie trumpeter Buck Clayton, Bob Dylan, the Rochester Philharmonic Orchestra and rock & roll pianist Sammy Price. She's also appeared in films—*The Last Time I Saw Paris* (1954), *Cinerama Holiday* (1955), *Sanctuary* (1960) and the TV movie *The Autobiography of Miss Jane Pittman*—as well as TV shows, playing characters or as herself, in both singing and dramatic roles.

In the mid-Seventies, the Public Broadcasting System aired a documentary about her. In early 1982, she appeared with Jackson Browne and others at a Santa Monica benefit show for Sing Out for Sight. Though she's never been a chart-making recording star, Odetta continued to tour indefatigably, and her status has by now become legendary.

OHIO EXPRESS

Formed 1968

Joey Levine, voc.; Dale Powers, gtr.; Doug Grassel, gtr.; Jim Pfayler, kybds.; Dean Kastran, bass; Tim Corwin, drums.

1968—*Beg Borrow and Steal* (Cameo) *Ohio Express* (Buddah) *Salt Water Taffy; Chewy Chewy* **1969**—*Mercy; Very Best of.*

Another studio bubblegum band like the 1910 Fruitgum Company (with whom they shared producers Kasenetz-Katz and vocalist Joey Levine), the Ohio Express hit in 1968 with the million-selling "Yummy Yummy Yummy" (#4) and "Chewy Chewy" (#15). They had scored some minor success in 1967 (on Cameo Records) with "Beg Borrow and Steal" (#29) and "Try It" (#83). In late 1968, they had a minor hit with "Down at Lulu's" (#33), followed in 1969 by "Sweeter Than Sugar" (#96), "Pinch Me" (#97), "Mercy" (#30) and "Sausalito" (#86) in 1969 before disbanding.

THE OHIO PLAYERS

Formed 1959, Dayton, Ohio

Lineup at height of popularity: Billy Beck, kybds.; Clarence Satchell, saxes, flute; Jimmy "Diamond" Williams, drums, percussion; Leroy "Sugar" Bonner, gtr., voc.; Marvin Pierce, trumpet; Marshall Jones, bass; Ralph "Pee Wee" Middlebrooks, trumpet.

1968—*First Impressions* (Trip) **1969**—*Observations in Time* (Capitol) *Ohio Players* **1972**—*Pain* (Westbound) **1973**—*Pleasure; Ecstasy* **1974**—*Skin Tight* (Mercury) *Fire* **1975**—*Greatest Hits* (Westbound) *Honey* (Mercury) **1976**—*Contradiction; Gold* **1977**—*Angel; Mr. Mean* **1978**—*Jass-Ay-Lay-Dee* **1979**—*Everybody Up* (Arista) **1980**—*Young and Ready* (Accord) **1981**—*Ouch!* (Boardwalk) *Tenderness.*

The Ohio Players enjoyed immense popularity during the mid-Seventies with a percussive funk style influenced greatly by Sly and the Family Stone.

The group was formed as Greg Webster and the Ohio Untouchables. For a time they were the backing band for the Falcons, whose lead singer was Wilson Pickett. (They can be heard on the Falcons' "I Found a Love.") The Untouchables became the Players following the recruitment of three musicians from a rival Ohio band. In 1967, they served as the studio band for Compass Records, using their free time to cut demo tapes. One of these tapes won them a contract with Capitol Records and the album *Observations in Time.*

The Players recorded for Detroit-based Westbound Records from 1971 to 1973, gaining a #1 R&B single with "Funky Worm" (#15 pop). By the time the band signed with Mercury Records in 1974, keyboardist Junie Morrison had split for a solo career. (He later joined Parliament/Funkadelic.) The Players then embarked on a three-year run of steady hits, beginning with "Jive Turkey" (#47 pop, #6 R&B) and "Skin Tight" (#13 pop, #2 R&B) from *Skin Tight* (1974).

The title song from the gold *Fire* album went #1 on the R&B and pop charts, while "I Want to Be Free" from that same album reached #6 R&B (#44 pop). The group's luck continued as the gold *Honey* yielded "Love Rollercoaster" (#1 pop, #1 R&B), "Sweet Sticky Thing" (#33 pop, #1 R&B) and "Fopp" (#9 pop, #9 R&B). "Who'd She Coo" in 1976 was the Players' last #1 R&B single (#18 pop). "O-H-I-O" (#45 pop, #9 R&B) in 1977 was the band's last big hit with Mercury. The Players cut an album for Arista Records before recording for Boardwalk Records in the early Eighties. At their peak, the Ohio Players were also renowned for their album covers, featuring half-clad, shaven-headed women in suggestive poses.

THE O'JAYS
Formed 1958, Canton, Ohio
Bobby Massey; Walter Williams (b. Aug. 25, 1942); Eddie Levert (b. June 16, 1942); Bill Isles; William Powell (d. May 26, 1977, Canton).
1965—*Comin' Through* (Imperial) (– Isles) **1967**—*Soul Sounds* (Minit) **1972**—(– Massey) *Greatest Hits* (Liberty) *Back Stabbers* (Philadelphia International) **1973**—*In Philadelphia; Ship Ahoy* **1974**—*Live in London* **1975**—*Survival; Family Reunion* **1976**—*Message in the Music* (+ Sammy Strain [b. Dec. 9, 1941]) *Travelin' at the Speed of Thought* **1977**—*Collectors' Items* (– Powell) **1978**—*So Full of Love* **1979**—*Identify Yourself* **1980**—*The Year 2000* **1982**—*My Favorite Person.*

The O'Jays were one of the most popular black vocal groups of the Seventies, when they were in effect the voice of producers Gamble and Huff.

Eddie Levert and Walter Williams sang together as a gospel duo before forming a doo-wop group, the Mascots, with William Powell, Bobby Massey and Bill Isles in 1958. In 1961, the Mascots made their recording debut with "Miracles" for the Wayco label. Cleveland DJ Eddie O'Jay liked the group and gave them advice on their career. As a gesture of appreciation, the Mascots became the O'Jays. They cut some songs with producer Don Davis for Apollo Records before signing with Los Angeles' Imperial label and working with producer/writer H. B. Barnum. They recorded for Imperial from 1963 to 1967 and had some minor success. "Stand in for Love" (#12 R&B, 1966) was their biggest seller of the period.

In 1965, Isles left, and the group became a quartet. They signed with Bell and had a hit, "I'll Be Sweeter Tomorrow" (#8 R&B) in 1967, but by then the members were growing discouraged and contemplating retirement when Kenny Gamble and Leon Huff signed them to their Neptune label the next year. The O'Jays released four hits, including "One Night Affair" (#15 R&B, 1969) and "Looky Looky (Look at Me, Girl)" (#17 R&B, 1970). After Neptune folded in 1971, Massey quit to start producing records.

Levert, Williams and Powell attempted self-production with a single for Saru Records, then signed with Gamble and Huff's new Columbia-distributed label, Philadelphia International.

With Gamble and Huff supplying social-commentary songs, the O'Jays began an impressive string of gold and platinum recordings. They had eight #1 R&B singles from 1972 to 1978, including "Back Stabbers" (#3 pop) in 1972; "Love Train" (#1 pop) in 1973; "Give the People What They Want" (#45 pop) and "I Love Music (Part 1)" (#5 pop) in 1975; "Livin' for the Weekend" b/w "Stairway to Heaven" (#20 pop), "Message in Our Music" (#49 pop) and "Darlin' Darlin' Baby" (#72 pop), in 1976; and "Used ta Be My Girl" (#4 pop) in 1978. Eight of their LPs of this period were certified gold, 1978's *So Full of Love* going platinum.

During this hot streak, Powell was debilitated by cancer and could no longer tour. In 1977, a year after coming off the road, he died in the O'Jays' hometown. Sammy Strain, a member of Little Anthony and the Imperials for 12 years, was Powell's replacement. *Identify Yourself* was certified platinum in 1979. On recent albums, like *My Favorite Person,* O'Jay members Levert and Williams have taken an active role in the production and writing.

MIKE OLDFIELD
Born May 15, 1953, Reading, England
1968—*Sallyangie* (with Sally Oldfield) (Transatlantic) **1973**—*Tubular Bells* (Virgin) **1974**—*Hergest Ridge* **1975**—*Ommadawn* **1976**—*Box Set* **1978**—*Incantations* **1979**—*Exposed; Platinum* **1980**—*QE 2; Airborn* **1982**—*Five Miles Out.*

Mike Oldfield's *Tubular Bells* was the first LP released by Virgin, and it got the new company off with a bang. It was a #1 LP in the U.K., and went to #3 on the U.S. LP charts and stayed there well over a year, eventually going platinum. In 1974, it won a Grammy for Best Pop Instrumental LP, after excerpts were used as the soundtrack for *The Exorcist.*

Tubular Bells was some nine months in the making, as Oldfield played virtually all 28 instruments—mainly various guitars, basses and keyboards—himself. The album was a more accessible reworking of ideas previously used by minimalist composers. Oldfield, however, used rock and folk motifs, layered in a controlled, ever-changing tapestry, achieving something of an artistic/commercial milestone in the arranging of a 48-minute "rock" composition.

Oldfield had launched his musical career at age 14 in an acoustic-folk duo with his sister Sally. After the duo had made an album, Oldfield formed a short-lived band, Barefeet, through which he met English singer/songwriter Kevin Ayers, who had just left Soft Machine. Ayers made Oldfield the bassist (later guitarist as well) in his band, the Whole World, for 1971's *Shoot the Moon.*

An edited version of *Tubular Bells,* known as "Mike Oldfield's Single" or "Theme from *The Exorcist,*" went to

#31 in the U.K. and #7 in the U.S. in 1974, but follow-up LPs were unsuccessful in the U.S. Oldfield did have several more U.K. hit singles: "In Dulce Jubilo/On Horseback" (#4, 1975), "Portsmouth" (#3, 1976), "Blue Peter" (#19, 1979) and "Guilty" (#22, 1979)—the last of which saw Oldfield mating his pop-folk harmonic progressions to a disco beat, an approach furthered on the *QE 2* LP. Oldfield also recorded a disco version of composer Philip Glass's "Noah Star."

In 1982, Oldfield received the Freedom of the City of London award, an ancient honor that was conferred after he gave a free concert on the eve of the royal wedding of England's Prince Charles, with music specially composed for the occasion. He also played his first highly successful tour of major U.S. concert halls that year. Sally Oldfield has also recorded as a solo act.

OLIVER

Born William Oliver Swofford, February 22, 1945, North Wilkesboro, North Carolina
1969—*Good Morning Starshine* (Crewe) **1970**—*Prisms* (United Artists).

Oliver was a folk-rock singer who had two gold record hits, "Good Morning Starshine" (#3 1969), from *Hair*, and Rod McKuen's "Jean" (#2, 1969), the theme song from the film *The Prime of Miss Jean Brodie*.

By the time he was a student at the University of North Carolina, Bill Swofford had formed a bluegrass-folk band, the Virginians, who toured the Southern campus-and-coffeehouse circuit before moving to New York. There they changed their name to the Good Earth. Soon they disbanded, leaving only Swofford (whom producer Bob

One-Hit Wonders

Long-lived groups and extended careers are important to the history of rock & roll, yet some of the best-remembered, best-loved and most influential music in rock was made by one-hit wonders, performers whose moment in the spotlight was as brief as it was dazzling. What follows is a list of some of the best-known one-hit wonders; some are great, some are funny, some are just bizarre. That's rock & roll.

"Abraham, Martin and John," Moms Mabley (#35, 1969)*
"Angel of the Morning," Merrilee Rush (#7, 1968)
"Ariel," Dean Friedman (#26, 1977)*
"The Astronaut (Parts 1 and 2)," Jose Jimenez (#19, 1961)*
"Baby Come Back," Equals (#32, 1968)*
"Baby It's You," Smith (#5, 1969)
"Baby Sittin' Boogie," Buzz Clifford (#6, 1961)*
"Barefootin'," Robert Parker (#7, 1966)
"The Blob," Five Blobs (#33, 1958)*
"Book of Love," Monotones (#5, 1958)*
"Bread and Butter," Newbeats (#2, 1964)

"Chain Gang," Bobby Scott (#13, 1956)*
"Chick-a-Boom," Daddy Dewdrop (#9, 1971)*
"Classical Gas," Mason Williams (#2, 1968)
"Come and Get Your Love," Redbone (#5, 1974)
"Cool Jerk," Capitols (#7, 1966)
"Crying in the Chapel," Orioles (#11, 1953)*
"Deep Purple," Nino Temple and April Stevens (#1, 1963)
"Desiderata," Les Crane (#8, 1971)*†
"Ding Dong! the Witch Is Dead," Fifth Estate (#11, 1967)*
"Dinner with Drac, Part 1," John "the Cool Ghoul" Zacherle (#6, 1958)*
"Dirty Water," Standells (#11, 1966)
"Dominique," Singing Nun (*Soeur Sourire*) (#1, 1963)*
"Don't Just Stand There," Patty Duke (#8, 1965)
"Double Shot (of My Baby's Love)," Swingin' Medallions (#17, 1966)
"Earth Angel (Will You Be Mine)," Penguins (#8, 1955)*
"Easier Said Than Done," Essex (#1, 1963)
"Elusive Butterfly," Bob Lind (#5, 1966)
"Farmer John," Premiers (#19, 1964)

"Foot Stomping, Part 1," Flares (#25, 1961)*
"Funky Nassau," Beginning of the End (#15, 1971)*
"Gallant Men," Senator Everett McKinley Dirksen (#29, 1967)*†
"Gee," Crows (#14, 1954)*
"Get a Job," Silhouettes (#1, 1958)*
"Gimme Dat Ding," Pipkins (#9, 1970)*
"Gimme Gimme Good Lovin'," Crazy Elephant (#12, 1969)*
"Girl Watcher," O'Kaysions (#9, 1968)
"Gonna Get Along Without You Now," Patience and Prudence (#11, 1956)
"Good Old Rock 'n' Roll," Cat Mother and the All Night News Boys (#21, 1969)
"Green-Eyed Lady," Sugarloaf (#3, 1970)
"Groovy Grubworm," Harlow Wilcox and the Oakies (#30, 1969)
"Guantanamera," Sandpipers (#9, 1966)
"Hello Hello," Sopwith Camel (#26, 1967)
"Here Comes Summer," Jerry Keller (#14, 1959)*
"He's Got the Whole World (in His Hands)," Laurie London (#1, 1958)*

"Hey Joe," Leaves (#31, 1966)*

"Hey Little Cobra," Rip Chords (#4, 1964)

"Hooked on a Feeling," Blue Swede (#1, 1974)

"Hot Smoke and Sassafrass," Bubble Puppy (#14, 1969)*

"If You Wanna Be Happy," Jimmy Soul (#1, 1963)

"I Know (You Don't Love Me No More)," Barbara George (#3, 1962)

"I'm Easy," Keith Carradine (#17, 1976)*

"I Was Kaiser Bill's Batman," Whistling Jack Smith (#20, 1967)*

"I Will Follow Him," Little Peggy March (#1, 1963)

"Jesus Is a Soul Man," Lawrence Reynolds (#28, 1969)

"Journey to the Center of the Mind," Amboy Dukes (#16, 1968)*

"Junk Food Junkie," Larry Croce (#9, 1976)*

"(Just Like) Romeo and Juliet," Reflections (#6, 1964)

"Just One Look," Doris Troy (#10, 1963)*

"Land of 1000 Dances," Cannibal and the Headhunters (#30, 1965)*

"Leader of the Laundromat," Detergents (#19, 1964)

"Let It Out (Let It All Hang Out)," Hombres (#12, 1967)*

"Liar, Liar," Castaways (#12, 1965)*

"Little Arrows," Leapy Lee (#16, 1968)*

"A Little Bit of Soap," Jarmels (#12, 1961)*

"Little Bit o' Soul," Music Explosion (#2, 1967)

"Little Girl," Syndicate of Sound (#8, 1966)

"Little Star," Elegants (#1, 1958)*

"Love (Can Make You Happy)," Mercy (#2, 1969)

"Love Grows (Where My Rosemary Goes)," Edison Lighthouse (#5, 1970)

"Ma Belle Amie," Tee Set (#5, 1970)*

"Martian Hop," Ran-Dells (#16, 1963)*

"May the Bird of Paradise Fly Up Your Nose," "Little" Jimmy Dickens (#15, 1965)*

"Me and You and a Dog Named Boo," Lobo (Kent Lavoie) (#5, 1971)

"Mixed-Up, Shook-Up Girl," Patty and the Emblems (#37, 1964)*

"More Today than Yesterday," Spiral Starecase (#12, 1969)

"Mr. Lee," Bobbettes (#6, 1957)

"Mr. Sandman," Chordettes (#1, 1954)*

"My Boomerang Won't Come Back," Charlie Drake (#21, 1962)*

"My Boy Lollipop," Millie Small (#2, 1964)

"My Pledge of Love," Joe Jeffrey Group (#14, 1969)*†

"Na Na Hey Hey Kiss Him Goodbye," Steam (#1, 1969)

"Navy Blue," Diane Renay (#6, 1964)

"No Matter What Shape (Your Stomach's In)," T. Bones (#3, 1966)

"Oh Julie," Crescendos (#5, 1958)*

"One Tin Soldier," Original Caste (#34, 1970)*

"An Open Letter to My Teenage Son," Victor Lundberg (#10, 1967)

"Party Lights," Claudine Clark (#5, 1962)*

"Penetration," Pyramids (#18, 1964)*

"Pictures of Matchstick Men," Status Quo (#12, 1968)

"Pipeline," Chantays (#4, 1963)

"Please Come to Boston," Dave Loggins (#5, 1974)

"Popsicles and Icicles," Murmaids (#3, 1964)

"Pretty Little Angel Eyes," Curtis Lee (#7, 1961)

"Psychotic Reaction," Count Five (#5, 1966)*

"Rama Lama Ding Dong," Edsels (#21, 1961)*

"Remember Then," Earls (#24, 1963)*

"Rosie Lee," Mello-Tones (#24, 1957)*

"Rubber Duckie," Ernie (#16, 1970)*

"Sally Go Round the Roses," Jaynetts (#2, 1963)*

"Seasons in the Sun," Terry Jacks (#1, 1974)

"Shape of Things to Come," Max Frost and the Troopers (#22, 1968)*

"Sh-Boom," Chords (#5, 1954)*

"Sh-Boom," Crew-Cuts (#1, 1954)

"Shout! Shout! (Knock Yourself Out)," Ernie Maresca (#6, 1962)*

"Silhouettes," Rays (#3, 1957)

"A Song of Joy," Miguel Rios (#14, 1970)*

"Sorry (I Ran All the Way Home)," Impalas (#2, 1959)

"Stranded in the Jungle," Cadets (#15, 1956)*

"Sukiyaki," Kyu Sakamoto (#1, 1963)

"Summertime, Summertime," Jamies (#26, 1958; #38, 1962)*

"Sunshine," Jonathan Edwards (#4, 1972)*

"Surfin' Bird," Trashmen (#4, 1964)

"Susie Darlin'," Robin Luke (#5, 1958)*

"Sweet Dreams," Tommy McLain (#15, 1966)*

"Swinging on a Star," Big Dee Irwin (with Little Eva) (#38, 1963)*

"Talk Talk," Music Machine (#15, 1966)

"Telstar," Tornadoes (#1, 1962)

"They're Coming to Take Me Away, Ha-Haaa!," Napoleon XIV (Jerry Samuels) (#3, 1966; #87, 1973)*

"Three Stars," Tommy Dee, Carol Kay and the Teen-Aires (#11, 1959)*

"Tighter, Tighter," Alive and Kicking (#7, 1970)

"Till Then," Classics (#20, 1963)*

"Time Won't Let Me," Outsiders (#5, 1966)

"Torture," Kris Jensen (#20, 1962)*

"Unchained Melody," Roy Hamilton (#9, 1955)*

"Venus," Shocking Blue (#1, 1970)

"Walkin' My Cat Named Dog," Norma Tanega (#22, 1966)*

"Walk Right In," Rooftop Singers (#1, 1963)

"We'll Sing in the Sunshine," Gale Garnett (#4, 1964)

"Western Union," Five Americans (#5, 1967)

"What Kind of Fool (Do You Think I Am)," Tams (#9, 1964)

"Winchester Cathedral," New Vaudeville Band (#1, 1966)

"You Can't Sit Down, Part 2," Philip Upchurch Combo (#29, 1961)*

"You've Got to Hide Your Love Away," Silkie (#10, 1965)*

"You Were on My Mind," We Five (#3, 1965)

(*Asterisk indicates that title is the performer's only single to ever reach the U.S. pop Hot 100.
†Dagger indicates that song won a Grammy Award.)

Crewe christened Oliver) and Jim Dawson, who went on to a folk-singing career of his own. Oliver also penned a minor hit for the Cryan Shames, "Young Birds Fly."

Under Crewe's guidance, Oliver recorded "Starshine" one evening in New York. The success of "Starshine" led to Oliver's recording of *The Prime of Miss Jean Brodie* theme. His last big hit was "Sunday Morning" (#35, 1969), though the *Starshine* LP sold well through much of 1970. In 1970, "Early Morning Rain" was a minor regional hit, after which Oliver resumed the name Bill Swofford and continued a modest folk-pop career for a few years.

ROY ORBISON
Born April 23, 1936, Wink, Texas
1962—*Greatest Hits* 1963—*Lonely and Blue* (London)
Crying; In Dreams 1964—*Oh Pretty Woman; More
Greatest Hits* 1966—*The Very Best of* 1970—*The
Original Sound* (Sun) 1973—*All Time Greatest Hits*
(Monument) 1979—*Laminar Flow* (Elektra).

One of the original Sun Records rockabilly artists, Roy Orbison went on to become one of the most distinctive singers of the early Sixties. In his peak period (1960–64), he vacillated between snarling blues rock and his mainstay, the romantic/paranoiac ballad with crescendoing falsetto and strings. These narratives were later given resonance by the personal tragedies that befell him (his wife Claudette was killed in a motorcycle accident in 1966; two of his three children died in a fire in his Nashville home in 1968).

With his twanging guitar and quavering bel-canto tenor, Orbison scored a number of hits: "Only the Lonely" (#2, 1960), "Running Scared" (#1, 1961), "Crying" (#2, 1961), "Dream Baby" (#4, 1962) and "Oh Pretty Woman" (#1, 1964). His songwriting, and especially his near-operatic singing, have been a prominent influence on Bruce Springsteen, among others. Orbison's ostensibly placid, introverted demeanor has always been offset by his trademark "look"—sunglasses, black leather and a slicked-back pompadour.

Like many other early rockers, Orbison came from country music to rock, then returned to country. Two of his friends were future stars; his college buddy at North Texas State University, Pat Boone, urged Orbison to experiment with more pop-oriented songwriting; and when Johnny Cash heard some of the results, he per-

suaded Orbison to send a tape to Sam Phillips of Sun Records. Though Orbison would later profess a greater liking at that time for slower country material than frenetic rock, the first song he sent Phillips—the hard-rocking "Ooby Dooby"—impressed Phillips, and became Orbison's first hit in 1956 (#59).

Orbison then moved to Nashville, where he wrote songs for Acuff-Rose Publishing. One of his first successes was "Claudette," named for his wife, which became a hit for the Everly Brothers. Then came the hits, starting with "Only the Lonely." Others included "Blue Angel" (#9, 1960), "I'm Hurtin' " (#27, 1961), "Candy Man" (#25, 1961), "The Crowd" (#26, 1962), "Leah" (#25, 1962), "In Dreams" (#7, 1963), "Falling" (#22, 1963), "Mean Woman Blues" (#5, 1963), "Blue Bayou" (#29, 1963, later covered by Linda Ronstadt), Willie Nelson's "Pretty Paper" (#15, 1963), "It's Over" (#9, 1964), "Goodnight" (#21, 1965) and "Ride Away" (#25, 1965).

Roy Orbison

Successful in the U.S., Orbison has also been a smash in Britain, where in 1963 he toured with the Beatles. Orbison's bands during the Sixties included guitarist Bobby Goldsboro and drummer Dewey Martin (later of Buffalo Springfield).

Following his wife's death in 1966, Orbison's career went on hold. But when he returned to the U.K. three years later, the adulation was overwhelming. He remarried that year, and as of this writing is still married with three children. In 1980, after steady but uneventful work through the Seventies (and open heart surgery in 1979), Orbison sang a duet with Emmylou Harris on the soundtrack of the film *Roadie* and then toured opening for the Eagles on the West Coast. A 1981 comeback show in New York City was a great commercial and critical success. In 1982, "Oh Pretty Woman" was a hit for Van Halen.

OREGON
Formed 1970
Ralph Towner (b. Mar. 1, 1940, Chehalis, Wash.), gtr., piano, French horn; Paul McCandless (b. Mar. 24, 1947, Indiana, Penn.), oboe, bass clarinet, English horn; Glenn Moore (b. Oct. 28, 1941, Portland, Ore.), bass, piano, wooden flute; Colin Walcott (b. 1945), tablas, percussion, sitar.
1973—*Music of Another Present Era* (Vanguard)
1974—*Distant Hills; Winter Light* 1975—*In Concert*
1976—*Oregon/Elvin Jones: Together* 1977—*Oregon/Friends* 1978—*Violin; Out of the Woods* (Elektra/Asylum).

An offshoot of the Paul Winter Consort, for whom Ralph Towner wrote "Icarus," Oregon has achieved moderate commercial success with its light, organic fusion of jazz improvising, folky arrangements and Indian raga inflections. Often taking on a pastoral tone, their music is largely acoustic, with only microphones used for amplification. One factor that has always differentiated Oregon from other such transcontinental fusion outfits is the band's long-standing refusal to use lyrics or exploit "utopian" philosophies usually associated with such music.

The members went separate ways in the late Seventies to pursue various ethnomusicological studies and solo and collaborative projects. Towner has made many albums for ECM, while Walcott has worked with modern jazz trumpeter Don Cherry in a group called Codona, which also record for ECM. Oregon has since regrouped on and off.

THE ORIOLES
Formed late 1940s, Baltimore
Sonny Til (b. Earlington Tilghman, Aug. 18, 1925; d. Dec. 9, 1981), lead voc.; George Nelson (d. late 1960s), second tenor; Alexander Sharp (d. *ca.* 1959), tenor; Johnny Reed, bass; Tommy Gaither (d. 1950), gtr.

1950—(− Gaither; + Ralph Williams) 1953—(− Nelson; + Gregory Carol; + Charlie Hayes).

The Orioles are cited by many rock historians as the first rhythm & blues vocal group and a harbinger of the Fifties doo-wop sound.

As teens, they were known as the Vibranaires, later changing the name to the bird associated with Baltimore and its sports teams. A local saleslady/songwriter, Deborah Chessler, managed the Orioles and landed them a spot on Arthur Godfrey's "Talent Scouts" television program in 1948. They lost, but became regulars on Godfrey's national broadcast.

The Orioles joined Natural Records in 1948, making the R&B chart with several singles. In 1949, they moved to Jubilee for several hits; "Tell Me So," #1 in 1949, is considered most significant because it used "a wordless falsetto doing a kind of obbligato to the lead vocal," according to critic/disc jockey Barry Hansen. This technique would later be a staple of doo-wop vocals. In 1953, the Orioles hit #1 on the R&B charts and #11 on the pop charts with "Crying in the Chapel." It was one of the first R&B songs to cross over to the pop market. The original Orioles disbanded in 1954, though over the years various groups have performed and recorded under the name. The year Sonny Til died, 1981, they had released independently *Sonny Til and the Orioles Visit Manhattan Circa 1950s*, new versions of doo-wop oldies.

TONY ORLANDO AND DAWN
Formed 1970, New York City
Tony Orlando (b. Michael Anthony Orlando Cassavitis, New York City), voc.; Telma Louise Hopkins (b. Oct. 28, 1948, Louisville, Ky.), voc.; Joyce Elaine Vincent-Wilson (b. Dec. 14, 1946, Detroit), voc.
1970—*Candida* (Bell) 1975—*Tony Orlando and Dawn/Greatest Hits* (Arista).

Tony Orlando and Dawn had many MOR hits in the early Seventies, including "Tie a Yellow Ribbon 'Round the Ole Oak Tree," the largest-selling single in 1973, which in 1981 became something of a theme song for the return of the U.S. hostages from Iran.

At age 16, Orlando auditioned for producer Don Kirshner, who teamed him up with songwriter Carole King. Kirshner produced and King wrote Orlando's first hits, all in 1961: "Halfway to Paradise" (#39), "Bless You" (#15) and "Happy Times (Are Here to Stay)" (#82). In a short while, though, Orlando stopped singing, in part because Kirshner sold his company to Screen Gems, who were more interested in publishing than recording. For a while Orlando worked in promotion, and in 1967 he became manager of April-Blackwood Music, the publishing arm of Columbia Records.

In early 1970, Bell Records producer Hank Medress (a former member of the Tokens) asked Orlando to sing lead over a demo he had received from Telma Louise Hopkins and Joyce Elaine Vincent, a duo calling themselves Dawn. The two Detroit-based singers had previously done backup vocals for Johnnie Taylor, Edwin Starr, Freda Payne, Frijid Pink and others. Hopkins had also been part of Isaac Hayes's Hot Buttered Soul and later sang on "Shaft." Orlando's voice was dubbed over the original, and "Candida" shot to #3 in 1970. (Supposedly, he didn't meet Dawn until after it hit.)

Orlando kept his day job until after their second single, "Knock Three Times," hit #1 in 1971. Then he signed with Bell, and the group (then called Dawn, featuring Tony Orlando) finally started touring in September 1971. In 1973, they returned with the #1 hit "Tie a Yellow Ribbon 'Round the Ole Oak Tree." Other hits included "Say, Has Anybody Seen My Sweet Gypsy Rose?" (#3, 1973), "Steppin' Out (Gonna Boogie Tonight)" (#7, 1974) and "He Don't Love You (Like I Love You)" (#1, 1975).

After that, their hits stopped, though they still had many concert dates and their 1974 summer television show. In July 1977, Orlando announced his retirement, claiming he was giving up show business for Jesus Christ. Orlando's decision followed the death of his sister and suicide of his close friend, comedian Freddie Prinze. Orlando also had a cocaine problem and suffered from manic depression. In November 1977, he made a solo comeback, playing Las Vegas, though only one chart hit, "Sweets for My Sweet" (#54, 1979), followed. He appeared on Broadway in *Barnum* in 1982.

The two women worked unsuccessfully as Dawn. Hopkins later went into acting.

ORLEANS
Formed 1972
Lance Hoppen (b. 1954, Bayshore, N.Y.), bass; Wells Kelly, organ, voc.; Larry Hoppen, voc., kybds., gtr.; Jerry Marotta, percussion, drums; John Hall (b. 1948, Baltimore), gtr., voc.
1973—*Orleans* (ABC) (re-released 1977 as *Before the Dance*) **1974**—*Let There Be Music* (Asylum) **1976**—*Waking and Dreaming* **1979**—*Forever* (Infinity) **1982**—*One of a Kind* (Radio/Atlantic).

John Hall solo: 1978—*John Hall* (Elektra/Asylum) **1979**—*Power* (Arc) *Action* (Columbia) **1981**—*All of the Above* (EMI America).

Orleans had a few pop hits in the mid-Seventies written by leader/guitarist John Hall and his wife, Johanna. The group was founded by John Hall, Larry Hoppen and Wells Kelly. Larry's brother Lance joined later in the year. Through the next year they became a popular East Coast club attraction. They signed with ABC in 1973 and cut their eponymous debut with producers Barry Beckett and Roger Hawkins at Alabama's Muscle Shoals studio.

In 1974, they recorded a self-produced album at Bearsville studio, but ABC rejected it and dropped them from the roster. Elektra-Asylum picked up Orleans and released their Chuck Plotkin–produced *Let There Be Music* late in the year. "Dance with Me" (#6) was the group's first big hit. *Waking and Dreaming* (1976) contained "Still the One" (#5), which the ABC television network used as its theme song for the year.

In 1977, Hall left to begin a solo career. He signed to Elektra Records and soon became a spokesman for the antinuclear power movement, playing a key role in organizing MUSE (Musicians United for Safe Energy) and writing its anthem, "Power."

Orleans continued on through various personnel changes and in 1979 had a moderate hit with "Love Takes Time" (#11) from *Forever*. By this time the band had moved to MCA's Infinity label, which in 1980 went bankrupt. The group stayed together and appeared in clubs through 1981, and in 1982 released *One of a Kind*.

OZZY OSBOURNE
Born December 3, 1948, Birmingham, England
1980—*Blizzard of Ozz* (Jet) **1981**—*Diary of a Madman* **1982**—*Speak of the Devil*.

Onetime lead singer with Black Sabbath, Ozzy Osbourne has traded on his former band's legacy of loud hard rock and mystical/occult trappings, and his own propensity for grossly outrageous acts.

"I'm *not* a musician," Osbourne once claimed, "I'm a ham." In 1981, at an L.A. meeting of Columbia Records

Grammy Awards

Mike Oldfield	Yoko Ono	Roy Orbison
1974 Best Instrumental Composition: "Tubular Bells (Theme from *The Exorcist*)"	1981 Album of the Year: *Double Fantasy* (with John Lennon)	1980 Best Country Performance by a Duo or Group with Vocal: "That Lovin' You Feelin' Again" (with Emmylou Harris)

executives, Ozzy bit the head off a live dove; a few months later, he bit the head off a bat tossed to him by a fan at a Des Moines concert. The latter incident resulted in Osbourne receiving a series of rabies shots.

Osbourne has said there was "a lot of insanity" in his family; that he'd made several suicide attempts, as early as age 14, "just to see what it would feel like"; that at one point he and Black Sabbath drummer Bill Wood took acid every day for two years; and that his last months with Black Sabbath in 1978 were ". . . very unhappy. I got very drunk and very stoned every single day."

Both of Osbourne's solo LPs have gone gold, and in 1981 "You Can't Kill Rock 'n' Roll" garnered heavy FM-AOR airplay. Osbourne was unhurt when, on March 19, 1982, near Orlando, Florida, his tour plane, which was buzzing his tour bus, hit a house. Osbourne and most of his band were in the bus; Osbourne's guitarist Randy Rhoads, hairdresser Rachel Youngblood and pilot/bus driver Andrew Aycock were all in the plane and were all killed. Rhoads was replaced within a few weeks, and the show went on. Later that year, Osbourne married his manager, Sharon Arden. He also recorded a live album at the Ritz in New York.

OSIBISA
Formed 1970, London
Teddy Osei (b. Ghana), saxes, flute, voc.; Sol Amarfio (b. Ghana), percussion; Mac Tontoh (b. Ghana), trumpet; Robert Bailey (b. Trinidad), kybds., drums; Wendell Richardson (b. Antigua), gtr., voc.; Spartacus R. (b. Grenada), bass; Loughty Lasisi Amao (b. Nigeria), saxes.
1970—*Osibisa* (MCA) 1972—*Woyaya* 1973—*Heads* (− Amao; + Kofi Ayivor [b. Ghana], drums; − R.; + Jean Dikota Mandengue [b. Cameroon], bass; − Richardson; + Gordon Hunte [b. Guyana], gtr., voc.) *Superfly TNT* (− Hunte) *Happy Children* (Warner Bros.) 1974—(+ Kiki Gyan [b. Ghana], kybds.; + Paul Golly [b. Cameroon], gtr.) *Osibirock* 1975—(− Richardson; + Mike Odumusu [b. Lagos, Nigeria], bass; + Kof Ayivor, percussion, voc.) 1976—*Welcome Home* (Antilles) (− Golly; − Gyan) *Ojah Awake* 1977—(− Bailey) *Black Magic Night* (disbanded) 1980—(+ Osei; + Amarfio; + Tontoh) *Mystic Nights* (Calibre).

Osibisa was by no means the first band to play a cross between Western pop and African traditional music, but it was the first to become more popular in the West than in Africa. The band was made up of both African and Caribbean musicians.

Teddy Osei's career began over a decade before he formed Osibisa in England; in the late Fifties and early Sixties, he played sax with a highlife band, the Comets, in Kumasi, Ghana. In 1962, he went to England on a Ghanaian government scholarship to study at the London Col-

lege of Music. He led a number of bands in London, among them Cat's Paw in the late Sixties, which included Ghanaian younger brother Mac Tontoh's longtime friend Sol Amarfio, with whom Osei recorded a film soundtrack in London in 1969. They formed a quartet with Nigerian drummer Remi Kabaka, until Kabaka joined Ginger Baker's Air Force.

By 1970, West Indians Wendell Richardson and Robert Bailey had joined and they named themselves with the West African Akan word for a certain dance rhythm. Spartacus R., a West Indian, and Loughty Amao, a West African, joined in time to record a demo tape which was aired on BBC radio before record companies heard it. The music was an original fusion of polyrhythmic African percussion, rock guitar and keyboard riffs, and R&B-styled horn charts; songs were in Akan and in English.

After a series of London club dates, Osibisa signed with MCA. Their debut album, produced by Tony Visconti, made the U.K. Top Ten and the U.S. Top Sixty. In the next year, Osibisa toured Europe, North America and Africa, and in the following year traveled to the Orient and Australia. Everywhere, the colorfully costumed band appeared on television; in Great Britain, the BBC devoted a special to them. Their music was further spread by their soundtrack to *Superfly TNT* and by Art Garfunkel's 1973 cover of Amarfio's "Woyaya."

By 1973, when Osibisa signed with Warner Bros., half the original group had left. Richardson sat in for Paul Kossoff on Free's 1973 U.S. tour, then made a solo album, *Pieces of a Jigsaw*, before rejoining Osibisa in 1975. In 1976, after moving to Island Records' Antilles label, they released their biggest hit, "Sunshine Day" (#17 U.K.), from *Welcome Home*, but they disbanded the following year. In 1980, Osei, Amarfio and Tontoh reunited for *Mystic Nights*, made with session musicians.

THE OSMONDS
Alan Osmond (b. June 22, 1949, Ogden, Ut.), voc., gtr.; Wayne Osmond (b. Aug. 28, 1951, Ogden, Ut.), voc., gtr., sax; Merrill Osmond (b. Apr. 30, 1953, Ogden, Ut.), voc., bass; Jay Osmond (b. Mar. 2, 1955, Ogden, Ut.), drums; Donny Osmond (b. Dec. 9, 1957, Ogden, Ut.), voc., kybds.; Marie Osmond (b. Oct. 13, 1959, Ogden, Ut.), voc.; Jimmy Osmond (b. Apr. 16, 1963, Canoga Park, Calif.), voc.
The Osmonds: 1971—*The Osmonds* (MGM) 1972—*Around the World Live in Concert* 1976—*Osmonds' Christmas Album* 1977—*The Osmonds' Greatest Hits.*
Donny Osmond: 1972—*Portrait of Donny; My Best to You.*
Marie Osmond: 1973—*Paper Roses* (MGM).
Donny and Marie: 1973—*I'm Leaving It All Up to You* (MGM) 1978—*Goin' Coconuts* (Polydor).

Between January 24, 1971, and November 6, 1978, the RIAA certified a total of 23 gold discs recorded either by the Osmonds or by Donny and Marie Osmond as solo acts or as a duo: five LPs and three singles by the Osmonds; four LPs and five singles by Donny; one single by Marie; four LPs and one single by Donny and Marie.

All of the Osmond progeny were taught music by their parents and raised in a strict Mormon environment. They began singing religious and barbershop-quartet songs. Their big break came when in 1962 the Osmond Brothers (at the time, Alan, Jay, Merrill and Wayne) went to Disneyland wearing identical suits and were invited to perform by the house barbershop quartet. On the recommendation of his father, Jay, Andy Williams auditioned them and invited them onto his TV show. In the mid-Sixties, the Osmonds (now with Donny) also did TV shows with Jerry Lewis and toured with Pat Boone and Phyllis Diller. By the time the boys began recording, they'd all learned to play instruments, and through diligent touring had become a mammoth MOR attraction.

Their 1971 debut LP went gold, as did Donny's million-selling debut single, "Sweet and Innocent" (#7). Earlier that year, the brothers scored a gold hit with the Jackson 5–style "One Bad Apple" (#1). Other 1971 hit singles for the Osmonds included "Double Lovin' " (#14), "I Can't Stop" (#96) and the million-selling "Yo-Yo" (#3); Donny hit gold again with "Go Away Little Girl" (#1). Their albums, for the most part, went gold as well.

The year 1972 brought more hits; Donny's "Hey Girl/I Knew You When" (#9) and the Osmonds' "Down by the Lazy River" (#4) both went gold. The Osmonds had further hits with "Hold Her Tight" (#14, 1972) and "Goin' Home" (#36, 1973). Donny hit with the singles "Puppy Love" (#3), "Why" (#13) and "Too Young" (#13) in 1972, and "The Twelfth of Never" and "A Million to One/Young Love" (#8, 1973).

At this time, Marie made her recording debut with the #1 country & western hit "Paper Roses" (#5 pop, 1973). Little Jimmy's debut LP and single, "Long Haired Lover from Liverpool," did well in the U.S. in 1972, but he was most successful in Japan, where the plump tyke was known affectionately as "Jimmy Boy."

Having achieved such overwhelming success, the Osmonds took it easy for the rest of the Seventies. Marie changed her image to something a little hipper in the late Seventies and wrote a book entitled *Marie Osmond's Guide to Beauty and Dating*. In the early Eighties, she and Donny were most visible doing Hawaiian Punch TV commercials. In early 1982, Donny appeared on Broadway in George M. Cohan's musical *Little Johnny Jones*, which closed on opening night.

GILBERT O'SULLIVAN

Born Raymond O'Sullivan, December, 1, 1946, Waterford, Ireland
1972—*Himself* (MAM) *Back to Front* **1973**—*I'm a Writer, Not a Fighter; A Stranger In My Own Back Yard.*

Gilbert O'Sullivan was a boyish-voiced pop singer/songwriter who burst onto the American charts in 1972 with two lilting but despairing MOR/McCartneyesque ballads—"Alone Again (Naturally)" (#1) and "Clair" (#2).

In his early days, he played in a local band called Rick's Blues with future Supertramp member Richard Davies, and he had his first solo British hit in November 1970 with "Nothing Rhymed" (#8). After his initial U.S. breakthrough, he enjoyed three more hits in 1973—"Out of the Question" (#17), "Get Down" (#7) and "Ooh Baby" (#25)—before dropping out of sight. He had hits in England through mid-1975, but then vanished there as well until 1983, when he won a major lawsuit against MAM for back royalties.

JOHNNY OTIS

Born December 8, 1921, Vallejo, California
1969—*Cold Shot* (Kent) **1970**—*Cuttin' Up* (Epic)
1971—*Live at Monterey; The Original Johnny Otis Show* (Savoy) **1981**—*The New Johnny Otis Show* (Alligator).

As a talent scout and bandleader Johnny Otis was a central figure in the development of rhythm & blues and rock & roll in the early Fifties.

Otis was born John Veliotes of Greek-American parents, but from his childhood he lived among blacks. In his Berkeley neighborhood, Otis became interested in blues, gospel and swing, and in his teens became an accomplished drummer, playing in the Bay Area and touring the Southwest with various swing bands. By the mid-Forties, Otis had his own big band, but when the Big Band format lost popularity he stripped his crew down to a nine-piece group with small horn and rhythm sections, which became a standard rhythm & blues lineup.

In 1948, Otis and a partner, Bardu Ali, opened a popular Watts nightclub, the Barrelhouse Club. He closed it in the early Fifties after he made a series of R&B hits featuring singers he had discovered in Los Angeles: Little Esther Phillips, Mel Walker, and the Robins, later known as the Coasters.

"Double Crossing Blues" (#1 R&B), "Mistrustin' Blues" (#1 R&B), "Deceivin' Blues" (#4 R&B), "Dreamin' Blues" (#8 R&B), "Wedding Boogie" (#6 R&B), "Far Away Christmas Blues" (#4 pop, #6 R&B) and "Rockin' Blues" (#21 pop, #2 R&B) were all hits in 1950. In 1952, "Sunset to Dawn," sung by Mel Walker, was a #10 R&B hit.

From 1950 to 1954, the Johnny Otis Rhythm and Blues Caravan touring revue traveled across the U.S. with then-unknown performers including Hank Ballard, Little Willie John, Big Mama Thornton and Jackie Wilson. Otis heard Jerry Leiber and Mike Stoller's "Hound Dog," and he produced Thornton's version of it. "Every Beat of My Heart," written by Otis in the early Fifties, became

Gladys Knight and the Pips' first hit in 1961, and has been covered regularly ever since.

In 1954, Otis quit the road for a DJ spot at Los Angeles' KFOX, later landing a television show in the late Fifties. But he hadn't given up music, and in 1958 he had his biggest hit with the Bo Diddley–styled "Willie and the Hand Jive" (#9 pop, #5 R&B). For most of the Sixties, Otis' musical career was dormant, though he was very active in the civil rights movement and politics. His mid-Sixties book, *Listen to the Lambs,* concerned the Watts riots.

With his guitarist son Shuggie, Johnny Otis returned to recording with *Cold Shot* (1969), *Cuttin' Up* (1970) and *The Johnny Otis Show Live at Monterey* (1971), a double album reuniting his old band and singers. *The New Johnny Otis Show* was released in 1981 on Alligator.

SHUGGIE OTIS
Born November 30, 1953, Los Angeles
1969—*Kooper Session: Al Kooper Introduces Shuggie Otis* (Columbia)   **1970**—*Here Comes Shuggie Otis* (Epic)   **1971**—*Freedom Flight*   **1975**—*Inspiration Information;   Omaha Bar-B-Q.*

Son of rhythm & blues pioneer Johnny Otis, Shuggie Otis is a blues-rock guitarist whose promising musical career was curtailed by personal problems in the Seventies.

By age 12, Shuggie was playing bass professionally with a jazz band in San Diego. Later that year, he began playing guitar in his father's band, painting a mustache on his upper lip in order to enter nightclubs closed to minors. By the time he turned 13, he was doing session work, playing guitar, bass, organ, piano and harmonica.

In 1968, Johnny Otis recorded *Cold Shot*, which featured Shuggie on guitar. The album brought him to the attention of Al Kooper, who teamed up with Shuggie for the loose jam of *Kooper Sessions*. This brought him a solo contract. He also began doing local session work, playing bass on Frank Zappa's *Hot Rats* and guitar on violinist Sugarcane Harris' first solo LP. He cut only three more albums before he retired in 1975 at age 22; later, his "Strawberry Letter 23" was a platinum hit for the Brothers Johnson. An appearance on *The New Johnny Otis Show* in 1981 was his first recording in several years, aside from session work on his father's Blues Spectrum label.

JOHN OTWAY
Born October 2, circa 1952, Aylesbury, England
1977—*John Otway + Wild Willy Barrett* (Polydor, U.K.)   **1978**—*Deep and Meaningless*   **1979**—*Where Did I Go Right?*   **1980**—*Way and Bar; Deep Thought* (Stiff)   **1982**—*All Balls and No Willy.*

John Otway, one of rock's great eccentrics, specializes in bizarre, paranoid humorous songs. With his very Cockney yammering vocals and totally whacked-out stage show (where he may spend more time running around the stage than actually singing), Otway has attracted only the most rarefied of cults. Yet some musicians have taken an interest in him. Paul McCartney once asked him to open a Wings tour (Otway had prior commitments), and his songs have been covered by others, including Rick Wakeman.

The Who's Pete Townshend helped Otway and constant partner Wild Willy Barrett get their first English record deal in 1974. He and Barrett cut four tracks, which flopped, and Otway spent the next 2½ years as a trash collector. In 1977, the two recorded and distributed their own album, which eventually got them a label deal with Polydor and the British #27 hit "Really Free." Since the punk revolution was going on at the time, Otway's extreme amateurism was appreciated, and he and Barrett went on to record three British LPs, the first with both their names, followed by *Deep and Meaningless* plus *Where Did I Go Right?*

Otway's debut release in the U.S. was 1980's *Deep Thought,* which was a compilation of the three British albums, including a pair of songs produced by Townshend in 1974. Also included was a weird update of "The Man Who Shot Liberty Valance" and a version of the Blues Project's "Cheryl's Going Home." Though the LP was billed as an Otway solo, Wild Willy played on it. A Stiff EP entitled *I Did It Otway,* mainly a jokey throwaway including a sendup of Tom Jones's hit "Green Green Grass of Home," was released in 1981. *All Balls and No Willy* was recorded without Barrett.

THE OUTLAWS
Formed 1974, Tampa, Florida
Hughie Thomasson, gtr., voc.; Billy Jones, gtr., voc.; Henry Paul, gtr., voc.; Frank O'Keefe, bass; Monte Yoho, drums.
1975—*The Outlaws* (Arista)   **1976**—*Lady in Waiting*   **1977**—(– O'Keefe; + Harvey Dalton Arnold, bass; + David Dix, drums)   *Hurry Sundown*   **1978**—(– Paul; + Freddie Salem, gtr., voc.)   *Bring It Back Alive; Playin' to Win*   **1979**—(– Salem)   *In the Eye of the Storm*   (– Arnold; + Rick Cua, bass, voc.)   **1980**—*Ghost Riders in the Sky*   **1981**—(– Jones)   **1982**—*Los Hombres Malo.*

Not to be confused with Ritchie Blackmore's early-Sixties British band of the same name, Tampa's Outlaws have built a solid audience by merging Eagles-style country rock and vocal harmonies (Eagles' producer Bill Szymczyk produced *Sundown*) and Allman Brothers–style twin-guitar Southern rock. The Outlaws were managed by Alan Walden, who felt it impropitious to enter a business relationship with his brother Phil, who ran Capricorn; they became Clive Davis' first Arista signing. Their name notwithstanding, the Outlaws were considerably smoother-sounding than fellow Southern rockers Molly Hatchet and .38 Special, with whom they shared an initial audience and a touring circuit; and the Outlaws began appearing regularly on the pop charts with "There Goes Another Love Song" (#34, 1975), several minor hits and "(Ghost) Riders in the Sky" (#31, 1980). Henry Paul led his own band after leaving the Outlaws in 1977, but in 1983 he announced plans to rejoin the group. *Ghost Riders*, *Bring It Back Alive* and *Outlaws* are gold.

OZARK MOUNTAIN DAREDEVILS

Formed 1973, Springfield, Missouri
John Dillon (b. 1947, Stuttgart, Ark.), gtr., dulcimer, mandolin, autoharp, piano; Steve Cash (b. 1946, Springfield, Mo.), voc., harmonica; Randle Chowning (b. 1950), gtr., mandolin, harmonica, voc.; Michael Granda (b. 1951, St. Louis), bass, voc.; Buddy Brayfield (b. 1951), piano; Larry Lee (b. 1947, Springfield, Mo.), drums, voc., gtr., piano.
1973—*Ozark Mountain Daredevils* (A&M)   1974—*It'll Shine When It Shines*   1975—*The Car over the Lake* 1976—(— Chowning; + Rune Walle [b. Norway], gtr., banjo)   *Men from Earth*   1977—(— Brayfield; + Ruell Chapell, kybds., voc.; + Jerry Mills, mandolin; + Steve Canday, gtrs., drums, voc.)   1978—*Don't Look Down; It's Alive*   1980—*Ozark Mountain Daredevils* (Columbia).

Growing out of a Springfield assemblage called Cosmic Corncob and his Amazing Mountain Daredevils, this is an unusually eclectic country-rock unit with original compositions ranging from Appalachian and hillbilly old-timey string-band music to Southern boogie and country pop. Their first three LPs sold well, and the Daredevils had a couple of hit singles: "If You Wanna Get to Heaven" (#25, 1974) from the debut LP, and "Jackie Blue" (#3, 1975) from *It'll Shine When It Shines*. Chowning left to pursue a solo career and in 1978 released *Hearts on Fire*.

P

AUGUSTUS PABLO

Born Horace Swaby, circa 1953, Kingston, Jamaica
1972—*This Is Augustus Pablo* (Kaya) **1974**—*King Tubby Meets Rockers Uptown* (Clocktower; reissued 1976 by Yard) **1975**—*Ital Dub* (Trojan) **1977**—*Pablo Nuh Jester* (City Line; reissued as *Dubbing in a Africa* 1981 by Abraham, and as *Thriller* 1981 by Echo) **1978**—*East of the River Nile* (Rockers; reissued 1981 by Message/Shanachie) **1979**—*Original Rockers* (Greensleeves) **1980**—*Rockers Meets King Tubby Inna Fire House* (Shanachie) **1982**—*Earth's Rightful Ruler* (Rockers).

One of the most distinguished names in reggae, dub producer/composer/arranger/keyboardist Augustus Pablo is equally renowned as the foremost exponent of the melodica, which has since been used by numerous reggae artists as well as by postpunks like Joe Jackson, the Clash and Gang of Four.

While still calling himself Horace Swaby, Pablo taught himself piano at Kingston College School and played the local church organ. One day he borrowed a melodica from a girlfriend and became fascinated by it. Bob Marley took young Swaby into his Kingston studios, where in 1969–70 he contributed melodica lines to Lee Perry–produced Wailers tracks such as "Sun Is Shining," "Kaya" and "Memphis." Pablo has also led backing bands for Jimmy Cliff and Burning Spear and was at one time a member of Sly Dunbar's Skin, Flesh and Bones Band.

In 1971 producer Herman Chin-Loy gave Swaby his nom de disc, and the following year Pablo had his first hit single, "Java," which established his distinctive sound: reggae rhythms supporting sinuous minor-key melodica and organ lines and exotic modalities which Pablo termed "Far Eastern." He claims the influence of jazz vibraphonist Milt Jackson's "sleepy vibrato and hang-glide sonics."

Around 1973, Pablo came under the sway of King Tubby, who with Lee Perry was one of the first dub producers. Pablo's *King Tubby Meets Rockers Uptown* is a landmark of dub—where tunes are remixed almost beyond recognition. Pablo's most formidable trait is his unique (within dub) obsession with melody; he has made a long-running practice of dubbing such pop tunes as "Fiddler on the Roof" (in *East of the River Nile*'s "Jah Light"), Rod McKuen's "Jean" (*Pablo Nuh Jester*'s "Fat Jean"), Bill Withers' "Ain't No Sunshine" (*Original Rockers*' "Thunder Clap") and "Old Man River" (*This Is Augustus Pablo*'s "Jah Rock"), as well as following standard dub practice revamping reggae hits.

PABLO CRUISE

Formed 1973, California
Dave Jenkins (b. Fla.), gtr., bass, voc.; Cory Lerios (b. Calif.), kybds., voc.; Bud Cockrell (b. Miss.), bass, voc.; Steve Price (b. Calif.), drums.
1975—*Pablo Cruise* (A&M) **1976**—*Life Line* **1977**—*A Place in the Sun* (− Cockrell; + Bruce Day [b. Calif.], bass, voc.) **1978**—*Worlds Away* **1980**—*Part of the Game* (− Day; + Angelo Rossi, gtr., voc.; + John Pierce, bass, voc.) **1981**—*Reflector*.

An immensely successful band with a string of tunes that have become favorites on AM and FM radio and TV, Pablo Cruise exemplifies the wholesome, ultra-smooth California sound. Indeed, their music has been called "music to watch sports by," and Pablo Cruise songs have been used as soundtracks for ABC's "Wide World of Sports," CBS's "Sports Spectacular" and NBC's "Sportsworld," as well as for a surfing documentary called *Free Ride*. The band has also contributed to the soundtracks of the films *An Unmarried Woman* and *Dreamer*.

Pablo Cruise comes by its California heritage honestly. Dave Jenkins, Cory Lerios and Steve Price were formerly with Stoneground, while Bud Cockrell came from It's a Beautiful Day. When Cockrell left to pursue a musical career with his wife, Patti Santos (ex–It's a Beautiful Day), he was replaced by Bruce Day, formerly of Santana. The band first drew attention for such instrumentals as "Ocean Breeze" (from their debut LP) and "Zero to Sixty in Five" (from *Life Line*), which both became FM radio favorites. The band's first big hit was "Whatcha Gonna Do?" (#6, 1977), but they really made it with *Worlds Away*, which contained three hit singles: "Love Will Find a Way" (#6, 1978), "Don't Want to Live Without It" (#21, 1978) and "I Go to Rio" (#46, 1979). The LP sold two million copies within a year of its release, as did *A Place in the Sun*. In 1981, Pablo Cruise scored again with the hit "Cool Love."

ROBERT PALMER

Born January 19, 1949, Batley, England
1974—*Sneakin' Sally through the Alley* (Island) **1975**—*Pressure Drop* **1976**—*Some People Can Do What They Like* **1978**—*Double Fun* **1979**—*Secrets* **1980**—*Clues* **1982**—*Maybe It's Live* **1983**—*Pride*.

White soul singer and sometime songwriter Robert Palmer is equally renowned for his taste in R&B cover songs and for his impeccably tailored suits.

Palmer spent most of his childhood on the island of Malta. Back in Britain as a teenager, he performed in a Yorkshire R&B band, the Mandrakes, then went professional with the Alan Bown Set in 1968. He joined Dada, which later became Vinegar Joe, the next year. Vinegar Joe's three albums (*Vinegar Joe* and *Rock 'n' Roll Gypsies* in 1972, *Six Star General* in 1973) included songs by Palmer and vocals shared by Palmer and Elkie Brooks. When the band broke up, Palmer went solo.

Sneakin' Sally through the Alley, recorded in New Orleans and New York, featured backup and songs by members of Little Feat and the Meters; the title track was by Allen Toussaint. Little Feat also had a hand in *Pressure Drop,* featuring the Toots and the Maytals' title cut and Palmer's own "Give Me an Inch," which received FM airplay but failed as a single. After making *Some People Can Do What They Like,* Palmer moved to Nassau in the Bahamas. He had his first U.S. hit with ex-Free Andy Fraser's "Every Kinda People" (#16, 1978) from *Double Fun,* followed by Moon Martin's "Bad Case of Loving You (Doctor, Doctor)" (#14, 1979) from *Secrets,* the first album Palmer produced himself.

Clues, with a backup band including Chris Frantz of Talking Heads and Gary Numan, and material by Numan, gave Palmer two more hits, both synthesizer-driven: "Johnny and Mary" and "Looking for Clues." Palmer produced albums in 1981 for reggae singer Desmond Dekker, synthesizer player Peter Baumann and rock songwriter Moon Martin. He followed his first Top Twenty British hit, "Some Guys Have All the Luck," with *Maybe It's Live,* half of which was recorded in concert. *Pride*'s first single was a cover of the System's "You Are in My System."

GRAHAM PARKER

Born 1950, London
1976—*Howlin' Wind* (Mercury) *Heat Treatment; Live at Marble Arch* (Vertigo, U.K.) 1977—*The Pink Parker* (Vertigo/Mercury); *Stick to Me* (Mercury) 1978—*The Parkerilla* 1979—*Squeezing Out Sparks* (Arista) 1980—*The Up Escalator* 1982—*Another Grey Area* 1983—*The Real Macaw.*

One of the most critically acclaimed graduates of the mid-Seventies British pub-rock scene, singer/songwriter Graham Parker has been compared to Bob Dylan, Bruce Springsteen and Elvis Costello for the best of his angry, eloquent songs. Yet the commercial success he's always seemed to deserve has remained, for the most part, just outside his grasp.

Until 1975, Parker lived off a succession of odd jobs—including gas-station attendant and breeder of mice and guinea pigs for a scientific institute—and fronted a number of unsuccessful London bands. He had also spent time in a cover band playing Gibraltar and Morocco in the late Sixties.

In 1975, Dave Robinson of London's fledgling independent Stiff Records label heard some Parker demos he liked and matched Parker with a backing band of pub-rock veterans, the Rumour, which included guitarist Brinsley Schwarz and keyboardist Bob Andrews from the band Brinsley Schwarz (which also included Nick Lowe, who produced Parker's first few LPs), guitarist Martin Belmont from Ducks Deluxe, bassist Andrew Bodnar and drummer Steve Goulding from Bontemps Roulez. Their first two LPs won mammoth critical acclaim but sold barely respectably in the U.S.

Parker had many run-ins with his label, Mercury, accusing them of poor distribution and promotion, resulting in the mediocre sales (*Heat Treatment* did best, selling some 60,000 copies). The poorly produced *Stick to Me*—which had to be quickly re-recorded after original tapes were mangled—met with the same results, hurt by the emergence of punk rock and Elvis Costello, and in 1978 Parker rushed out the live *Parkerilla* LP, reportedly in order to escape the Mercury contract.

Parker was the subject of an intense music-industry bidding war and finally signed with Arista. His first Arista LP, *Squeezing Out Sparks,* stands as probably his finest artistic/commercial achievement; it made the Top Forty and sold over 200,000 copies. Parker's star continued to rise with a cover of the Jackson 5's "I Want You Back" (never included on an album) that became a minor hit. But Parker has never been able to consolidate that incipient success. *The Up Escalator* (produced by Jimmy Iovine) and *Grey Area* (produced by Jack Douglas) met with mixed response and unexceptional sales; and by this time the Rumour had released a couple of LPs on their own. Various studio musicians and others, including Nicky Hopkins and Hugh McCracken, backed up Parker. Bruce Springsteen cowrote and sang on "Endless Night" on *Escalator.* Various Rumour members, meanwhile, worked with Nick Lowe and Garland Jeffreys.

JUNIOR PARKER

Born Herman Parker, March 3, 1927, West Memphis, Arkansas; died November 18, 1971, Blue Island, Illinois
1960—*Driving* (Duke) 1961—*Blues Consolidated* 1962—*Best of* 1964—*Junior Parker* (Bluesway) 1967—*Like It Is* (Mercury) 1970—*Outside Man* (Capitol) 1972—*Blue Shadows Falling* (Groove Merchant) *Good Things Don't Happen Everyday* 1973—*You Don't Have to Be Black . . .* (People) 1974—*Love Ain' Nothin' But Business* 1976—*Love My Baby* (EP) (Charly) 1978—*Legendary Sun Performers.*

A highly respected blues vocalist and harmonica player, Junior Parker may be best known as the author of Elvis Presley's 1955 classic "Mystery Train." But Parker had a long, noteworthy career of his own, which included stints with blues performers like Sonny Boy Williamson, Howlin' Wolf, B. B. King and Johnny Ace.

Junior Parker

Parker's career began in 1948 at a Sonny Boy Williamson show, where Parker responded to Williamson's request for a harmonica player from the audience; Parker ended up playing with Williamson for the rest of his tour, leading the band when Williamson had solo commitments. In 1949, Parker played with Howlin' Wolf and, two years later, after Wolf had temporarily retired, took over that band, which also included pianist Ike Turner and guitarist M. T. Murphy. Parker then moved to Memphis and joined the Beale Streeters, who also included B. B. King, Bobby Bland, Johnny Ace and Rosco Gordon. In 1952, Parker formed his own band, the Blue Flames, with whom he made his first recordings for Modern. He then moved to Sun Records, with whom he had a massive hit, "Feelin' Good," in 1953. His second Sun release, "Mystery Train," was a minor hit; Presley had much more success with it. In 1954, Parker began a four-year association with Houston's Duke Records.

Parker had joined the Johnny Ace Revue in 1953, which also included Big Mama Thornton. When Ace died (losing a game of Russian roulette) in 1954, Parker took over the Revue, renaming it Blues Consolidated, and toured with it through 1961. He also toured with Bobby Bland and Joe Hinton.

Among Parker's many R&B hits were "Next Time You See Me" (#7, 1957), "Driving Wheel" (#5, 1961), "In the Dark" (#7, 1961) and "Annie Get Your Yo-Yo" (#6, 1962). Some of his better-known earlier performances were "Mother-in-Law Blues" and "Barefoot Rock." On some of these early recordings, Parker's guitarist, Pat Hare, can be heard experimenting with unusually up-

tempo driving rhythms and distorted solos. As late as 1971, Parker was still having minor R&B hits, like "Ain't Gon' Be No Cutting Loose" and "Drowning on Dry Land," and had recorded for Blue Rock, Minit and Capitol. His death came after surgery for a brain tumor.

RAY PARKER, JR.
Born 1954, Detroit
1978—*Raydio* (Arista) **1979**—*Rock On* **1980**—*Two Places at the Same Time* **1981**—*A Woman Needs Love.*

First as a session guitarist/writer and currently as a performer/producer, Ray Parker has been an integral part of the Los Angeles pop music scene since the early Seventies. The group Raydio made its debut in 1978 as a vehicle for Parker's singing and writing. Although he cheerfully borrows arrangements from Sly and the Family Stone, Free and others, his man-about-town persona has made him a dependable hitmaker.

Parker was playing a number of instruments in elementary school before he picked up a guitar at age 12. At 16, he had appeared on a few Motown sessions. From 1969 to 1971, he played sessions for Holland-Dozier-Holland's Invictus Records. In 1972, he played on Stevie Wonder's *Talking Book* and accompanied Wonder on his tour with the Rolling Stones.

Before forming Raydio, he had been active in Los Angeles as a sideman and writer. Rufus' "You Got the Love," Barry White's "You See the Trouble with Me" and Herbie Hancock's "Keep On Doing It" were cowritten by Parker.

The first single from the *Raydio* debut, "Jack and Jill," was a major hit, reaching #5 on the R&B charts and #8 pop in 1978. By 1979, the band was known as Ray Parker and Raydio. "You Can't Change That" (#9 pop, #3 R&B) was another massive hit, making Parker one of the rare black stars of the late Seventies to receive immediate pop acceptance with each new release.

"Two Places at the Same Time" (#30 pop, #6 R&B) and the instrumental "For Those Who Like to Groove" (#14 R&B) were substantial black hits. The title cut from *A Woman Needs Love* (#4 pop, #1 R&B) continued Parker's crossover success. That record was recorded at Parker's Ameraycan Studios in Los Angeles, which, due to Parker's own achievements, became a popular recording site. During this period, Parker produced albums by the band Brick and by singer Cheryl Lynn. The latter resulted in a Top Ten soul single, "Shake It Up Tonight."

By 1982's platinum *The Other Woman*, Parker was recording as a solo act while still enjoying pop and black acceptance. With "The Other Woman," Parker moved into pop rock. He claims the idea for the song came while listening to Rick Springfield's "Jessie's Girl."

The group of musicians who backed Parker as Raydio circa 1979 were keyboardist/vocalist Arnell Carmichael, guitarist Darren Carmichael, drummer Larry Tolbert and guitarist Charles Fearing: all old buddies of Parker's from Detroit.

VAN DYKE PARKS

Born January 3, 1941, Mississippi or Alabama
1968—*Song Cycle* (Warner Bros.) 1972—*Discover America* 1975—*The Clang of the Yankee Reaper.*

Even by Hollywood standards, Van Dyke Parks is an oddball. His specialty—in his over two decades in the music business as songwriter, lyricist, arranger and producer—is dense aural and verbal montages, which are most easily sampled in his lyrics for the Beach Boys' "Heroes and Villains" or "Surf's Up."

He moved with his family to Hollywood at age 13 and became a child actor while studying classical piano and composition. In the early Sixties, he reportedly signed with MGM Studios to write soundtrack music for Walt Disney films. Instead, he began writing his own songs, one of which, "High Coin," has become a folk-rock standard and was covered by Bobby Vee, Harper's Bizarre and the Charlatans, among others. In the mid-Sixties, he produced such hits as the Mojo Men's cover of Stephen Stills's "Sit Down I Think I Love You" and Harper's Bizarre's cover of Cole Porter's "Anything Goes."

In 1966, Parks began collaborating with Brian Wilson of the Beach Boys on the never-released *Smile* LP; some of the songs appeared on later Beach Boys albums. He also produced for Judy Collins, Randy Newman, Ry Cooder, Phil Ochs, Arlo Guthrie and others, becoming something of a local L.A. legend for his mysterious, meticulous methods. His first solo LP, an ambitious and eclectic project four years in the making, earned him the reputation of "the first art-rocker."

Parks was made director of audio visual services for Warner Bros. in 1970, a post he quit a year later. He also played keyboards on sessions with Judy Collins and with the Byrds (on "Eight Miles High"), and in the score for Robert Altman's *Popeye*, in which he briefly appeared onscreen. His two other solo LPs showcased his love of calypso music; both featured the Esso Trinidad Steel Band. Parks remains an enigmatic figure.

PARLIAMENT/FUNKADELIC

George Clinton (b. July 22, 1940, Kannapolis, N.C.), voc.; Bernie Worrell (b. Apr. 19, 1944, N.J.), kybds.; Eddie Hazel (b. Apr. 10, 1950), gtr.; Raymond "Tiki" Fulwood (b. May 23, 1944), drums; Gary Shider, gtr.; "Junie" Morrison, kybds.
Funkadelic: 1970—*Funkadelic* (Westbound) *Free Your Mind and Your Ass Will Follow* 1971—*Maggot Brain* 1972—*America Eats Its Young* 1973—*Cosmic Slop* 1974—*Standing on the Verge of Getting It On* 1975— *Let's Take It to the Stage; Funkadelic's Greatest Hits*

1976—*Tales of Kidd Funkadelic; Hardcore Jollies* (Warner Bros.) 1977—*Best of the Early Years, Volume One* (Westbound) 1978—*One Nation under a Groove* (Warner Bros.) 1979—*Uncle Jam Wants You* 1981— *The Electric Spanking of War Babies.*
Parliament: 1970—*Osmium* (Invictus) 1974—*Up for the Down Stroke* (Casablanca) 1975—*Chocolate City* 1976—*Mothership Connection; Clones of Dr. Funkenstein; Get Down and Boogie* 1977—*Live; Funkentelechy Vs. the Placebo Syndrome* 1978— *Motor-Booty Affair* 1979—*Gloryhallastoopid—or Pin the Tale on the Funky* 1981—*Trombipulation.*
George Clinton solo: 1983—*Computer Games* (Capitol).

George Clinton (a.k.a. Dr. Funkenstein, a.k.a. Maggot Overlord) has, since 1955, headed a loose aggregation of musicians he now calls his "Parliafunkadelicment Thang," or "P-Funk All-Stars." Composed of members of two main groups, Parliament and Funkadelic, and various offshoot bands, the organization made some of black pop's most popular music in the mid-Seventies. Clinton's music was a mix of funk polyrhythms, psychedelic guitar, jazzy horns, vocal-group harmonies and often scatological imagery. One of its many mottoes was: "Free your ass and your mind will follow."

As a teenager in Plainfield, New Jersey, Clinton straightened hair working in a local barbershop, where he also founded a vocal group called the Parliaments. They struggled through the Fifties and most of the Sixties, by which time Clinton had moved to Detroit to work as staff writer for Motown.

In 1967, the Parliaments had a major hit with Clinton's "(I Just Wanna) Testify" (#20 pop, #3 R&B), a straight love song. The Parliaments' next charted single, "All Your Goodies Are Gone" (#21 R&B), suggested Clinton's future direction. Hanging out with Detroit hippies and listening to local hard-rock bands like the MC5 and the Stooges influenced Clinton's approach to music, and he began to contemplate making a radical change in the Parliaments' sound.

At the same time in 1967, a legal battle over the Parliament name ensued, so Clinton and the group's singers began recording with their backup band as Funkadelic for Westbound Records in 1968. After winning the lawsuit, Clinton would record Parliament (the "s" was dropped) and Funkadelic separately. Initially Parliament was more commercially oriented and Funkadelic more experimental and gritty, though as time went on these distinctions blurred.

Early Funkadelic albums built a cult audience. Parliament/Funkadelic concert appearances featured Clinton jumping out of a coffin, musicians running around in diapers and smoking marijuana and simulating sex acts. On both Parliament and Funkadelic albums, Clinton wrote about the dark realities of funk, utilizing negative imagery from the Process Church of Final Judgment and clear-

George Clinton of Parliament/Funkadelic

eyed wit; he wrote for denizens of "Chocolate City" surrounded by "vanilla suburbs."

Parliament's 1974 hit on Casablanca, "Up for the Down Stroke" (#63 pop, #10 R&B), introduced Clinton's concepts to a wider audience and helped Funkadelic get signed to Warner Bros. Over the years, the group attracted top R&B instrumentalists, including bassist Bootsy Collins (ex–James Brown), guitarists Eddie Hazel and Gary Shider, keyboardist Bernie Worrell, keyboardist Junie Morrison (ex–Ohio Players) and reedmen Fred Wesley and Maceo Parker (ex–James Brown).

Parliament's *Mothership Connection* and gold single "Tear the Roof Off the Sucker" (#15 pop, #5 R&B) made Clinton and company major concert attractions. With a weird, lengthy stage show that included a space ship descending on stage from a huge denim cap, the P-Funk crew rivaled Earth, Wind and Fire as black America's favorite band. From 1976 to 1981, Clinton's salesmanship and success landed recording contracts for many P-Funk offshoots: Bootsy's (Collins) Rubber Band, Eddie Hazel, the Horny Horns, Parlet, Bernie Worrell, the Brides of Funkenstein, Phillippe Wynne, Junie Morrison and Zapp.

Parliament's "Flash Light" (#16 pop, #1 R&B)—in which Worrell introduced the synthesized bass lines later imitated by many funk and new wave bands—and the platinum *Funkentelechy Vs. the Placebo Syndrome* in 1978; "Aqua Boogie" (#1 R&B) in 1979; and Funkadelic's funk anthems "One Nation under a Groove" (#28 pop, #1 R&B) in 1978 and "(not just) Knee Deep—Part I" (#77 pop, #1 R&B) in 1979, were Clinton's commercial peaks in the Seventies.

Beginning in 1980, internal strife and legal problems temporarily sapped Clinton's P-Funk tribe of its energy and key performers. And while P-Funk's sound got absorbed into mainstream funk, Clinton's many projects became entangled. Drummer Jerome Brailey left P-Funk to start his own group, Mutiny, which pointedly devoted its first album to imprecations against the "Mamaship." Other ex-sidemen actually recorded as Funkadelic, although their album (*Connections and Disconnections*, LAX Records) carried a sticker to the effect that Clinton was not involved. After Warner Bros. refused to release *The Electric Spanking of War Babies* (with guest Sly Stone) as a double album, Clinton cut it to a single LP and began proceedings to end his Warners contract. He recorded two singles, "Hydraulic Pump" and "One of Those Summers," with the P-Funk All-Stars on an independent label, Hump Records. Then he reemerged with a name that was not in litigation—his own—on a George Clinton solo album, *Computer Games*, which included P-Funk's core members and the hit single "Atomic Dog."

ALAN PARSONS PROJECT
Formed 1976
1976—*Tales of Mystery and Imagination* (Charisma, UK) **1977**—*I Robot* (Arista) **1978**—*Pyramid* **1979**—*Eve* **1980**—*The Turn of a Friendly Card* **1982**—*Eye in the Sky.*

Alan Parsons is mainly a producer/engineer. He worked on the Beatles' *Abbey Road*, Paul McCartney's *Wildlife* and *Red Rose Speedway*, and produced two successful art-rock LPs: Pink Floyd's *The Dark Side of the Moon* and Al Stewart's *Time Passages*. Parsons plays keyboards and sometimes sings with his Project, which is basically a loose collection of English session players interpreting Parsons' and lyricist/manager Eric Woolfson's arty, highly synthesized and orchestrated concepts.

Vocalists on his LPs have included Arthur Brown, Steve Harley of Cockney Rebel, Allan Clarke of the Hollies, and ex-Zombie Colin Blunstone. *Tales*, a Gothic-rock ode to E. A. Poe, and *Robot* have been his biggest successes, though *Card* (about gambling obsessions) also went gold, yielding hit singles in "Games People Play" and "Time." The title track from *Eye in the Sky* hit the Top Five in 1982.

GRAM PARSONS
Born Cecil Connor, November 5, 1946, Winterhaven, Florida; died, September 19, 1973, Joshua Tree National Monument, California
1972—*G.P.* (Reprise) **1973**—*Grievous Angel* **1976**—*Sleepless Nights* (A&M) **1979**—*Gram Parsons—The Early Years, Volume 1* (Sierra/Briar Records).

Singer/songwriter Gram Parsons was a major pioneer of country rock. He came up with the amalgam as far back as

1966 and then brought the style to the Los Angeles music community through his association with the Byrds and later the Flying Burrito Brothers in the late Sixties. He has achieved near-mythic status since his death at age 26 in 1973, under somewhat bizarre circumstances, and his eerie songs continue to be covered.

Cecil Connor spent his childhood in Waycross, Georgia. He played guitar starting in his early teens and was influenced by his father, Coon Dog Connor, a country singer/songwriter. When Cecil was 13, his father committed suicide. After his mother remarried, her new husband, Robert Parsons, adopted Cecil and legally changed his name to Gram Parsons. At age 14, Parsons ran away from home, eventually ending up in Greenwich Village. In 1964, he entered Harvard but dropped out.

He formed the International Submarine Band in 1966. They cut two unsuccessful singles, and then left Cambridge for the Bronx and later for Los Angeles. The band cut one LP, 1967's *Safe at Home,* now a major collector's item. Before the LP came out, Parsons met Chris Hillman and through him joined the Byrds in 1968. The Byrds' *Sweetheart of the Rodeo* included two Parsons songs, "Hickory Wind" (cowritten with Bob Bucannan of the International Submarine Band) and "One Hundred Years from Now."

After just three months in the Byrds, Parsons quit in summer 1968, refusing to join their tour of South Africa because of his opposition to apartheid. In late 1968, he and Hillman formed the Flying Burrito Brothers (an old Parsons phrase that the Byrds had considered using as the title of what became *The Notorious Byrd Brothers*). He played a strong role on the Burritos' first LP, but quit in April 1970, just before *Burritos Deluxe* came out.

In early 1970, Parsons was injured in a motorcycle accident and while recuperating met and became friends with Rolling Stones Mick Jagger and Keith Richards. He also spent some time with Richards at his home in Nellcote, France. Parsons did not record again until his 1972 solo debut, *G.P.,* which featured Emmylou Harris and backing from Rick Grech and three members of Elvis Presley's touring band.

Grievous Angel had just been completed when Parsons died in 1973. He was staying at a desert retreat, and, though the autopsy was inconclusive as to the cause of death, traces of morphine, cocaine, amphetamine and alcohol were found in his blood. Less than one week later, his coffin, en route to New Orleans for burial, was stolen by his manager Phil Kaufman and another friend and taken back to Joshua Tree (where he had died) and set afire. It was later revealed that Parsons had expressed a wish for cremation in the event of his death.

Parsons' legacy lived on as Emmylou Harris toured with his old Hot Band and covered and popularized his material, as did many others, including Elvis Costello on his country LP, *Almost Blue.* Costello also wrote liner notes for a 1982 British compilation of Parsons' work. Bernie Leadon's song "My Man," from the Eagles' 1974 *On the Border,* was a tribute to Parsons, and a song Richie Furay wrote about him in 1969, "Crazy Eyes," was the title track of a 1973 Poco LP. In 1979, Sierra/Briar Records released an album of early Parsons material when he was with a band called the Shilohs (circa 1962), titled *Gram Parsons—The Early Years, Volume 1.*

DOLLY PARTON
Born January 19, 1946, Sevierville, Tennessee
1970—*The Best of Dolly Parton* (RCA)   **1971**—*Coat of Many Colors*   **1973**—*My Tennessee Mountain Home* (RCA)   **1974**—*Love Is Like a Butterfly*   **1975**—*Bargain Store; The Best of Dolly Parton; Dolly*   **1976**—*All I Can Do*   **1977**—*New Harvest . . . First Gathering*   **1978**—*In the Beginning* (Monument)   *Heartbreaker* (RCA)   **1980**—*9 to 5 and Odd Jobs*   **1982**—*Heartbreak Express*   **1983**—*Burlap and Satin.*

Dolly Parton's girlish soprano and songs about old-time virtues made her a major country star as the Seventies began. Later in the decade, she wooed the pop audience and became a household name. Parton wrote many of her own hits, either alone or in collaboration with Bill Owens.

Parton grew up poor on a farm in Tennessee's Smoky Mountain foothills in a family with 12 children. Her sister Stella later became a singer as well, and five other siblings have worked as professional musicians. Parton sang in church as a girl, and at age six appeared on the Cas Walker TV show in Knoxville with members of her grade school class. She became a regular on Walker's radio show at age ten and stayed for the next eight years. Parton appeared at the Grand Ole Opry at age 13, and her first single, "Puppy Love," was released by the local blues-oriented label, Goldband. After graduating high school in 1964, she moved to Nashville and signed with Monument. Three years later, she joined singer Porter Wagoner and signed with RCA.

The duo had many hits on the country charts, including "Just Someone I Used to Know" (1969) and "Daddy Was an Old Time Preacher Man" (1970). Parton joined Wagoner as "Miss Dolly" on his syndicated television show, where she was known for her caricature of a buxom blond bombshell. (Her first solo chart single in 1967 was "Dumb Blonde.") While with Wagoner, she charted over a dozen solo country & western hits, including "Joshua" (#1, 1970) and "Coat of Many Colors" (#4, 1971).

In 1974, Parton left Wagoner completely, having released *Jolene,* the title track of which became her second #1 country hit and a minor pop crossover. Other singers began to take an interest in her work. Linda Ronstadt covered "I Will Always Love You" in 1975 on *Prisoner in Disguise;* Emmylou Harris sang "Coat of Many Colors"; and Maria Muldaur covered "My Tennessee Mountain

Home" on her first record. (There were plans for a Parton/Harris/Ronstadt joint record on Elektra in spring 1978, but it was never completed.) The covers encouraged Parton to bring her country to the pop market, which she did with *New Harvest*. The LP was more rock-oriented and included a version of "Higher and Higher." She also broke away from the country circuit to play rock clubs.

Parton's first major pop single was "Here You Come Again," which went gold and hit #3 in early 1978. The LP of the same name went platinum. She also hit the pop Top Twenty that year with "Two Doors Down." Parton had successfully crossed over; "Baby I'm Burning" (#25, 1979) even had some success in discos. By 1980, Parton was a regular headliner in Las Vegas. She also began working as an actress and starred with Jane Fonda and Lily Tomlin in *9 to 5* in 1980 (her recording of the title theme was a #1 hit in pop and country) and in *The Best Little Whorehouse in Texas* in 1982 with Burt Reynolds.

THE PARTRIDGE FAMILY

David Cassidy (b. Apr. 12, 1950, New York City); Shirley Jones (b. Mar. 31, 1934, Charleron, Penn.)

The Partridge Family, featuring teen idol David Cassidy, was more a marketing idea than a band. Their music was plugged on "The Partridge Family" TV series, which was about a family as traveling pop band (based loosely on the Cowsills), though only two of the actors actually sang on the group's many hit singles. The two real voices were Cassidy (who also played some guitar) and his stepmother, Shirley Jones, a veteran lead in many musicals, including *The Music Man*.

Rounding out the family on the TV show were Danny Bonaduce, Brian Foster and Suzanne Crough, plus ex-model Susan Dey. The show premiered on ABC on September 25, 1970, and weeks later their first single, "I Think I Love You," rose to #1 and went on to sell four million copies. Their debut, *The Partridge Family Album*, went gold in 1971. Cassidy (who played Keith Partridge) sang lead, and by 1972 he'd begun to tour and record solo as well as with "the band." Under the Partridge Family name there were three more 1971 hits: "Doesn't Somebody Want to Be Wanted" (#6), "I'll Meet You Halfway" (#9) and "I Woke Up in Love This Morning" (#13). They had three more Top Forty hits, two in 1972 and then, the next year, "Looking through the Eyes of Love" (#39). But their popularity had waned by that time and soon the show ended.

BILLY PAUL

Born December 1, 1934, Philadelphia
1970—*Ebony Woman* (Philadelphia International)
1971—*Going East*   **1973**—*360 Degrees of Billy Paul; Feelin' Good at the Cadillac Club; War of the Gods*
1974—*Live in Europe*   **1975**—*Got My Head on Straight;*
When Love Is New   **1976**—*Let 'Em In*   **1977**—*Only the Strong Survive.*

The success of singer Billy Paul's #1 pop and R&B hit "Me and Mrs. Jones" in 1972 helped establish Kenny Gamble and Leon Huff's then-young Philadelphia International Records and brought Paul's jazzy, unpredictable singing to its widest public.

Paul first appeared in public at age 11, when, encouraged by friend Bill Cosby, he sang on Philadelphia radio station WPEN. As a teen, Paul had extensive musical training (Temple University, West Philadelphia Music School, Granoff Music School) and had sung with the Flamingos and the Blue Notes. He recorded as a jazz singer for Jubilee Records.

One evening in the late Sixties, Paul met Gamble at Philadelphia's Cadillac Club. Paul would record for Gamble's ill-fated Neptune Records before working with him again at Philadelphia International. "Mrs. Jones," written and produced by Gamble and Huff, is regarded as one of their classic records.

Though Paul's later releases never matched "Mrs. Jones," he had several soul hits through 1980, including "Am I Black Enough for You" (#29 R&B) in 1973, "Thanks for Saving My Life" (#9 R&B) in 1974 and "Let's Make a Baby" (#18 R&B) in 1976.

LES PAUL

Born Lester Polfus, January 9, 1915, Waukesha, Wisconsin
1968—*Les Paul Now* (London)   **1974**—*Les Paul Story, Volumes 1 and 2* (Capitol, import)   **1975**—*Les and Mary* (Capitol)   **1977**—*Chester and Lester* (with Chet Atkins) (RCA)   **1978**—*Guitar Monsters.*

Though he had a long and successful pop-jazz career, both with and without singer Mary Ford (who was born Colleen Summer, July 7, 1928, Pasadena, and died September 30, 1977), guitarist Les Paul is of paramount importance to rock & roll as the creator of the solid-body electric guitar and as a pioneer in modern recording techniques like electronic echo and studio multitracking.

Having learned harmonica, guitar and banjo at age 13, Paul was playing with Midwestern semi-pro country & western bands. He moved to Chicago in his late teens and became a regular on WLS. He then concentrated on performing for a few years before taking over the house band at WJJD in 1934, and later became something of a hillbilly star under the pseudonym Hot Rod Red and later Rhubarb Red. He formed the Les Paul Trio—which included Chet Atkins' brother Jimmy on rhythm guitar and vocals and Ernie Newton on bass—in 1936, and with them moved to New York in 1937. They became regulars on bandleader Fred Waring's NBC radio show and stayed with Waring's Pennsylvanians orchestra for five years.

Around this time, Paul began seriously thinking about

revolutionizing the guitar. He had become interested in electronics at age 12, when he built a crystal radio set. He built his first guitar pickup from ham radio headphone parts in 1934, and by 1941, he had built the first prototypical solid-body electric guitar, a four-foot wooden board with strings, pickup and a plug, which he called the "Log," and which he still uses to test against other guitars.

Meanwhile, in New York, Paul's musical aspirations moved toward jazz. He jammed informally with such greats as Art Tatum, Louis Armstrong, Ben Webster and others, including electric (hollow-body) guitarist Charlie Christian. Paul left Waring in 1941, spent a year as music director for two Chicago radio stations, and moved to Los Angeles. In 1942, he was drafted and worked for the Armed Forces Radio Service, playing behind Bing Crosby, Rudy Vallee, Johnny Mercer, Kate Smith and others. Upon his discharge in 1943, he worked as a staff musician for NBC radio in L.A. He backed Bing Crosby with his trio and toured with the Andrews Sisters. With Crosby's encouragement, Paul built his first recording studio in his L.A. garage in 1945. There he began to pioneer such now-standard recording techniques as close microphone positioning ("close-miking"), echo delay and multitracking. In 1948, he broke his right elbow in an auto accident and had it reset at a special angle so he could still play guitar.

In the late Forties, he met and married singer Mary Ford, and they began recording together—unsuccessfully at first—for Decca and Columbia. After moving to Capitol, they had a long string of hits, including "Mockin' Bird Hill" (#3, 1951), "How High the Moon" (#1, 1951), "The World Is Waiting for the Sunrise" (#3, 1951) and "Vaya Con Dios" (#1, 1953). These recordings—among the earliest multitracked pop songs—featured Ford's voice answering Paul's "talking" guitar. Paul also had some instrumental hits on his own: "Nola" (#9, 1950), "Whispering" (#7, 1951), "Tiger Rag" (#6, 1952) and "Meet Mister Callaghan" (#5, 1952). Their hits stopped in 1961; two years later, Paul and Ford were divorced.

By that time, Paul's interests had shifted to experimenting and innovating. He built the Les Paul Recording Guitar in the early Fifties and used it on his own recordings, not allowing Gibson to market it until 1971. Since they were first marketed in May 1952, Les Paul Gibsons have been known for their "hot" pickups and sustaining capacity, as compared to the twangier electric guitars of Leo Fender.

In the early Fifties, Paul built the first eight-track tape recorder, which helped pioneer multitrack recording, and he invented "sound-on-sound" recording, which has since become known as overdubbing. His other inventions include the floating bridge pickup, the electrodynamic pickup (both patented), the guitar with dual pickups, the 14-fret guitar and various types of electronic transducers used both in guitars and recording studios.

In 1974, Paul returned to musicmaking, and in 1977 had a hit LP with *Chester and Lester,* with country guitarist Chet Atkins, which won a Grammy. A 1980 documentary, *The Wizard of Waukesha,* opened and closed with scenes of Les Paul in the late Seventies, still playing guitar, demonstrating his latest invention: a little box called the "Les Paulverizer," an invention that could record, play back and allow the musician to talk to anyone onstage, and which made his guitar sound like something that had inhaled laughing gas.

PAUL AND PAULA
Paul (b. Ray Hildebrand, Dec. 21, 1940, Joshua, Tex.);
Paula (b. Jill Jackson, May 20, 1942, Brownwood, Tex.)

Personifying the clean-cut optimism of early-Sixties Kennedy-era America, Paul and Paula had a smash hit with "Hey Paula" (#1, 1963) for Philips Records.

The pair had originally gotten together to sing for a radio station's charity drive in Texas. With their matching P-embroidered sweaters, they became a popular attraction. They had a few other hits—"Young Lovers" (#6, 1963), "First Quarrel" (#27, 1963), "Something Old, Something New" (#77, 1963) and "First Day Back at School" (#60, 1963)—in the same cute vein, but then quickly faded from view. They reunited in 1982 for a country single, "Any Way You Want Me," for Texas-based Lelam Records. The tune met with little public response.

TOM PAXTON
Born October 31, 1937, Chicago
1965—*Ramblin' Boy* (Elektra)   *Ain't That News*
1966—*Outward Bound*   1968—*Morning Again*
1969—*The Things I Notice Now*   1970—*Tom Paxton*
6   1971—*The Compleat Paxton; How Come the Sun*
(Reprise)   1972—*Peace Will Come*   1973—*New Songs for Old Friends*   1975—*Something in My Life* (Private Stock)   1977—*New Songs from the Briar Patch* (Vanguard)   1978—*Heroes*   1983—*Even a Gray Day* (Flying Fish).

Singer/songwriter Tom Paxton first came to prominence with his topical songs during the early-Sixties Greenwich Village folk revival along with performers like Bob Dylan, Phil Ochs and Joan Baez.

Paxton was raised in Oklahoma (his parents moved there when he was ten) and studied drama at the University of Oklahoma. He began writing songs, and after graduating in 1959 with a BFA he joined the Army. He later moved to New York City, where he played the folk circuit. The Gaslight Club issued his first (now out-of-print) album, but his first national major release wasn't until early 1965's *Ramblin' Boy.*

Paxton's albums mixed increasingly topical political songs (like "What Did You Learn in School Today," "Talking Vietnam Pot Luck Blues" and the later "Talking

Watergate") with occasional love songs (like "The Last Thing on My Mind") and children's songs. He recorded seven albums for Elektra and then switched to Reprise in 1971, when he moved to England and recorded three LPs, including *New Songs* with Ralph McTell.

Paxton's compositions are more popularly known in versions performed by others. Peter, Paul and Mary covered "Going to the Zoo" and were among the many who covered "The Last Thing on My Mind"; John Denver did "Forest Lawn" and "Whose Garden Was This?"; other songs have been covered by Judy Collins, the Kingston Trio and the Weavers. He continues to command a loyal following.

FREDA PAYNE
Born September 19, 1945, Detroit
1972—*The Best of Freda Payne* (Invictus).

Soul singer Freda Payne's greatest recording success came at Invictus Records in the early Seventies under the guidance of its owners/producers Lamont Dozier and Eddie and Brian Holland.

Payne's parents envisioned a career in the performing arts for both Freda and her sister Sherri (who later joined a latter-day version of the Supremes). Both studied voice and piano as children at the Detroit Institute of Musical Arts. Both later studied ballet. At 18, Payne moved to New York. Her best gig in the next two years was a stint in the chorus of a Pearl Bailey show. In 1965, she was the understudy for Leslie Uggams in the Broadway musical *Hallelujah, Baby!* There she met Quincy Jones, with whom she toured. For the rest of the Sixties, she worked as a jazz singer, performing with the top Big Bands, including Duke Ellington's.

After Eddie Holland left Motown, he persuaded Payne to join his new label and sing pop music. In 1970 and 1971, the Holland-Dozier-Holland production team furnished Payne with some neo-Motown music, including two gold singles, "Band of Gold" (#3 pop, #20 R&B, 1970) and "Bring the Boys Home" (#12 pop, #3 R&B, 1971). The latter was one of the era's rare black anti-Vietnam songs. Other popular Payne records of the period were "Deeper and Deeper" (#24 pop, #9 R&B, 1970), "Cherish What Is Dear to You (While It's Near to You)" (#99 pop, #11 R&B, 1971) and "You Brought the Joy" (#52 pop, #21 R&B, 1971).

Subsequently she recorded for ABC and Capitol Records. In the early Eighties, she hosted the syndicated television talk show "For You Black Woman," and she continues to perform as a singer.

PEACHES AND HERB
Herb Fame (b. circa 1943, Washington, D.C.); Peaches: Francine Barker (b. Francine Hurd, 1947, Washington, D.C.), 1966–68 and 1969–71; Marlene Mack (b. 1945, Va.), 1968–69; Linda Greene, 1977 to present.

N.A.—*Golden Duets* (Date) 1968—*Peaches and Herb's Greatest Hits* 1978—*2 Hot!* (Polydor) 1979—*Twice the Fire* 1980—*Worth the Wait* 1981—*Sayin' Something!* 1983—*Remember* (Columbia).

The Peaches and Herb story is a tale of three women, two careers and one Herb.

The original team of Francine Barker and Herb Fame formed in 1965 at the urging of producer Van McCoy. At the time, Barker was lead singer of a female vocal group, the Sweet Things, and Fame was a solo act on Date Records. The Sweet Things and Fame met while on tour together. McCoy suggested they form the duo, which he then produced.

The B side of their first single, "Let's Fall in Love" (#21 pop, #11 R&B), began a series of hits from 1967 to 1969 on Date: "Close Your Eyes" (#8 pop, #4 R&B), "For Your Love" (#20 pop, #10 R&B) and "Love Is Strange" (#13 pop, #16 R&B) in 1967; "United" (#46 pop, #11 R&B) in 1968; and "When He Touches Me" (#49 pop, #10 R&B) in 1969.

Marlene Mack filled in for Barker for one year, but by the time Barker returned, the duo's hits had stopped. After signing with Columbia in 1970, they suffered another dry spell and eventually quit the record business. During the Seventies, Fame was a D.C. police officer. For a time in the mid-Seventies, Fame and Barker released singles on their own BS label in Washington. But in 1977, Fame found a new Peaches, Linda Greene, and returned full-time to music. After a brief tenure with MCA Records, they signed to Polydor, where their "Shake Your Groove Thing" (#5 pop, #4 R&B, 1978) and the ballad "Reunited" (#1 pop, #1 R&B, 1979)—both from *2 Hot!* (#6 pop, #1 R&B)—were Herb's biggest hits yet.

PEARL HARBOUR AND THE EXPLOSIONS
Formed 1978, San Francisco
Pearl E. Gates (b. 1958, Germany), voc.; John Stench, drums; Hilary Stench, bass; Peter Bilt, gtr.
1980—*Pearl Harbour and the Explosions* (Warner Bros.).
Pearl Harbour solo: 1980—*Don't Follow Me, I'm Lost Too.*

Pearl Harbour and the Explosions were one of San Francisco's first nationally recognized new wave bands. Their focus was lead singer Pearl E. Gates (of American-Filipino heritage), who started her musical career as a dancer with the Tubes in 1976. She left the next year with another dancer from the band, Jane Dornacker, and formed the cabaret musical group Leila and the Snakes, which also included John and Hilary Stench. The Stenches and Gates then formed the Explosions with Bilt (who was in a local cover band).

Their first single, 1979's "Drivin'," became an underground hit, and with almost no promotion sold 10,000 copies, which prompted Warner Bros. to sign them. The band's self-titled album didn't sell, and they split in June of 1980. The two Stenches went on to become part of Jorma Kaukonen's Vital Parts, but first Hilary played awhile with Eddie Money, and John and Bilt did a stint with the Soul Rebels. Meanwhile, Pearl took the last name Harbour, went to London and hooked up with Otis Watkins (keyboardist for Shakin' Stevens) and Nigel Dixon (of the English rockabilly band Whirlwind) and formed a group. With their backing, Micky Gallagher (keyboardist for Ian Dury's Blockheads) produced her debut Warners solo LP, the rockabilly-style *Don't Follow Me, I'm Lost Too.* In mid-1983 it was revealed that Pearl and the Clash's Paul Simonon were married.

ANN PEEBLES
Born April 27, 1947, East St. Louis, Missouri
1971—*Part Time Love* (Hi) **1972**—*Straight from the Heart* **1974**—*I Can't Stand the Rain* **1976**—*Tellin' It* **1978**—*If This Is Heaven.*

Soul singer Ann Peebles is best known for her 1973 hit "I Can't Stand the Rain," but her grainy Memphis soul singing has influenced Bonnie Raitt, among others. Peebles began performing at age eight when she joined the Peebles Choir, a gospel group founded by her great-grandfather. After graduating from high school, she started working St. Louis nightclubs. In 1969, producer Willie Mitchell signed her to his Memphis-based Hi Records, where she worked with the same session band Al Green used. Her first single, "Walk Away," hit #22, and later hits like "Part Time Love" (#7 R&B), "I Pity the Fool" (#18 R&B) and "Breaking Up Somebody's Home" (#13 R&B) sold well, particularly in the South.

"I Can't Stand the Rain" (#6 R&B) was written by Peebles and her husband, Don Bryant. At the time of its release, John Lennon said of it, " 'Rain' is the greatest record I've heard in two years." The song has been covered by numerous performers, from rock bands to disco divas. Peebles continued recording through the late Seventies.

TEDDY PENDERGRASS
Born 1950, Philadelphia
1977—*Teddy Pendergrass* (Philadelphia International)
1978—*Life Is a Song Worth Singing* **1979**—*Teddy; Teddy Live! Coast to Coast* **1980**—*TP* **1981**—*It's Time for Love.*

Singer Teddy Pendergrass emerged as a major star and sex symbol after leaving Harold Melvin and the Blue Notes in 1976.

As a youngster, Pendergrass was ordained a minister; he was introduced to secular music by his mother, who worked at Skioles, a big Philadelphia nightclub popular in the early Sixties. Using the club's equipment, Pendergrass

Teddy Pendergrass

taught himself to play several instruments, and by 13 he was a capable drummer. He sang with a local group in his teens, but was disillusioned when a man claiming to be James Brown's brother recorded him in a New Jersey studio, then disappeared.

At age 19, Pendergrass became the drummer for a Philadelphia band called the Cadillacs, and a year later he became the Blue Notes' drummer. During a tour of the West Indies, Blue Notes lead singer John Atkins left the group and Pendergrass replaced him. Though in existence since 1956, the Blue Notes had their first substantial commercial success only after Pendergrass became their frontman in 1970; his shouting vocals and songs by Kenny Gamble and Leon Huff made the Blue Notes a chart staple in the mid-Seventies.

In 1976, Pendergrass quit the Blue Notes. With the release of his solo debut, he was marketed as a sex symbol and became known to his fans as Teddy Bear. "I Don't Love You Anymore" (#41 pop, #5 R&B, 1977) was the single from that platinum album. His next LP, *Life Is a Song Worth Singing,* was highlighted by the seductive "Close the Door" (#25 pop, #1 R&B, 1978), and the next summer the steamy tale continued with "Turn Off the Lights" (#48 pop, #2 R&B).

Backed by his Teddy Bear Orchestra, Pendergrass concerts were marked by intense female fan reaction. "For Women Only" concerts were instituted, with ladies given stuffed teddy bears to fondle during the show. Pendergrass' *TP* album contained another love song, "Love TKO" (#44 pop, #2 R&B, 1980) and a duet with Stephanie Mills on "Feel the Fire." They also collaborated on the single "Two Hearts" (#40 pop, #2 R&B, 1980).

In 1982, "You're My Latest, My Greatest Inspiration" (#4 R&B) made the charts. Pendergrass made his film debut in *Soup for One*. He also sang one song, "Dream Girl," on the Chic-produced soundtrack.

On March 18, 1982, Pendergrass' spinal cord was severely injured and he was paralyzed from the neck down when his car smashed into a highway divider outside Philadelphia.

THE PENGUINS

Formed 1954, Los Angeles
Cleveland Duncan (b. July 23, 1935), lead voc.; Curtis Williams (b. 1935), voc.; Dexter Tisby (b. 1936), voc.; Bruce Tate (b. 1935), voc.
N.A.—*Cool, Cool Penguins* (Dootone).

After attracting a strong local following in the early Fifties, the Penguins scored a big R&B hit with Curtis Williams' and Jesse Belvin's "Earth Angel." The song was #1 R&B, #8 pop in 1954, and had sold over four million copies by the mid-Sixties. Unfortunately, the Crew-Cuts covered that same song a year later and made it a bigger pop hit (something they'd earlier done with the Chords' "Sh-Boom").

The Penguins switched from Dootone to Mercury to Atlantic Records, never achieving follow-up success commensurate with their one and only hit. After making one release for Atlantic and one for Sun State Records, they returned to California nearly broke and split up. Lead singer Duncan re-formed the band several times. In 1963, they recorded a song written for them by Frank Zappa and Ray Collins (later of the Mothers of Invention), "Memories of El Monte." For some twenty years, the Penguins have made steady appearances at Fifties revival concerts.

PENTANGLE

Formed 1967, England
Bert Jansch (b. Nov. 3, 1943, Glasgow), gtr., voc.; John Renbourn (b. London), gtr.; Jacqui McShee (b. Dec. 25, London), voc.; Danny Thompson (b. Devon, Eng.), bass; Terry Cox (b. Buckinghamshire, Eng.), drums, percussion.
1968—*The Pentangle* (Reprise) *Sweet Child* **1969**—*Basket of Light* **1970**—*Cruel Sister* **1971**—*Reflections* **1972**—*Solomon's Seal; History Book* (Transatlantic, U.K.) **1973**—*Pentangling* **1975**—*Collection* **1978**—*Anthology*.

With the virtuoso acoustic guitars of Bert Jansch and John Renbourn, folksinger Jacqui McShee and the jazz-based rhythm section of Danny Thompson and Terry Cox (ex–Alexis Korner Blues Band), Pentangle achieved solid cult status with a unique repertoire that included traditional English folk songs, jazz, blues and occasional originals, all intricately arranged. They rarely used amplification until they used muted electric guitars on *Cruel Sister*. Their

debut LP did fairly well in the U.K. charts; the rest achieved modest U.S. and U.K. success.

Upon their breakup in 1972, Thompson worked with Nick Drake and John Martyn, while Jansch and Renbourn reunited (they'd made a duo LP, *Bert and John*, in 1966) for tours and LPs. Renbourn had begun making solo LPs while with Pentangle, and he has over a dozen of his own records out, including *Sir John—a Lot of Merrie Englandes* (1968) and *Faro Annie* (1972), the most recent being 1980's *Enchanted Garden* (all on Transatlantic). Jansch also recorded extensively on his own, notably with *Rosemary Lane* (Warner Bros.).

PERE UBU

Formed 1975, Cleveland, Ohio
David Thomas/Crocus Behemoth (b. circa 1953), voc.; Tom Herman, gtr., bass; Scott Krauss, drums; Peter Laughner (d. June 1977), gtr.; Dave Taylor, synth., organ; Tim Wright, bass; Alan Greenblatt, gtr.; Allen Ravenstine, synth.; Tony Maimone, bass.
1978—*The Modern Dance* (Blank/Mercury) (+ Greenblatt, gtr.) *Datapanik in the Year Zero* (EP) (Radar, U.K.) **1979**—*Datapanik in the Year Zero* (LP) (Hearthan) *Dub Housing* (Chrysalis) *New Picnic Time* (Chrysalis, U.K.) (– Herman; + Mayo Thompson, gtr., voc.) **1980**—*The Art of Walking* (Rough Trade) **1981**—*390 Degrees of Simulated Stereo* (recorded 1976-79) (– Maimone; – Krauss; + Anton Fier, drums) **1982**—*The Song of the Bailing Man*.
David Thomas solo: *The Sound of the Sand* (Rough Trade) **1982**—*Vocal Performances* (EP).

Pere Ubu's music is a unique mixture of control and anarchy, incorporating driving rock, industrial noises, falling-apart song structures and David Thomas' careening vocals and wide-eyed lyrics.

Founding members David Thomas and Peter Laughner were both rock journalists (Laughner with *Creem*) and formed the band to record Thomas' "30 Seconds over Tokyo" b/w "Heart of Darkness," released independently in 1975 on Hearthan and reissued on *Datapanik*. They named the band after the hero of *Ubu Roi*, a play by French absurdist Alfred Jarry, and Ubu became part of the fertile Ohio rock scene that also fostered Tin Huey and Devo. In early 1976, the initial Pere Ubu lineup recorded another two-sided single, "Final Solution"/"Cloud 149," then disbanded for three months. In July 1976, they regrouped as the quintet that recorded their first three albums. Tim Wright moved to New York and joined DNA. In 1977, Laughner died under mysterious circumstances; some speculated suicide, others a drug overdose.

The Modern Dance sold only 15,000 copies in the U.S., although it was more popular in England; by touring the U.S. and, in 1978, England, Pere Ubu became well known on the burgeoning new wave circuit. After their British shows, they signed with Chrysalis.

Herman left for solo work in 1979, making an album with some Cleveland avant-punk cohorts (*Frontier Justice*) before moving to Houston. He was replaced by Mayo Thompson, formerly of Texan avant-rockers Red Crayola, with whom Pere Ubu toured Europe; Ubu members appeared on Red Crayola's *Soldier Talk.* After *The Art of Walking,* Maimone and Krauss left to form their own group, House and Garden.

In 1981, Thomas, an avowed Jehovah's Witness, recorded a solo album, *The Sound of the Sand,* backed by British folk-rocker Richard Thompson among others, and did a few solo concerts in 1982 backed only by prerecorded tapes and Tin Huey saxophonist Ralph Carney. *The Song of the Bailing Man* was Pere Ubu's first album they didn't produce themselves.

CARL PERKINS

Born April 9, 1932, Lake City, Tennessee
1959—*Whole Lotta Shakin'* (Columbia)   **1968**—
Country Boy Dreams   **1969**—*On Top*   **1970**—*Boppin' the Blues* (with NRBQ)   **1976**—*Original Carl Perkins* (Charly)   **1979**—*Sun Story, Volume 3* (Sun).

Carl Perkins, the writer and singer of the 1956 #2 hit "Blue Suede Shoes" was, along with Jerry Lee Lewis, Johnny Cash and Elvis Presley, one of the seminal rockabilly artists on Sam Phillips' Sun label.

Perkins grew up poor in the only white sharecropping family on a West Tennessee plantation, where he heard both hillbilly country and Delta blues. He kicked off his career playing at local dances with his brothers Jay and Clayton and later performed on a local radio show, which led to the contract with Memphis' Sun Records in 1955. With his brothers providing backup, he recorded "Blue Suede Shoes," the first song to top the pop, country and R&B charts simultaneously.

Tragedy struck on March 21, 1956, when, driving to a television studio to tape a performance on Perry Como's show, Perkins was involved in a car accident that killed his brother Jay. It took Perkins nine months to recover from his own injuries, during which time Presley cut "Blue Suede Shoes" and sold even more than Perkins had. Perkins had several more minor rockabilly hits, on Sun and Columbia, but by the early Sixties he'd hit a low point.

On a British tour in 1963, he became friendly with the Beatles and oversaw the sessions where they recorded five of his songs—"Matchbox," "Honey Don't," "Your True Love," "Blue Suede Shoes" and "Everybody's Trying to Be My Baby." Ricky Nelson and Johnny Burnette also covered his songs. But Perkins turned to country material as the rockabilly trend died, and by 1964 he was part of Johnny Cash's touring troupe. When Cash got his national television show in 1969, Perkins became a regular guest. He also cut some country records and recorded an album with NRBQ. After the Cash show ended, he toured as Johnny's guitarist until 1975.

In late 1978, Perkins released a basic rock & roll LP called *Ol' Blue Suede's Back,* which sold 100,000 copies in England. He also toured then with his two sons, Stan and Greg, backing him. In 1981, he did some sessions for McCartney's *Tug of War*; and in early 1982, an album entitled *Survivors,* recorded live in Germany with Jerry Lee Lewis and Johnny Cash, was released. He also toured solo in the early Eighties, and many of his early recordings appeared on Epic's three-volume *Rockabilly Stars* compilations.

LEE "SCRATCH" PERRY

Born 1940, Jamaica
1971—*Africa Blood* (Trojan)   **1975**—*Scratch on the Wire* (Island)   **1976**—*Super Ape* (Mango)   *Roast Fish, Collie Weed and Corn Bread* (Lion of Judah)   **1977**—*Double Seven* (Trojan)   *Return of the Super Ape* (Mango)   **1981**—*The Upsetter Collection* (Trojan).

Under many names, disc jockey/producer/record businessman/songwriter/singer Lee Perry has been a guiding force in the development of reggae. He began his career in his teens as "Little Lee Perry," a DJ for Coxsone Dodd's Downbeat Sound System. When he made his recording debut with "The Chicken Scratch" on Dodd's Studio One label in the early Sixties, he became known as Scratch Perry. For most of the Sixties, he worked at Studio One as A&R director and producer of Jamaican hits for Justin Hines, Delroy Wilson and Shenley Dufus, among others; he also recorded his own material like "Trials and Crosses" and "Doctor Dick."

In 1968, Perry left Dodd and worked briefly—as producer and performer—with Joe Gibbs, Byron Lee and Clancy Eccles, until he built his Black Ark Studio in the

Carl Perkins

backyard of his Kingston home and founded his own record company.

With the success of Perry's first independent release, an instrumental called "The Upsetter," he acquired another sobriquet—the Upsetter. He named his label Upsetter and his studio band the Upsetters. That same year—1968—he had a hit with "People Funny Boy," billing himself as Lee "King" Perry. An unusually slow song for its time, "People Funny Boy" was one of the first real reggae hits. Most of Perry's late-Sixties hits, like "Clint Eastwood," "Live Injection" and "Return of Django" (#5 U.K., 1969), were instrumentals that set his spaghetti-Western-style themes in reggae as dry, spacious and ominous as the Western desert.

Perry was one of the pioneers of the reggae instrumental studio art known as dubbing—reworking a taped track by removing some parts and exaggerating others—and his work in the Seventies with toasters like U-Roy, Prince Jazzbo, I-Roy, Big Youth and Dennis Alcapone established him in the forefront of toasters' dub; he would make hit after hit from the same rhythm track until the tape wore out. Perry recorded his own toasting under the pseudonym of Jah Lion. He also recorded as Pipecock Jackson and under his own name; his most popular releases in the Seventies, "Station Underground News" and "Roast Fish and Corn Bread," were vocals.

In 1969, Perry began working with the Wailers. During the next three years, he oversaw their transformation from a ska vocal trio into a full-fledged five-piece reggae band—with bassist Aston "Family Man" Barrett and his drummer brother Carlton from the Upsetters—that would become the most acclaimed Jamaican group in the world. "Duppy Conqueror," "Small Axe," "Kaya" and "Sun Is Shining" were some of the Wailers' songs Perry wrote. The Wailers began producing themselves for their own label in 1971, but they were reunited with Perry for occasional sessions in the late Seventies. Perry also produced hits for Junior Byles, Max Romeo, the Heptones, Gregory Isaacs, Junior Murvin and the Clash.

THE PERSUASIONS

Formed 1962, Brooklyn, New York
Jerry Lawson (b. Jan. 23, 1944, Fort Lauderdale, Fla.);
Jayotis Washington (b. May 12, 1945, Detroit); Joseph "Jesse" Russell (b. Sep. 25, 1939, Henderson, N.C.);
Herbert "Tubo" Rhoad (b. Oct. 1, 1944, Bamberg County, S.C.); Jimmy Hayes (b. Nov. 12, 1943, Hopewell, Va.); Willie Daniels.
1968—A cappella (Straight) 1971—We Came to Play (Capitol) 1972—Street Corner Symphony; Spread the Word 1973—We Still Ain't Got No Band (MCA)
1974—More than Before (A&M) I Just Want to Sing with My Friends (− Washington; + Willie Daniels)
1977—Chirpin' (Elektra) (− Daniels; + Washington) 1979—Comin' at Ya (Flying Fish).

Since 1962, the Persuasions' unique brand of a cappella—they still perform without a band—has made them a popular live attraction and sought after as backup singers. Tenors Jesse Russell and Jayotis Washington, baritones Tubo Rhoad and Jerry Lawson, and nonpareil bass Jimmy Hayes started the group in Brooklyn, where all had migrated. Each had sung with gospel and secular vocal groups, and from the beginning the Persuasions have mixed doo-wop, soul and pop into their repertoire.

The Persuasions' first recording was a single on Minit/United Artist Records in 1966. In 1967, they were taped at a Jersey City performance by doo-wop fan David Dashev, who got the tape to Frank Zappa, who released it as A cappella in 1968 on his Straight Records. When Warner Bros. purchased Straight, they wanted to record the Persuasions with a band, but the group refused.

From 1971 to 1973, the Persuasions made three records for Capitol. With MCA Records in 1973, they cut one album, We Still Ain't Got No Band. The following year, Washington left the group and was replaced by Willie Daniels; Daniels left in 1975, Washington returned in 1977.

Two mid-Seventies albums with A&M, More Than Before and I Just Want to Sing with My Friends, included instrumental backing and resulted in two singles making the lower end of the R&B chart. From 1974 on, the Persuasions worked steadily as guest vocalists behind Stevie Wonder, Phoebe Snow, Ellen McIlwaine, Don McLean and others. They cut the critically acclaimed Chirpin' for Elektra in 1977, with Dashev producing. After backing Joni Mitchell on a 1979–80 tour, the Persuasions were featured on her Shadows and Light live album, including the single "Why Do Fools Fall in Love?" They continue a busy touring schedule.

PETER AND GORDON

Formed 1964, England
Peter Asher (b. June 22, 1944, London), voc., gtr.;
Gordon Waller (b. June 4, 1945, Braemar, Scot.), voc., gtr.
1964—A World without Love (Capitol) 1965—Peter and Gordon; True Love Ways 1966—The Best of Peter and Gordon 1967—Lady Godiva.

Peter and Gordon were an enormously successful British pop/folk team in the mid-Sixties. After their breakup, Gordon all but vanished into obscurity, but Peter Asher has kept his name in the limelight as a manager/producer of Linda Ronstadt, James Taylor and others.

Both Peter and Gordon came from upper-middle-class families and were products of private schools, the two meeting at Westminster School for Boys in London. They worked together as a campus duo, in an Everly Brothers vein, and decided to try the London club scene. Because of their school's 9 P.M. dorm curfew, they had to sneak over a 12-foot spiked fence to do it, which they managed successfully for around a year. Eventually they left school to concentrate on music, recording demos and making the record company rounds.

Asher and Waller landed a contract in 1963 and within a year had their first and biggest hit, "World without Love," written by Paul McCartney, who at the time was courting Asher's sister Jane. The tune went to #1 in the U.K. and the Top Ten in the U.S. in 1964. They became a big concert attraction in England and in America as well, touring the U.S. in 1964 and appearing on "The Ed Sullivan Show," "Hullabaloo" and "Shindig."

Between 1964 and 1967, the duo had a string of hit singles: "Nobody I Know" (#12) and "I Don't Want to See You Again" (#16) in 1964; Del Shannon's "I Go to Pieces" (#9), "True Love Ways" (#14) and "To Know You Is to Love You" (#24) in 1965; and "Woman" (#14) and "Lady Godiva" (#6) in 1966. "Knight in Rusty Armour" (#15) and "Sunday for Tea" (#31) in 1967 were their last big hits. For the most part, they found greater and more consistent success in the U.K. In 1968, they broke up. (See also: Peter Asher.)

PETER, PAUL and MARY
Formed 1961, New York City
Peter Yarrow (b. May 31, 1938, New York City), voc., gtr.; Paul Stookey (b. Nov. 30, 1937, Baltimore), voc., gtr.; Mary Travers (b. Nov. 7, 1937, Louisville, Ky.), voc.
1962—Peter, Paul and Mary (Warner Bros.) 1963—Peter, Paul and Mary—Moving; Peter, Paul and Mary—In the Wind 1965—Peter, Paul and Mary in Concert; A Song Will Rise; See What Tomorrow Brings 1966—The Peter, Paul and Mary Album 1967—Album 1700 1968—Late Again 1969—Peter, Paul and Mommy; Ten Years Together 1978—Reunion.

Peter, Paul and Mary became the most popular acoustic folk group of the Sixties. They were also the first to bring commercial success to Bob Dylan, by covering his "Blowin' in the Wind," a #2 hit in August 1963.

The trio were brought together in Greenwich Village in 1961 by manager Albert Grossman. Yarrow had had some success as a solo folk artist. After graduating in psychology from Cornell, he toured locally and appeared on the CBS special "Folk Sound U.S.A." in May 1960. Grossman spotted Yarrow there and arranged for him to perform at the Newport Folk Festival and make a national tour. Stookey was a stand-up comic in Greenwich Village and previously had led a high school rock & roll group.

Mary Travers had sung in school choruses and folk groups. She sang in the chorus of a 1957 Broadway flop called The Next President with Mort Sahl. In 1961, she met Stookey, who encouraged her to sing again, and Grossman decided she was right to round out the trio. They rehearsed for seven months, with Milt Okun crafting their arrangements. Soon after they played a special en-

gagement at New York's Bitter End, they signed with Warner Bros. Records.

The group's debut LP came out in May 1962, and in June "Lemon Tree" got to #35 on the singles chart. Their first big hit was in October with Pete Seeger's "If I Had a Hammer," which went to #10, bringing the folk and protest consciousness to the mainstream. They often toured college campuses and played at rallies.

After "Blowin' in the Wind" reached #2, their cover of Dylan's "Don't Think Twice It's Alright" hit #9 in 1963. In May of that year "Puff the Magic Dragon" (#2) stirred some controversy, since it was interpreted by some as a drug song. In fact it was just one of their many children's songs. (They released a whole LP of these in May 1969 called Peter, Paul and Mommy.) They were also known for love songs, like "Leavin' on a Jet Plane," which went to #1 in December 1969. They also did early covers of Gordon Lightfoot. His "Early Morning Rain" only went to #91 in 1965, but "For Lovin' Me" hit the Top Thirty.

The group decided to break up in 1970 and released a best-of collection that May. They all pursued solo album careers, with considerably less artistic and commercial success. Stookey's records (as Noël Paul Stookey) reflected his Christian religious convictions. His best-known solo song was "Wedding Song (There Is Love)," written for Yarrow's marriage. Yarrow also co-produced and wrote Mary MacGregor's 1977 hit "Torn between Two Lovers." In 1970 Yarrow pleaded guilty to charges of "taking immoral liberties" with a 14-year-old girl. He served a 3-month jail term. Travers had a radio talk show for a while. They reunited occasionally in the Seventies, at benefits such as the 1972 George McGovern campaign fund-raiser, which also brought back Simon and Garfunkel and Mike Nichols and Elaine May. In 1978, they got together and released an LP of new recordings and toured nationally. Other reunions have occurred, but no newer recordings to date.

RAY PETERSON
Born April 23, 1939, Denton, Texas

A late-Fifties singer with a 4½-octave voice, Ray Peterson specialized in ballads like "The Wonder of You" (a hit for Elvis Presley in 1970) and the classic death-rock song "Tell Laura I Love Her."

Peterson began singing while a polio patient in Warm Springs Foundation Hospital in Texas, to amuse the other patients. He started performing in local clubs and eventually moved to Los Angeles, where he was signed by Stan Shulman of RCA Records. His first record was 1958's "Let's Try Romance," followed by "Tail Light," a cover of the R&B standard "Fever" and the hard-rocking "Shirley Purley," none of which made the charts.

Peterson's first hit was "The Wonder of You" by Baker Knight (#25, 1959). He followed with "Tell Laura I Love

Her'' (#7, 1960), by Ellie Greenwich and Jeff Barry; the Phil Spector–produced "Corinna, Corinna" (#9, 1961); "Missing You" (#29, 1961); and "I Could Have Loved You So Well" (#57, 1962) by Gerry Goffin and Barry Mann. In 1961, Peterson had formed his own label, Dunes, which released all records after and including "Corinna, Corinna," and to which he signed Curtis "Pretty Little Angel Eyes" Lee. After some more discs for MGM failed, Peterson briefly tried a career as a country singer.

TOM PETTY AND THE HEARTBREAKERS

Formed 1975, Los Angeles
Tom Petty (b. 1952, Gainesville, Fla.), voc., gtr.; Mike Campbell, gtr.; Benmont Tench, kybds.; Ron Blair, bass; Stan Lynch, drums.
1976—*Tom Petty and the Heartbreakers* (Shelter)
1978—*You're Gonna Get It!* **1979**—*Damn the Torpedoes* (Backstreet) **1981**—*Hard Promises* **1982**—(– Blair; + Howie Epstein, bass) *Long after Dark.*

Tom Petty emerged in the Seventies with a distillate of FM-radio Sixties rock—chiming Byrds guitars, kicking Rolling Stones rhythms and his own more slurred version of Bob Dylan/Roger McGuinn vocals—and songs about long-suffering lovers. By the end of the decade, his albums regularly went platinum.

Petty, the son of a Florida insurance salesman, quit high school at 17 to join one of the state's top bands, Mudcrutch. (He'd previously played in a bar band called the Epics.) Mudcrutch also included future Heartbreakers Mike Campbell and Benmont Tench. In the early Seventies, the group sent Petty to L.A. to seek out a record contract, which they got with Denny Cordell's Shelter Records (co-owned with Leon Russell).

The band broke up soon after moving to L.A., and while Cordell offered to record Petty solo, nothing happened until 1975, when Petty heard a demo that Campbell and Tench were working on with Ron Blair and Stan Lynch. The fivesome became the Heartbreakers, inherited Petty's Shelter contract and released the self-titled debut in fall 1976. At first it sold poorly.

Then the Heartbreakers toured England, opening for Nils Lofgren. Within weeks, they were headlining and the LP was on the British charts. ABC then re-released the single "Breakdown" in the U.S., and it cracked the Top Forty nearly a year after its initial release. Another song on the LP, the very Byrdsy "American Girl," was recorded by ex-Byrd Roger McGuinn. The band's second LP boasted the singles "Listen to Her Heart" (#59, 1978) and "I Need to Know" (#41, 1978).

Just as Petty and the Heartbreakers' career seemed to be taking off, a legal battle arose when Petty tried to renegotiate his contract after ABC was sold to MCA; by mid-1979 he filed for bankruptcy. After nine months of litigation, Petty signed to Backstreet Records, a new MCA affiliate. His triumphant return LP, 1979's *Damn the*

Torpedoes, was a critical success, hitting #2, selling over 2½ million copies, and establishing Petty as a major star. He had two Top Twenty hits: "Don't Do Me Like That" (1979) and "Refugee" (1980).

But Petty again got into record company trouble in 1981 when he challenged his label's intention to issue *Hard Promises* with a $9.98 list price. After he threatened to withhold the LP (or entitle it *Eight Ninety Eight*) and organized fan protest letters, the album came out at $8.98. *Hard Promises* went on to platinum status as well, with the #19 hit "The Waiting." Also in 1981, Petty sang a duet with Stevie Nicks on her solo LP *Bella Donna*, "Stop Draggin' My Heart Around." The Heartbreakers also appeared on *Bella Donna*. That year Petty produced Del Shannon's 1981 comeback LP, *Drop Down and Get Me*. In late 1982, Petty had a hit with "You Got Lucky."

LITTLE ESTHER PHILLIPS

Born December 23, 1935, Galveston, Texas
1970—*Burnin'* (Atlantic) **1972**—*From a Whisper to a Scream* (Kudu) *Alone Again (Naturally)* **1973**—*Black Eyed Blues* **1974**—*Performance* **1975**—*What a Difference a Day Makes* **1976**—*For All We Know; Confessin' the Blues* (Atlantic) *Capricorn Princess* (Kudu) **1977**—*You've Come a Long Way Baby* (Mercury) **1978**—*All About Esther* **1979**—*Here's Esther . . . Are You Ready.*

Throughout her long career, singer Esther Phillips has covered blues, rhythm & blues and jazz, each in her own earthy style.

As a child in Texas, Phillips sang in churches before her family moved to Los Angeles in the late Forties. At 13, she won a talent show at Los Angeles' Barrelhouse Club, run by R&B impresario Johnny Otis. For the next three years, she recorded with Otis' orchestra as Little Esther Phillips and built a national following among black record buyers. Two duets with another Otis discovery, Mel Walker, resulted in Top Ten R&B hits "Cupid's Boogie" (#2 R&B, 1950) and "Ring-A-Ding-Doo" (#8 R&B, 1952). As a solo, Phillips had a #1 R&B hit record with "Double Crossing Blues" in 1950.

Because of illness, she retired in 1954 and settled in Houston. She returned to music in the early Sixties with New York's Lenox Records and in 1962 enjoyed international success with "Release Me" (#8 pop, #1 R&B), a reworking of a country hit. A 1963 duet with Big Al Downing on "You Never Miss Your Water (Until Your Well Runs Dry)" is well remembered, though it was not a hit at the time. She signed with Atlantic in the mid-Sixties and had success with a cover of the Beatles' "And I Love Her," done as "And I Love Him" (#11 R&B).

In the late Sixties, Phillips' recordings suffered as she battled a heroin addiction at Synanon. In 1971, she signed with Kudu Records, where she cut a series of bluesy jazz albums. Her chilling interpretation of Gil Scott-Heron's antidrug "Home Is Where the Hate Is" (#40 R&B) is considered by many to be one of her finest efforts. "I Never Found a Man (To Love Me Like You Do)" (#17 R&B) in 1972 showed that Phillips still had commercial appeal. This fact was further demonstrated by her 1975 disco hit "What a Difference a Day Makes" (#20 pop, #10 R&B). In 1981, an album on Mercury Records was produced by jazz trumpeter Benny Golson. In 1982, she duetted with Swamp Dogg on one song from his *I'm Not Selling Out, I'm Buying In*.

SAM PHILLIPS

Born January 5, 1923, Florence, Alabama

According to more than one observer, rock & roll music began at the Sun Studios in Memphis. Sun was founded by Sam Phillips, one of the first white men to record black blues and R&B artists like Howlin' Wolf, and the first to record the black-influenced music of such young white Southerners—and seminal rockabilly stars—as Elvis Presley, Jerry Lee Lewis and Carl Perkins.

Growing up on a farm in Alabama, Phillips first heard black music from an old blind sharecropper called Uncle Silas Payne, who told Sam stories and sang him blues and field hollers. He later frequented Memphis' blues clubs on Beale Street.

Phillips originally planned to become a criminal defense lawyer, but upon his father's death he became a teenaged disc jockey at WLAY in Muscle Shoals, Alabama. He earned certification as a radio engineer through a correspondence course and moved on to WLAC in Nashville, and by 1944 to WREC in Memphis.

Phillips built his own recording studio in a converted radiator shop on Memphis' Union Avenue and began recording local black performers. The studio was so small no business could be conducted there; money matters were discussed next door at Miss Taylor's Restaurant— "third booth from the window." Though his coworkers often greeted him with remarks like "You smell good today, guess you haven't been hanging around with those niggers," Phillips persevered and was soon leasing sides to Chess, Modern and RPM. In June 1951, his studio recorded what some consider the seminal rock & roll hit, Jackie Brenston's "Rocket 88"—which had a driving train-rhythm beat, hooting sax and a lyric extolling a car. In December of that year, Phillips quit WREC to start his own label, Sun Records, which used the same facilities as his Memphis Recording Service. His initial roster included mostly black artists like Rufus Thomas (who had a minor hit in 1953 on Sun with "Bear Cat"), Chester "Howlin' Wolf" Burnett (discovered by Ike Turner, then working for Phillips as a talent scout and bandleader), Junior Parker, Isaiah "Dr." Ross, Walter Horton and Jimmy DeBerry. With Sun, Phillips pioneered the echo-laden sound that became a hallmark of classic rockabilly.

By 1954, other black-music labels like Chess, Checker,

Grammy Awards

Dolly Parton
1978 Best Country Vocal Performance, Female:
Here You Come Again
1981 Best Country Vocal Performance, Female; Best Country Song:
"9 to 5"

Les Paul
1976 Best Country Instrumental Performance:
Chester and Lester (with Chet Atkins)

Peter, Paul and Mary
1962 Best Performance by a Vocal Group; Best Folk Recording:
"If I Had a Hammer"

1963 Best Performance by a Vocal Group; Best Folk Recording: "Blowin' in the Wind"
1969 Best Recording for Children:
Peter, Paul and Mommy

Pointer Sisters
1974 Best Country Vocal Performance by a Duo or Group:
"Fairytale"

Police
1980 Best Rock Instrumental Performance:
"Reggatta de Blanc"
1981 Best Rock Performance by a Duo or Group with Vocal:
"Don't Stand so Close to Me"
Best Rock Instrumental Performance:
"Behind My Camel"

Elvis Presley
1967 Best Sacred Performance:
"How Great Thou Art"
1972 Best Inspirational Performance:
"He Touched Me"
1974 Best Inspirational Performance:
"How Great Thou Art"

Billy Preston
1972 Album of the Year:
The Concert for Bangla Desh (with others)
Best Pop Instrumental Performance by an Instrumental Performer:
"Outa-Space"

Atlantic and Specialty had sprung up, so after much soul searching Phillips decided to forego black music in favor of producing the young whites from the area who sang in a distinctively black-influenced manner.

In August 1954, Elvis Presley recorded a demo at the Recording Service. Phillips later asked Presley to record some other demos, but it wasn't until over a year later that he signed him. In a year and a half, Presley made five smash singles with Phillips before RCA bought out his contract for $35,000.

Phillips also worked with Jerry Lee Lewis, Carl Perkins, Johnny Cash, Roy Orbison, Charlie Rich, Carl Smith and Billy Lee Riley, among many others. All these artists eventually left Sun, some complaining of lack of artistic control, but Phillips' place in history was assured.

Phillips finally sold Sun Records in 1969. With the recording royalties and his original shares in Holiday Inn stock, he was a wealthy man, though he continues to live in a modest Memphis home. In the mid-Seventies, the Amazing Rhythm Aces recorded several albums at Sun Studios; in 1979, John Prine recorded his *Pink Cadillac* there, with Phillips producing two tracks and his sons Knox and Jerry producing the rest.

BOBBY "BORIS" PICKETT
Born February 11, 1940, Somerville, Massachusetts
1962—*Monster Mash* (Garpax; reissued 1973 by London).

Bobby "Boris" Pickett's ticket to fame was an ability to imitate monster-movie star Boris Karloff, something he put to good use on the novelty hit "Monster Mash," a #1 in 1962 and #10 when reissued in 1973.

After three years in the Signal Corps in Korea, Pickett had drifted to Hollywood, where he attempted to establish himself as a comedian and actor. After joining a singing group called the Cordials, he and group member Leonard Capizzi wrote "Monster Mash." Gary Paxton—Flip of Skip and Flip fame and the lead singer on the Hollywood Argyles' novelty hit "Alley Oop"—released it on his own Garpax label. There were a few less successful followups: "Monster's Holiday" (#30, 1962), "Monster Motion" (1963) and "Graduation Day" (#88, 1963). Pickett has since worked as an actor.

WILSON PICKETT
Born March 18, 1941, Prattville, Alabama
1965—*In the Midnight Hour* (Atlantic)   **1966**—*The Exciting Wilson Pickett*   **1967**—*The Best of Wilson Pickett*   **1969**—*Hey Jude*   **1971**—*Best of Wilson Pickett, Volume 2*   **1973**—*Wilson Pickett's Greatest Hits*   **1974**—*Don't Knock My Love.*

Singer Wilson Pickett's rough, swaggering "wicked" style made him one of the Sixties' great soul singers.

After his family migrated from Alabama to Detroit in the Fifties, young Pickett formed a gospel group, the Violinaires, who were popular in local churches. In 1959, he was recruited by the R&B vocal group the Falcons. He wrote and sang lead on the Falcons' "I Found a Love" (#6 R&B in 1962). Falcons producer Robert Bateman suggested he go solo, and Pickett signed with Lloyd Price's Double L Records in 1963 and had hits with two of his songs, "If You Need Me" (#30 R&B) and "It's Too Late" (#17 R&B).

In 1964, Pickett signed with Atlantic. Following two unsuccessful singles, Atlantic executive/producer Jerry Wexler took Pickett to Memphis, where he recorded with Booker T. and the MGs. "In the Midnight Hour," credited to Pickett and guitarist/producer Steve Cropper, was a major breakthrough. Recording in a similar style with musicians in Memphis, Muscle Shoals and Miami, Pickett had a long series of R&B hits that occasionally crossed over to pop, including "634-5789" (#13 pop, #1 R&B) and "Land of 1,000 Dances" (#6 pop, #1 R&B) in 1966; "Funky Broadway" (#8 pop, #1 R&B) in 1967; "I'm a Midnight Mover" (#6 R&B) in 1968; and the tribute record "Cole, Cooke, and Redding" (#61 pop, #4 R&B) in 1970.

In March 1971, Pickett headlined a tour of American and African musicians in Ghana. The resulting film and album, *Soul to Soul*, featured Pickett prominently. Later that year, he recorded in Philadelphia with the Gamble and Huff production team, scoring with "Engine Number 9" (#14 pop, #3 R&B) and "Don't Let the Green Grass Fool You" (#17 pop, #2 R&B). Pickett's last three Atlantic hits were "Don't Knock My Love" (#13 pop, #1 R&B), "Call My Name, I'll Be There" (#10 R&B) and "Fire and Water" (#2 R&B).

Pickett signed to RCA Records in 1973, and in the early Eighties switched to EMI America. He continues to tour and record.

PINK FLOYD
Formed 1965, London
Syd Barrett (b. Roger Keith Barrett, Jan. 6, 1946, Cambridge, Eng.), gtr., voc.; Richard Wright (b. July 28, 1945, London), kybds., voc.; Roger Waters (b. Sep. 6, 1944, Surrey, Eng.), bass, voc.; Nick Mason (b. Jan. 27, 1945, Birmingham, Eng.), drums.
1967—*The Piper at the Gates of Dawn* (Tower)   **1968**—(+ David Gilmour [b. Mar. 6, 1944, Cambridge, Eng.], gtr., voc.)   *A Saucerful of Secrets; Tonight Let's All Make Love in London* (Instant Analysis) (soundtrack)   **1969**—(− Barrett)   *More* (soundtrack)   *Ummagumma*   **1970**—*Atom Heart Mother; Zabriskie Point* (MGM) (soundtrack)   **1971**—*Meddle; Relics*   **1972**—*Music from La Vallee: Obscured by Clouds* (soundtrack)   **1973**—*The Dark Side of the Moon;   A Nice Pair* (reissue of first two LPs)   **1975**—*Wish You Were Here* (Columbia)   **1977**—*Animals*   **1979**—*The*

Pink Floyd: Rick Wright, Dave Gilmour, Nicky Mason, Roger Waters

Wall **1981**—*A Collection of Great Dance Songs* (compilation) **1983**—*The Final Cut; Works* (Capitol).

With the release of 1973's *The Dark Side of the Moon,* one of the biggest-selling pop albums ever, Pink Floyd abruptly went from a moderately successful acid-rock band to one of rock's biggest acts.

As early as 1964, Pink Floyd's original members, except Syd Barrett, were together studying architecture and playing music at London's Regent Street Polytechnic School. With Barrett, an art student who named the group the Pink Floyd Sound after a favorite blues record by Pink Anderson and Floyd Council, they began playing R&B-based material for schoolmates. By 1967, the band had developed an unmistakably psychedelic sound: long, loud suite-like compositions that touched on hard rock, blues, country, folk, electronic and quasi-classical music. They added a slide and light show, one of the first in rock, and became a sensation among London's underground as a featured attraction at the UFO Club. Barrett, who was responsible for most of the band's earlier material, also had a knack for composing short singles-length bits of psychedelia, and Pink Floyd had British hits with two of them in 1967: "Arnold Layne" and "See Emily Play." However, space-epic titles like "Astronomy Dominé" and "Interstellar Overdrive" were more typical Pink Floyd.

In 1968, Barrett, allegedly because of an excess of LSD experimentation, began to exhibit ever more strange and erratic behavior. David Gilmour joined to help with the guitar work. Barrett appeared on only one track of *Secrets,* "Jugband Blues," which prophetically and aptly summed up his mental state: "I'm most obliged to you for making it clear/That I'm not really here." He left, entered a hospital and remained in seclusion. He later made two solo albums—recording odd, eerie ravings on guitar, with backup added afterward by Floyd members—and currently lives in the care of his mother. With his talent for

psychedelic singles gone, the band concentrated on the psychedelic epics.

From 1969 to 1972, the band made several film soundtracks—the most dramatic being *Zabriskie Point,* in which Antonioni's closing sequence of explosions was complemented by Floyd's "Careful with That Axe, Eugene"—and began using its "azimuth coordinated sound system" in concert, a sophisticated 360-degree PA they have used ever since.

Their commercial breakthrough came in 1973 with *The Dark Side of the Moon.* The themes were unremittingly bleak—alienation, paranoia, schizophrenia—and the music was doomy. Taped voices mumbling ominous asides (something the band had used before) surfaced at key moments. The album yielded a surprise hit single in "Money," but the biggest shock was the album's mammoth long-running sales success; it eventually sold over four million copies and in 1980 became the longest-charting rock LP in *Billboard*'s history at 303 weeks, eclipsing the previous record of 302 weeks set by Carole King's *Tapestry.* As late as 1983 it was still on the album chart.

The band's subsequent LPs have explored the same territory and Waters' songs have grown ever more bitter. *Wish You Were Here* was dedicated to Barrett. *The Wall* yielded a hit single, "Another Brick in the Wall," which was banned by the BBC. Meanwhile, Pink Floyd's stage shows had become increasingly elaborate. For the *Dark Side* and *Wish* tours, there were slide/light shows and animated films, plus a giant inflated jet that crashed into the stage; for *Animals,* huge inflated pigs hovered over the stadiums; for *The Wall* (performed only in New York, Los Angeles and London), there was all that plus an actual wall built, brick by brick, across the stage, eventually obscuring the band from audience view. For those tours, the band was also augmented by other musicians: guitarist Snowy White (later with Thin Lizzy) on the *Wall* tour, and several singers and players for the rest.

In 1978, there were two solo LPs by Pink Floyd members: Gilmour's *David Gilmour* and Wright's *Wet Dream.* Both sold moderately. Mason had begun a sideline career as a producer in 1974 with ex–Soft Machine Robert Wyatt's *Rock Bottom;* in 1976, he produced *Shamal* by French-English progressive-jazz-rock band Gong; in 1976, he produced an album of Edward Gorey songs sung by Wyatt; in 1981, he made *Fictitious Sports* with Carla Bley.

Two films related to the band have been made: the 1973 concert/studio/interview documentary *Pink Floyd Live at Pompeii* and *The Wall,* in 1982, which was mostly animation (Boomtown Rats lead singer Bob Geldof starred in the live action sequences) and featured music from Pink Floyd's LP of the same name. The first remains a cult film; the second was a massive commercial success.

The Final Cut, subtitled "a requiem for the post-war dream," was Waters' gloomiest work yet, and immediately hit the charts.

GENE PITNEY

Born February 17, 1941, Hartford, Connecticut
1962—*Only Love Can Break a Heart* (Musicor) **1963**—
World Wide Winners **1964**—*Big 16; It Hurts to Be in
Love* **1966**—*Big 16, Volume 2* **1968**—*Double Gold:
The Best of Gene Pitney* **1969**—*Sings Bacharach*.

Gene Pitney's long and varied career includes over twenty
chart-making singles, and just as many albums, spanning
rock, pop ballads, Italian-flavored country novelties, and
work and friendship with Phil Spector, the Rolling Stones
and country singer George Jones. Best known for singing
pop covers, Pitney also wrote many tunes himself. His
biggest hits include "Town without Pity" (#13, 1962),
"(The Man Who Shot) Liberty Valance" (#4, 1962),
"Only Love Can Break a Heart" (#2, 1962), "Half
Heaven—Half Heartache" (#12, 1963), "Mecca" (#12,
1963), "It Hurts to Be in Love" (#7, 1964) and "I'm
Gonna Be Strong" (#9, 1964).

Pitney studied piano, guitar and drums while at Rock-
ville High School in Connecticut, and by the time he
graduated had already written and published some songs.
He dropped out of the University of Connecticut, and for a
time enrolled in Ward's Electronic School. He began
performing as the male half of the duo Jamie and Jane,
then as a singer/songwriter under the name Billy Brian. By
1961, he had written "Hello Mary Lou" for Rick Nelson.
In 1962, he wrote "He's a Rebel" for the Crystals, and
became friends with producer Phil Spector. He also wrote
for Roy Orbison and Tommy Edwards.

Yearning for a hit of his own, Pitney locked himself in a
studio in 1961, played and overdubbed every instrument
and multitracked his vocals. The result was his first hit, "(I
Wanna) Love My Life Away" (#39, 1961). This attracted
the attention of the songwriting team of Burt Bacharach
and Hal David, who cowrote "Only Love Can Break a
Heart," "(The Man Who Shot) Liberty Valance" and "24
Hours from Tulsa" for him. Pitney's label, Musicor, was
primarily involved in country & western music, and Pitney began recording material in that vein, including an
album of duets with George Jones.

In 1964, Pitney's publicist was Andrew Loog Oldham,
and through him he met the Rolling Stones. He recorded
the Jagger-Richards composition "That Girl Belongs to
Yesterday" and with Phil Spector sat in on one of their
1964 recording sessions.

Though he was much more popular in England than in
America, Pitney remained a prolific recording artist, putting out numerous albums per year in the mid-Sixties. At
that time, in response to his tremendous popularity in
Italy, he began recording albums of country tunes sung in
Italian. His last U.S. chart appearance was in 1969, and he
continued to hit the U.K. charts until 1974.

THE PLASMATICS

Formed 1978, New York City
Wendy Orleans Williams (b. N.Y.), voc., chainsaw,
machine gun; Richard Stotts, lead and rhythm gtr.;
Jean Beauvoir, bass; Wes Beech, rhythm gtr.; Stu
Deutsch, drums.
1981—*New Hope for the Wretched* (Stiff) *Beyond the
Valley of 1984* (− Deutsch; − Beauvoir) **1982**—*Coup
d'Etat* (Capitol).

The Plasmatics are a sex-and-violence-touting heavy-
metal band that debuted in the New York punk clubs in
1978. They are fronted by barely dressed ex–topless
dancer Wendy O. Williams (W.O.W. for short), whose act
includes smashing televisions with a sledgehammer, blowing up Cadillac Coup de Villes, cutting guitars in half with
a chainsaw, and singing.

Essentially, the band is the brainchild of manager Rod
Swenson, a graduate of Yale with a master's degree in fine
arts. During the Seventies, he came to New York, dubbed
himself Captain Kink and began producing and promoting
live sex shows. One of his stars was Williams (who was
raised on a farm in upstate New York and ran away at 16).
After his work in porn, Swenson did videos for Patti Smith
and the Ramones, which inspired him to start a band, with
Williams fingering herself and demolishing things up front,
backed by a guitarist (Richard Stotts) with a blue Mohawk
cut who wore a nurse's uniform and sometimes a tutu,
plus other visual gimmicks. The band's music is all fast
and loud, and the lyrics are about murder, sex and fast
food.

The Plasmatics debuted at CBGB on July 26, 1978, and
immediately got lots of coverage for their antics. An
audience began to grow, especially in England, where
they stressed their connection to heavy metal. Williams
kept up her stunts, as on September 12, 1980, when she
jumped out of a brakeless car just before it plunged into
the Hudson River. The band's debut album sold margin-

**The Plasmatics: Wes Beech, Jean Beauvoir, Wendy O.
Williams, Richey Stotts**

ally, as did their followup, *Beyond the Valley of 1984*. On January 18, 1981, Williams was arrested on obscenity charges in Milwaukee and on similar charges in Cleveland the next day. She and Swenson were also charged with resisting arrest and disorderly conduct after an altercation with the police, which landed both in a Milwaukee hospital. They later sued and won their case. In 1982, the band signed with Capitol. Beauvoir joined Little Steven and the Disciples of Soul in 1982.

THE PLATTERS

Formed 1953, Los Angeles
Tony Williams (b. Apr. 15, 1928, Roselle, N.J.); David Lynch (b. 1929, St. Louis, Mo.; d. Jan. 2, 1981); Herbert Reed (b. Kansas City, Mo.); Alex Hodge.
1954—(+ Zola Taylor) **1955**—(− Hodge; + Paul Robi [b. New Orleans]) **1960**—*Encore of Golden Hits* (Mercury) (− Williams; + Sonny Turner [b. circa 1939, Cleveland]) **1966**—(− Robi; − Taylor; + Nate Nelson [b. New York City]; + Sandra Dawn [b. New York City]).

During the Platters' peak years (1955 to 1960) they were led by Tony Williams and enjoyed a series of massive crossover hits.

Original members Tony Williams, David Lynch, Alex Hodge and Herb Reed were signed by manager Buck Ram to Federal Records in 1953. After some unsuccessful efforts, Ram replaced Hodge with Paul Robi and added Zola Taylor. The Platters' last Federal single, "Only You," was their first regional hit. Along with another vocal group Ram managed, the Penguins, they were signed in a package deal to Mercury.

At Mercury they became one of the nation's top vocal groups and a major nightclub attraction. A new version of "Only You" along with "The Great Pretender" made 1955 a breakthrough year. In 1956, they appeared in two rock films, *The Girl Can't Help It* and *Rock around the Clock*.

Other major hits for the Platters were "The Magic Touch" (#4 pop and R&B) and "My Prayer" (#1 pop, #2 R&B) in 1956; "Twilight Time" (#1 pop and R&B) and "Smoke Gets in Your Eyes" (#1 pop, #3 R&B) in 1958. Williams went solo in 1960 and was replaced as lead singer by Sonny Turner.

Off the charts from 1961 to 1966, the Platters returned with Sandra Dawn replacing Taylor and Nate Nelson taking Robi's spot. At the Musicor label they had a limited comeback with "I Love You 1000 Times" (#31 pop, #6 R&B, 1966) and "With This Ring" (#14 pop, #12 R&B, 1967). There followed wholesale personnel changes and releases on United Artist before a return to Mercury in 1974. Williams and Ram battled in court during the Seventies over the rights to the name Platters; Ram won the case. Both have versions of the Platters performing in the U.S. and abroad.

POCO

Formed 1968, Los Angeles
Richie Furay (b. May 9, 1944, Yellow Springs, Oh.), gtr., voc.; Jim Messina (b. Oct. 30, 1947, Harlingen, Tex.), gtr., voc.; Rusty Young (b. Feb. 23, 1946, Long Beach, Calif.), pedal steel gtr.; George Grantham (b. Nov. 20, 1947, Cordell, Ok.), drums, voc.; Randy Meisner (b. Mar. 8, 1946, Scottsbluff, Neb.), bass, voc.
1969—*Pickin' Up the Pieces* (Epic) (− Meisner; Messina switches to bass) **1970**—(+ Timothy B. Schmit [b. Oct. 30, 1947, Sacramento, Calif.], bass, voc.; Messina back to guitar) *Poco* (− Messina; + Paul Cotton [b. Feb. 26, 1943], ld. gtr., voc.) **1971**—*Deliverin'* (Epic) *From the Inside* (Epic) **1972**—*A Good Feeling to Know* **1973**—*Crazy Eyes* (− Furay) **1974**—*Seven; Cantamos* **1975**—*Head over Heels; The Very Best of Poco* **1976**—*Live; Rose of Cimarron* (ABC) **1977**—*Indian Summer* (− Schmit; − Grantham; + Steve Chapman [b. Eng.], drums; + Charlie Harrison [b. Eng.], bass; + Kim Bullard [b. Atlanta, Ga.], kybds.) **1978**—*Legend* **1980**—*Under the Gun* (MCA) **1981**—*Blue and Gray* **1982**—*Cowboys and Englishmen; Ghost Town* (Atlantic).

Country-rock band Poco started out in August 1968 with great commercial promise. Their founders were from Buffalo Springfield, and the L.A. country-rock scene was just beginning to peak. But despite steady sales, Poco never quite reached a mass audience.

The two ex-Springfield originators of Poco were Richie Furay and Jim Messina. Poco was rounded out by Rusty Young, who had played in Boenzee Cryque, a Colorado band that went to L.A., where they broke up; Young met Furay and Messina when he played pedal steel guitar on sessions for Buffalo Springfield's "Kind Woman." Young was asked to join another L.A. country-rock band, the Flying Burrito Brothers, but chose Poco. George Grantham was also from Boenzee Cryque, and Randy Meisner came from a rival Colorado band, the Poor. Furay also auditioned Gregg Allman (then with Allman Joys) for the band, but it didn't work out.

The new band originally called itself Pogo, but Walt Kelly, the creator of the comic strip, sued, and they changed it to Poco. Within a month, Meisner quit (he later joined Ricky Nelson's Stone Canyon Band and then the Eagles in 1971). Several record companies were considering signing them following the band's live L.A. debut in November 1968. Furay's Springfield contract with Atlantic complicated things, but Poco was allowed to sign with Epic after the label traded Graham Nash to Atlantic (to form Crosby, Stills and Nash) in exchange for Poco.

Poco's 1969 debut sold over 100,000 copies. Following Meisner's departure, the band continued as a quartet until February 1970, when Tim B. Schmit (a veteran of local folk, surf and pop groups) joined. Schmit had originally auditioned for Poco in 1968 but lost out to Meisner. This new five-member Poco recorded *Poco* and the live *Deliverin'* before Messina quit, claiming he was tired of touring. (Messina then teamed with Kenny Loggins.)

Messina's replacement was Paul Cotton, former lead guitarist in a Buffalo Springfield–type band, the Illinois Speed Press. This lineup lasted for three LPs. Just after recording *Crazy Eyes*, Furay, frustrated with the band's poor financial prospects, left to form a quasi-supergroup, the Souther-Hillman-Furay Band, which disbanded after two LPs.

Furay's departure was expected to be fatal, but Poco's next four albums as a quartet through 1977 sold somewhat better than previous efforts. During these years, the Eagles dominated the field that Poco was expected to mine; and in 1977, after Meisner left that band, Schmit joined the Eagles to replace him.

With lone original member Young plus Cotton at the helm, the band finally hit in early 1979 with their fourteenth LP, the R&B/rock-influenced *Legend*. The band now included an English rhythm section, Steve Chapman and Charlie Harrison (who'd played together eight years with Leo Sayer and Al Stewart), plus keyboardist Kim Bullard, who'd backed Crosby, Stills and Nash. The new lineup hit #17 with "Crazy Love" and then had a Top Twenty hit that year with "Heart of the Night."

THE POINTER SISTERS
Formed Oakland, California
Ruth Pointer (b. 1946); Anita Pointer (b. 1948); Bonnie Pointer (b. 1950); June Pointer (b. 1954).
1973—*The Pointer Sisters* (Blue Thumb) 1974—*That's a Plenty; Live at the Opera House* 1975—*Steppin'* 1976—*Best of the Pointer Sisters* 1977—*Having a Party* 1978—*Energy* (Planet) 1979—*Priority* 1980—*Special Things* 1981—*Black and White* 1982—*So Excited.*

The four Oakland-born Pointer sisters are a vocal group whose repertoire spans pop, jazz, country and R&B, and has evoked comparisons to the Supremes and the Andrews Sisters.

Both of the Pointer parents were ministers at the West Oakland Church of God; the sisters were raised in a strict

The Pointer Sisters: Ruth Pointer, Anita Pointer, June Pointer

religious environment and heard very little secular music until adulthood. Singing in church was their only performing experience until Bonnie and June began singing in San Francisco clubs in 1969 as Pointers, a Pair. Anita quit her job as a legal secretary to join them, and eventually San Francisco producer David Rubinson hired them as background vocalists on several records. In 1971 Bill Graham became their manager. From 1971 to 1973, the trio sang behind Elvin Bishop, Taj Mahal, Tower of Power, Dave Mason, Sylvester, Boz Scaggs and Esther Phillips.

When the Pointers backed Elvin Bishop at Los Angeles' Whisky-a-Go-Go, Atlantic executive Jerry Wexler heard them and signed them. Two singles were cut with R&B veteran Wardell Quezergue; one, "Don't Try to Take the Fifth," was unsuccessfully released in 1972. That year, Ruth left her job as a keypunch operator to join her sisters. Rubinson helped the Pointers get out of contracts with Graham and Atlantic, and signed them to ABC's Blue Thumb label.

In 1973, their self-titled debut, featuring Allen Toussaint's "Yes We Can Can" (#11 pop, #12 R&B) and Willie Dixon's "Wang Dang Doodle" (#61 pop, #24 R&B), brought national recognition. The sisters' neo-nostalgic penchant for Forties clothes, plus their wide repertoire, landed them on the Merv Griffin, Flip Wilson, Mike Douglas and Carol Burnett television shows. On tour they became the first black women to play Nashville's Grand Ole Opry and the first pop act to perform at San Francisco's Opera House. In 1974, PBS filmed a documentary on the Pointer family.

That year "Fairytale," written by Anita and Bonnie Pointer, went to #13 on the pop charts (#37 C&W) and won a Grammy as Best Country Single of 1974. The sisters' first two LPs that year went gold.

The next year brought a #1 R&B hit, "How Long (Betcha' Got a Chick on the Side)" (#20 pop). But between 1975 and 1977, June suffered a nervous breakdown, the group filed a lawsuit against ABC/Blue Thumb for back royalties, Bonnie wanted to go solo, and the Pointer Sisters were still being identified (and categorized) as a nostalgia group.

In 1978, Bonnie signed a solo contract with Motown. She had top charting records there in 1978—"Free Me from My Freedom/Tie Me to a Tree (Handcuff Me)" (#58 pop, #10 R&B)—and in 1979, with "Heaven Must Have Sent You" (#11 pop, #52 R&B), but hasn't had a release since 1979 because of legal battles with Motown.

Her sisters signed with producer Richard Perry's Planet Records, where they have enjoyed steady pop success. A cover of Bruce Springsteen's "Fire" (#2 pop, #14 R&B, 1979) started a string continued by Toussaint's "Happiness" (#30 pop, #20 R&B, 1979), "He's So Shy" (#3 pop, #10 R&B) and "Could I Be Dreaming" (#22 R&B) in 1980; "Slow Hand" (#2 pop, #7 R&B) in 1981; and "Should I Do It" (#13 pop), "American Music" (#16 pop, #23 R&B) and "I'm So Excited" in 1982.

THE POLICE

Formed 1977, England
Stewart Copeland (b. July 16, 1952, Va.), drums; Sting
(b. Gordon Sumner, Oct. 2, 1951, Wallsend, Eng.),
bass, voc., saxes, kybds.; Andy Summers (b. Dec. 31,
1942, Blackpool, Eng.), gtr.
1978—*Outlandos d'Amour* (A&M)   **1979**—*Regatta de
Blanc*   **1980**—*Zenyatta Mondatta*   **1981**—*Ghost in the
Machine*   **1983**—*Synchronicity*.

The Police's canny, forward-looking combination of pop
hooks, exotic rhythms, blond good looks, adventurous
management and good timing won them a mass following
in America and around the world. Their distinctive
sound—songs centered on Sting's bass riffs and vocals,
with Andy Summers' atmospheric guitar and Copeland's
intricate drumming as a backdrop—has been the most
influential approach since punk. While the Police seemed
at first to be a white reggae band, they have since incorporated ideas from funk, minimalism, Arab, Indian and
African music.

Chief songwriter/singer/bassist Sting (so named because
of a yellow and black jersey he often wore) had been a
teacher, ditch digger and civil servant and had worked
with a jazz combo called Lost Exit in Newcastle, England,
before he met American drummer Stewart Copeland at a
local jazz club. Copeland, the son of a CIA agent, had
grown up in the Middle East, attended college in California, moved to England in 1975 and joined the English
progressive rock group Curved Air.

After Curved Air broke up in 1976, Copeland formed
the Police with Sting and guitarist Henri Padovani in 1977,
replacing Padovani with Summers after some months of
London club dates. Summers had played with numerous
groups since the mid-Sixties, including Eric Burdon and
the Animals, the Kevin Ayers Band, the Zoot Money Big
Roll Band and the Neil Sedaka Band; he had also studied
classical guitar in California.

From the start, the Police distinguished themselves for
their maverick business practices. Before recording anything, they portrayed a bleached-blonde punk-rock band
in a chewing gum TV commercial—a move that drew the
scorn of Britain's punks. But in punk style, their first
record, "Fall Out" (with Padovani) was homemade and
frenzied. Released in 1978 by the Illegal Records Syndicate (IRS)—an independent label founded by Stewart
Copeland and his brother Miles (also the group's manager)—the single sold about 70,000 copies in the U.K.

The following year, the Police signed with A&M after
negotiations concluded with a unique contract that
awarded the group a higher than usual royalty rate instead
of a large advance. The Police's next unorthodox move
was to tour America before they had released any records
in this country. Through Frontier Booking International
(FBI)—brother Ian Copeland's agency—they borrowed
equipment, rented a van and traveled cross-country to

The Police: Sting, Andy Summers, Stewart Copeland

play club dates. With this approach, they had a following
ready for their first American release, "Roxanne," which
went to #32 in 1979 (it was already a British hit).

Their first two albums made the U.S. Top Thirty, while
in the U.K. "Message in a Bottle" and "Walking on the
Moon" went to the top of the singles charts. The Police's
1980 world tour took them to Hong Kong, Thailand, India,
Egypt, Greece and Mexico—countries that rarely receive
foreign entertainers. *Zenyatta Mondatta*, which contained
"De Do Do Do, De Da Da Da" (#10, 1980) and "Don't
Stand So Close to Me" (#10, 1981), was their first U.S.
platinum album. It was followed by a second million-
seller, *Ghost in the Machine*, which secured the Police
among the big hitmakers of the early Eighties with "Every
Little Thing She Does Is Magic" (#3, 1981). *Synchronicity*
included the #1 hit "Every Breath You Take."

Each member of the Police has worked outside the
group in recent years. Sting has acted in dramatic roles in
Quadrophenia (1979), *Radio On* (1979) and *Brimstone and
Treacle*, which he also scored (1982), and performed solo
in *The Secret Policeman's Other Ball* (1982). Summers
collaborated with guitarist Robert Fripp on *I Advance
Masked* (1982). Copeland recorded with Peter Gabriel,
released a solo EP on IRS as *Klark Kent* and composed
the soundtrack for Francis Ford Coppola's movie
Rumblefish (1983).

DOC POMUS AND MORT SHUMAN

Jerome "Doc" Pomus, born June 27, 1925, Brooklyn,
New York; Mort Shuman, born November 12, 1936,
New York City.

The team of Doc Pomus and Mort Shuman wrote dozens
of enduring late-Fifties and early-Sixties pop, rock and

R&B hits, including "Save the Last Dance for Me," "This Magic Moment" and "Sweets for My Sweet" (the Drifters); "Teenager in Love" (Dion and the Belmonts); "(Marie's the Name) His Latest Flame," "Surrender," "Little Sister," "A Mess of Blues" and "Viva Las Vegas" (Elvis Presley); "Young Blood" (cowritten by Pomus with Leiber and Stoller for the Coasters); "Seven Day Weekend" (Gary "U.S." Bonds); and "Suspicion" (Terry Stafford).

While Shuman has pretty much retired from music, Pomus—despite being wheelchair-bound for some 17 years—has kept active, cowriting the title tune of B. B. King's 1982 *There Must Be a Better World Somewhere* and cowriting (with Willie DeVille) three tracks on Mink DeVille's 1980 *Le Chat Bleu* LP.

Doc Pomus began singing at age six at Brooklyn's Manhattan Beach bandshell. As a teenager, he sang the blues in black clubs, and began writing tunes. In 1955 he cowrote (with Reginald Ashby) a blues hit for Big Joe Turner, "Boogie Woogie Country Girl." That year he also recorded "Heartlessly" for Dawn Records; disc jockey Alan Freed pushed the tune, RCA picked it up, yet it inexplicably stopped selling, which effectively ended Pomus' singing career. He began writing songs with Shuman, a friend of his family's who'd been tagging along with Pomus to blues clubs for some time. At first Pomus wrote the bulk of the material, and they split their percentages 90/10. Within a year, they were 50/50 partners, Shuman writing most of the music, and Pomus the lyrics.

Songwriter Otis Blackwell brought them to the attention of Paul Case at Hill and Range Publishers. In early 1959, a few months after signing with Hill and Range, Pomus and Shuman had two Top Forty hits with Fabian's "I'm a Man" and Bobby Darin's "Plain Jane." Within two years, they had scored several Top Ten hits for a variety of performers. Though associated with the Brill Building songwriting school, Pomus and Shuman never actually worked for Aldon (Al Nevins and Don Kirshner) Publishers, whose stable the Brill Building was, because Aldon paid too little. They did, however, send singer/songwriter Neil Sedaka to Aldon, his first professional break.

With the mid-Sixties British Invasion, times changed and the Pomus-Shuman string of hits ran out. They went to England, where their tunes had been highly respected by managers and publishers, and there Pomus suffered a severe fall in 1965. He has been confined to a wheelchair ever since. Within a year, Shuman had left Pomus, at first teaming up with Jerry Ragavoy and writing a couple of 1966 hits for Howard Tate, "Get It While You Can" and "Look at Granny Run, Run," then moving to Paris, where he lived and for a time performed a one-man show. Pomus kept a low profile until 1978, when Dr. John coaxed him into working on two albums, *City Lights* and *Tango Palace*. In 1981, Pomus cowrote B. B. King's "There Must Be a Better World Somewhere," for which King won a Grammy in 1982. To this day, Pomus can still often be found in New York City clubs, in his wheelchair, scouting talent.

JEAN-LUC PONTY

Born September 29, 1942, Avranches, France
1967—*Sunday Walk* (MPS) **1968**—*Electric Connection* (Pacific Jazz) **1969**—*Experience* **1970**—*King Kong; Astrorama* (Far East) **1972**—*Open Strings* (MPS) *Live in Montreux* (Inner City) **1973**—*Ponty/Grappelli* (with Stephane Grappelli) (America) **1975**—*Upon the Wings of Music* (Atlantic) **1976**—*Imaginary Voyage; Cantaloupe Island* (Blue Note) **1977**—*Aurora* (Atlantic) *Enigmatic Ocean* **1979**—*Cosmic Messenger* **1980**—*Civilized Evil; Taste for Passion* **1982**—*Mystical Adventures.*

Jean-Luc Ponty is a jazz-rock-fusion violinist who has played both acoustic and amplified violin with Frank Zappa, the Mahavishnu Orchestra, Elton John and his own bands, as well as having worked on occasion with jazz violinists like Stephane Grappelli and Stuff Smith (he appeared with the latter two on the *Violin Summit* LP).

Ponty's father, a music teacher, gave him his first violin at age three, and the boy's classical studies began at age five. Ponty left school at 13 to study violin on his own, practicing six hours a day, and at 15 he entered the Conservatoire National Supérieur de Musique de Paris, graduating two years later at the head of his class. At age 18, he joined the Concerts Lamoureaux Symphony Orchestra for three years. In 1964, he gave up the classics for jazz, and played at the Antibes Jazz Festival the next year. He has since played most of the major jazz festivals—Newport, Montreux, Monterey—several times.

Ponty's first U.S. visit was in 1967, when he took part in a violin workshop at the Monterey Jazz Festival. In 1969, after having toured Europe for three years, he moved to America, touring and recording with the George Duke Trio. He returned to Europe in 1971 and formed the Jean-Luc Ponty Experience with guitarist Philip Catherine. Before leaving America, though, he had played on Zappa's *Hot Rats* LP and also recorded *King Kong*, an album of Zappa compositions (because of legal problems, Zappa did not get production credit).

Back in France, Ponty met Elton John, and in 1972 he contributed some violin work to *Honky Chateau*. In 1973, he came back to America and joined Zappa's Mothers of Invention for almost a year, then replaced Jerry Goodman as violinist with John McLaughlin's Mahavishnu Orchestra for a year. He then formed his own band and began recording a string of commercially successful fusion LPs, which have generally found his music leaning more toward rock than jazz.

POP

Pop is the melodic side of rock—the legacy of show tunes and popular songs of the prerock era. Pop's standards of what makes a well-constructed song still apply to much of rock, which strives for memorable tunes and clear sentiments; the tension between pop virtues (such as sophisticated chord structures and unusual melodic twists), and incantatory, formulaic blues elements animates much of the best rock, like that of the Beatles. "Pop" also connotes accessibility, disposability and other low-culture values, which rockers have accepted or rejected with varying degrees of irony.

IGGY POP AND THE STOOGES

Iggy Pop, born James Newell Osterberg, 1947, Ypsilanti, Michigan; The Stooges, formed 1967, Ann Arbor, Michigan
Ron Asheton, gtr.; Dave Alexander, bass; Scott Asheton, drums.
1969—*The Stooges* (Elektra)　**1970**—*Fun House* (group disbands)　**1972**—(+ James Williamson, gtr.; + Scott Thurston, bass, kybds.)　**1973**—*Raw Power* (Columbia)　**1976**—*Metallic K.O.* (Skydog)　**1978**—*Kill City* (Radar).
Iggy Pop solo: 1976—*The Idiot* (RCA)　**1977**—*Lust for Life*　**1978**—*TV Eye*　**1979**—*New Values* (Arista)　**1980**—*Soldier*　**1981**—*Party*　**1982**—*Zombie Birdhouse* (Animal).

For his outrageous, cathartic and at times dangerous stage antics, and for the relentlessly primitive and loud rock music that has accompanied them, Iggy Pop (a.k.a. Iggy Stooge) has come to be regarded, along with such figures as Lou Reed and the Velvet Underground and the New York Dolls, as an avatar of punk rock.

James Osterberg dropped out of the University of Michigan in 1966 and went to Chicago, where he listened to urban blues music on the South Side. He returned to Detroit as Iggy Stooge and, inspired by a Doors concert, formed the Stooges. They debuted on Halloween 1967 in Ann Arbor and were an appropriately frightening onstage sight: Iggy contorting his shirtless torso, letting out primal screams and guttural wails, rubbing peanut butter and raw steaks over his body, gouging his skin with broken glass, diving out into the audience; all while the Stooges played a raw, abrasive basic rock. Some thought Iggy and the Stooges were the embodiment and the future of rock; others were appalled that they were so unrepentantly primitive and gross.

Elektra, the Doors' label, gave them a contract in 1968. Their first two albums were later critically hailed as punk's predecessors but at the time of their release sold only moderately. The band broke up in 1970, with Iggy retiring for over a year to kick a heroin addiction. Around this time, he ran into David Bowie, who resolved to resurrect

Iggy Pop

Iggy's career. Bowie regrouped some of the Stooges and produced *Raw Power*, which was a critical success.

A dispute with Bowie's manager Tony DeFries forced Iggy and the re-formed Stooges onto the road without a manager. Through 1973, there was a return to drug addiction. Iggy spent 1974–75 in Los Angeles, trying to solve his legal problems. He committed himself to an L.A. mental hospital and was visited by Bowie (whose "Jean Genie" on the 1973 *Aladdin Sane* is said to be about Iggy), who in 1976 took Iggy with him on his European tour, after which they settled in Berlin. Bowie produced two more LPs for Iggy, *The Idiot* and *Lust for Life;* other LPs of this period, like *Metallic K.O.* and *Kill City*, were semi-bootleg issues of older Stooges-era material.

In 1977, Iggy toured the U.S. with Bowie (unannounced) playing keyboards; Blondie was their opening act. Iggy's autobiography, *I Need More*, was published in 1982, and a new LP, *Zombie Birdhouse*, produced by Chris Stein for his Animal label, was released that year as well. "China Girl," cowritten by Pop and David Bowie, appeared on Bowie's 1983 *Let's Dance.*

ELVIS PRESLEY

Born January 8, 1935, East Tupelo, Mississippi; died August 16, 1977, Memphis
1956—*Elvis Presley* (RCA)　*Elvis; Sun Sessions*　**1958**—*Elvis' Golden Records: 50,000,000 Elvis Fans Can't Be Wrong*　**1959**—*Elvis' Golden Records, volume 2; For LP Fans Only*　**1960**—*Elvis Is Back; His Hand in Mine*　**1967**—*How Great Thou Art*　**1968**—*Elvis* (TV special soundtrack)　**1969**—*From Elvis in Memphis*　**1970**—*From Memphis to Vegas/From Vegas to Memphis; Elvis*

Elvis Presley

in Person at the International Hotel in Las Vegas
1975—*The Elvis Presley Sun Collection* **1980**—*This Is
Elvis* (soundtrack) **1981**—*Elvis Aron Presley.*

Elvis Presley was the first real rock & roll star. A white
Southerner singing blues laced with country and country
tinged with gospel, he brought together American music
from both sides of the color line and performed it with a
natural hip-swiveling sexuality that made him a teen idol
and a role model for generations of cool rebels. He was
repeatedly dismissed as vulgar, incompetent and a bad
influence, but the force of his music and his image was no
mere merchandising feat. Presley signaled to mainstream
culture that it was time to let go.

Presley was the son of Gladys and Vernon Presley, a
sewing-machine operator and a truck driver. Elvis' twin
brother, Jesse Garon, was stillborn, and Presley grew up
an only child. When he was three, his father served an
eight-month prison term for writing bad checks, and afterwards Vernon Presley's employment was erratic, keeping
the family just above the poverty level. The Presleys
attended the First Assembly of God Church, and its
Pentecostal services always included singing.

In 1945, Presley won second prize at the Mississippi-
Alabama Fair and Dairy Show for his rendition of Red
Foley's "Old Shep." The following January, he received a
guitar for his birthday. In 1948, the family moved to
Memphis, and while attending L. C. Humes High School
there, Presley spent much of his spare time hanging
around the black section of town, especially on Beale
Street, where bluesmen like Furry Lewis and B. B. King
performed.

Upon graduation in June 1953, Presley worked at the
Precision Tool Company and then drove a truck for Crown

Electric. He planned to become a truck driver and had
begun to wear his long hair pompadoured, the current
truck-driver style. That summer, he recorded "My Happiness" and "That's When Your Heartaches Begin" at the
Memphis Recording Service, a sideline Sam Phillips had
established in his Sun Records studios where anyone
could record a ten-inch acetate for four dollars.

Presley was reportedly curious to know what he
sounded like and gravely disappointed by what he heard.
But he returned to the Recording Service again on January
4, 1954, and recorded "Casual Love Affair" and "I'll
Never Stand in Your Way." This time he met Phillips, who
called him later that spring to re-record a song that Phillips
had received on a demo, "Without You." Despite numerous takes, Presley failed miserably and at Phillips' request
just began singing songs in the studio. Phillips then began
to believe that he had finally found what he had been
looking for: "a white man with the Negro sound and the
Negro feel."

Phillips enlisted lead guitarist Scotty Moore and bassist
Bill Black, both of whom were then playing country &
western music in Doug Poindexter's Starlight Wranglers.
Though some sources cite the date of their first meeting as
July 4, 1954, the three had actually rehearsed for several
months, and on July 5, 1954, they recorded three songs: "I
Love You Because," "Blue Moon of Kentucky" and what
would become Presley's debut, Arthur "Big Boy" Crudup's "That's All Right."

Two days later, Memphis disc jockey Dewey Phillips
(no relation to Sam) played the song on his "Red Hot and
Blue" show on radio station WHBQ. Audience response
was overwhelming, and that night Presley came to the
studio for his first interview. Scotty Moore became Presley's manager, and "That's All Right" b/w "Blue Moon of
Kentucky" became his first local hit. After playing local
shows, Presley made his first—and last—appearance at
the Grand Ole Opry on September 25. Legend has it that
after his performance he was advised by the Opry's talent
coordinator to go back to driving trucks.

By October, Presley had debuted on "The Louisiana
Hayride," a radio program on which he appeared regularly
through 1955. He made his television debut on a local
television version of "Hayride" in March 1955. Meanwhile, "Good Rockin' Tonight" b/w "I Don't Care If the
Sun Don't Shine" were hits in the Memphis area.

In early 1955, Moore stopped managing Presley, although he would continue to play in Presley's band for
several years. Presley's new manager was Memphis disc
jockey Bob Neal. Colonel Thomas Parker first entered
Presley's career when he helped Neal make some tour
arrangements. Presley, still considered a country act,
continued to perform locally, and in April he traveled to
New York City, where he auditioned unsuccessfully for
Arthur Godfrey's "Talent Scouts" program. But on May
13, his performance in Jacksonville, Florida, started a
riot, Presley's first. "Baby, Let's Play House" b/w "I'm

Left, You're Right, She's Gone" was released and hit #10 on the national C&W charts in July.

That September, Presley had his first #1 country record, a version of Junior Parker's "Mystery Train" b/w "I Forgot to Remember to Forget." By this time, Colonel Parker, despite Presley's agreement with Neal, had become increasingly involved in his career. When RCA purchased Presley's contract from Sun for a then unheard-of $25,000, Hill and Range, a music publisher with whom Parker had some connections, purchased Sam Phillips' Hi-Lo Music for another $15,000. In addition, Presley received a $5,000 advance, with which he bought his mother a pink Cadillac.

Presley became a national star in 1956. He and Parker traveled to Nashville, where Presley cut his first records for RCA (including "I Got a Woman," "Heartbreak Hotel" and "I Was the One"), and on January 28, 1956, Presley made his national television debut on the Dorsey Brothers' "Stage Show," followed by six consecutive appearances. In March, Parker signed Presley to a managerial agreement for which he would receive 25 percent of Presley's earnings. The contract would last through Presley's lifetime and beyond.

Presley performed on the Milton Berle, Steve Allen and Ed Sullivan shows. The Colonel arranged Presley's debut at the New Frontier Hotel in Las Vegas that April, but the two-week engagement was canceled after one week of poor audience response. In August, he began filming his first movie, *Love Me Tender*, which was released three months later and recouped its cost—$1 million—in three days. Elvis' hit singles that year were all certified gold; they included "Heartbreak Hotel" (#1), "I Was the One" (#19), "I Want You, I Need You, I Love You" (#1), "Hound Dog" (#1), "Don't Be Cruel" (#1), "Love Me Tender" (#1) and "Anyway You Want Me (That's the Way I'll Be)" (#20). By early 1957, he was the idol of millions of teens and the perfect target for the wrath of critics, teachers, clergymen and even other entertainers (including many country performers), all of whom saw his style as too suggestive. Presley repeatedly claimed not to understand what all the criticism was about. On January 6, when Presley made his last of three appearances on Ed Sullivan's show, he was shown only from the waist up.

In March of 1957, Presley purchased Graceland, a former church that had been converted into a 23-room mansion; the next month, "All Shook Up" began an eight-week run at #1. *Loving You* was released in July, and "Teddy Bear" from its soundtrack hit #1 on the pop, country and R&B charts, as did "Don't Be Cruel," "All Shook Up" and "Jailhouse Rock," the title song from Presley's next movie, which featured Leiber and Stoller songs. In December, he received his draft notice, but was granted a sixty-day deferment to complete filming *King Creole*.

On March 24, 1958, Presley entered the Army. He took leave a few months later to be with his mother; Gladys Presley died the day after his arrival, on August 14, 1958. In later interviews, Presley would call her death the great tragedy of his life. He was shipped to Bremerhaven, West Germany, and in January 1960 was promoted to sergeant. He was discharged in March.

Colonel Parker, meanwhile, released singles Presley had recorded before his departure. One of them, "Big Hunk o' Love" (1959), hit #1, and in 1958 alone Presley earned over $2 million. Shortly after his return, he recorded his first stereo record, "Stuck on You" (#1), and later that month he taped a TV program with Frank Sinatra.

In July, Presley's father remarried. Vernon Presley's second wife, Davada "Dee" Stanley, and her three sons would later write *Elvis: We Love You Tender,* one of dozens of insiders' tell-all biographies that were published following his death. Also at this time, Presley gathered around him the friends, employees and hangers-on who would become known as the Memphis Mafia and would accompany him almost constantly until his death. Three of them, Red West, Sonny West and Dave Hebler, would write *Elvis—What Happened?* Published days before Presley's death, *What Happened* was the first book ever to allude to Presley's drug use and violent behavior.

G. I. Blues and *Flaming Star* were released in 1960, and "It's Now or Never" hit #1 in both the U.K. and the U.S. Presley had five #1 U.S. hits: "Stuck on You," "It's Now or Never," "Are You Lonesome Tonight" (1960); "Surrender" (1961); and "Good Luck Charm" (1962). On Christmas 1960, Priscilla Beaulieu, the teenaged daughter of an Army officer whom Presley had met in Germany, visited Graceland. In early 1961, she moved in to live, it was said, under the supervision of Presley's father and stepmother.

After a live performance on March 25, 1961, at a benefit for the U.S.S. *Arizona*, Presley left the concert stage and spent the next eight years making B movies: *Wild in the Country, Blue Hawaii* (1961); *Follow That Dream, Kid Galahad, Girls! Girls! Girls!* (1962); *It Happened at the World's Fair, Fun in Acapulco* (1963); *Kissin' Cousins, Viva Las Vegas, Roustabout* (1964); *Girl Happy, Tickle Me, Harum Scarum* (1965); *Frankie and Johnny, Paradise, Hawaiian Style, Spinout* (1966); *Easy Come, Easy Go, Double Trouble, Clambake* (1967); *Stay Away Joe, Speedway, Live a Little, Love a Little* (1968); *Charro!, The Trouble with Girls (and How to Get into It), Change of Habit* (1969). With a few exceptions, the soundtrack music was indisputably poor. But by the mid-Sixties Presley was earning $1 million per movie plus a large percentage of the gross. Each of the movies had a concurrently released soundtrack LP, nine of which went gold. Meanwhile, the younger rock audience heard Presley disciples like the Beatles more often than they heard Presley himself.

On May 1, 1967, Presley and Priscilla were wed in Las Vegas; on February 1, 1968, their only child, Lisa Marie, was born. Over the summer, he taped the surprisingly raw, powerful *Elvis* television special that was broadcast on December 3 to high ratings. Its soundtrack reached #8. It included his first performance before an audience in over seven years and (though many portions were taped without an audience), with that success behind him, Presley turned to performing in Las Vegas. His month-long debut at the International Hotel in Las Vegas began on July 26, 1969, and set the course for all of Presley's future performances. His fee for the four weeks was over $1 million. That October, "Suspicious Minds" became Presley's first #1 hit in seven and a half years and the last of his career. He toured the country annually, selling out showrooms, auditoriums and arenas, frequently breaking box-office records. There were two on-tour documentaries released, *Elvis: That's the Way It Is* (1970) and *Elvis on Tour* (1972), the latter of which won the Golden Globe Award for Best Documentary.

Presley was honored with countless Elvis Presley Days in cities around the country, and the U.S. Jaycees named him one of the ten most outstanding young men of America in 1970. His birthplace in Tupelo was opened to the public, and on January 18, 1972, the portion of Highway 51 South that ran in front of Graceland was renamed Elvis Presley Boulevard. That October, Presley had his last Top Twenty hit when "Burning Love" hit #2.

Meanwhile, Presley's personal life became the subject of countless tabloid headlines. Priscilla, from whom Presley had been separated since February 1972, refused to return to Graceland, and on his birthday in 1973 he filed for divorce. Less than a week later, the TV special "Elvis: Aloha from Hawaii" was broadcast via satellite to over a billion viewers in forty countries, an indication of his international appeal, although (with the exception of three dates in Canada in 1957 and an impromptu performance while on leave in Paris in 1959) Presley never performed outside the U.S. Through it all, his records continued to sell. During his career, Presley earned 94 gold singles, three gold EPs and over forty gold LPs. His movies grossed over $180 million, and millions were made by the merchandising of Elvis products that ranged from T-shirts to stuffed hound dogs and bracelets, the rights to which were controlled by Colonel Parker.

The offstage Elvis Presley was not so controlled. Soon after he left the Army, he became increasingly wary of the public and would often rent whole movie theaters and amusement parks to visit at night. By the late Sixties, he was nearly a total recluse. Although some evidence suggests that Presley may have begun taking drugs while in the service, his abuse of prescription drugs, including barbiturates, tranquilizers and amphetamines, increased during the last years of his life. Several painful physical conditions may have initiated this trend. Ironically, he remained devoutly religious, never drank alcohol and publicly denounced the use of recreational drugs. But toward the end he would babble incoherently onstage and

rip his pants, having grown quite obese, and on at least one occasion he collapsed onstage. Despite his clearly deteriorating health, he maintained a frantic tour schedule. His last live performance was on June 26, 1977, in Indianapolis.

On August 16, 1977—the day before his next scheduled concert—Presley was discovered by his girlfriend Ginger Alden dead in his bathroom at Graceland. Although his death was at first attributed to congestive heart failure (an autopsy also revealed advanced arteriosclerosis and an enlarged liver), later investigation revealed evidence that drug abuse may have been at least part of the cause of death. In September 1979, Presley's private physician, Dr. George Nichopoulos, was charged by the Tennessee Board of Medical Examiners with "indiscriminately prescribing 5,300 pills and vials for Elvis in the seven months before his death." He was later acquitted.

Thousands gathered at Graceland, where Presley lay in state before he was buried in a mausoleum at Forest Hill Cemetery in Memphis. After attempts were made to break into the mausoleum, Presley's body and that of his mother were moved to the Meditation Garden behind Graceland. Nearly two years later, his father, Vernon, died and was also buried there. With Vernon dead, all of Presley's estate passed on to Lisa Marie. Court battles over the estate ended in June 1983 after 21 months of litigation with a settlement that ended four lawsuits. One of the terms of the agreement called for Parker to turn over most of his interest in Presley's audio and visual recordings to RCA and the Presley family in return for a large monetary settlement. Claiming the funds were needed to maintain the property, Priscilla Presley opened Graceland to the public in fall 1982.

BILLY PRESTON

Born September 9, 1946, Houston
1966—*The Wildest Organ in Town* (Capitol)   **1967**—*Most Exciting Organ Ever* (VeeJay)   **1969**—*That's the Way God Planned It* (Apple)   *Encouraging Words* **1971**—*I Wrote a Simple Song* (A&M)   **1972**—*Music Is My Life*   **1973**—*Everybody Likes Some Kind of Music* **1974**—*The Kids and Me*   **1975**—*It's My Pleasure* **1976**—*Billy Preston*   **1977**—*A Whole New Thing.*

Though keyboardist/vocalist Billy Preston has recorded prolifically since he was a teenager, he may be best known for his performances as a sideman for Little Richard, Ray Charles, the Beatles and the Rolling Stones.

Preston's family moved to Los Angeles when he was two years old. At age ten, he had a cameo part in a film about W. C. Handy, *St. Louis Blues,* playing the composer as a child. Little Richard heard him in 1962 and invited him to appear on a European tour. There, backing Richard, Preston met Sam Cooke (who signed him to his SAR label) and the Beatles. After Cooke's death, Preston moved to

Vee Jay records, where he cut an instrumental gospel album, *The Most Exciting Organ Ever,* his first charted record.

Preston was playing in the house band of the television show "Shindig" when Ray Charles recruited him for his band. George Harrison spotted Preston on a BBC Ray Charles special and contacted him. Subsequently he was signed to the Beatles' Apple Records, where he cut two Harrison-produced albums, *That's the Way God Planned It* (whose title cut was a minor hit) and *Encouraging Words.*

Preston also became a valuable sideman for the Beatles, appearing on "Get Back" and "Let It Be." Following the Beatles' breakup, he performed on Harrison's *All Things Must Pass* and at the Bangladesh concert at Madison Square Garden in 1971.

With A&M records in the early Seventies, Preston had several hits, including the instrumental "Outa Space" (#2 pop, #1 R&B) in 1972; "Will It Go Round in Circles" (#1 pop, #10 R&B) and "Space Race" (#4 pop, #1 R&B) in 1973; and "Nothing from Nothing" (#1 pop, #8 R&B) in 1974. Each single went gold, and "Outa Space" won a Grammy as Best Pop Instrumental. In 1975, Preston wrote what became Joe Cocker's biggest solo hit, "You Are So Beautiful." That same year, Preston was featured on the Rolling Stones' tour; he later recorded with them.

Preston was active as a session musician through the late Seventies and into the Eighties, though his solo career declined. In 1979, he reached the top of the pop charts with "With You I'm Born Again," a duet with Syreeta Wright on a song from the film *Fastbreak.*

JOHNNY PRESTON

Born August 18, 1930, Port Arthur, Texas

An East Texas pop-rock singer, Johnny Preston had a #1 novelty hit in 1960 with "Running Bear," a tune inspired by a Dove Soap commercial. It was written by and featured the "oom-pah-pah" backing vocals of J. P. Richardson, also known as the "Big Bopper." The song became a hit not long after Richardson's death in the February 1959 plane crash that also killed Buddy Holly and Ritchie Valens.

Before returning to obscurity, Preston had a few follow-up hits: "Cradle of Love" (#7, 1960), a version of Shirley and Lee's "Feel So Good" called "Feel So Fine" (#14, 1960), a cover of Little Willie John's "Leave My Kitten Alone" (#73, 1961) and "Free Me" (#97, 1961).

THE PRETENDERS

Formed 1978, London
Chrissie Hynde (b. 1952, Akron, Oh.), voc., rhythm gtr.; Pete Farndon (b. 1953, Hereford, Eng.; d. Apr. 14, 1983, London), bass; James Honeyman-Scott (b. Nov. 4, 1957, Hereford, Eng.; d. June 16, 1982), gtr.; Martin Chambers (b. 1952, Hereford, Eng.), drums.

The Pretenders: Peter Farndon, Chrissie Hynde, Martin Chambers, James Honeyman-Scott

1980—*The Pretenders* (Sire)   1981—*Extended Play* (EP)   *The Pretenders II.*

The Pretenders, three Englishmen and an American woman, emerged at the close of the Seventies as one of the new wave's most commercially successful groups. Their focal point was Chrissie Hynde, the band's songwriter, lead singer and rhythm guitarist, whose tough songs and stage persona put feminist self-assertion into her own distinctive hard rock.

A single gig with an Akron band, Sat. Sun. Mat. (which included Mark Mothersbaugh, later of Devo), was Hynde's sole performing experience when, after three years of studying art at Kent State University, she left (with money earned as a waitress) for the rocker's life in London in 1973. She began writing savagely satiric reviews for *The New Musical Express;* but after playing cover girl for a story on Brian Eno, she moved to France to form a band. When nothing materialized, she returned to Akron, where she joined Jack Rabbit; it broke up, and Hynde returned to France and then to England by 1976, as punk rock was burgeoning. She tried to enlist a young guitarist, Mick Jones, into her would-be group, but Jones committed himself to another new group, the Clash.

She was then hired by punk fashion entrepreneur and Sex Pistols manager Malcolm McLaren (in whose boutique Hynde had worked when she'd first come to London) to play guitar in Masters of the Backside. After months of rehearsal, she was dismissed; the group turned into the Damned. Hynde played guitar or sang backup behind Johnny Moped, Chris Spedding, Johnny Thunders (the New York Dolls, the Heartbreakers) and Nick Lowe. With these contacts and a growing repertoire of original songs, she recorded a demo tape. Dave Hill, founder of Real Records, became her manager and advanced her the money to audition and hire a band.

Bassist Pete Farndon had lately returned to England from Australia, where he had played for two years with a popular Aussie group, the Bushwackers. He called James Honeyman-Scott, who had toured with several bands, notably Cheeks, a group led by ex–Mott the Hoople keyboardist Verdon Allen. Honeyman-Scott joined Hynde, Farndon and drummer Jerry Mcleduff to record two Hynde compositions—"Precious" and "The Wait"—and a 1964 Ray Davies (the Kinks) number, "Stop Your Sobbing." Nick Lowe pegged "Stop Your Sobbing" b/w "The Wait" for a hit and offered to produce a single, which he did in a single day in the fall of 1978. The next day the Pretenders left for Paris for their debut gig and a week-long club engagement.

Mcleduff was replaced by Cheeks' former drummer, Martin Chambers, then working as a drummer and driving instructor in London. In January 1979, "Stop Your Sobbing" was released in Britain. Soon it was in the Top Thirty. The followup, "Kid," written by Hynde and produced by Chris Thomas, did well, too. By spring, the Pretenders were selling out performances all over the U.K. In May, they began work on an album, with Thomas producing. *The Pretenders,* released worldwide in January 1980, was universally lauded. "Brass in Pocket" hit #1 in the U.K. and Australia, and reached #14 in the U.S. After whipping off another single, "Talk of the Town," for the British market, Hynde brought her band Stateside, where their album was rising through the Top Ten.

Live Pretenders songs from the first album, performed in December 1979, appeared on the *Concerts for Kampuchea* album in 1981; a five-song EP including more live songs and the two sides of the "Talk of the Town" single was released soon afterwards. Finally, in the summer of 1981, *Pretenders II* was released to mixed reviews. It included another tune by Ray Davies, "I Go to Sleep," and Hynde showed up so frequently on the Kinks tour that summer that her relationship with Ray Davies soon became public knowledge. A Pretenders tour of the U.S. was postponed when, in October 1981, Chambers badly injured his hand; the eventual tour was the last time the original Pretenders played together.

Farndon quit the group in 1982, and that June, Honeyman-Scott died of a drug overdose. Ex-Rockpile guitarist Billy Bremner, Hynde and Chambers recorded "Back on the Chain Gang," dedicated to Honeyman-Scott. In 1983, Farndon died of an apparent heart attack. Meanwhile, in January 1983 Hynde gave birth to a daughter.

THE PRETTY THINGS
Formed 1963, Kent, England
Phil May (b. Nov. 9, 1944, Kent), voc.; Dick Taylor, gtr., bass, voc.; Brian Pendleton, gtr.; John Stax, bass, harmonica; Peter Kitley, drums (replaced by Viv Andrews, who was replaced by Viv Prince).
1965—*The Pretty Things* (Fontana) *Get the Picture* (– Prince; + Skip Alan [b. Alan Ernest Skipper, June 11, 1948, London], drums) 1966—(– Pendleton; – Stax; + Wally Allen, bass, voc.; + John Povey [b. Aug.

20, 1944, London], kybds., voc.) 1967—*We Want Your Love; Emotions; Electric Banana* (De Wolf) 1968—(– Alan; + John "Twink" Alder, drums, voc.) *More Electric Banana* 1969—*S.F. Sorrow* (Rare Earth) *Even More Electric Banana* (De Wolf) (– Alder; – Taylor; + Alan; + Victor Unitt, gtr., voc.) 1970—*Parachute* (Rare Earth) (– Alan; – Unitt; + Peter Tolson [b. Sep. 10, 1951, Bishops Stortford, Eng.], gtr., voc.) 1971—(group disbands; re-forms: + Stuart Brooks, bass; + Gordon Edwards [b. Dec. 26, 1946, Southport, Eng.], kybds., gtr.) 1973—*Freeway Madness* (Warner Bros.) 1974—*Silk Torpedo* (Swan Song) 1975—(– Brooks; + Jack Green [b. Mar. 12, 1951, Glasgow], bass, voc.) *Savage Eye; Greatest Hits* (Philips) *Attention!* (Fontana) (compilation) 1976—*The Vintage Years* (Sire) (compilation) 1977—*The Singles* (Harvest) (compilation) 1978—*Live* (Jade) (compilation) 1979—*Real Pretty* (Rare Earth) (compilation) 1980—*Cross Talk* (Warner Bros.) (compilation).

The Pretty Things were a British pop-rock band who were highly regarded in the U.K. but scarcely made an impression in the U.S.

They were formed from lunchtime jam sessions at London's Sidcup Art College, where Phil May, Dick Taylor and Keith Richards were enrolled. Taylor, after playing bass with the original Rolling Stones, switched to guitar to form the Pretty Things with May. The band's performances of material by Chuck Berry, Jimmy Reed and Bo Diddley (they took their name from a Diddley song) were at first considered even more outrageous than the Stones', especially when their second U.K. chart single, "Don't Bring Me Down" (the first was "Rosalyn" in 1964), was banned in the U.S. in 1964 because of objectionable lyrics. Their last big U.K. hit was "Honey I Need" (#13, 1965).

But the Pretty Things took a lot longer to develop original material than the Stones, and it wasn't until 1969's *S.F. Sorrow* (based on May's short story) that the band attracted any interest in the U.S. (The album was originally released in England in 1968.) The album is one of the first "rock operas," and may have influenced Pete Townshend's writing of *Tommy.* It was a critical success, but a commercial failure, as was *Parachute,* which won *Rolling Stone*'s Album of the Year Award in 1969.

Meanwhile, founding member Taylor had left in 1970, first to produce Hawkwind in 1971 and then apparently to leave the music business. Pendleton had disappeared entirely after the first few albums; the band continued despite numerous personnel changes. One-time bassist Jack Green worked with T. Rex and released two solo LPs. When Pretty Things disbanded, May and Skip Alan formed Fallen Angels briefly, and other remaining members formed Metropolis. Fallen Angels released one LP. When Metropolis broke up in 1977, keyboardist Edwards briefly joined the Kinks.

DORY PREVIN

Born Dory Langdon, October 22, Woodbridge, New Jersey

1972—*Mythical Kings and Iguanas* (United Artists) *Reflections in a Mud Puddle; Mary C. Brown* **1973**— *On My Way to Where; Live at Carnegie Hall* **1974**— *Dory Previn* (Warner Bros.) **1976**—*Children of Coincidence* **1977**—*One A.M. Phone Calls* (United Artists).

More acclaimed as a songwriter than as a singer, Dory Previn has composed numerous themes for films, plays and TV shows, and her material has been covered by Judy Garland, Liza Minnelli, Dionne Warwick and Leontyne Price.

Previn's father, a semi-professional musician, pushed her into show business; at age four she began working as a singer/dancer in Perth Amboy, New Jersey, and for the next five years she performed in nightclubs. She left home at 16 to study acting at the American Academy of Dramatic Arts in New York City. Unable to afford her second year's tuition, she dropped out and hit the road in chorus lines, vaudeville shows and nightclubs. Previn's original songs brought her to the attention of an MGM producer who made her a house lyricist; from there she went to United Artists, where she wrote music for TV shows like "Zane Grey Theater," "The Millionaire" and "Dick Powell Theater." In 1959, she married Hollywood conductor André Previn.

In the early to mid-Sixties, she wrote words to music by Previn, David Raskin, Elmer Bernstein and others for such films as *Pepe, Two for the Seesaw, The Sterile Cuckoo, Inside Daisy Clover, Valley of the Dolls, Irma la Douce* and *Goodbye Charlie*. Her *Pepe* theme song, "The Faraway Part of Town" (sung by Judy Garland), was nominated for an Academy Award, as were "A Second Chance" (from *Seesaw*) and "Come Saturday Morning" (sung by Liza Minnelli) from *Cuckoo*.

In 1965, after she and her husband split up, she entered a mental institution. After her release, she wrote the theme from *Valley of the Dolls*, a million-selling hit for Dionne Warwick in 1967. In 1971, she published a collection of song lyrics and poems, *On My Way to Where*, and in 1976 published her memoirs, *Midnight Baby*. She also wrote two stage musicals, *Mary C. Brown and the Hollywood Sign* and *The Amazing Flight of the Gooney Bird*, as well as the original screenplay and music for the TV-movie *Third Girl from the Left*. She was moderately successful as a performer, writing angry, intimate confessional songs set to a rough folk-rock backup.

ALAN PRICE

Born April 19, 1942, County Durham, England

1966—*The Price to Play* (Decca) **1967**—*A Price on His Head; The Amazing* (EP) **1968**—*The Price Is Right* (Parrot) **1970**—*The World of . . .* (Decca) **1971**— *Fame and Price* (Columbia) **1973**—*O Lucky Man!* (soundtrack) (Warner Bros.) **1974**—*Between Yesterday and Today* **1975**—*Metropolitan Man* (Polydor) *Performing Price* **1976**—*Shouts Across the Street* **1977**—*Rainbow's End* (Jet) **1978**—*England My England; Alan Price* **1980**—*Rising Sun*.

Alan Price may be best known as the organist with the original Animals, but he was performing on his own some time before founding that band and continued his career long after its demise.

He formed his first group, the skiffle/blues Alan Price Combo, in 1958 while at Jarrow Grammar School and played small clubs in northeast England. This grew into the Animals, which he left in 1965. In 1966, he formed the Alan Price Set, a horn-laden band, and had some U.K. hit singles, like "I Put a Spell on You" (#9 U.K., #80 U.S.) and a cover of Randy Newman's "Simon Smith and His Amazing Dancing Bear" (#4 U.K.). He continued to record solo albums with various personnel. In the late Sixties, he teamed up with Georgie Fame for a series of British stage and television appearances, leading to a television series in 1970. Together Fame and Price released an LP and a British Top Twenty single, "Rosetta."

That year, British stage and film director Lindsay Anderson commissioned Price to score his London production of *Home*. Three years later, he scored Anderson's film *O Lucky Man!* and appeared in it as himself, singing songs that commented on the story. That score won Price the British Society of Film and Television Arts Award. The next year, the BBC did a television documentary on him to coincide with the release of his autobiographical *Between Yesterday and Today*, and in 1975 he starred in a second film, *Alfie Darling*, for which he won the British Film Award for Most Promising New Actor. His last big British hit was "Jarrow Song," #6 in 1974. He rejoined the Animals in 1983.

LLOYD PRICE

Born March 9, 1934, New Orleans

N.A.—*Sixteen Greatest Hits* (ABC) *Sixteen Greatest Hits* (Trip) *The ABC Collection* (ABC).

Singer/songwriter Lloyd Price was a major figure in the early years of New Orleans rock & roll. "Lawdy Miss Clawdy" (1952), written by Price as a commercial for a local radio station, was a #1 R&B hit.

In the next two years, Price had several Top Ten R&B singles, "Oooh-Oooh-Oooh" (#5), "Restless Heart" (#8) and "Ain't It a Shame" (#7), before serving in Korea from 1954 to 1956. Upon his discharge, he relocated to Washington, D.C., where he started KRC (Kent Record Company) and recorded "Just Because." Leased to ABC-Paramount in 1957, it reached R&B #4 and pop #20. Price soon signed to ABC and enjoyed his greatest success with "Stagger Lee" (#1 both R&B and pop), a reworking of the New Orleans folk song "Stagolee."

Price's subsequent ABC recordings shifted from the rocking New Orleans style to a mainstream pop sound, as reflected by "Personality" (#2 pop, #1 R&B), "I'm Gonna Get Married" (#3 pop, #1 R&B), "Where Were You (On Our Wedding Day)" (#23 pop) "Come into My Heart" (#2 R&B), in 1959; "Lady Luck" (#14 pop, #3 R&B) and "Question" (#9 pop, #5 R&B) in 1960. Price was an enterprising businessman during the Sixties, operating the Double L and Turntable labels, and a New York nightclub called the Turntable. On GSF Records in 1972 he released a new album, *To the Roots and Back*.

PRINCE

Born Prince Rogers Nelson, June 7, 1960, Minneapolis, Minnesota
1978—*For You* (Warner Bros.) **1979**—*Prince* **1980**—*Dirty Mind* **1981**—*Controversy* **1982**—*1999*.

Prince is a flamboyant and controversial performer/writer/producer with a flair for blatantly sexual lyrics and music that mixes rock and funk. His taut, keyboard-dominated "Minneapolis Sound" has been widely influential, not only on fellow Minneapolis bands like the Time, but throughout most early-Eighties dance music. Prince plays all the instruments on his albums and has produced himself since signing with Warner Bros. at age 18.

Prince's father was a mulatto bandleader in the Minneapolis area, and his white mother was the band's vocalist. Prince started playing piano at seven, guitar at 13 and drums at 14, all self-taught. At 12, he was in a band called

Prince

Grand Central, which later became Champagne. Four years later, a demo tape he made with engineer Chris Moon reached a local businessman Owen Husney. In 1978, Husney negotiated Prince's contract with Warner Bros.

"Soft and Wet" (#92 pop, #12 R&B) from *For You* introduced his erotic approach, while "I Wanna Be Your Lover" (#11 pop, #1 R&B) and "Why You Wanna Treat Me So Bad?" (#13 R&B) from *Prince* suggested his musical range.

Dirty Mind—a concept album including songs such as "Head," about oral sex, and "Sister, Sister," about incest—established Prince's image once and for all. One of its few songs that wasn't too obscene for airplay, "Uptown," went to #5 R&B, while "When You Were Mine" became Prince's most widely covered song and a minor comeback hit for Mitch Ryder in 1983.

Controversy had two substantial hits, the title cut (#3 R&B) and "Let's Work" (#9 R&B). *Prince, Dirty Mind* and *Controversy* were all gold albums. In Prince's concerts, backed by a six-piece band with black and white members and a female keyboardist, he would sometimes strip down to black bikini underpants, or finish the set doing "push-ups" on a brass bed.

A double album, *1999*, went platinum, bolstered by the Top Ten single "Little Red Corvette," which was also one of the first videos by a black performer to be played regularly on MTV.

Prince "discovered" another Minneapolis band, the Time, both of whose albums went gold; in turn, the Time supplied backup for Vanity 6, a female vocal trio that had a club hit with "Nasty Girl." Prince has denied that he is the "Jamie Starr" who produced albums by the Time and Vanity 6. He did tour with both bands, however.

JOHN PRINE

Born circa 1946, Maywood, Illinois
1971—*John Prine* (Atlantic) **1972**—*Diamonds in the Rough* **1973**—*Sweet Revenge* **1975**—*Common Sense* **1976**—*Prime Prine* (compilation) **1978**—*Bruised Orange* (Asylum) **1979**—*Pink Cadillac* **1980**—*Storm Windows*.

John Prine is a singer/songwriter who has gone from solo acoustic folk to hard country to rockabilly to soft rock, all the while maintaining his hard-headed vision of white proletarian America.

Prine learned guitar from his father and played the Chicago coffeehouse circuit while working at the post office. With his friend and sometime production cohort Steve Goodman, Prine graduated from the Chicago folk scene. Paul Anka liked some of Prine's Hank Williams–influenced songs, and was instrumental in landing him a recording contract. In 1971, Prine went to Memphis and cut his debut. That LP's most notable song may have been "Sam Stone," a bleak drug-addicted Vietnam-veteran's saga, which aptly demonstrated Prine's laconic, drawling delivery.

Though his own commercial success was meager, other artists began recording his songs: the Everly Brothers did "Paradise," and both Joan Baez and Bette Midler recorded "Hello in There." *Common Sense* saw Prine shocking his folk audience by using hard-rock rhythms and a guttural singing style. *Bruised Orange*, produced by Goodman, returned Prine to the acoustic format of *Diamonds in the Rough*, while *Pink Cadillac* was an electric rockabilly album produced by Sam Phillips and his son Knox at Sun Studios. Prine retains a cult following for his down-to-earth, unadorned insights.

P. J. PROBY
Born James Marcus Smith, November 6, 1938, Houston

P. J. Proby is a Presleyesque singer who was always more popular in England than in his native America. Proby's big break came when British TV producer Jack Good brought him to the U.K. for a Beatles special in 1964; he hit with the Good-produced "Hold Me" (#3 U.K.), a frantic revival of a 1939 ballad. Prior to that, Proby had been living in Hollywood, doing odd jobs, playing bit parts in films and recording demos like "Jet Powers." After "Hold Me," followups failed to generate comparable success, and he switched styles; he began singing melodramatic versions of tunes from the Broadway musical *West Side Story*, for example.

Proby toured England in 1965 with Cilla Black, but was expelled from the country later that year after a series of incidents in which he split his velvet trousers onstage. In 1967, his tour choreographer was Kim Fowley. That year, he had his biggest U.S. hit with "Niki Hoeky" (#23). By 1968, though, Proby was bankrupt. He was lured back to England by Good in 1971 to play Iago in *Catch My Soul*, a rock adaptation of *Othello*. After years as a steady-drawing revival act in England, Proby unexpectedly teamed up with the Dutch classical-rock band Focus in 1978 for the *Focus con Proby* LP. He's maintained a low profile since then.

PROCOL HARUM
Formed 1966, London
Gary Brooker (b. May 29, 1945, Eng.), piano, voc.; Matthew Fisher (b. Mar. 7, 1946, Eng.), organ; Ray Royer (b. Oct. 8, 1945, Eng.), gtr.; Dave Knights (b. June 28, 1945, Eng.), bass; Bobby Harrison (b. June 28, 1943, Eng.), drums.
1967—(– Royer; – Harrison; + Robin Trower [b. Mar. 9, 1945, Eng.], gtr.; + B. J. Wilson [b. Mar. 18, 1947, Eng.], drums) *Procol Harum* (Deram) 1968— *Shine on Brightly* (A&M) 1969—*A Salty Dog* 1970— (– Fisher; – Knights; + Chris Copping [b. Aug. 29, 1945, Eng.], bass, organ) *Home* 1971—*Broken Barricades* 1972—(– Trower; + Dave Ball [b. Mar.

30, 1950], gtr.; + Alan Cartwright [b. Oct. 10, 1945], bass) *Live in Concert* (– Ball; + Mick Grabham, gtr.) 1973—*Grand Hotel* 1974—*Exotic Birds and Fruit* 1975—*Procol Ninth* 1977—(– Cartwright; + Pete Solley, organ) *Something Magic*.

With the 1967 worldwide smash "A Whiter Shade of Pale"—a combination of mystical lyrics, a somber tempo and an organ line lifted directly from Bach's Suite No. 3 in D major—Procol Harum established itself, along with the Moody Blues, as an early British "classical rock" band. Though the band never matched that spectacular success again, "A Whiter Shade of Pale" has outlasted the Summer of Love. It has sold over six million copies worldwide and has been covered in soul, jazz and country versions.

The band—whose only other U.S. hit was an orchestrated 1972 reworking of 1967's "Conquistador"—included only one member with classical training: Matthew Fisher, who studied at the Guildhall School of Music. Procol Harum actually began as an R&B band, the Paramounts (Gary Brooker, Robin Trower, Chris Copping and B. J. Wilson) in London's Southend section in 1963. The Paramounts made several singles, but only a cover of "Little Bitty Pretty One" achieved any local success, and they broke up in 1966.

Later that year, Brooker met lyricist Keith Reid (who was always listed as a full-fledged band member on the group's albums) and they formed a band—with Fisher, Ray Royer, Dave Knights and Bobby Harrison—to record their songs. The name Procol Harum allegedly came from the name of a cat one of their friends owned (they often jokingly referred to themselves as the "Purple Horrors"); roughly translated from Latin, it means "beyond these things." The original Procol Harum ended up recording only one single, the crucial "A Whiter Shade of Pale" (on which sessionman Bill Eyden replaced Harrison).

In the wake of the single's success (repeated to a much lesser degree in the U.K. by "Homburg" in mid-1967), Royer and Harrison were replaced by Trower and Wilson, and this lineup recorded the first three Procol Harum albums.

In late 1969, Fisher and Knights departed (Fisher has since recorded three solo albums) and were replaced by Copping. *Home* saw Trower leading the band in a harder-rocking direction. The same held true for *Broken Barricades*, but Trower's hard-rock leanings were never fully integrated and seemed at odds with the band's stately pace and Reid's existential-visionary lyrics. Trower left in July 1971. He went on to form the short-lived Jude with British R&B singer Frankie Miller and then the highly successful Robin Trower Band, a Hendrixian power trio, whose 1973 debut, *Twice Removed from Yesterday*, was produced by Fisher.

With new guitarist Dave Ball, Copping concentrating on organ and new bassist Alan Cartwright, the band recorded *Live in Concert* with the Edmonton Symphony Orchestra and the Da Camera Singers. The success of the symphonic "Conquistador" remake caused a minor resurgence in sales, upon which the group failed to capitalize with *Grand Hotel*, a melange of orchestral epics and harder-rocking tunes. By the time of *Hotel*, Ball had left to form Bedlam and was replaced by ex-Cochise guitarist Mick Grabham. Two more albums, *Exotic Birds and Fruit* and *Procol Ninth*, went nowhere. After a two-year hiatus, the band tried one last time with *Something Magic*—produced by Leiber and Stoller—then broke up for good. After another two years, during which he played in the 1979 Concerts for Kampuchea, Brooker made a solo album, *No More Fear of Flying*, which was both a critical and commercial disappointment. In 1981, he played piano on Eric Clapton's LP *Another Ticket* and in 1982 he released *Lead Me to the Water*.

PROFESSOR LONGHAIR

Born Henry Roeland Byrd, December 19, 1918, Bogalusa, Louisiana; died January 30, 1980, New Orleans
1972—*New Orleans Piano* (Atlantic) 1975—*Rock 'n' Roll Gumbo* (Barclay) 1978—*Live on the Queen Mary* (Harvest) 1980—*Crawfish Fiesta* (Alligator).

Professor Longhair originated one of the classic styles of rock & roll piano playing, a New Orleans potpourri—ragtime, jazz, Delta blues, zydeco, West Indian and Afro-Cuban dances—distilled into boogie-woogie bass lines in the left hand and rolling arpeggios in the right. It was the style popularized by Fats Domino, Huey "Piano" Smith, Allen Toussaint, Dr. John and scores of others.

Henry Byrd first played piano when, as a boy, he discovered an abandoned upright in a New Orleans alley.

Producers

A producer's job is to make records—a process that can take minutes or years. In the early days of recording, the producer was the person who put the microphone somewhere near the musicians and turned on the tape recorder. Nowadays, with electronics and studio techniques that offer innumerable choices, those tasks are often left to engineers while the producer considers larger questions: Should the record sound like a documentary of the band playing live, or like a fantasy? And how, exactly, does the band sound?

Although some of the greatest blues and jazz recordings were made with decidedly primitive techniques, producers have been important from the beginning of rock & roll—partially because more of the musicians are amateurs, partially because records (more than live performances) are the way most rock is heard. As Jerry Leiber and Mike Stoller, who oversaw numerous early-Sixties pop recordings, claimed, "We didn't write songs, we wrote records."

Because rock is, for the most part, disseminated by radio, a distinctive recorded identity can be as important as a good stage show. Sam Phillips' liberal use of echo made Elvis Presley's first records stand out, but generally speaking, in the Fifties the job of the producer was to bring together the right musicians and get them to play at their best—a trickier proposition than it sounds. At Atlantic Records in the Fifties, for instance, Ahmet Ertegun and Jerry Wexler produced classic R&B records simply because they assembled tight, sophisticated bands; Dave Bartholemew and Allen Toussaint did the same in New Orleans.

As the Sixties began, producers began to gain recognition as collaborators, sometimes on an equal basis, with the acts they produced. Leiber and Stoller supplied songs, arrangements and technical expertise to the Coasters and others, including Elvis Presley. One of their students, Phil Spector, began to attract as much attention as the groups he produced: the Crystals, the Ronettes and the

Righteous Brothers. Leiber and Stoller had used pop trappings like strings and horns on R&B-style songs; Spector massed full orchestras, multiple pianos and percussionists and choruses behind his vocal groups to make a booming, amorphous roar he called the "Wall of Sound."

Meanwhile, in Los Angeles, young Brian Wilson managed to get an unusual recording contract under which he could produce his own band, the Beach Boys. He came up with a smooth, transparent sound that laid the groundwork for the perfectionism of virtually all the California rock that followed.

The advent of stereo in the early Sixties gave producers new leeway and new authority. Instruments could be placed anywhere in a 180-degree aural panorama, and multitracking (see Studio Techniques) gave producers the chance to add or subtract instruments at will. The Beatles and their producer, George Martin, experimented in the studio with all kinds of backup, with productions that grew increasingly more elaborate. The watershed of Sixties rock production was 1967's *Sgt. Pepper's Lonely Hearts Club Band*, which used strings, horns, brass bands, sound effects and all sorts of other noises in a dense collage, all assembled on a four-track tape. With *Sgt. Pepper* as an example, rock production took a turn for the baroque, as eclecticism ran rampant.

The most important production style of the Sixties, however, came from Motown Records, where "The Sound of Young America" was created by Berry Gordy, Jr., and a stable of producer/songwriters including Brian Holland, Lamont Dozier and Eddie Holland; Marvin Gaye; Smokey Robinson; Nick Ashford and Valerie Simpson; and later Norman Whitfield. The Motown Sound, which put equal emphasis on hard, danceable rhythms and melodic hooks, was applied to virtually every record, and producers, not singers, were in charge. When, in the Seventies, Stevie Wonder won the contractual right to produce his own records, it was a turning point.

In the psychedelic aftermath of the Beatles, many bands began to produce themselves, with results that were sometimes inspired (Sly and the Family Stone) and sometimes haphazard. But in the Seventies, as technology grew more complex and radio airplay got less automatic, producers reemerged as a new professional caste in rock. Some producers were sought after for their own styles: for hard rock, Jack Douglas or Bill Szymcyzk; for theatricalized hard rock, Bob Ezrin or Roy Thomas Baker; for singer/songwriters, Ted Templeman and Lenny Waronker or Peter Asher; for black pop, Quincy Jones or Thom Bell or Kenny Gamble and Leon Huff; for disco, Giorgio Moroder or Bernard Edwards and Nile Rodgers; for art rock, Brian Eno or Steve Lillywhite; for new wave, Nick Lowe.

With the recession of the early Eighties, production values shifted toward less elaborate, more live productions that could be done more quickly and cheaply, but producers were still important to provide an objective ear for the music.

Recalling everything he'd heard while dancing for tips outside of nightclubs and behind parade bands, he taught himself to play. It was not until he was thirty, however, that he began to work professionally as a musician; before then he'd had stints as a prizefighter, a gambler and a vaudeville dancer. In 1949, he formed a quintet called Professor Longhair and His Shuffling Hungarians, which included Robert Parker on tenor sax and recorded four songs—"She Ain't Got No Hair," "Mardi Gras in New Orleans," "Professor Longhair's Boogie" and "Bye Bye Baby"—on the Star Talent label.

The following year, the Professor was signed to Mercury and re-recorded "She Ain't Got No Hair" under the title "Baldhead," which reached #5 on *Billboard*'s R&B chart. Longhair later recorded on over a dozen labels, while a combination of poor health and mismanagement kept his career from being established. He received virtually nothing for "Go to the Mardi Gras," his 1959 remake of his own "Mardi Gras in New Orleans," which became a theme song of the annual carnival. Although "Big Chief" was a modest hit in the Louisiana area for him and Earl King in 1964, he soon afterwards left the music business and took up manual labor to support himself and his family.

In 1971, Longhair was rediscovered by talent scouts for the New Orleans Jazz and Heritage Festival; thereafter he performed at every New Orleans Festival until his death, and appeared on the 1976 live Festival album. His comeback also took him to the Newport Folk Festival in 1973 and to several festivals in Europe. In the last decade of his life, Atlantic released a collection of his vintage recordings, and he put out three newly recorded albums. Shortly before his death he was engaged to tour with the Clash.

PROGRESSIVE ROCK

Generally, "progressive" denotes a form of rock music in which electric instruments and rock-band formats are integrated with European classical motifs and orchestrations, typically forming extended, intricate, multisectional suites.

The progressive rock movement began in Britain in the late Sixties as an outgrowth of psychedelia's adventurism, and owes its lyrics' frequent use of cosmic themes to acid rock. But progressive rock is definitely a Seventies genre, accenting a daunting instrumental virtuosity and grandiosity over earthy directness.

One of the earliest and most influential progressive rock albums—in an album-oriented genre—is King Crimson's *In the Court of the Crimson King*, though that record pointed to the genre's prior influences, Procol Harum and the Moody Blues (for their churchy/symphonic classicism) and Jimi Hendrix (for his "cosmic," highly distorted guitar style). Progressive rock bands of the European classical virtuoso class—of wildly varying quality and popularity—include the Nice, King Crimson, Gentle Giant, Yes, Genesis, Emerson, Lake and Palmer, Focus, Kansas and Van der Graaf Generator.

Progressive rock is sometimes also known as "art rock"; though bands like Roxy Music, who rocked hard but made full, witty use of a self-conscious, ironic detachment that was less high-minded than Yes, ELP et al., are also known as "art-rockers," which can cause some confusion.

Ancillary to the British/European techno-flash movement was the whimsical jazz-rock-psychedelic fusion of Canterbury band Soft Machine, who begat a related school of more sedate, less grandiose chamber-oriented bands that were virtuosic in a more playfully jazzy manner—the Anglo/Gallic Gong (who later went the fusion route), Hatfield & the North and Caravan. This latter form of progressive rock has proven far less commercially successful than that of Yes, Genesis, ELP et al.

PSYCHEDELIC FURS

Formed 1977, London
Richard Butler (b. ca. 1953, Eng.), voc.; Tim Butler (b. ca. 1958, Eng.), bass; Duncan Kilburn (b. Eng.), sax; Roger Morris (b. Eng.), gtr.
1978—(+ John Ashton [b. Eng.], gtr.) **1979**—(+ Vince Ely [b. Eng.], drums) **1980**—*The Psychedelic Furs* (Columbia) **1981**—*Talk, Talk, Talk* (− Kilburn; − Morris; − Ely; + Phil Calvert, drums) **1982**— *Forever Now*.

Though their name may be psychedelic, the Furs' sound was very much a product of punk. The group began in early 1977 when leader/vocalist/songwriter Richard Butler joined with his younger brother Tim, Duncan Kilburn and Roger Morris. They decided on the name because it would stand out from all the S&M-named bands of the time and pay homage to their psychedelia-era idols like the Doors, the early Stooges and Velvet Underground.

Richard Butler had previously been an art student in college but around his graduation he decided to pursue music, although he knew little about playing. In November 1978, John Ashton joined on second guitar, and in the spring of 1979 they added drummer Vince Ely. The band's early dirges (which they describe as "beautiful chaos") were played by BBC disc jockey John Peel, which led to their signing with Columbia. Their debut was produced by Steve Lillywhite and Howard Thompson, with two tracks on the U.S. version produced by Martin Hannett. Though well received, it sold only moderately, as did their 1981 followup, *Talk, Talk, Talk*, despite its clearer lyrics and production (this time all by Lillywhite).

In 1982, several members left the band, protesting its new, more commercial direction. Their third album, *Forever Now*, was produced by Todd Rundgren and featured brass and strings; it included the Furs' first U.S. hit, "Love My Way."

PSYCHEDELIC ROCK

Also known variously as "acid rock" or the "San Francisco Sound," psychedelic music ostensibly intended to musically re-create the "trips" induced by mind-expanding drugs.

Many psychedelic bands, such as the Grateful Dead, Jefferson Airplane and Quicksilver Messenger Service, came out of San Francisco and its Haight-Ashbury district, the early center of hippie activity; concurrently, Britain produced Pink Floyd. Their music made use of electronic effects, extended forms and popular exotica like Middle Eastern modalities and Indian raga, and introduced extended improvisation into rock, often with musically dubious results but occasionally, as in the Grateful Dead's "Dark Star," with enough sustained invention and group interplay to stake a legitimate claim to the rock band as jazz ensemble. (The Grateful Dead are now the only major band still playing extended psychedelic jams in concert.)

This brand of psychedelia had some roots in the more adventurous forms of mid-Sixties American garage punk collated on albums like *Nuggets*, e.g. "It's a Happening" by the Magic Mushrooms or "Incense and Peppermints" by Strawberry Alarm Clock—both more poppish and naive than later psychedelia, but ultimately no more naive and outdated than most psychedelia soon became.

Nevertheless, all music that refers to drugs is not necessarily psychedelic, and all psychedelic music does not necessarily refer explicitly to drugs. Though psychedelia has become quaint and nostalgic, many of its innovations persisted through subsequent genres like progressive rock and some forms of fusion.

PUBLIC IMAGE LTD.

Formed 1978, England
John Lydon (a.k.a. Johnny Rotten, b. Jan. 31, 1956, Eng.), voc.; Keith Levene (b. Eng.), gtr., electronics; Jah Wobble (b. John Wordle, a.k.a. Dan MacArthur, Eng.), bass; Jim Walker (b. Canada), drums; Jeanette Lee, videos; Dave Crowe, business, finances.
1978—*Public Image Ltd.* (Virgin) **1979**—(− Walker; + Richard Dudanski, drums; − Dudanski; + Martin Atkins [b. Aug. 3, 1959, Coventry, Eng.], drums) **1980**—*Second Edition* (Virgin) *Paris au Printemps* (− Atkins, − Wobble) **1981**—(− Crowe) *Flowers of Romance* (Warner Bros.) (− Lee; + Pete Jones [b. Sep. 22, 1957], bass; + Atkins).

Public Image arose from the ashes of the Sex Pistols, attempting to be as much a reaction to that band as the Pistols were to Seventies rock & roll before them.

Former head Pistol Johnny Rotten took his real name, John Lydon, after the last Sex Pistols show on January 14, 1978. He conceived Public Image as a group organization to create "anti–rock & roll," to embody what the more conventionally rock-rooted Pistols only sang about. Lydon teamed up with Keith Levene, who was an early member of the Clash and also a classically trained guitarist and pianist, plus novice bassist Jah Wobble and drummer Jim Walker, from the Canadian group the Furys. Their original name was Carnivorous Buttock Flies, but they quickly changed to PIL (for Public Image Limited, the "Limited" since they professed to see themselves as a company rather than a rock band). Financial adviser Dave Crowe was credited as a band member.

PIL made their live debut in London on Christmas day 1978, just before their debut LP, *First Issue,* came out. It was not released in the U.S., and its slow, embittered songs got mostly negative reviews. Yet it soared to the top of the English charts. Critics caught on with 1979's *Second Edition,* released in England at first as a limited edition of 50,000, packaged as *Metal Box,* incorporating three 12-inch 45-rpm EPs in a film canister. It came out as a regular double LP in February 1980 in the U.S. to almost universal critical acclaim. *Second Edition* was characterized by a uniquely droning sound with prominent dublike bass, neopsychedelic guitar from Levene, oddly danceable rhythms and haunting echoed vocals. Levene's dissonant guitar influenced a whole range of bands, from Killing Joke and U2 to Gang of Four.

The band toured the U.S. in spring 1980 with new drummer Martin Atkins. At the end of the tour in June Atkins was fired (he joined the group Brian Brain), followed a few weeks later by Wobble. Wobble had released two solo LPs during his time in the band, and group members charged he used some PIL backing tracks on these without permission.

Later in 1980, a live LP from the band's Paris show the previous January, called *Paris au Printemps,* was issued in Europe only. In spring 1981, *The Flowers of Romance* came out. (The title was the name of late Sex Pistol Sid Vicious' first band.) Atkins as drummer-for-hire played on three tracks, with Levene and Lydon handling the rest. It was a stark, mostly percussion and vocals-oriented record with some Middle Eastern vocal influences. Its major connection to rock & roll may have been its audacity.

In May 1981, the band (Levene, Lydon and hired musicians) played New York's Ritz, using audio and video tapes and performing behind a screen, rendering them barely visible; they then verbally encouraged a bottle-throwing riot started by disappointed fans. The band videotaped the debacle for a future film project.

GARY PUCKETT AND THE UNION GAP

Formed 1967, San Diego, California
Gary Puckett (b. Oct. 17, 1942, Hibbing, Minn.), voc.; Dwight Bement (b. Dec. 1945, San Diego), sax; Kerry Chater (b. Aug. 7, 1945, Vancouver), bass; Mutha Withem (b. Aug. 22, 1946, San Diego), piano; Paul Wheatbread (b. Feb. 8, 1946, San Diego), drums.
1968—*Woman, Woman* (Columbia) *Young Girl; Incredible* **1970**—*Greatest Hits.*

Gary Puckett and the Union Gap had four big pop-soul soundalike hits within a year, beginning in late 1967 with "Woman, Woman."

The band formed in January 1967 in San Diego, where

they all had gone to school. They played the local circuit as the Outcasts but then took the name Union Gap from a small town in Washington State near where Puckett grew up. The only member with prior professional experience was Paul Wheatbread, who, after attending San Diego's Mesa College, became a regular on Dick Clark's "Where the Action Is." He had played with the Turtles, the Mamas and the Papas, Paul Revere and the Raiders, and Otis Redding.

The Union Gap's visual gimmick was to appear in blue and gold Civil War uniforms. After "Woman, Woman" the band hit #2 with both "Young Girl" and "Lady Willpower." The fourth big hit of 1968 was "Over You" (#7). "Young Girl" became a hit (#6) a second time in England in 1974. (It had been #1 there in 1968 as well.) In all, they released six LPs plus a best of, all produced by Fuller. But after 1968, their hits faded; they disbanded in 1971.

Puckett pursued an unsuccessful solo career and Chater, who had written many Union Gap songs, wrote tunes for Cass Elliot, Charlie Rich and Bobby Darin. He also did backup vocals for Sonny and Cher and "The Tonight Show" and recorded two solo LPs for Warner Bros.: *Part Time Love* and *Love on a Shoestring* (1978).

PUNK ROCK

The first punk rock was the aggressively amateurish, undecorous response of mid-Sixties middle-American garage bands to the more genteel British Invasion. This was the stuff of the *Nuggets* and *Wild Thing* compilations, tunes like ?(Question Mark) and the Mysterians' "96 Tears," Count Five's "Psychotic Reaction" and the Standells' "Dirty Water."

Now flash forward to mid-Seventies Britain: A generation of youth, disgusted with what it perceives as a corpulent, conservative, irrelevant and institutionalized rock establishment, creates punk rock. The music is raw, abrasive, basic and very fast, its rhythms forced and decidedly unfunky. The musicians are usually untrained, and make fashion statements with severely cropped hair, black leather and sadomasochistic bondage gear. Punk is an expression of postindustrial angst, nihilism and revulsion; its antecedents are such similarly abrasive, aggressive and minimally basic American bands as the Stooges, the MC5 and the New York Dolls.

Just before Britain's punk rock explosion, the Ramones had emerged from New York's more arty punk scene—alongside Talking Heads, Patti Smith and Television—with their stripped-down, hyperdriven remodelings of Sixties garage rock. They served as another inspiration to British punk bands like the Sex Pistols (with the first punk antihit "Anarchy in the U.K."), the Clash ("White Riot") and the Buzzcocks ("Boredom"). Soon, punk inevitably became an institution itself. It begat an acceptable corporate face in new wave, and caught on in America more through fashion advertisements than through music. The Sex Pistols broke up at the end of their brief first and only U.S. tour; the Clash matured into an ethnic-fusion band with political overtones; Buzzcocks turned to punky love songs, then broke up. There are more punk rock bands, and some lingering effects spurred by punk innovations, especially in the form of punk's introduction of female band members who shared equal footing with male counterparts.

By the early Eighties, though, punk had turned into American and British "hard-core" movements. The music was louder, harder and faster, the politics more nihilistic than ever and the use of dress codes (leather) and hairstyles (the Mohawk) was more pronounced than ever.

JAMES AND BOBBY PURIFY

James Purify, born May 12, 1944, Pensacola, Florida; Bobby Purify, born Robert Lee Dicky, September 2, 1939, Tallahassee, Florida .

James and Bobby Purify's 1966 debut, "I'm Your Puppet," was laid-back soul which charmed both black and white audiences, reaching #6 pop and #5 R&B. These cousins, who had been singing together just over a year before "Puppet," had previously been members of a Florida band, the Dothan Sextet. They subsequently charted with "Shake a Tail Feather" (#25 pop, #15 R&B), "I Take What I Want" (#41 pop, #23 R&B) and

"Let Love Come Between Us" (#23 pop, #18 R&B) in 1967. The Purifys signed with Casablanca Records in 1974 and cut "Do Your Thing" (#30 R&B).

FLORA PURIM

Born Rio de Janeiro
1974—*Butterfly Dreams* (Milestone)   1975—*Stories to Tell*   1976—*Open Your Eyes, You Can Fly*   1977—*Nothing Will Be As It Was . . . Tomorrow* (Warner Bros.).

Singer Flora Purim grew up in a middle-class Jewish family in Rio, married Brazilian jazz percussionist Airto Moreira and came with him to the U.S. in 1968. She worked with Moreira, Stan Getz and others, and sang on Chick Corea's *Return to Forever* LP and 1972's *Light as a Feather*.

Purim has a 6½-octave range and claims the childhood influence of Billie Holiday. She says that her highly developed scat-singing technique is partly attributable to language difficulties. In 1974, the same year she won *Downbeat*'s #1 Female Vocalist award, she was imprisoned for 18 months in Long Beach, California, for cocaine possession. She was finally freed, with some assistance from music industry figures, in December 1975. She continues to tour and record.

Q

QUARTERFLASH

Formed 1980, Portland, Oregon

Rindy Ross, voc., sax; Marv Ross, voc., gtr.; Jack
Charles, voc., gtr.; Rick DiGiallonardo, kybds.; Brian
David Willis, drums; Rick Gooch, bass.
1981—*Quarterflash* (Geffen)   **1983**—*Take Another
Picture.*

Quarterflash debuted in 1981 with two huge pop hits,
"Harden My Heart" (#3) and "Find Another Fool." The
band includes former members of two popular Portland
area bands, Seafood Mama and Pilot.

Seafood Mama, led by the husband-and-wife team
Rindy and Marv Ross, had landed a contract with Geffen
Records and traveled to Los Angeles to record with
producer John Boylan. In Portland, the Rosses recruited
Jack Charles, Rick DiGiallonardo, Brian David Willis and
Rick Gooch of Pilot to their new group. They came up
with the name, citing an Australian colloquialism "a quarter flash and three parts foolish." "Harden My Heart" had
been a #1 hit in the Portland area for Seafood Mama in
1980 before Quarterflash made their national hit version.

SUZI QUATRO

Born June 3, 1950, Detroit
1973—*Suzi Quatro* (Bell)   **1974**—*Quatro*   **1975**—*Your
Mama Won't Like Me* (Arista)   **1977**—*Aggro Phobia*
(RAK)   **1978**—*If You Knew Suzi* (RSO)   **1980**—*Greatest
Hits.*

Suzi Quatro was a pioneer female rocker who got a lot of
attention in her early-Seventies heyday with her leather
look and British glitter hard-pop sound. Fronting her own
band and playing hard sexual music, she was the prototype and idol of Joan Jett.

Born to a musical family (her father was a semi-pro jazz
bandleader), Quatro began playing bongos at age eight in
her father's jazz trio. Her sister Patti later played with the
all-female Fanny for a while, and brother Michael released
several "Jam Band" LPs in the mid-Seventies. Suzi quit
high school and formed her first band with sisters Patti,
Nancy and Arlene, an all-girl unit called Suzi Soul (her
stage name) and the Pleasure Seekers in 1965.

The group did some dates entertaining troops in Vietnam, and by the end of the Sixties they had changed their
name to Cradle. Mickie Most saw Cradle in Detroit, and
after the group disbanded, Suzi Quatro took up Most's
offer to come to England and sign with his RAK Records.
She wrote her own debut single, 1972's "Rolling Stone,"
but it didn't sell, so Most linked her up with the highly
commercial Nicky Chinn-Mike Chapman songwriting/pro-
ducing team, who gave her a string of British hits in the
bubble gum/hard rock vein of Slade, T. Rex and Gary
Glitter.

"Can the Can" (#1 U.K., over two million sold),
"Daytona Demon" (#14 U.K.) and "48 Crash" (#3 U.K.)
all hit in England in 1973, as did "Devil's Gate Drive" (#1
U.K., a million-seller) and "The Wild One" (#7 U.K.) in
1974. Quatro stressed her tough image ("She hasn't
owned a dress in years," claimed her bio). In 1974, Quatro
tried to repeat her European triumph in the U.S. with
tours that year and the next, opening for Alice Cooper.
But despite heavy media coverage, commercial success
was not forthcoming. "All Shook Up" and "Can the Can"
were minor hits in the U.S., but during her time Stateside
she soon lost her British fans.

In the fall of 1977, Quatro began appearing on the U.S.
TV show "Happy Days," as the one-season semi-regular
Leather Tuscadero, who fronted the hard-rock band
Leather and the Suedes. She got a new record deal with
RSO and released *If You Knew Suzi* (still produced by
Chapman), which yielded the #4 hit "Stumblin' In," a
duet with Chris Norman. She signed with Chapman's label
Dreamland in 1980 and had a minor U.S. hit, "Lipstick"
(#51, 1981).

QUEEN

Formed 1971, England
Freddie Mercury (b. Frederick Bulsara, Sep. 5, 1946,
Zanzibar), voc., piano; Brian May (b. July 19, 1947,
Hampton, Eng.), gtr.; John Deacon (b. Aug. 19, 1951,
Leicester, Eng.), bass; Roger Meadows-Taylor (b. July
26, 1949, Norfolk, Eng.), drums.
1973—*Queen* (Elektra)   **1974**—*Queen II; Sheer Heart
Attack*   **1975**—*A Night at the Opera*   **1976**—*A Day at
the Races*   **1977**—*News of the World*   **1978**—*Jazz*
1979—*Live Killers*   **1980**—*The Game; Flash Gordon*
(soundtrack)   **1981**—*Greatest Hits*   **1982**—*Hot Space.*

The enormously popular British band Queen is the epitome of pomp rock, with elaborate stage setups, smoke
bombs, flashpots, and lead singer Freddie Mercury's half-
martial, half-coy preening onstage, and highly produced,
much-overdubbed music on record.

Queen can be traced back to 1971, when Brian May and
Roger Taylor joined singer Tim Staffell in a group called
Smile. Staffell soon left to go solo, and the remaining two
Smiles teamed up with Freddie Mercury (from a group

Queen: Roger Taylor, Freddie Mercury, Brian May, John Deacon

called Wreckage) and later John Deacon. They played very few gigs at the start, avoiding the club circuit and rehearsing for two years while they all remained in college. (May has a Ph.D. in astronomy, Taylor in biology, Deacon a degree in electronics and Mercury in illustration and design.) They began touring in 1973, when their debut album was released. After a second LP, the band made its U.S. tour debut opening for Mott the Hoople.

Queen's sound combined showy glam rock, heavy metal and intricate vocal harmonies produced by multitracking Mercury's voice. May's guitar was also thickly overdubbed; one LP included "God Save the Queen" rendered as a chorale of lead guitar lines. (Until 1980, their albums boasted that "no synths" were used.) Queen's third LP, *Sheer Heart Attack,* featured "Killer Queen," their first U.S. Top Twenty hit. The LP also became their first U.S. gold.

Heavy-metal fans loved them (despite Freddie Mercury's onstage pseudo-dramatics, which had more to do with his admitted influence Liza Minnelli than Robert Plant), and their audience grew with their breakthrough LP, *A Night at the Opera,* containing the six-minute gold "Bohemian Rhapsody," including a Mercury solo episode of "mama mia" with dozens of vocal tracks. "Bohemian Rhapsody" stayed at #1 in England for nine weeks, breaking the record Paul Anka had held since 1957 for his "Diana."

Queen has had ten gold and four platinum records; only their second LP and their 1980 soundtrack to the film *Flash Gordon* failed to sell so impressively. They have remained productive over the years despite the success that has made them all millionaires. Each member writes

songs. Their U.S. hit singles include "Killer Queen" (#12), 1975; "Bohemian Rhapsody" (#9), "You're My Best Friend" (#16), "Somebody to Love" (#13), 1976; "Tie Your Mother Down" (#49), "We Are the Champions" b/w "We Will Rock You" (#4), 1977; "Fat Bottomed Girls" b/w "Bicycle Race" (#24), for which the group staged an all-female nude bicycle race, 1978; "Crazy Little Thing Called Love" (#1), 1979; "Play the Game" (#42), "Another One Bites the Dust" (#1), "Need Your Loving Tonight" (#44), 1980; "Flash" (#42), and "Under Pressure" with David Bowie (#29), 1982. At first, their hits were marchlike hard rock, but in the late Seventies the group began to branch out; their two biggest hits were the rockabilly-style "Crazy Little Thing Called Love" and the disco style "Another One Bites the Dust," a close relative of Chic's "Good Times" that went to #1 pop and R&B.

In 1981, Taylor released a solo album, *Fun in Space,* and later in the year the band recorded with an outsider for the first time, writing and singing with David Bowie on "Under Pressure," included on both their platinum *Greatest Hits* and *Hot Space.* One side of *Hot Space* was typically bombastic rock, while the other was funk followups to "Another One Bites the Dust."

?(QUESTION MARK) AND THE MYSTERIANS
Formed 1962, Flint, Michigan
Original lineup: Question Mark (b. 1945), voc.; Robert Martinez, drums; Larry Borjas, gtr. Later members included: Robert Balderrama (b. 1950), gtr.; Frank Rodriguez (b. 1951), kybds.; Frank Lugo (b. 1947), bass; Edward Serrato (b. 1947), drums.
1966—*96 Tears* (Cameo) *Action.*

Question Mark and the Mysterians' one song of consequence was not only a #1 hit but also epitomized a classic sound in rock & roll—that of the Farfisa organ. The song was "96 Tears" and with its famous organ line and leader ?'s gruff vocals it topped the charts in 1966.

The band's quick rise and fall were mirrored in the mystery surrounding the group. Their leader was never photographed without sunglasses, and he legally changed his name to simply ?. (The song is credited to Rudy Martinez, though ? refuses to say whether that's his name, and he has never revealed his background; it is believed that Martinez is a name he invented to collect royalties.) What *is* known is that all the major band members were born in Mexico and later moved to Detroit. Two original members, Robert Martinez and Larry Borjas, went into the Army before the band's big success. The group became local favorites in the Detroit area and their "96 Tears" was first cut for a small Flint, Michigan, record company. It became the most requested song on Flint's WTAC and Detroit's KCLW, leading to a national deal with Cameo Records, where it went on to sell over a million copies. Later in the year the band also hit #22 with "I Need Somebody," but their followups flopped, and by

1968 they called it quits. Mel Schacher, later bassist with Grand Funk, played in one of the later stages of the group.

In 1981, ? made a low-level comeback with an all-new group of Mysterians. They toured and played oldies plus new material, though the band featured a Vox instead of a Farfisa organ. The same year, Garland Jeffreys released a minor hit version of the old smash. (It had become very popular in new wave circles in the late Seventies, seen as an early punk nugget.) Joe "King" Carrasco also performed it live in 1980 and, in fact, built his entire sound around the Farfisa style that ? helped pioneer.

QUICKSILVER MESSENGER SERVICE
Formed 1965, San Francisco
Gary Duncan (b. Sep. 4, 1946, San Diego, Calif.), gtr., voc.; John Cipollina (b. Aug. 24, 1943, Berkeley, Calif.), gtr.; David Freiberg (b. Aug. 24, 1938, Boston), bass, voc.; Greg Elmore (b. Sep. 4, 1946, San Diego, Calif.), drums; Jim Murray, voc., harmonica.
1966—(− Murray) 1968—*Quicksilver Messenger Service* (Capitol) 1969—*Happy Trails* (− Duncan; + Nicky Hopkins [b. Feb. 24, 1944, London], kybds.) *Shady Grove* 1970—(+ Duncan; + Dino Valenti [b. Nov. 7, 1943, New York City], voc., gtr.) *Just for Love* (Capitol) (− Hopkins) 1971—(+ Mark Naftalin, piano) *What About Me* (− Cipollina; − Freiberg; + Mark Ryan, bass; − Naftalin; + Chuck Steales, organ) 1972—*Quicksilver* (Capitol) *Comin' Thru* (disbanded) 1973—*Anthology* (re-formed with Duncan, Cipollina, Elmore, Valenti, Freiberg) 1975—*Solid Silver.*

Quicksilver Messenger Service were one of the vintage acid-rock San Francisco bands of the late Sixties. Their early shows and albums (featuring the heavily tremoloed guitar work of John Cipollina plus that of second guitarist Gary Duncan) contributed some of the best-remembered instrumental jam music of the period. But as the Sixties ended, the band's popularity waned and they were never as popular nationally as their S.F. contemporaries, Jefferson Airplane and the Grateful Dead.

The group formed in 1965 with Gary Duncan, John Cipollina (whose godfather was classical pianist José Iturbi), David Freiberg and Greg Elmore plus Jim Murray. Their original guitarist was to have been Dino Valenti (a Greenwich Village folksinger and, under the name "Chester A. Powers," writer of "Hey Joe" and the Youngbloods' hit "Get Together"). But Valenti was arrested on a drug charge and jailed for 18 months.

In early 1966, the fivesome began playing the local circuit, but soon after, Jim Murray left to study the sitar. They recorded their debut as a quartet in December 1967, and it came out in May 1968, featuring jams like the 12-minute "The Fool." The band also provided two songs for the soundtrack of *Revolution,* out that year, and in late 1968 they recorded their part-live second LP, *Happy Trails.* After the second LP came out, though, in January 1969 Valenti got Duncan to move to New York and form a group with him; British sessionman Nicky Hopkins took Duncan's place, and was prominently featured on *Shady Grove.*

In early 1970, Duncan returned, bringing Valenti with him. Valenti finally joined Quicksilver three years late (though his "Dino's Song" appears on the debut LP). The new sextet issued *Just for Love,* and "Fresh Air" received FM airplay, helping to make the LP one of their biggest sellers (#27, 1970).

Hopkins left just before the release of *What about Me?,* and some of the tracks featured his replacement, Mark Naftalin. Cipollina also left around this time; he later formed Copperhead with early Quicksilverite Jim Murray, and in 1974 briefly played with the Welsh band Man. During 1971 Freiberg left. That year he was jailed for marijuana possession and then he did sessions with the Jefferson Airplane, whom he later joined in their Jefferson Starship incarnation in 1972. The remaining Quicksilver threesome—Duncan, Elmore and Valenti—produced two more LPs, *Quicksilver* and *Comin' Thru,* with Mark Ryan (bass) and keyboardist Chuck Steales, but these sparked little public interest. Quicksilver faded away but resurfaced in late 1975 for a brief reunion as a quintet including Freiberg and Cipollina.

R

EDDIE RABBITT

Born Edward Thomas, November 27, 1944, Brooklyn, New York

1975—*Eddie Rabbitt* (Elektra) **1976**—*Rocky Mountain Music* **1977**—*Rabbitt* **1978**—*Variations* **1979**— *Loveline; Best of Eddie Rabbitt* **1980**—*Horizon* **1981**—*Step by Step.*

After struggling on the outskirts of the Nashville country music community through much of the Seventies, Eddie Rabbitt emerged as a popular singer/songwriter in the early Eighties.

From East Orange, New Jersey, Edward Thomas migrated to Nashville in 1968 and landed a $37-a-week job as a staff writer at Hill and Range, a music publishing house.

His big break came in 1971, when Elvis Presley recorded his "Kentucky Rain," which became Presley's fiftieth gold record. (In 1973, Ronnie Milsap had a #1 hit with Rabbitt's "Pure Love.") Rabbitt's own singles—"Forgive and Forget," "Drinkin' My Baby (Off My Mind)," "Rocky Mountain Music" and "Two Dollars in the Juke-box"—established him with country audiences, and with his 1979 hit theme to Clint Eastwood's film *Every Which Way but Loose* he crossed over to the pop audience.

Rabbitt's later hits include "Suspicious" (#1 country, #13 pop, 1979), "Drivin' My Life Away" (#1 country, #5 pop, 1980), "I Love a Rainy Night" (#1 country, #1 pop, 1980) and "Step by Step" (#1 country, #5 pop, 1981). Rabbitt's 1981 *Horizon* went platinum, and both "Rainy Night" and "Step" were million-selling singles.

Radio

Rock and radio have evolved hand in hand, each molding the other. Radio airplay sells records; popular music pulls in listeners and makes commercial time more valuable. And like rock, radio programing goes through cycles of upset and innovation, followed by consolidation and formating.

As the advent of television killed radio drama, all-music (and talk and news) stations began to appear. The first major breakthrough for rock radio was Alan Freed's "Moondog Matinee" in the early Fifties, a program aimed at white teenagers, which played black R&B records. It attracted a huge audience, and stations across the country began to pick up both the idea and Freed's manic patter. Like the black disc jockeys and singers he had learned from, Freed used black and beatnik slang, onomatopoeia, shouts, giggles and anything else that came to mind. Each disc jockey made indepen-

dent decisions about what to play; those decisions occasionally suggested conflicts of interest. Since rock & roll was being blamed, by the end of the Fifties, for everything from juvenile delinquency to an increase in premarital motherhood, Freed and other disc jockeys were investigated for "payola"; Freed was hounded to his death.

In the meantime, the idea of a "format" had entered radio programing. A station would maintain a consistent mix of music, talk, identification jingles, etc., through the broadcast day, and its playlist would concentrate on proven hits, removing the disc jockey's choice (and corruptibility). KOWH in Omaha, Nebraska, had a format as early as 1949, and as pop hits became synonymous with rock & roll, Top Forty stations began to fit them into the format. Another factor was chain ownership of radio stations; more and more were

centrally programed as the Fifties progressed.

Although disc jockeys maintained their jivey "personalities" while giving the time every ten minutes, the weather every twenty minutes, the station ID between each song, or whatever the format called for, AM playlists grew gradually more restricted. From the Top Forty (with the most popular songs, perhaps the Top Ten, played more frequently than the rest) playlists shrank to twenty or fifteen records. As a result, fewer records were played frequently enough to benefit from radio exposure. Timid radio programing in the early Sixties helped choke back rock & roll performers in favor of the more clean-cut, malleable teen idols and pop singers that the old-line music and record business understood. But the early-Sixties folk revival reminded music fans that amateurs could make music, and the overwhelming success of the Beatles—who hit baby-boom teenagers as they became a majority—put the great unwashed back on the radio.

Stereo recording and FM radio, both of which made music more vivid, caught on during the Sixties; so did the notion that rock could be significant, and the idea of the album (rather than the single) as an artistic whole. In the mid-Sixties, the Federal Communications Commission ruled that jointly owned AM and FM stations had to present different programing, and suddenly the FM band opened up to rock records, a cheap source of program material. Rather than duplicate the Top Forty format, some programers assumed that FM listeners were likely to be more mature than AM listeners, and some stations—among them WOR-FM in New York City—began allowing disc jockeys to program "underground" rock as they saw fit. (Some stations, particularly college radio stations, went even further and allowed disc jockeys to mix rock, jazz, classical and whatever other program material seemed appropriate.)

"Underground" disc jockeys played songs that were unlikely to be released as singles and songs that were longer than three minutes; they also experimented with a less driven, more conversational tone of voice like that of the prerock DJs. "Underground" or "progressive" FM radio used longer, less predictable music segments, and also toyed with the segue—overlapping the end of one song with the beginning of the next—to connect records through musical similarities. In the late Sixties, progressive "free-form" commercial FM stations reached the burgeoning youth culture and became the medium of choice for advertising concerts, stereos, waterbeds, drug paraphernalia and other hip-capitalist products. And with FM rock radio as an outlet,

more musicians began to experiment with five- and seven-minute songs and ideas that could not be shaped into a bouncy, teen-accessible tune for the AM market.

During Richard Nixon's presidency, the FCC did not take kindly to FM radio becoming a seditious hippie intercom, and made vague noises threatening the licenses of stations that played obscene or drug-oriented lyrics in 1971. That scare, the huge increase in the number of albums released (spurred, of course, by their chance to be played on the radio) and the more cautious climate of the early Seventies relocated control over playlists in the hands of program directors; there was also competition between the increasing number of FM rock stations.

The solution was another format, which eventually became known as AOR (album-oriented radio). Once again, playlists were limited, this time to album cuts that program directors (or national programing consultants, like Lee Abrams) believed would not alienate their audiences. The songs might be seven minutes in length and more or less raunchy in content, but they were slotted into twenty-minute segments punctuated by time, weather, news, etc., at regular intervals. In city after city, reassuringly predictable AOR stations began earning higher ratings than free-form competitors, many of whom eventually adopted formats in self-defense. By the end of the Seventies, free-form radio was largely confined to college radio—and even there, some program directors in training made up their own pseudo-AOR formats.

The music that best fitted AOR formats was conservative, smooth and not radically different from the Rolling Stones, Beatles, Bob Dylan and Who songs that were staples of free-form radio. Yet tempos slowed imperceptibly, production values

grew more important and it became easier for baby-boomers to use AOR as background music. AOR playlists grew smaller and smaller through the Seventies, making it harder for new music that did not segue into the old favorites. Slowly, black music was ruled out of the format almost completely. AOR stations also began to play AM hits, which had begun to reflect FM-nurtured tastes.

Disco, and to a lesser extent punk, began to challenge AOR in the late Seventies, particularly in urban areas. Disco spoke directly to a black audience, and its steady pulse was just as effective a background-music metronome as AOR. In New York, a disco station topped the ratings over both AOR stations and Top Twenty AM formats, and some radio stations rushed to copy the format. AOR fans responded with a battle cry—"Disco sucks!"—that suggested both homophobia and racial hostility; disco radio was rejected outside big cities. Punk never made it into a radio format, but it affected musicians and club audiences. And the fallout from punk and disco—faster tempos and harder rhythms—crept onto AOR via AM radio (where disco had flourished) and through musicians' own interest.

In the early Eighties, the AOR format had clearly peaked. As ratings dropped and programers tried to further restrict playlists, other, more localized formats began to appear, from "urban contemporary" (danceable new wave and funk and disco) to "adult contemporary" (hip easy listening, all ballads and acoustic guitars) to a punk-influenced Top 40 FM to all-country, all-news and, on the flagship Top Twenty AM station of the ABC network, all-talk. As of 1982, some cities had stations that were broadcasting in AM stereo—a new variable.

GERRY RAFFERTY
Born in Scotland
1971—*Can I Have My Money Back?* (Transatlantic)
1974—*Revisited* 1978—*Gerry Rafferty* (Logo, import) *City to City* (United Artists) 1979—*Night Owl* 1980—*Snakes and Ladders.*

Though he had recorded a well-received 1971 solo album, it wasn't until five years after his former band, Stealers Wheel, had a hit with "Stuck in the Middle with You" that singer/songwriter Rafferty came into his own as a solo act. In 1978, his "Baker Street" was a huge international hit—it reached #2 in the U.S. at one point—and the album it came from, *City to City,* went gold. This success came after three years of post-Stealers Wheel management/record-label problems. Rafferty, who rarely performs live and then only in England and Europe, has never repeated that success, though *Night Owl* and its single "Days Gone Down" both made the Top Thirty in the U.S.

BONNIE RAITT
Born November 8, 1949, Los Angeles
1971—*Bonnie Raitt* (Warner Bros.) 1972—*Give It Up* 1973—*Takin' My Time* 1974—*Streetlights* 1975—*Home Plate* 1977—*Sweet Forgiveness* 1979—*The Glow* 1982—*Green Light.*

Singer/guitarist Bonnie Raitt's music incorporates blues, R&B, pop and folk. Though her albums have always sold respectably (averaging several hundred thousand copies), and she has been a headliner since the mid-Seventies, she has yet to achieve the great success critics have been predicting since she debuted in 1971.

The daughter of Broadway singer John Raitt (star of *Pajama Game* and *Carousel*), Bonnie Raitt started playing guitar at age 12 and was immediately attracted to the blues. In 1967, she left her L.A. home to enter Radcliffe, but she dropped out after two years and began playing the local folk and blues clubs. Dick Waterman, longtime blues aficionado and manager, signed her, and soon she was performing with Howlin' Wolf, Sippie Wallace, Mississippi Fred McDowell and other blues legends. Her reputation in Boston and Philadelphia led to a record contract with Warner Bros.

Raitt's early albums were critically acclaimed for her singing and guitar playing (she is one of the few women who play bottleneck) as well as her choice of material, which often included blues as well as pop and folk songs. Most of Raitt's repertoire consists of covers, and she has gone out of the way to credit her sources, often touring with them as opening acts. Her sixth album, *Sweet Forgiveness,* went gold and yielded a hit cover version of Del Shannon's "Runaway." *The Glow* (featuring her first original tunes since three on *Give It Up*) was produced by Peter Asher, but it didn't sell as well as its predecessor.

Raitt was a founder of M.U.S.E. (Musicians United for Safe Energy), which in September 1979 held a massive concert at Madison Square Garden, with other stars like Jackson Browne, James Taylor and the Doobie Brothers. It was later commemorated on a three-LP set. In 1982, she released her eighth LP, *Green Light,* which was a harder-rocking effort aided by her backup band, the Bump Band, which included veteran keyboardist Ian MacLagan (of the Faces and the Stones). They toured with Raitt in mid-1982, greeted by the usual critical acclaim. Her work also appeared on the platinum 1980 *Urban Cowboy* soundtrack, with the country song "Don't It Make You Wanna Dance." The one constant in Raitt's bands has been Freebo on bass and tuba.

THE RAMONES
Formed 1974, New York City
Joey Ramone (b. Jeffrey Hyman, 1952), voc.; Johnny Ramone (b. John Cummings, Long Island, N.Y.), gtr.; Dee Dee Ramone (b. Douglas Colvin, 1952, Va.), bass; Tommy Ramone (b. Tom Erdelyi, 1952, Budapest), drums.
1976—*Ramones* (Sire) *Ramones Leave Home* 1977—*Rocket to Russia* (− Tommy Ramone; + Marky Ramone [b. Mark Bell], drums) 1978—*Road to Ruin* 1979—*Rock 'n' Roll High School* (soundtrack) *It's Alive* (British import) 1980—*End of the Century* 1981—*Pleasant Dreams* 1983—*Subterranean Jungle.*

In the mid-Seventies, the Ramones shaped the sound of punk rock in New York: simple but fast songs with deadpan lyrics, no solos and a wall of guitar chords. Their influence stretched from Los Angeles to London.

The group formed in 1974, after the foursome graduated or left high school in Forest Hills, New York. The original lineup featured Joey on drums, Dee Dee sharing guitar with Johnny, and Tommy as manager, but they soon settled on their recording setup. Their name and pseudonym came via Paul McCartney, who had briefly called himself Phil Ramone back when the Beatles were Silver Beatles. The Ramones quickly gravitated toward the burgeoning scene at CBGB, where their twenty-minute sets of rapid-fire, under two-and-a-half minute songs earned them a recording contract before any of their contemporaries except Patti Smith.

In 1976, *Ramones* was a definitive punk statement, with songs like "Beat on the Brat," "Blitzkrieg Bop" and "Now I Wanna Sniff Some Glue"—13 of them, clocking in at under a half hour. The group traveled to England in 1976, giving the nascent British punk scene the same boost they had provided to New Yorkers. Before the year was out, *Ramones Leave Home* had been released. Then as now, the band toured almost incessantly.

With their next two singles, the group began to soften their sound slightly. "Sheena Is a Punk Rocker" and "Rockaway Beach" made explicit the influence that bub-

The Ramones: Johnny Ramone, Joey Ramone, Marky Ramone, Dee Dee Ramone

blegum and surf music had had on the Ramones from the start, and both made the lower reaches of the Top 100. They were included on 1977's *Rocket to Russia,* which also contained their first ballad, "Here Today, Gone Tomorrow." At this point, Tommy quit the band, preferring his behind-the-scenes activity as the band's coproducer, "disguised" as T. Erdelyi (his real name).

His replacement was Mark Bell, henceforth dubbed Marky Ramone. He was formerly one of Richard Hell's Voidoids and before that a member of Dust, who recorded a pair of albums during the Sixties. His first LP with the Ramones, *Road to Ruin,* was their first to contain only 12 songs and their first to last longer than thirty minutes. Despite their glossiest production yet, featuring acoustic guitars and real solos, its two singles, "Don't Come Close" and a version of the Searchers' "Needles and Pins," failed to break through to a mass audience. Neither did their starring role in Roger Corman's 1979 movie *Rock 'n' Roll High School.*

In the Eighties, the Ramones tried working with noted pop producers Phil Spector (*End of the Century*) and 10cc's Graham Gouldman (*Pleasant Dreams*), but commercial success remained elusive, while the band continued to draw full houses in concert.

RAP

Rap is a form of dance music in which vocalists—rappers—speak in rhythm and rhyme over prerecorded instrumental tracks. Radio and dance-club disc jockeys, concert emcees, reggae toasters and occasional R&B singers have talked over or chanted to music for many years, but rapping as a specialized style originated in the mid-Seventies in the discos of New York City's black neighborhoods, alongside such ghetto arts as freedom writing, break dancing and double-dutch jump-roping.

The progenitors of rap were spinners—disco DJs who segued songs for dancers. The first notable ghetto spin-

ners—Cool Herc, Afrika Bambaataa, Pete "DJ" Jones and others—began working discos in the Bronx around 1974. By 1977, young admirers like Grandmaster Flash, Deejay Hollywood and Dave D were spinning at street level—in playgrounds, at parties, at gym dances—for the mostly teenaged listeners known as b-boys and fly girls, who invented the part-mime, part-acrobatics dance style called break dancing.

For their tracks, the new generation preferred James Brown, Sly and the Family Stone, Chic and Funkadelic to newer disco hits. They experimented with turntable techniques like fast-break mixing to edit together snatches of songs; double tracking to repeat phrases or set them out of phase; and back spinning to elicit unexpected sounds from the grooves.

The younger spinners teamed up with rappers—Grandmaster Flash with the Furious Five, Dave D with Kurtis Blow. Initially, the role of the rapper was to encourage listeners to keep the beat going with handclaps while the spinner changed records. Before long, rappers had developed extensive routines: lines of lyrics, slogans, double-dutch rhymes, call-and-response exchanges with the audience, or the rhythmic doggerel called hip-hop. Solo rappers like Spoonie Gee extemporized much of their material, while groups like the Funky Four Plus One and Trouble Funk worked out arrangements of traded, overlapped and unison lines.

Dancing and partying and the romantic prowess of the rapper were the dominant themes of rap, but rap also had a political thrust, recalling the work of Gil-Scott Heron and the Last Poets. Such raps as Brother D's "How We Gonna Make the Black Nation Rise?" and Grandmaster Flash and the Furious Five's "The Message" were among the most overtly political statements from black musicians since the late Sixties.

The first rap records were not made until 1979, most of them for small independent labels like Enjoy, Sugarhill and Clappers. Very quickly, however, rap acquired widespread popularity. The Sugar Hill Gang, Fatback and Kurtis Blow had the first national rap hits. By 1980, rap had crossed racial lines, as white acts like Ian Dury, Blondie, the Clash and the Tom Tom Club adopted rap styles into their music.

RARE EARTH
Formed, 1969, Detroit
Gil Bridges, flute, sax, percussion, voc.; Pete Rivera, drums, voc.; John Persh, bass, trombone, voc.; Rob Richards, gtr., voc.; Kenny James, kybds.
1969—*Get Ready* (Rare Earth) **1970**—*Ecology* (− Richards; + Ray Monette, gtr.; − James; + Mark Olson, kybds.; + Ed Guzman, perc.) *One World* **1971**—*In Concert* (− Persh; + Mike Urso, bass, voc.; + Pete Hoorelbeke, drums, voc.) **1973**—*Willie Remembers; Ma* (− Rivera) **1975**—*Back to Earth*

1976—*Midnight Lady* 1977—*Rare Earth* (Prodigal)
1978—*Band Together; Grand Slam.*

Hard-rockers Rare Earth enjoyed several major hits with Motown Records in the early Seventies and were reportedly the first white act signed to the black-owned company. Founding members Pete Rivera, John Persh and Gil Bridges grew up in Detroit listening to and playing Motown hits in local bars as the Sunliners. In 1969, they became Rare Earth and added three new members. With the aid of Motown session guitarist Dennis Coffey they attracted the attention of the company and in 1969 were signed to a Motown subsidiary renamed Rare Earth.

Their first album, *Get Ready* (#12), was quite successful; and the title cut, a reworking of the Temptations' hit, was a #4 single. *Ecology* and *One World* in 1970 spawned "(I Know) I'm Losing You," another Temptations remake (#7 pop, #20 R&B), "Born to Wander" (#17 pop, #48 R&B), "I Just Want to Celebrate" (#7 pop, #30 R&B) and "Hey, Big Brother" (#19 pop, #48 R&B). Much of the group's material was produced by Motown staff producer Norman Whitfield.

After this peak period, they continued with Motown until they released *Rare Earth* on Prodigal Records in 1977.

THE RASCALS
Formed 1965, New York City

Felix Cavaliere (b. Nov. 29, 1944, Pelham, N.Y.), voc., kybds.; Eddie Brigati (b. Oct. 22, 1946, New York City), voc.; Gene Cornish (b. May 14, 1945, Ottawa), gtr.; Dino Danelli (b. July 23, 1945, New York City), drums.
1966—*The Young Rascals* (Atlantic) 1967—*Collections; Groovin'* 1968—*Once upon a Dream; Time Peace; Freedom Suite* 1969—*See* 1970—*Search and Nearness* 1971—(– Brigati; – Cornish; + Buzzy Feiten [b. New York City], gtr.; + Robert Popwell [b. Daytona, Fla.], bass; + Ann Sutton [b. Pittsburgh, Penn.], voc.) *Peaceful World* (Columbia) 1972—*The Island of Real.*

Felix Cavaliere solo:
1974—*Felix Cavaliere* (Bearsville) 1975—*Destiny* 1976—*Treasure* (Epic) 1980—*Castles in the Air.*

The term "blue-eyed soul" was coined for the Rascals (although none of them had blue eyes), whose approximation of mid-Sixties black pop crossed the color line.

Danelli began his career as a teenage jazz drummer (he played with Lionel Hampton's band) but switched to R&B while working in New Orleans, and he returned to New York to accompany such R&B acts as Little Willie John. There he met Brigati, a pickup singer on the New York R&B circuit.

Cavaliere had studied classical piano before becoming the only white member of the Stereos, a group based in his suburban hometown. While a student at Syracuse Univer-

sity, he formed a doo-wop group, the Escorts. After leaving school, Cavaliere moved to New York City where he met Danelli, and the two migrated to Las Vegas to try their luck with a casino house band. On their return to New York, Cavaliere joined Joey Dee and the Starlighters, which included Brigati and Cornish.

The Rascals came together in 1964 after Cavaliere, Brigati and Cornish left Dee and decided to form a quartet with Danelli. In February 1965, they began gigging in New Jersey and on Long Island.

By year's end, they had changed their name to the Young Rascals (after the old television series) and released their first Atlantic single, "I Ain't Gonna Eat Out My Heart Anymore," sung by Brigati. The group took a turn when Cavaliere sang the followup, "Good Lovin' " (#1, 1966), and gave the band one of the year's biggest hits. In the following two years, the group had nine more Top Twenty hits, including "You Better Run" (#20, 1966), "(I've Been) Lonely Too Long" (#16, 1967), "Groovin' " (#1, 1967) and "A Girl Like You" (#10, 1967), most of them Cavaliere-Brigati compositions. Other hits included "How Can I Be Sure" (#4, 1967), "A Beautiful Morning" (#3, 1968) and "People Got to Be Free" (#1, 1968).

Established hitmakers, the group tried to get serious in 1967, dropping the "Young" from their name and the Edwardian knickers from their onstage wardrobe. With *Freedom Suite*, their music took on elements of jazz; with *Search and Nearness*, their songs made room for lengthy instrumental tracks by jazzmen like Ron Carter, Hubert Laws and Joe Farrell. Record sales and concert attendance plummeted. In 1971, they signed to Columbia, but Brigati and Cornish left before their label debut. Filling their shoes were Buzzy Feiten (Butterfield Blues Band), fresh from sessions for Bob Dylan's *New Morning*; Robert Popwell, whose session credits included work for

The Rascals: Felix Cavaliere, Gene Cornish, Eddie Brigati, Dino Danelli

Dylan, Aretha Franklin, Eddie Floyd and Tim Hardin; and Ann Sutton, who had sung with various soul and jazz groups in Philadelphia. The band broke up in the early Seventies.

Cornish and Danelli started a group called Bulldog. Feiten joined Neil Larsen in a duo in 1980. Cavaliere has continued as a solo artist and producer (Laura Nyro, Deadly Nightshade). In 1982, Danelli joined Steve Van Zandt's Little Steven and the Disciples of Soul.

THE RASPBERRIES

Formed 1970, Cleveland, Ohio
Eric Howard Carmen (b. Aug. 11, 1949, Cleveland), voc., bass, gtr.; Wally Carter Bryson (b. July 18, 1949, Gastonia, N.C.), gtr.; Jim Alexander Bonfanti (b. Dec. 17, 1948, Windber, Penn.), drums; Dave Bruce Smalley (b. July 10, 1949, Oil City, Penn.), bass, gtr.
1972—*Raspberries* (Capitol) 1973—*Fresh; Side 3* (− Bonfanti; − Smalley; + Michael McBride, drums; + Scott McCarl, bass) *Starting Over* 1976—*Best of.*

The Raspberries, with their Beatles-like harmonies, mod-influenced suits and power pop, seemed very out of place when they first recorded in 1972, partly because the general trend in America at the time was toward longer FM-oriented tracks.

The band formed in Cleveland in 1970 from several local groups. Jim Bonfanti drummed on the Outsiders' hit "Time Won't Let Me" in the mid-Sixties. He was later in the Mods with Dave Smalley and Wally Bryson, who changed their name to the Choir. They became the most popular band in Cleveland, with a minor 1967 hit, "It's Cold Outside." Eric Carmen joined the local Cyrus Erie as lead singer and Bryson left the Choir to join Carmen's band. They recorded a few unnoticed singles for Epic; Carmen recorded with a band called the Quick and then went solo, writing and recording "Light the Way," later covered by Oliver.

At the turn of the decade, Carmen, Bryson, Bonfanti and Smalley finally united in the Raspberries. In mid-1971, their demos attracted the attention of future producer Jimmy Ienner, who got them a contract with Capitol. Their debut LP had a scratch-and-sniff sticker on the cover featuring the scent of the band's namesake. The second single, "Go All The Way," hit #5 and sold more than 1.3 million copies. The second LP included "I Want to Be with You" (#16, 1973). Carmen wrote and sang most of the hits.

After *Side Three*, internal problems developed. Bonfanti and Smalley resisted the group's teenybopper image, and by the end of the year they left, forming Dynamite with two ex-members of Freeport, another Cleveland band. They were replaced by Michael McBride, who had played in Cyrus Erie with Carmen, and Scott McCarl, who had sent an audition tape to Ienner. The new foursome

The Raspberries: Jim Bonfanti, Wally Bryson, Eric Carmen, Dave Smalley

released their fourth and final LP, *Starting Over*, a concept album about stardom, but "Overnight Sensation (Hit Record)" flopped and the band quit in frustration. Eric Carmen went on to an initially successful solo career.

GENYA RAVAN

Born Goldie Zelkowitz, 1942, Lodz, Poland
1972—*Genya Ravan with Baby* (Columbia) 1973— *They Love Me/They Love Me Not* (Dunhill) 1974— *Goldie Zelkowitz* (Janus) 1978—*Urban Desire* (20th Century–Fox) 1979—*And I Mean It.*

In two decades as a rock musician, Genya Ravan has led one of the first self-contained all-female rock bands, sung hits for Ten Wheel Drive, and later became the first female producer hired by a major record label.

Growing up in the Jewish ghetto on New York's Lower East Side, young Goldie Zelkowitz developed an interest in R&B. She ran with a teenage gang and dropped out of high school for a musical career, which began in a Brooklyn lounge when she walked onstage and began singing with Richard Perry's band, the Escorts, who made her their lead singer. She sang their #1 hit, "Somewhere."

In 1962, she formed Goldie and the Gingerbreads, probably the first girl group in which all the women played their own instruments. They stayed together until 1969, achieving their biggest successes in England, where they eventually relocated and later toured with the Rolling Stones, the Yardbirds, Manfred Mann and the Kinks.

In 1969 Zelkowitz changed her name to Genya Ravan and formed Ten Wheel Drive, an otherwise all-male jazz-blues band with a five-piece horn section in the mold of Blood, Sweat and Tears. She left them in 1971 to form her own band, Baby, which toured with Sly and the Family Stone and backed up Ravan on her first solo album. At that time, most of her material was written by Baby's guitarist, Mitch Styles, formerly of Diamond Reo.

In 1975, Ravan became the first woman producer hired by a major label when RCA had her produce cabaret act Gretchen Cryer and Nancy Ford (who wrote the feminist musical *I'm Getting My Act Together and Taking It on the Road*) and the debut album by Rosie (who later joined the Harlettes). A little over a year later, Ravan formed the short-lived Taxi. She also produced demos for CBGB's Hilly Kristal, including the Shirts, a popular band at the club, as well as the debut LP by the Dead Boys. She later sang on Blue Öyster Cult's *Mirrors* LP and did some production work with ex-Ronette Ronnie Spector. Lou Reed guested on *Urban Desire*, Ian Hunter on *And I Mean It;* both albums stuck to her hard-nosed rock vein, with many songs written by Ravan. In 1980, Ravan formed her own label, Polish Records. She appeared on *The Warriors* soundtrack.

THE RAVENS
Formed 1945, New York City
Warren Suttles, Jimmy Ricks, Leonard Puzey, Ollie Jones, Maithe Marshall, Tommy Evans.

The Ravens were an early R&B vocal group whose material ranged from Tin Pan Alley ballads to jive to doo-wop. Having begun in the smooth-harmony style of the Mills Brothers, the Ravens became one of the first vocal groups to feature a bass voice singing lead, something that happened by accident when bass singer Ricks nervously came in too soon with his part on "My Sugar Is So Refined" one night at Harlem's Apollo Theater. The crowd went wild. Ricks then sang "Old Man River," which went on to be a massive hit in 1946, selling over two million copies.

The Ravens never matched that success, but did have a long succession of R&B hits, including "I Don't Have to Ride No More" (1950), "Count Every Star" (1950), "Rock Me All Night Long" (1952) and "Green Eyes" (1954). The group went through various personnel changes: Warren Suttles was replaced by Joe Medlin in 1947, Bubba Ritchie in 1949 and Louis Heyward in 1950; Maithe Marshall (who'd replaced Ollie Jones) was followed by Richie Cannon in 1948; Jimmy Ricks, who briefly worked with Benny Goodman in 1950, by Tommy Evans; Leonard Puzey by Jimmy Stewart in 1952; Marshall, who'd returned in 1950, by Joe Van Loan in 1952. By the mid-Fifties, the group had been completely reshuffled, with Van Loan, his brothers Paul and James, and David Bowers forming the lineup. Ricks continued a successful solo career, Marshall sang with the Ink Spots, among others, and Van Loan went on to join the Du-Droppers, who had mid-Fifties hits with "I Wanna Know" and "I Found Out."

LOU RAWLS
Born December 1, 1935, Chicago
1963—*Black and Blue* (Capitol) 1966—*Lou Rawls Live; Pilgrim Travelers; Soulin'* 1967—*Too Much; That's Lou* 1968—*Feelin' Good; You're Good for Me; The Best of Lou Rawls* 1969—*The Way It Was/The Way It Is* 1971—*A Natural Man* (MGM) 1976—*All Things in Time* (Philadelphia International) 1977—*Unmistakably Lou; When You Hear Lou, You've Heard It All* 1978—*Lou Rawls Live* 1979—*Let Me Be Good to You* 1981—*Shades of Blue.*

Singer Lou Rawls has been a popular black MOR singer since the Fifties. He grew up on the South Side of Chicago, where he sang in church. In the mid-Fifties, he was in the Los Angeles–based Pilgrim Travelers gospel group before joining the Army in 1956. After returning, he toured with Sam Cooke; in 1958, Cooke and Rawls, traveling by car to a concert, were involved in an auto accident. Cooke wasn't badly hurt, but Rawls, who was initially pronounced dead, lay in a coma for five days before recovering.

In 1959, the Travelers broke up and Rawls began singing the blues in Los Angeles nightclubs. He also had a bit part in the popular "77 Sunset Strip" television series. For a time he was managed by Cooke, and he would later duet with Cooke on "Bring It on Home to Me." Rawls signed a solo contract with Capitol Records in 1962 and recorded with moderate success until 1966, when "Love Is a Hurtin' Thing" went to #13 pop, #1 R&B. It wasn't until the mid-Sixties, with hits that mixed spoken monologues and music—like the Grammy Award–winning "Dead End Street" (#29 pop, #3 R&B, 1967)—that Rawls reached white audiences. *Lou Rawls Live* was his first of several gold albums, and during the late Sixties he appeared regularly on television variety shows and in Las Vegas nightclubs.

In 1971, Rawls moved to MGM Records and cut the popular Grammy Award winner "A Natural Man" (#17 pop and R&B, 1971). He didn't have another major hit until he signed with Philadelphia International records in 1976. Under the guidance of producers Kenny Gamble and Leon Huff, Rawls recorded "You'll Never Find Another Love Like Mine" (#2 pop, #1 R&B) and "Groovy People" (#19 R&B) in 1976; "See You When I Git There" (#8 R&B) and "Lady Love" (#21 R&B) in 1977; and "Let Me Be Good to You" (#11 R&B, 1979). Rawls subsequently became known as the voice behind Budweiser beer ads, and in fact he recorded an album entitled *When You Hear Lou, You've Heard It All*, based on that company's slogan.

JOHNNIE RAY
Born January 10, 1927, Dallas, Oregon
1952—*Johnnie Ray* (Columbia) 1978—*Johnnie Ray— An American Legend.*

Though he had started to go deaf as a youngster, Johnnie Ray still managed to become one of America's most popular male vocalists of the early and mid-Fifties, with a dozen gold records. He left home for Hollywood, then ended up in Detroit in 1951. There he met blues singer LaVern Baker and her manager, Al Green (not the Memphis soul singer), who helped Ray work on his music. He was discovered by Detroit disc jockey Robin Seymour, and in 1951 he signed to Columbia's Okeh subsidiary. That year, his "Whiskey and Gin" was a minor hit in the Midwest.

Ray went to New York City, where, with Mitch Miller producing and the Four Lads backing, he recorded "Cry," a #1 ballad in 1952. Because he was so emotional during his performances, Ray is frequently cited as the first popular singer to break with the cool, professional stance of earlier pop crooners like Perry Como. Through the early to mid-Fifties, Ray had many pop hits, including "Please Mr. Sun," a cover of the Drifter's "Such a Night," "Just Walking in the Rain" and "You Don't Owe Me a Thing." In the following years, Ray popped up occasionally as an oldies act both on TV and in concerts.

REDBONE

Formed 1968, Los Angeles

Lolly Vegas (b. Fresno, Calif.), gtr., lead voc.; Pat Vegas (b. Fresno, Calif.), bass, voc.; Anthony Bellamy (b. Los Angeles), gtr.; Peter De Poe (a.k.a. Last Walking Bear, b. Neah Bay Reservation, Wash.), drums.

1970—*Redbone* (Epic) 1971—*Potlatch; Witch Queen from New Orleans; Message from a Drum* 1973— *Wovoka* 1974—(− De Poe; + Butch Rillera, drums) *Beaded Dreams* 1975—*Come and Get Your Redbone* 1978—*Cycles* (RCA).

Redbone were four American Indians (their name is a derogatory Cajun slang term for half-breed) who sometimes wore traditional dress onstage and played "swamp rock" (popularized by Creedence Clearwater) with some funk influences. "Come and Get Your Love," highlighted by Lolly Vegas' lead vocals, was their only hit (#5, 1974).

The band formed in California in 1968. The members had all grown up poor in migrant camps. In the mid-Sixties, brothers Pat and Lolly Vegas (the latter became Redbone's leader) played in a band on TV's "Shindig." They also did West Coast session work, backing Odetta and John Lee Hooker, and wrote "Niki Hoeky," which became a hit for P. J. Proby (#23, 1967).

Anthony Bellamy used to play flamenco guitar at his parents' restaurant and later performed with local L.A. rock & roll bands; Peter De Poe was a ceremonial drummer on the reservation where he was born. The band united on the L.A. club circuit, got a deal with Epic and released their debut in January 1970, including their own version of "Niki Hoeky."

Their albums never sold well, and while they did have some catchy soulful rock tracks like 1971's "Maggie" and 1972's "Witch Queen of New Orleans," they later explored more traditional Indian roots music. By the late Seventies, they had faded.

OTIS REDDING

Born September 9, 1941, Dawson, Georgia; died December 10, 1967

1965—*Pain in My Heart* (Atco) *Otis Blue* (Volt) 1966—*Dictionary of Soul* (Stax) *The Soul Album* 1967—*Live in Europe* (Atco) 1968—*Dock of the Bay* (Stax) *Immortal Otis Redding* (Atco) *In Person at the Whiskey-a-Go-Go* 1969—*Love Man; History of Otis Redding* 1970—*Tell the Truth* (Atlantic) *Otis Redding/Jimi Hendrix Experience* (Reprise) 1972—*The Best of Otis Redding* (Atlantic) 1982—*Recorded Live*.

Otis Redding's grainy voice and galvanizing stage shows made him one of the greatest male soul singers of the Sixties. At the time of his death, he was making his first significant impact on the pop audience after years as a favorite among blacks.

In his youth, Redding was influenced by both Little Richard and Sam Cooke. His "Shout Bamalama," released on a small Los Angeles–based label in 1960, was highly imitative of Little Richard. After taking odd jobs around the South, Redding worked as chauffeur and sometimes as singer for Johnny Jenkins and the Pinetoppers in 1962. One day, Redding drove Jenkins to Memphis for an audition with a then-new record label called Stax. Redding was determined to audition as well and at the end of the

Otis Redding

session was allowed to try two songs. One song was a Little Richard–style tune that Stax president Jim Stewart hated. But the other was a Redding tune called "These Arms of Mine," which was subsequently released on Stax's Volt label. It hit #20 on the R&B chart and established Redding as a recording artist. But it was his impassioned performances on the so-called chitlin' circuit that made him, next to James Brown, the most popular black entertainer of the mid-Sixties.

Redding wrote many of his own hits, including "Mr. Pitiful" (#41 pop, #10 R&B, 1965), "Fa-Fa-Fa-Fa-Fa" (#29 pop, #12 R&B, 1966) and "(Sittin' on) The Dock of the Bay" (#1 pop, #1 R&B, 1968), all co-credited to Stax session guitarist Steve Cropper; "I've Been Loving You Too Long" (#21 pop, #2 R&B, 1965) with Jerry Butler; "Respect" (#35 pop, #4 R&B, 1965), "I Can't Turn You Loose" (#11 R&B, 1965), "My Lover's Prayer" (#61 pop, #10 R&B, 1966). He also had hits with the Rolling Stones' "Satisfaction" (#31 pop, #4 R&B, 1966) and Sam Cooke's "Shake" (#47 pop, #16 R&B, 1967). Among his LPs, *Dictionary of Soul* is considered one of the best examples of the Memphis soul sound.

Redding also played an important role in the careers of other singers. In 1967, he cut a duet album with Carla Thomas, *King and Queen,* which had a hit in "Tramp" (#26 pop, #2 R&B). Redding produced Arthur Conley's tribute "Sweet Soul Music" (#2 pop and R&B) in 1967—an adaptation of Sam Cooke's "Yeah Man"—which became a soul standard. Redding also established his own label, Jotis.

Redding's appearance at the Monterey Pop Festival in 1967 introduced the singer to white rock fans. His intense performance (captured in the film *Monterey Pop* and on the LP *Otis Redding/Jimi Hendrix*) was enthusiastically received. As a gesture of thanks, Redding and Steve Cropper wrote "(Sittin' on) The Dock of the Bay." It would become his biggest hit, yet Redding never lived to see its release.

On December 10, 1967, his chartered plane crashed into a Wisconsin lake, killing Redding and four members of his backup band, the Bar-Kays. In early 1968, "The Dock of the Bay" hit #1 on both pop and R&B charts. Fourteen years later his two sons and a nephew formed their own group, called the Reddings, and covered "Dock of the Bay" (#55 pop, #21 R&B).

HELEN REDDY
Born October 4, 1942, Melbourne, Australia
1971—*I Don't Know How to Love Him* (Capitol)
1972—*Helen Reddy; I Am Woman*   **1973**—*Long Hard Climb.*

Among her many hits, singer Helen Reddy will no doubt be best remembered as the composer and singer of "I Am Woman," which went to #1 in 1972–73 and was nominated for a Grammy.

Reddy began performing at the age of four at the Tivoli Theatre in Perth, Australia, and she toured much of that country with her show-business parents. She left boarding school at age 15 to work with a road show, acting as well as singing. She eventually landed her own Australian TV show, "Helen Reddy Sings," and in 1966 won a trip to New York in the Australian Bandstand International contest, sponsored by Philips-Mercury Records.

Reddy had little success in New York, but she did meet Jeff Wald, an agent with the William Morris talent agency, whom she married a year later. In 1970, Wald arranged for her to perform on TV's "Tonight Show," and within a year she had her first hit, a version of "I Don't Know How to Love Him" (#13, 1971) from the Broadway rock musical *Jesus Christ Superstar.*

Reddy's other hits included "Crazy Love" and "No Sad Song" (1971); "Peaceful," "Delta Dawn" and "Leave Me Alone" (1973); "Keep on Singing," "You and Me Against the World" and "Angie Baby" (1974); "Emotion," "Bluebird" and "Ain't No Way to Treat a Lady" (1975); and "I Can't Hear You No More" (1976). In 1973, she had her own summer-replacement variety show on NBC-TV, and for most of the rest of the Seventies she was a hostess on NBC's late-night rock-variety show "The Midnight Special." In 1982, she sued Wald for divorce.

JERRY REED
Born Jerry Hubbard, March 20, 1937, Atlanta, Georgia
1972—*The Best of Jerry Reed* (RCA).

Jerry Reed is known mostly among musicians for his fast-pickin' country guitar style, and among the masses for his jokey, C&W-to-pop hits of the early Seventies. He got a record contract with Capitol in 1955 at age 18. He had been playing in country bands since his early teens and had worked in a cotton mill. Initially, Reed got attention as a songwriter, especially with "Crazy Legs" (which Gene Vincent recorded in 1956) and some covers by Brenda Lee.

From 1959 to 1961, Reed was in the Army, and upon release he moved to Nashville, where he had two minor country hits on Columbia, "Hully Gully Guitars" and "Goodnight Irene." Reed worked primarily as a session guitarist until 1965 when he signed to RCA. Elvis Presley began to record Reed's work, giving him his first pop chart exposure with 1968's "Guitar Man" (which became Reed's nickname; it was also a country hit for Reed the year before). Presley also cut Reed's "U.S. Male."

The guitarist's albums began to place on the C&W charts, and in 1970 he had his first gold single with his pop crossover debut, "Amos Moses," a swamp-rock song (#8 pop, #16 C&W). He became a household name with regular appearances on "Glen Campbell's Goodtime Hour" (1970–71). In 1971, he had a Top Ten pop and #1 country hit with the novelty number "When You're Hot You're Hot," which also won a Grammy. In 1973, he again hit #1 country with "Lord, Mr. Ford." Reed also won critical acclaim and a Grammy for a duet LP with Chet Atkins, *Me and Jerry.* He branched out into acting in the mid-Seventies with Southern roles, first in 1975's *W.W. and the Dixie Dance Kings,* and then *Gator* (1976), both with Burt Reynolds.

JIMMY REED

Born September 6, 1925, Dunleith, Mississippi; died August 29, 1976, Oakland, California
N.A.—*The Best of Jimmy Reed* (VeeJay).

Jimmy Reed, one of the most influential blues harpists and performers, was also composer of such standards as "Big Boss Man," "Honest I Do," "Bright Lights, Big City" and "Baby, What You Want Me to Do."

The son of a sharecropper, Reed began performing in the Chicago area in the late Forties to early Fifties, and in 1953 he signed with Vee Jay Records. His first big hit was "You Don't Have to Go" (#9 R&B) in 1955. The next year he scored with "Ain't That Lovin' You Baby" (#7 R&B). Between 1956 and 1961, he had 11 more Top Twenty R&B hits, including "Honest I Do" (#10, 1957) and "Baby, What You Want Me to Do" (#10, 1960), both of which crossed over to Top Forty pop success.

Reed's work has been covered by many others, including Elvis Presley ("Baby, What You Want Me to Do"), the Rolling Stones and Aretha Franklin, both of whom do versions of "Honest I Do." He died at age fifty of natural causes.

LOU REED

Born March 2, 1943, Brooklyn, New York
1972—*Lou Reed* (RCA)   *Transformer*   **1973**—*Berlin*
1974—*Rock 'n' Roll Animal;   Sally Can't Dance*
1975—*Lou Reed Live;   Metal Machine Music*   **1976**—*Coney Island Baby;   Rock and Roll Heart* (Arista)
1977—*Walk on the Wild Side* (RCA)   **1978**—*Street Hassle* (Arista)   *Live: Take No Prisoners*   **1979**—*The Bells*   **1980**—*Growing Up in Public;   Rock 'n' Roll Diary*   **1982**—*The Blue Mask* (RCA)   **1983**—*Legendary Hearts.*

As the lead singer and songwriter of the Velvet Underground in the late Sixties, Lou Reed was responsible for a body of work that was alienated from the optimism of the day and passionately bleak, and which remains highly influential today. His solo career, beginning in 1972, has been more idiosyncratic and marked by sudden turnabouts in image and sound, from self-consciously commercial product to white noise to unpredictable folk rock.

Before the formation of the Velvet Underground in 1965, Reed attended Syracuse University, studying poetry (under Delmore Schwartz, to whom Reed dedicated a song on the first Velvet Underground LP) and journalism. Reed's poems were published in *Fusion* magazine. (In

Lou Reed

1977 he earned an award from the Coordinating Council of Literary Magazines for his poem "The Slide.") After leaving Syracuse, Reed returned to New York City and worked for Pickwick Records, taking part in the studio group that recorded various Reed-penned songs, released by the Beachnuts and the Roughnecks. During this period, he met the musicians with whom he would subsequently form the Velvet Underground. With two of them he formed a band called the Primitives, which became the Warlocks and made one record.

Reed's 1970 departure from the Velvet Underground was bitter; he did not even stay to complete their fourth album, *Loaded.* He became a virtual recluse for nearly two years, until moving to England and beginning a solo career in 1971. *Transformer* was his pop breakthrough. Produced by Velvet Underground fan David Bowie, it yielded Reed's only Top Ten hit to date, "Walk on the Wild Side," an ode to the denizens of Andy Warhol's Sixties films. With Bowie's aid, Reed made the transition to the glitter rock of the period, camping up his presumed homosexuality with bleached-blond hair and black fingernail polish. Typically, the next record, *Berlin,* was as grim in tone as *Transformer* had been playful.

Reed's recordings have continued to be unpredictable. A pair of live albums drawn from the same set of concerts (including the gold *Rock 'n' Roll Animal*) featured streamlined heavy-metal versions of Velvet Underground material, while a later tour would pander to theatrics: Reed, for example, pretending to shoot up while performing the song "Heroin." *Sally Can't Dance* reached the Top Ten, and was repudiated by Reed almost on release. After another live LP, he followed with *Metal Machine Music,* four sides of grating instrumental noise, alternately considered high art worthy of RCA's classical division and a gambit to get off the label.

Reed moved to Arista Records in 1976 and at first made impeccably produced, harrowing music like the title cut of *Street Hassle.* He then entered a relatively peaceful phase, typified by album titles like *Rock and Roll Heart* and *Growing Up in Public.* He married Sylvia Morales on Valentine's Day 1980, and his songs about the seamy side of life began to appear alongside paeans to suburban life— "I'm an average guy," he sang on *The Blue Mask.*

Reed found affinity with some of rock & roll's romantics and mythologists: Bruce Springsteen appeared uncredited on 1978's *Street Hassle,* and Reed cowrote songs for Kiss and Nils Lofgren. Reed's sidemen over the years have included Jack Bruce (ex-Cream) and jazz trumpeter Don Cherry; for *The Blue Mask* and *Legendary Hearts,* he toured with an acclaimed band that included ex-Voidoids Robert Quine on guitar and Fred Maher on drums, and ex–Jean-Luc Ponty bassist Fernando Saunders.

REGGAE

Reggae was the name given in 1968 to the latest in a succession of Jamaican dance rhythms, but the term has come to refer to the various styles derived from Afro-Caribbean musics and American R&B that have flourished in Jamaica since the early Sixties.

The music popular with Jamaica's poor majority before the Forties was called "mento," sung and played on guitars and percussion by itinerant musicians who drew from Jamaica's African heritage, from local work songs and spirituals, and from the calypso, rhumba and merengue of neighboring islands. After World War II, music from the United States began to make an impression on Jamaicans via radio from Miami, New Orleans and Memphis and through "sound system" operators who imported the latest U.S. R&B records to play on their mobile discotheques. American R&B musicians like Louis Jordan, Roscoe Gordon, Johnny Ace, Amos Milburn and Fats Domino dominated Jamaican popular music throughout the Forties and Fifties.

When American records became scarce around 1960, sound-system moguls like Coxsone Dodd, Duke Reid and Prince Buster opened studios to record local talent. Kingston, Jamaica, suddenly became a recording center. Early hitmakers like Laurel Aitken, Owen Gray, Jackie Edwards and Derrick Morgan began by imitating American R&B, but rapidly developed an original sound by setting mento-styled songs to R&B-styled arrangements for horns, keyboards, drums and electric guitars and bass. The odd, bouncy rhythm that crossed the R&B backbeat with the characteristically Jamaican hesitation beat became known as "ska." Bands like the Skatalites, the Soul Vendors and the Ska Kings, and singers like Stranger Cole, Eric Morris, Jimmy Cliff, Justin Hines, the Maytals, the Blues Busters and the Wailers, made ska tremendously popular in Jamaica, particularly with the "rude boys"— the ghetto youth.

Sound systems continued to disseminate the music, giving rise to a ska offshoot called "toasting": sound-system disc jockeys would add vocal effects to the music or talk over it, reciting aphorisms and doggerel or mimicking singers and other DJs. Toasting, in turn, gave rise to "dub," the practice of manipulating playback controls to drop out or bring forward prerecorded tracks. Eventually, both these styles moved from the sound systems into the studios. King Stitt and U Roy had the first toaster hits in the late Sixties and early Seventies, followed by I Roy, Big Youth, Prince Jazzbo, Dillinger and others. Lee Perry, King Tubby and Augustus Pablo advanced from dubbing behind toasters to recording their own "dub-wise" instrumental records.

By that time, the music had gone through several stages beyond ska, roughly following the development of American R&B into the more gospel-inspired soul music of the mid-Sixties. Jamaica's heatwave of 1966 slowed down ska's tempos to what became known as "rock steady"; Alton Ellis, Delroy Wilson, Ken Boothe, the Heptones and the Paragons had hits with the relaxed, lilting rocksteady style. Rock steady was succeeded in 1968 by the looser, more upbeat "poppa-top" of the Pioneers and Desmond Dekker, and by the sparer, harder-driving reggae of the Slickers and the veteran Maytals. Reggae's distinctive sound was achieved by reversing instrumental roles: The guitar functioned mainly as a rhythm instrument, scratching chords on the offbeats, and the bass played a melodic counterpoint to the vocals; the drums provided complex cross rhythms and accents.

The ascetic, millenarian cult of Rastafari has been a presence in Jamaican music at least since the Fifties; some of the most influential ska musicians were Rastafarians, and by 1970, Rastafarianism was a crucial force in reggae. Groups like the Abyssinians, the Charmers, Burning Spear and the revived Wailers incorporated Rastafarian ritual "burra" drumming and chanting into their music, while their lyrics quoted Rasta scripture and the mystical-political teachings of Marcus Garvey. Rasta's influence— in the ethereal sound mixes, the narcotic tempos, the esoteric language and the Africanisms—pervaded the reggae of the Seventies.

In the second half of the decade, vocal trios like the Mighty Diamonds, Black Uhuru and the Itals, backed by ensembles like Sly and Robbie and the Roots Radics Band, hardened the reggae beat, honed instrumental tracks to their most skeletal, and floated the result in echo, arriving at "rockers." In a parallel—sometimes overlapping—development, Dennis Brown, Sugar Minott, Gregory Isaacs and other vocal stylists crooned more melodic, romantic songs in the "lovers' rock" mode.

While Jamaican music has had some popularity in the

U.S. since the ska era, it has never found the mass enthusiasm that it has enjoyed in Europe, Africa and South America. Millie Small, Desmond Dekker and Jimmy Cliff have each had one U.S. Top Forty hit, but a truer indication of reggae's impact is heard in Paul Simon's "Mother and Child Reunion," Johnny Nash's "I Can See Clearly Now," the J. Geils Band's "Give It to Me," Eric Clapton's "I Shot the Sheriff," Stevie Wonder's "Master Blaster," Blondie's "The Tide Is High" and numerous other covers and originals by the Rolling Stones, Ry Cooder, Joan Armatrading, the Clash, Elvis Costello, the Police, the Specials and the English Beat.

THE REMAINS

Formed 1965, Boston
Barry Tashian, gtr., voc.; Bill Briggs, kybds.; Vern Miller, bass, gtr., horns; N. D. Smart II, drums.
1967—*The Remains* (Spoonfed; reissued on Epic).

Formed by Barry Tashian along with fellow Boston University students, the Remains gained a loyal Boston following on the strength of live shows and one classic mid-Sixties garage-punk single, "Don't Look Back" (no relation to the Dylan film). In 1965, they opened local concerts by the Rolling Stones and in 1966 opened the Beatles' U.S. tour. But after no followup hits materialized, they broke up in 1967, with various members going to join the Flying Burrito Brothers, Kangaroo, Swallow and Mountain. "Don't Look Back" is included on the *Nuggets* collection. Tashian briefly regrouped the band in the mid-Seventies.

RENAISSANCE

Formed 1969, Surrey, England
Keith Relf (b. Mar. 23, 1943, Eng.; d. May 14, 1976, Eng.), voc., gtr.; Jim McCarty (b. July 25, 1943, Eng.), drums; Jane Relf (b. Eng.), voc.; John Hawken (b. Eng.), kybds.; Louis Cennamo, bass.
1969—*Renaissance* (Island) (− K. Relf; − McCarty, − J. Relf; − Hawken; + Rob Hendry, gtr.; + Jon Camp, bass; + John Tout, kybds.; + Terry Sullivan, percussion; + Annie Haslam, voc.) **1972**—*Prologue* (Capitol) (− Hendry; + Michael Dunford, gtr.)
1973—*Ashes Are Burning* **1974**—*Turn of the Cards* (Sire) **1975**—*Scheherazade and Other Stories* **1976**—*Live at Carnegie Hall* **1977**—*Novella* **1978**—*A Song for All Seasons* **1979**—*Azure d'Or* (− Sullivan; − Tout; + Peter Gosling, kybds.; + Peter Barron, drums) **1981**—*Camera Camera* (IRS) **1983**—*Time-Line*.

Though Keith Relf and Jim McCarty founded Renaissance shortly after leaving the Yardbirds, their reign did not last long, and the incarnation that came to some prominence in the U.S. in the mid-Seventies included neither of them. In 1969, Relf and McCarty joined Relf's sister Jane and John Hawken (ex–Nashville Teens, later with Strawbs) to form an eclectic band fusing folk, jazz and classical influences with rock. An eponymous LP on Island was released later in the year, but both Relf and McCarty quickly became dissatisfied with the venture. Relf and Louis Cennamo moved on to head a harder-rocking band called Armageddon. (Just before Relf's death, he, Jane and Hawken were forming Illusion. After Relf's death the group continued and recorded for Island.)

By the group's 1972 followup, *Prologue*, all of the members had changed. The album had a pop-classical, self-consciously refined art-rock feel highlighted by John Tout's piano and Annie Haslam's clear, high-flying soprano. The lyricist was poet Betty Thatcher, who resided in Cornwall and wrote the lyrics to fit Michael Dunford's sheet music, which she would receive by mail. *Prologue* got lots of U.S. FM airplay, and the group developed a strong following, particularly in New York. Before their followup, *Ashes Are Burning*, Rob Hendry left and was replaced by songwriter/guitarist Dunford. With *Turn of the Cards*, they switched to Sire, and their next LP (*Scheherazade*) featured an entire suite complete with strings. Their live LP, recorded with full orchestra on the East Coast, sold well; but their popularity was spotty elsewhere and nil in England. Haslam recorded the solo *Annie in Wonderland* (1977), produced by Roy Wood. In the Eighties, Haslam, Camp and Dunford (along with two new members) cut *Camera Camera* and *Time-Line* for IRS.

REO SPEEDWAGON

Formed 1967, Champaign, Illinois
Terry Luttrell, voc.; Greg Philbin, bass; Gary Richrath (b. Oct. 18, 1949, Peoria, Ill.), gtrs.; Neal Doughty (b. July 29, 1946, Evanston, Ill.), kybds.; Alan Gratzer (b. Nov. 9, 1948, Syracuse, N.Y.), drums.
1971—*REO Speedwagon* (Epic) (− Luttrell; + Kevin Cronin [b. Oct. 6, 1951, Evanston, Ill.], voc.) **1972**—*REO TWO* (− Cronin; + Michael Murphy, voc.)
1973—*Ridin' the Storm out* **1974**—*Lost in a Dream* **1975**—*This Time We Mean It* (− Murphy; + Cronin) **1976**—*REO* (− Philbin; + Bruce Hall [b. May 3, 1953, Champaign], bass) **1977**—*You Get What You Play For* **1978**—*You Can Tune a Piano but You Can't Tuna Fish* **1979**—*Nine Lives* **1980**—*A Decade of Rock 'n' Roll; Hi-Infidelity* **1982**—*Good Trouble*.

After more than a decade of touring and nine middling albums, this Midwestern journeyman hard-pop quintet sold over six million copies of *Hi-Infidelity*.

REO Speedwagon (named after a high-speed fire engine) was formed by Neal Doughty and Alan Gratzer while both were students at the University of Illinois in 1968. They became a popular local club attraction. Irving Azoff, who later managed the Eagles and Steely Dan, handled the group in the early Seventies, getting them dates opening for other popular Midwestern acts like Bob Seger and Kansas. REO and Azoff severed their relationship in 1977.

Throughout the early Seventies, REO Speedwagon's records sold unspectacularly as they continued to tour. REO went through relatively few personnel changes, the most significant being vocalist Kevin Cronin's departure in 1972 and return in 1975. After briefly pursuing a solo career as a singer/songwriter, Cronin returned to REO; his songwriting and singing would be crucial to the band's ascendance.

REO was their least successful LP, but their seventh (*You Get What You Play For*) and eighth LPs (*You Can Tune a Piano but You Can't Tuna Fish*) were breakthroughs. With Cronin and Richrath coproducing, REO began to develop a distinctive sound, a mix of rock riffs and pop hooks. *Tuna* contained the band's first chart single, "Roll with the Changes" (#58, 1978), and was its first to sell a million copies thanks to touring. *Nine Lives* in 1979 continued in this pop-rock direction.

Hi-Infidelity in 1980 was a phenomenally successful album, climbing to #1 on the *Billboard* chart three separate times between its release and the winter of 1981. Its sales eventually topped six million. Three singles charted from *Infidelity*: "Keep On Lovin' You" (#1, 1980), "Take It on the Run" (#5, 1981) and "In Your Letter" (#20, 1981). A best-of collection, *A Decade of Rock 'n' Roll: 1970 to 1980*, appeared in 1980. In the summer of 1982, *Good Trouble* was released, and the singles "Keep the Fire Burnin' " and "Don't Let Him Know" reached the Top Twenty.

THE RESIDENTS
Formed 1974, San Francisco
1974—*Meet the Residents* (Ralph)   **1976**—*Third Reich 'n' Roll; Fingerprince*   **1978**—*Not Available; Duck Stab/ Buster and Glen*   **1979**—*Eskimo; Nibbles* (Virgin) (compilation)   **1980**—*Commercial Album* (Ralph) **1981**—*Mark of the Mole*   **1982**—*Tunes of Two Cities; Intermission* (EP).

The Residents have never identified themselves by name, nor have they ever appeared in photos without some kind of mask (skulls; neo-KKK hoods and robes made from newspapers; huge bloodshot-eyeball masks to go with top hats and tails). Until 1982 they had given only one public concert, in 1976 at Berkeley, California, and then they appeared wrapped in mummylike coverings and played behind an opaque screen. The Residents have made several surrealistic short films, which, like their albums, cryptically elaborate a deliberately perverse antipop vision.

About all that is known is that there are four of them and that they emigrated from northern Louisiana to San Francisco in the early Seventies. They were named when Warner Bros. sent back an anonymous tape to "Residents" at their return address. On record they use a broad sonic palette, encompassing acoustic chamberlike instrumentation, tonal and atonal quasi jazz, electronics, noisy distortion and intentionally whiny-nasal vocals. Until the mid-Seventies, their albums were available only on the mail-order Ralph label.

The jacket of their debut album originally featured a grotesque dadaesque parody of *Meet the Beatles*. Threatened with legal action, the Residents changed it to depict Beatle-suited figures with crayfish heads and Beatle-like names (i.e., "Paul McCrawfish"; "Ringo Starrfish" had a starfish head). *Not Available* features modern-classical suites; *Eskimo* purports to be an Arctic cultural documentary with its otherworldly windswept sounds and native-Eskimo chants; and *Commercial Album* fits forty songs lasting a minute or less (like commercials) on one LP. As of 1982, there were rumors that the Residents would celebrate the tenth anniversary of Ralph Records with their first U.S. concert tour—though, as Residents spokesman Jay Clem put it, such a move would "run counter to the Residents' Theory of Obscurity." In October 1982, the Residents played five shows in San Francisco and Los Angeles. Adhering to their "Theory of Obscurity," the Residents were veiled and behind screens throughout the multimedia show, which included props and dancers enacting the "Mark of the Mole" story line.

PAUL REVERE AND THE RAIDERS
Formed early 1960s, Portland, Oregon
Paul Revere (b. 1942, Boise, Id.), kybds.; Mark Lindsay (b. Mar. 9, 1942, Cambridge, Id.), voc., sax; Phil "Fang" Volk, bass; Michael "Smitty" Smith, drums; Drake Levin, gtr.   **Later personnel included:** Jim "Harpo" Valley, gtr.; Joe Correro, Jr. (b. Nov. 19, 1946, Greenwood, Miss.), drums; Charlie Coe, bass; Freddy Weller (b. Sep. 9, 1947, Ga.), gtr.; Keith Allison, bass. **1967**—*Greatest Hits* (Columbia)   **1972**—*All-Time Greatest Hits*.

Paul Revere and the Raiders emerged from the rock & roll scene of the Northwest to become national pop successes, trading on the enormous teenybopper appeal of ponytailed lead singer Mark Lindsay.

The Raiders began early in the Sixties as the Downbeats, a raunchy rock & roll band. Lindsay played saxophone, leading the band through raucous, honking numbers like their first record, "Like, Long Hair" (1961), an independent single heard in Portland, Oregon, and nowhere else. They changed their name in mid-1962 and started wearing pseudo-Revolutionary War costumes. Columbia signed the group after hearing an unsolicited tape, and in mid-1963 the Raiders' version of "Louie Louie" was released. Though once again popular in the Northwest, their version was beaten out across America by the Kingsmen's hit. Sometime in 1964, Lindsay left the band; in early 1965, the Raiders moved to California and began to focus on a cleaner, more pop-oriented sound. Lindsay returned shortly thereafter.

"Steppin' Out" was their first national hit single (#46,

1965), aided by the band's prominence on Dick Clark's daily television rock program, "Where the Action Is." By 1967, they were known as Paul Revere and the Raiders featuring Mark Lindsay, which served as acknowledgment that Lindsay was cowriting most of their hits.

The group's hits during these years included "Just Like Me" (#11, 1965), "Kicks" (#4, 1966), "Hungry" (#6, 1966), "Ups and Downs" (#22, 1967) and "Him or Me—What's It Gonna Be?" (#5, 1967). Their one apparent problem was constantly fluctuating personnel. Drake Levin had been drafted and was replaced by Jim Valley. When Levin returned from the Army, he, Michael Smith and Phil Volk formed Brotherhood. Valley left for a solo career. Replacements included Freddy Weller, destined for a highly successful solo career as a country singer, and Joe Frank, later one-third of Hamilton, Joe Frank and Reynolds, who had hit records with "Fallin' in Love" (#1, 1975) and "Don't Pull Your Love" (#4, 1971). Another latter-day member, Keith Allison, was a minor teen idol in his own right, mainly thanks to his many appearances as a regular on "Action."

In 1969, Lindsay began to make solo records in addition to his work with the Raiders. Both enjoyed success early in the Seventies with "Arizona" (Lindsay) (#10, 1970) and "Indian Reservation" (Raiders) (#1, 1971), but little afterward. Paul Revere and the Raiders—that is Paul Revere, Mark Lindsay and whoever else they can round up—continue to play their oldies on the rock & roll revival circuit and were especially visible during the American bicentennial in 1976.

RHINOCEROS

Formed 1968, Los Angeles
Original lineup: John Finley, voc.; Michael Fonfara, kybds.; Danny Weis, gtr.; Alan Gerber, piano, voc.; Doug Hastings, gtr.; Jerry Penrod, bass; Billy Mundi, drums.
1968—*Rhinoceros* (Elektra)   **1969**—*Satin Chicken*
1970—*Better Times Are Coming*.

Like Blind Faith on a smaller scale, Rhinoceros were a manufactured "supergroup" devised by Elektra record producer Paul Rothchild in 1968. That summer, Rothchild got the idea to build a group out of castoffs from proven bands, though the numbers he eventually settled on had not really been prime movers in the name bands they came from. Doug Hastings had briefly played in Buffalo Springfield; Billy Mundi, who'd spent time with the Los

Grammy Awards

Lou Rawls
1967 Best R&B Vocal Performance, Male:
"Dead End Street"
1971 Best R&B Vocal Performance, Male:
"A Natural Man"
1977 Best R&B Vocal Performance, Male:
Unmistakably Lou

Otis Redding
1968 Best R&B Vocal Performance, Male; Best R&B Song:
"(Sittin' on) The Dock of the Bay" (with Steve Cropper)

Helen Reddy
1972 Best Pop Vocal Performance, Female:
"I Am Woman"

Jerry Reed
1970 Best Country Instrumental Performance:
Me and Jerry (with Chet Atkins)
1971 Best Country Vocal Performance, Male:
"When You're Hot, You're Hot"

Lionel Richie
1982 Best Pop Vocal Performance, Male:
"Truly"

Jeannie C. Riley
1968 Best Country Vocal Performance, Female:
"Harper Valley P.T.A."

Kenny Rogers
1977 Best Country Vocal Performance, Male:
"Lucille"

1979 Best Country Vocal Performance, Male:
"The Gambler"

Linda Ronstadt
1975 Best Country Vocal Performance, Female:
"I Can't Help It (If I'm Still in Love with You)"
1976 Best Pop Vocal Performance, Female:
Hasten Down the Wind

Rufus
1974 Best R&B Vocal Performance by a Duo, Group or Chorus:
"Tell Me Something Good"

Leon Russell
1972 Album of the Year:
The Concert for Bangla Desh (with others)

Angeles Philharmonic, had also worked for 2½ years as one of Frank Zappa's Mothers of Invention; Danny Weis and Jerry Penrod had played in the early Iron Butterfly; and Michael Fonfara had been with Jon and Lee and the Checkmates and the Electric Flag.

Elektra initially invested $80,000 in them (a large amount for the time). Their debut included "Apricot Brandy," a minor hit. Soon after the debut LP, Penrod left, briefly replaced by Weis's brother Steve, formerly the band's equipment manager. But before recording *Satin Chicken*, bassist Peter Hodgson took over. The band got only marginal public support, though, and soon Mundi, Gerber and Hastings left. *Better Times Are Coming* was recorded with new members, but very soon afterward the band fell apart completely. Fonfara later played on Lou Reed's *Street Hassle* and coproduced Reed's *Growing Up in Public*.

RHYTHM & BLUES/R&B

R&B is a euphemism with a grain of truth for black pop from the Forties to the Sixties; it replaced "race music" and gave way to soul, funk, disco and simply "black" styles. Small rhythm & blues combos revved up Tin Pan Alley pop tunes with rhythms derived from swing jazz and vocals reflecting the blues. They linked the Big Band jump blues of the Forties with early rock & roll. Early rock & roll hits were often covers by white singers of R&B hits, like Elvis Presley's version of Roy Brown's "Good Rockin' Tonight."

CHARLIE RICH

Born December 14, 1932, Colt, Arizona
N.A.—*The Early Years* (Sun)   *Classic Rich, volumes 1 and 2* (Epic)   **1972**—*Best of*   **N.A.**—*Greatest Hits*.

One of the original Sun rockabilly artists, gray-haired Charlie Rich (known as the "Silver Fox") is a country and blues singer, songwriter and pianist. His career was fitfully successful until his MOR country and pop crossover singles "Behind Closed Doors" and "The Most Beautiful Girl" hit in 1973.

Rich grew up listening to gospel music and learned piano from his missionary Baptist mother; he also sang in the church choir. In high school, he met the woman whom he married upon graduation, and who later became his songwriting partner, Margaret Ann Rich. Rich played in dance bands and jazz combos, then spent a year studying music at Arkansas University in 1950.

He joined the Air Force in 1951, and while stationed in Oklahoma formed his own jazz unit and then a pop band, the Velvetones, who had their own local television show. Though Rich felt he should restrict music to weekends and support his family by farming, his wife pushed his musical aspirations and eventually got him signed to Sun Records,

where he wrote songs and played sessions for Johnny Cash, Roy Orbison and others. His third solo single, "Lonely Weekends," was a chart hit through mid-1960.

Rich went to Mercury's Smash subsidiary in 1965, when "Mohair Sam" became his next Top Forty hit. He went to RCA in 1967, achieving a minor hit with "Big Boss Man," then went to Hi and finally Epic. He grew depressed and developed problems with pills and alcohol. At Epic, Rich teamed with Nashville producer Billy Sherrill.

Things finally clicked when Rich covered Kenny O'Dell's "Behind Closed Doors," which went gold and was a hit for much of 1973. The followup, "The Most Beautiful Girl" (by Sherrill, Norro Wilson and Rory Bourke), was #1 in December 1973, and it too was a gold record. The *Most Beautiful Girl* LP went gold as well. Thus was born the country-pop sound known as "countrypolitan." In 1978 Rich appeared in the Clint Eastwood film *Every Which Way but Loose*.

CLIFF RICHARD

Born Harry Roger Webb, October 14, 1940, Lucknow, India
1959—*Cliff* (Columbia)   *Cliff Sings*   **1960**—*Me and My Shadows*   **1961**—*Listen to Cliff*   **1963**—*Hit Album*   **1969**—*The Best of Cliff Richard*   **1974**—*Help It Along* (EMI)   **1976**—*I'm Nearly Famous*   **1977**—*Every Face Tells a Story;   My Kind of Life*   **1978**—*Small Corners; Green Light*   **1979**—*Rock 'n' Roll Juvenile; Thank You Very Much*   **1981**—*Wired for Sound*.

Cliff Richard has had roughly 75 hits in England since the late Fifties, although his first sustained U.S. success came as late as 1976. In Britain, Richard first gained popularity as something of an English Elvis Presley in such beatnik/rocker films as *Expresso Bongo* and by singing with the Ventures-like backup band the Shadows. In the mid-Sixties, he became a clean-cut pop idol, and by the Seventies he was a born-again Christian singing easy-listening rock and vaguely evangelical pop.

Harry Webb's parents were British subjects in India—his father born in Burma, his mother in India—who didn't see England until 1947. He learned guitar and sang with skiffle groups near his Herefordshire home, and formed a short-lived vocal group, the Quintones, with one other boy and three girls in 1957. He next joined the Dave Teague Skiffle Group, and worked for a short time as a credit control clerk in a TV factory.

In 1958, he put together a backup band, the Drifters, and changed his name to Cliff Richard for the Drifters' first demo, "Lawdy Miss Clawdy." In 1959, the Drifters became the Shadows to avoid confusion with the American R&B Drifters. The group's first hit was "Livin' Doll" in 1959 (#30 U.S.), followed in the U.K. by "Travellin' Light" (1959), "Please Don't Tease" (1960), "The Young Ones" (1962), "The Next Time" (1962), "Summer Holiday" (1963) and "The Minute You're Gone" (1965). With the Shadows dancing in formation behind Richard, they became a major live draw in Britain.

The Shadows had a few instrumental hits in England; meanwhile, only a few of Richard's songs made it onto the U.S. charts. (In 1968, "Congratulations" reached #99.) Richard made his film debut in 1958 in *Serious Charge*. He also appeared in *The Young Ones* (1961), *Summer Holiday* (1962), *Wonderful Life* (1964) and *Finders Keepers* (1967).

Richard's British hits continued in the Seventies with "Goodbye Sam, Hello Samantha" and "I Ain't Got the Time Anymore" (1970); "Sunny Honey Girl," "Silver Rain," "Jesus" and "Sing a Song of Freedom" (1972). He hosted a variety show on British television, and in 1970 he performed in Czechoslovakia and Romania. In 1970, Richard also made his stage acting debut in *Five Finger Exercise*.

By 1976, when Richard's "Devil Woman" became a Top Ten hit in the U.S., he had declared himself a born-again Christian; that same year he also toured the U.S.S.R. "We Don't Talk Anymore," a #1 hit in the U.K., went into the U.S. Top Ten in 1980, and that year he toured America for the first time since 1963. He was also named an officer of the Order of the British Empire (like the Beatles in 1965). In 1981, Richard's autobiography was published; he claimed not to have slept with a woman in more than 16 years, and also denied that he was homosexual. In 1982, he had a British hit with "Daddy's Home" and toured the Far East. (See also: The Shadows)

JONATHAN RICHMAN/MODERN LOVERS

Jonathan Richman, born 1952, Boston
1976—*Modern Lovers* (Beserkley)   **1977**—*Jonathan Richman and the Modern Lovers; Rock & Roll with the Modern Lovers; Modern Lovers Live*   **1978**—*Back in Your Life*   **1979**—*Modern Love Songs.*

Jonathan Richman is easily one of rock's quirkiest figures. He dreams up songs like "I'm a Little Aeroplane" or "I'm Nature's Mosquito" and croons them in a tone of boyish wonder, with no irony or cynicism intended. Those neo-nursery rhymes are far removed from the singer/songwriter/guitarist's early days with the original incarnation of the Modern Lovers, the group he formed in New England.

The Lovers—who also featured Jerry Harrison and Dave Robinson, who later joined the Talking Heads and the Cars, respectively—were inspired by the Velvet Underground and wrote songs like "Roadrunner," "Pablo Picasso" and "Hospital." But Richman's tolerance for loud music decreased, and he began to tone down the Modern Lovers; when David Robinson's drum kit was reduced to a single snare drum covered with a towel, he quit. The group also had run-ins with its record company, Warner Bros., and disbanded in 1972. Richman went on to

cut a series of albums for the independent Beserkley label (including the 1976 release *Modern Lovers*, an anthology of Warner demos from the early Seventies).

In 1977, Richman's instrumental tune "Egyptian Reggae"—taken from *Rock & Roll with the Modern Lovers*—became a hit in England, Holland and Germany, where he enjoys large cult followings. A period of self-imposed obscurity in New England was broken in 1980, when Richman began touring fairly regularly. Richman has yet to achieve mass acceptance. His sheer unpredictability and artistic risk-taking keep him outside the mainstream. In 1982, he was searching for a new record label.

RIGHTEOUS BROTHERS

Bill Medley, born September 19, 1940, Santa Ana, California; Bobby Hatfield, born August 10, 1940, Beaver Dam, Wisconsin
1965—*You've Lost That Lovin' Feelin'* (Philles)   **1966**—*Soul and Inspiration: Best of the Righteous Brothers* (Moonglow)   **1967**—*Greatest Hits* (Verve)   *Greatest Hits, volume 2.*

Bill Medley and Bobby Hatfield's close-harmony ballads came to exemplify white soul. Medley performed with the Paramours until he teamed up with Hatfield in 1962. They became the Righteous Brothers reportedly after a black fan referred to them as "righteous," a popular black slang term. In 1963, they had a hit on Moonglow Records with "Little Latin Lupe Lu" (#49 pop).

Phil Spector signed them to his Philles Records in 1964, where they cut "You've Lost That Lovin' Feelin'." The Barry Mann-Cynthia Weil-Spector song went to #1 pop, #3 R&B, and was successfully revived by Hall and Oates in 1980. Spector had other significant hits with the Righteous Brothers—"Unchained Melody" (#4 pop, #3 R&B, 1965), "Ebb Tide" (#5, 1965) and "Just Once in My Life" (#9, 1965)—before the duo moved to Verve Records in 1966. That year another Mann-Weil song, "(You're My) Soul and Inspiration," went to #1 pop, #13 R&B for Medley and Hatfield.

In 1968, they broke up and Medley recorded solo. Hatfield kept the Righteous Brothers name and performed with Jimmy Walker. That year, Medley had two minor chart singles on his own, "Brown Eyed Woman" (#43) and "Peace Brother Peace" (#48), on MGM Records.

In 1974, Medley and Hatfield reunited to record a tribute to dead rock stars, "Rock and Roll Heaven" (#3 pop), but little came of further collaborations. They did appear on an "American Bandstand" anniversary television special in 1981, where they performed a substantially reworked version of the song as a tribute to John Lennon. Medley signed with Planet Records in 1982 and released *Right Here and Now*, produced by Richard Perry and featuring a title track by Barry Mann and Cynthia Weil. In 1983, Medley and Hatfield toured together again.

BILLY LEE RILEY
Born Pocahontas, Arkansas
N.A.—*Funk Harmonica* (Crescendo)   1977—*Billy Lee Riley* (EP) (Charly)   1978—*Legendary Sun Performers; Sun Sounds Special.*

Billy Lee Riley, an adept multiinstrumentalist on guitar, harmonica, piano and drums, came to Memphis' Sun Studios in 1955 and became a session musician for Jerry Lee Lewis, Roy Orbison, Charlie Rich and others. In the mid-Fifties, he gathered some Sun musicians together and recorded two high-energy rockabilly singles, "Red Hot" and "Flying Saucers Rock 'n' Roll." The former featured what at the time were daring lyrics; the latter concerned little green men from outer space who visit Earth to enjoy some rock & roll. Both tunes were revived in 1978 by Robert Gordon and Link Wray.

The success of "Flying Saucers" gave Riley a brief solo career—his band was called the Little Green Men—but despite his good looks and stage moves, he was soon back in the Sun studio band. In the Sixties, Riley worked as a sessionman and producer in Memphis, Nashville and Los Angeles, recording under a number of aliases for several labels. In 1973, he returned to Arkansas to work as an interior designer. In 1978, he came back to Memphis and recorded some country and rock tracks at the refurbished Sun Studios with Sam Phillips' son Knox producing. Except for British reissues on the Charly label, he hasn't been heard from since.

JEANNIE C. RILEY
Born October 19, 1945, Anson, Texas
1968—*Harper Valley PTA* (Plantation)   N.A.—*Jeannie C. Riley's Greatest Hits.*

In 1968, Jeannie C. Riley was working as a secretary in Nashville, still trying to get her career as a country singer off the ground. Everything changed when her recording of "Harper Valley PTA" hit #1 on both pop and country charts, selling 5½ million copies globally, though in the long run it did more for its author, Tom T. Hall, than it did for Riley.

Subsequent singles—"The Girl Most Likely," "There Never Was a Time" and "Good Enough to Be Your Wife"—hit the country & western Top Ten, but only reached the lower regions of the pop charts. She had C&W hits through 1974. "Harper Valley PTA," on the other hand, made an impression so lasting that it inspired a nighttime TV series 13 years after its release.

TERRY RILEY
Born 1935, Colfax, California
1967—*Reed Streams* (Mass Art)   1969—*Keyboard Studies* (BYG)   1970—*In C* (Columbia)   1971—*Church of Anthrax* (with John Cale)   *A Rainbow in Curved Air*   1972—*Persian Surgery Dervishes* (Shandar)   1975—*Le Secret de la Vie* (Philips)   1980—*Shri Camel* (Columbia)   1982—*Descending Moonshine Dervishes* (Kuckuck).

An avant-garde musician/composer who first attracted attention in post-psychedelic San Francisco, keyboardist/reedman Riley is one of the original proponents of the minimalist school of modern classical music, which includes other influential figures like Steve Reich and Philip Glass. Such music uses the layered repetition of simple modular melodies to build up a rich, hypnotic fabric of sound.

Riley worked his way through Berkeley by playing ragtime piano at a San Francisco saloon. After getting his MA in composition, he toured France and Scandinavia with a floor show and various "happenings" and street theater projects. He worked with the early minimalist La Monte Young, and became known for all-night concerts of live and electronic music.

Riley's best-known records include *In C* (where a large number of musicians and singers perform the same melodies in staggered sequence, to make a slowly evolving, pulsing chord), *A Rainbow in Curved Air* and *Church of Anthrax* (the latter recorded with ex–Velvet Underground John Cale).

Through the Seventies, while he was on the faculty of Mills College, Riley's compositions turned increasingly improvisational; he would use preplanned motifs for solo performances on electric organ with a delay-repeat system. He also studied with Indian vocalist Pandit Pran Nath. In 1982, he gave a concert at Town Hall in New York featuring organ improvisations, Indian-influenced songs and a new string quartet.

The influence of the Riley/Reich/Glass school can be found in middle-period Soft Machine, Mike Oldfield's *Tubular Bells*, Robert Fripp's solo guitar performances, the Talking Heads of *Remain in Light* and the work of Eighties performance artist Laurie Anderson.

MINNIE RIPERTON
Born November 8, 1947, Chicago; died July 12, 1979, Los Angeles
1970—*Come to My Garden* (Janus)   1974—*Perfect Angel* (Epic)   1975—*Adventures in Paradise*   1977—*Stay in Love*   1979—*Minnie* (Capitol)   1980—*Love Lives Forever.*

Singer Minnie Riperton's angelic five-octave voice made her one of pop's most distinctive singers.

After studying opera as a child, Riperton decided she wanted a career in pop music when she reached her teens. She got a job as a receptionist at Chess Records. There she joined a vocal group called the Gems that sang backup behind Fontella Bass, Etta James and other Chess acts. In 1967, she sang with a black psychedelic pop band, Rotary Connection, that cut four albums on Cadet. "Amen" from their 1968 debut album was an FM staple for many years.

Rotary Connection split up in 1970, and that year Riperton recorded an unsuccessful solo album for Janus, *Come to My Garden.* She sang with Stevie Wonder's backup band Wonderlove before signing with Epic Records in 1974. *Perfect Angel,* with two tracks coproduced by Wonder, was her most successful album. It was certified gold and contained Wonder's "Lovin' You" (#1 pop, #3 R&B).

In 1976, Riperton had a mastectomy and then spent much of her time as a spokeswoman for the American Cancer Society. Two years later she moved to Capitol Records, where she recorded her last album, *Minnie.* Her condition gradually worsened, and she died of cancer in Los Angeles. *Love Lives Forever* is a posthumous collection consisting of Riperton's previously unreleased vocal tracks with completely new backing.

THE RITCHIE FAMILY
Formed 1974, New York City
N.A.—*Arabian Nights* (Marlin) *Life Is Music; African Queens; American Generation.*

Innumerable trios of anonymous studio singers have performed under the Ritchie Family banner since its inception in 1974. Jacques Morali and Henri Belolo, who later formed the Village People, utilized Philadelphia singers and session musicians (see MFSB) to cut "Brazil" (#11 pop, #13 R&B), a disco version of the 1943 Xavier Cugat hit. Similar disco versions of prerock hits (e.g., "Tangerine") filled early albums. In 1982, the current edition of the Ritchie Family had a hit with "I'll Do My Best" (#27 R&B).

JOHNNY RIVERS
Born John Ramistella, November 7, 1942, New York City
1966—*Johnny Rivers' Golden Hits* (Imperial) 1968—*Realization* 1969—*A Touch of Gold* 1978—*Outside Help* (Big Tree).

In addition to Johnny Rivers' major achievements behind the scenes (discovering talent like the Fifth Dimension and Jimmy Webb, bringing together top studio musicians as a regular band), his own singles have sold over 25 million copies in the last 18 years.

John Ramistella grew up in Baton Rouge, Louisiana, and there began playing in high school bands. On a summer trip to New York he met disc jockey Alan Freed, who changed Ramistella to Rivers and got him a contract with Gone Records. Nothing happened, though, and Rivers concentrated on songwriting in New York and L.A. One song, "I'll Make Believe," became a B side to a big Ricky Nelson hit in 1958.

In 1963, Rivers landed a gig at the new Whisky-a-Go-Go on the Sunset Strip, soon becoming the club's regular

star attraction. His 1964 debut Imperial LP, *Johnny Rivers Live at the Whisky-a-Go-Go,* yielded the #2 hit "Memphis." He recorded other live Whisky LPs over the years. His hits throughout the Sixties were usually covers, but they sold well, including "Seventh Son," which went to #7 in 1965, "Poor Side of Town" (#1, 1966), "Secret Agent Man" (#3, 1966) and two Motown covers, "Baby I Need Your Lovin' " (#3, 1967) and "The Tracks of My Tears" (#10, 1967). He covered Van Morrison's "Into the Mystic" in 1970.

In 1966, Rivers was approached by manager Marc Gordon with a group called the Hi-Fis, previously the Versatiles. Rivers liked the band, renamed them the Fifth Dimension, signed them to his newly established record company, Soul City, and linked them with his friend songwriter Jimmy Webb. Rivers played guitar on the Fifth Dimension's records and organized a regular band of studio musicians, including Hal Blaine (drums), Larry Knechtel (keyboards) and Joe Osborn (bass).

He continued to enjoy chart success as a performer in the Seventies with a remake of Huey "Piano" Smith's Fifties hit "Rockin' Pneumonia and the Boogie Woogie Flu" (#6, 1972) and the gold "Swayin' to the Music (Slow Dancin')" (#10, 1977). In 1975, he coaxed Brian Wilson out of retirement to do backups on his version of the Beach Boys' "Help Me Rhonda" (#22).

THE RIVINGTONS
Formed Los Angeles
Carl White (b. 1932; d. Jan. 7, 1980); Sonny Harris (b. Tex.); Al Frazier (b. Calif.); Rocky Wilson, Jr. (b. Pensacola, Fla.).

The Rivingtons were a Southern California vocal quartet of the early Sixties who hit it big twice with novelty records. In the summer of 1962, "Papa-Oom-Mow-Mow" reached the Top Fifty; its successor, "Mama-Oom-Mow-Mow" failed to hit the charts. The following year, "The Bird's the Word" propelled them to #27. From then on, the Rivingtons met with hard luck.

In 1963, a Minneapolis band called the Trashmen combined "Papa-Oom-Mow-Mow" and "The Bird's the Word" and came up with a smash, "Surfin' Bird." The Rivingtons filed suit, as they would again when the Oak Ridge Boys used the syllables "papa-oom-mow-mow" in "Elvira" in 1981. Little is known about the band except that prior to their days as the Rivingtons the foursome had worked as the Sharps, their membership drawn from two earlier groups, the Lamplighters and the Tenderfoots.

SMOKEY ROBINSON AND THE MIRACLES
Formed 1957, Detroit
William "Smokey" Robinson (b. Feb. 19, 1940); Ronnie White (b. Apr. 5, 1939); Bobby Rogers (b. Feb. 19, 1940); Pete Moore (b. Nov. 19, 1939); Claudette Rogers Robinson (b. 1942).

1965—*Greatest Hits from the Beginning* (Tamla)
1968—*Greatest Hits, Volume 2* 1974—*Anthology*
(Motown).
Smokey Robinson solo: 1973—*Smokey* (Tamla) 1974—
Pure Smokey 1975—*Quiet Storm* 1976—*Smokey's*
Family Robinson 1977—*Deep in My Soul* 1978—
Love Breeze; Smokin' 1979—*Where There's Smoke*
1981—*Being with You* 1982—*Touch the Sky*.

Soon after his debut with the Miracles, Smokey Robinson became known as one of the premier songwriter/singers in pop music. His delicate falsetto and his way with a metaphor—as in "Let Me Be the Time (on the Clock of Your Heart)"—have been hugely influential.

Robinson founded the Miracles—all Detroit born—while attending that city's Northern High School. As the Matadors, they played locally, usually performing Robinson originals. In 1957, they met Berry Gordy, Jr., while they were auditioning for Jackie Wilson's manager. Gordy, who had written songs for Wilson, was impressed by their material. "Got a Job," an answer to the #1 hit "Get a Job" by the Silhouettes, attracted local attention in 1958. In 1959, "Bad Girl" was distributed locally by Motown, nationally by Chicago's Chess Records. It hit #93 on the pop chart and convinced Motown to go national. In 1960, "Shop Around" established both the group and the company when it went to #1 on the R&B chart, #2 on pop.

Throughout the Sixties, Robinson wrote songs for many other Motown acts, including the Marvelettes ("Don't Mess with Bill," "The Hunter Gets Captured by the Game" and "My Baby Must Be a Magician"); Marvin Gaye ("I'll Be Doggone," with Warren Moore and Marvin Tarplin, "Ain't That Peculiar," with Moore); Mary Wells ("My Guy," "The One Who Really Loves You" and "You Beat Me to the Punch," with Ronald White); and the Temptations ("Get Ready," "Don't Look Back" and "My Girl," with White; "The Way You Do the Things You Do," with Bobby Rogers; "It's Growing," with Moore).

Though the Miracles made numerous uptempo singles such as "Mickey's Monkey" (#8 pop, #3 R&B) in 1963 and "Going to a Go-Go" (#11 pop, #2 R&B) in 1966, they are best known for their ballads, including "You've Really Got a Hold on Me" (#8 pop, #1 R&B, 1963), "Ooo Baby Baby" (#16 pop, #4 R&B, 1965), "The Tracks of My Tears" (#16 pop, #2 R&B, 1965), "More Love" (#23 pop, #5 R&B, 1967—by which time they had become Smokey Robinson and the Miracles), "I Second That Emotion" (#4 pop, #1 R&B, 1967) and "Baby, Baby Don't Cry" (#8 pop, #3 R&B, 1969). Their last big hit together was the uptempo "The Tears of a Clown," a #1 hit in England and on both the R&B and pop charts in the U.S. in 1970. A great deal of their work in these years featured Marv Tarplin on guitar; he even appeared on a few album covers looking like a sixth member.

In 1972, Robinson left the group to record on his own, to

Smokey Robinson and the Miracles: Pete Moore, Ronnie White, Smokey Robinson, Bobby Rogers

spend more time with his wife (former Miracle Claudette) and to continue duties as a Motown vice-president. He continued to work frequently with Tarplin. *Quiet Storm* (1975) is regarded as his best early solo album. While always a popular concert attraction, his record sales during the Seventies fluctuated. It wasn't until 1979's "Cruisin' " (#4 pop, #4 R&B) that Robinson again enjoyed mass success. His #1 R&B single "Being with You" (#2 pop) in 1981 continued his performing comeback.

But Robinson's music had never gone away. Linda Ronstadt with "Ooo Baby Baby" and "The Tracks of My Tears" and Kim Carnes with "More Love" are just two of the singers who have had Top Thirty singles with his compositions.

The Miracles continued to perform after Robinson's departure, replacing him with Billy Griffin. While they continued to chart through 1978, only three singles had significant chart status: "Do It Baby" (#13 pop, #14 R&B) and "Don't Cha Love It" (#4 R&B) in 1974, and their early-1976 #1 pop hit "Love Machine (Part 1)" (#5 R&B).

THE TOM ROBINSON BAND/SECTOR 27
Formed 1977, England
Tom Robinson (b. circa 1951, Cambridge, Eng.), bass, voc.; Danny Kustow, gtr., voc.; Mark Ambler, organ, piano; Brian "Dolphin" Taylor, drums.
1978—*Power in the Darkness* (Harvest) (− Taylor; − Ambler; + Nick Plytas, kybds.; − Plytas; + Ian "Quince" Parker, kybds.; + Preston Keyman [b. U.S.], drums) **1979—*TRB Two*** (disbanded; in late 1979 formed Sector 27: Robinson, voc., gtr.; Jo Burt, bass; Stevie B., gtr.; Derek Quinton, percussion, drums) **1980—*Sector 27* (I.R.S) 1982—*North by Northwest*.**

Singer/songwriter Tom Robinson—one of rock's few openly gay performers—is also the only successful one to musically treat his sexual preference as a political issue, as in his "Glad to Be Gay." Robinson first came to public attention during the early days of British punk in 1977. The Tom Robinson Band, like the early Clash, played rousing battle-cry rock & roll.

Robinson claimed he was first drawn to rock & roll as an angry counterpoint to his father's love of classical music. At 17 Robinson was shipped off to Finchden Manor, a home for "maladjusted boys." In his six years there he met guitarist Danny Kustow and the two became friendly. He left for London in 1973 and there formed Cafe Society, a cabaret, folk-harmony band, with two old friends, Herewood Kaye and Raphael Doyle. Ray Davies signed them to his Konk label in 1973 and produced their one album in 1975. (Robinson and Davies had a falling out, later obliquely chronicled in "Don't Take No for an Answer" on TRB's debut.)

In 1976, Robinson left Cafe Society, and he formed the Tom Robinson Band in January 1977. In October, TRB's "2-4-6-8-Motorway" went Top Ten in the U.K. The band became press darlings in England, especially after the *Rising Free* EP in early 1978, which included "Glad to Be Gay." That press attention was soon repeated in the U.S., leading to the release of their American debut, *Power in the Darkness*. "Glad to Be Gay" got nearly as much radio play on the big-city U.S. stations as "2-4-6-8-Motorway." Robinson also plugged Rock Against Racism on the back of the album cover and included the New York and L.A. gay switchboard numbers on the inner sleeve of the U.S. version.

The band went through some personnel changes before their second LP, which was produced by Todd Rundgren. Despite several U.S. tours, neither LP sold well. The album was poorly received in England also, and Robinson began to feel that TRB's style was no longer new, so he broke it up in July 1979. Earlier that year, Robinson had written a few songs with Elton John, including one for Gay Pride Week.

Robinson's new band, Sector 27, appeared later in the year, influenced by the harsher wave of post-punk bands like Gang of Four, XTC and the Cure. The band toured England and then the U.S. in the summer of 1980. The self-titled LP got good reviews but failed to sell, and Sector 27 fell apart. In mid-1982, Robinson resurfaced with a solo record, *North by Northwest*.

THE ROCHES

Formed 1976, New York City
Maggie Roche (b. Oct. 26, 1951, Detroit), voc., gtr.; Suzzy Roche (b. Sep. 29, 1956, Bronxville, N.Y.), voc., gtr.; Terre Roche (b. Apr. 10, 1953, New York City), voc., gtr.
1975—*Seductive Reasoning* (Columbia) **1979**—*The Roches* (Warner Bros.) **1980**—*Nurds* **1982**—*Keep on Doing*.

By the time their critically acclaimed debut album was released, the three Roche sisters had been singing together for some time, Maggie and Terre as a duo, and the trio of sisters in New York clubs. With Suzzy's sweet-and-sour voice, Terre's pliant upper register and Maggie's near-baritone, they came out of New York's folk/feminist/bohemian traditions, mingling barbershop quartet, Irish traditional, Andrews Sisters, doo-wop and other vocal-group styles in songs—most of them by Maggie—full of wordplays and unexpected twists. Onstage, they inevitably wear an eccentric array of thrift shop clothes and sporting gear.

Maggie and Terre had begun singing professionally in the late Sixties. Soon Maggie had dropped out of Bard College and Terre left high school so that the duo could tour. In 1970, they met Paul Simon, and in 1972 they sang backup harmonies on his *There Goes Rhymin' Simon*. Simon's lawyer got the duo a contract with Columbia, which resulted in *Seductive Reasoning*, an album that went largely unnoticed. Maggie and Terre retreated to a friend's Kung Fu temple in Hammond, Louisiana, but eventually drifted back north, performing again for the first time in June 1976 at the Women's Music Festival in Champaign, Illinois. Within a few months Suzzy, who'd been attending the State University of New York in Purchase, joined them and they became fixtures in Greenwich Village folk clubs. After amassing local critical raves, they recorded their trio debut LP, produced by Robert Fripp. The album sold 200,000 copies and contained "The Married Men" (later covered by Phoebe Snow) but failed to yield a hit. Terre performed some vocals on Fripp's 1979 *Exposure* solo LP, and the trio sang backup for Loudon Wainwright III's "Golfin' Blues." In late 1980, augmented with the rhythm section of ex-Television bassist Fred Smith and Patti Smith drummer Jay Dee Daugherty, they recorded *Nurds*. In mid-1982, Fripp produced their third album, *Keep on Doing*, which featured members of King Crimson although the album was primarily acoustic.

ROCKABILLY

Rockabilly was Elvis Presley's music, the hybrid of blues and country that became rock & roll. It emerged from Sam Phillips' Sun Studios in Memphis, were Phillips recorded small bands—slapping string bass, twanging lead guitar, acoustic rhythm guitar—with plenty of echo while singers made astonishing yelps and gulps and hiccups and stutters. Rockabilly's original manic burst of activity ended with the Fifties. Its leading lights—Jerry Lee Lewis, Johnny Cash, Carl Perkins—moved into country music. But every generation of rockers has revived and rediscovered rockabilly—from Creedence Clearwater Revival to

Elvis Costello to the Stray Cats to X—and its guitar licks and high spirits inform all kinds of rock.

ROCK & ROLL

The term is a blues euphemism for sexual intercourse.

ROCKPILE
Formed 1976, London
Dave Edmunds (b. Apr. 15, 1944, Cardiff, Wales), voc., gtr.; Nick Lowe (b. March 25, 1949, Eng.), voc., bass; Terry Williams (b. 1948), drums; Billy Bremner (b. 1947, Scot.), gtr., voc.
1980—*Seconds of Pleasure* (Columbia).

Though they recorded only one album under the name Rockpile, the band had made four previous U.S. tours and its members had appeared on most solo LPs by the group's best-known members: Nick Lowe (who specializes in ironic pop) and Dave Edmunds (known for his revitalized rockabilly). Ex–Love Sculpture guitarist Edmunds called his first solo album *Rockpile* (1972), and his band, which toured to support that album, was also christened Rockpile, though the only member of the more recent group was Terry Williams, who'd done substitute drumming on one of Love Sculpture's U.S. tours. Williams had also played with Deke Leonard and Martin Ace, whom he later joined in Man.

This initial Rockpile helped kick off England's pub-rock movement, which included other no-frills bands like Ducks Deluxe and Brinsley Schwarz. Nick Lowe of the Brinsley band met Williams and Edmunds on the pub circuit, and Edmunds produced the final Brinsley LP in 1974. On Edmunds' next solo LP, 1975's *Subtle As a Flying Mallet,* Lowe played and contributed songs.

Rockpile: Terry Williams, Nick Lowe, Dave Edmunds, Billy Bremner

In mid-1976, Rockpile solidified their new lineup for a brief American tour with Bad Company, rounded out by Billy Bremner, a sessionman who'd backed everyone from Duane Eddy to Lulu. Their sets offered a furiously paced mixtured of Lowe's tuneful ditties and Edmunds' more rocking outbursts. In late 1980, the band's two leaders were both signed to the same label and Rockpile released its one and only LP, which included an EP of Lowe and Edmunds duetting on Everly Brothers tunes. Rockpile toured the U.S. that winter, but in February of 1981 they had a bitter split. In 1982, Bremner was a temporary replacement for the late James Honeyman-Scott in the Pretenders, but he then rejoined Dave Edmunds' band.

JIMMIE RODGERS
Born September 8, 1897, Meridian, Mississippi; died May 26, 1933, New York City
1962—*Country Music Hall of Fame* (RCA) **1965**—*Best of the Legendary Jimmie Rodgers* **N.A.**—*This Is Jimmie Rodgers* **1975**—*My Rough and Rowdy Ways* **1978**—*A Legendary Performer* (RCA).

Though his recording career only lasted seven years (from 1927 until his death in 1933), Jimmie Rodgers established himself as the father of modern country music, mixing black blues with folk and traditional hillbilly country.

Rodgers first played the guitar and banjo while working as a water carrier on the M&O Railroad, where he picked up blues influences from the black fellow laborers. He later worked as a brakeman until ill health forced him to quit in 1925. (He always had health problems; his mother died of TB when he was four.)

Rodgers had long been an amateur performer, but following his forced retirement he pursued music full-time, becoming a black-face performer in a medicine show. In 1926, he appeared as a yodeler and later that year formed his own band, the Jimmie Rodgers Entertainers. The group soon split. Rodgers got a solo contract with Victor Records and released "The Soldier's Sweetheart" and "Sleep Baby Sleep" in 1927, around the same time the Carter Family made their recording debut. His song "Blue Yodel" became a million-seller, making Rodgers the first country superstar. "Brakeman's Blues" also sold a million, and in 1929 he made the movie short *The Singing Brakeman;* its title became his nickname.

Even during the Depression, Rodgers' records sold well, but his health was deteriorating. Though he was critically ill (and had to cancel shows), he continued to record up until his death. His final song, "Fifteen Years Ago Today," was completed the same day he hemorrhaged and lapsed into a coma. The next day, he died. In 1961, Rodgers, along with Frank Rose and Hank Williams, became one of the first persons elected to the Country Music Hall of Fame.

TOMMY ROE

Born May 9, 1942, Atlanta
1969—*12 in a Roe—Tommy Roe's Greatest Hits* (ABC).

At the peak of his career, in the late Sixties, singer/songwriter Tommy Roe could do no wrong. Though probably one of the oldest bubblegum singers, he had two #1 records, starting with a remake of his first hit, "Sheila," in 1962 and "Dizzy" in 1969. He also scored big with "Sweet Pea" (#8, 1966), "Hooray for Hazel" (#6, 1966) and "Jam Up and Jelly Tight" (#8, 1969). Even a version of Lloyd Price's hit from 1959, "Stagger Lee," reached the Top Thirty.

At the age of 16, Roe was living in Atlanta, leading his own group, the Satins. In 1960, he recorded one of his own songs, a bald rewrite of Buddy Holly's "Peggy Sue" called "Sheila." Two years later, Roe was signed to ABC. His first single there seemed destined for failure until disc jockeys flipped over "Save Your Kisses" and found "Sheila" (in its second version), which became a huge success.

Follow-up records didn't fare so well. But Roe was doing much better in England, where he relocated for a while in the Sixties. Today he continues to perform, alternating between the oldies circuit and country shows.

KENNY ROGERS

Born August 21, 1941, Houston
Kenny Rogers and the First Edition: 1968—*First Edition* (Reprise)   **1971**—*Greatest Hits.*
Kenny Rogers solo: 1974—*Love Lifted Me* (United Artists)   **1975**—*Kenny Rogers*   **1976**—*Daytime Friends*   **1978**—*The Gambler; Ten Years of Gold*   **1979**—*Kenny*   **1980**—*Gideon; Greatest Hits*   **1981**—*Share Your Love.*

Though usually dismissed by critics, Kenny Rogers has had well over a decade and a half of success with folk pop (with the New Christy Minstrels), mild psychedelia and country rock (with the First Edition) and country-pop ballads (as a solo act).

Rogers began singing in a high school band, the Scholars, who had a regional Texas hit with "That Crazy Feeling." At the University of Houston, he joined a jazz group, the Bobby Doyle Trio, as a vocalist and recorded with them for Columbia. He then joined the New Christy Minstrels in 1966.

The First Edition was formed by ex-Minstrels in 1967, making their debut at Ledbetter's in Los Angeles, a club owned by another ex-Minstrel, Randy Sparks. There they were brought to the attention of musician/comedian Tommy Smothers, who put Rogers and the First Edition on his TV show. This led to their Reprise contract, and they had their first hit with the quasi-psychedelic "Just Dropped In (To See What Condition My Condition Was In)," #5 in 1968. This success was followed by hits in a more countryish vein, like "Ruby Don't Take Your Love to Town" (#6) and the Kingston Trio's "Reuben James" (#26), both in 1969. More hits followed, including the harder-rocking "Something's Burning" (#11) and the gospelish "Tell It All Brother" (#17) in 1970 and "School Teacher" in 1972. In late 1971, the First Edition had its own syndicated TV show, "Rollin' on the River."

After the breakup of the First Edition, Rogers switched to an MOR-country style and chalked up a string of big hits like "Lucille" (#5, 1977), "The Gambler" (#16, 1979), "Don't Fall in Love with a Dreamer" (#4, 1980, a duet with Kim Carnes), Lionel Richie's "Lady" (his first #1 hit), "I Don't Need You" (#3) and "Through the Years."

Between 1977 and 1979, Rogers sold over $100 million worth of records. In 1980, Rogers starred in a TV movie, *The Gambler,* based on his 1979 hit.

THE ROLLING STONES

Formed July, 1962, London
Mick Jagger (b. Michael Phillip Jagger, July 26, 1943, Dartford, Eng.), voc.; Keith Richards (b. Dec. 18, 1943, Dartford), gtr., voc.; Brian Jones (b. Lewis Brian Hopkins-Jones, Feb. 28, 1942, Cheltenham, Eng.; d. July 3, 1969, London), gtr.; Bill Wyman (b. Oct. 24, 1936, London), bass; Charlie Watts (b. June 2, 1941, Islington, Eng.), drums.
1964—*The Rolling Stones* (Decca, U.K.)   *England's Newest Hitmakers* (London)   **1965**—*Rolling Stones Two* (Decca, U.K.)   *12 X 5* (London)   *Rolling Stones Now; Out of Our Heads; December's Children*   **1966**—*Aftermath; High Tide and Green Grass; Got Live If You Want It*   **1967**—*Between the Buttons; Flowers; Their Satanic Majesties Request*   **1968**—*Beggar's Banquet*   **1969**—(− Jones; + Mick Taylor [b. Jan. 17, 1948, Hertfordshire, Eng.], gtr.)   *Through the Past Darkly; Let It Bleed*   **1970**—*Get Yer Ya-Ya's Out!*   **1971**—*Sticky Fingers* (Rolling Stones/Atlantic)   *—Hot Rocks* (London)   **1972**—*Exile on Main Street* (Rolling Stones/Atlantic)   *More Hot Rocks: Big Hits and Fazed Cookies* (London)   **1973**—*Goat's Head Soup* (Rolling Stones/Atlantic)   *No Stone Unturned* (Decca, U.K.)   **1974**—*It's Only Rock 'n' Roll*   **1975**—*Made in the Shade* (− Taylor; + Ron Wood [b. June 1, 1947, London], gtr., voc.)   **1976**—*Black and Blue*   **1977**—*Love You Live*   **1978**—*Some Girls*   **1980**—*Emotional Rescue*   **1981**—*Sucking in the Seventies; Tattoo You*   **1982**—*Still Life.*

The Rolling Stones began calling themselves the "World's Greatest Rock & Roll Band" in the late Sixties, and few disputed the claim. The Stones' music, based on Chicago blues, has continued to sound vital through the decades, and the Stones' attitude of flippant defiance has come to seem as important as their music.

The Rolling Stones: Charlie Watts, Bill Wyman, Mick Taylor, Keith Richards, Mick Jagger

In the 1964 British Invasion, they were promoted as bad boys, but what began as a gimmick has stuck as an indelible image, and not just because of incidents like Brian Jones's death in 1969 and a violent murder during their set at Altamont. In their music, the Stones pioneered British rock's tone of ironic detachment and wrote about offhand brutality, sex as power and other taboos. Jagger was branded a "Lucifer" figure, thanks to songs like "Sympathy for the Devil." In the Eighties, the Stones have lost their dangerous aura while still seeming "bad"—they've become icons of an elegantly debauched, world-weary decadence. But Jagger remains the most self-consciously assured appropriator of black performers' up-front sexuality; Keith Richards' Chuck Berry–derived riffing defines rock rhythm guitar (not to mention rock guitar rhythm); the stalwart Wyman-Watts rhythm section holds its own with any band's; and Jagger and Richards continue to write telling songs.

Jagger and Richards first met at Dartford Maypole County Primary School. When they ran into each other ten years later in 1960, they were both avid fans of blues and American R&B, and they found they had a mutual friend in guitarist Dick Taylor, a fellow student of Richards' at Sidcup Art School. Jagger was attending the London School of Economics and playing in Little Boy Blue and the Blue Boys, with Taylor. Richards joined the band as second guitarist; soon afterward, he was expelled from Dartford Technical College for truancy.

Meanwhile, Brian Jones had begun skipping school in Cheltenham to practice be-bop alto sax and clarinet. By the time he was 16, he had fathered two illegitimate children and run off briefly to Scandinavia, where he began playing guitar. Back in Cheltenham, he joined the Ramrods, then drifted to London with his girlfriend and child. He began playing with Alexis Korner's Blues, Inc.,

then decided to start his own band; an ad attracted pianist Ian Stewart.

As Elmo Lewis, Jones began working at the Ealing Blues Club, where he ran into a later, loosely knit version of Blues, Inc., which at the time included drummer Charlie Watts. Jagger and Richards began jamming with Blues, Inc., and while Jagger, Richards and Jones began to practice on their own, Jagger became featured singer with Blues, Inc.

Jones, Jagger and Richards began to share a tiny, cheap London apartment, and with Tony Chapman they cut a demo tape, which was rejected by EMI. Taylor left to attend the Royal College of Art; he eventually formed Pretty Things. Ian Stewart's job with a chemical company kept the rest of the group from starving. By the time Taylor left, they began to call themselves the Rolling Stones, after a Muddy Waters song.

On July 12, 1962, the Rolling Stones—Jagger, Richards, Jones, a returned Dick Taylor on bass and Mick Avory, later of the Kinks, on drums—played their first show at the Marquee. Avory and Taylor were replaced by drummer Tony Chapman and bassist Bill Wyman, from the Cliftons. Chapman didn't work out, and the band spent months recruiting a cautious Charlie Watts, who worked for an advertising agency and had left Blues, Inc. when its schedule got too busy. In January 1963, Watts completed the band.

Local entrepreneur Giorgio Gomelsky booked the Stones for his Crawdaddy Club for an eight-month, highly successful residency; he was also their unofficial manager until Andrew Loog Oldham, with financing from Eric Easton, signed them as clients. By then, the Beatles were a British sensation, and Oldham decided to promote the Stones as their nasty opposites. He eased out the mild-mannered Stewart, who subsequently became a Stones roadie and frequent session and tour pianist.

In June 1963, the Stones released their first single, Chuck Berry's "Come On." After the band played on the British TV rock show "Thank Your Lucky Stars"—its producer reportedly told Oldham to get rid of "that vile-looking singer with the tire-tread lips"—the single reached #21 on the British charts. The Stones also appeared at the first annual National Jazz and Blues Festival in London's borough of Richmond and in September were part of a package tour with the Everly Brothers, Bo Diddley and Little Richard. In December 1963, the Stones' second single, "I Wanna Be Your Man" (written by John Lennon and Paul McCartney), made the British Top Fifteen. In January 1964, the Stones did their first headlining British tour, with the Ronettes, and released a version of Buddy Holly's "Not Fade Away," which made #3.

"Not Fade Away" also made the U.S. singles charts (#48), and by this time the band had become a sensation in Britain, with the press gleefully reporting that bandmembers had been seen urinating in public. In April 1964, their first album was released in the U.K., and two months later they made their first American tour. Their cover of the Bobby Womack/Valentinos song "It's All Over Now" was a British #1, their first. Their American tour was a smashing success; in Chicago, where they'd stopped off to record the *Five by Five* EP at the Chess Records studio, riots broke out when the band tried to give a press conference. Their version of the blues standard "Little Red Rooster," which had become another U.K. #1, was banned in the U.S. because of its objectionable lyrics. Jagger and Richards had now begun composing their own tunes (at first using the "Nanker Phelge" pseudonym for group compositions).

In January 1965, their "The Last Time" became another U.K. #1 and their first U.S. Top Ten hit. Their second LP (*Two* in Britain, *12 X 5* in America) took off, as did "Satisfaction" (#1, U.S. and U.K.). Jagger and Richards continued to write hits: "Get Off My Cloud" (#1, 1965), "Time Is on My Side" (#1, 1964), "As Tears Go By" (#6, 1965) and "Tell Me" (#24, 1964).

Aftermath, the first Stones LP of all original compositions, came out in 1966, though its impact was minimized by the simultaneous release of the Beatles' *Revolver* and Bob Dylan's *Blonde on Blonde.* The Eastern-tinged "Paint It Black" and "Ruby Tuesday," a ballad, were both U.S. #1 hits in 1966–67. By this time, the Stones had also appeared on "The Ed Sullivan Show" (1965) and had released *Got Live If You Want It.* The band had already chalked up more international hits in "Mother's Little Helper" (#8, 1966), "19th Nervous Breakdown" (#2, 1966), "Have You Seen Your Mother, Baby (Standing in the Shadows)" (#9, 1966) and "Lady Jane" (#24, 1966).

In January 1967, the Stones caused another sensation when they performed "Let's Spend the Night Together" on the Sullivan show and Jagger mumbled the title lines after threats of censorship (some claimed that the line was censored; others that Jagger actually sang "Let's spend some time together"; Jagger later said "When it came to that line, I sang mumble"). In February, Jagger and Richards were arrested on drug possession charges in Britain; in May, Brian Jones too was arrested. The heavy jail sentences they received were eventually suspended on appeal. The Stones temporarily withdrew from public appearances; Jagger and his girlfriend, singer Marianne Faithfull, went to India with the Beatles to meet the Maharishi; and the band recorded a psychedelic answer record to the Beatles' *Sgt. Pepper* in *Their Satanic Majesties Request.* The Stones had a minor hit single in "We Love You" (on which Lennon and McCartney sang backup vocals). By the time that "Dandelion" and *Satanic Majesties'* "She's a Rainbow" had also become hits, Allen Klein was the Stones' manager.

May 1968 saw the release of "Jumping Jack Flash," a #3 hit. After five months of delay provoked by controversial album-sleeve photos, the eclectic *Beggar's Banquet* was released and was hailed by critics as the band's finest achievement. On June 9, 1969, Brian Jones, the Stones'

most musically adventurous member, who had lent sitar, dulcimer and, on "Under My Thumb," marimba to the band's sound, and who had been in Morocco recording nomadic Joujouka musicians, left the band with the explanation that "I no longer see eye-to-eye with the others over the discs we are cutting." Within a week he was replaced by ex–John Mayall guitarist Mick Taylor. Jones announced that he would form his own band, but on July 3, 1969, he was found dead in his swimming pool; the coroner's report cited "death by misadventure." At an outdoor concert in London's Hyde Park a few days after Jones's death, Jagger read an excerpt from Shelley and released thousands of butterflies over the park. On July 11, the day after Jones was buried, the Stones released "Honky Tonk Women."

By this time, every Stones album went gold in short order, and *Let It Bleed* (a sardonic reply to the Beatles' *Let It Be*) was no exception. "Gimme Shelter" received constant airplay. Jones appeared on most of the album's tracks, though Taylor also made his first on-disc appearances.

After going to Australia to star in the film *Ned Kelly,* Jagger rejoined the band for its 1969 American tour, their biggest and most successful yet. But the Stones' Satanic image came home to roost at a free thank-you-America concert at California's Altamont Speedway. In the darkness just in front of the stage, a young black, Meredith Hunter, was stabbed to death by members of the Hell's Angels motorcycle gang, whom the Stones—on advice of the Grateful Dead—had appointed to work security for the event. The incident was captured on film by the Maysles brothers in their feature-length documentary *Gimme Shelter.* Public outcry that "Sympathy for the Devil" had in some way incited the violence led the Stones to drop the tune from their stage shows for the next six years.

After another spell of inactivity, the *Get Yer Ya-Ya's Out!* live album was released and quickly went gold. In 1970, the Stones formed their own Rolling Stones Records, an Atlantic subsidiary. The band's first album for its own label, *Sticky Fingers*—which introduced their Andy Warhol–designed lips-and-lolling-tongue logo—yielded hits in "Brown Sugar" (#1, 1971) and "Wild Horses" (#28, 1971). Jagger, who had starred in Nicolas Roeg's 1970 *Performance* (the soundtrack of which yielded "Memo from Turner"), married Nicaraguan fashion model Bianca Perez Morena de Macias, and the pair became international jet-set favorites. Though many interpreted Jagger's acceptance into high society as yet another sign that rock was dead, or that at least the Stones had lost their spark, *Exile on Main Street,* a double album, was another critically acclaimed hit, yielding successful singles like "Tumbling Dice" (#7, 1972) and "Happy" (#22, 1972). By this time, the Stones were touring the U.S. only once every three years; their 1972 extravaganza, like those in 1975, 1978 and 1981, was a sold-out affair.

Goat's Head Soup was termed the band's worst effort

since *Satanic Majesties* by critics, yet it contained "Angie" (#1, 1973) and "Heartbreaker" (#15, 1974). *It's Only Rock 'n' Roll* yielded hits in the title tune and a cover of the Temptations' "Ain't Too Proud to Beg" (#17, 1974). Mick Taylor left the band after that album; and after trying out scores of sessionmen (many of whom showed up on the next LP, *Black and Blue*), the Stones settled on Ron Wood, then still nominally committed to Rod Stewart and the Faces (who disbanded soon after Wood joined the Stones). In 1979, Richards and Wood, with Meters drummer Ziggy Modeliste and fusion bassist Stanley Clarke, toured as the New Barbarians.

Black and Blue sold as well as ever, with hits like the discofied "Hot Stuff" and "Fool to Cry" (#10, 1976). Wyman, who had released a 1974 solo album in *Monkey Grip*, recorded another, *Stone Alone*. Jagger guested on "I Can Feel the Fire" on Wood's solo first LP, *I've Got My Own Album to Do*.

Some Girls was the Stones' biggest-selling LP yet, with hits like "Miss You" (another disco crossover, #1, 1978) and "Shattered" (#31, 1978), while the title tune's ethnic-stereotype lyrics provoked public protest (the last outcry had been in 1976 over *Black and Blue*'s battered-woman advertising campaign). Richards and his long-time commonlaw wife, Anita Pallenburg, were arrested in March 1977 in Canada for heroin possession, but he subsequently kicked his habit and in 1978 was given a suspended sentence.

In 1981, *Tattoo You* outsold *Some Girls,* yielding hits like "Start Me Up" (#2, 1981) and "Waiting on a Friend" (#13, 1981), featuring jazz great Sonny Rollins on tenor saxophone. Even *Still Life,* an uneven live album from the tour, was snapped up by young, eager Stones fans. The movie of that tour—the largest-grossing tour in rock & roll—*Let's Spend the Night Together* (directed by Hal Ashby), was only moderately successful.

ROMEO VOID
Formed 1979, San Francisco
Debora Iyall (b. ca. 1956), voc.; Frank Zincavage, bass; Peter Woods, gtr.; Jay Derrah, drums; Ben Bossi, sax.
1980—(− Derrah; + John Stench, drums) **1981**—*It's a Condition* (415) (− Stench; + Larry Carter, drums) **1982**—*Benefactor* (415/Columbia).

Debora Iyall's sung-spoken songs for Romeo Void explore the empty consequences of love over a solid post-punk dance beat. The critically acclaimed band was formed in San Francisco in 1979, with most members coming from an art-school background.

Iyall, a Cowlitz Indian, wanted to become a poet as a teenager growing up in Fresno. In 1977, while studying at the San Francisco Art Institute, she sang with a Sixties-style pop revival band, the Mummers and the Poppers, and later met Frank Zincavage, a sculpture student. They formed the band with other locals Jay Derrah, Peter

Woods (both from the M&Ps) and later Ben Bossi. Their debut, *It's a Condition,* featuring "Myself to Myself," received massive critical praise. Playing drums on the LP was John Stench of Pearl Harbour and the Explosions, taking over for Derrah; both were later replaced by Larry Carter. Iyall's tough, unsentimental stance on love was compared to Pretender Chrissie Hynde's, and her sexy deadpan-to-pouty voice also drew attention on their 1981 EP *Never Say Never,* coproduced by Ric Ocasek of the Cars. *Benefactor,* including "Never Say Never," was a dance-floor favorite.

THE RONETTES
Formed 1959, New York City
Veronica Bennett (later Ronnie Spector, b. Aug. 10, 1943, New York City), voc.; Estelle Bennett (b. July 22, 1944, New York City), voc.; Nedra Talley (b. Jan. 27, 1946, New York City), voc.
1964—*The Fabulous Ronettes Featuring Veronica* (Philles).

The Ronettes, a classic mid-Sixties girl group, were one of producer Phil Spector's greatest successes. Before Spector discovered them, they had been singing since high school in 1959. They were all related; the two Bennetts are sisters and Talley is their cousin. By 1963, they became featured vocalists in the Peppermint Lounge's chain of clubs, performing a song-and-dance routine inspired by Hank Ballard and Chubby Checker's "Twist."

Spector caught one of their shows and signed them to his Philles label in 1963. His first Wall of Sound production for them was a song he cowrote with Ellie Greenwich and Jeff Barry, "Be My Baby." In 1963, it hit #2 and sold over a million copies.

The Ronettes had many other less successful hits: "Baby I Love You" (#24, 1963), "(The Best Part of) Breakin' Up" (#39, 1964), "Walking in the Rain" (#23, 1964), "Do I Love You?" (#34, 1964), "Is This What I Get for Lovin' You?" (#75, 1965) and "I Can Hear Music" (#100, 1966).

In 1968, lead singer Ronnie Bennett married Phil Spector. They were divorced in 1974, and she later pursued a solo career, inspired by the fact that so many Seventies musicians (including Bruce Springsteen and Billy Joel, who wrote "Say Goodbye to Hollywood" for her) cited her as an influence. She sang on Southside Johnny's debut LP and then cut a solo album in 1980 entitled *Siren.*

MICK RONSON
Born Hull, England
1974—*Slaughter on Tenth Avenue* (RCA) **1975**—*Play Don't Worry.*

After having played sessions with Michael Chapman and David Bowie producer Gus Dudgeon, Ronson came to attention as the guitarist with Bowie's early-Seventies

Spiders from Mars backing band. Upon Bowie's temporary retirement from performing in 1973, Ronson launched an unsuccessful solo career. He joined Mott the Hoople in its last days, and continued a partnership with Mott's Ian Hunter, in both the Hunter-Ronson Band and on Hunter's solo LPs. In late 1975, Ronson was a surprise member of Bob Dylan's Rolling Thunder Revue. He has since gone on to help produce Roger McGuinn's *Cardiff Rose*, David Johansen's *In Style* and Ellen Foley's *Night Out*.

LINDA RONSTADT

Born July 15, 1946, Tucson, Arizona
1969—*Hand Sown . . . Home Grown* (Capitol)   **1970**—
Silk Purse   **1972**—*Linda Ronstadt*   **1973**—*Don't Cry
Now* (Asylum)   **1974**—*Different Drum* (Capitol)   *Heart
Like a Wheel*   **1975**—*Prisoner in Disguise* (Asylum)
1976—*Hasten Down the Wind; Greatest Hits*   **1977**—
Simple Dreams (Asylum)   *A Retrospective* (Capitol)
1978—*Living in the U.S.A.*   **1980**—*Greatest Hits,
Volume 2; Mad Love*   **1982**—*Get Closer.*

Linda Ronstadt

During her 15-year recording career, Linda Ronstadt has covered much of America's popular and folk music and appealed to a mass audience who, but for her, might never have heard the work of Buddy Holly, Chuck Berry or Elvis Costello.

Ronstadt is half Mexican, half German. She grew up singing Hank Williams and Elvis Presley favorites with her siblings and Mexican folk songs with her father, who played his guitar. While in high school, Linda performed around Tucson with her brother and sister. Local Bob Kimmel invited her to go with him to L.A. She declined the invitation until after a semester at the University of Arizona, and by the end of 1964 she was in L.A., where she joined the Stone Poneys, a folk group with Kimmel and guitarist Kenny Edwards.

The trio landed a gig at the Troubadour, where promoter Herb Cohen offered Ronstadt a solo management contract. She refused the offer out of loyalty to the trio and doubts about going it alone (earlier, the three had turned down Mercury's offer to make them into a surf music group to be called the Signets). But when the Stone Poneys failed to attract further interest, they split up and Ronstadt signed with Cohen, whom she later persuaded to manage the trio.

Cohen got them a recording contract in 1966 and hired Nick Venet to produce three albums. The first was a failed attempt to present the Poneys as a sort of Hollywood Peter, Paul and Mary. The second included one number on which L.A. session musicians backed Ronstadt—"Different Drum," written by Mike Nesmith of the Monkees—which was a Top Twenty hit in 1967. It induced Capitol to send the Stone Poneys on tour as an opening act, but Edwards soon quit. (He was reunited with Ronstadt in 1974 and was her bassist for the following five years.) Kimmel and Ronstadt stayed together for a while, using pickup musicians for another tour and recording a few tracks for the third album, but soon Kimmel dropped out, leaving Ronstadt with a contractual obligation to finish using session musicians. It sold so poorly that it wasn't until *Heart Like a Wheel* went gold seven years later that Ronstadt began to collect royalties.

Solo, Ronstadt floundered for most of the next five years. She went through a succession of managers, producers and backup musicians (including in the last category the four original Eagles). Onstage she was often devastatingly timid, and in the studio her voice was undermined by inappropriate material and arrangements. She attracted brief notice as a country singer—playing the Grand Ole Opry in Nashville, making TV appearances on "The Johnny Cash Show" and a Glen Campbell special—and reached the Top Thirty in the summer of 1970 with "Long, Long Time" off *Silk Purse*. But by the end of 1972 she was in debt and paying commissions to two managers—Cohen, who still owned her contract, and John Boylan, her current producer. *Don't Cry Now*, her first album on Asylum (although it turned out she owed another to Capitol), was predictably bogged down unfinished in the studio.

The catalyst to Ronstadt's popularity and acclaim was Peter Asher. A former half of the British pop duo Peter and Gordon, he had gone from performing in the mid-Sixties to producing and managing. Under Asher's direction, *Don't Cry Now* was completed after a year in the works, $150,000 and three producers. Despite its flaws, the album sparked Ronstadt's career and prompted Capitol to market a collection of her early songs under the title *Different Drum*.

With Asher as producer and manager, Ronstadt made *Heart Like a Wheel,* which established her best-selling mix of oldies covers and contemporary songs. In addition to astute song choices, high standards of studio craft became Ronstadt and Asher's trademarks. Released shortly before Christmas 1974, *Heart Like a Wheel* was a gold record on its way to #1 by the next spring. "You're No Good" rocked to #1 on the pop singles chart while its flip side, Hank Williams' "I Can't Help It If I'm Still in Love with You," hit #2 on the country & western chart and won the Grammy Award for Best Female Country Vocal that year. "When Will I Be Loved" reached #2 on pop charts and #1 on the C&W charts. Although still hampered by stage fright, Ronstadt became a popular concert attraction and something of a sex symbol.

With a 1976 tour of Europe—her first outside the U.S.—she extended her popularity to the world market. *Heart Like a Wheel* was the first of ten gold albums. She won a second Grammy in 1976. Her albums retained a California sensibility with songs by Souther and Warren Zevon, but she also expanded her repertoire to R&B (the Holland-Dozier-Holland Motown classic "Heat Wave," a couple by Smokey Robinson), show tunes (Hammerstein-Romberg's "When I Grow Too Old to Dream"), traditional folk ballads ("I Never Will Marry," "Old Paint"), reggae (Jimmy Cliff's "Many Rivers to Cross") and even cocky rock & roll (Jagger-Richards' "Tumbling Dice"). Her covers of Buddy Holly ("That'll Be the Day" and "It's So Easy") brought his music to a new audience.

Ronstadt's success gave a substantial boost to other female performers. She was the first to record songs by Karla Bonoff. Maria Muldaur, Wendy Waldman, Emmylou Harris and Dolly Parton are a few of the female singers who have harmonized with Ronstadt in the studio and onstage; and she was instrumental in the careers of Valerie Carter and Nicolette Larson. With these women, Ronstadt formed tight friendships and a sort of professional support system. In 1977 and 1978 Ronstadt, Harris and Parton worked on a trio album, but the project was shelved before completion.

At the end of the decade, Ronstadt was at the height of her popularity—*Living in the U.S.A.* was a platinum #1 album in late 1978 and early 1979. She was also highly visible as the constant companion of California Governor Jerry Brown, with whom she shared the cover of *Time.* Ronstadt's *Mad Love,* her fifth platinum LP, included new wave rock. Working with a self-styled L.A. new wave group, the Cretones, she put three songs by group member Mark Goldenberg alongside three by Elvis Costello (whose "Alison" she had covered on her previous album). The response from Ronstadt's audience was decidedly mixed, but "How Do I Make You" was a Top Ten hit.

Rather than return to the studio, Ronstadt tried something new—the role of Mabel in Gilbert and Sullivan's 19th-century light opera *The Pirates of Penzance.* Ronstadt performed at Central Park's Delacorte Theater in New York City through the summer of 1980 and later appeared in the film version.

In late 1982, she released *Get Closer,* her least successful LP of the last five years.

ROSIE AND THE ORIGINALS

Rosie Hamlin was a self-taught pianist and songwriter. While living in San Diego, she met a group called the Originals and soon became their lead singer. Her "Angel Baby" was a big hit in 1961 (#5 pop, #5 R&B). It caught the attention of singer Jackie Wilson, who introduced her to his manager, and in turn his record label, Brunswick, where she launched a solo career that produced only one minor single, "Lonely Blue Nights" (#61, 1961).

DIANA ROSS

Born March 26, 1944, Detroit
1970—*Diana Ross* (Motown)   *Everything Is Everything*   1971—*Surrender*   1972—*Lady Sings the Blues* (soundtrack)   1975—*Mahogany*   1977—*Baby, It's Me*   1978—*Ross*   1979—*The Boss*   1981—*Diana: All the Great Hits; Why Do Fools Fall in Love?* (RCA)   1982—*Silk Electric.*

Diana Ross's tender, cooing voice brought her to prominence as the lead singer of the Supremes in the Sixties. Since leaving the Supremes in December 1969, she has established herself on records, in films and on television. Ross's career shift was carefully planned by Motown president Berry Gordy, Jr., and was foreshadowed when in the late Sixties he changed the group's name from simply the Supremes to Diana Ross and the Supremes.

Ross's initial solo recordings were produced by the husband-and-wife team of Nick Ashford and Valerie Simpson. "Reach Out and Touch (Somebody's Hand)" in 1970 (#20 pop, #7 R&B) was her first solo single. Her next release, a new version of the Marvin Gaye-Tammi Terrell hit "Ain't No Mountain High Enough" (by Ashford and Simpson), reached #1 pop and R&B.

In 1971, Ross released four singles, none of which was a major hit. Most of her attention was taken up with a television special and preparations for playing Billie Holiday in the first Motown film production, *Lady Sings the Blues.* The 1972 film was a commercial success, spawning a popular soundtrack of Ross singing Holiday, and garnering Ross an Oscar nomination for Best Actress.

The title songs from her next two albums, *Touch Me in the Morning* and *Last Time I Saw Him,* were both Top Twenty pop singles, the former hitting #1. In 1973, she recorded an album of duets with Marvin Gaye, *Diana and Marvin.* Her next film, *Mahogany,* directed by Berry Gordy, failed to match either the commercial or artistic accomplishments of *Lady.* The soundtrack, however, did have the MOR ballad "Do You Know Where You're

Going To" (#1 pop, #14 R&B, 1976). Her *Diana Ross* of 1976 was highlighted by "Love Hangover," a ballad-cum-disco dance song that went #1 with pop and black audiences. But Ross was about to enter a trying period. She played Dorothy in the film version of the black musical *The Wiz*, for which she was severely criticized. Her 1977 *Baby, It's Me*, produced by Richard Perry, sold disappointingly, as did *Ross* in 1978.

She returned to Ashford and Simpson for 1979's *The Boss* and was rewarded with her best sales in years. The title song (#19 pop, #10 R&B) reestablished Ross with the black audience. *Diana* updated her approach. Produced by Nile Rodgers and Bernard Edwards of Chic, the 1980 platinum album went to #1 on the soul charts, #2 on the pop charts and had two big singles, "Upside Down" (#1 pop, R&B) and "I'm Coming Out" (#5 pop, #6 R&B). In 1981, Ross duetted with Commodores lead singer Lionel Richie on the #1 theme from the film *Endless Love*. It was the year's most popular single, selling well over two million copies. But it proved to be her last hit for Motown. In 1981, she ended her twenty-year tenure with the company and signed with RCA Records. That fall she released her self-produced *Why Do Fools Fall in Love* and had a hit with the title cut, a remake of the Frankie Lymon and the Teenagers hit, and in 1982 with "Mirror, Mirror." During this period, Motown released a double album entitled *All the Greatest Hits*. In 1982, Ross released her second RCA LP, *Silk Electric*, which featured the hit single "Muscles" (written and produced by Michael Jackson).

THE ROSSINGTON-COLLINS BAND
Formed 1979, Jacksonville, Florida
Gary Rossington, lead, rhythm and slide gtrs.; Allen Collins, lead and rhythm gtrs.; Billy Powell, kybds.; Leon Wilkeson, bass; Barry Harwood (b. Ga.), lead, rhythm and slide gtrs., voc.; Derek Hess, drums; Dale Krantz (b. Ind.), lead voc.
1980—*Anytime, Anyplace, Anywhere* (MCA) 1981— *This Is the Way.*

The Rossington-Collins Band was formed by four of the five surviving members of Lynyrd Skynyrd. Nearly two years after the plane crash that killed Skynyrd lead singer Ronnie Van Zant, guitarist Steve Gaines and backup vocalist Cassie Gaines, Jacksonville natives Gary Rossington, Allen Collins, Billy Powell and Leon Wilkeson (all of whom had been injured in the crash) decided to regroup.

Of the surviving Skynyrds, only drummer Artimus Pyle declined to join the new band. He went on to form his own five-piece Artimus Pyle Band in 1979 with members of the Marshall Tucker Band producing. Rossington-Collins also solidified in late 1979. Female vocalist Dale Krantz, who sang in church gospels as a child, had played with Leon Russell in L.A. after graduating college and in 1977 joined

Ronnie Van Zant's brother Donnie's .38 Special as a backup singer. Her hoarse vocals and tough persona surprised many and delighted critics. The group also included Barry Harwood, who completed the three-guitar lineup (in the Skynyrd tradition). He also came from Jacksonville, and had done session work with Joe South and Melanie and had played on three Skynyrd LPs. The last member was Derek Hess, also from Jacksonville, who had played in some local bands with Harwood.

The group's self-produced debut, *Anytime, Anyplace, Anywhere*, came out in June 1980 and went gold. Soon after the LP's release, Collins' wife, Katy, died. Their second album, *This Is the Way*, in late 1981, was dedicated to her. Though the band seemed to have a promising future, they disbanded in 1982. Collins has since formed the Allen Collins Band with Powell, Wilkeson, Harwood and Hess. Krantz and Rossington were rumored to be starting a band of their own.

ROXY MUSIC
Formed 1971, London
Bryan Ferry (b. Sep. 26, 1945, Washington, Eng.), voc., kybds.; Graham Simpson, bass; Brian Eno (b. May 15, 1948, Woodbridge, Eng.), synth., treatments; Andy Mackay (b. July 23, 1946, Eng.), sax, oboe; Dexter Lloyd, drums; Roger Bunn, gtr.
1971—(– Lloyd; – Bunn; + Paul Thompson [b. May 13, 1951, Jarrow, Eng.], drums; + David O'List, gtr.)
1972—(– O'List; + Phil Manzanera [b. Jan. 31, 1951, London], gtr.) *Roxy Music* (Atco) (– Simpson; + Rik Kenton [b. Oct. 31, 1945, Eng.], bass; – Kenton; + John Porter, bass; – Porter; + Sal Maida, bass)
1973—*For Your Pleasure* (– Eno; + Eddie Jobson [b. Apr. 28, 1955, Billingham, Eng.], violin, synth.; – Maida; + John Gustafson, bass) 1974—*Stranded;*

Roxy Music: Andy Mackay, Bryan Ferry, Eddie Jobson, Rick Wills, Phil Manzanera, Paul Thompson

Country Life 1975—(− Gustafson; + John Wetton [b. 1949, Bournemouth, Eng.], bass) *Siren* (− Wetton; + Rick Wills, bass) 1976—*Viva!* (disbanded) 1977—*Greatest Hits* 1978—(+ Ferry; + Mackay; + Manzanera; + Thompson; + Gary Tibbs, bass; + David Skinner, kybds.; + Paul Carrack, kybds.; + Alan Spenner, bass) 1979—*Manifesto* 1980—(− Thompson; + Andy Newmark, drums) *Flesh and Blood* 1982—*Avalon* (Warner Bros.) 1983—*The High Road* (EP).
Bryan Ferry solo: 1973—*These Foolish Things* (Atlantic) 1974—*Another Time, Another Place* 1976—*Let's Stick Together* 1977—*In Your Mind* 1978—*The Bride Stripped Bare.*

Roxy Music defined the tone of Seventies art rock by coupling Bryan Ferry's elegant, wistful romantic irony with initially anarchic and later subdued, stately rock. The band has never been as popular in America as it has in England and on the Continent, perhaps because their detachment and understatement baffled American tastes. But Ferry's hoping-against-hopelessness persona and Brian Eno's happy amateurism filtered into the late-Seventies new wave while Roxy Music itself was in suspension.

Ferry and bassist Graham Simpson began searching for bandmates around November 1970. Ferry, who would write almost all of Roxy's songs, is the son of a coalminer. He attended the University of Newcastle, where he studied art for three years with pop-conceptual artist Richard Hamilton. At school, he sang in a more rock-oriented band, the Banshees, before joining an R&B band called the Gas Board with Simpson. He also taught art.

In January 1971, Andy Mackay joined the fledgling band; he had played oboe as a teenager with the London Symphony Orchestra and saxophone at Reading University. Mackay brought Eno with him. The earliest lineup also included classical percussionist Dexter Lloyd, who left by June, and guitarist Roger Bunn, who soon returned to session work. Drummer Paul Thompson had played with a local band, Smokestack, and guitarist Davy O'List had been with the Nice. O'List left after five months and was replaced by Phil Manzanera from the experimental band Quiet Sun.

Simpson decided to give up music; Roxy Music recorded its debut album with Rik Kenton, and has never had a full member on bass. Their debut album, produced by King Crimson lyricist Peter Sinfield, went Top Ten in England in 1972, and "Virginia Plain" went to #4 in Britain, where their Fifties-style retro-chic costumes fit in with the glam-rock fad, although their music was far more sophisticatedly primitive. The U.S. audience had no interest in Roxy Music when they toured in December 1972 as an opening act for Jethro Tull in arenas.

The second Roxy Music album, *For Your Pleasure*, met with a similar reaction; its strangeness was popular in Britain and ignored in America. In July 1973, Eno left for a solo career—perhaps inevitably since he was a songwriter himself, and Roxy Music was Ferry's outlet. Ferry cut his first solo album in 1974; *These Foolish Things* treated Lesley Gore and Bob Dylan songs with equal camp disengagement.

Teenage multiinstrumentalist Eddie Jobson, formerly with Curved Air, replaced Eno for *Stranded*, which also included writing credits for Manzanera and Mackay. But 1974's *Country Life* was Roxy's first U.S. success; it went to #37, although its cover, with a glimpse of pubic hair through panties, was banned in some record stores, covered with an opaque wrapper elsewhere and finally replaced with an inoffensive forest photo. Eno's departure had focused the music on Ferry's singing rather than the band's counterpoint; the band toured the U.S. in 1975 with bassist John Wetton, formerly of King Crimson and Family, and later with Uriah Heep, U.K. and Asia. After their most singlemindedly danceable record, *Siren*—which included Roxy's first U.S. hit single, "Love Is the Drug" (#30)—Roxy disbanded, leaving the live LP *Viva!* and *Greatest Hits* in its wake.

Ferry released another album of covers (excepting Ferry's title tune)—*Another Time, Another Place* (1974)—and *Let's Stick Together* (1976). *In Your Mind* (1977), an album of originals, was the occasion for a world tour by Ferry with Roxy's Manzanera, Wetton and Thompson. For *The Bride Stripped Bare*, Ferry recorded with Los Angeles sessionmen and several Roxy regulars.

Mackay released solo albums and wrote music for the British TV series "Rock Follies." Manzanera recorded and toured briefly with a band called 801, featuring Eno; he also re-formed Quiet Sun for a short time and played sessions for John Cale, Eno, Nico and others.

In 1978, after the appearance of groups like the Cars that showed Roxy's influence, the group reunited for *Manifesto*, minus Jobson, who had joined U.K.; Jobson later recorded with Frank Zappa and Jethro Tull. *Manifesto* became their highest-charting U.S. album at #23. Roxy Music embarked on a world tour with guest keyboardist Paul Carrack (formerly of Ace, later with Squeeze and Nick Lowe's Noise to Go) and two bassists, including Gary Tibbs, formerly of the Vibrators and later of Adam and the Ants. Just prior to that tour, Thompson broke his thumb in a motorcycle accident and left the band.

For 1980's *Flesh and Blood*, Roxy Music was down to a threesome—Ferry, Manzanera and Mackay—plus sessionmen; it was their most subdued album, and became their second #1 album in England (after *Stranded*) and went to #35 in the U.S. *Avalon* continued in the same vein, and yielded the Top Ten British hit "More Than This." It went Top 40 in the U.S. Roxy Music members seem content to divide their efforts between Roxy albums in alternate years and solo projects, such as Manzanera's 1982 release, *Primitive Guitars*. In 1983, Roxy Music toured the U.S. as an eight-piece band plus three backup singers, concurrent with a live EP by that group, *The High Road*.

ROYAL GUARDSMEN

Formed mid-1960s, Ocala, Florida
Billy Taylor, organ; Barry Winslow, voc., rhythm gtr.; Chris Nunley, lead voc.; Tom Richards, lead gtr.; Bill Balogh, gtr.; John Burdette, drums.
1967—*Snoopy vs. the Red Baron* (Laurie) *Snoopy and His Friends* **1968**—*Snoopy for President.*

"Snoopy vs. the Red Baron" hit #2, sold three million singles for this sextet in 1966–67, and gave them a lease on life that they exploited to the hilt. "The Return of the Red Baron" (#15) and "Snoopy's Christmas" followed in 1967, with decreasing success. The next year, the failure of "Snoopy for President" signaled that the gimmick had run its course, and the Royal Guardsmen eventually broke up (1967's unpopular 45 "Airplane Song" having already established that their only big hits would come with Snoopy records). Winslow was the Guardsman who bore the nickname Snoopy.

ROYAL TEENS

Formed late 1950s, New York City
Bob Gaudio (b. Nov. 17, 1942, Fort Lee, N.J.), piano; Joe Villa (b. Brooklyn), voc.; Tom Austin (b. Fort Lee, N.J.), drums; Bill Crandall (b. Fort Lee, N.J.), sax; Bill Dalton, bass; − Crandall; + Larry Qualaino, sax; − Dalton; + Al Kooper, bass.

In 1958, the Royal Teens caused a brief sensation with their #3 singsong novelty, "Short Shorts." For two years, they tried in vain to repeat their success with such tunes as "Big Name Button," "Harvey's Got a Girl Friend" and "Believe Me." Al Kooper, later of the Blues Project, Blood Sweat and Tears and myriad solo projects, joined a later version of the group. Pianist and "Short Shorts" coauthor Bob Gaudio would later score countless hit records as the mastermind behind the Four Seasons. Today, the "Short Shorts" melody is part of a commercial jingle for Nair depilatory cream.

DAVID RUFFIN

Born January 18, 1941, Whyknot, Mississippi
1969—*My Whole World Ended* (Motown) *Feelin' Good* **1973**—*David Ruffin* **1974**—*Me 'n' Rock 'n' Roll Are Here to Stay* **1975**—*Who Am I?* **1976**—*Everything's Coming Up Love* **1977**—*In My Stride* **1979**—*So Soon We Change* (Warner Bros.) **1980**—*Gentleman Ruffin.*

After his years as the Temptations' primary lead singer (1964–1968), David Ruffin embarked on a solo career in 1969. His first single, "My Whole World Ended (the

Moment You Left Me)" (#2 R&B, #9 pop), was his biggest solo hit. In 1969, he had two other Top Twenty soul singles, "I've Lost Everything I've Ever Loved" (#11 R&B) and "I'm So Glad I Feel You" (#18 R&B), but he soon hit hard times. "Walk Away from Love" (#1 R&B, #9 pop), produced by Van McCoy, revived Ruffin's career and was followed by Top Ten R&B hits, including "Heavy Love" and "Everything's Coming Up Love" (1976) and "Break My Heart" (1979). In 1982, he and another original Temptation, Eddie Kendricks, rejoined the group for a tour and album, *Reunion*. It was the most popular Temptations release in years and contained "Standing on the Top" (#66 pop, #6 R&B).

RUFUS (See Chaka Khan)

THE RUMOUR

Formed 1975, England
Bob Andrews, kybds.; Stephen Goulding, drums; Andrew Bodnar, bass; Brinsley Schwarz, gtr.; Martin Belmont, gtr.
1977—*Max* (Mercury) **1979**—*Frogs, Sprouts, Clogs and Krauts* (Stiff) **1980**—(− Andrews) **1981**—*Purity of Essence* (Hannibal).

The Rumour, five veterans of England's pub-rock scene of the early Seventies, are best known as Graham Parker's backup band on his first six LPs. But they've also recorded their own albums and backed up and produced performers other than Parker.

The Rumour were first heard from in 1976 on Parker's *Howlin' Wind*. Bob Andrews and Brinsley Schwarz came from the group Brinsley Schwarz (as did the LP's producer, Nick Lowe); Martin Belmont was originally in Ducks Deluxe; Andrew Bodnar and Stephen Goulding were the former rhythm section of Bontemps Roulee.

While working with Parker, members of the Rumour played on Lowe's *Pure Pop for Now People* and on debut LPs by Rachel Sweet and Carlene Carter (the latter produced by Andrews and Schwarz); and they recorded the albums *Max* (in reply to Fleetwood Mac's *Rumours*) and *Frogs*. . . .

Andrews left the group in 1980, with the band continuing as a four-piece, recording *Purity of Essence* with that lineup. They left Graham Parker a year later. Since then, they've backed Garland Jeffreys on tour.

THE RUNAWAYS

Formed 1975, Los Angeles
Joan Jett (b. Sep. 22, 1960, Philadelphia), gtr., voc.; Sandy West (b. 1960), drums; Micki Steele, bass, voc.; − Steele; + Cherie Currie (b. 1960, Los Angeles), lead voc.; + Lita Ford (b. 1959, London), lead gtr.; + Jackie Fox (b. 1960), bass.
1976—*The Runaways* (Mercury) **1977**—*Queens of*

Noise (− Fox; − Currie; + Vicki Blue, bass) *Waitin'
for the Night* 1979—*And Now the Runaways!* 1981—
Little Lost Girls (Rhino) 1982—*Best of the Runaways.*

The Runaways were an all-female hard-rock band who
suffered from hype, manipulation and being slightly ahead
of their time. Formed on the Sunset Strip in late 1975 by
Kim Fowley, they were presented as five hot, tough high-
school-age girls out for sex and fun (a fairly novel idea in
pre-punk days). But with their musical deficiencies, the
stigma of Fowley-as-Svengali, and a blatantly sexual presentation—lead singer Cherie Currie wore lingerie onstage—they often seemed more like tease objects than real
musicians.

The group started when Fowley met 13-year-old lyricist
Kari Krome at a party. He liked her three-minute lyrics
about sex; and when she suggested girls a few years older
than herself to play her songs, Fowley was interested.
First they got Krome's acquaintance Joan Jett and then,
through some local ads, Micki Steele and Sandy West.
They were going to be a threesome; but after Steele left,
Lita Ford, Cherie Currie and Jackie Fox joined. Only Ford
had been in a band before.

The Runaways signed to Mercury, and their Alice
Cooper–influenced debut (with much material cowritten
by Fowley and the band) came out in May 1976 to
universal pans and snickers. Their only real audience was
in Japan, where they earned three gold records for their
debut and for *Queens of Noise* (where Currie and Jett split
lead vocals) and *Live in Japan*. But after some internal
conflict, Currie and Fox left in mid-1977. Jett took over the
lead (she already did the most writing in the band). Vickie
Blue was added on bass. Currie went on to become an
actress, playing a major role in *Foxes* and the 3-D splatter
film *Parasite*. She later recorded an LP with her sister
Marie entitled *Messin' with the Boys.*

Waitin' for the Night did no better than the early
albums, and though the band turned in good performances
as U.S. openers for the Ramones' tour of 1978, they
played their last show on New Year's Eve 1978 in San
Francisco. Jett felt that their last LP, *And Now the
Runaways!* (out in Europe only; released in the U.S. as
Little Lost Girls in 1981), was too heavy metal, and so at
the start of 1979 she quit and the band died. Afterwards
Jett took part in a B movie based loosely on the group
called *We're All Crazy Now*, after the Slade song. It has
yet to be released. Jett then went on to a successful solo
career, and in 1983 Lita Ford released a solo LP.

TODD RUNDGREN/UTOPIA

Born June 22, 1948, Upper Darby, Pennsylvania
With the Nazz: Rundgren, gtr., voc.; Robert Antoni
(Stewkey) (b. Nov. 17, 1947, R.I.), kybds., voc.; Carson
Van Osten (b. Sep. 24, 1946, N.J.), bass; Thom Mooney
(b. Jan. 5, 1948, Penn.), drums.
1968—*Nazz* (SGC) **1969**—*Nazz Nazz* **1970**—*Nazz 3.*

Todd Rundgren solo: 1970—*Runt* (Bearsville) 1971—
Ballad of Todd Rundgren 1972—*Something/Any-
thing* 1973—*A Wizard/A True Star* 1974—*Todd*
1975—*Initiation* 1976—*Faithful* 1978—*Hermit of
Mink Hollow; Back to the Bars* 1981—*Healing*
1983—*The Ever Popular Tortured Artist Effect.*

With Utopia (formed 1974): Rundgren, gtr., voc.;
Mark "Moogy" Klingman, kybds.; Ralph Shuckett,
kybds.; Roger "M. Frog" Powell, synth.; John Siegler,
bass; John Wilcox, drums; Kevin Elliman, perc.
1974—*Todd Rundgren's Utopia* (Bearsville) **1975**—
Another Live **1976**—(− Klingman; − Shuckett; −
Siegler; − Elliman; + Kasim Sulton, bass) **1977**—
RA; Oops, Wrong Planet **1979**—*Adventures in
Utopia* **1980**—*Deface the Music* **1982**—*Swing to the
Right; Utopia* (Network).

An eclectically accomplished musician and studio virtuoso, Todd Rundgren has been recording for over a decade.
His musical career has gone from simple pop that never
brought the success some critics felt he deserved (only one
gold LP, *Something/Anything*) to the more complex progressive rock of Utopia, which, though despised by critics, did gain Rundgren a devoted cult following. Through
it all, Rundgren has maintained a prolific sideline career as
a producer and is also a pioneer of rock-video.

Rundgren began playing in a high school band, Money,
then went on to play with Woody's Truckstop in the mid-
Sixties; the latter makes a brief appearance (on tape) on
Something/Anything. In 1967, he formed the Nazz, who,
contrary to then-prevailing West Coast psychedelic
trends, tried to replicate the look of Swinging London in
their clothes, mod haircuts and Beatlesish pop sound. In
some ways, the Nazz were ahead of their time, especially
in terms of Rundgren's studio facility and the band's
musical sophistication. But they remained a local Philadelphia phenomenon, with one minor hit single, the original
version of "Hello It's Me." They broke up in 1969, at
which point Rundgren formed the studio band Runt, who
hit the Top Twenty in early 1971 with the single "We Gotta
Get You a Woman."

By this time, Rundgren had become associated with
manager Albert Grossman, who let him produce for his
new Bearsville label. By 1972, Rundgren had taken over
production of Badfinger's *Straight Up* LP from George
Harrison (who was involved with his Bangladesh concerts) and had engineered the Band's *Stage Fright* and
Jesse Winchester's self-titled 1971 LP, as well as produced
records by the Hello People, bluesman James Cotton, the
Paul Butterfield Blues Band, and Halfnelson (who later
became Sparks). He would go on to produce the New
York Dolls' debut LP, Grand Funk Railroad's *We're an
American Band* and Fanny's *Mother's Pride*, all in 1973.

For many, *Something/Anything* is the high-water mark
of Rundgren's solo career. On it he played nearly all the
instruments, overdubbed scores of vocals, and managed

to cover pop bases from Motown to Hendrix, from the Beach Boys to the Beatles. The album yielded hit singles in "Hello It's Me" and "I Saw the Light" and eventually went gold.

A Wizard, while in much the same vein, was more of a critical than commercial success. However, by then Rundgren's cult following was growing. In the liner notes of *Wizard* he asked fans to send their names to him for inclusion in a poster to be included in his next LP; when *Todd* came out, there was a poster with some 10,000 names printed on it in very small type.

By that time, Rundgren had unveiled his cosmic/symphonic progressive-rock band Utopia, which gradually expanded his following to mammoth proportions. Utopia was a more democratic band, in which Rundgren shared songwriting and lead singing with other members. In the mid-Seventies, Utopia played bombastic suites with "cosmic" lyrics and used pyramids as a backdrop, but in the Eighties they returned to Beatles/Nazz/new-wave-style pop.

In 1975, Rundgren produced Gong guitarist Steve Hillage's *L,* on which Utopia played backup. A trip to the Middle East in 1978 led Rundgren to a brief flirtation with Sufism; that same year *Hermit of Mink Hollow* yielded his first hit single in several years in "Can We Still Be Friends?" and Rundgren produced Meat Loaf's *Bat Out of Hell.* In 1979, he produced Tom Robinson's *TRB Two,* the Tubes' *Remote Control* and Patti Smith's *Wave.* In 1980, he produced Shaun Cassidy's *Wasp.*

By that time, Rundgren had taken a strong interest in the emerging field of rock-video. By 1981, he had built his own computer-video studio in Woodstock, New York, and was making technically advanced surrealistic videotapes. Also in 1981, he produced the debut LP by Meat Loaf's lyricist Jim Steinman, Utopia's Beatle-parody LP, *Deface the Music,* and his own solo album, *Healing,* on which he played all instruments. In 1982, Rundgren embarked on a one-man tour, playing both solo-acoustic sets and backed by taped band arrangements, with his computer-graphic videos being shown as well. He still concentrated on production (with the Psychedelic Furs, among others) and video art as well, and entered negotiations to escape his Bearsville contract. Kasim Sulton embarked on a brief solo career before returning to Utopia.

RUSH
Formed 1969, Toronto
Alex Lifeson (b. Aug. 27, 1953, Surnie, B.C.), gtr.;
Geddy Lee (b. July 29, 1953, Toronto), voc., bass, gtr., kybds.; John Rutsey, drums.
1974—*Rush* (Moon/Mercury) (− Rutsey; + Neil Peart [b. Sep. 12, 1952, Hamilton, Ont.], drums) **1975**—*Fly By Night; Caress of Steel* **1976**—*2112; All the World's a Stage* **1977**—*A Farewell to Kings* **1978**—*Archives* (compilation) *Hemispheres* **1980**—*Permanent*

Rush: Geddy Lee, Neil Peart, Alex Lifeson

Waves **1981**—*Moving Pictures; Exit . . . Stage Left* **1982**—*Signals.*

This Canadian progressive power trio has earned several gold records since their 1974 debut. Critics have suggested that singer Geddy Lee's high-pitched vocals, Alex Lifeson's major-chord guitar heroics and Neil Peart's heavy but adroit drumming in usually epic-length melanges of intricate musical structures and apocalyptic lyrics (by Peart) are highly reminiscent of vintage Yes. The albums *2112, All the World's a Stage, A Farewell to Kings, Permanent Waves, Moving Pictures, Exit . . .* and *Signals* all went gold in the U.S., and the band has twice won Canadian Juno Awards for Best Group (1978, 1979). *Waves* marked something of a departure with its shorter compositions; it too went gold. By 1982, *2112, Pictures, All the World's* and *Signals* had gone platinum. Rush's success was based on diligent touring, as they established themselves first in Canada and the Northern U.S. and expanded their following despite limited airplay, especially in their early years.

In 1982, Lee proved they had a sense of humor by appearing on "Take Off" by Bob and Doug McKenzie, the Canadian-bumpkin satire by Dave Thomas and Rick Moranis from the Canada-based TV comedy show "SCTV." Thanks in part to Rush's music and Lee's vocals on the tune, the Bob and Doug McKenzie single and LP (*"Great White North"*) were in the Top Ten in America for much of the year.

TOM RUSH
Born February 8, 1941, Portsmouth, New Hampshire
1963—*Got a Mind to Ramble* (Prestige) *Blues Songs and Ballads* **1965**—*Blues and Folk* (Transatlantic) *Tom Rush* (Elektra) **1966**—*Take a Little Walk with Me* **1968**—*The Circle Game* **1970**—*Tom Rush* (Columbia) *Wrong End of a Rainbow; Merrimack County* **1974**—*Ladies Love Outlaws.*

Singer and occasional songwriter Tom Rush came to prominence while working the Cambridge, Massachusetts, coffeehouse circuit (he holds a BA from Harvard) in the early Sixties. He was eclectic from the beginning, experimenting with blues, jazz, classical arrangements and electric instrumentation.

Circle Game, one of pop's first concept albums, yielded Rush's two best-known performances: his own "No Regrets" and the album's title cut, written by Joni Mitchell. Rush was performing songs by Mitchell, Jackson Browne and James Taylor before any of them were well known. *Merrimack County* presaged a two-year period of self-imposed retirement, broken only by the more commercially oriented *Ladies Love Outlaws.* He continues to tour regularly.

JIMMY RUSHING
Born August 26, 1903, Oklahoma City; died June 8, 1972, New York City

Known as "Mr. Five by Five" for his short and wide physique, Jimmy Rushing was arguably the best male blues-based vocalist of the swing era, during which he was a featured attraction with Count Basie's orchestra (1935–50). His tenor voice and his phrasing easily fit jazz, blues, pop and shouting R&B.

Born to musical parents, Rushing studied violin, piano and theory as a child, and he sang in church, school glee clubs and opera-hall pageants. As a teenager, he hoboed through the Midwest before moving to California, where he occasionally sang with Jelly Roll Morton and worked solo as a barroom singer/pianist. In the late Twenties, he was with the seminal Kansas City swing band Walter Page's Blue Devils; and from 1929 to 1935 he was vocalist with another important early Kansas City big band, Bennie Moten's Kansas City Orchestra.

Rushing then worked with Count Basie, often sharing the microphone with Billie Holiday. In 1946, he recorded with Johnny Otis, and in the early Fifties he led his own septet at New York's Savoy Ballroom. He had a resurgence in popularity in the late Fifties, and in 1964 he toured Australia and Japan with Eddie Condon's All Stars. He also toured with Benny Goodman's orchestra, appeared on TV in several specials and in 1969 had a singing and acting role in the film *The Learning Tree.* In 1972, he died from leukemia. He was an immensely influential vocalist on generations of blues, jazz, R&B, pop and rock singers; and his performances are available on a number of albums under both his own and Basie's names.

LEON RUSSELL
Born Hank Wilson, April 2, 1941, Lawton, Oklahoma
1968—*Asylum Choir: Looking Inside* (Smash) **1970**—*Leon Russell* (A&M/Shelter) **1971**—*Asylum Choir II* (Shelter) *Leon Russell and the Shelter People* **1972**—*Carny* **1973**—*Hank Wilson's Back; Leon Live*

1974—*Stop All That Jazz* **1975**—*Will o' the Wisp; Live in Japan* **1976**—*The Wedding Album* (Paradise) *Best of* (Shelter) **1977**—*Make Love to the Music* (Paradise) **1978**—*Americana* **1979**—*Willie and Leon* (with Willie Nelson) (Columbia) *Live and Love* (Paradise) **1981**—*Leon Russell and New Grass Revival Live* (Warner Bros.).

Leon Russell is perhaps best known as one of the first supersessionmen, having worked for everyone from Jerry Lee Lewis and Phil Spector to Joe Cocker, Bob Dylan and the Rolling Stones. He has also maintained a solo career as a countryish blues-gospel performer.

A multiinstrumentalist, Russell studied classical piano from ages 3 to 13. At 14, he learned trumpet and formed his own band in Tulsa (where he grew up) and lied about his age to land a job at a Tulsa nightclub, where he played with Ronnie Hawkins and the Hawks (who later became the Band). Soon after, Jerry Lee Lewis took Russell's band on tour.

In 1958, Russell moved to Los Angeles, where he learned guitar from Presley sideman James Burton and did studio work with Dorsey Burnette, Glen Campbell and others. Russell played on nearly all of Phil Spector's hit sessions. He also played on Bob Lind's "Elusive Butterfly," Herb Alpert's "A Taste of Honey" and the Byrds' "Mr. Tambourine Man." In 1965–66 he arranged some hit records by Gary Lewis and the Playboys, including the gold "This Diamond Ring." He became a close friend of Delaney and Bonnie Bramlett and in 1967 built his own studio. He appeared on the TV rock show "Shindig!" occasionally in the Shindogs band. He also played on Gene Clark's 1967 album, and arranged Harper's Bizarre's 1967 *Feelin' Groovy* LP.

In 1968, Russell teamed up with guitarist Marc Benno to make the critically acclaimed but commercially unsuccessful *Asylum Choir* LP. He then went on the road with Delaney and Bonnie's Friends tour, during which time Joe Cocker recorded Russell's "Delta Lady" at Russell's studio, where Booker T. (of MGs fame) was also working. In 1969, Russell and A&M producer Denny Cordell founded Shelter Records. In 1970, Russell organized the backing band for Cocker's Mad Dogs and Englishmen tour, an event and film that eventually made him as much of a star as Cocker. When Mercury seemed reluctant to release the second *Asylum Choir* LP, Russell bought the master tapes and released them himself on Shelter. He played piano on Bob Dylan's "Watching the River Flow" and "When I Paint My Masterpiece" and played at George Harrison's Concert for Bangladesh in 1971.

From then on, Russell devoted his energies to his solo career, though he toured with the Rolling Stones in the early Seventies. He also helped out his wife, singer Mary McCreary, who appeared with him on *The Wedding Album* and released her own *Butterflies in Heaven* LP on Shelter in 1973. His first U.K. solo tour, in 1970, found him backed by the ex–Cocker Grease Band. That year, he also played on Dave Mason's *Alone Together* LP. In the fall of 1970, Russell hosted a highly praised hour-long music special on public TV station WNET in New York. *Leon Russell and the Shelter People* went gold, while *Carny* also went gold on the strength of its Top Twenty single "Tight Rope." *Leon Live* also went gold, and in 1976 Russell's "This Masquerade" (as performed by George Benson) won a Grammy. More recently, Russell has returned to his Southwestern roots, recording and performing with Willie Nelson and leading a bluegrass band, the New Grass Revival.

BOBBY RYDELL
Born Robert Ridarelli, April 26, 1942, Philadelphia

In the late Fifties and early Sixties, there was a preponderance of clean-cut American boys smoothing out the threatening rock & roll beat. The most successful of these was Pat Boone, but the center for this sound was Philadelphia, home of Dick Clark's "American Bandstand," Frankie Avalon, Fabian and Bobby Rydell.

Unlike many of the others, who were literally no more than pretty faces, Rydell was a genuine musician. He began playing drums at the age of six and was a nightclub attraction at seven. At nine, he entered Paul Whiteman's local "Teen Club" amateur TV show and remained as a regular for three years (Whiteman shortened Bobby's surname to Rydell). In 1957, Rydell became the drummer for local rock & roll combo Rocco and His Saints (who also featured Frankie Avalon on trumpet), but soon struck out on his own. Three major labels turned him down, and Rydell's first two singles for his manager Frankie Day's label flopped. He recorded three more failed singles for Cameo-Parkway.

In 1959, "Kissin' Time" became a huge hit, launching a four-year period in which Rydell scored 19 Top Thirty smashes, including "Volare" (#4), "Sway" (#14), "Swingin' School" (#5), "Wild One" (#2), in 1960, and "Forget Him" (#4, 1964). Beatlemania ended his career, as presaged by the film *Bye Bye Birdie*, in which he appeared as Hugo Peabody.

MITCH RYDER AND THE DETROIT WHEELS
Formed 1965, Detroit
Mitch Ryder (b. William Levise, Jr., 1945), voc.; James McCarty (b. 1947), gtr.; Joseph Cubert (b. 1947), gtr.; Earl Elliot (b. 1947), bass; John Badanjek (b. 1948), drums.

1966—*Jenny Take a Ride* (New Voice) *Breakout* **1967**—*Sock It to Me; What Now My Love* (Dynavoice) **1968**—*Mitch Ryder Sings the Hits* (New Voice) **1969**—*The Detroit Memphis Experience* (Dot) **1971**—*Detroit* (Paramount) **1978**—*How I Spent My Vacation* (Seeds and Stems) **1983**—*Never Kick a Sleeping Dog* (Riva).

Mitch Ryder was a white soul shouter from Detroit who reached his peak of popularity in the late Sixties while fronting the Detroit Wheels. His career began well before that, though. Ryder had sung with local combos the Tempest and the Peps before forming Billy Lee and the Rivieras. In 1965 their stage act (opening for the Dave Clark Five) caught the attention of Four Seasons producer Bob Crewe, who signed them and gave Ryder the name he became famous with (supposedly picked out of a phone book) and rechristened the Rivieras the Detroit Wheels.

Their first single combined Little Richard's "Jenny Jenny" and Chuck Willis' "C. C. Rider" into "Jenny Take a Ride," which became a #10 hit in 1966, inspiring follow-up medleys "Devil with a Blue Dress On" and "Good Golly Miss Molly" (#4, 1966) and "Too Many Fish in the Sea" and "Three Little Fishes" (#24, 1967). Ryder's next big hit came with "Sock It to Me Baby" (#6, 1967), a hard-rocking tune whose success was due in part to the fact that it had been banned in some markets for being too suggestive.

Ryder's first attempt at a solo career met with less success, though with "What Now My Love" (#30, 1967) he tried to re-create the controversy that had boosted the sales of "Sock It to Me Baby." He re-formed the original group. They shortened their name to Detroit and backed Ryder on the critically acclaimed LP *Detroit*. A cover of Lou Reed's "Rock and Roll" was a minor FM hit.

By 1973, Ryder had quit music and moved to Denver. He made a comeback in the late Seventies with several albums, all containing his own songs, a few of which alluded to homosexual experiences. Ryder then toured sporadically to mixed reviews.

Former Detroit wheels Rusty Day and Jim McCarty went on to form Cactus with Tim Bogert and Carmine Appice. McCarty and John Badanjek later joined the Rockets. In recent years, the memory of the Detroit Wheels has been kept alive by Bruce Springsteen, whose "Detroit Medley" reprises two Mitch Ryder hit singles. Another fan, John Cougar, produced Ryder's major label comeback in 1983.

S

STAFF SERGEANT BARRY SADLER
Born 1941, New Mexico

Wounded in Vietnam, Staff Sergeant Barry Sadler had the #1 single of 1966 with his patriotic novelty song "The Ballad of the Green Berets." The song, inspired by Robin Moore's best-selling book *The Green Berets* (Sadler's face is on the cover of the paperback edition), was written by Moore (lyrics) and Sadler (music). The LP of the same name contained such Sadler compositions as "Letter from Vietnam," "Saigon," "Trooper's Lament" and "Salute to the Nurses." Both the single and the LP were certified gold soon after their release.

Sadler wasn't heard from again until December 1978, when he was involved in a Nashville shooting incident that left local songwriter Lee Bellamy, 51, dead. The fracas was apparently over a woman; no charges were filed against Sadler. In mid-1981, Sadler was involved in another shooting incident, in Memphis, though the victim—an ex-business partner of Sadler's—wasn't killed. Sadler, in fact, justified his innocent plea by explaining, "I'm a Green Beret. If I'd shot him, he'd be dead."

CAROLE BAYER SAGER
Born circa 1947, New York City
1977—*Carole Bayer Sager (Elektra)* 1978—*. . .Too.*

Lyricist Carole Bayer Sager has penned several big MOR hits alone or in collaboration with Peter Allen, Melissa Manchester, Albert Hammond, Marvin Hamlisch, Bruce Roberts and others. Her best-known hits are the James Bond theme "Nobody Does It Better" (for Carly Simon, written with Hamlisch), "Midnight Blue" (for and with Melissa Manchester), "A Groovy Kind of Love" (for the Mindbenders), "You're Movin' Out Today" (for and with Bette Midler and Bruce Roberts), "With You" (a Top Twenty R&B for the Moments), "When I Need You" (for Leo Sayer, with Albert Hammond) and "Break It to Me Gently" (for Aretha Franklin, with Marvin Hamlisch).

At 15, while she was a student at New York's High School of Music and Art, a teacher helped her publish a song she'd written with a friend. This led to a contract with Screen Gems, headed by Don Kirshner, for whom she wrote "A Groovy Kind of Love" with Toni Wine in 1966. Still, unlike fellow Screen Gems writer Neil Sedaka (with whom she wrote some unsuccessful pieces), her material never fared well, and in 1970 she left after writing lyrics for the Broadway musical *Georgy*, which closed after five performances.

Sager's breakthrough came in 1975 when Melissa Manchester's "Midnight Blue" hit. She pursued Manchester after hearing her singing backups for Bette Midler, and the two went on to write most of Manchester's debut 1973 LP together. After the LP, Manchester used her less and Sager branched out. By 1978, her songs had been recorded by Frank Sinatra, Dolly Parton, Shaun Cassidy and many others. In 1976, friend and producer Richard Perry coaxed her into going solo. Both her eponymous debut and . . . *Too* were greeted with minimal public response. In 1979, she wrote the words to Marvin Hamlisch's music for the hit Broadway Neil Simon play *They're Playing Our Song*—about the love life of a songwriting team (roughly based on her own relationship with Hamlisch). She married Burt Bacharach in 1982. In 1981, she had collaborated with Peter Allen, Bacharach and Christopher Cross on the Oscar-winning hit "Arthur's Theme."

BUFFY SAINTE-MARIE
Born February 20, 1941, Maine
1964—*It's My Way* (Vanguard) 1965—*Many a Mile* 1966—*Little Wheel Spin* 1967—*Fire, Fleet and Candlelight* 1968—*I'm Gonna Be a Country Girl Again* 1970—*Illuminations* 1971—*She Used to Wanna Be a Ballerina* 1972—*Moon Shot* 1973—*Quiet Places; Best of* 1974—*Natural North American Child; Best of, Volume 2; Buffy* (MCA) 1975—*Changing Woman* 1976—*Sweet America* (ABC).

Born of Cree Indian parents and adopted as an infant, Buffy Sainte-Marie was at least as well known through other artists' versions of her songs as for her own wide-vibratoed vocal delivery. She was discovered singing in a Boston coffeehouse by Vanguard producer Maynard Soloman. Her debut LP contained the protest song "Universal Soldier," which became a classic of the genre, mainly through well-known cover versions by Donovan and Glen Campbell. Elvis Presley had a Top Forty hit in 1972 (#5 in the U.K.) with her "Until It's Time for You to Go."

Initially a solo folksinger, as her career progressed Sainte-Marie infused rock, classical, orchestral and native-Indian styles into her albums. The *Ballerina* LP featured backing from Ry Cooder and Neil Young and Crazy Horse.

She appeared on the 1983 Academy Awards telecast to pick up the award for Best Song, "Up Where We Belong," from *An Officer and a Gentleman*.

SAM AND DAVE
Samuel Moore, born October 12, 1935, Miami;
David Prater, born May 9, 1937, Ocilla, Georgia
1966—*Sam and Dave* (Roulette) *Hold On I'm Comin'*

(Stax) *Double Dynamite* **1967**—*Soul Man* **1968**—*I Thank You* (Atlantic) **1969**—*The Best of Sam and Dave* **1975**—*Back Atcha* (United Artists).

Sam Moore and Dave Prater's string of soul and pop hits made them the Sixties' most successful black vocal duo.

Both had grown up singing in church, and each was a regular solo performer in Southern clubs before they met in the early Sixties. They became a popular club attraction in the Miami area and soon signed to Roulette. They moved to Stax in 1965 and quickly became the favorite foil of the production/songwriting team of Isaac Hayes and David Porter. Their first single, "You Don't Know Like I Know" (#7 R&B), in 1966, began a string of high-powered gospelly soul hits. Later in 1966, "Hold On! I'm a Comin' " went to #1 on the R&B chart (#21 pop), while "Said I Wasn't Gonna Tell Nobody" (#8 R&B) and "You Got Me Hummin' " (#7 R&B) rounded out a successful year.

In 1967, Sam and Dave gained their widest exposure with "When Something Is Wrong with My Baby" (#2 R&B) and the epochal "Soul Man" (#2 pop, #1 R&B). In 1968, they scored with their last major hit, "I Thank You" (#9 pop, #4 R&B).

Over the next decade, Sam and Dave broke up and reunited often. In 1979, the Blues Brothers' success with "Soul Man" rekindled interest in them, and the duo received booking at many clubs nationally. But in 1982, they broke up again.

In a 1983 interview with the *Los Angeles Herald Examiner*, Moore admitted that he had been a drug addict for twelve years and that the main reason for his feud with Dave Prater was that he "lost respect" for him after Prater shot his own wife.

SAM THE SHAM AND THE PHARAOHS

Formed early 1960s, Texas
Sam the Sham (Domingo Samudio),(b. Dallas), voc., organ; David Martin, bass; Ray Stinnet, gtr.; Jerry Patterson, drums; Butch Gibson, sax.
1965—*Wooly Bully* (MGM) **1966**—*Li'l Red Riding Hood* **1967**—*Best of Sam the Sham and the Pharaohs* **1970**—*Sam, Hard and Heavy* (Atlantic).

Sam the Sham and his turban-clad Pharaohs achieved brief but massive success in the mid-Sixties with their rollicking Tex-Mex rock & roll. Following the moderately successful independent single "Haunted House," Sam the Sham moved to MGM, where he hit it big with his second record, "Wooly Bully." The record sold three million copies in 1965, rising to #2 on the chart.

For the next two years, the Pharaohs continued to rack up hit singles: "Juju Hand" (#22, 1966), "Oh That's Good, No That's Bad" (#54, 1967) and the million-selling "Li'l Red Riding Hood" (#2, 1966) among them. In 1967, Sam broke up the band and went solo, reverting to his given name, Domingo Samudio.

Though his years of stardom may be behind him, he did win a Grammy Award in 1970 for his liner notes to the LP *Sam, Hard and Heavy*. He resurfaced in 1981, providing two original songs, sung in Spanish, to the soundtrack of *The Border*. "Wooly Bully" remains a bar-band standard and was recorded in 1981 by Joan Jett.

SANTANA

Formed 1967, San Francisco
Original lineup: Carlos Santana (b. July 20, 1947, Autlán de Navarro, Mex.), gtr., voc., percussion; Gregg Rolie, kybds.; David Brown, bass; Michael Shrieve, drums; Mike Carabello, percussion; José Chepito Areas, percussion.
1969—*Santana* (Columbia) **1970**—*Abraxas* *Santana III; Caravanserai* **1973**—*Welcome* **1974**—*Greatest Hits; Borboletta* **1976**—*Amigos; Festival;* **1977**—*Moonflower* **1978**—*Inner Secrets* **1979**—*Marathon* **1981**—*Zebop!* **1982**—*Shangó.*
Carlos Santana solo:
1972—*Carlos Santana with Buddy Miles Live* (Columbia) **1973**—*Love, Devotion, Surrender* **1974**—*Illuminations* **1979**—*Oneness; Silver Dreams—Golden Reality* **1980**—*The Swing of Delight* **1983**—*Havana Moon.*

Through a long, erratic career laden with personnel changes, Santana has maintained popularity and critical respect with what was in the beginning an innovative fusion of rock, fiery Afro-Latin polyrhythms and contrasting cool, low-key vocals. In time, guitarist Carlos Santana was drawn to jazz-rock fusion and worked outside the band with John McLaughlin, Stanley Clarke and others. Though the mid-Seventies saw Santana becoming involved in spiritual mysticism (he affixed "Devadip" before his name), by the late Seventies the Santana band was back in hard-driving rhythmic form and chalked up several hit dance singles.

The band evolved in San Francisco's Latin district from jam sessions between Santana, David Brown and Gregg Rolie. With original drummer Rod Harper and rhythm guitarist Tom Frazer, they became the Santana Blues Band. Though the soft-spoken Santana felt uncomfortable as leader, he lent his name to the group because the local musicians union required that each band have a designated leader. Their 1968 debut at San Francisco's Fillmore West (by which time the band was known simply as Santana) won them a standing ovation; and the band became so popular locally that they won a spot in the 1969 Woodstock Festival, where they stopped the show (their "Soul Sacrifice" is one of the high points of the *Woodstock* album).

Their overwhelming success at the festival led to a deal with Columbia Records, and within a few weeks of its November 1969 release their debut LP was #1 in America and eventually went double platinum. That album's "Evil

Ways" was a Top Forty hit single. Their next two albums went gold. *Abraxas* yielded such Top Forty hits as "Black Magic Woman" (previously recorded by Fleetwood Mac), and "Oye Como Va" (by veteran salsa bandleader Tito Puente). *Santana III* contained the hit singles "Everybody's Everything" and "No One to Depend On." The live album with Buddy Miles was dismissed by critics but sold well, eventually going gold.

Caravanserai went gold, as did *Welcome;* both LPs saw Santana's music stretching out into jazzier directions, and the band's personnel changed considerably with every album. In 1973, Santana made his first recording outside the band, the fusion supersession *Love, Devotion, Surrender* with McLaughlin, Jan Hammer and Billy Cobham of the Mahavishnu Orchestra; Stanley Clarke of Return to Forever; and Larry Young of the Tony Williams Lifetime. Guitarist Neal Schon, who had joined the band after *Abraxas,* and keyboardist Gregg Rolie went on to found Journey; drummer Michael Shrieve played various sessions, including Stomu Yamashta's *Go* series, and formed Automatic Man. In 1974, Santana collaborated with Alice Coltrane and ex–Miles Davis jazz bassist David Holland, among others, for the string-dominated *Illuminations;* it didn't sell as well as *Love, Devotion, Surrender,* which had gone gold.

Borboletta featured contributions from Clarke and Brazilian musicians Airto Moreira and Flora Purim. *Lotus* stands out in Santana's mid-Seventies period; it was recorded in Japan and long unavailable in America except as a costly import (it's a three-record set). Those who did hear it raved about it, and it became an instant cult item, finally gaining U.S. release in the late Seventies. By that time, Santana had tightened up his band into a funkier direction, and had hit singles with a cover of the Zombies' mid-Sixties hit "She's Not There" (from *Moonflower*) and "Dance Sister Dance" (from *Amigos*). After two more jazz-fusion solo LPs, *Oneness* and *The Swing of Delight*—the latter featuring such fusion stars and former Miles Davis sidemen as Herbie Hancock, Tony Williams, Ron Carter and Weather Report reedman Wayne Shorter—the Santana band's *Zebop!* became a big seller on the strength of a Top Twenty hit single, "Winning," written by ex-Argent Russ Ballard. *Havana Moon* featured guests Willie Nelson and the Texas blues band the Fabulous Thunderbirds.

SAVOY BROWN
Formed 1966, London
Kim Simmonds, gtr., voc.; Bryce Portius, voc.; Martin Stone, gtr.; Ray Chappell, bass; Leo Mannings, drums; Bob Hall, kybds.
1967—*Shake Down* (Decca, U.K.)   1968—(– Portius; + Chris Youlden, voc.; + "Lonesome" Dave Peverett, gtr.; – Chappell; – Mannings; + Rivers Jobe, bass; + Roger Earl, drums)   *Getting to the Point* (Parrot)

1969—*Blue Matter*   (– Jobe; + Tone Stevens, bass) *A Step Further*   1970—(– Hall)   *Raw Sienna* (– Youlden);   *Looking In*   1971—(– Peverett; – Stevens; – Earl; + Paul Raymond, kybds.; + Dave Walker, voc.; + Andy Silvester, bass; + Dave Bidwell, drums)   *Street Corner Talking*   1972—*Hellbound Train*   1973—(– Silvester; + Andy Pyle, bass)   *Lion's Share*   (– Bidwell; – Pyle; + Jackie Lynton, voc.; + Ron Berg, drums)   *Jack the Toad*   (group disbands) 1974—(re-formed: Simmonds; Miller Anderson, gtr., voc.; Stan Webb, gtr., voc.; + Jimmy Leverton, bass; + Eric Dillon, drums)   *Boogie Brothers*   1975—(– Webb; – Dillon; – Anderson)   1976—*Wire Fire; Skin 'n' Bone*   1978—*Savage Return;   Blues Roots* (Decca, U.K.)   1981—*Rock 'N' Roll Warriors* (Town House).

This workmanlike blues-rock band became a favorite with American audiences while never achieving popularity at home in Britain. Though the group never had a hit single, their albums sold respectably, thanks to dogged touring. The only constant in the band's membership was guitarist Kim Simmonds, who ruled the group with an iron hand and hired and fired members regularly.

Savoy Brown was formed originally as the Savoy Brown Blues Band. In 1968, drummer Bill Bruford (Yes, King Crimson, U.K.) joined them for about a week before moving on to Yes. As the British blues boom wound down in the early Seventies, Savoy Brown edged toward a more hard-rock boogie style. Around this time, they also began to concentrate almost exclusively on the U.S. In 1971, Dave Peverett, Roger Earl and Tone Stevens left the band to form another rock-boogie outfit, Foghat. Over the years, Simmonds re-formed the band, drawing on personnel from such defunct British blues bands as Chicken Shack (Walker, Raymond, Silvester, Bidwell, Webb) and the Keef Hartley Band (Anderson).

In 1973, Simmonds announced that Savoy Brown was no more, but the following year he formed yet another version of it. This group was also known (parenthetically) as the Boogie Brothers, and lasted for only one album. Simmonds continued to record with groups called Savoy Brown through the early Eighties.

LEO SAYER
Born Gerard Hugh Sayer, May 21, 1948, Shoreham-by-Sea, England
1973—*Silverbird* (Warner Bros.)   1974—*Just a Boy* 1975—*Another Year*   1976—*Endless Flight*   1977—*Thunder in My Heart*   1978—*Leo Sayer*   1979—*The Very Best of;   Here*   1980—*Living in a Fantasy; World Radio.*

Singer/songwriter Leo Sayer has enjoyed sporadic American success, and at one point, in 1977, he had three top singles and a platinum album.

While attending Worthington Art College, Sayer formed his first band, Terraplane Blues. He later moved to London and headed a group called Patches. Sayer then began writing songs with David Courtney. Courtney linked the group up with singer/actor Adam Faith, who became their manager. After Patches' debut single sold only 55 copies, Sayer decided to go solo. Faith's wife, Jackie, renamed him Leo, thinking he looked like a lion. Faith and Courtney produced the debut Sayer LP, *Silverbird,* at Roger Daltrey's studio in Sussex, with Sayer writing the words and Courtney the music. Daltrey liked their songs so much he recorded his debut solo with all material written by the two unknowns, making their "Giving It All Away" a #1 British hit in early 1973. *Silverbird* came out a short time later, and in keeping with the glitter trend, the cover featured Leo in a Pierrot clown costume (which he also wore live). The LP established Sayer as a big British star in his own right and yielded the #1 English hit "The Show Must Go On."

For *Just A Boy,* Sayer gave up the clown image, which had been ridiculed in the U.S. The album became a British gold LP and featured his first U.S. hit single, "Long Tall Glasses." In 1975, he split with Courtney, who wanted to go solo (he later reunited with Sayer for *Here*). On *Another Year,* Sayer wrote the songs with Frank Farrell. The single "Moonlighting" went #1 in the U.K., but was ignored in the U.S.

Sayer next linked up with Richard Perry, who suggested more covers and new songwriting alliances for 1976's *Endless Flight. Flight* was Sayer's platinum U.S. breakthrough, and yielded three hit singles: "How Much Love," "You Make Me Feel Like Dancing" and "When I Need You." *Thunder in My Heart* went gold in the U.K. but flopped in the U.S. Soon his British audience dwindled as well. Though he produced some respectable surface pop in this period, he did not return to the U.S. charts until late 1980, with a cover of Bobby Vee's "More Than I Can Say," produced by Alan Tarney.

BOZ SCAGGS

Born William Royce Scaggs, June 8, 1944, Ohio
1965—*Boz* (Polydor, U.K.) **1969**—*Boz Scaggs* (Atlantic) **1971**—*Moments; Boz Scaggs and His Band* (Columbia) **1972**—*My Time* **1974**—*Slow Dancer* **1976**—*Silk Degrees* **1977**—*Down Two, Then Left* **1980**—*Hits; Middle Man.*

After over a decade of trying to make it as a solo act, singer/songwriter Boz Scaggs hit with a five-million-seller, *Silk Degrees.*

Scaggs grew up in Oklahoma and Texas, and while at St. Mark's Preparatory School in Dallas he met Steve Miller. He joined Miller's band, the Marksmen, as lead vocalist while Miller taught him guitar. Scaggs followed Miller to the University of Wisconsin, where they played together in a blues-rock band known as the Ardells or the Fabulous Knight Trains. Returning to Texas in 1963, Scaggs joined an R&B band, the Wigs. The next year, Scaggs and two of the Wigs—John Andrews and Bob Arthur— went to England. Finding little success, they broke up (most of the Wigs eventually forming Mother Earth), while Scaggs roved Europe as a street singer, recording his debut LP in Stockholm. He returned to the U.S. in 1967 and moved to San Francisco, where he reunited with Steve Miller for two albums with the Steve Miller Band *(Children of the Future* and *Sailor).*

Jann Wenner, editor of *Rolling Stone,* helped arrange for Scaggs's U.S. solo debut with Atlantic, *Boz Scaggs.* It was released to some critical acclaim but almost no sales. The album gained most of its fame from the tune "Loan Me a Dime," which featured a memorable Duane Allman guitar solo; bluesman Fenton Robinson later successfully sued for composer credit on the song. Scaggs's second and third U.S. LPs were produced by Glyn Johns. On *My Time,* he dispensed with a backing band in favor of studio musicians. Also at this time his vocals began to show more of a soul influence. This became even more pronounced on *Slow Dancer,* produced by ex-Motown producer Johnny Bristol, which was again critically hailed but not commercially successful.

Then came *Silk Degrees,* with its #3 hit, "Lowdown," and other smashes like "Lido Shuffle" (#11, 1977). His studio band for much of the Seventies included the nucleus of what became Toto. Though Scaggs has never quite matched that success, *Middle Man* yielded minor hits with "Breakdown Dead Ahead" (#15, 1980) and "Jo Jo" (#17, 1980). Scaggs also appeared on the soundtrack of the film *Urban Cowboy* (1980). In San Francisco, Scaggs became known for his annual black-tie concerts on New Year's Eve.

TOM SCOTT

Born May 19, 1948, Los Angeles

Though he was known in jazz circles since the late Sixties, saxophonist Tom Scott didn't become widely recognized in pop until the mid-Seventies for studio work with Carole King, Joni Mitchell, Steely Dan, Blondie, Paul McCartney, Barbra Streisand and countless others.

Scott's mother was a classical pianist and his father a film and television theme composer. At eight, he took up the clarinet, but switched to baritone sax in junior high. He left college after one semester in 1966 and started playing the L.A. clubs with Don Ellis' band and then Roger Kellaway's quartet. His work with Oliver Nelson's band led to a contract with Impulse, who released his first solo album, *Honeysuckle Breeze.* He recorded another LP for Impulse, 1968's *Rural Still Life,* and then two for Flying Dutchman. He also did sessions, playing on *Phil Ochs Greatest Hits* in 1970, and began composing TV scores, first for "Dan August" in 1969. (He later wrote the themes for "Starsky and Hutch," "The Streets of San Francisco" and many more. He has also done movie scores for *Stir Crazy, Neighbors* and others.)

In 1971, Scott got a contract with A&M, and on his first LP for the label, *Great Scott,* he did a version of Joni Mitchell's "Woodstock" which so impressed Mitchell that she invited him to play on her *For the Roses* (1972). After that LP, Scott began to develop a band, an informal, ever-shifting group that became the L.A. Express, a pop-jazz band. Ode Records released *Tom Scott and the L.A. Express,* which got more attention than usual, especially after he was featured on Carole King's tour and soloed on her 1974 single "Jazzman."

A new Express played on Joni Mitchell's *Court and Spark* and on her live *Miles of Aisles.* Scott later toured with George Harrison and Ravi Shankar and added sax to Wings' hit "Listen to What the Man Said." In 1978, Scott recorded an album with Billy Cobham, Alphonso Johnson and Steve Kahn called *Alivemutherfoya.* He continues to do solo LPs, movie soundtracks and session work, and in the summer of 1982 he served as musical director for an Olivia Newton-John tour and released a solo LP called *Desire.*

GIL SCOTT-HERON

Born 1950, Chicago
1972—*Small Talk at 125th and Lenox* (Flying Dutchman) *Free Will* 1973—*Pieces of a Man* 1975—*Winter in America* (Strata/East) *The Revolution Will Not Be Televised* (Flying Dutchman) *The First Minute of a New Day* (Arista) 1975—*From South Africa to South Carolina* 1976—*It's Your World* 1977—*Bridges* 1978—*Secrets; The Mind of Gil Scott-Heron* 1980—*1980; Real Eyes* 1981—*Reflections* 1982—*Moving Target.*

Writer-turned-singer Gil Scott-Heron stresses his literate, politically conscious lyrics as much as his funk and jazz-based music.

His mother was a librarian (his father a pro soccer player), and Scott-Heron wrote detective stories as an early teen. At 19, he published his first novel, *The Vulture,* followed by a book of rap verse called *Small Talk at 125th and Lenox* and a second novel, *The Nigger Factory.* Scott-Heron believed he could reach more people through music so he began to collaborate with a friend from Pennsylvania's Lincoln University, Brian Jackson. They each played piano, and at first Jackson wrote music to Scott-Heron's words, but soon they began to collaborate on the music.

The two cut three LPs for Flying Dutchman, first a mostly verbal version of his verse, *Small Talk . . . ,* followed by two more musical albums, *Pieces of a Man,* which included the militant poem "This Revolution Will Not Be Televised" (popularized by Labelle on their *Pres-*

sure Cookin' LP) and *Free Will. Winter in America* contained Scott-Heron's first minor hit, "The Bottle." In 1974, he became the first signing to the new Arista label, releasing *The First Minute of a New Day.* It was also the debut of Scott-Heron and Jackson's jazzy backup group, the Midnight Band.

His followup, 1975's *From South Africa to South Carolina,* included his big hit "Johannesburg." Scott-Heron's music has gotten generally good reviews, though some have said his lyrics tend to be didactic. He appeared at the antinuclear MUSE benefit at Madison Square Garden in September of 1979, where he performed his own atomic warning, "We Almost Lost Detroit." He also recorded "Shut 'Em Down" on the same subject. He has been writing on his own, without Jackson, since the late Seventies.

SEALS AND CROFTS

Jim Seals (b. 1940, Sidney, Tex.), gtr., sax, fiddle, voc.;
Dash Crofts (b. 1940, Cisco, Tex.), drums, voc., mandolin, kybds., gtr.
1970—*Seals and Crofts* (TA) *Down Home* 1972—*Year of Sunday* (Warner Bros.) *Summer Breeze* 1973—*Diamond Girl* 1974—*Unborn Child* 1975—*I'll Play for You; Greatest Hits* 1976—*Get Closer; Sudan Village* 1977—*One on One* 1978—*Takin' It Easy.*

Jim Seals and Dash Crofts were a commercially successful soft-rock pop duo through the Seventies. They first achieved success in the late Fifties with the Champs, who had the huge 1958 Latin-rock instrumental hit "Tequila" (though at that time only Seals, who'd won a Texas state fiddling championship at age nine, was in the band). They remained with the Champs until the mid-Sixties, then formed the Dawnbreakers, who broke up a short time later when all the members became converts to the Baha'i faith. They reemerged as a duo in 1970 with two little-known albums, then signed to Warner Bros., after which most of their albums went gold.

Their hits include "Summer Breeze" (#6, 1972), "Diamond Girl" (#6, 1973), "We May Never Pass This Way (Again)" (#21, 1973), the anti-abortion song "Unborn Child" (#66, 1974), "I'll Play for You" (#18, 1975) and "Get Closer" (#6, 1976). The latter, and the LP *Sudan Village,* found them working with black singer Carolyn Willis, formerly of Bobb B. Soxx's Blue Jeans and Honey Cone. In 1974, "Summer Breeze" was a hit for the Isley Brothers.

THE SEARCHERS

Formed 1961, Liverpool, England
John McNally (b. Aug. 30, 1941, Liverpool), gtr., voc.;
Mike Pender (b. Mar. 3, 1942, Liverpool), gtr., voc.;
Tony Jackson (b. July 16, 1940, Liverpool), bass, voc.;
Chris Curtis (b. Aug. 26, 1942, Oldham, Eng.), drums, voc.

1963—*Meet the Searchers* (Pye, U. K.)
1964—(− Jackson; + Frank Allen [b. Dec. 14, 1943, Hayes, Eng.], bass, voc.) 1965—(− Curtis; + John Blunt, drums) 1967—*Smash Hits, Volumes 1 and 2* (Marble Arch) 1970—(− Blunt; + Billy Adamson, drums, voc.) 1971—*Needles and Pins* (Hallmark) 1972—*Golden Hour with* (Pye) *Second Take* (RCA) 1973—*Golden Hour, Volume 2* (Pye) 1977—*Searchers File* 1980—*The Searchers* (Sire) 1981—*Love's Melodies.*

The Searchers were one of the best of the Liverpool pop bands to emerge in the wake of the Beatles. Their sound matched their clean-cut looks: pretty, gentle, with perfect close-harmony vocals and ringing guitar lines that presaged the Byrds.

The Searchers, originally formed to back up British singer Johnny Sandon, took their name from the John Ford-John Wayne film. They went to Hamburg to play the Star Club after the Beatles' success there, and then returned to Liverpool. A&R man Tony Hatch offered them a recording contract after they had established a residency at Liverpool's Iron Door club. Their first U. K. hit came in 1963 with their cover of the Drifters' "Sweets for My Sweet." "Needles and Pins," written by Sonny Bono and Jack Nitzsche, was #1 in Britain in 1964 (#13 U.S.); it eventually sold over a million copies.

The Searchers toured America, Australia and New Zealand that year. Their only subsequent U.S. successes were "Don't Throw Your Love Away" (#16, 1964) and "Love Potion Number 9" (#3, 1965). In Britain, their Top Twenty success continued through 1965, with "Sugar and Spice" (1963), "Someday We're Gonna Love Again," "When You Walk in the Room," "What Have They Done to the Rain" (1964) and "Goodbye My Love" and "He's Got No Love" (1965). They then became stalwart club and cabaret performers for many years before resurfacing on Sire in 1979. None of their recent albums sold spectacularly.

JOHN SEBASTIAN

Born March 17, 1944, New York City
1970—*John B. Sebastian* (Reprise) 1971—*Cheapo-Cheapo Productions Presents the Real Live John Sebastian; The Four of Us* 1974—*The Tarzana Kid* 1976—*Welcome Back.*

Though John Sebastian's solo sales never matched those of the Lovin' Spoonful, his solo career took off almost immediately after breaking up his old group. He appeared in an unscheduled set at Woodstock and captured the audience with songs like "I Had a Dream" and a persona that was the epitome of the tie-dyed hippie.

John B. Sebastian, his first solo album, featured "I Had a Dream," as well as a remake of the Spoonful's "You're a Big Boy Now," and though it produced no hit singles, it

became the best-selling album of Sebastian's solo career.

Cheapo-Cheapo Productions Presents the Real Live John Sebastian was meant to counter an unauthorized live set released and quickly deleted by his old label, MGM, and it relied largely on previously recorded material. Sebastian's fortunes were temporarily reversed with his first hit single in close to ten years, "Welcome Back" (#1, 1976), the title song of the TV show "Welcome Back, Kotter." Sebastian's current live performances largely skip over his solo period and emphasize the songs he wrote for the Lovin' Spoonful. In 1982–83 he appeared in concerts and on an LP with NRBQ.

NEIL SEDAKA

Born March 13, 1939, Brooklyn, New York
1962—*Neil Sedaka Sings His Greatest Hits* (RCA) 1974—*Sedaka's Back* (MCA/Rocket) 1975—*The Hungry Years* 1976—*Steppin' Out* 1977—*A Song* (Elektra) 1981—*Now.*

Neil Sedaka began in the late Fifties as a writer of hit songs, became a hitmaking performer himself, then returned to songwriting until the early Seventies, when Elton John helped him resume a singing career that briefly propelled him back into the spotlight. He has since written hits for the Captain and Tennille and others.

Both of Sedaka's parents played piano, and his grandmother had been a concert pianist. As a teenager, he was selected by Arthur Rubinstein to play on a show on New York's classical music station, WQXR. By that time he had become strongly attracted to popular music as well, and he began writing songs at age 13 to lyrics by his high school friend Howard Greenfield. He formed a backing band, the Tokens, who later had a hit of their own, "The Lion Sleeps Tonight."

While on a two-year scholarship to the Juilliard School in New York City, Sedaka sold his first tune, "Stupid Cupid," a hit for Connie Francis in 1958, as was his "Fallin'" later that year. He also sold Sedaka/Greenfield songs to Jerry Wexler at Atlantic Records, who placed them with R&B singer LaVern Baker. On the advice of Doc Pomus, Sedaka signed up with Al Nevins and Don Kirshner's Aldon Publishing. They felt Sedaka's own high-pitched voice was worth consideration and got him signed with RCA as a singer. In 1959, he had two hits for RCA, "The Diary" (#14) and "I Go Ape" (#42). More Sedaka/Greenfield hits followed: "Oh! Carol" (#9) in 1959; "Stairway to Heaven" (#9) in 1960; "Calendar Girl" (#4), "Little Devil" (#11) and "Happy Birthday, Sweet Sixteen" (#6) in 1961; "Breaking Up Is Hard to Do" (#1) and "Next Door to an Angel" (#5) in 1962.

Sedaka's performing career slowed in 1963. However, through the Sixties and early Seventies he and Greenfield continued to write hits for others, including the Fifth Dimension's "Workin' on a Groovy Thing," Tom Jones's "Puppet Man" and Davy Jones's "Rainy Jane." Greenfield, in the meantime, had also found success collaborating with Carole King; together they wrote "Crying in the Rain" for the Everly Brothers. Sedaka and Greenfield split up in 1973, after Sedaka had begun a performing comeback in England.

After Sedaka made three LPs in Britain with Graham Gouldman of 10cc coproducing, Elton John helped him get back onto the U.S. charts, first by reissuing cuts from the three British LPs on one U.S. package (Sedaka's Back), then by having him record for his Rocket label. Sedaka's Back and The Hungry Years were both top-selling LPs. "Laughter in the Rain" was a #1 hit for Sedaka in 1975, and his "Love Will Keep Us Together" (cowritten with Greenfield) was a #1 smash for the Captain and Tennille, winning a 1975 Grammy as Record of the Year.

Sedaka's second recording streak culminated with a #1 hit, "Bad Blood," in 1975 and a bluesy reworking of "Breaking Up Is Hard to Do" (#8, 1976). Since then, Sedaka and Greenfield have collaborated regularly, and Sedaka has become a moderately successful MOR ballad singer and has made numerous TV appearances. In 1980, he and his daughter Dara recorded "Should've Never Let You Go," which reached #19 on the pop chart.

THE SEEDS
Formed 1965, Los Angeles
Sky Saxon (b. Richard Marsh), voc.; Jan Savage, gtr.; Daryl Hooper, kybds.; Rick Andridge, drums.
1966—The Seeds (GNP); Web of Sound 1967—Future.

On the cusp of the early-to-mid-Sixties garage-rock boom and the mid-to-late-Sixties flower-power era came the Seeds. Their Top Forty hit of 1967, "Pushin' Too Hard," matched their scruffy looks with a nasty, threatening drive and ominous lyrics. This product of the L.A. teen scene had a few more minor hits—"Mr. Farmer," "Can't Seem to Make You Mine" and "Thousand Shadows"—later that year; all were very much in the vein of "Pushin'," though their sound gradually became more psychedelic. The group disbanded soon after. Lead singer Sky Saxon attempted a very brief Seventies comeback and hasn't been heard from since.

PETE SEEGER
Born May 3, 1919, New York City
1955—Original Talking Union (Folkways) 1957—Pete Seeger Sings American Ballads 1958—Pete Seeger with Sonny Terry at Carnegie Hall 1959–1962—American Favorite Ballads, Volumes 1 to 5 1960—Pete Seeger with Memphis Slim and Willie Dixon at the Village Gate 1964—Songs of Struggle and Protest 1966—Dangerous Songs? (Columbia) 1967—Pete Seeger Sings Woody Guthrie (Folkways); Pete Seeger's Greatest Hits (Columbia); Waist Deep in the Big Muddy and Other Love Songs 1969—Young vs.

Old 1972—The World of Pete Seeger 1975—Together in Concert (with Arlo Guthrie) (Warner Bros.) 1982—Precious Friend (with Arlo Guthrie).

Pete Seeger has been a major folk-music figure for longer than many current folksingers have been alive. He is perhaps the foremost folk archivist and popularizer of American folk music. From his pop-folk successes with the Weavers in the late Forties, through the Fifties, when he was blacklisted by the government, through the Sixties, when he became a culture hero, Seeger has remained an indomitable, resourceful and charming performer. He has also written folk standards: "If I Had a Hammer" (with Lee Hays) and "Where Have All the Flowers Gone?"

Seeger's interest in music began early. His father was a musicologist, his mother a violin teacher. He had learned banjo, ukulele and guitar by his teens, when he developed an interest in America's folk-music legacy. He worked with noted folk archivist and field recorder Alan Lomax before traveling around the country as a hobo, absorbing rural music. He attended Harvard University and served in the Army in World War II. In the Forties, he became a friend and singing associate of Woody Guthrie before forming the Weavers, an enormously popular folk quartet who popularized such folk chestnuts as "On Top of Old Smokey" and Leadbelly's "Goodnight Irene."

In the Fifties, Seeger's sympathies with humanitarian socialism led him to be blacklisted by the House Un-American Activities Committee; still Seeger continued to perform wherever he could. He recorded for Folkways and signed with John Hammond and Columbia Records in the early Sixties. With the arrival of the Vietnam War protests, Seeger was rediscovered by a younger audience. In 1965, the Byrds had a #1 hit with Seeger's "Turn! Turn! Turn!"—a Biblical passage set to music.

From the mid-Seventies on, Seeger has worked regularly with Woody Guthrie's son Arlo. He has crusaded for ecology with the sloop Clearwater, giving concerts along the Hudson River. In the Seventies, he performed in China and Siberia and has continued to be active in political and social causes into the Eighties.

BOB SEGER
Born May 6, 1945, Ann Arbor, Michigan
1969—Ramblin' Gamblin' Man (Capitol); Noah 1970—Mongrel 1971—Brand New Morning 1972—Smokin' OP's (Reprise) 1973—Back in '72 1974—Seven 1975—Beautiful Loser (Capitol) 1976—Live Bullet; Night Moves; Get Out of Denver (EP) (Reprise) 1978—Stranger in Town (Capitol) 1980—Against the Wind 1981—Nine Tonight 1983—The Distance.

For years, singer and songwriter Bob Seger remained a local Michigan rock hero. His music brought together Detroit's two legacies—hard-rock and soul—while a se-

Bob Seger

ries of bad breaks denied him the nationwide audience critics thought his hard-driving workingman's rock deserved. But he came into his own in the mid-Seventies with the gold *Live Bullet* and platinum *Night Moves* LPs.

Seger's father had been a Big Band leader who quit music to work in a factory, then left the family when Seger was 12, leaving Seger to live in near-poverty with his mother and brother. (His father died in a fire in 1968.) In 1961, he led a three-piece band, the Decibels, then joined another local Michigan band, the Town Criers, before going on to Doug Brown's Omens. Seger recorded "East Side Story" with members of the Town Criers and the Omens; the tune had previously been a failure for the Underdogs, who included Michael and Suzi Quatro and future Eagle Glenn Frey, but Seger's version was a local hit in 1966. He later produced Frey's first solo single, "Such a Lonely Child."

In the late Sixties, Seger had strong followings in the Midwest and Florida as well as more big local hits, such as "Nutbush City Limits," "Ramblin' Gamblin' Man" and, most notably, "Heavy Music," which had begun climbing the national chart before dropping when Seger's record company, Cameo, folded. He also recorded an answer record to Staff Sergeant Barry Sadler's "The Ballad of the Green Berets"—"Ballad of the Yellow Beret," for Are You Kidding Me Records in 1966.

Seger signed with Capitol in 1969, but left music in 1970 to go back to college. Within a year, though, he was back on the road with a group called Teegarden and Van

Winkle, a partnership resulting in Seger's first Reprise LP, *Smokin' OP's. Back in '72,* partly recorded at Muscle Shoals and including J. J. Cale backing on some cuts, was yet another commercial failure, as was *Seven,* which yielded the failed single "Get Out of Denver" (later covered by Dave Edmunds).

After moving back to Capitol, things slowly began to click with *Beautiful Loser,* which introduced Seger's own backup unit, the Silver Bullet Band (Drew Abbott, guitar; Robyn Robbins, keyboards; Alto Reed, sax; Chris Campbell, bass; Charlie Allen Martin, drums), and included another local Detroit hit, "Katmandu." The *Live Bullet* double album, recorded in Detroit, stayed on the U.S. chart for over a year and eventually went platinum, as have all of Seger's subsequent albums.

Night Moves established Seger on ballads as well as hard rock, with the hit title tune (#8, 1977) and "Rock and Roll Never Forgets." The four-million-selling *Stranger in Town* also yielded two major hits, "Still the Same" (#4, 1978) and "Hollywood Nights" (#12, 1978). The three-million-selling *Against the Wind* had a hit title cut (#5, 1980). *The Distance* quickly sold 1½ million copies, spurred by a hit cover of Rodney Crowell's "Shame on the Moon" (#2, 1983). In 1983, Seger returned to the road with a slightly revamped Silver Bullet Band, including ex–Grand Funk Railroad drummer Don Brewer.

THE SELECTER
Formed 1979, Coventry, England
Noel Davies, gtr.; Charley Anderson, bass; Pauline Black, voc.; Charley "H" Bembridge, drums; Compton Amanor, gtr.; Arthur "Gaps" Hendrickson, voc.; Desmond Brown, kybds.
1980—*Too Much Pressure* (Chrysalis) **1981**—*Celebrate the Bullet.*

Along with the Specials, Madness and the English Beat, the Selecter was one of the main bands in the ska-influenced two-tone trend that broke big in England in 1979. Like the other bands in this "movement," the Selecter used the old mod two-tone fashion style as a visual aid. Their music was an upbeat blend of ska (quicker and less brooding than reggae, the latter also an influence in their music), rock and soul, with socially conscious unification lyrics, backed up by the band's own racially and sexually integrated personnel.

Like the Specials, the members of Selecter all hail from the industrial city of Coventry, about eighty miles northwest of London. Noel Davies had written a song called "The Selecter" that he tried to sell to various record companies, without success. Davies and the Specials financed their own label, 2-Tone, and issued a single, "Gangsters" b/w "The Selecter," with Davies playing guitar. The single went British Top Ten in 1979 and Davies formed a band.

Charley Anderson, Charley Bembridge, Arthur Hen-

The Selecter: Charley Anderson, Noel Davis, Charley Bembridge, Compton Amanor, Pauline Black, Desmond Brown, Arthur "Gaps" Hendrickson

drickson and Compton Amanor had been playing in the Coventry roots-reggae band Hard Top 22; the band was completed with Pauline Black and Desmond Brown, who were working in another local rock-reggae outfit. Their 2-Tone went on to become England's most successful independent record company since Stiff, and the band's debut, *Too Much Pressure*, came out in America on Chrysalis in spring 1980. Highlighted by Black's lead vocals, the sound was fast-paced and politically charged. It was the rage for a short while in England (their single "Three Minute Hero" went Top Ten there) but it did not go over in America despite positive press and a strong summer tour. They released a second LP in 1981, *Celebrate the Bullet*, and were featured in the film and soundtrack that year to *Dance Craze*, chronicling all the 2-Tone bands, but broke up in late 1981. Black pursued a solo career on Chrysalis.

THE SEX PISTOLS
Formed 1975, London
Johnny Rotten (b. John Lydon, Jan. 31, 1956), voc.; Steve Jones, gtr.; Glen Matlock, bass; Paul Cook, drums.
1977—(− Matlock; + Sid Vicious [b. John Ritchie or Beverly; d. Feb. 2, 1979, New York City], bass)   *Never Mind the Bollocks, Here's the Sex Pistols* (Warner Bros.)   **1979**—*The Great Rock 'n' Roll Swindle* (Virgin).

The Sex Pistols were the brainchild of young entrepreneur Malcolm McLaren. Unabashedly crude, intensely emotional, calculated either to exhilarate or to offend, their music and stance were in direct opposition to the star trappings and complacency which they felt had rendered rock & roll irrelevant to the common bloke. The owner of a London clothes boutique, Sex, which specialized in "anti-fashion," McLaren had conceived the idea of a rock & roll act that would challenge every established notion of propriety when, early in 1975, he found himself managing the New York Dolls in their final months as a group. A part-time employee of Sex, Glen Matlock played bass with Paul Cook and Steve Jones; he let McLaren know they were looking for a singer. McLaren approached John Lydon, whom he had seen hanging around the juke box at Sex and who was known mainly for his rudeness.

Lydon had never sung before, but he accepted the invitation and thoroughly impressed the others with his scabrous charisma. McLaren had found his act; he named the group the Sex Pistols. Allegedly, Lydon's disregard for personal hygiene prompted Jones to dub him Johnny Rotten.

Ten minutes into their first gig at a suburban art school dance on November 6, 1975, the school's social programmer unplugged their amplifiers. In the early months of 1976, McLaren's carefully cultivated word-of-mouth about the Sex Pistols made them leaders of the nascent punk movement. Their gigs inspired the formation of the Clash, the Buzzcocks, X-Ray Spex and countless other rebel groups in the second half of the Seventies.

The press and record industry ignored the Sex Pistols at first, but by the end of the summer the uproar—both acclamatory and denunciatory—was too loud to be ignored. In November, EMI outbid Polydor with a recording contract worth £40,000. The Sex Pistols' first single, "Anarchy in the U.K.," was released in December. That month, the band used the word "fucker" in a nationally televised interview; the consequent outrage led promoters and local authorities to cancel all but five of the dates scheduled on the group's national tour and EMI to withdraw "Anarchy in the U.K."—#38 on the U.K. chart in January 1977—from circulation and to terminate their contract with the Sex Pistols.

In March, Matlock left to form the Rich Kids and was replaced by John Ritchie (or Beverly), a previously nonmusical friend of Rotten, who named him Sid Vicious. That same month, A&M signed up the Pistols for £150,000; the next week they fired them for a balance payment of £75,000. In May, Virgin signed the Pistols and released their second record, "God Save the Queen," in time to spite the Queen's Silver Jubilee that June. The song was immediately banned from airplay in England. Nonetheless it was a top-selling single in the summer of 1977 (cited as a blank at the #2 position on official charts, listed as #1 on independent charts).

When no hall in Britian would book the Sex Pistols, they went abroad—to the Continent in July and to the U.S. in December, by which time their album had been released. In America they found themselves the object of a little adulation, considerable hostility, but mostly uncomprehending curiosity, which turned to scoffing when the Pistols made only halfhearted attempts to live up to their reputation for savagery. Rotten was characteristically critical of the sensationalism and opportunism that had been attached to the Sex Pistols (for which he blamed

McLaren), and on January 14, 1978, immediately after a concert in San Francisco, he announced the breakup of the group.

Jones and Cook remained active in the punk movement and formed the Professionals. Vicious initiated a solo career, which ended when he was imprisoned in New York on charges of murdering his girlfriend Nancy Spungen; he died of a heroin overdose before he could be tried. Dismissing the Sex Pistols as "a farce" and reverting to his given name, Lydon formed Public Image Ltd.

Grammy Awards

Sam and Dave
1967 Best R&B Group Performance, Vocal or Instrumental (2 or more): "Soul Man"

Leo Sayer
1977 Best R&B Song: "You Make Me Feel Like Dancing" (with Vini Poncia)

Boz Scaggs
1976 Best R&B Song: "Lowdown" (with David Paich)

Tom Scott
1974 Best Arrangement Accompanying Vocalists: "Down to You" (with Joni Mitchell)

Bob Seger and the Silver Bullet Band
1980 Best Rock Performance by a Duo or Group with Vocal: *Against the Wind*

Ravi Shankar
1967 Best Chamber Music Performance: *West Meets East* (with Yehudi Menuhin)
1972 Album of the Year: *The Concert for Bangla Desh* (with others)

Silver Convention
1975 Best R&B Instrumental Performance: "Fly, Robin, Fly"

Simon and Garfunkel (see also: Paul Simon)
1968 Record of the Year; Best Contemporary Pop Performance, Vocal, Duo or Group: "Mrs. Robinson"

1970 Record of the Year: "Bridge over Troubled Water" Album of the Year: *Bridge over Troubled Water*

Carly Simon
1971 Best New Artist of the Year

Paul Simon (see also: Simon and Garfunkel)
1968 Best Original Score Written for a Motion Picture or TV Special: *The Graduate*
1970 Song of the Year; Best Contemporary Song; Best Arrangement: Accompanying Vocalist(s): "Bridge over Troubled Water"
1975 Album of the Year; Best Pop Vocal Performance, Male: *Still Crazy After All These Years*

Frank Sinatra
1959 Album of the Year; Best Vocal Performance, Male: *Come Dance With Me*
1965 Album of the Year: *September of My Years* Best Vocal Performance, Male: "It Was a Very Good Year"
1966 Record of the Year; Best Vocal Performance, Male: "Strangers in the Night" Album of the Year: *Sinatra: A Man and His Music*

The Singing Nun (Soeur Sourire)
1963 Best Gospel or Other Religious Recording (Musical): "Dominique"

Joe South
1969 Song of the Year; Best Contemporary Song: "Games People Play"

Rick Springfield
1981 Best Rock Vocal Performance, Male: "Jessie's Girl"

Starland Vocal Band
1976 Best New Artist of the Year; Best Arrangement for Voices: "Afternoon Delight"

Ringo Starr (see also: the Beatles)
1970 Best Original Score Written for a Motion Picture or TV Special: *Let It Be*
1972 Album of the Year: *The Concert for Bangla Desh* (with others)

April Stevens
1963 Best Rock & Roll Recording: "Deep Purple" (with Nino Tempo)

Barrett Strong
1972 Best R&B Song: "Papa Was a Rolling Stone"

Donna Summer
1978 Best R&B Vocal Performance, Female: "Last Dance"
1979 Best Rock Vocal Performance, Female: "Hot Stuff"

Survivor
1982 Best Rock Performance by a Duo or Group with Vocal: "Eye of the Tiger"

THE SHADOWS

Formed 1958 as the Drifters, London
Hank B. Marvin (b. Oct. 28, 1941, Newcastle, Eng.),
gtr., voc.; Bruce Welch (b. Nov. 2, 1941, Bognor Regis,
Eng.), gtr., voc.; Ian Samwell, bass; Terry Smart,
drums; Ken Payne, gtr.; − Samwell; + Jet Harris (b.
July 6, 1939), bass; − Smart; + Tony Meehan (b. Mar.
2, 1942, London), drums; − Meehan; + Brian Bennett
(b. Feb. 9, 1940, London), drums.
1962—*The Shadows* (Columbia, U.K.) (− Harris; −
Bennett; + "Licorice" Locking, bass) **1963**—*Greatest
Hits* (− Locking; + John Rostill [b. June 16, 1942,
Birmingham, Eng.; d. Nov. 26, 1973], bass) **1965**—
More Hits **1968**—(− Welch; + Adam Hawkshaw,
gtr., voc.) **1972**—(− Hawkshaw; + Welch; + John
Farrar, bass, gtr., voc.) **1973**—*Specs Appeal* (EMI)
1976—*Rarities* **1977**—*The Best of the Shadows; 20
Golden Greats.*

While still backing British teen idol Cliff Richard in the late Fifties, the Shadows began to branch out into a successful instrumental-rock career of their own, which made everbespectacled lead guitarist Hank B. Marvin one of the most influential British rock guitarists.

Marvin, whose twanging guitar leads were the group's hallmark, took up banjo and guitar as a youth, and by 14 he and schoolmate Bruce Welch were playing together in skiffle groups. They moved to London's Soho section, and after a few months of living in poverty, they joined Richard's touring band, which already included Terry Smart and Ian Samwell (the latter wrote Richard's first hit, "Move It").

They were originally called the Drifters, but changed their name to the Shadows to avoid confusion with the American vocal group. They stayed with Richard through 1968, despite their own long string of hits. They appeared with Richard in films like *Expresso Bongo, The Young Ones, Summer Holiday* and *Finders Keepers,* and despite several personnel changes, they always maintained their trademark sound. Their first single, 1959's "Feelin' Fine," wasn't a hit, but their fourth, 1960's "Apache," was a long-running #1 in the U.K. In 1981, it was revived in a rap-funk version by the Sugar Hill Gang.

Most of their twenty-plus follow-up hits—"F.B.I.," "Kon Tiki," "Atlantis," "Frightened City" (1961); "Shindig" (1963); "Don't Make My Baby Blue" (1965)—were instrumentals and were mainly U.K. successes, including thirteen Top Ten hits.

In 1962, Tony Meehan and Jet Harris performed as a duo and had three 1963 hits in Britain: "Diamonds" (#1), "Scarlet O'Hara" (#2) and "Applejack" (#4). After Harris was involved in a car crash, Meehan returned to songwriting and production work.

Welch finally quit in 1968, precipitating the first of several Shadows breakups. Within two years, though, he and Marvin were back together with Bennett and Australian guitarist John Farrar. They recorded two LPs as Marvin, Welch and Farrar. Ex-bassist Rostill had gone on to play with Tom Jones, to record a few solo singles and to write tunes for Engelbert Humperdinck, the Family Dogg and others, and was fatally electrocuted by his guitar in 1973.

Meanwhile, the Shadows had split up again in 1969—when Welch fell ill—and they re-formed several times through the Seventies.

The title of 1973's *Specs Appeal* referred to Marvin's glasses. In 1977, the *20 Golden Greats* album was #1 in Britain, and the Shadows re-formed again to tour by popular demand. Bennett, Welch, Farrar and Marvin have done session and production work; Welch has worked with Cliff Richard and Farrar with Olivia Newton-John.

THE SHAGGS

Betty Wiggin (b. Fremont, N.H.), voc., gtr.; Dorothy
Wiggin (b. Fremont, N.H.), gtr.; Helen Wiggin (b.
Fremont, N.H.), drums.
1969—*The Philosophy of the World* (re-released 1980
by Red Rooster) **1982**—*The Shaggs' Own Thing* (Red
Rooster).

The Shaggs' *Philosophy of the World* was one of the most curious collectors' records of the Seventies.

Dorothy Wiggin was the group's songwriter; she and her two sisters played the music; their father paid for the studio time, for which they traveled from their New Hampshire home to Boston. By most standards, the Shaggs were horrible, but their utter originality and boundless enthusiasm were undeniable. Their record became a valued item in the homes of such personages as NRBQ's Terry Adams. Adams arranged for the album's reissue in 1980 on NRBQ's Red Rooster label (distributed by Rounder), increasing the Shaggs' cult by leaps and bounds and whetting the appetite for more Shaggs, in the form of *The Shaggs' Own Thing.* A third Shaggs LP is in the works.

SHALAMAR

Formed 1977, Los Angeles
Jeffrey Daniels (b. Aug. 24, 1957, Los Angeles), voc.;
Jody Watley (b. Jan. 30, 1961, Chicago), voc.; Howard
Hewett (b. Oct. 1, 1957, Akron, Oh.), voc.
1978—*Disco Gardens* (Solar) **1979**—*Big Fun* **1981**—
Three for Love; Go for It.

This good-looking vocal trio were black teen idols of the late Seventies and early Eighties. The original Shalamar was made up of several Los Angeles session singers convened in 1977 by concert promoter Dick Griffey to record a medley of Motown dance hits, "Uptown Festival" (#25 pop, #10 R&B, 1977). With producer Leon

Sylvers III, they had a dance hit with "Take That to the Bank" (#11 R&B, 1978), a lively number that was the model for other hits on Griffey's new Solar ("Sound of Los Angeles Records") label.

For a touring group, Griffey recruited Jeffrey Daniels and Jody Watley, two dancers from "Soul Train," the television show produced by his friend and sometime business partner Don Cornelius. Howard Hewett joined after the original third member, Gerald Brown, left. "The Second Time Around" (#8 pop, #1 R&B, 1979) established them as stars; they followed up with "Right in the Socket" (#22 R&B, 1980), "Full of Fire" (#24 R&B, 1980) and "Make that Move" (#6 R&B, 1981).

Adding to their teen appeal was a real-life love triangle between Daniels, Watley and singer Stephanie Mills. The two Shalamar singers had been childhood sweethearts, but after meeting Mills in New York, Daniels married the Broadway star; less than a year later, they were divorced—all of which was dramatically reported in teen magazines.

In 1981, Shalamar released "This Is for the Lover in You" (#17 R&B, 1981) and "Sweeter as the Days Go By" (#19 R&B, 1981).

SHA NA NA
Original lineup: Johnny Contardo, voc.; Scott Powell, voc.; Frederick Dennis "Denny" Greene, voc.; Don York, voc.; Bruce Clarke, bass; John "Jocko" Marcellino, drums; Ritchie Joffe, voc.; Elliot Cahn, gtr.; Henry Gross, gtr.; Chris Donald, gtr.; Screamin' Scott Simon, piano, bass; John "Bowser" Baumann, piano, voc.; Lennie Baker, sax.
1969—Rock & Roll Is Here to Stay (Kama Sutra) *1971—Sha Na Na 1972—The Night Is Still Young 1973—The Golden Age of Rock 'n' Roll; From the Streets of New York 1974—Hot Sox 1975—Sha Na Now 1976—Best of Sha Na Na.*

Sha Na Na were forerunners of the Fifties revival craze that eventually spawned shows like "Happy Days" and *Grease.*

They began while students at Columbia University, making frequent appearances at the Fillmore East. Lennie Baker, who had played saxophone on Fifties hits, was their claim to authenticity. Their big break was a booking at the Woodstock festival in 1969. The band's humor, choreography and costuming caught on, and though never particularly successful on record, Sha Na Na became a popular live attraction, first on the rock & roll circuit, later in nightclubs. Their popularity reached unprecedented heights starting in 1977, when they began a syndicated TV show. Over the years, personnel has been fluid, the most notable change being the departure of original guitarist Henry Gross in 1970 for a solo career, which was highlighted by the 1976 hit single "Shannon."

THE SHANGRI-LAS
Formed 1964, Queens, New York
Mary Ann Ganser, Marge Ganser, Betty Weiss, Mary Weiss.
1964—Leader of the Pack (Red Bird) *1965—Shangri-Las '65 1966—I Can Never Go Home Anymore; Golden Hits* (Mercury) *1976—Remember (Walking in the Sand)* (EP) (Charly, U.K.).

Of the early-Sixties girl vocal groups who rose meteorically to fame and disappeared nearly as quickly, one of the few white units was the Shangri-Las: two sets of sisters (the Gansers were twins) who first started singing together at Andrew Jackson High School in Queens.

In early 1964, they attracted the attention of writer/ producer George "Shadow" Morton, who got the new Red Bird label (for which he was a producer) off the ground with the first Shangri-Las hit, his "Remember (Walkin' in the Sand)." A few months later, they recorded the motorcycle-gang melodrama "Leader of the Pack"—a typically showy Morton production complete with sound effects and talk-over sections—which was #1. It inspired an answer record, the Detergents' "Leader of the Laundromat," and several transparent imitations. Their other hits included "Maybe" (#91) and "Give Him a Great Big Kiss" (#18) in 1964; "Out in the Streets" (#53), "Give Us Your Blessings" (#29), "Right Now and Not Later" (#99) and "I Can Never Go Home Anymore" (#6) in 1965; and "Long Live Our Love" (#33), "He Cried" (#65) and "Past, Present and Future" (#59) in 1966.

The group, despite several in-and-out personnel shifts, was a top concert attraction in the U.S. and the U.K. in those years; but when the girl groups were eclipsed by progressive rock, the Shangri-Las faded.

DEL SHANNON
Born Charles Westover, December 30, 1939, Coopersville, Michigan
1961—Runaway (Big Top) *1963—Little Town Flirt 1965—Handy Man* (Amy) *Sings Hank Williams; 1,661 Seconds 1966—This Is My Bag* (Liberty) *Total Commitment 1967—Best of* (Dot) *1968—Further Adventures of Charles Westover 1970—Del Shannon Sings* (Post) *1973—Live in England* (United Artists) *Best of* (Polydor) *1975—Vintage Years* (Sire) *1981— Drop Down and Get Me* (Elektra).

With hit songs like "Runaway" and "Hats Off to Larry," Del Shannon was one of the few early rockers who wrote his own material.

Shannon was 14 when he learned guitar and began performing in school shows. After graduating high school, he took his stage name from those of a friend (Mark Shannon) and his boss's car (a Cadillac Coupe de Ville). In early 1960, a Grand Rapids area disc jockey passed live tapes of Shannon on to manager/publishers Harry Balk and Irving Micahnik, who then signed Shannon to Detroit's Big Top label. Big Top sent him to New York to record, but not much came of it.

On a second trip to New York, Shannon recorded "Runaway," which—with its galloping beat, Max Crook's proto-synthesizer Musitron solo and Shannon's nearly hiccuping falsetto vocals—went to #1 in 1961. He followed up with "Hats Off to Larry" (#5), "So Long Baby" (#28) and "Hey! Little Girl" (#38) in 1961; and "Little Town Flirt" (#12) in 1962. He first toured England in 1962 and the next year met the Beatles there. His version of Lennon-McCartney's "From Me to You" made Shannon the first American to cover a Beatles tune.

In 1963, Shannon had legal problems with Balk and Micahnik; the action instituted that year dragged on for the next decade. Still, he had more hits with "Keep Searchin' " (#9) and "Stranger in Town" (#30) in 1965. That year, Peter and Gordon recorded Shannon's "I Go to Pieces." In 1966, Shannon signed to Liberty, where producer Snuff Garrett and arranger Leon Russell tried to mold him into a teen idol.

When Tommy Boyce asked Shannon to record "Action," the theme for the TV rock show "Where the Action Is," Shannon turned him down and gave the song instead to Freddy Cannon. The *Total Commitment* LP, belying its title, was almost all covers. In England in 1967, Shannon recorded an album with Andrew Loog Oldham called *Home and Away* (Nicky Hopkins and John Paul Jones played on it).

With his career on the wane, Shannon left Liberty in 1969 and concentrated on production work. He arranged Smith's 1969 hit "Baby It's You" and produced Brian

Hyland's 1970 hit "Gypsy Woman." In England, he recorded tracks with Jeff Lynne of the Electric Light Orchestra (including "Cry Baby Cry"). In 1974, Dave Edmunds produced Shannon's "And the Music Plays On." The next year, Shannon signed to Island and released a cover of the Zombies hit "Tell Her No."

During 1976 and 1977, Shannon suffered from alcoholism, but beginning in 1979 he returned to music. He recorded material under the production supervision of longtime fan Tom Petty, with Petty's band the Heartbreakers backing him. The album included "Sea of Love," which hit #33 in early 1982.

SHEP AND THE LIMELITES
Formed Queens, New York
James "Shep" Sheppard (d. Jan. 24, 1970); Clarence Bassett; Charles Baskerville.

As lead singer of the Heartbeats, James Sheppard wrote and recorded "A Thousand Miles Away," which, though it only hit #5 on the R&B chart and #53 on the pop chart, remains one of the best-remembered doo-wop ballads of the era. In 1961, he formed Shep and the Limelites and hit big with "Daddy's Home" (#2 pop, #4 R&B). Over the next year and a half, they hit the Hot 100 with five more entries, but none went higher than #42. Sheppard was found dead in 1970 in his automobile on the Long Island Expressway after having been robbed and beaten. In 1982, with "A Thousand Miles Away" featured on the soundtrack of *Diner,* Sheppard's Limelites played some doo-wop revival concerts at places like the Bottom Line in New York City.

BOBBY SHERMAN
Born 1944, Santa Monica, California
1972—*Greatest Hits* (Metromedia).

Bobby Sherman was a teenybopper heartthrob who had talent. Besides singing and acting, Sherman also played guitar, piano, trumpet, trombone, French horn, drums and sitar. He'd begun performing in school, but rather than going into show business, he first entered college in California to major in psychology. He later told an interviewer, "I gave up psychology because I realized I was a schizo and belonged in show business with the rest of them."

Sherman began writing tunes and making record company rounds, eventually getting some work as a record producer. He landed a regular spot on the TV rock show "Shindig!," where his good looks and singing attracted a teenybopper following. When "Shindig!" was canceled, Sherman went on to star in the ABC series "Here Come the Brides." His first hit was 1969's "Little Woman," which made #3 and earned a gold record. In the fall of 1969, he won another gold record for the #9 "La La La (If I Had You)."In early 1970, the *Bobby Sherman* LP went

Del Shannon

gold, and his next two LPs were in the Top Twenty. "Easy Come, Easy Go" (#9, 1970) was followed by hits like "Hey Mister Sun" (#24) and "Julie, Do Ya Love Me" (#5) in 1970. That year, he played a documentary filmmaker in the ABC-TV movie *Zoom*, and then became a real-life filmmaking buff.

In 1971, Sherman had a couple of hit singles, "The Drum" (#29) and "Cried Like a Baby" (#16), but his sales were beginning to fall off. His last bubblegum hit was 1972's "Together Again."

THE SHIRELLES

Formed 1958, Passaic, New Jersey
Shirley Owens Alston (b. June 10, 1941, Passaic, N.J.), lead voc.; Micki Harris (b. Jan. 22, 1940, Passaic, N.J.; d. June 10, 1982, Los Angeles), voc.; Doris Coley Kenner (b. Aug. 2, 1941, Passaic, N.J.), voc.; Beverly Lee (b. Aug. 3, 1941, Passaic, N.J.), voc.
1961—*Tonight's the Night* (Scepter); *The Shirelles Sing* 1962—*Baby It's You; Greatest Hits* 1964—*Foolish Little Girl* 1972—*The Shirelles* (RCA) **N.A.**—*The Very Best of* (United Artists).

One of the first of the late-Fifties and early-Sixties girl groups and among the few to write their own hits, the Shirelles were also one of the most lasting.

The four girls began singing together at school shows and parties. A classmate, Mary Jane Greenberg, heard them singing one of their compositions, "I Met Him on a Sunday." Mary Jane convinced them to bring the song to her mother, Florence, who was in the music business. The Shirelles auditioned in Florence Greenberg's living room and were signed to Greenberg's Tiara label. In early 1958, "I Met Him on a Sunday" had garnered so much airplay that Decca Records bought it; it was on the pop chart for over two months, reaching #49.

Greenberg formed her own independent Scepter Records and in 1959, she released the Shirelles' cover of the Five Royales' "Dedicated to the One I Love." Without a national distributor, the disc only reached #83 on the pop chart. In 1960, the Shirelles scored with "Tonight's the Night" (#39 pop, #14 R&B), a song cowritten by lead vocalist Shirley Owens and produced by her cowriter, Luther Dixon, formerly of the Four Buddies.

Within a year, the Shirelles had their first #1 pop hit (#2 R&B) with the Carole King-Gerry Goffin composition "Will You Love Me Tomorrow?" Scepter re-released "Dedicated to the One I Love," and it joined "Will You" in the Top Ten for a while early in 1961.

The Shirelles became regulars on disc jockey Murray the K's Brooklyn all-star rock shows. In mid-1961 "Mama Said" (by Dixon and W. Denson) reached #4 pop, #2 R&B, and early in 1962 "Baby It's You" (by Burt Bacharach, Hal David and Barney Williams) went to #8 pop, #3 R&B. A few months later, "Soldier Boy," a first take

recorded initially as album filler, became their second #1 pop single (#3 R&B) and their biggest seller. Then Dixon (who had cowritten "Soldier Boy") left Scepter, precipitating the Shirelles' decline, although their first post-Dixon single, "Foolish Little Girl," went to #4 pop, #9 R&B in 1963.

In 1963, the Beatles covered the Shirelles' "Baby It's You" and "Boys" on their first U.K. LP. The Shirelles continued to perform and record, finally breaking up in the late Sixties, then re-forming in the early Seventies to play revival concerts, which they have continued to do sporadically into the Eighties. In 1977, Shirley Alston recorded a solo LP, *Lady Rose*.

SHIRLEY AND LEE/SHIRLEY AND COMPANY

Shirley Goodman, born Shirley Pixley, 1937; Leonard Lee, born June 29, 1935
Shirley and Lee: 1960—*Let the Good Times Roll* (Warwick; reissued 1975 by United Artists).
Shirley and Company: 1975—*Shame, Shame, Shame* (Vibration).

Shirley and Lee, who recorded "Let the Good Times Roll" in 1956, were known as "the sweethearts of the blues." Many of their records were supposed to tell the continuing story of their on-again, off-again romance. Long after the duo had gone separate ways and had stopped making New Orleans R&B hits, Shirley resurfaced in 1975 with the disco hit "Shame, Shame, Shame" (#12 pop, #1 R&B).

Shirley Goodman and Leonard Lee were discovered by New Orleans studio owner Cosimo Matassa when thirty local children, including Shirley and Lee, collected nickels to make a two-dollar demo record of "I'm Gone" at Matassa's studio. Matassa dispatched Eddie Mesner of Aladdin Records to track down the teenaged Shirley and Lee, and they re-recorded "I'm Gone" with ace New Orleans producer Dave Bartholomew. The tune was a #2 R&B hit in 1952. Their love-story songs were minor early-Fifties R&B hits, but the big hit was "Let the Good Times Roll," a #2 R&B hit that also did well on the pop chart (#20) in 1956 and eventually sold over a million copies. Despite Shirley's unique quavery soprano, the duo didn't catch on with white audiences, and their only followup was "I Feel Good" (#38 pop, #5 R&B, 1956).

In 1960, they began recording for Warwick and had three Top 100 hits, including a 1960 remake of "Let the Good Times Roll" (#48). They split up in 1963, and Shirley briefly worked with West Coast singer Jesse Hill (of "Ooh Poo Pah Doo" fame) as Shirley and Jesse. She later did sessions for New Orleans-based performers like Harold Battiste and Dr. John. Lee recorded a few singles as Leonard Lee for Imperial and Broadside in the mid-Sixties. In 1972, the pair reunited for one of Richard Nader's Rock & Roll Revival shows.

In 1975, Shirley teamed up with an anonymous crew of studio musicians to record the smash hit "Shame, Shame, Shame," one of the first disco songs. It was cowritten and produced by Sylvia Robinson of Mickey and Sylvia.

SIMON AND GARFUNKEL

Paul Simon (b. Oct. 13, 1942, Newark, N.J.), gtr., voc.; Arthur Garfunkel (b. Nov. 5, 1942, New York City), voc. **1966**—*Wednesday Morning, 3 A.M.* (Columbia); *Sounds of Silence; Parsley, Sage, Rosemary and Thyme* **1968**—*Bookends; The Graduate* (soundtrack) **1970**—*Bridge over Troubled Water* **1972**—*Greatest Hits* **1982**—*The Concert in Central Park.*

When they were in the sixth grade together in Forest Hills, New York, Simon and Garfunkel found they could harmonize. The first songs they sang together were doo-wop hits, but soon they were singing Simon's songs. One of those was "Hey, Schoolgirl," which the duo recorded in 1957. An agent of Big Records present at the session signed them on the spot. Calling themselves Tom and Jerry ("Tom Graph" and "Jerry Landis"), they had a Top Fifty hit with "Hey, Schoolgirl" and appeared on "American Bandstand." Garfunkel estimates the record sold 150,000 copies. When the followup flopped, Tom and Jerry split up.

When they met again in 1962, Garfunkel was studying architecture after trying to record as Arty Garr, and Simon was studying English literature but devoting most of his time to writing and selling his songs. In 1964, Simon, who had just dropped out of law school and quit his job as a song peddler for a music publishing company, took one of his originals to Columbia Records producer Tom Wilson. Wilson bought the song and signed the duo.

Wednesday Morning, 3 A.M.—a set that combined traditional folk songs with Simon's originals and Dylan anthems like "The Times They Are A-Changin'," performed only by the two singers accompanied by Simon's acoustic guitar—was lost in the glut of early Dylan imitations. Simon went to work the folk circuit in London, where in May 1965 he recorded a solo album. Several months later, he was gigging around England and the Continent when he received the news that one of the songs on *Wednesday Morning*—"Sounds of Silence"—was the #1 single in the United States.

It was not quite the song Simon and Garfunkel had recorded. Wilson (who had played a part in electrifying Dylan's music) had added electric guitars, bass and drums to the original track. The remixed single was at the vanguard of "folk rock." Simon returned to hit the college circuit with Garfunkel and to record a second duo album.

Along with the redubbed "Sounds of Silence," the album of that name comprised folk-rock remakes of many of the songs from Simon's U.K. solo album. The production was elaborate, an appropriate setting for Simon's self-

consciously poetic songs, and Simon and Garfunkel turned out to be acceptable to both teenagers (who found them relevant) and adults (who found them intelligent). In 1966, they placed four singles and three albums in the Top Thirty (the revived *Wednesday Morning, Sounds of Silence* and *Parsley, Sage, Rosemary and Thyme*). "Homeward Bound" (#5), "I Am a Rock" (#3) and *Parsley, Sage* reached the Top Five.

Simon was not a prolific writer—most of the material on the first three Simon and Garfunkel albums had been composed between 1962 and 1965—and once *Parsley, Sage* was completed, the duo's output slowed considerably. They released only two singles in 1967: "At the Zoo" (#16) and "Fakin' It" (#23). Simon was developing the more colloquial, less literary style he would bring to his later solo work; the first sign of it was the elliptical "Mrs. Robinson," composed for the soundtrack of *The Graduate*. The film and the soundtrack album were followed within two months by *Bookends;* "Mrs. Robinson" hit #1 in June, *Bookends* soon afterward.

Simon and Garfunkel produced *Bookends* with engineer Roy Halee, who had worked on every Simon and Garfunkel session. (With *Parsley, Sage,* Halee had taken a major role in the arranging; it was Columbia's first album recorded on eight tracks.) "The Boxer" (#7), Simon and Garfunkel's only release in 1969, was Columbia's first song recorded on 16 tracks.

Bridge over Troubled Water took almost two years to make, as the duo began to separate. They often worked separately in the studio, and as their music became more complex they performed less often on stage; their only appearance in 1969 was on their own network television special. Garfunkel's role in the creation of the duo's music, always small compared to Simon's, shrank further when he began to work as an actor. While Simon and Halee were working on *Bridge* in Los Angeles, Garfunkel was on the film set of *Catch-22* in Mexico; he returned to L.A. only to add his vocal tracks. Soon after the record's release, Simon and Garfunkel staged a brief but very successful tour, which quieted rumors about a breakup, but by the time Garfunkel's second movie, *Carnal Knowledge,* and Simon's first solo album came out at around the end of 1971 it was clear that their individual solo careers were taking precedence.

They left their joint career at its peak. After reaching #1 in spring 1970, *Bridge over Troubled Water* rode the charts for over a year and a half. Eventually it sold nine million copies worldwide. The LP yielded three hit singles—the title song (a #1 hit, the biggest seller of their career), "Cecelia" (#4) and "El Condor Pasa" (#18)—and won six Grammys. In 1977, it was given the British Britannia Award as Best International Pop Album of the past 25 years, and the title song received the equivalent award as a single.

Since 1970, the Forest Hills classmates have gotten together on a few notable occasions. The first was a

Art Garfunkel and Paul Simon

benefit concert for presidential candidate George McGovern at Madison Square Garden, New York, in June 1972. (That occasion also saw the reunions of Peter, Paul and Mary and the comedy team of Mike Nichols and Elaine May.) In 1975, Simon and Garfunkel had a Top Ten hit single with "My Little Town," a song Simon wrote for Garfunkel and sang with him, which appeared on solo LPs by both. Garfunkel joined Simon to perform a selection of their old hits on Simon's 1977 television special, and the two got together again the next year in a studio with James Taylor to record a trio rendition of Sam Cooke's "(What a) Wonderful World." In late September 1981, Simon and Garfunkel gave a free concert for an estimated 400,000 fans in New York's Central Park, and in 1982, a double album, *The Concert in Central Park*, went gold.

CARLY SIMON

Born June 25, 1945, New York City
1971—*Carly Simon* (Elektra); *Anticipation* (first 2 LPs reissued in 1975) **1972**—*No Secrets* **1973**—*Hot-cakes* **1974**—*Playing Possum* **1975**—*Best of* **1976**—*Another Passenger* **1978**—*Boys in the Trees* **1979**—*Spy* **1980**—*Come Upstairs* (Warner Bros.) **1981**—*Torch*.

Born into an affluent, musical family (her father, a co-founder of Simon and Schuster publishers, played classical piano in his spare time; one sister, Lucy, is a folksinger; another, Joanna, is an opera singer), Carly Simon became a successful folk-pop singer/songwriter.

She left Sarah Lawrence College to work as a folk duo with Lucy. They played New York City clubs as the Simon Sisters, breaking up when Lucy got married. The

Simon Sisters cut an LP for Kapp and had a minor hit in 1964 with "Winken, Blinken and Nod." Carly continued as a solo act; eventually manager/producer Albert Grossman took her into a New York studio in 1966 for a planned debut album with sessionmen like Robbie Robertson, Rick Danko and Richard Manuel (of the Band), Al Kooper and Mike Bloomfield. One of the tracks to be included was a version of Eric Von Schmidt's "Baby Let Me Follow You Down," with lyrics rewritten for Simon by Bob Dylan. The album never was completed because of differences between Simon and Grossman, and Simon kept a low profile for the rest of the decade.

She reemerged in 1970, and a single from her debut LP, "That's the Way I've Always Heard It Should Be," made #10 in the summer of 1971. In late 1971, the title cut of her second LP, *Anticipation,* was a #13 hit, and the album was also a best seller. In 1972, she had two more hits, "Legend in Your Own Time" (#50) and the mammoth smash "You're So Vain" (#1) allegedly inspired by and sung to either Warren Beatty or Mick Jagger (who appears on it as a backup vocalist). The *No Secrets* LP went gold later that year.

In 1972, she married James Taylor, and in 1974 their duet cover of "Mockingbird" was a #5 single; the album it came from, *Hotcakes,* went gold. Simon's next few LPs failed to yield any big hits and sold only moderately. In 1977 the theme song from the James Bond movie *The Spy Who Loved Me,* "Nobody Does It Better" (#2), went gold and in 1978 she had a #6 hit with "You Belong to Me." Simon suffers from stage fright and rarely performs in public. In 1979, she made a rare appearance in New York City at the MUSE "No Nukes" benefit concerts. In 1981, she released *Torch,* consisting of pop standards by Hoagy Carmichael, Rodgers and Hart and others, and she filed for divorce from Taylor.

PAUL SIMON

Born October 13, 1942, Newark, New Jersey
1965—*The Paul Simon Song Book* (CBS, U.K.) **1972**—*Paul Simon* (Columbia) **1973**—*There Goes Rhymin' Simon* **1974**—*Live Rhymin'* **1975**—*Still Crazy After All These Years* **1977**—*Greatest Hits, Etc.* **1980**—*One Trick Pony* (Warner Bros.).

Paul Simon as solo artist has never been able to persuade the world to forget Simon and Garfunkel, although he has had both artistic and commercial success on his own. Simon's terse, exquisitely crafted songs have drawn on reggae, salsa, jazz, gospel, blues and New Orleans music, and while they are artfully composed, they are also hugely popular. Simon and Garfunkel broke up in 1970 after recording *Bridge over Troubled Water.*

Simon had recorded solo in England between Simon and Garfunkel's first and second albums. His first solo album after breakup, *Paul Simon,* was a more varied record than any of Simon and Garfunkel's, made in studios around the world. One tune featured jazz violinist Stephane Grappelli; the first single, "Mother and Child Reunion," was cut in Jamaica. It became a hit (#4) in 1972, as did the followup, "Me and Julio down by the Schoolyard" (#22).

Simon's second album was an even greater commercial success. *There Goes Rhymin' Simon* boasted two hits: the gospel-tinged "Loves Me Like a Rock" (#2) (featuring the Dixie Hummingbirds on backup) and "Kodachrome" (#2). It also included "American Tune" (#35). *Live Rhymin'* featured backup by the Dixie Hummingbirds and the Peruvian folk group Urubama.

But Simon never completely severed ties with Garfunkel. The pair reunited to perform at a fund-raiser for George McGovern in 1972 and Garfunkel was a frequent guest at Simon's concerts. In 1975, they made their first record together since *Bridge over Troubled Water*, the single "My Little Town" (#9), which turned up on both Garfunkel's *Breakaway* and Simon's *Still Crazy After All These Years*. The latter LP also featured another pair of hits: a duet with Phoebe Snow, "Gone at Last" (#23) and "50 Ways to Leave Your Lover" (#1).

Next Simon played a small non-singing part in Woody Allen's *Annie Hall* in 1977, and he started working in television, hosting "Saturday Night Live" and his own special. His *Greatest Hits* package yielded the late 1977 #5 hit "Slip Slidin' Away." In 1980, Simon starred in *One Trick Pony*, for which he wrote the screenplay and soundtrack. An ambitious story of a journeyman rock & roller, *Pony* received a mixed reaction critically and was a flop at the box office, although the salsa-influenced "Late in the Evening" became yet another hit single (#6). In 1981, Simon reunited with Art Garfunkel again in Central Park for a concert that also became a live album.

NINA SIMONE
Born Eunice Waymon, February 21, 1933, Tryon, North Carolina
N.A.—*Nina Simone Sings the Blues* (RCA) **1967**—*Silk and Soul* **1968**—*'Nuff Said* **1970**—*Black Gold* **1972**—*Emergency Ward; It Is Finished* **1978**—*Baltimore* (CTI).

Singer Nina Simone's music has gone from gospel, to jazz, to pop, to R&B, to blues, to a raging black protest that moved her off the supper-club circuit and into political rallies and soul concerts. Since the late Fifties, when she had her first hits, she has been known as the "High Priestess of Soul."

Simone began singing in her church choir as a girl, and had taught herself piano and organ by the time she was seven. She took classical keyboard lessons and attended New York's Juilliard School, then began playing clubs and concerts on the East Coast. Her first hit was a 1959 version of Gershwin's "I Loves You Porgy," which earned her a gold record.

In the Sixties, she moved toward R&B, recording Screaming Jay Hawkins' "I Put a Spell on You" and "Don't Let Me Be Misunderstood" before the Animals did. This led to sizable popularity in England, where she had hits with "Ain't Got No—I Got Life" (from the rock musical *Hair*) in 1968 and the Bee Gees' "To Love Somebody" in 1969. By that time she had become deeply involved in the growing black-power movement. Politically oriented tracks like "Four Women" (on an out-of-print Philips LP) alienated her white audience. She became even more intense, and more unpredictable, in her concert appearances, and despite continuing critical acclaim gradually lost her commercial powers. She quit the music business altogether in 1974, then came back in 1978 with *Baltimore*. Since that time, she has made sporadic concert appearances, including 1983 club dates in New York.

FRANK SINATRA
Born Francis Albert Sinatra, December 12, 1915, Hoboken, New Jersey
1955—*In the Wee Small Hours* (Capitol) **1958**—*Come Fly with Me; Only the Lonely* **1959**—*Come Dance with Me* **1960**—*Nice 'n' Easy* **1961**—*Ring-a-Ding Ding* (Reprise) **1962**—*Sinatra and Basie* **1965**—*September of My Years;   Sinatra—A Man and His Music* **1966**—*Sinatra at the Sands;   That's Life* **1968**—*Frank Sinatra's Greatest Hits* **1969**—*My Way* **1972**—*Frank Sinatra's Greatest Hits, Volume 2* **1973**—*Ol' Blue Eyes Is Back* **1974**—*Sinatra–The Main Event Live* **1980**—*Trilogy* **1981**—*She Shot Me Down* **1982**—*The Dorsey/Sinatra Sessions 1940–1942* (RCA).

Frank Sinatra is a pop singer whose closest approach to rock is an occasional Beatles or Sonny and Cher cover. But his poised trombone-like phrasing, his nearly 100 hit singles and his career trajectory—from riot-inducing teen idol to movie star to pop elder statesman—have been the model and envy of rockers from the beginning.

Sinatra, an only child of a family with Sicilian roots, grew up in Hoboken, and sang in the glee club of Demarest High School. His break came in 1937, when he and three instrumentalists, billed as the Hoboken Four, won on the "Major Bowes Original Amateur Hour." After some touring, the group disbanded.

Harry James signed Sinatra to sing with his orchestra, and on July 13, 1939, two weeks after his debut as a Big Band vocalist at the Hippodrome Theatre in Baltimore, Sinatra cut his first disc, "From the Bottom of My Heart," with the orchestra. Of the ten sides he recorded with them, the biggest seller, "All or Nothing at All," sold just over 8,000 copies upon release. In 1943, when Sinatra and James had both become national figures, it was re-released and became the first of Sinatra's many million-sellers, hitting #2 on the charts.

In 1940, Tommy Dorsey's lead singer, Jack Leonard, quit and Sinatra began a two-year stay with the Dorsey band, developing his phrasing by studying Dorsey's technique on the trombone. During those years, the Dorsey band consistently hit the Top Ten (15 entries in 1940–41 including their first, the #1 hit "I'll Never Smile Again"). His radio work with Dorsey was the springboard for Sinatra's solo career.

During the war years, Sinatra sang love songs to his mostly female audiences, notably on Lucky Strike's "Hit Parade," and between 1943 and 1946 had 17 Top Ten chart singles. With the GIs back in the U.S., the public taste shifted away from these songs and Sinatra's popularity waned. At Columbia, producer Mitch Miller burdened Sinatra with inappropriate novelty songs (washboard accompaniment on one, barking dogs on another), and his sales slipped to an average of 30,000 per record. In the early Fifties, he was dropped by Columbia and by his talent agent, and he lost his motion picture contract with MGM. To rescue his popularity he begged to be cast as Maggio in the film of *From Here to Eternity.* His first non-singing role, it won him the 1953 Best Supporting Male Actor Oscar and brought him back into the limelight. (His film debut had been with the Tommy Dorsey Orchestra in 1941's *Las Vegas Nights.*)

The fledgling Capitol Records signed him in 1953 and, with ex-Dorsey trombonist and arranger Nelson Riddle, Sinatra moved into the next phase of his recording career with a new emphasis: booze ballads and swing tunes. With Capitol, he concentrated on making albums, although he once again began charting in the singles Top Ten, notably with "Young at Heart" (#2, 1954), "Learnin' the Blues" (#1, 1955), "Hey! Jealous Lover" (#3, 1956), "All the Way" (#2, 1957) and "Witchcraft" (#6, 1958). His best albums of the period were arranged by Riddle, Billy May or Gordon Jenkins.

Through the Fifties, Sinatra was equally well known as a movie star, winning especially high praise for his role of a drug addict in *The Man with the Golden Arm* (1955). Beginning in 1959, his singles failed to hit the Top Thirty, and in 1961 he left Capitol to establish his own recording company, Reprise, signing Bing Crosby, Dean Martin and Sammy Davis, Jr., among his first acts. (In 1963, he sold Reprise to Warner Bros. and became a vice president and consultant of Warner Brothers Picture Corp.)

Sinatra decided to try once again to become a Top Forty singles artist. "The Second Time Around" hit #50 in 1961; subsequent releases charted lower. But in the mid-Sixties he recouped. He was the triumphant headliner of the final evening of the 1965 Newport Jazz Festival in a twenty-song set accompanied by Count Basie's orchestra, conducted by Quincy Jones. His 1965 Thanksgiving TV special, "Frank Sinatra: A Man and His Music," a review of his 25-year career, won an Emmy and set the precedent for numerous other TV specials, including one each in the

four next years. In 1966–67, he charted three of his biggest hits in the Top Ten: "Strangers in the Night" (#1, 1966), "That's Life" (#4, 1966) and "Somethin' Stupid" (a duet with daughter Nancy, #1, 1967).

In the Sixties, he made his Las Vegas debut at the Sands and continues to be a main attraction at Caesars Palace. In 1968, he recorded Las Vegas regular Paul Anka's song "My Way." While it was a modest hit in the U.S. (#27), it was an overwhelming smash in the U.K., staying in the Top Fifty an unprecedented 122 weeks. (Sex Pistol Sid Vicious later recorded a sarcastic version.)

In 1970, Sinatra announced his retirement and was honored with a gala farewell on June 13, 1971, at the Los Angeles Music Center. He reversed that decision in 1973 with the release of *Ol' Blue Eyes Is Back,* a TV special of the same name, and a performance at the Nixon White House at a state dinner for visiting Italian Premier Giulio Andreotti. In 1974, he mounted an eight-city, thirteen-date sold-out U.S. tour and performed in Japan and Australia. In Australia, he once again aggravated the paparazzi with his anti-journalist harangues: through the years he has referred to the males as parasites, and the females as everything from "a buck-and-a-half hooker" to "two-dollar broads."

In the mid-Seventies, Sinatra's career slowed somewhat but in mid-1980, after a five-year recording hiatus, he released *Trilogy,* which included his version of "Theme from *New York, New York*" (#32), a version that city has fervently adopted.

Into the Eighties, Sinatra continues to perform sell-out concerts in major halls, to star in movies and TV specials, and to spark controversy for his business and political associations. (His 1972 appearances before the House Select Committee on Crime investigating criminal infiltration into horseracing were front-page news.)

The most acclaimed and influential pop stylist of his generation, he continues to record standards. While his staples have been the songs of Cole Porter, Irving Berlin, Jerome Kern and George and Ira Gershwin, he has also recorded pop and rock songs by Stevie Wonder, George Harrison, Paul McCartney, Jimmy Webb, Jim Croce, Neil Diamond and Billy Joel.

NANCY SINATRA

Born June 8, 1940, Jersey City
1966—*Boots* (Reprise) **1968**—*Nancy and Lee* (with Lee Hazlewood) **1970**—*Greatest Hits* **1972**—*Nancy and Lee—Encore* (RCA).

Frank Sinatra's daughter Nancy had several late-Sixties hits, including "These Boots Are Made for Walkin' " and "How Does That Grab You, Darlin'?"

At an early age Nancy Sinatra began studying dance, acting, singing and piano. She made her national TV debut in 1960, in a special featuring her father and Elvis Presley.

She dropped out of the University of Southern California in 1960 after marrying singer/actor Tommy Sands, and did not resume her career until they divorced in 1965.

Her first few singles, "Like I Do," "Tonight You Belong to Me" and "Think of Me," were hits in England, Europe and South Africa, but were ignored in the U.S. Then, in 1966, came the #1 hit and million-selling "These Boots." She followed it up with the gold "Sugar Town/Summer Wine" (#5).

In 1967, Nancy Sinatra's country & western version of "Jackson" (#14) sold well, as did her title tune from the James Bond film *You Only Live Twice* (#44). That year she also earned her third gold record for the #1 duet with her father, "Somethin' Stupid." By that time, she was working with singer/songwriter/producer Lee Hazlewood. She appeared on TV rock shows like "Hullabaloo" and "American Bandstand," and acted in episodes of TV series like "The Virginian" and "Burke's Law." She also appeared in films: *For Those Who Think Young, Get Yourself a College Girl, Bikini Party in a Haunted House* and *Last of the Secret Agents;* she played herself in *The Oscar* and the Elvis Presley film *Speedway.* In 1968, she made the first of two albums with Hazlewood, and a year later had her last chart singles.

SIOUXSIE AND THE BANSHEES
Formed 1976, London
Siouxsie Sioux (b. Susan Dallion, Chislehurst, Eng.), voc.; Sid Vicious (b. John Ritchie or Beverly; d. Feb. 2, 1979, New York City), drums; Steve Havoc (b. Steve Severin), bass; Marco Pirroni, gtr.; − Vicious; + Kenny Morris, drums; − Pirroni; + John McKay, gtr. **1978**—*The Scream* (Polydor); *Join Hands* **1979**— (− Morris; + Budgie, drums; − McKay; + John McGeoch, gtr.) **1981**—*Kaleidoscope* (PVC); *Juju.*

Siouxsie and the Banshees began as Sex Pistols fans; shortly after their formation, original member Sid Vicious became a Pistol himself. In the end, the Banshees outlived their fandom and the Pistols, going on to spend a few years in the avant-punk forefront of British rock.

Of the founding four, only Siouxsie Sioux and Steve Severin were still around when their debut single, "Hong Kong Garden," and the LP *The Scream* came out (although Marco Pirroni would be heard from again as one of Adam's Ants). The two records set standards the Banshees found difficult to live up to with their next album, *Join Hands.* Unlike its predecessor, it never received an American release, and the group dissolved back to its two leaders, replacements coming in the form of ex-Magazine guitarist John McGeoch and Budgie, formerly of Big in Japan and the Slits. The new group was more focused and more tuneful, as attested by their British hits "Christine" and "Happy House." McGeoch joined the British Electric Foundation (ex–Human Leaguers Martyn Ware and Ian Marsh) and continued working with his other band, Visage.

SIR DOUGLAS QUINTET
Formed 1964, California
Original lineup: Doug Sahm (b. Nov. 6, 1941, Tex.), gtr., voc.; Augie Meyer (b. May 31, 1941), kybds.; Francisco Moran (b. Aug. 13, 1946), sax; Harvey Kagan (b. Apr. 18, 1946), bass; Johnny Perez (b. Nov. 8, 1942), drums. **1965**—*Best of Sir Douglas Quintet* (Tribe) **1968**—*Honkey Blues* (Smash) **1969**—*Mendocino* **1970**—*Together After Five; 1 + 1 + 1 = 4* (Philips) **1971**—*The Return of Doug Saldana* **1973**—*Texas Tornado* (Atlantic) **1976**—*Texas Rock for Country Rollers* (ABC/Dot) **1981**—*Border Wave* (Takoma).
Doug Sahm solo:
1973—*Doug Sahm and Band* (Atlantic); *Rough Edges* (Mercury) **1974**—*Groovers Paradise* (Warner Bros.) **1980**—*Hell of a Spell* (Takoma).

"Mendocino" and "She's about a Mover" were Doug Sahm and the Sir Douglas Quintet's commercial peaks, but they were only part of Sahm's long, varied career.

Sahm grew up around San Antonio, Texas, where he absorbed the strains of music that would show up in his bands: country, blues, Western swing, jazz and the polkas of Mexican *conjunto* bands. He began performing (as Little Doug Sahm) at age six, playing steel guitar. When rock & roll arrived in the mid-Fifties, he started forming his own bands and had hits around San Antonio while still in high school.

In 1960, Sahm moved to California and continued to have local hits. In 1964, as the British Invasion got under way, he called his newest band (featuring Augie Meyer on Vox organ) the Sir Douglas Quintet. "She's about a Mover," featuring a recurring organ line reminiscent of *conjunto* accordion, went into the Top Twenty, spurring a short wave of Tex-Mex hits (by Sam the Sham and ? and the Mysterians). "The Rains Came" reached the Top Twenty in 1966.

With the blues revival and psychedelia, a shifting Quintet played loose-limbed blues around San Francisco; Meyer rejoined in 1968 and the group cut its last big hit, "Mendocino" (#27, 1969). The group's albums grew more experimental and spacier, and didn't sell.

Sahm returned to Texas in 1971 to cut an album of San Antonio barroom honky-tonk, then he temporarily gave up the Sir Douglas monicker. His first solo album featured Dr. John, *conjunto* accordionist Flaco Jimenez, jazz saxophonist David "Fathead" Newman and Bob Dylan, who wrote a country-flavored song, "Wallflower," for Sahm. Mercury capitalized on Sahm's expected stardom with *Rough Edges,* a collection of Quintet outtakes, but *Doug Sahm and Band* never caught on.

Sahm continued to record through the Seventies—under his own name, as the Sir Douglas Band (1973) and as Sir Douglas and the Texas Tornadoes (1976)—with his mixture of Texans, Mexicans and Californians. *Groovers Paradise* featured Creedence Clearwater's rhythm section, Stu Cook and Doug Clifford. In the late Seventies, Sahm was part of the "cosmic cowboy" scene in Austin. Meanwhile, new wave bands—particularly Elvis Costello and the Attractions—were rediscovering the organ-pumping sound of Tex-Mex. As the Eighties began, Sahm resurrected the Quintet with Meyer and Perez to make *Border Wave*, and he has since toured with them in a band that also includes his son.

THE SKATALITES

Formed 1963, Kingston, Jamaica
Don Drummond (d. April 21, 1971), trombone; Rico Rodriguez, trombone; Baba Brooks, trumpet; Johnny "Dizzy" Moore, fluegelhorn, trumpet; Raymond Harper, trumpet; Bobby Ellis, trumpet; Lester Sterling, alto sax; Karl Bryan, alto sax; Roland Alphonso, tenor sax; Tommy McCook, trumpet, tenor sax; Ernest Ranglin, gtr.; Jah Jerry, gtr.; Lloyd Brevette, bass; Jackie Mittoo, kybds.; Theophilus Beckford, kybds.; Gladstone Anderson, kybds.; Lloyd Nibbs, bass, perc.; Drumbago, drums; Hugh Malcolm, drums.
1963–67—*Ska Authentic* (Studio One); *Ska Authentic, Volume II; Best of the Skatalites* **1975**—*Legendary Skatalites* (Top Ranking) **1977**—*African Roots* (United Artists).

From 1963 to 1967, the Skatalites played on nearly every session recorded in Jamaica. Leader Don Drummond virtually invented ska, and the ranks of his band were filled with stars of that and later eras.

Drummond was a music teacher at a Catholic boys' school in West Kingston when he formed his band; some members had been his students. With varying numbers according to the demands of the session, they recorded for all of the Jamaican producers, but especially for Coxsone Dodd at his Studio One, and they backed Eric Morris, the Charms, Justin Hines, Derrick Morgan, the Maytals, the Wailers and the Heptones. They issued instrumental records from their own sessions as well, scoring Jamaican hits with "Ball o' Fire," "Independent Anniversary Ska," "Confucius" and "Dick Tracy."

One of the first Jamaican acts signed to Island Records and marketed in the U.K., they made the British Top Forty with "Guns of Navarone" in 1967. They also recorded, in various aggregations, as the Don Drummond All Stars, Roland Al and the Soul Brothers, Tommy McCook and the Supersonics, the Baba Brooks Band, the Karl Bryan Orchestra, Jackie Mittoo and the Soul Vendors, Drumbago's All Stars, Sir Coxsone's All Stars and Roland Alphonso's Alley Cats.

By 1967, the Skatalites were no longer recording under that name, although most of the members were active in Jamaican music into the Eighties. Some moved to England, where—like Ernest Ranglin—they maintained careers as session musicians or—like Rico Rodriguez—they began making solo records. Drummond, who had won international jazz trombonist awards, died in 1971 after

years of steadily worsening mental illness. In 1975, Tommy McCook, Roland Alphonso, Lloyd Nibbs and Lester Sterling briefly reunited as the Skatalites under Lloyd Brevette's leadership.

SKIFFLE

The name for England's equivalent of America's late-Fifties folk revival, which involved enthusiastic amateur performances of old novelty songs, New Orleans jazz and jug-band music, was skiffle. Lonnie Donegan was skiffle's major hitmaker ("Rock Island Line"), but the impact of the craze was that it encouraged amateur musicians to start playing and performing. A number of Sixties rockers, including John Lennon and George Harrison of the Beatles, got started in skiffle bands.

SLADE

Formed 1968, Wolverhampton, England
Noddy Holder (b. June 15, 1950, Walshall, Eng.), gtr., voc.; Dave Hill (b. Apr. 4, 1952, Fleet Castle, Eng.), gtr.; Jimmy Lea (b. June 14, 1952, Wolverhampton, Eng.), bass, piano; Don Powell (b. Sep. 10, 1950, Bilston, Eng.), drums.
1969—*Beginnings* (Fontana) **1970**—*Play It Loud* (Cotillion) **1972**—*Slade Alive* (Polydor) *Slayed* **1973**—*Sladest* (Reprise) **1974**—*Old, New, Borrowed and Blue* (Polydor) **1975**—*In Flame* (Warner Bros.) **1977**—*Whatever Happened to Slade?* (Polydor, U.K.).

Distinguished by Noddy Holder's harsh screaming, a crudely thunderous rhythm section and song titles that recast the English language ("Gudbuy T'Jane," "Cum On Feel the Noize," "Skweeze Me Pleeze Me"), Slade breathed life into early Seventies hard rock.

Hailing from Wolverhampton, an industrial city near Birmingham, the quartet started as the In Betweens. They changed their name to Ambrose Slade and were spotted one night by Chas Chandler, the former Animal and former manager/producer of Jimi Hendrix. Chandler dropped the Ambrose and became the group's manager and producer, giving them their first British hit in 1971, a cover of Little Richard's "Get Down and Get With It," followed by the #1 record "Coz I Love You."

The key to Slade's primitive attack was Chandler's live-in-the-studio production. Appearing onstage at first with closely cropped haircuts, blue jeans, suspenders and construction boots—trademarks of England's working-class skinhead movement—Slade was as noisy as the Who and generated an unrestrained "Slademania." Fans stomped, clapped, rushed the stage, fainted and tossed bras and panties onstage. Slade gradually switched its visual image, becoming one of rock's most gaudily outfitted groups. The four rockers dressed in the unlikely combination of silver sci-fi gear and high-fashion platform boots.

Their hits from this period included "Take Me Bak 'Ome" (#1, 1972, U.K.), "Mama Weer All Crazee Now"

(#1, 1972, U.K.), "Gudbuy T'Jane" (#2, 1972, U.K.) and "Cum On Feel the Noize" (#1, 1973, U.K.), which were generally ignored in the U.S. In 1974, Slade starred in the film *Flame*, in which the members appeared as rock stars on the way to the top. At the same time, Slade's popularity was slipping, with decreasing sales of albums like *Slade in Flame*, which underlined the group's maturing hard-rock style. Slade have carried on since, but were never able to regain the momentum of their peak period, when they sold more than ten million records worldwide. In 1981, they had a British hit with "Lock Up Your Daughters."

PERCY SLEDGE

Born 1941, Leighton, Alabama
1966—*When a Man Loves a Woman* (Atlantic) *Warm and Tender Soul* **1967**—*The Percy Sledge Way* **1968**—*Take Time to Know Her* **1969**—*The Best of Percy Sledge* **1974**—*I'll Be Your Everything* (Capricorn).

In the mid-Sixties, singer Percy Sledge was performing throughout Mississippi and Alabama as a member of the Esquires Combo. His career took a dramatic turn for the better in 1966, when he quit to go solo and scored a #1 pop and R&B hit with his debut single, "When a Man Loves a Woman." Sledge remained a popular singer through the end of the decade, working in the same intense balladeering style of "When a Man."

His successes included "Warm and Tender Love" (#17 pop, #5 R&B) and "It Tears Me Up" (#20 pop, #7 R&B) in 1966; "Out of Left Field" (#25 R&B) in 1967; "Sudden Stop" (#41 R&B) in 1968; "Any Day Now" (#35 R&B) in 1969; and especially "Take Time to Know Her" (#11 pop, #6 R&B) in 1968. Sledge's career stalled in the Seventies, save for a brief resurgence with the R&B hits "Sunshine" (#89 R&B, 1973) and "I'll Be Your Everything" (#15 R&B, 1974).

SISTER SLEDGE

Formed late 1950s, Philadelphia
Joni Sledge (b. circa 1957); Kathy Sledge (b. circa 1959); Kim Sledge (b. circa 1958); Debbie Sledge (b. circa 1955).
1975—*Circle of Love* (Atco) **1979**—*We Are Family* (Cotillion) **1980**—*Love Somebody Today* **1981**—*All American Girls* **1983**—*Bet Cha Say That to All the Girls*.

This vocal quartet of Philadelphia-born sisters enjoyed considerable success as the Seventies ended.

The Sledge sisters made their performing debut at Philadelphia's Second Macedonia Church in the late Fifties. Their parents had both been entertainers, and their grandmother, Viola Williams, was an opera singer. Before they attended elementary school, the four girls entertained at parties as "Mrs. Williams' Grandchildren."

In 1971, they recorded "Time Will Tell" for the Money label. It was produced by Marty Bryant and the band Slim and the Boys, the team behind the Stylistics' first hit. While attending college they worked as background singers on several Kenny Gamble and Leon Huff productions, and in 1973 they were signed to Atlantic Records. All four have since graduated from Temple University.

From 1973 to 1978, Sister Sledge recorded in New York and Philadelphia without any significant success. It wasn't until the gold *We Are Family* in 1979, written and produced by Nile Rodgers and Bernard Edwards of Chic, that they became a chart presence. "He's the Greatest Dancer" (#9 pop, #1 R&B) and "We Are Family" (#2 pop, #1 R&B) were dance hits. The latter became the theme song of the Pittsburgh Pirates, the 1979 baseball champions, and later the anthem of gays marching on Washington, D.C., that year. In 1981, they recorded "He's Just a Runaway," a tribute to the late Bob Marley. The next year, Sister Sledge had a hit with a cover of the Mary Wells oldie "My Guy."

PHILIP (P.F.) SLOAN

P. F. Sloan LPs: 1965—*Songs of Our Time* (Dunhill) **1966**—*12 More Times* **1968**—*Measure of Pleasure* (Atco) **1972**—*Raised on Records* (Epic, U.K.).
Fantastic Baggies LP: *Tell 'Em I'm Surfin'* (Imperial).

Though he had his own career as a Dylan-styled singer/songwriter, P. F. Sloan is best known for his songwriting, particularly Barry McGuire's 1965 smash "Eve of Destruction."

Prior to "Eve," Sloan and his partner Steve Barri had written surf rock hits, and even recorded a few of them disguised as the Fantastic Baggies on the album, *Tell 'Em I'm Surfin'*.

In the years that followed, Sloan and Barri worked extensively with the Grass Roots, provided the Turtles with a hit record, "You Baby," and wrote songs for the Searchers, Herman's Hermits and many others. Because of the groups he was involved with, Sloan's work tended to be dismissed—a situation addressed by Jimmy Webb in his song "P. F. Sloan." Barri remains active as a pop-rock producer.

SLY AND ROBBIE

Formed 1975, Kingston, Jamaica
Sly "Drumbar" Dunbar (b. Lowell Fillmore Dunbar, May 10, 1952, Kingston), drums; Robbie "Basspeare" Shakespeare (b. Sep. 27, 1953, Kingston), bass.
1981—*Sly and Robbie Present Taxi* (Mango); *60s, 70s, 80s* **1982**—*Sly-Go-Ville* **1983**—*Crucial Reggae Driven by Sly and Robbie*.

Sly Dunbar and Robbie Shakespeare began their careers as teenaged session musicians. They teamed up to become one of Jamaica's most celebrated rhythm sections, and continued their partnership as bandleaders, producers and record businessmen.

Dunbar started out in the Yardbrooms, a reggae band of the late Sixties that nurtured several of Jamaica's leading instrumentalists. In the early Seventies, Dunbar was with Skin, Flesh and Bones, who recorded their own records and backed various singers.

Shakespeare studied with Aston "Family Man" Barrett (bassist with the Upsetters, who went on to join the Wailers) and played sessions for Burning Spear, Bunny Wailer and others. He first played with Dunbar behind Peter Tosh in 1975, and the following year—after Dunbar had returned from touring the U.K. with the Mighty Diamonds—the two formed the Revolutionaires, a leading dub band of the Seventies.

Concurrently until 1979, Dunbar and Shakespeare led Peter Tosh's band, Word, Sound and Power, in the studio and on tours of North America and Europe. Their sound exemplified the "rockers' riddims" of late-Seventies reggae. (Shakespeare played a cameo role in *Rockers,* the 1977 film inspired by that sound.)

In 1978, they set up their own record company, Taxi Productions, formed the Taxi All-Stars from the ashes of the Revolutionaires and Word, Sound and Power, and began working as producers. Taxi's first release was Black Uhuru's "Observe Life." It was followed by numerous albums for Black Uhuru, for established artists like Gregory Isaacs, Max Romeo, Prince Far-I and Dennis Brown, and for newer acts like the Tamlins, the Wailing Souls, Jimmy Riley and General Echo. In addition, Sly and Robbie (as they are invariably billed) issued their own duo and solo recordings on Taxi. In 1980, they entered into a worldwide distribution agreement with Island Records. Most of their U.S. releases have been anthologies of Taxi artists. In the early Eighties, they worked with such reggae veterans as Jimmy Cliff, Desmond Dekker and the Paragons, and also with artists not usually associated with reggae—Ian Dury, Joan Armatrading, Grace Jones, Manu Dibango, Robert Palmer and Joe Cocker. They regularly took their "riddims" on the road with Black Uhuru.

SLY AND THE FAMILY STONE
Original lineup: Sly Stone (b. Sylvester Stewart, Mar. 15, 1944, Dallas), gtr., kybds., voc.; Freddie Stone (b. Fred Stewart, June 5, 1946, Dallas), gtr., voc.; Larry Graham, Jr. (b. Aug. 14, 1946, Beaumont, Tex.), bass, voc.; Cynthia Robinson (b. Jan. 12, 1946, Sacramento, Calif.), trumpet; Greg Errico (b. Sep. 1, 1946, San Francisco), drums; Rosie Stone (b. Mar. 21, 1945, Vallejo, Calif.), piano; Jerry Martini (b. Oct. 1, 1943, Colo.), sax.
1967—*A Whole New Thing* (Epic)   **1968**—*Dance to the Music; Life*   **1969**—*Stand*   **1970**—*Greatest Hits*   **1971**—*There's a Riot Goin' On*   **1973**—*Fresh*   **1974**—*Small Talk*   **1975**—*High Energy* (reissue of *A Whole New Thing* and *Dance to the Music*)   *High on You*   **1978**—*Heard You Missed Me*   **1979**—*Back on the Right Track* (Warner Bros.)   **1983**—*Ain't but the One Way.*

In the late Sixties, Sly and the Family Stone fused black rhythms and a psychedelic sensibility into a new pop/soul/rock hybrid that drew both white and black audiences. The Family Stone's music predated disco and inspired the many black self-contained bands that emerged in the Seventies; along with James Brown, the Family Stone virtually invented Seventies funk.

Sylvester Stewart's family moved from Texas to the San Francisco area in the Fifties. At age four, he began singing gospel music and at age 16 made a local hit, "Long Time Away." Stewart studied trumpet, music theory and composition at Vallejo Junior College and while in school became active on the Bay Area music scene. With his brother, Fred, he formed several short-lived groups like the Stewart Bros. He was a disc jockey at soul station KSOL, and at Autumn Records he produced records by the Beau Brummels, Bobby Freeman, the Mojo Men and Grace Slick's first band, the Great Society. He later worked for KDIA.

In 1966, Sly formed a short-lived group called the Stoners, which included female trumpeter Cynthia Robinson. With her he started his next band, Sly and the Family Stone. Sly, Robinson and Fred Stewart were joined by Larry Graham, Jr. (see separate entry), Greg Errico and Jerry Martini, all of whom had studied music and worked in numerous amateur groups. Rosie Stone joined the group soon after. Working around the Bay Area in 1967, this multiracial band made a strong impression. They recorded their debut single, "I Ain't Got Nobody" b/w "I Can't Turn You Loose," on the local Loadstone label.

The Family Stone's debut LP, *A Whole New Thing,* flopped. Its followup, *Dance to the Music,* included the hit title cut (#8 pop, #9 R&B). *Life* sold fewer copies than their previous albums, but their next release, a double-sided single, "Everyday People" b/w "Sing a Simple Song," was #1 on both the R&B and pop charts.

Stand mixed hard-edged politics with the Family's ecstatic dance music. It rose to #13 on the pop chart, and contained Sly standards like the title song, "Don't Call Me Nigger Whitey," "Sex Machine," "Somebody's Watching You" and "I Want to Take You Higher" (#38 pop, #24 R&B). Fiery versions of "Dance to the Music" and "Higher," heard on the *Woodstock* soundtrack album, established them as one of the finest live bands of the late Sixties.

Singles like "Hot Fun in the Summertime" (#2 pop, #3 R&B) and "Thank You Falettinme Be Mice Elf Agin" b/w "Everybody Is a Star" (#1 pop and R&B), were the band's commercial peak, and the success of *Greatest Hits* (#2 pop) reflected their immense popularity. By then, *Stand* had been on the charts over eighty weeks, and most of the Family's Top Ten singles had gone gold, as had most of their post–*Dance to the Music* LPs.

After 1970, Sly became somewhat notorious for arriving late or missing concerts, and it was generally known that he was suffering from drug problems. The group's turning point came in 1971, when *There's a Riot Goin' On* went to #1. It was nothing like any of their previous efforts. Its darkly understated sound, violent imagery and controversial militant stance were a sharp contrast to the optimism of earlier works. From that album came "Family Affair" (#1 pop and R&B), Sly's last across-the-board hit.

By 1972, the Family Stone were growing restless. Key members Larry Graham and drummer Greg Errico left and were replaced by Rusty Allen and Andy Newmark. From *Fresh*, "If You Want Me to Stay" (#12 pop, #3 R&B) did fairly well, and a blues version of "Que Sera Sera" got some airplay, particularly when rumors of a romance between Sly and Doris Day emerged. *Small Talk* fared moderately well. It took advertising of Sly's public wedding ceremony to Kathy Silva at Madison Square Garden in 1974 to sell it out. "I Get High on You" (R&B #3) did respectably, but subsequent albums failed. Meanwhile, disco had emerged, and in 1979 Epic issued *Ten Years Too Soon*, a compilation album on which the quirky original rhythm tracks were erased and a disco beat dubbed in. By the mid-Seventies, stories of drug problems and arrests were part of the Sly Stone legacy.

By 1979, he was with Warner Bros. attempting to make the comeback many observers felt would be as natural as James Brown's, given the current interest in and popularity of funk. In 1981, he assisted on Funkadelic's *Electric Spanking of War Babies*. He toured with George Clinton and the P-Funk All-Stars and on his own in the early Eighties.

THE SMALL FACES
Formed 1965, London
Steve Marriott (b. Jan. 30, 1947, London), gtr., voc.; Jimmy Winston (b. Eng.), kybds.; Ronnie Lane (b. Apr. 1, 1948, London), bass; Kenney Jones (b. Sep. 16, 1948, London), drums.
1965—(– Winston; + Ian McLagan [b. May 12, 1946, Hounslown, Eng.], kybds.) **1966**—*The Small Faces* (Decca) **1967**—*From the Beginning* **1968**—*Ogden's Nut Gone Flake* (Immediate) (– Marriott) **1969**—*Autumn Stone* **1970**—*In Memoriam* **1975**—*The Vintage Years* (Sire) **1977**—(Marriott; McLagan; Jones; Rick Wills, bass; Joe Brown, gtr., voc.) *Playmates* (Atlantic) **1978**—(– Brown; + Jimmy McCulloch [b. 1953, Glasgow; d. Sep. 27, 1979, London], gtr.) *78 in the Shade.*

The Small Faces got their name for two reasons: They were small, under five feet six inches tall, and they were "faces," as in the Who's "I'm the Face," a declaration of mod-era hipness. When the Small Faces first hit the

The Small Faces: Steve Marriott, Jimmy Winston, Kenney Jones, Ronnie Lane

British singles charts in 1965 with "Whatcha Gonna Do About It?" (recorded six weeks after their formation), they were seen by British youth as East London's answer to West London's Who. Led by Steve Marriott, the Small Faces became as big an attraction in Britain for their mod clothing as for their basic, raw R&B-inspired music.

Marriott, a former child actor, formed the band with Ronnie Lane, who had already played with several local bands and was writing his own tunes. McLagan was recruited when original keyboardist Jimmy Winston left immediately after the Faces' first hit single. Rounding out the lineup was drummer Kenney Jones, who had studied drums but had never played with a professional band. Though Marriott has said that he could barely play guitar at the time, he and Lane began writing songs together. After attracting a following with fevered London club performances, and the success of their first single, the Small Faces were signed to Andrew Loog Oldham's Immediate label and appeared frequently in the British singles charts for the next few years with "Sha La La La Lee," "Hey Girl," "All or Nothing" and "My Mind's Eye" (1966); "Here Comes the Nice" and "Tin Soldier" (1967); and "Lazy Sunday" and "The Universal" (1968). The only one of their early hits to gain any attention in America was "Itchycoo Park" (#16) in 1967, a piece of psychedelia that featured one of the earliest uses of studio "phase-shifting" production.

By 1968, the band was becoming frustrated with its image as a singles band. That changed somewhat in 1968, when they released the concept album *Ogden's Nut Gone Flake*. Still, internal tensions grew, and in 1969 Marriott left to form Humble Pie. It seemed a crucial blow at the time, but with the addition of Rod Stewart and Ronnie Wood the Faces were Small no more. The band later reunited, minus Lane and with the addition of Jimmy McCulloch and Ricky Wills. (See also: the Faces.)

HUEY "PIANO" SMITH

Born January 26, 1934, New Orleans
N.A.—*Havin' a Good Time* (Ace); *For Dancing; 'Twas Night before Christmas; Rock 'n' Roll Revival* 1978—*Rockin' Pneumonia.*

New Orleans R&B pianist Huey Smith, together with his vocal group, the Clowns, recorded some of the R&B classics of the Fifties.

Smith began playing professionally at age 15 with Guitar Slim. In the early Fifties, after a stint with Earl King, he played sessions for Lloyd Price, Smiley Lewis and Little Richard. Meanwhile, he began writing songs and recording for Savoy. A weak singer, he was unsuccessful as a soloist. Consequently, he recruited the Clowns, originally Junior Gordon, Dave Dixon and Roland Cook. When he signed with Ace they included Bobby Marchan, "Scarface" John Williams and James Black. They had their first hit: "Rockin' Pneumonia and the Boogie Woogie Flu" (#52 pop, #9 R&B, 1957). A gold record, it was followed by the even bigger "Don't You Just Know It" (#9 pop, #4 R&B, 1958), with Gerri Hall, Eugene Francis and Billy Roosevelt singing behind Marchan.

Famous for their stage shenanigans and comic dancing, Smith and the Clowns were a popular live attraction throughout the U.S., but they had no more big hits after "Don't You Just Know It." Their best known record is probably one not credited to the group: Frankie Ford's 1959 hit "Sea Cruise," with Ford's vocal over a Clowns backup. The Clowns' own "Don't You Know Yockomo" reached #56 pop in 1959 before Marchan left the Clowns—to be replaced by Curley Moore—and Smith moved to Imperial. He returned to Ace with "Pop-Eye" (#51 pop, 1962) before the Clowns broke up.

Smith continued to work through the rest of the decade, but his success was local at best. He formed his own label, Pity-Pat, and recorded as the Hueys and Shindig Smith and the Soulshakers. In the early Seventies, he retired from show business.

PATTI SMITH

Born December 31, 1946, Chicago
1975—*Horses* (Arista) 1976—*Radio Ethiopia* 1978—*Easter* 1979—*Wave.*

In the early Seventies, painter-turned-poet and sometime playwright (*Cowboy Mouth,* with Sam Shepard) Patti Smith began to set her poems to the electric guitar backup of rock critic Lenny Kaye, who compiled the garage-band anthology *Nuggets.* By the end of the decade, she had proved remarkably influential, releasing what may be the first punk-rock record (the independent single "Hey Joe" b/w "Piss Factory," 1974) and claiming the rock-musician-as-shaman role previously reserved by males.

When she made "Hey Joe," Smith was working with only Kaye and pianist Richard Sohl. Along with Televi-

sion, she helped put New York's punk-rock landmark CBGB on the map, and her music grew toward rock & roll. Ivan Kral was added on guitar, and Jay Dee Daugherty left Lance Loud (of *"An American Family"*) and his group, the Mumps, to play drums. This lineup made *Horses,* produced by John Cale, an original mixture of exhortatory rock & roll ("Gloria," "Land of 1000 Dances"), Smith's poetry, vocal mannerisms copped from Mick Jagger, and the band's energetically rudimentary playing. Aerosmith producer Jack Douglas oversaw the Patti Smith group's second album, *Radio Ethiopia,* and the result was a more bombastic guitar-heavy record, tempered by the title cut, the height of Smith's improvised free rock.

A fall from a Florida stage hospitalized Smith in early 1977, during which time she wrote her fourth book of poetry, *Babel* (*Seventh Heaven, Witt* and *Kodak* preceding it). When able to perform again, the result was her most commercial LP, *Easter,* and her only Top Forty hit, "Because the Night," written by Bruce Springsteen and revised by Smith. She then began her withdrawal from rock & roll—her last album, *Wave,* was overtly religious. Soon after its release, Smith moved to Detroit to live with her new husband, Fred "Sonic" Smith (ex-MC5), and except for rare local appearances, dropped out of the music scene altogether.

Since the breakup of the Patti Smith Group, Daugherty has played with a variety of people, from folkies like the Roches and Willie Nile, to Tom Verlaine. Ivan Kral put in a stint with Iggy Pop (on the LP *Soldier*). Lenny Kaye leads the Lenny Kaye Connection and released an independent 45, "Child Bride," in 1981, while continuing to write occasionally for print.

PHOEBE SNOW

Born Phoebe Laub, July 17, 1952, New York City
1974—*Phoebe Snow* (Shelter/A&M) 1976—*Second Childhood* (Columbia) *It Looks Like Snow* 1978—*Never Letting Go; Against the Grain* 1981—*Rock Away* (Mirage).

With her supple contralto voice and melismatic jazz-scat abilities, Phoebe Snow burst onto the music scene with an impressive debut LP on Leon Russell's Shelter label that yielded the Top Five single "Poetry Man."

She had moved with her family from New York to Teaneck, New Jersey, at age three and did not take up music seriously until the late Sixties. A shy performer, she began to play Greenwich Village clubs in the early Seventies, singing blues, jazz and torch songs, as well as folk and pop. After her debut LP, she toured with Paul Simon and sang with him on his hit gospel single "Gone at Last." Her second LP did not match its predecessor's success although it did go Top Ten in the U.S. Since then, her LPs have fared moderately with both critics and audiences.

SOFT MACHINE

Formed 1966, Canterbury, England
Mike Ratledge, kybds.; Robert Wyatt (b. Robert
Ellidge, Bristol, Eng.), drums, voc.; Kevin Ayers (b.
Aug. 16, 1945, Kent, Eng.), gtr., voc., bass; Daevid
Allen (b. Austral.), gtr., voc.
1967—(− Allen; + Larry Nolan [b. Calif.], gtr.; −
Nolan) 1968—*The Soft Machine* (Probe) (− Ayers; +
Hugh Hopper, bass, gtr.) *Volume 2* (Columbia)
1970—(+ Elton Dean, sax; + Marc Charig, trumpet;
+ Nick Evans, trombone; + Lyn Dobson, flute, sax; +
Rob Spall, violin; − Evans) *Third* 1971—(− Charig;
− Dobson; − Spall) *Fourth* 1972—(− Wyatt; +
Phil Howard, drums; − Howard; + John Marshall,
drums) *Fifth* 1973—(− Dean; + Karl Jenkins, sax,
kybds.) *Sixth* (− Hopper; + Roy Babbington,
bass) *Seventh* 1975—(+ Allan Holdsworth, gtr.)
Bundles (Harvest) (− Holdsworth) 1976—(−
Ratledge; + John Etheridge, gtr.; + Alan Wakeman,
sax) *Softs* 1977—*Triple Echo* 1978—(− Bab-
bington; + Steve Cook, bass) *Alive and Well in
Paris* 1980—(− Etheridge; − Cook; + Jack Bruce [b.
May 14, 1943, Glasgow], bass, voc.; + Dick Morisey,
sax; + Alan Parker, gtr.) 1981—*Land of Cockayne*
(EMI).

The original Canterbury progressive British rock band
(along with Caravan, Gong, Hatfield and the North, National Health, Henry Cow), Soft Machine lasted through
seemingly endless personnel changes to become one of
Britain's most durable progressive-fusion units.

Actually, *the* original Canterbury band was the Wilde
Flowers, who got together at Canterbury's Simon
Langton School, where Mike Ratledge, Hugh Hopper,
Robert Wyatt and Caravan's David Sinclair were schoolmates. The Wilde Flowers existed in varying lineups from
1963 to 1965, usually gathering at the home of Wyatt's
mother, a writer and disc jockey who introduced her son
to modern jazz. (One writer later described a car ride with
Wyatt in which he whistled Charlie Parker's "Donna Lee"
solo note for note). Wyatt enrolled in the Canterbury
College of Art but dropped out to travel in Europe. There
he met beatnik/hippie and fellow avant-gardist Daevid
Allen. Hopper soon joined them. Upon their return to
Canterbury, they opened up the Wilde Flowers' jazz rock
to include more free-form experimentations and "pa-
taphysics," a sort of winsome absurdity derived from
French playwright Alfred Jarry. Ratledge came back to
Canterbury next from Oxford University; Hopper went
with Sinclair, Pye Hastings and Richard Coughlan to form
another version of the Wilde Flowers, which quickly
became Caravan. Ratledge formed Soft Machine with
Wyatt, Ayers and Allen; they got the name from the
William Burroughs novel.

After some rehearsal, Soft Machine went to London

and played with Pink Floyd at the psychedelic UFO club.
At this point guitarist Andy Summers (later with the
Police) occasionally played with them. In London they
met producer Kim Fowley, with whom they recorded two
songs, "Feelin' Reelin' Squealin' " and "Love Makes
Sweet Music" (reissued on *At the Beginning*); Jimi Hendrix, who was recording "Hey Joe" in the same studio,
played some rhythm guitar. The records made little impact
in England, and Soft Machine went back to France,
settling in St. Tropez, where they soon attracted much
notoriety as the center of "happenings" surrounding Alan
Zion's production of the Picasso play *Désir Attrapé par la
Queue*. When they finally returned to Britain late in 1967,
Allen had visa problems; he went back to Paris and later
founded Gong.

Soft Machine played some shows as a trio and opened
Hendrix's 1968 U.S. tour (Wyatt painted a suit and tie on
his bare torso on that tour). In New York, they recorded
their debut LP with producer Tom Wilson.

After the tour and recording sessions, Soft Machine
temporarily disbanded. Ayers went to Ibiza, then Majorca, to write before forming his own band, the Whole
World; Ratledge went to London; and Wyatt stayed in the
U.S. The record company pressured Wyatt to reassemble
the group. Ayers was replaced by Hopper. The new band
recorded *Volume Two*, less a concept album than a stream-
of-consciousness LP, with 17 tracks bleeding into each
other over two sides and jazz influences ranging from
cocktail to avant-garde. Toward the end of a long U.K.
tour, they added a horn section from Keith Tippett's
Centipede Orchestra for *Third*, sax player Elton Dean
stayed on to help on *Fourth*, a double LP of four side-long
compositions (including Wyatt's magnum opus, "Moon in
June"), which again won heavy critical acclaim but sold
only moderately.

In 1971, Wyatt began to grow disenchanted with Soft
Machine, as the band became more and more formulaic.
He left after recording *Fourth* and formed Matching Mole,
who recorded two LPs. He went on to have a critically
respected career as a solo performer, though an accident
left him paralyzed from the waist down. With Ratledge's
fuzz organ the sole sonic link with the band's past, and
Wyatt apparently taking the band's verbal wit with him,
Soft Machine gradually devolved into just another jazz-
rock fusion band, recruiting members from other such
British units as Nucleus (whence came John Jenkins and
Karl Marshall).

Hopper went on to record solo concept LPs like *1984*, to
form a band called Isotope and to work with reedman
Elton Dean in Soft Heap. Ayers maintained a respectable
solo-singer/songwriter career of his own. Marshall and
Babbington have returned to the jazz and jazz-rock
scenes. Ratledge quit Soft Machine in 1976 (replaced by
Rick Wakeman's brother Alan), leaving the band with *no*
original members.

SONNY AND CHER

Salvatore Bono, born February 16, 1935, Detroit;
Cherilyn Sarkasian LaPier, born May 20, 1946, El
Centro, California
1965—*Baby, Don't Go* (Reprise) *Look at Us* (Atco)
1966—*Wondrous World of Sonny and Cher* 1967—*In Case You're in Love; Good Times; Best of Sonny and Cher* 1971—*Live* (Kapp) 1972—*All I Ever Need Is You* 1973—*Live in Las Vegas, Volume 2* (MCA) *Mama Was a Rock and Roll Singer, Papa Used to Write All Her Songs* 1974—*Greatest Hits.*
Cher solo: 1965—*All I Really Wanna Do* (Imperial)
1966—*Cher* 1967—*With Love* 1968—*Backstage*
1969—*3614 Jackson Highway* (Atco) 1971—*Cher* (Kapp) 1972—*Foxy Lady* 1973—*Half-Breed* (MCA) *Bittersweet White Light* 1974—*Dark Lady; Cher's Greatest Hits* 1975—*The Very Best of, Volume II* (United Artists) *Stars* (Warners) 1976—*I'd Rather Believe in You* 1979—*Take Me Home* (Casablanca)
1980—*Black Rose* 1982—*I Paralyze* (Columbia).

Sonny and Cher were a husband-and-wife team who enjoyed a brief period of success as wildly garbed pop singers, followed by a slightly longer stretch when their Vegas-style singing and stand-up comedy found favor with a nationwide TV audience. The partnership ended in divorce, and Cher went on to a solo career as singer, actress and garishly gowned celebrity.

Bono spent years trying to break into the music business as a songwriter. In 1957, he placed "High School Dance" on the B side of Larry Williams' "Short Fat Fannie." When Sonny's tune reached #90 in its own right, he became a staff producer at Specialty, where he also began recording under the name Don Christy. He had no particular success until 1964, when "Needles and Pins," which he cowrote with Jack Nitzsche, became a big hit for the Searchers. By this time, Sonny was working for Phil Spector as writer and backup vocalist.

In 1963, he met Cher singing backup on some of Spector's sessions. They married in 1964 and made a couple of unsuccessful singles under various names (Caesar and Cleo) for Vault and Reprise before signing to Atco in 1965. Their first chart entry was the million-seller "I Got You Babe" (#1, 1965). Then came "Baby Don't Go" (#8, 1965), "The Beat Goes On" (#6, 1967) and "solo" hits like Sonny's "Laugh at Me" (#10, 1965) and Cher's "All I Really Wanna Do" (#15, 1965), "Bang Bang (My Baby Shot Me Down)" (#2, 1966) and "You Better Sit Down Kids" (#9, 1967). The pair also made two movies: *Good Times* (1967) and *Chastity* (1969, written by Sonny, starring Cher, named for their daughter). The pop hits slowed at the end of the Sixties.

Produced by Snuff Garrett, Sonny and Cher bounced back in 1971–72 with a pair of Top Ten hits: "All I Ever Need Is You" (#7, 1971) and "A Cowboy's Work Is Never Done" (#8, 1972). These led to the TV series (1971–75) that made them household names, even as their marriage was breaking up. During and after the split, both tried solo careers and had solo TV shows. Cher, the more successful one, had four Top Ten hits in this period, including three #1s—"Gypsys, Tramps and Thieves" (1971), "Half-Breed" (1973) and "Dark Lady" (1974) and "The Way of Love" (#7, 1972). Cher began some highly publicized liaisons: with Gregg Allman (whom she married, had a son by, and made an album—*Allman and Woman: Two the Hard Way* [1977]—with); Kiss's Gene Simmons; and Les Dudek, with whom she made her latest attempt at a comeback with the hard-rock band Black Rose. In 1982, Cher made her Broadway debut in the Robert Altman–directed play *Come Back to the 5 and Dime, Jimmy Dean, Jimmy Dean,* which was also released as a movie.

SOUL

A merger of gospel-charged singing, secular subject matter and funk rhythms, soul grew out of Fifties rhythm & blues, spurred by Ray Charles' eclectic, decidedly secular late-Fifties hits. In soul's mid-Sixties heyday, there were distinctive regional styles: gritty, gospelly shouting over a stripped-down backup in Memphis (Otis Redding, Sam and Dave, Wilson Pickett); smoothly orchestrated pop-soul in Chicago (the Impressions, Jerry Butler); architectonic, dramatic mini-epics at Motown in Detroit (Marvin Gaye, the Temptations, Smokey Robinson, the Supremes); and a little of them all in New York (Aretha Franklin). There's no clear division between late-Sixties soul and the black pop that followed it; but at some point, music for dancing—funk, later disco—and music for listening—pop ballads—moved decisively apart.

"Soul" was also a black slang term for authenticity and sincerity, but after it moved into the mainstream vocabulary in the late Sixties the term became diluted and, eventually, unhip.

SOUL SURVIVORS

Formed 1966, New York City
Kenneth Jeremiah, voc.; Richard Ingui, voc.; Charles Ingui, voc.; Paul Venturini, organ; Edward Leonetti, gtr.; Joey Forigone, drums.

Kenneth Jeremiah and the Ingui brothers were a New York vocal trio, the Dedications, until meeting Paul Venturini, Edward Leonetti and Joey Forigone. They changed their name to the Soul Survivors and relocated to Philadelphia, where they hooked up with Gamble and Huff, who wrote and produced "Expressway to Your Heart." It became a Top Five hit on both the pop and R&B charts in 1967, but turned out to be their last success. When it was discovered that the group was white, R&B airplay slowed. When their next two singles failed, pop radio lost interest as well. The band broke up a few years later and a 1974 comeback proved unsuccessful.

JOE SOUTH
Born February 28, 1942, Atlanta
1968—*Introspect* (Capitol) (reissued as *Games People Play*) **1969**—*Don't It Make You Want to Go Home* **1971**—*So the Seeds are Growing* **1975**—*Midnight Rainbows* (Island).

Joe South was a successful sessionman who went on to become a hit songwriter and performer, crossing over from country to pop in the early Seventies.

At age 11, South got his first guitar, and a year later he was appearing regularly on Atlanta country music station WGST. In 1957, he joined the band of Pete Drake, the famed country pedal steel guitar player, and in the early Sixties he recorded some unsuccessful solo singles, including "Purple People Eater Meets the Witch Doctor." He also worked for a while as a country disc jockey.

South became a regular session guitarist in Nashville and Muscle Shoals, backing up country artists like Marty Robbins and Eddy Arnold, in addition to Bob Dylan and Aretha Franklin. He appears on Simon and Garfunkel's "Sounds of Silence." South had also begun to do some songwriting, and in the mid-Sixties he wrote hits for the Tams ("Untie Me"), Billy Joe Royal ("Down in the Boondocks") and early Deep Purple ("Hush"). By 1968, South was recording his own material.

Introspect at first sold marginally, but when other performers began to cover "Games People Play," Capitol reissued the LP in 1969 under that title. They also released the song as a single, and both album and single went gold. It also won a Grammy as Song of the Year. *So the Seeds Are Growing* included his 1970 hit "Walk a Mile in My Shoes" (#12). His "I Never Promised You a Rose Garden" became an international country and pop hit for Lynn Anderson (#3, 1971). In 1971, South took time off, in part to recuperate from a hectic schedule and also because of the death of his brother Tommy. He lived awhile in the jungles of Maui, Hawaii, and did not record again until 1975, when *Midnight Rainbows* was released on Island.

THE SOUTHER-HILLMAN-FURAY BAND
Formed 1973, Los Angeles
John David Souther (b. Detroit), gtr., voc.; Richie Furay (b. May 9, 1944, Yellow Springs, Oh.), gtr., voc.; Chris Hillman (b. Dec. 4, 1942, Los Angeles), bass, gtr., mandolin, voc.; Paul Harris (b. New York City), kybds.; Al Perkins, steel gtr.; Jim Gordon, drums.
1974—*Souther-Hillman-Furay Band* (Asylum) (− Gordon; + Ron Grinel, drums) **1975**—*Trouble in Paradise*.

Formed at the instigation of Asylum Records chief David Geffen as a ready-made Crosby Stills and Nash–type country-rock band, Souther-Hillman-Furay claimed connections with just about every other notable country-rock band: Richie Furay had been in Buffalo Springfield and Poco; Chris Hillman in the Byrds, the Flying Burrito Brothers and Stephen Stills's Manassas; J. D. Souther in Longbranch Pennywhistle with the Eagles' Glenn Frey, as well as having made one solo album and writing songs for other artists, including Bonnie Raitt and Linda Ronstadt. Al Perkins had also been with the Burritos and Manassas, and the others were experienced sessionmen.

Despite great expectations and a massive promotional campaign, the chemistry was wrong. Though their first LP went gold, the second was not nearly so well received, and SHF disbanded shortly after its release, each member going on to a solo career.

SOUTHSIDE JOHNNY AND THE ASBURY JUKES
Formed 1974, Asbury Park, New Jersey
Southside Johnny (b. John Lyon, Dec. 4, 1948, Neptune, N.J.), voc., harmonica; Billy Rush (b. Aug. 26, 1952), gtr.; Kevin Kavanaugh (b. Aug. 27, 1951), kybds., voc.; Al Berger (b. Nov. 8, 1949), bass, voc.; Kenny Pentifallo (b. Dec. 30, 1940), drums; Carlo Novi (b. Aug. 7, 1949, Mexico City), tenor sax; Eddie Manion (b. Feb. 28, 1952), baritone sax; Tony Palligrosi (b. May 9, 1954), trumpet; Ricky Gazda (b. June 18, 1952), trumpet; Richie "La Bamba" Rosenberg, trombone.
1976—*I Don't Wanna Go Home* (Epic) **1977**—*This Time It's for Real* (− Pentifallo; − Novi) **1978**—*Hearts of Stone* (+ Steve Becker, drums; + Joe Gramalin, gtr.) **1979**—*The Jukes* (Mercury) **1980**—*Love Is a Sacrifice* (− Berger; + Gene Bacia, bass) **1981**—*Live/Reach Up and Touch the Sky*.

Southside Johnny and the Asbury Jukes are an R&B-influenced rock band who graduated from the Asbury Park bar-band scene soon after Bruce Springsteen's massive success.

Johnny Lyon, Springsteen and Springsteen guitarist Miami Steve Van Zandt played together in the late Sixties in Asbury Park bands like the Sundance Blues Band and Dr. Zoom and the Sonic Boom. Lyon got his nickname because he liked blues from the South Side of Chicago. After migrating to Richmond, Virginia, with a band called Studio B, Lyon returned to Asbury Park and formed a duo with Van Zandt called Southside Johnny and the Kid, which became the Bank Street Blues Band with keyboardist Kevin Kavanaugh. In 1974, Van Zandt left again to go on the road with the Dovells (of "Bristol Stomp" fame), whose backing band also included bassist Al Berger. Lyon then joined the Blackberry Booze Band, which included drummer Kenny Pentifallo. With the addition of a horn section, they became the Asbury Jukes. Van Zandt briefly rejoined them before moving on to Springsteen's band.

The Jukes became mainstays at Asbury Park's top barroom, the Stone Pony. After Springsteen's successful

1975 U.S. and European tours, Van Zandt became the Jukes' manager/producer and landed them a recording contract. Their debut LP, which included two Springsteen tunes and guest appearances by Ronnie Spector and Lee Dorsey, sold well. *This Time* featured more Van Zandt and Springsteen tunes and included guest shots by members of the Coasters, the Drifters and the Five Satins.

Their third LP, with guest appearances by Van Zandt and E Street Band drummer Max Weinberg, still contained many Van Zandt and Springsteen titles. On their self-titled fourth LP, the Jukes declared their independence from the Springsteen imprimatur by writing all their own material (Lyon and Rush are the main composers). While their albums began to sell less well, they remain a successful touring unit.

BOB B. SOXX AND THE BLUE JEANS
Formed 1963, New York City
Bob B. Soxx (b. Robert Sheen); Darlene Love (b. Darlene Wright); Fanita James.
1963—*Zip-A-Dee Doo-Dah* (Philles).

Out of Phil Spector's Wall of Sound stable came vocal group Bob B. Soxx and the Blue Jeans in 1963, with their only big hit a revamped swinging version of "Zip-A-Dee Doo-Dah" (#8), a tune from the Disney film *Song of the South*. The LP also included covers of tunes like "This Land Is Your Land," "Let the Good Times Roll" and "The White Cliffs of Dover."

Spector had been initially attracted to Robert Sheen (a.k.a. Bob B. Soxx) because his voice reminded him of Clyde McPhatter's. All of the Blue Jeans had been singing since their early teens. Though they only had three chart hits, the group was a mainstay of the rock-concert circuit between 1963 and 1965. Darlene Love went on to have some hits of her own for Spector.

THE SPANIELS
Formed 1952, Gary, Indiana
James "Pookie" Hudson; Gerald Gregory; Opal Courtney, Jr.; Ernest Warren; Willis C. Jackson.
1954—(− Courtney, Warren, Jackson; + Donald Porter, Carl Rainge, James Cochran)   **1956**—*Goodnight, It's Time to Go* (Vee Jay).

A mid-Fifties doo-wop vocal group, the Spaniels had several big R&B hits but never crossed over into pop-chart success.

They had begun as street singers in the Gary, Indiana, ghetto, and attracted the attention of local disc jockey Vivian Carter, who became their manager and with James Bracken formed Vee Jay Records to release their material. The Spaniels' first single was "Baby, It's You," a Top Ten R&B hit in 1953, which established both the band and Vee Jay Records (whose roster would later include Jimmy Reed and Jerry Butler, among others).

In early 1954, their "Goodnite, Sweetheart, Goodnite" was a #5 R&B hit (covered on the pop chart by the McGuire Sisters); in 1973 it was used as the closing theme for the film *American Graffiti*. The Spaniels became a top live attraction on the national R&B circuit, but in 1954 the original group disbanded. With three new members, the re-formed group continued to chart, notably with "Everyone's Laughing" (#69 pop, #13 R&B, 1957). The Spaniels began fading in the late Fifties, and in 1961 they broke up again. In 1969, "Pookie" re-formed the Spaniels. They toured the revival circuit and in 1970 released "Fairy Tales" on Lloyd Price's Calla label (#45 R&B).

SPANKY AND OUR GANG
Formed 1966, Chicago
Elaine "Spanky" McFarlane (b. June 19, 1942, Peoria, Ill.), voc.; Malcolm Hale (b. May 17, 1941, Butte, Mont.; d. 1968), gtr., voc.; Kenny Hodges (b. Jacksonville, Fla.), gtr., voc., bass; Nigel Pickering (b. June 15, 1929, Pontiac, Mich.), bass, gtr., voc.; Lefty Baker (b. Eustace Britchforth, Roanoke, Va.), gtr., banjo, voc.; John Seiter (b. Aug. 17, 1944, St. Louis, Mo.), drums, voc.
1967—*Spanky and Our Gang* (Mercury)   **1968**—*Like to Get to Know You; Without Rhyme or Reason*   **1970**—*Spanky's Greatest Hits; Live*   **1975**—*Change* (Epic).

Along with the Mamas and the Papas, Spanky and Our Gang were part of the late-Sixties folk/pop vocal-group movement, with major pop hits like "Lazy Days," "Sunday Will Never Be the Same," "Like to Get to Know You" and "Give a Damn." In 1982, Spanky joined the re-formed Mamas and the Papas.

Elaine McFarlane had met Mama Cass Elliot in the early Sixties, and then joined "an electric comedy-jug band," the New Wine Singers, which included Malcolm Hale. "Spanky" met Nigel Pickering, Kenny Hodges and Lefty Baker while vacationing in Florida. As a quartet they debuted at the Mother Blues club and were an immediate success; they were signed by Chicago-based Mercury Records. Malcolm Hale and John Seiter then joined. They took their name from the "Little Rascals" TV series.

The Gang began racking up a string of soft-rock/folk-pop hits like "Sunday Will Never Be the Same" (#9), "Making Every Minute Count" (#31) and "Lazy Day" (#14) in 1967; "Like to Get to Know You" (#17) and "Sunday Morning" (#30) in 1968. They were often featured on network TV variety shows, though in 1969 their ghetto-consciousness protest song "Give a Damn" was banned on many radio stations. Though Hale had died of cirrhosis in 1968 during the mixing of *Without Rhyme or Reason*, they retained the rest of the original lineup until the hits stopped in 1970.

In 1975 McFarlane and Pickering re-formed the band

with three new members, playing Texas bars until 1980; McFarlane also appeared on Roger McGuinn's solo debut album. Then came the Mamas and the Papas reunion, with McFarlane even being called "Mama Spanky" by the rest of the group. Their initial concert tour was a success, but as of this writing they haven't released any recordings.

THE SPECIALS
Formed 1977, Coventry, England
Jerry Dammers, kybds.; Horace Panter, bass; Lynval Golding, gtr.; Roddy Byers, gtr.; Terry Hall, voc.; Neville Staples, voc.; John Bradbury, drums.
1979—*The Specials* (Chrysalis)   **1980**—*More Specials*.

The Specials were the prime movers behind England's short-lived two-tone movement of 1979-81, which also included Madness, the Selecter, the English Beat and several other bands. (The original fans often sported two-tone clothes and the band was racially mixed; ergo the title of the "movement.")

Coming together from mid-1977 to early 1978 in Coventry, the Specials initially played both fast punk and slower roots reggae. But they were unable to bring the two sounds together into a recognizable package, so they reoriented themselves toward ska, an upbeat precursor to reggae that was fashionable in England among mods and skinheads in the mid-Sixties.

By early 1979, after a 1978 tour with the Clash, the Specials cut an independent single, "Gangsters," but for its B side they used a cut by another struggling band, the Selecter. Pressed on the band's 2-Tone label, the single soared to #6 on the British charts. That led to a distribution deal with Chrysalis in June 1979. Soon their 2-Tone label gave British hits to a whole movement of bands—the Selecter, the Beat and Madness—making it for a while the most successful independent English label since Stiff.

The Specials' debut LP, out in the U.S. in early 1980, was produced by Elvis Costello. Like that of most neo-ska bands, the music was danceable and charged with anti-racist sentiment. Most of the music was by leader Jerry Dammers, but it also included the 1967 ska anthem "A Message to You Rudy."

The Specials were stars in England but made little impression in America, except with critics. Their follow-up LP confused even the few fans they had here. Released in late 1980, *More Specials* had elements of cocktail jazz, cabaret theatricality, odd pop and not much ska. The 2-Tone label soon fell apart, with the Beat, the Selecter and Madness all going to other companies. But the Specials hit a poignant high point in England in the summer of 1981 when they released "Ghost Town." It was inspired by the unemployment and racial tensions in England, and its release coincided with black-white riots in Brixton and Liverpool. (Black guitarist Golding was himself a victim of a racial attack, having his throat slashed and requiring 27

stitches.) The single went #1 in England, although it was banned from airplay by the BBC.

Soon after that, though, in October, the band fell apart after vocalists Hall and Staples plus Golding quit to form Fun Boy Three. That band released an eponymous LP in 1982 on Chrysalis. Their second album, *Waiting*, was produced by David Byrne of Talking Heads.

PHIL SPECTOR
Born December 25, 1940, Bronx, New York
1963—*A Christmas Gift to You* (Philles) (reissued 1967 by Spector as *Phil Spector's Christmas Album*)   **1977**—*Phil Spector's Greatest Hits* (Warner Bros.) (compilation).

Twenty years after its heyday, Phil Spector's Wall of Sound still stands as a milestone in recording history. It changed the course of pop record producing and left some of rock's best-loved music. Spector raised pop production's ambition and sophistication by overdubbing scores of musicians—five or six guitars, three or four pianos, and an army of percussion, including multiple drum kits, castanets, tambourines, bells and timpani—to create a massive roar. Spector called it "a Wagnerian approach to rock & roll: little symphonies for the kids."

Spector was raised in the Bronx but moved with his mother to Los Angeles at age twelve after his father died. He began learning guitar and piano while at Fairfax High School, and at 16 played with local jazz combos. In high school, Spector met Marshall Lieb, and in 1957 the two began writing songs. In early 1958, another friend, Annette Bard, joined them to form the trio the Teddy Bears. In short order they had a Top Ten U.S. and U.K. hit with Spector's first production, "To Know Him Is to Love Him," taken from the inscription on Spector's father's gravestone ("To Know Him Was to Love Him"). The Teddy Bears appeared on national television, but did not produce a follow-up hit and disbanded in 1959.

Spector then enrolled in UCLA, and also worked as a part-time court stenographer. He dropped out and moved back to New York, where he hoped to become a U.N. interpreter in French. But he soon returned to L.A., where he decided to reenter the record business. The 18-year-old Spector approached independent producers Lester Sill and Lee Hazlewood and persuaded them to take him under their wing. At this time, he formed another group, the Spectors Three, but after several flops they disbanded and Spector concentrated on producing.

In 1960, Sill and Hazlewood sent Spector to New York, where he worked with hitmakers Jerry Leiber and Mike Stoller. With Leiber he cowrote "Spanish Harlem," a mammoth 1960 hit for Ben E. King. Spector also played the guitar break in the Drifters' "On Broadway." He became staff producer for Dunes Records and produced Ray Peterson's "Corinna, Corinna," a Top Ten hit. By this time he was also a freelance producer and A&R man at Atlantic Records as well as an independent producer. He produced Gene Pitney's "Every Breath I Take" and Curtis Lee's "Pretty Little Angel Eyes." Back on the West Coast, the Paris Sisters' "I Love How You Love Me" and the Ducanes' "Little Did I Know" followed. The youthful Spector was becoming an industry sensation.

While these late-1961 hits were still on the charts, Spector returned to New York and with Sill formed Philles (from Phil and Les) Records. He began recording a girl group called the Crystals, who hit in early 1962 with "There's No Other (Like My Baby)." Their next Spector-produced hit, "Uptown," was an even bigger success; and then came "He Hit Me (And It Felt Like a Kiss)," which was banned in some markets because of its lyrics, and the million-selling "He's a Rebel." Spector bought out Sill's part of Philles in late 1962.

At 21, Spector was a millionaire. He began recording on the West Coast, where he crafted his Wall of Sound in earnest, using such sessionmen as guitarists Glen Campbell, Sonny Bono and Barney Kessel, pianist Leon Russell and drummer Hal Blaine. Within three years, Spector had twenty consecutive smash hits, including the Crystals' "Da Doo Ron Ron," "Then He Kissed Me" and "He's Sure the Boy That I Love"; the Ronettes' "Be My Baby," "Baby I Love You," "The Best Part of Breaking Up" and "Walking in the Rain"; Darlene Love's "Today I Met the Boy I'm Gonna Marry" and "Wait Till My Bobby Gets Home"; and Bob B. Soxx and the Blue Jeans' "Zip-a-Dee Doo-Dah." The Righteous Brothers' "You've Lost That Lovin' Feeling" sold over two million copies. In 1963, Spector made a Christmas album, featuring Darlene Love's "Christmas (Baby Please Come Home)" and the Ronettes' "Santa Claus Is Coming to Town."

By this time, however, Spector had made more enemies than friends in the record business. In 1966 came the turning point, with Ike and Tina Turner's "River Deep, Mountain High." Spector considered it his greatest production to date, but it became a hit only in England.

Embittered, Spector went into seclusion for two years, during which time reports of strange, near-psychotic behavior on his part filtered out of his 23-room Hollywood mansion: Spector allegedly mentally abused his wife, Ronnie (formerly of the Ronettes); Spector carried a gun. Except for a cameo appearance as a dope pusher in the film *Easy Rider* and some hits for Sonny Charles and the Checkmates—"Love Is All I Have to Give," "Black Pearl" and "Proud Mary" (the latter employed some 300 musicians)—he remained inactive through the late Sixties.

In 1969, Spector was brought in to do a remix on the Beatles' *Let It Be*. He proved he could adapt to more minimal arrangements with Lennon's "Imagine," which he coproduced, and he returned to the Wall of Sound style for George Harrison's *All Things Must Pass* LP. In 1971, Spector oversaw production of Harrison's *The Concert*

for Bangladesh and produced the studio sides of John Lennon and Yoko Ono's *Some Time in New York City*. In 1973, he formed Warner-Spector Records with Warner Bros., but little came of the association. In 1974 and 1975, he survived two near-fatal auto accidents, and in late 1975 formed Spector International, which reissued the *Christmas Album* and *Greatest Hits* packages, and found Spector working with Cher, Dion, Harry Nilsson, Darlene Love and Spector's latest "discovery," Jerri Bo Keno, still using L.A.'s Gold Star Studios, where he'd made his classics. More recently, Spector produced Leonard Cohen's *Death of a Ladies' Man* and the Ramones' *End of the Century*.

RONNIE SPECTOR
Born Veronica Bennett, August 10, 1943, New York City
1981—Siren (Polish).

With her sultry image and throbbing voice, Ronnie Spector first came to prominence as a protegée of pop producer Phil Spector in the Ronettes, the vocal group (including her sister Estelle and their cousin Nedra Talley) that Spector named after her.

The group had first gotten together as a dancing team doing the Twist in the early Sixties at the Peppermint Lounge clubs in New York City and Miami Beach, and then, with Spector, had a string of mid-Sixties pop hits including "Be My Baby" and "Walking in the Rain." Veronica Bennett married Spector in 1967, lived with him in a 23-room California mansion in the late Sixties during Spector's period of reclusion, had their son Donte in 1969, and was divorced from Spector in 1974.

In 1971, she recorded a failed comeback single, "Try Some Buy Some," coproduced by Spector and George Harrison. In 1977, another comeback, "Say Goodbye to Hollywood," written by Billy Joel and produced by Miami Steve Van Zandt and featuring Bruce Springsteen's E Street Band, made the U.S. Top Forty. She made several live appearances with the Asbury Jukes. In late 1980, with Genya Ravan producing, she made an album and a single, "Darlin'," which sold poorly. She continues to tour.

CHRIS SPEDDING
Born June 17, 1944, Sheffield, England
1970—Backwood Progression (Harvest, import)
1972—The Only Lick I Know   1976—Chris Spedding
(RAK)   **1977—Hurt   1979—Guitar Graffiti   1980—I'm
Not Like Everybody Else.**

Chris Spedding is one of the most widely experienced session guitarists in rock.

Spedding first learned violin as a youngster, but by his early teens gave it up for guitar. He joined a hometown band, the Vulcans, in the late Fifties, went with them to London and then joined a country band that toured U.S. Army bases for three years. In 1964, he spent a year on the ship *Himalaya* entertaining passengers; upon his return to London, he worked with ex-Animal Alan Price and ex-Manfred Mann vocalist Paul Jones. In 1967, he formed Battered Ornaments with Pete Brown, through whom Spedding met ex-Cream bassist Jack Bruce (for whom Brown wrote lyrics). When Battered Ornaments disbanded in 1969, Spedding took his first session job on Bruce's *Songs for a Tailor* LP. He then briefly worked with Ian Carr's jazz-fusion band Nucleus and has since played fusion with Keith Tippett, Mike Westbrook and Mike Gibbs.

For the next few years, Spedding became one of Britain's busiest session guitarists, working with Lulu, Gilbert O'Sullivan, Dusty Springfield, David Essex, Donovan (he wrote string arrangements on Donovan's *Cosmic Wheels* LP) and John Cale, among many more. During this period he recorded two solo LPs.

In 1972, Spedding and ex-Free bassist Andy Fraser formed the hard-rock band Sharks (which included session bassist, Busta Jones, who went on to play with Brian Eno, Talking Heads and Gang of Four). They made two albums, then broke up in 1974; Spedding worked with Jones on Eno's 1974 *Here Come the Warm Jets*. In 1975, Spedding joined session bassist Dave Cochran and ex-Yes/King Crimson drummer Bill Bruford to form the backing band Trigger for British folk-rock singer/songwriter Roy Harper. Trigger backed Harper on what many consider his best album, *HQ* (reissued as *When an Old Cricketer Leaves the Crease* in the U.S.), and on a 1975 U.K. tour, then disbanded. Spedding then teamed with British pop producer Mickie Most for his next solo album. Spedding's eponymous 1976 solo album yielded the Top Ten U.K. hit "Motorbikin'," and included "Guitar Jamboree," in which Spedding imitated just about every famous rock guitarist in rapid succession. During the Seventies, Spedding reportedly turned down an offer to join the Rolling Stones.

Spedding also played sessions with Roxy Music singer Bryan Ferry (on *Let's Stick Together* and *In Your Mind*) and British punk band the Vibrators. He also reportedly played power chords for the first Sex Pistols singles.

In 1979, Spedding teamed up with ex-Tuff Darts singer Robert Gordon. In 1980, he played with the New York band the Necessaries, and in 1981 formed a New York trio with Busta Jones and drummer David Van Tieghem, who had worked with minimalist composer Steve Reich and Brian Eno, among others.

THE SPINNERS

Formed 1957, Detroit
Bobby Smith (b. Apr. 10), tenor voc.; Pervis Jackson (b. May 16), bass voc.; Henry Fambrough (b. May 10), baritone voc.; Billy Henderson (b. Aug. 9), tenor-baritone voc.; George W. Dixon, tenor voc.
1962—(– Dixon; + Edgar Edwards, tenor voc.)

1967—*The Original Spinners* (Motown) (– Edwards; + G. C. Cameron, tenor voc.) 1972—(– Cameron; + Phillipe Wynne [b. April 3,], tenor voc.) 1973—*Spinners* (Atlantic) 1974—*Mighty Love; New and Improved Spinners* 1975—*Pick of the Litter; Spinners Live!* 1976—*Happiness Is Being with the Spinners* 1977—*Yesterday, Today and Tomorrow* (– Wynne; + John Edwards [b. St. Louis], tenor voc.) 8 1978—*The Best of the Spinners; From Here to Eternally* 1979—*Dancin' and Lovin'* 1980—*Love Trippin'* 1981—*Superstar Series, Volume 9* (Motown) *Labor of Love* (Atlantic) *Can't Shake This Feeling*.

The Spinners' got started in the late Fifties, when singer/producer Harvey Fuqua organized a group of young singers to replace the original Moonglows (who had included Marvin Gaye). When Fuqua founded his own Tri-Phi records, the group's name was changed to the Spinners. The first Spinners single, "That's What Girls Are Made For" (#5 R&B) in 1961, featured Fuqua singing lead. Over the next several years, there was a complete turnover in personnel, with Henry Fambrough, Pervis Jackson, Billy Henderson, Edgar Edwards and Bobby Smith performing under the name Bobby Smith and the Spinners. They cut several singles on the Time label before joining Motown in 1965 as the Detroit Spinners.

Although the group had some hits at Motown, such as "I'll Always Love You" (#8 R&B) in 1965, "Truly Yours" (#16 R&B) in 1966, "We'll Have It Made" (#20 R&B) in 1971 and the Stevie Wonder–produced-and-penned "It's a Shame" (#14 pop, #4 R&B) in 1970, the company never considered them a major act. G. C. Cameron was lead singer for much of the late Sixties, and Edwards had left.

In 1972, the Spinners moved to Atlantic Records and were teamed with Philadelphia producer Thom Bell. Newcomer Phillipe Wynne was now handling most of the lead vocals, and from 1972 to 1979 the Spinners' close-harmony ballads regularly topped the R&B and pop charts. Their hits included "I'll Be Around" (#3 pop, #1 R&B) and "Could It Be I'm Falling in Love" (#4 pop, #1 R&B), 1972; "One of a Kind (Love Affair)" (#11 pop, #1 R&B) and "Ghetto Child" (#4 R&B), 1973; "Mighty Love, Part I" (#20 pop, #1 R&B), "I'm Coming Home" (#18 pop, #13 R&B) and, with Dionne Warwick, "Then Came You" (#1 pop, #2 R&B), 1974; "Sadie" (#7 R&B) and "They Just Can't Stop It (the Games People Play)" (#5 pop, #1 R&B), 1975; "Wake Up Susan" (#11 R&B) and "The Rubberband Man" (#2 pop, #1 R&B), 1976; "You're Throwing a Good Love Away" (#5 R&B), 1977; and "If You Wanna Do a Dance" (#17 R&B), 1978.

In 1977, Wynne left for a solo career (he also toured with Parliament-Funkadelic) and was replaced by John Edwards. In 1979, the Spinners returned to the charts with a remake of the Four Seasons' "Working My Way Back to You" (#2 pop, #6 R&B). They continue to tour and record.

SPIRIT

Formed 1967, Los Angeles
Randy California (b. Feb. 20, 1951, Los Angeles), gtr.,
voc.; Jay Ferguson (b. John Arden Ferguson, May 10,
1947, Burbank, Calif.), gtr., kybds., voc.; John Locke
(b. Sep. 25, 1943, Los Angeles), kybds., voc.; Mark
Andes (b. Feb. 19, 1948, Philadelphia), bass, voc.; Ed
Cassidy (b. May 4, 1931, Chicago), drums.
1968—*Spirit* (Ode) *The Family That Plays Together*
1969—*Clear Spirit* **1970**—*The Twelve Dreams of Dr.
Sardonicus* (Epic) **1971**—(− Ferguson; − Andes;
− California; + Chris Staehely [b. Tex.], gtr., voc.; +
Al Staehely [b. Tex.], bass, voc.) *Feedback* **1974**—
(group re-forms: California; Cassidy; Barry Keene,
bass) **1975**—*Spirit of 76* (Mercury) (+ John Locke,
kybds., voc.) **1976**—*Son of Spirit* (+ Andes; + Matt
Andes, gtr.) *Farther Along* **1977**—*Future Games (A
Magical Kahvana Dream)* (− Locke; − Andes; −
Andes; + Larry Knight, bass) *Live* (made in Germany)
(Potato) **1981**—*Journey to Potatoland* (Beggar's
Banquet/Rhino).

Though they did have one hit single, "I Got a Line on
You," Spirit were known primarily for their albums: an
ambitious, eclectic blend of hard rock, blues, country folk
and pre-fusion jazz.

Shaven-headed drummer Ed Cassidy met Randy California while he was dating the latter's mother (whom he
later married) when Randy was 13. He joined Randy's
band, the Red Roosters, which had been formed in 1965
and featured most of the original Spirit lineup. Previously,
Cassidy had drummed for jazzmen Thelonious Monk, Art
Pepper, Cannonball Adderley and Gerry Mulligan on the
West Coast in the mid-Fifties, and in the early Sixties had
formed his own New Jazz Trio. In 1965, he joined Rising
Sons with Ry Cooder and Taj Mahal, but was forced to
leave the group after injuring his hand.

John Locke, who claimed to be a direct descendant of
the British philosopher of the same name, first encountered Cassidy in the New Jazz Trio. At UCLA, he later
met Mark Andes and Jay Ferguson, who had grown up
together in the San Fernando Valley. Andes' band, the
Marksmen, had played sessions with Bobby "Boris"
Pickett, among others. Ferguson had met California while
with a bluegrass band, the Oat Hill Stump Straddlers. In
1965, Cassidy joined California, Ferguson and Andes in
the Red Roosters, but they broke up in 1966.

In New York, Cassidy and California played in sessions, and joined numerous bands. Meanwhile, Ferguson
formed Western Union with Mark and his brother Matt
Andes; the band gained some local popularity before Mark
Andes left to briefly join Canned Heat. In late 1966,
Cassidy and California returned to the state of California
and, with Locke, formed Spirits Rebellious, which with
the addition of Ferguson and Mark Andes became Spirit.

Their LPs rarely sold better than moderately well, but

Spirit were critically well received. Their biggest success
critically and commercially was *Sardonicus*, the last LP
by the original lineup. In mid-1971, Andes and Ferguson
left to form Jo Jo Gunne, with Cassidy and Locke bringing
in the Staehely brothers from Texas. After recording
Feedback, however, the two original members quit, leaving the Staehelys to take their own "Spirit" on the road.

Randy California then went to England, where he
played sessions with British art-rocker Peter Hammill of
Van der Graaf Generator. He suffered an accident in late
1971, which sidelined him until 1973, when he released a
solo LP, *Kaptain Kopter and the Twirlybirds*. When California and Cassidy re-formed Spirit in 1974, Chris
Staehely went to Jo Jo Gunne.

In 1973, Spirit toured Europe and America successfully.
In 1975, they played some West Coast reunion dates with
Mark Andes, who'd left Jo Jo Gunne and would go on to
join Firefall and, later, Heart. Ferguson, in the meantime,
had hits on his own ("Thunder Island") and became an
active West Coast sessionman and producer. Spirit continued recording and touring until 1981.

SPLIT ENZ

Formed 1972, New Zealand
Tim Finn, voc., piano; Phil Judd, voc., gtr., mandolin;
Eddie Rayner, kybds.; Wally Wilkinson, gtr.; Jonathan
Michael Chunn, bass; Emlyn Crowther, drums; Noel
Crombie, perc., spoons
1975—*Mental Notes* (Mushroom) **1976**—*Second
Thoughts* **1977**—(− Judd; + Neil Finn, gtr., voc.;
− Chunn; − Crowther; + Nigel Griggs, bass; +
Robert Gillie, sax; + Malcolm Green, drums)
Dizrythmia (+ Judd; − Judd; − Gillie) **1979**—
Frenzy (−Wilkinson) **1980**—*True Colours* (A&M)
Beginning of the Enz **1981**—(− Green) *Waiata*
1982—*Time and Tide*.

When the New Zealand band Split Enz began playing in
the mid-Seventies, they had a lot of trouble being taken
seriously because of their weird appearance, complete
with glaring clownlike costumes and hairdos that made
them look like parrots. Their music was an eclectic art-
pop amalgam with innovative song structures swinging
from ballads to cabaret to heavy pop. They later
reemerged with neo-Beatles pop songs and well-made
video clips to gain a larger audience.

The band went to Australia in 1975 as a seven-piece
outfit and recorded their debut, *Mental Notes*, there in
May and June; it was released only in Australia. They
came to the attention of Roxy Music's Phil Manzanera,
who produced *Second Thoughts* in England, which was
mostly new versions of material from the first record.
England became their home base, and they went through
many personnel changes, including the loss of major

songwriter Phil Judd. (The other writer is Tim Finn.) Their records sold well only in Australia.

In 1976, they made an attempt to reach Americans with a brief tour, including a date at New York's Bottom Line, opening for Henny Youngman. In January 1977, Chrysalis released their debut U.S. LP, a compilation under the title *Mental Notes.* In 1978, Judd briefly rejoined, but he left again and the group soon lost their contract. Judd went on to start his own band, the Swingers.

With Finn in charge, the group made itself more accessible. They groomed themselves as a pop band, performing Beatles-influenced songs that, like 10cc's, masked droll undertones with winsome melodies. The band broadened its Australian following, and returned to the U.S. market with *True Colours* in 1980; new anti-counterfeiting technology allowed the record to be pressed in laser-etched vinyl with rainbow patterns. "I Got You" gave the band its first taste of U.S. airplay; the single was #1 in Australia for ten weeks and the album sold 200,000 copies there.

Split Enz had made rock videos in its early, more eccentric form, and with the advent of cable-cast rock video in the early Eighties they got wide exposure for clips based on their newer songs.

SPOOKY TOOTH
Formed 1967, England
Mike Harrison (b. Sep. 3, 1945, Carlisle, Eng.), voc., kybds.; Gary Wright (b. Apr. 26, 1945, Englewood, N.J.), kybds., voc.; Luther Grosvenor (b. Dec. 23, 1949, Worcestershire, Eng.), gtr.; Greg Ridley (b. Oct. 23, 1947), bass; Mike Kellie (b. Mar. 24, 1947, Birmingham, Eng.), drums.
1968—*It's All About . . .* (Island; reissued in U.S. in 1970 as *Tobacco Road*) 1969—*Spooky Two* (− Ridley; + Andy Leigh, bass) *Ceremony* 1970—(− Wright; + Henry McCullough, gtr.; + Chris Stainton, kybds.; + Alan Spenner, bass) *The Last Puff* 1972—(− Kellie; − McCullough; − Stainton; + Spenner; − Grosvenor; + Mick Jones, gtr.; + Chris Stewart, bass; + Bryson Graham, drums) *You Broke My Heart, So I Busted Your Jaw* 1973—*Witness* 1974—(− Harrison; − Stewart; + Mike Patto [d. 1979, Eng.], kybds., voc.; + Val Burke, bass, voc.) *The Mirror* 1976—*Best of.*

Though they never had a hit single or a best-selling LP, Spooky Tooth remained a bastion of Britain's hard-rock scene. Gary Wright made hits after leaving the band.

Mike Harrison had worked as a clerk before joining the VIPs, which became the group Art in the mid-Sixties, with Mike Kellie. Gary Wright had been a child actor (in "Captain Video" and TV commercials) and a psychology student in New Jersey before attending college in Berlin. Spooky Tooth's first two albums, produced by Jimmy Miller, sold respectably in the U.K.; U.S. bassist Greg Ridley left for Humble Pie after the second and was replaced by Andy Leigh for *Ceremony,* a surprising U.S. chart success.

Wright brought in French electronic-music pioneer Pierre Henry to add processed musique concrète overdubs. Wright then left to form the short-lived Wonderwheel and reemerged a few years later on his own. Harrison brought in Henry McCullough, Chris Stainton and Alan Spenner from Joe Cocker's Grease Band for *Last Puff.* Grosvenor left after that LP, later to join Mott the Hoople, and Spooky Tooth entered suspended animation, with Harrison pursuing a short solo career with an LP, *Smokestack Lightning.* Wright and Harrison reformed the band in 1972, with future Foreigner guitarist Mick Jones.

Their next two albums sold fairly well, especially *You Broke My Heart.* Harrison left again to pursue a solo career in 1973; in 1974 Spooky Tooth re-formed yet again, with Mike Patto on vocals and keyboards. (He would work with a few more bands before dying of throat cancer in 1979.) They broke up for good a year later. Kellie, who in 1970 had briefly played with the British supergroup Balls (which also included Denny Laine and Steve Gibbons), resurfaced in the late Seventies with the Only Ones.

DUSTY SPRINGFIELD
Born Mary O'Brien, April 16, 1939, London.
1964—*The Dusty Springfield Album* (Philips) 1966—*You Don't Have to Say You Love Me; Golden Hits* 1967—*Look of Love* 1968—*Stay Awhile* (Mercury) 1969—*Dusty in Memphis* (Atlantic) 1970—*A Brand New Me* 1971—*For You, Love, Dusty* (Philips) 1973—*Cameo* (Dunhill) 1978—*It Begins Again* (United Artists) 1979—*Living Without Your Love* 1982—*White Heat* (Casablanca).

Dusty Springfield's husky voice made her one of Britain's best-selling pop-rock singers in the Sixties. She and her brother Tom began harmonizing with radio hits as children, and in their teens—while Dusty/Mary was hearing a broad range of music working in a record store—they formed a folk trio, the Springfields, with Tim Field. The group, a British equivalent of Peter, Paul and Mary, had U.K. chart hits in 1962–63 with "Island of Dreams" and "Say I Won't Be There," and hit the American Top Twenty in 1962 with "Silver Threads and Golden Needles." That year, Field quit, replaced by Mike Hurst (who later produced Cat Stevens), before the trio disbanded.

Springfield continued on her own, and in late 1963 had a British Top Ten hit with "I Only Want to Be with You," which went to #12 in the U.S. in early 1964 and eventually went gold. The tune has since been covered by many other performers. That song was Springfield's first flirtation with Motown-style soul, a sound to which she would often return. She toured the world and had British hits through 1964–65 with Bacharach-David's "I Just Don't Know What to Do with Myself" and "Wishin' and Hopin'," and with Goffin-King's "Some of Your Lovin' " and "Goin' Back." In 1966, "You Don't Have to Say You Love Me" was #1 in the U.K. and #4 in the U.S.

She continued to tour extensively and made TV appearances with Tom Jones, Engelbert Humperdinck, and on the "Ed Sullivan Show." In 1969, she recorded *Dusty in Memphis,* which yielded the Top Ten international hit single "Son of a Preacher Man." In 1970, she moved back toward pop with the *Brand New Me* LP, which contained "Land of Make Believe," "Silly Silly Fool" and the title cut. In England, her popularity declined, though "How Can I Be Sure" was a 1970 Top Forty hit in the U.K.

Between 1973 and 1978, Springfield lived reclusively in America and did not record, except for some backup vocals on Anne Murray's *Together* LP. In 1978, Springfield recorded two comeback albums on the West Coast. The first, produced by Roy Thomas Baker (of Queen and Cars fame), fared poorly both critically and commercially; the second, *Living Without Your Love,* produced by David Wolfert, fared slightly better. In the fall of 1980, Springfield played some New York club dates, her first in eight years.

RICK SPRINGFIELD
Born August 23, 1949, Sydney, Australia
1972—*Beginnings* (Capitol)   **1974**—*Comic Book Heroes* (Columbia)   **1976**—*Wait for the Night* (Chelsea)   **1981**—*Working Class Dog* (RCA)   **1982**—*Success Hasn't Spoiled Me Yet*   **1983**—*Living in Oz.*

Rick Springfield first became a household name as an actor, playing Dr. Noah Drake on the television soap opera "General Hospital." Later that same year (1981) he became a platinum-selling recording star as well with the #1 single "Jessie's Girl."

Springfield grew up in both Australia and England, where his father was a lieutenant colonel in the Army. He got his first guitar at 13 and three years later formed his first band, the Jordy Boys. He was later in a band called Rock House, which once played to U.S. troops in Vietnam. Springfield performed his first original material with Zoot, who became a top teen idol band in Australia with a #1 hit, "Speak to the Sky." He got a U.S. solo deal with Capitol, for whom he recorded *Beginnings* in London in 1972. His remake of "Speak to the Sky" reached the Top Fifteen that year in America.

The label promoted Springfield as a teen star, which got him lots of fanzine coverage but kept him from being taken seriously, a situation exacerbated by immigration problems, which kept him from touring. His next album, *Comic Book Heroes,* also flopped. Legal tangles kept Springfield out of circulation for two years, after which he signed to the small Chelsea label and released *Wait for the Night.* In 1974, he had been originally cast as lead in *The Buddy Holly Story,* but the role went to Gary Busey.

In 1976, Chelsea folded and Springfield turned to acting.

He made guest appearances on "The Six Million Dollar Man" and "Wonder Woman" while still making demos, and in early 1980 signed with RCA. *Working Class Dog,* which contained "Jessie's Girl," was released as Springfield became a regular on "General Hospital." The album went platinum, as did *Success Hasn't Spoiled Me Yet,* with the hits "I've Done Everything for You" (#8, 1981) and "Don't Talk to Strangers" (#2, 1982). In February 1983, he began filming his first starring movie role for Universal, as a rock star in a film directed by Ray Stark; a few months later, he released *Living in Oz.*

BRUCE SPRINGSTEEN
Born September 23, 1949, Freehold, New Jersey
1973—*Greetings from Asbury Park, New Jersey* (Columbia)   *The Wild, the Innocent and the E Street Shuffle*   **1975**—*Born to Run*   **1978**—*Darkness on the Edge of Town*   **1980**—*The River*   **1982**—*Nebraska.*

To his dedicated fans, Bruce Springsteen is the embodiment of the romantic myths he writes about: the working-class everyman with a heart of gold, the doomed urban lover, the spirit of rock & roll. To skeptics, he's a songwriter with a limited musical vocabulary and a tendency toward operatic bathos, overly obsessed with cars and darkness. He is, indisputably, one of the most energetic performers in the history of rock, and his showmanship is as heartfelt as his songs.

Springsteen, of Irish-Italian ancestry, grew up in Freehold, New Jersey. He took up the guitar when he was 13, and joined the Castiles a year later. In 1966, the Castiles recorded (but never released) two songs cowritten by Springsteen, and they worked their way up to a string of dates at New York City's Cafe Wha in 1967. During the summer after his graduation from high school, Springsteen was working with Earth, a Cream-style power trio, and hanging out in Asbury Park, New Jersey. He entered Ocean County Community College in the fall, but dropped out when a New York producer promised him a contract; he never saw the producer again.

While in college, he had formed a group with some local musicians, including drummer Vini "Mad Dog" Lopez and keyboardist Danny Federici. Called Child, then Steel Mill, the group worked the Atlantic coast down to Virginia. In summer 1969, Steel Mill visited California (where Springsteen's parents had moved); club dates in San Francisco led to a show at Bill Graham's Fillmore and a contract offer from Graham's Fillmore Records, which Steel Mill turned down because the advance was too small. The band returned East, and was joined by an old friend of Springsteen's, Miami Steve Van Zandt, on bass.

Springsteen disbanded Steel Mill in early 1971, intending to put together a band with a brass section and several singers. Meanwhile, he formed Dr. Zoom and the Sonic Boom, which played only three dates. Eventually, the Bruce Springsteen Band was formed with Lopez, Fe-

Bruce Springsteen

derici, Van Zandt (on guitar), pianist and guitarist David Sancious, bassist Garry Tallent and a four-piece brass section. After the group's first show, the brass section was dropped and Clarence Clemons, a football-player-turned-tenor-saxophonist (a knee injury aborted his pro career), joined the band. The group didn't last; by autumn 1971 Springsteen was working solo.

Springsteen had auditioned for Laurel Canyon Productions, a.k.a. Mike Appel and Jim Cretecos, who had written a hit for the Partridge Family and produced an album by a band called Sir Lord Baltimore. In May 1972, Springsteen signed a long-term management contract and an agreement giving Laurel Canyon exclusive rights to his songs. Royalty rates effective for five albums were set at a low 3 percent of retail price.

Appel arranged for his new client to audition for John Hammond, who had signed Bob Dylan to Columbia Records; after hearing Springsteen sing in his office, Hammond set up a showcase for CBS executives at the Gaslight and supervised a demo session. In June 1972, Columbia president Clive Davis signed a ten-album contract with Appel that gave Laurel Canyon about a 9 percent royalty.

Within the month, Springsteen completed *Greetings from Asbury Park, N.J.* Some of Springsteen's word-crammed songs were set to acoustic singer/songwriter backup, and some to the R&B-inflected rock of the reconstituted Bruce Springsteen Band. Released in January 1973 and touted as one more "new Dylan" effort, *Greetings* initially sold about 25,000 copies, largely to Jersey Shore fans. Springsteen and the band toured the Northeast, playing extended sets that earned him followings in Boston and Philadelphia. A string of dates opening for Chicago, who limited his sets to a half-hour, convinced Springsteen not to open for other bands.

The Wild, the Innocent and the E Street Shuffle was Springsteen's most experimental album. With the band, he integrated lyrics and instrumental passages into long romantic narratives; the average track was over seven minutes. The album sold as poorly as its predecessor, and Springsteen decided to concentrate on his stage show. Replacing Lopez with Ernest "Boom" Carter on drums, he tightened up what's now known as the E Street Band, hired expensive light and sound crews and rehearsed them to theatrical precision. He made up elaborate stories, often involving bandmembers, to introduce his songs, dramatized the songs as he sang them, and capped his sets with fervently rendered oldies.

In spring of 1974, critic Jon Landau saw a Springsteen show in Cambridge, Massachusetts, and wrote in the *Real Paper,* "I saw rock & roll's future and its name is Bruce Springsteen." Columbia used the quote in an ad campaign, and rave reviews of Springsteen concerts and belated notices of *The Wild* began showing up in print. By November 1974 the album had sold 150,000 copies.

Springsteen and a revamped E Street Band (pianist Roy Bittan and drummer Max Weinberg replaced Sancious and Carter, who had formed their own fusion group, Tone; Van Zandt joined as second guitarist) were bogged down by an ambitious third album. Landau, who had been visiting the studio with suggestions, became coproducer with Springsteen and Appel. Far from toning down Springsteen's histrionics, Landau inflated them with dramatic arrangements. While the album was being mastered, Springsteen wanted to scrap it in favor of a concert album. But that plan was dropped, and in October 1975 *Born to Run* was released.

Advance sales put the album on the chart a week before its release date, and it made the Top Ten shortly afterward. Within the month, it hit #3—and gold—while Springsteen started his first national tour. *Time* and *Newsweek* simultaneously ran cover stories on him. Yet Springsteen was still a cult figure—the album didn't stay on the charts long.

In spring of 1976, an independent auditor's report called Appel's management "unconscionable exploitation." And when Appel refused permission for Landau to produce the next album, Springsteen sued his manager in July 1976, alleging fraud, undue influence and breach of trust. Appel's countersuit asked for an injunction to bar Springsteen from working with Landau, which the court granted. Springsteen rejected the producer Appel chose, and the injunction prevented Springsteen from recording until May 1977. An out-of-court settlement gave Springsteen rights to his songs and he was allowed to work with Landau, while his Columbia contract was upgraded. Appel reportedly received a lump sum.

During the legal imbroglio, Springsteen toured and E

Streeters did session work: Bittan with David Bowie and Meat Loaf, Van Zandt with Southside Johnny and the Asbury Jukes.

While not recording, Springsteen toured in 1976 and 1977. Van Zandt produced the debut album by Southside Johnny and the Asbury Jukes, *I Don't Want to Go Home,* which featured several Springsteen compositions. Other Springsteen songs provided hits for the Hollies ("Sandy"), Manfred Mann ("Blinded by the Light," a #1 single in 1977), Robert Gordon ("Fire"—later a smash for the Pointer Sisters) and Patti Smith ("Because the Night," to which she contributed some lyrics). And Springsteen continued to write new songs, several of which were chosen for *Darkness on the Edge of Town.*

Work on *The River* began in April 1979 and went on for a year and a half. Springsteen appeared on stage only twice in that period, at the Musicians United for Safe Energy (MUSE) antinuclear benefit concerts in New York which were filmed as *No Nukes.* Coproduced by Springsteen, Landau and Van Zandt, *The River,* with shorter songs than previous albums, sold over two million copies. A single, "Hungry Heart," was Springsteen's first Top Ten hit.

On the eve of *The River*'s release in October 1980, Springsteen kicked off a tour that crisscrossed the United States twice, took him to over twenty European cities and to Japan and Australia; every one of his four-hour shows was sold out. In the fall, he played six benefit concerts in Los Angeles for Vietnam war veterans.

In 1981, Springsteen persuaded Gary "U.S." Bonds (whose "Quarter to Three" was a favorite Springsteen encore) to return to recording, on an album produced by Van Zandt that included Springsteen material. Members of the E Street Band played sessions for Garland Jeffreys, Joan Armatrading, Ian Hunter and others. Van Zandt continued producing Southside Johnny and the Asbury Jukes, and Bittan produced an album for rock singer Jimmy Mack.

In 1982, Springsteen made *Nebraska,* a stark, gloomy album recorded (initially as demo tapes) on a four-track machine at home. The album reached #3.

SQUEEZE

Formed 1974, London
Chris Difford (b. Apr. 11, 1954, London), gtr., voc.; Glenn Tilbrook (b. Aug. 31, 1957, London), gtr., voc.; Julian "Jools" Holland, kybds., voc.; Harry Kakoulli, bass; Gilson Lavis (b. June 27, 1951, Bedford, Eng.), drums.
1978—*U.K. Squeeze* (A&M) **1979**—(− Kakoulli; + John Bentley [b. Apr. 16, 1951, London], bass) *Cool for Cats* **1980**—*Argybargy* **1981**—(− Holland; + Paul Carrack [b. Apr. 1951, Sheffield, Eng.], kybds., voc.) *East Side Story* **1982**—(− Carrack; + Don Snow [b. Jan. 13, 1957, Kenya], kybds., voc.) *Sweets from a Stranger* **1983**—*Singles—45's and Under.*

Though they had garnered some critical acclaim and a few minor commercial successes in the late Seventies, pop-rockers Squeeze broke through in 1981 with *East Side Story,* which yielded a hit U.S. single in "Tempted" and was one of the most highly praised albums of the year. Squeeze's songwriting team, Chris Difford and Glenn Tilbrook, had been writing and performing together since 1973, and claim to have written some 600 songs together to date, Difford writing the lyrics, Tilbrook the music.

They were initially formed as Squeeze, but affixed a "U.K." to avoid confusion with a preexisting American band called Tight Squeeze; when the latter disbanded, they went back to Squeeze. The title tune from *Cool for Cats,* featuring Jools Holland's eccentric guttural vocals, was a #2 U.K. hit and achieved some dance floor success in the U.S.; "Up the Junction" from the same LP fared similarly. *Argybargy* yielded near-hits like "Pulling Mussels (from the Shell)," "Another Nail in My Heart" and "If I Didn't Love You." In late 1980, Holland left to form his own band, the Millionaires. He was replaced by Paul Carrack, formerly of Ace; he'd sung Ace's hit "How Long," which Squeeze included in its live concerts, and sang "Tempted," a #49 hit in America, where the Elvis Costello–coproduced *East Side Story* sold well.

Carrack left to join Carlene Carter's band, then to work with her husband Nick Lowe's Noise to Go. He was replaced by ex-Sincero Don Snow for *Sweets,* another well-received LP, which yielded FM hits in "Black Coffee in Bed" and "I Can't Hold On." Difford became involved in England's antinuclear movement and wrote what he called the band's "first protest song," "Apple Tree," which was to be included on *Sweets* but, for unknown reasons, was not. That year Difford also co-wrote "Boy with a Problem" with Elvis Costello for Costello's *Imperial Bedroom* LP (Tilbrook had appeared on Costello's *Trust* earlier), and Squeeze played its first Madison Square Garden concert. In the fall of 1982 the group broke up, although Difford and Tilbrook continued to collaborate.

BILLY SQUIER

Born May 12, 1950, Wellesley Hills, Massachusetts
1980—*The Tale of the Tape* (Capitol) **1981**—*Don't Say No* **1982**—*Emotions in Motion.*

After more than a decade of performing, heavy-metal guitarist Billy Squier hit it big in 1981 with "The Stroke."

Squier grew up in an affluent Boston suburb, and after graduating high school he moved to New York City, where he and several friends formed Magic Terry and the Universe. Squier later returned to the Boston area, where he studied at the Berklee School of Music, planning to become a music teacher. But he soon returned to New York, where in 1973 he joined the pop group the Sidewinders (he does not appear on their LP). Next he joined Piper, but after two LPs (*Piper* and *Can't Wait*) the group disbanded and Squier began a solo career. After a lackluster debut, he hit #5 on the LP chart with *Don't Say No,* which featured "The Stroke" and "My Kinda Lover." By mid-1982, Squier had a Top Ten hit, "Everybody Wants You," from the platinum *Emotions in Motion* LP.

THE STAPLES
Formed 1953, Chicago
Roebuck "Pop" Staples (b. Dec. 2, 1915, Winona, Miss.; Mavis Staples (b. Chicago); Cleo Staples (b. Miss.); Pervis Staples (b. Miss.); Yvonne Staples (b. Chicago).
1968—*Soul Folk in Action* (Stax) *We'll Get Over* **1969**—(– P. Staples) **1971**—*Heavy Makes You Happy* **1972**—*Bealtitude: Respect Yourself* **1973**—*Be What You Are* **1974**—*City in the Sky* **1975**—*Best of the Staple Singers* **1976**—*Pass It On* (Warner Bros.) **1977**—*Family Tree* **1978**—*Unlock Your Mind.*

First as gospel singers and then as a soul-pop group, the Staples family has maintained a strong following and had several pop and soul hits, usually fronted by Mavis Staples' breathy vocals.

The Staples go back to Mississippi, where as a young man Roebuck Staples played guitar and sang in local choirs. In the mid-Thirties, he and his wife, Oceola, traveled up the Mississippi River to Chicago in search of work, like many of his contemporaries. The Staples had three daughters, each of whom sang from an early age. They put together a family gospel act and by the mid-Fifties were considered one of the finest vocal groups in the field. They recorded many sides for Chicago's Vee Jay Records, including their rendition of "Amazing Grace."

In the early Sixties, they made their first pop (secular) recordings for Epic, but had no commerical success. They signed to Stax in 1968. Their new material reflected the Staples' commitment to making secular music with a message, but not until 1972's gold *Bealtitude: Respect Yourself* did they make the approach commercial. The Staples' first secular hit was "Heavy Makes You Happy" (#27 pop, #6 R&B); and their next two hits, "Respect Yourself" (#12 pop, #2 R&B) and "I'll Take You There" (#1 pop and R&B), went gold. The Staples had succeeded in meshing Memphis soul shuffles with their own messages. The group appeared in 1971's *Soul to Soul,* a documentary of a concert in Ghana, and in *Wattstax* (1973) and *The Last Waltz* (1978).

"If You're Ready (Come Go with Me)" was a #1 R&B hit in 1973, and in 1974 the Staples had a #1 pop and R&B hit with Curtis Mayfield's "Let's Do It Again," a movie theme song.

The Staples continued to record through the early Eighties on 20th Century–Fox Records, and Mavis Staples also recorded solo, but without comparable success.

EDWIN STARR
Born Charles Hatcher, January 21, 1942, Nashville, Tennessee
1969—*Soul Master* (Gordy) *25 Miles* **1970**—*War and Peace* **1971**—*Involved* **1978**—*Clean* (20th Century–Fox) **1979**—*Happy Radio* **1980**—*Stronger Than You Think I Am.*

Singer Edwin Starr's rough, powerful voice has made him a memorable but erratic hitmaker since the mid-Sixties, though he is best known for his 1970 #1 protest song "War."

Starr sang in high school and began his professional career on Ric-Tic Records, a Detroit-based label that copied the sound of its crosstown rival, Motown, in many of its releases. On Ric-Tic, Starr had hits with "Agent Double O Soul" (#21 pop, #8 R&B, 1965) and "Stop Her on Sight (S.O.S.)" (#9 R&B, 1966). In 1968, Ric-Tic was purchased by Motown. The gritty "Twenty-five Miles" (#6 pop and R&B, 1969) is regarded as a soul classic. "I'm Still a Strugglin' Man" (#27 R&B) was the followup.

With producer Norman Whitfield, Starr had success in 1970 with two social commentary songs, "War" (#1 pop, #3 R&B) and "Stop the War Now" (#26 pop, #5 R&B). The next year brought "Funky Music Sho Nuff Turns Me On" (#6 R&B). During the late Seventies, Starr recorded for 20th Century–Fox Records. His most successful single of the period was 1979's "Contact" (#13 R&B), a mix of soul and disco. In 1982, he cut a comical commentary song, "Tired of It," for Montage Records.

RINGO STARR
Born Richard Starkey, July 7, 1940, Liverpool, England
1970—*Sentimental Journey* (Apple) *Beaucoups of Blues* **1973**—*Ringo* **1974**—*Goodnight Vienna* **1975**—*Blast from Your Past* **1976**—*Rotogravure* (Atlantic) **1977**—*Ringo the Fourth* **1978**—*Bad Boy* **1981**—*Stop and Smell the Roses* (Boardwalk).

While some accused Ringo Starr of being a clumsy drummer, many more agreed with George Harrison's assessment: "Ringo's the best backbeat in the business." And while many in the wake of the Beatles' breakup predicted that Starr would be the one without a solo career, he proved them wrong not only by releasing several LPs (the first came out before the Beatles disbanded) and hit singles. He's also the only Beatle to establish a film-acting career for himself outside of the band's mid-Sixties movies.

Young Richard Starkey's parents had divorced when he was three, and he was raised by his mother and step-father, a Liverpool house painter his mother married eight years later. By the time he was 13, he'd been in and out of the hospital several times with pleurisy, and once, at age six, with appendicitis. After leaving the hospital in 1955, too old to return to school, he became a messenger boy for

British Railways. In 1959, while working as an apprentice engineer, he got his first drum set as a Christmas present, and he joined the Ed Clayton Skiffle Group soon after. By 1961, he was playing drums in Rory Storme's Hurricanes. It was while on tour with that band in Hamburg, Germany, in 1961 that he met John Lennon, Paul McCartney and George Harrison. A year later, when drummer Pete Best was ousted from the Beatles, Starr agreed to join them. (See the Beatles.) The Ringo stage name came from his penchant for wearing lots of rings.

Beginning with "Boys" on the Beatles' first British album, Starr was given the occasional lead vocal, usually on covers of country tunes such as Carl Perkins' "Honey Don't" and "Matchbox" and Buck Owens' "Act Naturally." Later, he sang the lead on "Yellow Submarine" and "With a Little Help from My Friends," songs written for him by Lennon and McCartney. *The Beatles* in 1968 featured Starr's first songwriting credit, "Don't Pass Me By."

After appearing in three films with the Beatles, in 1967 Starr made his solo film debut playing a Mexican gardener in the film of Terry Southern's *Candy*. He appeared in *The Magic Christian* (1969, also from a Southern book); in 1970 he costarred with David Essex in *That'll Be the Day;* in 1973 he documented the success of glitter-rock star T. Rex by directing *Born to Boogie;* in 1975 he costarred again with Essex in *Stardust;* and in 1981 he starred in the moderately successful U.S. feature *Caveman* (in April of that year he married his *Caveman* costar Barbara Bach; it was his second marriage).

Starr's solo recording career began in 1970, just prior to the Beatles' breakup, with *Sentimental Journey,* a collection of Tin Pan Alley standards (allegedly to please his mother) produced by George Martin, with a different arranger for each track. *Beaucoups of Blues,* released later that year, was a country-music collaboration with guitarist Pete Drake and other Nashville sessionmen. It fared better than its predecessor, but failed to yield a hit. In 1971, Starr appeared on Lennon's *Plastic Ono Band* and Harrison's *All Things Must Pass* LPs, and recorded two hit singles, the hard-rocking "It Don't Come Easy" (#4) and "Back Off Boogaloo" (#9).

Starr appeared at Harrison's Concerts for Bangladesh and in 1972 sat in on Peter Frampton's *Wind of Change* LP. In 1973, he recorded *Ringo,* with Richard Perry producing. The LP included three Top Ten singles—"Photograph" (#1), "You're Sixteen" (#1) and "Oh My My" (#5)—and featured songs and playing by the other Beatles; Lennon contributed "I'm the Greatest," McCartney "Six O'Clock" and Harrison "Sunshine Life for Me."

Goodnight Vienna yielded hit singles in Hoyt Axton's "No No Song" (#3) and "Only You" (#6). While co-managing a furniture-designing business with his brother in London, Starr in 1975 started his own label, Ring O' Records, and signed to Atlantic; none of his subsequent albums, however, have made much of an impression. In 1976, he played at the Band's San Francisco farewell concert and appeared in the film of the event, *The Last Waltz.* In 1977, he contributed to an LP by British skiffle pioneer Lonnie Donegan. In late 1981, Starr had a Top Forty hit with "Wrack My Brain," from *Roses,* a tune written and produced by George Harrison.

STATUS QUO
Formed 1962, London
Francis Rossi (b. Apr. 29, 1949, London), gtr., voc.; Richard Parfitt (b. Oct. 12, 1948, London), gtr., voc.; Alan Lancaster (b. Feb. 7, 1949, London), bass; John Coghlan (b. Sep. 19, 1946, London), drums.
1968—*Picturesque Matchstickable* (Pye, U.K.) *Spare Parts* **1969**—*Status Quotation* (Marble Arch, U.K.) **1970**—*Ma Kelly's Greasy Spoon* (Pye, U.K.) **1971**—*Dog of Two Heads* **1972**—*Best of* **1973**—*Pile Driver* (A&M) **1974**—*Hello; Quo* **1975**—*On the Level* **1976**—*Status Quo* (Vertigo, U.K.) *Blue for You* **1977**—*Live* (Capitol) *Pictures of Matchstick Men* (Hallmark) *Rockin' All Over the World* (Capitol) **1978**—*If You Can't Stand the Heat . . .* (Vertigo, U.K.) **1979**—*In My Chair* (Mode, France) *Whatever You Want* (Vertigo, U.K.) *Mean Girl* (Mode, France) *Just for the Record* (Pye, U.K.) **1980**—*Just Supposin'* (Vertigo, U.K.) *Gold Bars* **1981**—*Never Too Late* **1982**—*Rock 'n' Roll.*

Britain's longest-running hard-rock boogie band, Status Quo have actually had only one U.K. #1 single, "Down Down" in 1975, and one U.S. hit single, the psychedelic-pop "Pictures of Matchstick Men" in 1968 (also a Top Ten U.K. hit).

They began playing together as the Spectres while still schoolmates, and in 1966 recorded two singles for Pye Records. In 1967, they became Traffic Jam, releasing another single, then Status Quo. By 1970, they'd dropped their high-harmony pop style for heavy-metal boogie, and their albums became consistent big sellers in the U.K., though never in the U.S., which they toured several times in the Seventies. *Rock 'n' Roll* was a Top Ten LP in the U.K. in 1982.

STEALERS WHEEL
Formed 1972, London
Gerry Rafferty, gtr., voc.; Joe Egan, kybds., voc.; Rab Noakes, gtr.; Ian Campbell, bass; Roger Brown, drums, voc.
1973—(− Noakes; − Campbell; − Brown; + Paul Pilnick, gtr.; + Tony Williams, bass; + Rod Coombes, drums) *Stealers Wheel* (A&M) **1974**—(− Pilnick; − Williams; − Coombes; + Gary Taylor, bass; + Joe Jammer, gtr.; + Andrew Steele, drums) *Ferguslie Park* **1975**—(+ Bernie Holland, gtr.; + Dave Win-

tour, bass) *Right or Wrong* **1976**—*Stuck in the Middle with You* (compilation) **1981**—*Best of* (MFP, import).

One of the most critically respected pop groups of the mid-Seventies, Stealers Wheel were so ridden with internal turmoil they were never able to capitalize on their one big hit, "Stuck in the Middle with You," from their Leiber–Stoller–produced debut LP, which made #6 in the U.K. and #2 in the U.S. in 1973.

Gerry Rafferty, after working with Scottish comic folkies Billy Connolly and Tam Harvey in the Humblebums, and recording a solo LP (*Can I Have My Money Back?*), formed the original Stealers Wheel, which never recorded. The band regrouped with Rafferty, Joe Egan and guitarist Paul Pilnick (formerly of Liverpool band the Big Three; Pilnick later worked with Badger) and drummer Rod Coombes, later of the Strawbs. Stealers Wheel's debut included "Stuck in the Middle with You," but Rafferty had quit before it was released, and only rejoined the band after it had become a hit.

Leiber and Stoller produced *Ferguslie Park*—for which the band included ex–Spooky Tooth guitarist Luther Grosvenor, who would go on to Mott the Hoople—and though the album was again critically acclaimed, it yielded only a Top Thirty U.S. single in "Star" and sold poorly. Rafferty and Egan, the obvious nucleus of Stealers Wheel, fell out with Leiber and Stoller before recording a third LP. Mentor Williams produced *Right or Wrong*, but its release was held up for 18 months because of managerial problems, and by the time it came out the public had apparently forgotten Stealers Wheel. Rafferty and Egan were reportedly no longer speaking to each other after the LP's release. Rafferty went on to have a briefly spectacular solo career with the mammoth hit single "Baker Street," while Egan has not been heard from since the band's breakup.

TOMMY STEELE
Born Thomas Hicks, December 17, 1936, London.

Tommy Steele, England's first rock & roll star, was a teenaged merchant seaman when a young entrepreneur from New Zealand, John Kennedy, spotted him strumming a guitar and singing in a club in London's Soho district. Kennedy became Steele's manager and began intensively promoting the youngster as a British Elvis Presley. By early 1957, Steele had had a few top chart hits and was a big-selling teen idol in Britain and much of Europe. Within a year or so, however, Steele became dissatisfied with his image and began studying dance and acting, which led to theatrical roles in London's West End (including stints with the Old Vic company).

In the early Sixties, Steele starred in a British hit musical, *Half a Sixpence*, which in 1965 went to Broadway with similar success and yielded a top-selling

soundtrack album. Steele continued acting in musical comedies.

STEELEYE SPAN
Formed 1969, England
Ashley Hutchings, bass; Maddy Prior, voc.; Tim Hart, gtr., voc., dulcimer; Gay Woods, voc., concertina; Terry Woods, gtr.
1970—*Hark! The Village Wait* (Chrysalis) (− G. Woods; − T. Woods; + Martin Carthy, gtr.; + Peter Knight, fiddle, mandolin, voc.) **1971**—*Please to See the King; Ten Man Mop* (− Hutchings) **1972**—(− Carthy; + Rick Kemp, bass, voc.; + Bob Johnson, lead gtr., voc.) *Below the Salt* **1973**—*Parcel of Rogues* **1974**—(+ Nigel Pegrum, drums) *Now We Are Six* **1975**—*Commoner's Crown* **1976**—*All Around My Hat; Rocket Cottage* **1977**—(+ John Kirkpatrick, voc., accordion; + Carthy) *Storm Force 10; Original Masters* **1978**—*Live at Last* (− Knight; − Johnson; disbanded) **1980**—(+ Prior; + Hart; + Kemp; + Johnson; + Pegrum; + Knight) *Sails of Silver* (Takoma).

Steeleye Span were formed in 1969 with the idea of introducing electric instruments to traditional British folk music—updating mainly 17th- and 18th-century works found in the journals of the English Folk Dance and Song Society.

Founder Ashley Hutchings, formerly bassist for tradrockers Fairport Convention, left that band after their *Liege and Lief* LP. Hutchings sought out more purely history-obsessed musicians and came up with two teams: Maddy Prior and Tim Hart (who had performed locally in St. Albans, England, and recorded three traditional albums) plus Gay and Terry Woods (a married couple who were part of the folk-rock group Sweeney's Men). The new fivesome took their name from a character in the Lincolnshire ballad "Horkston Grange" and recorded *Hark! The Village Wait* in 1970. A few months later the Woodses left, and Hart brought in Martin Carthy, another folk scene regular, and Peter Knight.

The new lineup recorded two LPs in 1971, *Please to See the King* and *Ten Man Mop*, which included more amplification on their all-traditional pieces. They began to attract attention, especially for Maddy Prior's vocals. The group were appearing in a play written for them called *Carunna*, by Keith Dewhurst, when Hutchings lost confidence in the project and, in 1971, left to form the very traditional Albion Country Band; Carthy also left. Their replacements were the more rock-oriented Rick Kemp (who had worked with Mike Chapman and spent a week once in King Crimson) and Bob Johnson (who had played in a folk duo with Knight). This lineup gave Steeleye their first real success. *Below the Salt* in 1972 was their U.S. debut and the Latin a cappella song "Gaudete" became a British hit in 1973.

By now, Hart, Carthy and Prior were doing solo work. In 1973 the band released *Parcel of Rogues,* with its first drummer, ex-Gnidgrolog member Nigel Pegrum. He joined full time in 1974, making them a six-piece band, inspiring the title of their next LP, *Now We Are Six,* produced by Jethro Tull's Ian Anderson. The band now began to write their own songs and settings for traditional lyrics. Their popularity increased in the U.K. with the gold hit single "Thomas the Rhymer." The LP also featured David Bowie playing sax on "To Know Him Is to Love Him." *Commoner's Crown* in 1975 featured actor Peter Sellers playing ukulele on "New York Girls," and the even more commercial *All Around My Hat* gave them a big British hit with the title track, and also their first U.S. charting. A cult began to grow in America, drawn to the band's live show, which featured Prior's nimble jigs. In 1976, Prior recorded the album *Silly Sisters* with traditional singer June Tabor, and the two toured England.

That solo outlet was indicative of the band's splintering, though. After *Rocket Cottage* failed to sell even in England, Knight and Johnson produced a duo album, *The King of Elfland's Daughter.* In 1977, with the newly rejoined Carthy and Kirkpatrick, Knight and Johnson announced their departure, but first the band gave a farewell concert on March 7, 1978, captured on *Live at Last.*

In early 1981, the band resurfaced with the most popular lineup—Prior and Hart plus Johnson, Kemp, Knight and Pegrum, on *Sails of Silver.*

STEELY DAN

Formed 1972, Los Angeles
Walter Becker (b. ca. 1951, Queens, N.Y.), bass, gtr., voc.; Donald Fagen (b. ca. 1950, Passaic, N.J.), kybds., voc.; Denny Dias, gtr.; Jim Hodder, drums.
1971—*You Gotta Walk It Like You Talk It* (soundtrack) (Spark) 1972—(+ David Palmer, kybds., voc.; + Jeffrey "Skunk" Baxter [b. Dec. 13, 1948], gtr.) *Can't Buy a Thrill* (ABC) 1973—(– Palmer) *Countdown to Ecstasy* 1974—(– Hodder; + Michael McDonald, voc., kybds.; + Jeff Porcaro, drums) *Pretzel Logic* 1975—(– Baxter; – McDonald; + various sessionmen, including Elliot Randall [gtr.], Larry Carlton [gtr.], David Paich, Michael Omartian [kybds.], Wilton Felder [bass], Victor Feldman [percussion, kybds.]) *Katy Lied* 1976—(– Porcaro; + sessionmen) *The Royal Scam* 1977—*Aja* 1978—*Greatest Hits* 1979—(– Dias; + sessionmen) 1980—*Gaucho* (MCA).
Donald Fagen solo: 1982—*The Nightfly* (Warner Bros.).

Less a band than a concept, Steely Dan was one of the most respected, advanced, successful and mysterious pop units of the Seventies. They have several hit singles and gold LPs to their credit and an unmistakable sound based on jazz-derived harmonies and cryptic lyrics. Because of the perfectionism of the band's founders, Donald Fagen and Walter Becker, the group rarely toured, and toward the end, was composed almost entirely of session musicians, while Becker and Fagen began to play less and less on their own albums. The band's producer, Gary Katz, has become Steely Dan's "third member," as much because of Becker-Fagen's insistence on state-of-the-art sound quality as for Katz's role in forming the band.

Becker and Fagen met at Bard College in upstate New York. There they played together in several college bands, ranging from jazz to rock to pop to progressive rock; one of their groups (the Bad Rock Group) included Chevy Chase of "Saturday Night Live" on drums. Becker and Fagen began composing songs together and, after leaving Bard, toured as backing musicians with Jay and the Americans. They also wrote and recorded the soundtrack for the film *You Gotta Walk It Like You Talk It,* produced by Kenny Vance of Jay and the Americans. They tried, unsuccessfully, to start a Long Island band with guitarist Denny Dias, then they moved to New York City to try to sell their tunes to publishers, but had little success. They did, however, meet independent producer Gary Katz, who placed them at ABC Records in L.A. as staff songwriters as a stipulation to accepting his own contract as ABC staff producer. It was Katz who first hatched the idea for what would become Steely Dan. Steely Dan was the name of a dildo in William Burroughs' novel *Naked Lunch.*

Steely Dan's debut LP yielded two hit singles, "Do It Again" and "Reeling in the Years" (which featured guitarist Elliot Randall); it sold well and was hailed by critics. Put off by a singles-oriented audience, as well as inadequate rehearsals, Becker, Fagen and Katz considered Steely Dan's first tour a total disaster. Their next LP contained no hit singles—possibly because of the absence of singer David Palmer, who had left to form the abortive Big Wha-Koo; this forced Fagen's distinctive vocals to the fore.

For their next LP, Steely Dan were joined by singer/keyboardist and future Doobie Brother Michael McDonald, who sang mostly backup vocals. *Pretzel Logic* contained the single "Rikki Don't Lose That Number" (#4, 1974). That album had more pronounced jazz leanings; the opening of "Rikki" was a nod to hard-bop pianist Horace Silver, and "Parker's Band" was a salute to be-bop sax giant Charlie Parker. In 1974, Steely Dan made their last tour. Hodder returned to session work; Baxter and then McDonald left to join the Doobie Brothers; Dias, though he continued to work with Becker and Fagen for some time, also returned to session work. Becker and Fagen amassed enormous debts by spending lengthy spells in the studio with high-priced sessionmen. *Katy Lied,* in effect the first Steely Dan LP by Becker and Fagen plus session players, contained "Black Friday" (# 37) and featured a solo on "Dr. Wu" by jazz alto saxophonist Phil Woods. The DBX noise-reduction system used to enhance the LP's sound malfunctioned, and the album's sleeve contained a lengthy apology for this from Becker, Fagen and Katz; still, it sounded cleaner than most contemporary releases. A scheduled tour was scrapped during rehearsals.

The Royal Scam, like most Steely Dan albums, sold well. *Aja*, which included FM favorites like the title tune and "Deacon Blues," was a Top Five album within three weeks of its release, and became the band's first platinum album.

In 1978, jazz bandleader Woody Herman's Thundering Herd Big Band recorded five Becker-Fagen songs, selected by and under the supervision of Becker and Fagen. A subsequent contractual dispute with MCA (which had absorbed ABC Records) delayed the release of *Gaucho*, which also went platinum and yielded another minor hit single in "Hey Nineteen." The B side of the single was Steely Dan's only live recording, "Bodhissatva," from the 1974 tour. In the summer of 1980, Becker suffered a broken leg and other injuries when a car hit him while he was walking in Manhattan.

In June 1981, Becker and Fagen announced that they would go separate ways, though their management denied it would be a permanent separation. In 1982, *Gaucho* won a Grammy for Best Engineered Album, as did *Aja* in 1978. *The Nightfly*, Fagen's first solo album, went to #11 and became a gold LP.

STEPPENWOLF

Formed 1967, Los Angeles
John Kay (b. Joachim F. Krauledat, Apr. 12, 1944, Tilsit, Ger.), gtr., voc.; Michael Monarch (b. July 5, 1950, Los Angeles), gtr.; Goldy McJohn (b. May 2, 1945), organ; Rushton Moreve (b. circa 1948, Los Angeles; d. July 1, 1981, Los Angeles), bass; Jerry Edmonton (b. Oct. 24, 1946, Canada), drums.
1968—(– Moreve; + John Russell Morgan, bass) *Steppenwolf* (Dunhill) *The Second* **1969**—*Early Steppenwolf* (– Monarch; – Morgan; + Larry Byrom [b. Dec. 27, 1948, U.S.], gtr.; + Nick St. Nicholas [b. Sept. 28, 1943, Hamburg, Ger.], bass) *At Your Birthday Party* **1970**—(– St. Nicholas; + George Biondo [b. Sep. 3, 1945, Brooklyn, N.Y.], bass) *Monster; Live; Seven* **1971**—*Gold* (compilation with earlier lineups) (– Byrum; + Kent Henry, gtr.) *For Ladies Only* **1972**—*Rest in Peace* **1974**—*Greatest Hits* (– Henry; + Bobby Cochran [b. Minn.], gtr.) *Slow Flux* (Epic) **1975**—(– McJohn; + Wayne Cook, kybds.) *16 Great Performances* (ABC); *Hour of the Wolf* (Epic) **1976**—*Skullduggery; The ABC Collection* (ABC) **1977**—*Born to Be Wild* (Epic) **1982**—*Wolf Tracks* (Nautilus).

Though tangentially identified with late-Sixties West Coast psychedelia, Steppenwolf's music was hard rock,

and the term "heavy metal" was popularized in their hit, "Born to Be Wild."

Leader John Kay, never seen without sunglasses, escaped from East Germany to Toronto, Canada, with his family in 1958. There he formed a blues-rock band, Sparrow, which eventually traveled to Los Angeles and became Steppenwolf—named, at a producer's suggestion, after the Hermann Hesse novel. Some Steppenwolf members had also played in a band called the Mynah Birds, which also included Neil Young and Rick James.

Their hard-rock won them favor with local audiences, and their debut LP yielded "Born to Be Wild" (#2). Despite the tough image that song gave them, Steppenwolf were an unabashedly political band—Kay ran for a Los Angeles city council seat at one point—with their politics most clearly articulated on 1969's *Monster. The Second* yielded another massive hit single in "Magic Carpet Ride" (# 3, 1968). "Born to Be Wild" and "The Pusher" were featured in the film *Easy Rider*.

Other hits of the period included "Rock Me," from the film *Candy* (# 10, 1969) and "Move Over" (# 31, 1969). Michael Monarch left to do session work with Janis Joplin and Deep Purple's Roger Glover. In early 1972, the band announced its first breakup. Kay launched a solo career, releasing *Forgotten Songs and Unsung Heroes* and *My Sporting Life* for Dunhill, while Edmonton and the classically trained McJohn formed Manbeast. Kay had a minor hit single in 1972 with "I'm Movin' On."

In 1974, Steppenwolf re-formed and put "Straight-Shootin' Woman" at #29, but by that time had lost most of its audience. Their lineup included guitarist Bobby Cochran, who had worked with the Flying Burrito Brothers and with the Grateful Dead's Bob Weir. The band broke up again in 1976, after which Michael Monarch resurfaced in the heavy-metal band Detective. Kay recorded another solo album, *All in Good Time*, for Mercury in 1978, and in 1980 he formed an entirely new band with whom he toured the U.S. billed as John Kay and Steppenwolf. In the summer of 1981, Moreve was killed in an auto accident.

CAT STEVENS

Born Steven Georgiou, July 21, 1947, London
1967—*Matthew and Son* (Deram) **1968**—*New Masters* **1970**—*World of* (Decca) *Mona Bone Jakon* (A&M) *Cats Cradle* (London) (compilation) **1971**—*Tea for the Tillerman* (A&M) *Teaser and the Firecat* **1972**—*Very Young and Early Songs* (Deram) (compilation) *Catch Bull at Four* (A&M) **1973**—*Foreigner* **1974**—*Buddah and the Chocolate Box* **1975**—*Numbers; Greatest Hits* **1977**—*Izitso* **1978**—*Back to Earth*.

Cat Stevens was one of the most successful singer/songwriters of the first half of the Seventies. After eight gold albums in a row, his star began to fade, and in the late Seventies he became a Muslim and dropped out of music.

The son of a Greek father and Swedish mother, Stevens

Cat Stevens

spent his early youth developing a love of Greek folk songs and dances. By the time he entered secondary school, he had also taken an interest in rock & roll and English and American folk music. While attending Hammersmith College in the mid-Sixties, he began writing his own songs and performing solo.

In 1966, independent producer Mike Hurst (formerly with the Springfields) produced Stevens' first U.K. hit single, "I Love My Dog." In 1967, "Matthew and Son" went to #2 on the British chart. Meanwhile, Stevens' tunes were British hits for other performers as well. P. P. Arnold hit with "The First Cut Is the Deepest" (later covered by Rod Stewart), the Tremeloes with "Here Comes My Baby." Stevens toured England and Europe, becoming something of a teen idol, and shared bills with Jimi Hendrix and Engelbert Humperdinck, among others.

But Stevens became disenchanted with what he considered the shallowness of his ventures. After his 1968 hit "I'm Gonna Get Me a Gun" (#6 U.K.), he tried to work ambitious classical arrangements into his tunes, to his producers' chagrin. Stevens' career then came to a standstill when he contracted tuberculosis in late 1968 and was confined to a hospital for a year. He took that time to work on his new material, which was unveiled in *Mona Bone Jakon*, a critical success that yielded a British hit single in "Lady D'Arbanville" (#13 U.K.). The muted accompaniment was by flutist Peter Gabriel (who went on to form Genesis), percussionist Harvey Burns and perennial Stevens collaborator, guitarist Alun Davies.

Stevens' next album, *Tea for the Tillerman*, hit the U.S. Top Ten and stayed on the charts for well over a year, yielding the hit "Wild World." Stevens was now a highly successful concert performer as well. The next album was another hit; *Teaser and the Firecat* went to #3, then gold, and contained the hits "Morning Has Broken" (#6), "Peace Train" (#7) and "Moon Shadow" (#30).

Though his next two albums, *Catch Bull at Four* and *Foreigner,* went gold, they yielded no big hits. At that time, unbeknownst to many of his fans, Stevens was living in Brazil, donating much of his earnings to charities like UNESCO. With *Buddah and the Chocolate Box,* featuring "Oh Very Young" (#10), and *Numbers,* Stevens' sales dropped off.

In late 1979, Stevens converted to the Muslim religion, changing his name to Yosef Islam and marrying Fouzia Ali. In late 1981, he announced, "I'm no longer seeking applause and fame," and auctioned off all his material possessions, including his gold records.

AL STEWART

Born September 5, 1945, Glasgow
1967—*Bedsitter Images* (Columbia, U.K.)   **1969**—*Love Chronicles* (Epic)   **1970**—*Zero She Flies* (Columbia, U.K.)   **1972**—*Orange*   **1974**—*Past, Present and Future* (Janus)   **1975**—*Modern Times*   **1976**—*The Year of the Cat*   **1978**—*The Early Years; Time Passages* (Arista)   **1980**—*24 Carrots*   **1981**—*Live/Indian Summer.*

British folk-rocker Al Stewart sold many records in the late Seventies with a sound influenced by mid-period Dylan, and some distinctive name-dropping lyrics that focused on historical themes from Napoleonic invasions to Nostradamus.

Stewart, who moved to London with his widowed mother when he was three, first played in rock bands in Bournemouth beginning at age 16. But after hearing Bob Dylan, he started performing his own softer compositions at small London folk clubs in the mid-Sixties. Of his first four albums, Columbia allowed only one to be released in the U.S., 1969's *Love Chronicles*. It featured Jimmy Page on guitar and was voted Folk Album of the Year by *Melody Maker;* it included a lengthy confessional song about women Stewart had known.

Stewart signed with Janus Records in 1974 and released *Past, Present and Future.* Unlike his four previous LPs (which he's since repudiated) this record traded first-person love songs for historical sagas. This LP won him his first American FM airplay.

Modern Times, improved the style with catchier melodies and harder-rocking music, helping it to reach the U.S. Top Thirty. His breakthrough came in late 1976 with *The Year of the Cat.* The title single became a Top Ten hit and the LP went platinum. Stewart then switched to Arista, sparking a complicated lawsuit.

Time Passages, produced by Alan Parsons like its predecessor, was Top Ten and platinum. The LP *24 Carrots,* in 1980, rocked harder but was a commercial disappointment, as was *Live/Indian Summer.*

BILLY STEWART
Born Washington, D.C.; died January, 17, 1970
1982—*The Greatest* (Chess).

Billy Stewart qualifies as a unique entry in that he is rock's only high-powered scat man (hence his nickname "Motor-mouth"), using his outrageous trill to rip the stuffing out of such standards as "Summertime," "Secret Love" and "Every Day I Have the Blues" (#74, 1967).

Son of a piano teacher who had her own gospel group, the Stewart Gospel Singers (Billy was a member during his late teens), he won an amateur contest in Washington with a rendition of "Summertime" from *Porgy and Bess*. This led to club bookings and later to his discovery by Bo Diddley, with whose band he played for two years. Meanwhile he cut his first single, "Billy's Blues (Parts 1 and 2)," and later sang with the Rainbows, who included in their quartet Don Covay.

Stewart then signed with the Okeh label (he is included on 1982's *Okeh Rhythm and Blues* compilation with "Baby, You're My Only Life"). In 1961, he returned to Chess, and in 1966 he hit the Top 100 (his sixth entry) with the scorching "Summertime" (#10), followed that same year by his equally dynamic cover of Fain and Webster's "Secret Love" (#29). Four years later, he and two members of his band were killed when their car plunged into the Neuse River in North Carolina.

JOHN STEWART
Born September 5, 1939, San Diego, California
1968—*Signals through the Glass* (Capitol) **1969**—*California Bloodlines* **1970**—*Willard* **1971**—*The Lonesome Picker Rides Again* (Warner Bros.) **1972**—*Sunstorm* **1973**—*Cannons in the Rain* (RCA) **1974**—*Phoenix Concerts Live* **1975**—*Wingless Angels* **1977**—*Fire in the Wind* (RSO) **1979**—*Bombs Away Dream Babies* **1980**—*Dream Babies Go Hollywood; In Concert* (RCA) *Forgotten Songs*.

Despite a fairly successful solo career, singer/songwriter John Stewart is probably best remembered as the composer of the Monkees' hit "Daydream Believer" and as a member of the Kingston Trio.

At Pomona College in the mid-Fifties, Frank Zappa taught Stewart the chords to "Streets of Laredo." Stewart went on to form a garage-rock band, the Furies, who recorded a single in the late Fifties. Two of Stewart's tunes had been recorded by the Kingston Trio, and when the trio's manager, Frank Werber, told Stewart he was looking for a similar act to sign, Stewart formed the Cumberland Three, which included his former glee-club teacher, Gil Robbins.

In July 1961, Stewart replaced Dave Guard in the Kingston Trio, staying on as a salaried member until 1967. Before leaving, Stewart had tried unsuccessfully to form a band with John Phillips (later of the Mamas and the Papas)

and Scott McKenzie. He had also formed a short-lived duo with John Denver before either had gained any fame. "Daydream Believer" spurred Stewart on to a solo career. His debut LP flopped commercially, but *Bloodlines*, recorded in Nashville, received some critical acclaim and fared slightly better.

Despite his general lack of commercial success, Stewart has maintained pockets of loyal cultists around the country, especially in Phoenix, where his live LP was recorded in 1974. He finally had some success in 1979 with *Bombs Away Dream Babies*, produced by Fleetwood Mac's Lindsey Buckingham and featuring Mac's Stevie Nicks on backing vocals on the hit single "Gold," which went to #5 in the U.S.

ROD STEWART
Born January 10, 1945, London
1969—*The Rod Stewart Album* (Mercury) **1970**—*Gasoline Alley* **1971**—*Every Picture Tells a Story* **1972**—*Never a Dull Moment* **1973**—*Sing It Again, Rod* **1974**—*Smiler* **1975**—*Atlantic Crossing* (Warner Bros.) **1976**—*A Night on the Town* **1977**—*Best of Rod Stewart, volume I* (Mercury) *Best of Rod Stewart, volume II; Foot Loose and Fancy Free* (Warner Bros.) **1978**—*Blondes Have More Fun* **1979**—*Greatest Hits, volume I* **1980**—*Foolish Behaviour* **1981**—*Tonight I'm Yours* **1982**—*Absolutely Live* **1983**—*Body Wishes*.

Gritty-voiced singer and sometime songwriter Rod Stewart earned the tag "vocals extraordinaire" during his first stint with the Jeff Beck Group, and maintained it during his subsequent solo career and with the Faces.

The son of a Scottish shopkeeper, Stewart was born and raised in London but considers himself a Scot. By the time he left secondary school, he longed to be a professional soccer player. He erected fences and dug graves until he signed as an apprentice to a pro soccer team. But after a year of bench-warming and odd jobs, Stewart took up with English bohemian folksinger Wizz Jones. Jones supposedly taught Stewart guitar and banjo, and the two performed on Continental streetcorners until they were arrested for vagrancy in Spain and deported to England in 1963.

In London, Stewart began hanging out at the R&B clubs. He played harmonica with Jimmy Powell and the Five Dimensions, and the following year he joined the Hoochie Coochie Men. That group (with Stewart and Long John Baldry sharing vocals) lasted a year, during which time Stewart moonlighted as a session musician (he played harmonica on Millie Small's "My Boy Lollipop") and recorded a single, "Good Morning Little Schoolgirl." His apparel earned him the nickname "Rod the Mod."

Baldry disbanded the Hoochie Coochie Men in 1965 to form Steampacket with Brian Auger and Julie Driscoll, and once again called on Stewart to share the vocals. *(Rod*

Stewart and Steampacket, compiling various obscure recordings, was later released on Springboard.) Stewart left the group in 1966 following a dispute with Baldry, although he later coproduced Baldry's 1971 solo album *It Ain't Easy* with Elton John. He joined Shotgun Express, which included future Fleetwood Mac guitarist Peter Green and drummer Mick Fleetwood. Modeled after Steampacket, the Express couldn't shake that group's shadow, and broke up within a year.

In 1967, Jeff Beck enlisted Stewart as lead vocalist for the Jeff Beck Group. Beck was especially popular in America, where the new group first toured in 1968. Petrified by the first-night audience at New York's Fillmore East, Stewart sang the opening number from backstage. Two albums, *Truth* (1968) and *Beck-Ola* (1969), established Stewart as a vocal stylist, and his tenure with Beck taught him to phrase his sandpaper voice around the lead instrument.

In 1969, while still with Beck, Stewart signed a solo contract with Mercury Records. His solo debut, *The Rod Stewart Album* (originally titled *An Old Raincoat Won't Ever Let You Down*), was recorded with Mick Waller and Ron Wood of the Jeff Beck Group, plus Small Faces keyboardist Ian McLagan and guitarist Martin Quittenton. Stewart's solo material was a grab bag of gentle folk songs, bawdy drinking songs, a taste of soul and a couple of barrelhouse rockers. The album sold modestly—Jeff Beck Group fans considered it too subdued—but critics were impressed by Stewart's five original songs.

Planning to form a new group with Stewart and the Vanilla Fudge's Tim Bogert and Carmine Appice, Beck disbanded his group. That group finally materialized in 1972, long after Stewart and his buddy Wood had joined the Small Faces, soon redubbed the Faces. Stewart spent the next seven years dividing his time between that group and his solo career, recording a Faces album for each solo LP.

In 1970, the Faces recorded *The First Step,* Stewart recorded *Gasoline Alley,* and together they toured the United States twice. In the studio with the Faces, Stewart was but one of a quintet of equals merrily banging out rock & roll. Alone in the studio, Stewart was different; the moody *Gasoline Alley* amplified his reputation as a singer and storyteller.

When *Every Picture Tells a Story* came out in June 1971, the response was swift and strong. In October, the album was simultaneously #1 in America and Britain, the first record to do so. The first single from the album, "Maggie May," a Stewart-Quittenton song, was the second record to do the same. Before "Maggie May" had faded, Stewart followed up with a gritty version of the Temptations' hit "(I Know) I'm Losing You" (#24, 1971). *Never a Dull Moment,* with "You Wear It Well" (#13, 1972), was also a hit album.

With two gold albums, Stewart's role in the Faces

became strained. The group's records were neither as lucrative nor as popular as Stewart's, and more than the occasional gig was undermined by the group's sodden sloppiness. Bassist Ronnie Lane quit the group in 1973, to be replaced by Tetsu Yamauchi, and legal battles were waged between Mercury and Warners (with whom Stewart had signed a new solo contract) over control of the Faces. While court proceedings kept him out of the studio, Mercury released a greatest-hits compilation, *Sing It Again, Rod.* The next year, the disputing companies jointly issued *Coast to Coast Overture and Beginnings,* a live album billed under "The Faces/Rod Stewart." Late in 1974, Mercury released *Smiler,* Stewart's last album for the label.

Stewart hired veteran American producer Tom Dowd and Muscle Shoals session musicians to record his Warner Bros. debut, *Atlantic Crossing.* In 1975, he moved to Los Angeles to escape British taxes and was soon the toast of the Beverly Hills celebrity set. His romance with Swedish movie starlet Britt Ekland (which ended in 1979 and added juice to her autobiography *True Britt*) made him a gossip column staple.

Stewart retained Dowd and the American studio musicians for *A Night on the Town* and came up with a better-selling album than *Every Picture,* largely on the strength of the biggest single of 1976, "Tonight's the Night," which topped the U.S. chart for eight weeks. Two other singles, Cat Stevens' "The First Cut Is the Deepest" (#21, 1977) and "The Killing of Georgie" (#30, 1977), a song about a homosexual friend's murder, rode the charts through 1977 and made Stewart a star in the previously indifferent international market.

The Faces had by now fallen apart, and Wood was a full-fledged Rolling Stone. Stewart formed a new, American touring band. The hits kept coming—raunchy rockers like "Hot Legs" (#28, 1978), romantic ballads like "You're in My Heart" (#4, 1978) and even a #1 pop hit with "Da Ya Think I'm Sexy" (1979). Stewart even recaptured the critics with 1981's *Tonight I'm Yours* and the worldwide tour that followed. He had a hit with "Young Turks" (#5) in 1982, and *Body Wishes* included the hit "Baby Jane."

STONE THE CROWS

Formed 1969, Glasgow
Maggie Bell, voc.; Les Harvey (b. circa 1947; d. May 3, 1972, Swansea, Wales), gtr.; Jon McGinnis, kybds.; Jim Dewar, bass; Colin Allen, drums.
1970—*Stone the Crows* (Polydor)   *Ode to John Law*
1971—(− Dewar; − McGinnis; + Steve Thompson, bass; + Ronnie Leahy, kybds.)   *Teenage Licks*
1972—(+ Jimmy McCulloch [b. 1953, Glasgow; d. Sep. 27, 1979, London], gtr.)   *'Ontinuous Performance.*

A Scottish-English soul band, Stone the Crows (the name comes from a Scottish curse meaning "the hell with it") is perhaps most significant for introducing Maggie Bell, a blues singer in the style of Janis Joplin, who went on to a solo career.

Young Maggie Bell had gotten onstage to sing in Glasgow with Alex Harvey (who in the early Seventies led the Sensational Alex Harvey Band), earning two pounds. Harvey introduced her to his brother Les, who was leading the Kinning Park Ramblers. Within a few years Bell and Les Harvey were leading Power, which played clubs and U.S. Army bases in Europe. When Led Zeppelin manager Peter Grant discovered them, he renamed them Stone the Crows. Their first two albums were critically acclaimed but sold few copies.

Jim Dewar eventually left to join ex–Procol Harum guitarist Robin Trower, and Steve Thompson was recruited from John Mayall; with *Teenage Licks* the band seemed on the verge of success. In 1972, Bell won Britain's Top Girl Singer Award for the first of many times, but that year also saw Les Harvey electrocuted by a microphone wire during a show at Swansea University. Jimmy McCulloch came in to finish the sessions for *'Ontinuous*, but the band soon broke up. McCulloch later joined Paul McCartney's Wings, and Bell released several solo LPs. Colin Allen went on to join Focus.

STORIES
Formed 1972, New York City
Michael Brown (b. Apr. 25, 1949, Brooklyn, N.Y.), kybds., voc.; Steve Love, gtr., voc.; Ian Lloyd, bass, voc., kybds.; Bryan Madey, drums, voc.
1972—*Stories* (Kama Sutra) 1973—*About Us* (– Brown; – Love; – Lloyd; – Madey; + Kenny Aaronson [b. Apr. 14, 1952, Brooklyn], bass; + Rich Ranno, drums) *Travelling Underground.*

Formed by ex–Left Banke mentor Michael Brown, Stories had a #1 hit in 1973 with "Brother Louie." The tune was written by Errol Brown of British soul group Hot Chocolate, who released a competing version of it in 1973.

Brown left after their second LP to become the guiding spirit, writer and producer of the Beckies (though he never actually played with them). Bassist Kenny Aaronson went on to work with Hall and Oates, Leslie West, Rick Derringer and Billy Squier. At a 1976 Ian Lloyd solo-album session, Mick Jones met Ian MacDonald, and the pair went on to form Foreigner.

THE STRANGELOVES
Formed 1965, Brooklyn, New York
Richard Gottehrer, Robert Feldman, Jerry Goldstein.
1965—*I Want Candy* (Bang).

The Strangeloves' big hit was 1965's "I Want Candy" (#11). The song was treated to some bizarre versions in the early Eighties by Lydia Lunch's 8 Eyed Spy and Bow Wow Wow. The Strangeloves were originally a studio-based writer-production trio, and even worked on some outside projects while they were recording their own band. Before they'd taken their name and become a group, they worked for the Angels (creating "My Boyfriend's Back") and the McCoys ("Hang on Sloopy").

After 1966, the band broke up and each member went back to full-time producing. Richard Gottehrer became a partner in Sire Records in 1970, and along with the two other original Strangeloves recorded unsuccessfully for the label under the name the Strange Brothers Show. In 1976, he produced the debut Blondie LP and in 1981 he coproduced the Go-Go's' first album, which went platinum.

THE STRAWBERRY ALARM CLOCK
Formed 1967, Santa Barbara, California
Ed King, gtr., voc.; Lee Freeman, gtr., bass, horns, drums, voc.; Mark Weitz, kybds.; Gary Lovetro, bass, voc.; George Bunnel, bass, special effects; Randy Seol, drums.
1967—*Incense and Peppermints* (Uni) 1968—*Wake Up, It's Tomorrow; World in a Sea Shell* 1969— (– Seol; – Bunnel; + Jimmy Pitman, gtr., voc.; + Gene Gunnels, drums) *Good Morning Starshine* 1970—*Psych Out; Best of; Changes.*

This one-hit wonder surfaced in 1967 with the #1 hit and flower-power anthem "Incense and Peppermints." Though it would fade quickly from view, the band was renowned for its psychedelic stage show (drummer Randy Seol played bongos with his hands on fire) and for the presence of two bassists. Subsequent releases included "Sit with the Guru." Ed King later resurfaced with Lynyrd Skynyrd.

In the summer of 1982, Lee Freeman happened to spot an ad for Strawberry Alarm Clock at an L.A. nightclub; intrigued, he went in and discovered the ad was a fake, designed to draw in original Alarm Clock members for a reunion. Freeman told *Rolling Stone* he planned to assemble most of the original personnel—minus King, who by that time was working with a New Jersey gospel group—plus new singer Leo Gaffney, to record all new material.

THE STRAWBS
Formed as Strawberry Hill Boys, 1967, Leicester, England
Dave Cousins, voc., gtr., banjo, dulcimer; Tony Hooper, gtr., voc.; Arthur Phillips, mandolin.
1968—(– Phillips; + Ron Chesterman, bass; + Sandy Denny [b. Jan. 6, 1941, Wimbledon, Eng.; d. Apr. 21, 1978, London], voc.) 1969—(– Chesterman; – Denny; + Rick Wakeman [b. May 18, 1949 London], kybds.; + John Ford, bass, voc.; + Richard Hudson, drums) *Strawbs* (A&M) 1970—(+ Claire Deniz, cello) *Dragonfly* (– Deniz) *Just a Collection of*

Antiques and Curios **1971**—*From the Witchwood*
1972—*Grave New World* (− Hooper; − Wakeman; +
Dave Lambert, gtr.; + Blue Weaver, kybds.) **1973**—
Bursting at the Seams; All Our Own Work (Hallmark)
(reissue) **1974**—(− Ford; − Hudson; − Weaver; +
John Hawken, kybds.; + Chas Cronk, bass; + Rod
Coombes, drums) *Hero and Heroine* (A&M) *By
Choice* (compilation) **1975**—*Ghosts* (− Hawken; +
John Mealing, kybds.; + Robert Kirby, kybds.)
Nomadness **1976**—*Deep Cuts* (Oyster) **1977**—
Burning for You **1978**—(− Coombes; + Tony Fernan-
dez, drums) *Deadlines* (Arista) *Best of* (A&M).

Through a long career laden with personnel changes, the
Strawbs have kept in touch with both their British folk
roots and the Seventies progressive-rock movement.

Dave Cousins, the band's main songwriter, and Tony
Hooper formed the Strawberry Hill Boys (named for the
London district where they rehearsed) in 1967, singing
traditional British and American folk music, then recorded
with Sandy Denny (who went on to Fairport Convention)
before becoming the Strawbs with the addition of Richard
Hudson and John Ford, from Velvet Opera. Their debut
LP won great acclaim in British folk circles, but the
second, which saw them turning to a keyboard-dominated
progressive sound (Nicky Hopkins guested on it), left
them between audiences.

Royal Academy of Music graduate Rick Wakeman's
classical arpeggios took the band decisively away from
folk and into progressive rock. Wakeman left in 1971 to
join Yes. His replacement was Blue Weaver, who had
played with Andy Fairweather-Low's Amen Corner and,
with Dave Mason, had had a minor solo career under the
name Wynder K. Frogg. Shortly after Wakeman's departure, internal disagreements between Cousins and Hudson
and Ford led to Cousins' temporary departure, placing the
band in limbo in late 1971. Cousins recorded a solo LP,
Two Weeks Last Summer; Strawbs then regrouped and
had their first British hit singles with "Lay Down" in 1972,
and in 1973 with Hudson-Ford's "Part of the Union."

After a traumatic 1973 U.S. tour, Hudson and Ford left
to work as a team, with three LPs and a 1974 U.S. tour.
Weaver also left, and Cousins recruited John Hawken
(from Nashville Teens, Vinegar Joe and Renaissance),
Chas Cronk and Rod Coombes (of Stealers Wheel). At this
time the band's audience base shifted from the U.K. to the
U.S. Though they never became a truly major American
attraction, they toured the U.S. constantly and hardly
ever played the U.K. After middling success with a series
of progressively more commercial late-Seventies LPs, the
group disbanded.

THE STRAY CATS
Formed 1979, Massapequa, New York
Brian Setzer (b. 1959), gtr., voc.; Slim Jim Phantom (b.

Jim McDonell, 1961), drums; Lee Rocker (b. Lee
Drucker, 1961), string bass, voc.
1981—*Stray Cats* (Arista, U.K.) **1982**—*Gonna Ball;
Built for Speed* (EMI America).

The Stray Cats' cartoonish version of classic Fifties rockabilly proved one of the surprise successes of 1982. The
group was formed in a New York suburb by Brian Setzer
(an ex-member of the Bloodless Pharaohs), Slim Jim
Phantom and Lee Rocker. After playing the Long Island
club circuit for several months, the group moved to
London with their manager in the summer of 1980.

Although New Romanticism and new wave dominated
the British scene, the Stray Cats soon became a popular
club act. The group signed with Arista U.K. and Dave
Edmunds produced their debut single, "Runaway Boys."
Released in England in November 1980, "Runaway
Boys" hit the British Top Ten as did their two subsequent
singles, "Stray Cat Strut" and "Rock This Town." The
Stray Cats opened three dates on the Rolling Stones 1981
North American tour; by that time their debut LP had
become a top-selling import in the U.S. Their second LP,
Gonna Ball, was not as well received as their debut, and
by 1982 there were management problems as well. Nonetheless, the group signed to EMI America, which released
their U.S. debut, *Built for Speed,* containing material from
the two British albums. Within months, the Stray Cats'
"Rock This Town" and "Stray Cat Strut" videos were in
heavy rotation on MTV; "Rock This Town" was a Top Ten
hit and the LP sold over 2 million copies.

BARRETT STRONG
Born February 5, 1941, Mississippi
1976—*Live and Love* (Capitol).

Barrett Strong's career as a singer/songwriter began on a
very promising note with "Money" in 1960. One of Berry
Gordy's first hits (#23 pop, #2 R&B), it was covered by a
wide variety of acts, from the Beatles to the Flying
Lizards. But Strong's singing career was soon overshadowed by his songwriting duties. As a Motown staff writer,
he collaborated with Norman Whitfield on some of the
songs that revolutionized Motown's sound in the late
Sixties and early Seventies: "Ball of Confusion," "Papa
Was a Rolling Stone," "Psychedelic Shack" and "I Wish
It Would Rain" for the Temptations, and "War" for Edwin
Starr. In the mid-Seventies, he tried unsuccessfully to
revive his singing career.

STUDIO TECHNIQUES

The growth of rock coincided with—and stimulated—the
development of recording technology. Early recordings
simply involved putting a microphone in front of the
musicians and turning on the tape recorder. With two-
channel stereo recording, careful placement of micro-

phones could create various spatial illusions on two independent channels. Since the mid-Sixties, the number of independent channels that can be mixed into a rock recording has proliferated; at last count, a 64-track tape recorder was in use, which meant that up to 64 separate instruments or groups of instruments could be combined, and any one of those 64 tracks could be changed without affecting the rest of the tape. If, for instance, a singer backed by a full orchestra misses a note, the singer's track can be redone without bringing back the whole orchestra. Or if the singer wants to sing more than one part, he can record one on top of the other, in a process called multitracking.

A modern rock record can be painstakingly assembled note by note, track by track. Some musicians, including Paul McCartney, Steve Winwood, Stevie Wonder, Lindsey Buckingham, Todd Rundgren and Prince, have turned themselves into one-man rock bands through multitracking.

Like a camera, a tape recorder can lie. Wrong notes can be erased and replaced; instrumental sounds can be altered electronically, used for only a moment (as in reggae dub mixes) or mixed in "impossible" proportions. On a typical rock record, for instance, the singer is louder than a full band. Other studio effects include electronic reverberation (like the slap-echo of Elvis Presley's early vocals), filtering and compression (which radically alter tone quality) and tape tricks such as running the tape backward (as in the Beatles' "Rain" and "Strawberry Fields Forever") and splicing for sudden, shocking changes. Every record producer has private tricks and techniques; most insist, however, that all the gimmicks in the world can't replace a good song.

Studio Musicians

Studio musicians provide a specialized kind of hired help. They are freelancers who earn union wages (or, for an elite, double or triple scale) to give professional instrumental and vocal performances. They are sometimes credited on records, but the bulk of their work is anonymous: jingles, background music, soundtracks. They work in a high-pressure environment—the recording studio, where every minute costs someone money—and are expected to deliver perfect performances in as few takes as possible. The best-paid session musicians are adaptable and dependable; they fit into virtually any musical context. At worst, session players know which musical cliché goes in any given spot, and at best they add a subtle personal touch to someone else's music.

Session musicians were taken for granted before rock & roll subsumed pop. While blues and R&B musicians might tour and record with the same band, pop singers were regularly matched with tunes, arrangements and musicians in the studio. Early rock

& rollers had to demand the right to record with their own bands, although many of the finest Fifties rock records were made by putting a good singer in front of a crack studio band (which might play gigs on its own ouside the studio), like the one Dave Bartholomew maintained in New Orleans, including drummer Earl Palmer and tenor saxophonist Lee Allen.

As the Sixties began studio musicians galore worked on the orchestral pop of Phil Spector and his less adventurous colleagues. But with the advent of the Beatles, the image of the self-contained band began to dominate rock—although the Beatles used a session drummer on their first singles, and session players augmented many British Invasion bands. Guitarist Jimmy Page can be heard on records by Herman's Hermits and Donovan, for example.

Since amateur musicians were obviously making best-selling discs, record companies allowed them to do sessions that were sloppier but perhaps more unpredictable than those using session players. Meanwhile, soul music remained the province of

singers hooked up with studio bands, notably Stax-Volt's Booker T. (Jones, an organist) and the MGs (or Memphis Group: Duck Dunn on bass, Steve Cropper on guitar and Al Jackson on drums), who backed Sam and Dave, Wilson Pickett and Otis Redding. In Detroit, Motown Records' studio band was anchored by bassist James Jamerson; at Muscle Shoals studios in Sheffield, Alabama, tenor saxophonist King Curtis and the Kingpins backed Aretha Franklin and others.

As recording became a more entrenched business, studio elites arose in major recording centers, including New York, Los Angeles, Nashville, Miami, London and (for reggae) Kingston, Jamaica. Singer/songwriters like Paul Simon would go studio-hopping to get the local "feel" on the appropriate songs. Simon was one of many singers to use the Muscle Shoals house band from the late Sixties onward; the group generally included keyboardist Barry Beckett, guitarist Pete Carr, bassist David Hood and drummer Roger Hawkins.

Sooner or later, top session musicians tend to get the urge to express themselves in their own bands, which may simply record under a group name or actually take a sabbatical from lucrative studio jobs to go on the road. Some of those aggregates include the Section (bassist Leland Sklar, keyboardist Craig Doerge, drummer Russ Kunkel and guitarist Danny Kortchmar, based in Los Angeles), Stuff (drummers Steve Gadd and Chris Parker, guitarists Cornell Dupree and Eric Gale, bassist Gordon Edwards and keyboardist Richard Tee, in New York), Area Code 615 (from Nashville: Mac Gayden, Kenny Buttrey), Attitudes (drummer Jim Keltner), MFSB (Gamble and Huff's Sigma Sound Studios orchestra, from Philadelphia) and Ronin (Los Angeles guitarist Waddy Wachtel, drummer Rick Marotta, keyboardist Stanley Sheldon, bassist Dan Dugmore). When the right offer comes along, studio musicians sometimes hit the road as a touring band for the likes of Linda Ronstadt, James Taylor or Paul Simon.

Probably the most successful band of ex–studio musicians are Toto, who played sessions for Aretha Franklin, Steely Dan and numerous others before finding a vocalist and writing their own hits. The Eagles, the Doobie Brothers, the Mahavishnu Orchestra and numerous other bands have included studio veterans. Other studio musicians who made their own names as solo acts—employing other session players for records—include pianist Leon Russell, saxophonist David Sanborn, guitarist Larry Carlton and singer Luther Vandross. And some studio players work their way up to becoming producers, such as Sly Dunbar and Robbie Shakespeare in Jamaica, or Chic's Bernard Edwards and Nile Rodgers in New York.

As rock has become more professional ever since the late Sixties, it is rarer and rarer to find a record that does not use studio musicians. And there are probably hundreds of these musicians whose work will always remain anonymous.

STUFF

Formed mid-Seventies
Steve Gadd, drums; Richard Tee, kybds.; Cornell Dupree, gtr.; Chris Parker, drums; Eric Gale, gtr.
1977—*Stuff* (Warner Bros.) **1978**—*More Stuff* **1979**—*Stuff It.*

Stuff is an aggregation of top New York studio musicians who performed at West Side clubs, especially Mikell's, before recording several albums for Warner Bros. Gordon Edwards, the driving force behind Stuff, had a group of session players, Encyclopedia of Soul, on and off for ten years before forming Stuff. In 1975, he appeared on two Grammy Award–winning records, Paul Simon's *Still Crazy After All These Years* and Van McCoy's "The Hustle." Stuff backed Joe Cocker on *Stingray* in 1976, and most of Stuff appeared in Paul Simon's film *One Trick Pony*.

Cornell Dupree was part of King Curtis and His King Pins. Richard Tee is a gospel-based keyboardist. Chris Parker made a reputation with Paul Butterfield's Better Days. Steve Gadd has appeared in every context, from pop to funk to jazz.

Stuff's members split up to perform in other group projects in the early Eighties. Edwards revived Encyclopedia of Soul in 1981 and performed in a number of New York City clubs.

STYLISTICS

Formed 1968, Philadelphia
Russell Thompkins, Jr., Airrion Love, James Smith, Herbie Murrell, James Dunn.

1971—*The Stylistics* (Avco) **1972**—*Round 2* **1973**—*Rockin' Roll Baby* **1974**—*Let's Put It All Together; Heavy* **1975**—*Best of the Stylistics; Thank You Baby; You Are Beautiful* **1976**—*Fabulous* (Hugo and Luigi) *Wonder Woman* **1979**—*Love Spell* (Mercury) **1980**—*Hurry Up This Way Again* (TSOP).

Led by Russell Thompkins, the Stylistics were leading practitioners of the lush "Philadelphia sound" of the mid-Seventies.

They came together in 1968, a union of two Philadelphia vocal groups. Herbie Murrell and James Dunn came from the Percussions; Thompkins, Airrion Love and James Smith joined from the Monarchs. Robert Douglas, a member of their backing band Slim and the Boys, and road manager Marty Bryant wrote "You're a Big Girl Now" for the Stylistics. It began as a hit on the small Sebring Records in the Philadelphia area before being picked up by Avco Records and hitting the national R&B chart at #7.

Philadelphia producer/writer Thom Bell then took control of the Stylistics' music. Collaborating with songwriter Linda Creed, Bell created "Stop, Look, Listen (to Your Heart)" (#39 pop, #6 R&B) and "You Are Everything" (#9 pop, #10 R&B) in 1971; "Betcha By Golly, Wow" (#3 pop, #2 R&B), "People Make the World Go Round" (#25 pop, #6 R&B) and "I'm Stone in Love with You" (#10 pop, #4 R&B) in 1972; "Break Up to Make Up" (#5 pop and R&B), "You'll Never Get to Heaven" (#23 pop, #8 R&B) and "Rockin' Roll Baby" (#14 pop, #13 R&B) in 1973; and "You Make Me Feel Brand New" (#2 pop, #5 R&B) in 1974.

After their relationship with Bell ended, the Stylistics' sales in America declined. They remained popular in

Europe both on record and in nightclubs throughout the Seventies. They signed to Philadelphia International Records in 1980.

STYX

Formed 1963, Chicago

James Young, gtr., voc.; John Curulewski, gtr.; Dennis DeYoung, kybds., voc.; Chuck Panozzo, bass, voc.; John Panozzo, drums.

1972—*Styx* (Wooden Nickel) 1973—*Styx II; The Serpent Is Rising* 1974—*Man of Miracles* 1975—*Equinox* (A&M) (− Curulewski; + Tommy Shaw, gtr., voc.) 1976—*Crystal Ball* 1977—*The Grand Illusion* 1978—*Pieces of Eight* 1979—*Cornerstone* 1981—*Paradise Theatre* 1983—*Kilroy Was Here*.

One of the leading exemplars of the FM radio–oriented hard pop known as "pomp rock," Styx also claim the distinction of having been named (in a 1979 Gallup Poll) the most popular rock band among American fans aged 13 to 18.

Twins Chuck and John Panozzo, along with Dennis DeYoung and Tom Nardini, worked the Chicago area bar circuit from 1963 until 1969, when Nardini left the group and the Panozzos and DeYoung entered Chicago State University. There they met John Curulewski, with whom they formed TW4. James Young joined a year later, and they changed their name to Styx (after the river that flows through Hades in Greek mythology).

After incessant touring, their national break came in 1975 with the #6 single "Lady," featuring the blaring vocal triads that are a Styx trademark. Since 1977, every one of their releases has sold platinum or better, and their concerts are invariably sold out. Their 1978 hit singles included "Come Sail Away" (#8), "Fooling Yourself (the Angry Young Man)" (#29) and "Blue Collar Man (Long Nights)" (#21). In 1979, they had a #1 hit single with "Babe," followed by "The Best of Times" (#3) and "Too Much Time On My Hands" (#9) in 1981. They toured 3,000-seat halls in 1983 with a theatrical presentation of *Kilroy Was Here,* a concept album that included the hit singles "Mr. Roboto" and "Don't Let It End."

THE SUGAR HILL GANG

Formed 1977, New York City

Master Gee (b. Guy O'Brien, 1963, New York City), voc.; Wonder Mike (b. Michael Wright, 1958, Montclair, N.J.), voc.; Big Bank Hank (b. Henry Jackson, 1958, Bronx, N.Y.), voc.

1979—*Rapper's Delight* (Sugarhill) 1981—*The 8th Wonder.*

Before the Sugar Hill Gang's "Rapper's Delight," rap was confined to the clubs and house parties in the New York City area. Following the record's release in the summer of 1979, rap became a part of the pop music vocabulary.

In 1979, Sylvia and Joe Robinson's independent label All Platinum was awash in lawsuits and losing money; the husband-and-wife team (Sylvia had been a hitmaking singer as half of Mickey and Sylvia and as a soloist) expected to quit the record business. At a party for her sister in Harlem, she heard guests chanting rhymes over the instrumental breaks in disco records. Using her son Joey as talent scout, she rounded up three youngsters from the New York area to rap over a rhythm track adapted from Chic's "Good Times," and chartered a new label, Sugarhill, to carry the record, "Rapper's Delight."

According to Sugarhill, the record sold two million copies in America. It placed #4 R&B in the U.S., made the Top Five in the U.K., Israel, South Africa and other countries, and went to #1 in Canada. It proved to be the Sugar Hill Gang's only big hit, although "8th Wonder" (#15 R&B, 1981) and "Lover in You" were chart singles.

SUICIDE

Formed 1972, New York City

Alan Vega, voc.; Martin Rev, kybds., percussion.

1978—*Suicide* (Red Star) 1980—*Suicide* (includes live-in-Brussels flexi-disc) *Suicide* (Ze).

When artist/sculptor Alan Vega and keyboardist Martin Rev formed Suicide in 1972 and began performing at New York's Mercer Arts Center in the wake of the success of the New York Dolls, they were ahead of their time. Suicide based its music on Rev's repetitive wall-of-noise keyboards and pneumatic rhythm machines, with Vega's Presleyish vocals providing a link to rock & roll tradition. But Vega also brought a form of performance art onstage. He hit himself in the face with his microphone, he whispered and screamed, he strode into the audience seeking to incite involvement or confrontation.

Some found Suicide fascinating; others thought them brilliant and important; more seemed to enjoy them as some sort of joke; and most simply hated them. Suicide opened for the Clash and Elvis Costello on 1978 British tours, where audiences regularly flung beer bottles at the stage, and a few fights broke out. On the live-in-Brussels flexi-disc, one can hear audience members grabbing the microphone from the stage and passing it around, hurling epithets at the band the whole time.

In 1980, Ric Ocasek of the Cars revealed himself as Suicide's most famous fan. The Cars' *Candy-O* includes a direct allusion to Suicide in "Shoo-Be-Doo." Ocasek got Suicide to open the Cars' 1980 U.S. tour (in L.A. Suicide nearly caused riots, and the concert promoters unsuccessfully tried to have them taken off the bill), included Suicide on a Cars-hosted "Midnight Special," and produced Suicide's 1980 Ze album. Since that album, Rev released a solo-instrumental LP for Lust/Unlust Records in 1980 and Vega has recorded *Alan Vega* and *Collision Drive* for Ze and *Saturn Strip* (produced by Ocasek) for Elektra.

DONNA SUMMER

Born Donna Gaines, December 31, 1948, Boston
1975—*Love to Love You* (Oasis) **1976**—*A Love Trilogy;
The Four Seasons of Love* **1977**—*I Remember Yesterday* (Casablanca) *Once upon a Time* **1978**—*Live and More* **1979**—*Bad Girls; On the Radio—Greatest Hits* **1980**—*The Wanderer* (Geffen) **1982**—*Donna Summer* **1983**—*She Works Hard for the Money* (Mercury).

Donna Summer was the biggest star to emerge from the mid-Seventies disco explosion and has since pursued a successful pop career.

She sang in Boston churches as a child, occasionally as a lead vocalist. In 1967, she made her professional debut at Boston's Psychedelic Supermarket. Later that year, at age 18, she landed a role in the Munich, Germany, production of *Hair*. While in Germany, she married Austrian actor Helmut Sommer, later divorcing him but keeping the Anglicized surname. For a time she sang in a Vienna Folk Opera version of *Porgy and Bess*.

Working as a backup singer at Munich's Musicland Studios, Summer met producers Giorgio Moroder and Pete Bellotte. Together the trio created a string of European pop hits for Moroder's Oasis label. In 1975, Moroder licensed Oasis to America's Casablanca Records. The orgasmic 17-minute "Love to Love You Baby" first became a major disco hit, and by year's end had crossed over to pop and R&B charts as well (#2 pop, #3 R&B).

Many thought Summer would be a typical one-hit disco act, but Moroder, Bellotte and Casablanca president Neil Bogart were determined to make her a consistent record seller. Her *Love Trilogy* solidified her disco following, while *The Four Seasons of Love* and "Spring Affair" (#47 pop, #24 R&B) expanded her pop audience.

With 1977's *I Remember Yesterday,* Moroder expanded the music's stylistic range. The album yielded the influential synthesizer pop hit "I Feel Love" (#6 pop, #9 R&B). For the disco fairy-tale concept LP *Once upon a Time* Summer contributed lyrics to most of the material. The *Live and More* album in 1978 provided Summer with her first pop #1, a cover of Jimmy Webb's "MacArthur Park." That year she also appeared in the disco film *Thank God It's Friday*. "Last Dance" from the soundtrack album won two Grammy Awards—one for Summer, one for songwriter Paul Jabara—and an Oscar for Jabara.

Bad Girls broke down any lingering critical resistance to Summer. The rocking title track (#1 pop, #1 R&B) and "Hot Stuff" (#1 pop, #3 R&B) made her popular with disco, pop and rock fans. That year, Barbra Streisand duetted with Summer on "No More Tears (Enough Is Enough)" (#1 pop, #20 R&B). Two other crossover hits rounded out Summer's biggest year: "Heaven Knows" (#4 pop, #10 R&B) and "Dim All the Lights" (#2 pop, #13 R&B).

But success also brought problems. In 1980, she sued

Donna Summer

her manager, Joyce Bogart, and husband Neil for $10 million for mismanagement. She was thus able to end her Casablanca contract and to sign with Geffen Records.

The Wanderer was her first Geffen release, the title track becoming a strong-selling single (#3 pop, #13 R&B), although the album didn't live up to sales expectations. (*The Wanderer* also included Summer's first born-again-Christian message song.) In 1980, she married Bruce Sudano, lead singer of Brooklyn Dreams, with whom she had recorded "Heaven Knows"; they named their daughter Brook Lyn.

Donna Summer was released in 1982. The Quincy Jones–produced album was a replacement for an LP Giorgio Moroder had produced but Geffen Records had rejected. A track from that unreleased album appears on the *Fast Times at Ridgemont High* soundtrack. As of 1982, Summer has garnered eight gold LPs, two platinum LPs, ten gold singles and two platinum singles.

SUPERTRAMP

Formed 1969, England
Roger Hodgson (b. Mar. 21, 1950, Portsmouth, Eng.), gtr., voc., bass; Richard Davies (b. July 22, 1944, Eng.), kybds., voc.; Richard Palmer, gtr.; Bob Miller, drums.
1970—*Supertramp* (A&M) (− Palmer; − Miller; + Dave Winthrop [b. Nov. 27, 1948, N.J.], sax; + Frank Farrell [b. Birmingham, Eng.], bass; + Kevin Currie [b. Liverpool, Eng.], drums **1971**—*Indelibly Stamped*

1973—*Extremes* (soundtrack) (Deram)   1974—(−
Winthrop; − Farrel; − Currie; + John Anthony
Helliwell [b. circa 1945, Eng.], sax; + Dougie Thomson
[b. 1951, Scot.], bass; + Bob C. Benberg, drums)
Crime of the Century (A&M)   1975—*Crisis? What
Crisis?*   1977—*Even in the Quietest Moments*   1979—
Breakfast in America   1980—*Paris*   1982—
". . . famous last words . . .".

Supertramp began as the wish fulfillment of a millionaire
rock fan. By the late Seventies, their blend of keyboard-
heavy progressive rock and immaculate pop had given
them several hit singles and a few platinum LPs.

In the late Sixties, Dutch millionaire Stanley August
Miesegaes heard Rick Davies in a band called the Joint.
When that band broke up, Miesegaes offered to bankroll a
band if Davies would handle the music. Davies placed
classified ads in London newspapers for a band. The first
response was from Roger Hodgson, who was to split
songwriting and singing with Davies in Supertramp, the
name they took from W. H. Davies' 1938 book, *The
Autobiography of a Supertramp.* Drummer Bob Miller
suffered a nervous breakdown after their first LP's release; he was replaced by Kevin Currie for the next, but
like the first, it flopped.

After a disastrous tour, the band (except Davies and
Hodgson) broke up. Davies and Hodgson recruited Bob
Benberg from pub rockers Bees Make Honey, and John
Helliwell and Dougie Thomson from the Alan Bown Set,
and A&M sent them to a rehearsal retreat at a 17th-
century farm. Their next LP, *Crime of the Century,* was
the subject of a massive advertising/promotional campaign, and went to #1 in the U.K. but didn't take off
commercially in the U.S., though it did sow the seeds of a
cult following.

In 1975, the singles "Dreamer" and "Bloody Well
Right" from *Crime* achieved some chart success in both
the U.K. and the U.S. Supertramp toured the U.S. as
headliners, with A&M giving away most of the tickets.
Crisis? failed to yield a hit single, but was heavily played
on progressive FM radio and solidified the band's audience base, as did *Quietest Moments.* Their breakthrough
was *Breakfast in America,* a #1 worldwide LP, which
eventually went platinum and contained hit singles in
"The Logical Song" (#6), "Goodbye Stranger" (#15) and
"Take the Long Way Home" (#10). The *Paris* live double
LP hit #8; and *". . . famous last words . . ."* included
another hit, "It's Raining Again." In early 1983, Hodgson
announced he was leaving the group for a solo career.

THE SUPREMES
Formed 1960, Detroit
Diana Ross (b. Mar. 26, 1944, Detroit); Florence Ballard
(b. June 30, 1943, Detroit; d. Feb. 22, 1976, Detroit);
Mary Wilson (b. Mar. 6, 1944, Detroit).
1967—(− Ballard; + Cindy Birdsong [b. Dec. 15, 1939,
Camden, N.J.])   1969—(− Ross; + Jean Terrell [b.
Nov. 26, ca. 1944, Tex.])   1972—(− Birdsong; + Lynda
Laurence)   1973—(− Terrell; + Sherri Payne [b. Nov.
14, 1944])   1967—*Diana Ross and the Supremes'
Greatest Hits* (Motown)   1969—*Diana Ross and the
Supremes' Greatest Hits, Volume 2*   1972—*Diana Ross
and the Supremes' Greatest Hits, Volume 3*   1974—
Anthology.

With twelve #1 pop singles, numerous gold recordings,
sold-out concerts and regular television appearances, the
Supremes were the most commercially successful female
group of the Sixties. Fronted by Diana Ross during their
peak years, they epitomized Holland-Dozier-Holland's
Motown sound and realized Berry Gordy's dreams of
creating the ultimate crossover group.

The original Supremes—Diana Ross, Mary Wilson and
Florence Ballard—grew up together in Detroit's Brewster
housing project. They began singing together in their
teens. Ballard was the most enthusiastic about pursuing a
music career. While in high school, they became friendly
with members of the Temptations, then known as the
Primes, and named themselves the Primettes. Through the
Temptations they met Berry Gordy, and upon graduation
from high school in 1961, were signed to Motown. Ballard
suggested they change their name to the Supremes.

Gordy groomed all his groups but paid special attention
to the Supremes. The girls took classes in dance, charm
and singing while recording sporadically. "Let Me Go the

The Supremes: Diana Ross, Mary Wilson, Florence Ballard

Right Way" (#26 R&B) in 1962 and "When the Lovelight Starts Shining through His Eyes" (#23 pop) in 1963 were early efforts.

It wasn't until their tenth single, "Where Did Our Love Go," hit #1 in 1964 that producers Eddie and Brian Holland and Lamont Dozier found the right formula. It sold over two million copies and was followed that year by "Baby Love" (#1 pop) and "Come See About Me" (#1 pop, #3 R&B).

The Supremes' big singles of 1965 were "Stop! In the Name of Love" (#1 pop, #2 R&B), "Back in My Arms Again" (#1 pop and R&B) and "I Hear a Symphony" (#1 pop, #2 R&B). "You Can't Hurry Love" and "You Keep Me Hangin' On" were #1 on both the pop and R&B charts in 1966. "Love Is Here and Now You're Gone" (#1 pop and R&B), "The Happening" (#1 pop, #12 R&B) and "Reflections" (#2 pop, #4 R&B) hit in 1967. "Reflections" was the first single credited to Diana Ross and the Supremes.

Some personal problems (particularly a rivalry between Ross and Ballard) led Ballard to quit the Supremes in 1967. (According to some sources, Gordy fired her.) She attempted a solo career with another label, then unsuccessfully brought suit against Gordy and Ross, alleging she was forced out. Ballard also lost the few royalties Motown paid her through an attorney. Ross and Wilson had always credited her with founding the Supremes. Nine years later, she died of cardiac arrest in Detroit at 32. At the time of her death, she and her three children were living on welfare.

Ballard was replaced by a former member of Patti La-Belle and the Blue Belles, Cindy Birdsong. "Love Child" (#1 pop, #2 R&B) was the Supremes' biggest hit of 1968, along with their group duet with the Temptations, "I'm Gonna Make You Love Me" (#2 pop). The two groups also filmed a television special together. Rumors of Ross going solo were by then quite common. "I'm Livin' in Shame" (#10 pop, #8 R&B) and "I'll Try Something New," cut with the Temptations (#8 R&B), followed in 1969. Late in the year Ross's departure was announced, and the soaring "Someday We'll Be Together" (#1 pop and R&B) marked the end of the Supremes' golden era. Ross went on as a hugely successful solo act.

With boxer Ernie Terrell's sister, Jean Terrell, taking Ross's place, the Supremes continued to chart. The year 1970 brought "Up the Ladder to the Roof" (#10 pop, #5 R&B) and the group's last #1 hit, "Stoned Love" (#7 pop, #1 R&B). Along with the Four Tops, the Supremes cut an updated version of "River Deep—Mountain High" (#14 pop, #7 R&B) in 1970. "Nathan Jones" (#16 pop, #8 R&B) was the Supremes' only major hit in 1971, while "Floy Joy" (#16 pop, #5 R&B) was considered their best effort of 1972.

Subsequently, Mary Wilson and Cindy Birdsong would both leave the group, to be replaced by Lynda Laurence and Sherri Payne and, in subsequent incarnations, Susaye

Green and Karen Jackson. In 1976, the Supremes had a minor hit with "You're My Drivin' Wheel" (#85 pop, #50 R&B), but by the late Seventies the group had disbanded; Wilson performed with a pair of back-up singers as Mary Wilson and the Supremes. The 1981 Broadway hit *Dreamgirls* is based largely on the Supremes' story.

THE SURFARIS

Formed circa 1963, Southern California
Pat Connolly, voc., bass; Jim Fuller, gtr.; Bob Berryhill, gtr.; Ron Wilson, drums; Jim Pash, sax, clarinet, gtr.

The Surfaris rode the wave of the early-Sixties surf music boom, often appearing at Southern California teen dances and beach parties with surf outfits like the Crossfires, who later became the Turtles. The Surfaris had only one big hit record, the immortal 1963 instrumental "Wipeout," which contained one of rock's first and most influential drum solos. The single hit #2 in 1963 and recharted at #16 in 1966. After surf music went out of vogue, the Surfaris adjusted to the folk-rock trend.

SURF MUSIC

A Southern Californian genre of the early Sixties, surf rock celebrated not just catching the perfect wave but such carefree adolescent phenomena as the sun, beach parties, girls and hot rods.

Surf music had two strains, vocal and instrumental. Jan and Dean started surf vocal music off in 1959 with their hit "Baby Talk" and followed with such genre classics as "Surf City" and "Deadman's Curve," all featuring their trademark high harmony vocals and bouncy denatured Chuck Berry guitar riffs. The Beach Boys came along soon after and scored a series of mammoth national hits, and soon eclipsed Jan and Dean in both popularity and significance, not to mention durability.

Instrumental surf music featured throbbing tribal tom-tom tattoos and trebly, metallic, twanging guitar riffs: the Ventures' "Walk Don't Run," the Duals' "Stick Shift," Dick Dale and the Del-Tones' "Pipeline." Thanks in large part to the prolific Ventures, instrumental surf rock has proven one of rock's most influential subgenres. The influence of surf rock can be heard in the music of contemporary bands like Blondie, the Go-Go's, the Raybeats and many others.

SUTHERLAND BROTHERS AND QUIVER

Formed 1973, London
Ian Sutherland, gtr., voc., kybds.; Gavin Sutherland, gtr., bass, voc.; Peter Wood, kybds.; Tim Renwick, gtr.; Willie Wilson, drums; Bruce Thomas, bass.
1973—*Dream Kid* (Island/Columbia) 1974—*Beat of the Street* (− Thomas) 1975—*Lifeboat* (Island) (− Wood); *Reach for the Sky* (Columbia) 1976—*Sailing* (compilation) *Slipstream* 1977—*Down to Earth*

1978—(— band; + I. Sutherland; + G. Sutherland; + various sessionmen) **1979—When the Night Comes Down.**

The Sutherland Brothers had made two folk-rock LPs for Island in the early Seventies: *Sutherland Bros. Band* and *Lifeboat* (the latter not to be confused with the U.K. *Lifeboat* compilation). Quiver had made two of their own rock albums for Warner Bros.: *Quiver* and *Gone in the Morning*. The two groups merged and, despite some critical admiration, had only one hit single, "(I Don't Want to Love You But) You Got Me Anyway," which went to #48 in the U.S. in 1973 and got the band a spot opening for Elton John's 1973 U.S. tour.

Little happened for them after that until 1975, when Rod Stewart, a longtime admirer of the Sutherlands' songwriting, had a massive U.K. hit with their "Sailing." This sparked some interest in the group's next LP, *Reach for the Sky*, which yielded the U.K. Top Ten single "Arms of Mary." When *Slipstream* failed to achieve any commercial success, guitarist Tim Renwick (who had played on David Bowie's "Space Oddity") quit halfway through the *Down to Earth* sessions, with ex–Procol Harum Mick Grabham filling in on some tracks. After the rest of Quiver quit, the Sutherlands carried on for one more album.

SWAMP DOGG
Born Jerry Williams, 1942, Portsmouth, Virginia
1970—Total Destruction to Your Mind (Canyon)
1971—Rat On! (Elektra) **1972—Cuffed, Collared and Tagged** (Cream) **1973—Gag a Maggot** (Stone Dogg)
1974—Have You Heard This Story? (Island) **1976—Swamp Dogg's Greatest Hits** (Stone Dogg) **1981—I'm Not Selling Out, I'm Buying In!** (Takoma) **1982—Best of Swamp Dogg** (Solid Smoke).

Singer/songwriter/producer Swamp Dogg has had a varied career, during which his work has resulted in hits for other artists but rarely for himself.

His musical career began in the Sixties, when as Jerry Williams he was a moderately successful soul singer. He had a couple of minor hits, "I'm a Lover Man" and "You're My Everything Baby." In 1970, he became chief producer for Wally Roker's Canyon Records. Encouraged by Roker to stretch out musically, Williams became Swamp Dogg and released *Total Destruction to Your Mind,* a psychedelically eccentric soul album influenced by Sly and the Family Stone and the Mothers of Invention. "Mama's Baby, Daddy's Maybe" was a minor hit (#33 R&B).

With Canyon Records about to go under, Williams signed with Elektra, but *Rat On!* was a commercial and artistic failure. In 1972, he signed with Cream Records, releasing *Cuffed, Collared and Tagged*, which included a tribute to Sly Stone called "If It Hadn't Been for Sly" and the John Prine song "Sam Stone." Soon after the album's release, Cream went out of business.

As a producer, Jerry Williams fared better. He wrote Gene Pitney's 1968 hit "She's a Heartbreaker," produced the Commodores' first single, "I Keep On Dancing," while an Atlantic staff member, and Doris Duke's Top Ten soul hit, "I'm the Other Woman to the Other Woman," in 1970. In 1971, his song "She's All I Got" was a Top Forty pop hit for Freddie North and a #1 country song for Johnny Paycheck. Williams also had soul hits sung by Z. Z. Hill, Irma Thomas and Charlie Whitehead.

Still Swamp Dogg struggled. *Gag a Maggot*, distributed by T.K. Records, and a single, "Ebony and Jet," on Brut Records, were his only releases in 1973. *Have You Heard This Story?* was released on Island records in 1974. In the late Seventies, he cut *Finally Caught Up with Myself* and *Swamp Dogg* for Wizard. In 1981, *I'm Not Selling Out, I'm Buying In!* appeared on Takoma Records, featuring Swamp Dogg and Esther Phillips duetting on "The Love We Got Ain't Worth Two Dead Flies." The next year Solid Smoke put out a *Best of Swamp Dogg* collection.

BILLY SWAN
Born May 12, 1944, Cape Girardeau, Missouri
1974—I Can Help (Columbia) **1975—Rock 'n' Roll Moon 1976—Billy Swan 1977—Four 1978—You're OK, I'm OK** (A&M) **1978—Billy Swan at His Best** (Monument).

Billy Swan, a Nashville journeyman, emerged seemingly from nowhere with one of 1974's biggest hits, the strolling organ-heavy "I Can Help." A #1 on both the pop and country & western charts, "I Can Help" differed almost completely from Swan's usual output, which leaned toward rockabilly.

Swan had his first success when his song "Lover Please," which he had written at age 16 for his band Mirt Mirley and the Rhythm Steppers, became a nationwide hit in 1962 for Clyde McPhatter. Swan lived off that song's royalties for a time, then moved to Nashville at age 21, where his pursuit of a music career led him to replace Kris Kristofferson as janitor at Columbia's Nashville studios.

Within a few years Swan was producing Tony Joe White's first three LPs (including White's hit "Polk Salad Annie"). He also lived for a time in Elvis Presley's uncle's house; in fact, after Presley covered "I Can Help," he gave Swan a pair of his socks. In 1970, Swan played in Kristofferson's band at the Isle of Wight Festival, and in 1973 he worked with comic country singer Kinky Friedman; in 1975 the latter covered "Lover Please" (Kristofferson has, too).

After the international success of "I Can Help," Swan's debut album yielded a minor U.K. hit in a cover of Otis Blackwell's "Don't Be Cruel." *Rock 'n' Roll Moon*, another critically acclaimed album, contained another minor hit in "Everything's the Same." It was Swan's last pop success, but through 1975 and 1976 he embarked on successful worldwide tours, playing with Nashville session stars like Kenny Buttrey and Charlie McCoy in Paris in 1975, and with Willie Nelson in Britain in 1976.

SWEET

Formed 1968, London
Brian Connolly (b. Oct. 5, 1948, Middlesex, Eng.), voc.; Mick Tucker (b. July 17, 1948, Middlesex, Eng.), voc., drums; Andy Scott (b. July 30, 1949, Wexham, Wales), gtr., kybds., voc.; Steve Priest (b. Feb. 23, 1950, Middlesex, Eng.), bass, voc., harmonica.
1971—*Funny How Sweet Co-Co Can Be* (RCA)   **1972**— *Biggest Hits*   **1973**—*Sweet* (Bell)   **1974**—*Sweet Fanny Adams* (RCA)   **1975**—*Desolation Boulevard* (Capitol) *Strung Up* (RCA)   **1976**—*Give Us a Wink* (Capitol) **1977**—*Off the Record; Golden Greats* (RCA, import) **1978**—*Level Headed* (Capitol) (− Connolly)   *The Sweet* (Camden)   **1979**—*A Cut Above the Rest* **1980**—*Sweet Six.*

One of the leading British hard-rock/bubblegum bands in the Chinnichap stable of British writer/producers Nicky Chinn and Mike Chapman, Sweet had hits in the U.K. and later in America as well.

The band was originally formed by Brian Connolly and Mick Tucker as Wainwright's Gentlemen in 1968. As Sweet, they recorded four unsuccessful singles that flopped before Chinnichap took over in 1971. Their U.K. hits that year included "Co-Co" and "Funny Funny." In 1972 came "Poppa Joe," "Little Willy" (also Top Ten in America in 1973) and "Wig Wam Bam"; and in 1973, "Blockbuster," "Hell Raiser" and "Ballroom Blitz" (Top Ten in the U.S. two years later).

By 1973, the blatant nature of many of Sweet's lyrics and overt stage antics led some British clubs to ban the group. They subsequently tried to abandon their bubblegum image and left inamicably from Chinnichap. They went on to hit in 1976 in both the U.K. and the U.S. with the Top Ten single "Fox on the Run," but they didn't really change their sound until 1978's *Level Headed* LP, which yielded the worldwide smash "Love Is Like Oxygen" (#8).

RACHEL SWEET

Born circa 1962, Akron, Ohio
1979—*Fool Around* (Stiff/Columbia)   **1980**—*Protect the Innocent* (Columbia)   **1981**—*And Then He Kissed Me*   **1982**—*Blame It on Love.*

Rachel Sweet was 18 when rock fans first heard her on Stiff Records' *Akron Compilation*, with a big twangy voice that elicited comparisons to Linda Ronstadt and Brenda Lee.

Sweet had begun performing at age five, when she won first prize at an Akron talent contest with a rendition of "I Am a Pretty Little Dutch Girl." She went on to perform in summer stock theater, in TV commercials and in club shows with Mickey Rooney and Bill Cosby. At age 11, she cut a minor country & western hit single for Derrick Records in Nashville.

A few years later, producer Liam Sternberg (a friend of Sweet's father) asked her to sing on a demo of his songs, which he sent to Stiff. Sweet was attending Firestone High School in Akron when "Who Does Lisa Like" became a minor hit in England and New York City. A cover of Carla Thomas' "B-A-B-Y," from Sweet's debut album, also generated some attention, as did her segments in the 1979 Be Stiff tour and her own tour backed by British band Fingerprintz. With her second album, Sweet parted ways with Sternberg and Stiff, and has since been searching for a major pop hit. She reached the Top Fifty with "Everlasting Love," a duet with Rex Smith; it appeared on *And Then He Kissed Me*. Sweet herself wrote and produced the album *Blame It on Love*, and in 1982 she worked on a 3D horror film, *Rock 'n' Roll Hotel.*

SWEET INSPIRATIONS

Formed 1960s
Emily "Cissy" Drinkard Houston, Sylvia Sherwell, Myrna Smith, Estelle Brown.
1968—*Sweet Inspirations* (Atlantic)   *What the World Needs Now Is Love.*

In the six years before they recorded on their own, the Sweet Inspirations sang backing vocals on hundreds of songs recorded for Atlantic Records in Memphis, Muscle Shoals and New York. They were featured prominently on some of Aretha Franklin's best work. Led by Cissy Houston, they recorded two critically acclaimed albums in 1968, and had a hit single with "Sweet Inspiration" (#18 pop, #5 R&B).

After Houston left for a solo career, the remaining three continued recording into the Seventies. They provided the backing on Elvis Presley's 1969 hit "Suspicious Minds" and toured with him into the mid-Seventies. Former Sweet Inspiration Myrna Smith cowrote the bulk of the material on Beach Boy Carl Wilson's eponymous 1981 solo album.

THE SWINGIN' BLUE JEANS

Formed 1963, Liverpool, England
Ray Ennis (b. May 26, 1942, Eng.), gtr., voc.; Ralph Ellis (b. Mar. 8, 1942, Eng.), gtr.; Les Braid (b. Sep. 15, 1941, Eng.), bass; Norman Kuhlke (b. June 12, 1942, Eng.), drums.
1964—(+ Terry Sylvester [b. Jan. 8, 1945, Liverpool], gtr., voc.)   *Tutti Frutti* (Regal Zonophone)   *Blue Jeans a-Swinging* (HMV)   *Hippy Hippy Shake* (Imperial) *Shaking Time* (Electrola)   **1965**—*Hey Hey Hey Hey* **1966**—*The Swinging Blue Jeans* (MFP)   **1974**—(Reformed without Sylvester)   *Brand New and Faded* (Dart)   **1978**—*Swinging Blue Jeans* (EMI).

In 1963, just as England's Merseybeat sound was coming together, the Swingin' Blue Jeans emerged with one of the wildest rock raveups of the era, a cover of Chan Romero's "Hippy Hippy Shake." It went to #2 in the U.K. In 1964, their cover of Little Richard's "Good Golly Miss Molly" hit #11, and their cover of Betty Everett's "You're No Good" (a hit for Linda Ronstadt over a decade later) made it to #3. Though they continued to record and perform, and even re-formed in the early Seventies, no further successes came. Terry Sylvester later joined the Hollies.

S-Z

Formed 1978, New Haven, Connecticut
Ed Polenka (b. Oct. 25, 1953, Waterloo, Ia.), voc.; Sandra Nesbitt (b. June 20, 1954, Gloucester, Mass.), gtr.; Dave Zelman (b. Nov. 15, 1951, Brooklyn, N.Y.), bass; Owen Selfridge (b. Dec. 7, 1946, Los Alamos, N.M.), drums; Ruben All-Media (b. Ruben Almeida, Jan. 13, 1948, Los Angeles), percussion, voc.
1978—*Just Texting* (Sign) **1979**—*Signifiers* (− Selfridge; + Linda McIntyre [b. May 18, 1955, London], drums) **1980**—*Deconstruction*.

With the avowed purpose of "deconstructing" rock, this group of Yale graduate students (Ruben Almeida, Ed Polenka and Sandra Nesbitt) and New Haven residents began working together shortly after final exams in spring of 1978. They named themselves after Roland Barthes' book on semiotics, and rehearsed in Yale's music rooms until complaints about excessive volume drove them out. Owen Selfridge's wealthy parents lent the band enough money to record *Just Texting* on their own label, and that album helped them get booked in New Haven, New York and Boston's nascent new wave clubs.

Their music was intricate and unpredictable, full of sudden contrasts. Polenka prided himself on going "from a whisper to a scream" within a single phrase, and Nesbitt provided a counterpoint of classical guitar filigree and Hendrix-style feedback. *Signifiers* consolidated their cult following, but the music they composed in its wake was so complicated and unswinging that gigs dried up. Selfridge decided to finish his long-dormant Ph.D. thesis, and Linda McIntyre, who had played with a British punk band called Lotus Position, provided a more basic beat (her drum kit included bottles for smashing) on the band's final album. Polenka and Nesbitt went on to form an avant-funk band, the Hermeneutics.

TALKING HEADS

Formed 1975, New York City

David Byrne (b. May 14, 1952, Dunbartin, Scot.), voc., gtr.; Tina Weymouth (b. Nov. 22, 1950, Coronado, Calif.), bass, synth.; Chris Frantz (b. May 8, 1951, Ft. Campbell, Ky.), drums; Jerry Harrison (b. Feb. 21, 1949, Milwaukee, Wis.), kybds., gtr.

1977—*77* (Sire) **1978**—*More Songs About Buildings and Food* **1979**—*Fear of Music* **1980**—*Remain in Light* **1982**—*The Name of This Band Is Talking Heads* **1983**—*Speaking in Tongues.*

Talking Heads is a band of smart, self-conscious white musicians intrigued by the rhythms and the spirit of black music. They have drawn on funk, classical minimalism and African rock to create some of the most adventurous, original and danceable new wave music.

David Byrne and Chris Frantz met at the Rhode Island School of Design, where they were part of a quintet called, variously, the Artistics and the Autistics. With Tina Weymouth, Frantz's girlfriend, they shared an apartment in New York and formed Talking Heads as a trio in 1975; they played their first shows at CBGB that June. Their music was never conventional punk rock; it was more delicate and contrapuntal, and their early sets included covers of the 1910 Fruitgum Company. Jerry Harrison, a Harvard alumnus who had been a Modern Lover with Jonathan Richman until 1974 and had also backed Elliott Murphy, completed the band in 1977.

Talking Heads: Tina Weymouth, Jerry Harrison, Chris Frantz, David Byrne

Talking Heads toured Europe with the Ramones before recording their first album, and once it was released they began constant touring of the U.S. and Europe. Their first album contained "Psycho Killer," which typecast them as eccentrics, an impression confirmed by Byrne's nervous, wild-eyed stage presence. The album reached the Top 100, and every subsequent album has reached the U.S. Top Forty.

With *More Songs About Buildings and Food,* Talking Heads began a four-year relationship with producer Brian Eno, an experimentalist who toyed with electronically altered sounds and shared their growing interest in Arabian and African music.

More Songs included a cover of Al Green's "Take Me to the River," which was the band's first hit (#26 pop, 1978). *Fear of Music* was a denser, more ominous record, but its followup, *Remain in Light,* was a complete shift in tone—it used rhythm tracks improvised by Eno and the band in the studio that were then layered with vocals and solos, a mixture of African communalism and Western technology.

After *Remain in Light,* Talking Heads toured the world with an expanded band: keyboardist Bernie Worrell of Parliament-Funkadelic; guitarist Adrian Belew, who had played with Frank Zappa and David Bowie; bassist Busta Jones; percussionist Steven Scales; and singers Nona Hendryx, formerly of Labelle, and Dollett McDonald.

Band members then turned to solo projects. Byrne scored a ballet for Twyla Tharp, *The Catherine Wheel,* and finished a collaboration begun with Eno before *Remain in Light*—*My Life in the Bush of Ghosts,* a collage of found voices and studio rhythm tracks. In 1981, Byrne also had a classical piece given its premiere at the New Music America Festival. Harrison made *The Red and the Black;* and Frantz and Weymouth recorded as the Tom Tom Club, scoring a major disco hit with "Genius of Love," which made the album go platinum. In 1982, the Heads ended their association with Eno; they released a compilation of live performances by all versions of the band and toured the U.S. and Europe as an eight-piece group. Byrne produced an EP, *Mesopotamia,* for the B-52's, and in 1983 produced *Waiting* for Fun Boy Three.

Speaking in Tongues, the first album of new Heads songs in three years, was released in 1983; its cover was designed by Robert Rauschenberg. They toured with an expanded band including Alex Weir, a guitarist with the Brothers Johnson.

TANGERINE DREAM

Formed 1967, Germany
Edgar Froese, synth., kybds., gtr.; Klaus Schulze, synth., kybds.; Conrad Schnitzler, flute.
1970—*Electronic Meditation* (Ohr)   1971—(— Schulze; — Schnitzler + Christophe Franke, synth.; + Steve Schroyder, organ)   *Alpha Centauri* (Ohr; reissued 1975 by Polydor)   1972—(+ Peter Baumann, synth., kybds., flute)   *Zeit* (Ohr; reissued 1976 by Virgin)   (— Schroyder)   *Atem* (Ohr; reissued 1974 by Polydor)   1974—*Phaedra* (Virgin)   1975—*Rubycon; Live*   1976—*Atem Alpha Centauri; Ricochet; Stratosfear*   1977—*Sorcerer* (soundtrack) (MCA)   1978—*Cyclone* (Virgin)   *Force Majeure*   (+ Johannes Schmelling, synth., kybds.)   1980—*Tamgram*   1981—*Thief* (soundtrack) (— Baumann)   1982—*Exit*.

This German ensemble has been responsible for some of the "spaciest" exploratory synthesizer music. Though many critics have dismissed them as mere self-absorbed post-psychedelic electro-doodlers, others have praised them as sonic painters, and they have always had a large, tenacious cult following.

They started out as a rock band featuring Edgar Froese (a classical music student, as was Christophe Franke), but as they became more and more enamored of far-flung improvisations, they abandoned guitars and drums in favor of an almost completely electronic keyboard/synthesizer setup. Original member Klaus Schulze went on to a career of his own, in much the same musical vein.

In 1974, the group gained further attention by playing a concert at Rheims Cathedral in France, at which some 6,000 fans tried to jam into the 2,000-capacity church to hear Tangerine Dream's always-improvised and often arhythmic, protoplasmic electronics.

In 1975, they went to Britain for the first time, again playing in cathedrals wherever possible. The tour was sold out, and featured Michael Hoenig replacing Baumann, who was busy working on his first solo album, *Romance '76*. By that time, Froese had recorded his first solo album, *Aqua*. He also made *Epsilon in Malaysian Pale* (1975), *Electronic Dreams* (1976), *Ages* (1977), *Macula Transfer* (1978) and *Stunt Man* (1979).

In the mid-Seventies, Tangerine Dream achieved some degree of cult success in the U.S., though never on the scale they enjoyed in England and Europe. Baumann left in 1981 to pursue a solo career, releasing *Repeat Repeat* in 1982, the title cut of which was a minor hit in rock dance clubs.

TAVARES

Formed circa 1959, New Bedford, Massachusetts
Ralph Tavares (b. Dec. 10, 1948); Arthur "Pooch" Tavares (b. Nov. 12, 1949); Feliciano "Butch" Tavares (b. May 18, 1953); Perry Lee "Tiny" Tavares (b. Oct. 24, 1954); Antone "Chubby" Tavares (b. June 2, 1950).
1974—*Check It Out* (Capitol)   *Hard Core Poetry*   1975—*In the City*   1976—*Sky High!*   1977—*Love Storm; The Best of Tavares*   1978—*Future Bound*   1979—*Madam Butterfly*   1980—*Supercharged; Love Uprising*   1981—*Loveline*.

Throughout the Seventies, the harmonizing Tavares brothers had several R&B and disco hit singles. Their hit version of Hall and Oates's "She's Gone" paved the way for that duo's later success.

The group's grandparents were from the Cape Verde Islands (a Portuguese province in the Atlantic Ocean), and as children the five brothers learned to sing island folk songs and doo-wop favorites from their older brother, John. In 1963, they turned pro as Chubby and the Turnpikes, playing clubs throughout New England. By the time they signed with Capitol in 1973, they had changed their group name to Tavares.

Tavares' first album was produced by Johnny Bristol, the second two by the Brian Potter/Dennis Lambert team. The group had hits with two ballads, "Check It Out" (#35 pop, #5 R&B, 1973) and "She's Gone" (#50 pop, #1 R&B, 1974).

Ex-Motown producer Freddie Perren took over on *Sky High!* and the group had the first of a string of pop-disco hits, which include "It Only Takes a Minute" (#10 pop, #1 R&B, 1975), "Heaven Must Be Missing an Angel" (#15 pop, #3 R&B, 1976) and "Whodunit" (#22 pop, #1 R&B, 1977). Major public exposure came when their "More Than a Woman" (#32 pop, #36 R&B) was included on the multimillion-selling *Saturday Night Fever* soundtrack album.

JAMES TAYLOR

Born March 12, 1948, Boston
1968—*James Taylor* (Apple)   1970—*Sweet Baby James* (Warner Bros.)   1971—*James Taylor and the Original Flying Machine, 1967* (Euphoria 2)   *Mud Slide Slim and the Blue Horizon* (Warner Bros.)   1972—*One Man Dog*   1974—*Walking Man*   1975—*Gorilla*   1976—*In the Pocket; Greatest Hits*   1977—*J.T.* (Columbia)   1979—*Flag*   1981—*Dad Loves His Work*.

James Taylor was the archetypal "sensitive" singer/songwriter of the Seventies. His songs, especially his early ones, were tales of inner torment delivered in low-key tunes featuring Taylor's understated tenor and his intricate acoustic guitar accompaniments that drew on folk and jazz. Taylor came across as relaxed, personable and open; he was imitated by a horde of would-be confessionalists, although his best songs were as artful as they were emotional. They weren't folk songs; they were pop compositions with folk's dynamics, and in them Taylor put across more bitterness and resignation than reassurance. As he continued to record, Taylor split his albums between cover singles that were hits ("Handy Man," "You've Got a Friend") and his own songs.

Born into a wealthy family, Taylor grew up in Boston. The family subsequently lived in Chapel Hill, North Carolina, where James's father became dean of the medical school of the University of North Carolina, and on Martha's Vineyard off the coast of Cape Cod. Everyone in the family was musical; James initially played the cello. His older brother Alex introduced him to folk and country music, and James soon took up the guitar. When he was 15, summering on Martha's Vineyard, he met another budding guitarist, Danny Kortchmar. As a duo they won a Vineyard hootenanny contest. The prize was a coffeehouse gig with the Reverend Gary Davis.

Taylor attended high school at a private academy outside Boston. Lonely away from his family, he took off a term in his junior year to return to Chapel Hill, where he played local gigs with Alex's rock band. In 1965 he committed himself to a mental institution—McLean Psychiatric Hospital in Belmont, Massachusetts—to which his sister Kate and brother Livingston would later be admitted. There he began writing songs.

After ten months, he discharged himself and went to New York City, where Kortchmar was putting together a rock & roll group, the Flying Machine. The group played Greenwich Village coffeehouses and recorded two Taylor originals, "Night Owl" and "Brighten Your Night with My Day," in early 1967 before breaking up. Their demo tape was released as an album after Taylor became popular.

One reason for the group's breakup was Taylor's addiction to heroin. Escaping from the city where he had developed his habit, Taylor traveled for a few months and in early 1968 went to England. In London, he recorded a tape of his material and sent it to Peter Asher (Kortchmar had backed Peter and Gordon on American appearances). As an A&R man for the Beatles' Apple Records, Asher encouraged Paul McCartney to sign him. In mid-1968, Taylor recorded his debut album in London; Asher produced and McCartney and George Harrison sat in on one cut. Despite the Beatles connection, the LP attracted little attention, and Taylor, still hooked on heroin at the end of the year, returned to America and signed himself into another mental institution, Austin Riggs in Stockbridge, Massachusetts. During Taylor's five-month stay, with Apple in disarray, Asher—who became Taylor's producer and manager—negotiated a contract between Taylor and Warner Bros. Before Taylor was released, his solo stage debut at L.A.'s Troubadour had been arranged. From there he went to the Newport Folk Festival, where he met Joni Mitchell (she sang on *Mud Slide Slim,* and he played guitar on her autobiographical *Blue*).

Taylor and Asher rounded up Kortchmar, bassist Lee Sklar, drummer Russ Kunkel and pianist Carole King to back him on his second album. *Sweet Baby James,* released in early 1970, attracted little initial attention. Eventually, however, the album's air of quiet desperation began to find an audience. "Fire and Rain" reached #3 in September.

Sweet Baby James reached the Top Ten in November 1970 and stayed on the LP chart into 1972. Taylor's Apple debut was re-released, entering the charts in October with the single "Carolina in My Mind." Taylor appeared on a March 1971 cover of *Time* magazine. *Time* hailed his ascent to stardom as a turn toward maturity and restraint in pop music but at the same time publicized his drug abuses and other skeletons in his and his family's closet. The article also alluded to a possible dynasty of Taylor-made pop stars. Livingston Taylor had launched his singing and songwriting career before his older brother had become famous, but Alex and Kate, while unquestionably musical, were more or less shoved into the spotlight.

Within two months of its release, *Mud Slide Slim* was the nation's #2 album. Taylor's version of Carole King's "You've Got a Friend" hit #1 in June 1971, the same year that King's version came out on *Tapestry.* Taylor toured with both the album band and as a solo. In 1971, he costarred with Dennis Wilson of the Beach Boys in the film *Two-Lane Blacktop.*

Then, almost as suddenly as he had emerged into public attention, he retreated from it. Except for a few benefit concerts for George McGovern's 1972 presidential campaign, he did not perform for another three years. He married Carly Simon in November 1972.

Taylor continued to make and sell albums, but he didn't score a Top Ten single between "You've Got a Friend" and "How Sweet It Is" in 1975. ("Mockingbird," a duet, was released by Simon in 1974.) *One Man Dog* featured the Section (Kortchmar, Kunkel, Sklar and pianist Craig Doerge), but had no hits. *Walking Man,* produced by guitarist David Spinozza with New York session players, was even less popular.

A month-long tour in 1974 signaled Taylor's reemergence as a performer. He returned to the charts with *Gorilla,* produced by Lenny Waronker and Russ Titelman. Taylor's cover of Holland-Dozier-Holland's "How Sweet It Is (To Be Loved by You)" hit #5 in 1975.

J.T., including a Top Five cover of the Jimmy Jones-Otis Blackwell "Handy Man," was Taylor's first release on Columbia. *Greatest Hits,* for which he re-recorded "Carolina in My Mind" and "Something in the Way She Moves," fulfilled his obligations to Warners; he signed Columbia's lucrative contract before *Hits* was released. *J.T.* also marked Asher's return as producer.

Taylor's albums since *J.T.* have not repeated its success, but they have sold consistently. In 1978, he joined Paul Simon and Art Garfunkel on a Top Twenty cover of Sam Cooke's "Wonderful World," released by Garfunkel. In 1979, he wrote a couple of songs for a Broadway musical, *Working.* He has continued to support a variety of causes with benefit concerts. He campaigned for Jimmy Carter in 1976 and for John Anderson in 1980; in 1979 he participated in the MUSE anti-nuclear rally concerts at Madison Square Garden and appeared in the concert film *No Nukes*. Also in 1979, he gave a concert in New York's Central Park to raise money for the Parks Commission, and the following year he performed at the city's South Street Seaport Museum, joining his siblings Alex, Kate, Liv and Hugh for the debut public performance of the Taylor clan.

Taylor's 1981 album, *Dad Loves His Work*, yielded a hit single duet with J. D. Souther, "Her Town Too" (#11), released amid rumors that his marriage to Simon was ending. In 1982, Simon sued Taylor for divorce.

JOHNNIE TAYLOR

Born May 5, 1938, Crawsfordsville, Arkansas
1968—*Wanted: One Soul Singer* (Stax) **1969**—*Who's Makin' Love; Raw Blues; JT Philosophy Continues* **1970**—*Greatest Hits* **1971**—*One Step Beyond* **1973**—*Taylored in Silk* **1974**—*Super Taylor* **1976**—*Eargasm* (Columbia) **1977**—*Rated Extraordinaire* **1978**—*Ever Ready; Disco 9000; The Johnnie Taylor Chronicle* (Stax) *Reflections* (RCA).

Johnnie Taylor's gritty soul vocals made him a steady mid-Sixties hitmaker and gave him one mammoth disco hit in 1976. Taylor made his recording debut with a Vee Jay doowop group, the Five Echoes, in 1955. In 1957, he became lead singer of the Soul Stirrers, replacing Sam Cooke in the influential gospel quintet. After leaving the Soul Stirrers in 1963, Taylor signed with Cooke's Sar label. Although he abandoned gospel music, songs like "Rome (Wasn't Built in a Day)" reflected his deep religious roots.

Taylor hit his commercial stride after signing with Stax records in 1965. Two 1966 releases, "I Had a Dream" (#19 R&B) and "I Got to Love Somebody's Baby" (#15 R&B), were minor hits. With "Who's Making Love" (#5 pop, #1 R&B) in 1968, Taylor replaced the late Otis Redding as Stax's leading male singer. "Take Care of Your Homework" (#20 pop, #2 R&B), "Testify (I Wanna)" (#4 R&B), "I Could Never Be President" (#10 R&B), "Love Bones" (#4 R&B) in 1969; "Steal Away" (#3 R&B), "I Am Somebody, Part II" (#3 R&B) in 1970; and "Jody's Got Your Girl and Gone" (#1 R&B), "Hi-Jackin' Love" (#10 R&B) in 1971 continued the streak. "I Believe in You" (#1 R&B) and "Cheaper to Keep Her" (#15 pop, #2 R&B) were his last big hits for Stax.

By 1975, Stax was in turmoil, and its distributor, CBS, took over Taylor's contract. The next year, Taylor's "Disco Lady" (#1 pop and R&B) was one of the first platinum singles ever.

KOKO TAYLOR

Born Cora Walton, September 28, 1935, Memphis, Tennessee

1975—*I Got What It Takes* (Alligator) *Southside Baby* (Black & Blue) **1978**—*Earthshaker* (Alligator) **1981**—*From the Heart of a Woman*.

A mighty-voiced urban blues singer, Koko Taylor began singing in her local church choir in her teens and soon moved to Chicago, where she began performing with the Buddy Guy/Junior Wells Blues Band. She began recording in Chicago in 1963, and has toured the U.S., Britain and Europe extensively since. She recorded several albums for Chicago's Chess Records.

In 1970, she appeared in the film *The Blues Is Alive and Well in Chicago*, and she played the Montreux Jazz and Blues Festival in 1972 with Muddy Waters. Taylor began recording for Alligator, a Chicago-based independent label specializing in blues, in 1974, and the following year formed her own band, the Blues Machine.

LIVINGSTON TAYLOR

Born November 21, 1950, Boston
1970—*Livingston Taylor* (Capricorn) **1971**—*Liv* **1973**—*Over the Rainbow* **1978**—*3-Way Mirror* (Epic).

Brother of James, Kate and Alex, the musically inclined offspring of University of North Carolina School of Medicine Dean Dr. Isaac Taylor, Livingston Taylor was writing and performing his own songs while in his teens, before James had recorded his first album.

Like James and Kate, Liv did some voluntary time in hospital psychiatric wards. While in McLean Hospital in 1968 for "adolescent turmoil," he met music critic Jon Landau through a music therapist. After his discharge from McLean, Taylor played Boston folk clubs and then, on Landau's suggestion, auditioned for record companies. After several unsuccessful tries, Landau finally hooked Taylor up with Phil Walden, who had just formed Capricorn Records. Landau produced his debut LP, which sold well and yielded a minor hit single, "Carolina Day."

The second LP was another moderate chart success, with the single "Get Out of Bed" making the U.S. Top 100. Taylor's third LP also sold respectably, but he then kept out of the studios for five years, touring constantly, especially on the East Coast. In 1978, he signed with Epic Records; his LP for Epic yielded his only Top Thirty hit, "I Will Be in Love with You."

TELEVISION

Formed 1973, New York City
Tom Verlaine (b. Thomas Miller, N.J.), gtr., voc.; Richard Lloyd, gtr., voc.; Richard Hell (b. Richard Myers, Oct. 2, 1949), bass; Billy Ficca, drums.
1975—(− Hell, + Fred Smith, bass) **1977**—*Marquee Moon* (Elektra) **1978**—*Adventure* **1982**—*The Blow-Up* (ROIR).
Tom Verlaine solo: 1980—*Tom Verlaine* (Elektra) **1981**—*Dreamtime* (Warner Bros.) **1982**—*Words from the Front*.

Richard Lloyd solo: 1980—*Alchemy* (Elektra).

Television appeared at the same time and place as punk rock, in the mid-Seventies at CBGB. But while the band's harsh attack and their obvious affection for the Velvet Underground linked them to the rest of punk, Television's trademark chiming guitars, and the tendency of lead guitarist (and main songwriter) Tom Verlaine and rhythm guitarist Richard Lloyd to spur each other on long jams evoked psychedelic-era bands like the Byrds and the Grateful Dead. (Verlaine cited the Rolling Stones, classical composer Maurice Ravel and jazz musicians Miles Davis and Albert Ayler as influences.) Television had a devout following in New York City and had a major effect on post–punk rock in Britain, but its albums were virtually ignored by the mass market.

Tom Miller (who renamed himself Verlaine after the French Symbolist poet) had dropped out of high school in Wilmington, Delaware, and had left colleges in South Carolina and Pennsylvania before coming to New York in 1968. Richard Hell was a onetime boarding school roommate. With Billy Ficca they formed a short-lived band, the Neon Boys, in 1973. When Lloyd joined in late 1973, they became Television, and were one of the first bands to play at CBGB, along with the Patti Smith Group (Verlaine and Smith collaborated on a book of poetry, *The Night*). The first Television lineup made an independent single, "Little Johnny Jewel," but Hell soon left to form the Heartbreakers with ex–New York Doll Johnny Thunders, and later he led the Voidoids. Dee Dee Ramone auditioned as bassist, but the gig went to Fred Smith. The new lineup played frequently in New York, to critical raves.

In late 1975, Brian Eno produced some demo recordings of the band, which were never released; though the band continued to enlarge its cult following, it wasn't until 1977 that its debut album was released. *Marquee Moon* sold poorly, but it made many critics' Ten Best lists that year. *Adventure* was softer, more reflective and restrained than the debut, and sold a bit better. In 1978, Television broke up.

Verlaine has released three solo albums, and though he has established a solid cult following he's still more a critical than commercial success. Lloyd released one solo album, *Alchemy*, in 1980, and a single of mid-Sixties Rolling Stones covers in 1981. In 1980, Ficca resurfaced with the Waitresses, a New York–Ohio band who had a hit with "I Know What Boys Like" in 1981. Smith played with the Roches and Willie Nile in 1980, then rejoined Verlaine's touring and studio bands.

THE TEMPTATIONS

Formed 1962, Detroit
Otis Williams (b. Otis Miles, Oct. 30, 1949, Texarkana, Tex.); Eddie Kendricks (b. Dec. 17, 1939, Birmingham, Ala.); Paul Williams (b. July 2, 1939, Birmingham, Ala.; d. Aug. 17, 1973, Birmingham); Melvin Franklin (b.

David English, Oct. 12, 1942, Montgomery, Ala.); Eldridge Bryant.
1963—(− Bryant; + David Ruffin [b. Jan. 18, 1941, Meridian, Miss.]) **1964**—*Meet the Temptations* (Gordy) **1965**—*Temptations Sing Smokey* **1966**—*Greatest Hits* **1967**—*Temptations Live!* (− Ruffin; + Dennis Edwards [b. Feb. 3, 1943, Birmingham, Ala.]) **1968**—*I Wish It Would Rain* **1969**—*Cloud Nine; Puzzle People* **1970**—*Psychedelic Shack; Greatest Hits, Volume 2* **1971**—(− Kendricks; + Damon Harris [b. July 3, 1950, Baltimore]; − Williams; + Richard Street [b. Oct. 5, 1942, Detroit]) **1972**—*Solid Rock* **1973**—*All Directions; Masterpiece* **1974**—*Anthology; A Song for You* **1975**—*House Party* (− Harris; + Glenn Leonard [b. Washington, D.C.]) **1976**—*Wings of Love; Do the Temptations* **1977**—(− Edwards) *Hear to Tempt You* (Atlantic) **1978**—*Bare Back* **1979**—(+ Edwards) **1980**—*Power* (Gordy) **1981**—*The Temptations* **1982**—(+ Ruffin; + Kendricks) *Reunion*.

The Temptations were the most successful male vocal group of the Sixties and the early Seventies. Their rough-edged leads and urgent harmonies and their precise choreography made the most of Motown's best material and production. By 1982, the group had sold an estimated 22 million records worldwide.

The original Temptations came together from a variety of vocal groups. Otis Williams, Eldridge Bryant and Melvin Franklin had been in a series of Detroit groups, including the Questions, the Elegants and Otis Williams and the Distants. Eddie Kendricks and Paul Williams belonged to a Birmingham, Alabama, trio, the Primes. Kendricks, Williams, Franklin and Bryant formed the Elgins in 1959, and —renamed the Primes—began recording for Motown Records in 1960. By the time Bryant quit and was replaced by David Ruffin the group was calling itself the Temptations.

Soon after Ruffin joined, the group began working with writer/producer Smokey Robinson. Beginning in 1964 with Robinson's "The Way You Do the Things You Do" (#11 pop), the Temptations had an almost unbroken run of R&B and pop hits that extended into the early Seventies. In 1965, their hits included "My Girl" (#1 pop, #1 R&B), "It's Growing" (#18 pop, #3 R&B), "Since I Lost My Baby" (#17 pop, #4 R&B) and "Don't Look Back" (#13 pop, #4 R&B).

The following year, the hits continued with "Get Ready" (#29 pop, #1 R&B) and the Norman Whitfield-Brian Holland productions "Ain't Too Proud to Beg" (#13 pop, #1 R&B), "Beauty's Only Skin Deep" (#3 pop, #1 R&B) and "(I Know) I'm Losing You" (#8 pop, #1 R&B). By 1967, Whitfield had become the group's sole producer. They had new hits in 1967 with "All I Need" (#8 pop, #2 R&B), "You're My Everything" (#6 pop, #3 R&B) and "(Loneliness Made Me Realize) It's You That I Need" (#14 pop, #3 R&B), but the most significant event

The Temptations: Dennis Edwards, Melvin Franklin, Damon Harris, Richard Street, Otis Williams

for the group was Ruffin's departure. Citing dissatisfaction with the compensation Motown musicians received, he left to begin a solo career.

With Dennis Edwards (formerly of the Contours) replacing Ruffin, the Temptations continued to record briefly in the accustomed style, hitting with "I Wish It Would Rain" (#4 pop, #1 R&B), "I Could Never Love Another (After Loving You)" (#13 pop, #1 R&B) and "Please Return Your Love to Me" (#26 pop, # 4 R&B). But with Ruffin gone, Whitfield began to change the group's direction from romantic pop ballads to the "psychedelic" soul sound popularized by Sly and the Family Stone. "Cloud Nine" (#6 pop, #2 R&B) introduced this new direction in 1968. By 1969, many of the Temptations' hits dealt with social issues. This trend—illustrated by "Run Away Child, Running Wild" (#6 pop, #1 R&B), "Don't Let the Joneses Get You Down" (#20 pop, #2 R&B), 1969; "Psychedelic Shack" (#7 pop, #2 R&B) and "Ball of Confusion" (#3 pop, #2 R&B), 1970—was broken in 1971 with the vintage Temptations' last record, "Just My Imagination (Running Away with Me)" (#1 R&B and pop). Kendricks quit to start a fitfully successful solo career. Later that year, Williams also left the group because of poor health; two years later he was dead.

With new replacements Damon Harris and Richard Street, Whitfield moved the band away from ballads toward songs like "Papa Was a Rollin' Stone" (#1 pop, #5 R&B, 1972), "Hey Girl (I Like Your Style)" (#35 pop, #2 R&B, 1973), "The Plastic Man" (#40 pop, #8 R&B, 1973) and "Masterpiece" (#7 pop, #1 R&B, 1973).

In the mid-Seventies, the Temptations left Motown for Atlantic, where they recorded two disco albums, *Bare Back* and *Hear to Tempt You*. In 1980, Berry Gordy, Jr., lured them back to Motown, where he cowrote and produced their first hit single in seven years, "Power" (#43 pop, #11 R&B). In 1982, Ruffin and Kendricks rejoined the group for the *Reunion* album and mini-tour. "Standing on the Top" was written and produced by Rick James.

10cc

Formed 1972, Manchester, England
Eric Stewart (b. Jan. 20, 1945, Manchester), gtr., voc.; Lol Creme (b. Sep. 19, 1947, Manchester), gtr., voc., kybds., bass; Graham Gouldman (b. May 10, 1946, Manchester), gtr., voc., bass, kybds.; Kevin Godley (b. Oct. 7, 1945, Manchester), drums, voc., kybds.
1973—*10cc* (U.K.) 1974—*Sheet Music* 1975—*100cc; The Original Soundtrack* (Mercury) (+ Paul Burgess, drums) 1976—*How Dare You* 1976—(− Godley; − Creme) 1977—*Deceptive Bends* (+ Rick Fenn, voc., gtr.; + Tony O'Malley, kybds.; + Stuart Tosh, drums, voc., percussion) *10cc Live and Let Live* 1978—*Bloody Tourists* 1979—*Greatest Hits, 1972–78* 1980—*Look Hear?* 1982—*Ten Out of 10.*

Composed of four prolific singer/player/songwriters, 10cc won critical acclaim for its witty and melodic "art pop." The band began scoring pop hits as it moved closer to the boundary between parody and romantic pop.

Graham Gouldman had played with Manchester bands like the Mockingbirds, as well as a later version of Wayne Fontana's Mindbenders. He wrote such Top Ten mid-Sixties British rock hits as "For Your Love," "Heart Full of Soul" and "Evil Hearted You" (by the Yardbirds); "Look Through Any Window" and "Bus Stop" (by the Hollies); and "No Milk Today" (by Herman's Hermits). He had left the Mindbenders in 1968 to go to New York City, where he worked unsuccessfully for bubblegum producers Kasenetz and Katz and released the late Sixties solo LP *The Graham Gouldman Thing*. In 1970, he formed Hotlegs, which included Lol Creme, Kevin Godley and Eric Stewart.

Working out of Strawberry Studios in England, which Stewart partly owned, Hotlegs had a #2 U.K. hit with 1970's "Neanderthal Man." Stewart had also been in the Mindbenders with Gouldman; when Wayne Fontana left the group, Stewart became frontman. Godley and Creme had attended art school together (they designed 10cc's debut album cover) and played together in a few local bands, then played sessions at Strawberry Studios.

Like Hotlegs, 10cc would be primarily a studio group (though Hotlegs did tour with the Moody Blues on the heels of their hit single); while fooling around in Strawberry Studios with the Godley-Creme song "Donna," they transformed it into a sharp-edged satire of late-Fifties teen-idol hits and had 10cc's first demo.

They took the tape of "Donna" to British impresario Jonathan King; he claims he rechristened Hotlegs as 10cc (the name supposedly derives from the 9 cubic centimeters of semen ejaculated by the average male). Within weeks of its 1972 release, "Donna" was at #2 on the British singles chart. In 1973 came "Rubber Bullets" and "The Dean and I," both of which were Top Five U.K. hits, followed by "I'm Not in Love" and "Art for Art's Sake." However, despite critical acclaim, they'd had no U.S. hit singles, though "Rubber Bullets" became a novelty sensation on FM radio.

That changed with the late-blooming American success of the lush "I'm Not in Love" (#2, 1975), followed in 1977 by "The Things We Do for Love" (#5). After the success of "I'm Not in Love," Godley and Creme left, to record together and to work on their guitar-modification device, the Gizmo (it clips on over the bridge, and using continuous-motion rotary plectrums, effects infinite sustain and string-section sounds).

Stewart and Gouldman made *Deceptive Bends,* which featured "The Things We Do for Love," basically as a duo, then added several new members, including drummer/vocalist Stuart Tosh, formerly of British teenybopper hitmakers Pilot. *Live and Let Live* was more or less a flop, but *Bloody Tourists* yielded "Dreadlock Holiday."

While Godley and Creme continued to record and produce promotional videos for other bands (they refuse to tour), and even had a Top Ten U.K. single in 1982 with "Wedding Bells," Stewart and Gouldman weren't heard from again until 1982's 10cc LP *Ten Out of 10,* for which ex–Linda Ronstadt guitarist Andrew Gold cowrote and coproduced three songs.

TEN YEARS AFTER/ALVIN LEE
Formed 1967, Nottingham, England
Alvin Lee (b. Dec. 19, 1944, Nottingham), gtr., voc.; Chick Churchill (b. Jan. 2, 1949, Flintshire, Eng.), kybds.; Leo Lyons (b. Nov. 30, 1944, Bedfordshire, Eng.), bass; Ric Lee (b. Oct. 20, 1945, Staffordshire, Eng.), drums.
1967—*Ten Years After* (Deram) 1968—*Undead* 1969—*Stonedhenge; Sssh* 1970—*Cricklewood Green; Watt* 1971—*A Space in Time* (Columbia) 1972—*Alvin Lee & Co.; Rock 'n' Roll Music to the World* 1973—*Recorded Live* 1974—*Positive Vibrations* 1975—*Goin' Home* 1976—*Anthology* 1977—*Classic Performances* 1981—*Hear Me Calling* (Decca) (compilation).

Ten Years After was a dependably hard-rocking blues-based band for many years, best remembered for the sped-up blues solos of guitarist Alvin Lee, whose supersonic version of "Goin' Home" was a smash hit at the 1969 Woodstock Festival and in the *Woodstock* film.

Alvin Lee and Leo Lyons grew up together in Nottingham. Lee was playing guitar by age 13; and Lyons began performing publicly at age 15. By the early Sixties, both were involved in blues groups. Lee performed in a John Lee Hooker show at London's Marquee; Lyons appeared at a Windsor Jazz Festival; both were also studio musicians. They got together in 1964 as Britain's Largest Sounding Trio (with Lyons on drums), which toured England and the Continent and was quite successful in Hamburg. In 1967, Ric Lee (no relation to Alvin) and Chick Churchill joined, completing what was now called Ten Years After.

Alvin Lee's speed made the band a popular concert attraction, and, despite a lack of hits, their first few LPs sold well. By 1968, Ten Years After were regulars at New York's The Scene—where they jammed with Jimi Hendrix, Janis Joplin and Larry Coryell—and at San Francisco's Fillmore West. *A Space in Time* eventually went gold. By that time the band had chalked up its first hit single, "I'd Love to Change the World," a dreamy song that made the U.S. and U.K. charts in 1971. They followed with "Baby Won't You Let Me Rock 'n' Roll You" in 1972 and "Choo Choo Mama" in 1973.

After *Rock 'n' Roll Music to the World,* the band took a break from touring. Lee built a studio in his 15th-century Berkshire home and recorded *On the Road to Freedom* with Mylon LeFevre; the album also featured guest appearances from Steve Winwood, Jim Capaldi, George Harrison (credited as Harry Georgeson) and Ron Wood. Churchill recorded a solo album, *You and Me.*

In early 1974, with the band's status in doubt, Lee organized a nine-piece band, including reedman Mel Collins and drummer Ian Wallace (both formerly with King Crimson), who played a show at London's Rainbow Theatre before Ten Years After's scheduled appearance. Lee's band was recorded on *Alvin Lee and Company in Flight.* Ten Years After did end up playing the Rainbow, and it turned out to be their last British concert. *Positive Vibrations* was the band's final album.

Later in 1974, Lee announced plans for a worldwide tour with a band featuring Collins, Wallace and keyboardist Ronnie Leahy and bassist Steve Thompson of Stone the Crows. Though Ten Years After seemed officially defunct, the band's management denied the split. In May 1975, Alvin Lee declared the group to be through and it was announced that Ric Lee had formed his own band. Ten Years After then regrouped for one last American tour. The band's demise has never been made official.

Since that last tour, Alvin Lee has released solo LPs: *Pump Iron, Saguitar, The Alvin Lee Band* and *Free Fall.* Chick Churchill is a professional manager for Chrysalis Publishing. Leo Lyons produced some mid-Seventies albums by British heavy-metal band UFO. Ric Lee formed his own production company.

TAMMI TERRELL
Born 1946, Philadelphia; died March 16, 1970
1969—*Irresistible* (Tamla).

Tammi Terrell is best known for a series of duets she recorded with Marvin Gaye, some of which were written and produced by Valerie Simpson and Nick Ashford.

Terrell grew up in Philadelphia, where she began singing as a child. She studied psychology and pre-med at the University of Pennsylvania, until she quit in her sophomore year to sing. She recorded for several labels in the early Sixties before signing to Motown in 1965. Terrell's first hits with Motown came with "This Old Heart of Mine" and "Come On and See Me." Then the popularity of "Ain't No Mountain High Enough" (#19 pop, #3 R&B), sung with Marvin Gaye, changed her career direction.

All her subsequent chart singles were duets with Gaye, including "Your Precious Love" (#5 pop, #2 R&B) and "If I Could Build My Whole World Around You" b/w "If This World Were Mine" (#10 pop, #27 R&B) in 1967; "Ain't Nothing Like the Real Thing" (#8 pop, #1 R&B), "You're All I Need to Get By" (#7 pop, #1 R&B) and "Keep on Lovin' Me Honey" (#24 pop, #11 R&B) in 1968; "Good Lovin' Ain't Easy to Come By" (#30 pop, #11 R&B) and "What You Gave Me" (#6 R&B) in 1969; and "The Onion Song" (#50 pop, #18 R&B) in 1970.

While performing with Gaye in the summer of 1967, Terrell collapsed in his arms. It was discovered that she had a brain tumor and, after a series of operations, she died in 1970. "The Onion Song" was a posthumous hit in 1970.

SONNY TERRY AND BROWNIE McGHEE
Teddell Saunders "Sonny" Terry (born October 24, 1911, Greensboro, North Carolina); Walter Brown "Brownie" McGhee (born November 30, 1915, Knoxville, Tennessee)
1962—*Live at the 2nd Fret* (Prestige) **N.A.**—*Back to New Orleans* (Fantasy) *Midnight Special.*

Sonny Terry and Brownie McGhee are Southern blues musicians with church roots. They paired up in the early Forties and became a popular and influential folk-blues team, despite the fact that both suffered crippling childhood diseases.

Terry was blind, the result of two separate accidents in 1922 and 1927. He spent his early years playing harmonica around North Carolina, slowly achieving a wider reputation in the late Thirties, thanks to performances with Leadbelly and Blind Boy Fuller.

McGhee contracted polio at the age of four, though he made a substantial recovery that left him only with a limp. His entire family was musical, and he was performing with them by the age of eight. He quit school at 13 to become a full-time musician, and had just begun his recording career when he was introduced to Sonny Terry.

They were a steady duo after that, although they worked apart extensively as well, McGhee under pseudonyms like Spider Sam, Big Tom Collins, Henry Johnson and Blind Boy Williams. After being discovered by folk revivalists in the Fifties, notably Pete Seeger, they went on to perform in clubs, in colleges, and at jazz and blues festivals around the world. They've made dozens of records. As of 1983, McGhee was touring with his own band.

JOE TEX
Born Joseph Arrington, Jr., August 8, 1933, Rogers, Texas; died Joseph Arrington Hazziez, August 12, 1982, Navasota, Texas
1965—*The Best of Joe Tex* (Parrot) *Hold on to What You've Got* (Atlantic) *New Boss* **1966**—*The Love You Save* **1968**—*Live and Lovely; Soul Country* **1969**—*Happy Soul; You Better Get It* **1972**—*I Gotcha* (Dial) **1977**—*Bumps and Bruises* (Epic) **1978**—*Rub Down.*

Soul singer Joe Tex recorded in a variety of styles but is best known for his dance hits. Tex first recorded for King from 1955 to 1957, and from 1958 to 1960 for Ace. He was a journeyman performer through most of the early Sixties, recording occasionally, but with no success. His first break came in 1961 when James Brown recorded his "Baby You're Right." In 1964, Tex signed to Buddy Killen's Dial Records, a Nashville soul label.

Recording at what would later become the famous Muscle Shoals studio, Tex broke through in 1965 with "Hold What You've Got" (#5 pop, #2 R&B). Through soul's mid- to late-Sixties heyday, Tex had several big hits including "I Want to (Do Everything for You)" (#1 R&B), "A Sweet Woman Like You" (#1 R&B) and "The Love You Save" (#10 pop, #2 R&B) in 1965; and the comedic "Skinny Legs and All" (#10 pop, #2 R&B) in 1967.

In 1967, Tex, along with Otis Redding, Wilson Pickett, Don Covay, Solomon Burke and Ben E. King became part of the Soul Clan, a prefabricated "superstar" grouping engineered by Atlantic Records. Redding died before the group recorded. Later, with Arthur Conley substituting for Pickett, they released "Soul Meeting" b/w "That's How I Feel." (A 1981 Soul Clan "reunion" folded after a single show in New York City.)

In 1972, Tex had a big hit with the lecherous "I Gotcha" (#2 pop, #1 R&B). A year later he left Atlantic and through the Seventies recorded for numerous companies, although always under the guidance of Buddy Killen. In 1977, Tex had his last major hit, another comedy record, "Ain't Gonna Bump No More (with No Big Fat Woman)" (#12 pop, #7 R&B). During his later years he had become a Muslim minister and adopted the surname Hazziez. He died of a heart attack at age 49. Among the pallbearers at his funeral were Buddy Killen, Wilson Pickett, Ben E. King, Don Covay and Percy Mayfield.

THEM
Formed 1963, Belfast, Northern Ireland
Original lineup: Billy Harrison, gtr.; Jackie McAuley,

kybds.; Alan Henderson, bass; Ronnie Millings, drums; Van Morrison (b. Aug. 21, 1945, Belfast), voc., sax, harmonica.
1965—*Angry Young Them* (Decca, U.K.) *Them* (Parrot) 1966—*Them Again* 1972—*Them* 1977—*Story of Them* (London).

In the early days of singer Van Morrison's recording and performing career, he was backed by Them, a young Belfast garage band. Morrison and Them had major U.K. hits in 1965 with "Baby Please Don't Go" (#10) and "Here Comes the Night" (#2). Their U.S. hits were "Here Comes the Night" (#24) and "Mystic Eyes" (#33) in 1965; and "Gloria" (#71) in 1966. The latter was beaten on the U.S. chart by the Shadows of Knight's version.

Morrison toured Europe and the American West Coast with Them in 1966 (the Doors opened the West Coast shows). When Morrison returned home after the tour, he took a lot of time off before planning his next career move; after a short time, Them disbanded. During its brief career, its personnel changed often, at various times including guitarist Jimmy Page and keyboardist Peter Bardens (who went on to form Camel).

THIN LIZZY
Formed 1970, Dublin, Ireland
Philip Lynott (b. Aug. 20, 1951, Dublin) bass, voc.; Brian Downey, drums; Eric Bell, gtr.
1971—*Thin Lizzy* (Decca) 1972—*Shades of a Blue Orphanage* 1973—*Vagabonds of the Western World* (London) 1974—(− Bell; + Gary Moore, gtr.; − Moore; + Brian Robertson, gtr.; + Scott Gorham [b. Los Angeles], gtr., voc.) *Nightlife* (Mercury) *Fighting* 1976—*Jailbreak; Johnny the Fox* 1977—*Bad Reputation* (− Robertson; + Moore) 1978—*Live and Dangerous* 1979—*Black Rose* (− Moore; + Midge Ure, gtr.; − Ure; + Snowy White, gtr., voc.) 1980—*Chinatown* 1982—*Renegade* (+ Darren Wharton, kybds; − White) 1983—*Thunder and Lightning*.

Fronted by Phil Lynott, a black Irishman, Thin Lizzy is a hard-nosed rock & roll band whose music is mostly distinguished by the strongly masculine-to-macho themes of Lynott's songs, which often celebrate male camaraderie and comic-book heroism. Thin Lizzy's finest hour was unquestionably 1976's *Jailbreak*, whose power chords and

Grammy Awards

A Taste of Honey
1978 Best New Artist of the Year

Tavares
1978 Album of the Year:
Saturday Night Fever (with others)

James Taylor
1971 Best Pop Vocal Performance, Male:
"You've Got a Friend"
1977 Best Pop Vocal Performance, Male:
"Handy Man"

Nino Tempo
1963 Best Rock & Roll Recording: "Deep Purple" (with April Stevens)

The Temptations
1968 Best R&B Performance by a Duo or Group, Vocal or Instrumental:
"Cloud Nine"

1972 Best R&B Performance by a Duo, Group or Chorus; Best Instrumental Performance: "Papa Was a Rolling Stone"

B. J. Thomas
1977 Best Inspirational Performance:
"Home Where I Belong"
1978 Best Inspirational Performance:
Happy Man
1979 Best Inspirational Performance:
You Gave Me Love (When Nobody Gave Me A Prayer)
1980 Best Gospel Performance, Contemporary or Inspirational:
The Lord's Prayer (with others)
1981 Best Inspirational Performance:
Amazing Grace

Toto
1982 Record of the Year: "Rosanna"
Album of the Year:
Toto IV

Trammps
1978 Album of the Year:
Saturday Night Fever (with others)

Ike and Tina Turner
1971 Best R&B Vocal Performance by a Group:
"Proud Mary"

Conway Twitty
1971 Best Country Vocal Performance by a Group:
"After the Fire Is Gone" (with Loretta Lynn)

R&B undertones established the band as a major act in Britain and gave them their greatest American success with the LP's single "The Boys Are Back in Town" (#12).

After being formed in Ireland by Lynott with his boyhood friend, drummer Brian Downey, Thin Lizzy relocated to England in 1971, subsequently scoring a hit single, "Whisky in a Jar" (#6 U.K., 1973). Eric Bell quit the band after the third LP, suffering exhaustion. Indifferent record sales followed until Thin Lizzy released *Jailbreak*.

Since that LP, the group continued to record a series of uneven albums (excepting 1978's *Live and Dangerous*) and failed to become a superstar attraction as was once predicted. Lynott, who earned the respect of the new wave elite in 1978 by forming a spare-time group, the Greedy Bastards, with Rat Scabies of the Damned, released a solo album in 1980, *Solo in Soho*, which sold disappointingly. With Thin Lizzy, Lynott continued his thematic style of songwriting on albums like *Chinatown* and *Renegade*, which also spotlit the twin lead guitar work of Scott Gorham and new member Snowy White, Pink Floyd's ex-stage guitarist. Lynott has published two books of poetry, *Songs for While I'm Away* and *Philip*. Lynott continued to make solo LPs; White and Garry Moore have also made solo albums.

Rock in Theater

Rock reaches Broadway in two forms: as concerts (a prestigious version of an extended club engagement) and in the scores of "rock musicals." For Broadway concerts, see individual entries for George Benson, Bette Midler, Harry Chapin. *Tommy,* the "rock opera" by the Who, was made into a movie by Ken Russell in 1975, but was only performed as a concert in the U.S. Here are the most important Broadway rock musicals:

HAIR
Music, Galt McDermot; lyrics, James Rado and Gerome Ragni.
Hair opened October 17, 1967, as part of the New York Shakespeare Festival and moved to Broadway in 1968; the Broadway production closed July 1, 1972. Meanwhile, it toured 25 countries and was translated into 14 languages. Numerous rockers, including Meat Loaf, Donna Summer and Joan Armatrading, participated in various productions. The original cast album sold three million copies, with songs including "Good Morning Starshine," "Aquarius," "Let the Sun Shine In," "Easy to Be Hard" and the title song. The Fifth Dimension had a hit with a medley from the show. In 1979, Milos Forman made a movie version.

JESUS CHRIST SUPERSTAR
Music, Andrew Lloyd Webber; lyrics, Tim Rice.
Based on the gospels of Matthew, Mark and Luke, *Jesus Christ Superstar* began as an album with a cast including Ben Vereen and Yvonne Elliman. Its Broadway run was from October 20, 1971, to July 1, 1973. The original album included a hit single, Elliman's "I Don't Know How to Love Him."

GREASE
Music and lyrics, Jim Jacobs and Warren Casey.
A musical with a Fifties rock score, *Grease* opened Off Broadway on February 14, 1972, moved to Broadway later that year and closed in 1980. The 1977 film version, directed by Randal Kleiser, included two additional songs, Barry Gibb's "Grease" (a hit for Frankie Valli) and John Farrar's "You're the One That I Want" (a platinum hit for Olivia Newton-John and John Travolta).

YOUR ARMS TOO SHORT TO BOX WITH GOD
Music and lyrics, Vinnette Carroll.
A Broadway revival of this gospel musical ran from September 1982 to November 7, 1982, with a cast including Al Green and Patti LaBelle.

THE WIZ
Music, Charlie Smalls; book, William F. Brown.
This all-black remake of *The Wizard of Oz* had a disco-ish score and ran from January 1975 to January 28, 1979. The cast album included "Ease on Down the Road," sung by Stephanie Mills. A 1978 film version featured Diana Ross and Michael Jackson.

THE ROCKY HORROR SHOW
Music, book and lyrics, Richard O'Brien.
This campy cult phenomenon opened in London in July 1973 and played in Los Angeles before it came to Broadway for a short run from March 10 to April 19, 1975. Author Richard O'Brien had played in London companies of *Hair* and *Jesus Christ Superstar*. The London production introduced Tim Curry; the Los Angeles and Broadway productions added Meat Loaf. Both of them also appeared in the 1975 film *The Rocky Horror Picture Show,* directed by Jim Sharman. The film's devoted following still shows up for weekly midnight screenings on Fridays and Saturdays dressed up as their favorite characters.

.38 SPECIAL

Formed 1975, Jacksonville, Florida.
Donnie Van Zant, voc.; Don Barnes, gtr., voc.; Jeff
Carlisi, gtr.; Ken Lyons, bass; Jack Grondin, drums;
Steve Brookins, drums.
1977—*.38 Special* (A&M)   **1978**—*Special Delivery* (−
Lyons; + Larry Junstrom, bass, gtr.)   **1979**—*Rockin'
into the Night*   **1981**—*Wild-Eyed Southern Boys*
1982—*Special Forces*.

One of the many Southern-rock groups to take its cue
from the Allman Brothers Band, .38 Special specializes in
blues-based rock & roll that showcases twin lead guitarists
and two drummers. Featuring lead vocalist Donnie Van
Zant, brother of Lynyrd Skynyrd's Ronnie Van Zant, .38
Special recently altered its sound somewhat to accommodate a more melodic approach. This resulted in "Hold On
Loosely" (#27, 1981) and the band's first Top Ten single,
"Caught Up in You," taken from *Special Forces*. The
group cut two albums filled with competent Southern rock
and toured extensively before racking up a hit album with
Rockin' into the Night, followed by 1981's platinum *Wild-
Eyed Southern Boys*.

B. J. THOMAS

Born August 27, 1942, Houston, Texas
1969—*Greatest Hits* (Scepter)   **1971**—*Greatest Hits,
Volume 2*.

For about six years, starting in 1966, B. J. Thomas had a
run of hit singles, spotlighting his easy vocal style and
MOR arrangements, most notable of which were the gold
records "Raindrops Keep Fallin' on My Head" (#1, 1970)
and "Hooked on a Feeling" (#5, 1968). Other successes
of this period include "I'm So Lonesome, I Could Cry"
(#8) and "Billy and Sue" (#34) in 1966; "The Eyes of a
New York Woman" (#28, 1968); "I Just Can't Help
Believing" (#9, 1970); "No Love at All" (#16, 1971); and
"Rock and Roll Lullaby" (#15, 1972).

Before achieving fame on his own, Thomas belonged to
a Houston combo the Triumphs, who had a number of
regional hits. In 1975, he returned to the #1 spot on the
pop charts with the country tune "(Hey Won't You Play)
Another Somebody Done Somebody Wrong Song" (also
#1 C&W). This was followed by a 1977 Top Twenty cover
of the Beach Boys hit "Don't Worry Baby." In recent
years, he has become a born-again Christian, and he
released Grammy Award–winning gospel-pop LPs in 1979
and 1980.

CARLA THOMAS

Born 1942, Memphis, Tennessee
1961—*Gee Whiz* (Atlantic)   **1966**—*Comfort Me*
(Stax)   *Carla*   **1967**—*King and Queen* (with Otis
Redding)   *Queen Alone*   **1969**—*The Best of Carla
Thomas* (Atlantic)   **1971**—*Love Means* (Stax).

Before Aretha Franklin, Carla Thomas was black music's
reigning Queen of Soul. Her "Gee Whiz (Look at His
Eyes)" in 1961 was, in fact, the first Memphis soul record
to make a national impact (#10 pop, #5 R&B); its success
resulted in the foundation of Stax Records.

The daughter of Memphis music veteran Rufus Thomas,
Carla Thomas made her recording debut in 1960, when she
duetted with her father on "Cause I Love You" while on
summer vacation from college. After "Gee Whiz" succeeded, her education took a back seat to an active
performing career.

Throughout the Sixties, Thomas was a star member of
the Stax roster, scoring with "I'll Bring It Home to You"
(#41 pop, #9 R&B) in 1962; "Let Me Be Good to You"
(#62 pop, #11 R&B) and "B-A-B-Y" (#14 pop, #3 R&B)
in 1966; with Otis Redding on "Tramp" (#26 pop, #2
R&B) and "Knock on Wood" (#30 pop, #8 R&B) and
"I'll Always Have Faith in You" (#85 pop, #11 R&B) in
1967; and "I Like What You're Doing (to Me)" (#9 R&B)
in 1969. After Stax's demise in the mid-Seventies, Thomas
stopped recording, but still performs on the club circuit.

RUFUS THOMAS

Born March 26, 1917, Casey, Mississippi
1964—*Walking the Dog* (Stax)   *May I Have Your Ticket,
Please?*   **1970**—*Funky Chicken; Live at PJs Doing the
Push and Pull*   **1972**—*Did You Hear Me?*   **1973**—
Crown Prince of Dance   **1977**—*If There Were No
Music* (AVI).

Singer Rufus Thomas has been a fixture on the Memphis
music scene since the Forties. He enjoyed his greatest
record sales with his mid-Sixties and early-Seventies
dance hits.

While Thomas was attending Memphis' Booker T.
Washington High School in the Thirties, Professor Nat D.
Williams, a history teacher and emcee of a talent show at
the Palace Theater, selected him to become his sidekick in
a comedy act. Upon graduation from high school, Thomas
toured the South with the Rabbit Foot Minstrels, telling
jokes, tap dancing and singing. He performed at tent
shows until 1940, when he married. Later that year, he
would replace Williams as emcee at the Palace talent
shows.

When he left the talent shows 11 years later, Thomas
worked three other jobs—day worker at a textile plant,
emcee at a local club and DJing on WDIA, where he
befriended another popular disc jockey, B. B. King. During the early Fifties he recorded for Sam Phillips and his
infant Sun Records. Thomas had his first national hit in
1953 with "Bear Cat" (#3 R&B), an answer record to Big
Mama Thornton's "Hound Dog."

Rufus and his daughter Carla were early stars of Stax
Records. His two 1963 dance hits, "The Dog" (#22 R&B)
and "Walking the Dog" (#10 pop, #5 R&B), helped
establish that company. In the early Seventies, Thomas

would have another hot streak with "Do the Funky Chicken" (#28 pop, #5 R&B) and "(Do the) Push and Pull" (#31 pop, #1 R&B) in 1970, and "The Breakdown" (#2 R&B) in 1971. Into the Seventies, Thomas worked at WDIA. When Stax went bankrupt, his recording career ended, though he still tours occasionally.

RICHARD AND LINDA THOMPSON
Richard Thompson (b. Apr. 3, 1949, London), gtr., voc., mandolin, dulcimer; Linda Thompson (b. Linda Peters), voc.
1974—*I Want to See the Bright Lights Tonight* (Island, U.K.) *Hokey Pokey* **1975**—*Pour Down Like Silver* **1977**—*Live (more or less)* **1978**—*First Light* (Chrysalis) **1979**—*Sunnyvista* (Chrysalis, U.K.) **1982**—*Shoot Out the Lights* (Hannibal).
Richard Thompson solo: **1972**—*Henry the Human Fly* (Warner Bros.) **1976**—*(guitar, vocal)* (Island, U.K.) **1981**—*Strict Tempo!* (Elixir, U.K.) **1983**—*Hand of Kindness* (Hannibal).

Richard Thompson, a founding member of the British folk-rock group Fairport Convention, left that band in 1971 for a solo career that in many ways fulfilled Fairport's goals: to link Celtic folk music to rock. Thompson's gallows-humored, fatalistic songs, whose outlook owes something to his Sufi-Muslim religion, are steeped in the jigs and reels and marches of British folk music, although they are often played on electric instruments.

After leaving Fairport, Thompson first sat in as a guitarist on British folk-rock albums like Mike and Lal Waterson's *Bright Phoebus*. He joined a loose aggregation of Fairport and folk-scene veterans, including drummer Dave Mattacks, singer Sandy Denny and bassist Ashley Hutchings under the name the Bunch to record an album of pop oldies, *Rock On*. On that album, a friend of Sandy Denny's named Linda Peters sang "The Loco-motion," and she married Thompson soon afterward. Thompson also sat in on Hutchings' first solo project, *Morris On*.

In 1972, Thompson began his solo career with the brilliant, eccentric *Henry the Human Fly*, which juxtaposed Chuck Berry riffs with old-English concertinas on Thompson's original songs. Linda Peters Thompson sang a few backup vocals, but she didn't get full billing until *I Want to See the Bright Lights Tonight,* which was belatedly released in the U.S. as half of the double album *Live (more or less)*. Although Richard Thompson wrote all the duo's material (except for a song on their final album cowritten by Linda), he shared lead vocals with her on the albums they made together, and Linda's emotive mezzo-soprano was widely praised. In 1974, the Thompsons put together an electric band called Sour Grapes, with ex-Fairport guitarist Simon Nicol and a rhythm section, but after a tour opening for Traffic the group broke up. In 1974, the Thompsons converted to Sufism.

The pair toured Britain in 1975 with a band that included ex-Fairports Dave Pegg on bass and Dave Mattacks on drums, plus button accordionist John Kirkpatrick. Afterward, they retreated to the English countryside to start a Sufi community. They returned in 1978 with *First Light,* which used a U.S. rhythm section. *Strict Tempo!,* released on Thompson's own label, was an album of instrumentals on which he played all the instruments except percussion (by Mattacks); it included traditional jigs, reels and polkas and a Duke Ellington tune. He also sat in on the first solo album by David Thomas of Pere Ubu.

Thompson toured the U.S. as an acoustic solo act before *Shoot Out the Lights* was released, and afterward toured with Linda and a band including Nicol, Mattacks and bassist Pete Zorn. But during that tour, the marriage broke up. While Linda sought a solo contract, Thompson recorded an album of country-and-Celtic breakup songs, *Hand of Kindness*.

BIG MAMA THORNTON
Born Willie Mae Thornton, December 11, 1926, Montgomery, Alabama
1966—*In Europe* (Arhoolie) **1967**—*Chicago Blues* **1968**—*Ball and Chain* **1969**—*Stronger Than Dirt* (Mercury) **1971**—*She's Back* (Backbeat) **1975**—*Jail* (Vanguard) *Sassy Mama* **1978**—*Mama's Pride.*

A singer/songwriter who also plays harmonica and drums, Willie Mae "Big Mama" Thornton is a blueswoman who, in spanning the decades from country to city blues, has carried forward the legacy of such seminal blueswomen as Bessie Smith, Ma Rainey, and Memphis Minnie. She is the originator of two songs later made famous by rock & roll superstars: "Hound Dog" (by Elvis Presley), written by Leiber and Stoller, and her own "Ball and Chain" (a hit for Janis Joplin).

Thornton was one of seven children; her father was a minister, her mother a church singer. She became interested in music at an early age and won first prize in a local talent show in her teens. From 1941 to 1948, she toured the south as a singer/dancer/comedienne with Sammy Greene's Hot Harlem Revue. She settled in Houston, Texas, in 1948 and began recording there in 1951. In 1952, she worked with Johnny Otis' band on his Rhythm and Blues Caravan tour, and appeared in package shows with Junior Parker and Johnny Ace during 1953 and 1954. She recorded for small labels like Kent and Baytone.

In 1965, Thornton toured England and Europe with the American Folk Blues Festival, and in 1967 she appeared at one of John Hammond's Spirituals to Swing concerts at Carnegie Hall, and appeared in the PBS documentary *Black White and Blue*. A year later, she appeared at the Monterey Jazz Festival, and in 1969 played the Newport Folk Festival and the Chicago and Ann Arbor Blues festivals. In 1971, she appeared on the Dick Cavett talk show on ABC-TV, and recorded material for the soundtrack of the film *Vanishing Point*. In 1974, she appeared on NBC-TV's rock show "Midnight Special," and in 1980 appeared on the "Blues Is a Woman" bill with such other veteran blueswomen as Sippie Wallace at the Newport Jazz Festival.

Thornton began recording her currently available albums with *In Europe*. *Chicago Blues*, featuring such blues giants as Muddy Waters and Otis Spann, is considered one of her best. *Jail* contains her versions of "Hound Dog" (originally an R&B hit for her in 1953, before Presley's version), "Ball and Chain" and "Little Red Rooster."

GEORGE THOROGOOD AND THE DESTROYERS

Formed 1973, Delaware
Original lineup: George Thorogood (b. Wilmington, Del.), gtr., voc.; Ron Smith, gtr.; Billy Blough, bass; Jeff Simon, drums.
1977—*George Thorogood and the Destroyers* (Rounder) **1978**—*Move It On Over* **1979**—*Better Than the Rest* (MCA) **1980**—(+ Hank Carter, sax) *More* (Rounder) **1982**—*Bad to the Bone* (EMI).

The son of a white-collar British immigrant and a onetime semi-pro baseball player, George Thorogood is a spirited recreator of the driving, raucous urban slide-guitar blues pioneered by Chicago greats like Elmore James.

Thorogood did not become seriously involved with music until 1970, when he saw a show by another blues archivist, John Paul Hammond. Thorogood went to California, where he was soon opening shows for Bonnie Raitt and bluesmen Sonny Terry and Brownie McGhee. In late 1978, Thorogood had a big hit single with his raw adaptation of Hank Williams' "Move It On Over," which stayed on the chart into 1979—the first single on the folk-oriented Rounder label. Although Thorogood publicly repudiated *Better than the Rest*, a demo tape he had signed away, it also charted. In 1980, he spent the summer playing semi-pro baseball; and in 1981, he and the Destroyers opened several dates on the Rolling Stones' U.S. tour. He later played a tour of all fifty states in two months.

THREE DOG NIGHT

Formed 1968
Danny Hutton (b. Sep. 10, 1946, Buncrana, Ire.), voc.; Chuck Negron (b. June 8, Bronx, N.Y.), voc.; Cory Wells (b. Feb. 5, circa 1944, Buffalo, N.Y.), voc.; Mike Allsup (b. March 8, Modesto, Calif.), gtr.; Jimmy Greenspoon (b. Feb. 7, Los Angeles), kybds.; Joe Schermie (b. Feb. 12, Madison, Wis.), bass; Floyd Sneed (b. Nov. 22, Calgary, Can.), drums.
1969—*Three Dog Night* (Dunhill) *Suitable for Framing* **1970**—*Captured Live at the Forum; It Ain't Easy* **1971**—*Naturally; Golden Biscuits; Harmony* **1972**—*Seven Separate Fools* **1973**—(− Schermie; + Jack Ryland, bass; + Skip Konte, kybds.) *Around the World* **1973**—*Cyan* **1974**—*Hard Labor; Greatest Hits;*

Dog Style **1975**—*Coming Down Your Way* (ABC) *American Pastime*.

In the late Sixties to early Seventies, Three Dog Night were one of the most popular bands in America, with 18 consecutive Top Twenty hits, nine gold singles and 14 gold LPs—their entire album catalogue up through 1973's *Cyan*. Their music—always ridiculed by critics as crassly commercial—was singles-oriented, soul-influenced pop-rock, and almost always consisted of covers. Still, Three Dog Night provided exposure for songwriters Randy Newman, Elton John and Bernie Taupin, Harry Nilsson, Laura Nyro, Hoyt Axton, Leo Sayer and others.

The band centered on three lead singers—Cory Wells, Danny Hutton and Chuck Negron—with four backup musicians—Mike Allsup, Jimmy Greenspoon, Joe Schermie and Floyd Sneed. Wells knew Hutton from the mid-Sixties, when the latter produced Wells's band, the Enemies, for MGM. Hutton, born in Ireland but raised in the U.S., worked as a producer from age 18, and in 1965 he wrote, arranged and produced as a solo the single "Roses and Rainbows" for Hanna-Barbera Records (the cartoon company), which became a small hit. In the fall of that year, he auditioned unsuccessfully for the Monkees. Hutton also recorded for MGM, where he had the minor hit "Big Bright Eyes."

It was Hutton who first hit on the three-vocalist-band idea, rounded out by old friends Wells and Negron, who used to sing regularly at the Apollo and had recorded unsuccessfully with Columbia in the mid-Sixties. Negron also sang backup on one of Hutton's first singles.

By 1968, the lineup was a firm seven-piece. Schermie had been with the Cory Wells Blues Band, which broke up the year before. Sneed had backed José Feliciano, and Greenspoon had done many L.A. sessions. After some initial consultation with Van Dyke Parks and Brian Wilson, Gabriel Mekler, a Hungarian-born classical pianist, who had worked with Steppenwolf, became their producer.

Three Dog Night's 1968 debut contained three singles. First "Nobody" gained initial interest, followed by the Top Thirty cover of Otis Redding's "Try a Little Tenderness." Their big breakthrough came in 1969 with "One," a Harry Nilsson song that soared to #5, their first gold. *Suitable for Framing* gave them hits with "Easy to Be Hard" (#4, 1969, gold) from *Hair*; "Eli's Coming" (#10, 1969) by Laura Nyro, and "Lady Samantha," the first stateside success for Elton John and Bernie Taupin.

On *It Ain't Easy*, they covered Randy Newman's "Mama Told Me Not to Come" (#1, 1970). They later made Hoyt Axton's "Joy to the World" #1 in 1971. They also gave Leo Sayer his first writing hit here by covering "The Show Must Go On" (#14, 1974). Their other hits include Russ Ballard's song for Argent, "Liar" (#7, 1971), "One Man Band" (#19, 1970), "An Old Fashioned Love Song" (#4, 1971), "Never Been to Spain" (#5, 1972),

"Black and White" (#1, 1972) and B. W. Stevenson's "Shambala" (#3, 1973).

By 1974, though, their commercial magic had finally waned. Their 13th LP, *Coming Down Your Way,* was the first not to go gold. In 1976, after the *American Pastime* LP, Hutton was replaced by Jay Gruska, and the band got three new musicians, all former members of Rufus—Al Ciner, Denny Belfield and Ron Stocker. Hutton began managing punk bands in the later Seventies, including L.A.'s Fear. In June of 1981, the three original vocalists reunited.

THUNDERCLAP NEWMAN
Formed 1969, England
Andy Newman (b. circa 1943, Eng.), kybds.; Jimmy McCulloch, (b. 1953, Scot.; d. Sep. 27, 1979), gtr.; John "Speedy" Keen (b. Eng.), voc., drums; and later, Jim Avery (b. Eng.), bass; Jack McCulloch (b. Scot.), drums.
1970—*Hollywood Dream* (Track, U.K.).

Thunderclap Newman was a group haphazardly assembled by Pete Townshend in 1969. The group had one hit, "Something in the Air," and then disbanded.

Andy Newman was a 26-year-old eccentric, a barrelhouse jazz pianist who had previously worked as a post office engineer. Townshend first heard a tape of Newman back in 1963. Townshend ran into Jimmy McCulloch during a Who gig where 13-year-old Jimmy's Cowsill-type family opened the show. Townshend knew ex-Mayall roadie "Speedy" Keen from the early Who days; Keen's "Armenia City in the Sky" wound up on *The Who Sell Out.*

Townshend made the three members into a regular band and, as producer and bass player (under the pseudonym Bijou Drains), recorded Keen's "Something in the Air." It went to #1 in England, got much FM airplay in America, but only hit #37. It was also used in the films *The Magic Christian* and *Strawberry Statement.* Keen wrote the hit and most of the other material on *Hollywood Dreams.*

The band toured England to support the single, with Jim Avery on bass and Jimmy McCulloch's brother Jack on drums (to free Keen for the front vocal spot), but it didn't work out and they disbanded in 1970.

Keen went on to make two solo albums, *Previous Convictions* (Track) and *Y'know Wot I Mean?* (Island). Newman had his own solo, *Rainbow* (Track), and then briefly joined ex–Bonzo Dog Band member Roger Spear in Kinetic Wardrobe. McCulloch played with Stone the Crows (with Maggie Bell), John Mayall and Blue, and then Paul McCartney's Wings from 1975 until 1978; he died the following year.

JOHNNY TILLOTSON
Born April 20, 1939, Jacksonville, Florida

Johnny Tillotson's smooth pop-country songs made him a forerunner of commercialized C&W that crossed over to the pop charts.

He began performing around the age of nine, and in 1958 was signed by Cadence Records. After a few minor singles, he had his biggest-selling hit, "Poetry in Motion" (#2), in late 1960. Through 1965, Tillotson continued to score hit singles, including "Without You" (#7) in 1961; "It Keeps Right on a-Hurtin'" (#3) and "Send Me the Pillow You Dream On" (#17) in 1962; "You Can Never Stop Me Loving You" (#18) and "Talk Back Trembling Lips" (#7) in 1963; and "Heartaches by the Number" (#35) in 1965. In the Seventies, Tillotson remained active on the country circuit.

TINY TIM
Born Herbert Khaury, April 12, 1925, New York City
1968—*God Bless Tiny Tim* (Reprise)   *Tiny Tim's Second Album*   **1969**—*For All My Little Friends.*

With his strange voice (a trembling falsetto), unique appearance (big nose, stringy hair and bag-man clothes) and sweet demeanor, Tiny Tim became a highly successful camp novelty artist in the late Sixties to early Seventies.

The budding singer had a strong record-collector's interest in the fluffy comedic pop of the Twenties—particularly Rudy Vallee—and he first performed these little-known oldies to mostly uninterested audiences in Greenwich Village. He accompanied himself on ukulele and used such pseudonyms as Darry Dover and Larry Love.

By the mid-Sixties, he began to gather a cult audience. He played often at Steve Paul's Scene, and eventually got booked on "The Tonight Show," where he became an instant national celebrity of sorts.

By 1968, rock audiences at places like the Fillmores East and West liked his act as much as older nightclub crowds. In spring 1968, his first LP on Reprise came out. He became a frequent guest on "Laugh-In" as well as the Carson show. On the latter, he was married to 17-year-old Victoria May Budinger (Miss Vicky, as he called her) on December 17, 1969. Their daughter was named Tulip, after Tiny's one major hit, "Tiptoe through the Tulips" (#17, 1968). Tim and Miss Vicky first filed for divorce in early 1972, at which point he was out of public favor and broke. The divorce was final in 1977. He continued to perform occasionally in the Seventies and Eighties.

THE TOKENS
Formed 1958, New York City
Phil Margo (b. April 1, 1942, Brooklyn, N.Y.), bass voc.; Hank Medress (b. Nov. 19, 1938, Brooklyn, N.Y.), first tenor; Jay Siegel (b. Oct. 20, 1939, Brooklyn, N.Y.), lead baritone; Joseph Venneri (b. 1937, Brooklyn, N.Y.); Mitchel Margo (b. May 25, 1947, Brooklyn, N.Y.), second tenor and baritone.

The Tokens, all formerly small-time Brooklyn singer/musicians, were first brought together in 1958 by Neil Sedaka to act as his backup group for live performances and in the studio. Their best-known achievement upon leaving him was their doo-woplike smash hit "The Lion Sleeps Tonight" (#1, 1961). The song, which is derived from a Zulu folk melody originally titled "Wimoweh," was first popular a decade earlier sung in Zulu by Miriam Makeba on Victor Records. The Tokens' souped-up English version sold over two million copies.

Their first single, on Warwick, had been "Tonight I Fell in Love," which sold 700,000 copies in the U.S. and 300,000 in Canada and Europe. All their post–"Lion Sleeps" material, though, fell on deaf ears. The band soon disintegrated, though the members continued in the music business.

Hank Medress produced another version of "Lion Sleeps" for Robert John on Atlantic, which also became a Top Ten smash in 1972. Medress also worked as a staff producer at Bell Records in the early Seventies, and teamed up Dawn with Tony Orlando. Jay Siegel and the Margo brothers became Cross Country and recorded for Atlantic in 1973. The original Tokens continued to sing together on occasion, doing commercials for Pan Am and Clairol. They got a new record contract and released the *Both Sides Now* LP for Buddah in 1971.

TOOTS AND THE MAYTALS
Formed 1962, Kingston, Jamaica
Frederick "Toots" Hibbert (b. 1946, Maypen, Jamaica), lead voc.; Nathaniel "Jerry" Matthias (b. ca. 1945, Jamaica), harmony voc.; Ralphus "Raleigh" Gordon (b. ca. 1945, Jamaica), harmony voc.
1971—*Monkey Man* (Trojan) 1972—*From the Roots*
1973—*Funky Kingston* 1974—*In the Dark* 1975—
Funky Kingston (Island) 1976—*Reggae Got Soul*
1978—*The Maytals* (State) 1979—*The Best of Toots and the Maytals* (Trojan) *Pass the Pipe* (Island)
1980—*Just Like That* 1981—*Live!* 1982—*Knockout* (Mango).

For over two decades, Toots Hibbert's exhortatory vocals and evangelistic stage delivery have charged Jamaican popular music with the fervor of American gospel-rooted soul singers like Otis Redding, Solomon Burke and Wilson Pickett.

Toots Hibbert spent his first 15 years in a small town in the Jamaican countryside; he sang in the local Baptist church. He left home for Kingston in 1962 and formed a vocal trio with Jerry Matthias and Raleigh Gordon.

Coxsone Dodd produced their first Jamaican hits—"Hallelujah" (1963) and "Six and Seven Books of Moses" (1963)—when they called themselves the Vikings. They left Dodd for Prince Buster in 1964 and recorded "Little Slea" as the V. Maytals before deciding to work as the Maytals. In the next two years they worked mainly with

Toots

Byron Lee and his Ska-Kings band. With hits like "If You Act This Way" (1964) and "John and James" (1965), they became a leading group of the ska era.

In 1966, they won the Jamaican Song Festival prize with Hibbert's "Bam Bam." That same year, Hibbert was jailed for possession of marijuana. After his release 12 months later, the Maytals recorded "54-46," commemorating his prison experience, for Leslie Kong's Beverley's label. Among the Maytals' other Beverley's sides was "Do the Reggay" (sic), the 1968 song usually credited with coining the term "reggae."

By that time, Kong was releasing Maytals singles in Britain; "Monkey Man" was the first Maytals song to chart overseas (U.K. #47, 1970). Following Kong's death in 1971, the Maytals worked with his former partner Warwick Lynn and established a following.

The 1972 release of *The Harder They Come* introduced the Maytals to the U.S.; the film's soundtrack featured "Sweet and Dandy" (winner of the 1969 Jamaican Song Festival prize) and "Pressure Drop." Later that year, the Maytals won their third Jamaican Song Festival prize with another Hibbert original, "Pomps and Pride."

In 1975, now known as Toots and the Maytals, they signed their first major contract with Island Records. Island released *Funky Kingston*—a collection culled from Trojan's *Funky Kingston* and *In the Dark*—which contained the Maytal's unique interpretations of John Denver's "Country Roads," in which "West Virginia" became "West Jamaica." Also in 1975, Toots and the Maytals made their first tour of the U.S., opening shows for the Who. Since then, their unreconstructed soul-style reggae has made them one of the Jamaican acts most popular with Americans.

THE TORNADOES
Formed 1962
George Bellamy (b. Oct. 8, 1941), gtr.; Heinz Burt (b.

July 24, 1942), gtr.; Alan Caddy (b. Feb. 2, 1940), gtr., violin; Clem Cattini (b. Aug. 28, 1939), drums; Roger Laverne Jackson (b. Nov. 11, 1938), kybds.
1963—*Telstar* (London).

The Tornadoes were assembled by British songwriter/entrepreneur Don Meek in 1962 to back up vocalists who would sing his songs.

After working with small-time singers John Leyton and Don Charles, the Tornadoes were hooked up with English teen idol Billy Fury. Later in the year, Meeks, inspired by developments in the space program, composed an instrumental for the Tornadoes to record. "Telstar" (the name of the first U.S. communications satellite) became a #1 hit single. The group had just one other minor success, 1963's "Ridin' the Wind."

PETER TOSH
Born Winston Hubert MacIntosh, October 9, 1944, Westmoreland, Jamaica
1976—*Legalize It* (Columbia)   **1977**—*Equal Rights*
1978—*Bush Doctor* (Rolling Stones)   **1979**—*Mystic Man*   **1981**—*Wanted Dread and Alive*   **1983**—*Mama Africa* (EMI America).

Peter Tosh first became known (in Jamaica in the early Sixties and in Europe and America in the early Seventies) as the baritone vocalist of the Wailers.

Through his years with the Wailers, however, he also maintained a solo career. From 1964 to 1967, he released numerous singles in Jamaica on Coxsone Dodd's Studio One and Coxsone labels, variously calling himself Peter Mackingtosh, Peter MacIntosh, Peter Tosh or—most often—Peter Touch. Among his solo recordings (which often featured Wailers Bob Marley and Bunny Livingston as backup singers) were early versions of "I'm the Toughest" and "400 Years," songs he was later to popularize beyond Jamaica.

Some 1969 sessions with Leslie Kong resulted in British releases on the Bullet and Unity labels, and in 1971 and 1972, recordings cut with Joe Gibbs were released in the U.K. on the Bullet, Punch and Pressure Beat labels. In 1971, Tosh founded his own Jamaican label, Intel-Diplo H.I.M., on which he began issuing self-produced solo singles.

Since he left the Wailers in 1973 (complaining that Marley was attracting an undue share of attention overseas), Intel-Diplo H.I.M. has been his sole Jamaican outlet, and he has leased his recordings to foreign companies for world distribution. Columbia got U.S. rights to *Legalize It*, on which Tosh prosyletized for the many uses of marijuana, and *Equal Rights*, which contained his perennially popular "Stepping Razor."

In 1978, Mick Jagger and Keith Richards signed Tosh to Rolling Stones Records and sat in on *Bush Doctor*, which featured the Temptations' "(Got to Walk and) Don't Look Back" in a duet version by Tosh and Jagger (#81 pop). Tosh and his Word, Sound and Power band toured America with the Stones that year, and Jagger joined Tosh on his "Saturday Night Live" appearance. Since then, he has returned to the U.S. regularly, including a 1982 tour with Jimmy Cliff. *Mama Africa* included a reggae remake of Chuck Berry's "Johnny B. Goode."

Tosh has had a history of confrontations with the law. He was jailed for possession of marijuana in the mid-Sixties. In 1978, performing for a Kingston crowd of 30,000 that included the Jamaican Prime Minister, he smoked a "spliff" onstage and berated the Prime Minister for thirty minutes for not legalizing "ganja." Later that year, he was arrested in his studio, taken to a police station and beaten almost to death before he was released.

TOTO
Formed 1978, Los Angeles
David Paich, kybds., voc.; Steve Lukather, gtr., voc.; Bobby Kimball, voc.; Steve Porcaro, kybds.; David Hungate, bass; Jeff Porcaro (b. 1954), drums.
1978—*Toto* (Columbia)   **1979**—*Hydra*   (+ Joe Porcaro, percussion)   **1981**—*Turn Back*   **1982**—*Toto IV* (+ Mike Porcaro, bass).

A studio band assembled by experienced sessionmen, Toto purvey a smooth, glossy power-pop sound that has netted them several hit singles and top-selling LPs. Their debut album and the self-produced *Toto IV* were their biggest sellers.

Most of the bandmembers had met around 1972 at Grant High School in Southern California, and they kept meeting on sessions for albums by Steely Dan, Cheap Trick, Pink Floyd, Earth Wind and Fire and others.

In 1976, Jeff Porcaro, David Hungate and David Paich performed on Boz Scaggs's *Silk Degrees* LP, for which Porcaro wrote several songs, including "Lowdown" and "Lido Shuffle." Their debut album sold over two million copies by 1979, during which year they also had a two-million-selling #5 single, "Hold the Line." Their other Top Forty hits include "I'll Supply the Love" (#45, 1979), "Georgy Porgy" (#48, 1979), "99" (#26, 1979) and "Africa" (1983).

Toto members cowrote the Tubes' 1982 Top Forty hit "Talk to You Later." In 1983, the group won seven Grammy Awards, including Album of the Year for *Toto IV* and Song of the Year for "Rosanna," written for actress Rosanna Arquette.

ALLEN TOUSSAINT
Born Jan. 14, 1938, New Orleans
1958—*The Wild Sounds of New Orleans by Tousan* (RCA)   **1971**—*Toussaint* (Tiffany)   **1972**—*Love, Life and Faith* (Reprise)   **1975**—*Southern Nights*   **1978**—*Motion* (Warner Bros.).

Singer/pianist/songwriter/arranger/producer Allen Toussaint was as important to the music of New Orleans in the Sixties as Dave Bartholomew had been in the Fifties. In the Seventies, musicians from the rest of the United States and abroad came to his city to record with him.

He began playing piano, emulating Professor Longhair, while in grade school. He made his professional debut with the Flamingos when he was in his early teens. In the mid-Fifties, he began working as a studio keyboardist for Dave Bartholomew (he played piano on some Fats Domino sessions), and in 1958 he recorded his first solo album, calling himself Tousan. One of his first compositions, "Java," was a hit for Al Hirt in 1964.

When Minit Records was founded in 1960, Toussaint became the label's house songwriter, arranger and producer for songs like Jessie Hill's "Ooh Poo Pah Doo," Ernie K-Doe's "Mother-in-Law," Chris Kenner's "I Like It Like That," Lee Dorsey's "Ya Ya," Barbara George's "I Know" and records for Aaron Neville, Irma Thomas, Clarence "Frogman" Henry and Benny Spellman. Toussaint established himself as a hitmaker with the definitive New Orleans sound of the Sixties—jaunty dance music characterized by a dialogue of rolling piano licks and horn riffs. His regular studio band included tenor saxophonist Nat Perrilliat, baritone saxophonist Clarence Ford, guitarist Roy Montrell, bassist Peter "Chuck" Badie and drummers John Boudreaux and James Black.

After producing records for the Instant, Fury and AFO labels, in 1963 Toussaint went into the Army. Even as a serviceman he remained a musician, forming the Stokes to record "Whipped Cream" for Instant; the song became a hit for Herb Alpert and the Tijuana Brass. Discharged from the Army in 1965, Toussaint returned to Minit, but the label was sold to Liberty later that year. He and another New Orleans producer, Marshall Sehorn, then founded Sansu Enterprises, which included Marsaint Music Publishers and the Sansu, Amy and Deesu labels.

In the second half of the Sixties, Toussaint wrote and produced hits for Lee Dorsey, Maurice Williams, Ernie K-Doe, Wilbert Harrison and Sansu's studio band, the Meters. After Sansu opened Sea-Saint Studios in 1972, artists such as Paul Simon, Paul McCartney and Wings, Sandy Denny, and the Mighty Diamonds recorded there; Toussaint produced sessions by Dr. John, Labelle (including their 1975 bestseller, "Lady Marmalade"), Badger, John Mayall and Joe Cocker. He was also responsible for the horn arrangements on the Band's 1972 live album, *Rock of Ages*, and the period music for the 1978 soundtrack to Louis Malle's *Pretty Baby*.

Toussaint records his own albums and appears live only occasionally, but his songs have been covered by the Rolling Stones ("Fortune Teller"), Herman's Hermits ("A Certain Girl"), Betty Wright ("Shoorah, Shoorah"), Three Dog Night ("Brickyard Blues"), Frankie Miller ("High Life"), Glen Campbell ("Southern Nights"), the Yardbirds, the Pointer Sisters, Maria Muldaur, Little Feat, Boz Scaggs, Bonnie Raitt, Robert Palmer, Ringo Starr and Warren Zevon.

TOWER OF POWER

Formed late 1960s, Oakland, California
Lineup, circa 1973: Lenny Williams (b. Pine Bluff, Ark.), voc.; Lenny Pickett, sax, flute, piccolo; Emilio Castillo, sax; Steve Kupka, sax, English horn; Greg Adams, trumpet, voc., flugelhorn; Mic Gillette, trumpet, trombone, flugelhorn; Bruce Conte, gtr., voc.; Chester Thompson, kybds., voc.; Francis Rocco Prestia, bass; David Garibaldi, drums; Brent Byars, congas.
1970—*East Bay Grease* (San Francisco) **1972**—*Bump City* (Warner Bros.) **1973**—*Power* **1974**—*Back to Oakland* **1975**—(+ Hubert Tubbs, voc.; − Williams) *In the Slot.*

This integrated Oakland-based R&B band reached its commercial peak between 1973 and 1975, when Lenny Williams sang lead. Emerging from the early-Seventies Bay Area club scene, the band made its recording debut with *East Bay Grease* on Bill Graham's San Francisco Records in 1971.

The next year, signed to Warner Bros., they scored with "You're Still a Young Man" (#29 pop), with Rich Stevens as lead vocalist. Williams joined Tower of Power for their third album, *Power*, and continued fronting the band on *Back to Oakland* and *Urban Renewal*. During this period, the band had hits with "So Very Hard to Go" (#17 pop, #11 R&B) and "What Is Hip?" (#91 pop, #31 R&B). Williams left to sign with ABC as a solo; his R&B hits include "Choosing You" (#62) and "Shoo Doo Fu Fu Ooh!" (#31), both 1977. Hubert Tubbs succeeded him and sang lead on "You Ought to Be Having Fun" (#68 pop, #62 R&B) in 1976, when Tower was signed to Columbia.

Throughout the Seventies, the Tower of Power's ultraprecise horn section worked as studio musicians on other acts' recordings. Among them were Elton John, Elvin Bishop, Santana and José Feliciano. In 1983, Pickett was heard in avant-grade music concerts in New York.

THE TOYS

Formed early 1960s, Jamaica, New York
June Montiero (b. July 1, 1946, Queens, N.Y.), voc.; Barbara Harris (b. Aug. 18, 1945, Elizabeth, N.J.), voc.; Barbara Parritt (b. Oct. 1, 1944, Wilmington, N.C.), voc.
1966—*A Lover's Concerto* (Attack).

The Toys were an R&B girl group whose big hit was "A Lover's Concerto," a refashioning of a Bach piece (#2, 1965).

The three members met as teenagers at Woodrow Wilson High School in Queens, New York, and continued to sing after their graduation. In 1964, they were signed by the publishing firm Genius Inc., who teamed them with the songwriting duo Sandy Linzer and Denny Rendell. Their big single went #4 R&B, crossed over to pop and also became a #5 hit in England. During 1965, the song sold over a million copies. The Toys appeared on television rock shows like "Shindig!", and toured with Gene Pitney. They also appeared in the film *The Girl in Daddy's Bikini.* They had a less successful hit in 1966 with "Attack" (#18). By the next year they were gone from the charts, but continued to do session work separately.

TRAFFIC
Formed 1967, England
Steve Winwood (b. May 12, 1948, Birmingham, Eng.), voc., kybds., gtr.; Chris Wood (b. June 24, 1944, Birmingham, Eng.; d. July 12, 1983, London), sax, flute; Dave Mason (b. May 10, 1947, Worcester, Eng.), gtr., voc.; Jim Capaldi (b. Aug. 24, 1944, Evesham, Eng.), drums, voc.
1967—*Mr. Fantasy* (United Artists) (–Mason; + Mason) 1968—*Traffic* (– Mason) 1969—*Last Exit* 1970—*John Barleycorn Must Die* (+ Rick Grech [b. Nov. 1, 1946], bass) 1971—(+ Jim Gordon, drums; + Reebop Kwaku Baah [b. Konongo, Ghana], percussion; + Dave Mason, gtr., voc.) *Welcome to the Canteen* (– Mason) *The Low Spark of High-Heeled Boys* (Island) (– Grech; – Gordon; + Roger Hawkins, drums; + David Hood, bass) 1973—*Shoot Out at the Fantasy Factory* 1974—*On the Road* (– Hawkins; – Hood; + Rosco Gee, bass) *When the Eagle Flies.*

Traffic had two phases. At first it was a winsomely psychedelic pop band that blended blues, folk, rock and R&B and was fronted by Steve Winwood and Dave Mason. After Mason left, the band became Steve Winwood's vehicle for longer, moodier excursions that leaned closer to jazz and soul. Traffic was popular in both incarnations.

When the band formed in 1967, Steve Winwood was its best-known member because of his lead vocals with the Spencer Davis Group. Winwood left that band to found Traffic and with friends Chris Wood, Jim Capaldi and Dave Mason wrote and rehearsed in a cottage in the English countryside. Traffic's debut LP, *Mr. Fantasy,* contained two British hits, "Paper Sun" (U.K. #5) and "Hole in My Shoe." But conflicts between Mason's pop style and Winwood's jazz ambitions flared up and in late 1967 Mason split, first joining up with Delaney and Bonnie Bramlett before pursuing a solo career. A film called *Here We Go Round the Mulberry Bush* in 1968 contained some of Traffic's music, and the theme song was a minor hit.

Despite differences with Winwood, Mason helped cut *Traffic,* contributing the often covered "Feelin' Alright." But by 1968 he had left again. It looked like Traffic was

finished in 1969, when Winwood joined Blind Faith with Eric Clapton, Ginger Baker and Rick Grech.

However, Blind Faith proved short-lived, and after a stint in Ginger Baker's Air Force in 1970 Winwood began recording his first solo album, the working title of which was *Mad Shadows.* Capaldi and Wood sat in on some sessions, and the LP became Traffic's fifth and most commercially successful album, *John Barleycorn Must Die,* a staple of "progressive" FM radio. The group then added Grech. The next year, before recording *Welcome to the Canteen,* Reebop Kwaku Baah was added on percussion. In addition, that live album featured Jim Gordon augmenting Capaldi on drums and a guest appearance by Mason. Despite the success of the gold album *The Low Spark of High-Heeled Boys* in 1972, Gordon and Grech departed.

Winwood was then stricken with peritonitis, and so the band was temporarily sidelined. Capaldi cut a solo album (*Oh! How We Danced*) in Muscle Shoals, Alabama, and in the process he recruited session players bassist David Hood and drummer Roger Hawkins into the band. They appeared on *Shoot Out at the Fantasy Factory* and with another Muscle Shoals musician, keyboardist Barry Beckett, on the live *On the Road.* By the sessions for *When the Eagle Flies,* only the original trio of Winwood, Wood, and Capaldi plus bassist Rosco Gee were left. After its release, Winwood and Capaldi started their solo careers in earnest. Wood died in 1983 in his London apartment after a long illness. (See also: Steve Winwood.)

THE TRAMMPS
Formed mid-1960s, Philadelphia
Key personnel: Earl Young, drums, bass voc.; Jimmy Ellis, voc.; Robert Upchurch, voc.; Stanley Wade, bass, voc.; Harold Wade, gtr., voc.
1975—*Trammps* (Golden Fleece) *The Legendary Zing Album* (Buddah) 1976—*That's Where the Happy People Go* (Atlantic) *Disco Inferno* 1977—*Trammps III* 1978—*The Best of the Trammps* 1980—*Slipping Out.*

While the Trammps had their first recording success in 1965 with "Storm Warning," when they were known as the Volcanoes, it was not until a 1975 contract with Atlantic Records, several personnel changes and the rise of disco music that they became a celebrated recording and touring act. Their peak popularity came through the inclusion of their blazing rendition of "Disco Inferno" on the *Saturday Night Fever* soundtrack in 1977.

Basing their vocal style on that of the Coasters (a lead and bass vocal combination), their earliest success as the Trammps came on the Buddah label with a rendition of "Zing Went the Strings of My Heart" (#17 R&B), featuring Earl Young's bass vocal.

Young, a top Philadelphia session musician and co-owner of the Philadelphia publishing and production company Golden Fleece (with producers Norman Harris and Ronnie Baker) brought the Trammps to that label after their Buddah contract expired. Their association with Golden Fleece yielded an early disco hit, "Love Epidemic" (#75 R&B), in 1973. In 1975, they signed on with Atlantic Records and had the first of a string of hits with the uptempo love plea "Hooked for Life" (#70 R&B). This was followed by "Hold Back the Night" (#35 pop, #10 R&B) in 1975; "That's Where the Happy People Go" (#27 pop, #12 R&B), in 1976; and "Disco Inferno" (#11 pop, #9 R&B) in 1977. That proved to be their last major hit, and as the disco phase drew to a close, the Trammps faded from sight.

THE TREMELOES

Formed 1959, Dagenham, England
Brian Poole (b. Nov. 3, 1941), voc.; Alan Blakely (b. Apr. 1, 1942), rhythm gtr.; Alan Howard, bass; Dave Munden (b. Dec. 2, 1943), drums; Rick Westwood (b. May 7, 1943), lead gtr.
1966—(− Poole; − Howard; + Len "Chip" Hawkes [b. Nov. 2, 1946], bass)   1967—*Here Comes My Baby* (Columbia) *Even the Bad Times Are Good; Suddenly You Love Me*   1968—*58/68 World Explosion*   1974—*Shiner* (DMJ).

The Tremeloes began their career as the backup band for British vocalist Brian Poole, and with him had a number of U.K. hit records in 1963 and 1964, including the #1 single "Do You Love Me." When Poole left them in 1966, they brought in Len Hawkes and proceeded to eclipse their former frontman with a trio of British Top Five hit records: "Silence Is Golden," "Even the Bad Times Are Good" and "Here Comes My Baby," all in 1967. All except the second hit the U.S. Top Twenty as well. Even when the hits stopped, the Tremeloes remained a viable nightclub attraction, and they continue to this day, though a car accident forced Hawkes to quit in 1974, and Blakely left on his own the following year.

T. REX/TYRANNOSAURUS REX/MARC BOLAN

Formed 1967, England
Marc Bolan (b. Mark Feld, Sep. 30, 1948, London; d. Sep. 16, 1977, London)
1968—*My People Were Fair and Had Sky in Their Hair But Now They're Content to Wear Stars on Their Brows* (Regal/Zonophone, U.K.) *Prophets, Seers and Sages, The Angels of the Ages*   1969—*Unicorn* (Blue Thumb)   1970—*Beard of Stars* (Regal/Zonophone, U.K.) *T. Rex* (Reprise)   1971—*Electric Warrior*   1972—*The Slider*   1973—*Tanx*   1974—*Zinc Alloy and the Hidden Riders of Tomorrow*   1975—*Zip Gun Boogie* (EMI, U.K.)   1976—*Futuristic Dragon*   1977—*Dandy in the Underworld.*

T. Rex: Mickey Finn and Marc Bolan

With his Botticelli face and curls and whimsically glamorous image, Marc Bolan fronted T. Rex, a British group that generated a fan hysteria reminiscent of Beatlemania and produced eleven successive U.K. Top Ten hits between 1970 and 1974. Among these were "Bang a Gong (Get It On)" (#1), "Jeepster" (#2) and "Telegram Sam" (#1). But T. Rex could hardly duplicate its British success in America. Its sole major hit was the Top Ten smash "Bang a Gong."

T. Rex had its beginnings when the group—known as Tyrannosaurus Rex until the 1970 success of "Ride a White Swan"—was formed by Bolan in 1967 with Steve Peregrine Took. A well-known scene-making Mod in the early Sixties, Bolan released two singles in the mid-Sixties on Decca—"Hippy Gumbo" and "The Wizard"—which failed to establish him as a solo artist. But with the group John's Children, Bolan enjoyed two minor U.K. hits in 1967—"Desdemona" and "Go Go Girl."

One year later, Tyrannosaurus Rex recorded its debut album (produced by Tony Visconti), which blended acoustic textures with such instruments as the Chinese gong and talking drums and accented Bolan's lyrics—a blend of myth, fantasy and magic. As a British flower-power band, Tyrannosaurus Rex earned a sizable underground following and toured the U.S. in 1969.

The band began to achieve widespread success by embracing a full-blown rock attack on albums like *Electric Warrior*. During the height of T. Rex mania in 1973, Ringo Starr directed a documentary on the group's success, *Born to Boogie*. T. Rex's popularity declined shortly thereafter, and Bolan declared the group extinct in 1975, leaving his wife and exiling himself to America. He returned to England in 1976 and began living with American singer Gloria Jones. Respected by followers of the then-burgeoning new wave scene, Bolan brought the Damned on tour with his newly re-formed T. Rex in 1977 as a support act.

But his solo career never took off in the U.S., partially because of his haphazard personal life. "I was living in a twilight world of drugs, booze and kinky sex," he told *Rolling Stone*. Bolan died in a crash on September 16, 1977, in a car driven by Jones. In 1980, Steve Peregrine Took died from choking.

THE TROGGS
Formed circa 1966, Andover, England
Reg Presley (b. Jun. 12, 1943, Andover, Eng.), voc.; Chris Britton (b. Jun. 21, 1945, Watford, Eng.), lead gtr.; Peter Staples (b. May 3, 1944, Andover, Eng.), bass; Ronnie Bond (b. May 4, 1943, Andover, Eng.), drums.
1976—*The Troggs* (Pye)   *The Original Troggs Tapes* (Private Stock)   *Vintage Years* (Sire).

Though their popularity only lasted a short time, the Troggs were initially one of the most successful mid-Sixties British Invasion bands, most known for their five-million-selling seminal punk hit "Wild Thing" (#1, 1966).

The foursome formed in Hampshire in the mid-Sixties, taking their name from the term "troglodyte." "Wild Thing" was their debut single. The song was so popular and so frequently covered that it spawned a parody version sung by two people imitating Robert Kennedy and Senator Everett Dirksen. The Troggs' other hits in 1966 were "With a Girl Like You" (#29) and "I Can't Control Myself" (#43).

Their roots-of-power-pop sound, featuring Reg Presley's wispy vocals, also got them a Top Ten hit with "Love Is All Around" (#7, 1968). Though their hits dried up at that point, they continued to tour Europe. They didn't record, though, for several years. In 1976, Pye released *The Troggs*, which featured "Summertime," a double-entendre-laden song that also got U.S. FM airplay.

In 1976, Sire released *Vintage Years*, a retrospective, and Private Stock put out *The Original Troggs Tapes*, which was all new material. In 1980, there was the *Live at Max's Kansas City* album including older hits and newer songs. It garnered only cult interest. There was also a French import album in 1981 called *Black Bottom*, again with new and old material. The group continues to tour.

ROBIN TROWER
Born March 9, 1945, London
1973—(Trower, gtr.; James Dewar [b. Scot.], bass, voc.; Reg Isadore [b. West Indies], drums) *Twice Removed from Yesterday* (Chrysalis)   **1974**—*Bridge of Sighs*   **1975**—(– Isadore; + Bill Lordan, drums) *For Earth Below; Live*   **1976**—*Long Misty Days*   **1977**—(+ Rusty Allen, bass)   *City Dreams*   **1978**—*Caravan to Midnight*   **1980**—(– Allen)   *Victim of Fury*   **1981**—(– Dewar, + Jack Bruce [b. May 14, 1943, Glasgow], bass, voc.)   *BLT*   **1982**—*Truce*.

In his early years with Procol Harum, Robin Trower's piercing, distorted guitar sound was more often than not compared to that of Eric Clapton. But on Procol's "Whiskey Train" (on *Home*) and "Song for a Dreamer" (on *Broken Barricades*) Trower exhibited a strong Jimi Hendrix influence; "Song for a Dreamer" was dedicated to Hendrix.

By the time of *Barricades*, it was obvious that Trower's hard-rocking style was at odds with Procol's classical-rock direction, and he left after that album, at first forming the abortive Jude with ex–Jethro Tull drummer Clive Bunker, ex–Stone the Crows bassist Jim Dewar and Scottish blues singer Frankie Miller. When that venture ran aground, Trower took a year off to re-form a Hendrix-style power trio with Dewar and drummer Reg Isadore. They debuted with 1973's *Twice Removed from Yesterday*, which was produced by ex-Procol Matthew Fisher.

With *Bridge of Sighs* and heavy American touring, Trower came into his own as a guitar hero with U.S. audiences. After that album, Isadore was replaced by Bill Lordan, formerly with Sly and the Family Stone. Meanwhile, Trower took some guitar lessons from another pioneer of electronically modified guitar, Robert Fripp, who had just disbanded King Crimson. *For Earth Below* and *Live* were top-selling LPs, and through the Seventies Trower continued to ably demonstrate his love for Hendrix, usually with solid commericial results. In 1981, Trower began collaborating with ex-Cream bassist and singer Jack Bruce, for two well-received albums.

THE TUBES
Formed late 1960s, Phoenix, Arizona
Fee Waybill (b. John Waldo, Sep. 17, 1950, Omaha, Neb.), lead voc.; Bill Spooner (b. Apr. 16, 1949, Phoenix, Ariz.), gtr.; Roger Steen (b. Nov. 13, 1949, Pipestone, Minn.), gtr.; Vince Welnick (b. Feb. 21, 1951, Phoenix, Ariz.), kybds.; Michael Cotten (b. Jan. 25, 1950, Kansas City, Mo.), kybds.; Prairie Prince (b. May 7, 1950, Charlotte, N.C.), drums; Rick Anderson (b. Aug. 1, 1947, St. Paul, Minn.), bass; Re Styles (b. Mar. 3, 1950), voc.
1975—*The Tubes* (A&M)   **1976**—*Young and Rich*   **1977**—*Now*   **1978**—*What Do You Want From Live?*   **1979**—*Remote Control*   **1981**—*The Completion Backward Principle* (Capitol)   *Trash* (A&M)   **1983**—*Outside/Inside* (Capitol).

From the mid-Seventies on, the Tubes' mixture of rock, theater and satire has proved more capable of achieving notoriety than sales. Despite one of the wildest stage shows in the business (verging at times on soft-core pornography) and critical acclaim for their records, their five LPs for A&M were flops (even though the first was produced by Al Kooper and the last by Todd Rundgren). The Tubes came close to hits during this period with a pair of radio staples—the heavy-metal parody "White Punks on Dope" (featuring Waybill in the guise of Quay Lewd) and the mock-girl-group song "Don't Touch Me There."

Bill Spooner, Rick Anderson and Vince Welnick started embryonic versions of the Tubes in their hometown of Phoenix in the late Sixties, though they wouldn't come to be known as the Tubes until they moved to San Francisco in 1972. Early performances were generally reviled, and it took the group three years to build a cult following sufficient to justify a recording contract.

But as each LP became another commercial setback, the Tubes began to streamline their act, and by 1980 they were down to six, after experimenting with a propless all-music live show. Even then, when their self-conscious attempt at a hit record, "Don't Want to Wait Anymore," proved successful, the only Tubes present were Waybill and Prince. That song, along with the AOR hit "Talk to You Later," made the Tubes' Capitol debut, *The Completion Backward Principle,* a big seller. Later that year, the group appeared in the movie *Xanadu.* In 1983, "She's a Beauty" reached the Top Ten.

TANYA TUCKER

Born October 10, 1958, Seminole, Texas
1972—*Delta Dawn* (Columbia)   1973—*What's Your Mama's Name*   1974—*Would You Lay With Me*
1975—*Greatest Hits; Tanya Tucker* (MCA)   1976—
Lovin' and Learnin'; Here's Some Love   1977—*Ridin' Rainbows*   1978—*TNT*   1981—*Should I Do It?*
1982—*Live.*

Three things made Tanya Tucker a major country-pop star at age 14: a fine voice, Billy Sherrill's MOR-Nashville production, and an image as a pubescent sexpot.

Tucker got into music through her construction-worker father, who took her to country shows after the family had moved to Wilcox, Arizona, and then to Phoenix. At age 13, she appeared in the film *Jeremiah Johnson.* Her first country hit was 1972's "Delta Dawn," followed by two #1 country hits: "What's Your Mama's Name" and "Blood Red and Goin' Down." At age 16 she made the #1 country single "Would You Lay With Me (in a Field of Stone)."

After she reached the age of consent, Tucker left Columbia and producer Billy Sherrill and signed with MCA. In the late Seventies, she briefly tried to become a rock singer, wearing red tights (for *TNT*) and adding fuzz-tone guitars, but she soon retreated into country music. A liaison with country-pop crooner Glen Campbell included some duet recordings, but it ended in 1981, and Tucker continued to work the country circuit on her own.

IKE AND TINA TURNER

Ike Turner, born November 5, 1931, Clarksdale, Mississippi; Tina Turner, born Annie Mae Bullock, November 26, 1938, Brownsville, Tennessee

1966—*River Deep, Mountain High* (A&M)   1969—*The Hunter* (Blue Thumb)   1970—*Her Man, His Woman* (Capitol)   1971—*Nuff Said* (United Artists)   1972—
Feel Good   1973—*Nutbush City Limits*   1976—*Very Best of*   1977—*Delilah's Power.*
Ike Turner solo: 1972—*Blues Roots* (United Artists)
1978—*I'm Tore Up* (Red Lightnin').
Tina Turner solo: 1975—*Acid Queen* (United Artists)
1979—*Rough.*

Guitarist Ike Turner and his wife Tina are best known for their late-Sixties and early-Seventies recordings and their soul revue. Ike Turner was also a seminal figure in the early years of rock & roll as both a performer and talent scout, and Tina remains one of the most flamboyant, overtly sexual performers in rock, singing in a blues rasp and suggestively caressing her microphone.

Ike Turner's career began when, at age 11, he backed local bluesmen like Sonny Boy Williamson and Robert Nighthawk on piano in Mississippi clubs. He formed his first band, the Kings of Rhythm, while still in high school. In 1951, his band recorded "Rocket '88" at Sam Phillips' Sun studio in Memphis. The lead vocal was by saxophonist Jackie Brenston, but Turner ran the session. "Rocket '88," released under Brenston's name, went on to become a #1 R&B hit on the Chess label, and over the years it has been frequently cited as the first rock & roll record.

Turner went on to become a top session guitarist, talent scout and producer through the Fifties. The sessions he recorded with Junior Parker and Howlin' Wolf, B. B. King, Roscoe Gordon and Johnny Ace were leased to Chess, Modern and RPM Records.

In 1956, Turner and the Kings of Rhythm went to St. Louis, where they played a number of night spots. Annie Mae Bullock and her sister were regulars at one such club. Bullock repeatedly asked Turner if she could sing with his band; he said that she could but never called her to the stage. One night Bullock, who had never sung professionally but had been appearing in talent shows since childhood, simply grabbed the microphone and sang. Turner later hired her, and in 1958, they married. Soon after, he changed her name to Tina.

They first recorded as Ike and Tina Turner in 1960 after a singer failed to appear for a session. Tina stood in for the missing singer, and the song, "A Fool in Love," became a hit in 1960 (#27 pop, #2 R&B). Ike then developed an entire revue around Tina. With nine musicians and three scantily clad female background singers called the Ikettes, the Ike and Tina Turner Revue became a major soul act.

In 1961, they charted with "It's Gonna Work Out Fine" (#14 pop, #2 R&B) and "I Idolize You" (#5 R&B). The following year, "Poor Fool" (#38 pop, #4 R&B) and "Tra La La La La" (#9 R&B) were hits. In the late Sixties, they became major stars in England, and in 1966 Phil Spector produced what proved to be his last Wall of Sound

Ike and Tina Turner

single, "River Deep, Mountain High." It went to #3 in England, but did so poorly in the U.S. that Spector did not produce again until 1969.

The Turners continued to make pop hits into the late Sixties. They opened for the Rolling Stones on their 1969 tour. They were especially successful into the early Seventies with steamy cover songs like "Come Together" (#57 pop, #21 R&B), "I Want to Take You Higher" (#34 pop, #25 R&B) and "Proud Mary" (#4 pop, #5 R&B), featuring Tina's "We never do *anything* nice and easy" spoken intro. In 1973, "Nutbush City Limits" (written by Tina) hit #4 in England and #13 R&B and #22 pop in the U.S. Three years later, Tina and Ike divorced.

Ike Turner retired to his studio in Inglewood, California, and released two solo LPs. The studio was destroyed by fire in 1982. Tina, after several years of not performing, made something of a comeback in 1981, touring clubs and appearing on Rod Stewart's satellite-broadcast concert late that year; she also opened some arena shows for the Rolling Stones. Although she had released solo albums through the Seventies, her work received little attention, save for her frenzied performance as the Acid Queen in Ken Russell's film of the Who's *Tommy*.

JOE TURNER
Born May 18, 1911, Kansas City, Missouri
1956—*The Boss of the Blues* (Atlantic)   **1971**—*His Greatest Recordings* (ALCO).

Big Joe Turner is one of rock & roll's forefathers, with jump-blues staples including "Shake, Rattle and Roll,"

"Honey Hush," "Sweet Sixteen," "Chains of Love" and "Flip, Flop and Fly." He had been singing for over twenty years when he recorded those songs in the early Fifties. And in the early Eighties he was still performing.

Turner got his start as a singing bartender in a Kansas City cabaret in the late Twenties. He was already known as one of the most powerful blues singers west of the Mississippi when he teamed up with boogie-woogie pianist Pete Johnson and became one of the originators of "blues shouting."

In 1938, talent scout John Hammond brought Turner and Johnson to New York to appear at the Carnegie Hall concert that sparked the boogie-woogie craze of the late Thirties and early Forties. As their engagement at Cafe Society—a New York jazz club—extended into a four-year run, boogie-woogie bumped its way into mainstream white pop for the first time. Turner sang jazz-style slow blues with pianist Art Tatum, but he also shouted boogie-woogie fast blues with Johnson, and the propulsive rhythms and extroverted vocals of songs like "Roll 'em Pete" showed the stirrings of the rhythm & blues that became popular in the years after World War II.

In 1941, Turner went to Hollywood to appear in Duke Ellington's "Jump for Joy" revue. He was based on the West Coast for most of the Forties, joined occasionally by Johnson and pianist Albert Ammons. In 1951, he returned to New York to play the Apollo Theater with Count Basie. There he met Ahmet Ertegun and Jerry Wexler, who brought him to Atlantic Records, where Ertegun's "Chains of Love" gave him a #2 R&B hit. (Pat Boone had a #10 pop hit with the song five years later.)

It was the first of a string of R&B hits on Atlantic between 1951 and 1956, each of which is a rock & roll classic: "Sweet Sixteen" (#4, 1952), "Honey Hush" (#2, 1953; reissued in 1960, it made the pop Top Sixty), "T.V. Mama" (#9, 1954, recorded in Chicago with Elmore James and his band), "Shake, Rattle and Roll" (#2, 1954, a big hit for Bill Haley later that year in a bowdlerized form), "Flip, Flop and Fly" (#3, 1955, covered by Johnnie Ray), "The Chicken and the Hawk" (#13, 1956), "Corrina, Corrina" (#3, 1956; at #41, his biggest pop hit) and "Rock a While" (#12, 1956). In addition to Ertegun's songs, his own, and his brother Lou Willie Turner's, he recorded material by Doc Pomus and Leiber and Stoller.

While he never had the pop success of his imitators, who often cleaned up the sexual metaphors and took some of the energy out of the songs, Turner continued to work through good times and bad. He toured Europe several times in the Fifties; and in the Sixties and Seventies he appeared and recorded with the Johnny Otis Show, Eddie "Lockjaw" Davis, Milt Jackson, Roy Eldridge, Dizzy Gillespie and Pee Wee Crayton. In 1974, he was featured with Count Basie in *The Last of the Blue Devils*, a film about the Kansas City music scene. In 1982, he continued to appear in clubs, his vocal powers undiminished by age and arthritis.

THE TURTLES
Formed 1963, Inglewood, California
Original lineup: Howard Kaylan (b. June 22, 1945, Calif.), voc.; Mark Volman (b. Apr. 19, 1944, Calif.), voc., gtr.; Al Nichol (b. Mar. 31, 1945), gtr.; Chuck Portz (b. Mar. 28, 1945), bass; Donald Ray Murray (b. Nov. 8, 1945), drums.
1965—*It Ain't Me Babe* (White Whale) **1966**—*You Baby* **1967**—*Happy Together; Golden Hits* **1968**—*The Turtles Present the Battle of the Bands* **1969**—*Turtle Soup* **1970**—*More Golden Hits; Wooden Head* **1975**—*Happy Together Again* (Sire).

The Turtles were a successful pop group of the Sixties, but they were dissatisfied with "mere" hit singles. Their aspirations to more profound statements broke up the band, with lead singers Mark Volman and Howard Kaylan joining up with Frank Zappa and then embarking on a duo career as the Phlorescent Leech (Flo) and Eddie.

The name Turtles came from White Whale Records. Prior to the band's signing in 1965, the L.A.-based combo had been known as the Nightriders, and later as the Cross Fires. Their local singles during that time were uniformly unsuccessful. Once under contract, they were converted from a surf group (White Whale astutely noting that that trend was on the wane) to folk rock, then in vogue thanks to Bob Dylan, the Byrds, et al.

Their debut single, Dylan's "It Ain't Me Babe," went Top Ten in 1965 and launched the band on a brief string of hits: "Let Me Be" (#20, 1965), "You Baby" (#20, 1966), "Grim Reaper of Love " (#81, 1966) and "Can I Get to Know You Better" (#89, 1966).

The Turtles weren't content, however, and were about to break up; but first they released "Happy Together," which proved to be their biggest hit, and one of 1967's Top Ten records. With their career reinvigorated, "She'd Rather Be with Me" (#3, 1967) and "You Know What I Mean" (#12, 1967) were follow-up hits; but they stalled the internal dissatisfaction only temporarily.

Though it included their last two hit 45s, "Elenore" and "You Showed Me," *The Turtles Present the Battle of the Bands* was an ambitious reflection of the group's desire to be more than AM radio material. Each song was meant to sound completely different from the others, literally as if performed by a different group. The gatefold sleeve presented the Turtles dressed in eleven guises, including the Cross Fires. The next album, *Turtle Soup*, was produced by the Kinks' Ray Davies when he was at his least commercial. The band split up then.

The Turtles had fluid personnel; only lead guitarist Al Nichol was with them from Cross Fires to breakup. After some of the original members quit, replacements were found in ex-Leaves (who had one hit with "Hey Joe") bassist Jim Pons and drummer John Barbata. After Barbata quit the group, he drummed with Crosby, Stills, Nash and Young and the Jefferson Starship. Pons stuck with Volman and Kaylan into Zappa's band and the initial Flo and Eddie group (the alias was devised when White Whale forced the group into litigation while they were breaking up). Other temporary Turtles included onetime Monkees producer Chip Douglas and former Spanky and Our Gang drummer John Seiter.

TV Rock

Ever since Ed Sullivan's camera crews were ordered not to shoot Elvis Presley's lower half, television has been wary of rock. At the same time, the music is vastly popular, so periodic attempts have been made to present rock on TV. As popular entertainers, rock musicians have shown up with some frequency on variety shows, from Ed Sullivan to "The Smothers Brothers Comedy Hour" to "Saturday Night Live" to "Uncle Floyd," and there have been six cartoon series with rock bands as characters: The Beatles, the Beagles, the Banana Splits, the Archies, the Jackson 5 and Josie and the Pussycats.

At various times, pop musicians have also been given their own variety shows, including Sonny and Cher, Tom Jones, the Jacksons, Bobby Darin, the Captain and Tennille, the Everly Brothers, Helen Reddy and Donny and Marie Osmond. And there were two situation comedies based on rock acts, the Monkees and the Partridge Family. TV stars have also had occasional hits, mostly novelties, although Rick Springfield of "General Hospital" had an unsuccessful rock career before he took the role and only later began to sell millions of records.

But the most important rock shows on TV are those that center on the music and its incidental behavior. The longest running one is "American Bandstand," in which teenagers dance to current hits, rate them, and dance around live musicians who are lip-synching their latest efforts. Over 8,500 guests have appeared since the program was started as "Bandstand" on WFIL-TV, Philadelphia, in 1952, by Bob Horn and Lee Stewart. Dick Clark became host in 1956, and in 1957 ABC began broadcasting it nationally as "American Bandstand." After a two-month run in 1957 on Saturday nights, it moved to the Saturday-afternoon slot it still holds.

The folk revival of the early

Sixties showed up on ABC's "Hootenanny" from April to September of 1963. Taped at different college campuses and hosted by Jack Linkletter, with regulars including the Chad Mitchell Trio, the show carefully steered away from any of the left-wing implications still clinging to the folk movement after the McCarthy era; such folk stalwarts as Pete Seeger did not appear.

With the British Invasion came two variety shows devoted to rock exclusively. ABC's "Shindig!" began in September 1964; NBC answered it with "Hullabaloo" in January 1965. Both were half-hour shows with dancers including "Hullabaloo"'s go-go girl in a cage, Lada Edmund, Jr. "Shindig!" was hosted by Jimmy O'Neal, and its house band, the Shindogs, included Leon Russell and Delaney Bramlett. The hosts of "Hullabaloo" included Paul Anka, Jack Jones, Annette Funicello and Jerry Lewis with his son Gary. Guests on both included British Invasion acts and American hitmakers. For its first three months "Hullabaloo" included a London segment hosted by the Beatles' manager, Brian Epstein, although the Beatles never appeared. "Shindig!" was canceled in January 1966; "Hullabaloo" ended that August.

From July 1965 to April 1967, Dick Clark had a daytime show every weekday on ABC, "Where the Action Is," with a theme song by Freddie Cannon. Regulars included Paul Revere and the Raiders; it was like a Mickey Mouse Club for teenagers, with bouncy music and comedy schtick. "Malibu U.," also on ABC, was a weekly beach movie, hosted by "Dean" Rick Nelson with girls called the Malibeauties. It lasted from July to September 1967.

Slightly greater social significance was attached to ABC's "The Music Scene," a 45-minute weekly show that lasted from September 1969 to January 1970. Its six hosts included comics David Steinberg and Lily Tomlin, and it showed live segments and film clips of the Beatles, James Brown, Tom Jones, Janis Joplin, Stevie Wonder, Sly and the Family Stone and others.

The Seventies brought the late-night "concert" format, in which bands would perform more than one song to cheering audiences; concert shows also included some segments staged without an audience and some film and video clips. The first was Don Kirshner's "In Concert" which ran on ABC from January 1973 to January 1976; it was an hour and a half long and, in some cities, simulcast in stereo by cooperating FM radio stations. Kirshner also started "Rock Concert," at first in syndication, then in September 1973 on ABC, and later on NBC with a similar format; it is still running. Mean-

while, NBC came up with "Midnight Special," with Wolfman Jack, a former disc jockey, as announcer, and various guest hosts. "Midnight Special" tended to use shorter segments, spreading one performance taping throughout a show. It, too, was an hour and a half long and had some stereo simulcasts. As the Seventies continued, rockers leaned to use TV more carefully, and the number of genuinely live performances dropped while film clips, post-synched vocals and video clips rose.

The Public Broadcasting System offers two eclectically programed music series. "Soundstage," from Chicago, began in 1974 and has offered folk, jazz, rock and country performers, usually ones less popular than the concert shows. "Austin City Limits" offers country, rock and blues.

But television's most effective purveyor of rock has been Warner-Amex's cable channel, Music Television (MTV), a 24-hour all-music service that is effectively a visual radio format. It broadcasts prerecorded video clips and short personality and music news segments by "video jockeys," who do not have to choose the clips; there are also occasional concerts and rock movies. Other cable companies also use the prerecorded clips, which are financed and distributed by record companies.

DWIGHT TWILLEY
Born June 6, circa 1952, Tulsa, Oklahoma
1976—*Sincerely* (Shelter) 1977—*Twilley Don't Mind* (Arista) 1979—*Twilley* 1982—*Scuba Divers* (EMI America).

Dwight Twilley has made a career out of trying to fuse Elvis Presley's rockabilly with the Beatles' pop, and he never came closer than on his very first single. He and partner Phil Seymour became overnight sensations when "I'm On Fire" came out of nowhere and went Top Twenty in 1975. But since then, Twilley has been bogged down by a split with Seymour, erratic live appearances and myriad troubles with record companies.

As the Dwight Twilley Band, Tulsa natives Twilley and Seymour laid down nearly all the parts on their two LPs, *Sincerely* and *Twilley Don't Mind*. Though they were popular with critics, neither album was a commercial success, in part because of the shaky condition of Shelter Records. There was no LP to capitalize on "I'm On Fire" for over a year. Twilley freed himself of Shelter and got into a new struggle with his next label, Arista. Following the release of *Twilley* and the 45 "Somebody to Love" some months later, Arista rejected his second solo album.

After a lengthy battle, Twilley put out *Scuba Divers* on a new label, EMI, in 1982, complete with a redone version of "Somebody to Love."

Seymour, meanwhile, went on to an initially successful solo career, helped along by a pair of Twilley compositions, one of which, "Looking for the Magic," appeared originally on *Twilley Don't Mind*. In early 1982, 150 of Twilley's paintings and drawings were displayed at the Museum of Rock Art in Los Angeles.

CONWAY TWITTY
Born Harold Jenkins, September 1, 1933, Friars Point, Mississippi
1961—*Greatest Hits* (MGM) **1970**—*Hello Darlin'* (Decca) **1971**—*We Only Make Believe* (with Loretta Lynn) *Fifteen Years Ago* **1979**—*Very Best of Loretta and Conway* (MCA).

Like Charlie Rich, Conway Twitty began as a rockabilly singer, then moved more profitably into country and country-pop music. The lost-love sentimentality that's made him a country giant was manifested in his first big hit single, 1958's "It's Only Make Believe," which he cowrote.

In the Forties, under his given name, Harold Jenkins formed a country band called the Phillips County Ramblers. By the mid-Fifties, after Jenkins had finished a two-year Army stint, they had changed their name to the Rockhousers and their repertoire to a harder-hitting mix of country, boogie-woogie and R&B. In 1955, they cut demos for Sun Records in Memphis; by this time Jenkins had adopted the names of two towns he had passed through and became Conway Twitty. He had a minor rockabilly hit with "I Need Your Lovin' " (#93) in 1957 before "Make Believe" became a #1 pop smash. In 1960, Twitty followed with "Lonely Blue Boy" (#6). Twitty was now a pop star and appeared on TV shows and in college- and teen-oriented films. But by 1962 his pop star had waned.

He organized a country band in 1964, and with constant touring he built a huge following in the South and Southwest. In 1966, when he signed with Decca, he began churning out hits. In 1968, he had a country best seller with "Next in Line" (#1 C&W) and followed in 1969 with "To See My Angel Cry" (#1 C&W) and "I Love You More Today" (#1 C&W). In 1970, he hit with "That's When She Started to Stop Loving Me" (#3 C&W) and one of the five best-selling country singles of the year, "Hello Darlin' " (#60 pop, #1 C&W). In 1971, he teamed with Loretta Lynn for the first of many duets, producing the Top Ten country hit "After the Fire Is Gone" (#56 pop, #1 C&W). Twitty himself also hit that year with "Wonder What She'll Think About Me Leaving" (#4 C&W). In 1972 came the country hits "I Can't See Me Without You" (#4), "She Needs Someone to Hold Her" (#1), "I Can't Stop Loving You" (#1) and "(Lost Her Love) On Our Last Date" (#1). Since that time, his hit singles and albums have continued to reach #1 on the country chart, where he is the all-time sales champ. Fans flock to his Twitty City souvenir store in Nashville.

TYMES
Formed 1959, Philadelphia
George Hilliard, Donald Banks, George Williams, Albert Berry, Norman Burnett.

The Tymes didn't have their first hit until four years after they got together, when "So Much in Love" went to #1 on the pop charts, #4 R&B, on the local independent Parkway label. Utilizing a similar sweet soul style, they had a trio of followup successes: "Wonderful! Wonderful!" (#7 pop, #23 R&B), "Somewhere" (#19 pop) and "To Each His Own" (#78 pop). During the mid-Sixties, the group struggled once more, releasing flops on their own Winchester label (co-owned by Leon Huff, prior to his own massive success) and MGM, before rebounding in 1968 with "People" (#39 pop, #33 R&B) and in 1974 with "You Little Trustmaker" (#12 pop, #20 R&B).

U

UFO

Formed 1971, England

Phil Mogg (b. 1951, London), voc.; Mick Bolton, gtr.; Peter Way (b. London), bass; Andy Parker, drums. **1973**—*UFO/Flying* (Beacon) **1974**—(− Bolton; + Michael Schenker [b. Ger.], gtr.) *Phenomenon* (Chrysalis) **1975**—*Force It* **1976**—(+ Danny Peyronel [b. 1953, Buenos Aires], kybds.) *No Heavy Petting* **1977**—(− Peyronel; + Paul Raymond, kybds.) *Lights Out* **1978**—*Strangers in the Night; Obsessions* (− Schenker; − Raymond; + Paul Chapman, gtr.) **1979**—*No Place to Run* **1980**—(+ Neil Carter, gtr., kybds., voc.) **1981**—*The Wild, the Willing, and the Innocent* **1982**—*Mechanix*.

This British hard-rock band has gone virtually unnoticed in its home country but has gradually made inroads into the U.S. market. They were first a hit in France, Germany and Japan; in 1972 they had a Japanese hit single with their version of Eddie Cochran's "C'mon Everybody," and they went there to record a live LP (*UFO Land in Tokyo*) released only in Japan.

In 1974, Michael Schenker came into the band from the German heavy-metal band Scorpions. Their next three albums, all produced by ex–Ten Years After Leo Lyons for Chrysalis, saw them denting the American market, even as critics reviled them both at home and abroad. Schenker left in 1979 to form his own band, which has also released albums on Chrysalis. By early 1982, UFO had finally scored something of a hit single with "Back into My Life," and was opening shows for Ozzy Osbourne.

U.K.

Formed 1977, England

Eddie Jobson (b. Apr. 28, 1955), kybds., violin; John Wetton (b. June 12, 1949, Eng.), bass, voc.; Allan Holdsworth, gtr.; Bill Bruford (b. May 17, 1948, London), drums. **1978**—*U.K.* (Polydor) **1979**—(− Holdsworth; − Bruford; + Terry Bozzio, drums) *Danger Money*.

A British art-rock supergroup, U.K. drew together such respected veterans of the progressive-rock genre as Bill Bruford (Yes, King Crimson), John Wetton (King Crimson, Roxy Music, Uriah Heep), Eddie Jobson (Roxy Music) and Allan Holdsworth (Jon Hiseman's Tempest, Tony Williams' Lifetime, Gong, Soft Machine).

When U.K. was formed, Bruford and Wetton had last worked together in King Crimson; Holdsworth had played on Bruford's first solo album, which was released just prior to U.K.'s formation. U.K. became an immediate hit with progressive-rock fans, and their first album and U.S. tour did respectably sales-wise.

As the band featured Jobson's keyboards most prominently, Holdsworth's fluid, jazzy guitar seemed like icing on the cake, and he and Bruford soon left to work together on more jazz-fusion projects. The focus shifted decisively to Jobson as the band became a trio with the addition of drummer Terry Bozzio, fresh from a stint with Frank Zappa's Mothers of Invention. U.K.'s music became simpler and heavier, as Bozzio was less inclined toward dauntingly tricky, cracklingly precise meters than Bruford was.

After *Danger Money* had been on the LP charts for a while, U.K. disbanded. Jobson went on to tour with Jethro Tull; Wetton cofounded another art-rock supergroup, Asia; Bruford and Holdsworth continued to work together and separately. Bruford resurfaced in 1981 with the re-formed King Crimson, while Holdsworth came back in 1982 with a solo album and a brief low-level U.S. tour, and began working on an album produced by a fan, Eddie Van Halen. Bozzio cofounded Missing Persons.

JAMES "BLOOD" ULMER

Born 1942, St. Matthews, South Carolina

1980—*Are You Glad to Be in America?* (Rough Trade) *Tales of Captain Black* (Artist House) **1982**—*Free Lancing* (Columbia) *Black Rock*.

James "Blood" Ulmer came into his own at the outset of the Eighties, hailed as the most innovative guitarist of his day. Combining a background of ten years of hard roadwork on the R&B circuit and a grounding in "harmolodic" theory (harmony-movement-melodic) from its developer Ornette Coleman, Ulmer's sound has roots in blues, hard rock and avant-garde jazz.

In the years prior to *Tales of Captain Black*, his first album as a leader, Ulmer recorded with jazz organist Larry Young (Khalid Yasim) and tenor saxophonist Joe Henderson, as well as with Coleman in a series of extensive though mostly unreleased sessions (Coleman appears on *Captain Black*). During the early years of this decade, Ulmer has released four more albums, backed by the cream of the younger jazz players, including drummer Ronald Shannon Jackson (who leads his own band, the Decoding Society) and highly regarded saxophonists Oliver Lake and David Murray. Ulmer's crossover into rock has been meager so far, despite being picked by Public Image Ltd. to open their first New York concert and being signed to Columbia. Ulmer continues to perform frequently, usually with a Jimi Hendrix–style trio.

THE ULTIMATE SPINACH

Formed 1967, Boston
Original lineup: Geoffrey Winthrop, gtr., voc.; Barbara Hudson, gtr., voc.; Ted Myers, gtr., voc.; Ian Bruce Douglas, voc.; Richard Nese, bass; Keith Lahteinen, drums, voc.
1968—*The Ultimate Spinach* (MGM) *Behold and See* **1969**—*Ultimate Spinach.*

In the late Sixties, a post-psychedelic upsurge of rock activity in Boston led critics and record companies to create the "Bosstown Sound," which was built around bands like Earth Opera, the Beacon Street Union, the Big Three and the Ultimate Spinach. The movement never really took hold and was soon laughed at as one of the first great music-industry "hypes." Today the Ultimate Spinach albums, replete with flower-power and canyons-of-your-mind lyrics and heavy on the Farfisa organ, are rare collectors' items. Only Jeffrey "Skunk" Baxter (later with Steely Dan and the Doobie Brothers) from a later version of Spinach, and the Rowan Brothers from Earth Opera, have gone on to any further fame and accomplishment.

ULTRAVOX

Formed 1974, London
John Foxx (b. Dennis Leigh, Eng.), voc., synth.; Steve Shears, kybds., voc.; Billy Currie, kybds., synth., violin; Chris Cross, bass; Warren Cann, drums.
1977—*Ultravox!* (Island, U.K.) **1978**—(– Shears; + Robin Simon, gtr.) *Systems of Romance* (Antilles) **1980**—*Three Into One* (Island) (compilation) (– Foxx; – Simon; + Midge Ure, gtr., voc.) **1981**—*Vienna* (Chrysalis) *Rage in Eden* **1983**—*Quartet.*

Important precursors of the early-Eighties British "electro-pop" movement, Ultravox was one of the first modern post-punk bands to dispense with guitars in favor of synthesizers.

The band was formed by and around John Foxx, who had become interested in music while dabbling in synthesizers and tapes at school. Foxx went to London in 1974, began writing songs and soon formed Ultravox, who had a minor British hit in 1977 with "My Sex" and made three critically acclaimed albums (the first produced by Brian Eno) before he left to pursue a solo career, which has so far yielded two albums, *Metamatic* (1980) and *John Foxx* (1982).

Ultravox regrouped with the addition of Midge Ure, formerly with Scottish popsters Slik and a late version of the ex–Sex Pistol Glen Matlock's Rich Kids. With a more dramatic lead singer and a slightly less foreboding sound, *Vienna* yielded a minor hit single in "Sleepwalk." Electro-popper Gary Numan, among others, has often cited Ultravox's influence on his own work, and Ultravox's Billy Currie has toured with Numan.

URIAH HEEP

Formed 1970, London
David Byron (b. Jan. 29, 1947, Essex, Eng.), voc.; Mick Box (b. June 8, 1947, London), gtr.; Ken Hensley (b. Aug. 24, 1945, Eng.), kybds., voc.; Paul Newton, bass; Alan Napier, drums.
1970—*Very 'eavy, Very 'umble* (Mercury) **1971**—(– Napier; + Keith Baker, drums) *Salisbury* (– Baker; + Lee Kerslake, drums; + Mark Clarke [b. July 25, 1950, Liverpool, Eng.], bass) *Look at Yourself* (Mercury) **1972**—(– Newton; – Clarke; + Gary Thain [d. Mar. 19, 1976], bass) *Demons and Wizards; The Magician's Birthday* **1973**—*Live* (Warner Bros.) *Sweet Freedom* **1974**—*Wonderworld* **1975**—(– Thain; + John Wetton [b. Jul. 12, 1949, Derby, Eng.], bass, voc.) *Return to Fantasy; Best of* (Mercury) **1976**—*High and Mighty* (Warner Bros.) (– Byron; – Wetton; + John Lawton, voc.; + Trevor Bolder, bass) **1977**—*Fire Fly; Innocent Victim* **1978**—*Fallen Angel* **1982**—*Abominog.*

"If this group makes it, I'll have to commit suicide," wrote one rock critic, expressing the typical critical opinion of Uriah Heep, who did indeed make it for much of the Seventies with a blend of heavy metal and hard art rock.

The band's roots were in a London outfit called the Stalkers, which Mick Box joined in 1964. They were later joined by David Byron, who had sung on anonymous hit-cover albums alongside Elton John. Box and Byron then formed Spice with bassist Paul Newton of the Gods (which also included Ken Hensley, formerly with Kit and the Saracens and the Jimmy Brown Sound, and Mick Taylor, the latter going on to John Mayall and the Rolling Stones). Hensley worked briefly with Cliff Bennett's Toe Fat band, then joined Spice, who renamed themselves Uriah Heep after Charles Dickens' conniving paragon of "humility." They cut their hard-rock debut LP, then landed a regular drummer in Keith Baker.

The debut and *Salisbury*, for which the band was augmented by an orchestra on some cuts, found only minor European success, though Uriah Heep was already an established concert attraction in Britain. *Look at Yourself* made the band a success in both the U.S. and U.K., and they consolidated their status with *Demons and Wizards, The Magician's Birthday* and *Live*, which all went gold in Britain and America. Uriah Heep also made the singles chart in 1972 and 1973 with "Stealin'," "Easy Living" and "Blind Eye/Sweet Lorraine."

In 1974, dissent plagued the band. Bassist Gary Thain suffered a near-fatal electric shock onstage in Dallas, Texas, and later complained that the band was inconsiderate of his physical well-being. Personal problems and drug use furthered Thain's conflicts with the rest of the band, and in early 1975 he was "invited" to leave; he died of a drug overdose a year later. He was replaced by John Wetton, formerly of Family and King Crimson, who stayed with the band for two albums before further internal squabbles resulted in the firing of David Byron in July 1976. Wetton soon left to record a solo album and eventually joined art-rock supergroups U.K. and Asia.

Hensley in the meantime had recorded two solo albums, 1973's *Proud Words on a Dusty Shelf* and 1975's *Eager to Please*. With new vocalist John Lawton and bassist Trevor Bolder, from David Bowie's Spiders from Mars band, Uriah Heep continued plowing its heavy-metal furrow for a few more albums before disbanding in late 1978, only to re-form in 1982.

U2

Formed 1978, Dublin, Ireland
Bono Vox (b. Paul Hewson, May 10, 1960), voc.; Dave "The Edge" Evans (b. Aug. 8, 1961), gtr.; Larry Mullen (b. Oct. 31, 1961), drums; Adam Clayton (b. Mar. 13, 1960), bass.
1980—*Boy* (Island) **1981**—*October* **1983**—*War*.

In the wake of punk, U2 stormed out of Ireland in the early Eighties with a sound that made something new out of punk and heavy metal. Over a pummeling rhythm section, "The Edge" might play only one or two keening notes at a time, while Bono Vox's vocals sound both triumphant and fearful. Their songs tend to be about existential hopes and terrors, from growing up *(Boy)* to impending apocalypse *(War)*, rather than hard rock's earthy egotism or punk rock's nihilism. Lyricist Vox is a practicing Christian.

The band members were all teenagers when, with their parents' approval and support, they began rehearsing together. They quickly became a sensation in Ireland, and recorded independently before signing with Island. *Boy*, like their next two albums, was produced by Steve Lillywhite and received U.S. airplay with "I Will Follow." A tour of new wave clubs generated further U.S. interest. Even Lillywhite admitted that the material on *October* was weak, but with *War* U2 returned to form while retaining their aura of sincerity, expanding their U.S. following with a Top Fifty single ("New Year's Day"), a Top Ten (and gold) album and a headlining tour.

V

RITCHIE VALENS

Born Richard Valenzuela, May 13, 1941, Pacoima,
California; died February 3, 1959, near Mason City,
Iowa
N.A.—*Ritchie Valens* (Del-Fi) **1979**—*Ritchie Valens*
(London).

The first of several Latin rockers of the late Fifties and
early Sixties (others included Chan Romero, Chris Mon-
tez, Eddie Quinteros, Sunny and the Sunglows and Cannibal and the Headhunters), Ritchie Valens started playing
guitar as a child, and at Pacoima High (near L.A.) he
formed his own band, the Silhouettes.

In the spring of 1958, Valens signed with Del-Fi Records
and later that year had a Top Fifty hit with "Come On,
Let's Go," later covered by early-Sixties British teen idol
Tommy Steele. In early 1959, Valens hit #2 on the charts
with his two-sided single "Donna" and "La Bamba."
Valens appeared on nationwide TV and in package tours.
On one such tour the stars' plane crashed in a snowstorm,
killing Valens, Buddy Holly and the Big Bopper.

VAN DER GRAAF GENERATOR/PETER HAMMILL

Formed 1967, Manchester, England
Peter Hammill (b. Nov. 5, 1948, London), gtr., kybds.,
voc.; Hugh Banton, kybds.; Chris Judge Smith, drums;
Keith Ellis, bass; Guy Evans, drums.
1968—(− Smith) *The Aerosol Grey Machine* (Mer-
cury) **1969**—(− Ellis; + Nic Potter, bass; + David
Jackson, sax) *The Least We Can Do Is Wave* (Cha-
risma) **1970**—*H to He Who Am the Only One*
1971—(− Potter) *Pawn Hearts* **1973**—*The Long
Hello* **1975**—*Godbluff* **1976**—*Still Life; World
Record* **1977**—*The Quiet Zone* **1978**—(+ Potter; +
Graham Smith, violin) *Vital/Live.*
Peter Hammill solo: 1972—*Fools Mate* (Charisma)
Chameleon in the Shadows of Night **1974**—*The Silent
Corner and the Empty Stage; In Camera* **1975**—
Nadir's Last Chance **1977**—*Over* **1978**—*The Future
Now* **1979**—*PH 7.*

One of the few top-rank British art-rock bands that never
achieved more than cult success in America, Van der
Graaf Generator constructed stately sepulchers of Gothic
sound with Hugh Banton's churchy Hammond organ and
Guy Evans' virtuosic drumming framing the intensely
existential verse and tortured vocals of Peter Hammill.
Hammill's relentlessly bleak visions were later cited by

some members of Britain's late-Seventies punk-rock
movement as their inspiration, and in fact Hammill in 1975
created a "Rikki Nadir" persona for a solo album that
presaged punk.

Van der Graaf Generator formed and split up and re-
formed several times, usually with the same core personnel, and played only one U.S. concert, in 1976 in New
York. Hammill, however, has conducted several solo
American tours, selling out club dates.

The band first came together at Manchester University
in 1967. Founding member Chris Judge Smith gave the
band its name (taken from a device that creates static
electricity) but soon left, and the band broke up in late
1968. Hammill played solo concerts and recorded material
with the Van der Graaf core intended as a solo album, but
when the band came back together before its release, *The
Aerosol Grey Machine* was issued under Van der Graaf's
aegis. Robert Fripp of King Crimson sat in on *H to He*.
After the elaborate *Pawn Hearts*, the band broke up again
for three years, during which time Hammill pursued his
solo career in earnest. Fripp sat in on *Fools Mate* (Hammill returned the favor on Fripp's *Exposure*), ex-Spirit
guitarist Randy California on *Silent Corner*.

In 1975, upon the release of the proto-punk *Nadir's Last
Chance*, Van der Graaf re-formed again, with a sound that
was tighter and more powerful than before. In 1978, with
Van der Graaf apparently broken up for keeps, Hammill
began small-scale U.S. club tours, sometimes playing
solo, sometimes accompanied by violinist Graham Smith.
Neither Hammill nor Van der Graaf has ever had a genuine
hit single or album, but they remain a significant cult
phenomenon.

LUTHER VANDROSS

Born New York City
1981—*Never Too Much* (Epic) **1982**—*Forever, for
Always, for Love.*

Luther Vandross emerged from jingles and background
singing to become one of black pop's most successful
performer/producer/writers in the early Eighties.

Throughout the Seventies, Vandross sang on numerous
commercials (from ads for the U.S. Army to local Burger
Kings). His singing was distinguished by his impeccable
phrasing and vocal control. He first came to the attention
of the pop world through his writing and singing on David
Bowie's *Young Americans* (1975). With other singers,
Vandross cut two little-noted albums under the name
Luther, and sang on "Dance, Dance, Dance" and "Every-

body Dance'' for Chic. He continued his highly lucrative jingles career.

Following his lead vocal appearances on "Searchin' " and "Glow of Love" (from Change's hit album *Glow of Love*), several labels expressed interest in signing Vandross as a solo act. In 1981, he signed with Epic Records, who allowed him to write and produce.

His *Never Too Much* was a #1 R&B album and the title cut was a #1 R&B single (#33 pop); the album went platinum. He produced Aretha Franklin's *Jump to It!* in 1982; the title cut and the album went to #1 on the R&B chart. He also produced Franklin's 1983 *Get It Right*. Vandross produced Cheryl Lynn's 1982 LP *Instant Love*, which contained their duet "If This World Were Mine," a cover of a Marvin Gaye/Tammi Terrell hit. His million-selling *Forever, for Always, for Love* album was released in 1982 and contained the hit single "Bad Boy/Having a Party."

VANGELIS

Born Vangelis Papathanassiou, Greece
Aphrodite's Child: 1968—*End of the World/Rain and Tears* (Vertigo, U.K.)   **1969**—*It's Five O'Clock*   **1970**—*Aphrodite's Child* (Mercury)   **1972**—*666—Apocalypse of John* (Vertigo, U.K.)   **1975**—*Best of* (Mercury).
Vangelis solo: 1971—*The Dragon* (Charly, U.K.)   **1973**—*L'Apocalypse des Animeaux* (Polydor)   **1974**—*Earth* (Vertigo, U.K.)   **1975**—*Heaven and Hell* (RCA)   **1976**—*Albedo .39*   **1977**—*Spiral*   **1978**—*Beaubourg; Hypothesis* (Affinity)   *Best of* (RCA)   **1979**—*China* (Polydor)   **1980**—*See You Later*   **1981**—*Chariots of Fire*.

Vangelis was in France at the time of the 1968 student riots; unable to return to Greece, he formed a band with Demis Roussos. That band, Aphrodite's Child, released a series of unremarkable progressive-rock albums, and had one European hit single with "Rain and Tears." Roussos went on to become an international MOR singing star. Vangelis turned to a solo career and began composing film scores with *L'Apocalypse des Animeaux*.

In 1974, Vangelis was rumored to be the replacement for Yes's departed keyboard whiz Rick Wakeman. Though he never did join Yes, Vangelis formed a lasting association with Yes singer Jon Anderson, and has worked with him on his solo projects. Vangelis also made albums on his own, such as *Beaubourg*, which were pastiches of electronic music and pop and jazz. In 1982, Vangelis finally made his commercial breakthrough with the score to the film *Chariots of Fire*. The movie theme was on the singles chart for 15 weeks and went as high as #6, while the score won an Oscar. His follow-up single, "Titles," failed to match that success, but the *Chariots* theme did inspire numerous soundalikes for American TV commercials.

VAN HALEN

Formed 1974, Pasadena, California
David Lee Roth (b. Oct. 10, 1955, Bloomington, Ind.), voc.; Edward Van Halen (b. Jan. 26, 1957, Nijmegen, Neth.), gtr., voc.; Alex Van Halen (b. May 8, 1955, Nijmegen, Neth.), drums; Michael Anthony (b. Jun. 20, 1955, Chicago), bass.
1978—*Van Halen* (Warner Bros.)   **1979**—*Van Halen II*   **1980**—*Women and Children First*   **1981**—*Fair Warning*   **1982**—*Diver Down*.

Since their national debut in 1978, Van Halen have become one of the most popular American heavy-metal bands. Fronted by the flamboyant and ever-quotable David Lee Roth and featuring the highly original guitar pyrotechnics of Eddie Van Halen, Van Halen have garnered a loyal mass following and several gold and platinum LPs.

The Van Halen brothers' father was a jazz musician in the Netherlands, where they lived until moving to Pasadena in 1968. As children, Eddie and Alex Van Halen studied piano and had received extensive classical music training, but upon their arrival in America, both took an interest in rock & roll. Eddie learned to play drums and Alex learned to play guitar; eventually they traded instruments and started a band called Mammoth. Michael Anthony, then a leader of a rival teen band, joined them. A

Van Halen: Alex Van Halen, David Lee Roth, Eddie Van Halen, Michael Anthony

few months later Roth, the scion of a wealthy Midwestern family, joined them. The group considered calling themselves Rat Salade before deciding on Van Halen.

Van Halen played the Pasadena/Santa Barbara bar circuit for over three years. Their sets initially consisted primarily of cover material ranging from disco to pop, but they eventually introduced original songs and were soon one of the most popular groups in California. In 1976, Kiss's Gene Simmons spotted them in an L.A. club and financed a demo tape. After seeing the group at the Starwood Club in L.A. and upon hearing Simmons' recommendation, Warner Bros. Records' Mo Ostin and staff producer Ted Templeman signed them.

Their self-titled debut album hit the Top Twenty and eventually sold over two million copies; the debut single, a cover of the Kinks' 1964 hit "You Really Got Me," hit #36. The followup, "Runnin' with the Devil," hit #84. Each of their subsequent LPs went platinum, and every tour was a sellout. Roth's swaggering good looks and extroverted persona, not to mention pithy statements on the sex-drugs-and-rock-&-roll lifestyle he claims to espouse, assured press coverage.

The band's albums and singles have consistently charted in the Top Thirty and include *Van Halen II* (#6, 1979), *Women and Children First* (#6, 1980), *Fair Warning* (#5, 1981), *Diver Down* (#3, 1982), "Dance the Night Away" (#15, 1979) and a stomping cover of Roy Orbison's "Oh Pretty Woman."

VANILLA FUDGE

Formed 1966, New York City
Vince Martell (b. Nov. 11, 1945, Bronx, N. Y.), gtr., voc.; Mark Stein (b. Mar. 1947, Bayonne, N. J.), kybds., voc.; Tim Bogert (b. Aug. 1944, New York City), bass, voc.; Carmine Appice (b. Dec. 15, 1946, Staten Island, N. Y.), drums, voc.
1967—*The Vanilla Fudge* (Atlantic) 1968—*The Beat Goes On; Renaissance* 1969—*Near the Beginning* 1970—*Rock 'n' Roll* 1982—*Greatest Hits*.

One of the first heavy-rock bands, Vanilla Fudge were also pioneers of the "long version." The band evolved from New York bar bands like the Pigeons and the Vagrants. The Pigeons included Tim Bogert, Mark Stein (who had played and sung on TV shows as a child and teenager, and who recorded in 1959 for Cameo Records) and, eventually, Vince Martell and Carmine Appice (who had been voted "most musically inclined" in high school).

They named themselves Vanilla Fudge in early 1967 and began practicing their "psychedelic-symphonic rock." They made their New York concert debut July 22, 1967, at the Village Theater with the Byrds and the Seeds. By the end of the year they were signed by Atlantic Records. Their first single was an extended version of the Supremes' "You Keep Me Hangin' On," complete with half-speed tempo, Gothic organ and quasi-raga guitar. The single was a Top Ten hit, and Vanilla Fudge's debut LP, which contained similarly treated versions of "Eleanor Rigby," "Ticket to Ride," "People Get Ready" and "Bang Bang," went gold.

The follow-up LP sold fairly well, but is chiefly remembered as one of the most ludicrous concept albums of all time; it purported to be a musical history of the previous 25 years, and included a 12-minute cut that contained the entire history of music. Their third album was even less popular and contained nine minutes of Donovan's "Season of the Witch."

The band finally broke up after their fifth, and least successful, album. Appice and Bogert went on to form heavy-metal band Cactus, and later teamed up with Jeff Beck in the Beck, Bogert and Appice power trio. Appice has since become a sought-after session drummer, and has often backed Rod Stewart, among others. Stein formed Boomerang, and Martell's whereabouts were unknown until 1982, soon after the release of a greatest-hits package, when the group re-formed.

DAVE VAN RONK

Born June 30, 1936, Brooklyn, New York
1959—*Sings Earthy Ballads and Blues* (Folkways) 1960—*Black Mountain Blues* 1962—*Inside* (Prestige) 1963—*Folksinger* 1964—*In the Tradition; Dave Van Ronk and the Ragtime Jug Stompers* (Mercury) *Dave Van Ronk* 1967—*No Dirty Names* (Verve/ Folkways) 1968—*Dave Van Ronk and the Hudson Dusters* (Verve) 1974—*Songs for Aging Children* (Cadet) 1976—*Sunday Street* (Philo).

With his bawdy, gruff yet tender singing style and considerable blues-archivist skills, Dave Van Ronk became one of the most respected members of New York's early Sixties folk boom. Though he's never been a commercial success, he remains influential in folk circles.

While in high school in Brooklyn, Van Ronk became avidly interested in traditional jazz and played with New York–area jazz groups upon graduation. In 1957, he performed with Odetta, an experience that spurred him on to an in-depth investigation of blues and folk music, resulting in his becoming an avid fan of Josh White. He began performing on the folk circuit.

In 1958, Van Ronk formed a jug band with his friend and frequent collaborator Sam Charters and recorded an album for Lyrichord Records. By 1959, he had played folk festivals and been signed to Folkways. While his next few albums for Folkways and Prestige stuck with his folk-blues mode, in 1964 he performed at the Newport Folk Festival with a jazz-flavored jug band; and soon after the festival he formed the Ragtime Jug Stompers, again with Charters.

By this time, Van Ronk had long been a close friend of

Bob Dylan, who in the early Sixties had frequently stayed at Van Ronk's Greenwich Village apartment. In May 1974, he appeared with Dylan and others at a New York City benefit for Chilean political prisoners. Van Ronk, though recording only sporadically through most of the Seventies, has continued to perform and to teach guitar.

BOBBY VEE

Born Robert Velline, April 30, 1943, Fargo, North Dakota
1960—*Devil or Angel* (Liberty) **1963**—*Meets the Ventures; The Night Has a Thousand Eyes* **1964**—*I Remember Buddy Holly* **1967**—*Come Back When You Grow Up* **1972**—*Robert Thomas Velline* **1975**—*Very Best of* (United Artists).

One of the longest-lasting teen idols of the early Sixties, Bobby Vee got his lucky break when he and his band the Shadows filled in for the late Buddy Holly at a 1959 Mason City, Iowa, concert days after Holly had died in a plane crash. The Shadows then managed to get their song "Suzie Baby" recorded locally, and it became a hit. Producer Snuff Garrett signed the band to Liberty Records in 1959, releasing "Suzie Baby" (#77) nationally.

At Liberty, Vee was quickly (and literally) groomed for solo success, under Garrett's supervision. First, Garrett had Vee cover British teen-idol Adam Faith's "What Do You Want?," which flopped at #93 in the spring of 1960. But later that year a cover of the Clovers' R&B hit "Devil or Angel" hit #6 on the U.S. singles chart. "Rubber Ball" was a Top Ten hit in the U.S. (#6) and the U.K., and for the next few years the clean-cut Vee, in his high school letter sweater, sang sweetly of the ups and downs of sexless romance from the top of the charts with hits like "Take Good Care of My Baby" (#1) and "Run to Him" (#2) in 1961; "Punish Her" (#20) in 1962; and "The Night Has a Thousand Eyes" (#8) and "Charms" (#13) in 1963.

Vee was just as enormously popular in Britain as in America, and he toured both countries frequently. In the midst of his big-hit years, Vee cut a Buddy Holly tribute album with the Crickets, as well as one other album simply backed by Holly's onetime band. The mid-Sixties were fallow years for Vee, but he returned to the charts in 1967 with the million-selling "Come Back When You Grow Up" (#3). In 1972, he cut an album under his real name.

VELVET UNDERGROUND

Formed 1965, New York City
Lou Reed (b. Mar. 2, 1944, Long Island, N.Y.), voc., gtr.; John Cale (b. Dec. 3, 1940, Wales), viola, bass, kybds., voc.; Nico (b. Christa Päffgen, Cologne, W. Ger.), voc; Sterling Morrison, bass, gtr.; Maureen Tucker, drums.
1967—*The Velvet Underground and Nico* (MGM/ Verve) (− Nico) **1968**—*White Light, White Heat* (− Cale; + Doug Yule, bass, voc.) **1969**—*The Velvet Underground* (MGM) **1970**—*Loaded* (Atlantic) (− Tucker; + Billy Yule, drums; − Reed; + Walter Powers, voc.) **1971**—(− Morrison; + Willie Alexander, gtr.) **1972**—*Squeeze* (Polydor) **1974**—*The Velvet Underground; Live at Max's Kansas City.*

The Velvet Underground never sold many records, but, as one critic put it, it seemed that every Velvets fan went out and started a band. While their songs were constructed on the same three chords and 4/4 beat employed by most groups of the late Sixties, the Velvets were unique in their intentional crudity, in their sense of beauty in ugliness and in their lyrics. In the age of flower power they spoke in no uncertain terms of social alienation, sexual deviancy, drug addiction, violence and hopelessness. Both in their sound and in their words, the songs evoked the exhilaration and destructiveness of modern urban life. The group's sound and stance were of seminal importance to David Bowie, the New York Dolls, Patti Smith, Mott the Hoople, Roxy Music, the Sex Pistols, the Cars and countless others of the proto-punk, punk and post-punk movements.

In 1964, John Cale met Lou Reed in New York City. Both had been classically trained—Cale as a violist and theorist, Reed as a pianist—but by the time of their first meeting Cale was experimenting in the avant-garde with La Monte Young and Reed was writing poems about down-and-out streetlife. Cale, Reed, Sterling Morrison (recently of the King Hatreds) and Angus MacLise (percussionist in Young's ensemble) formed a group that played under various names—the Warlocks, the Primitives, the Falling Spikes—in galleries and at poetry readings around lower Manhattan. As the Primitives, they recorded a series of singles on Pickwick Records, for which Reed had once worked as house songwriter. In 1965, MacLise abruptly packed up and went to India (he died of malnutrition in Nepal in 1979 at the age of 41). Maureen Tucker was enlisted to take his place on a per diem basis, which became permanent when she constructed her own drum kit out of tambourines and garbage-can lids.

On November 11, 1965, the group played their first gig as the Velvet Underground, opening for the Myddle Class at a high school dance in Summit, New Jersey. Within a few months, they had taken up residency at the Cafe Bizarre in Greenwich Village, where they met pop artist Andy Warhol. When the group was fired by the Bizarre's management for performing "Black Angel's Death Song" immediately after being told not to, Warhol invited them to perform at showings of his film series, *Cinematique Uptight*, and then employed them as the aural component of his traveling mixed-media show, the Exploding Plastic Inevitable. For the latter, he augmented their lineup with singer/actress Nico, whom he gave equal billing on the group's first album, although she sang only a couple of

songs. The album was recorded in 1966, and two singles—
"I'll Be Your Mirror" b/w "All Tomorrow's Parties" and
"Sunday Morning" b/w "Femme Fatale"—appeared.
The album, which included Reed's "Heroin" and "Venus
in Furs" (a song about sado-masochism), was not released
for almost a year. Sporting a Warhol cover with a peelable
illustration of a banana, the album sold more copies than
any other Velvets record.

The group ended their association with Warhol when
they performed in Boston minus Nico and the rest of the
Inevitable troupe and took on Steve Sesnick as their
manager. Without Warhol's name and knack for generat-
ing publicity, the Velvet Underground faded from public
attention. Their following was reduced further when the
uncompromisingly noisy *White Light/White Heat* came
out. It had been recorded in a single day after a tour of
mostly empty theaters. Cale quit the group. Rather than
find another electric violist, the remaining members enlisted Doug Yule, who had played with a Boston folk-rock
group, the Grass Menagerie. The third album, recorded in
Los Angeles with Yule, was much softer than either of its
predecessors, and it cost the group all but the most loyal of
their following. MGM dropped them and it was some
months before Atlantic signed them.

Upon their return to New York to record in the summer
of 1970, the Velvet Underground played a month-long
engagement at Max's Kansas City (with Billy Yule depu-
tizing for Tucker, who was pregnant). These were the
group's first appearances in New York since 1967, and
they rekindled some interest. But soon after *Loaded* was
finished, Reed, at odds with Sesnick, left the group and
moved to England, where he lived for two years before
reemerging as a solo performer. Although he denounced
Loaded, claiming it was remixed after his departure (a
charge Yule and Morrison denied), the album introduced
"Sweet Jane" and "Rock and Roll."

With Doug Yule and Powers sharing lead vocals, the
group toured the East Coast before Morrison dropped out
in 1971 to teach English at the University of Texas in
Austin. Tucker, Yule, Walter Powers and Willie Alexander
(later of the Boom-Boom Band) recorded an album for
MGM, but when MGM decided against releasing it,
Tucker also moved to the Southwest—to Phoenix, Arizona—where she raised a family and in 1980 recorded a
single for Spy Records. Doug Yule retained the Velvet
Underground name until 1973, recording what amounted
to a solo album, *Squeeze*, which was released only in
Britain.

With the success of Reed's solo career and, to lesser
extents, Cale's and Nico's, the Velvet Underground generated more interest in the Seventies than it had during the
group's existence. Two live albums were released in 1974:
The Velvet Underground, recorded in 1969 in Texas and
California, and *Live at Max's Kansas City*, recorded the
night of Reed's last appearance with the group.

THE VENTURES

Formed 1960, Seattle, Washington
Bob Bogle (b. Jan. 16, 1937, Portland, Ore.), gtr., bass;
Don Wilson (b. Feb. 10, 1937, Tacoma, Wash.), gtr.;
Nokie Edwards (b. Okla.), gtr., bass; Howie Johnston
(b. Wash.), drums.
1960—*Walk Don't Run* (Liberty) **1961**—*Another
Smash; The Colorful Ventures* **1962**—*Dance Party*
1963—(− Johnston; + Mel Taylor [b. New York City],
drums) *Surfing; Let's Go!* **1964**—*The Fabulous
Ventures* **1965**—*Ventures a Go Go; Christmas with the
Ventures* **1967**—(− Edwards; + Jerry McGee, gtr.)
Guitar Freakout; Super Psychedelics; Genius (Sunset)
Golden Greats (Liberty) **1968**—(+ Johnny Durrill [b.
Houston, Tex.], kybds.) **1969**—*More Golden Greats;
Hawaii Five-O* **1970**—(− McGee; + Edwards) *Best
of; Tenth Anniversary Album.*

The Ventures were one of the first, best, most lasting and
influential of instrumental guitar-based rock combos (rivaled only by Britain's Shadows). Their trademark
sound—driving mechanical drums, metallic guitars twanging out simple, catchy pop tunes—has filtered down
through the years to gain prominence in the sounds of
bands like Blondie, the B-52's, the Go-Go's and many
more. Often classified as a surf-rock band, the Ventures
actually predated surf music and lasted well beyond its
early-Sixties boom. Some twenty years after their formation, they still play to receptive audiences.

Founding member Bob Bogle had started playing guitar
by his teens. In his mid-teens, he supported himself by
bringing wet cement to bricklayers, and he moved to
Seattle to work. There he met Don Wilson, who had
learned piano and trombone as a child, and bass and guitar
in the Army. By mid-1959 they had begun playing in local
clubs. They soon added Nokie Edwards on lead guitar
(Bogle switching to bass) and Howie Johnston on drums.
They sent their first demo, "Walk Don't Run," to various
record labels. When nobody responded, Don Wilson's
mother released it as a single on her own Blue Horizon
label. It became an instant regional hit in 1960, and in late
summer was picked up for distribution by Dolton Records
(distributed by Liberty).

In August 1960, "Walk Don't Run" became a #2 hit.
The Ventures followed it with a rock version of "Ghost
Riders in the Sky," then "Perfidia," "Lullaby of the
Leaves," "Diamond Head" and "2,000 Pound Bee," all of
which were big hits through the early and mid-Sixties.

In 1963, Johnston was hurt in an auto accident and left
the group. He was replaced by Mel Taylor. The hits kept
on coming, with versions of "Lonely Bull" and "I Walk
the Line" in 1963 and a surf remake of "Walk Don't Run"
in 1964. For the next few years, their albums still sold and
they continued to tour. In 1967, Edwards was replaced by
Jerry McGee, who left in 1969 to record with Delaney and

Bonnie Bramlett, after which Edwards returned. By that time, keyboardist Johnny Durrill had expanded the unit to a quintet, and the Ventures had delved into fuzz-tone and wah-wah guitar modification as well as blues, calypso and Latin material.

In 1969, they hit the charts again with a version of the theme from the TV show "Hawaii Five-O." In 1981, with Bogle, Wilson, Edwards and Taylor, they released a regional West Coast single, "Surfin' and Spyin' " (written by Go-Go Charlotte Caffey), and embarked on successful tours of the U.S. and Japan, where they had long been a star attraction.

VILLAGE PEOPLE

Formed late 1970s, New York City
Victor Willis, David Hodo, Felipe Rose, Randy Jones, Glenn Hughes, Alex Briley.
1977—*Village People* (Casablanca)   1978—*Macho Men*   1979—(– Willis; + Ray Simpson)   *Cruisin'; Go West*   1981—*Renaissance* (RCA)   1982—(– Simpson; + Miles Jay).

Under the direction of disco producer Jacques Morali, this campy vocal group had massive late-Seventies pop hits with double-entendre songs like "Macho Man" and "Y.M.C.A."

In 1978, Morali, with business partners Henri Belolo, lyricist Phil Hurtt and Peter Whitehead, composed self-consciously gay-themed disco songs like "Fire Island" and "San Francisco." With actor/singer Victor Willis handling vocals, the songs became favorites of both gay and straight club audiences. Backed by Casablanca Records president Neil Bogart, Morali formed a group of singer/actors dressed as a cross section of gay clichés: a beefy biker, a construction worker, a policeman, an Indian chief, a GI and a cowboy. As Tom Smucker wrote, they "were gay goofs to those who got the joke, and disco novelties to those who didn't."

With major hits like "Macho Man" (#25 pop) in 1978 and "Y.M.C.A." (#2 pop) in 1979, the Village People had six gold and four platinum records, sold out major concert halls and appeared on numerous television talk shows. During their short-lived stardom, they reportedly sold over 20 million singles and 18 million albums worldwide.

In 1979, Ray Simpson, Valerie Simpson's brother, replaced Willis as lead singer. By then, however, the bubble had burst. On their 1981 release *Renaissance*, the group briefly traded in its gay outfits for the "new romantic" look of English new wave bands. They then released *Fox in the Box* (not in the U.S.) with their old look.

GENE VINCENT

Born Eugene Vincent Craddock, February 11, 1935, Norfolk, Virginia; died October 12, 1971, Los Angeles
N.A.—*Gene Vincent and the Blue Caps* (Capitol)
1967—*Best of Gene Vincent*   1969—*Best of Gene Vincent, Volume 2*   1974—*The Bop That Won't Stop*.

One of the first American rockers, Gene Vincent began singing while in the Navy in the early Fifties. After being discharged in 1955, he performed regularly on live country music radio shows in Norfolk. In 1956, he recorded a demo of a song he and "Sheriff" Tex Davis had written—"Be-Bop-A-Lula"—and sent it to Capitol Records. Capitol heard an Elvis Presley soundalike in his rockabilly stutter-and-hiccup style and signed him to a long-term

The Village People

Gene Vincent and the Blue Caps

contract. "Be-Bop-A-Lula," re-recorded by Vincent and his group, the Bluecaps (guitarists Cliff Gallup and Willie Williams, bass player Jack Neal and drummer Dickie Harrell), in Capitol's imitation–Sam Phillips echo chamber, was a hit nationwide (#7).

Vincent's looks—darker, tougher, greasier than Elvis', all blue denim and black leather—were featured in the 1956 movie *The Girl Can't Help It* and were imitated widely. Fans even affected his limp, the result of a Navy motorcycle accident that forced him to wear a metal brace on one leg. For several years Gene Vincent and the Bluecaps were among the most popular rock & roll acts in America ("Lotta Lovin' " was a #13 hit in 1957).

When, by the end of the decade, the record industry began to favor cleaned-up, tuned-down pop stars, Vincent went abroad and found huge followings in Australia, Japan and Europe, wherever "real American rockers" were in demand. He toured England with Eddie Cochran and was critically injured in the car crash that killed Cochran in April 1960. Although he recovered from his injuries, his career never regained momentum. For most of the Sixties, he lived in England, where, playing the pub circuit, he retained a small following of latter-day Teddy boys. A "comeback" album in 1969 failed to attract much attention. Broke and suffering from a bleeding ulcer, he returned to America in September 1971 and died a month later. "Be-Bop-A-Lula" had, by that time, sold nine million copies worldwide.

BUNNY WAILER

Born Neville O'Reilly Livingston, April 10, 1947, Kingston, Jamaica

1976—*Blackheart Man* (Island) **1977**—*Protest* **1979**—*Struggle* (Solomonic) **1980**—*Bunny Wailer Sings the Wailers* (Island) *In I Father's House* (Solomonic) **1981**—*Rock 'n' Groove; Tribute to the Late Hon. Robert Nesta Marley, O.M.* **1982**—*Hook, Line and Sinker.*

Bunny Livingston—better known as Bunny Wailer—left the Wailers less than a year after the group made its first tours of the U.K. and the U.S. His aversion to traveling was one reason for his departure, and since then he has not left Jamaica. International acclaim accrued to Bob Marley and Peter Tosh (the other original Wailers), while Bunny Wailer's following was—until recently—small even by Jamaican standards.

In his ten years with the Wailers, he was considered the equal of Marley and Tosh as a singer and as a songwriter. "Let Him Go," "Who Feels It," "Jail House" and "Pass It On" are among the songs associated with him. He founded his own record company, Solomonic, in 1972, and recorded his first solo singles—"Life Line," "Bide Up" and "Arab Oil Weapon"—before quitting the Wailers in 1973. Between then and 1976, he retired from the record business and lived in the Jamaican countryside. When he resumed recording, he secured a distribution arrangement with Island Records and released *Blackheart Man* (backed up by Marley, Tosh and the Wailers band) in America and Europe.

Darker and denser than Marley's, less strident than Tosh's, Wailer's music found less acceptance from most quarters, and his records were usually not released in the U.S. Since 1980, as his music has become lighter and more upbeat, he has become a hitmaker in Jamaica. "Ballroom Floor," "Galong So" and "Collie Man" were big hits in 1981, while "Cool Runnings" topped the Jamaican charts that year and "Rock and Groove" followed suit in 1982.

THE WAILERS (See Bob Marley and the Wailers)

LOUDON WAINWRIGHT III

Born September 5, 1946, Chapel Hill, North Carolina

1970—*Album I* (Atlantic) **1971**—*Album II* **1972**—*Album III* (Columbia) **1973**—*Attempted Mustache* **1975**—*Unrequited* **1976**—*T Shirt* (Arista) **1978**—*Final Exam* **1980**—*A Live One* (Rounder) **1983**—*Fame and Wealth.*

Folksinger/songwriter Loudon Wainwright III, the son of an American writer, has gained considerable critical respect and a modicum of sales for his self-lacerating humor, deadpan irony and deliberate tastelessness, complemented by a comic rubber-faced stage presence.

Wainwright began playing the club and college circuit in the late Sixties, attracting a following with his offbeat wit. His first albums included just vocals and guitar and were simultaneously stark confessionals and a mockery of the whole idea, presenting Wainwright as a sort of insensitive singer/songwriter. With *Album III*, Wainwright mellowed his approach until it resembled slapstick more than anything else, and he crossed over into the pop chart with the Top Twenty single "Dead Skunk."

Attempted Mustache played things almost completely for laughs and failed to appreciably increase his sales, but *Unrequited* was received as a welcome return to form. For *T Shirt* and *Final Exam*, Wainwright was backed by a five-piece rock band called Slow Train for such tunes as "Watch Me Rock, I'm Over Thirty." In the early Seventies, Wainwright had married Kate McGarrigle of the McGarrigle sisters, and he recorded her song "Come a Long Way," but they were separated in 1977. Wainwright appeared in the play *Pump Boys and Dinettes* and had a small role in the TV series "M.A.S.H." In 1982, he and Suzzy Roche were the parents of Lucy Roche. Wainwright continues to tour as a solo performer.

TOM WAITS

Born December 7, 1949, Pomona, California

1973—*Closing Time* (Asylum) **1974**—*Heart of a Saturday Night* **1975**—*Nighthawks at the Diner* **1976**—*Small Change* **1977**—*Foreign Affairs* **1978**—*Blue Valentine* (Elektra) **1980**—*Heartattack and Vine* (Asylum).

Singer/songwriter Tom Waits is a one-man Beatnik revival. He generally appears with a cap pulled over his brow, a cigarette dangling from his stubbled face, talksinging and/or mumbling jive in a cancerous growl to the accompaniment of cool saxophone jazz; he also writes romantic ballads, which have been covered by the Eagles, Rickie Lee Jones and others.

Waits claims he was born in a moving taxi. He grew up in California, preferring Bing Crosby, Stephen Foster parlor songs and George Gershwin to, say, the Beach Boys and the Grateful Dead. He also developed an intense admiration for, and identification with, such Beat writers as Jack Kerouac and Charles Bukowski. As a teenager,

Waits was living out of a car and working as a doorman at the L.A. nightclub the Heritage when he decided he should be performing and began writing songs based on overheard snatches of conversation. He first played at L.A.'s Troubador club in 1969, where Herb Cohen, who had managed Frank Zappa, heard him and offered to manage him. With Cohen's financial help, Waits moved out of his car and into L.A.'s Tropicana Hotel (a favorite of visiting rock stars).

Waits built up a strong cult following as an opening act. Working solo, he merged humorous Beatnik free-verse raps with his own compositions. In 1972, he was signed to Elektra/Asylum Records, and his debut album was produced by ex–Lovin' Spoonful Jerry Yester. Though the album sold poorly, one of its songs, "Ol' 55," was covered by the Eagles on their *On the Border* LP. In 1973, Waits toured with a sax-bass-drums trio, often opening for Zappa and the Mothers and usually drawing extremely adverse audience receptions. His second album, produced by Bones Howe, sold a little better than the first.

By 1975, Waits had built a small nationwide cult following and was still opening shows, but he had to cut his trio for financial reasons. Later that year, Waits and Howe assembled a sax-led quartet and an audience to record *Nighthawks at the Diner*. In 1976, he conducted American and European tours, which were mildly received. In London that year, he composed tunes for his next album, *Small Change*, which sold poorly, as did *Foreign Affairs* (which contained his duet with Bette Midler, "I Never Talk to Strangers") and *Blue Valentine*, on which Waits introduced electric guitar for the first time.

Waits appeared as a honky-tonk pianist in Sylvester Stallone's film *Paradise Alley,* in 1979. By this time, he was involved with Rickie Lee Jones, whose picture appeared on the back cover of *Valentine.* They broke up in 1980. In 1982, Waits's soundtrack for Francis Ford Coppola's *One from the Heart* featured him in a number of duets with Crystal Gayle.

WENDY WALDMAN

Born circa 1951, Los Angeles
1973—*Love Has Got Me* (Warner Bros.) **1974**—*Gypsy Symphony* **1975**—*Wendy Waldman* **1976**—*The Main Refrain* **1978**—*Strange Company* **1982**—*Which Way to Main Street* (Epic) **1983**—*I Can See.*

A school of folk-pop singers developed in the early Seventies on America's West Coast that included Linda Ronstadt, Emmylou Harris, Karla Bonoff, Maria Muldaur and Wendy Waldman, among others.

Waldman spent part of her childhood in Mexico, and began performing at age 16 in L.A., first as a solo singer/guitarist and then with a local jug band. In 1969, she formed a folk-rock unit called Bryndle with guitarist Andrew Gold (who later worked with Ronstadt and then went solo) and Bonoff. They broke up a year later.

In 1973, as Waldman recorded her debut LP, Maria Muldaur sang two Waldman tunes, "Mad Mad Me" and "Vaudeville Man," on her own debut. Soon, Waldman, Ronstadt, Harris and Muldaur were appearing on and contributing material to each other's albums. Waldman sang backup on Ronstadt's *Don't Cry Now* and *Heart Like a Wheel,* and Muldaur covered Waldman's "Gringo in Mexico" on *Waitress in a Donut Shop.* Judy Collins covered Waldman's "Pirate Ships," as did Kim Carnes and ex-Eagle Randy Meisner.

Waldman has found it hard to break through commercially, perhaps because of the ironic surplus of West Coast folk-pop singers like herself. In 1978, she recorded and toured with a rock band promoting her *Strange Company* LP. On her Epic albums, she cowrote songs with Eric Kaz, and in 1983 she collaborated with Bette Midler. She has also appeared as a backup singer with Linda Ronstadt.

THE WALKER BROTHERS

Formed 1964, London
Original lineup: John Maus (b. Nov. 12, 1943, New York City), gtr., voc.; Scott Engel (b. Jan 9, 1944, Hamilton, Oh.), bass, voc., gtr., kybds.; Gary Leeds (b. Sep. 3, 1944, Glendale, Calif.), drums, voc.
1965—*The Walker Brothers* (Star Club) **1966**—*Portrait* (Philips) **1967**—*Images* (Star Club) **1975**—*Spotlight On* (Philips) *No Regrets* (GTO) **1976**—*Lines* **1978**—*Nite Flights.*

Though born in America, the Walker Brothers were usually thought of as a British Invasion group because they went to Britain in 1964 after failing to achieve any success in the U.S. In the U.K., pop producer/entrepreneur Jack Good hooked John Maus and Scott Engel up with ex–P. J. Proby drummer Gary Leeds and renamed them the Walker Brothers. Within a year, they had a minor British hit, "Love Her," which set their style: dramatic Spectorian arrangements featuring harmony vocals.

In late 1965, they scored their first big international pop hit with "Make It Easy on Yourself," and followed it up in 1966 with "The Sun Ain't Gonna Shine (Anymore)," their biggest American Top Forty hit. The Walkers were teen sensations in England, but aside from their singles successes still couldn't really crack the American market. They split up after the *Images* album, with Scott Engel (still referring to himself as Scott Walker) going on to a somewhat successful solo career in the U.K. In 1975, the original Walkers, with many sessionmen aboard, reformed, but after one comeback hit in the U.K. with Tom Rush's "No Regrets," they faded from view.

JERRY JEFF WALKER

Born March 16, 1942, Oneonta, New York
1968—*Mr. Bojangles* (Atco) **1969**—*Driftin' Way of Life* (Vanguard) *Five Years Gone* (Atco) **1970**—*Bein' Free* **1972**—*Jerry Jeff Walker* (MCA) **1973**—*Viva*

Terlingua **1974**—*Walker's Collectibles* **1975**—*Ridin' High* **1976**—*It's a Good Night for Singing* **1977**—*A Man Must Carry On* **1978**—*Contrary to Ordinary; Jerry Jeff* (Elektra) **1979**—*Too Old to Change.*

Though he first came to prominence with the psychedelic band Circus Maximus ("The Wind") and has long enjoyed a moderately successful solo career as a "cosmic cowboy" in the Austin, Texas, area, Jerry Jeff Walker is best known for writing "Mr. Bojangles," a song covered by everyone from Sammy Davis, Jr., to the Nitty Gritty Dirt Band.

Walker became attracted to folk music in his youth, and by the mid-Fifties, he had begun performing traditional songs. By his late teens, he was playing in East Coast clubs and coffeehouses. He left home after graduating high school in 1959 and became a wandering minstrel, playing the East Coast and more often the West and Southwest and writing. In Austin, Texas, Walker met singer/songwriter Bob Bruno, and together they returned to New York and formed Circus Maximus, an East Coast answer to San Francisco's psychedelic sound. The band merged Walker's characteristic country folk with jazz rock and other exotica and became a favorite attraction in the Northeast. Their one minor hit was the jazzy "The Wind," which later became a staple of progressive FM radio. Disputes between Walker and Bruno about musical direction led to a breakup in 1968.

New York radio DJ Bob Fass of WBAI-FM had taped "Mr. Bojangles" (about an old street dancer Walker had met in a New Orleans jail) during a broadcast by Walker and David Bromberg, and he aired the much-requested tape while Walker sought a solo contract.

None of Walker's Atco albums sold well, despite the immense popularity of "Mr. Bojangles." Walker then moved to Austin and signed with MCA. He formed the Four-Man Deaf Cowboy Band and recorded *Viva Terlingua* in a mobile truck parked in the middle of Luckenbach, Texas. He then formed the Lost Gonzo Band, who recorded an album of their own in 1975 and have toured and recorded with and without Walker since. *It's a Good Night for Singing* was recorded in Nashville, and featured material by Walker and Austin songwriter Guy Clark.

Walker has since enjoyed steady if unspectacular sales and has toured regularly all over the U.S.

JR. WALKER AND THE ALL STARS
Formed 1961, Detroit
Original lineup: Junior Walker (b. Autry DeWalt Walker, Jr., 1942, Blytheville, Ark.), sax., voc.; Vic Thomas, kybds.; Willie Woods, gtr.; James Graves, drums.
1965—*Shotgun* (Soul) **1966**—*Soul Session; Road Runner* **1967**—*Live!; Home Cookin'; Greatest Hits; What Does It Take to Win Your Love?* **1970**—*A Gasssss* **1971**—*Rainbow Funk; Moody Jr.* **1973**—

Peace and Understanding **1974**—*Anthology* **1976**—*Whopper Bopper Show Stopper* **1978**—*Smooth Soul.*

Jr. Walker's perky, bluesy tenor sax and raspy voice, backed by his band the All Stars, made him one of Motown's more idiosyncratic performers. In the Seventies, studio musicians like Tom Scott and David Sanborn openly imitated Walker's tone and attack.

Walker was a naturally gifted musician, and played both piano and sax as a teen. He worked as a sideman in the late Sixties with several R&B bands. With the original All Stars he recorded "Shotgun" (#4 pop, #1 R&B) and started a string of party hits that included "Do the Boomerang" (#10 R&B) and "Shake and Fingerpop" (#7 R&B) in 1965; "How Sweet It Is (to be Loved by You)" (#18 pop, #3 R&B), "I'm a Road Runner" (#20 pop, #4 R&B) in 1966; "Pucker Up Buttercup" (#3 pop, #11 R&B) and "Come See About Me" (#24 pop, #8 R&B) in 1967; and "Hip City, Part 2" (#7 R&B) in 1968.

With Walker singing more, he enjoyed success with the mellow "What Does It Take (to Win Your Love)" (#4 pop, #1 R&B) and "These Eyes" (#16 pop, #3 R&B) in 1969; "Gotta Hold on to This Feeling" (#21 pop, #2 R&B) and "Do You See My Love (for You Growing)" (#32 pop, #3 R&B) in 1970; and "Walk in the Night" (#46 pop, #10 R&B) in 1972.

Walker continued recording during the Seventies, but was never as commercially successful. In the early Eighties, he was still active on the rock club circuit, playing his Motown hits, and he played on Foreigner's big 1981 hit, "Urgent."

T-BONE WALKER
Born Aaron Thibeaux Walker, May 28, 1910, Linden, Texas; died March 16, 1975, Los Angeles
1968—*The Truth* (Brunswick) *Stormy Monday Blues* (Stateside; reissued 1978 by Charly, U.K.) **1969**—*T-Bone Walker* (Capitol) *Funky Town* (Stateside; reissued 1973 by Bluesway) **1970**—*Good Feelin'* (Polydor) *Well Done* (Home Cooking) **1972**—*Feelin' the Blues* (B&B) **1973**—*Dirty Mistreater* (Bluesway) *I Want a Little Girl* (Delmark) **1974**—*Very Rare* (Warner Bros.) **1975**—*T-Bone Blues* (Atlantic) **1976**—*Classics of Modern Blues* (Blue Note) **1980**—*Jumps Again* (Charly, U.K.).

As the first bluesman to exploit the electric guitar, T-Bone Walker stands as an exceptionally important and influential figure. Walker was indispensable to the birth of urban electric blues and its descendants, R&B and rock & roll. His use of finger-vibrato and piercing electric-guitar sustain influenced scores of subsequent blues guitarists such as B. B. King, Freddie King, Buddy Guy, Albert Collins, Albert King, Lowell Fulson, J. B. Hutto and Otis Rush. Walker's gritty chordal style on fast numbers eventually gave birth to Chuck Berry's archetypal rock guitar riffs.

Born to musical parents (he had a Cherokee Indian grandmother), Aaron Thibeaux Walker moved with his family to Dallas at age two. Through his church choir and street-singing stepfather, Marco Washington, he became interested in music. He acquired the nickname T-Bone early on; it was a corruption of his mother's pet name, T-Bow, from Thibeaux. By the time he was ten, Walker was accompanying his stepfather at drive-in soft drink stands. Soon after he became "lead boy" for the legendary Blind Lemon Jefferson, probably the most popular and influential country bluesman of the Twenties. From 1920 through 1923, Walker led Jefferson down Texas streets.

By late 1923, Walker had taught himself guitar and he began entertaining at Dallas parties. He soon was ready to leave home and tour Texas with Dr. Breeding's Big B Tonic Medicine Show. In 1925, he joined blues singer Ida Cox's road show, which toured the South. Back in Dallas in 1929, Walker began recording acoustic country blues as Oak Cliff T-Bone. He continued touring the South and Southwest until 1934, when he moved to the West Coast. A year later, he married a woman named Viola Lee, for whom he wrote his "Viola Lee Blues" (later covered by the Grateful Dead, among others).

For the next ten years, Walker worked with both small groups and Big Bands (from Les Hite's to Fletcher Henderson's), both on the West Coast and on tours through the Midwest and to New York. As early as 1935, he had begun playing primitive electric guitar models, using a sprung-rhythm, single-string lead style derived from Blind Lemon Jefferson's acoustic picking. By the time he first recorded as T-Bone Walker, in 1942, he was quite proficient on the electric guitar and made an instant impression on dozens of other bluesmen. In 1943, he had his biggest blues hit with the immortal "Call It Stormy Monday," which as "Stormy Monday Blues" or just "Stormy Monday" has become one of the most-often-covered blues songs.

Through the Forties and Fifties, Walker recorded often and toured frequently (usually with smaller groups). He appeared on TV shows from the Fifties through the Seventies, toured all over the world, played jazz and blues festivals from Monterey to Montreux and in 1972 appeared in the French Film *Jazz Odyssey*. In 1970, Walker won a Grammy for Best Ethnic/Traditional Recording with *Good Feelin'*. He became inactive in 1974, when he was hospitalized with bronchial pneumonia, which felled him a year later.

JOE WALSH
Born November 20, 1947, Wichita, Kansas
1972—*Barnstorm* (Dunhill) 1973—*The Smoker You Drink, the Player You Get* 1974—*So What* 1975—*You Can't Argue with a Sick Mind* (ABC) 1978—*But Seriously Folks* (Asylum) *Best of* (ABC) 1981—*There Goes the Neighborhood* (Asylum) 1983—*You Bought It, You Name It* (Full Moon/Warner Bros.).

Hard rock guitarist and songwriter Joe Walsh went solo after leaving his first band, the James Gang, in 1971, and later joined the Eagles. He added some punch to the Eagles' sound, while his solo albums mixed spacious guitar production with offhandedly cheerful lyrics.

Walsh's first solo album, which refined the hard-rock approach of the James Gang with vocal harmonies and more intricate arrangements, sold respectably. His second went gold on the strength of the #23 single "Rocky Mountain Way." *So What* featured Walsh's Barnstorm band (which had included bassist Kenny Passarelli and drummer Joe Vitale as well as former members of Stephen Stills's Manassas) on only a few cuts, with backing on the rest by J. D. Souther, Dan Fogelberg and the Eagles.

In 1974, Walsh produced and played on Fogelberg's top-selling *Souvenirs* LP, and a year later guested on the first solo album by ex-Spirit Jay Ferguson. For the live *You Can't Argue with a Sick Mind* LP, Walsh's band included ex–Beach Boys drummer Ricky Fataar, but by the time of its release Walsh had replaced Bernie Leadon in the Eagles, making his debut with them on *Hotel California*. Walsh continued sporadic solo work, and his *But Seriously Folks* lived up to its title and became a top seller on the strength of the deadpan "Life's Been Good" (#12, 1978), an account of rock-star decadence. In 1979, Walsh further endeared himself to critics and audiences with a semi-serious campaign for the presidency. His platform included "Free gas for everyone"; his qualifications, "Has never lied to the American public." He continued to record after the Eagles broke up.

WAR
Formed 1969, Long Beach, California
Harold Brown (b. Mar. 17, 1946, Long Beach, Calif.), drums; Papa Dee Allen (b. July 19, 1931, Wilmington, Del.), percussion; B. B. Dickerson (b. Aug. 3, 1949, Torrance, Calif.), bass; Lonnie Jordan (b. Nov. 21, 1948, San Diego, Calif.), kybds., voc.; Charles Miller (b. June 2, 1939, Olathe, Kan.), reeds; Lee Oskar (b. Mar. 24, 1948, Copenhagen, Den.), harmonica; Howard Scott (b. Mar. 15, 1946, San Pedro, Calif.), gtr., voc.
1971—*War* (United Artists) *All Day Music* 1972—*The World Is a Ghetto* 1973—*Deliver the Word* 1974—*War Live* 1975—*Why Can't We Be Friends?* 1976—*War's Greatest Hits; Love Is All Around* (MCA) 1977—*Platinum Jazz* (Blue Note) *Galaxy* (MCA) 1978—*Youngblood* (United Artists) (−Dickerson; + Luther Rabb, bass) 1979—*Music Band; Music Band 2* 1982—*Outlaw* (RCA).

War's distinctive mix of funk, Latin and jazz has kept them on the charts since their 1969 debut as ex-Animal Eric Burdon's backup band.

Burdon met Lee Oskar in 1969, and together they set out to form a band. They saw a group called Night Shift at a Los Angeles club and recruited them. At the time, the band was backing football star Deacon Jones's ill-fated efforts as a singer. Burdon changed the band's name to War and, backed by this mostly black band (Oskar was white), began a lengthy tour. The band recorded two albums with Burdon, and "Spill the Wine" was their biggest hit (#3, 1970).

While on tour in Europe in 1971, Burdon split and left War on their own. They continued to tour and to fulfill their commitments. Later that year, they released *War*. The gold *All Day Music* helped establish their identity as a band apart from Burdon, and it contained "Slippin' into Darkness" (#16 pop, #12 R&B, 1972). Subsequent releases were equally successful: "The World Is a Ghetto" (#17 pop, #3 R&B, 1973); *Deliver the Word* contained "The Cisco Kid" (#2 pop, #5 R&B, 1973), "Gypsy Man" (#8 pop, #6 R&B, 1973) and "Me and Baby Brother" (#15 pop, #18 R&B, 1973); and *Why Can't We Be Friends?* boasted hits in "Low Rider" (#1 pop, #7 R&B, 1975) and the title cut (#6 pop, #7 R&B, 1975). *Greatest Hits* included one new song, "Summer" (#7 pop, #4 R&B, 1976).

In 1977, War moved to MCA Records, and the title cut from *Galaxy* was a disco hit. Subsequent albums had neither the commercial nor artistic impact of their early- and mid-Seventies releases. But War's 1982 debut on RCA, *Outlaw,* proved something of a comeback, boasting "You Got the Power" and the title cut.

BILLY WARD AND THE DOMINOES
Formed circa 1950, New York City
1956—*Billy Ward and the Dominoes* (Federal).

Founder Billy Ward was the only constant in the ever-changing personnel of this important, popular Fifties R&B vocal group. Notable performers who were once Dominoes include Clyde McPhatter, Jackie Wilson and Louisiana zydeco blues accordionist Clifton Chenier.

Ward had begun studying music in Los Angeles as a child, and at age 14 won a national contest for his composition "Dejection," the award presented by conductor Walter Damrosch. During and after an Army stint in the early Forties, Ward became a boxer, and after his discharge he moved east as sports editor and columnist for *Transradio Press.* He still loved music and was a vocal coach in the Carnegie Hall building. By the late Forties, Ward had his own voice teaching studio on Broadway, and eventually he got the idea to start a singing group with his students. Thus were born the Dominoes.

In 1950, 17-year-old Clyde McPhatter joined as lead tenor, and in 1951 the group had three Top Ten R&B singles: "Do Something for Me" (#6), "I Am with You" (#8) and "60-Minute Man" (#1). In 1952, their "Have

Mercy Baby" was an R&B #1 for several weeks running. They again hit the Top Ten in 1965—as Billy Ward and the Dominoes—with "The Bells" (#6), "I'd Be Satisfied" (#8), "Rags to Riches" (#3) and "These Foolish Things" (#5).

McPhatter then left to form the Drifters. His place was taken by Jackie Wilson, who remained with the Dominoes until 1956. The group that made the above album included Ward, Gene Mumford, Milton Merle, Milton Grayson and Cliff Owens, and they had a hit single in 1957 with a cover of Hoagy Carmichael's standard "Star Dust," a pop (#12) and R&B (#5) hit in the U.S. and U.K. (#13). It eventually sold over a million copies worldwide. It was their last big hit, but the group remained popular as a concert attraction into the early Sixties.

DIONNE WARWICK
Born December 12, 1941, East Orange, New Jersey
1967—*Dionne Warwick's Golden Hits, Part One* (Scepter) **1969—***Dionne Warwick's Golden Hits, Part Two* **1972—***Dionne* (Warner Bros.) **1973—***Just Being Myself* **1975—***Then Came You; Track of the Cat* **1979—***Dionne* (Arista) **1980—***No Night So Long* **1981—***Hot! Live and Otherwise* **1982—***Friends and Love; Heartbreaker.*

Since her debut in 1962, Dionne Warwick has been one of the most successful American pop singers, particularly in the years when she was the voice of Bacharach-David.

Warwick grew up in a family of gospel singers and received considerable vocal training as a girl, singing with the Drinkard Singers, a group managed by her mother and including her sister Dee Dee. She attended Hartt College of Music in Hartford, Connecticut, and after singing background on some recording sessions, she was signed to Scepter Records in 1962 to work with the production and writing team of Burt Bacharach and Hal David.

"Don't Make Me Over" (#21 pop, #5 R&B) in late 1962 was the first of many Bacharach-David compositions Warwick would record, including "Anyone Who Had a Heart" (#8 pop), 1963; "Walk On By" (#6 pop) and "You'll Never Get to Heaven" (#34 pop), 1964; "I Just Don't Know What to Do with Myself" (#26 pop, #20 R&B) and "Message to Michael" (#8 pop, #5 R&B), 1966; "I Say a Little Prayer" (#4 pop, #8 R&B) and "Alfie" (#18 pop, #5 R&B), 1967.

In the 1968–69 period, she had four huge hits: "Do You Know the Way to San Jose" (#10 pop, #23 R&B), "Valley of the Dolls" (#2 pop, #13 R&B), "This Girl's in Love with You" (#7 pop and R&B) and "I'll Never Fall in Love Again" (#6 pop, #17 R&B) from the Bacharach-David musical *Promises, Promises.*

In 1971, Warwick moved to Warner Bros. Records and left Bacharach/David behind. She couldn't duplicate her success, although she worked with a number of fine producer/writers. *Just Being Myself* was written by the Brian Holland and Lamont Dozier team, and *Track of the Cat* (1975) by Thom Bell. In 1974, she had a Bell-produced hit, "Then Came You," with the Spinners (#1 pop, #2 R&B). "Once You Hit the Road" (#5 R&B) with Bell did well in 1975. In the early Seventies, on the advice of a numerologist, she added an "e" to her surname, but dropped it in 1975. A 1977 live album with Isaac Hayes, *A Man and a Woman,* was well received.

In 1979, she returned to the charts with "I'll Never Love This Way Again" (#5 pop, #18 R&B), produced by Barry Manilow, and "Déjà Vu" (#15 pop, #25 R&B). In 1982, Barry Gibb of the Bee Gees coproduced and wrote songs for Warwick's *Heartbreaker,* which had hits in the title cut and "Take the Short Way Home."

DINAH WASHINGTON
Born Ruth Jones, August 29, 1924, Tuscaloosa, Alabama; died December 14, 1963, Detroit
1957—*Sings Fats Waller* (Mercury) **1958**—*Sings Bessie Smith* **1960**—*The Two of Us* (with Brook Benton) **1963**—*The Dinah Washington Story.*

Dinah Washington was the most popular black female singer of the Fifties; her sinuous, nasal, penetrating vocals were marvelously effective on blues, jazz or straight pop songs.

Growing up in Chicago, she gave gospel recitals on the South Side, accompanying herself on piano. At 15, she won an amateur contest at the Regal Theater and began appearing at local nightclubs. But in 1940, she returned to the church at the urging of Sallie Martin, a powerful figure in the gospel world who helped young Ruth Jones polish her talent.

In 1942, she became immersed in secular music after agent Joe Glaser heard her sing. He suggested she change her name to Dinah Washington and recommended her to Lionel Hampton, with whom she sang from 1943 to 1946. Jazz writer Leonard Feather arranged for her to cut two of his songs for Keynote Records in 1943, "Evil Gal Blues" and "Salty Papa Blues," backed by Hampton's band.

During the mid-Fifties, Washington was known as the "Queen of the Harlem Blues," partially because of her sales consistency, and because her style of blues was much more complex than that of Chicago-area singers. Among her Top Ten R&B hits were "Baby Get Lost" (#1 R&B) in 1949; "Trouble in Mind" (#4 R&B) in 1952; "What a Diff'rence a Day Makes" (#8 pop, #4 R&B) in 1959; and "This Bitter Earth" (#24 pop, #1 R&B) in 1960. Also in 1960 Washington cut two popular duets with Brook Benton, "Baby (You've Got What It Takes)" (#5 pop, #1 R&B) and "A Rockin' Good Way" (#7 pop, #1 R&B). After 18 years with Mercury, Washington went to Roulette Records in 1961. She died in 1963 after consuming weight-reduction pills and alcohol.

GROVER WASHINGTON, JR.
Born December 12, 1943, Buffalo, New York
1971—*Inner City Blues* (Kudu) **1972**—*All the King's Horses* **1973**—*Soul Box* **1974**—*Mister Magic* **1975**— *Feels So Good* **1976**—*A Secret Place* **1977**—*Live at the Bijou* **1978**—*Reed Seed* (Motown) **1979**— *Paradise* (Elektra) *Skylark* (Motown) **1980**—*Winelight* (Elektra) **1981**—*Come Morning.*

Grover Washington, Jr.'s recordings, which feature his soulful tenor sax backed by supple, funky grooves, have made him one of the most commercially successful pop jazzmen of the Seventies and Eighties.

Washington has been playing saxophone since he was ten. His family was musically inclined; his father plays tenor sax, his mother sings in a choir and his brother is a drummer. At 16 Washington left home to tour with a Columbus, Ohio–based band, the Four Clefs. While in the Army from 1965 to 1967, he gigged in Philadelphia with organ trios and rock bands. Washington also played in New York occasionally with drummer Billy Cobham. After playing on a number of albums in the early Seventies as a sideman, he was signed to Kudu Records by pop-jazz mogul Creed Taylor. His gold *Mister Magic* (1974), arranged by Bob James, established Washington's profitable style. This was the first of seven Washington albums to go #1 on the jazz charts and the first to go gold. Washington's most successful release was the platinum *Winelight,* which contained "Just the Two of Us," featuring Bill Withers' vocal.

MUDDY WATERS
Born McKinley Morganfield, April 4, 1915, Rolling Fork, Mississippi; died April 30, 1983, Chicago
1962—*Fathers and Sons* (Chess) **1964**—*Folk Singer* **1966**—*Real Folk Blues* (French import) **1968**—*Sail On* (Chess) **1970**—*They Call Me Muddy Waters* **1971**— *McKinley Morganfield; Muddy Waters Live* **1972**—*The London Muddy Waters Sessions* **1973**—*Can't Get No Grindin'* **1977**—*Hard Again* (Blue Sky) **1978**—*I'm Ready* **1982**—*Rolling Stone* (Chess).

Muddy Waters was the leading exponent of Chicago blues in the Fifties. With him, the blues came up from the Delta and went electric, and his guitar licks and repertoire have fueled innumerable blues bands.

Waters was the son of a farmer and, following his mother's death in 1918, was raised by his grandmother. He picked up his nickname because he fished and played regularly in a muddy creek. He learned to play harmonica, and as a teen he led a band that frequently played Mississippi Delta clubs. His singing was influenced by the style of local bluesman Son House. At 17, Waters began playing guitar by studying Robert Johnson records. In 1940, he traveled to St. Louis and in 1941 joined the Silas Green tent show as a singer and harmonica player. Sometime around 1941–42, Waters was recorded by folk archivist/ researchers Alan Lomax and John Work in Mississippi for the Library of Congress.

In 1943, he moved to Chicago, where he found employment in a paper mill. In 1944, Waters got an electric guitar and began performing at South Side clubs and rent parties. He cut several sides in 1946 for Columbia's Okeh subsidiary, but none were released until 1981, when they appeared on a Columbia blues reissue, *Okeh Chicago Blues*.

In 1946, bluesman Sunnyland Slim helped Waters get signed to Aristocrat Records, where he cut several singles. None were particularly successful, and Waters continued playing clubs seven nights a week and driving a truck six days a week.

In 1948, the Chess brothers changed Aristocrat to Chess. Waters' first single on the new label was "Rollin' Stone," a major blues hit. "I Can't Be Satisfied" and "I Feel Like Going Home" from that year secured his position as a major blues performer. Most of Waters' early recordings featured him on electric guitar, Big Crawford or writer/producer Willie Dixon on bass and occasionally Little Walter on harmonica. By 1951, he was supported by a complete band with Otis Spann on piano, Little Walter on harmonica, Jimmie Rodgers on second guitar and Elgin Evans on drums.

"Honey Bee" in 1951; "She Moves Me" (#10 R&B) in 1952; "I'm Your Hoochie Coochie Man" (#8 R&B), "I Just Wanna Make Love to You" (#4 R&B), "I'm Ready" (#5 R&B) and "Got My Mojo Working" in 1954; and "Mannish Boy" (#9 R&B) in 1955 are all regarded as blues classics and have been recorded by numerous rock groups. During the Fifties, many of the top Chicago bluesmen passed through Waters' band, including Walter Horton, Junior Wells, Jimmie Rodgers, James Cotton and Buddy Guy. In addition, Waters was helpful in the early stages of both Howlin' Wolf's and Chuck Berry's careers.

During his peak years as a record seller, most of Waters' sales were confined primarily to the Mississippi Delta, the New Orleans area and Chicago. But his reputation and music were internationally known, as the attendance at concerts on his 1958 English tour revealed. The Rolling Stones named themselves after his song, "Rollin' Stone."

After the mid-Fifties, Waters never had another Top Ten R&B single, but his albums began to reach rock listeners. Into the Sixties, Waters appeared at concerts and festivals nationally, such as the 1960 Newport Jazz Festival, where *Muddy Waters at Newport* was cut. In the late Sixties and early Seventies, he recorded several albums either with rock musicians or in a rock direction, the best of which were the *London Muddy Waters Sessions* and *Fathers and Sons*, the latter with many of the players he had influenced. In 1971, Waters won the first of several Grammys with *They Call Me Muddy Waters*.

In the early Seventies, Waters left Chess and sued Chess's publishing arm for back royalties. He signed with Steve Paul's Blue Sky records in 1976, the year he appeared at the Band's farewell concert. Using members of his Fifties bands and producer/guitarist Johnny Winter, Waters made two of his best-selling albums, *Hard Again* and *I'm Ready*. Winter and Waters frequently performed together in the Seventies and Eighties. Waters died of a heart attack.

JOHNNY "GUITAR" WATSON
Born February 3, 1935, Houston, Texas
1966—*Bad* (Okeh) **1967**—*Two for the Price of One*
1968—*In the Fats Bag* **1973**—*Gangster of Love* (Fantasy) **1976**—*I Don't Want to be Alone, Stranger; Captured Live* (DJM) *Ain't That a Bitch* **1977**—*A Real Mother for Ya; Funk Beyond the Call of Duty* **1978**—*Giant* **1979**—*What the Hell Is This* **1980**—*Love Jones*.

Johnny "Guitar" Watson enjoyed great popularity in the mid-Seventies with several hit singles and LPs, but his work has been known in blues circles since the Fifties. His playing style was influential on Jimi Hendrix, among others, and his "Gangster of Love" was recorded by Steve Miller in 1968.

Watson's father taught him to play piano, and at age 11 his grandmother gave him his grandfather's guitar, which he taught himself to play. He moved to Los Angeles in 1950, where he began working as a sideman in various bands and recording as a solo artist for Federal Records. Among the bands he played in through the Fifties were those led by Amos Milburn, Bumps Blackwell and Big Jay McNeely. In 1961, he began recording for King. His late-Fifties and early-Sixties hits include "Three Hours Past Midnight," "Those Lonely Lonely Nights" and "Space Guitar," which was one of the first recorded songs to use reverb and feedback.

Through the Sixties and Seventies, Watson performed around the U.S. and occasionally in Europe. In the early to mid-Sixties, he often toured with Larry Williams. Recording for DJM in the mid-Seventies, Watson had funk hits with "A Real Mother for Ya," "I Don't Wanna Be a Lone Ranger" and "It's Too Late." Later releases on A&M and Mercury were not as well received.

WEATHER REPORT
Formed 1970
Josef Zawinul (b. July 7, 1932, Vienna, Austria), kybds., synth.; Wayne Shorter (b. Aug. 25, 1933, Newark, N.J.), saxes; Miroslav Vitous (b. Dec. 6, 1947, Prague, Czechoslovakia), bass; Alphonse Mouzon (b. Nov. 21, 1948, Charleston, S.C.), drums; Airto Moreira (b. Aug. 5, 1941, Brazil), percussion.
1971—*Weather Report* (Columbia) (− Mouzon; + Eric Gravatt, drums; − Moreira; + Dom Um Romao,

percussion) **1972**—*I Sing the Body Electric* **1973**—*Streetnighter* (− Gravatt; + Ishmael Wilburn, drums; + Alphonso Johnson [b. Feb. 2, 1951, Philadelphia], bass) **1974**—*Mysterious Traveller* (− Vitous; − Wilburn; + Alyrio Lima, drums; − Romao; + Ndugu [b. Leon Chancler], percussion) **1975**—*Tale Spinnin'* (− Lima; + Chester Thompson, drums; − Ndugu) **1976**—*Black Market* (− Johnson; + Jaco Pastorius [b. Dec. 1, 1951, Norristown, Penn.], bass; − Thompson; + Alejandro Neciosup Acuna, percussion; + Manola Badrena [b. Puerto Rico], percussion, voc.) **1977**—*Heavy Weather* (− Acuna; − Badrena) **1978**—*Mr. Gone* (+ Peter Erskine [b. May 5, 1954, Somers Point, N.J.], drums) **1979**—*8:30* **1980**—*Night Passages* **1982**—(− Erskine; − Pastorius; + Victor Bailey, bass; + Jose Rossy, percussion; + Omar Hakim, drums) **1983**—*Procession*.

Since its inception in 1970, Weather Report has been the premier electric jazz ensemble. Born of the Miles Davis groups of the late Sixties that also spawned many other fusion bands, Weather Report is one of the very few groups that has managed to win commercial success while going their own way. Their music has the drive of rock, the harmonic sophistication of jazz, the formal ingenuity of classical music and hints of Brazilian, African and Oriental traditions. The best-known Weather Report tunes, like "Birdland," sound like electrified global carnivals.

Josef Zawinul and Wayne Shorter have been the only constants of Weather Report. The first music Zawinul heard and played was the Gypsy folk music of his family; his first instrument was an accordion. At about the age of 12, when he was living in Nazi-occupied Vienna, he began studying classical piano. In the postwar years, he played jazz at U.S. Army clubs and Viennese cabarets. On the basis of a record he cut in a local studio, he was awarded a scholarship to study at the Berklee School of Music in Boston, and he arrived in the United States in 1959. Three weeks after classes had begun, he dropped out and went to New York, where he met Shorter.

Shorter had been in the city since 1951, when he entered New York University to study music. After graduating, he played tenor saxophone with Horace Silver before joining Maynard Ferguson's band. Through Shorter, Zawinul began playing with Ferguson as well. Not long after that, however, Shorter moved on to Art Blakey's Jazz Messengers, where he stayed five years. Zawinul also left Ferguson. He led Dinah Washington's band for over a year and played sessions behind Joe Williams, Yusef Lateef, Ben Webster and a very young Aretha Franklin. He played the electric piano extensively during nine years in the Cannonball Adderley Quintet, which he joined in 1961, and for whom he wrote "Mercy Mercy Mercy."

Shorter joined the Miles Davis Quintet (with Hancock, drummer Tony Williams and bassist Ron Carter) in 1964.

Shorter's work with Davis and on a half-dozen solo albums had established him as one of the outstanding saxophonists of the John Coltrane school, although he later tempered the Coltrane influence with his own lyricism. Shorter was also an outstanding composer; his "Nefertiti" (the title track of a 1967 Miles Davis Quintet album) convinced Zawinul that the two of them should join forces. Meanwhile, Davis decided to experiment with a large electrified ensemble, which Zawinul joined. A Zawinul composition, "In a Silent Way," became the title track of the album, recorded in 1968. Zawinul continued to play with Adderley, but he joined the Davis aggregation again in 1969 to record the landmark *Bitches Brew*, to which Zawinul and Shorter contributed compositions.

Shorter left Davis soon after the *Bitches Brew* sessions, and Zawinul left Adderley the following year. Each recorded solo albums before forming a group to experiment with electric jazz. They recruited Czechoslovak bassist Miroslav Vitous, who had recently played on a Zawinul date. After studying classical composition at the Prague Conservatory, Vitous—like Zawinul—had come to the United States on a scholarship from the Berklee School of Music. His jazz credits included work with Stan Getz, Sonny Rollins, Art Farmer, Herbie Mann, Larry Coryell and Miles Davis. Clive Davis reportedly signed the group without even listening to their demo tape. With Brazilian percussionist Airto Moreira and drummer Alphonse Mouzon they recorded their highly experimental debut album.

Moreira, who left Weather Report to join Chick Corea, was replaced by another Brazilian, Dom Um Romao, formerly of Sergio Mendes and Brazil 66. Mouzon joined the McCoy Tyner Quartet and was replaced in Weather Report by Tyner's drummer, Eric Gravatt. One side of *I Sing the Body Electric* was excerpted from a double live album released only in Japan. On their third album, *Streetnighter*, Zawinul began using synthesizers as lead instruments and sticking to a funkier beat. *Streetnighter* sold 200,000 copies, quite a number for a record of instrumentals. *Mysterious Traveller* went further toward dance music with fixed rhythms, riffs and figures repeated in unison by the bass, saxophone and synthesizers. *Traveller* introduced Alphonso Johnson, formerly with Chuck Mangione. By *Tale Spinnin'*, Johnson had taken over from Vitous.

Tale Spinnin' featured Zawinul's ARP 2600, one of the most advanced of the monophonic synths. On *Black Market*, he introduced the Oberheim polyphonic, and the effect was dramatic. Weather Report's music became almost orchestral in texture. But as Zawinul's arsenal of sounds expanded, Wayne Shorter's role diminished on records, although in Weather Report's concerts he took ample solos. In 1973, Shorter made an album with Brazilian songwriter Milton Nascimento.

Black Market included one cut on which the bassist was

Jaco Pastorius. Pastorius had introduced himself to Zawinul after a Weather Report concert in Miami in 1975 and given him tapes of his playing. The son of a professional drummer, he had started as a drummer at the age of 13, before taking up the bass. He toured with Wayne Cochran's C.C. Riders for one year and played with Ira Sullivan's big band, the Baker's Dozen, for three. As a freelance bassist in New York and Boston, he worked with Paul Bley and Pat Metheny, and his solo debut album was released concurrently with *Black Market,* introducing his busily contrapuntal fretless bass style. By the *Heavy Weather* sessions, he was a full member of the group, a contributing composer and coproducer (with Zawinul). While devoting most of his efforts to Weather Report, he also recorded and toured with Joni Mitchell.

Heavy Weather was Weather Report's most commercially successful album. It sold over 500,000 copies—the first gold album for the group—and Zawinul's "Birdland" was given considerable airplay (a vocal rendition by the Manhattan Transfer was popular three years later).

Mr. Gone did not depart far from the rich orchestral sound of *Heavy Weather,* but the group no longer included a percussionist. With the addition of Pete Erskine they remained a four-piece unit for almost four years. A double album, *8:30,* comprised three sides recorded at two dates at the culmination of the 1979 tour, and one side recorded in Zawinul's home studio. Pastorius left Weather Report in 1982 and formed his own band, Word of Mouth. *Procession,* with a new lineup, included the first Weather Report song with lyrics (sung by Janis Siegel of Manhattan Transfer), and Shorter announced plans to record another album with Milton Nascimento.

THE WEAVERS
Formed 1949
Original lineup: Pete Seeger (b. May 3, 1919, New York City), gtr., banjo, voc.; Ronnie Gilbert, voc.; Fred Hellerman, voc., gtr.; Lee Hays (d. Aug. 26, 1981), voc., gtr.
1956—*At Carnegie Hall* (Vanguard) **1957**—*Greatest Hits* **1963**—*Reunion at Carnegie Hall Parts 1 and 2* **1965**—*Songbook.*

The Weavers were the most important and influential early American folk revivalists, as well as one of the most commercially successful. They disbanded for a time in the early Fifties because of anti-Communist government blacklisting, but regrouped in 1955; through the Fifties they scored hits with Leadbelly's "Goodnight Irene," the traditional "On Top of Old Smokey," "When the Saints Go Marching In" and "Kisses Sweeter Than Wine."

Pete Seeger left to go solo in 1958 and was replaced in succession by Erik Darling, Frank Hamilton and, in 1963, Bernie Krause. After Seeger's departure, scores of imitators appeared, and the Weavers' legacy went on to heavily influence the early-Sixties folk boom. The four original members were reunited in 1981 for a concert that was filmed for the documentary *Wasn't That a Time.*

JIMMY WEBB
Born August 15, 1946, Elk City, Oklahoma
1968—*Jim Webb Sings Jim Webb* (Epic) **1970**—*Words and Music* (Reprise) **1971**—*And So On* **1972**—*Letters* **1974**—*Land's End* (Asylum) **1977**—*El Mirage* (Atlantic) **1982**—*Angel Heart.*

At age 21, Jimmy Webb was a millionaire, having written such pop hits as Glen Campbell's "By the Time I Get to Phoenix" and the Fifth Dimension's "Up, Up and Away," both of which were Grammy nominees in 1967 for Best Song ("Up, Up and Away" won). Other often-covered Webb songs include "Wichita Lineman," "MacArthur Park," "Galveston" and "The Moon Is a Harsh Mistress."

The son of a Baptist minister, Webb grew up in rural Oklahoma, learning piano and organ. When he moved with his family to San Bernardino, California, in 1964, he was already writing songs. In 1966, he enrolled in San Bernardino Valley College, but dropped out shortly thereafter when his mother died. He moved to Los Angeles and began making the rounds of the record business. For a time he earned $50 a week working at one recording studio. He also worked for Motown's publishing company, Jobete Music, which in 1965 published Webb's "Honey Come Back." Singer and record executive Johnny Rivers recorded a Webb tune he liked, "By the Time I Get to Phoenix." Though Rivers didn't have a hit with it, he recommended Webb's work to the Fifth Dimension, who had a 1967 hit with "Up, Up and Away." That year Glen Campbell covered "Phoenix." After TWA airlines used "Up, Up and Away" as a commercial theme, Webb formed a company that provided jingles for Chevrolet, Doritos tortilla chips and Hamm's beer.

In 1968, the Brooklyn Bridge hit with Webb's "The Worst That Could Happen." That year Richard Harris (for whom Webb had written the entire LP *A Tramp Shining*) scored a #2 pop hit with Webb's melodramatic "MacArthur Park," which was later covered by Waylon Jennings (who won a Grammy with it in 1969) and Donna Summer. Glen Campbell had a gold hit with "Wichita Lineman."

Meanwhile, in 1968, Epic had issued an album of Webb singing his own demos, without Webb's consent. Webb had previously made his singing debut with an obscure group called Strawberry Children in 1967, on the single "Love Years Coming." In 1969, he also composed music for the films *Tell Them Willie Boy Is Here* and *How Sweet It Is* and worked on a semi-autobiographical Broadway musical, *His Own Dark City.*

Webb's solo concert debut in Los Angeles in February 1970 was poorly received, despite a capacity audience;

none of his solo albums have been popular. In 1972, Webb produced a Supremes album, and in 1973 he found his hitmaking touch again, as Art Garfunkel (who called Webb "the best songwriter since Paul Simon") hit with Webb's "All I Know."

Webb went on to produce Cher's *Stars* LP, an album by his sister Susan in 1975 and a failed Fifth Dimension reunion LP, *Earthbound*, in 1976. His own solo albums continued to meet with little acclaim, and he began taking three- and four-year intervals between recordings. *El Mirage* was produced by Beatles producer George Martin.

JUNIOR WELLS
Born Amos Blackmore, December 9, 1934, Memphis, Tennessee
1966—*On Tap* (Delmark) *It's My Life Baby* (Vanguard) *South Side Jam* (Delmark) *Hoodoo Man Blues* **1967**—*Blues Hit the Big Town* **1968**—*Comin' At You* (Vanguard) *You're Tuff Enough* (Mercury) *Sings at the Golden Bear* (Blue Rock) **1971**—*In My Younger Days* (Red Lightning) **1972**—*Buddy Guy and Junior Wells Play the Blues* (Atlantic) **1973**—*I Was Walking Through the Woods* (Chess) (with Buddy Guy) **1979**—*Got to Use Your Head* (Blues Ball) (with Buddy Guy).

One of the more noted Chicago blues singers and harmonica players, Junior Wells was inspired by the blues harp of Sonny Boy Williamson and Little Walter Jacobs.

In the early Fifties, Wells replaced Little Walter in Muddy Waters' band, with whom he cut his first solo hit, "Hoodoo Man." Wells's other best-known hit was "Messin' with the Kid," later covered by Rory Gallagher.

In the late Sixties, Wells began a long-running touring and recording partnership with Chicago blues guitarist Buddy Guy. Their 1972 album together, *Play the Blues*, featured guest appearances by Eric Clapton, Dr. John and the J. Geils Band. In the Seventies Guy and Wells opened tour dates for the Rolling Stones, and they still tour together frequently.

MARY WELLS
Born May 13, 1943, Detroit, Michigan
1961—*Bye Bye Baby* (Motown) **1962**—*One Who Really Loves You* **1963**—*Mary Wells Live on Stage; Two Lovers* **1964**—*Mary Wells' Greatest Hits; Together* (with Marvin Gaye) *My Guy* **1965**—*Mary Wells* (20th Century–Fox) *In and Out of Love* (Epic).

Mary Wells was one of Motown's first stars. At age 16, she met Berry Gordy, Jr.'s assistant, Robert Bateman. She had written a song she wanted Jackie Wilson to record and had Bateman introduce her to Gordy, who had been writing material for Wilson. Unable to write her song down, she sang the tune for Gordy. He signed her, and

Motown released that song as her debut single, "Bye Bye Baby" (#45 pop, #8 R&B, 1960).

After teaming up with Motown performer/writer/producer Smokey Robinson in 1962, her singing style became more pop. The Wells-Robinson team scored a string of hits including "The One Who Really Loves You" (#8 pop, #2 R&B), "You Beat Me to the Punch" (#9 pop, #1 R&B) and "Two Lovers" (#7 pop, #1 R&B) in 1962; "Laughing Boy" (#15 pop, #6 R&B), "Your Old Stand By" (#40 pop, #3 R&B) and "What's Easy for Two Is So Hard for One" b/w "You Lost the Sweetest Boy" (#22 pop, #8 R&B) in 1963. In 1964, Wells had her biggest Motown hit, "My Guy" (#1 pop), followed by two duets with Marvin Gaye, "What's the Matter with You Baby" (#17 pop) and "Once Upon a Time" (#19 pop).

Wells signed with Atco in late 1965, where she had the 1966 hit "Dear Lover" (#51 pop, #6 R&B), but none of her subsequent releases were as successful as her Motown recordings. "Dig the Way I Feel" (#35 R&B) on Jubilee in 1969 was a minor hit. Subsequently Wells left recording to raise a family, but returned in the early Eighties.

WESTERN SWING

One of the original forms of "fusion" music, Western swing merged country and western string bands with the horn arrangements of Dixieland and Big Band jazz. The genre began when string bands like Milton Brown's Musical Brownies began adding jazz and pop standards, and even blues, to their repertoires. Onetime Brownie Bob Wills formed his Texas Playboys in the mid-Thirties. Within a few years, Wills had expanded his outfit into a bona fide Big Band, with a horn section as well as banjos, fiddles, guitars and pedal steel guitars. Wills's Texas Playboys remain the best-remembered of Western swing dance bands. Its anything-goes hybridizing and its early use of the electric guitar made Western swing an important precursor of rock, and along with Western swing revivalists like Asleep at the Wheel, country singers including Merle Haggard and Willie Nelson carry on Western swing's jazz-and-country experiments.

WET WILLIE
Formed circa 1970, Mobile, Alabama
Jimmy Hall, voc., sax, harmonica; Ricky Hirsch, gtr., voc.; John Anthony, kybds., voc.; Jack Hall, bass, voc.; Lewis Ross, drums.
1971—*Wet Willie* (Capricorn) **1972**—*II* **1973**—(+ Ella Avery, voc.; + Donna Hall, voc.) *Drippin' Wet* **1974**—*Keep on Smilin'* **1975**—*Dixie Rock* **1976**—*The Wetter the Better* **1977**—*Left Coast Live; Greatest Hits* **1978**—(– Hirsch; – Ross; + Larry Bernwald, gtr., voc.; + Marshall Smith, gtr., voc.; + Theophilus Lively, drums, voc.) *Manorisms* (Epic) **1979**—*Which One's Willie*.

588 / JERRY WEXLER

Originally known as Fox while performing in Mobile, Alabama, Wet Willie became yet another Southern boogie-rock band signed to Capricorn Records in the wake of the success of the Allman Brothers Band. Their first two albums were produced by Eddie Offord, who had worked with Emerson, Lake and Palmer and Yes. Their third album, a live recording of a 1972 New Year's Eve concert in New Orleans, broke them in U.S. album charts, and the title cut of *Keep on Smilin'* was a hit single (it was also a semi-reggae venture outside their guitar-heavy boogie style). No more hits were forthcoming, and they disbanded in 1980.

JERRY WEXLER
Born January 10, 1917

Jerry Wexler was one of the seminal soul producers of the Sixties.

He grew up in Manhattan and was exposed to black music in Harlem and Greenwich Village clubs. After

Grammy Awards

T-Bone Walker
1970 Best Ethnic or Traditional Recording:
Good Feelin'

Dionne Warwick
1968 Best Contemporary Pop Vocal Performance, Female:
"Do You Know the Way to San Jose"
1970 Best Contemporary Vocal Performance, Female:
"I'll Never Fall in Love Again"
1979 Best Pop Vocal Performance, Female:
"I'll Never Love This Way Again"
Best R&B Vocal Performance, Female:
"Déjà Vu"

Dinah Washington
1959 Best R&B Performance:
"What a Difference a Day Makes"

Muddy Waters
1971 Best Ethnic or Traditional Recording:
They Call Me Muddy Waters
1972 *The London Muddy Waters Sessions*
1975 *The Muddy Waters Woodstock Album*
1977 *Hard Again*
1978 *I'm Ready*
1979 *Muddy "Mississippi" Waters Live*

Weather Report
1979 Best Jazz Fusion Performance, Vocal or Instrumental:
8:30

Mason Williams
1968 Best Contemporary Pop Performance, Instrumental;
Best Instrumental Theme:
"Classical Gas"

Paul Williams
1977 Song of the Year:
"Love Theme for *A Star Is Born* (Evergreen)" (with Barbra Streisand)
1979 Best Recording for Children:
The Muppet Movie (with Jim Henson)

Wings (see also: Paul McCartney)
1979 Best Rock Instrumental Performance:
"Rockestra Theme"

Bill Withers
1971 Best R&B Song:
"Ain't No Sunshine"
1981 Best R&B Song:
"Just the Two of Us" (with others)

Stevie Wonder
1973 Album of the Year:
Innervisions
Best Pop Vocal Performance, Male:
"You Are the Sunshine of My Life"

Best R&B Vocal Performance, Male; Best R&B Song:
"Superstition"
1974 Album of the Year; Best Pop Vocal Performance, Male:
Fulfillingness' First Finale
Best R&B Vocal Performance, Male:
"Boogie On Reggae Woman"
Best R&B Song:
"Living for the City"
1976 Album of the Year; Best Producer of the Year;
Best Pop Vocal Performance, Male:
Songs in the Key of Life
Best R&B Vocal Performance, Male:
"I Wish"

Betty Wright
1975 Best R&B Song:
"Where Is the Love" (with others)

Tammy Wynette
1967 Best Country & Western Solo Vocal Performance, Female:
"I Don't Wanna Play House"
1969 Best Country Vocal Performance, Female:
Stand by Your Man

serving in the Army, Wexler got a journalism degree from Kansas State University in 1946. He worked briefly for the music publishing association BMI before joining *Billboard,* where he worked as a staff reporter from 1948 to 1951. He left when, during the McCarthy era, he was asked to compile a dossier on Pete Seeger and the Weavers. For a year and a half he worked as a publicist for MGM publishing.

In June 1953, Wexler became a co-owner of Atlantic Records, where he helped shape rhythm & blues into soul. He gave both Bert Berns and Phil Spector early encouragement as producers, and he helped produce and choose songs for early rhythm & blues stars LaVern Baker, Solomon Burke, Ivory Joe Hunter, the Clovers and Ray Charles. Wexler, Atlantic president Ahmet Ertegun and songwriter Jesse Stone provided the background shouts on Joe Turner's "Shake, Rattle and Roll."

Wexler's most important contribution was matching Aretha Franklin and Wilson Pickett to studio bands in Memphis and Muscle Shoals in the Sixties, thus introducing the Southern soul sound to a mass audience. In the Seventies, often in tandem with Tom Dowd and Arif Mardin, Wexler produced Dr. John, Dusty Springfield, José Feliciano, Jackie DeShannon and others.

In 1978, he joined Warner Bros. as senior vice president, although he continued to produce albums, including Dire Straits' *Communiqué* and Bob Dylan's *Saved.*

THE WHISPERS
Formed 1965, Los Angeles
Walter Scott, Wallace Scott (both b. Sep. 3, 1943, Fort Worth); Nicholas Caldwell (b. Apr. 5, 1944, Loma Linda, Cal.); Marcus Hutson (b. Jan. 8, 1943, L.A.); Gordy Harmon.
N.A.—*Greatest Hits* (Janus)   1974—(– Harmon; + Leaveil Degree [b. July 31, 1948, New Orleans])   1976—*One for the Money* (Soul Train)   1978—*Headlights* (Solar)   1979—*Whisper in Your Ear; Happy Holidays to You*   1980—*The Whispers; Imagination*   1981—*This Kind of Lovin'*   1982—*Best of; Love Is Where You Find It.*

In 1980, after years of minor hits, the Whispers became one of black music's most popular vocal groups. Twin brothers Walter and Wallace Scott formed the group in Los Angeles with Nicholas Caldwell, Marcus Hutson and Gordy Harmon. They cut a few singles in the mid-Sixties on the Dore label before they met producer Ron Carson. Carson produced Whispers singles for Canyon/Soul Clock Records, including "Planets of Life," which became a staple of their live show, and their first chart singles, "Time Will Come" (#17 R&B) and "Seems Like I Gotta Go Wrong" (#6 R&B). When Canyon folded they recorded for Janus.

In 1974, they went to Philadelphia to work with producer/guitarist Norman Harris and the MFSB rhythm section. "Bingo" and "A Mother for My Child" did well. By then, Leaveil Degree had replaced Harmon.

In the late Seventies, the band signed with Dick Griffey's Solar label and began to climb in popularity. "(Olivia) Lost and Turned Out," a song about prostitution, hit #13 on the R&B chart. They followed with "And the Beat Goes On" (#1 R&B) and "Lady" (#3 R&B) from *The Whispers* in 1980 and "It's a Love Thing" (#2 R&B) in 1981.

IAN WHITCOMB
Born July 10, 1941, Woking, England
1965—*You Turn Me On* (Tower)   1966—*Ian Whitcomb's Mod, Mod Music Hall*   1967—*Yellow Underground*   1968—*Sock Me Some Rock*   1970—*World Record Club—On the Pier*   1972—*Under the Ragtime Moon* (UA)   1973—*Hip Hooray For Neville Chamberlain* (Argo)   1976—*Crooner Tunes* (Great Northwest Music Co.)   1977—*Ian Whitcomb's Red Hot Blue Heaven* (First American)   *Treasures of Tin Pan Alley* (Audiophile)   1980—*Pianomelt* (Sierra Brier)   1981—*At the Ragtime Ball* (Audiophile)   *Instrumentals* (First American)   *The Rock 'n' Roll Years*   1982—*Don't Say Goodbye, Miss Ragtime* (Stomp Off)   *In Hollywood!* (First American).

Ian Whitcomb's third single, a falsetto-voiced novelty song called "You Turn Me On," became a Top Ten hit in 1965; it was banned in various American cities, partially because of the heavy breathing and sighing on the record and the title itself. The followup, "N-E-R-V-O-U-S!," was modeled on the hit, but only reached #59 on the charts, and Whitcomb's rock & roll career tailed off.

He has never stopped recording, however, making albums that span the entire history of pop music, as chronicled in his 1972 book *After the Ball—Pop Music from Rag to Rock.* Around that same time, Whitcomb produced *Great Balls of Fire* by Mae West, and Goldie Hawn's single "Pitta Patta."

BARRY WHITE
Born September 12, 1944, Galveston, Texas
1973—*I've Got So Much to Give* (20th Century–Fox)   *Stone Gon'*   1974—*Can't Get Enough*   1975—*Just Another Way to Say I Love You; Barry White's Greatest Hits*   1976—*Let the Music Play; Is This Watcha Wont?*   1977—*Barry White Sings for Someone You Love*   1978—*The Man*   1979—*The Message Is Love* (Unlimited Gold).

With his deep, husky voice, lush musical arrangements and songs that usually dealt with love, singer/songwriter/producer Barry White—despite a somewhat chubby physique—became a sex symbol during the Seventies. White was also one of the pioneering producers in disco, often using large orchestras on his records.

White made his singing debut in a Galveston church choir at age eight. Two years later, he was church organist and served as part-time choir director. At 16, White joined the Upfronts, a Los Angeles R&B band, as a singer/pianist, and two years later he wrote "The Harlem Shuffle," which was recorded by Bob and Earl. The recording used a twenty-piece orchestra and was a hit in 1963.

White developed his writing and production skills and in 1966 went to work as an A&R man for Bronco Records. There he discovered a female vocal trio called Love Unlimited (Diana Taylor, Linda and Glodean James) and produced their gold single, 1972's "Walking in the Rain with the One I Love" (#14 pop, #6 R&B) for Uni Records.

In 1973, White signed with 20th Century–Fox Records and made his national recording debut with "I'm Gonna Love You Just a Little More Baby" (#3 pop, #1 R&B), "Never, Never, Gonna Give Ya Up" (#7 pop, #2 R&B) and "I've Got So Much to Give" (#32 pop, #5 R&B). Also that year he started to write for the Love Unlimited Orchestra, with whom he had a string-laden instrumental disco hit, "Love's Theme" (#1 pop, #10 R&B). Love Unlimited's *Under the Influence* was also a big hit. In 1973 alone, White wrote, produced or performed on records whose total sales exceeded over $16 million.

Among his gold records are *Rhapsody in White* by the Love Unlimited Orchestra (#8 pop), *Can't Get Enough* (#1 pop), "Can't Get Enough of Your Love, Baby" (#1 pop and R&B), "You're the First, the Last, My Everything" (#2 pop, #1 R&B, 1974); *Just Another Way to Say I Love You* (#17 pop) and *Barry White's Greatest Hits* (#23 pop). In 1977, *Barry White Sings for Someone You Love* (#8 pop) went platinum and "It's Ecstasy When You Lay Down Next to Me" (#4 pop, #1 R&B) went gold. At his peak, White toured with an all-female orchestra.

By the late Seventies, White's appeal had begun to cool, though he had minor hits with a cover of Billy Joel's "Just the Way You Are" (#44 R&B, 1979) and in 1982 with the title track from *Change*.

BUKKA WHITE

Born Booker T. Washington White, November 12, 1906, Houston, Mississippi; died February 26, 1977, Memphis, Tennessee
1963—*Bukka White* (Sonet)   1964—*Bukka White* (Columbia)   1966—*Memphis Hot Shots* (Blue Horizon)   1969—*Mississippi Blues* (Takoma)   1970—*Big Daddy* (Biograph)   1975—*Sky Songs, volumes 1 and 2* (Arhoolie).

A cousin of blues guitarist B. B. King (who lived with White when he first moved to Memphis in the late Forties), Bukka White was, after Robert Johnson, a widely heard Delta bluesman. White's guitar playing (usually on an acoustic guitar) has influenced B. B. King and many others; his singing has influenced Richie Havens, among others.

White learned guitar as a child from his father, and at age ten began traveling up and down the Mississippi River as a musician. He also worked as a boxer and a baseball player in the Negro leagues. He began recording in Memphis in 1930 for Victor. In 1937, he recorded his first blues hit, the often-covered "Shake 'Em on Down," for Vocalion in Chicago. But before he could record a followup, he was jailed for two years in Mississippi's Parchman Farm Prison on an assault charge. He was recorded by the Library of Congress while in prison in 1939; pressure from his record company helped win him parole.

Upon his release, White recorded twelve of his most famous sides for the Okeh label, but he found his rough-hewn country blues were out of style. He labored in obscurity until the early Sixties, when John Fahey heard a recording of his "Aberdeen Mississippi Blues," tracked White down in Memphis and recorded him for his own Takoma label.

White's career was revived, and he toured the U.S. and Europe, making occasional film and television appearances. He suffered ill health in the mid-Seventies, entered the City of Memphis Hospital and died of cancer there. The Takoma album and the two *Sky Songs* LPs are considered his best work.

TONY JOE WHITE

Born July 23, 1943, Oak Grove, Louisiana
1968—*Black and White* (Monument)   1969—*Continued*   1970—*Tony Joe*   1971—*Tony Joe White* (Warner Bros.)   1972—*The Train I'm On*   1973—*Home Made Ice Cream*   1977—*Eyes* (20th Century–Fox)   *Tony Joe White*.

One of the prime practitioners of the late-Sixties country-rock style known as bayou rock, Tony Joe White was the only one who actually came from the Louisiana bayous and rose to national prominence.

White began playing music at age 16 and formed Tony and the Mojos. His next band, Tony and the Twilights, went to Texas, where White remained as a solo singer/songwriter after the group disbanded. He then moved to Nashville, made the rounds of music publishers and eventually hooked up with Billy Swan, who produced White's first three albums.

White's first two singles, "Georgia Pines" and "Watching the Trains Go By," went unnoticed. "Soul Francisco" was a big European hit in 1967, and White continued to be a major recording and performing star in Europe for the next five years (in 1972 he toured Europe with Creedence Clearwater). In 1969, he hit the Top Ten with the single "Polk Salad Annie," which showcased White's deep, gruff voice and the stylized guitar technique White called "whomper stomper."

Despite frequent TV appearances, it was White's last hit in the U.S. However, several White songs were hits for other artists: Elvis Presley covered "Polk Salad Annie" (as did Tom Jones) and "I've Got a Thing About You Baby." In 1969, Dusty Springfield had a minor hit with White's "Willie and Laura Mae Jones"; and a year later Brook Benton made it to the Top Five with "A Rainy Night in Georgia."

THE WHO

Formed 1964, London
Peter Dennis Blandford Townshend (b. May 19, 1945, London), gtr., voc.; Roger Harry Daltrey (b. Mar. 1, 1944, London), voc.; John Alec Entwistle (b. Oct. 9, 1944, London), bass, French horn, voc.; Keith Moon (b. Aug. 23, 1947, London; d. Sep. 7, 1978, Eng.), drums.
1965—*My Generation* (MCA)   1966—*Happy Jack*
1967—*The Who Sell Out*   1968—*On Tour; Magic Bus*   1969—*Tommy*   1970—*Live at Leeds*   1971—
Who's Next; Meaty, Beaty, Big and Bouncy   1973—
Quadrophenia (Track)   1974—*Odds and Sods*   1975—
The Who by Numbers   1978—*Who Are You*

The Who: Roger Daltrey, Pete Townshend, John Entwistle, Keith Moon

1979—*The Kids Are Alright* (soundtrack) (− Moon)
Quadrophenia (soundtrack) (Polydor)   (+ Kenney Jones [b. Sep. 16, 1948, London], drums)   1981—*Face Dances* (Warner Bros.)   1982—*It's Hard.*
Pete Townshend solo: 1972—*Who Came First* (Decca)
1977—*Rough Mix* (MCA) (with Ronnie Lane)   1980—
Empty Glass (Atco)   1982—*All the Best Cowboys Have Chinese Eyes*   1983—*Scoop.*
Baba Society: 1970—*Happy Birthday*   1972—*I Am*
1976—*With Love* (on three songs).
John Entwistle solo: 1971—*Smash Your Head Against the Wall* (Decca)   1972—*Whistle Rymes*   1973—*John Entwistle's Rigor Mortis Sets In* (MCA)   1975—*John Entwistle's Ox: Mad Dog*   1981—*Too Late the Hero* (Atco).
Keith Moon solo: 1975—*Two Sides of the Moon* (MCA).
Roger Daltrey solo: 1973—*Daltrey* (MCA)   1975—*Ride a Rock Horse*   1977—*One of the Boys*   1980—*McVicar* (soundtrack) (Polydor)   1982—*Best Bits* (MCA).

The Who showed up with blasts of power chords and shouts of adolescent rage, acting out teen aggression by smashing their instruments after concerts. Guitarist and main songwriter Pete Townshend took on the mantle of spokesman for "My Generation" and declared, "Hope I die before I get old," but the Who have stayed together as Townshend has aged, expanding their songs into rock operas like *Tommy* and *Quadrophenia*, texturing their guitar-based attack with keyboards and synthesizers and trying to stay relevant to "the kids" without fooling themselves.

All four band members grew up around London—Townshend, Roger Daltrey and John Entwistle in the working-class area Shepherd's Bush. Townshend and Entwistle knew each other at school in the late Fifties and played in a Dixieland band when they were in their early teens, with Townshend on banjo and Entwistle on trumpet. They played together in a rock band, but Entwistle left in 1960 to join Roger Daltrey's band, the Detours. When they needed to replace their rhythm guitarist, Entwistle suggested Townshend, and Daltrey switched from lead guitar to vocals when the original singer left.

In late 1963, the Detours came under the wing of managers Helmut Gorden and Pete Meaden, who renamed them the High Numbers and gave them a better-dressed Mod image. They replaced drummer Doug Sanden with Keith Moon, formerly with a surf band, the Beach Combers. The High Numbers released an unsuccessful single, "I'm the Face" b/w "Zoot Suit" (both written by Meaden), then got new managers, former small-time film directors Kit Lambert and Chris Stamp.

The High Numbers became the Who, and with Lambert and Stamp's encouragement they became an even more Mod band, with violent stage shows and a repertoire including blues, James Brown and Motown, because the

Mods were soul fans. The Who's demo of "I Can't Explain," with sessionman Jimmy Page adding guitar, brought them to producer Shel Talmy (who had also worked with the Kinks) and got them a record deal. When "I Can't Explain" came out in January 1965, it was ignored until the band appeared on the TV show "Ready, Steady, Go." Townshend smashed his guitar, Moon overturned his drums and the song eventually reached #8 in Britain.

"Anyway, Anyhow, Anywhere" also reached the British Top Ten, followed in November 1965 by "My Generation." It went to #2 in Britain, but only reached #75 in the U.S. But the Who were already stars in Britain, having established their sound—with Townshend's power chords serving as both rhythm and lead guitar, and Moon thrashing wildly at his cymbals—and their personae. Townshend played guitar with full-circle windmilling motions, Daltrey strutted like a bantam fighter, Entwistle (whose occasional songwriting effort revealed a macabre sense of humor) just stood there unmoved and Moon was all over his drum kit.

After the Who's fourth hit single, "Substitute" (#5 U.K.), Lambert replaced Talmy as producer. Their second album, *A Quick One* (*Happy Jack* in the U.S.), included a ten-minute mini-opera as the title track, shortly before the Beatles' concept album *Sgt. Pepper.* The Who also began to make inroads in the U.S. with "Happy Jack" (#24, 1967) and a tour including the performance filmed at the Monterey Pop Festival in June.

The Who Sell Out featured mock-advertisement songs and genuine jingles from offshore British pirate radio stations; it also contained another mini-opera, "Rael," and a Top Ten hit in England and the U.S., "I Can See for Miles." In October 1968, the band released *Magic Bus,* a compilation of singles and B sides, while Townshend worked on his 90-minute rock opera, *Tommy.* The band performed the opera only twice in its entirety—at London's Coliseum in 1969 and the Metropolitan Opera House in 1970—although excerpts were thereafter part of the live show. Its story—about a deaf, dumb and blind boy who becomes a champion pinball player and then a totalitarian guru—was variously considered profound and pretentious, but "Pinball Wizard" became a hit and *Tommy* caught on.

Troupes mounted productions of it around the world (the Who's performances had been concert versions), and Townshend oversaw a new recording of it in 1972, backed by the London Symphony and featuring Rod Stewart, Steve Winwood, Sandy Denny, Richard Burton and others. In 1975, Ken Russell directed the film version, which included Tina Turner as the Acid Queen and Elton John singing "Pinball Wizard." Moon and Daltrey appeared in the film. Daltrey went on to play Franz Liszt in Russell's *Lisztomania;* he also appeared in *Sextet, The Legacy* and *McVicar.*

In 1972, Townshend privately released his first solo album, a birthday tribute to guru Meher Baba. Bits of *Tommy* turned up on *Live at Leeds,* a juggernaut live set, which was followed by *Who's Next,* a staple of FM rock radio. It included Townshend's first experiments with synthesizers ("Baba O'Reilly," "Bargain," "Won't Get Fooled Again") and sold in the millions.

In October 1973, Townshend unveiled the Who's second double-album rock opera, *Quadrophenia,* a tribute to the tortured inner life of the Mods. It, too, was a hit and became a movie directed by Franc Roddam in 1979, with Sting of the Police in a wordless role. In 1973, Daltrey released his first solo album, with the first recordings of Leo Sayer songs and a big British hit, "Just a Boy."

While the Who were hugely popular, *Quadrophenia* signaled that Townshend was now a generation older than the fans he had initially spoken for. As he agonized over his role as an elder statesman of rock—as he would do for much of the rest of his career—the Who released *Odds and Sods,* a compilation of the previous decade's outtakes. *The Who by Numbers* was the result of Townshend's self-appraisal; it lacked the Who's usual vigor, but yielded a hit single in "Squeeze Box." The band could dependably pack arenas wherever it went, but it took some time off the road after *By Numbers.* Moon released a novelty solo disc, *Two Sides of the Moon.* Entwistle recorded solo LPs with bands called Ox (with whom he toured) and Rigor Mortis, and produced the debut album by the semi-popular Fabulous Poodles. Daltrey also recorded solo, and Townshend collaborated with ex-Faces Ronnie Lane on the mostly acoustic *Rough Mix.*

Meanwhile, punk was burgeoning in Britain, and the Sex Pistols among others were brandishing the Who's old power chords. Townshend's continuing identity crisis showed up in the title of *Who Are You,* but the title song became a hit single (#14) and the album went platinum.

It was the last album by the original band. On September 7, 1978, Keith Moon died of an overdose of a sedative, Heminevrin, that had been prescribed to curb his alcoholism. In 1979, the Who oversaw a concert documentary of their early years, *The Kids Are Alright,* and worked on the soundtrack version of *Quadrophenia.* Kenney Jones, formerly of the Small Faces, replaced Moon, and session keyboardist John "Rabbit" Bundrick began working with the Who. The new lineup toured, but its reception was marred when 11 concertgoers were killed—trampled to death or asphyxiated—in a rush for "festival seating" spots at Cincinnati's Riverfront Coliseum in December 1979.

After 15 years with Decca/MCA, the Who signed a band contract with Warner Bros., and Townshend got a solo deal with Atco. His *Empty Glass* included an angry reply ("Rough Boys") to Jimmy Pursey of Sham 69, who had insulted the Who during an interview. Townshend also appeared solo with an acoustic guitar at a benefit for Amnesty International, recorded as *The Secret Police-*

man's Ball. Classical guitarist John Williams played a duet with him on "Won't Get Fooled Again."

Face Dances was produced by Bill Szymczyk, who had worked with the Eagles; it included the hit single "You Better You Bet," but Townshend later called the new band's debut a disappointment. Entwistle's 1981 solo album *Too Late the Hero* featured Eagle Joe Walsh. One month after *Face Dances* came out, the Who's former producer/manager, Kit Lambert, died after falling down a flight of stairs; he was 45.

Townshend released the wordy *All the Best Cowboys Have Chinese Eyes* early in 1982, and soon followed it with the group's *It's Hard*. After that album was released, the Who played what they said was their last tour, ending with a concert in Toronto on December 17, 1982; they did not, however, rule out further concerts or recordings. And in 1983, Townshend released *Scoop*, a double album of his demo tapes, ranging from early basement recordings to his 16-track home studio productions.

HANK WILLIAMS

Born Hiram Williams, September 17, 1923, Mount Olive, Alabama; died January 1, 1953, Oak Hill, West Virginia
1972—*I Saw the Light* (MGM)   **N.A.**—*Hank Williams Sr.'s Greatest Hits; Very Best of*   **1976**—*Home in Heaven; Live at the Grand Ole Opry*   **1977**—*24 of Hank Williams' Greatest Hits.*

Hank Williams was perhaps the most influential of all country & western musicians. His unique vocal style (he called it "moanin' the blues") and magnetic stage presence led the way for the nationwide popularity of country music. His many C&W #1 records, including "Cold, Cold Heart," "Jambalaya," "Your Cheatin' Heart" and "Hey, Good Lookin'," are still popular today, and his songs have been recorded by countless country and pop musicians.

Hiram "Hank" Williams was born in a two-room sharecropper's shack in southeastern Alabama. His father was shell-shocked from World War I and committed himself to a veterans' hospital when Hank was seven. Williams' mother supported him and his sister. She played organ in the local Baptist church, where Hank sang in the choir, and she bought him a guitar for $3.50. When he was 11, Williams moved in with relatives in a railroad camp and began frequenting the Saturday night dances, where he learned about country music and moonshine. The following year, he moved with his family to the larger town of Greenville and began learning blues songs from a black street singer named Rufe "Tee-Tot" Payne. Williams played on streetcorners with Tee-Tot, sold peanuts and shined shoes.

In 1937, the family moved to Montgomery, Alabama. Hank won an amateur contest by performing his "W.P.A. Blues" and, dubbed the Singing Kid, he secured a twice-weekly radio show on local station WSFA. Soon after, he formed the Drifting Cowboys and began playing the Alabama roadhouse circuit, with his mother as booking agent and driver.

By December 1944, Williams had played nearly every roadhouse in Alabama and had married Audrey Mae Sheppard. Two years later, he signed a songwriting contract with Nashville publishers Acuff-Rose, and he recorded in Nashville on the small Sterling label. Soon after, he got a recording contract with newly formed MGM and began his successful collaboration with producer/arranger Fred Rose. That summer (1948), Williams joined the popular KWKH country music radio program "Louisiana Hayride" in Shreveport. His records starting making the C&W charts, and he finally hit big with "Lovesick Blues," which became the #1 country record of 1949.

On June 11, 1949, Williams played at the Grand Ole Opry for the first time and received an unprecedented six encores. His fame grew along with his touring schedule of one-nighters across the country. Besides recording his bluesy C&W records, he also recorded gospel-influenced songs under the name Luke the Drifter. By 1952, his drinking had gotten out of hand, his health had deteriorated and his marriage ended in divorce.

Williams' chronic back problems had resulted in his dependence on painkillers, and in August he was fired from the Grand Ole Opry because of frequent no-shows. Four months later, at the age of 29, he died of a heart attack in the back of his Cadillac on the way to a show in Canton, Ohio. Many years later reports were issued that he actually died in a Knoxville, Tennessee, hotel room after excessive alcohol and drug consumption.

After his death, his records sold more than ever, and he hit #1 twice more with "Kaw-Liga" and "Take These Chains from My Heart." His son Hank Williams, Jr., recorded his father's songs for the biographical film *Your Cheatin' Heart* (MGM, 1964).

HANK WILLIAMS, JR.

Born Randall Hank Williams, Jr., May 26, 1949, Shreveport, Louisiana
1964—*Your Cheatin' Heart* (soundtrack) (MGM)
1973—*Living Proof* (Warner Bros.)   **1976**—*Hank Williams Jr. and Friends* (MGM)   *14 Greatest Hits*
1977—*The New South* (Warner Bros./Curb)   *One Night Stands*   **1979**—*Family Tradition* (Elektra/Curb)
1981—*Rowdy*   **1982**—*A Country Boy Can Survive.*

Hank Williams' son has carved out a country-rock career of his own.

Young Williams was just 2½ when his father died. He learned to play from his father's friends and associates, who included Jerry Lee Lewis, Johnny Cash, Ray Charles and Brenda Lee. He changed his name to Hank Williams, Jr., and with his mother guiding his career, made his debut at age eight in Swainsboro, Georgia. He made his first appearance at the Grand Ole Opry in 1960 and cut his first record at age 14, "Long Gone Lonesome Blues." His formal concert debut came soon after, at Cobo Hall in Detroit.

Williams then quit school and began touring, also appearing on TV. At 16, he became the youngest songwriter ever to earn a BMI citation; he also had a #1 C&W hit, "Stand in the Shadows." On tour, he mainly performed his father's material, with a band called the Cheatin' Hearts. His *Your Cheatin' Heart* soundtrack LP went gold. He later wrote soundtracks for *Time to Sing* and *Kelly's Heroes*. By age 25, he'd been married and divorced twice, and suffered from drug and alcohol problems.

In 1974, Williams grew disenchanted with Nashville and with living up to his father's legacy, and he temporarily stopped performing. On August 8, 1975, he had a climbing accident in which he fell 490 feet, resulting in injuries so severe that his entire face had to be reconstructed surgically. A year and a half later, he came back in the more rock-oriented "outlaw" mold; fellow "outlaw" Waylon Jennings produced *New South*.

In 1979, Williams' autobiography, *Living Proof*, was published by Putnam. He also recorded in the late Sixties and Seventies as Luke the Drifter, Jr. In 1981, he had one of his biggest country hits with "All My Rowdy Friends (Have Settled Down)."

LARRY WILLIAMS
Born May 10, 1935, New Orleans; died January 2, 1980, Los Angeles
N.A.—*Here's Larry Williams* (Specialty) *Greatest Hits* (Okeh) *The Larry Williams Show* (Decca) **1965**—*Live* (Sue) *Missing and Unissued Sides* (Specialty) **1978**—*That Larry Williams* (Fantasy).

Larry Williams scored important hits in 1957–58 with "Short Fat Fanny" (#5 pop, #2 R&B), "Bony Moronie" (#14 pop, #9 R&B) (later covered by John Lennon on *Rock 'n' Roll*) and "Dizzy Miss Lizzy" (#69, 1958) (later covered by the Beatles). Their alliterative titles and frantic shouting performances made him a momentary rival to Little Richard. Little Richard was the star performer of Specialty Records, the label that discovered Williams when he was playing piano on R&B sessions for performers like Lloyd Price, Roy Brown and Percy Mayfield.

Williams' first record for Specialty, a cover of Lloyd Price's "Just Because," was a flop, but was followed by his three big hits of 1957–58. When the hits stopped coming, Williams turned to record production for a time, and he grew more and more obscure before his poorly received funk-oriented comeback album for Fantasy in 1978. Two years later, he was found dead in his Los Angeles home, a gunshot wound in his head. The verdict was suicide.

MAURICE WILLIAMS AND THE ZODIACS
Formed 1955, Lancaster, South Carolina
Maurice Williams (b. Apr. 26, 1938); Henry Gasten; Willie Bennet; Charles Thomas.

Maurice Williams and the Zodiacs had only one major hit, "Stay," but it has kept reappearing. In 1960, after being together for five years, first as the Charms, then the Gladiolas, the Excellos and finally the Zodiacs, the group hit with "Stay," a #1 record that sold well over a million copies. Williams wrote the song as he had "Little Darlin'," an unsuccessful single by the Gladiolas but a hit a couple of years later for the Diamonds. In 1963, "Stay" became one of the Hollies' early U.K. hits, and in 1978 Jackson Browne recorded it on *Running on Empty*, as well as performing the number with Bruce Springsteen on the 1979 *No Nukes* LP.

OTIS WILLIAMS AND THE CHARMS
Formed 1954, Cincinnati, Ohio
Otis Williams (b. June 2, 1936), lead voc.; Roland Bradley; Joe Penn; Richard Parker; Donald Peak.

The Charms, a Fifties vocal group from Cincinnati, began a string of Top Ten R&B hits in 1955 with their debut disc, "Hearts of Stone" (#15 pop, #1 R&B). That year, they also scored with "Ling, Ting, Tong" (#26 pop, #6 R&B) and "Two Hearts" (#9 R&B). In 1956, Williams took top billing. Two more Top Ten R&B hits followed—"Ivory Tower" (#11 pop, #9 R&B) in 1956 and "United" (#5 R&B) in 1957—and the group remained together until 1964 without any further chart success.

After they disbanded, Williams continued to record solo, first on Okeh and then for Stop, where he and his group sang country-style tunes billed as Otis Williams and the Midnight Cowboys.

PAUL WILLIAMS
Born September 19, 1940, Omaha, Nebraska
1970—*Someday Man* (Reprise) **1971**—*Just an Old Fashioned Love Song* (A&M) **1973**—*Life Goes On* **1974**—*Here Comes Inspiration; A Little Bit of Love* **1975**—*Phantom of the Paradise; Ordinary Fool; Bugsy Malone.*

Singer/songwriter Paul Williams started out as a set painter and stunt man in films. In *The Loved One* in 1964, 24-year-old Williams was cast as a ten-year-old child genius. In 1965, he appeared with Marlon Brando in *The Chase*, as another punk kid.

While on the set of *The Chase*, Williams first tried his hand at songwriting. He wrote songs with Biff Rose and comedy sketches for Mort Sahl before teaming up in 1967 with lyricist Roger Nichols. Together they wrote such million-selling MOR pop hits as the Carpenters' "We've Only Just Begun" (which started out as a commercial jingle for a bank) and "Rainy Days and Mondays," and

Three Dog Night's "Just an Old Fashioned Love Song" and "Out in the Country."

Despite his limited voice, Williams became a successful singer in his own right, and has long been a regular on the talk show and Las Vegas circuits. In 1975, Williams teamed up with lyricist Ken Ascher. A year later, he starred in the title role of the rock film *Phantom of the Paradise*, for which he wrote the soundtrack. The next year, he scored Alan Parker's child-gangster film *Bugsy Malone* and contributed songs to the Barbra Streisand-Kris Kristofferson remake of a *A Star Is Born*. His brother Mentor Williams is a country record producer and wrote "Drift Away."

THE TONY WILLIAMS LIFETIME

Formed 1969
Tony Williams (b. Dec. 12, 1945, Chicago), drums; John McLaughlin (b. Jan. 4, 1942, Yorkshire, Eng.), gtr.; Larry Young, organ.
1969—*Emergency* (Polydor)   (+ Jack Bruce [b. May 14, 1943, Glasgow, Scot.], bass, voc.)   1970—*Turn It Over*   1971—(− McLaughlin; − Bruce; + Ted Dunbar [b. Jan 17, 1937, Port Arthur, Texas], gtr.; + Warren Smith [b. May 14, 1934, Chicago], percussion; + Don Alias, percussion; + Juni Booth, bass)   *Ego*   (− Young; − Dunbar; − Smith; + Webster Lewis, organ; + David Horowitz, kybds.; + Tequila, gtr., voc.; + Tillmon Williams, tenor sax; + Herb Bushler, bass)
1972—*The Old Bum's Rush*   (disbanded; re-formed 1975: Allan Holdsworth, gtr.; Alan Pasqua, kybds.; Tony Newton, bass, voc.)   1976—*Believe It* (Columbia)   *Million Dollar Legs*.
Tony Williams solo: 1979—*The Joy of Flying*.

Tony Williams' shifting accents helped define the sound of the Miles Davis Quintet of the Sixties, a group Williams joined when he was 17. In 1969, after playing with Davis and on numerous Blue Note jazz sessions, he left to form one of the first jazz-rock fusion bands, the Tony Williams Lifetime, with organist Larry Young, guitarist John McLaughlin (who also worked with Davis at the time) and ex-Cream bassist Jack Bruce.

Lifetime played highly complex hard rock, presaging the late-Seventies "punk-funk-jazz" of Ornette Coleman and James "Blood" Ulmer, but after its first two albums the original Lifetime disbanded. Williams freelanced as a jazz drummer and tried making a more conventional funk album, *The Old Bum's Rush,* on which he sang. He joined fellow Davis quintet veterans under Herbie Hancock's leadership in VSOP, with whom he has continued to tour and to record.

In the mid-Seventies, Williams organized another version of Lifetime, featuring guitarist Allan Holdsworth, formerly of Soft Machine and Gong. Like the first Lifetime, the group was critically acclaimed but sold poorly and broke up again. Williams' 1979 solo LP featured both

fusion players and a duet with avant-garde pianist Cecil Taylor. Williams continues to work in a variety of groups.

SONNY BOY WILLIAMSON

Sonny Boy No. 1: born John Lee Williamson, March 30, 1914, Jackson, Tennessee; died June 1, 1948, Chicago
Sonny Boy No. 2: born Aleck "Rice" Miller, December 5, 1899, Glendora, Mississippi; died May 25, 1965, Helena, Arkansas
Sonny Boy No. 1: N.A.—*Sonny Boy Williamson* (RCA) *Bluebird Blues; Sonny Boy, volume 1, 2 and 3* (Blues Classics).
Sonny Boy No. 2: 1962—*Bummer Road* (Chess)   **1963**—*Sonny Boy and Memphis Slim* (Vogue)   **1965**—*This Is My Story* (Chess)   **1966**—*Sonny Boy Williamson* (Storyville)   **1967**—*The Original* (Blues Classics)   **1975**—*And the Animals* (Charly, U.K.)   **1976**—*King Biscuit Time* (Arhoolie).

There were two Sonny Boy Williamsons. The first was John Lee Williamson, who recorded very little and is known mainly as a major influence on such blues-harp giants as Little Walter Jacobs and Junior Wells. The second was Rice Miller, by far the better known.

The first Sonny Boy worked with Sleepy John Estes and Homesick James as a teenager. He moved to Chicago in 1937, where he recorded "Good Morning, Little School-girl" and "Sugar Mama" for RCA/Bluebird and played in a small group featuring Big Bill Broonzy. He was killed in a brutal attack and robbery.

The second Sonny Boy was the author of such blues standards as "One Way Out" (covered by the Allman Brothers Band), "Bye Bye Bird" (covered by the Moody Blues), "Help Me" (covered by Van Morrison), "Eyesight to the Blind" (covered by the Who on *Tommy*), "Fattening Frogs for Snakes" and "Don't Start Me Talking."

He first came to prominence, still known as Rice Miller, singing and playing blues harp on the popular radio show "King Biscuit Time," broadcast from Helena, Arkansas. At that time, Miller appropriated the name Sonny Boy Williamson (something the confusion surrounding the "race record" market of the time allowed him to get away with, as did his undoubted prowess on the harmonica). He first recorded in 1951 for the Jackson, Mississippi, Trumpet label, then went to Chicago in 1955 to begin recording blues hits for Chess, backed at times by the Muddy Waters band.

Rice Miller made his first British tour in 1963, causing a sensation with a two-tone suit and bowler hat. In subsequent U.K. tours, he appeared on the British rock TV show "Ready, Steady, Go" and recorded live albums with British Invasion bands the Yardbirds and the Animals. Shortly before his death, Williamson jammed with an early version of the Band, then called Levon and the Hawks. He died of tuberculosis.

CHUCK WILLIS
Born January 31, 1928, Atlanta, Georgia; died April 10,
1958, Atlanta
1980—*Chuck Willis—My Story* (Columbia).

Chuck Willis was a blues singer/songwriter best remembered as the "King of the Stroll."

As a teen, Willis was a popular R&B singer around Atlanta. A local DJ, Zenus "Daddy" Sears, took him to Columbia Records in 1952, where he cut a few minor releases for their Okeh label. Oft-recorded Willis tunes include "I Feel So Bad" (Foghat, Delbert McClinton) and "Hang Up My Rock 'n' Roll Shoes" (the Band, Jerry Lee Lewis). Willis, wearing turbans on stage—at one point he owned 54 of them—was often introduced to audiences as the "Sheik of the Shake."

In 1956, Jerry Wexler signed Willis to Atlantic Records, and the next year Willis cut the blues standard "C.C. Rider" (#12 pop, #3 R&B). It was a major hit and established him as the "King of the Stroll." But within the year, Willis died in a car accident near Atlanta. Posthumously, "What Am I Living For?" (#9 pop, #3 R&B) became his biggest crossover hit. In 1980, Columbia reissued his Okeh recordings on *Chuck Willis—My Story*.

BOB WILLS AND HIS TEXAS PLAYBOYS
Formed 1935, Tulsa, Oklahoma
Bob Wills (b. March 6, 1905, Limestone, Texas; d. May 13, 1975)
1958—*Bob Wills and His Texas Playboys* (MCA)
1963—*Bob Wills Sings and Plays* (Liberty) **1968**—*King of the Western Swing* (MCA) **1969**—*The Best of Bob Wills and His Texas Playboys; Living Legend* **1971**—*In Person* **1973**—*Anthology* (Columbia) **1974**—*For the Last Time* (United Artists) **1975**—*Fathers and Sons* (Epic) **1976**—*Remembering . . .* (Columbia).

Fiddler/bandleader Bob Wills helped change the course of country and pop music in the Thirties with his Texas Playboys, a Western swing band numbering anywhere from 13 to 18 members, who fused country & western, pop, blues and Big Band swing. This seminal unit introduced horns, drums and electric guitars to country music.

The eldest of ten children of a fiddle-playing father, Wills moved with his family to Memphis in 1913 and began playing fiddle and mandolin in square-dance bands. He moved to Fort Worth in 1929. A year later, Wills joined the Light Crust Dough Boys with Milton Brown, and they began recording in 1932. Wills was fired from the band in 1933 for excessive drinking and personality conflicts with leader W. Lee O'Daniel. Wills left with banjoist Johnnie Lee Wills to form the Playboys, and they soon became regulars on radio broadcasts by WACO in Waco, Texas.

They moved to Tulsa, Oklahoma, and became regulars on KVOO. As Bob Wills and His Texas Playboys, they began recording for Brunswick in 1935. In April 1940, they recorded the million-selling "San Antonio Rose" (his biggest hit), which also became a million-seller for Bing Crosby. In the late Thirties, Wills's daughter Laura Lee became lead singer with the band; she also wrote songs, and later married Texas Playboys guitarist Dick McBride.

Wills maintained the Texas Playboys through the early Sixties. In 1962, his health began to deteriorate and he suffered a series of heart attacks. In 1968, he was named to the Country Music Hall of Fame. In 1973, during his last recording session, he suffered a stroke from which he never recovered, entering a coma that lasted until his death in 1975. A year later, the Texas Playboys reunited for some memorial concerts.

JACKIE WILSON
Born June 9, 1934, Detroit
1983—*The Jackie Wilson Story* (Epic).

Jackie Wilson was one of the premier black vocalists of the late Fifties and the Sixties.

Wilson grew up in a rough section of Detroit. In the late Forties, he lied about his age, entered the Golden Gloves and won in his division. He later quit at his mother's request. He had sung throughout his childhood, and after high school, he began performing in local clubs. He was discovered by Johnny Otis at a talent show in 1951.

In 1953, Wilson successfully auditioned for Billy Ward and the Dominoes, replacing Clyde McPhatter, who had joined the Drifters. In 1956, he went solo, signing with Brunswick Records. His first single, "Reet Petite" (#62 pop, #11 R&B), written by his friend Berry Gordy, Jr., appeared in 1957.

In 1958, Wilson began making his mark with "To Be Loved" (#22 pop, #11 R&B) and "Lonely Teardrops" (#7 pop, #1 R&B), another Gordy tune. He hit his commercial stride in 1959 with "That's Why" (#13 pop, #2 R&B), "I'll Be Satisfied" (#20 pop, #6 R&B), "You Better Know It" (#37 pop, #1 R&B) and "Talk That Talk" (#34 pop, #3 R&B). His success continued in 1960 with "Night" b/w "Doggin' Around" (#4 pop, #1 R&B), "All My Love" and "Am I the Man" b/w "Alone at Last" (#8 pop, #10 R&B). His stage show was as athletic as James Brown's, and the sexual hysteria surrounding Wilson at this time was such that his audiences were often worked up into a frenzy. In 1961 he was shot and seriously wounded by a female fan in a New York hotel. That year he hit big with "My Empty Arms" (#9 pop, #10 R&B).

With the exception of the frenzied "Baby Workout" (#5 pop, #1 R&B) in 1963, Wilson's next few years yielded few hits. Then in 1966 he was matched with veteran producer Carl Davis, with whom he scored two hits: "Whispers" (#11 pop, #5 R&B) and "(Your Love Keeps Lifting Me) Higher and Higher" (#6 pop, #1 R&B). Unfortunately, these were Wilson's last great recordings, although he continued to chart singles as a pop style

Jackie Wilson

crooner through 1972. By 1975 he was playing the oldies circuit. On September 25, 1975, at a Dick Clark revue in the Latin Casino in Cherry Hill, New Jersey, he suffered a heart attack on stage and has been hospitalized and in a coma ever since.

JESSE WINCHESTER
Born May 17, 1944, Shreveport, Louisiana
1971—*Jesse Winchester* (Ampex; reissued 1976 by Bearsville) **1972**—*Third Down, 110 to Go* (Bearsville) **1974**—*Learn to Love It* **1976**—*Let the Rough Side Drag* **1977**—*Nothin' but a Breeze* **1978**—*A Touch on the Rainy Side.*

Singer/songwriter Jesse Winchester's early albums were tales of exile from a Southerner who had moved to Canada to avoid the draft. His later work, after he was granted amnesty, has leaned toward easygoing love songs, but Winchester still has a distinctive voice and a style that encompasses acoustic folk and Memphis rockabilly.

Winchester grew up in Memphis and played piano and sang with his church choir. He also learned guitar, and as a teenager he joined various unsuccessful rock bands. In 1967, he went to study in Munich, Germany, and when he found out that his draft notice had arrived at home, he went to Canada, where he's kept a residence ever since.

In 1970, Winchester met Robbie Robertson of the Band, who got him a management contract with Albert Gross-man. Robertson produced and played on Winchester's debut LP, which included the much-covered songs "Biloxi," "The Brand New Tennessee Waltz" and "Yankee Lady." Todd Rundgren produced part of Winchester's second album (the title refers to Canadian football) and, like the debut, it garnered rave reviews.

Winchester became a Canadian citizen in 1973, and didn't tour the U.S. until after President Carter declared amnesty for draft evaders in 1977. Since then, he has appeared regularly in U.S. clubs, both with a band and as a solo performer.

EDGAR WINTER
Born December 28, 1946, Beaumont, Texas
1970—*Entrance* (Epic) **1971**—*White Trash* **1972**— *Road Work* **1973**—*They Only Come Out at Night* **1974**—*Shock Treatment* **1975**—*Jasmine Nightdreams* (Blue Sky) *With Rick Derringer* **1976**—*With Johnny Winter: Together* **1977**—*Recycled* **1979**—*Edgar Winter Album.*

Vocalist/keyboardist/saxophonist Edgar Winter is Johnny Winter's younger brother. After Edgar and Johnny played together in their teens in the Black Plague, the two pursued solo careers in the early Sixties. Edgar was playing in a jazz group around the time that Johnny rose suddenly to fame in the late Sixties. Edgar joined his brother's band, playing sax and keyboards, then left to pursue a solo career.

On his debut, Edgar played many instruments himself; though it was critically well received, it sold poorly. For his next two albums, he formed the jazz/R&B horn band White Trash, which became a popular concert attraction (they played the closing night of New York's Fillmore East). Edgar broke the band up, however, and next formed the experimental hard-rock quartet the Edgar Winter Band, which featured bassist/vocalist Dan Hartman and guitarist Ronnie Montrose. Their first release was a single, "Hangin' Around," backed by an instrumental called "Frankenstein."

An edited "Frankenstein" became the A side of the single; it went to #1 in the U.S. and sold platinum worldwide, as did the Edgar Winter Band's first album, *They Only Come Out at Night.*

In late 1973, as "Free Ride" became another smash hit single, Rick Derringer, who'd produced *White Trash* and *They Only,* joined Edgar's band, replacing Jerry Weems, who'd replaced Montrose. They became a major concert attraction, and the *Shock Treatment* album, featuring Derringer, sold well. Edgar then recorded a solo LP, *Jasmine Nightdreams,* but returned to the group for the more rock-oriented *With Rick Derringer.* Edgar appears on Johnny Winter's *Johnny Winter* and *Second Winter,* Derringer's *All American Boy* and *Spring Fever,* Dan Hartman's first three solo LPs and Bette Midler's *Songs for the New Depression.* In 1976, Edgar cut an album of oldies with brother Johnny. Except for two subsequent solo albums, he has been fairly inactive since.

JOHNNY WINTER
Born February 23, 1944, Leland, Mississippi
1969—*Progressive Blues Experiment* (Liberty)   *Johnny Winter* (Columbia)   **1970**—*Second Winter* (Columbia)   **1971**—*Story* (GRT)   *And* (Columbia)   *And Live; About Blues* (Janus)   *Early Times*   **1973**—*Still Alive and Well* (Columbia)   **1974**—*Saints and Sinners; John Dawson Winter III* (Blue Sky)   **1976**—*With Edgar Winter: Together; Captured Live*   **1977**—*Nothin' but the Blues*   **1978**—*White Hot and Blue*   **1980**—*Raisin' Cain; Johnny Winter Story.*

Johnny Winter came to fame as a much-heralded white blues guitarist and was popular in the Seventies with blues-based hard rock. In recent years he returned even more strongly to his blues roots by backing up Muddy Waters on concert tours and some recordings.

Winter grew up in Beaumont, Texas, the son of a banjo- and saxophone-playing father and a piano-playing mother. Both he and his younger brother Edgar—who are both albinos—learned several instruments, and in their teens they formed local rock bands with names like It and Them and the Black Plague, playing mainly blues and rock. After graduating high school, Johnny enrolled in Lamar Technical College, but soon dropped out.

He hitchhiked to Louisiana, where he backed up local blues and rock musicians, and in the early Sixties he traveled to Chicago, where he frequented blues clubs. In 1962, Winter played with Mike Bloomfield and Barry Goldberg, among others (they went on to form Electric Flag). Winter eventually returned to Texas, where he played with various journeyman blues bands.

After a few years of garnering local raves on the Georgia-Florida circuit, a 1968 *Rolling Stone* article, in which Winter was described as a "cross-eyed albino with long fleecy hair, playing some of the gutsiest fluid blues guitar you've ever heard," brought Winter to national attention. New York club owner Steve Paul read the article and flew out to Texas to sign Winter. Paul installed him as a regular attraction at his club, the Scene, in New York, and within weeks Winter was attracting capacity audiences.

Winter's debut album for Columbia sold well; concurrent with its release came *Progressive Blues Experiment,* an album of demo tapes Winter had been peddling around before he got signed. *Second Winter,* recorded in Nashville, won even more ecstatic raves and bigger sales than the debut. After that album, Winter assembled a new band (his previous one had been with him since his Texas-journeyman days), including his brother Edgar, guitarist Rick Derringer, bassist Randy Hobbs and drummer Randy Zehringer from the McCoys, who'd had a massive hit a few years earlier with "Hang On Sloopy." This band

Johnny Winter, Randy Hobbs, Richard Hughes

recorded *And,* after which Bobby Caldwell replaced Zehringer for *And Live.* While both albums were successful, Winter's heavy touring schedule and mounting heroin problems forced him to retire for a time.

Winter came back in 1973 with *Still Alive and Well,* which featured a song Mick Jagger and Keith Richards had written for Winter, "Silver Train." Critically, it and *Saints and Sinners* are considered Winter's last great albums. In 1976, he worked with brother Edgar for the first time in several years on *Together;* by that time, Edgar's popularity had eclipsed Johnny's. For *Nothin' but the Blues,* Winter was joined by Muddy Waters and his band, but the set received only moderate critical reaction and went largely unnoticed. Since then, Winter has toured and frequently played festivals as a member of Waters' backing band, as well as touring on his own. He produced and sat in on Waters' late-Seventies LPs *Hard Again, I'm Ready* and *Live.*

STEVE WINWOOD
Born May 12, 1948, Birmingham, England
1977—*Steve Winwood* (Island)   **1980**—*Arc of a Diver*
1982—*Talking Back to the Night.*

Keyboardist/singer Steve Winwood has found his own hugely successful blend of pop and R&B after years of working with blues, pop and experimental bands.

Winwood began playing piano as a child, and picked up bass, guitar and drums as a teenager. At 15, he was a member of his older brother Muff Winwood's jazz band, and a year later the two joined the Spencer Davis Group. Stevie Winwood's lead vocals and insistent organ riffs gave the band hits with "Gimme Some Lovin' " and "I'm a Man."

At 18, Winwood participated in a studio group, Powerhouse, that included Eric Clapton on guitar; their tracks appeared on *What's Shakin'*, an Elektra Records sampler. Winwood then went on to form Traffic, while Clapton worked with Cream. During Traffic's on-again, off-again existence (1967–74), Winwood appeared with Clapton in the short-lived supergroup Blind Faith and with Ginger Baker's Air Force.

In 1970, Winwood began work on a solo album to be called *Mad Shadows,* but it eventually became the reformed Traffic's *John Barleycorn Must Die.* After Traffic's final album, *When the Eagle Flies,* Winwood worked with Japanese percussionist Stomu Yamashta and German synthesizer player Klaus Schulze in 1976, resulting in an album, *Go,* and a concert at Royal Albert Hall in London.

Winwood's 1977 solo debut, which used a backup band, was a modest success. But 1980's *Arc of a Diver,* on which Winwood played all the instruments but sang lyrics written by others (including Viv Stanshall of the Bonzo Dog Band and Will Jennings), went platinum, with a Top Ten single, "While You See a Chance." *Talking Back to the Night,* made with the same method, was also a hit album. Winwood has also appeared on the soundtrack of *They Call It an Accident.* When not recording, he works on his farm near Gloucester, where the studios he built are located.

BILL WITHERS

Born July 4, 1938, Slab Fork, West Virginia
1971—*Just As I Am* (Sussex)   **1972**—*Still Bill*   **1973**— *Live at Carnegie Hall*   **1974**—+*'Justments*   **1975**—*The Best of Bill Withers; Making Music* (Columbia)   **1976**— *Naked and Warm*   **1978**—*Menagerie; 'Bout Love* **1980**—*Best of* (Columbia).

Singer/songwriter Bill Withers, whose understated hits mix folk and soul music, was nearly thirty years old before he sought a career in music.

Withers graduated high school and worked as a mechanic. In 1967, he moved to Los Angeles and, while working in an aerospace factory, began recording demos of his songs, which got no response.

Withers had just learned to play guitar, but was considering giving up songwriting when he met Booker T. Jones in 1970. Later that year, Jones produced Withers' debut LP (*Just As I Am*) and the gold single "Ain't No Sunshine." In 1971, the record hit #3, and Withers made his performing debut in Los Angeles. His followup, "Grandma's Hands," hit #42 pop (#18 R&B) and has since been recorded by a number of other singers. *Still Bill* in 1972 was even more successful, containing "Lean on Me" (#1 pop and R&B, 1972) and "Use Me" (#2 pop and R&B, 1972). Other hits included "Let Us Love" (#17 R&B, 1972), "Kissing My Love" (#12 R&B, 1973) and "Friend of Mine" (#25 R&B, 1973).

Withers signed with Columbia in 1975, and there he recorded four albums. *Making Music* (1975) contained "Make Love to Your Mind" (#10 R&B), and *Menagerie* (1977) had "Lovely Day" (#30 pop, #6 R&B), but subsequent releases were not nearly as successful as his early albums. He sang on Grover Washington, Jr.'s *Winelight* in 1981 and cowrote and sang "Just the Two of Us" (#2 pop, #3 R&B), one of that year's most popular singles.

BOBBY WOMACK

Born March 4, 1944, Cleveland, Ohio
1972—*Understanding* (United Artists)   **1973**—*Communication; Facts of Life*   **1974**—*Looking for a Love Again*   **1975**—*Greatest Hits; I Don't Know What the World's Coming To*   **1976**—*Safety Zone; BW Goes C&W; Home Is Where the Heart Is* (Columbia) *Pieces*   **1979**—*Roads of Life* (Arista)   **1981**—*The Poet* (Beverly Glen).

As a writer and performer, guitarist Bobby Womack has been one of the most important black musicians of the last 15 years.

Womack and his four brothers formed a gospel group, the Womack Brothers, in the late Fifties. On the gospel circuit, they met the Soul Stirrers and lead singer Sam Cooke, who later recruited Womack for his own pop band. Cooke then signed the Womack Brothers to his Sar label,

Bobby Womack

where, as the Valentinos, they cut two R&B classics, "It's All Over Now" and "Lookin' for a Love" (#8 R&B, 1962). The former would be a major hit for the Rolling Stones, the latter for the J. Geils Band.

After Cooke's death and the Valentinos' breakup, Womack became a top session guitarist. He also continued writing. His "I'm a Midnight Mover" and "I'm in Love" were hits for Wilson Pickett. Reviving his solo career in the late Sixties, Womack had a few moderate soul hits on the Minit label, but really picked up when he moved to United Artists. His solo career took off in the early Seventies with "That's the Way I Feel About 'Cha" (#27 pop, #2 R&B) in 1971; "Woman's Got to Have It" (#1 R&B) and "Harry Hippie" (#8 R&B) in 1972; and "Nobody Wants You When You're Down and Out" (#2 R&B) in 1973. His albums with Columbia and Arista saw Womack in a commercial decline. But in 1981 he made a tremendous comeback with the #1 R&B LP *The Poet* and a #3 R&B single, "If You Think You're Lonely Now."

STEVIE WONDER

Born Steveland Judkins or Morris, May 13, 1950, Saginaw, Michigan

1963—*Little Stevie Wonder, the 12 Year Old Genius* (Tamla) **1966**—*Up-Tight* **1967**—*Down to Earth; I Was Made to Love Her* **1968**—*Stevie Wonder's Greatest Hits; For Once in My Life* **1969**—*My Cherie Amour* **1970**—*Stevie Wonder Live; Signed, Sealed and Delivered* **1971**—*Where I'm Coming From; Stevie Wonder's Greatest Hits, volume II* **1972**—*Music of My Mind; Talking Book* **1973**—*Innervisions* **1974**—*Fulfillingness' First Finale* **1976**—*Songs in the Key of Life* **1978**—*Looking Back* **1979**—*Journey Through the Secret Life of Plants* **1980**—*Hotter Than July* **1982**— *Original Musiquarium I.*

Stevie Morris' prodigious musical talents were recognized when Ronnie White of the Miracles heard the ten-year-old boy, blind from birth, playing the harmonica for his children, and introduced him to Berry Gordy, Jr., of the Hitsville U.S.A.—soon Motown—organization. Gordy named him Little Stevie Wonder. His third single, "Fingertips (Part 2)," was a #1 pop and R&B hit eight months later. Both on records and in live shows he was featured playing harmonica, drums, piano and organ, as well as singing—sometimes all in one number.

During his first three years in show business, Wonder was presented as an R&B screamer in the Ray Charles mold; much was made of the fact that both were blind. In 1964, he appeared on the screen in *Muscle Beach Party* and *Bikini Beach*. *Up-Tight* (#3 pop, #1 R&B, 1965) included upbeat numbers like "I Was Made to Love Her" (#2 pop, #1 R&B, 1967), "For Once in My Life" (#2 pop, #2 R&B, 1968) and "Shoo-Be-Doo-Be-Doo-Da-Day" (#9 pop, #1 R&B, 1968). The Wonder style broadened to include Bob Dylan's "Blowin' in the Wind" (#9 pop, #1 R&B, 1966), the optimistic "A Place in the Sun" (#9 pop, #3 R&B, 1968) and an instrumental version of Burt Bacharach's "Alfie." In 1969, he hit the upper regions of the charts with "My Cherie Amour" (#4 pop, #4 R&B) and "Yester-Me, Yester-You, Yesterday" (#7 pop, #5 R&B).

As his adolescence came to an end, Wonder took charge of his career. By the time of *Signed, Sealed and Delivered,* he was virtually self-sufficient in the studio, serving as his own producer and arranger, playing most of the instruments himself and writing material with his wife, Syreeta Wright. In this phase, he scored three more hit singles: "Signed, Sealed, Delivered I'm Yours" (#3 pop, #1 R&B), "Heaven Help Us All" (#9 pop, #2 R&B) and "If You Really Love Me" (#8 pop, #4 R&B).

When he reached his 21st birthday in 1971, he negotiated a new contract with Motown that gave him complete artistic control; he was the first Motown artist to win such freedom. While his singles upheld the company tradition of snappy, hook-happy radio fare, they distinguished themselves with subjects such as ghetto hardship and political disenfranchisement, especially in evidence in "Living for the City" (#8 pop, #1 R&B, 1973). His albums, beginning with *Music of My Mind,* on which he played most of the instruments, were devoted to his more exotic musical ideas (which incorporated gospel, rock & roll, jazz and African and Latin American rhythms). To his panoply of instruments he added synthesizers, which became the signature of his sound.

Wonder's 1972 tour of the United States with the Rolling Stones introduced him to a huge white audience, which helped make #1 pop hits of two singles released within the next year—"Superstition" (#1 R&B) and "You Are the Sunshine of My Life" (#3 R&B)—from *Talking Book.*

In the four years and three albums following *Talking Book,* Wonder made three more #1 pop and R&B singles ("You Haven't Done Nothin'," "I Wish" and "Sir Duke"), sold millions of each and received 15 Grammy Awards. *Innervisions* also included "Higher Ground" (#4 pop, #1 R&B) while *Fulfillingness* yielded "Boogie On Reggae Woman" (#3 pop, #1 R&B). His songs were covered widely, and he was an acknowledged influence on musicians from Jeff Beck to Bob Marley to George Benson. Working with B. B. King, the Jacksons, Minnie Riperton, Rufus and Syreeta Wright, he established himself as a major producer and songwriter. *Songs in the Key of Life* (a package of two LPs and a 45 released after he had signed a $13 million contract with Motown) was a tour de force.

Journey Through the Secret Life of Plants, three years in the making, was ostensibly the soundtrack to an unreleased film of the same name; it was predominantly instrumental and failed to catch on with the public. But *Hotter Than July* contained little of the esoterica that had been

Stevie Wonder

unknown in the U.S. Hit records like "See My Baby Jive" and "I Wish It Could Be Christmas Everyday" showed off Wood's talent for mimicking Phil Spector. The second solo LP, *Eddy and the Falcons,* was an imitator's tour de force, ranging from Elvis Presley to Del Shannon.

When Wizzard disbanded, Wood continued a solo career begun during the latter days of the Move (literally solo—he played all the instruments, including oboe, bassoon and bagpipes) and put together Wizzo. Wood had become linked with the British glitter movement of the early Seventies, thanks to his outlandish garb and face makeup, and as that era waned, so did his career. Late singles were unsuccessful even in England, and his latest group, the Helicoptors, has been roundly ignored. In addition to his records, Wood produced an album for Annie Haslam of Renaissance in 1977, *Annie in Wonderland,* and an album by British doo-wop revivalists Darts.

LINK WRAY
Born circa 1930, Fort Bragg, North Carolina
1960—*Link Wray and the Wraymen* (Epic) **1963**—*Jack the Ripper* (Swan) **1971**—*Link Wray* (Polydor) **1973**—*There's Good Rockin' Tonight* (Union Pacific) **1979**—*Bullshot* (Charisma/Visa,U.K.) **1980**—*Live at the Paradiso.*

One of the more influential rock guitarists of the Fifties, Link Wray introduced the distorted fuzz-tone guitar sound on his million-selling single "Rumble." For that tune, Wray and his band the Wraymen wanted to approximate the effect of a brawl that took place in a dance hall where they were performing. Wray punctured the speaker in his amplifier with a pencil, which added the crackling, burry fuzz-tone sound to a brooding, ominous mid-tempo riff, anticipating heavy metal by more than a decade.

Wray, who is part American Indian, learned bottleneck guitar as a youth, after moving with his family to Arizona. He formed a country band in his late teens with his brothers Doug and Vernon (who sometimes sang under the name Ray Vernon), playing bars, juke joints and brothels. Allegedly in 1954, Wray recorded "Rumble," cowritten by Wray and local DJ Milt Grant; by 1958 it had sold over a million copies and had reached #16 that year.

By that time, Wray had also played on sessions backing his brother Vernon and with Fats Domino and Ricky Nelson on Milt Grant's Washington, D.C., TV show. In 1959, Wray had another instrumental hit with the rockabilly-style "Rawhide." Several similar followups failed to hit, however, and by the mid-Sixties Wray had retired to a family farm commune in Maryland, where he built a three-track studio in a shed, playing live only occasionally in local bars. He recorded in his shed quite often, though; word has it that when his backup musicians could not afford drums, Wray had them stomp on the floor and rattle pots, pans and beer cans instead. Many of Wray's three-

encroaching on his recent albums, returning to the street-dancing spirit of earlier periods (updated in contemporary idioms such as reggae and rap). That album yielded "Master Blaster (Jammin')" (#5 pop, #1 R&B) and his plea for an international holiday in remembrance of Martin Luther King, "Happy Birthday." By 1982, fans, still waiting for another album of new material, were placated with hit singles: "That Girl" (#4 pop), "Do I Do" (#13 pop), a duet with Paul McCartney—"Ebony and Ivory" (#1 pop)—and his thematically programed greatest-hits album *Musiquarium.*

ROY WOOD
Born Ulysses Adrian Wood, November 8, 1946, Birmingham, England
1973—*Boulders* (United Artists) *Wizzard's Brew* (Harvest) **1974**—*See My Baby Jive; Introducing Eddy and the Falcons* (United Artists) **1975**—*Mustard* (Jet) **1976**—*The Roy Wood Story* (Harvest) **1977**—*Super Active Wizzo* (Warner Bros.) **1979**—*On the Road Again.*

Roy Wood enjoyed substantial commercial success in England as the leader of the Move, but he longed to form the Electric Light Orchestra and pick up where "I Am the Walrus" left off. Eventually he did, but ended up leaving that group after just one album to form Wizzard. Like the Move, they were very successful in England and largely track recordings were issued on the 1971 *Link Wray*, a critically acclaimed LP that sold little and was largely made possible by the acclaim Wray had garnered from rock stars like Pete Townshend of the Who, Jeff Beck, Bob Dylan and the Kinks.

Wray followed the 1971 LP with several more unsuccessful albums. In 1977, Wray began working with neorockabilly singer Robert Gordon. Wray stayed with Gordon until 1978, and a year later recorded *Bullshot*, which was unspectacularly received.

BETTY WRIGHT

Born December 21, 1953, Miami, Florida
1968—*My First Time Around* (Atco)   **1971**—*I Love the Way You Love Me* (Alston)   **1974**—*Danger: High Voltage*   **1976**—*Explosion*   **1977**—*This Time for Real*   **1978**—*Betty Wright Live*   **1979**—*Traveling in the Wright Circle*   **1981**—*Betty Wright* (Epic).

Betty Wright's fiery soul vocals made her a strong presence on Miami's black music scene of the Seventies. She continues to make regular appearances on the R&B chart.

Wright started as a gospel singer but soon turned to R&B. At 13, she cut "Paralyzed" for a local label after being discovered singing along to Billy Stewart's "Summertime." Two years later, at 15, her "Girls Can't Do What the Guys Do" (#33 pop, #15 R&B) began an association with Miami's T.K. Records stable (including the Alston label) that would continue until that company's demise in the late Seventies. She was 18 when her spunky late 1971 hit "Clean Up Woman" (#6 pop, #2 R&B) was certified gold. In 1975, she won a Grammy for "Where Is the Love." She also contributed background vocals to T.K. disco hits by K. C. and the Sunshine Band and Peter Brown in the Seventies.

In 1981, Wright's first Epic album included the single "What Are You Going to Do with It," a collaboration between Wright and Stevie Wonder. Later that summer, she contributed the feisty rap to Richard "Dimples" Fields's "She's Got Papers on Me" that helped make it a major black hit.

GARY WRIGHT

Born April 26, 1943, Creskill, New Jersey
1970—*Extraction* (A&M)   **1971**—*Foot Print*   **1972**—*Ring of Changes* (with Wonderwheel)   **1975**—*The Dream Weaver* (Warner Bros.)   *Light of Smiles*   **1977**—*Touch and Gone*   **1979**—*Headin' Home*.

Gary Wright, ex–Spooky Tooth member and successful late-Seventies solo act, started out as a child actor, debuting on the "Captain Video" TV show in New York at age seven. He also appeared in TV and radio commercials and in the Broadway play *Fanny*, all the while studying piano

and organ. He joined various high school rock bands, went to college to study psychology in New York and then to Berlin, Germany.

In Europe, Wright met Mike Harrison, and the two began performing together, leading to the formation of Spooky Tooth. When Spooky Tooth temporarily disbanded in 1970, Wright turned to a solo career, forming the band Wonderwheel. His solo work attracted little attention, though, and in 1973 he returned to the re-formed Spooky Tooth. When the band broke up for good in 1974, Wright again embarked on solo ventures, this time with much more success.

The mellow synthesizer-dominated *Dream Weaver* yielded #2 hit singles in the title tune and "My Love Is Alive," and the LP went platinum. No more hit singles were forthcoming, but Wright's subsequent albums won heavy airplay on FM radio.

O. V. WRIGHT

Born Overton Vertis Wright, October 9, 1939, Memphis, Tennessee
1965—*O. V. Wright* (Backbeat)   **1966**—*Nucleus of Soul*   **1970**—*Ace of Spades*   **1971**—*A Nickel and a Nail*   **1973**—*Memphis Unlimited*   **1975**—*Into Something I Can't Shake* (Hi)   **1978**—*The Bottom Line*.

A Memphis soul singer with a dark and moody voice, Wright has never attained the level of success some critics believe he deserves. His commercial frustrations began in 1965, when Otis Redding hit before Wright did with Wright's "That's How Strong My Love Is."

Wright did have several R&B hits of his own, including "You're Gonna Make Me Cry" (#6, 1965), "Eight Men, Four Women" (#4, 1967), "Ace of Spade" (#11, 1970), "A Nickel and a Nail" (#19, 1971) and "I'd Rather Be Blind, Crippled and Crazy" (#33, 1973). But despite high critical praise and the chilling quality of songs like "Ace of Spade," popular acclaim has continued to elude Wright.

SYREETA WRIGHT

Born Pittsburgh, Pennsylvania
1972—*Syreeta* (Mowest)   **1974**—*Stevie Wonder Presents Syreeta*   **1977**—*One to One* (Tamla)   *Rich Love, Poor Love* (Motown) (with G. C. Cameron)   **1983**—*The Spell* (Tamla).

As a performer, Syreeta Wright has had only one major hit, a duet with Billy Preston on "With You I'm Born Again" (#4 pop) in 1980. But as a writer she contributed to a number of artists, most significantly to her ex-husband, Stevie Wonder.

She cut a single, "Can't Give Back the Love," in 1968. After it flopped, she worked as a Motown secretary and occasional background singer. She met Wonder and began songwriting as a result. Her first two albums, *Syreeta* (1972) and *Stevie Wonder Presents Syreeta* (1974), were produced by Wonder. She was married to Wonder during the period he first sought and achieved artistic independence from Motown.

Wright cowrote songs on Wonder's *Music of My Mind, The Secret Life of Plants* and *Talking Book.* On *Talking Book,* she cowrote "Blame It on the Sun" and "Lookin' for Another Pure Love." She has continued recording for Motown; *The Spell* was produced by Jermaine Jackson.

X

X

Formed 1977, Los Angeles
John Doe (b. 1954, Decatur, Ill.), bass, voc.; Exene (b. Christine Cervenka), voc.; Billy Zoom, gtr.; Don J. Bonebrake (b. N. Hollywood, Calif.), drums.
1980—*Los Angeles* (Slash) **1981**—*Wild Gift* **1982**—*Under the Big Black Sun* (Elektra).

In 1980, X emerged from the L.A. punk scene as the most critically lauded American band of the early decade. X helped to vindicate the West Coast scene, which had lagged behind New York and London's early punk and new wave movements. But while X's music was influenced by punk, their lyrics were more sophisticated. And for all the speed and thrust of their playing, X claims roots in rockabilly and old-time country music, which echoes in the vocal harmonies and husband-wife duets of John Doe and Exene.

The band began in 1977, when John Doe and Billy Zoom met through classified ads in a local publication. Doe's family had moved all around America when he was growing up, and he settled in L.A. in 1976. Zoom had played guitar and sax with Gene Vincent for a while in the Seventies and also fronted his own rockabilly band, who had cut several songs. Exene first met Doe at a poetry workshop in Venice, California, and the two soon became lovers and bandmates. The couple, who later married, also write all the band's lyrics. With Don Bonebrake, they began playing at the Masque, Hollywood's seminal punk club. A local following grew quickly, and in 1979, after seeing a performance at the Whisky, ex-Door Ray Manzarek became their producer.

Their debut LP, *Los Angeles*, out on local Slash Records in 1980, sold over 60,000 copies, an incredible number for a small label, and 1981's *Wild Gift* sold equally well. In L.A., they were considered superstars. Their music touched on rockabilly, heavy metal, punk and country, plus a bit of the Doors with Manzarek's organ and their sped-up version of the Door's "Soul Kitchen." Both records were highlighted by Exene and Doe's minor-key vocal harmonies and by the incisive lyrics. Both LPs topped critics' year-end best-of lists; and in 1981 the band was also featured in two concert films: Penelope Spheeris' punk documentary *The Decline . . . of Western Civilization* and *Urgh! A Musical War.*

X also toured the U.S., finding appreciative audiences along the punk/new wave circuit. In December of 1981, the band signed with Elektra, who released their third LP, *Under the Big Black Sun,* in July 1982. During the year, Exene also worked on a book of poetry with Lydia Lunch for Grove Press called *Adulterers Anonymous.* X sang the title tune of *Breathless* as remade by Jim McBride in 1983.

X: Billy Zoom, John Doe, Exene Cervenka, D. J. Bonebrake

XTC

Formed 1977, Swindon, England
Andy Partridge (b. Swindon, Eng.), gtr., voc., synth.;
Colin Moulding (b. Swindon, Eng.), bass, voc.; Terry
Chambers (b. Eng.), percussion; John Perkins (b.
Eng.), kybds.; − Perkins; + Barry Andrews (b. Eng.),
kybds.
1978—*White Music* (Virgin, U.K.) *Go 2* (− Andrews;
+ Dave Gregory [b. Eng.], gtr., synth.) **1979**—*Drums
and Wires* **1980**—*Black Sea* **1983**—*English Settle-
ment* (Epic).

XTC's dense, quirky art pop, with its innovative jerky
rhythms and odd melodic twists, has earned them critical
respect and a cult following in the U.S., and hits in Britain.

In 1973, they were known as the Helium Kidz, a New
York Dolls–type glitter band that played straight-ahead
rock & roll in their hometown of Swindon, some 75 miles
out of London. The group then included XTC's later
leader, Andy Partridge, plus second writer Colin Moulding and drummer Terry Chambers. In 1976, they became
XTC and reorganized around Partridge's material.

The band then included John Perkins on keyboards,
who was replaced by Barry Andrews before the foursome
recorded their debut LP, *White Music*. That LP and 1978's
Go 2 were initially released in England only. They became
available in the U.S. shortly after their 1979 U.S. debut,
Drums and Wires. By then Andrews had left; he later
toured with Iggy Pop, joined Robert Fripp's short-lived
League of Gentlemen and cofounded Shriekback with
Dave Allen of Gang of Four.

In late 1980, *Black Sea* went to the U.S. Top Fifty. It
was less frenetic, but featured their usual jolting rhythms
and strangely perched hooks plus several songs about war.
English Settlement got rave reviews but didn't sell in
America. It did better in England, yielding the hit "Senses
Working Overtime." It was a double LP in the U.K., with
four songs not included on the U.S. edition. The band
began a spring U.S. tour to promote the record, but
Partridge became ill, which put future touring and the
band's ultimate unity in serious question. During this
period, the group's videos were in moderate rotation on
MTV.

THE YARDBIRDS

Formed 1963, London

Keith Relf (b. Mar. 22, 1943, Richmond, Eng.; d. May 14, 1976, Eng.), voc., harmonica; Chris Dreja (b. Nov. 11, 1946, Surbiton, Eng.), gtr.; Jim McCarty (b. July 25, 1943, Liverpool, Eng.), drums; Paul Samwell-Smith (b. May 8, 1943, Eng.), bass; Anthony "Top" Topham (b. Eng.), gtr. **1963**—(− Topham; + Eric Clapton [b. Mar. 30, 1945, Surrey, Eng.], lead gtr.) **1965**—*For Your Love* (Epic) *Sonny Boy Williamson and the Yardbirds* (Fontana, released 1966) (− Clapton; + Jeff Beck [b. June 24, 1944, Surrey, Eng.], gtr.) *Having a Rave Up with the Yardbirds* (Epic) **1966**—*Over Under Sideways Down* (− Samwell-Smith; + Jimmy Page [b. Jan. 9, 1944, Middlesex, Eng.], bass, later lead gtr.; Dreja to bass; − Beck) **1967**—*Little Games; Greatest Hits.*

The Yardbirds virtually wrote the book on guitar-oriented blues-based rock & roll. They were a crucial link between mid-Sixties British R&B and late-Sixties psychedelia, setting the groundwork for heavy metal. This seminal band spawned three major guitar heroes of the Sixties—Eric Clapton, Jimmy Page and Jeff Beck—who, with the Yard-birds, pioneered almost every technical guitar innovation of the era, including feedback and fuzz tone.

The Yardbirds formed in June 1963 with Keith Relf, Chris Dreja, Paul Samwell-Smith, Jim McCarty and guitarist Anthony "Top" Topham, who was replaced in October by Eric Clapton. Originally called the Most Blueswailing Yardbirds, the fivesome initially played all strict blues covers of Chess/Checker/Vee Jay material. They began to attract a large cult audience, especially when they took over the Rolling Stones' residency at the Crawdaddy Club in Richmond. They soon toured Europe with American bluesman Sonny Boy Williamson; a joint LP under both their names was issued in 1965. (It was re-released in 1975.) The band's first "solo" album in America was *For Your Love* in August 1965, yielding the hit title track written by Graham Gouldman, later of 10cc. (In the U.K., their first LP was titled *Five Live Yardbirds* and was out in 1964. The band's British records had different lineups of songs, album titles and release dates than the U.S. versions.)

The Yardbirds' second U.S. LP, *Having a Rave Up*, featured Clapton on only four cuts. He quit in 1965 because he objected to the band's increased pop-commer-

The Yardbirds: Chris Dreja, Eric Clapton, Paul Samwell-Smith, Keith Relf, Jim McCarty

cial direction. In order to stick with purist blues, he joined John Mayall's band. His replacement was Jeff Beck, and the band soon enjoyed two more hits by Gouldman—"Heart Full of Soul," with its pre-psychedelic guitar fuzz licks, and "Evil Hearted You," which charted in the U.K. only. In 1966, the band had two more hits—"Shapes of Things" and "Over Under Sideways Down"—but then Samwell-Smith bowed out to become a producer full-time. (He had coproduced the band's records.)

His replacement on bass was Jimmy Page, who moved to lead guitar as soon as rhythm guitarist Dreja learned bass. By summer 1966, Page and Beck were coleads. (Page was earlier asked to be Clapton's replacement but declined, recommending Beck instead.) This lineup only lasted until November, but appeared in the rock club sequence in *Blow-Up*. Beck had been missing many shows because of illness, and at the end of the year he suffered a full breakdown. The band floundered from there. They put out one LP in 1967 called *Little Games*, produced by Mickie Most, but it was filled with old demos and bad leftover tracks. It came out only in the U.S. More singles were released, but they didn't go far, and in July 1968 the band finally broke up.

Relf and McCarty formed a folk duo called Together, followed by the classical-rock Renaissance and later the heavy Armageddon—none of which were successful. Relf died of an electric shock at home on May 14, 1976. Dreja became a photographer, and Jimmy Page formed the New Yardbirds, which soon became Led Zeppelin. Several repackagings of Yardbirds tracks were released through the Eighties. In 1971, the *Live Yardbirds* LP (recorded at New York's Anderson Theater on March 30, 1968) was issued, without the band's consent. The group was supposed to have had the right to refuse release, and after hearing the LP they had it withdrawn. It later appeared as a bootleg.

YES

Formed 1968, London
Jon Anderson (b. Oct. 25, 1944, Lancashire, Eng.), voc., percussion; Peter Banks, gtr., voc; Tony Kaye, kybds.; Chris Squire (b. Mar. 4, 1948, London), bass, voc; Bill Bruford (b. May 17, 1948, London), drums.
1969—*Yes* (Atlantic) **1970**—*Time and a Word* **1971**—(− Banks; + Steve Howe [b. Apr. 8, 1947, London], gtr., voc.) *The Yes Album* (− Kaye; + Rick Wakeman [b. May 18, 1949, London], kybds.) *Fragile;* **1972**—*Close to the Edge* (− Bruford; + Alan White [b. June 14, 1949, Durham, Eng.], drums) **1973**—*Yessongs; Tales from Topographic Oceans* **1974**—(− Wakeman; + Patrick Moraz [b. June 24, 1948, Morges, Switz.], kybds.) *Relayer* **1975**—*Yesterdays* (compilation) **1976**—(− Moraz; + Wakeman) **1977**—*Going for the One* (Atlantic) **1978**—*Tormato* **1980**—*Yesshows* (− Anderson; − Wakeman; + Trevor

Yes: Bill Bruford, Rick Wakeman, Chris Squire, Jon Anderson, Steve Howe

Horn, voc.; + Geoff Downes, kybds.) *Drama* **1982**—*Classic Yes* (compilation).
Jon Anderson solo: 1976—*Olias of Sunhillow* (Atlantic) **1980**—*Song of Seven* **1982**—*Animation* **With Vangelis: 1980**—*Short Stories* (Mercury) **1982**—*Friends of Mr. Cairo*.
Bill Bruford solo: 1978—*Feels Good to Me* (Polydor) **1979**—*One of a Kind* **1980**—*Gradually Going Tornado*.
Steve Howe solo: 1975—*Beginnings* (Atlantic) **1979**—*Steve Howe Album*.
Chris Squire solo: 1975—*Fish Out of Water* (Atlantic).
Rick Wakeman solo: 1973—*The Six Wives of Henry VIII* (A&M) **1974**—*Journey to the Center of the Earth* **1975**—*The Myths and Legends of King Arthur; Lisztomania* (soundtrack) **1976**—*No Earthly Connection; White Rock* **1977**—*Criminal Record* **1978**—*Best Known Works* (compilation) **1980**—*Rhapsodies*.

One of the preeminent and most phenomenally successful progressive-rock bands of the Seventies, Yes combined virtuosic musicianship, suitelike neoclassical structures and Crosby, Stills and Nash–style three-part high vocal harmonies to form an elaborate whole that critics called irrelevant, high-flown indulgence—and that audiences loved.

Yes was formed after Jon Anderson met Chris Squire at a London music-industry bar in 1968. Anderson had spent the previous 12 years in various bands, including his brother Tony's unit, the Warriors. Squire, a self-taught bassist, had been in the Syn. With guitarist Peter Banks, keyboardist Tony Kaye and drummer Bill Bruford (who'd played three shows with Savoy Brown), they formed Yes. One of their first engagements was opening for Cream's London farewell concert in November 1968. The band won instant critical acclaim in Britain, and by the time of their debut album, which mixed originals with covers, they were being hailed as "the next supergroup." *Time and a Word,* which used an orchestra to flesh out intricately shifting arrangements, was somewhat less well received.

At this point, the band had yet to break through in America, and was informed by Atlantic Records that the next album might be its last. The departure of Banks to form his band Flash and the arrival of Steve Howe proved decisive. Howe had been with the Syndicate, the In Crowd, Bodast and Tomorrow (who had a minor psychedelic-era hit with "My White Bicycle"). His playing and composing helped make *The Yes Album* their breakthrough, with continual FM airplay making it a gold LP and yielding a minor hit single in "Your Move/I've Seen All Good People."

In 1971, Tony Kaye left to form Badger (he later did sessions with David Bowie, and he joined Detective and the late-Seventies re-formed Badfinger). His replacement was Rick Wakeman, who had garnered acclaim with the Strawbs. *Fragile* further consolidated the band's success. An edited version of "Roundabout" became a Top Fifteen U.S. single, and *Fragile* went gold.

With *Close to the Edge,* Yes's ambitious eclecticism attained new heights. It consisted of three extended cuts, with a four-movement title suite, and it too went gold in short order. After recording that album, Bruford left to join King Crimson (whose leader, Robert Fripp, had once been approached to replace Peter Banks). His replacement was sessionman Alan White, who had played in John Lennon's Plastic On   and had recently been in the Balls with Denny Laine and Steve Gibbons.

The live *Yessongs* was followed by the critically derided *Tales from Topographic Oceans.* The album sold well, however, and the band continued to be a top-drawing concert attraction in the U.S. and U.K. But *Tales* brought to a head the internal conflicts between Wakeman, an extroverted meat-eating beer drinker, and the rest of the band, who were sober vegetarians. Wakeman openly expressed his bewilderment and disillusionment with the album and the band, and soon left.

Wakeman's replacement was Patrick Moraz (like Wakeman, classically trained), of progressive-rock band Refugee, and he debuted on *Relayer,* which like *Close to the Edge* featured a side-long suite on one side and two ten-minute cuts on the other. With the release of the *Yesterdays* compilation (including the full-length Yes cover of Paul Simon's "America," which had been a minor hit single in edited form), the band took a year off to allow each member to pursue solo projects.

After Yes had made a successful world tour with Moraz, Wakeman rejoined the band. Both *Going for the One* and *Tormato* returned to shorter, tighter song structures. But though Yes continued to sell albums and fill arenas, its days seemed numbered. Wakeman left again, followed by Anderson, who had written most of Yes's lyrics. Trevor Horn and Geoff Downes of the new wave band the Buggles (who had had a hit with "Video Killed the Radio Star") debuted on *Drama.* After that album, Yes broke up.

Though an era seemed over, another similar one was just beginning. Howe and Downes joined with Carl Palmer of Emerson, Lake and Palmer and John Wetton to form the progressive-rock supergroup Asia, who debuted in 1982 with a massively successful album. Anderson has continued to make solo albums. Squire and White were forming a band that was tentatively called Cinema. But in mid-1983, Anderson, Kaye, Squire, White and Trevor Rabin announced plans to re-form Yes.

NEIL YOUNG
Born November 12, 1945, Toronto, Canada
1969—*Neil Young* (Reprise)   *Everybody Knows This Is Nowhere*   **1970**—*After the Goldrush*   **1972**—*Harvest; Journey through the Past*   **1973**—*Time Fades Away* **1974**—*On the Beach*   **1975**—*Tonight's the Night; Zuma*   **1976**—*Long May You Run* (with Stephen Stills)   **1977**—*American Stars and Bars*   **1978**—*Decade; Comes a Times*   **1979**—*Rust Never Sleeps; Live Rust* **1980**—*Hawks and Doves*   **1981**—*Re•ac•tor*   **1983**— *Trans; Everybody's Rockin'.*

Singer/songwriter Neil Young is sometimes visionary, sometimes flaky, sometimes both at once. He has maintained a large following since the early Seventies with music in three basic styles—solo acoustic ballads, sweet country rock and lumbering hard rock, all topped by his high voice—and he veers from one to another in unpredictable phases. His subject matter also shifts from personal confessions to allusive stories to bouncy throwaways. A dedicated primitivist, Young is constantly proving that simplicity is not always simple.

As a child, Young moved with his mother to Winnipeg after she divorced his father, a well-known sports journalist. He played in several high school rock bands. In the Sixties, he moved back to Toronto and worked in folk clubs, where he met Steve Stills, Richie Furay and Joni

Neil Young

Mitchell. Mitchell wrote "The Circle Game" for Young after hearing his "Sugar Mountain."

Young formed another rock band, the Mynah Birds (which included Rick James), and after that fizzled he and that band's bassist, Bruce Palmer, drove to Los Angeles in Young's Pontiac hearse. Young and Palmer ran into Stills and Furay out west and formed Buffalo Springfield (see separate entry), one of the most important of the new folk-country-rock bands, who recorded Young's "Broken Arrow," "I Am a Child," "Mr. Soul" and "Nowadays Clancy Can't Even Sing." But friction developed between Stills and Young, and in May 1968 the band split up.

Young acquired Joni Mitchell's manager, Elliot Roberts, and released his debut solo LP in January 1969, co-produced by Jack Nitzsche. While making the album, Young met a West Coast band called the Rockets, whom he renamed Crazy Horse. They were Ralph Molina (drums), Billy Talbot (bass) and Danny Whitten (guitar). Crazy Horse backed Young on *Everybody Knows This Is Nowhere,* recorded in two weeks, which includes three of Young's most famous songs—"Cinnamon Girl," "Down by the River" and "Cowgirl in the Sand."

The LP began to sell rapidly, going gold (and much later platinum), but Young decided to split his time between Crazy Horse and Crosby, Stills and Nash, whom he joined in June. In March 1970, his presence was first felt on CSN&Y's *Déjà Vu.* Young's third solo, the gold (and utterly pessimistic) *After the Goldrush,* included Crazy Horse and 19-year-old guitarist Nils Lofgren. It and the CSN&Y album made Young a superstar singer/songwriter. *Harvest* was another platinum LP, with the #1 single "Heart of Gold."

Young has yet to make an album as commercial and predictable as *Harvest.* CSN&Y had broken up after the release of the live album *Four Way Street* in spring 1971. Young made a movie and soundtrack, *Journey through the Past,* and confused fans further with *Time Fades Away,* a rough-hewn live album recorded with the Stray Gators, including Nitzsche (keyboards), Ben Keith (pedal steel guitar), Tim Drummond (bass) and John Barbata (drums).

In June 1975, Warners consented to release a bleak, ragged album recorded two years earlier, *Tonight's the Night.* The album's dark tone reflected Young's emotional upheaval following the drug deaths of Crazy Horse's Danny Whitten in 1972 and CSN&Y roadie Bruce Berry in the summer of 1973. In November, Young released the harder-rocking *Zuma.* Crazy Horse now included Talbot, Molina and Frank Sampedro (rhythm guitar). In September 1976, Young recorded *Long May You Run* with Steve Stills, which went gold, but he left Stills halfway through a tour.

In June 1977, Young was back on his own with the gold *American Stars and Bars,* again a more accessible effort, with Linda Ronstadt doing backup vocals along with newcomer Nicolette Larson. *Decade* was a carefully chosen, not entirely hit-centered compilation. *Comes a Time* was folkish and went gold.

In the fall of 1978, Young did an arena tour called "Rust Never Sleeps." He played old and new music, performing half the show by himself on piano or guitar, and the other half with Crazy Horse, amid giant mockups of microphones and speakers. In June 1979, he released *Rust Never Sleeps,* with songs previewed on the tour, including "Out of the Blue," dedicated to Johnny Rotten and the Sex Pistols. The album also featured "Sedan Delivery" and "Powderfinger," which Young had once offered to Lynyrd Skynyrd, though they didn't record them. (Back in 1974, Skynyrd had written "Sweet Home Alabama" as an answer to Young's "Southern Man.") In November of 1979, Young released the gold *Live Rust* LP, culled from the fall 1978 shows and the soundtrack to a film of the tour (directed by Young) entitled *Rust Never Sleeps.*

Right before Presidential election week 1980, Young issued *Hawks and Doves,* an enigmatic state-of-the-union address, with one side of odd acoustic pieces and the other of rickety country songs. Exactly one year later, he released *Re•ac•tor,* an all-hard-rock LP, which, despite its title, seemed to have little to do with nuclear power. *Trans* introduced what Young called "Neil 2"; he fed his voice through a computerized vocoder and sang songs like "Sample and Hold." He toured arenas as a solo performer when the album was released, singing his most-requested songs, covering "backstage" action on a large video screen, and singing along with his vocoderized video image on songs from *Trans*. *Everybody's Rockin'* was a rockabilly-style album.

THE YOUNGBLOODS
Formed 1965, Boston
Jesse Colin Young (b. Perry Miller, Nov. 11, 1944, New York City), voc., bass, gtr.; Jerry Corbitt (b. Tifton, Ga.), gtr., voc.; Joe Bauer (b. Sep. 26, 1941, Memphis Tenn.), drums; Banana (b. Lowell Levinger, 1946, Cambridge, Mass.), gtr., kybds.
1967—*The Youngbloods* (RCA)   *Earth Music*   1969— *Elephant Mountain*   (− Corbitt)   1970—*Rock Festival* (Raccoon)   *The Best of the Youngbloods* (RCA)   *Two Trips* (Mercury)   1971—*Ride the Wind* (Raccoon) *Sunlight* (RCA)   (+ Michael Kane, bass)   *Good and Dusty* (Raccoon)   1972—*High on a Ridgetop*.
Jesse Colin Young solo:
1964—*The Soul of a City Boy* (Capitol)   *Youngblood* (Mercury)   1972—*Together* (Warner Bros.)   1973— *Song for Juli*   1975—*Songbird*   1976—*On the Road* 1977—*Love on the Wing*   1978—*American Dreams* (Elektra).

The Youngbloods were a folk-rock group led by Jesse Colin Young. Though they had a jazzy, mellow West Coast sound, their roots were in Boston and New York.

Young started out playing the folk circuit in Greenwich Village, where he met Bobby Scott, a composer/singer/ pianist who had played with Bobby Darin, among others. Scott financed and produced Young's debut, *Soul of a City Boy*. Reputedly cut in four hours, the solo LP of Young and acoustic guitar was released on Capitol in 1964. He began to play the Boston clubs and then cut *Youngblood* for Mercury, again with Scott producing, this time with a backup band including friend John Sebastian.

Inspired by the Beatles, Young decided to form a group, beginning with Massachusetts folkie Jerry Corbitt and then adding Joe Bauer and Lowell "Banana" Levinger, the last being the most accomplished musician of the band. In late 1965, the new Youngbloods cut some tracks for Mercury, but these were not released until years later on *Two Trips*. Their official debut was *Youngbloods*, released in 1967. It included the hit "Grizzly Bear" and "Get Together," written by Dino Valenti, later a singer for Quicksilver. It was first a regional hit, and it didn't take off nationally until it was re-released two years later in July 1969 after it had been used on a TV public service ad for brotherhood. In 1969, it hit #5 and went gold. RCA later renamed the first album after the single.

The band moved to Marin County, California, in late 1967. Their next two LPs were produced in New York by Felix Pappalardi before they went west. The third, *Elephant Mountain*, was overseen by Charlie Daniels. Corbitt left the band during *Elephant Mountain*, and they continued as a trio, signing to Warner Bros., who gave them their own label, Raccoon, in 1970. RCA began to repackage all their older work, including a *Best of* that year, also re-releasing for the third time "Darkness Darkness," previously out in August 1968 and March 1969. It was later covered by Mott the Hoople on their *Brain Capers* LP.

The Youngbloods' first two Warners/Raccoon albums were live recordings—*Rock Festival* (1970) and *Ride the Wind* (1971). In early 1971, they added bassist Michael Kane, freeing Young to play guitar. The band issued two more LPs—*Good and Dusty* and *High on a Ridgetop*— before disbanding in 1972.

Bauer and Banana made solo albums; Corbitt had previously cut two; all of these went nowhere. Bauer, Banana and Kane briefly united to form the band Noggins, doing one LP, *Crab Tunes*, for Raccoon in 1972. Young was the only musician to successfully carry on, releasing his first solo, *Together*, in 1972. His album had the same breezy feel of the Youngbloods, again highlighted by his light, supple vocals. He recorded and toured through the Seventies.

Z

FRANK ZAPPA/MOTHERS OF INVENTION

Formed 1965, Los Angeles
Frank Zappa (b. Dec. 21, 1940, Baltimore), gtr., voc., miscellaneous.
1966—*Freak Out* (Verve) **1967**—*Absolutely Free;
We're Only in It for the Money; Lumpy Gravy* **1968**—
Cruisin' with Ruben and the Jets **1969**—*Mothermania;
Uncle Meat* (Bizarre) **1970**—*Weasels Ripped My Flesh;
Chunga's Revenge; Hot Rats; Burnt Weeny Sandwich*
1971—*Mothers Live at the Fillmore* **1972**—*Just Another Band from L.A.; 200 Motels* (United Artists)
The Grand Wazoo (Bizarre) *Waka Jawaka*
1973—*Overnight Sensation* (Discreet)
1974—*Apostrophe; The Roxy and Elsewhere; One Size
Fits All* **1975**—*Bongo Fury* **1976**—*Zoot Allures*
1978—*In New York; Studio Tan* **1979**—*Sleep Dirt;
Orchestral Favorites; Sheik Yerbouti* (Zappa) **1980**—
Joe's Garage, Act I; Joe's Garage, Acts 2 and 3 **1981**—
Tinseltown Rebellion (Barking Pumpkin) *Shut Up 'n'
Play Yer Guitar; Shut Up 'n' Play Yer Guitar Some More;
Return of the Son of Shut Up 'n' Play Yer Guitar; You
Are What You Is* **1982**—*Ship Too Late to Save a
Drowning Witch.*

One of rock's most consistently controversial figures, composer/arranger/guitarist/bandleader Frank Zappa has cultivated two seemingly opposed images. One is the serious composer who pioneered fusions of jazz and classical with rock music, and the outspoken and incisive satirist. The other is the smutty, sneering crowd pleaser whose hyperintricate music has been called by critics a gratuitous display of advanced technique. Nevertheless, by pursuing the latter course since the early Seventies, Zappa has secured a large and devout following.

The son of a guitar-playing government scientist, Frank Zappa moved with his family at age ten to California, eventually settling in Lancaster. He played in school orchestras and bands and began teaching himself a variety of instruments, mainly guitar. While at school, he became an avid collector of Fifties rock and R&B singles, and began listening to modern classical composers like Stravinsky and his avowed favorite, Edgard Varèse. In high school around 1957 or 1958, he formed the Blackouts and began adding country blues to his record collection. He met Don Van Vliet, another Lancaster resident, and allegedly christened him Captain Beefheart. In 1959, he attended Chaffey College in Alta Loma, California, and studied music theory before dropping out after six months.

In 1960, Zappa played cocktail music in local lounges, and he worked on his first recordings and the score for a B movie called *The World's Greatest Sinner*. He also appeared on Steve Allen's TV show, performing a "bicycle concerto" (plucking the spokes, blowing through the handlebars.) In 1963, Zappa wrote his second film score, for a Western called *Run Home Slow*, and with the money built a studio in Cucamonga, California. He befriended future Mothers Ray Collins and Jim "Motorhead" Sherwood, and formed a band with Beefheart called the Soots.

Zappa was lured into making some sort of sex tape by the San Bernardino Vice Squad, and as a result spent ten days in jail and three years on probation. The girl involved was bailed out of jail with royalties from the song "Memories of El Monte," which Zappa and Collins had written for the doo-wop group the Penguins.

In 1964, Zappa joined the Soul Giants, with Collins (vocals), Dave Coronada (sax), Roy Estrada (bass) and Jimmy Carl Black (drums). Zappa renamed the band the Muthers, then the Mothers, and moved the band onto L.A.'s proto-hippie "Freak" circuit. Coronada quit, replaced by guitarist Elliot Ingber. The band played club dates for two years, mixing romantic pop with social-protest tunes like "Who Are the Brain Police?". In early 1966, producer Tom Wilson signed them to MGM/Verve and recorded *Freak Out!* MGM, wary of the band's already outrageous reputation, forced Zappa to add "of Invention" to the Mothers. Though Zappa advertised the album in underground papers and comics and earned critical respect for the album's obvious musical and lyrical distinction, it ended up losing money.

Ingber joined Fraternity of Man (for whom he wrote "Don't Bogart That Joint," which appeared on the *Easy Rider* soundtrack); he later joined Captain Beefheart's Magic Band as Winged Eel Fingerling. The Mothers lineup expanded to include saxophonists Bunk Gardner and Motorhead Sherwood, keyboardist Don Preston and drummer Billy Mundi. Released in 1967, *Absolutely Free* further satirized "straight" America with arrogant tunes like "Brown Shoes Don't Make It" and "Plastic People." *We're Only in It for the Money*, a parody of the Beatles' *Sgt. Pepper*, found Zappa relentlessly savaging the "hip underground." Zappa's montage production techniques—mingling tape edits, noise, recitative, free-form outbursts and Varèse-like modern classical music with rock—were coming into their own. In 1967 Zappa and the Mothers also recorded *Lumpy Gravy*, with a fifty-piece orchestra, including many Mothers, and *Cruisin' with Ruben and the Jets*, a straightforward homage to Fifties rock.

Frank Zappa

While recording *Money,* Zappa and the band had moved to New York City's Greenwich Village, where they began a long residency at the Garrick Theater. There they pioneered rock theater with a series of often-spontaneous audience-participation skits.

Billy Mundi left after *Lumpy Gravy;* he joined Rhinoceros and, later, Earth Opera. While recording *Ruben and the Jets,* the Mothers also began recording *Uncle Meat,* a double album for a never-completed movie. It is the first full-blown example of Zappa's trademark complex-meter jazz-rock fusion.

After making *Uncle Meat,* Zappa moved the band back to L.A. and married his second wife, Gail; they have four children—daughters Moon Unit and Diva, and sons Dweezil and Ahmet Rodan. In L.A., Zappa moved into movie cowboy Tom Mix's Log Cabin Ranch, where he put together the increasingly complex *Burnt Weeny Sandwich* and *Weasels Ripped My Flesh.* By this time, the band had

come to include second guitarist Lowell George and drummer Art Tripp III.

In late 1968, Zappa and his manager Herb Cohen had moved to Warner/Reprise, where they formed their own Straight and Bizarre labels. Zappa recorded such acts as the groupie collective the GTO's (Girls Together Outrageously), onetime L.A. street-singer Wild Man Fischer, Alice Cooper and Captain Beefheart (whose *Trout Mask Replica* remains Zappa's most memorable production). By the time *Weasels* was released in 1970, Zappa had temporarily disbanded the Mothers because of overwhelming expenses and public apathy. Lowell George and Roy Estrada went on to form Little Feat; Art Tripp III joined Beefheart and became Ed Marimba (Estrada later joined Beefheart as well, as Orejon); Gardner and Black formed Geronimo Black.

Zappa began composing the soundtrack for *200 Motels.* He also recorded his first solo album, *Hot Rats,* a jazz-rock guitar showcase that featured Beefheart and jazz violinists Jean-Luc Ponty and Don "Sugarcane" Harris. *Hot Rats* was released to great critical response in 1970, as was Ponty's *King Kong,* an album of Zappa compositions (for legal reasons, Zappa's name couldn't be listed on the album as producer and guitarist). In 1970, Zappa also performed the *200 Motels* score with Zubin Mehta and the L.A. Philharmonic at a sold-out L.A. concert. That summer, Zappa re-formed the Mothers, retaining keyboardist/reedman Ian Underwood and adding ex-Turtles Howard Kaylan and Mark Volman (the singers then known as the Phlorescent Leech and Eddie) and Jim Pons (bass), jazz keyboardist George Duke and British rock drummer Aynsley Dunbar. With this lineup and other session players, Zappa recorded *Waka Jawaka* and *Chunga's Revenge* as solo LPs and the Mothers' *Live at the Fillmore East* and *Just Another Band from L.A.*

At this point, critics began accusing the Mothers of becoming a cynical, scatological joke. In 1971, the *200 Motels* film, which featured Theodore Bikel and Ringo Starr as surrogate Zappas, as well as the Mothers, was released to mixed response. In May 1971, Zappa appeared at one of the last Fillmore East concerts with John Lennon and Yoko Ono; the performance appears on Lennon/Ono's *Some Time in New York City.* As the Mothers personnel began to change more and more often, they embarked on a disastrous 1971 European tour in which the band's equipment was destroyed in a fire at Switzerland's Montreux Casino (immortalized in opening act Deep Purple's "Smoke on the Water") and Zappa was injured when a fan pushed him from the stage of London's Rainbow. A year later, the Mothers were banned from Royal Albert Hall for "obscenity."

The Grand Wazoo, with numerous auxiliary players added, was a Big Band fusion album. But in 1973, Zappa and the Mothers also recorded *Overnight Sensation,* on which Zappa streamlined and simplified his music and kept his lyrics in a scatological-humorous vein (as in "Don't Eat the Yellow Snow"). Album sales picked up. *Apostrophe* featured an extended jam with ex-Cream bassist Jack Bruce, as well as by-now-typical dirty jokes and satires. Sometime around 1973, Zappa produced the now-obscure Ruben and the Jets LP *For Real.*

From this point on, Zappa prolifically churned out albums, his critical reputation sinking as he was accused of constantly resorting to smarmy sarcasm backed by simple boogie riffs and/or music as showily and tortuously technical as British art rock.

The 1975 *Bongo Fury* album reunited Zappa with Beefheart. The latter had fallen out with Zappa after *Trout Mask,* accusing Zappa of marketing him like "a freak."

After producing Grand Funk Railroad's *Good Singin', Good Playin'* in 1976, Zappa filed a lawsuit against Herb Cohen in 1977, and he severed his ties with Warner Bros., moving to Mercury two years later, where he set up Zappa Records and retired the Mothers name, calling all later groups Zappa. Since then, he has gained frequent notoriety for ethnic stereotype songs. *Sheik Yerbouti* (a pun on K.C. and the Sunshine Band's "Shake Your Booty") caused a sensation with the song "Jewish Princess," for which the B'nai B'rith Anti-Defamation League filed a complaint with the FCC against Zappa. That album also yielded a surprise hit single, "Dancin' Fool," which made fun of the disco crowd (*Sheik* peaked at #22 on album charts, Zappa's best showing). *Joe's Garage, Act I,* the first installment of a three-record rock opera, included "Catholic Girls."

In 1980, Zappa recorded a single, "I Don't Wanna Get Drafted," which Mercury refused to release, prompting him to leave the label and eventually establish Barking Pumpkin, distributed by CBS. In 1980, Zappa also released the film *Baby Snakes,* a melange of concert footage, dressing-room slapstick and clay-figure animation. The late-Seventies Zappa bands included guitarist Adrian Belew (later of Talking Heads and King Crimson) and drummer Terry Bozzio (who later with his wife Dale founded Missing Persons).

In 1981, Zappa released his first Barking Pumpkin LP; and that year, some ex-Mothers, including Jimmy Carl Black, Don Preston and Bunk Gardner, united to form the Grandmothers. They toured and recorded, playing all-Zappa material from the Mothers' vintage late-Sixties period. In April 1981, Zappa produced and hosted a New York City concert of music by Edgard Varèse. Zappa also released a limited-edition mail-order-only, three-album series, *Shut Up 'n' Play Yer Guitar.*

In 1982, Zappa parlayed stereotype satire into success once more with "Valley Girl," from the *Drowning Witch* LP. The song parodied the daughters of entertainment-industry folk, specifically those in the San Bernardino Valley city of Encino, and featured an inspired rap by then-14-year-old Moon Unit Zappa, whose precisely ap-

proximated California drawl introduced such West Coast colloquialisms as "Gag me with a spoon" and "Bag your face" to the nation. The song was a big novelty hit, and seemed to ensure that Zappa's satiric legacy would survive for a long time.

WARREN ZEVON
Born January 24, 1947, Chicago
1969—*Wanted—Dead or Alive* (Imperial) 1976—*Warren Zevon* (Asylum) 1978—*Excitable Boy* 1980—*Bad Luck Streak in Dancing School; Stand in the Fire*
1982—*The Envoy.*

Singer/songwriter Warren Zevon's ironic tales of physical and psychological mayhem have earned him a cult following and comparisons to figures as diverse as Dorothy Parker, Raymond Chandler, Sam Peckinpah and Martin Scorsese.

The son of Russian immigrants, Zevon grew up in Arizona and California. He studied music briefly, and after meeting Igor Stravinsky during his junior high school years, Zevon taught himself to play guitar and began writing songs. He played in local bands and at age 16 moved to New York City, then to the Bay Area. He wrote songs (including "She Quit Me Man," used in the film *Midnight Cowboy*) and released his debut LP, *Wanted—Dead or Alive.* It was poorly received, and he went to work writing jingles (for Ernest and Julio Gallo wine ads) and as pianist and bandleader for the Everly Brothers shortly before their breakup. Over the next couple of years he continued to work with each brother separately.

In 1976, Linda Ronstadt covered Zevon's "Hasten Down the Wind" on *Hasten Down the Wind.* In 1977, two more of Zevon's songs appeared on *Simple Dreams:* "Carmelita" and "Poor Poor Pitiful Me," the latter of which was a hit for Ronstadt in 1978. Zevon, who had been living in Spain, was persuaded by his friend Jackson Browne to return to the U.S. and record. Browne produced *Warren Zevon,* which was released to critical acclaim, as all of Zevon's LPs have been since.

In 1978, Zevon had a Top Ten single with "Werewolves of London." But his career was temporarily set back by his alcoholism. He did not record for two years, and his live performances were few and erratic. His two 1980 releases, *Bad Luck Streak* and the live *Stand in the Fire,* represented something of a comeback for Zevon. In 1982, he announced he had given up alcohol and he released *The Envoy,* the title track written about U.S. envoy to the Mideast Philip Habib.

THE ZOMBIES
Formed 1963, Hertfordshire, England
Colin Blunstone (b. June 24, 1945, Hatfield, Eng.), voc.;
Paul Atkinson (b. Mar. 19, 1946, Cuffley, Eng.), gtr.;
Rod Argent (b. June 14, 1945, St. Albans, Eng.), kybds.,

voc.; Hugh Grundy (b. Mar. 6, 1945, Winchester, Eng.), drums; Paul Arnold (b. Eng.), bass.
1963—(− Arnold; + Chris White [b. Mar. 7, 1943, Barnet, Eng.], bass) **1965**—*Begins Here* (Decca) **1968**—*Odyssey and Oracle* (Date) **1973**—*Time of the Zombies* (Epic).

Though the Zombies had several major hits, their career was a frustrating one. Paul Atkinson, Rod Argent and Hugh Grundy met at St. Albans School, and they soon linked up with Colin Blunstone and bassist Paul Arnold. Six months later Arnold was replaced by Chris White. After winning a rock band contest held by a local newspaper, they got an audition with British Decca in 1964. In July, the electric-piano-centered "She's Not There" was released and it became a worldwide smash, going #2 in America. Their debut LP came out on Parrot/Decca in late 1964. A second single, "Leave Me Be," failed, but "Tell Her No" went Top Ten, their last hit for some time. They also contributed songs to the movie *Bunny Lake Is Missing.*

In 1967, they recorded a final LP, *Odyssey and Oracle* (the only album the band themselves approve of). But they broke up two weeks after it was completed, in December, 1967. Columbia staff producer Al Kooper fought to have the album issued; when it was, in late 1968, it yielded another #1 gold hit in "Time of the Season." The band declined to re-form, although sizable sums were offered.

Argent already was moving ahead on plans for his eponymous band (see separate entry) and most of the rest were fed up with the music business.

Blunstone had first gone back to working in an insurance office, then began working as a singer under the name Neil MacArthur. With that pseudonym he had a 1970 hit with a remake of "She's Not There." He made several solo LPs under his own name for Epic, beginning in 1971 with *One Year* (produced by Argent and White). In 1978, he tried again, unsuccessfully, with *Never Even Thought* on Rocket Records.

Atkinson first went into programing computers but later was in A&R, working for Columbia in New York for several years. Grundy also worked in Columbia A&R, but in the Eighties he was running a horse transport business near London. White cowrote songs and produced for Argent, and in the Seventies he helped discover Dire Straits. Original bassist Arnold became a doctor in Scotland. Epic released a two-record "best of," *Time of the Zombies,* in 1973.

ZZ TOP
Formed 1970, Texas
Billy Gibbons, gtr., voc.; Dusty Hill, bass, voc.; Frank Beard, drums.
1970—*First Album* (London) **1972**—*Rio Grande Mud* **1973**—*Tres Hombres* **1975**—*Fandango!* **1976**—

Z.Z. Top: Dusty Hill, Frank Beard, Billy Gibbons

Tejas **1977—***Best of ZZ Top* (all reissued on Warner Bros.) **1979—***Deguello* (Warner Bros.) **1983—***Eliminator.*

ZZ Top is a rough and ready power trio from Texas who were a huge mid-Seventies concert attraction. The group is built around guitarist Billy Gibbons. His career started with the popular Southwestern band Moving Sidewalk, whose "99th Floor" was a regional hit. They opened one night for Jimi Hendrix, and he later mentioned Gibbons on the "Tonight Show" as one of America's best young guitarists. After Moving Sidewalk broke up, Gibbons and manager/producer Bill Ham recruited Beard and Hill from a Dallas band, American Blues.

Beginning with the release of *First Album* in 1970, ZZ Top has toured constantly, building a national following that has made all the band's albums gold or platinum. A year-long tour in 1976, the Worldwide Texas Tour, was one of the largest-grossing tours in rock. Onstage with the band were snakes, longhorn cattle, buffalo, cactus and other Southwestern paraphernalia. The group sold over one million tickets. They didn't record for the next three years, until 1979's *Deguello*. Despite a lack of hit singles (except for "Tush" in 1975 and "Gimme All Your Lovin' " in 1983), ZZ Top's LPs have consistently reached the Top Forty.

ABOUT THE CONTRIBUTORS

KEN BRAUN has written biographies of musicians for the *Annual Obituary* and is a contributor to *The Rolling Stone Rock Almanac*. He currently contributes to the *Record*.

JIM FARBER is a music and film critic whose work has appeared in the *New York Times*, the *Village Voice*, *Rolling Stone* and many other publications.

NELSON GEORGE is a black-music editor at *Billboard*. He has contributed to *Musician*, the *Village Voice*, *Essence*, *Rolling Stone* and the *Record*, and is the author of *Top of the Charts*, a look back at pop music in the Seventies. He is currently writing a book on Michael Jackson.

JEFF HOWREY is a freelance writer.

IRA KAPLAN is a New York–based freelance writer.

JOHN MILWARD writes for many national magazines, including *Rolling Stone*, the *Village Voice* and *Penthouse*. He is the former music critic for the late *Chicago Daily News* and the *Chicago Reader*.

JON PARELES has written for virtually every major music publication since 1977, when his work first appeared in *Crawdaddy*. He has been music editor at *Crawdaddy*, *Rolling Stone* and the *Village Voice*, and is currently a critic for the *New York Times*.

PATRICIA ROMANOWSKI is the editor of Rolling Stone Press.

MITCHELL SCHNEIDER is a Los Angeles–based freelance writer. He has written reviews and features for *Rolling Stone*, *Crawdaddy*, *Circus*, *New York Rocker*, *High Fidelity*, *Good Times*, *L.A. Weekly*, the *Los Angeles Herald-Examiner* and *BAM*, for which he is a contributing editor.

MICHAEL SHORE, a former editor of *SoHo Weekly News* and *Home Video*, has written about music, video and related matters for the *Village Voice*, *Omni*, *Musician*, *Music Sound Output*, *ARTnews* and *Popular Computing*.